EDUCATIONAL RESEARCH

D1214782

EDUCATIONAL RESEARCH

Competencies for Analysis and Applications

TWELFTH EDITION

Geoffrey E. Mills
Southern Oregon University

L. R. Gay
Late of Florida International University

 Pearson

330 Hudson Street, NY NY 10013

Director and Portfolio Manager: Kevin M. Davis
Content Producer: Janelle Rogers
Sr. Development Editor: Carolyn Schweitzer
Media Producer: Lauren Carlson
Portfolio Management Assistant: Casey Coriell
Executive Field Marketing Manager: Krista Clark
Executive Product Marketing Manager: Christopher Barry
Procurement Specialist: Carol Melville
Full Service Project Management: Katie Ostler, Cenveo Publisher Services
Cover Designer: Cenveo Publisher Services
Cover Image: © FatCamera/Getty Images
Composition: Cenveo Publisher Services
Printer/Binder: LSC Communications
Cover Printer: LSC Communications
Text Font: 10/12 ITC Garamond Std

Credits and acknowledgments for material borrowed from other sources and reproduced, with permission, in this textbook appear on the appropriate page within the text.

Every effort has been made to provide accurate and current Internet information in this book. However, the Internet and information posted on it are constantly changing, so it is inevitable that some of the Internet addresses listed in this textbook will change.

Copyright © 2019, 2016, 2012 by Pearson Education, Inc. or its affiliates. All Rights Reserved. Manufactured in the United States of America. This publication is protected by Copyright, and permission should be obtained from the publisher prior to any prohibited reproduction, storage in a retrieval system, or transmission in any form or by any means, electronic, mechanical, photocopying, recording, or likewise. For information regarding permissions, request forms, and the appropriate contacts within the Pearson Education Global Rights & Permissions department, please visit www.pearsoned.com/permissions.

PEARSON and ALWAYS LEARNING are exclusive trademarks in the U.S. and/or other countries owned by Pearson Education, Inc. or its affiliates.

Library of Congress Cataloging-in-Publication Data

CIP is on file with the Library of Congress.

6 2021

ISBN 10:   0-13-478422-7
ISBN 13: 978-0-13-478422-9

Preface

NEW TO THIS EDITION

Like the 11th edition, the 12th edition reflects a combination of both unsolicited and solicited input. Positive feedback suggested aspects of the text that should not be changed—the writing style and the focus on ethical practice, for example. Those aspects remain. Part I, Foundational Concepts and Processes, retains the same six chapters from the 11th edition and adds a seventh chapter on ethics. Part II, Research Designs, includes all of the research design chapters that were covered in the 11th edition. Part III, Working with Quantitative and Qualitative Data, brings together discussions of descriptive statistics, inferential statistics, and qualitative data collection and analysis. New for this edition is the introduction of open source statistics software—R. Part IV, Reporting and Critiquing Research, effectively remains the same.

Content changes reflect the inclusion of new topics and the expansion or clarification of existing topics. There are many improvements in this edition, and we describe the more significant highlights here:

- Chapter 2 is new for this edition with the chapter dedicated to ethics in educational research. This chapter adds to the existing content on informed consent and protection from harm with a new and expanded section on action research and Institutional Review Boards (IRBs) that will be especially helpful for classroom-based, and school-based educational researchers.
- Chapter 4 has undergone significant revision because of the way technology has affected the literature review process. The use of online and digital technologies is growing in popularity and effectiveness for researchers in the field of education and other disciplines. Changes include an expanded Digital Research Tools feature that covers annotation, brainstorming, citation management, organization, and writing management.

- Chapter 7 has been significantly revised to provide an up-to-date discussion of selecting measuring instruments especially as it relates to the use of personality and affective tests in schools.
- Chapter 12 on single-subject experimental research has been updated and expanded to include a classroom-based special education example that breathes life in to the research process for classroom teachers.
- Chapters 18 and 19 on descriptive and inferential statistics have been updated, and new for this edition is the introduction of open-sourced statistical software R. R is a little different than Excel and SPSS in that it is open-source (read: free) but in order to operate R you need some very basic coding skills. This may frighten some readers from the start, but don't worry. We are going to send the reader off with a nice start to R programming and offer suggestions for future reading that will enhance one's skillset.

In addition, we have added new tables and figures throughout the text. Every chapter has been edited and updated. References have been updated as well.

MyLab for Education

One of the most visible changes in the new edition, also one of the most significant, is the expansion of the digital learning and assessment resources embedded in the etext and the inclusion of *MyLab* in the text. *MyLab for Education* is an online homework, tutorial, and assessment program designed to work with the text to engage learners and to improve learning. Within its structured environment, learners practice what they learn in the etext, test their understanding, and receive feedback to guide their learning and ensure their mastery of key learning outcomes. The *MyLab* portion of the new edition of *Educational Research* is designed to help learners (1) understand the basic vocabulary of educational research, (2) get hands-on experiences in reading and evaluating research articles, and (3) get guided practice in planning and developing a research proposal and in collecting and analyzing research data. The resources in *MyLab for Education* with *Educational Research: Competencies for Analysis and Applications*, 12th edition include:

- *Self-Check* assessments with feedback throughout the etext help readers assess how well they have mastered content.
- Two kinds of *Application Exercises*, all with feedback, either help students learn how to read, understand, and evaluate research articles or give students opportunities to practice specific research tasks like collecting and analyzing research data or planning and writing up a proposal.

PHILOSOPHY AND PURPOSE

This text is designed primarily for use in the introductory course in educational research that is a basic requirement for many graduate programs. Because the topic coverage of the text is relatively comprehensive, it may be easily adapted for use in either a senior-level undergraduate course or a more advanced graduate-level course.

The philosophy that guided the development of the current and previous editions of this text was the conviction that an introductory research course should be more oriented toward skill and application than toward theory. Thus, the purpose of this text is for students to become familiar with research mainly at a "how-to" skill and application level. The authors do not mystify students with theoretical and statistical jargon. They strive to provide a down-to-earth approach that helps students acquire the skills and knowledge required of a competent consumer and producer of educational research. The emphasis is not just on what the student knows but also on what the student can do with what he or she knows. It is recognized that being a "good" researcher involves more than the acquisition of skills and knowledge; in any field, important research is usually produced by those who through experience have acquired insights, intuitions, and strategies related to the research process. Research of any worth, however, is rarely conducted in the absence of basic research skills and knowledge. A fundamental assumption of this text is that the competencies required of a competent consumer of research overlap considerably with those required of a competent producer of research. A person is in a much better position to evaluate the work of others after she or he has performed the major tasks involved in the research process.

ORGANIZATION AND STRATEGY

The overall strategy of the text is to promote students' attainment of a degree of expertise in research through the acquisition of knowledge and by involvement in the research process.

Organization

In the 12th edition, Part I, Foundational Concepts and Processes, includes discussion of the scientific and disciplined inquiry approach and its application in education. The main steps in the research process and the purpose and methods of the various research designs are discussed. In Part I, each student selects and delineates a research problem of interest that has relevance to his or her professional area. Throughout the rest of the text, the student then simulates the procedures that would be followed in conducting a study designed to investigate the research problem; each chapter develops a specific skill or set of skills required for the execution of such a research design. Specifically, the student learns about the application of the scientific method in education (Chapter 1) and the ethical considerations that affect the conduct of any educational research (Chapter 2), identifies a research problem and formulates hypotheses (Chapter 3), conducts a review of the related literature (Chapter 4), develops a research plan (Chapter 5), selects and defines samples (Chapter 6), and evaluates and selects measuring instruments (Chapter 7). Throughout these chapters are parallel discussions of quantitative and qualitative research constructs. This organization, with increased emphasis on ethical considerations in the conduct of educational research and the skills needed to conduct a comprehensive review of related literature, allows the student to see the similarities and differences in research designs and to understand more fully how the nature of the research question influences the selection of a research design. Part II, Research Designs, includes description and discussion of different quantitative research designs, qualitative research designs, mixed methods research designs, and action research designs. Part III, Working with Quantitative and Qualitative Data, includes two chapters devoted to the statistical approaches and the analysis and interpretation of quantitative data, and two chapters describing the collection, analysis, and interpretation of qualitative data. Part IV, Reporting and Critiquing Research, focuses on helping the student prepare a research report, either for the completion of a degree requirement or for publication in a refereed journal, and an opportunity for the student to apply the skills and knowledge acquired in Parts I through III to critique a research report.

Strategy

This text represents more than just a textbook to be incorporated into a course; it is a total instructional system that includes stated learning outcomes, instruction, and procedures for evaluating each outcome. The instructional strategy of the system emphasizes the demonstration of skills and individualization within this structure. Each chapter begins with a list of learning outcomes that describes the knowledge and skills that the student should gain from the chapter. In many instances, learning outcomes may be assessed either as written exercises submitted by students or by tests, whichever the instructor prefers. In most chapters, a task to be performed is described next. Tasks require students to demonstrate that they can perform particular research skills. Because each student works with a different research problem, each student demonstrates the competency required by a task as it applies to his or her own problem. With the exception of Chapter 1, an individual chapter is directed toward the attainment of only one task (occasionally, students have a choice between a quantitative and qualitative task).

Text discussion is intended to be as simple and straightforward as possible. Whenever feasible, procedures are presented as a series of steps, and concepts are explained in terms of illustrative examples. In a number of cases, relatively complex topics or topics beyond the scope of the text are presented at a very elementary level, and students are directed to other sources for additional, in-depth discussion. There is also a degree of intentional repetition; a number of concepts are discussed in different contexts and from different perspectives. Also, at the risk of eliciting more than a few groans, an attempt has been made to sprinkle the text with touches of humor—a hallmark of this text spanning four decades—and perhaps best captured by the pictures and quotes that open each chapter. Each chapter includes a detailed, often lengthy summary with headings and subheadings directly parallel to those in the chapter. The summaries are designed to facilitate both the review and location of related text discussion. Finally, each chapter (or part) concludes with suggested criteria for evaluating the associated task and with an example of the task produced by a former introductory educational research student. Full-length articles, reprinted from the educational research literature, appear at the ends of all chapters presenting research designs and serve as illustrations of "real-life" research using that design. For the 12th edition all of these articles have been annotated with descriptive and evaluative annotations.

SUPPLEMENTARY MATERIALS

The following resources are available for instructors to download from **www.pearsonhighered .com/educator**. Enter the author, title of the text, or the ISBN number, then select this text, and click on the "Resources" tab. Download the supplement you need. If you require assistance in downloading any resources, contact your Pearson representative.

Instructor's Resource Manual With Test Bank

The *Instructor's Resource Manual with Test Bank* is divided into two parts. The *Instructor's Resource Manual* contains, for each chapter, suggested activities that have been effectively used in Educational Research courses, strategies for teaching, and selected resources to supplement the textbook content. The test bank contains multiple-choice items covering the content of each chapter, newly updated for this edition, and can be printed and edited or used with TestGen®.

TestGen®

TestGen is a powerful test generator available exclusively from Pearson Education publishers. You install TestGen on your personal computer (Windows or Macintosh) and create your own tests for classroom testing and for other specialized delivery options, such as over a local area network or on the Web. A test bank, which is also called a Test Item File (TIF), typically contains a large set of test items, organized by chapter, and ready for your use in creating a test based on the associated textbook material. Assessments may be created for both print and testing online.

The tests can be downloaded in the following formats:

TestGen Testbank file—PC
TestGen Testbank file—MAC
TestGen Testbank—Blackboard 9 TIF
TestGen Testbank—Blackboard CE/Vista
  (WebCT) TIF
Angel Test Bank (zip)
D2L Test Bank (zip)
Moodle Test Bank
Sakai Test Bank (zip)

PowerPoint® Slides

The PowerPoint® slides highlight key concepts and summarize text content to help students understand, organize, and remember core concepts and ideas. They are organized around chapter learning outcomes to help instructors structure class presentations.

ACKNOWLEDGMENTS

I sincerely thank everyone who provided input for the development of this edition. The following individuals made thoughtful and detailed suggestions and comments for improving the 12th edition: Jacqueline Swank, University of Florida; Raymond W. Francis, Central Michigan University; Robin Lund, University of Northern Iowa; Alane Starko, Eastern Michigan University; Vivian Ikpa, Temple University; Christian Kimm, California State University, Los Angeles. These reviewers contributed greatly to the 12th edition and their efforts are very much appreciated.

I would also like to acknowledge the staff at Pearson, without whose guidance (and patience!) this text would not have become a reality. In particular, I thank Kevin Davis, Director & Portfolio Manager, for working with me on the 12th edition of the text so as to build on what we achieved with the previous editions. Kevin has been my friend and mentor since he offered my first textbook contract in 1997, and I am indebted to him for his encouragement and support of my writing. Kevin worked diligently to ensure a quality, user-friendly, academically coherent text and patiently kept me on track in order to meet publication deadlines. His feedback on chapter drafts was insightful and important to the development of this 12th edition. Kevin has taught me a great deal about writing, and I will always be indebted to him for trusting me with stewardship of this wonderful text. The publication of this 12th edition also coincides with the end of my tenure at my academic home for the past 29 years: Southern Oregon University. I am now officially an Emeritus Professor and looking forward to dedicating more time to writing without the time commitment of teaching full time. At the risk of embarrassing Kevin, I can state with confidence that the past 20 years of my professorial career exceeded all of my expectations because of the opportunities Kevin has given me. Thank you.

This edition benefited from the efforts of my Developmental Editor Carolyn Schweitzer. This is my first collaboration with Carolyn and I am looking forward to working with her on future editions of *Educational Research* and *Action Research*. While we have never met face-to-face, I trust and respect all the contributions she has made to my work and benefit greatly from Carolyn's creative thinking about how to make an educational research textbook meaningful and fun. Also at Pearson, Janelle Rogers ably shepherded the manuscript through development and production. An author does not take on the task of a major revision of a text of this magnitude without the commitment and support of excellent editors. Kevin and Carolyn were instrumental in the development of this edition and I sincerely thank them for their professionalism, patience, caring, and sense of humor.

I believe that I have made a positive contribution to this text, now my fifth edition, and added to the wisdom of earlier editions by L. R. Gay and Peter Airasian. Long-time users of the text will still "hear"

Lorrie Gay's voice throughout the text, but increasingly there is an Aussie accent and sense of humor creeping its way into the pages!

I wish to thank my friend and colleague Dr. Adam Jordan (Associate Professor, University of North Georgia) for his thoughtful work on revising the descriptive and inferential statistics chapters and feedback and contributions on other quantitative chapters in the text. Similarly, my friend and colleague at Southern Oregon University, Dr. Dale Vidmar, was instrumental in the revision of the reviewing the literature chapter.

Finally, I want to thank my best friend and wife, Dr. Donna Mills (Emeritus Professor, Southern Oregon University), and my son, Jonathan, for their love, support, and patience. Their commitment to my work is always appreciated and never taken for granted. The completion of this edition signals another new era in my life as my son Jonathan has now graduated from college, and Donna and I prepare for retirement after long university careers.

Geoff Mills
Emeritus Professor
Southern Oregon University

Brief Contents

Contents

Research Articles

EDUCATIONAL RESEARCH

CHAPTER ONE

Introduction to Educational Research

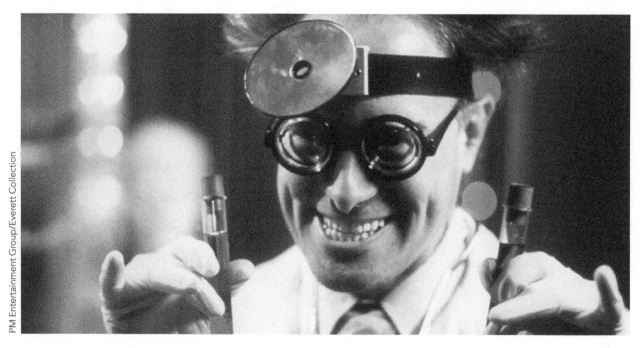

PM Entertainment Group/Everett Collection

Little Heroes 3, 2002

"Despite a popular stereotype that depicts researchers as spectacled, stoop-shouldered, elderly gentlemen...who endlessly add chemicals to test tubes, every day thousands of men and women of all ages and postures conduct educational research in a wide variety of settings." (p. 3)

LEARNING OUTCOMES

After reading Chapter 1, you should be able to do the following:

1.1 Briefly describe the reasoning involved in the scientific method.

1.2 Explain why researchers would use quantitative, qualitative, mixed methods, or action research designs to address a specific research problem.

1.3 Briefly define and state the major characteristics of these research designs: survey, correlational, causal–comparative, experimental, single-subject, narrative, ethnographic, case study, mixed methods, and action research.

1.4 Explain the purposes of basic research, applied research, evaluation research, research and development (R&D), and action research.

Completing Chapter 1 should enable you to perform the following tasks:

TASKS 1A, 1B

Identify and briefly state the following for both research studies at the end of this chapter:

1. The research design
2. The rationale for the choice of the research design
3. The major characteristics of the research design, including research procedures, method of analysis, and major conclusions (See Performance Criteria, p. 23.)

TASK 1C

Classify given research studies based on their characteristics and purposes. (See Performance Criteria, p. 23.)

WELCOME!

If you are taking a research course because it is required in your program of studies, raise your right hand. If you are taking a research course because it seems like it will be a really fun elective, raise your left hand. We thought you may not be here of your own free will. Although you may be required to take this course, you are not the innocent victim of one or more sadists. Your professors have several legitimate reasons for believing this research course is an essential component of your education.

First, educational research findings contribute significantly to both educational theory and educational practice. As a professional, you need to know how to find, understand, and evaluate these findings. And when you encounter research findings in professional publications or in the media, you have a responsibility, as a professional, to distinguish between legitimate and ill-founded research claims. Second, although many of you will be primarily critical consumers of research, some of you will decide to become educational researchers. A career in research opens the door to a variety of employment opportunities in universities, research centers, and business and industry.

Despite a popular stereotype that depicts researchers as spectacled, stoop-shouldered, elderly gentlemen (a stereotype I am rapidly approaching!) who endlessly add chemicals to test tubes, every day thousands of men and women of all ages and postures conduct educational research in a wide variety of settings. Every year many millions of dollars are spent in the quest for knowledge related to teaching and learning. For example, in 2017 the U.S. Department of Education budget was $69.4 billion, which included an allocation of $180 million for "[e]ducation innovation and research" (www2. ed.gov/about/overview/budget/budget17/budget-factsheet.pdf). Educational research has contributed many findings concerning principles of behavior, learning, and retention of knowledge—many of which can also be applied to curriculum, instruction, instructional materials, and assessment techniques. Both the quantity and the quality of research are increasing, partly because researchers are better trained. Educational research classes have become core components of preservice teacher education programs, as well as the cornerstone of advanced degree programs.

We recognize that educational research is a relatively unfamiliar discipline for many of you. Our first goals, then, are to help you acquire a general understanding of research processes and to help you develop the perspective of a researcher. We begin by examining the scientific method.

THE SCIENTIFIC METHOD

What is knowledge? And how do we come to "know" something? Experience is certainly one of the fundamental ways we come to know about and understand our world. For example, a child who touches something hot learns that high heat hurts. We know other things because a trusted authority, such as a parent or a teacher, told us about them. Most likely, much of your knowledge of current world events comes secondhand, from things you have read or heard from a source you trust.

Another way we come to know something is through thinking, through reasoning. Reasoning refers to the process of using logical thought to reach a conclusion. We can reason *inductively* or *deductively*. **Inductive reasoning** involves developing generalizations based on observation of a limited number of related events or experiences. Consider the following example of inductive reasoning:

Observation: An instructor examines five research textbooks. Each contains a chapter about sampling.
Generalization: The instructor concludes that all research textbooks contain a chapter about sampling.

Deductive reasoning involves essentially the reverse process—arriving at specific conclusions based on general principles, observations, or experiences (i.e., generalizations)—as shown in the next example.

Observations: All research textbooks contain a chapter on sampling. The book you are reading is a research text.
Generalization: This book must contain a chapter on sampling. (Does it?)

Although people commonly use experience, authority, inductive reasoning, and deductive reasoning to learn new things and draw new conclusions from that knowledge, each of these approaches to understanding has limitations when used in isolation. Some problems associated with experience and authority as sources of knowledge are graphically illustrated in a story told about Aristotle. According to

the story, one day Aristotle caught a fly and carefully counted and recounted the legs. He then announced that flies have five legs. No one questioned the word of Aristotle. For years his finding was accepted uncritically. Unfortunately, the fly that Aristotle caught just happened to be missing a leg! Whether or not you believe the story, it illustrates the limitations of relying on personal experience and authority as sources of knowledge.

The story also points out a potential problem with inductive reasoning: Generalizing from a small sample, especially one that is atypical, can lead to errors. Deductive reasoning, too, is limited by the evidence in the original observations. If every research text really does have a chapter on sampling, and if this book really is a research text, then it follows that this book must have a chapter on sampling. However, if one or more of the premises is false (perhaps some research texts do not have a chapter on sampling), your conclusion may also be wrong.

When we rely exclusively on these common approaches to knowing, the resulting knowledge is susceptible to error and may be of limited value to understanding the world beyond our immediate experience. However, experience, authority, and inductive and deductive reasoning are very effective when used together as integral components of the scientific method. The **scientific method** is an orderly process entailing a number of steps: recognition and definition of a problem, formulation of hypotheses, collection of data, analysis of data, and statement of conclusions regarding confirmation or disconfirmation of the hypotheses (i.e., a researcher forms a **hypothesis**—an explanation for the occurrence of certain behaviors, phenomena, or events—as a way of predicting the results of a research study and then collects data to test that prediction). These steps can be applied informally to solve everyday problems such as the most efficient route to take from home to work or school, the best time to go to the bank, or the best kind of computer to purchase. The more formal application of the scientific method is standard in research; it is more efficient and more reliable than relying solely on experience, authority, inductive reasoning, and deductive reasoning as sources of knowledge.

Limitations of the Scientific Method

The steps in the scientific method guide researchers in planning, conducting, and interpreting research studies. However, it is important to recognize some limitations of the method. First, the scientific method cannot answer all questions. For example, applying the scientific method will not resolve the question "Should we legalize euthanasia?" The answers to questions like this one are influenced by personal philosophy, values, and ethics.

Second, application of the scientific method can never capture the full richness of the individuals and the environments under study. Although some applications of the method lead to deeper understanding of the research context than others, no application—and in fact no research approach—provides full comprehension of a site and its inhabitants. No matter how many variables one studies or how long one is immersed in a research context, other variables and aspects of context will remain unexamined. Thus, the scientific method and, indeed, all types of inquiry give us a simplified version of reality.

Third, our measuring instruments always have some degree of error. The variables we study are often proxies for the real behavior we seek to examine. For example, even if we use a very precisely constructed multiple-choice test to assess a person's values, we will likely gather information that gives us a picture of that person's beliefs about his or her values. However, we aren't likely to have an adequate picture of how that person acts, which may be the better reflection of the person's real values.

More broadly, all educational inquiry, not just the scientific method, is carried out with the cooperation of participants who agree to provide researchers with data. Because educational researchers deal with human beings, they must consider a number of ethical concerns and responsibilities to the participants. For example, they must shelter participants from real or potential harm. They must inform participants about the nature of the planned research and address the expectations of the participants. These factors can limit and skew results. All these limitations will be addressed in later sections of this book.

Application of the Scientific Method in Education

Research is the formal, systematic application of the scientific method to the study of problems; **educational research** is the formal, systematic application of the scientific method to the study of educational problems. The goal of educational research is essentially the same as the goal of all science: to describe, explain, predict, or control phenomena—in this case, educational phenomena. As we mentioned previously, it can be quite difficult to describe, explain, predict, and control situations involving human beings, who are by far the most complex of all organisms. So many factors, known and unknown, operate in any educational environment that it can be extremely difficult to identify specific causes of behaviors or to generalize or replicate findings. The kinds of rigid controls that can be established and maintained in a biochemistry laboratory, for instance, are impossible in an educational setting. Even describing behaviors, based on observing people, has limits. Observers may be subjective in recording behaviors, and people who are observed may behave atypically just because they are being watched. Chemical reactions, on the other hand, are certainly not aware of being observed! Nevertheless, behavioral research should not be viewed as less scientific than natural science research conducted in a lab.

Despite the difficulty and complexity of applying the scientific method in educational settings, the steps of the scientific method used by educational researchers are the same as those used by researchers in other more easily controlled settings:

1. *Selection and definition of a problem.* A problem is a question of interest that can be tested or answered through the collection and analysis of data. Upon identifying a research question, researchers typically review previously published research on the same topic and use that information to hypothesize about the results. In other words, they make an educated guess about the answer to the question.
2. *Execution of research procedures.* The procedures reflect all the activities involved in collecting data related to the problem (e.g., how data are collected and from whom). To a great extent, the specific procedures are dictated by the research question and the variables involved in the study.
3. *Analysis of data.* Data are analyzed in a way that permits the researcher to test the research hypothesis or answer the research

question. Analysis usually involves application of one or more statistical technique. For some studies, data analysis involves verbal synthesis of narrative data; these studies typically involve new insights about the phenomena in question, generate hypotheses for future research, or both.

4. *Drawing and stating conclusions.* The conclusions, which should advance our general knowledge of the topic in question, are based on the results of data analysis. They should be stated in terms of the original hypothesis or research question. Conclusions should indicate, for example, whether the research hypothesis was supported or not. For studies involving verbal synthesis, conclusions are much more tentative.

MyLab Education **Self-Check 1.1**

MyLab Education **Application Exercise 1.1:** Understanding the Scientific Method

---

DIFFERENT APPROACHES TO EDUCATIONAL RESEARCH

All educational inquiry ultimately involves a decision to study or describe something—to ask some question and seek an answer. All educational inquiry necessitates that data of some kind be collected, that the data be analyzed in some way, and that the researcher come to some conclusion or interpretation. In other words, all educational inquiry shares the same four basic actions we find in the scientific method. However, it is not accurate to say that all educational research is an application of the scientific method. Important differences exist between the types of problems researchers investigate and the questions they ask, the types of data they collect, the form of data analysis, and the conclusions that the researcher can draw meaningfully and with validity.

The Continuum of Research Philosophies

Historically, educational researchers used approaches that involved the use of the scientific method. However, over the last four decades, researchers have adopted diverse philosophies toward their research. Now, there are certain philosophical assumptions that underpin an educational researcher's decision to conduct research. These philosophical assumptions address issues related to the nature of reality (ontology), how researchers know what they know (epistemology), and the methods used to study a particular phenomenon (methodology), with an emphasis on quantitative or qualitative methods. As Creswell[1] notes, historically, researchers compared the philosophical assumptions that underpinned qualitative and quantitative research approaches in order to establish the legitimacy of qualitative research, but given the evolution of qualitative and quantitative research over the past four decades, there is no longer any need to justify one set of philosophical assumptions over another set of assumptions.

Quantitative Research

Educational researchers have also followed well-defined, widely accepted procedures for stating research problems, carrying out the research process, analyzing the resulting data, and verifying the quality of the study and its conclusions. Often, these research procedures are based on what has come to be known as a quantitative approach to conducting and obtaining educational understandings. The quantitative framework in educational research involves the application of the scientific method to try to answer questions about education. At the end of this chapter you will find an example of quantitative research published in *Child Development* (a refereed journal): "Can Instructional and Emotional Support in the First-Grade Classroom Make a Difference for Children at Risk of School Failure?" (Hamre & Pianta, 2005). As this title suggests, this research investigates the ways in which children's risk of school failure may be moderated by instructional and emotional support from teachers.

Quantitative research is the collection and analysis of numerical data to describe, explain, predict, or control phenomena of interest. Part II of the text will address in detail specific quantitative research designs that satisfy the assumptions

---

[1] *Qualitative Inquiry & Research Design: Choosing Among Five Approaches* (4th ed.) by J. W. Creswell and C. N. Poth, 2018, Thousand Oaks, CA: Sage.

underpinning a quantitative approach to research. A quantitative research design entails more than just the use of numerical data. At the outset of a study, quantitative researchers state the hypotheses to be examined and specify the research procedures that will be used to carry out the study. They also maintain control over contextual factors that may interfere with the data collection and identify a sample of participants large enough to provide statistically meaningful data. Many quantitative researchers have little personal interaction with the participants they study because they frequently collect data using paper-and-pencil, noninteractive instruments. The analysis of numerical data can be complex but addressed systematically it can be manageable and Part III of the text will provide a detailed description for how to work with quantitative data.

Underlying quantitative research methods is the philosophical belief or assumption that we inhabit a relatively stable, uniform, and coherent world that we can measure, understand, and generalize about. This view, adopted from the natural sciences, implies that the world and the laws that govern it are somewhat predictable and can be understood by scientific research and examination. In this quantitative perspective, claims about the world are not considered meaningful unless they can be verified through direct observation.

Qualitative Research

Qualitative research is the collection, analysis, and interpretation of comprehensive narrative and visual (i.e., non-numerical) data to gain insights into a particular phenomenon of interest. Part II of the text will address in detail specific qualitative research designs that satisfy the underpinning assumptions of a qualitative approach to research. Qualitative research designs are based on different beliefs and purposes than quantitative research designs. For example, qualitative researchers do not necessarily accept the view of a stable, coherent, uniform world. They argue that all meaning is situated in a particular perspective or context, and because different people and groups often have different perspectives and contexts, the world has many different meanings, none of which is necessarily more valid or true than another.

Qualitative research designs tend to evolve as understanding of the research context and participants deepens (think back to the discussion of inductive reasoning). As a result, qualitative researchers often avoid stating hypotheses before data are collected, and they may examine a particular phenomenon without a guiding statement about what may or may not be true about that phenomenon or its context. However, qualitative researchers do not enter a research setting without any idea of what they intend to study. Rather, they commence their research with "foreshadowed problems."[2] This difference is important—quantitative research usually tests a specific hypothesis; qualitative research often does not.

Additionally, in qualitative research, context is not controlled or manipulated by the researcher. The effort to understand the participants' perspectives requires researchers using qualitative methods to interact extensively and intimately with participants during the study, using time-intensive data collection methods such as interviews and observations. As a result, the number of participants tends to be small, and qualitative researchers analyze the data inductively by categorizing and organizing it into patterns that produce a descriptive, narrative synthesis.

Qualitative research differs from quantitative research in two additional ways: (1) Qualitative research often involves the simultaneous collection of a wealth of narrative and visual data over an extended period of time, and (2) as much as is possible, data collection occurs in a naturalistic setting. In quantitative studies, in contrast, research is most often conducted in researcher-controlled environments under researcher-controlled conditions, and the activities of data collection, analysis, and writing are separate, discrete activities. Because qualitative researchers strive to study people and events in their naturalistic settings, qualitative research is sometimes referred to as naturalistic research, naturalistic inquiry, or field-oriented research.

These two characteristics of qualitative research, the simultaneous study of many aspects of a phenomenon and the attempt to study things as they exist naturally, help in part to explain the growing enthusiasm for qualitative research in education, especially in applied teacher practitioner–oriented

---

[2] *Argonauts of the Western Pacific* (p. 9), by B. Malinowski, 1922, London: Routledge.

research. Some researchers and educators feel that certain kinds of educational problems and questions do not lend themselves well to quantitative methods, which use principally numerical analysis and try to control variables in very complex environments. As qualitative researchers point out, findings should be derived from research conducted in real-world settings to have relevance to real-world settings.

At the end of this chapter, you will find an example of qualitative research published in *Action in Teacher Education* (a refereed journal): "Developing Teacher Epistemological Sophistication about Multicultural Curriculum: A Case Study" (Sleeter, 2009). This research investigates how teachers' thinking about curriculum develops during a teacher preparation program and how the lessons from the case study might inform teacher education pedagogy. And, of course, the use of the word *epistemological* in the title introduces you to the language of educational research!

Mixed Methods Research

Mixed methods research combines quantitative and qualitative designs by including both quantitative and qualitative data in a single study. The purpose of mixed methods research is to build on the synergy and strength that exists between quantitative and qualitative research designs to understand a phenomenon more fully than is possible using either quantitative or qualitative approaches alone. Chapter 16 will describe in detail six mixed methods research designs (convergent-parallel, explanatory, exploratory, experimental, social justice, and multistage evaluation). However, the basic differences among the designs are related to the priority given to the following areas:

- The type of data collected (i.e., qualitative and quantitative data are of equal weight, or one type of data has greater weight than the other)
- The sequence of data collection (i.e., both types of data are collected during the same time period, or one type of data is collected in each sequential phase of the project)
- The analysis techniques (i.e., either an analysis that combines the data or one that keeps the two types of data separate)

Characteristics of Quantitative and Qualitative Research Approaches

Earlier in this chapter, we presented four general, conceptual research steps used in the scientific method. In this section, we expand the number of steps to six, which are followed by both quantitative researchers and qualitative researchers. As we discuss in subsequent chapters in Part II, however, the application of the steps differs depending on the research design. For example, the research procedures in qualitative research are often less rigid than those in quantitative research. Similarly, although both quantitative and qualitative researchers collect data, the nature of the data differs. Figure 1.1 compares the six steps of qualitative and quantitative research approaches and lists traits that characterize each approach at every step:

1. *Identifying a research topic*
2. *Reviewing the literature*
3. *Selecting participants*
4. *Collecting data*
5. *Analyzing and interpreting data*
6. *Reporting and evaluating the research*

Table 1.1 provides another snapshot of quantitative and qualitative research characteristics. Despite the differences between them, you should not consider quantitative and qualitative research approaches to be oppositional. Taken together, they represent the full range of educational research designs. The terms *quantitative* and *qualitative* are used to differentiate one approach from the other conveniently. If you see yourself as a positivist—the belief that qualities of natural phenomena must be verified by evidence before they can be considered knowledge—that does not mean you cannot use or learn from qualitative research methods. The same holds true for nonpositivist, phenomenologist qualitative researchers. Depending on the nature of the question, topic, or problem to be investigated, one of these approaches will generally be more appropriate than the other, although selecting a primary approach does not preclude borrowing from the other. In fact, both may be utilized in the same studies, as when the administration of a (quantitative) questionnaire is followed by a small number of detailed (qualitative) interviews to obtain deeper explanations for the numerical data.

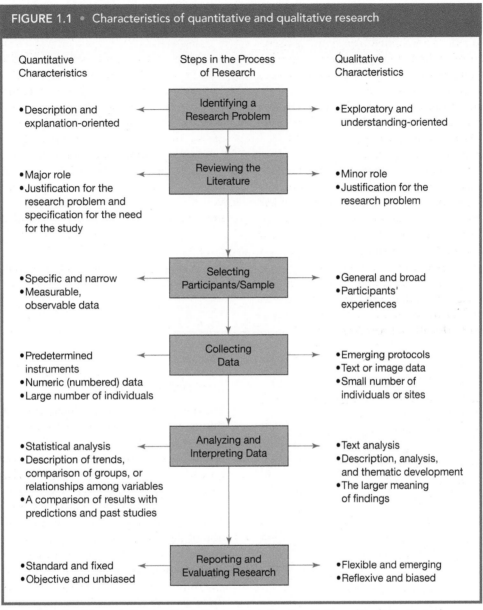

FIGURE 1.1 • Characteristics of quantitative and qualitative research

Quantitative Characteristics	Steps in the Process of Research	Qualitative Characteristics
•Description and explanation-oriented	Identifying a Research Problem	•Exploratory and understanding-oriented
•Major role •Justification for the research problem and specification for the need for the study	Reviewing the Literature	•Minor role •Justification for the research problem
•Specific and narrow •Measurable, observable data	Selecting Participants/Sample	•General and broad •Participants' experiences
•Predetermined instruments •Numeric (numbered) data •Large number of individuals	Collecting Data	•Emerging protocols •Text or image data •Small number of individuals or sites
•Statistical analysis •Description of trends, comparison of groups, or relationships among variables •A comparison of results with predictions and past studies	Analyzing and Interpreting Data	•Text analysis •Description, analysis, and thematic development •The larger meaning of findings
•Standard and fixed •Objective and unbiased	Reporting and Evaluating Research	•Flexible and emerging •Reflexive and biased

Source: Educational Research: Planning, Conducting, and Evaluating Quantitative and Qualitative Research (5th ed.), (pp. 20, 464, 504, 541), by John W. Creswell, © 2015. Reprinted by permission of Pearson Education, Inc., Upper Saddle River, NJ.

MyLab Education **Self-Check 1.2**

MyLab Education **Application Exercise 1.2:** Evaluating Research Articles: Recognizing the Characteristics of Quantitative and Qualitative Research

MyLab Education **Application Exercise 1.3:** Evaluating Research Articles: Identifying Steps in the Research Process Part 1

MyLab Education **Application Exercise 1.4:** Evaluating Research Articles: Identifying Steps in the Research Process Part 2

TABLE 1.1 • Overview of qualitative and quantitative research characteristics

	Quantitative Research	Qualitative Research
Type of data collected	Numerical data	Non-numerical narrative and visual data
Research problem	Hypothesis and research procedures stated before beginning the study	Research problems and methods evolve as understanding of topic deepens
Manipulation of context	Yes	No
Sample size	Larger	Smaller
Research procedures	Relies on statistical procedures	Relies on categorizing and organizing data into patterns to produce a descriptive, narrative synthesis
Participant interaction	Little interaction	Extensive interaction
Underlying belief	We live in a stable and predictable world that we can measure, understand, and generalize about.	Meaning is situated in a particular perspective or context that is different for people and groups; therefore, the world has many meanings.

CLASSIFICATION OF RESEARCH BY DESIGN

A research design comprises the overall strategy followed in collecting and analyzing data. Although there is some overlap, most research studies follow a readily identifiable design. The largest distinction we can make in classifying research by design is the distinction between quantitative and qualitative approaches. Quantitative and qualitative research approaches, in turn, include several distinct types or designs with a focus on unique research problems.

Quantitative Approaches

Quantitative research approaches are applied to describe current conditions, investigate relations, and study cause–effect phenomena. Survey research is often designed to describe current conditions. Studies that investigate the relations between two or more variables are correlational research. Experimental studies and causal–comparative studies provide information about cause–effect outcomes. Studies that focus on the behavior change an individual exhibits as a result of some intervention fall under the heading of single-subject research.

Survey Research

Survey research determines and reports the way things are; it involves collecting numerical data to test hypotheses or answer questions about the current status of the subject of study. One common type of survey research involves assessing the preferences, attitudes, practices, concerns, or interests of a group of people. A pre-election political poll and a survey about community members' perception of the quality of the local schools are examples. Survey research data are mainly collected through questionnaires, interviews, and observations.

Although survey research sounds very simple, there is considerably more to it than just asking questions and reporting answers. Because researchers often ask questions that have not been asked before, they usually have to develop their own measuring instrument for each survey study. Constructing questions for the intended respondents requires clarity, consistency, and tact. Other major challenges facing survey researchers are participants' failure to return questionnaires, their willingness to be surveyed over the phone, and their ability to attend scheduled interviews. If the response rate is low, then valid, trustworthy conclusions cannot be drawn. For example, suppose you are doing a study to determine the attitudes of principals toward research in their schools. You send a questionnaire to 100 principals and include the question "Do you usually cooperate if your school is asked to participate in a research study?" Forty principals respond, and they all answer "Yes." It's certainly a mistake to conclude that principals in general cooperate. Although all those who responded said yes, those 60 principals who did not respond may never cooperate with researchers. After all, they didn't cooperate with you! Without more responses, it is not possible to make generalizations about how principals feel about research in their schools.

Following are examples of questions that can be investigated in survey research studies, along with typical research designs:

- *How do second-grade teachers spend their teaching time?* Second-grade teachers are asked to fill out questionnaires, and results are presented as percentages (e.g., teachers spent 50% of their time lecturing, 20% asking or answering questions, 20% in discussion, and 10% providing individual student help).
- *How will citizens of Yourtown vote in the next school board election?* A sample of Yourtown citizens complete a questionnaire or interview, and results are presented as percentages (e.g., 70% said they will vote for Peter Pure, 20% named George Graft, and 10% are undecided). Survey research is described in more detail in Chapter 8.

Correlational Research

Correlational research involves collecting data to determine whether, and to what degree, a relation exists between two or more quantifiable variables. A **variable** is a placeholder that can assume any one of a range of values; for example, intelligence, height, and test score are variables. At a minimum, correlational research requires information about at least two variables obtained from a single group of participants.

The purpose of a correlational study may be to establish relations or use existing relations to make predictions. For example, a college admissions director may be interested in answering the question "How do the SAT scores of high school seniors correspond to the students' first-semester college grades?" If students' SAT scores are strongly related to their first-semester grades, SAT scores may be useful in predicting how students will perform in their first year of college. On the other hand, if there is little or no correlation between the two variables, SAT scores likely will not be useful as predictors.

Correlation refers to a quantitative measure of the degree of correspondence. The degree to which two variables are related is expressed as a **correlation coefficient,** which is a number between +1.00 and −1.00. Two variables that are not related have a correlation coefficient near 0.00. Two variables that are highly correlated will have a correlation coefficient near +1.00 or −1.00. A number near +1.00 indicates a positive correlation: As one variable increases, the other variable also increases (e.g., students with high SAT scores may also have high grade point averages [GPAs]). A number near −1.00 indicates a negative correlation: As one variable increases, the other variable decreases (e.g., a high GPA may correlate negatively with the likelihood of dropping out). Because very few pairs of variables are perfectly correlated, predictions based on them are rarely +1.0 or −1.0.

It is very important to note that the results of correlational studies do not suggest cause–effect relations among variables. Thus, a positive correlation between, for example, self-concept and achievement does not imply that self-concept causes achievement or that achievement causes self-concept. The correlation indicates only that students with higher self-concepts tend to have higher levels of achievement and that students with lower self-concepts tend to have lower levels of achievement. We cannot conclude that one variable is the cause of the other.

Following are examples of research questions tested with correlational studies:

- *What is the relation between intelligence and self-esteem?* Scores on an intelligence test and a measure of self-esteem are acquired from each member of a given group. The two sets of scores are analyzed, and the resulting coefficient indicates the degree of correlation.
- *Does an algebra aptitude test predict success in an algebra course?* Scores on the algebra aptitude test are correlated with final exam scores in the algebra course. If the correlation is high, the aptitude test is a good predictor of success in algebra.

Correlational research is described in detail in Chapter 9.

Causal–Comparative Research

Causal–comparative research attempts to determine the cause, or reason, for existing differences in the behavior or status of groups of individuals.

The cause is a behavior or characteristic believed to influence some other behavior or characteristic and is known as the **grouping variable.** The change or difference in a behavior or characteristic that occurs as a result—that is, the effect—is known as the **dependent variable.** Put simply, causal–comparative research attempts to establish cause–effect relations among groups.

Following are examples of research questions tested with causal–comparative studies (note that the word is *causal*, not *casual*):

■ *How does preschool attendance affect social maturity at the end of the first grade?* The grouping variable is preschool attendance (i.e., the variable can take one of two values—students attending preschool and students not attending); the dependent variable, or effect, is social maturity at the end of the first grade. The researcher identifies a group of first-graders who attended preschool and a group who did not, gathers data about their social maturity, and then compares the two groups.

■ *How does having a working mother affect a child's school absenteeism?* The grouping variable is the employment status of the mother (again with two possible values—the mother works or does not work); the dependent variable is absenteeism, measured as number of days absent. The researcher identifies a group of students who have working mothers and a group whose mothers do not work, gathers information about their absenteeism, and compares the groups.

A weakness of causal–comparative studies is that, because the cause under study has already occurred, the researcher has no control over it. For example, suppose a researcher wanted to investigate the effect of heavy smoking on lung cancer and designs a study comparing the frequency of lung cancer diagnoses in two groups, long-time smokers and nonsmokers. Because the groups are preexisting, the researcher did not control the conditions under which the participants smoked or did not smoke (this lack of researcher control is why the variable is known as a grouping variable rather than an independent variable). Perhaps a large number of the long-time smokers lived in a smoggy, urban environment, whereas only a few of the nonsmokers were exposed to those conditions. In that case, attempts to draw cause–effect conclusions in the study would be tentative at best. Is it smoking that causes higher rates of lung cancer? Is it living in a smoggy, urban environment? Or is it some unknown combination of smoking and environment? A clear cause–effect link cannot be obtained.

Although causal–comparative research produces limited cause–effect information, it is an important form of educational research. True cause–effect relations can be determined only through experimental research (discussed in the next section), in which the researcher maintains control of an independent variable; but in many cases, an experimental study is inappropriate or unethical. The causal–comparative approach is chosen precisely because the grouping variable either cannot be manipulated (e.g., as with gender, height, or year in school) or should not be manipulated (e.g., as with smoking or prenatal care). For example, to conduct the smoking study as an experiment, a researcher would need to select a large number of participants who had never smoked and divide them into two groups, one directed to smoke heavily and one forbidden to smoke. Obviously, such a study is unethical because of the potential harm to those forced to smoke. A causal–comparative study, which approximates cause–effect results without harming the participants, is the only reasonable approach. Like descriptive and correlational studies, however, causal–comparative research does not produce true experimental research outcomes.

Causal–comparative research is described in detail in Chapter 10.

Experimental Research

In **experimental research,** at least one independent variable is manipulated, other relevant variables are controlled, and the effect on one or more dependent variables is observed. True experimental research provides the strongest results of any of the quantitative research approaches because it provides clear evidence for linking variables. As a result, it also offers **generalizability,** or applicability of findings to settings and contexts different from the one in which they were obtained.

Unlike causal–comparative researchers, researchers conducting an experimental study can control an independent variable. They can select the participants for the study, divide the participants into two or more groups that have similar characteristics at the start of the research experiment, and then apply different treatments to the selected groups. They can also control the conditions in the research setting, such as when the treatments will be applied, by whom, for how long, and under what circumstances. Finally, the researchers can select tests or measurements to collect data about any changes in the research groups. The selection of participants from a single pool of participants and the ability to apply different treatments or programs to participants with similar initial characteristics permit experimental researchers to draw conclusions about cause and effect. The essence of experimentation is control, although in many education settings it is not possible or feasible to meet the stringent control conditions required by experimental research.

Following are examples of research questions that are explored with experimental studies:

■ *Is personalized instruction from a teacher more effective for increasing students' computational skills than computer instruction?* The independent variable is type of instruction (with two values: personalized instruction and computer instruction); the dependent variable is computational skills. A group of students who have never experienced either personalized teacher instruction or computer instruction are selected and randomly divided into two groups, each taught by one of the methods. After a predetermined time, the students' computational skills are measured and compared to determine which treatment, if either, produced higher skill levels.

■ *Is there an effect of reinforcement on students' attitude toward school?* The independent variable is type of reinforcement (with three values: positive, negative, or no reinforcement); the dependent variable is attitude toward school. The researcher randomly forms three groups from a single large group of students. One group receives positive reinforcement, another negative reinforcement, and the third no reinforcement. After the treatments are applied for a predetermined time, student attitudes toward school are measured and compared for each of the three groups.

Experimental research is described in detail in Chapter 11.

Single-Subject Research

Rather than compare the effects of different treatments (or treatment versus no treatment) on two or more groups of people, experimental researchers sometimes compare a single person's behavior before treatment to behavior exhibited during the course of the experiment. They may also study a number of people together as one group, rather than as individuals. **Single-subject experimental designs** are those used to study the behavior change that an individual or group exhibits as a result of some intervention or treatment. In these designs, the size of the **sample**—the individuals selected from a population for a study—is said to be one.

Following are examples of published studies that used single-subject designs:

■ *The effects of a training program with and without reinforced directed rehearsal as a correction procedure in teaching expressive sign language to nonverbal students with intellectual disabilities.* Ten students with moderate to severe intellectual disabilities were studied.[3]

■ *The effects of instruction focused on assignment completion on the homework performance of students with learning disabilities.* A single-subject experiment design was used to determine how instruction in a comprehensive, independent assignment completion strategy affected the quality of homework and the homework completion rate of eight students with learning disabilities.[4]

Single-subject experimental research is described in detail Chapter 12.

Qualitative Approaches

Qualitative research seeks to probe deeply into the research setting to obtain in-depth understandings about the way things are, why they are that way, and how the participants in the context perceive them. To achieve the detailed understandings they seek, qualitative researchers must undertake sustained in-depth, in-context research that allows them to uncover subtle, less overt, personal understandings. The field of qualitative research uses a variety of common qualitative research designs. For example,

---

[3] "Effects of Reinforced Directed Rehearsal on Expressive Sign Language Learning by Persons with Mental Retardation," by A. J. Dalrymple and M. A. Feldman, 1992, *Journal of Behavioral Education*, 2(1), pp. 1–16.

[4] "Effects of Instruction in an Assignment Completion Strategy on the Homework Performance of Students with Learning Disabilities in General Education Classes," by C. A. Hughes, K. L. Ruhl, J. B. Schumaker, and D. D. Deshler, 2002, *Learning Disabilities Research and Practice*, 17(1), pp. 1–18.

some qualitative researchers focus on the exploration of phenomena that occur within a bounded system (e.g., a person, event, program, life cycle; in a *case study*); some focus in depth on a group's cultural patterns and perspectives to understand participants' behavior and their context (i.e., using *ethnography*); some examine how multiple cultures compare to one another (i.e., *ethology*); some examine people's understanding of their daily activities (i.e., *ethnomethodology*); some derive theory using multiple steps of data collection and interpretation that link actions of participants to general social science theories or work inductively to arrive at a theory that explains a particular phenomenon (i.e., *grounded theory*); some ask about the meaning of this experience for these participants (i.e., *phenomenology*); some look for common understandings that have emerged to give meaning to participants' interactions (i.e., *symbolic interaction*); some seek to understand the past by studying documents, relics, and interviews (i.e., *historical research*); and some describe the lives of individuals (i.e., *narrative*). Overall, a collective, generic name for these qualitative approaches is *interpretive research*.[5]

Narrative Research

Narrative research is the study of how different humans experience the world around them; it involves a methodology that allows people to tell the stories of their "storied lives."[6] The researcher typically focuses on a single person and gathers data by collecting stories about the person's life. The researcher and participant then construct a written account, known as a narrative, about the individual's experiences and the meanings the individual attributes to the experiences. Because of the collaborative nature of narrative research, it is important for the researcher and participant to establish a trusting and respectful relationship. Another way to think of narrative research is that the narrative is the story of the phenomenon being investigated, and narrative is also the method of inquiry being used by the researcher.[7] One of the goals of narrative research in education is to increase understanding of central issues related to teaching and learning through the telling and retelling of teachers' stories.

Following is an example of the narrative research approach:

> Kristy, an assistant professor of education, is frustrated by what she perceives as the gender-biased distribution of resources within the School of Education (SOE). Kristy shares her story with Winston, a colleague and researcher. In the course of their lengthy recorded conversations, Kristy describes in great detail her view that the SOE dean, George, is allocating more resources for technology upgrades, curriculum materials, and conference travel to her male colleagues. Kristy also shares with Winston her detailed journals, which capture her experiences with George and other faculty members in interactions dealing with the allocation of resources. In addition, Winston collects artifacts—including minutes of faculty meetings, technology orders, and lists of curriculum materials ordered for the library at the university—that relate to resource allocation.
>
> After collecting all the data that will influence the story, Winston reviews the information, identifies important elements and themes, and retells Kristy's story in a narrative form. After constructing the story with attention given to time, place, plot, and scene, he shares the story with Kristy, who collaborates on establishing its accuracy. In his interpretation of Kristy's unique story of gender bias, Winston describes themes related to power and influence in a hierarchical school of education and the struggles faced by beginning professors to establish their career paths in a culture that is remarkably resistant to change.

Narrative research is described in detail in Chapter 13.

Ethnographic Research

Ethnographic research, or ethnography, is the study of the cultural patterns and perspectives of participants in their natural settings. Ethnography focuses on a particular site or sites that provide the researcher with a context in which to study both the setting and the participants who inhabit it. An ethnographic setting can be defined as anything from a bowling alley to a neighborhood, from a nomadic group's traveling range to an elementary principal's office. The participants are observed as they take part in naturally occurring activities within the setting.

---

[5] For a discussion, see *Qualitative Evaluation and Research Methods* (4th ed.), by M. Q. Patton, 2015, Thousand Oaks, CA: Sage.
[6] "Stories of Experience and Narrative Inquiry," by F. M. Connelly and D. J. Clandinin, 1990, *Educational Research, 19*(5), p. 2.
[7] "Stories," Connelly and Clandinin, pp. 2–14.

The ethnographic researcher avoids making interpretations and drawing conclusions too early in the study. Instead, the researcher enters the setting slowly, learning how to become accepted by the participants and gaining rapport with them. Then, over time, the researcher collects data in waves, making initial observations and interpretations about the context and participants, then collecting and examining more data in a second wave of refining the initial interpretation, then collecting another wave of data to further refine observations and interpretation, and so on, until the researcher has obtained a deep understanding of both the context and its participants' roles in it. Lengthy engagement in the setting is a key facet of ethnographic research. The researcher organizes the data and undertakes a cultural interpretation. The result of the ethnographic study is a holistic description and cultural interpretation that represents the participants' everyday activities, values, and events. The study is written and presented as a narrative, which, like the study from which it was produced, may also be referred to as an ethnography.

Following is an example of an ethnographic approach to a research question:

> *What is the Hispanic student culture in an urban community college?* After selecting a general research question and a research site in a community college that enrolls many Hispanic students, the researcher first gains entry to the college and establishes rapport with the participants of the study. Building rapport can be a lengthy process, depending on the characteristics of the researcher (e.g., non-Hispanic versus Hispanic; Spanish speaking versus non-Spanish speaking). As is common in qualitative approaches, the researcher simultaneously collects and interprets data to help focus the general research question initially posed.

Throughout data collection, the ethnographic researcher identifies recurrent themes, integrates them into existing categories, and adds new categories as new themes or topics arise. The success of the study relies heavily on the researcher's skills in analyzing and synthesizing the qualitative data into coherent and meaningful descriptions. The research report includes a holistic description of the culture, the common understandings and beliefs shared by participants, a discussion of how these beliefs relate to life in the culture, and discussion of how the findings compare to literature already published about similar groups. In a sense, the successful researcher provides guidelines that enable someone not in the culture to know how to think and behave in the culture.

Ethnographic research is described in detail in Chapter 14.

Case Study Research

Case study research is a qualitative research approach to conducting research on a unit of study or bounded system (e.g., an individual teacher, a classroom, or a school can be a case). Case study research is an all-encompassing method covering design, data collection techniques, and specific approaches to data analysis.[8] A case study is also the name for the product of case study research, which is different from other field-oriented research approaches such as narrative research and ethnographic research.

Following is an example of a study that used the case study research approach:

> Mills (1988)[9] asked, "How do central office personnel, principals, and teachers manage and cope with multiple innovations?" and studied educational change in one American school district. Mills described and analyzed how change functioned and what functions it served in this district. The function of change was viewed from the perspectives of central office personnel (e.g., superintendent, director of research and evaluation, program coordinators), principals, and teachers as they coped with and managed multiple innovations, including the introduction of kindergartens to elementary schools, the continuation of a program for at-risk students, and the use of the California Achievement Test (CAT) scores to drive school improvement efforts. Mills used qualitative data collection techniques including participant observation, interviewing, written sources of data, and nonwritten sources of data.

Case study research is described in detail in Chapter 14.

MyLab Education **Self-Check 1.3**

---

[8] *Case Study Research: Design and Methods* (5th ed.) by R. K. Yin, 2014., Thousand Oaks, CA: Sage.
[9] *Managing and Coping with Multiple Educational Changes: A Case Study* by G. E. Mills, 1988, unpublished doctoral dissertation, University of Oregon, Eugene.

CLASSIFICATION OF RESEARCH BY PURPOSE

Research designs can also be classified by the degree of direct applicability of the research to educational practice or settings. When purpose is the classification criterion, all research studies fall into one of two categories: basic research and applied research. Applied research can be subdivided into evaluation research, research and development (R&D), and action research.

Basic and Applied Research

It is difficult to discuss basic and applied research separately because they are on a single continuum. In its purest form, **basic research** is conducted solely for the purpose of developing or refining a theory. Theory development is a conceptual process that requires many research studies conducted over time. Basic researchers may not be concerned with the immediate utility of their findings because it may be years before basic research leads to a practical educational application. For example, one of the articles listed at the end of this chapter focuses on basic research to develop and refine theories of children's adaptation to new school settings (Hamre & Pianta, 2005).

Applied research, as the name implies, is conducted for the purpose of applying or testing a theory to determine its usefulness in solving practical problems. A teacher who asks, "Will the theory of multiple intelligences help improve my students' learning?" is seeking an answer to a practical classroom question. This teacher is not interested in building a new theory or even generalizing beyond her classroom; instead, she is seeking specific helpful information about the impact of a promising practice (i.e., a teaching strategy based on the theory of multiple intelligences) on student learning. For example, one of the articles listed at the end of this chapter focuses on how a beginning teacher integrates university coursework on multicultural education into her classroom teaching and the decision-making process related to the implementation of a multicultural curriculum (Sleeter, 2009).

Educators and researchers sometimes disagree about which end of the basic–applied research continuum should be emphasized. Many educational research studies are located on the applied end of the continuum; they are more focused on what works best than on finding out why it works as it does. However, both basic research and applied research are necessary. Basic research provides the theory that produces the concepts for solving educational problems. Applied research provides data that can help support, guide, and revise the development of theory. Studies located in the middle of the basic–applied continuum seek to integrate both purposes. Figure 1.2 illustrates the educational research continuum.

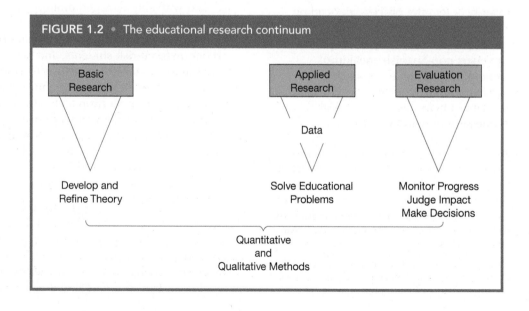

FIGURE 1.2 • The educational research continuum

Evaluation Research

At the applied end of the research continuum is evaluation research, an important, widely used, and explicitly practical form of research. **Evaluation research** is the systematic process of collecting and analyzing data about the quality, effectiveness, merit, or value of programs, products, or practices. Unlike other forms of research that seek new knowledge or understanding, evaluation research focuses mainly on making decisions—decisions about those programs, products, and practices. For example, following evaluation, administrators may decide to continue a program or to abandon it, to adopt a new curriculum or to keep the current one. Some typical evaluation research questions are "Is this special science program worth its costs?" "Is the new reading curriculum better than the old one?" "Did students reach the objectives of the diversity sensitivity program?" and "Is the new geography curriculum meeting the teachers' needs?"

Evaluations come in various forms and serve different functions.[10] An evaluation may be either formative or summative, for example. **Formative evaluation** occurs during the design phase when a program or product is under development and is conducted during implementation so that weaknesses can be remedied. **Summative evaluation** focuses on the overall quality or worth of a completed program or product.

Research and Development (R&D)

Research and development (R&D) is the process of researching consumer needs and then developing products to fulfill those needs. The purpose of R&D efforts in education is not to formulate or test theory but to develop effective products for use in schools. Such products include teacher-training materials, learning materials, sets of behavioral objectives, media materials, and management systems. R&D efforts are generally quite extensive in terms of objectives, personnel, and time to completion. Products are developed according to detailed

specifications. Once completed, products are field-tested and revised until a prespecified level of effectiveness is achieved. Although the R&D cycle is expensive, it results in quality products designed to meet specific educational needs. School personnel who are the consumers of R&D endeavors may, for the first time, really see the value of educational research.

Action Research

Action research in education is any systematic inquiry conducted by teachers, principals, school counselors, or other stakeholders in the teaching–learning environment to gather information about the ways in which their particular schools operate, the teachers teach, and the students learn. Its purpose is to provide teacher-researchers with a method for solving everyday problems in their own settings. Because the research is not characterized by the same kind of control evident in other categories of research, however, study results cannot be applied to other settings. The primary goal of action research is the solution of a given problem, not contribution to science. Whether the research is conducted in one classroom or in many classrooms, the teacher is very much a part of the process. The more research training the teachers have had, the more likely it is that the research will produce valid results. Action research can use quantitative, qualitative, or mixed methods research designs depending on the nature of the research problem.

Following are examples of action research:

- *A study to determine how mathematics problem-solving strategies are integrated into student learning and transferred to real-life settings outside the classroom.* An elementary teacher conducts the study in his or her own school.
- *A study on how a school grading policy change affects student learning.* A team of high school teachers works collaboratively to determine how replacing number and letter grades with narrative feedback affects student learning and attitudes toward learning.

The value of action research is confined primarily to those conducting it. Despite this limitation, action research represents a scientific approach to problem solving that is considerably better than change based on the alleged effectiveness of

[10] See *Evaluation Models: Viewpoints on Educational and Human Services Evaluation*, by D. Stufflebeam, G. Madaus, and T. Kellaghan, 2000, Norwell, MA: Kluwer Academic; *The Program Evaluation Standards: A Guide for Evaluators and Evaluation Users* (3rd ed.), by Yarbrough, D.B., Shulha, L.M., Hopson, R.K., and Caruthers, F.A., by Joint Committee on Standards for Educational Evaluation, 2011, Thousand Oaks, CA: Sage.

untried procedures and infinitely better than no change at all. It is a means by which concerned school personnel can attempt to improve the educational process, at least within their environment.

Action research is described in detail in Chapter 17.

This chapter has provided a general introduction to fundamental aspects of the scientific method, along with examples of both quantitative and qualitative approaches. Included are overviews of educational research methods and research purposes. If the number of new terms and definitions seems overwhelming, remember that most will be revisited and reviewed in succeeding chapters. In those chapters we present more specific and detailed features needed to carry out, understand, and conduct useful educational research.

MyLab Education **Self-Check 1.4**

MyLab Education **Application Exercise 1.5:** Explaining the Purpose of Different Research Methods

---

WRITE LIKE A RESEARCHER!

Sometimes educational researchers are criticized for being incredibly boring, especially in the way they write about their research (not engaging like this textbook!). After all, while the content of our research is perhaps far more "black and white" than E. L. James's *Fifty Shades of Grey*, perhaps it is still possible to write in a style that is consistent with meeting the requirements of the scientific method while still being engaging for our readers. After all, how many of us can claim that we have recently completed a real "page turner" of a research paper?! Like some of the pages of this text, I suspect that we ultimately find ourselves trapped with the writing conventions of the academy, but I encourage you not to give up the goal of writing about your research in an engaging fashion.

If we look at the characteristics of the scientific method presented in this chapter, we can start to think about writing an initial research narrative that includes the following four sections and compare what we may write with what the authors of the research articles at the end of this chapter have written:

1. *Selection and definition of a problem.* A problem is a question of interest that can be tested or answered through the collection and analysis of data.
   - "The current study was designed to extend work related to school effects by following children identified in kindergarten as being at risk of school failure and examining whether the classroom environment to which they were exposed during the first grade moderated these risks by the end of the first grade" (Hamre & Pianta).
   - "To examine the relationship between a teacher's learning and my teaching strategies in the university" (Sleeter)

2. *Execution of research procedures.* The procedures reflect all the activities involved in collecting data related to the problem (e.g., how data are collected and from whom).
   - "Children included in this study took part in the National Institute of Child Health and Human Development (NICHD) Study of Early Child Care. The children's mothers were recruited from hospitals located in or near Little Rock, AK; Irvine, CA; Lawrence, KS; Boston, MA; Philadelphia, PA; Pittsburgh, PA; Charlottesville, VA; Morganton, NC; Seattle, WA; and Madison, WI. In 1991, research staff visited 8,986 mothers giving birth in these hospitals. Of these mothers, 5,416 met eligibility criteria and agreed to be contacted after returning home from the hospital. A randomly selected subgroup (with procedures to ensure economic, educational, and ethnic diversity) were contacted and enrolled in the study. This resulted in a sample of 1,364 families with healthy newborns. Details of this selection procedure are published in the study manuals (NICHD ECCRN, 1993)" (Hamre & Pianta).

- "Case study research typically uses a variety of methods to collect data, with an objective toward triangulating findings across methods (Creswell, 2008; Stake, 2000). Data for this study included (1) several papers that Ann completed during the course, including a unit that she designed as a course requirement; (2) a journal that I kept after each class session; (3) notes on two observations of Ann teaching the unit that she designed after the course had ended; and (4) a 40-minute recorded interview with Ann following my observations" (Sleeter).

3. *Analysis of data.* Data are analyzed in a way that permits the researcher to test the research hypothesis or answer the research question.

   - "In order to establish whether instructional and emotional support in the first grade may moderate risk, we first had to establish two preconditions: (1) the existence of a natural experiment, in which children with varying risk backgrounds in kindergarten would sort into first-grade classrooms offering different levels of emotional and instructional support, and (2) whether the hypothesized risk factors were associated with poorer outcomes in first grade. The first precondition was assessed through examining the distribution of children in each risk group into classrooms offering high, moderate, and low support. The second precondition was assessed by conducting ANCOVAs in which risk status was used to predict first-grade outcomes, after adjusting for children's previous performance on these outcomes measures" (Hamre & Pianta).

   - "Early in the semester (September), I guided teachers in analyzing epistemological assumptions in various documents related to curriculum, such as curriculum standards and school reform proposals available on the Internet. Teachers examined documents in relationship to questions such as the following: *Who produced this document (if it is possible to tell)? How is it intended to be used? By whom? What is its purpose? Whose view of the world does it support? Whose view does it undermine or ignore? Whose knowledge isn't here?* In addition, they analyzed textbooks from their classrooms, with guidance from a textbook analysis instrument" (Sleeter).

4. *Drawing and stating conclusions.* The conclusions, which should advance our general knowledge of the topic in question, are based on the results of data analysis.

   - "The study provides evidence that across two important domains of child functioning in the early grades of school, achievement, and relationships with teachers, the quality of everyday classroom interactions in the form of instructional and emotional support moderates the risk of early school failure" (Hamre & Pianta).

   - "This case study showed how one novice teacher began to question institutionalized assumptions in the context of a graduate course and how she began to think more complexly. The case study reinforced for me the importance of creating contexts in which teachers can examine their own backgrounds and beliefs, interact with one another, and interact with ideas that stretch them intellectually. Of course, no two teachers bring the same prior experiences, beliefs, and commitments. The challenge for an instructor lies in planning a course that activates a variety of experiences and enables uncomfortable questions and disagreements to take place so that teachers can grow. This inquiry into learning has helped me make sense of that challenge" (Sleeter).

Are there characteristics of each of these papers that you find engaging? If so, what are they and how might they find their way into your own writing about your research? Are you up to the challenge? Chapter 22 contains considerable details about guidelines for writing a research report, and formats and styles for theses, dissertations, and journal articles.

SUMMARY

THE SCIENTIFIC METHOD

1. The goal of all scientific endeavors is to describe, explain, predict, and/or control phenomena.
2. Compared to other sources of knowledge, such as experience, authority, inductive reasoning, and deductive reasoning, application of the scientific method is the most efficient and reliable.
3. The scientific method is an orderly process that entails recognition and definition of a problem, formulation of hypotheses, collection and analysis of data, and statement of conclusions regarding confirmation or disconfirmation of the hypotheses.

Limitations of the Scientific Method

4. Four main factors put limitations on the use of a scientific and disciplined inquiry approach: inability to answer some types of questions, inability to capture the full richness of the research site and the complexity of the participants, limitations of measuring instruments, and the need to address participants' needs in ethical and responsible ways.

Application of the Scientific Method in Education

5. Research is the formal, systematic application of the scientific method to the study of problems; educational research is the formal, systematic application of the scientific method to the study of educational problems.
6. The major difference between educational research and some other types of scientific research is the nature of the phenomena studied. It can be quite difficult to explain, predict, and control situations involving human beings, by far the most complex of all organisms.
7. The research process usually comprises four general steps:
   a. Selection and definition of a problem
   b. Execution of research procedures
   c. Analysis of data
   d. Drawing and stating conclusions

DIFFERENT APPROACHES TO EDUCATIONAL RESEARCH

The Continuum of Research Philosophies

8. Certain philosophical assumptions underpin an educational researcher's decision to conduct research. These philosophical assumptions address issues related to the nature of reality (ontology), how researchers know what they know (epistemology), and the methods used to study a particular phenomenon (methodology).

Quantitative Research

9. Quantitative research is the collection and analysis of numerical data to explain, predict, and/or control phenomena of interest.
10. Key features of quantitative research are hypotheses that predict the results of the research before the study begins; control of contextual factors that may influence the study; collection of data from sufficient samples of participants; and use of numerical, statistical approaches to analyze the collected data.
11. The quantitative approach assumes that the world is relatively stable, uniform, and coherent.

Qualitative Research

12. Qualitative research is the collection, analysis, and interpretation of comprehensive narrative and visual (nonnumeric) data to gain insights into a particular phenomenon of interest.
13. Key features of qualitative research include defining the problem, but not necessarily at the start of the study; studying contextual factors in the participants' natural settings; collecting data from a small number of purposely selected participants; and using nonnumeric, interpretive approaches to provide narrative descriptions of the participants and their contexts.
14. An important belief that underlies qualitative research is that the world is not stable, coherent, or uniform, and therefore there are many truths.

Mixed Methods Research

15. Mixed methods research combines quantitative and qualitative approaches by including both quantitative and qualitative data in a single study. The purpose of mixed methods research is to build on the synergy and strength that exists between quantitative and qualitative research approaches to understand a phenomenon more fully than is possible using either quantitative or qualitative approaches alone.

Characteristics of Quantitative and Qualitative Research Approaches

16. Qualitative and quantitative researchers follow the same basic six steps in conducting research, although application of the steps may differ depending on the research design.

CLASSIFICATION OF RESEARCH BY DESIGN

Quantitative Approaches

17. Quantitative research approaches are intended to describe current conditions, investigate relations, and study cause–effect phenomena.

18. Survey research involves collecting numerical data to answer questions about the current status of the subject of study.

19. Correlational research examines the relation between two or more variables. A variable is a placeholder—such as age, IQ, or height—that can take on different values.

20. In correlational research, the degree of relation is measured by a correlation coefficient. If two variables are highly related, one is not necessarily the cause of the other.

21. Causal–comparative research seeks to investigate differences between two or more different programs, methods, or groups. The activity thought to make a difference (e.g., the program, method, or group) is called the grouping variable. The effect is called the dependent variable.

22. In most causal–comparative research studies, the researcher does not have control over the grouping variable because it already has occurred or cannot be manipulated. Causal–comparative research is useful in those circumstances when it is impossible or unethical to manipulate an independent variable.

23. True experimental research investigates causal relations among variables.

24. The experimental researcher controls the selection of participants by choosing them from a single pool and assigning them at random to different causal treatments. The researcher also controls contextual variables that may interfere with the study. Because participants are randomly selected and assigned to different treatments, experimental research permits researchers to make true cause–effect statements.

25. Single-subject experimental designs are a type of experimental research that can be applied when the sample is one individual or group. This type of design is often used to study the behavior change that an individual or group exhibits as a result of some intervention or treatment.

Qualitative Approaches

26. Qualitative approaches include narrative research, ethnographic research, and case study research. The focus of these methods is on deep description of aspects of people's everyday perspectives and context.

27. Narrative research is the study of how individuals experience the world. The researcher typically focuses on a single person and gathers data through the collection of stories.

28. Ethnographic research is the study of the cultural patterns and perspectives of participants in their natural setting. Ethnography focuses on a particular site or sites that provide the researcher with a context in which to study both the setting and the participants who inhabit it.

29. Case study research is a qualitative research approach to conducting research on a unit of study or bounded system (e.g., classroom, school).

CLASSIFICATION OF RESEARCH BY PURPOSE

Basic and Applied Research

30. Basic research is conducted to develop or refine theory, not to solve immediate practical problems. Applied research is conducted to find solutions to current practical problems.

Evaluation Research

31. The purpose of evaluation research is to inform decision making about educational programs and practices.

Research & Development

32. The major purpose of R&D efforts is to develop effective products for use in schools.

Action Research

33. The purpose of action research is to provide teacher-researchers with a method for solving everyday problems in their own settings.

PERFORMANCE CRITERIA   TASK 1

Tasks 1A and 1B

Reprints of two published research reports appear on the following pages (Task 1A Quantitative Example and Task 1B Qualitative Example). Read the reports and then state the following for each study:

- Research design
- Rationale for the choice of the design
- Major characteristics of the design including: research problems, methods of data analysis, and major conclusions

One sentence should be sufficient to describe the research design and the rationale for the choice of the design. For the major characteristics of the design, one or two sentences will usually be sufficient to state the research problems and the method of data analysis. You are expected only to identify the analysis, not explain it. The major conclusion that you identify and state (one or two sentences should be sufficient) should directly relate to the original topic. Statements such as "more research is needed in this area" do not represent major conclusions.

Suggested responses to these tasks appear in Appendix B of this text. If your responses differ greatly from those suggested, study the reports again.

Task 1C

Brief descriptions of five research studies follow these instructions. Read each description and decide whether the study represents a survey, correlational, causal–comparative, experimental, single-subject, narrative, ethnographic, or case study approach. State the research approach for each topic statement, and indicate why you selected that approach. Your reasons should be related to characteristics that are unique to the type of research you have selected.

1. In this study, researchers administered a questionnaire to determine how social studies teachers felt about teaching world history to fifth-graders.
2. This study was conducted to determine whether the Acme Interest Test provided similar results to the Acne Interest Test.
3. This study compared the achievement in reading of fifth-graders from single-parent families and those from two-parent families.
4. This study divided fifth-grade students in a school into two groups at random and compared the results of two methods of conflict resolution on students' aggressive behavior.
5. This study examined the culture of recent Armenian emigrants in their new setting.

Suggested responses appear in Appendix B.

Can Instructional and Emotional Support in the First-Grade Classroom Make a Difference for Children at Risk of School Failure?

BRIDGET K. HAMRE
University of Virginia

ROBERT C. PIANTA
University of Virginia

ABSTRACT   This study examined ways in which children's risk of school failure may be moderated by support from teachers. Participants were 910 children in a national prospective study. Children were identified as at risk at ages 5–6 years on the basis of demographic characteristics and the display of multiple functional (behavioral, attention, academic, social) problems reported by their kindergarten teachers. By the end of first grade, at-risk students placed in first-grade classrooms offering strong instructional and emotional support had achievement scores and student–teacher relationships commensurate with their low-risk peers; at-risk students placed in less supportive classrooms had lower achievement and more conflict with teachers. These findings have implications for understanding the role that classroom experience may play in pathways to positive adaptation.

Application of the scientific method: selection and definition of a problem—whether experiences in high-quality classrooms can help close the gap between children at risk of school failure and their low-risk peers in the early grades.

(01)   Identifying the conditions under which experiences in school settings can alter the early trajectories of children's social or academic functioning has important implications for understanding pathways to children's positive adaptation. Of particular interest is whether experiences in high-quality classrooms can help close the gap between children at risk of school failure and their low-risk peers, particularly in the early grades when small increments in achievement play a large role in eventual outcomes (Alexander, Entwisle, & Kabbani, 2001; Ferguson, 1998; Phillips, Crouse, & Ralph, 1998; Ross, Smith, Slavin, & Madden, 1997). Two bodies of work are relevant to this question. The first examines everyday classroom interactions between teachers and children that predict more positive development for all children (Brophy & Good, 1986; Gage & Needel, 1989; Howes et al., 2005; NICHD ECCRN, 2003; Pianta, LaParo, Payne, Cox, & Bradley, 2002; Rimm-Kaufman, LaParo, Pianta, & Downer, in press; Ritchie & Howes, 2003; Skinner & Belmont, 1993; Stipek et al., 1998). The second area of research provides evidence of specific

The work reported herein was supported in part by the National Institute of Child Health and Human Development (NICHD) Study of Early Child Care (U10-HD25449), NICHD R21-43750 and by American Psychological Association/Institute of Education Sciences Postdoctoral Education Research Training fellowship under the Department of Education, Institute of Education Sciences grant number R305U030004.

Correspondence concerning this article should be addressed to Bridget K. Hamre, University of Virginia, PO Box 800784, Charlottesville, VA 22908-0784. Electronic mail may be sent to bkh3d@virginia.edu.

© 2005 by the Society for Research in Child Development, Inc. All rights reserved. 0009-3920/2005/7605-0001]

school-based interventions that may alter trajectories for students with various risk factors (Battistich, Schaps, Watson, & Solomon, 1996; Durlak & Wells, 1997; Elias, Gara, Schuyler, Branden-Muller, & Sayette, 1991; Greenberg et al., 2003; Weissberg & Greenberg, 1998; Wilson, Gottfredson, & Najaka, 2001). At the intersection of these areas of education and developmental science is the question of whether students' everyday instructional and social interactions with teachers in the classroom may themselves ameliorate the risk of school failure. If this were the case, focused efforts related to teacher training and support, curriculum implementation, and assessments of classroom settings could be used more strategically to counter the tendency toward poor outcomes for such children (see Pianta, in press, for a discussion). The current study used data from a large, national prospective study of children and families to examine ways in which risk of school failure may be moderated by strong support from teachers in the first-grade classroom. Specifically, we examined whether children at risk of early school failure experiencing high levels of instructional and emotional support in the first grade displayed higher achievement and lower levels of student–teacher conflict than did their at-risk peers who did not receive this support.

Everyday Classroom Interactions and Student Outcomes

Research on everyday classroom processes that may alter trajectories for students at risk has its foundations in the process–product research from the 1960s to 1980s that focused attention on observable teacher behaviors (Brophy & Good, 1986; Gage & Needel, 1989) and in developmentally informed theories of schooling that focus attention on socio-emotional, motivational (Connell & Wellborn, 1991; Deci & Ryan, 1985; Eccles, 1993; Wentzel, 2002) and instructional (e.g., Resnick, 1994; Stevenson & Lee, 1990) experiences in classrooms that trigger growth and change in competence. Although it posited the type of interactions between student characteristics and teacher behaviors that are now beginning to be reported in the literature (e.g., Morrison & Connor, 2002; Rimm-Kaufman et al., 2002) and has resulted in frameworks for describing classroom processes that inform educational research (e.g., Brophy, 2004), the process–product research tradition did not yield a body of empirical findings that provide a strong case for classroom effects, particularly in relation to issues such as moderation of child characteristics. Reviews of the contribution of this literature in large part note the lack of grounding in developmental and psychological research as well as the complex and interactive nature of student's classroom experiences (Gage & Needel, 1989; Good & Weinstein, 1986). Within developmental psychology, the focus on proximal processes in ecological models (Bronfenbrenner & Morris, 1998; Lerner, 1998; Sameroff, 1995, 2000) and the extension of these perspectives to school settings (Connell & Wellborn, 1991; Pianta, 1999; Resnick, 1994; Stevenson & Lee, 1990) have advanced efforts to understand the interactive processes through which children and adolescents experience, the classroom environment (Pianta, in press). Roeser, Eccles, and Sameroff (2000) extend the linkage between developmental studies and education, even further when arguing, with respect to understanding middle school effects, for research "linking the study of adolescents' experience, motivation, and behavior in school with the study of their teachers' experience, motivation, and behavior at school" (p. 466). This explicit need to focus on the interaction of child characteristics with types or categories of resources available in classroom (and school) settings is consistent with Rutter and Maughan's (2002) analysis of shortcomings in the school-effects literature. However, if such an approach is to yield more fruitful results than the process–product work, it is in large part predicated on more sophisticated understandings of the developmental needs of children vis-à-vis experiences in school (e.g., Reid, Patterson, & Snyder, 2002) and parallel efforts to understand and measure developmentally relevant assets in school environments (see Morrison & Connor, 2002; Rimm-Kaufman et al., 2002, as recent examples).

(02)

(03)   One avenue for advancing the understanding of schooling as a moderator of child (or background) characteristics is the assessment of variation in the nature, quality, and quantity of teachers' interactions with students (e.g., Burchinal et al., 2005). Recent large-scale observational studies indicate that these types of interaction within classrooms are highly variable (e.g., National Institute of Child Health and Human Development, Early Child Care Research Network (NICHD ECCRN), 2002b, in press). Even the most well-described, manualized, standardized, scientifically based classroom intervention programs are enacted in practice in ways that vary widely from child to child or classroom to classroom (e.g., Greenberg, Doitrovich, & Bumbarger, 2001). In descriptions of less-tightly prescribed classroom interactions, the degree to which classroom teachers make productive use of time or classrooms are well-managed ranges across the full spectrum of possibilities, even though kindergartens and first-grade classes appear, on average, to be positive and supportive social settings (NICHD ECCRN, 2002b, in press; Pianta et al., 2002).

(04)   In recent large-scale observational studies of pre-k to elementary classrooms, two dimensions consistently emerge: instructional support and emotional support (NICHD ECCRN, 2002b, in press; Pianta et al., 2002; Pianta, LaParo, & Hamre, 2005). Interestingly, these two dimensions, to some extent, predict differentially children's social and academic outcomes, confirming theoretical views that various developmental needs of children may interact differentially with the qualities of school settings (Connell & Wellborn, 1991; Morrison & Connor, 2002; Rutter & Maughan, 2002). For example, when evaluated in the same prediction model, instructional support for learning predicts achievement outcomes to a significantly greater degree than emotional support predicts these same outcomes (Howes et al., 2005). On the other hand, children's anxious behavior reported by mothers (but not academic performance) is predicted by the degree of classroom structure and instructional press in the first grade (NICHD ECCRN, 2003), while higher levels of emotional support predict a very broad range of social and task-oriented competencies such as following directions (Howes et al., 2005). Morrison and Connor (2002) argue that the effects of schooling on development have to be modeled at the level of specific forms of input and resource that are matched to specific child needs, abilities, and skills. Thus, according to Morrison and Connor (2002), it is not only necessary to conceptualize and measure the classroom setting (or school) in terms of specific aspects of instructional or social environment, but also to gauge the effects of those experiences relative to how well they match the child's capacities and skill. In this view, school effects are predominantly in the form of interactions between specific inputs from the classroom and the characteristics of the child.

(05)   These two broad dimensions of everyday teacher–student classroom interactions—emotional and instructional support—with theoretical and empirical links to student development, can be a starting point for examining interactions with child and background characteristics, particularly attributes that place children at risk for school failure. In global observations reported in the literature, emotional support encompasses the classroom warmth, negativity, child-centeredness as well as teachers' sensitivity and responsivity toward specific children (NICHD ECCRN, 2002b, in press). This should not be surprising as a number of developmentally informed theories suggests that positive and responsive interactions with adults (parents, teachers, child-care providers) contribute to regulation of emotional experience and social behavior, the development of skills in social interactions, and emotional understanding (Birch & Ladd, 1998; Connell & Wellborn, 1991; Eccles, 1993; Howes, 2000; Howes, Matheson, & Hamilton, 1994; Pianta, 1999; Wentzel, 2002). Confirming this perspective are results indicating that exposure to positive classroom climates and sensitive teachers is linked to

greater self-regulation among elementary and middle school students (Skinner, Zimmer-Gembeck, & Connell, 1998), greater teacher-rated social competence (Burchinal et al., 2005; Howes, 2000; Pianta et al., 2002), and decreases in mother-reported internalizing problems from 54 months to the end of the first grade (NICHD ECCRN, 2003).

From a somewhat different theoretical perspective, teachers' emotional (06) support directly provides students with experiences that foster motivational and learning-related processes important to academic functioning (Crosnoe, Johnson, & Elder, 2004; Greenberg et al., 2003; Gregory & Weinstein, 2004; Pianta et al., 2002; Rimm-Kaufman et al., in press; Roeser et al., 2000; Zins, Bloodworth, Weissberg, & Walberg, 2004). Theories of motivation suggest that students who experience sensitive, responsive, and positive interactions with teachers perceive them as more supportive and are more motivated within the academic contexts of schooling (Connell & Wellborn, 1991; Deci & Ryan, 1985; Eccles, 1993). In the early grades, Pianta et al. (2002) found that when teachers offered a more child-centered climate, kindergarten children were observed to be more often on-task and engaged in learning. Among older students, perceptions of positive relatedness to teachers predict gains in student engagement over the course of the school year (Furrer & Skinner, 2003), increased motivation to learn (Roeser et al., 2000), and greater academic achievement (Crosnoe et al., 2004; Gregory & Weinstein, 2004). Consistent with this link between motivation and support from adults, teacher support was related to sixth graders' school and class-related interests and pursuit of social goals (Wentzel, 2002), which in turn predicted pursuit of social goals and grades in the seventh grade. For children at risk of problems in school, Noam and Herman's (2002) school-based prevention approach emphasizes the primary importance of relationships with a school-based mentor (Noam, Warner, & Van Dyken, 2001), based explicitly on the rationale that such relationships function as resources and resilience mechanisms in counteracting the effects of risk mechanisms attributable to problems in family relationships.

Notwithstanding the importance of relationships and social support, the (07) nature and quality of instruction is of paramount importance for the value of classroom experience that is intended to produce gains in learning; in elementary school, instruction is under great scrutiny as a result of standards and performance evaluations (Pianta, in press). Although the apparent dichotomy between child-centered and direct instruction has for some years dominated discussions of learning in the early grades (see Stipek et al., 1998), there is accumulating evidence that teachers' instructional interactions with children have the greatest value for students' performance when they are focused, direct, intentional, and characterized by feedback loops involving student performance (Dolezal, Welsh, Pressley, & Vincent, 2003; Juel, 1996; Meyer, Wardrop, Hastings, & Linn, 1993; Pianta et al., 2002; Torgesen, 2002). Torgesen (2002) provides an explicit example of this type of instruction applied to the area of reading by suggesting three primary ways in which everyday teaching can contribute to growth in reading skills: the provision of explicit teaching experiences and practice (i.e., phonemic skills, vocabulary); more productive classroom time in which there are more opportunities for teaching and learning; and intensive scaffolding and feedback to students about their progress. The value of intentional, focused interaction and feedback is not limited to reading, but appears to be a key component in other skill domains such as writing (Matsumura, Patthey-Chavez, Valdes, & Garnier, 2002) that may extend to cognition and higher order thinking (Dolezal et al., 2003).

In addition, these instructional inputs are also associated with more pos- (08) itive and fewer negative interactions between students and teachers, and higher levels of attention and task-oriented behavior (NICHD ECCRN, 2002a; Pianta et al., 2002). Yet, as was the case for emotional support in classrooms, large-scale studies document great variation in the frequency and quality of these instructional procedures within early elementary school classrooms (Meyer et al., 1993; NICHD ECCRN, 2002a, in press). For example, within the NICHD Study of Early Child Care sample (NICHD ECCRN, 2002b, in press), teachers provided specific academic instruction in an average of 8% of all observed intervals over the course of a morning-long observation. However, the range was remarkable, with some classrooms providing no explicit instruction and others providing this instruction in almost 70% of observed intervals. This variability provides an opportunity to examine ways in which exposure to these classroom processes may impact student achievement.

(09)   Taken together, research on the nature and quality of early schooling experiences provides emerging evidence that classroom environments and teacher behaviors are associated in a "value-added" sense with student outcomes. Yet, until recently, few researchers have specifically examined the possibility that these everyday processes in elementary school classrooms may help close (or increase) the gap in student achievement observed among students at risk of school failure because of demographic characteristics (low income, minority status) or functional risks such as serious behavioral and emotional problems. Although there is increasing evidence from well-designed and highly controlled studies that school-based interventions that prescribe certain desired teacher–child interactions can succeed in ameliorating some risks (Catalano et al., 2003; Greenberg et al., 2001; Ialongo et al., 1999; Walker, Stiller, Severson, Feil, & Golly, 1998), there is little available evidence on whether features of classrooms and child–teacher interactions such as emotional or instruction support, present in everyday classroom interactions in naturally varying samples, are sufficiently potent to counteract risk for school failure.

Everyday Interactions and Risk for Early School Failure

(10)   Recent evidence from developmentally informed studies of naturally occurring variation in classroom environments directly tests the hypothesis that everyday experiences within elementary classrooms may moderate outcomes for children at risk (Peisner-Feinberg et al., 2001). In one such study, Morrison and Connor (2002) demonstrate that children at risk of reading difficulties at the beginning of the first grade (identified on the basis of test scores) benefited from high levels of teacher-directed explicit language instruction—the more teacher-directed, explicit instruction they received, the higher were their word-decoding skills at the end of the first grade. In contrast, teacher-directed explicit instruction made no difference in decoding skills for children with already high skills on this dimension upon school entry. These highly skilled children made the strongest gains in classrooms, with more child-led literacy-related activities.

(11)   In another study providing evidence of the moderating effect of teachers' classroom behaviors on outcomes for at-risk children, Rimm-Kaufman et al. (2002) examined whether teacher sensitivity predicted kindergarten children's behavior for groups of socially bold and wary children, with the bold children demonstrating high levels of off-task behavior and negative interactions with peers and teachers. Although there was no relation between teachers' sensitivity and child classroom behavior among the socially wary children, socially bold children who had more sensitive teachers were more self-reliant and displayed fewer negative and off-task behaviors than did bold children with less sensitive teachers. Similarly, two recent studies suggest that student–teacher conflict is a stronger predictor of later problems for children who display significant acting out behaviors than for their peers who do not display these behavior problems (Hamre & Pianta, 2001; Ladd & Burgess, 2001). Taken together, these studies suggest that positive social and instructional experiences within the school setting may help reduce children's risk, while negative interactions between teachers and children may

be particularly problematic for those children displaying the highest risk of school failure. In the present study, we follow and extend the work of Morrison and Connor (2002) and Rimm-Kaufman et al. (2002) to examine effects of two dimensions of classroom process (instructional and emotional quality) on moderating the association(s) between two forms of risk for failure in achievement and social adjustment in the first grade.

Defining School-Based Risk

Although conceptualizations of risk vary, two central categories of children's (12) risk for early school failure relate to *demographic* and *functional* risks. Prior to entering school, it is largely family and demographic factors that place children at risk of failure. One of the most robust of these demographic risk indicators is low maternal education (e.g., Christian, Morrison, & Bryant, 1998; Ferguson, Jimerson, & Dalton, 2001; NICHD ECCRN, 2002a; Peisner-Feinberg et al., 2001; Shonkoff & Phillips, 2000). One reason posited for this is that children of mothers with low levels of education are less likely to be exposed to frequent and rich language and literacy stimulation (Bowman, Donovan, & Burns, 2001; Christian et al., 1998; Hart & Risley, 1995; U.S. Department of Education, 2000) and thus may come to kindergarten with fewer academic skills (Pianta & McCoy, 1997). These early gaps are often maintained throughout children's school careers (Alexander et al., 2001; Entwisle & Hayduk, 1988; Ferguson et al., 2001).

In addition to demographic factors that signal risk, indicators reflecting (13) children's general functioning and adaptation in the classroom as they enter school (behavioral, attention, social, and academic problems) are established predictors of success or failure in the next grade(s). Children identified by their teachers as displaying difficulties in these domains in the early school years are at higher risk of problems throughout their school careers (Alexander et al., 2001; Flanagan et al., 2003; Hamre & Pianta, 2001; Ladd, Buhs, & Troop, 2002; Lewis, Sugai, & Colvin, 1998). Although problems in individual domains of functioning predict future difficulties, research suggests that the accumulation of multiple risks is typically a much stronger indicator of later problems (Gutman, Sameroff, & Cole, 2003; Seifer, Sameroff, Baldwin, & Baldwin, 1992) and therefore our approach to conceptualizing and assessing functional risk will rely on multiple indicators.

Current Study

The current study was designed to extend work related to school effects (14) by following children identified in kindergarten as being at risk of school failure and examining whether the classroom environment to which they were exposed during the first grade moderated these risks by the end of the first grade. Rutter and Maughan (2002) suggest that effectively testing environmental influences on child development requires attending to several methodological issues. First, they suggest using longitudinal data to measure change within individuals. We were interested in assessing achievement and relational functioning in first grade as a function of the support these children received from teachers; therefore, we needed to adjust for previous performance on these outcomes. Ideally, we would adjust for performance at the beginning of the first-grade year; however, because multiple assessments were not available within the first-grade year, we adjusted for earlier performance on the outcomes (completed at either 54 months or kindergarten). Secondly, Rutter and Maughan (2002) suggest using some form of a *natural experiment* that "pulls apart variables that ordinarily go together" (p. 46). Within this study, the classroom process itself served as the natural experiment, in which children with differing risk backgrounds in kindergarten were placed in first-grade classrooms offering varying levels of emotional and instructional support. Their third recommendation suggests quantified measurement of the postulated causal factor; here we use observations of

Selection of a problem—identification of children in kindergarten as being at risk of school failure and examining whether the classroom environment to which they were exposed during first grade moderated these risks by the end of first grade.

Classification of research by approach— "a natural experiment"—or causal– comparative research.

Causal–comparative research "grouping variable" is the classroom process offering varying levels of emotional and instructional support.

teachers' instructional and emotional support conducted within classrooms, a notable difference from most previous research on classroom effects, which relies on structural features of the classroom or teacher-reported practices. Two of Rutter and Maughan's (2002) last three recommendations, testing for a dose response gradient and controlling for social selection, initial level, and self-perpetuating effects, were also attended to within this study. The last recommendation, explicitly testing the hypothesized mechanism against some competing explanations, was beyond the scope of this study, although the implications of not testing competing explanations are addressed in the discussion.

(15) Because of an interest in examining both academic and social functioning, we examined two major outcomes—performance on an individually administered, standardized achievement battery, and first-grade teacher ratings of conflict with the student. Although student–teacher conflict could be viewed as a classroom process, when assessed via the teachers' perspective, it is best conceptualized as an outcome derived in part from the teachers' social or instructional interactions toward the child. Teachers' rating of their relationship with children measure the extent to which students are able to successfully use the teacher as a resource in the classroom. Thus, although teachers' interactions with students are expected to influence relationships in important ways, these relationships are themselves key indicators of school adaptation. This conceptualization of relationships as outcomes was validated by a study showing that kindergarten teachers' perceptions of conflict with students were stronger predictors of behavioral functioning through the eighth grade than were these same teachers' ratings of behavior problems (Hamre & Pianta, 2001).

> Dependent variables are "performance on an individually administered standardized achievement battery" and "first-grade teacher ratings of conflict with the student."

(16) Globally, we expected that children in the risk groups would be more likely than children at low risk to benefit from placement in classrooms offering high levels of support and that placement in high-quality classrooms would help at-risk students catch up to their low-risk peers. More specific hypotheses require a consideration of the mechanisms through which we expect the risk factors to operate. For example, children whose mothers have low levels of education tend to have less exposure to pre-academic experiences within the home (Bowman et al., 2001; U.S. Department of Education, 2000); thus, we expected that these children would benefit academically from high levels of instructional support within the classroom. In contrast, children displaying behavioral and social problems in kindergarten may require higher levels of emotional support to adjust to the demands of the first grade. However, by responding to children's social and emotional needs, teachers may not only help children adapt socially, but may allow these children to more successfully access the instructional aspects of classrooms; thus, we expected that high levels of emotional support would be associated with more positive academic experiences and lower levels of teacher–child conflict for children displaying multiple functional risks in kindergarten.

Method

Participants

(17) Children included in this study took part in the NICHD Study of Early Child Care. The children's mothers were recruited from hospitals located in or near Little Rock, AK; Irvine, CA; Lawrence, KS; Boston, MA; Philadelphia, PA; Pittsburgh, PA; Charlottesville, VA; Morganton, NC; Seattle, WA; and Madison, WI. In 1991, research staff visited 8,986 mothers giving birth in these hospitals. Of these mothers, 5,416 met eligibility criteria and agreed to be contacted after returning home from the hospital. A randomly selected subgroup (with procedures to ensure economic, educational, and ethnic diversity) were contacted and enrolled in the study. This resulted in a sample of 1,364 families

> Scientific method, Selection of a sample.

with healthy newborns. Details of this selection procedure are published in the study manuals (NICHD ECCRN, 1993).

Classroom observations were conducted in the children's second year of (18) school, which for the majority was the first grade. Of the original sample of 1,364 children, 910 had complete data and were included in the current study. Analyses comparing the children included in this investigation with the entire sample indicate selected attrition: among all children who began the study, White children and those with mothers with higher education were more likely to have data collected in the first grade, $\chi^2(3, N = 1,364) = 18.14, p < .001$ and $\chi^2(3, N = 1,364) = 16.75, p < .001$, respectively. Among the children in the present study, 49% were female. The majority were White ($n = 723$), followed in frequency by African American ($n = 96$), Hispanic ($n = 50$), and Other ($n = 39$). Maternal education ranged from 7 to 21 years, with a mean of 14.45 years. The income-to-needs ratio, used to measure income relative to the number of household members, was average across the period of study (54 months, kindergarten, and first grade) and ranged from .15 to 33.77, with an average of 3.73. These factors indicate a largely nonpoverty sample, although there was considerable range.

Overview of Data Collection

Children in this study were followed from birth through the first grade. (19) Maternal education and child ethnicity were reported when children were one-month old. Child outcomes and measures of classroom process were collected in the spring of the children's first-grade year. The 827 classrooms were distributed across 747 schools, in 295 public school districts, in 32 states. Earlier assessments, conducted when the children were 54 months and in kindergarten, provided measures of children's risk status as well as a measure of children's prior functioning on the outcomes of interest. Further documentation about all data collection procedures, psychometric properties of measures, and descriptions of how composites were derived are documented in the Manuals of Operations of the NICHD Study of Early Child Care (NICHD ECCRN, 1993).

Risk Indicators

Children in this study were grouped based on their status on *functional* and (20) *demographic* indicators of risk. Functional indicators of risk included measures of children's attention, externalizing behavior, social skills, and academic competence. The last three measures were collected through teacher report when the study children were in kindergarten. Unfortunately, individual child assessments were not conducted when children were in kindergarten. Because of an interest in including a non-teacher-reported risk variable and based on data showing the links between sustained attention and school failure (Gordon, Mettelman, & Irwin, 1994), the attention risk variable used in this investigation was collected during child assessments conducted when children were 54 months old. Students whose mothers had less than a 4-year college degree were placed in the demographic risk group. Information on the measures and procedures used to identify children at risk of school failure is provided below.

Functional Risk

Sustained attention. Sustained attention was assessed using a continuous (21) performance task (CPT) based on the young children's version described by Mirsky, Anthony, Duncan, Aheani, and Kellam (1991). This measure consisted of a computer-generated task in which children are asked to push a button each time a target stimulus appears. The number of omission errors was used as the unit of analysis for this study. The CPT has adequate test–retest reliability ($r = .65 - .74$) and has high content and predictive validity (Halperin, Sharman, Greenblat, & Schwartz, 1991).

(22)   *Externalizing behaviors.* Externalizing behaviors were assessed with the teacher report form (TRF; Achenbach, 1991), a widely used measure of problem behaviors that has been standardized on large samples of children. This measure lists 100 problem behaviors and has teachers rate them as not true (0), somewhat true (1), or very true (2) of the student. The externalizing problems standard score was used for these analyses. This scale contains teachers' reports on children's aggressive (e.g., gets in many fights; cruelty, bullying, or meanness to others; physically attacks people), attention (e.g., cannot concentrate; fails to finish things he/she starts), and defiant behaviors (e.g., defiant, talks back to staff; disrupts class discipline). The reliability and validity of the TRF has been widely established (see Bérubé & Achenbach, 2001, for a review).

(23)   *Social skills and academic competence.* Students' social skills and academic competence were assessed with the social skills rating system–teacher form (SSRS; Gresham & Elliot, 1990). This measure consists of three scales: social skills, problems behaviors, and academic competence. Because the TRF is a more established measure of problem behaviors, only the social skills and academic competence scales were used in these analyses. The social skills composite asks teachers to rate the frequency of classroom behaviors (0 = never, 1 = sometimes, two = very often) in three areas related to positive social adjustment in school settings: cooperation (e.g., paying attention to instructions, putting away materials properly), assertion (e.g., starting conversations with peers, helping peers with classroom tasks), and self-control (e.g., responding to peer pressure appropriately, controlling temper). Within this sample, the coefficient α for the social skills composite was .93. The academic competence composite asks teachers to judge children's academic or learning behaviors in the classroom on a 5-point scale that corresponds to the percentage clusters of the students in the class (1 = lowest 10%, 5 = highest 10%). Within this sample, the coefficient α for this scale was .95. Scores are standardized based on norms from a large, national sample of children. The SSRS has sufficient reliability and has been found to correlate with many other measures of adjustment (Gresham & Elliot, 1990).

(24)   *Functional risk status.* Students' risk status was determined for each of these four indicators. Children with standardized scores at least one standard deviation below the mean (85 or lower) on the social skills and academic competence scales were placed in the social risk ($n = 83$; 10%) and academic risk groups ($n = 112$; 13%), respectively. Similarly, children who fell one standard deviation above the mean on the number of omission errors on the CPT were included in the attention risk group ($n = 144$; 17%). Consistent with recommendations in the TRF manual (Achenbach, 1991), children in the externalizing problems risk group had T scores at or above 62 on the externalizing problems factor ($n = 80$; 9%). Given previous research indicating that multiple, rather than isolated, risks are most predictive of later problems (Gutman et al., 2003; Seifer et al., 1992), each child was given a risk score created by summing the number of risks. The children were then split into two groups, those with zero or one risk ($n = 811$; 89%), referred to within the remainder of this report as displaying "low functional risk," and those with multiple risks ($n = 99$; 11%), referred to as displaying "high functional risk." Among children in the low functional risk group, 73% had no risk factors and 25% had one risk factor. Among children in the high functional risk group, 73% had two risk factors, 21% had three risk factors, and 6% had all four risk factors. Among this high functional risk group, academic problems were most common (72%), followed by social skills problems (63%), attention problems (59%), and externalizing problems (36%).

Demographic Risk

(25)   We were also interested in following the trajectory of children who have typically been identified as at risk of school failure—children whose mothers

have low levels of education. Among this sample, 249 children (27%) had mothers with less than a 4-year college degree. This cutpoint was chosen to provide an adequate sample size and is validated as a risk indicator in later analyses; implications of the moderate level of risks in this sample are included in the discussion. Ways in which school processes may moderate this risk factor were hypothesized to differ from the functional risk factor; thus, rather than composting demographic risk with those manifest in child behavior or skills, demographic risk was maintained as a separate indicator. Although low maternal education children were more likely than other children to display functional risks, the majority (78%) of those with low maternal education were in the low functional risk group.

Child Outcomes

Achievement. Children's achievement was assessed with the Woodcock–Johnson Psycho-educational Battery-Revised (WJ-R; Woodcock & Johnson, 1989), a standardized measure of young children's academic achievement with excellent psychometric properties (Woodcock & Johnson, 1989). At each assessment point, several subtests were given out of the cognitive and achievement batteries. The cognitive battery included an assessment of long-term retrieval (Memory for Names), short-term memory (Memory for Sentences), auditory processing (Incomplete Words), and comprehensive knowledge (Picture Vocabulary). The achievement battery included measures of reading (Letter–Word Identification and Word Attack) and mathematics (Applied Problems). Memory for Names and Word Attack were only administered in first grade; all other tests were given at both 54 months and first grade. Because of the high levels of association between measures of cognitive ability and achievement, all subtests were composited at each time point, and are referred to for the remainder of this report as achievement scores. The coefficient α at 54 months was .80, and at first grade it was .83. Descriptives on the achievement battery are provided in Table 1.

(26)

> Scientific method, Execution of research procedures. Data collection strategies are used to measure three dependent variables: (1) children's achievement, (2) student-teacher relationships, and (3) classroom processes.

Student–Teacher Relationships. Children's relational functioning was assessed with the Student–Teacher Relationship Scale (Pianta, 2001), a 28-item rating scale, using a Likert-type format, designed to assess teachers' perceptions of their relationship with a particular student. This scale has been used extensively in studies of preschool-age and elementary-age children (e.g., Birch & Ladd, 1997, 1998; Hamre & Pianta, 2001; Howes & Hamilton, 1992). The conflict scale assesses the degree of negative interactions and emotions involving the teacher and child and contains items such as, "This child easily becomes angry at me" and "This child and I always seem to be struggling with each other." Coefficient α for conflict was .93 among this sample. Descriptives on the conflict scores are provided in Table 1.

(27)

Table 1

Mean (Standard Deviation) on Academic Achievement (Woodcock–Johnson) and Student–Teacher Conflict by Time and Risk Status

	Kindergarten functional risk		Demographic risk (maternal education)	
	Low (n = 881)	High (n = 99)	Low (n = 661)	High (n = 249)
Woodcock–Johnson composite				
54 months	100.40 (10.79)	87.81 (10.42)	101.56 (10.50)	92.33 (11.24)
First	106.45 (9.78)	94.93 (10.42)	107.39 (9.58)	99.37 (10.54)
Student–teacher conflict				
K	9.80 (4.47)	15.74 (7.15)	10.00 (4.76)	11.74 (6.05)
First	10.28 (4.63)	14.59 (6.19)	10.32 (4.67)	11.91 (5.64)

(28) **Classroom Process.** Classroom process was measured using the Classroom Observation System for First Grade (COS-1; NICHD ECCRN, 2002b). Trained data collectors observed each classroom on 1 day during the spring of the first-grade year. Classrooms were observed for approximately 3 hr during a morning-long period beginning with the official start of the school day on a day the teacher identified as being focused on academic activities. Observers made global ratings of classroom quality and teacher behavior using a set of 7-point rating scales. Some of the scales focused on global classroom quality and others focused specifically on the teacher's interaction with the study child. Global ratings of classroom-level dimensions included overcontrol, positive emotional climate, negative emotional climate, effective classroom management, literacy instruction, evaluative feedback, instructional conversation, and encouragement of child responsibility. Rating scales for the teacher's behavior toward the target child included sensitivity/responsivity, instrusiveness/overcontrol, and detachment/disengagement. A summary of these ratings is provided in Table 2. A rating of 1 was assigned when that code was "uncharacteristic," a 3 was assigned when the description was "minimally characteristic," a 5 was assigned when the description of the code was "very

Table 2

Summary of COS-1 Rating of Emotional and Instructional Climate

Composite Construct	Description (at high end)
Emotional support	
Teacher sensitivity	The sensitive teacher is tuned in to the child and manifests awareness of the child's needs, moods, interests, and capabilities, and allows this awareness to guide his/her behavior with the child
Intrusiveness (reversed)	An intrusive teacher imposes his/her own agenda on the child and interactions are adult-driven, rather than child-centered
Detachment (reversed)	A detached teacher shows a lack of emotional involvement and rarely joins in the child's activities or conversations
Positive climate	A positive classroom is characterized by pleasant conversations, spontaneous laughter, and exclamations of excitement. Teachers demonstrate positive regard and warmth in interactions with students
Classroom management	In a well-managed classroom, the teacher has clear yet flexible expectations related to the classroom rules and routines. Children understand and follow rules and the teacher does not have to employ many control techniques
Negative climate (reversed)	A negative classroom is characterized by hostile, angry, punitive, and controlling interactions in which the teacher displays negative regard, disapproval, criticism, and annoyance with children
Over-control (reversed)	The over-controlled classroom is rigidly structured and children are not given options for activities but instead must participate in very regimented ways
Instructional support	
Literacy instruction	This rating captures the amount of literacy instruction in the classroom. At the high end, the teacher frequently reads and teaches phonics and comprehension
Evaluative feedback	This rating focuses on the quality of verbal evaluation of children's work comments or ideas. At the high end feedback focuses on learning, mastery, developing understanding, personal improvement, effort, persistence, or trying new strategies
Instructional conversation	This scale focuses on the quality of cognitive skills or concepts elicited during the teacher-led discussions. At the high end children are encouraged to engage in conversations and expand on their ideas and perceptions of events. Teachers ask open-ended questions such as "what do you think?"
Encouragement of child responsibility	Children in classrooms high on this scale are encouraged to take on jobs, asked to offer solutions to classroom problems, and take responsibility for putting away materials, etc.

characteristic" of the classroom, and a 7 was assigned under circumstances in which the code was "extremely characteristic" of the observed classroom or teacher–child interactional pattern.

Observers from all 10 sites trained on practice videotapes using a standardized manual that provided extensive descriptions of codes and anchor points. They trained on these videotaped observations prior to attending a centralized training workshop. After the training workshop, coders returned to their sites, conducted pilot observations, and trained on one to two more videotaped cases. All observers had to pass a videotaped reliability test involving six cases. Criteria for passing were an 80% match (with 1 scale point) on the global rating scales. All coders passed at these levels on a reliability test before being certified to conduct observations in the field. (29)

These scales were factor analyzed and averaged into two composite indicators of the classroom environment: emotional support and instructional support. The emotional support composite included ratings of over-control (reflected), positive emotional climate, negative emotional climate (reflected), effective classroom management, teacher sensitivity, intrusiveness (reflected), and detachment (reflected). The instructional support composite included ratings of literacy instruction, evaluative feedback, instructional conversation, and encouragement of child responsibility. These two composites are moderately associated with one another ($r = .57$). Table 2 provides a summary of these scales. For details on these composites and the training of observers, refer to NICHD ECCRN (2002b). Of note is the fact that, although only one observation was made for the majority of classrooms (one visit per child enrolled in the study), for almost 60 classrooms there was more than one child enrolled and hence more than one observation was conducted. For these classrooms, the correlations between pairs of the global ratings described above was, on average, higher than .70, indicating that these ratings reflect quite stable features of the classroom environment (NICHD ECCRN, 2004). (30)

The COS-1 composites were used to categorize classrooms into offering high, moderate, and low support (using 33% cutpoints). We used these cut-offs, rather than continuous measures of classroom process, because of our interest in creating a natural experiment and decided on cutting the sample in thirds to capture adequate range while allowing for ease of interpretation and analysis. For emotional support, the 303 classrooms in the Low category ranged from a score of 15.33 to 38.83 ($M = 33.15$; $SD = 5.16$), the 313 in the Moderate category ranged from a score of 39 to 44 ($M = 41.83$; $SD = 1.58$), and the 294 in the High category ranged from a score of 44.33 to 49.00 ($M = 46.53$; $SD = 1.45$). For instructional support, the 289 classrooms in the Low category ranged from a score of 4 to 13 ($M = 11.13$; $SD = 1.76$), the 328 in the Moderate category ranged from a score of 14 to 17 ($M = 15.41$; $SD = 1.07$), and the 293 in the High category ranged from a score of 18 to 28 ($M = 20.47$; $SD = 2.15$). (31)

Results

Data Analysis Plan

In order to establish whether instructional and emotional support in the first grade may moderate risk, we first had to establish two preconditions: (1) the existence of a natural experiment, in which children with varying risks backgrounds in kindergarten would sort into first-grade classrooms offering different levels of emotional and instructional support, and (2) whether the hypothesized risk factors were associated with poorer outcomes in first grade. The first precondition was assessed through examining the distribution of children in each risk group into classrooms offering high, moderate, and low support. The second precondition was assessed by conducting ANCOVAs in which risk status was used to predict first-grade outcomes, after adjusting for children's previous performance on these outcomes measures. (32)

Scientific method: Analysis of the data

(33)   Following these analyses, we turned to answering the main questions of this study: does classroom support moderate children's risk of school failure? First, the instructional and emotional support variables were entered into the ANCOVA models to assess whether classroom support had a main effect on children's outcomes. Next, following the recommendations of Kraemer, Stice, Kazdin, Offord, and Kupfer (2001) regarding testing the moderation of risk, a series of interactions were added to the model to test whether functional and demographic risks were moderated by classroom support variables. The relatively small *n*s among the risk groups provides for unbalanced ANCOVA designs. This situation may inflate Type I errors and thus increase the likelihood that true effects are not statistically significant (Keselman, Cribbie, & Wilcox, 2002). Although not ideal, this analytic approach was determined to be most appropriate for testing the natural experiment described above and provides a stringent test of potential effects for placement in high-quality classrooms. Further details on these analyses are provided below.

Selection into High- and Low-Support Classrooms

(34)   The distribution of classroom support among the risk groups is presented in Table 3. Children displaying high functional risk in kindergarten were as likely as those with low functional risk to be in classrooms offering high instructional or emotional support. Children of mothers with less than a 4-year college degree were somewhat more likely than their peers to be in first-grade classrooms offering low instructional or emotional support. Despite this differential placement based on maternal education levels, there were enough low and high maternal education students placed in each of the three levels of classrooms to exploit a natural experiment. The implication of this differential placement will be considered in the discussion.

Risks as Indicators of First-Grade Achievement and Relational Functioning Achievement

(35)   In order to provide a robust test of associations between risk and outcomes, we adjusted for children's prior scores on outcomes. Descriptive information on both previous and first-grade outcomes are presented for each risk group in Table 1. Consistent with hypotheses, results of ANCOVAs suggest that after adjusting for children's achievement at 54 months, children whose mothers had less than a 4-year college degree and those with high functional risk in kindergarten had lower achievement scores at the end of first grade (see Table 4). This suggests that not only do children at risk start school behind their low-risk peers, but the gap increases by the end of the first-grade year.

Table 3

Percentage Placement in First-Grade Classroom Support (Instructional and Emotional) by Risk Status

	Kindergarten functional risk			Demographic risk (maternal education)		
	Low ($n = 881$)	High ($n = 99$)	χ^2	Low ($n = 661$)	High ($n = 249$)	χ^2
Instructional support						
Low	31.6	33.3	0.28	28.6	40.2	11.76**
Moderate	36.5	32.3		37.1	33.3	
High	31.9	34.3		34.3	26.5	
Emotional support						
Low	32.4	40.4	3.54	29.8	42.6	13.87**
Moderate	35.3	27.3		35.6	31.3	
High	32.3	32.3		34.6	26.1	

*$p < .05$. ** $p < .01$. *** $p < .001$.

Table 4

Results of ANCOVAs Predicting First-Grade Achievement, Controlling for Previous Performance, From Risk and Classroom Process

	Achievement Woodcock–Johnson[a] ($n = 908$)				Teacher–child conflict[b] ($n = 881$)			
	Main effects		Moderation		Main effects		Moderation	
	F	Partial η^2	**F**	Partial η^2	**F**	Partial η^2	**F**	Partial η^2
Corrected model	152.17***	.57	78.45***	.58	31.38***	.22	22.03***	.23
Intercept	389.85***	.30	389.39***	.30	415.75***	.32	396.41***	.31
54 months WJ/K conflict	774.03***	.46	789.39***	.47	103.68***	.11	106.14***	.11
Female	12.80***	.01	13.59***	.01	20.77***	.02	20.64***	.02
Risk factors								
Maternal education— some college or less	8.97**	.01	8.335**	.01	0.74	.00	0.77	.00
High functional risk—kindergarten	14.92***	.02	13.20***	.02	23.58***	.03	19.27***	.02
Classroom process								
Instructional support	0.34	.00	0.13	.00	0.03	.00	0.60	.00
Emotional support	1.29	.00	3.20*	.01	2.30	.00	5.69**	.01
Risk: classroom process								
Maternal education: instructional support			6.68**	.02				
Maternal education: emotional support			1.82	.00				
Functional risk: instructional support			1.22	.00			0.69	.00
Functional risk: emotional support			4.57*	.01			3.62*	.01

*$p \le .05$. ** $p \le .01$. *** $p \le .001$.

To test whether these risks may operate differently for boys and girls, (36) interactions between each risk and child gender were initially included in the ANCOVA model. Because none of these interactions were statistically significant at the $p < .05$ level, they were removed from the model.

Relational Functioning

An identical set of analyses was performed to assess children's relational (37) adjustment at the end of the first grade. Risk status was used to predict first-grade teachers' ratings of conflict with children, adjusting for kindergarten teacher ratings on this measure. Children in the high functional risk group had higher levels of teacher-rated conflict at the end of the first grade (see Table 4). Low maternal education did not arise as a significant risk factor for poor relational adjustment. As in the case of analyses on achievement, associations between risk and outcomes were not different between boys and girls and therefore these interactions were not included in the final model.

These analyses provide support for the conceptualization of risk within (38) this study. Even after controlling for previous performance, children at risk were not performing as well by the end of the first grade as were their peers without these risks, suggesting that these are indicators of increasing gaps between children at risk and those who are not at risk. Furthermore, the analyses provide evidence of the independence of each domain of risk; in the case of achievement, both functional and demographic risk independently predicted poorer outcomes. Only functional risk predicted higher rates of conflict with first-grade teachers.

Role of Instructional and Emotional Support in Moderating Risk Achievement

(39)   Results presented in Table 4 suggest that neither support variable had a significant main effect on children's achievement. Because both risk indicators significantly predicted poorer achievement in the first grade, interactions between maternal education and functional risk status with each of the classroom support variables were entered into the final ANCOVA model. The two-way interactions between instructional support and maternal education and between emotional support and functional risk status both explained significant variance in the final model (Table 4). Effect sizes (partial η^2) were small; however, an examination of the estimated marginal means, presented in Figures 1 and 2, suggests that differences were meaningful, particularly considering that these models controlled for previous performance on very stable measures of academic functioning and are attributable to a relatively short period of time, that is, 1 school year. Figure 1 shows that, consistent with hypotheses, among children whose mothers had less than a 4-year college degree, those in classrooms with moderate and high instructional support had achievement performance in the first grade (controlling for 54-month achievement) equal to their peers whose mothers had more education. In contrast, children at high demographic risk who were in low instructionally supportive classrooms were performing significantly below their peers with low demographic risk.

(40)   The main effect for the presence of high functional risk on achievement was moderated by the level of emotional support in the first-grade classroom (Table 4). Among children displaying high functional risk in kindergarten, those who were in highly emotionally supportive first-grade classrooms had similar scores on the first-grade Woodcock–Johnson as did their peers with low functional risk (see Figure 2). Children displaying high functional risk in kindergarten who were in low or moderately emotionally supportive classrooms had lower Woodcock–Johnson scores than did children in the low functional risk group.

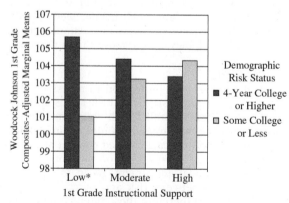

Figure 1.   Woodcock–Johnson first-grade composites, adjusted for 54-month performance, by demographic risk status and first-grade instructional support.

*Estimated means at this level have 95% confidence intervals that do not overlap.

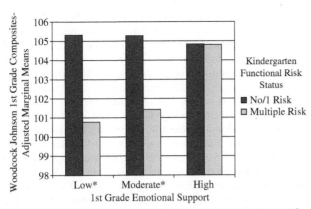

Figure 2. Woodcock–Johnson first-grade composites, adjusted for 54-month performance, by kindergarten functional risk status and first-grade emotional support.

*Estimated means at this level have 95% confidence intervals that do not overlap.

Relational Functioning. As in predicting achievement, classroom support variables did not have a main effect on changes in student–teacher conflict ratings from kindergarten to first grade (Table 4). However, in support of hypotheses regarding the moderating role of classroom process on risk, the interaction between emotional support and child functional risk explained significant variance in the final model. Again, effect sizes (partial η^2) were small. Among children displaying high functional risk in kindergarten, those in highly or moderately emotionally supportive first-grade classrooms had similar levels of conflict with teachers (adjusted for kindergarten conflict levels) as did their low-risk peers, while high-risk children in low emotional support classrooms had higher levels of conflict with teachers (Figure 3).

(41)

> Scientific method: drawing and stating conclusions: (1) The study provides evidence that across two important domains of child functioning in the early grades of school, (a) achievement and (b) relationships with teachers, the quality of everyday classroom interactions in the form of instructional and emotional support moderates the risk of early school failure.

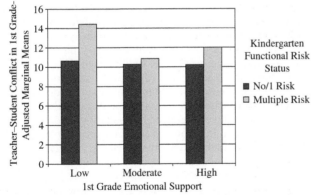

Figure 3. Teacher–student conflict in first grade, adjusted for kindergarten conflict, by kindergarten functional risk status and first-grade emotional support.

*Estimated means have 95% confidence intervals that do not overlap.

Discussion

The current study provides evidence that across two important domains of child functioning in the early grades of school, achievement, and relationships with teachers, the quality of everyday classroom interactions in the form of instructional and emotional support moderates the risk of early school

(42)

failure. In contrast to much of the research on school effectiveness, which has focused on structural indicators of classroom quality such as class size and teacher–student ratio (Rutter & Maughan, 2002), this study adds to the growing body of work documenting ways in which specific classroom processes facilitate children's development (e.g., Connell & Wellborn, 1991; Hamre & Pianta, 2001; Ladd & Burgess, 2001; Morrison & Connor, 2002; Peisner-Feinberg et al., 2001; Stevenson & Lee, 1990; Wentzel, 2002).

(43)   Children within this study who were identified as at risk of school failure on the basis of displaying multiple problems within the kindergarten classroom, as well as children whose mothers had less than a 4-year college degree, all displayed lower levels of achievement at the end of first grade than did their low-risk peers, even after adjusting for achievement performance at 54 months. These findings are consistent with others that suggest that children at risk of school failure may fall further behind academically with each successive year in school (Alexander et al., 2001; Entwisle & Hayduk, 1988). Yet not all children displaying early risk displayed academic problems at the end of the first grade, and both instructional and emotional support offered by first-grade teachers may be important in closing the gap in achievement between high-risk and low-risk children.

(44)   Consistent with recent views of effective teaching that focus on explicitness and intentionality (Dolezal et al., 2003; Matsumura et al., 2002; Morrison & Connor, 2002), high-quality instructional support in this study was observed when teachers made frequent and effective use of literacy instruction, evaluative feedback, instructional conversations, and encouragement of child responsibility. Among children in this study whose mothers had less than a 4-year college degree, those who were placed in first-grade classrooms offering high-to-moderate instructional support displayed similar levels of achievement at the end of the first grade as their peers with more educated mothers. In contrast, students with less educated mothers who were placed in classrooms offering low instructional support displayed significantly lower achievement at the end of the first grade than their low-risk peers, even after adjusting for prior (54 months) performance on the standardized achievement battery. Thus, just as Morrison and Connor (2002) found evidence that explicit teaching benefited students with reading difficulties more than it did students who did not display these early problems, this study suggests that focused literacy instruction, high-quality feedback, and the engagement of students in discussion of academic concepts may be particularly important in facilitating achievement gains for children with fewer socioeconomic resources. Stevenson and Lee (1990) report the value of similar focused, active teaching for achievement in older elementary students. This finding is also consistent with research on preschool settings, which generally finds the most significant cognitive effects of high-quality child care among children of fewer socioeconomic resources (e.g., Peisner-Feinberg & Burchinal, 1997), but is among the first to document a similar effect for natural variation (i.e., not the consequence of targeted interventions) in instructional processes in elementary classrooms. That effects on achievement were attributable to instructional support for children in the low maternal education group may reflect compensation for lower levels of language stimulation and experiences with learning materials often reported in lower socioeconomic groups (Alexander et al., 2001; Hart & Risley, 1995).

(45)   Among children at high functional risk (those who displayed some combination of early behavioral, attentional, social, and/or academic problems), academic achievement in the first grade was highest for those in classrooms offering high emotional support. In these classrooms, teachers were aware of and responsive to individual students' needs, offered effective and proactive behavior management, and created a positive classroom climate in which teachers and students enjoyed each other and their time in the classroom. High functional risk children in these emotionally supportive classrooms

had similar scores on the first-grade Woodcock–Johnson as their low functional risk peers, while high functional risk children in classrooms offering low or moderate emotional support displayed significantly lower levels of achievement than did their low-risk peers. Academic performance for students at high functional risk was not significantly moderated by the level of instructional support in the classroom. This finding is consistent with other work indicating that among children who have displayed difficulties adjusting to the classroom environment, having teachers who attend to their social and emotional needs may be as or more important to academic development than specific instructional practices (Burchinal et al., 2005; Hamre & Pianta, 2001; Noam & Herman, 2002; Pianta, 1999; Wentzel, 2002).

Theories seeking to explain the potential mechanisms of this connection (46) between students' social and academic lives include social-motivation theories as well as work on student–teacher relationships. Wentzel (1998, 2002) has argued that positive interactions with teachers and peers can increase students' motivation and pursuit of academic goals. In this view, students who see teachers as supportive are more likely to pursue goals valued by teachers, such as engagement in academic activities. Consistent with this view is work on student–teacher relationships, which has suggested that stressful aspects of students' relationships with adults can lead to lower classroom participation and achievement (Ladd, 1989), while supportive relationships can help engage students in school (Furrer & Skinner, 2003). The current study extends these findings by suggesting that naturally occurring variation in teachers' emotional support can be important in enabling some children to make academic gains in early elementary school.

Beyond academic achievement, children's ability to develop a strong (47) relationship with their teachers, characterized by low levels of conflict, is a key indicator of positive school adjustment both concurrently and in the future (e.g., Hamre & Pianta, 2001; Ladd & Burgess, 1999; Ladd et al., 2002). This study provides evidence that for children who struggled in the prior year, their risk of developing conflictual relationships with teachers in the first grade is moderated by the quality of emotional support they received within their first-grade classrooms. Arnold, McWilliams, and Arnold (1998) have described ways in which interactions between teachers and children may resemble the coercive cycles between parents and children studies by Patterson and colleagues (Patterson & Fisher, 2002; Reid et al., 2002), with child misbehavior being influenced by and resulting in less positive interactions with teachers. Therefore, it is not surprising to find that, consistent with previous studies (Ladd & Burgess, 1999), children who have displayed multiple indicators of functional problems in kindergarten were more likely to develop poor relationships with teachers in the first grade. But when these children displaying high functional risk were placed with teachers offering high-to-moderate levels of emotional support, they did not differ significantly from their better-adjusted peers in levels of teacher-reported conflict. In contrast, children displaying high functional risk in kindergarten who were placed in classrooms characterized by low emotional support appeared to be particularly vulnerable to developing conflictual relationships with teachers in the first grade. This finding underscores the important role that teachers may play in interrupting cycles of coercive interactions with students (Arnold et al., 1998) and teacher–child relationships as a particularly important asset for children with social or relational challenges (Gregory & Weinstein, 2004; Noam & Herman, 2002). Future research may examine whether children at risk who are able to develop positive relationships with teachers show fewer behavioral and social problems in later school years.

There are several notable limitations to this research resulting from (48) the fact that it was conducted using a large, existing data set, rather than data developed specifically to address the research questions. Most notably, although this study successfully identified children at risk of school difficulties, the fact that the overall sample was not highly at risk constrains our ability to generalize findings and may have led to smaller effect sizes than would be observed in a more highly at-risk sample. These results need to be replicated among other high-risk groups before more conclusive statements regarding the role of instructional and emotional support in moderating risk of school failure can be made. Secondly, the global composites used to define classroom process prohibit more specific statements about the types of interactions between teachers and children that may moderate risk. Global measures offer the benefit of allowing a more simplified characterization of classroom quality, but limit our understanding of the specific interactional processes that may be most important in classrooms.

(49)   Among their methodological recommendations for studying environmental effects on children's outcomes, Rutter and Maughan (2002) suggest directly testing competing hypotheses. One competing hypothesis not tested within this study concerns the direction of causality. This is a particular issue in the analysis on functional risk, as it could be argued that children displaying more behavioral, attention, academic, and social problems draw different types of interactions from teachers (e.g., Arnold et al., 1998). Although there was evidence that first-grade classroom support was independent of students' functional risk status, it is possible that children who ended up in first-grade classrooms offering higher support had made positive gains in the period not measured, between fall of kindergarten and the beginning of first grade. Having multiple measurements within each school year would enable more careful analysis of change across time.

(50)   Taken together, these findings provide evidence of the potential for schools to moderate children's risk of academic and relational problems. Although the effect sizes are small, the findings are notable given that these effects (a) were not because of a focused intervention but rather because of natural variation in everyday interactions, as observed on only 1 school day; (b) were observed over a relatively short period of time (1–2 years); and (c) were controlled for previous functioning on outcomes known to have high-to-moderate stability. Unfortunately, although these findings suggest possible pathways to reduce gaps between children in school performance, recent evidence suggests great variability in the quality of classroom environments as well as in the stability of quality from year to year, even within the same school (NICHD ECCRN, in press). If children are not systematically exposed to high levels of classroom support across time, the effects of such positive placements are likely to be short-lived. This is particularly concerning given the finding that students with lower levels of maternal education tend to be exposed to lower quality classroom environments.

(51)   Just as developmental psychopathology has focused on using knowledge about underlying processes of adaptation to inform clinical practice (Hinshaw, 2002), school and educational psychologists, as well as developmental psychologists interested in school settings, would benefit from an increased focus on the processes underlying children's school adaptations (Pianta, in press). Research on these processes may be used to inform school-based interventions at the individual level, through working with teachers to improve the quality of their interactions with a specific student (e.g., Ladd et al., 2002; Pianta & Hamre, 2001), or at a more global level, through providing schools with professional development and measurement tools based on strong empirical evidence connecting specific classroom processes to more positive child outcomes. Furthermore, as school-based prevention and intervention efforts increasingly target improvements in the social and emotional climate of classrooms and schools as a means of facilitating children's development across academic, behavioral, and social domains (Greenberg et al., 2003), inclusion of measures of observed classroom processes will continue to expand our knowledge about specific classroom processes that are amenable to change and are associated with more positive outcomes for students.

Finally, from a theoretical perspective, the results of this study provide evidence of the benefit of understanding schools not only as a place to measure children's outcomes, but as an important context for children's development (Connell & Wellborn, 1991; Eccles, 1993; Pianta, in press; Roeser et al., 2000). Modeling the ways in which school experiences can add to, mediate, and moderate established trajectories of development allows for a more comprehensive understanding of children's adaptation (Cicchetti & Aber, 1998). Absent information on the process of schooling, and it is difficult to evaluate the legacy of early experience in the light of the possibility that school experience mediates or moderates the effects of prior history or concurrent experience at home. Given increasing evidence of the contribution of classroom process to school-age outcomes in the short term (e.g., Brody, Corsey, Forehand, & Armisted, 2002; Morrison & Connor, 2002; NICHD ECCRN, 2002b; Pianta et al., 2002; Rimm-Kaufman et al., 2002), not modeling such effects could lead to overestimating the linear, direct association between early experience, and children's long-term outcomes. Integrating methodologies for measuring classroom process in programs of longitudinal research, conceptually and functionally, is essential to the advancement of increasingly comprehensive models of development.

(52)

Classification of research by purpose: Basic research to develop and refine theories of children's adaptation.

REFERENCES

Achenbach, T. M. (1991). *Manual for the child behavior checklist/4–18 and profile*. Burlington: Department of Psychiatry, University of Vermont.

Alexander, K. L., Entwisle, D. R., & Kabbani, N. S. (2001). The dropout process in life course perspective: Early risk factors at home and school. *Teachers College Record, 103*, 760–822. Retrieved from blackwellpublishers.co.uk/asp/journal.asp?ref=0161-4681

Arnold, D. H., McWilliams, L., & Arnold, E. H. (1998). Teacher discipline and child misbehavior in day care: Untangling causality with correlational data. *Developmental Psychology, 34*, 276–287.

Battistich, V., Schaps, E., Watson, M., & Solomon, D. (1996). Prevention effects of the Child Development Project: Early findings from an ongoing multisite demonstration trial. *Journal of Adolescent Research, 11*, 12–35.

Bérubé, R. L., & Achenbach, T. M. (2001). *Bibliography of published studies using ASEBA instruments: 2001 edition*. Burlington: Research Center for Children, Youth, & Families, University of Vermont.

Birch, S. H., & Ladd, G. W. (1997). The teacher–child relationship and children's early school adjustment. *Journal of School Psychology, 35*, 61–79.

Birch, S. H., & Ladd, G. W. (1998). Children's interpersonal behaviors and the teacher–child relationship. *Developmental Psychology, 34*, 934–946.

Bowman, B. T., Donovan, M. S., & Burns, M. S. (2001). *Eager to learn: Educating our preschoolers. [Full report and executive summary.]* Washington, DC: National Academy Press.

Brody, G. H., Dorsey, S., Forehand, R., & Armistead, L. (2002). Unique and protective contributions of parenting and classroom processes to the adjustment of African American children living in single-parent families. *Child Development, 73*, 274–286.

Bronfenbrenner, U., & Morris, P. A. (1998). The ecology of developmental processes. In W. Damon & R. M. Lerner (Eds.), *Handbook of child psychology: Vol. 1. Theoretical models of human development* (5th ed., pp. 993–1029). New York: Wiley.

Brophy, J. (2004). *Teaching. Educational practices series—1*. Switzerland: PCL, Lausanne, International Academy of Education, International Bureau of Education.

Brophy, J. E., & Good, T. L. (1986). Teacher behavior and student achievement. In M. L. Wittrock (Ed.), *Handbook of research on teaching* (3rd ed., pp. 133–275). Indianapolis, IN: Macmillan Publishing.

Burchinal, M., Howes, C., Pianta, R. C., Bryant, D., Early, D., Clifford, R., et al. (2005). Predicting child outcomes at the end of kindergarten from the quality of pre-kindergarten teaching, instruction, activities, and caregiver sensitivity: Manuscript under review.

Catalano, R. F., Mazza, J. J., Harachi, T. W., Abbott, R. D., Haggerty, K. P., & Fleming, C. B. (2003). Raising healthy children through enhancing social development in elementary school: Results after 1.5 years. *Journal of School Psychology, 41*, 143–164.

Christian, K., Morrison, F. J., & Bryant, F. B. (1998). Predicting kindergarten academic skills: Interactions among child care, maternal education, and family literacy environments. *Early Childhood Research Quarterly, 13*, 501–521.

Cicchetti, D., & Aber, J. L. (1998). Editorial: Contextualism and developmental psychopathology. *Development and Psychopathology, 10,* 137–141.

Connell, J. P., & Wellborn, J. G. (1991). Competence, autonomy, and relatedness: A motivational analysis of self-system processes. In R. Gunnar & L. A. Sroufe (Eds.), *Minnesota symposia on child psychology* (Vol. 23. pp. 43–77). Hillsdale, NJ: Erlbaum.

Crosnoe, R., Johnson, M. K., & Elder, G. H. (2004). Intergenerational bonding in school: The behavioral and contextual correlates of student–teacher relationships. *Sociology of Education, 77,* 60–81.

Deci, E. L., & Ryan, R. M. (1985). *Intrinsic motivation and self-determination in human behavior.* New York: Plenum.

Dolezal, S. E., Welsh, L. M., Pressley, M., & Vincent, M. M. (2003). How nine third-grade teachers motivate student academic engagement. *The Elementary School Journal, 103,* 239–269.

Durlak, J., & Wells, A. (1997). Primary prevention mental health programs for children and adolescents: A meta-analytic review. *American Journal of Community Psychology, 25,* 115–152.

Eccles, J. S. (1993). School and family effects on the ontogeny of children's interests, self-perceptions, and activity choices. In J. Jacobs (Ed.), *Nebraska symposium on motivation: Vol. 40. Developmental perspectives on motivation* (pp. 145–208). Lincoln: University of Nebraska Press.

Elias, M. J., Gara, M. A., Schuyler, T. F., Branden-Muller, L. R., & Sayette, M. A. (1991). The promotion of social competence: Longitudinal study of a preventative school-based program. *American Journal of Orthopsychiatry, 61,* 409–417.

Entwisle, D. R., & Hayduk, L. A. (1988). Lasting effects of elementary school. *Sociology of Education, 61,* 147–159.

Ferguson, R. F. (1998). Teachers' perceptions and expectations and the Black–White test score gap. In C. Jencks & M. Phillips (Eds.), *The Black–White test score gap* (pp. 273–317). Washington, DC: Brookings Institution.

Ferguson, P., Jimerson, S. R., & Dalton, M. J. (2001). Sorting out successful failures: Exploratory analyses of factors associated with academic and behavioral outcomes of retained students. *Psychology in the Schools, 38,* 327–341.

Flanagan, K. S., Bierman, K. L., Kam, C., Coie, J. D., Dodge, K. A., Foster, E. M., et al. (2003). Identifying at-risk children at school entry: The usefulness of multibehavioral problem profiles. *Journal of Clinical Child and Adolescent Psychology, 32,* 396–407.

Furrer, C., & Skinner, E. (2003). Sense of relatedness as a factor in children's academic engagement and performance. *Journal of Educational Psychology, 95,* 148–162.

Gage, N. L., & Needels, M. C. (1989). Process–product research on teaching: A review of criticisms. *Elementary School Journal, 89,* 253–300.

Good, T. L., & Weinstein, R. S. (1986). Schools make a difference: Evidence, criticisms, and new directions. *American Psychologist, 41,* 1090–1097.

Gordon, M., Mettelman, B. B., & Irwin, M. (1994). Sustained attention and grade retention. *Perceptual and Motor Skills, 78,* 555–560.

Greenberg, M. T., Domitrovich, C., & Bumbarger, B. (2001). The prevention of mental disorders in school-aged children: Current state of the field. *Prevention and Treatment, 4* Article 0001a. Retrieved April 15, 2005, from journals.apa.org/prevention/volume4/pre0040001a.html

Greenberg, M. T., Weissberg, R. P., O'Brien, M. U., Zins, J. E., Fredericks, L., Resnik, H., et al. (2003). Enhancing school-based prevention and youth development through coordinated social, emotional, and academic learning. *American Psychologist. Special Issue: Prevention that Works for Children and Youth, 58,* 466–474.

Gregory, A., & Weinstein, R. S. (2004). Connection and regulation at home and in school: Predicting growth in achievement for adolescents. *Journal of Adolescent Research, 19,* 405–427.

Gresham, F. M., & Elliot, S. N. (1990). *The social skills rating system.* Circle Pines, MN: American Guidance Service.

Gutman, L. M., Sameroff, A. J., & Cole, R. (2003). Academic growth curve trajectories from 1st grade to 12th grade: Effects of multiple social risk factors and preschool child factors. *Developmental Psychology, 39,* 777–790.

Halperin, J. M., Sharman, V., Greenblatt, E., & Schwartz, S. T. (1991). Assessment of the continuous performance test: Reliability and validity in a nonreferred sample. *Psychological Assessment: Journal of Consulting and Clinical Psychology, 3,* 603–608.

Hamre, B. K., & Pianta, R. C. (2001). Early teacher–child relationships and the trajectory of children's school outcomes through eighth grade. *Child Development, 72,* 625–638.

Hart, B., & Risley, T. (1995). *Meaningful differences in the everyday experience of young American children.* Baltimore: Brookes Publishing.

Hinshaw, S. P. (2002). Process, mechanism, and explanation related to externalizing behavior in developmental psychopathology. *Journal of Abnormal Child Psychology, 30,* 431–446.

Howes, C. (2000). Social–emotional classroom climate in child care, child–teacher relationships and children's second grade peer relations. *Social Development, 9,* 191–204.

Howes, C., Burchinal, M., Pianta, R. C., Bryant, D., Early, D., Clifford, R., & Barbarin, O. (in press). Ready to learn? Children's pre-academic achievement in pre-kindergarten programs. *Developmental Psychology.*

Howes, C., & Hamilton, C. E. (1992). Children's relationships with child care teachers: Stability and concordance with parental attachments. *Child Development, 63,* 867–878.

Howes, C., Matheson, C. C., & Hamilton, C. E. (1994). Maternal teacher, and child care history correlates of children's relationship with peers. *Child Development, 65,* 264–273.

Ialongo, N. S., Werthamer, L., Kellam, S. G., Brown, C. H., Wang, S., & Lin, Y. (1999). Proximal impact of two first-grade preventive interventions on the early risk behaviors for later substance abuse, depression, and antisocial behavior. *American Journal of Community Psychology, 27,* 299–641.

Juel, C. (1996). What makes literacy tutoring effective? *Reading Research Quarterly, 31,* 268–289.

Keselman, H. J., Cribbie, R. A., & Wilcox, R. (2002). Pair-wise multiple comparison tests when data are nonnormal. *Educational and Psychological Measurement, 62,* 420–434.

Kraemer, H. C., Stice, E., Kazdin, A., Offord, D., & Kupfer, D. (2001). How do risk factors work together? Mediators, moderators, and independent, overlapping, and proxy risk factors. *American Journal of Psychiatry, 158,* 848–856.

Ladd, G. W. (1989). Children's social competence and social supports: Precursors of early school adjustment? In B. H. Schneider & G. Attili (Eds.), *NATO Advanced Study Institute on Social Competence in Developmental Perspective, July 1988, Les Arcs, France; Social competence in developmental perspective. NATO Advanced Science Institutes series. Series D: Behavioural and social sciences, Vol. 51; Social competence in developmental perspective* (pp. 277–291). New York: Kluwer Academic/Plenum Publishers.

Ladd, G. W., Buhs, E. S., & Troop, W. (2002). Children's interpersonal skills and relationships in school settings: Adaptive significance and implications for school-based prevention and intervention programs. In P. K. Smith & C. H. Hart (Eds.), *Blackwell handbook of childhood social development. Blackwell handbooks of developmental psychology* (pp. 394–415). Malden, MA: Blackwell Publishers.

Ladd, G. W., & Burgess, K. B. (1999). Charting the relationship trajectories of aggressive, withdrawn, and aggressive/withdrawn children during early grade school. *Child Development, 70,* 910–929.

Ladd, G. W., & Burgess, K. B. (2001). Do relational risks and protective factors moderate the linkages between childhood aggression and early psychological and school adjustment? *Child Development, 72,* 1579–1601.

Lerner, R. M. (1998). Theories of human development: Contemporary perspectives. In W. Damon & R. M. Lerner (Eds.), *Handbook of child psychology: Vol. 1. Theoretical models of human development* (5th ed., pp. 1–24). New York: Wiley.

Lewis, T. J., Sugai, G., & Colvin, G. (1998). Reducing problem behavior through a school-wide system of effective behavioral support: Investigation of a school-wide social skills training program and contextual interventions. *School Psychology Review, 27,* 446–459.

Matsumura, L. C., Patthey-Chavez, G. G., Valdes, R., & Garnier, H. (2002). Teacher feedback, writing assignment quality, and third-grade students' revision in higher and lower achieving schools. *The Elementary School Journal, 103,* 3–25.

Meyer, L. A., Wardrop, J. L., Hastings, C. N., & Linn, R. L. (1993). Effects of ability and settings on kindergarteners' reading performance. *Journal of Educational Research, 86,* 142–160.

Mirsky, A., Anthony, B., Duncan, C., Aheani, M., & Kellam, S. (1991). Analysis of the elements of attention. *Neuro-psychology Review, 2,* 109–145.

Morrison, F. J., & Connor, C. M. (2002). Understanding schooling effects on early literacy: A working research strategy. *Journal of School Psychology, 40,* 493–500.

National Institute of Child Health and Human Development, Early Child Care Research Network (NICHD ECCRN). (2005). A day in third grade: A large-scale study of classroom quality and teacher and student behavior. *Elementary School Journal, 105,* 305–323.

NICHD ECCRN. (1993). *The NICHD study of early child care: A comprehensive longitudinal study of young children's lives.* ERIC Document Reproduction Service No. ED 353 0870.

NICHD ECCRN. (2002a). The interaction of child care and family risk in relation to child development at 24 and 36 months. *Applied Developmental Science, 6,* 144–156.

NICHD ECCRN. (2002b). The relation of first grade classroom environment to structural classroom features, teacher, and student behaviors. *Elementary School Journal, 102,* 367–387.

NICHD ECCRN. (2003). Social functioning in first grade: Prediction from home, child care and concurrent school experience. *Child Development, 74,* 1639–1662.

NICHD ECCRN. (2004). Does class size in first grade relate to changes in child academic and social performance or observed classroom processes? *Developmental Psychology, 40,* 651–664.

Noam, G. G., & Hermann, C. A. (2002). Where education and mental health meet: Developmental prevention and early intervention in schools. *Development and Psychopathology, 14,* 861–875.

Noam, G. G., Warner, L. A., & Van Dyken, L. (2001). Beyond the rhetoric of zero tolerance: Long-term solutions for at-risk youth. *New Directions for Youth Development, 92,* 155–182.

Patterson, G. R., & Fisher, P. A. (2002). Recent developments in our understanding of parenting: Bidirectional effects, causal models, and the search for parsimony. In M. H. Bornstein (Ed.), *Handbook of parenting: Vol. 5: Practical issues in parenting* (2nd ed., pp. 59–88). Mahwah, NJ: Lawrence Erlbaum Associates.

Peisner-Feinberg, E. S., & Burchinal, M. R. (1997). Relations between preschool children's child-care experiences and concurrent development: The Cost, Quality, and Outcomes Study. *Merrill–Palmer Quarterly, 43*, 451–477.

Peisner-Feinberg, E. S., Burchinal, M. R., Clifford, R. M., Culkin, M. L., Howes, C., Kagan, S. L., et al. (2001). The relation of preschool child-care quality to children's cognitive and social developmental trajectories through second grade. *Child Development, 72*, 1534–1553.

Phillips, M., Crouse, J., & Ralph, J. (1998). Does the Black–White test score gap widen after children enter school? In C. Jencks & M. Phillips (Eds.), *The Black–White test score gap* (pp. 229–272). Washington, DC: Brookings Institution.

Pianta, R., La Paro, K., & Hamre, B. K. (2005). *Classroom Assessment Scoring System (CLASS).* Unpublished measure, University of Virginia, Charlottesville, VA.

Pianta, R. C. (1999). *Enhancing relationships between children and teachers.* Washington, DC: American Psychological Association.

Pianta, R. C. (2001). *Student–teacher relationship scale.* Lutz, FL: Psychological Assessment Resources Inc.

Pianta, R. C. (in press). Schools, schooling, and developmental psychopathology. In D. Cicchetti (Ed.), *Handbook of developmental psychopathology* (Vol. 2), New York: John Wiley & Sons.

Pianta, R. C., & Hamre, B. (2001). *Students, teachers, and relationship support [STARS]: User's guide.* Lutz, FL: Psychological Assessment Resources Inc.

Pianta, R. C., La Paro, K. M., Payne, C., Cox, M. J., & Bradley, R. (2002). The relation of kindergarten classroom environment to teacher, family, and school characteristics and child outcomes. *Elementary School Journal, 102*, 225–238.

Pianta, R. C., & McCoy, S. J. (1997). The first day of school: The predictive validity of early school screening. *Journal of Applied Developmental Psychology, 18*, 1–22.

Reid, J. B., Patterson, G. R., & Snyder, J. (2002). *Antisocial behavior in children and adolescents: A developmental analysis and model for intervention.* Washington, DC: American Psychological Association.

Resnick, L. (1994). Situated rationalism: Biological and social preparation for learning. In L. A. Hirschfeld & S. A. Gelman (Eds.), *Mapping the mind: Domain specificity in cognition and culture* (pp. 474–493). New York: Cambridge University Press.

Rimm-Kaufman, S. E., Early, D. M., Cox, M. J., Saluja, G., Pianta, R. C., Bradley, R. H., et al. (2002). Early behavioral attributes and teachers' sensitivity as predictors of competent behavior in the kindergarten classroom. *Journal of Applied Developmental Psychology, 23*, 451–470.

Rimm-Kaufman, S. E., LaParo, K. M., Downer, J. T., & Pianta, R. C. (2005). The contribution of classroom setting and quality of instruction to children's behavior in the kindergarten classroom. *Elementary School Journal, 105*, 377–394.

Ritchie, S., & Howes, C. (2003). Program practices, caregiver stability, and child-caregiver relationships. *Journal of Applied Developmental Psychology, 24*, 497–516.

Roeser, R. W., Eccles, J. S., & Sameroff, A. J. (2000). School as a context of early adolescents' academic and social–emotional development: A summary of research findings. *Elementary School Journal, 100*, 443–471.

Ross, S. M., Smith, L. J., Slavin, R. E., & Madden, N. A. (1997). Improving the academic success of disadvantaged children: An examination of success for all. *Psychology in the Schools, 34*, 171–180.

Rutter, M., & Maughan, B. (2002). School effectiveness findings 1979–2002. *Journal of School Psychology, 40*, 451–475.

Sameroff, A. J. (1995). General systems theories and psychopathology. In D. Cicchetti & D. Cohen (Eds.), *Developmental psychopathology* (Vol. 1), New York: Wiley.

Sameroff, A. J. (2000). Developmental systems and psychopathology. *Development and Psychopathology, 12*, 297–312.

Seifer, R., Sameroff, A. J., Baldwin, C. P., & Baldwin, A. L. (1992). Child and family factors that ameliorate risk between 4 and 13 years of age. *Journal of the American Academy of Child and Adolescent Psychiatry, 31*, 893–903.

Shonkoff, J. P., & Phillips, D. A. (2000). *From neurons to neighborhoods: The science of early childhood development.* Washington, DC: National Academy Press.

Skinner, E. A., & Belmont, M. J. (1993). Motivation in the classroom: Reciprocal effects of teacher behavior and student engagement across the school year. *Journal of Educational Psychology, 85*, 571–581.

Skinner, E. A., Zimmer-Gembeck, M. J., & Connell, J. P. (1998). Individual differences in the development of perceived control. *Monographs of the Society for Research in Child Development, Serial No. 254, Vol. 63.* Chicago: University of Chicago Press.

Stevenson, H. W., & Lee, S. (1990). Contexts of achievement. *Monographs of the Society for Research in Child Development, Serial No. 221, Vol. 55.* Chicago: University of Chicago Press.

Stipek, D. J., Feiler, R., Byler, P., Ryan, R., Milburn, S., & Salmon, J. (1998). Good beginnings: What difference does the program make in preparing young children for school? *Journal of Applied Developmental Psychology, 19*, 41–66.

Torgesen, J. K. (2002). The prevention of reading difficulties. *Journal of School Psychology, 40*, 7–26.

U.S. Department of Education. (2000). *America's kindergartens: Findings from the early childhood longitudinal study, kindergarten class of 1998–99, Fall 1998*. Washington, DC: National Center for Education Statistics.

Walker, H. M., Stiller, B., Severson, H. H., Feil, E. G., & Golly, A. (1998). First step to success: Intervening at the point of school entry to prevent antisocial behavior patterns. *Psychology in the Schools, 35*, 259–269.

Weissberg, R. P., & Greenberg, M. T. (1998). School and community competence-enhancement and prevention programs. In I. E. Siegel & K. A. Renninger (Eds.), *Handbook of child psychology: Child psychology in practice* (Vol. 4., 5th ed., pp. 877–954). New York: John Wiley.

Wentzel, K. (1998). Social relationships and motivation in middle school: The role of parents, teachers, and peers. *Journal of Educational Psychology, 90*(2), 202–209.

Wentzel, K. (2002). Are effective teachers like good parents? Teaching styles and student adjustment in early adolescence. *Child Development, 73*, 287–301.

Wilson, D. B., Gottfredson, D. C., & Najaka, S. S. (2001). School-based prevention of problem behaviors: A meta-analysis. *Journal of Quantitative Criminology, 17*, 247–272.

Woodcock, R. W., & Johnson, M. B. (1989). *Woodcock–Johnson psycho-educational battery–revised*. Allen, TX: DLM.

Zins, J. E., Bloodworth, M. R., Weissberg, R. P., & Walberg, H. (2004). The scientific base linking social and emotional learning to school success. In J. E. Zins, R. P. Weissberg, M. C. Wang, & H. J. Walberg (Eds.), *Building academic success on social and emotional learning: What does the research say?* New York: Teachers College Press.

Source: From "Can Instructional and Emotional Support in the First-Grade Classroom Make a Difference for Children at Risk of School Failure?," by B. K. Hamre and R. C. Pianta, 2005, *Child Development, 76,* pp. 949–967. Copyright 2005 by Blackwell Publishing. Reproduced by permission.

Developing Teacher Epistemological Sophistication About Multicultural Curriculum: A Case Study

CHRISTINE SLEETER
California State University, Monterey Bay

ABSTRACT Teachers are significant curriculum decision makers in their classrooms. How does teachers' thinking about curriculum develop in the context of teacher education coursework, and how might an analysis of a novice teacher's learning to think more complexly inform teacher education pedagogy? This article presents a case study of a 2nd-year teacher who was in a graduate-level Multicultural Curriculum Design course, which was designed to develop the complexity with which teachers understand and plan curriculum. Data—which included student papers, a reflective journal, classroom observation of the teacher, and an interview—are analyzed using a rubric that differentiates novice, developing, and accomplished teachers' thinking about multicultural curriculum.

(01)   Teachers are significant curriculum decision makers in their classrooms, although curriculum is given far less attention in professional development for novice teachers than are other classroom concerns (Clayton, 2007). How does teachers' thinking about curriculum develop in the context of teacher education coursework? And how might an analysis of a novice teacher's learning to think more complexly inform teacher education pedagogy? This article presents a case study of a 2nd-year teacher who enrolled in my graduate-level Multicultural Curriculum Design course, which was designed to develop the complexity with which teachers understand and plan curriculum. As a teacher educator, I attempt to (1) disrupt common novice assumptions that there is a "right" way to design and teach multicultural curriculum and that there is a body of "correct" knowledge and attitudes to teach and (2) help teachers develop more sophisticated epistemological perspectives about the nature of knowledge and their work as teachers. This case study teases out factors that appeared to prompt the growth of one teacher.

Teachers' Epistemological Beliefs

(02)   Working with multiple perspectives, frames of reference, and funds of knowledge is at the heart of designing and teaching multicultural curriculum (Banks, 2004). Developing curriculum that is intellectually rich and relevant to diverse students, in contexts already furnished with a fairly prescribed curriculum, requires teachers to judge what is most worth teaching and learning and to identify space in which they can invite students' knowledge and interests. Making such judgments requires evaluating knowledge in terms of its sociopolitical moorings and intellectual basis. These are issues of epistemology—beliefs about how people know what they know, including assumptions about the nature of knowledge and the process of coming to know (Clayton, 2007).

Address correspondence to Christine Sleeter, 118½ Dunecrest Avenue, Monterey, CA 93940. E-mail: christine_sleeter@csumb.edu

Schommer (1990) describes three epistemological dimensions of knowledge that have relevance to teachers: certainty, source, and structure. *Certainty* refers to the extent to which one sees knowledge as being based on a fixed reality that is "out there" and unchanging. *Source* refers to where valid knowledge can come from (established external authorities, personal experience, etc.) and how one evaluates the relative strength of various sources and forms of evidence. *Structure* refers to the extent to which one sees knowledge as having, on one hand, its own internal structure and hierarchy or, on the other, an organic relationship to context, knowers, and everyday life. Research on teachers' and college students' epistemological beliefs suggests growth along a continuum (Schommer, 1998; White, 2000). At one end are those who hold absolutist beliefs, seeing knowledge as being fixed and certain, outside the knower, and established by authority figures. At the other end are reflective individuals who see knowledge as being situated within the context in which people create it: Problems have multiple solutions, and truth claims can be evaluated on the basis of the veracity of evidence on which they rest. In the middle are relativists, who reject anchoring knowledge in established authorities but, not knowing how to evaluate it otherwise, assume that all perspectives are equally valid. (03)

Assumptions that teachers make about the certainty, source, and structure of knowledge affect what they do with curriculum in general and multicultural curriculum in particular. Powell (1996) compares how two teachers with different epistemologies approached multicultural curriculum. One teacher held a developmentalist approach, seeing students' needs and interests as the basis on which academic knowledge should be built. The other saw the structure of his discipline (science) as being fundamental, and he judged students' learning abilities in relationship to their mastery of disciplinary content. The first teacher saw multicultural curriculum as being relevant; the second did not. (04)

So, to help teachers plan and teach intellectually sound multicultural curriculum that engages their students, one should prompt them to question their beliefs about the certainty, source, and structure of knowledge. Teaching a course in higher education, I have 15 weeks in which to do this—a relatively short time in which to disrupt assumptions built over many years of experiencing conventional schooling. (05)

The purpose of this case study was to examine the relationship between a teacher's learning and my teaching strategies in the university, as coupled with visitation to the teacher's classroom. (06)

> The scientific method—selection and definition of a problem: "to examine the relationship between a teacher's learning and my teaching strategies in the university...."

Methodology for a Case Study

According to Stake (2000), "a case study is expected to catch the complexity of a single case" (p. xi). Stake maintains that case study research is useful to education because, although school settings, teachers, and students share similarities, they are unique and complex. We cannot fully understand shared patterns without seeing the uniqueness of individual cases. (07)

This case study is drawn from a larger study of teachers working with multicultural curriculum (Sleeter, 2005). Why did I select Ann (pseudonym) for a case study? Stake (2000) recommends selecting cases that "maximize what we can learn" (p. 4). Beginning teachers in racially or ethnically diverse classrooms are commonly involved in induction programs and thus of interest to many teacher educators (Achinstein & Athanases, 2005; Chan & East, 1998). (08)

> Case study research is focused on a "unit of study" or "bounded system," that is, a beginning teacher new to multicultural education.

Therefore, I wanted to focus my attention on a beginning teacher who was relatively new to multicultural education, open to learning, and teaching in a diverse classroom. Of the teachers in my course (veterans as well as new teachers, in varying classroom settings), Ann best fit these criteria. She was a 2nd-year teacher who had moved to California from the East Coast about 2 years previously. A young White woman, she taught fifth grade in an (09)

	elementary school that serves a diverse, largely low-income student population. She expressed interest in multicultural education, even though it was new to her.
Applied research focused on how a beginning teacher integrates university coursework on multicultural education into her classroom teaching and the decision—making process related to the implementation of a multicultural curriculum.	**(10)** Case study research typically uses a variety of methods to collect data, with an objective toward triangulating findings across methods (Creswell, 2008; Stake, 2000). Data for this study included (1) several papers that Ann completed during the course, including a unit that she designed as a course requirement, (2) a journal that I kept after each class session, (3) notes on two observations of Ann teaching the unit that she designed after the course had ended, and (4) a 40-minute tape-recorded interview with Ann following my observations.
Scientific method: execution of research procedures: (1) sample selection, (2) curriculum unit, (3) journal, (4) field notes, and (5) interviews.	**(11)** As a heuristic tool for reflection and analysis, I developed a rubric that appears in Table 1, which describes a rough progression of levels in learning to think complexly about multicultural curriculum at novice, developing,

Table 1

Thinking Complexly About Multicultural Curriculum

Task definition

Novice. Assumes a "right" way to design and teach curriculum. Assumes that one already understands multicultural curriculum and that "new learning" involves adding onto that. Ignores, sees as irrelevant, or lacks confidence to examine what puzzles, feels threatening, or seems impractical.

Developing. Recognizes more than one "right" way that good curriculum could be designed and taught. Willing to question things that one thought one understood and to explore dimensions that are puzzling or new.

Accomplished. Assumes that multiple ways of designing and teaching curriculum emanate from diverse ideologies; able to own and work with one's ideology. Continually tries to recognize new dimensions of curriculum and to figure out the most ethical and practical balance among competing demands.

Perspective taking

Novice. Assumes there is a body of "correct" knowledge or attitudes to teach; tends to interpret and dismiss other perspectives or critical questions as opinion, personal criticism, or simply impractical.

Developing. Willing to consider multiple and possibly conflicting definitions of what is most worth knowing; able to acknowledge how one's viewpoint, identity, and social location shapes one's perspective; willing to own one's judgments about what is best.

Accomplished. Actively seeks multiple perspectives; makes explicit effort to learn from perspectives different from one's own, especially those that have been historically subjugated. Able to articulate own perspective as one of many; able to invite dialogue and discussion across divergent perspectives.

Self-reflexivity

Novice. Strives for certainty, assumes that questioning oneself is the same as questioning one's competence; seeks approval for one's thinking from authority figures.

Developing. Willing to acknowledge uncertainty, at least tentatively; occasionally asks what is most worth teaching and why; recognizes need to attend to practical consequences of one's teaching while maintaining some level of critical questioning.

Accomplished. Views uncertainty as tool for learning. Consistently monitors, questions, and evaluates practical and ethical impacts of one's work on students. Questions how one's own positionality, experiences, and point of view affect one's work but can move forward while doing so.

Locus of decision making

Novice. Either looks to external authorities (such as the state, well-known people in the field, texts) to find out what and how to teach or ignores them entirely; assumes that educational decision making flows top-down.

Developing. Attends to external authorities but also willing to seek input from students, parents, community members, or other teachers; explores how to make decisions in a way that satisfies authorities and invites bottom-up input.

Accomplished. Negotiates decision making in a way that consciously places well-being of students at the center; regularly engages students and their communities in collaborative decision making while attending to external expectations; able to take ownership for the consequences of one's decisions.

and accomplished levels. In developing the rubric, I drew from research comparing teachers' thinking at novice, developing, and expert levels, which generally finds that expert teachers, compared to novice teachers, make more distinctions among aspects of curriculum and instruction and bring to bear more elaborated thinking about their judgments (e.g., Cushing, Sabers, & Berliner, 1992; Krull, Oras, & Sisack, 2007; Swanson, O'Connor, & Cooney, 1990). I also drew from my experience planning and teaching multicultural curriculum, as well as collaborating with several colleagues who were investigating the development of cognitive complexity among their students.

The rubric includes four dimensions along which epistemological beliefs (12) can be examined: task definition, perspective taking, self-reflexivity, and locus of decision making. Assumptions labeled *novice* correspond to what White (2000) characterizes as absolutist thinking. Those labeled *developing* correspond to relativist thinking, and those labeled *accomplished*, to reflective thinking. I used the rubric to guide my analysis of the case study data (presented later). I also used it with teachers in the Multicultural Curriculum Design course as a reflective tool. Ann used the rubric in a paper to reflect on her own growth, which I read after I had made my preliminary analysis of her growth. Her self-analysis was quite similar to mine. Ann also read an earlier draft of this article, offering a few comments while confirming its consistency with her analysis of her growth.

Case Study of Ann

Ann had enrolled voluntarily in Multicultural Curriculum Design. When I (13) asked how she came to be interested in it, she replied,

> I [student-taught] in Eastern London; it was all primarily Afghani and Pakistani descent students. And I was just fascinated with the Arabic that they spoke and the writing and it was so different. . . .
>
> And when I came home, I taught this fifth grade about the cultures I learned over there, and they had no idea what Arabic was, what Muslim, what Mohammed, nothing. And I think it's really important to teach about the different cultures and religions. I think a lot of times ignorance brings hate. (January 28, 2004)

On the 1st day of the course, I asked teachers to write their definition of (14) *curriculum*. Ann wrote, "Curriculum is what the teacher is required to teach to the students" (September 8, 2003). About 3 weeks later, I had them write about the extent to which their curriculum is determined by authorities such as the state and about any concerns that they might have about what they are expected to teach. Ann wrote,

> I have concerns with teaching the history textbook content. As a public school teacher, though, you really can't go outside of your prescribed literature and academic standards. So, I believe at this moment that it is my job as a teacher to try and guide the students to question and look at the text differently than what they read in the chapter.... So, the dilemma is how to tactfully incorporate other multicultural views in a school-adopted textbook and be able to cover all the standards the state and government expects of you at the same time. (September 30, 2003)

These responses suggest that Ann entered the course with an absolutist (15) perspective about curriculum. A novice, she accepted the legitimacy of external authorities to determine curriculum; she believed that she could tweak it a bit to make it multicultural; and she was looking for strategies and ideas to use.

My task, however, was not to simply offer her strategies and ideas but to (16) slow down her learning process so that she could reflect more deeply on her beliefs and assumptions. Throughout the semester, I used various strategies to do this: analyzing epistemological and ideological assumptions in documents, reading works that reflect multiple ideological perspectives, engaging in personal interactions that challenge thinking, engaging in reflective writing, and developing a curriculum unit one can teach. I examine these in relationship to Ann's growth.

Analyzing Epistemological and Ideological Assumptions in Documents

(17) Early in the semester (September), I guided teachers in analyzing epistemological assumptions in various documents related to curriculum, such as curriculum standards and school reform proposals available on the Internet. Teachers examined documents in relationship to questions such as the following: *Who produced this document (if it is possible to tell)? How is it intended to be used? By whom? What is its purpose? Whose view of the world does it support? Whose view does it undermine or ignore? Whose knowledge isn't here?* In addition, they analyzed textbooks from their classrooms, with guidance from a textbook analysis instrument (see Grant & Sleeter, 2009).

(18) Ann elected to analyze her social studies textbook. As she explained near the end of the semester, this analysis caused her to realize that

> history is told overwhelmingly in the white European male perspective…. The history text teaches the story of American history as "We the People" as a succession. All the chapters from 30,000 B.C. to 1600 are never rethought after colonization…. The broader ideology that is being supported in the text is that it is natural for Europeans to succeed prior races without accepting or studying their culture. (December 8, 2003)

(19) She coupled this analysis with interviews with some of her students, for another short paper. She asked her students what they knew about indigenous people of the United States and the history of colonization. She was surprised to discover that they thought that there are no Native Americans left. Ann discovered that "they knew very little about the colonization period of the United States. Looking at my student perspectives paper, the pieces of information that they did know were mostly filled [with] myth and false facts" (December 15, 2003).

> Scientific method: analysis of data. This is an iterative process in case study research that involves the analysis of qualitative data and leads to statements of the themes that have emerged from the data.

(20) Coupling document analysis with student interviews helped Ann see that U.S. history is told from a perspective that excludes indigenous perspectives; as a result, her students were coming to believe that indigenous people no longer exist. By October, Ann began to question her earlier assumption that a teacher's job is to teach what the state demands.

Reading from Multiple Ideological Perspectives

(21) Readings that engage teachers with various ideological perspectives can prompt reflection when used in conjunction with discussion and reflective writing. To that end, we read Macedo's *Literacies of Power* (1994), which examines curriculum, ideology, and power from a critical ethnic studies perspective, and we read online selections from *Rethinking Schools* (rethinkingschools.org), a newspaper written from critical perspectives, mainly by classroom teachers. The readings offered a language that many of the teachers had not previously encountered.

(22) As Ann read *Literacies of Power,* she made connections between its critique of schooling and her own belief system. She wrote that she is a registered Democrat with leanings "toward liberal, green, and democratic ideals"; she also described her coteachers as dismissing conspiracy theories and as being attached to "their Republican government and books and standards" (October 13, 2003). She was not put off by Macedo's radical questioning of dominant beliefs about schools, because his questions supported her

disagreements with coworkers and her new awareness that history texts reflect dominant points of view. At the same time, she realized that she did not understand some of Macedo's ideas. Halfway through the semester, in a class discussion, Ann commented that after listening to classmates of color, she better understood Macedo's ideas.

Her reactions to Macedo suggest that Ann sought connections between (23) his ideas and life experience—her own and that of people whom she knew. Because she was able to make those connections, she gradually took up questions that he raised about how dominant groups shape what happens in schools. By November, she was interested in connecting his analysis of power and curriculum with global power. Ann participated in a small-group discussion of an article in which a fifth-grade teacher describes how he helped his students develop a sense of solidarity with struggles of workers across the globe (Peterson, 2000/2001). Ann asked me what the term *globalize* means, whether it is positive or negative. I explained that the author was referring to the process of large corporations' incorporating Third World economies into a capitalist global economy. Ann commented that she was not sure what the term meant. Two weeks later, she wanted to discuss this article, along with another (Bigelow, 2002) that examined how school knowledge constructs Third World peoples from highly Westernized points of view rather than from Third World points of view. These seemed to be new ideas that she wanted to further explore because they appeared to resonate with her political beliefs and, possibly, with her student teaching experience.

To acquire background for a curriculum unit that was the course's cul- (24) minating project, teachers were to identify a concept that they could teach, and they were to research it from points of view found in the intellectual scholarship of one historically marginalized group. In early October, as Ann became aware that her textbook virtually ignores indigenous people and the impact of colonization on them, she decided to pursue the topic of colonization from indigenous perspectives. She initially suggested starting with the question, what are Native American perspectives on colonization? I advised that she narrow her question to a specific period, place, and tribe or nation; she decided to focus on the Iroquois during the 17th century. Over the next 2 months, she read *Lies My Teacher Told Me* (Loewen, 1995) and *Rethinking Columbus* (Bigelow & Peterson, 1998), as well as work by indigenous authors such as LaDuke (1999) and Churchill (2002). As she read, she focused on the Haudenosaunee (Iroquois), Wampanoag, and Pequot during the late 17th century. She came to see that books by indigenous scholars present an opposing perspective from that in the school's history text. She was initially confused, commenting in class, "Topics just kept spinning off each other and it was hard to stop or to figure out what to actually use" (journal notes, December 8, 2003). She struggled with how to rethink her curriculum because she realized that she could not simply add information to it. Later I show how she resolved this dilemma. But it was clear to me that readings grounded in a different perspective prompted her over the semester to recognize and question the perspective in her curriculum and textbooks.

Engaging in Personal Interactions

Throughout the semester, I had teachers engage in various structured and (25) semistructured interactions to simulate their thinking and self-analysis. The fact that they were from diverse backgrounds produced rich discussions all semester. They were mainly women. About one third were White; one third, Latino; and the rest included an African American, a Korean, two Africans, two Greeks, and some biracial students who identified as Asian American.

A powerful interaction involved sharing from each teacher's life. They (26) were asked to bring one or two objects that reflect membership in a sociocultural group (e.g., based on race or ethnicity, gender, sexual orientation, language) and a struggle for rights or identity related to membership in that group. The objects should prompt sharing about how they have claimed identity, space, and rights (Flores, 2003). Ann is of Italian American descent, as were several other teachers in the class. They discussed the centrality of food to family gatherings and the position of women in traditional Italian families (as well as Mexican families). Ann discussed being a vegetarian, which her family saw as a rejection of Italian food and family; she had struggled to help her family see that one can be an Italian vegetarian. Although her struggle was less intense than those of some of the teachers of color, it gave Ann a basis for hearing where others were coming from. After this session, she commented that Macedo's critique of schooling in the U.S. made more sense to her.

Engaging in Reflective Writing

(27)   Throughout the semester, teachers wrote reflections about various teaching dilemmas that they had experienced, such as how they handled conflicts between the demands placed on them as teachers and their political or pedagogical beliefs. Ann found that reflective writing enabled her to link insights from readings with some of her core beliefs about schooling that conflicted with what she was told to do.

(28)   In one reflection, teachers were to identify and analyze a teaching practice that they favored and had tried but that did not work or was rejected by their students. Ann wrote about her experiences using small-group activities:

> The students did not respond to my group activities as well as when practiced in my student teaching. When given manipulatives in math, they were thrown sometimes. In language arts we worked in writing workshop groups, and more times than not there were disagreements and fights. The science experiments resulted in many referrals and suspensions. (November 3, 2003)

(29)   Her new-teacher mentor told her that she was giving the students too much freedom, "that this kind of population needs seatwork and a definite routine every day…. As a result, I backed off on these activities and have a whole class teaching method instead of learning centers." On reflection, Ann realized, "I gave up too easily." She went on to write,

> My theory on this is that students tend to talk out and voice expressions when interested in a certain subject matter. . . . I feel that some cultures need to be heard, literally, more than others. The quote from Macedo "education so as not to educate" makes me think, is this the type of teaching that I've adopted from my mentor, just silencing students that probably need to speak out? My dilemma here is how to have a classroom where students speak out, learn in different ways and in group settings, without having troublesome discipline problems. (November 3, 2003)

(30)   For Ann, writing reflectively about the intersection between her experiences, beliefs, readings, and discussions seemed to prompt self-analysis. In the process, she questioned the basis on which experienced teachers recommended teaching practices, seeing limitations in her coworkers' advice and reclaiming her beliefs about teaching and learning.

Developing a Curriculum Unit

(31)   The course is organized around a culminating assignment: developing a multicultural curriculum unit that one can actually teach. I use this assignment to provide teachers with a way of working through the questions, dilemmas, and new insights they grapple with over the semester. As noted earlier, Ann

grappled with two major problems: how to address the fact that "indigenous people's history stops after Columbus is introduced" (December 8, 2003) and how to engage students in active learning without losing control over the class.

To resolve the problem of how to teach history from two opposing per- (32) spectives, Ann used a teacher's suggestion of organizing the unit around a trial. It focused on the Wampanoag nation's frustrations with colonists who were misusing natural resources—particularly, overkilling the deer population. It was based on the Haudenosaunee Great Law of Peace and Good Mind, which uses a trial process as a tool for building consensus about solutions to community problems. The trial structure helped her figure out how to engage students in active learning.

To prepare this unit for teaching, Ann needed to learn a good deal more. (33) For example, it was not enough to know that the Haudenosaunee had a well-developed democratic governmental and legal system; she also had to be able to accurately describe some of its features. She commented on the amount of time that it took her to research background material:

> Just when I was planning this lesson, I went and spent another few hours finding those words and finding all the Native American names.... I spent time on Native American websites. And researching this is something I'm kind of interested in. I mean, I've looked up some different Native American beliefs and traditions just for my own personal knowledge. (interview, January 28, 2004)

As a 2nd-year teacher, Ann was overwhelmed with preparing lessons for (34) state standards in all the content areas. She recognized that preparing such a unit entailed work above and beyond that required by the state curriculum. Because Native Americans disappear from the social studies curriculum as it traces the story of Europeans and Euro-Americans, she could elect not to teach the unit and be in full compliance with state requirements. But she believed that the unit was too important to drop.

Ann's completed unit included three 45-minute lessons. I visited her class- (35) room in January while she was teaching the second and third lessons. During the third lesson, students role-played the trial, which Ann entitled "The Case of the Missing Deer." In a fictitious trial set in Massachusetts during the 17th century, the Wampanoag tribe sued the European colonists for misusing natural resources. Ann had given each student a role card that included a name, a designation as a Wampanoag or colonist, and role in the trial. She showed who would sit where: defendants at one table, plaintiffs at another, jury at another table, and judges at the circular table at the front (there were five judges: two colonists, two Wampanoag, and one from another tribe who would act as a tiebreaker, if needed). Ann directed everyone into his or her place, then passed out worksheets appropriate to each role. When students received their worksheets, they started filling them out. Ann stressed the need for quiet in the courtroom; the students looked very engaged, with only a little fidgety off-task behavior.

Then the trial started. The Wampanoag witnesses were followed by colo- (36) nist witnesses. Most students stuck to the lines on their role cards, but a few knew their lines and extemporized. After witnesses for both sides had testified, additional witnesses contradicted some of the testimony. Then Ann took the jurors out of the room and gave them 2 minutes to render a verdict. While they were deliberating, she had the rest of the class finish answers on their worksheets. The jury returned and found the colonists guilty.

The judges then left the room to deliberate sentencing. While they were (37) out, Ann asked the colonists what they thought about the verdict. When a boy suggested planting vegetables, Ann pointed out that the colonists came from England and probably did not know what would grow in Massachusetts. After a small amount of silliness, the children started constructive brainstorming, such as suggesting that the colonists could learn from the Indians what grows in the local geography. The judges returned, sentencing the colonists to share all the deer with the Wampanoag people for 2 years. Ann led a whole-class discussion of the trial and verdict, asking students to consider whether the decisions were fair. She also asked students to consider whether the Native Americans would teach the colonists how to hunt deer without killing them off.

(38)   When I interviewed Ann after the unit had concluded, I realized that she was not yet connecting students' engaged behavior with her careful planning for their active involvement. While teaching, she usually expended considerable energy keeping students on task, but during the simulation, she did not need to do so. She initially attributed their on-task behavior to external factors such as the weather, but by prompting her to reflect on the structure of the unit, I helped her see how her planning offered students a way to become involved and interested in the academic lesson.

Implications for Teacher Education

(39)   Over a 5-month period, Ann moved from a novice level to a developing level in planning multicultural curriculum. She no longer defined the task of curriculum design as finding the "right" way; rather, she sorted through multiple possibilities to plan curriculum that embodied more than one perspective. She no longer accepted the authority of the state and the textbook companies to define what to teach; rather, she considered the scholarship of indigenous people, the perspectives of students, the experiences of teachers of color, and her own experiences with culture and gender. She was supported in working with uncertainty and investing time in reading and thinking to make decisions that she could defend. Her growth, with the kind of support that she received, was similar to that documented in other studies of new teachers in urban schools, in which coursework and mentoring challenge beginning teachers' beliefs—particularly, those related to race, ethnicity, and poverty—focus on pedagogy, and examine tensions between perspectives of new teachers and responses of their students (Achinstein & Athanases, 2005; Chan & East, 1998).

(40)   By carefully reflecting on Ann's learning in the context of my teaching, I learned that the following can help guide teacher educators: First, reflective discussions and writings, as embedded in teachers' classroom work, prompt thinking that can dislodge novice assumptions (Clayton, 2007; Krull et al., 2007). This was a graduate course for practicing classroom teachers; as such, the document analyses, reflective writings, and personal interactions asked them to reflect on their work. For Ann, continued connection between the course and her everyday teaching was fruitful. Analyzing one of her textbooks and interviewing her students prompted her realization that state-defined knowledge assumes a perspective that needs to be questioned. This realization caused her to question where curriculum decision making should be located. Furthermore, the reflective writings helped Ann to name some of her questions and struggles, such as how to build active engagement without losing control over the class.

(41)   Second, to facilitate development beyond novice thinking, it is essential to provide space and support for uncertainty. Ann brought a capacity to self-reflect and live with uncertainty; I could not give her this capacity, but I could work with it. In addition to encouraging reflection in written work and discussions, I made a reasonable attempt to allow students to wonder, to make statements that could be considered naïve, and to disagree with one another and with me. As I examined the journal that I had kept over the semester, I identified Ann's expressions of uncertainty all semester, as well as evidence of her pursuit of questions that interested her. Sometimes in multicultural education courses, students feel shut down and unable to say what they think for fear of offending other students or the professor. This

case study shows how important it is to work on creating a climate in which students can ask questions, express their thoughts, and disagree, as long as they do so respectfully. Without creating space for uncertainty, as well as support for questioning and disagreeing, it is unlikely that an instructor will help teachers develop epistemological sophistication.

Third, teachers value opportunities to learn from peers in contexts of guided inquiry (e.g., Jennings & Smith, 2002). I had structured the course to provide multiple opportunities for peer learning, particularly inviting novice teachers to learn from more-experienced teachers. In addition to having regular small-group discussions that asked teachers to link readings with their teaching experience, I used many readings written by classroom teachers (articles from *Rethinking Schools* in particular), and I invited an experienced multicultural educator as a guest speaker. These opportunities helped Ann to envision viable possibilities for teaching, which broadened her definition of the task of multicultural curriculum design. In a reflection paper, for example, she mentioned that some of the readings from *Rethinking Schools* had been especially helpful to her because they linked political issues with real-world classroom teaching. It appeared to me that opportunities to learn from more-experienced teachers helped novice teachers such as Ann to see possibilities that they might not otherwise see. (42)

Opportunities to learn from perspectives across racial, ethnic, and cultural boundaries stretched teachers' beliefs, sometimes painfully. As mentioned earlier, the teachers in the course were highly diverse; there was no racial or ethnic majority. Furthermore, I chose readings to reflect points of view usually absent or silenced in predominantly White, mainstream contexts. Many class sessions provided various kinds of opportunities for teachers to dialogue about their diverse life experiences and to reflect on their experiences in relationship to people of backgrounds different from their own. Some of these discussions became heated and painful; as instructor, my role was to organize such discussions, then to mediate as needed. For Ann, the process of learning across cultural boundaries enabled her to reject her coworkers' beliefs that "this kind of population needs seatwork" and to hear Macedo's (1994) assertion that students such as those in her classroom need an education that enables them to think and speak out. As she read viewpoints of indigenous writers, she briefly experienced a crisis: She recognized that there is no one "correct" body of knowledge to teach; she then gradually took responsibility for trying to make multiple perspectives visible in her curriculum. The process of hearing perspectives across cultural boundaries also helped her to see the limitations in her textbook's point of view and summon the time and energy to construct an alternative. (43)

Deepening teachers' epistemological thinking in one course is a challenging task. Teacher education courses generally last 10 to 15 weeks, and they are usually located on the college campus rather than in the classrooms where teachers work. Both conditions limit the potential potency of coursework. Because of her participation in this study, I maintained a relationship with Ann after the course had ended in order to visit her classroom. There, I was able to offer guidance and coaching—particularly, reflection about the unit's structure and how it increased students' engagement and decreased discipline problems. This study emphasizes the extent to which teachers weigh the viability of new insights in relationship to their feasibility and their impact on students in the classroom. Rather than plan discrete courses for the development of teachers' epistemological complexity, we should plan entire teacher education programs to that end. (44)

Conclusion

In today's standards-based context, schools tend to reinforce novice assumptions about knowledge by defining what to teach and expecting teachers to accept the state as the main authority over knowledge. When I teach, I (45)

Scientific method: drawing and stating conclusions.

intentionally disrupt that expectation, tapping into historically marginalized points of view about what is worth knowing and into teachers' beliefs about what schooling could be. As Clayton (2007) argues in her case studies of beginning teachers, teachers ultimately need to figure out how to resolve tensions between (1) an institutionalized press toward standardizing knowledge and treating students as passive knowledge consumers and (2) alternative visions of what is worth knowing and what constitutes teaching and learning.

(46)   This case study showed how one novice teacher began to question institutionalized assumptions in the context of a graduate course and how she began to think more complexly. The case study reinforced for me the importance of creating contexts in which teachers can examine their own backgrounds and beliefs, interact with one another, and interact with ideas that stretch them intellectually. Of course, no two teachers bring the same prior experiences, beliefs, and commitments. The challenge for an instructor lies in planning a course that activates a variety of experiences and enables uncomfortable questions and disagreements to take place so that teachers can grow. This inquiry into learning has helped me make sense of that challenge.

REFERENCES

Achinstein, B., & Athanases, S. Z. (2005). Focusing new teachers on diversity and equity. *Teaching and Teacher Education, 21*(7), 843–862.

Banks, J. A. (2004). Race, knowledge construction, and education in the United States. In J. A. Banks & C. A. M. Banks (Eds.), *Handbook of research on multicultural education* (2nd ed., pp. 228–239). San Francisco: Jossey-Bass.

Bigelow, B. (2002). Rethinking primitive cultures: Ancient futures and learning from Ladakh. In B. Bigelow & B. Peterson (Eds.), *Rethinking globalization* (pp. 308–315). Milwaukee, WI: Rethinking Schools.

Bigelow, B., & Peterson, B. (1998). *Rethinking Columbus.* Milwaukee, WI: Rethinking Schools.

Chan, S. M., & East, P. (1998). Teacher education and race equality: A focus on an induction course. *Multicultural Teaching, 16*(2), 43–46.

Churchill, W. (2002). *Struggle for the land.* San Francisco: City Lights.

Clayton, C. D. (2007). Curriculum making as novice professional development: Practical risk taking as learning in high-stakes times. *Journal of Teacher Education, 58*(3), 216–230.

Creswell, J. W. (2008). *Research design: Qualitative, quantitative, and mixed methods approaches.* Thousand Oaks, CA: Sage.

Cushing, K. S., Sabers, D. S., & Berliner, D. C. (1992). Olympic gold: Investigations of expertise in teaching. *Educational Horizons, 70*, 108–114.

Flores, J. (2003). *Dismantling the master's house: Using whose tools?* Unpublished master's thesis, California State University, Monterey Bay.

Grant, C. A., & Sleeter. C. E. (2009). *Turning on learning* (4th ed.). New York: Wiley.

Jennings, L. B., & Smith, C. P. (2002). Examining the role of critical inquiry for transformative practices. *Teachers College Record, 104*(3), 456–481.

Krull, E., Oras, K., & Sisack, S. (2007). Differences in teachers' comments on classroom events as indicators of their professional development. *Teaching and Teacher Education, 23*(7), 1038–1050.

LaDuke, W. (1999). *All our relations: Native struggle for land and life.* Minneapolis, MN: Honor the Earth.

Loewen, J. W. (1995). *Lies my teacher told me.* New York: New Press.

Macedo, D. (1994). *Literacies of power.* Boulder, CO: Westview.

Peterson, B. (2000/2001). Planting the seeds of solidarity. *Rethinking Schools, 15*(2). Retrieved June 1, 2003, from rethinkingschools.org/archive/15_02/Seed152.shtml

Powell, R. R. (1996). Epistemological antecedents to culturally relevant and constructivist classroom curricula: A longitudinal study of teachers' contrasting worldviews. *Teaching and Teacher Education, 12*(4), 365–384.

Schommer, M. (1990). Effects of beliefs about the nature of knowledge on comprehension. *Journal of Educational Psychology, 82*, 498–504.

Schommer, M. (1998). The role of adults' beliefs about knowledge in school, work, and everyday life. In M. C. Smith & T. Pourchot (Eds.), *Adult learning and development: Perspectives from educational psychology* (pp. 127–143). Mahwah, NJ: Erlbaum.

Sleeter, C. E. (2005). *Un-standardizing curriculum: Multicultural teaching in the standards-based classroom.* New York, NY: Teachers College Press.

Stake, R. E. (2000). *The art of case study research.* Thousand Oaks, CA: Sage.

Swanson, H. L., O'Connor, J. E., & Cooney, J. B. (1990). An information processing analysis of expert and novice teachers' problem solving. *American Educational Research Journal, 27*(3), 533–556.

White, B. C. (2000). Pre-service teachers' epistemology viewed through perspectives on problematic classroom situations. *Journal of Education for Teaching, 26*(3), 279–306.

Christine Sleeter is professor emerita in the College of Professional Studies at California State University, Monterey Bay. Her research focuses on antiracist multicultural education and multicultural teacher education.

CHAPTER TWO

Ethics in Educational Research

RGR Collection/Alamy Stock Photo

Karate Kid, 1984

"Research studies are built on trust between the researcher and the participants, and researchers have a responsibility to behave in a trustworthy manner, just as they expect participants to behave in the same manner." (p.61)

LEARNING OUTCOMES

After reading Chapter 2, you should be able to do the following:

2.1 Explain the ethical obligations that educational researchers have (particularly those involving informed consent) and describe the codes they must follow to ensure they adhere to them.

2.2 Understand the ethical issues prevalent in qualitative research and understand how to navigate those issues.

2.3 Understand the issues facing action researchers for IRB approval.

2.4 Describe the issues involved in gaining access to sites to conduct educational research.

Completing Chapter 2 should enable you to perform the following task:

TASK 1D

Identify and briefly state the following for both research studies at the end of Chapter 1:

1. Ethical issues the authors experienced and how they were addressed. (See Performance Criteria, p. 75.)

ETHICAL CODES

Ethical considerations play a role in all research studies, and all researchers must be aware of and attend to the ethical considerations related to their studies. In research, the ends do not justify the means, and researchers must not put the need or desire to carry out a study above the responsibility to maintain the well-being of the study participants. Research studies are built on trust between the researcher and the participants, and researchers have a responsibility to behave in a trustworthy manner, just as they expect participants to behave in the same manner (e.g., by providing responses that can be trusted). The two overriding rules of ethics are that participants should not be harmed in any way—physically, mentally, or socially—and that researchers obtain the participants' informed consent, as discussed in the following sections.

To remind researchers of their responsibilities, professional organizations have developed codes of ethical conduct for their members. The general principles from the Ethical Principles of Psychologists and Code of Conduct adopted by the American Psychological Association (June 1, 2010 and March 1, 2016) provides guidelines and contains specific ethical standards in 10 categories, which are not limited to research: (1) Resolving Ethical Issues, (2) Competence, (3) Human Relations, (4) Privacy and Confidentiality, (5) Advertising and Other Public Statements, (6) Record Keeping and Fees, (7) Education and Training, (8) Research

and Publication, (9) Assessment, and (10) Therapy. You may read the full text online at the website for the American Psychological Association (apa.org).

The American Educational Research Association (AERA) approved a code of ethics in February 2011 (for a comprehensive discussion see *Educational Researcher*, *40*[3], 145–156). The code of ethics of AERA outlines a set of values on which educational researchers should build their research practices. Included in the code of ethics are five principles and 22 ethical standards. The principles are intended to serve as a guide for education researchers in determining ethical behavior in various contexts and include: (a) Professional Competence; (b) Integrity; (c) Professional, Scientific, and Scholarly Responsibility; (d) Respect for People's Rights, Dignity, and Diversity; and (e) Social Responsibility. The 22 ethical standards set forth the rules for ethical conduct by education researchers and, while not intended to be an exhaustive list, aims to cover most situations encountered by education researchers. The list is as follows:

1. Scientific, Scholarly, and Professional Standards
2. Competence
3. Use and Misuse of Expertise
4. Fabrication, Falsification, and Plagiarism
5. Avoiding Harm
6. Nondiscrimination
7. Nonexploitation
8. Harassment

9. Employment Decisions
10. Conflicts of Interest
11. Public Communications
12. Confidentiality
13. Informed Consent
14. Research Planning, Implementation, and Dissemination
15. Authorship Credit
16. Publication Process
17. Responsibilities of Reviewers
18. Teaching, Training, and Administering Education Programs
19. Mentoring
20. Supervision
21. Contractual and Consulting Services
22. Adherence to the Ethical Standards of the American Educational Research Association

Of particular importance is the ethical standard of informed consent, and AERA provides considerable guidance for how and when informed consent with children should be sought (cf. pp. 151–152). This will be discussed further in the section on ethical guidelines. Educational researchers should consider membership in the American Educational Research Association; membership information and benefits can be found at aera.net.

The similarity among the ethical codes is not coincidental; they are based in the same history. In 1974, the U.S. Congress passed the **National Research Act of 1974,** which authorized the creation of the National Commission for the Protection of Human Subjects of Biomedical and Behavioral Research. This commission was charged with developing an ethical code and guidelines for researchers. The need for a standard set of guidelines was prompted by a number of studies in which researchers lied to research participants or put them in harm's way to carry out their studies. For example, in a study on the effects of group pressure conducted in the 1960s, researchers lied to participants, telling them to apply high levels of electric shock to another (unseen) person who was apparently in agony, although no shock was really applied and the unseen person was simply pretending.[1] In another study lasting four decades, men known to be infected with syphilis were not treated for their illness because they were part of a control group in a comparative study.[2]

Today, these types of studies would not be federally funded and could not be conducted at universities, research institutes, and medical centers that adhere to the current ethical guidelines. Most hospitals, colleges, and universities have a review group, usually called the Human Subjects Review Committee (HSRC) or Institutional Review Board (IRB). This board should consist of at least five members, not all of one gender; include one nonscientist; and include at least one member who is mainly concerned with the welfare of the participants. People who may have a conflict of interest (e.g., the researcher of a particular study, a member of the funding organization) are excluded.

INFORMED CONSENT AND PROTECTION FROM HARM

Perhaps the most basic and important ethical issues in research are concerned with protection of participants, broadly defined, which requires that research participants not be harmed in any way (i.e., physically, mentally, or socially) and that they participate only if they freely agree to do so (i.e., give informed consent).

Researchers obtain *informed consent* by making sure that research participants enter the research of their free will and with understanding of the nature of the study and any possible dangers that may arise as a result of participation. This requirement is intended to reduce the likelihood that participants will be exploited by a researcher persuading them to participate when they do not fully know the requirements of the study. Participants who are not of legal age or are not mentally capable cannot give informed consent; in these cases, permission must be given by parents or legal guardians. Even if permission is granted from a guardian, all participants still retain the right to decline to participate—the researcher must provide to each participant, in language appropriate to the individual's developmental level, basic information about the task, and the participant must agree to participate.

[1] "Group Pressure and Action Against a Person," by S. Milgram, 1964, *Journal of Abnormal and Social Psychology, 69* 137–143.

[2] *The Tuskegee Syphilis Experiment*, by J. H. Jones, 1998, New York: Free Press.

Researchers ensure *freedom from harm* first by not exposing participants to undue risks. This requirement involves issues related to personal privacy and confidentiality (i.e., protecting participants from embarrassment or ridicule). Collecting information about participants or observing them without their knowledge or without appropriate permission is not ethical. Furthermore, any information or data that are collected, either from or about a person, should be strictly confidential, especially if it is personal. In other words, access to data should be limited to people directly involved in conducting the research. An individual participant's performance should not be reported or made public using the participant's name, even for a seemingly innocuous measure such as an arithmetic test.

The use of anonymity to ensure confidentiality and avoid privacy invasion and potential harm is common. Study participants have complete **anonymity** when their identities are kept hidden from the researcher. It is often confused with **confidentiality;** researchers protect confidentiality when they know the identities of study participants but do not disclose that information. If the researcher knows participants' identities, the participants should be assured of confidentiality but not anonymity. Removing names from data sheets or coding records is one common way to maintain anonymity. When planning a study, researchers tell participants whether they will provide confidentiality (i.e., the researcher knows but won't tell) or anonymity (i.e., researcher will not know the participants' names); good researchers make sure they know the difference. Sometimes researchers seek access to data from a previous study to examine new questions based on the old data. In such cases, the original researcher has the responsibility to maintain the confidentiality or anonymity promised the participants of the original study.

When research is conducted in the classroom, concerns about confidentiality and anonymity are frequently raised. The **Family Educational Rights and Privacy Act of 1974,** usually referred to as the Buckley Amendment, was designed to protect the privacy of students' educational records. Among its provisions is the specification that data that identify a student may not be made available unless written permission is acquired from the student (if of legal age) or a parent or legal guardian. The permission form must indicate what data may be disclosed, for what purposes, and to whom. If a study requires obtaining information from individual elementary students' school record files, the researcher must obtain written permission from each student's parent or guardian, not a blanket approval from the school principal or classroom teacher. In contrast, researchers interested in using class averages (in which no individual student was identified) can usually seek permission only from the principal. However, if a researcher planned to calculate the class average him- or herself by using information provided in individual student records, permission from each student is required.

There are some exceptions to this requirement for written consent. For example, school personnel with a legitimate educational interest in a student would not need written consent to examine student records (e.g., a teacher conducting action research in his or her own classroom). In other cases, the researcher could request that a teacher or guidance counselor either remove names from students' records completely or replace them with a coded number or letter. The researcher could then use the records without knowing the names of the individual students.

Deception

A common ethical dilemma in research with human subjects occurs when a researcher wants to study a topic that he or she cannot disclose completely to potential participants without influencing or changing the participants behavior or responses. Studies concerned with participants' attitudes about things like race, gender, or culture are often susceptible to such influences. In such instances researchers can be tempted to hide the true nature of the topic of study. A common example where this dilemma can surface in research on teaching and classrooms are studies on teachers' interactions with or attitudes towards students. Teachers' responses on a survey or their behaviors during an observation may be affected if the teachers know the aim of the study and change their normal behaviors as a result. When deception occurs, participants cannot truly give informed consent.

This type of deception is a form of lying, and studies in which the researcher plans to deceive participants must be carefully scrutinized on ethical grounds. Some researchers believe that any study that requires deceitful practice should not be carried out. Others recognize that some important studies cannot be undertaken without deception. We recommend that you do your initial research studies on topics that do not require deception. If you choose a topic that involves deception, your adviser and the HSRC or IRB at your institution will provide suggestions for ethical ways to carry out your research plan. Remember that all researchers, even student-researchers, are responsible for maintaining ethical standards in the research.

MyLab Education **Self-Check 2.1**

MyLab Education **Application Exercise 2.1:**
Evaluating Research Articles: Understanding Research Ethics

MyLab Education **Application Exercise 2.2:**
Reflecting on Ethics in Educational Research

ETHICAL ISSUES UNIQUE TO QUALITATIVE RESEARCH

The ethical issues and responsibilities discussed thus far pertain to both quantitative and qualitative research plans. However, some features of qualitative research raise additional issues not typically encountered in quantitative research.

Qualitative research differs from quantitative research in at least two major ways that produce additional ethical concerns. First, qualitative research plans typically evolve and change as the researcher's immersion in and understanding of the research setting grow. In a real sense, the research plan is only generally formed when presented to the IRB. As the plan evolves with added understanding of the context and participants, unanticipated and un-reviewed ethical issues can arise and need to be resolved on the spot. For example, as participants become more comfortable with the researcher, they often ask to see what has been written about them. They feel entitled to this information, even though seeing what has been written may cause personal distress for them or data collection problems for the researcher. Second,

qualitative researchers typically are personally engaged in the research context. Interviews, observations, and debriefings bring the researcher and participants in close, personal contact. The closeness between participants and researcher helps to provide deep and rich data, but it may also create unintended influences on objectivity and data interpretation.

Another professional organization that provides guidance for qualitative researchers is the American Anthropological Association (AAA) that adopted a Code of Ethics in 2012. These guidelines are helpful for ethnographic researchers in particular, and qualitative researchers in general. As Glesne (2016) acknowledges, "The AAA Code of Ethics includes directives on the researcher's responsibilities to scholarship, the public, employees, students and trainees, and to applied work" (p. 172). These directives can be summarized as follows:

1. Avoidance of harm
2. Open, honest, and transparent conduct of the research process
3. Ongoing informed consent of research participants
4. Accessibility of results
5. Accurate reporting of results taking into consideration the social and political implications of the research

For a comprehensive discussion of the AAA Code of Ethics visit www.aaanet.org/profdev/ethics and Glesne[3] pp. 158–182.

The focus on immersion and detailed knowledge of the research context, more common in qualitative than quantitative research, may result in the researcher observing behavior that may otherwise be hidden, such as illegal or unprofessional activities. The qualitative researcher may observe theft, emotional cruelty and ridicule, or narcotics use, for example. In these and other similar situations, the researcher must make a choice—report the observations, knowing that to do so likely will end the study because participants will no longer be certain of the researcher's promise of confidentiality, or keep silent on the assumption that the system will eventually identify and correct the problems. In educational research, if the researcher perceives

---

[3] *Becoming Qualitative Researchers: An Introduction.* (5th Ed.) by C. Glesne, 2016, Upper Saddle River, NJ: Pearson

physical or psychological danger, he or she has a strong mandate to inform the school authorities.

Unfortunately, not all situations present ethically clear actions. To respond appropriately and to make ethical decisions, qualitative researchers must ensure that their professional ethical perspectives are closely aligned with their personal ethical perspectives. This statement may seem obvious, except for this caveat: Qualitative researchers may find themselves in situations that require an immediate response—the very essence of which may threaten the success of the research. If your personal and research ethical perspectives are aligned, you will in all likelihood respond to ethical challenges in an appropriate, professional fashion that will not threaten the ongoing conduct of your research.

Considering ethics before commencing qualitative research is one way to ensure that you will be prepared to respond in an ethical, caring manner if difficult situations arise. The role of ethics in qualitative research can be considered in terms of how we treat the individuals with whom we interact in research settings. The nature of the qualitative research enterprise provides the potential for conflict and harm, and it is critical that everyone involved has a clear understanding of the intimate and open-ended nature of the research process so that participants are not injured in the name of research.

To summarize, qualitative research is intimate because there is little distance between researchers and their study participants. Qualitative research is open-ended because the direction of the research often unfolds during the course of the study. As a result, qualitative researchers often cannot obtain participants' informed consent, the principle that seeks to ensure that all human research participants retain autonomy and the ability to judge for themselves whether risks are worth taking for the purpose of furthering scientific knowledge.

Navigating Ethical Issues in Qualitative Research

The following commonsense ethical guideposts, adapted from Smith,[4] may help qualitative researchers respond appropriately when faced with ethical

[4] "Ethics in Qualitative Field Research," by L. M. Smith, 1990, in *Qualitative Inquiry in Education: The Continuing Debate*, by E. W. Eisner and A. P. Peshkin (Eds.), New York: Teachers College Press.

decisions before, during, and after a qualitative research inquiry.

1. *A researcher should have an ethical perspective with regard to the research that is very close to his or her personal ethical position.* Qualitative researchers may find themselves in situations that seem foreign. For example, consider a collaborative action research project focused on how a new math problem-solving curriculum affects student achievement and attitude. Teachers distribute student attitude surveys in their classrooms, which are later analyzed by a team of teacher-researchers representing different grades in the school. During the analysis, it becomes clear that students in one of the groups are very unhappy with their math instruction and have supported their assertions with negative comments about the teacher. What will you do with the data? Should they be shared in an unedited form with the teacher? Who stands to be hurt in the process? What potential good can come from sharing the data? What assurances of confidentiality were given to the participants before collecting the data?

   This scenario is not meant to scare you away from doing qualitative research but rather to illustrate the unexpected outcomes that occasionally face qualitative researchers. Smith's guidepost is an important one. You will more likely avoid such awkward situations if you clarify your ethical perspectives at the outset. A values clarification activity that can be undertaken individually or collectively may be helpful. It is worthwhile to reflect on how you would want to be treated as a participant in a research study. How would you feel if you were deceived by the researchers? What action would you take? How can you prevent research participants from feeling exploited? Again, there are no simple answers to these ethical questions. The point is this: Be prepared to respond in a manner that is comfortable and natural for you.

2. *Informed consent should take the form of a dialogue that mutually shapes the research and the results.* Be clear about whether you need to seek permission from

participants in the study by discussing the research project with a school administrator or central office person who can describe instances that require written permission, and check the requirements of your IRB. For example, if you are collecting photographs or digital recordings as data and intend to use these artifacts in a public forum, such as a presentation at a conference, make sure that you know whether written permission is necessary.

Thinking about the relation between confidentiality and informed consent helps to clarify some of these issues. Confidentiality is important for protecting research informants from stress, embarrassment, or unwanted publicity as well as for protecting participants should they reveal something to a researcher that could be used against them by others interested in the outcomes of the research. In some qualitative research efforts, assigning pseudonyms to conceal identities is not enough because other details can lead to identification of the individuals or specific research settings. Researchers must consider whether participants would have consented to the study had they known about the type of data collected and the way in which results would be distributed, and they must take steps to ensure that participants' right to privacy is not violated. Informed consent should take the form of an ongoing dialogue that shapes the research and the results.

3. *Researchers should also think beyond the methods they plan to use; they must identify broader social principles that are integral parts of who they are as researchers and as contributing members of the communities in which they live.* These broader social principles dictate one's ethical stance. For example, a researcher studying schools in Ferguson, Missouri following the shooting of Michael Brown, an unarmed black teenager by a white police officer, may have faced social justice, equality, and emancipation issues in a politically volatile environment. The researcher was struggling with the ethical challenges of being in a community and how her insider lens (to neighborhood listservs, etc.) gave her access to data that she was not explicitly granted permission to use. She was struggling with the public/private realm of neighborhood sites like Nextdoor, Facebook, and so on, and whether those conversations could be analyzed by a researcher engaged in a community-based development project (personal communication, Arend, 2017).

4. *Qualitative researchers are morally bound to conduct their research in a manner that minimizes potential harm to those involved in the study.* A broader view of this concept suggests that qualitative researchers need to convey with confidence that research participants will not suffer harm as the result of their involvement in the research effort.

5. *Even though an action may bring about good results, it is not ethical unless that action also conforms to ethical standards such as honesty and justice.* From this perspective, acting ethically may be viewed in terms of doing unto others as you would have them do unto you. For example, it is unethical to treat participants as research pawns or as means to an end.

6. *The qualitative researcher must remain attentive to the relationship between the researcher and the participants, a relationship determined by "roles, status, language, and cultural norms."*[5] The lesson for qualitative researchers who are proponents of this perspective is to pay attention to the research processes of giving information, reciprocity, and collaboration and to be sensitive to how these processes are viewed by other participants in the research. Again, this perspective forces us to confront the socially responsive characteristics of our research efforts as being democratic, equitable, liberating, and life-enhancing.

The purpose of this discussion on ethics in qualitative research has been to prepare you to think about a range of issues that face any researcher. Carefully consider how you will respond when confronted with difficult questions from colleagues, parents, students, and administrators. Taking time to clarify your values and ethical perspectives will help you respond in a professional, personal, and caring fashion.

---

[5] "In Search of Ethical Guidance: Constructing a Basis for Dialogue," by D. J. Flinders, 1992, *Qualitative Studies in Education,* 5(2), p. 108.

As you embark on your qualitative research journey, remember that, in matters of ethics, there are few absolutes. Working through issues related to confidentiality, anonymity, informed consent, and rational judgment before you begin will help you to avoid or resolve potentially difficult situations that may arise in implementing a qualitative research effort.

Action Research and IRBs

Another group of qualitative researchers who face unique challenges are classroom-based, school-based researchers using an action research design. Specifically, action researchers conducting research as part of a university program face unique challenges associated with obtaining IRB approval and must meet standards that go beyond what most schools and school districts require as part of their own research protocols. IRBs are charged by universities to ensure the ethical conduct of research involving human subjects. The key issue for action researchers studying their own practices (for example, teachers conducting action research) and, hence, collecting data based primarily on student outcomes relates to the fact that they are acting not only as researchers but also as the change agents who have the power and authority to bring about change in their classrooms. According to Nolen and Vander Putten,[6] "These potentially conflicting roles can confound the individual's primary objective in the classroom or school: student learning" (p. 402). Given this potential conflict, Nolen and Vander Putten raise a number of questions, the answers to which provide guidance for school-based researchers seeking to obtain IRB approval:

- At what point does teaching become research?
- Where does the accountability for this research lie?
- Are teachers properly trained to see the possible ethical pitfalls in such research?
- How are the rights and freedoms of the research participants (the students) protected?

For example, given the emancipatory nature of action research, it is clear that the answer to the

first question is that teaching and research are intertwined. For action researchers studying their own practices and their impact on student outcomes, the inquiry lens of action research pervades the teaching process: Teacher researchers are the data collection instruments constantly monitoring what is going on in their classrooms. The accountability for this research lies not only with the teacher researcher but also, in a university context, with the researcher's mentor/teacher, who must ensure that proposed action research studies are ethical in their conduct. As such, it is the responsibility of the university instructor to teach neophyte teacher researchers about the potential ethical pitfalls associated with classroom/school-based action research.

In many ways, the most complex issue action researchers face is how to safeguard the rights and freedoms of the students in the classrooms. How do teachers negotiate informed consent with students (and their parents)? Are students really in a position to opt out of any research their classroom teachers are conducting? Similarly, this question raises concerns about the role of power and authority in a classroom environment and whether students can reasonably be expected to opt out of a study without being concerned about possible censure by the classroom teacher. It should be noted that these kinds of concerns are not new to action researchers or any other qualitatively oriented community-based researchers. IRBs often struggle with social science research proposals that invariably focus on "insider" research, where the research process is inherently open ended and intimate. Teacher researchers are active participant observers of their classrooms, continually monitoring and adjusting their teaching based on formal and informal observations of their students.

Given this context, we offer the following recommendations for action researchers wishing to obtain IRB approval (adapted from Nolen and Vander Putten, 2007):

- Action researchers should provide IRBs with all the necessary university-based IRB requirements (which vary slightly from university to university).
- Action researchers should provide IRBs, school district administrators, and parents with data collection plans that clearly minimize data sources

[6] "Action research in education: Addressing gaps in ethical principles and practices," by A. L. Nolen and J. Vander Putten, 2007, *Educational Researcher, 36*(7), 401–407.

that could be construed as providing evidence that could be used in a coercive manner.

- Action researchers should provide IRBs, school district administrators, and parents with cover letters that explain their studies and include statements about the dual role of teacher and researcher and the sensitivity it takes to conduct research into one's own practice.
- Action researchers should provide IRBs, school district administrators, and parents with parental consent forms that clearly state how they will guarantee that students will be protected from harm, that is, that students will not be penalized for not participating in a study.

Action researchers should include in all data collection instruments a final "yes or no" option, such as "Please include my answers in the study," which unobtrusively allows the student to opt out of the study while appearing to participate. It is the burden of the action researcher to provide the IRB with evidence that the proposed study clearly addresses issues of informed consent, protection from harm, student autonomy, and the potentially coercive nature of action research. The National Research Act of 1974 was also designed to protect the privacy of students' educational records. Among its provisions is the specification that data that actually identify students may not be made available unless written permission is acquired from the students (if of age) or a parent or legal guardian. The consent must indicate what data may be disclosed, for what purposes, and to whom. If part of your study requires obtaining information from individual elementary students' record files, you would need to obtain written permission from each student's parent or guardian, not a blanket approval from the school principal or classroom teacher. Note that if you are interested in using only class averages (in which no individual student is identified), individual consent from the principal would likely suffice. If you calculate the class average from individual student records, however, individual permission would be necessary because you have access to individual records.

There are some exceptions that may not require written consent. For example, school personnel with a "legitimate educational interest" in a student would not need written consent to examine student records. In other cases, the researcher could request that a teacher or guidance counselor either remove names from students' records completely or replace them with a coded number or letter. The researcher can then use the records without knowing the names of the individual students. Again, this adherence to providing anonymity offers other instructional challenges for the teacher researcher who wishes to use formative and summative evaluation data to develop specific instructional interventions designed to meet students' needs.

It is also worth noting that some IRBs do not require IRB approval for action research conducted as part of a university course. Be sure to check with your instructor and/or IRB to determine if IRB approval is required at your university. Sometimes the determining factor in this decision relates to whether the outcomes of the proposed study will be published or presented at a professional conference. See Figure 2.1 for a summary of ethical guidelines for action researchers.

MyLab Education **Self-Check 2.2**

MyLab Education **Self-Check 2.3**

MyLab Education **Application Exercise 2.3:** Obtaining IRB Approval for Action Researchers

---

FIGURE 2.1 • Ethical guidelines for action researchers

_____ Determine whether you require IRB approval and/ or school district approval.

_____ If necessary, obtain IRB approval.

_____ Seek your research participants' informed consent.

_____ Consider confidentiality, anonymity, and avoidance of harm.

_____ Deception is unacceptable.

_____ Develop an ethical research perspective that is close to your personal, ethical position.

_____ Determine the broader social principles that affect your ethical stance.

_____ Ensure that you accurately record data.

Source: Action Research: A Guide for the Teacher Researcher (6th ed.) by G. E. Mills, 2018, Upper Saddle River, NJ: Pearson.

GAINING ENTRY TO A RESEARCH SITE

Very rarely is it possible to conduct educational research without the cooperation of other people. An initial step in acquiring the needed cooperation is to identify and follow required procedures for gaining approval to conduct the study in the chosen site. In schools, research approval is usually granted by the superintendent, school board, or some other high-level administrator, such as the associate superintendent for instruction. In other settings, such as hospitals or industry, an individual or a committee is typically charged with examining and then approving or denying requests to do research at the site. Regardless of the site, the researcher must complete one or more forms that describe the nature of the research, the specific request being made of the site personnel, and the benefits to the site. Before the request is approved, the researcher may need to obtain permission from others as well; for example, a superintendent or school board may require that permission be granted from the principal or principals whose schools will be involved. Even if such approval is not required, it should be sought, both as a courtesy and for the sake of a smoothly executed study. Of course, as discussed earlier, all participants must agree to be part of the study. Depending on the nature of the study, permission, or at least acceptance, should be obtained from the teachers who will participate in the study. If students under age 18 are to be involved, written parental permission will be needed.

Given the potential complexity of obtaining permission to conduct your research at the chosen site or sites, you should not assume that permission will be granted easily (e.g., often researchers hear, "we're too busy") or quickly (i.e., bureaucracies move slowly). Thus, you should think carefully about how to explain your study to all those who must provide permission and approval. The key to gaining approval and cooperation is good planning, and the key to good planning is a well-designed, carefully thought-out study and research plan. Some superintendents and principals are hesitant about research in their schools because of previous bad experiences. They don't want anyone else running around their schools, disrupting classes, administering poorly constructed questionnaires, or finding problems. It is up to you to convince school personnel that what you are proposing is of value, that your study is carefully designed, and that you will work with teachers to minimize inconvenience.

Achieving full cooperation, beyond approval on paper, requires that you invest as much time as is necessary to discuss your study with the principals, the teachers, and perhaps even parents. These groups have varying levels of knowledge and understanding regarding the research process. Their concerns will focus mainly on the perceived value of the study, its potential impact on participants, and the logistics of carrying it out. The principal, for example, will probably be more concerned with whether you are collecting any data that may be viewed as objectionable by the community than with the specific design you will be using. All groups will be interested in what you may be able to do for them. You should fully explain any potential benefits to the students, teachers, or principals as a result of your study. Your study, for example, may involve special instructional materials that are given to the teachers after the data collection ends. Even if all parties are favorably impressed, however, the spirit of cooperation will quickly dwindle if your study involves considerable extra work or inconvenience on their part. Bear in mind that principals and teachers are accommodating you; they are helping you complete your study without relief from their normal responsibilities. If asked, you should make any changes you can in the study to better preserve participants' normal routines, as long as you do not adversely affect your work or its results. No change should be made solely for the sake of the compromise without considering its impact on the study as a whole.

It is not unusual for principals or teachers to want something in return for their participation. The request may be related to your study, as when a principal asks to review your final report for accuracy, asks you to return to the school to describe your findings to teachers, or requests that your results not be disseminated without the principal's approval. The first two requests are more easily agreed to than the third, which probably should be refused in favor of an offer to discuss

FIGURE 2.2 • Principal's letter to parents concerning a proposed research study

THE SCHOOL BOARD OF KNOX COUNTY, MASSACHUSETTS

Oak Street Elementary School
Gwen Gregory, Principal
113 Oak Street
Clover, Massachusetts
555-555-5555

January 23, 2005

Dear Parent/Guardian:

Oak Street Elementary School has been chosen to participate in a research study. Our school was selected out of the entire country as a result of our outstanding students and computer program. All third- and fifth-grade students will be able to participate. The results of this study will enable our teachers and parents to discover and understand the learning styles of our students. This knowledge will enable teachers and parents to provide special instruction and materials to improve student learning. It will also provide valuable information for the future development of effective professional computer software.

This study will take place from January 29 to March 30, 2005. It will be conducted by Mrs. Joleen Levine, a recognized and experienced computer educator. She has been Director of Computer Education at Northern University for six years. During that time she has participated in many projects in Knox County that involved teacher training, computer curriculum development, and computer assisted instruction implementation.

I have reviewed this research study and feel that it is a very worthwhile endeavor for our students and school. Please review the information on the following page in order to make a decision concerning permission consent for your child to participate in this study.

Sincerely,

Gwen Gregory

Gwen Gregory
Principal

the principal's concerns, if any. It is also common for principals to ask the researcher to provide a session or two of professional development for teachers in the school.

Figure 2.2 presents a letter written by a principal to inform parents of a doctoral student's proposed study. The doctoral student appears to have shared the potential benefits of the study with the principal and, as a result, secured not only the principal's permission but also her strong support and cooperation. The parental permission form that accompanied the letter, shown in Figure 2.3, addresses many of the ethical and legal concerns discussed in this chapter.

Clearly, human relations are an important factor in conducting research in applied settings. That you should be your usual charming self goes without saying, but you should keep in mind that

---

FIGURE 2.3 • Parental permission form for a proposed research study

PARENTAL PERMISSION FORM

The information provided on this form and the accompanying cover letter is presented to you in order to fulfill legal and ethical requirements for Northwest Eaton College (the institution sponsoring this doctoral dissertation study) and the Department of Health and Human Services (HHS) regulations for the Protection of Human Research Subjects as amended on March 26, 1989. The wording used in this form is utilized for all types of studies and should not be misinterpreted for this particular study.

The dissertation committee at Northern University and the Research Review Committee of Knox County Public Schools have both given approval to conduct this study, "The Relationships Between the Modality Preferences of Elementary Students and Selected Instructional Styles of CAI as They Affect Verbal Learning of Facts." The purpose of this study is to determine the effect on achievement scores when the identified learning styles (visual, audio, tactile/kinesthetic) of elementary students in grades 3 and 5 are matched or mismatched to the instructional methods of specifically selected computer assisted instruction (CAI).

Your child will be involved in this study by way of the following:

1. Pretest on animal facts.
2. Posttest on animal facts.
3. Test on learning styles.
4. Interaction with computer-assisted instruction (CAI-software on the computer)—visual, audio, tactile CAI matching the student's own learning style.

All of these activities should not take more than two hours per student. There are no foreseeable risks to the students involved. In addition, the parent or researcher may remove the student from the study at any time with just cause. Specific information about individual students will be kept *strictly confidential* and will be obtainable from the school principal if desired. The results that are published publicly will not reference any individual students since the study will only analyze relationships among groups of data.

The purpose of this form is to allow your child to participate in the study, and to allow the researcher to use the information already available at the school or information obtained from the actual study to analyze the outcomes of the study. Parental consent for this research study is strictly voluntary without undue influence or penalty. The parent signature below also assumes that the child understands and agrees to participate cooperatively.

If you have additional questions regarding the study, the rights of subjects, or potential problems, please call the principal, Ms. Gwen Gregory, or the researcher, Ms. Joleen Levine (Director of Computer Education, Northern University, 555-5554).

_____

Student's Name

_____   _____

Signature of Parent/Guardian   Date

---

you are dealing with sincere, concerned educators who may not have your level of research expertise. Therefore, you must make a special effort to discuss your study in plain English (it is possible!) and never give school personnel the impression that you are talking down to them. Also, your task is not over once the study begins. The feelings of involved persons must be monitored and responded to throughout the duration of the study if the initial level of cooperation is to be maintained.

The sources and advice noted in this chapter will help you conceive and conduct ethical studies, and to successfully gain access to your research site/s. The suggestions do not cover all the ethical issues you are likely to encounter in your research. Perhaps the fundamental ethical rule is that participants should not be harmed in any way, real or possible, in the name of science. Respect and concern for your own integrity and for your participants' dignity and welfare are the bottom lines of ethical research.

MyLab Education **Self-Check 2.4**

MyLab Education **Application**
Exercise 2.4: Understanding Considerations in Accessing Research Sites

SUMMARY

ETHICAL CODES

1. Ethical considerations play a role in all research studies, and all researchers must be aware of and attend to ethical considerations in their research.

2. The two overriding rules of ethics are that participants should not be harmed in any way—physically, mentally, or socially—and that researchers must obtain the participants' informed consent.

3. Professional organizations develop ethical principles for their members, and the federal government has enacted laws to protect research participants from harm and invasion of privacy.

4. Probably the most definitive sources of ethical guidelines for researchers are the Ethical Principles of Psychologists and Code of Conduct adopted in 2010 by the American Psychological Association, the Code of Ethics approved by the American Educational Research Association in 2011, and the ethical guidelines adopted by the American Anthropological Association in 2012.

5. The National Research Act of 1974 led to the creation of a standard set of federal guidelines for the protection of human research participants.

6. Most hospitals, colleges, and universities require that proposed research activities involving human participants be reviewed and approved by an IRB prior to the execution of the research, to ensure protection of the participants.

INFORMED CONSENT AND PROTECTION FROM HARM

7. Researchers obtain informed consent by making sure that research participants enter the research of their free will and with understanding of the nature of the study and any possible dangers that may arise as a result of participation.

8. Study participants are assured of confidentiality; researchers promise not to disclose participants' identities or information

that could lead to discovery of those identities. Confidentiality differs from anonymity; the identities of anonymous participants are hidden from the researcher as well.

9. The Family Educational Rights and Privacy Act of 1974, referred to as the Buckley Amendment, protects the privacy of the educational records of students. It stipulates that data that identify participants by name may not be made available to the researcher unless written permission is granted by the participants.

Deception

10. Studies involving deception of participants are sometimes unavoidable but should be examined critically for unethical practices.

ETHICAL ISSUES UNIQUE TO QUALITATIVE RESEARCH

11. Qualitative researchers, because of their closeness to participants, must pay special attention to ethical issues and view informed consent as a process that evolves and changes throughout the study. Qualitative researchers may witness dangerous or illegal behavior and may have to make ethical decisions on the spot.

Navigating Ethical Issues in Qualitative Research

12. A researcher should have an ethical perspective with regard to the research that is very close to his or her personal ethical position.

13. Informed consent should take the form of a dialogue that mutually shapes the research and the results.

14. Researchers should also think beyond the methods they plan to use; they must identify broader social principles that are integral parts of who they are as researchers and as contributing members of the communities in which they live.

15. Qualitative researchers are morally bound to conduct their research in a manner that minimizes potential harm to those involved in the study.

16. Even though an action may bring about good results, it is not ethical unless that action also conforms to ethical standards such as honesty and justice.

17. The qualitative researcher must remain attentive to the relationship between the researcher and the participants, a relationship determined by roles, status, language, and cultural norms.

Action Research and IRBs

18. Action researchers should provide IRBs with all the necessary university-based IRB requirements (which vary slightly from university to university).

19. Action researchers should provide IRBs, school district administrators, and parents with data collection plans that clearly minimize data sources that could be construed as providing evidence that could be used in a coercive manner.

20. Action researchers should provide IRBs, school district administrators, and parents with cover letters that explain their studies and include statements about the dual role of teacher and researcher and the sensitivity it takes to conduct research into one's own practice.

21. Action researchers should provide IRBs, school district administrators, and parents with parental consent forms that clearly state how they will guarantee that students will be protected from harm; that is, that students will not be penalized for not participating in a study.

GAINING ENTRY TO A RESEARCH SITE

22. It is rarely possible to conduct research without the cooperation of other people. The first step in acquiring needed cooperation is to follow required procedures in the chosen site.

23. A formal approval process usually involves the completion of one or more forms describing the nature of the research and the specific request being made of the school or other system.

24. The key to gaining approval and cooperation is good planning and a well-designed, carefully constructed study.

25. After formal approval for the study is granted, you should invest the time necessary to explain the study to the principal, the teachers, and perhaps even parents. If these groups do not cooperate, you will likely not be able to do your study.

26. If changes in the study are requested and can be made to accommodate the normal routine of the participants, these changes should be made unless the research will suffer as a consequence.

27. The feelings of participants should be monitored and responded to throughout the study if the initial level of cooperation is to be maintained. Human relations are important when conducting research in applied research settings.

PERFORMANCE CRITERIA   TASK 1D

Reprints of two published research reports appeared at the end of Chapter 1. Read the reports and describe any potential ethical dilemmas faced by the researchers. If the authors do not explicitly state ethical dilemmas they faced during the conduct of the study, make an inference about possible dilemmas and challenges based on the description of the research. One or two sentences should be sufficient to describe potential ethical challenges. See Appendix B for possible challenges faced by the authors.

CHAPTER THREE

Selecting and Defining a Research Problem

Everett Collection

Doctor's Orders, 1930

"Some graduate students spend many anxiety-ridden days and sleepless nights worrying about where they are going to find a problem to address in their theses or dissertations." (p. 78)

LEARNING OUTCOMES

After reading Chapter 3, you should be able to do the following:

3.1 Describe the importance of selecting and defining a good research problem.
3.2 Identify a research problem.
3.3 Formulate and state a hypothesis.

Completing Chapter 3 should enable you to perform the following task:

TASK 2

1. Identify a general subject area that is related to your area of expertise and is of particular interest to you.

2. State whether the general subject area is related to an educational theory, personal experience (problem of practice), replication of a study that interests you, the result of a library search, or the outcome of participation in an electronic forum.
3. State your research problem.
4. State your research questions (See Performance Criteria p. 93.)

THE RESEARCH PROBLEM

Selecting and defining a research problem is the first step in applying the scientific method. Before you read more about this first step, a few comments about the research process seem appropriate. Textbooks tend to present the research process and its steps in a simple, linear form: Do this and then this and then this, and ultimately you'll get to where you want to be. Although a linear format provides a necessary template for student learning, the reality of educational research is that progress is seldom so straightforward. Educational research is truly a process of trial and error. As you investigate and refine a research problem, for instance, you will find things that don't fit as expected, ideas that are not as clear on paper as they were in your head, and ideas that require considerable rethinking and rewriting. That is the reality of research. However, your ability to work through these challenges is an important and satisfying measure of your understanding. Remember this as you embark on this learning experience.

The research problem provides focus and structure for the remaining steps in the scientific method; it is the thread that binds everything together. Selecting and defining a problem should entail considerable thought. An initial problem that is broad and complex often proves unmanageable for study, and the researcher must narrow its scope

to implement or complete the study. When properly defined, the research problem reduces a study to a manageable size.

The research problem that you ultimately select is the problem you will work with in succeeding chapters of this text. Therefore, it is important that you select a problem relevant to your area of study and of particular interest to you. The Chapter 3 outcomes are for you to identify and define a meaningful problem and to state a testable hypothesis. A problem statement and a hypothesis are components of both a written research plan and a research report.

> MyLab Education **Self-Check 3.1**

IDENTIFYING A RESEARCH PROBLEM

Throughout our school careers, we are taught to solve problems of various kinds. Ask people to list the 10 most important outcomes of education, and most will mention problem-solving skills. Now, after many years of emphasis on solving problems, you face a research task that asks you to find, rather than solve, a problem. If you are like most people, you have had little experience finding problems. For beginning researchers, selection of a problem is the most difficult step in the research process. Some graduate students spend many anxiety-ridden days and sleepless nights worrying about where they are going to find a problem to address in their theses or dissertations.

The first step in selecting a research problem is to identify a general subject area that is related to your area of expertise and is of particular interest to you. Remember, you will be spending a great deal of time reading about and working with your chosen problem. Having one that interests you will help you maintain focus during the months of conducting your study.

Sources of Research Problems

You may be asking yourself, "Where do research problems come from? Where should I look to ferret out problems to study?" The four main sources of research problems are theories, personal experiences, previous studies that can be replicated, and library searches. Additional sources are discussed in the section on digital research tools for the 21st century and include: RSS feeds, Facebook, Twitter, blogs, and electronic mailing lists.

Theories

The most meaningful problems are generally those derived from theories. A **theory** is an organized body of concepts, generalizations, and principles that can be investigated. Educationally relevant theories, such as theories of learning and behavior, can provide the inspiration for many research problems. For example, Jean Piaget posited that children's thinking develops in four stages: the sensorimotor stage (birth to approximately age 2 years), preoperational stage (approximately age 2 to 7 years), concrete operational stage (approximately age 7 to 11 years), and formal operational stage (approximately age 11 years and older). Piaget described tasks and behaviors that children can and cannot do at each stage. Whether aspects of Piaget's theory operate as suggested is a good basis for many possible research problems. For example, a researcher may explore certain factors that may affect the length of time children take to pass from one stage to the next.

Research focused on aspects of a theory is not only conceptually rich; such research also provides information that confirms or disconfirms one or more of those aspects and may suggest additional

studies to test the theory further. Take a moment now to think of two other theories that are popular in education and, from them, identify a few problems to investigate.

Personal Experiences

Another common way to identify research problems is to examine some of the questions we often ask ourselves about education. Questions may arise when we participate in class discussion, read articles in local newspapers and educational journals, or interact with others. When we observe or read about schools, teachers, and programs, we should ask ourselves questions such as "Why does that happen?" "What causes that?" "What would happen if…?" and "How would a different group respond to this?" Normally we think only briefly about such questions before returning to our everyday business, but such questions are probably the most common source of research problems because they capture our interest. It is hard to imagine an educator who has never had a hunch about a better way to do something (e.g., increase learning or improve student behavior) or asked questions about a program or materials whose effectiveness was untested (e.g., questioning why a writing program was successful or why science materials were not). A possible research problem based on personal experience could be "What is the impact of the Every Student Succeed Acts (ESSA) testing requirements on the ways teachers teach?" For classroom practitioners, another source of a research problem would be daily classroom life and the effects of teaching practices on student outcomes—the starting place for action research.

Studies That Can Be Replicated

An additional source of research problems is previously published studies, many of which can be replicated. A **replication** is a repetition of a study using different subjects to retest its hypothesis. No single study, regardless of its focus or breadth, provides the certainty needed to assume that similar results occur in all or most similar situations. Progress through research usually comes from accumulated understandings and explanations, and replication is a tool to provide such accumulated information.

In most cases, the method of a replication is not identical to the original study. Rather, some feature or features of the original study are altered in an attempt to stretch or move beyond the original findings. For example, the researcher may select a different sample of participants for the replication in the hope of determining whether the results are the same as those found in the original study. Or the researcher may examine a different kind of community or student, use a different questionnaire, or apply a different method of data analysis. There are many different interesting and useful ways to replicate studies in the many domains of education. For example, a possible replication study may focus on how students' use of computers in classrooms affects their achievement, and the study may extend original studies in the area by providing computers to children who have not previously had access to such technology.

Library Searches

Another commonly cited source for a research problem is a library search. Many students are encouraged to immerse themselves in the library and read voraciously in their areas of study until research problems emerge. Although some research problems may emerge from library immersion, they are considerably fewer than those emerging from theories, personal experiences, and previous studies. Trying to identify a problem amid the enormous possibilities in a library is akin to looking for a needle in a haystack—sometimes we find it, but not very often. Clearly libraries are essential sources of information in the research process, but the library is most useful to the researcher after a problem has been narrowed. Then library resources can provide

information to place the problem in perspective, reveal what researchers have already learned about the problem, and suggest methods for carrying out a study.

Electronic Mailing Lists

Researchers frequently use e-mail to solicit advice and feedback and conduct dialogue with peers and experts in their fields. The most common way to do so is by subscribing to electronic mailing lists as part of membership to professional organizations. Electronic mailing lists are designed by organizations or special interest groups to facilitate communication among their members. Through these lists, you can expect to receive announcements and bulletins related to your area of interest. In addition, you can post comments or questions to the mailing list. Your messages will be read by members of the list, who may respond to you personally or to the mailing list as a whole.

An electronic mailing list is a good resource to consult when you are devising a research problem. You can ask list members what they think of a particular problem, if they know of other research pertaining to your problem, or for links (electronic or otherwise) to resources of interest. You can also bounce ideas off other list members at each stage of your research. You can even ask for volunteers to read your work in progress! To subscribe to an electronic mailing list, you are generally required to send a short e-mail message to the list address. When you are subscribed, you will receive detailed information about how to post messages, how to unsubscribe, and rules for use.

Digital Research Tools

DEVELOPING RESEARCH PROBLEMS

Many efficiency-based digital tools are available to educational researchers, primarily in the realm of assisting with reviewing the literature, data collection, data analysis, and publishing (these will be discussed in the chapters that deal with these topics). We suggest the following digital research tools to assist with the development of your research problem or questions.

Rich Site Summary (RSS) Feeds

Staying current in your area of interest (or challenge) will help you stay on top of what other professionals in the field are researching and contributing to the existing body of knowledge. Arguably, one of the best digital tools to assist with the development of your research problem is the use of Rich Site Summary (RSS) feeds (also known as

(Continued)

web feeds or channels). RSS feeds allow you to subscribe to a content distributor (e.g., publisher, professional organization, and individual educational researcher) and to receive regular updates on everything from a specific journal's table of contents to upcoming podcasts and an individual's blog posting.

Getting started is as simple as selecting a free RSS service (e.g., NetNewsWire for Mac users or SharpReader for Windows users) and subscribing to RSS feeds of interest to you. A simple Google search of "educational research RSS feeds" resulted in millions of hits, so you probably want to be selective about the feeds you choose, for example, professional journals and organizations in your area of interest, and government-sponsored feeds.

One advantage of subscribing to RSS feeds is that your e-mail inbox will not be inundated with regular postings from publishers and professional organizations—your RSS reader will simply indicate whenever you have updates to read. Similarly, many of the updates provided to you will include web links to journal abstracts and full online versions of articles that have become available. And in an era in which we must all be concerned about identity theft, subscription to RSS feeds does not require disclosure of personal e-mail addresses that may make you vulnerable to spam, viruses, and phishing.

Facebook

Facebook is a social networking website that allows users to maintain an updated personal profile and to notify friends and colleagues about themselves. Users can also join (and form) networks, which are increasingly being formed by schools and colleges. Universities have turned to using Facebook as a recruiting tool as well as a way to notify their current students and faculty members about changes at the university. Educational research organizations such as the American Educational Research Association (AERA) use Facebook as a tool to connect divisions within the organization, thus creating a mechanism that connects like-minded scholars. Participation in one of these groups is one way to connect to other researchers investigating your current area of interest.

Twitter

Twitter is another social networking website that allows users to send short (140-character) messages to subscribers (followers). These short messages are referred to as tweets and have become the short message service (SMS) of the Internet. Twitter has also become popular with schools, colleges, and universities as a way of connecting with Millennial (also known as Generation Y) potential students. However, Twitter has also become a popular tool with researchers and with journals as yet another way of providing educational researchers with the ability to subscribe to live tweets about interesting problems or individuals. As was reported at one website, the "edublogosphere" is way too big to try and capture in a 140-character tweet; however, Twitter serves as another potentially valuable way of connecting with like-minded educational researchers.

Blogs

Blogs are another way of tracking what educational researchers are investigating at any given time and provide followers with another way of connecting with individual researcher's journeys. For example, I used a blog to track my work experiences of teaching educational research in Greenland (millsingreenland@blogspot.com) and was surprised by the number of followers who tracked my journey and who wanted to engage in conversations, especially about the challenges of teaching educational research in a setting where English is a distant third language.

A useful website to consult in your search for appropriate electronic mailing lists is lsoft.com/lists/listref.html. This site, sponsored by L-Soft International, contains a catalog of more than 63,000+ public electronic mailing lists. At this site, you can browse public lists on the Internet, search for mailing lists of interest, and get information about host sites. A recent search for education lists yielded hundreds of electronic mailing lists. Appropriately, this site is called CataList! Additional digital sources for research problems are included in the feature "Digital Research Tools."

Narrowing the Problem

For most quantitative researchers and some qualitative researchers, the general problem area must be narrowed to a more specific, researchable one. A problem that is too broad can lead to grief. First, a broad problem enlarges the task of reviewing the related literature, likely resulting in many extra hours spent in the library. Second, broad problems complicate the organization of the literature review itself. Finally, and most important, a problem that is too broad tends to result in a study that is general, difficult to carry out, and difficult to interpret. Conversely, a well-defined, manageable problem results in a well-defined, manageable study.

Note that the appropriate time to narrow a problem differs for quantitative and qualitative approaches. Quantitative research typically requires that the researcher spell out a specific and manageable problem at the start of the research process. For most qualitative research, the researcher often enters the research setting with only a general problem in mind. Following observation over a period of time, the qualitative researcher formulates a narrower research problem.

For ideas on narrowing your problem, you may begin by talking to your faculty advisers and to specialists in your area to solicit specific suggestions for study. You may also want to read sources that provide overviews of the current status of research in your problem area and search through handbooks that contain many chapters focused on research in a particular area (e.g., *Handbook of Research in Educational Administration, The Handbook of Educational Psychology, Handbook of Research on Curriculum, Handbook of Research on Teacher Education, Handbook of Sport Psychology, International Handbook of Early Child Education, International Handbook of Self-Study of Teacher Education Practices*, and many more). You can also check the *Encyclopedia of Educational Research* or journals such as the *Review of Educational Research*, which provide reviews of research in many areas. These sources often identify what may be called *next-step studies*, or those that need to be conducted. For example, following a study investigating the effectiveness of computer-assisted instruction in elementary arithmetic, the researcher may suggest the need for similar studies in other curriculum areas. At this stage in the research process, look for general research overviews that describe the nature of research in an area and can suggest more specific problems in your chosen area.

In narrowing your problem, you should select an aspect of the general problem area that is related to your area of expertise. For example, from the general problem area, "the use of reviews to increase retention," you may generate many specific problems, such as the comparative effectiveness of immediate versus delayed review on the retention of geometric concepts and the effect of review games on the retention of vocabulary words by second-graders. In your efforts to delineate a problem sufficiently, however, be careful not to get carried away—a problem that is too narrow is just as bad as a problem that is too broad. A study on the effectiveness of preclass reminders in reducing instances of pencil sharpening during class time, for example, would probably contribute little, if anything, to the education knowledge base. Table 3.1 provides examples of broad and narrow research statements focused on the same problem.

TABLE 3.1 • Comparison of broad and narrow research problems	
Broad Research Problem	**Narrow Research Problem**
1. How is passing through Piaget's four stages of cognitive development related to success at college?	1. What factors affect the length of time children take to pass from one Piagetian stage to the next?
2. How do the requirements of Every Student Succeeds Act (ESSA) legislation affect whether or not children become good citizens?	2. What is the impact of the Every Student Succeeds Act (ESSA) testing requirements on the ways teachers teach?
3. How is use of the Internet by elementary-school-age children related to success at college?	3. How does providing computers to children who have not previously had access to such technology affect their achievement?

Characteristics of Good Problems

Selecting a good problem is well worth the time and effort. As mentioned previously, there is no shortage of significant educational problems that need to be studied; there is really no excuse for selecting a trite, overly narrow problem. Besides, it is generally to your advantage to select a worthwhile problem because you will certainly get a great deal more out of it professionally and academically. If the subsequent study is well conducted and reported, not only will you make a contribution to the existing knowledge base but you may also find your work published in a professional journal. The potential personal benefits to be derived from publication include increased professional status and job opportunities, not to mention tremendous self-satisfaction.

Working with an interesting problem helps a researcher stay motivated during months of study. Being interesting, however, is only one characteristic of a good research problem. A research problem, by definition, is an issue in need of investigation, so it follows that a fundamental characteristic of a good problem is that it is researchable. A researchable problem is one that can be investigated through collecting and analyzing data. Problems dealing with philosophical or ethical issues are not researchable. Research can assess how people feel about such issues, but it cannot resolve them. In education, many issues make great problems for debate (e.g., "Should prayer be allowed in public schools?"), but they are not researchable problems; there is no way to resolve these issues through collecting and analyzing data. Generally, problems or questions that contain the word *should* cannot be answered by research of any kind because they are ultimately matters of opinion.

However, a slight wording change can turn an unresearchable problem into a researchable one. For example, studies that examine the effects of school prayer on teachers and students, the effects of grouping practices on classroom learning, or the consequences of being held back in a grade can be carried out. Such studies, as worded, can tell us about the varied consequences of these practices. The decisions that any school or teacher makes regarding those practices can then be based in part on those studies, but ultimately those decisions also involve issues that go beyond any research study.

A third characteristic of a good research problem is that it has theoretical or practical significance. People's definitions of *significance* vary, but a general rule of thumb is that a significant study is one that contributes in some way to the improvement or understanding of educational theory or practice.

A fourth characteristic of a good problem is that the research is ethical. That is, the research must not potentially harm the research participants. Harm encompasses not only physical danger but emotional danger as well.

A fifth important characteristic is that the problem is manageable *for you*. Choosing an interesting problem in an area in which you have expertise is not sufficient. You must choose a problem that you can investigate adequately, given your current level of research skill, the resources available to you, and the time you can commit to carrying out the study. The availability of appropriate participants and measuring instruments, for example, is an important consideration.

The characteristics of a good research problem are summarized in Table 3.2. As you assess a problem for its appropriateness and feasibility, you may want to consult your faculty advisers for their opinions.

Stating the Research Problem

After you have selected and narrowed your research problem, you should draft a written statement of that problem. The way in which a problem is stated varies according to the type of research undertaken and the preferences of the researcher. As with other parts of the research process, the approach differs somewhat for quantitative and qualitative studies.

Stating Quantitative Research Problems

For a quantitative study, a well-written **problem statement** generally describes the variables of interest, the specific relations among those variables, and (ideally) important characteristics of the participants (e.g., gifted students, fourth-graders with learning disabilities, teenage mothers). An example of a problem statement is: "The problem to be investigated in this study is the effect of positive reinforcement on the quality of 10th-graders' English compositions." It is clear that the variables in this study are positive reinforcement and quality

TABLE 3.2 • Choosing a good research problem

1. Your problem is interesting. It will hold your interest throughout the entire research process.
2. Your problem is researchable. It can be investigated through the collection and analysis of data and is not stated as an effort to determine what should be done.
3. Your problem is significant. It contributes in some way to the improvement or understanding of educational theory or practice.
4. Your problem is ethical. It does not involve practices or strategies that may embarrass or harm participants.
5. Your problem is manageable. It fits your level of skill, the available resources, and the time restrictions.

of English compositions, and the participants will be 10th-graders.

Other possible problem statements include the following:

■ "The problem to be investigated in this study is secondary teachers' attitudes toward required after-school activities."
■ "The purpose of this study is to investigate the relation between school entrance age and reading comprehension skills of primary-level students."
■ "The problem to be studied is the effect of wearing required school uniforms on the self-esteem of socioeconomically disadvantaged sixth-grade students."

Try to identify the variable or variables in each example and suggest the quantitative research approach that would likely be employed to carry out the study.

Stating Qualitative Research Problems

At this point in the research process, qualitative research problems are often stated in more general language than quantitative ones because, in many cases, the qualitative researcher needs to spend time in the research context for the focus of the study to emerge. Remember, the qualitative researcher usually is much more attuned to the specifics of the context in which the study takes place than is the quantitative researcher. Qualitative problem statements eventually narrow as the researcher learns more about the research context and its inhabitants, and these more precise statements appear in the research report. Following are examples of general

statements that may be drafted in the early stages of the qualitative research process:

■ "The purpose of this study is to describe the nature of children's engagement with mathematics. The intention is to gather details about children's ways of entering into and sustaining their involvement with mathematics."
■ "This qualitative study examines how members of an organization identify, evaluate, and respond to organizational change. The study examines the events that members of an organization identify as significant change events and whether different events are seen as significant by subgroups in the organization."
■ "The purpose of this research is to study the social integration of children with disabilities in a general education third-grade class."

Developing Research Questions

Developing research questions breathes life into the research problem statements. To use a teaching analogy, it is like taking the aims of the lesson (the problem statement, broad statement of outcomes) and developing the instructional objectives for the lesson (the research questions; bite-size, narrow questions). These research questions also validate that you have a workable way to proceed with your research. (See Figure 3.1.) There is a direct connection between the research question and the data collection strategies that the researcher will use to answer the question. The research questions add another level of specificity to the development of the research and provide the researcher with an action plan for the development and identification of research instruments.

Following are examples of research questions developed from the earlier quantitative research problems:

■ "The problem to be investigated in this study is secondary teachers' attitudes toward required after-school activities."

FIGURE 3.1 • Framework for conceptualizing research questions

Activity	Characteristics
Identifying a problem	Theories Personal experiences Replication studies Library searches RSS Feeds Twitter Blogs Electronic mailing lists
Narrowing the problem	Talk with faculty advisors. Consult overviews of current research in your problem area. Select a general problem area related to your area of expertise.
Developing a good problem	The problem is interesting. The problem is researchable. The problem is significant. The problem is ethical. The problem is manageable.
Stating the research problem	A well-written problem statement generally describes the variables of interest and, ideally, important characteristics of the participants.
Developing research questions	Breathes life into the research problem statements and validates that you have a workable way to proceed with your research. Provides direction for the development of research instruments.

Research questions: What are secondary teachers' attitudes toward varsity athletics programs? What instructional strategies do secondary teachers use to accommodate student-athletes? How do these instructional strategies affect student achievement?

■ "The purpose of this study is to investigate the relation between school entrance age and reading comprehension skills of primary-level students."

Research question: What is the correlation between student entrance age at the beginning of primary school and students' performance in reading comprehension at the end of first grade?

■ "The problem to be studied is the effect of wearing required school uniforms on the self-esteem of socioeconomically disadvantaged sixth-grade students."

Research question: What is the effect of mandatory school uniforms on the self-esteem of socioeconomically disadvantaged sixth-grade students?

Following are examples of research questions developed from the earlier qualitative research problems:

■ "The purpose of this study is to describe the nature of children's engagement with mathematics. The intention is to gather details about children's ways of entering into and sustaining their involvement with mathematics."

Research question: What strategies do children use to engage in learning mathematics? How do these strategies sustain student involvement in learning mathematics? How does being engaged with mathematics content affect student attitudes toward mathematics?

■ "This qualitative study examines how members of an organization identify, evaluate, and respond to organizational change. The study examines the events that members of an organization identify as significant change events and whether different events are seen as significant by subgroups in the organization."

Research questions: What are the unintended consequences of teacher involvement in the schoolwide reform efforts? How do the school administrators involve teachers, students, and community members in the schoolwide reform efforts? What are the major challenges facing school administrators in building teacher support for the schoolwide reform efforts?

■ "The purpose of this research is to study the social integration of children with disabilities in a general education third-grade class."

Research questions: What instructional strategies do regular education teachers use to integrate children with learning disabilities into their general education third-grade class? How do regular education students accommodate children with learning disabilities in their regular classroom activities?

These examples illustrate the importance of translating qualitative and quantitative research problems into specific research questions that provide the researcher with a methodological road map for how to proceed with the development of the research proposal (discussed in detail in Chapter 5).

Placement and Nature of the Problem Statement in a Study

It's helpful to understand how the problem statement is used in later stages of the research process. A statement of the problem is the first component of both a research plan and the completed research report, and it gives direction to the remaining aspects of both the plan and report. The statement is accompanied by a presentation of the background of the problem, a justification for the study (i.e., a discussion of its significance), and often limitations of the study. The background includes information needed by readers to understand the nature of the problem.

To provide a justification of the study, the researcher must explain how investigation of the research problem can contribute to educational theory or practice. For example, consider an introduction that begins with this problem statement: "The purpose of this study is to compare the effectiveness of salaried paraprofessionals and nonsalaried parent volunteers with respect to the reading achievement of first-grade children." This statement may be followed by a discussion of (1) the role of paraprofessionals; (2) the increased utilization of paraprofessionals by schools; (3) the expense involved; and (4) the search for alternatives, such as parent volunteers. The significance of the problem is that, if parent volunteers and paid paraprofessionals are equally effective, volunteers can be substituted for salaried paraprofessionals at great savings. Any educational practice that may increase achievement at no additional cost is certainly worthy of investigation!

Thinking about the significance of your problem will help you develop a tentative hypothesis, which is a prediction about the research findings. A researcher typically uses the tentative hypothesis as a guiding hypothesis during the process of reviewing literature related to the research problem. In the example just given, a tentative hypothesis is that parent volunteers are equally as effective as salaried paraprofessionals. The tentative hypothesis is likely to be modified, even changed radically, as a result of the review of the literature, but it gives direction to the literature search and helps the researcher narrow the scope of the search to include only relevant problems. Clearly, it is important to develop a guiding hypothesis prior to starting your literature review.

MyLab Education **Self-Check 3.2**

MyLab Education **Application Exercise 3.1:** Identifying Research Problems in Research Reports Part 1

MyLab Education **Application Exercise 3.2:** Evaluating Research Articles: Identifying Research Problems in Research Reports Part 2

FORMULATING AND STATING A HYPOTHESIS

A **hypothesis** is a researcher's prediction of the research findings, a statement of the researcher's expectations about the relations among the variables in the research problem. Many studies contain a number of variables, and it is not uncommon to have more than one hypothesis for a research problem. The researcher does not set out to prove a hypothesis but rather collects data that either support or do not support it. A written statement of your hypothesis is part of your research plan and report.

Both quantitative and qualitative researchers deal with hypotheses, but the nature of each approach differs. We first discuss the quantitative use of hypotheses and then discuss the qualitative counterpart.

Definition and Purpose of Hypotheses in Quantitative Studies

Hypotheses are essential to all quantitative research studies, with the possible exception of some survey studies whose purpose is to answer certain specific questions. A quantitative researcher formulates a hypothesis before conducting the study because the nature of the study is determined by the hypothesis. Every aspect of the research is affected, including participants, measuring instruments, design, procedures, data analysis, and conclusions.

Hypotheses are typically derived from theories or from knowledge gained while reviewing the related literature, which often leads the researcher to expect a certain finding. For example, studies finding white chalk to be more effective than yellow chalk in teaching mathematics may lead a researcher to expect white chalk to be more effective in teaching physics as well, if there are no other findings to the contrary. Similarly, a theory suggesting that the ability to think abstractly is quite different for 10-year-olds than for 15-year-olds may lead a researcher to propose a hypothesis that 10- and 15-year-olds perform differently on tests of abstract reasoning.

Although all hypotheses are based on theory or previous knowledge and are aimed at extending knowledge, they are not all of equal worth. A number of criteria can be, and should be, applied to determine the value of a hypothesis. The following guidelines help ensure that you develop a good research hypothesis:

1. *A hypothesis should be based on a sound rationale. It should derive from previous research or theory, and its confirmation or disconfirmation should contribute to*

educational theory or practice. Therefore, a major characteristic of a good hypothesis is that it is consistent with theory or previous research. The chances are slim that you'll be a Christopher Columbus of educational research who shows that something believed to be flat is really round! Of course, in areas of research where results are conflicting, your hypothesis won't be consistent with every study, but it should follow from the rule, not from the exception.

2. *A good hypothesis provides a reasonable explanation for the predicted outcome.* If your television and Internet are not working at home, you may hypothesize that gophers have chewed through the underground cables to your house, but such a hypothesis does not provide a reasonable explanation. More reasonable hypotheses are that you forgot to pay your bill or that a repair crew is working outside. As another example, a hypothesis suggesting that schoolchildren with freckles attend longer to tasks than schoolchildren without freckles does not provide a reasonable explanation for children's attention behavior. A hypothesis suggesting that children who eat a nutritious breakfast pay attention longer than children who have no breakfast is more reasonable.

3. *A good hypothesis states as clearly and concisely as possible the expected relation (or difference) between variables and defines those variables in operational, measurable terms.* A simple but clearly stated hypothesis makes the relation easier for readers to understand, is simpler to test, and facilitates the formulation of conclusions. A relation between variables may be expressed as a correlational or a causal one. For example, in a study focused on the relation between anxiety and math achievement, the hypothesis may be that anxiety and math achievement are negatively correlated, such that students who are highly anxious also have low math achievement, and students with higher math achievement have low anxiety. In a causal study addressing the same variables, a researcher may hypothesize that anxiety causes poor performance on a math test.

This example illustrates the need for **operational definitions** that clearly describe variables in measurable ways. Operational definitions clarify important terms in a study so that all readers understand the precise meaning the researcher intends. To define the variables in these studies, a researcher must ask such questions as "How can we measure math achievement?" "What does 'poor performance' mean?" "What observable behaviors define high anxiety?" In this example, "high anxiety" may be a score on the Acme Anxiety Inventory in the upper 30% of student scores, and "low anxiety" may be a score in the lowest 30% of students. "Poor" performance on a math test may be operationally defined in terms of certain math subtest scores on the California Achievement Test.

If you can operationally define your variables within the hypothesis statement without making it unwieldy, you should do so. If not, state the hypothesis and define the appropriate terms immediately afterward. Of course, if all necessary terms have already been defined, either within or immediately following the problem statement, repeating the definitions in the statement of the hypothesis is not necessary. The general rule of thumb is to define terms the first time you use them, but it does not hurt to remind readers of these definitions occasionally.

4. *A well-stated and well-defined hypothesis must also be testable—and it will be testable if it is well formulated and stated.* It should be possible to test the hypothesis by collecting and analyzing data. It is not possible to test a hypothesis that some students behave better than others because some have an invisible little angel on their right shoulders and some have an invisible little devil on their left shoulders; a researcher would have no way to collect data to support the hypothesis.

A good hypothesis should normally be testable within some reasonable period of time. For example, the hypothesis that first-grade students who read after lunch every day will have bigger vocabularies at age 60 would obviously take a very long time to test, and the researcher would very likely be long gone before the study was completed. A more manageable hypothesis with the same theme is that first-grade children who read after

TABLE 3.3 • Characteristics of a good hypothesis
1. A good hypothesis is based on sound reasoning that is consistent with theory or previous research.
2. A good hypothesis provides a reasonable explanation for the predicted outcome.
3. A good hypothesis clearly states the expected relation or difference between defined variables.
4. A good hypothesis is testable within a reasonable time frame.

lunch every day will have bigger vocabularies at the end of the first grade than those who don't read daily.

See Table 3.3 for a summary of the characteristics of a good hypothesis.

Types of Hypotheses

Hypotheses can be classified in terms of how they are derived (i.e., inductive versus deductive hypotheses) or how they are stated (i.e., directional versus null hypotheses). If you recall the discussion of inductive and deductive reasoning in Chapter 1, you may guess that an **inductive hypothesis** is a generalization based on specific observations. The researcher observes that certain patterns or associations among variables occur in a number of situations and uses these tentative observations to form an inductive hypothesis. For example, a researcher observes that, in some eighth-grade classrooms, students who take essay tests appear to show less test anxiety than those who take multiple-choice tests. This observation could become the basis for an inductive hypothesis. A **deductive hypothesis,** in contrast, is derived from theory and provides evidence that supports, expands, or contradicts the theory.

A research hypothesis states an expected relation or difference between variables. In other words, the quantitative researcher specifies the relation he or she expects to test in the research study. Research hypotheses can be nondirectional or directional. A **nondirectional hypothesis** states simply that a relation or difference between variables exists. A **directional hypothesis** states the expected direction of the relation or difference.

For example, a nondirectional hypothesis may state the following:

The achievement of 10th-grade biology students who are instructed using interactive multimedia is significantly different than the achievement of those who receive regular instruction only.

The corresponding directional hypothesis may read:

Tenth-grade biology students who are instructed using interactive multimedia achieve at a higher level than those who receive regular instruction only.

The nondirectional hypothesis predicts a difference between the groups, whereas the directional hypothesis predicts not only the difference but also that the difference favors interactive media instruction. A directional hypothesis should be stated only if you have a basis for believing that the results will occur in the stated direction. Nondirectional and directional hypotheses involve different types of statistical tests of significance, which are examined in Chapter 19.

Finally, a **null hypothesis** states that there is no significant relation or difference between variables. For example, a null hypothesis may be stated as follows:

The achievement level of 10th-grade biology students who are instructed using interactive multimedia is not significantly different than the achievement level of those who receive regular instruction.

The null hypothesis is the hypothesis of choice when a researcher has little research or theoretical support for a hypothesis. Also, statistical tests for the null hypothesis are more conservative than they are for directional hypotheses. The disadvantage of null hypotheses is that they rarely express the researcher's true expectations based on literature, insights, and logic. Given that few studies can be designed to test for the nonexistence of a relation, it seems logical that most studies should not be based on a null hypothesis.

Stating the Hypothesis

A good hypothesis is stated clearly and concisely, expresses the relation or difference between variables, and defines those variables in measurable terms. A general model for stating hypotheses for experimental studies is as follows:

P who get X do better on Y than P who do not get X (or get some other X).

In the model,

P = the participants
X = the treatment, the causal or independent variable (IV)
Y = the study outcome, the effect or dependent variable (DV)

Although this model is an oversimplification and may not always be appropriate, it should help you to understand the statement of a hypothesis. Further, this model, sometimes with variations, is applicable in many situations.

Study the following problem statement, and see if you can identify P, X, and Y:

The purpose of this study is to investigate the effectiveness of 12th-grade mentors on the absenteeism of low-achieving 10th-graders.

In this example,

P = low-achieving 10th-graders
X = presence or absence of a 12th-grade mentor (IV)
Y = absenteeism, measured as days absent or, stated positively, days present (DV)

A review of the literature may indicate that mentors are effective in influencing younger students. Therefore, the directional hypothesis resulting from this problem may read as follows:

Low-achieving 10th-graders (P) who have a 12th-grade mentor (X) have less absenteeism (Y) than low-achieving 10th-graders who do not.

As another example, consider this problem statement:

The purpose of the proposed research is to investigate the effectiveness of different conflict resolution techniques in reducing the aggressive behaviors of high school students in an alternative educational setting.

For this problem statement,

P = high school students in an alternative educational setting
X = type of conflict resolution—punishment or discussion (IV)
Y = instances of aggressive behaviors (DV)

The related nondirectional hypothesis may read as follows:

> For high school students in an alternative educational setting, the number of aggressive behaviors will be different for students who receive punishment than for students who engage in discussion approaches to conflict resolution.

Of course, in all these examples, the terms require operational definition (e.g., "aggressive behaviors").

Got the idea? Let's try one more. Here is the problem statement:

> This study investigates the effectiveness of token reinforcement, in the form of free time given for the completion of practice worksheets, on the math computation skills of ninth-grade general math students.

> P = ninth-grade general math students
> X = token reinforcement in the form of free time for completion of practice worksheets
> Y = math computation skills

The directional hypothesis may be written as follows:

> Ninth-grade general math students who receive token reinforcement in the form of free time when they complete their practice worksheets have higher math computation skills than ninth-grade general math students who do not receive token reinforcement for completed worksheets.

The null hypothesis may take this form:

> There is no difference on Y (the outcome of the study) between P_1 (treatment A) and P_2 (treatment B).

> P_1 (treatment A) = free time
> P_2 (treatment B) = no free time

See if you can write the null hypothesis for the following problem statement:

> The purpose of this study is to assess the impact of formal versus informal preschool reading instruction on children's reading comprehension at the end of the first grade.

Testing the Hypothesis

You will use your hypothesis as you conduct your research study. The researcher selects the sample, measuring instruments, design, and procedures that will enable him or her to collect the data necessary to test the hypothesis. During the course of a research study, those data are analyzed in a manner that permits the researcher to determine whether the hypothesis is supported. Remember that analysis of the data does not lead to a hypothesis being proven or not proven, only supported or not supported for this particular study. The results of analysis indicate whether a hypothesis is supported or not supported for the particular participants, context, and instruments involved.

Many beginning researchers have the misconception that if the hypothesis is not supported by the data, then the study is a failure and, conversely, if the hypothesis is supported, then the study is a success. Neither of these beliefs is true. If a hypothesis is not supported, a valuable contribution may be made through the development of new research methods or even a revision of some aspect of a theory. Such revisions can generate new or revised hypotheses and new and original studies. Thus, hypothesis testing contributes to education primarily by expanding, refining, or revising its knowledge base.

Definition and Purpose of Hypotheses in Qualitative Studies

The aims and strategies of qualitative researchers may differ substantially from those of quantitative researchers. Typically, qualitative researchers do not state formal hypotheses before conducting studies; rather, they seek to understand the nature of their participants and contexts before stating a research focus or hypothesis. As noted earlier, however, qualitative researchers may develop **guiding hypotheses** for the proposed research. Rather than testing hypotheses, qualitative researchers are much more likely to generate new hypotheses as a result of their studies. The inductive process widely used in qualitative research is based on observing patterns and associations in the participants' natural setting without prior hunches or hypotheses about what researchers will study and observe. Qualitative researchers' reluctance to identify variables and predictions immediately stems from the view that contexts and participants differ and must be understood on their own terms before a researcher can begin hypothesizing or judging. Thus, qualitative researchers have more discretion in determining when and how to examine or narrow a problem.

Identifying patterns and associations in the setting often helps a researcher discover ideas and questions that lead to new hypotheses. For example, the repeated observation that, early in the school year, first-grade students can accurately identify the "smart" and the "not smart" students in class may suggest a hypothesis about how teachers' actions and words communicate students' status in the classroom. In simple terms, it is generally appropriate to say that a strength of qualitative research is in generating hypotheses, not testing hypotheses.

Having identified a guiding hypothesis, the qualitative researcher may operationalize the hypothesis through the development of research questions that provide a focus for data collection. Qualitative research questions encompass a range of problems, but most focus on participants' understanding of meanings and social life in a particular context. However, these general problems must

necessarily be more focused to become useful and researchable questions. For example, the problem "What are the cultural patterns and perspectives of this group in its natural setting?" can be narrowed by asking, "What are the cultural patterns and perspectives of teachers during lunch in the teachers' lounge?" Similarly, the problem "How do people make sense of their everyday activities to behave in socially acceptable ways?" may be narrowed by asking, "How do rival gang members engage in socially acceptable ways when interacting with each other during the school day?" Clearly, there are many ways to restate these questions to make them viable and focused research questions. In most cases, the purpose of narrowing questions is to reduce aspects of the problem, much as a hypothesis does for quantitative research, because most researchers overestimate the proper scope of a study.

MyLab Education **Self-Check 3.3**

MyLab Education **Application Exercise 3.3:**
Evaluating Research Articles: Identifying Hypotheses

MyLab Education **Application Exercise 3.4:**
Evaluating Research Articles: Developing a Hypothesis

SUMMARY

IDENTIFYING A RESEARCH PROBLEM

1. The first step in selecting a research problem is to identify a general subject that is related to your area of expertise and is of particular interest to you.

Sources of Research Problems

2. The five main sources of research problems are theories, personal experiences, previous studies that can be replicated, electronic mailing lists, and library searches.
3. Theories are organized bodies of concepts, generalizations, and principles. Researchers often study particular aspects of a theory to determine its applicability or generalizability.
4. A researcher's personal experiences and concerns often lead to useful and personally rewarding studies. Common questions, such as "Why does that happen?" and "What would happen if…?" can be rich problem sources.
5. Existing studies are a common source of research problems. Replication of a study usually involves changing some feature from the original study.
6. Library searches are generally not efficient ways to identify research problems. Handbooks, encyclopedias, and yearbooks that cover many problems briefly are more useful. Library resources are invaluable, however, after you have identified a problem to study.
7. Electronic mailing list services are designed by organizations to facilitate communication (usually via the Internet) among their members. Other digital tools such as RSS feeds, Facebook, Twitter, and blogs keep researchers updated on what others are investigating.

Narrowing the Problem

8. After an initial problem is identified, it often needs to be narrowed and focused into a manageable problem to study.
9. Quantitative research problems are usually narrowed quickly at the start of a study.

Qualitative research problems are not usually narrowed until the researcher has more information about the participants and their setting.

Characteristics of Good Problems

10. Two basic characteristics of a good research problem are that it is of interest to the researcher and that it is researchable using the collection and analysis of data. Problems related to philosophical and ethical issues (i.e., *should* questions) are not researchable.
11. A good problem has theoretical or practical significance; its solution contributes in some way to improving the educational process.
12. A good problem is one that is ethical and does not harm participants in any way.
13. A good problem *for you* must be a problem that can be adequately investigated given your current level of research skill, the available resources, and time and other restrictions.

Stating the Research Problem

14. The problem statement is the first item in the introduction to a research plan and the introduction to the final research report. It provides direction for the remaining aspects of both.
15. A well-written problem statement for a quantitative study generally indicates the variables of interest, the specific relations among those variables, and (ideally) the characteristics of the participants. Qualitative research problems are usually stated in general language because qualitative researchers need to become attuned to the research context before narrowing their problem.

Developing Research Questions

16. Developing research questions breathes life into the research problem statements.
17. The research questions add another level of specificity to the development of the research problem and provide the researcher with

an action plan for the development and identification of research instruments.

FORMULATING AND STATING A HYPOTHESIS

18. A hypothesis is a researcher's prediction of the research findings.
19. Researchers do not set out to prove a hypothesis but rather collect data that either support or do not support it.

Definition and Purpose of Hypotheses in Quantitative Studies

20. A hypothesis in a quantitative study is formulated based on theory or on knowledge gained while reviewing the related literature.
21. A critical characteristic of a good hypothesis is that it is based on a sound rationale. A hypothesis is a reasoned prediction, not a wild guess. It is a tentative but rational explanation for the predicted outcome.
22. A good hypothesis states clearly and concisely the expected relations or differences between variables. Variables should be stated in measurable terms.
23. A well-stated and well-defined hypothesis must be testable.

Types of Hypotheses

24. An inductive hypothesis is a generalization made from a number of observations. A deductive hypothesis is derived from theory and is aimed at providing evidence that supports, expands, or contradicts aspects of a given theory.
25. A research hypothesis states the expected relation or difference between variables, which the researcher expects to test through the collection and analysis of data.

26. A nondirectional hypothesis predicts only that a relation or difference exists; a directional hypothesis indicates the direction of the difference as well. A null hypothesis predicts that there is no significant relation or difference between variables.

Stating the Hypothesis

27. A general paradigm, or model, for stating hypotheses for experimental studies is P who get X do better on Y than P who do not get X (or get some other X). P refers to participants, X refers to the treatment or independent variable (IV), and Y refers to the outcome or dependent variable (DV).

Testing the Hypothesis

28. The researcher selects the sample, measuring instruments, design, and procedures that will enable him or her to collect the data necessary to test the hypothesis. Those data are analyzed to determine whether or not the hypothesis is supported.

Definition and Purpose of Hypotheses in Qualitative Studies

29. Typically, qualitative researchers do not state formal hypotheses prior to the study. However, a qualitative researcher may develop guiding hypotheses for the proposed research.
30. Having identified a guiding hypothesis, the qualitative researcher may operationalize the hypothesis through the development of research questions that provide a focus for data collection. Qualitative researchers are likely to generate new hypotheses as a result of their studies.

PERFORMANCE CRITERIA

TASK 2

One sentence should be sufficient to describe your general subject area. One sentence should be sufficient to describe whether your subject area is related to an educational theory, personal experience (problem of practice), replication of a study that interests you, the result of a library search, or the outcome of participation in an electronic forum. One sentence should be sufficient to state your research problem in the form of "The purpose of this study is to. . . ." The number of research questions you state will depend on your problem. As an example of this completed task consider the following example from Mills (2000) *"Come to My Web (Site)," Said the Spider to the Fly: Reflections on the Life of a Virtual Professor.*

1. Identify a general subject area that is related to your area of expertise and is of particular interest to you. *I am interested in the effects of teaching action research online on student outcomes and attitudes.*

2. State whether the general subject area is related to an educational theory, personal experience (problem of practice), replication of a study that interests you, the result of a library search, or the outcome of participation in an electronic forum. *This general subject is related to a personal experience of teaching online in the role of a virtual professor.*

3. State your research problem. *The purpose of this study is to describe the effects of web-based instruction teaching action research on student outcomes and attitudes.*

4. State your research questions. *(i) What is the effect of online instruction on students' communication with each other? With the instructor? (ii) How do students' learning styles affect their success in an online class? (iii) How do online resources meet students' needs to access course materials?*

CHAPTER FOUR

Reviewing the Literature

Everett Collection

Real Genius, 1985

"Too often the review of related literature is seen as a necessary evil to be completed as fast as possible so that one can get on with the 'real research.'" (p. 95)

LEARNING OUTCOMES

After reading Chapter 4, you should be able to do the following:

4.1 Define the purpose and scope of a review of related literature.

4.2 Describe the role of the literature review in qualitative research.

4.3 Identify keywords and identify, evaluate, and annotate sources.

4.4 Describe the steps involved in analyzing, organizing, and reporting a review of the literature.

4.5 Define *meta-analysis* and describe the process for conducting a meta-analysis.

4.6 Identify digital research methods and tools to assist in the research process.

The chapter outcomes form the basis for Tasks 3A and 3B, which require you to:

1. Identify 10 to 15 good references (sources) that relate directly to a problem of interest. The references should include a variety of source types (e.g., books, articles, Internet reports, etc.).

2. Evaluate and abstract those references.

3. Write an introduction for a research plan, including a complete review of the literature that supports a testable hypothesis.

TASK 3A

Write an introduction for a quantitative research plan. Include a statement of the research problem, a statement concerning the importance or significance of the problem, a brief review of related literature, and a testable hypothesis regarding the outcome of your study. Include definitions of terms where appropriate (see Performance Criteria, p. 124).

TASK 3B

Write an introduction for a qualitative research plan. Include a statement of the research problem, a statement concerning the importance or significance of the problem, a brief review of related literature, and a guiding hypothesis for your study. Include definitions of terms where appropriate (see Performance Criteria, p. 124).

REVIEW OF RELATED LITERATURE: PURPOSE AND SCOPE

Having happily found a suitable problem, the beginning researcher is usually raring to go. Too often the review of related literature is seen as a necessary evil to be completed as fast as possible so that one can get on with the "real research." This perspective reflects a lack of understanding of the purposes and importance of the review and a feeling of uneasiness on the part of students who are not sure how to report the literature. Nonetheless, the review of related literature is as important as any other component of the research process and can be conducted quite painlessly if approached in an orderly manner. Some researchers even find the process quite enjoyable!

The **review of related literature** involves the systematic identification, location, and analysis of documents containing information related to the research problem. The term is also used to describe the written component of a research plan or report that discusses the reviewed documents.

These documents can include articles, abstracts, reviews, books, dissertations, government publications, and other research reports. The major purpose of reviewing the literature is to determine what has already been done that relates to your problem. This knowledge not only prevents you from unintentionally duplicating another person's research but also gives you the understanding and insight you need to place your problem within a logical framework. Previous studies can provide the rationale for your research hypothesis and indicate what needs to be done to help you justify the significance of your study. Put simply, the review tells you what has been done and what needs to be done.

Another important purpose of reviewing the literature is to discover research strategies and specific data collection approaches that have or have not been productive in investigations of problems similar to yours. This information will help you avoid other researchers' mistakes and profit from their experiences. It may suggest approaches and procedures that you previously had not considered.

For example, suppose your problem involved the comparative effects of a brand-new experimental method versus the traditional method on the achievement of eighth-grade science students. The review of literature may reveal 10 related studies that found no differences in achievement. Several of the studies, however, may suggest that the brand-new method is more effective for certain kinds of students than for others. Thus, you may reformulate your problem to involve the comparative effectiveness of the brand-new method versus the traditional method on the achievement of a subgroup of eighth-grade science students—such as those with low aptitude.

Being familiar with previous research also facilitates interpretation of your study results. The results can be discussed in terms of whether or how they agree with previous findings. If the results contradict previous findings, you can describe differences among your study and the others, providing a rationale for the discrepancy. If your results are consistent with other findings, your report should include suggestions for the next step; if they are not consistent, your report should include suggestions for studies that may resolve the conflict.

Beginning researchers often have difficulty determining how broad and comprehensive their literature reviews should be. At times, all the literature will seem directly related to the problem, so it may be difficult to determine when to stop. Determining if an article is truly relevant to the problem is complicated and requires time. Unfortunately, there is no simple formula to solve the problem. You must decide using your own judgment and the advice of your teachers or advisers. The following general guidelines can assist you:

- *Avoid the temptation to include everything you find in your literature review.* Bigger does not mean better. A smaller, well-organized review is definitely preferred to a review containing many studies that are only tangentially related to the problem.
- *When investigating a heavily researched area, review only those works that are directly related to your specific problem.* You will find plenty of references and should not have to rely on less relevant studies. For example, the role of feedback for verbal and nonverbal learning has been studied extensively in both nonhuman animals and human beings for a variety of different learning tasks. Focus on those using similar subjects or similar variables—for example, if you were concerned with the relation between frequency of feedback and chemistry achievement, you would probably not have to review feedback studies related to nonhuman animal learning.
- *When investigating a new or little-researched problem area, review any study related in some meaningful way to your problem.* Gather enough information to develop a logical framework for the study and a sound rationale for the research hypothesis. For example, suppose you want to study the effects of an exam for non-English-speaking students on grade point average (GPA). The students must pass the exam to graduate. Your literature review would probably include any studies that involved English as a second language (ESL) classes and the effects of culture-specific grading practices as well as studies that identified strategies to improve the learning of ESL students. In a few years, there will probably be enough research on the academic consequences of such an exam on non-English-speaking students to permit a much more narrowly focused literature review.

A common misconception among beginning researchers is that the worth of a problem is directly related to the amount of literature available about it. This is not the case. For many new and important areas of research, few studies have been published. The relationship between instructional leadership, teacher collaboration, and student test scores is one such area. The very lack of such research often increases the worth of its study. On the other hand, the fact that a thousand studies have already been done in a given problem area does not mean there is no further need for research in that area. Such an area will generally be very well developed, and subproblems that need additional research will be readily identifiable.

MyLab Education **Self-Check 4.1**

MyLab Education **Application Exercise 4.1:** Explaining the Function of the Literature Review

QUALITATIVE RESEARCH AND THE REVIEW OF RELATED LITERATURE

Both qualitative and quantitative researchers conduct literature reviews. Unlike quantitative researchers, however, who spend a great deal of time examining the research on their problems at the outset of the study, some qualitative researchers do not delve deeply into their literature until the problem has emerged over time. Qualitative researchers disagree about the role of the literature review in the research process. Some qualitative researchers have argued that reviewing the literature curtails inductive analysis—using induction to determine the direction of the research—and should be avoided at the early stages of the research process.[1] Others suggest that the review of related literature is important early in the qualitative research process because it serves the following functions:[2]

- The literature review demonstrates the underlying assumptions (i.e., propositions) behind the research questions that are central to the research proposal.
- The literature review provides a way for the novice researcher to convince the proposal reviewers that he or she is knowledgeable about the related research and the intellectual traditions that support the proposed study.[3]
- The literature review provides the researcher with an opportunity to identify any gaps that may exist in the body of literature and to provide a rationale for how the proposed study may contribute to the existing body of knowledge.
- The literature review helps the researcher to refine the research questions and embed them in guiding hypotheses that provide possible directions the researcher may follow.

We recommend that qualitative researchers conduct a review of related literature but also recognize that the review serves a slightly different

---

[1] *Qualitative Research for Education: An Introduction to Theory and Methods* (3rd ed.), by R. C. Bogdan and S. K. Biklen, 1998, Boston, MA: Allyn & Bacon.
[2] *Designing Qualitative Research* (2nd ed.), by C. Marshall and G. Rossman, 1995, Thousand Oaks, CA: Sage.
[3] Ibid., p. 28.

TABLE 4.1 • Conducting a literature review
1. Identify and make a list of keywords to guide your literature search.
2. Search appropriate databases using your keywords and identify authoritative subject headings to locate primary and secondary sources pertaining to your research problem.
3. Evaluate your sources for quality.
4. Abstract your sources.
5. Analyze and organize your sources using a literature matrix.
6. Write the literature review.

purpose than the one outlined for quantitative researchers.

Conducting a literature review follows a basic set of steps for both quantitative and qualitative research. Table 4.1 outlines the basic process to take when reviewing the literature.

MyLab Education **Self-Check 4.2**

MyLab Education **Application Exercise 4.2:** Conducting Literature Reviews in Qualitative Research

---

IDENTIFYING KEYWORDS AND IDENTIFYING, EVALUATING, AND ANNOTATING SOURCES

Identifying Keywords

The words you select for your searches will dictate the success of your research. Before you begin your research, make a list of possible keywords to guide your literature search. As you progress through your searching, add keywords and subject headings related to your search. Most of the initial source works you consult will have an alphabetical subject index or thesaurus to help you generate words to describe your research problem. You can look in these indexes for the keywords you have selected. Another option is to search databases such as the Education Resources Information Center (ERIC) and Education Full Text to generate subject headings or descriptors from the search results.

For example, if your research topic concerns the effect of interactive multimedia on the achievement of 10th-grade biology students, the logical keywords would be *interactive multimedia* and *biology*. When beginning with a keyword search for *interactive multimedia* in a database such as ERIC, however, you will see a list of possible subject headings such as *multimedia instruction, computer-assisted instruction, multimedia materials, games*, or *hypermedia*. These subject headings may also be called *descriptors*. It is important that you understand the difference between the keyword search and a subject heading—and perhaps, more importantly, why you want to connect to the subject headings.

Every article indexed in a database such as ERIC or Education Full Text is read by a human being who determines what topics are addressed in the article. The topics are listed as subject headings or descriptors in the article citation. Therefore, a subject search is more precise than a keyword search that searches for the words anywhere in the complete record of an article. If the words appear one time in the full text of an article, you will retrieve that article even though it may not be very relevant to your search. Subject headings or descriptors connect you with concepts that you are searching for, not just the words. You may have to mix and match your search terms to retrieve more accurate and relevant results. At times, the keywords and subject headings will be obvious for some searches such as biology. For others you may have to play detective. Giving a bit of thought to possible keywords and subject headings should facilitate an efficient beginning to an effective search. As you progress through your search, try to identify additional keywords and subject headings that you can use to reformulate a search to produce different and more relevant results or results that address specific aspects or subheadings about the topic.

Identifying Your Sources

For your review, you will examine a range of sources that are pertinent to your topic. To start, it is best to consult educational encyclopedias, handbooks, and annual reviews found in libraries. You may also search the Internet for government publications or organizational sites that address your research topic. These resources provide summaries of important topics in education and reviews of research on various topics. They allow you to get a picture of your topic in the broader context and help you understand where it fits in the field. You may also find these sources useful for identifying search terms and aspects related to your topic that you may not have considered.

The following are some examples of handbooks, encyclopedias, and reviews relevant to educational research:

- *International Encyclopedia of Education*
- *Encyclopedia of Curriculum Studies*
- *Handbook of Research on Teacher Education: Enduring Questions in Changing Contexts*
- *Handbook of Research on the Education of Young Children*
- *Handbook of Latinos and Education: Theory, Research, and Practice*
- *Handbook of Research on Practices and Outcomes in E-Learning: Issues and Trends*
- *Handbook of Reading Disability Research*
- *Handbook of Research on the Education of School Leaders*
- *Handbook of Research on New Media Literacy at the K–12 Level: Issues and Challenges*
- *Handbook of Research on Children's and Young Adult Literature*
- *Handbook on the Research of Teaching the English Language Arts*
- *Handbook of Education Finance and Policy*
- *Handbook of Research on School Choice*
- *Handbook of Research on Literacy and Diversity*
- *Handbook of Education Finance and Policy*
- *Research in the Social Foundations of Education*
- *Handbook of Research on Schools, Schooling, and Human Development*

It is important to distinguish between two types of sources used by educational researchers: primary and secondary sources. A **primary source** contains firsthand information, such as an original document or a description of a study written by the person who conducted the study. The data are factual rather than interpretive, so the study is more valued than secondary research. Research reports, dissertations, experiments, surveys, conference proceedings, letters, and interviews are some examples of primary sources. There is a difference between the opinion of an author and the results of an empirical study. The latter is more valued in a review.

A **secondary source** is a source that interprets or analyzes the work of others—either a primary source or another secondary source, such as a brief description of a study written by someone other than the person who conducted it. Secondary sources are often used to review what has already been written or studied. Education encyclopedias, handbooks, and other reference works typically contain secondhand information summarizing research studies conducted on a given topic. Secondary sources usually give complete bibliographic information for the references cited, so they can direct you to relevant primary sources, which are preferred over secondary sources. In fact, a primary source may have a literature review section that contains secondary source information. A good researcher can use the literature review to track down the original primary research.

Searching for Books on Your Research Topic in the Library

Having identified your keywords and some potential resources, you are ready to make an initial foray into your university library. Because the library will be a second home to you, at least for a while, you should become familiar with it. The time you spend here initially will save more in the long run. You should learn about the references available and where they are located. You should be able to completely navigate your library's website and know how to access resources from any location with Internet. Most libraries, especially university libraries, provide help and education in the uses of their resources. Libraries also provide access to materials through interlibrary loan for articles and to collective library catalogs to find books that are available from other institutions. You should be familiar with services offered by the library as well as the rules and regulations regarding the use of library materials.

Most university libraries have a librarian on duty to help with requests. More importantly, there also is a librarian who is the liaison to the education department and specializes in research within the discipline. This librarian has experience in both K–12 and graduate education and is very skilled in helping track down resources. Most libraries offer 24/7 online chat reference to assist you with your research if you are not in the building. Librarians usually are very willing to help you, but you should also learn to navigate the library on your own. The librarian is available to work with you, not to do your research.

With or without a librarian's help, you should take advantage of the resources available from the library, such as the online catalog, databases like ERIC and Education Full Text, and government publications. Most libraries have subject-specific online research guides that help organize the resources for a specific discipline. Also, learn to browse the stacks to search for books on your problem. Most of all, make a point to know the education librarian. Generally, if you are taking more than 15 to 20 minutes trying to finding something, then you should ask for assistance. You may even want to set up an appointment with the education librarian before you get started.

Using Library Catalogs. In today's academic libraries, card catalogs of previous generations have been replaced with online catalogs. These online catalogs provide access to the resources in the library as well as to collective catalogs accessing materials from other libraries within a particular region as part of a library's consortium agreement with other institutions. For students, getting books through the collective catalog and having them delivered to a particular library is generally free. These electronic catalogs are extremely user-friendly and provide a good place to start your search for literature related to your area of focus. In addition, electronic books are becoming increasing popular both for their immediate availability and ease of use.

To locate books, videos, and other materials such as government documents, you need to conduct a search of the library catalog. To search by topic, begin with a keyword search. In library catalogs, a keyword search will search the entire record of an item that includes the content notes—the chapter headings or titles of essays within a book. For example, to find summaries of research previously conducted in an area of psychology, you may enter the keywords *handbook* and *psychology*, or *encyclopedia* and *psychology*. If you search for a particular topic such as transformative learning, enter that term as a keyword search. The keyword search is important when you are looking for books because the search retrieves items with your keywords in the title, subject heading, and content notes. Since the content notes provide a listing of essays and chapter headings within a book, a keyword search could retrieve an essay about transformative learning in a book about adult learning. Always check the subject headings of any relevant item that you locate. You will find the subject headings important for finding similar items and further information. If you know a title of a book, then you can also search for the specific title.

If you are at the beginning of your search for primary sources, add search terms slowly and thoughtfully. Refrain from searching phrases such as "developing active learning activities in the classroom." Choose the main concepts from your research question—"active learning" and "classroom activities." Add additional search terms concept-by-concept depending on the amount of materials you retrieve and how narrow you want your search to be. If you need a relatively small number of references and a significant amount of research has been published about your topic, a narrow search will likely be appropriate. If you need a relatively large number of references and very little has been published about your topic, a broad search will be better. If you do not have a sense of what is available, your best strategy is to start narrow and broaden as necessary. For example, if you find very few references related to the effect of interactive multimedia on the achievement of 10th-grade biology students, you can broaden your search by including all sciences or all secondary students.

A useful way to narrow or broaden a keyword search is to use Boolean operators, words that tell the computer the keywords you want your search results to include or exclude. Common Boolean operators are the words AND, OR, and NOT. Put simply, using the connector AND or NOT between keywords narrows a search, whereas using the connector OR broadens one. Searching "multiple intelligences AND music" will provide a list of references that refer to both multiple intelligences and music. Searching "multiple intelligences NOT music" will retrieve references pertaining to multiple intelligences but will exclude references pertaining to music. A search for "multiple intelligences OR music" retrieves references that relate to either or both concepts. By using various combinations of the AND and OR connectors, you can vary your search strategy as needed. Note that it is difficult to develop a search model that can be followed in every library and every catalog or database. You must get acquainted with the unique search strategies and methods that are successful within your library environment. It is a good idea to check with the education librarian to determine if additional Boolean operator strategies are best suited to your search.

Another feature of current library catalogs is federated or discovery searching which allows you to simultaneously search across various resources available in the library. This type of search enables you to retrieve books, articles, videos, and government publications by searching not only the library catalog, but by searching the available article databases (for example, the **Education Resources Information Center, Education Full Text, and PsycINFO**) at the same time. A federated or discovery search has the advantage of enabling you to explore a wide range of materials in a broad way. However, the disadvantage is that you are sometimes inundated with sources that are less relevant and you cannot make use of the specific search features of the databases you are accessing. If you venture down the path of federating or discovery searching, do so carefully and thoughtfully.

Browsing the Stacks. With access to online catalogs, many new researchers may not consider an older strategy for locating books: browsing the stacks. This strategy is similar to the kind of activity you undertake at a public library when looking for a new fiction book to read. When the area of the library with books related to your area of focus is located, it can be productive to browse and pull interesting books off the shelves. You may also find leads to related materials if you initiate your search on the computer. Remember, libraries try to organize like objects with like objects. Accordingly, when you spot a relevant item on the shelves or in the results of an online search, always look at the other items nearby.

Steps for Searching Online Databases

The online catalog found in a library is an example of a database—a sortable, analyzable collection of records representing books, documents, DVDs, and videos. Other types of subject specific databases also are used in research to search indexes for scholarly and peer reviewed journal articles—some of which are available in fulltext, abstracts, or other

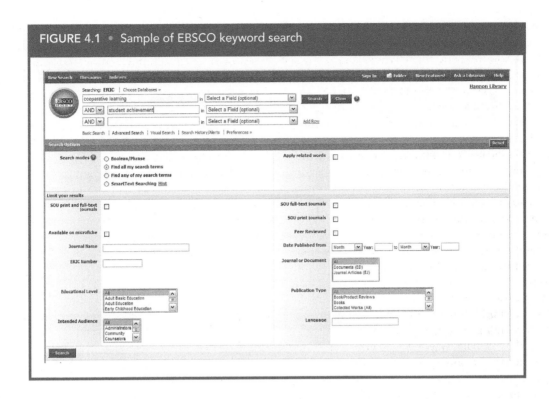

FIGURE 4.1 • Sample of EBSCO keyword search

documents. These databases such as the Education Resources Information Center (ERIC), Education Full Text, PsycINFO, and others provide an excellent way to identify primary sources and secondary sources.

The steps involved in searching a research database are similar to those involved in a book search, except that it is more critical to identify appropriate subject headings or descriptors to retrieve highly relevant material:

1. Identify keywords related to your topic.
2. Select the appropriate databases—some databases using the same interface may allow you to search multiple databases simultaneously.
3. Initiate a search using your keywords selectively. Some databases will map to subject headings or descriptors, requiring you to build your search, term by term. Other databases will provide a list of subject headings or descriptors based on the results of your search. In Figure 4.1, you can see an example of a keyword search using *cooperative learning* and *student achievement* with a possible 1,761 articles listed in the results in Figure 4.2. These initial "hits" will require additional sorting to determine their relevancy for your review of related literature.

4. Reformulate your search using appropriate subject headings or descriptors, combining terms as appropriate. Remember that combining too many terms may result in few or no retrieved items. If this occurs, mix and match search terms or broaden the search to produce better results. For example, in Figure 4.2 the subject term *academic achievement* is used instead of *student achievement*. By reformulating your search using *cooperative learning* with *academic achievement* and choosing to search both of the terms as subject headings or SU Subject Descriptors as in Figure 4.2 at the bottom, the search results in a more targeted list of references. In other words, articles identified by a human reader as being about cooperative learning and academic achievement.
5. Once you have found a relevant article, check the item record for links to additional subject headings or descriptors, author(s), cited references, times cited in the database, or other references for finding additional related items using the features within the database. For example, the record in Figure 4.3 gives all the descriptors used to classify the article and these descriptors can link to other articles

FIGURE 4.2 • Sample of ERIC/EBSCO search: reformulating with subject descriptors

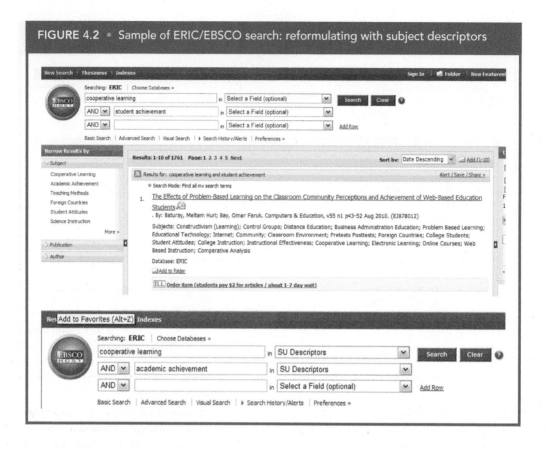

FIGURE 4.3 • Sample ERIC/EBSCO: sample record

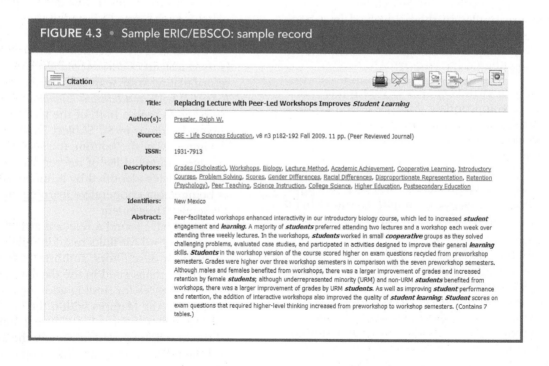

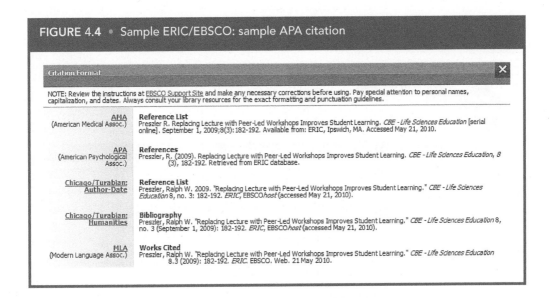

FIGURE 4.4 • Sample ERIC/EBSCO: sample APA citation

in the database about any of the descriptors. Also, by clicking the name of the author, you can find any other articles written and published by the same author.

6. Most databases provide a link that will create a citation in various formats, including APA. Although the citations still need to be checked for correctness, they provide an excellent start to creating your list of references. It is highly recommended that you begin your list of references and populate the list with citations from any relevant articles as you search and retrieve relevant articles. This will save you time in either going back later to retrieve citations or in creating citations after your paper is written. For example, in Figure 4.4, ERIC/EBSCO allows you to create and save your references in APA, AMA, Chicago, or MLA formats. There are a number of digital technologies that can help you manage your citations including:

■ BibMe—www.bibme.org/—enables researchers to create citation lists in MLA, APA, Chicago, and Turabian.

■ Citation Machine—http://www.citationmachine.net/—helps researchers generate citations in MLA, APA, Chicago, Turabian, and more.

■ Citefast—http://www.citefast.com/—helps researchers generate bibliography, in-text citations, and a title page in MLA, APA, and Chicago.

■ Easy Bib—http://www.easybib.com/—helps researchers generate citations and works cited pages in MLA, APA, and Chicago formats. Includes citation guides for the various formats.

7. Many databases allow you to create an account within the database, so you can log in to save and manage your searches and your relevant research articles. This feature is an important part of using a particular database to not only retrieve relevant research but to manage your sources by organizing them into folders. For example, in Figure 4.5 you can return to your MyEBSCO account at any time to copy your references, which can finally be moved into your review of related literature documents. When you write your review of related literature, you will be very thankful that you have created this account, so you can access your work more readily. There are also a number of other digital technologies that can help you manage your citations and references including:

■ Citavi—www.citavi.com/en/index.html— helps researchers manage reference, integrate .pdfs and other documents, evaluate content, organize content, and cite sources.

■ Colwiz—www.colwiz.com—helps researchers store files, maintain a reference library, annotate documents, and cite references.

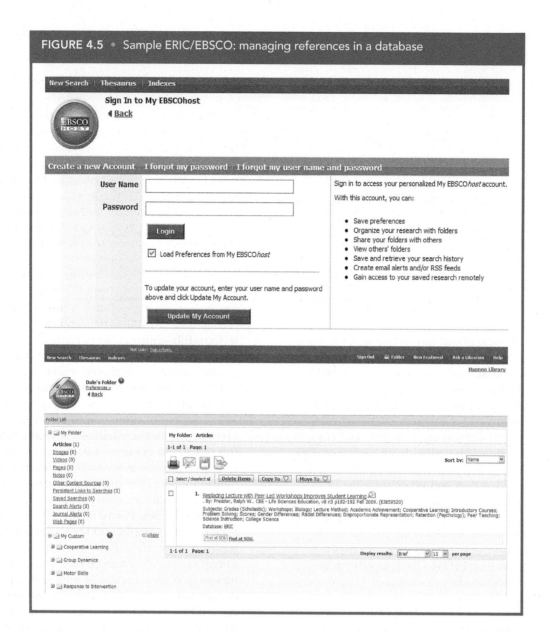

FIGURE 4.5 · Sample ERIC/EBSCO: managing references in a database

- Endnote—endnote.com/—is a commercial online research and reference management tool that can store documents, organizes information, create notes to annotate and tag documents, cite references, and construct bibliographies.
- Mendeley—www.mendeley.com/—helps researchers create a personal library of research. Search, sort, annotate, create sticky notes, and cite using appropriate style.
- Qiqqa—www.qiqqa.com/—helps researchers manage references, read,

annotate, tag, search, and cite .pdfs and other documents.
- ReadCube—www.readcube.com—is a PDF manager that stores documents and creates a searchable database including annotations, notes, highlighting, and more.
- RefWorks—www.refworks.com/refworks2— is a commercial online research and reference management tool that allows you to import data directly from most commercial databases and saved text files, organize and store information into custom

folders, generate citations, and create bibliographies.

- Zotero—www.zotero.org—is a suite of tools that creates a searchable personal library of sources, indexes the full-text, and cites references.

Education Databases. The following sections describe some of the commonly used databases for searches of education literature.

- *Education Resources Information Center (ERIC)*
ERIC, the largest digital library of education literature in the world, was established in 1966 by the National Library of Education as part of the United States Department of Education's Office of Educational Research and Improvement and is now sponsored by Institute of Education Sciences (IES) of the U.S. Department of Education. The online database provides information on subjects ranging from early childhood and elementary education, to education for gifted children and rural and urban education. ERIC is used by more than 500,000 people each year, providing access to more than 1.6 million bibliographic records of journal articles, research reports, curriculum and teaching guides, dissertations, theses, conference papers, books, and technical reports. ERIC indexes content published by more than 1,000 selected centers, agencies, programs, associations, non-profit organizations, and initiatives.

  The ERIC database is available at almost every academic library or via the ERIC website at http://www.eric.ed.gov. The website uses the most up-to-date retrieval methods for the ERIC databases, but it is no match for the database interfaces provided by your academic library. Given a choice, search ERIC via the interface available through your library—such as EBSCO or ProQuest. Doing so will allow you to automatically link to full-text articles when they are available through your library, save your articles, and cite the articles in the appropriate style guide such as APA. Regardless of whether you use your library's database interfaces or the government-sponsored ERIC website, ERIC is a formidable database for searching educational materials that is relatively quick and easy to search.

  When you search ERIC, you may notice that documents are categorized with an ED or EJ designation. An ED designation is generally used for unpublished documents, such as reports, studies, and theses. Usually, ED references are available in academic libraries as full-text on-line documents or via microfiche, if they are very old. An EJ designation is used for articles published in scholarly or professional journals as well as discipline-related magazines. EJ articles are often available in full text from the ERIC database at an academic library. If you are using the ERIC collection on the Web at www.eric.ed.gov/, the full text may not be available and must be tracked down in the periodicals collection of a library or purchased from article reprint companies.

  ERIC is the largest computer database for searches of education literature, but it is not the only source available. Other commonly used databases in education are described next.

- *Education Full Text*
The Education Full Text database contains articles historically available within the Wilson Education Index and references articles published in educational periodicals since 1983. The database provides references to many full-text articles that are not available in the ERIC database, so it is important to search both databases for more comprehensive research. In addition to article abstracts, the database includes citations for yearbooks and monograph series, videotapes, motion picture and computer program reviews, and legal cases.

- *Education Source*
Education Source is a more comprehensive database that duplicates the Education Full Text database with additional full-text journals previously not available in other databases. Coverage dates back to 1929 with full-text for more than 2,000 journals, 550 books, and 1,200 education-related conference papers encompassing all levels of education from early childhood to higher education including adult education, continuing education, distance learning, multicultural education, social issues, counseling, and vocational education.

- *PsycINFO*
The PsycINFO database is the online version of *Psychological Abstracts,* a former print source that presented summaries of completed psychological research studies (see apa.org/psycinfo) PsycINFO contains full-text and

abstracting of journal articles, technical reports, book chapters, and books in the field of psychology. Approximately 90% of the articles are from peer-reviewed sources. The database centers on psychology but also explores the interdisciplinary aspects of behavioral and social science literature including clinical case reports, empirical studies, and some dissertations. PsycINFO is organized by subject according to the Thesaurus of Psychological Index Terms codes, a controlled vocabulary describing the content of articles within in the database. The classification codes are available at www.apa.org/pubs//databases/training/class-codes.aspx. These classification codes allow you to retrieve abstracts for studies in a specific category— for example, Learning and Memory (2343), Developmental Disorders and Autism (3250), or Speech and Language Disorders (3270).

- *Dissertation Abstracts*
  Dissertation Abstracts contains bibliographic citations and abstracts from all subject areas for doctoral dissertations and master's theses completed at more than 1,000 accredited colleges and universities worldwide. The database dates back to 1861, with abstracts included from 1980 forward. If after reading an abstract you want to obtain a copy of the complete dissertation, check to see if it is available in your library. If not, speak to a librarian about how to obtain a copy. You can request a dissertation from your library through interlibrary loan. Be aware that there may be charges to get the dissertation from the lending library. Dissertations may be able to be obtained by searching the Internet for an online copy or by contacting the author.

Searching the Internet

An abundance of educational materials is available on the Web—from primary research articles and educational theory, to lesson plans and research guides. Currently, a proficient researcher can access information in a variety of formats such as video, images, multimedia, PowerPoint presentations, screen captures, tutorials, and more. Blogs, RSS feeds, podcasts, wikis, e-mail, and other Web 2.0 tools offer researchers a variety of alternative means for finding information. Also, as search engines develop to include more sophisticated methods for finding research, both "digital

natives" and traditional researchers can find primary sources using tools such as Google Scholar, Google Books, and more. Even Wikipedia can provide background information to help a researcher understand fundamental concepts and theory that lead to better keywords and strategies for searching. For further discussion of using Google, see the feature "Digital Research Tools."

Internet search engines are structured and function differently than databases. The essential difference is a search engine is compiled and organized through programming. Search results are retrieved using complex algorithms that establish an essential relevancy for each site or page. No person reads or reviews the list of sites compiled within a search engine. This somewhat explains why an Internet search breaks down after the second or third page and begins to contain more and more irrelevant information. A research database like ERIC or Education Full Text is also compiled through programming, but it is organized by humans who have read the contents, such as the articles. It is essential to connect with the human organization of a database by using the appropriate subject headings and descriptors that are not present in an Internet search engine. On the Internet, using multiple keywords and experimenting with search terms is essential for successfully retrieving useful information. It is also important to specify a date range when searching a source like Google Scholar because the algorithms of Internet search tools do not use date of publication as a criteria for relevancy.

The resources you can find on the Web are almost limitless. More and more print material is being digitized and new sites are constantly being developed and tested to provide more and more access to information. Academic social network sites like *ResearchGate*, *Academia*, and other sites are providing an online space for scientists and researchers to connect and share publications and other works for free. With just a few clicks, you can access electronic educational journals that provide full-text articles, bibliographic information, and abstracts. You can obtain up-to-the-minute research reports and information about educational research activities undertaken at various research centers, and you can access education sites with links to resources that other researchers have found especially valuable. But be warned— there is little quality control on the Internet and at times the sheer volume of information can be overwhelming. Some Internet sites post research articles selected specifically to promote or encourage a particular point of view or even an educational product. Blogs and wikis provide excellent modes of creating and manipulating content to share and communicate ideas and concepts, but they are not always as robust as peer-reviewed academic research. Make sure you understand the strengths and limits of the sources you use.

The following websites are especially useful to educational researchers:

- CSTEEP: The Center for the Study of Testing, Evaluation, and Educational Policy (www .bc.edu/research/csteep.html). The website for this educational research organization contains information on testing, evaluation, and public policy studies on school assessment practices and international comparative research.

- National Center for Education Statistics (nces. ed.gov). This site contains statistical reports and other information on the condition of U.S. education. It also reports on education activities internationally.
- TeachersFirst: State Education Standards (www .teachersfirst.com/statestds.cfm). This site contains a wealth of up-to-date information regarding state-by-state educational standards and curriculum frameworks.
- U.S. Department of Education (www.ed.gov/). This site contains links to the education databases supported by the U.S. government (including ERIC). It also makes available full-text reports on current findings on education and provides links to research offices and organizations as well as research publications and products.

Digital Research Tools

SEARCH TOOLS

Google Books (books.google.com/)

Google Books searches for books and the content of books in Google's digital book collection. The searchable collection of digitized books contains full-text as well as limited selections, previews, or snippet views of the content—including front cover, table of contents, indexes, and other relevant information like related books, posted reviews, and key terms. As such, Google Books offers an alternative search mechanism to the library online catalog for finding and previewing books and information inside books. Google Books searches full-text content, so a search can often retrieve more specific information that a library catalog will not retrieve.

In most cases, however, Google Books does *not* replace the full text of all the books that it finds, so it is best used in conjunction with a library catalog or the collective catalog from a consortium of libraries. For example, you may search Google Books and find a relevant book. After reviewing information such as the table of contents and the limited preview of the book, you may want to search your library catalog to obtain the book. On the other hand, you may find an item record of a book using your library catalog that does not

contain much information about the book--that is, you may not be able to see the table of contents or any information other than the title and the subject headings. As an alternative, you could search the title of the book in Google Books to find additional information such as the table of contents or even a preview of the contents of the book.

Google Books began in 2004, and as more and more content is digitized into the Google Books database, its usefulness to researchers will continue to expand. You may want to consider limiting the publication date of a search using the advanced feature to retrieve more current materials. The default search is set to relevancy, but the most relevant material may be too old for the research you are doing.

Google Scholar (http://scholar.google .com/)

Google Scholar offers simple and free access to scholarly information. Originally released in a beta version in November 2004, Google Scholar searches for full-text articles, citations, and abstracts. It also searches the Google Books database for books. To take full advantage of Google Scholar, you should click on Scholar Preferences and set the Library Links feature to access your library. This will allow you to obtain the full text of the articles you find through your library and your library databases. You may also want to set your preferences to retrieve only articles. Google Scholar also includes links to other articles that have cited a specific article and related articles.

Again, for finding scholarly and peer-reviewed journal articles, you will ultimately want to use your library's access to the ERIC or Education Full Text databases. Google Scholar, however, often can help you tease out the correct descriptors or subject headings for finding articles in your library databases. This is especially true if you find the full text of an article in a database from your library. If you are familiar with searching Google, then searching Google Scholar allows you to find relevant information using the simple and familiar search strategies you use to search the Web. However, you should set the time range to ensure you are retrieving current research. Your initial search can start with Scholar, which can ultimately lead you to more sophisticated searching in library databases.

USA.gov (usa.gov)

USA.gov is a powerful online search tool for finding U.S. federal government and state government information. For education research, USA.gov refines a typical search by limiting the results to information from federal and state domains. For example, you may search for "standards aligned curriculum" to determine what activities are happening in various states. You can also limit a search to a particular state, such as Oregon, to retrieve information specifically from sites such as the Oregon Department of Education. Because so much educational information and decision-making can be found on government sites, a USA.gov search is a good option for finding relevant primary information not found in books and journal articles.

Becoming a Member of Professional Organizations

Another way to find current literature related to your research topic is through membership in professional organizations. The following list gives the names of a few U.S.-based professional organizations that can be valuable resources for research reports and curriculum materials. In countries other than the United States, similar organizations likely can also be accessed through an Internet search. This list of professional organizations is not intended to be comprehensive because there are as many professional organizations as there are content areas (e.g., reading, writing, mathematics, science, social studies, music, health, and physical education) and special interest groups (e.g., Montessori education). Search the Education Resource Organizations Directory to discover and learn about some of the associations that support teachers and specific disciplines in education.

ASCD: Association for Supervision and Curriculum Development. (www.ascd.org). Boasting 160,000 members in more than 135 countries, ASCD is one of the largest educational organizations in the world. ASCD publishes books, newsletters, audiotapes, videotapes, and some excellent journals that are valuable resources for teacher researchers, including Educational Leadership and the Journal of Curriculum and Supervision.

NCTM: National Council of Teachers of Mathematics. (www.nctm.org). With more than 80,000 members and 230 affiliates in the U.S. and Canada, NCTM is dedicated to the teaching and learning of mathematics and offers vision and leadership for mathematics educators at all age levels. NCTM provides regional and national professional development opportunities and publishes the following journals: *Teaching Children Mathematics, Mathematics Teaching in the Middle School, Mathematics Teacher, Mathematics Teacher Education*, and the *Journal for Research in Mathematics Education*.

NCSS: National Council for the Social Studies. (www.socialstudies.org/). The NCSS supports and advocates for social studies education to prepare students for civic life. The NCSS serves elementary, secondary, and college teachers of the social sciences both in the classroom and through curriculum design. Its resources for educators include the journals *Social Education* and *Social Studies and the Young Learner*.

NEA: National Education Association. (www.nea.org/). The mission of the NEA is to advance the cause of public education and to advocate for education professionals. The NEA seeks to fulfill the promise of public education, campaign for the rights of children, and to prepare students to succeed in a diverse and interdependent world.

NSTA: National Science Teachers Association. (www.nsta.org/). The NSTA, with more than 55,000 members, provides many valuable resources for science teachers. It develops the National Science Education Standards and publishes the journals *Science and Children, Science Scope, The Science Teacher*, and *Journal of College Science Teaching*.

ILA: International Literacy Association. (www.literacyworldwide.org/). The ILA provides resources to an international audience of reading teachers through its publication of the journals *The Reading Teacher, Journal of Adolescent and Adult Literacy*, and *Reading Research Quarterly*.

U.S. Department of Education—Educational State Contacts. (www2.ed.gov/about/contacts/state/index.html). This U.S. Department of Education site lists a variety of state-by-state educational departments and contacts, the higher education agency, special education agency, and adult education agency.

Evaluating Your Sources

After you have retrieved a list of sources, you will need to evaluate them to determine not only whether these sources are relevant, but also whether they are reliable and legitimate. Good researchers must be able to discern the quality and limitations of a source, so good research requires excellent judgment. The statements in Table 4.2 can serve as a rubric for evaluating your sources regardless of whether those sources are from scholarly journals, magazines, or websites. A note of caution: Anyone can post a "professional"

looking website on the Internet. Do not be fooled by looks. Apply the same criteria for evaluating web-based materials that you would use for print materials. Critically evaluating your sources will save you time and energy reading and annotating sources that may contribute little to your understanding of a research topic. This section includes an evaluation rubric using the categories of relevancy, author, source, methodology, date, validity, and references.

Relevancy

What was the purpose or problem statement of the study? Obviously, the first thing to do is to determine whether the source really applies to your research topic and qualifies to be included in a review of related literature. Does the title of the source reflect research related to your work? Is there a well-refined question or statement of purpose? The problem statement is often found in the abstract and will allow you to determine the relevance of the research to your own research.

Author

Who was the author? What are the qualifications, reputation, and status of the author? In most databases, the name of the author links to any other published works in the database. Check to determine what other works, if any, have been published by the author and if any of the other works are related to your research. Is the subject matter a primary interest in the published works of the author? Is the author affiliated with any institution or organization? Most importantly, can you contact the author? Does the author have a personal website with vitae?

Source

Where was the source published? Does the information come from a scholarly or peer-reviewed journal, an education-related magazine, a popular magazine, or a website? Is the information personal opinion, a review of a research study, or the result of a research study? Clearly, sources of different types merit different weight in your review. For instance, did you find your source in a refereed or a nonrefereed journal? In a refereed journal, articles are reviewed by a panel of experts in the field and are more scholarly and trustworthy

TABLE 4.2 • Rubric for evaluating print and Internet resources

Dimension	Evaluation Criteria				
	1 Poor	2 Below Average	3 Average	4 Above Average	5 Excellent
Relevancy	The source does not address the research interests of your study.	The source addresses one of the research interests of your study.	The source addresses most of the research interests of your study.	The source meets all of the research interests of your study.	The source meets all of the research interests of your study and provides a conceptual framework for a study that is replicable.
Author	Unclear who authored the study.	Author name and contact information is provided.	Author name, contact information, and some credentials are included in the article.	Author name, contact information, and full credentials are included in the article.	Author is a well-known researcher in the research area under investigation and provides links to other research related to the current study.
Source	Source is not a scholarly nor a peer-reviewed journal and is a summary of the author's opinion.	Source is not a scholarly nor a peer-reviewed journal and must be closely examined for bias, subjectivity, intent, accuracy, and reliability before inclusion in the review of related literature.	Source is a scholarly or peer-reviewed journal, an education-related magazine, or a popular magazine.	Source is a scholarly or peer-reviewed journal.	Source is a scholarly or peer-reviewed journal with links to related literature by same author(s) and ability to download fully online versions of articles.
Methodology	It is not possible to determine from the description of the study whether or not an appropriate methodology was used to investigate the research problem.	The description of the methodology does not include sufficient information to determine if the sample size was acceptable given the research problem.	The source includes a full description of the research problem and the appropriateness of the methodology to investigate the problem.	The source includes a full description of the research problem and the appropriateness of the methodology to investigate the problem. The results are presented objectively and can be connected to the data presented in the study.	The source includes a full description of the research problem and the appropriateness of the methodology to investigate the problem. Issues of validity and reliability are discussed along with limitations of the study. There is sufficient information in the source to enable a replication of the study.
Date	No date of publication is included in the source.	Date of publication is included but is too old to be helpful for the current research problem.	Current date of publication.	Current date of publication with a list of references consulted by the author.	Current date of publication with a list of references consulted by the author including links to fully online articles.

than articles from nonrefereed or popular journals. Research articles in refereed journals are required to comply with strict guidelines regarding format and research procedures. Review the submission guidelines at the journal website to determine the criteria for publication. Special care and caution must also be taken when evaluating websites because anyone can post information on the Internet. Websites must be closely examined for bias, subjectivity, intent, accuracy, and reliability. These important quality-control questions will help you determine whether or not a source is worthy of inclusion in your review of related literature.

Methodology

How was the study conducted? It is important to verify that the information presented in a particular source is objective and impartial. What methodology was used to investigate the problem or test the hypothesis? Was an appropriate method used? Can the research be replicated by others? Was the sample size suitable for the research? Does the source add to the information you have already gathered about your topic? Is the information presented in the source accurate? It is important to verify that the information presented in a particular source is objective and impartial. Does the author present evidence that supports the interpretations? Does the content of the article consist mainly of opinion, or does it contain appropriately collected and analyzed data? How accurate are the discussion and conclusions of the findings? Do the findings present any contrary data or assumptions?

Date

When was the research conducted? The date of publication is of primary importance in evaluating a source. Look at the copyright date of books and the dates when articles were published. Websites should always include a reference to the last updated or revised date, but in general, web search tools do not incorporate date as a relevancy factor. Research in areas of current interest and continuing development generally requires recent, up-to-date references. Searching for recent references does not mean disregarding older research. Oftentimes, older research as opposed to out-of-date research is pertinent to your worldview as an educator and is still relevant. The importance of seminal theoretical works is evident throughout this text, such as the theoretical work conducted in educational psychology by Jean Piaget.

Cited References

What other sources were referenced? Check the bibliography of a source to help determine the quality of the research. Do the references reflect current, scholarly, or peer-reviewed research? Are they robust enough for the subject matter? Do they reflect original sources and alternative perspectives? Who are the authors? The list of references can yield an abundance of information when evaluating the quality of a source. Remember, the quality of your research will also be judged by the references you choose, so you should be careful to select the best research to support your work.

Conducting effective library and Internet searches will yield an abundance of useful information about your topic. By using multiple search methods and strategies, you can collect information that is current, accurate, and comprehensive. As you become more experienced, you will learn to conduct more efficient and effective searches, identifying better sources that focus on your topic and accurately represent the information needed for your research. For the most part, articles published in databases that access primary, scholarly and peer-reviewed sources will produce high quality information and therefore should be the emphasis of your research.

Annotating Your Sources

After you have identified the primary references related to your topic, you are ready to move on to the next phase of a review of related literature—annotating the references. Many databases include an abstract or summary of a study that describes the hypotheses, procedures, and conclusions. An abstract is descriptive in nature and does not assess the value or intent of the source. An annotation assesses the quality, relevance, and accuracy of a source. Additionally, the annotation describes how the source relates to the topic and its relative importance. Basically, annotating involves reviewing, summarizing, and classifying your references. Students sometimes ask why it is necessary to read and annotate original, complete articles or reports if they already have perfectly good abstracts. By assessing the quality and usefulness of a source, annotations articulate your response to a source and why the source is important to your research. After completing annotations, many students discover that these same annotations contributed heavily to the writing of their review of related literature.

To begin the annotation process, arrange your articles and other sources in reverse chronological order. Beginning with the latest references is a good research strategy because the most recent research is likely to have profited from previous research. Also, recent references may cite preceding studies that you may not have identified. For each reference, complete the following steps:

1. If the article has an abstract or a summary, as most do, read it to determine the relevance of the article to your problem.

2. Skim the entire article, making mental notes of the main points of the study.

3. If you were searching research databases, then you should have a document already that contains a complete bibliographic reference for the work. Include the library call number if the source work is from a book. This step can be tedious but is important. You would spend much more time trying to find the complete bibliographic information for an article or book that you failed to annotate completely than you will spend annotating it in the first place. If you know that your final report must follow a particular editorial style, such as that described in the *Publication Manual* of the American Psychological Association (APA), put your bibliographic reference in that form. Remember, most databases put the citation of a source in a citation style. For example, an APA-style reference for a journal article looks like this:

Snurd, B. J. (2016). The use of white versus yellow chalk in the teaching of advanced calculus. *Journal of Useless Findings, 105*(5) 465–477.

In this example, "2016" is the date of publication, "105" is the volume number of the journal, "5" is the issue number, and "465–477" are the page numbers. A style manual provides reference formats for all types of sources. Whatever format you select, use it consistently

and be sure your bibliographic references are accurate. You never know when you may have to go back and get additional information from an article.

4. Classify and code the article according to some system, and then add the code to the annotation in a conspicuous place, such as an upper corner. The code should be one that can be easily accessed when you want to sort your notes into the categories you devise. Any coding system that makes sense to you will facilitate your task later when you have to sort, organize, analyze, synthesize, and write your review of the literature. You may use abbreviations to code variables relevant to your study (e.g., SA in the upper corner of your abstract may signify that the article is about student achievement). Coding and keeping track of articles is a key to organization. Programs such as RefWorks, EndNote, and others can help you manage, organize, annotate, and create bibliographic citations. They also allow you to add keywords or descriptors to your citations. Database vendors such as ProQuest and EBSCO allow you to create an account to store references from the ERIC and Education Full Text databases. To manage citation with ProQuest's My Research or MyEBSCO, you must create a profile account that allows you to save individual citation records, create folders to organize citations, and save searches. In addition, you can request RSS feeds and search alerts that automatically retrieve newer articles that meet your search criteria.

5. Annotate the source by summarizing the central theme and scope of the reference, why the source is useful, strengths and limitations, the author's conclusions, and your overall reaction to the work. If the work is an opinion article, write the main points of the author's position—for example, "Jones believes parent volunteers should be used because [list the reasons]." If it is a study, state the problem, the procedures (including a description of participants and instruments), and the major conclusions. Make special note of any particularly interesting or unique aspect of the study, such as use of a new measuring

FIGURE 4.6 • Literature matrix					
Authors' names	Relevancy	Author	Source	Methodology	Date

instrument. Double-check the reference to make sure you have not omitted any pertinent information. If an abstract provided at the beginning of an article contains all the essential information (and that is a big if), by all means use it.

6. Indicate any thoughts that come to your mind, such as points on which you disagree (e.g., mark them with an X) or components that you do not understand (e.g., mark with a ?). For example, if an author states that he or she used a double-blind procedure and you are unfamiliar with that technique, you can put a question mark next to that statement in your database entry, on your index card, or on a photocopy of the page. Later, you can find out what it is.

7. Indicate any statements that are direct quotations or personal reactions. Plagiarism, intentional or not, is an absolute no-no with the direst of consequences. Put quotation marks around direct quotations and add the in-text citation information, or you may not remember later which statements are direct quotations. You must also record the exact page number of the quotation in case you use it later in your paper. You will need the page number when citing the source in your paper. Direct quotations should be kept to a minimum in your research plan and report. Use your own words, not those of other researchers. Occasionally, a direct quotation may be quite appropriate and useful.

Whatever approach you use, guard your notes and digital records carefully. Save more than one copy so that you will not lose your work. Also,

when your annotations are complete, save the information for future reference and future studies (nobody can do just one!). There are a number of popular digital technologies that can help you manage your annotations including:

- A.nnotate—a.nnotate.com/—allows you to store and share comments on PDF files, Microsoft Office documents, images, and Internet sites. It includes the ability to create notes anywhere on an item and share them with others.
- Scribe—http://chnm.gmu.edu/tools/scribe/—is a note-taking program that can manage research notes, comments, and ideas, so they can be indexed, searched, and cross referenced like an online index card that is searchable.
- ReadCube—www.readcube.com—is a tool that imports and manages searchable references, and makes inline notes and highlights while reading.

Literature Matrix

A helpful way to keep track of your annotations is to record them on a matrix (see Figure 4.6). The matrix is a powerful organizer when you are committing your thoughts to text. Along the Y-axis list the authors' names. Along the X-axis list the dimensions used for evaluating your sources: relevancy, author, source, methodology, and date. The matrix will provide you with a mental map of what you are reading and what the studies share in common. Figure 4.7 is a brief sample matrix for the annotated review of related literature from "'Come to My (Web) Site,' Said the Spider to the Fly: Reflections of a Virtual Professor."

FIGURE 4.7 • Example of literature matrix					
Authors' names	Relevancy	Author	Source	Methodology	Date
Berge, Z.	Relevant	European perspective	Refereed journal	Surveys and interviews	1999
Daugherty, M., & Funke, B. L	Relevant	Experienced online instructors	Refereed journal	Surveys and interviews	1998
Harasim, L	Relevant	Experience with computer mediated instruction	Refereed journal	Interviews, surveys, observations	1987
Levin, D.	Relevant	Experience in distance education	Eric Document institutional report. Non refereed	Instructor reflections on institutional development of online courses	1997
Schrum, L.	Highly relevant drescription of online pedgagogies	Extensive background in online teaching	Refereed quarterly journal	Qualitative, interviews	1998

MyLab Education **Self-Check 4.3**

MyLab Education **Application Exercise 4.3:** Identifying Primary and Secondary Sources

MyLab Education **Application Exercise 4.4:** Narrowing a Keyword Search

ANALYZING, ORGANIZING, AND REPORTING THE LITERATURE

For beginning researchers, the hardest part of writing the literature review for a plan or report is thinking about how hard it is going to be to write the literature review. More time is spent worrying about doing it than actually doing it. This hesitancy stems mostly from a lack of experience with the type of writing needed in a literature review—a technical form of writing unlike most of the writing we do. In technical writing, facts must be documented and opinions substantiated. For example, if you say that the high school dropout percentage in Ohio has increased in the last 10 years, you must provide a source for this information. Technical writing is precise, requiring clarity of definitions and consistency in the use of

terms. If the term *achievement* is important in your review, for example, you must indicate what you mean by it and be consistent in using that meaning throughout the written review. Figure 4.8 summarizes these and other important technical writing guidelines useful in a literature review.

If you have annotated the literature related to your problem efficiently, and if you approach the task in an equally systematic manner, then analyzing, organizing, and reporting the literature will be relatively painless. To get warmed up, you should read quickly through your annotations and notes to refresh your memory and identify references that no longer seem sufficiently related to your topic. Do not force references into your review that do not really fit. The review forms the background and rationale for your hypothesis and should contain only references that serve this purpose. The following guidelines—based on experience acquired the hard way—should be helpful to you.

Make an Outline

Don't groan! Your eighth-grade teacher was right about the virtues of an outline. However you construct it, an outline will save you time and effort in the long run and will increase the probability of having an organized review. The outline will

---

FIGURE 4.8 • Guidelines for technical writing

1. *Document facts and substantiate opinions.* Cite references to support your facts and opinions. Note that facts are usually based on empirical data, whereas opinions are not. In the hierarchy of persuasiveness, facts are more persuasive than opinions. Differentiate between facts and opinions in the review.

2. *Define terms clearly, and be consistent in your use of terms.*

3. *Organize content logically.*

4. *Direct your writing to a particular audience.* Usually the literature review is aimed at a relatively naïve reader, one who has some basic understanding of the topic but requires additional education to understand the topic or issue. Do not assume your audience knows as much as you do about the topic and literature! They don't, so you have to write to educate them.

5. *Follow an accepted manual of style.* The manual indicates the style in which chapter headings are set up, how tables must be constructed, how footnotes and bibliographies must be prepared, and the like. Commonly used manuals and their current editions are *Publication Manual of the American Psychological Association*, sixth edition, and *The Chicago Manual of Style*, sixteenth edition.

6. *Evade affected verbiage and eschew obscuration of the obvious.* In other words, limit big words and avoid jargon.

7. *Start each major section with a brief overview of the section.* The overview may begin like this: "In this section, three main issues are examined. The first is . . ."

8. *End each major section with a summary of the main ideas.*

---

also help you organize the research that you are using. The outline does not have to be excessively detailed. Begin by identifying the main topics and the order in which they should be presented. For example, the outline of the review for a problem concerned with salaried paraprofessionals versus parent volunteers may begin with these headings: "Literature on Salaried Paraprofessionals," "Literature on Parent Volunteers," and "Literature Comparing the Two." You can always add or remove topics in the outline as your work progresses. The next step is to differentiate each major heading into logical sub-headings. The need for further differentiation will be determined by your topic; the more complex it is, the more subheadings you will require. When you have completed your outline, you will invariably need to rearrange, add, and delete topics. It is much easier, however, to reorganize an outline than it is to reorganize a document written in paragraph form. There are also a number of popular digital technologies that can help you brainstorm your outline including:

- Bubbl.us—bubbl.us—is a visual thinking tool that creates a graphical mind map of ideas and concepts to structure information.
- Gliffy—www.gliffy.com—enables researchers to collaborate on flowcharts, diagrams, technical drawings, and organizational charts that can be shared from the cloud or a local drive.
- Mindmeister—www.mindmeister.com—is a collaborative mind mapping and brainstorming tool to help organize your thoughts.
- MindMup—www.mindmup.com/—enables researchers to brainstorm and create mind maps, presentations, and outlines to help focus ideas and collaborate with others. Converts mind maps to PDF, PowerPoint, and other programs.
- VUE—vue.tufts.edu/—is a visual understanding environment (VUE) that provides a concept and content map to visually organize digital files.

Analyze Each Reference in Terms of Your Outline

In other words, determine the subheading under which each reference fits. Then sort your references into appropriate piles. If you end up with references without a home, there are three logical possibilities: (1) Something is wrong with your outline, (2) the references do not belong in your review and should be discarded, or (3) the references do not belong in your review but do belong somewhere else in your research plan and report introduction. Opinion articles or reports of descriptive research often are useful in the introduction, whereas formal research studies are most useful in the review of related literature.

Analyze the References under Each Subheading for Similarities and Differences

If three references say essentially the same thing, you will not need to describe each one; it is much better to make one summary statement and cite the three sources, as in this example:

Several studies have found white chalk to be more effective than yellow chalk in the teaching of advanced mathematics (Snurd, 2016; Trivia, 2014; Ziggy, 2015).

Give a Meaningful Overview of Past Research

Don't present a series of abstracts or a mere list of findings (Jones found A, Smith found B, and Brown found C). Your task is to organize and summarize the references in a meaningful way. Do not ignore studies that are contradictory to most other studies or to your personal bias. Analyze and evaluate contradictory studies and try to determine a possible explanation. For example:

Contrary to these studies is the work of Rottenstudee (2015), who found yellow chalk to be more effective than white chalk in the teaching of trigonometry. However, the size of the treatment groups (two students per group) and the duration of the study (one class period) may have seriously affected the results.

Discuss the References Least Related to Your Problem First and Those Most Related to Your Problem Just Before the Statement of the Hypothesis

Think of a big V. At the bottom of the V is your guiding hypothesis; directly above your hypothesis are the studies most directly related to it, and so forth. The idea is to organize and present your literature in such a way that it leads logically to a tentative, testable conclusion, namely, your hypothesis. Highlight or summarize important aspects of the review to help readers identify them. If your problem has more than one major aspect, you may have two Vs or one V that logically leads to two tentative, testable conclusions.

Conclude the Review with a Brief Summary of the Literature and Its Implications

The length of this summary depends on the length of the review. It should be detailed enough to clearly show the chain of logic you have followed in arriving at your implications and tentative conclusions.

There are also a number of popular digital technologies that can help you organizing, writing, and editing your review of literature including:

- Evernote—evernote.com/—helps researchers create texts, photos, and audio notes and enables researchers to synchronize notes on different devices.
- WorkFlowy—workflowy.com—is an organizational tool used to create lists, take notes, and write collaboratively.
- Wunderlust—www.wunderlist.com—is a tool that helps researchers create and organize lists, tasks, reminders, or ideas and collaborate with others.
- Scrivener—www.literatureandlatte.com/scrivener.php—is a word processing and project management tool that allows researchers to compose, structure, and revise long documents.
- Q10—www.baara.com/q10/—is a full screen, customizable, text editor that supports paragraph formatting, spell checker, timed alarm, word and character counter, text substitution, and auto-correct.
- Write! —https://wri.tt/—is a text editor that automatically cloud saves and has a variety of features such as auto-complete, unlimited undo, spell checker, and productivity counters, and a dark/light mode that focuses the light on the current paragraph.
- Grammarly—www.grammarly.com—helps researchers to check grammar, writing style, spelling and other aspects of writing including plagiarism.
- Hemingway App—http://www.hemingwayapp.com/—is an application that highlights lengthy, complex sentences and common errors to help write more concise and clear sentences. Allows the researcher to paste text into the app or write something directly.

Sample Brief Annotated Review of Related Literature

Mills, G. E. (2000). "'Come to My Web (Site),' Said the Spider to the Fly: Reflections on the Life of a Virtual Professor." Paper presented at the Self-Study of Teacher Education Practices Conference, Herstmonceux, England.

Research Questions

1. What is the effect of web-based instruction on students' communication with each other? With the instructor?
2. How do students' learning styles affect their success in a web-based class?
3. How do on-line resources meet students' needs to access course materials?

Review of Related Literature

As an expatriate Australian, I am positively predisposed to distance learning. As a young teacher in a small rural "outback" town in Australia, my only option for continuing my education was via correspondence education. In the United States, correspondence education is not widely accepted as an acceptable form of education by those of us working in universities. But why is this the case when other developed countries (like Australia!) have wide acceptance of distance learning via correspondence? I believe that this issue gets to the heart of the propositions many of us hold about effective pedagogy, whether it is in a live or web-based learning environment, and provides the framework for the related literature to be considered here.

Context for the study

There is a dearth of literature that addresses what is for me one of the most critical aspects of classroom learning environments—the nature and quality of the interaction between teachers and students, and between students and other students. This pedagogical concern can be viewed in broader terms to include "the identification of learning goals, philosophical changes in teaching and learning, reconceptualization of the teacher's role, evaluation of student and instructor, and the stimulation of interactivity" (Schrum, 1998, p. 56). In order to foster interaction in a virtual classroom, Berge (1999) points out that teachers must utilize interactions of a synchronous (communication occurs in real time) or asynchronous (technologically mediated in time) nature. I taught my action research class based on an asynchronous model—students who registered for the class could take it anywhere, anytime—although they were encouraged to follow a 10-week outline of tasks and activities. Similarly, the class was characterized by asynchronous communication—there was never the expectation that the class would meet in "real time" or with any face-to-face interaction. But as I will discuss later in this paper, this kind of communication provided me with a significant challenge in the way I developed rapport with my students. Levin (1997) characterizes this challenge in the following way:

Overview of past research

Reference least related to the research problem

Reference most related to the research problem

Research most related to the research problem

> I can neither see the puzzlement in an online learner's eyes or the "aha" twinkle when a student gets the point. One of the attractions of asynchronous computer mediated communication also poses another challenge: anytime, anywhere, but alone. If you believe as I do that learning should be viewed as the social construction of meaning and knowledge, then this isolation poses a stiff challenge to learning. Online learning is conducted largely within text. (p. 6)

As you will see, I find this inability to see the twinkle of my students' eyes a drawback in my ability to develop a rapport and understanding of the complex worldviews they bring to the learning environment. However, there is little evidence in the literature to suggest that students of web-based instruction (WBI) classes perform differently compared with traditional classes.

Teachers and students who participate in WBI classes appear to hold somewhat contrasting views of the distance learning experience that are challenging to reconcile. For example, faculty are consistently concerned about the quality of the teaching/learning experience and the degree of interactivity that occurs. Alternatively, students are generally positive about the experience and report that the convenience of this medium meets the needs of the nontraditional (distance learning) student who balances work, family, and study (Daugherty & Funke, 1998). The same study reports that faculty perceptions of WBI can be categorized as follows: lack of technical support, lack of software/adequate equipment, lack of faculty/administrative support, the amount of preparation time required to create and grade assignments, and student lack of knowledge and resistance to the technology. Alternatively, students tend to acknowledge the utility of the Internet and the "discovery" learning that occurred through the use of Internet resources and, according to Daugherty and Funke (1998), "appeared genuinely impressed by the variety and quality of the learning materials offered via the Web" (p. 30). In an earlier study, Harasim (1987) reported an even greater list of perceived advantages of on-line learning, from an increased interaction in quantity and intensity to motivational aspects related to text-based communication (p. 124). Students value being able to communicate in a text-based environment to a far greater degree than they would in a traditional live class—a finding that is supported in my own study and to which I will speak later in this paper.

> Brief summary of the literature and its implications

REFERENCES

Berge, Z. (1999). Interaction in post-secondary web-based learning. *Educational Technology, 39*(1), 5–11.

Daugherty, M., & Funke, B. L. (1998). University faculty and student perceptions of web-based instruction. *Journal of Distance Education, 13*(1), 21–39.

Harasim, L. (1987). Teaching and learning on-line: Issues in computer-mediated graduate courses. *CJCE, 16*(2), 117–135.

Levin, D. (1997). Institutional concerns: Supporting the use of Internet discussion groups. ED 416481.

Schrum, L. (1998). On-line education: A study of emerging pedagogy. *New Directions for Adult and Continuing Education, 78*, 53–61.

MyLab Education **Self-Check 4.4**

MyLab Education **Application Exercise 4.5:**
Writing a Literature Review

META-ANALYSIS

One way to summarize the results of the literature is to conduct a meta-analysis. A **meta-analysis** is a statistical approach to summarizing the results of many quantitative studies that have investigated basically the same problem. It provides a numerical way of expressing the composite (i.e., "average") result of a group of studies.

As you may have noticed when you reviewed the literature related to your problem, numerous problems have been the subject of literally hundreds of studies (e.g., ability grouping is one such problem). Traditional attempts to summarize the results of many related studies have involved classifying the studies in some defined way, noting the number of studies in which a particular variable showed a significant effect, and drawing one or more conclusions. For example, a summary statement may say something like, "In 45 of 57 studies, the Warm-Fuzzy approach resulted in greater student self-esteem than the No-Nonsense approach, and therefore the Warm-Fuzzy approach appears to be an effective method for promoting self-esteem."

WRITING ABOUT RESEARCH

Neophyte researchers often ask the question: "When should I start writing about my research?" The simple answer is "It's never too soon!" As you embark on the research process, regardless of the method you use to investigate your problem, you should start writing about your research. Create electronic folders that correspond with the major headings of a research article or capstone degree thesis. For example, at this stage of the research process, you are ready to create the following folders and start to make entries that will eventually be edited into your final project, whether it is a journal article submission or thesis:

- Abstract: An abstract is a brief (usually 250–500 words) summary of the contents of the article or thesis you are writing. Even though you have not yet implemented your research plan, you can write a brief description about the problem under investigation and the themes that emerged from the review of related literature. Later in the research process, you will be able to return to this *draft* abstract and continue to add important information such as participants, method, findings, conclusions, and implications of the research.
- Introduction: The article or thesis will open with an introduction (I know, this is a statement of the obvious!) that describes the problem under investigation (if you write this first you can cut and paste it in to your abstract) and the design you have used. You might have some naïve assumptions about the appropriate design to use to investigate your problem; after all, you have another 10 chapters to read in this book to help you decide the design that best fits your research problem! The introduction also provides you with an opportunity to write about the following:

- Why is this problem important?
- How does this study relate to previous research? (Sounds like a review of related literature!)
- What are the theoretical and practical implications of the proposed study?

For a complete discussion of these and other elements, consult the *Publication Manual of the American Psychological Association*. Remember, you are still early in the research process, but we hope that you will seriously consider the benefits of starting to write about your research *early*. (Perhaps EARLY could be an acronym for "eventually all research leaves you" if you don't write about it!) You do not want to wait until the end of the process to start writing. If you start to write early, you will be able to seek feedback from your professors and peers and to learn how best to present your work to the scholarly community.

Two major problems are associated with the traditional approach to summarizing studies. The first is that subjectivity is involved. Different authors use different criteria for selecting the studies to be summarized, use different review strategies, and often come to different (sometimes opposite) conclusions. For example, some reviewers may conclude that the Warm-Fuzzy method is superior to the No-Nonsense method, whereas other reviewers may conclude that the results are inconclusive. The second problem is that, as the number of research studies available about a problem increases, so does the difficulty of the reviewing task. During the 1970s, the need for a more efficient and more objective approach to research integration, or summarization, became increasingly apparent.

Meta-analysis is the alternative that was developed by Gene Glass and his colleagues.[4] Although much has been written on the subject, Glass's *Meta-Analysis in Social Research* remains the classic work in the field. It delineates specific procedures for finding, describing, classifying, and coding the research studies to be included in a meta-analytic review and for measuring and analyzing study findings.

A central characteristic that distinguishes meta-analysis from more traditional approaches is the emphasis placed on making the review as inclusive as possible. Reviewers are encouraged to include results typically excluded, such as those presented in dissertation reports and unpublished works. Critics of meta-analysis claim that this strategy results in the inclusion in a review of a number of "poor" studies. Glass and his colleagues countered that no evidence supports this claim; final conclusions are not negatively affected by including the studies. Evidence suggests that, on average, dissertations exhibit higher design quality than many published journal articles. Glass and his colleagues also noted that experimental effects reported in journals are generally larger than those presented in dissertations; thus, if dissertations are excluded, effects may appear to be greater than they actually are.

The key feature of meta-analysis is that the results from each study are translated into an effect size. *Effect size* is a numerical way of expressing the strength or magnitude of a reported relation, be it causal or not. For example, in an experimental study, the effect size expresses how much better (or worse) the experimental group performed on a task or test compared to the control group.

After effect size has been calculated for each study, the results are averaged, yielding one number that summarizes the overall effect of the studies. Effect size is expressed as a decimal number; although numbers greater than 1.00 are possible,

they do not occur very often. An effect size near .00 means that, on average, experimental and control groups performed the same; a positive effect size means that, on average, the experimental group performed better; and a negative effect size means that, on average, the control group did better. For positive effect sizes, a larger number indicates a more effective experimental treatment.

Although there are no hard and fast rules, it is generally agreed that an effect size in the twenties (e.g., 0.28) indicates a treatment that produces a relatively small effect, whereas an effect size in the eighties (e.g., 0.81) indicates a powerful treatment. Walberg,[5] for example, reported an effect size of 0.76 for cooperative learning studies. This finding indicates that cooperative learning is a very effective instructional strategy. Walberg also reported that the effect size for assigned homework is 0.28, and for graded homework, 0.79. These findings suggest that homework makes a relatively small difference in achievement but that graded homework makes a big difference. (Many of you can probably use this information to your advantage!) Marzano, Waters, and McNulty[6] provide another educational example of a research meta-analysis based on 35 years of research on school leadership that indicates that school leadership has a substantial effect on student achievement and identifies 21 "responsibilities" that make a difference in the effectiveness of school leaders.

As suggested earlier, meta-analysis is not without its critics. It must be recognized, however, that despite its perceived shortcomings, it still represents a significant improvement over traditional methods of summarizing literature. Further, it is not a fait accompli but rather an approach in the process of refinement.

MyLab Education **Self-Check 4.5**

MyLab Education **Self-Check 4.6**

MyLab Education **Application Exercise 4.6:** Conducting a Meta-Analysis

---

[4] *Meta-Analysis in Social Research*, by G. V. Glass, B. McGaw, and M. L. Smith, 1981, Beverly Hills, CA: Sage.

[5] "Improving the Productivity of America's Schools," by H. J. Walberg, 1984, *Educational Leadership*, 41(8), pp. 19–27.

[6] R. J. Marzano, T. Waters, and B. A. McNulty. (2005). *School Leadership That Works: From Research to Results*. Alexandria, VA: ASCD.

SUMMARY

REVIEW OF RELATED LITERATURE: PURPOSE AND SCOPE

1. The review of related literature involves systematically identifying, locating, and analyzing documents pertaining to the research problem.

2. The major purpose of reviewing the literature is to identify information that already exists about your research problem.

3. The literature review can point out research strategies, procedures, and instruments that have and have not been found to be productive in investigating your research problem.

4. A smaller, well-organized review is preferred to a review containing many studies that are less related to your research problem.

5. Heavily researched areas usually provide enough references directly related to a problem to eliminate the need for reporting less-related or secondary studies. Little-researched problems usually require review of any study related in some meaningful way so that the researcher may develop a logical framework and rationale for the study.

QUALITATIVE RESEARCH AND THE REVIEW OF RELATED LITERATURE

6. Qualitative researchers are more likely to construct the review after starting their study, whereas quantitative researchers are more likely to construct the review prior to starting their study.

7. The qualitative research review of related literature may demonstrate the underlying assumptions behind the research questions, convince proposal reviewers that the researcher is knowledgeable about intellectual traditions, provide the researcher with an opportunity to identify any gaps in the body of literature and how the proposed study may contribute to the existing body of knowledge, and help the qualitative researcher to refine research questions.

IDENTIFYING KEYWORDS AND SUBJECT TERMS, AND IDENTIFYING, EVALUATING, AND ANNOTATING SOURCES

Identifying Keywords

8. Most sources have an alphabetical subject index or a thesaurus to help you locate information on your research problem. In addition, most databases generate subject headings or descriptors with the search results. Maintaining a list of keywords should guide your literature search.

Identifying Your Sources

9. A good way to start a review of related literature is with a narrow search of pertinent educational encyclopedias, handbooks, and annual reviews found in libraries. These resources provide broad overviews of issues in various subject areas. Consult with the subject librarian who specializes in your discipline to learn what sources are available and how to access and retrieve needed information.

10. An article or report written by the person who conducted the study is a primary source. A brief description of a study written by someone other than the original researcher is a secondary source. Primary sources are preferred in the review.

11. Most libraries use an online catalog system as well as collective catalogs to access materials from other libraries. You should familiarize yourself with your library, the library website, and the resources available within and beyond your library.

12. A keyword search uses terms or phrases pertinent to your research problem to search for and identify potentially useful sources.

13. Keyword searches can be focused by using the Boolean operators AND, OR, and NOT. Using AND or NOT narrows a search and reduces the number of sources identified; using OR broadens the search and increases the number of sources. It is often best to start with a narrow search.

14. Identify keywords related to your research problem.

15. Select the appropriate databases—some databases using the same interface may allow you to search more than one database simultaneously.

16. Initiate a search using your keywords selectively.

17. Reformulate your search using appropriate subject headings or descriptors, combining terms as needed.

18. Once you have found a relevant article, check the item record for links to additional subject headings or descriptors, author(s), cited references, times cited in database, or other references for finding additional related items using the features within the database. Remember that most databases provide a citation feature that allows you to begin your list of references in the appropriate style, such as APA, MLA, or Chicago.

19. The Internet links organizations and individuals all over the world. An abundance of educational materials is available on the Web—from primary research articles and educational theory to lesson plans and research guides in a variety of formats, including video, presentations, screen captures, podcasts, and so on.

20. Internet search tools and resources continue to develop to include more primary sources and background information. Good research goes beyond simply googling a problem to searching Google Scholar, Google Books, YouTube EDU, blogs, wikis, RSS feeds, discussion groups, and more.

21. The available resources on the World Wide Web are almost limitless, so it is important to learn how to use the Internet in conjunction with databases and online catalogs to access the full text of articles or contact information for an author.

22. Internet search engines are structured and function differently than databases. The essential difference is a search engine is compiled and organized through programming. A database is also compiled through programming, but it is organized by humans who have read the contents, such as the articles. It is essential to connect with the human organization of a database by using the appropriate subject headings and descriptors that are not present in an Internet search engine.

23. The websites for professional organizations maintain links to current research in a particular discipline.

24. Popular professional organizations include Association for Supervision and Curriculum Development, National Council of Teachers of Mathematics, National Council for the Social Studies, National Science Teachers Association, and the International Reading Association.

Evaluating Your Sources

25. It is important to evaluate all literature sources by determining the following: What is the problem statement of the study? Is the study relevant given your research interests? Who or what are the sample groups studied? Where was the study published? When was the study conducted? How was the study conducted?

Annotating Your Sources

26. Annotating your sources involves creating summaries by locating, reviewing, summarizing, and classifying your references. Annotations assess the quality, relevance, and accuracy of a source; articulate your response to a source; and indicate why the source is important to your research.

27. The main advantage of beginning with the latest references on your research problem is that the most recent studies are likely to have profited from previous research. References in recent studies often contain references to previous studies you have not yet identified.

28. For each source work, list the complete bibliographic record, including author's name, date of publication, title, journal name or book title, volume number, issue number, page numbers, and library call number. Briefly list main ideas. Put quotation marks around quotes taken from the source, and include page numbers. Keep all references in the citation format required for research reports or dissertations. Remember, most databases have a citation feature that will help you format your citation in the proper style format. Although you will have to check the accuracy of these or any other citation maker, you will find these immeasurably helpful in creating your reference list.

29. Make a copy of your references and put it in a safe place.

30. A helpful way to keep track of the literature is to use a matrix.

ANALYZING, ORGANIZING, AND REPORTING THE LITERATURE

31. Describing and reporting research call for a specialized style of writing. Technical writing requires documenting facts and substantiating opinions, clarifying definitions and using them consistently, using an accepted style manual, and starting sections with an introduction and ending them with a brief summary.

32. When organizing a review, make an outline; sort references by problem; analyze the similarities and differences between references in a given subheading; give a meaningful overview in which you discuss references least related to the problem first; and conclude with a brief summary of the literature and its implications.

META-ANALYSIS

33. Meta-analysis is a statistical approach to summarizing the results of many quantitative studies addressing the same problem. It provides a numerical way of expressing the composite result of the studies.

34. A central characteristic of meta-analysis is that it is as inclusive as possible.

35. An effect size is a numerical way of expressing the strength or magnitude of a reported relation. In meta-analysis, an effect size is computed for each study, and then the individual effect sizes are averaged.

PERFORMANCE CRITERIA — TASK 3

The introduction that you develop for Tasks 3A or 3B will be the first part of the research report required for Task 11 (Chapter 22). Therefore, it may save you some revision time later if, when appropriate, statements are expressed in the past tense (e.g., "the problem investigated was" or "it was hypothesized"). Your introduction should include the following subheadings and contain the following types of information:

- Introduction (background and significance of the problem)
- Statement of the Problem (problem statement and necessary definitions)
- Review of the Literature (don't forget the big V)
- Statement of the Hypothesis(es) or, for a qualitative study, Statement of a Guiding Hypothesis.

As a guideline, three typed pages is generally a sufficient length for Task 3. Of course, for a real study, you would review not just 10 to 15 references but all relevant references, and the introduction would be correspondingly longer.

One final note: The hypothesis you formulate and include in Task 3 after the review of literature now influences all further tasks—that is, who will be your participants, what they will do, and so forth. On this topic, the following is an informal observation based on the behavior of thousands of students, not a research-based finding. All beginning research students fall somewhere on a continuum of realism. At one extreme are the Cecil B. Demise students who want to design a study involving a cast of thousands, over an extended period of time. At the other extreme are the Mr. Magi students who will not even consider a procedure unless they are certain that they could actually execute it in their work setting, with their students or clients. You do not have to execute the study you design, so feel free to operate in the manner most comfortable for you. Keep in mind, however, that there is a middle ground between Demise and Magi.

The Task 3 example that follows illustrates the format and content of an introduction that meets the criteria just described. This task example, with few modifications, represents the task as submitted by a former student (Sara Jane Calderin of Florida International University) in an introductory educational research course. Although an example from published research could have been used, the example given more accurately reflects the performance that is expected of you at your current level of expertise.

1

Effect of Interactive Multimedia on the Achievement of 10th-Grade Biology Students

Introduction

One of the major concerns of educators and parents alike is the decline in student achievement (as measured by standardized tests). An area of particular concern is science education where the high-level thinking skills and problem solving techniques so necessary for success in our technological society need to be developed (Smith & Westhoff, 1992).

Research is constantly providing new proven methods for educators to use, and technology has developed all kinds of tools ideally suited to the classroom. One such tool is interactive multimedia (IMM). IMM provides teachers with an extensive amount of data in a number of different formats including text, sound, and video, making it possible to appeal to the different learning styles of the students and to offer a variety of material for students to analyze (Howson & Davis, 1992).

When teachers use IMM, students become highly motivated, which results in improved class attendance and more completed assignments (O'Connor, 1993). Students also become actively involved in their own learning, encouraging comprehension rather than mere memorization of facts (Kneedler, 1993; Reeves, 1992).

Statement of the Problem

The purpose of this study was to investigate the effect of interactive multimedia on the achievement of 10th-grade biology students. Interactive multimedia was defined as "a computerized database that allows users to access information in multiple forms, including text, graphics, video and audio" (Reeves, 1992, p. 47).

Review of Related Literature

Due to modern technology, students receive more information from visual sources than they do from the written word, and yet in school the majority of information is still transmitted through textbooks. While textbooks cover a wide range of topics superficially, IMM provides in-depth information on essential topics in a format that students find interesting (Kneedler, 1993). Smith and Westhoff (1992) note that when student interest is sparked, curiosity levels are increased and students are motivated to ask questions. The interactive nature of multimedia allows the students to seek out their own answers and by so doing they become owners of the concept involved. Ownership translates into comprehension (Howson & Davis, 1992).

Many science concepts are learned through observation of experiments. Using multimedia, students can participate in a variety of experiments that are either too expensive, too lengthy, or too dangerous to carry out in the laboratory (Howson & Davis, 1992; Leonard, 1989; Louie, Sweat, Gresham, & Smith, 1991). While observing the experiments the students can discuss what is happening and ask questions. At the touch of a button teachers are able to replay any part of the proceedings, and they also have random access to related information that can be used to completely illustrate the answer to the question (Howson & Davis, 1992). By answering students' questions in this detailed way the content will become more relevant to the needs of the student (Smith & Westhoff, 1992). When knowledge is relevant students are able to use it to solve problems and, in so doing, develop higher-level thinking skills (Helms & Helms, 1992; Sherwood, Kinzer, Bransford, & Franks, 1987).

A major challenge of science education is to provide students with large amounts of information that will encourage them to be analytical (Howson & Davis, 1992; Sherwood et al., 1987). IMM offers electronic access to extensive information allowing students to organize, evaluate and use it in the solution of problems (Smith & Wilson, 1993). When information is introduced as an aid to problem solving, it becomes a tool with which to solve other problems, rather than a series of solitary, disconnected facts (Sherwood et al., 1987).

Although critics complain that IMM is entertainment and students do not learn from it (Corcoran, 1989), research has shown that student learning does improve when IMM is used in the classroom (Sherwood et al., 1987; Sherwood & Others, 1990). A 1987 study by Sherwood et al., for example, showed that seventh- and eighth-grade science students receiving instruction enhanced with IMM had better retention of that information, and O'Connor (1993) found that the use of IMM in high school mathematics and science increased the focus on students' problem solving and critical thinking skills.

Statement of the Hypothesis

The quality and quantity of software available for science classes has dramatically improved during the past decade. Although some research has been carried out on the effects of IMM on student achievement in science, due to promising updates in the technology involved, further study is warranted. Therefore, it was hypothesized that 10th-grade biology students whose teachers use IMM as part of their instructional technique will exhibit significantly higher achievement than 10th-grade biology students whose teachers do not use IMM.

References

Corcoran, E. (1989, July). Show and tell: Hypermedia turns information into a multisensory event. *Scientific American, 261,* 72, 74.

Helms, C. W., & Helms, D. R. (1992, June). Multimedia in education (Report No. IR-016-090). Proceedings of the 25th Summer Conference of the Association of Small Computer Users in Education. North Myrtle Beach, SC (ERIC Document Reproduction Service No. ED 357 732).

Howson, B. A., & Davis, H. (1992). Enhancing comprehension with videodiscs. *Media and Methods, 28,* 3, 12–14.

Kneedler, P. E. (1993). California adopts multimedia science program. *Technological Horizons in Education Journal, 20,* 7, 73–76.

Lehmann, I. J. (1990). Review of National Proficiency Survey Series. In J. J. Kramer & J. C. Conoley (Eds.), *The eleventh mental measurements yearbook* (pp. 595–599). Lincoln: University of Nebraska, Buros Institute of Mental Measurement.

Leonard, W. H. (1989). A comparison of student reaction to biology instruction by interactive videodisc or conventional laboratory. *Journal of Research in Science Teaching, 26,* 95–104.

Louie, R., Sweat, S., Gresham, R., & Smith, L. (1991). Interactive video: Disseminating vital science and math information. *Media and Methods, 27,* 5, 22–23.

O'Connor, J. E. (1993, April). Evaluating the effects of collaborative efforts to improve mathematics and science curricula (Report No. TM-019-862). Paper presented at the Annual Meeting of the American Educational Research Association, Atlanta, GA (ERIC Document Reproduction Service No. ED 357 083).

Reeves, T. C. (1992). Evaluating interactive multimedia. *Educational Technology, 32,* 5, 47–52.

Sherwood, R. D., Kinzer, C. K., Bransford, J. D., & Franks, J. J. (1987). Some benefits of creating macro-contexts for science instruction: Initial findings. *Journal of Research in Science Teaching, 24,* 417–435.

Sherwood, R. D., & Others (1990, April). An evaluative study of level one videodisc based chemistry program (Report No. SE-051-513). Paper presented at a Poster Session at the 63rd. Annual Meeting of the National Association for Research in Science Teaching, Atlanta, GA (ERIC Document Reproduction Service No. ED 320 772).

Smith, E. E., & Westhoff, G. M. (1992). The Taliesin project: Multidisciplinary education and multimedia. *Educational Technology, 32,* 15–23.

Smith, M. K., & Wilson, C. (1993, March). Integration of student learning strategies via technology (Report No. IR-016-035). Proceedings of the Fourth Annual Conference of Technology and Teacher Education. San Diego, CA (ERIC Document Reproduction Service No. ED 355 937).

CHAPTER FIVE

Preparing and Evaluating a Research Plan

Everett Collection

Willy Wonka and the Chocolate Factory, 1971

"Part of good planning is anticipating potential problems and then doing what you can to prevent them." (p. 130)

LEARNING OUTCOMES

After reading Chapter 5, you should be able to do the following:

5.1 Define and discuss the purpose of a research plan.

5.2 Describe each component of a quantitative research plan.

5.3 Describe each component of a qualitative research plan.

5.4 Describe ways in which a research plan can be revised and improved.

The chapter outcomes form the basis for the following tasks, which require you to develop a complete research plan for a quantitative study (Task 4A) or a qualitative study (Task 4B).

TASK 4A

For the hypothesis you have formulated (Task 3A), develop the remaining components of a research plan for a quantitative study you would conduct to test that hypothesis. Create brief sections using the following components from Figure 5.1 (p. 130) in your plan. In addition, include assumptions, limitations, and definitions where appropriate (see Performance Criteria, p. 142).

TASK 4B

Formulate a research problem and develop a research plan for a qualitative study you would conduct. Include the components from Figure 5.2 (p. 142) in your plan. In addition, include assumptions, limitations, and definitions where appropriate (see Performance Criteria, p. 142).

DEFINITION AND PURPOSE OF A RESEARCH PLAN

A **research plan** is a detailed description of a study proposed to investigate a given problem. Research plans, regardless of whether they are for quantitative or qualitative studies, generally include an introduction that includes the review of related literature, a discussion of the research design and procedures, and information about data analysis. A research plan may be relatively brief and informal or very lengthy and formal, such as the proposals submitted to obtain government and private research funding.

Most colleges and universities require that a proposal be submitted for approval before the execution of a thesis or dissertation study. Students are expected to demonstrate that they have a reasonable research plan before being allowed to begin the study. Playing it by ear is all right for the piano, but not for conducting research.

After you have completed a review of related literature and formulated a hypothesis, problem statement, and research question(s), you are ready to develop the rest of the research plan. In quantitative research, the hypothesis is the basis for determining the participant group, measuring instruments, design, procedures, and

statistical techniques used in your study. In qualitative research, the researcher's questions are the basis for gaining entrance to the research context, identifying research participants, spending time in the field, determining how to gather data, and interpreting and narrating those data. In this chapter, we describe, in general, how these tasks fit into the research plan; succeeding chapters provide details about conducting the tasks.

The research plan serves several important purposes. First, it forces you to think through every aspect of the study. The very process of getting the details down on paper usually helps you think of something you may otherwise have overlooked. A second purpose of a written plan is that it facilitates evaluation of the study, by you and others. Sometimes great ideas do not look so great after they have been written down and considered. In creating the plan, you may discover certain problems or find that some aspect of the study is infeasible. Others, too, can identify flaws and make suggestions to improve the plan. A third and fundamental purpose of a research plan is that it provides detailed procedures to guide the study. If something unexpected occurs that alters some phase of the study, you can refer to the plan to assess the overall impact on the rest of the study. For example, suppose you order 60 copies of a test to administer on May 1. If on April 15 you receive a letter saying that, due to a shortage of available tests, your order cannot be filled until May 15, your study may be seriously affected. At the least, it would be delayed several weeks. The deadlines in your research plan may indicate that you cannot afford to wait. Therefore, you may decide to use an alternative measuring instrument or to contact another vendor.

A well-thought-out plan saves time, provides structure for the study, reduces the probability of costly mistakes, and generally results in higher quality research. If your study is a disaster because of poor planning, you lose. If something that could have been avoided goes wrong, you may have to salvage the remnants of a less-than-ideal study somehow or redo the whole study. Murphy's law states, essentially, "If anything can go wrong, it will, and at the worst possible time." Our law states, "If anything can go wrong, it will—unless you make sure that it doesn't."

Part of good planning is anticipating potential problems and then doing what you can to prevent them. For example, you may anticipate that some principals will be less than open to your including their students as participants in your study (a common occurrence). To deal with this contingency, you should develop the best but most honest sales pitch possible. Do not ask, "Hey, can I use your kids for my study?" Instead, tell principals how the study will benefit their students or their schools. If you encounter further opposition, you may tell principals that central administration is enthusiastic about the study, assuming that you've spoken with them and they are in fact enthusiastic. To avoid many problems and to obtain strategies for overcoming them, it is extremely useful to talk to more-experienced researchers.

You may get frustrated at times because you cannot do everything the way you would like due to real or bureaucratic constraints. Don't let such obstacles exasperate you; just relax and do your best. On the positive side, a sound plan critiqued by others is likely to result in a sound study conducted with a minimum of grief. You cannot guarantee that your study will be executed exactly as planned, but you can guarantee that things will go as smoothly as possible.

MyLab Education **Self-Check 5.1**

COMPONENTS OF THE QUANTITATIVE RESEARCH PLAN

Although the headings may go by other names, quantitative research plans typically include an introduction, a method section, a description of proposed data analyses, a time schedule, and sometimes a budget. The basic format for a typical research plan is shown in Figure 5.1. Other headings may also be included, as needed. For example, if special materials are developed for the study or special equipment will be used (such as computer terminals), then subheadings such as "Materials" or "Apparatus" may be included under "Method" and before "Design."

Introduction Section

If you have completed Task 3A, you are very familiar with the content of the introduction section: a statement of the research problem, a review of related literature, and a statement of the hypothesis.

Statement of the Problem

Because the problem sets the stage for the rest of the plan, it should be stated as early as possible. The statement should be accompanied by a description of the background of the problem and a rationale for its significance.

FIGURE 5.1 • Components of a quantitative research plan

1. Introduction
   a. Statement of the research problem
   b. Statement of research questions
   c. Review of related literature
   d. Statement of the hypothesis (if appropriate)
2. Method
   a. Participants
   b. Instruments
   c. Design
   d. Procedure
3. Data Analysis
4. Time Schedule
5. Budget (if appropriate)

Statement of Research Questions

Include the research questions that breathe life into your problem statement and help provide a focus for your data collection.

Review of Related Literature

The review of related literature should provide an overview of the research problem and present references related to what is known about the problem. The literature review should lead logically to a testable hypothesis. The review should conclude with a brief summary of the literature and its implications.

Statement of the Hypothesis

For research plans that have one or more hypotheses, each hypothesis should have an underlying explanation for its prediction. That is, some literature should support the hypothesis. The hypothesis should clearly and concisely state the expected relation or difference between the variables in your study, and either in the statement itself or leading up to it, you should define those variables in operational, measurable, or common-usage terms. The people reading your plan and especially those reading your final report may not be as familiar with your terminology as you are. In addition, each hypothesis should be clearly testable within a reasonable period of time.

Method Section

In general, the method section includes a description of the research participants, measuring instruments, design, and procedure, although the specific method used in your study will affect the format and content. The method section for an experimental study, for example, typically includes a description of the experimental design, whereas the design and procedure sections may be combined in a plan for a descriptive study.

Research Participants

The description of participants should identify the number, source, and characteristics of the sample. It should also define the **population,** that is, the larger group from which the sample will be selected. In other words, what are members of the population like? How large is the population? For example, a description of participants may include the following:

> Participants will be selected from a population of 157 students enrolled in an Algebra I course at a large urban high school in Miami, Florida. The population is tricultural, being composed primarily of Caucasian non-Hispanic students, African American students, and Hispanic students from a variety of Latin American backgrounds.

In general, quantitative research samples tend to be large and broadly representative.

Instruments

An **instrument** is a test or tool used for data collection, and the instruments section of a research plan describes the particular instruments to be used in the study and how they will measure the variables stated in your hypothesis. If you use instruments that are published, such as a standardized test, you should provide information about the appropriateness of the chosen instruments for your study and sample; the measurement properties of the instruments, especially their validity and reliability;[1] and the process of administering and scoring the instruments. If you plan to develop your own instrument, you should describe how the instrument will be developed, what it will measure, how you plan to evaluate its validity and reliability, and how it relates to your hypothesis and participants.

Of course, if more than one instrument is used—a common occurrence in many studies—each should be described separately and in detail. At this stage in your research, you may not yet be able to identify by name or fully describe the instrument you will use in your study. Consequently, in Task 4A, you should describe the kind of instrument you plan to use rather than name a specific instrument. For example, you may say that your instrument will be a questionnaire about teacher unions that will allow teachers to express different degrees of agreement or disagreement in response to statements about teacher unions. While planning or conducting your research, you may discover that an appropriate instrument for

---

[1] Validity is concerned with whether the data or information gathered is relevant to the decision being made; reliability is concerned with the stability or consistency of the data or information. Both concepts are discussed fully in Chapter 6.

collecting the needed data is not available, and you will need to decide whether to alter the hypothesis, change the selected variable, or develop your own instrument.

In some cases, the instrument section is small or omitted. For research plans that do not include a separate instrument section, relevant information about the instrument is presented in the procedure section.

Materials/Apparatus

If special materials (such as booklets, training manuals, or computer programs) are to be developed for use in the study, they should be described in the research plan. Also, if special apparatus (such as computer terminals) will be used, they should be described.

Design

A **design** is a general strategy or plan for conducting a research study. The description of the design indicates the basic structure and goals of the study. The nature of the hypothesis, the variables involved, and the constraints of the environment all contribute to the selection of the research design. For example, if a hypothesis involves comparing the effectiveness of highlighting textbooks versus outlining textbooks, the design may involve two groups receiving different instructions for studying, followed by a comparison of the test scores for each group. If the participants were randomly assigned to classes using particular study methods, the design of the study is experimental; if they were already in such classrooms before the study, the design is causal–comparative. You can select from a number of basic research designs, each one having a number of variations. Part II of the text describes different quantitative research designs in detail.

Procedure

The procedure section describes all the steps in collecting the data, from beginning to end, in the order in which they will occur. This section typically begins with a detailed description of the technique to be used to select the study participants. If the design includes a pretest, the procedures for its administration—when it will be administered and how—are usually described next. Any other measure to be administered at the beginning of the study should also be discussed. For example,

a researcher studying the effect of a music-reading strategy may administer a pretest on current skill in reading music as well as a general musical achievement test to ensure that the experimental groups do not differ prior to treatment. An example of the procedure section for a study designed to compare two different methods of teaching reading comprehension to third-graders may include the following statement:

> In September, one week following the first day of school, the *Barney Test of Reading Comprehension,* Form A, will be administered to both reading method groups.

The remainder of the section describes procedures for carrying out all the other major components of the study, including procedures for gaining entry to the research site and those for collecting and storing data. The nature of the procedures, however, depends greatly on the kind of research study planned. The procedures for conducting an experiment are different from those for conducting a survey or a historical study. These differences are examined in detail in later chapters.

The procedure section should also include any assumptions and limitations that have been identified by the researcher. An **assumption** is an assertion presumed to be true but not actually verified. For example, in a study involving reading instruction for preschool children, a researcher may assume that, given the population, none of the children had received reading instruction at home. A **limitation** is some aspect of the study that the researcher cannot control but believes may negatively affect the results of the study. Two common limitations are less-than-ideal sample size and the length of the study. Limitations may be stated as follows:

> Only one class of 30 students will be available for participation.
>
> Ideally, participants should be exposed to the experimental treatment for a longer period of time to assess its effectiveness more accurately; however, the researcher has permission to be in the school for a maximum of two weeks.

Such limitations should be openly and honestly stated so readers can judge for themselves how seriously the limits may affect the study results.

The appropriateness of the procedures permits readers to judge the quality of the study. The procedure section should therefore be as detailed as possible, and any new terms should be defined. The writing should be so precise that a person reading your plan would be able to conduct the study exactly as you intended it to be conducted. Without detailed information about how a study will be carried out, external readers cannot make reasonable judgments about the usefulness of the potential results.

Data Analysis

The research plan must include a description of the technique or techniques that will be used to analyze the data collected during the study. For certain descriptive studies, data analysis may involve little more than simple tabulation and presentation of results. For most studies, however, one or more statistical methods will be required. Identification of appropriate analysis techniques is extremely important. Very few situations cause as much weeping and gnashing of teeth as collecting data only to find that no appropriate analysis exists or that the appropriate analysis requires sophistication beyond the researcher's level of competence. After the data are collected, it usually is too late to resolve the problem, so you should submit a detailed description of your analysis in the research plan.

The hypothesis of a study determines the nature of the research design, which in turn determines the analysis. An inappropriate analysis does not permit a valid test of the research hypothesis. The analysis technique should be selected based on a number of factors, such as how the groups will be formed (e.g., by random assignment, by using existing groups), how many different treatment groups will be involved, how many variables will be involved, and the kind of data to be collected (e.g., counts of the number of times fifth-grade students fail to turn in their homework on time, a student's test score, or students' placement into one of five socioeconomic categories). Although you may not be familiar with a variety of specific analytic techniques, you probably can describe in your research plan the kind of analysis you need. For example, you may say,

> An analysis will be used that is appropriate for comparing the achievement, on a test of reading comprehension, of two randomly formed groups of second-grade students.

By the time you get to Task 8, you will know exactly what you need (honest!).

Time Schedule

A realistic time schedule is equally important for beginning researchers working on a thesis or dissertation and for experienced researchers working under the deadlines of a research grant or contract. Researchers rarely have unlimited time to complete a study. The existence of deadlines typically necessitates careful budgeting of time. Basically, a time schedule includes a list of major activities or phases of the proposed study and an expected completion time or date for each activity. Such a schedule in a research plan enables the researcher to assess the feasibility of conducting a study within existing time limitations. It also helps the researcher to stay on schedule during the execution of the study.

In developing a time frame, do not make the mistake of cutting it too thin by allocating a minimum amount of time for each activity. Allow yourself more time than you initially planned to account for unforeseen delays (some people call research a process designed to take 3 to 6 months longer than the researcher thinks it will)—perhaps your adviser is not available when needed, your computer malfunctions and takes days or weeks to be repaired, or the teacher who agreed to let you collect data in her class becomes ill and is out for a month. You should plan to set the completion date for your study sometime before your final deadline. Also recognize that your schedule will not necessarily be a series of sequential steps that require one activity to be completed before another is begun. For example, while you are analyzing data, you may also be working on the first part of the research report.

Budget

Proposals submitted to governmental or private agencies for research support almost always require a tentative budget. Researchers not seeking external funding for their research are not required to create a budget; however, it is useful to anticipate costs that may be incurred in the study.

For example, costs related to computer programs, travel, printing, and mailing are common research expenses. Although you do not need a detailed budget for these and similar expenses, you should recognize that conducting your study will require some personal expenditures.

MyLab Education **Self-Check 5.2**

MyLab Education **Application Exercise 5.1:**
Preparing a Quantitative Research Plan

COMPONENTS OF THE QUALITATIVE RESEARCH PLAN

A qualitative research plan is a much less structured document than a quantitative research plan. Because qualitative research is an intimate and open-ended endeavor that must be responsive to the context and setting under study, the plan must be flexible. Flexible does not mean, however, that the qualitative researcher is excused from creating a plan in the first place! The qualitative researcher must be able to craft a conceptually sound and persuasive (if not elegant) document that provides reviewers with an argument for supporting the proposed study. As Bogdan and Biklen[2] warn, plans for qualitative research sometimes place graduate students and contract researchers at odds with Institutional Review Boards (IRBs) and funding agencies who are more accustomed to dealing with quantitative proposals. Therefore, writing a qualitative research plan requires skill in crafting a document that ultimately provides the "intellectual glue"[3] for the entire proposal and research process.

Prior Fieldwork

Qualitative researchers disagree about the need to undertake some kind of preliminary fieldwork, or data collection (discussed further in Chapter 15), before writing a research plan. The purpose of such preproposal fieldwork is to provide background that will prepare researchers for what they may expect to find in the research setting. At a very practical level, however, it may be difficult for a qualitative researcher to obtain permission from a school district to conduct fieldwork when the researcher has not yet received approval from the IRB to undertake research in public schools (or elsewhere). Furthermore, preproposal fieldwork conflicts with the traditions established in universities—institutions that are not well recognized for being responsive to change!

Our recommendation is for the researcher to undertake some informal preproposal fieldwork that will yield a better understanding of the sociocultural context of the research setting, if possible. Otherwise, the researcher will have to rely on the literature review and life experiences to gain a perspective from which to craft the proposal.

A well-written qualitative research proposal includes details under the headings shown in Figure 5.2.

Title

In qualitative research, the title of a study provides the researcher with a frame of reference for continuous reflection. As qualitative researchers immerse themselves in the contexts of their studies, they become increasingly attuned to key issues of their research—issues they may have been unaware of before starting the research. This perspective may lead a researcher to shift the focus of the research and, as a result, change the title of the study to reflect the new focus more accurately.

Similarly, the title serves as a "conceptual point of reference"[4] for readers of the study. By conveying the key concepts of the study in the title, the researcher attracts the attention of interested readers and enables the work to be catalogued correctly based on the title alone.[5]

Introduction Section

The introduction section of the research plan should include subsections that give the purpose

---

[2] *Qualitative Research for Education: An Introduction to Theory and Methods* (5th ed.), by R. C. Bogdan and S. K. Biklen, 2007, Boston, MA: Allyn & Bacon.
[3] *Designing Qualitative Research* (5th ed., p. 82), by C. Marshall and G. Rossman, 2011, Thousand Oaks, CA: Sage.

[4] *Conceptualizing Qualitative Inquiry: Mindwork for Fieldwork in Education and the Social Sciences* (2nd ed.) (p. 112), by T. H. Schram, 2006, Upper Saddle River, NJ: Merrill/Prentice Hall.
[5] *Writing Up Qualitative Research* (3rd ed.), by H. F. Wolcott, 2009, Thousand Oaks, CA: Sage.

FIGURE 5.2 • Components of a qualitative research plan

1. Title of the Study
2. Introduction to the Study
   a. Describe the purpose of the research study
   b. Frame the study as a larger theoretical, policy, or practical problem
   c. Pose initial research questions
   d. Describe related literature that helps to frame the research questions
3. Research Procedures
   a. Overall approach and rationale for the study
   b. Site and sample selection
   c. The researcher's role (entry to the research site, reciprocity, and ethics)
   d. Data collection methods
   e. Data management strategies
   f. Data analysis strategies
   g. Trustworthiness features
   h. Ethical considerations
4. Potential Contributions of the Research
5. Limitations of the Study
6. Appendixes (one or more of the following, if needed)
   a. Timeline for the research
   b. Proposed table of contents for the study
   c. Consent forms, IRB approval
   d. Samples of structured surveys or questionnaires

Sources: *Qualitative Research for Education: An Introduction to Theory and Methods* (5th ed.), by R. C. Bogdan and S. K. Biklen, 2007, Boston, MA: Allyn & Bacon; *Designing Qualitative Research* (5th ed.), by C. Marshall and G. Rossman, 2011, Thousand Oaks, CA: Sage; and *Conceptualizing Qualitative Inquiry: Mindwork for Fieldwork in Education and the Social Sciences* (2nd ed.), by T. H. Schram, 2006, Upper Saddle River, NJ: Merrill/Prentice Hall.

of the research study; a frame for the study as a larger theoretical, policy, or practical problem; initial research questions; and related literature that helps to support the research questions.

Problem Statement

The problem statement sets the stage for everything that follows in the research plan. It should be written as clearly as possible and be a bite-size statement that can be retained by the reader and researcher alike.

Framing the Study

In this subsection, the researcher should demonstrate the relevance of the proposed study using a frame of reference that the reader will be able to relate to. Where appropriate, the researcher should indicate how the proposed study will contribute to existing theory, educational policy, or the solution of a practical problem.

Statement of Research Questions

Posing initial research questions (which may include guiding hypotheses) in a qualitative research plan can be tricky business if the researcher is to maintain the flexibility inherent in qualitative research. We suggest that these initial questions be closely linked to theories, policies, and practical problems outlined in the previous discussion of framing the study. They should also be linked clearly to the related literature.

Review of Related Literature

The review of related literature should describe the assumptions and theories that underlie your initial research questions and proposed study. In these descriptions, you should persuade the reader of your preparedness to undertake a qualitative study, identify potential gaps in the existing literature that may be filled by the proposed study, and, if appropriate, suggest a promising educational practice to address an identified teaching or learning need. As discussed earlier, the review of related literature helps the researcher refine the research questions and embed the questions in guiding hypotheses that provide possible directions for the researcher to follow.

Research Procedures Section

The procedure section in a qualitative study may have varying forms and degrees of specificity depending on whether the researcher has completed any preproposal fieldwork. In general, however, this section includes a description of the overall approach and rationale for the study, the site and sample selection, the researcher's role, data collection methods, data management strategies, data analysis strategies, trustworthiness features, ethical considerations, potential contributions of the research, and limitations of the study.

Overall Approach and Rationale for the Study

This part of the procedure section provides the researcher with an opportunity to classify the overall qualitative research approach (e.g., narrative research, ethnographic research, case study research) to be used in the research; to provide a rationale for why the particular approach is appropriate, given the purpose of the study (e.g., action research, evaluation research); and to provide a link to the appropriate literature on research methods. For example, Mills[6] linked his proposed study of educational change to the literature on educational change as well as to the anthropological literature on cultural change. At the same time, he provided a rationale for the appropriateness of an ethnographic approach to studying the processes and functions of educational change.

Site and Sample Selection

In contrast to quantitative research, qualitative research samples tend to be small and not necessarily broadly representative of the phenomena under investigation. For example, it is not uncommon for qualitative researchers to claim a sample size of one—although the sample may be one classroom of children or one school district. In this subsection, the qualitative researcher should briefly describe the rationale for choosing a particular sample. The researcher should explain why a site was chosen, specifically noting the likelihood of gaining entry to the site and of building sound relationships with the study participants.

In his research plan, for example, Mills[7] discussed the selection of a single school district as his sample; the rationale behind choosing three specific case study sites from among the 15 elementary schools in the district; his access to the site made possible by personal relationships with district administrators, teachers, and student–teachers;

and the expectation that the study would yield credible data. The sites were discussed in terms of the representativeness of the schools in the district, but no claims were made as to the generalizability of the findings of the study.

The Researcher's Role

In this part of the procedure section, the researcher should describe any negotiations that must be undertaken to obtain entry to the research site, any expectations of reciprocity that the research participants may have, and any ethical dilemmas that may face the researcher. Marshall and Rossman[8] suggested that these issues can be sorted into technical ones that address entry to the research site and interpersonal ones that deal with the ethical and personal dilemmas that arise in qualitative research, although rarely are the technical and interpersonal issues mutually exclusive. For example, to gain entry to McKenzie School District, Mills[9] met with the administrative team at the district, explained the purpose of the proposed study and how his role in the district would be defined, and answered questions from principals and central office personnel. Interpersonal issues were an important aspect of this presentation—the researcher had to convince the administrators that he was trustworthy, sensitive to ethical issues, and a good communicator. In qualitative research, where the researcher is the instrument (i.e., is the observer in the field with the participants), it is critical to the success of the study that the researcher establish that he or she will fit in comfortably with the participants.

Data Collection Methods

This part of the procedure section provides the qualitative researcher with an opportunity to describe the specific fieldwork techniques or tools that will be used to collect data to answer the research questions. The researcher should provide examples of the data sources for each research question, including samples of structured interview schedules, survey questions, and other measures that may be used in the study. In short, the researcher must convince the reader that he or she has a sensible plan and valid instruments for collecting the data.

---

[6] *Managing and Coping with Multiple Educational Change: A Case Study and Analysis*, by G. E. Mills, 1988, unpublished doctoral dissertation, University of Oregon, Eugene.
[7] Ibid.

[8] *Designing Qualitative Research*, (p. 112), Marshall and Rossman.
[9] *Managing and Coping*, Mills.

Data Management Strategies

One of the pervasive images of qualitative researchers is that they are literally buried knee deep in data, surrounded by field notes, transcriptions of recorded interviews, artifacts, video-recordings, portfolios, and the like. For this reason, it is important for qualitative researchers to provide some insights into how they intend to manage various data sources. The research plan should describe when materials will be collected, giving dates and times, if appropriate (e.g., "Video-recording will be collected from classrooms weekly") and how field notes (see Chapter 15), audio-recordings, video-recordings, or photographs will be stored. The importance of attention to detail in managing data will become evident to the qualitative researcher when it's time to write the research report.

Data Analysis Strategies

Qualitative research sometimes combines qualitative and quantitative data (e.g., test scores) in studies, resulting in the need for statistical analysis. However, most qualitative research is heavily weighted toward interpretive rather than statistical data analysis. The researcher analyzes the qualitative data from interviews, field notes, and observations by organizing and interpreting the data. Thus, in the research plan, the qualitative researcher should describe the procedures for collating the various forms of data and the manner in which they will be categorized, often by emergent themes. For example, you may state that you will use an analysis that allows field notes and interview data to be organized into a limited number of categories or issues.

Trustworthiness Features

In qualitative research, trustworthiness features consist of any efforts by the researcher to address the more traditional quantitative issues of validity (i.e., the degree to which something measures what it purports to measure) and reliability (i.e., the consistency with which the same results can be replicated over time or by different observers). For example, you may address the trustworthiness of your data collection through the use of triangulation, which is the use of multiple data sources to address each of your research questions.

Ethical Considerations

The qualitative researcher is well advised to include a discussion of ethics in the research plan. Sensitivity to possible ethical issues that may arise during the study is critical to the success of the research. In qualitative research, the most pervasive ethical issues relate to informed consent and the researcher's ability to have closely aligned personal and professional ethical perspectives. Therefore, you should include in your research plan a description of the process you will use to obtain informed consent, including any forms participants will complete, as well as a statement describing your personal and professional ethical perspectives for addressing difficult issues that may arise.

Addressing ethical issues can be tricky business. For example, in his study of educational change, Mills[10] was surprised to find himself questioned by principals about the teaching effectiveness of individual teachers participating in the study—they must have thought that, because he was from the university, he must be an expert on teaching! Commenting on the instructional practices would have been an obvious violation of the participants' right to confidentiality. It was critical for the researcher to respond sensitively to the requests while educating the principals about the researcher's role in the district and revisiting the conditions under which the conduct of the study had been negotiated.

Potential Contributions of the Research

In this section of the plan, the researcher should be prepared to answer the question "So what?"—a common challenge to a qualitative researcher who has just explained that a proposed study will contribute to one's so-called understanding of the phenomenon under investigation. In elaborating on the significance of your study, you have an excellent opportunity to link the possible implications of your research back to the broader ideas about theory, policy, and practical solutions discussed in the review of related literature. If you are tempted to make claims about the generalizability of your potential findings, you should think again about the specificity of your research context. It is usually prudent to make modest claims about how a qualitative study will contribute to the existing body of knowledge.

[10] Ibid.

TABLE 5.1 • Comparison of quantitative and qualitative research components

	Quantitative Research	Qualitative Research
Problem statement	Problem stated at the beginning to guide the research process.	Problem statement may be preceded by fieldwork to learn context of the research; purpose guides study; study framed as part of theoretical, policy, or practical problem; narrower problem may emerge after immersion in setting.
Research questions	Research questions breathe life into the study and provide direction for the development of data collection strategies.	
Review of the literature	Review conducted early in the study to identify related research, potential hypotheses, and methodological approaches.	Review may lead to guiding hypotheses and/or promising practices and links study to underlying assumptions and theories; if not needed for a research plan, may be conducted after study onset.
Hypotheses	Hypothesis is usually related to review of literature, states researcher's hunches about the relations between the study variables in operational terms, is more specific than the problem statement.	Formal hypothesis rarely stated; initial research questions used in plan are closely linked to theories, policies, and practical problems; understanding is ongoing, shifting.
Research participants	Participants chosen from a defined population, usually randomly, at the start of the study; samples often large.	Small group of participants purposefully selected from research context; participants provide detailed data about themselves and life in context.
Data collection and instruments	Data consist of results from tests, questionnaires, and other paper-and-pencil instruments; collection requires little direct interaction between researcher and participants.	Data consist of notes from observations, interviews, examination of artifacts; collection requires substantial interaction between researcher and participants; researcher must manage variety of data sources.
Special materials or apparatus	Chosen and used as needed.	
Research design	Clear, well-ordered sequence of steps used to conduct research. Research designs may include both quantitative and qualitative methods; the two approaches are not totally independent of each other.	
Research procedures	Procedures describe what occurs in a study; despite many different emphases, most procedures are pertinent to both quantitative and qualitative research.	
Time schedule	Research usually completed in relatively short time; data collected and analyzed relatively quickly; planning of time schedule very useful.	Research usually occupies lengthy time period; much time needed to collect data in the field and to interact with participants over time; planning of time schedule very useful.
Budget	Budget depends on the nature of study and the researcher's resources, including time; realistic assessment of budget will help guide choice of a reasonable research problem.	
Data analysis	Quantitative methods used to collect primarily numerical data; analysis based on numerical and statistical analyses; validity and reliability measures ensure data trustworthiness.	Qualitative methods used to collect primarily descriptive narrative and visual data; analysis based on identifying themes and patterns; triangulation used to ensure trustworthiness of data.
Final report	Report heavily focused on statistical analyses.	Report heavily focused on narrative description.

Limitations of the Study

The limitations section of the research plan need not be extensive. You should focus your discussion on any perceived limitations over which you have no control and that may affect your ability to conduct the proposed research. For example, if the research participants with whom you negotiated entry to the setting leave, you may find yourself without a place to conduct your research. Discuss possible roadblocks to your work in an open and honest fashion so that the readers of your plan can judge for themselves whether the limitations may affect the results of the study.

Appendixes

The appendixes of a qualitative research plan typically include one or more of the following: a time line for the research, a proposed table of contents for the research report (it's never too early to start writing!), sample consent forms to be given to research participants, a letter specifying IRB approval if already obtained, and samples of structured surveys or questionnaires to be used in the research. You should consider including in your research plan any material that will help the reader determine your preparedness to conduct the research.

Table 5.1 provides a comparison of the two approaches based on the components of the research process and written plan. As you read the table, note the similarities and differences among the components.

MyLab Education **Self-Check 5.3**

MyLab Education **Application Exercise 5.2:** Preparing a Qualitative Research Plan

REVISING AND IMPROVING THE RESEARCH PLAN

Judging the adequacy of a research plan can involve both informal and formal assessment. Informally, a research plan should be reviewed by at least one skilled researcher and at least one expert in the area of investigation. Any researcher, no matter how long she or he has been a researcher, can benefit from the insight of others. Rereading your own plan several days after having written it can help you identify flaws or weaknesses.

To assess your plan formally, you can field-test some aspects in a **pilot study,** a small-scale trial of a study conducted before the full-scale study. Think of the pilot study as a dress rehearsal. For all or part of the study, follow every procedure exactly as planned to identify unanticipated problems or issues. Your research plan will almost always be modified as a result of the pilot study, and in some cases it may be substantially overhauled. One reason, aside from time, that more large-scale pilot studies are not conducted is lack of available participants, but any pilot study—even a small one—should be considered a very worthwhile use of your time.

Table 5.2 contains guidelines for critiquing your own research plan.

MyLab Education **Self-Check 5.4**

MyLab Education **Application Exercise 5.3:** Evaluating a Research Plan

MyLab Education **Application Exercise 5.4:** Reviewing and Revising a Research Proposal

---

TABLE 5.2 • Critiquing your research plan

1. Read your research plan to ensure that you have included all the major headings for either a quantitative or a qualitative research plan (e.g., introduction, problem statement, review of literature, statement of hypothesis, method, data analysis, time schedule, and budget).

2. Check that your research plan includes sufficient detail to allow another reader (e.g., colleague or adviser) to understand what you plan to study (i.e., problem statement), why you plan to study it (i.e., review of literature, context), how you plan to study it (i.e., method including participants, instruments, design, and procedure), how you plan to make sense of the data you collect (i.e., data analysis), when you plan to do it (i.e., time line), and any external support (i.e., budget) you may require to conduct the research.

3. Ask a trusted friend or colleague to read your proposal with a critical eye and to spend time discussing the proposal with you before you submit your proposal to your adviser. A reader not involved in your research can often see gaps in your logic.

SUMMARY

DEFINITION AND PURPOSE OF A RESEARCH PLAN

1. A research plan is a detailed description of a proposed study; it includes a literature review that justifies the study and its hypotheses, a description of the steps that will be followed in the study, and information about the analysis of the collected data. The plan provides a guide for conducting the study.

2. Most quantitative studies test a hypothesis that influences decisions about the participation, measuring instruments, design, procedures, and statistical techniques used in the study. Qualitative plans focus on gaining entry to the research context, identifying research participants, spending time in the field, determining how to gather data, and interpreting and narrating the data.

3. A written research plan helps you to think through the aspects of your study, facilitates evaluation of the proposed study, and generally improves the quality of the research.

4. Part of good planning is anticipation. Try to anticipate potential problems that may arise, do what you can to prevent them, and plan your strategies for dealing with them if they occur.

COMPONENTS OF THE QUANTITATIVE RESEARCH PLAN

5. Quantitative research plans typically include an introduction, a method section, a data analysis description, and a time schedule.

Introduction Section

6. The introduction includes a statement of the problem, research question(s), a review of related literature, and a statement of the hypothesis with variables stated in operational terms.

Method Section

7. The method section generally includes a description of the research participants, measuring instruments, design, and procedure.

Research Participants

8. The description of participants should include the number, source, and characteristics of the sample, as well as the population the sample was drawn from.

Instruments

9. This subsection should provide a description of the particular tests or tools used for data collection as well as a rationale for the specific selection of the instruments.

10. If you are developing your own instrument, describe how the instrument will be developed, what it will measure, and how you plan to determine its validity and reliability.

Design

11. A design is a general strategy for conducting a research study, determined by the nature of the hypothesis, variables involved, and any environmental constraints.

Procedure

12. The procedure section describes all the steps in collecting the data, in the order in which they will occur. It typically begins with a description of the strategy for selecting the sample or samples and then addresses the administration of any treatments or tests.

13. The procedure section should also include any identified assumptions and limitations. An assumption is an assertion presumed to be true but not verified, whereas a limitation is an aspect of the study that the researcher believes may alter the results.

14. The procedure section should be precise to the point that someone else could read your plan and execute your study exactly as you intended it to be conducted.

Data Analysis

15. The research plan must include a description of the techniques that will be used to analyze study data.

16. The hypothesis in a quantitative study determines the design, which in turn determines the data analysis.

Time Schedule

17. A time schedule listing major research activities and their corresponding expected completion date is a useful planning aid.

Budget

18. Describe anticipated costs that may be incurred in the study.

COMPONENTS OF THE QUALITATIVE RESEARCH PLAN

19. A qualitative research plan is much less structured than a quantitative plan because the research must be responsive to the context and setting under study.

Prior Fieldwork

20. If possible, qualitative researchers should undertake some informal preproposal fieldwork to understand the sociocultural context of the research setting.

Title

21. The title of a study provides a frame of reference for the researcher and for readers of the study.

Introduction Section

22. The introduction includes the purpose of the study, its relation to a larger problem, the initial research questions, a guiding hypothesis (if appropriate), a review of related literature, and any appendixes.

Research Procedures Section

23. The research procedures section includes a description of the overall approach for the study, the site and sample, the researcher's role, data collection methods, data management strategies, data analysis strategies, trustworthiness features, ethical considerations, potential contributions of the research, and study limitations.

Appendixes

24. Appendixes should include any material that will help the reader determine your preparedness to conduct the research, such as sample consent forms, samples of surveys or questionnaires, or a letter specifying IRB approval.

REVISING AND IMPROVING A RESEARCH PLAN

25. A research plan should be reviewed by at least one skilled researcher and at least one expert in the area of investigation.

26. If possible, a researcher should carry out a small-scale pilot study to help in refining or changing planned procedures.

PERFORMANCE CRITERIA   TASK 4

The purpose of Task 4 is to have you construct brief research plans for a quantitative (Task 4A) and a qualitative (Task 4B) study. For a quantitative study, you have already created the introduction section of the plan (Task 3). You should now provide information about the methods you will employ to carry out your study, including information on the research participants (i.e., sample), instruments (e.g., questionnaires, surveys), design, and procedure; a short statement about the way in which data will be analyzed; and a time schedule. For a qualitative study, you will need to develop a research problem. You can then complete a preliminary plan that includes the components outlined in Figure 5.1 (p. 130).

Although each of your plans should contain all the required components, your plans need not be extensive or technically accurate. In later chapters, you will learn new ways to formulate each component. Feedback from your instructor will also help you identify and critique your research plan.

An example that illustrates the performance called for by Task 4A appears on the following pages (see Task 4A Example). The task in the example was submitted by the same student whose Task 3 work was presented in Chapter 4. Thus, in this example, the research plan is a continuation of the introduction. Keep in mind that the proposed activities described in this example do not necessarily represent an ideal research procedure. Research plans are usually more detailed. The example given, however, represents what you ought to be able to do at this point.

1

Effect of Interactive Multimedia on the Achievement of 10th-Grade Biology Students

Method

Participants

Participants for this study will be 10th-grade biology students in an upper-middle-class, all-girl Catholic high school in Miami, Florida. Forty students will be selected and divided into two groups.

Instrument

The effectiveness of interactive multimedia (IMM) will be determined by comparing the biology achievement of the two groups as measured by a standardized test, if there is an acceptable test available. Otherwise, one will be developed.

Design

There will be two groups of 20 students each. Students in both groups will be posttested in May using a test of biology achievement.

Procedure

At the beginning of the school year, 40 10th-grade biology students will be selected from a population of approximately 200. Selected students will be divided into two groups, and one group will be designated to be the experimental group. The same teacher will teach both classes.

During the school year, the nonexperimental group of students will be taught biology using traditional lecture and discussion methods. The students in the experimental group will be taught using IMM. Both groups will cover the same subject matter and use the same text. The groups will receive biology instruction for the same amount of time and in the same room, but not at the same time, as they will be taught by the same teacher.

Academic objectives will be the same for each class and all tests measuring achievement will be identical. Both classes will have the same homework reading assignments. In May, a biology achievement test will be administered to both classes at the same time.

Data Analysis

The scores of the two groups will be compared statistically.

	August	September . . . April	May	June
		Time Schedule		
Select Participants	_____			
Pretest	_____			
Execute Study		_____		
Posttest			_____	
Analyze Data				_____
Write Report			_____	

CHAPTER SIX

Selecting a Sample

"… [E]very individual has the same probability of being selected, and selection of one individual in no way affects selection of another individual." (p. 149)

LEARNING OUTCOMES

After reading Chapter 6, you should be able to do the following:

6.1 Define sampling in quantitative research and how to use random and nonrandom sampling techniques to obtain an appropriate sample.

6.2 Define sampling in qualitative research and how to use purposive sampling approaches to obtain an appropriate sample.

The chapter learning outcomes form the basis for the following tasks, which require you to describe the sample appropriate for the research plan you developed in the previous chapters.

TASK 5A

Having selected a problem and having formulated one or more testable quantitative hypotheses (Task 3A), describe a sample appropriate for evaluating your hypotheses. Include the following in your description:

1. A description of the population from which the sample will be drawn
2. The procedural technique for selecting the sample and, if necessary, for assigning participants to groups
3. Expected sample size
4. Possible sources of sampling bias (See Performance Criteria, p. 164).

TASK 5B

Having selected a problem and formulated initial research questions (Task 4B), describe the process and context for selecting a purposive sample for a qualitative research study (see Performance Criteria, p. 164).

In a research study, a *sample* is a group of individuals, items, or events that represents the characteristics of the larger group from which the sample is drawn. Testing a sample, especially in a quantitative study, allows the researcher to make inferences about the performance of the larger group, which is known as the *population*. The process of selecting a sample is known as *sampling*.

Although all research involves the use of samples, the nature, size, and method of selecting samples can vary with the research aim. The goals of Chapter 6 are to explain the importance of selecting an appropriate sample and to introduce you to various sampling techniques. The first section of the chapter deals with quantitative sampling, the second with qualitative sampling.

SAMPLING IN QUANTITATIVE RESEARCH

Quantitative researchers generally do not gather data from the entire population—it's rarely necessary and even more rarely feasible, especially if the population of interest is large or geographically scattered. If a sample is well selected, the results of a study testing that sample should be **generalizable** to the population. That is, the results of the research will be applicable to other samples selected from the same population.

To see an example of generalization from a sample, consider a situation in which the superintendent of a large school system wants to find out how the 5,000 teachers in that system feel about teacher unions. Would the teachers join one? What reasons would they give for their choices? The superintendent wants to conduct interviews with the teachers, but clearly it would take much too long to interview every teacher—if each interview took 15 minutes, the superintendent would spend, at minimum, 1,250 hours (more than 31 full-day workweeks) to collect data from all 5,000 teachers. On the other hand, if he interviews 10%, or 500, of the teachers, he would spend only 125 hours, or about 3 weeks, collecting data. If the sample of 500 teachers is selected correctly, the conclusions based on their interviews should be the same or very close to the conclusions based on interviews of all the teachers.

Note, however, that a sample must be selected correctly. In this example, selecting and interviewing 500 elementary teachers would not be satisfactory for at least two reasons: First, elementary teachers may feel differently about unions than teachers in the upper grades; and second, the percentage of teachers in the elementary grades who are female is much higher than the overall percentage of female teachers in the district. Male teachers may feel differently about unions than females.

How, then, can we obtain an adequate sample? Several relatively simple sampling techniques can be applied to select what is known as a *representative sample*. These procedures do not guarantee that the sample will be perfectly representative of the population, but they definitely increase the odds. By following the procedures for defining a population, selecting a random sample, determining sample size, avoiding sampling error and bias, and selecting a nonrandom sample, all of which are described in the sections that follow, the superintendent in this example should feel confident that his results reflect those of his population of teachers.

Defining a Population

The first step in sampling is to define the population to which results will be generalizable. Examples of populations are:

- All 10th-grade students in the United States
- All gifted elementary school children in Utah
- All first-grade students in Utopia County who have physical disabilities and have participated in preschool training

These examples illustrate two important points about populations. First, populations may be any size and may cover almost any geographical area. Second, the entire group of interest to the researcher is rarely available. Thus, a distinction is made between the population to which the researcher would ideally like to generalize study results, the **target population,** and the population from which the researcher can realistically select subjects, which is known as the **accessible population** or *available population*.

In most studies, the chosen population is generally a realistic choice (i.e., the accessible population), not an ideal one (i.e., the target population). For example, consider a study of high school principals' opinions about a 6-day-a-week class schedule. Ideally, the results should generalize to all high school principals in the United States. Given the difficulty of getting information from every high school principal in the United States, a representative sample of all U.S. principals is the next optimal choice, but obtaining even this sample would be a difficult, time-consuming, and expensive effort.

A more realistic approach is to study only principals in one state. By selecting from a more narrowly defined population, a researcher saves time and money but also loses the ability to generalize about the target population. The results will be directly generalizable to all high school principals in the target state but not necessarily to all high school principals in the United States. The key is to define the population in enough detail that others can determine how applicable the findings are to their own situations.

A description of the sample you ultimately choose should include the number of participants and demographic information about the sample (e.g., average number of years teaching, percentage of each gender or racial group, level of education, achievement level). The type of demographic information reported depends on the sample; the information used to describe a sample of teachers is different from that used to describe a sample of students, parents, or administrators.

Selecting a Random Sample

In quantitative research, a good sample is one that is representative of the population from which it was selected, and selecting a representative sample is not a haphazard process. Several techniques for selecting a sample are appropriate, and selection depends on the situation because the techniques do not all provide the same level of assurance concerning representativeness. However, as with populations, we sometimes have to compromise the ideal for what is feasible.

The following sections describe four basic techniques or procedures for selecting a random sample: simple random sampling, stratified sampling, cluster sampling, and systematic sampling. These techniques are known as **probability sampling** techniques because they permit the researcher to specify the probability, or chance, that each member of a defined population will be selected for the sample. Each technique requires the same basic steps: identify the population, determine the required sample size, and select the sample.

Simple Random Sampling

Simple random sampling is the process of selecting a sample so that all individuals in the defined population have an equal and independent chance of selection for the sample. The selection of the sample is completely out of the researcher's control; instead, a random, or chance, procedure selects the sample. In other words, every individual has the same probability of being selected, and selection of one individual in no way affects selection of another individual. To understand random sampling, consider a situation that is not random—in physical education class, a teacher forms teams by having the class line up and count off by twos: one, two, one, two, and so on. With this method, the team assignment for any one student is determined by that person's place in line and the team of the student next in line. If selection of teams had been random, any student would have had an equal (50-50) chance of being on either team, regardless of the team assignment for the person next in line.

Random sampling is the best way to obtain a representative sample. Although no technique, not even random sampling, guarantees a representative sample, the probability of achieving one is higher for this procedure than for any other. In most cases, the differences between the random sample and the population from which it's drawn are small. For example, the sample may not have the exact same ratio of males to females as found in the population, but random sampling assures that the ratio will be close and that the probability of having too many females is the same as the probability of having too many males. Differences that occur are a result of chance and are not the result of the researcher's conscious or unconscious bias in selection.

Another point in favor of random sampling is that it is required for many statistical analyses. These analyses permit the researcher to make inferences about a population based on the behavior of a sample.[1] If samples are not randomly selected, then a major assumption of many statistical analyses is violated, and inferences made from the research are suspect.

Steps in Simple Random Sampling. In general, random sampling involves defining the population, identifying each member of the population, and selecting individuals for the sample on a completely chance basis. One way to do this is to write each individual's name on a separate slip of paper, place all the slips in a hat or other container, shake the container, and select slips from the container until the desired number of participants is selected. This procedure is not exactly satisfactory if a population has 1,000 or more members. One would need a very large hat—and a strong writing hand! A much more satisfactory approach is to use a **table of random numbers,** also called a *table of random digits*. In essence, a table of random numbers selects the sample for you, with each member selected on a purely random or chance basis. Such tables are included in the appendix sections of most statistics books and some educational research books; they usually consist of columns of five-digit numbers that have been randomly generated by a computer to have no defined patterns or regularities (see Table 6.1). By the way, there are a number of websites that let you generate sets of random numbers. See, for example, stattrek.com/Tables/Random.aspx.

Using a table of random numbers to select a sample involves the following specific steps:

1. Identify and define the population.
2. Determine the desired sample size.
3. List all members of the population.
4. Assign all individuals on the list a consecutive number from zero to the required number, for example, 000 to 799 or 00 to 89. Each individual must be assigned a value with the same number of digits as each other individual.
5. Select an arbitrary number in the table of random numbers (close your eyes and point!).
6. For the selected number, look only at the number of digits assigned to each population member. For example, if a population has 800 members, look at the last 3 digits of the number in the table; if a population has 90 members, look at the last 2 digits.
7. If the number corresponds to a number assigned to an individual in the population, then that individual is in the sample. For example, if a population has 500 members and the number selected is 375, the individual assigned 375 is in the sample; if a population has only 300 members, then 375 is ignored.
8. Go to the next number in the column, and repeat steps 6 and 7 until the desired number of individuals has been selected for the sample.

---

[1] In Chapter 19 you will learn how to select and apply several commonly used inferential statistics. (Don't you dare groan. You will be amazed at how easy it is.)

TABLE 6.1 • Random numbers

	00–04	05–09	10–14	15–19	20–24	25–29	30–34	35–39	40–44	45–49
00	19581	97814	00760	44812	13577	23449	58034	07168	34131	49085
01	10373	28790	40280	61239	01828	25327	95014	21054	93283	48421
02	11441	09305	21718	85401	37076	66579	10632	79397	62711	23854
03	08236	14645	03964	39471	31331	69379	90337	30926	54425	97555
04	17850	98623	30667	77261	75124	87537	51221	02896	32399	49894
05	89010	46689	50557	37335	43744	33063	42012	33872	71920	92878
06	02087	02491	17445	83669	64443	96487	43080	40944	53357	17041
07	15972	61643	16782	18109	75788	53098	39876	46285	35603	44553
08	47757	57630	92214	41349	68311	83265	49489	30263	62307	08900
09	99287	22786	92474	18513	90742	45880	20650	78329	82197	42417

After the sample has been selected, it may be used for descriptive or correlational studies, and it can be randomly subdivided into two or more subgroups for use in experimental studies. To divide a sample into two subgroups, a researcher can simply flip a coin—heads for one group, tails for the other.

An Example of Simple Random Sampling. It is now time to help the long-suffering superintendent who wants to select a sample of teachers and assess their attitudes toward unions. We apply the steps to select a sample for the superintendent:

1. The population is all 5,000 teachers in the superintendent's school system.
2. The desired sample size is 10% of the 5,000 teachers, or 500 teachers.
3. The superintendent has supplied a directory that lists all teachers in the system.
4. The teachers in the directory are each assigned a number from 0000 to 4999.
5. A table of random numbers is entered at an arbitrarily selected number, such as the one underlined here.

59058
11859
<u>53634</u>
48708
71710
83942
33278 (and so on)

6. The population has 5,000 members, so we are concerned only with the last four digits of the number, 3634.
7. There is a teacher assigned the number 3634; that teacher is therefore in the sample.
8. The next number in the column is 48708. The last four digits are 8708. There are only 5,000 teachers, so there is no teacher assigned the number 8708. The number is therefore skipped.
9. Applying these steps to the remaining random numbers shown, we select teachers 1710, 3942, and 3278. This procedure should be continued in succeeding columns until 500 teachers are selected.

At the completion of this process, the superintendent should have a representative sample of all the teachers in the system. The 500 selected teachers should represent all relevant subgroups of teachers, such as elementary teachers, older teachers, male teachers, and so on.

With simple random sampling, representation of specific subgroups is probable but not guaranteed. For example, if you flip a quarter 100 times, the probable outcome is 50 heads and 50 tails. The coin may fall 53 times heads and 47 tails, or 45 heads and 55 tails, but most of the time you can expect to get close to a 50-50 split. Other, more deviant outcomes are possible but relatively infrequent—85 heads and 15 tails is a possible but low-probability outcome. Similarly, if 55% of the 5,000 teachers were female and 45% were male, we would expect roughly the same percentages in the random sample of 500. Just by chance, however, the sample may include 30% females and 70% males.

Stratified Sampling

The superintendent in this example may not be willing to leave accurate representation to chance. If the superintendent believes that one or more variables are highly related to attitudes toward unions, a different sampling approach may be better. For example, teaching level (i.e., elementary, middle, high) may be an important variable because elementary teachers may feel differently toward unions than middle school or senior high school teachers. The superintendent may thus want a sample that reflects the representation of the three teaching levels in his district. To select this sort of sample, he would probably use stratified sampling rather than simple random sampling.

Stratified sampling is a way to guarantee desired representation of relevant subgroups within the sample. In other words, some populations can be subdivided into subgroups, known as *strata* (one is called a *stratum*). Stratified sampling involves strategically selecting participants from each subgroup. When a research goal is to compare the behavior of participants from different subgroups of the population, stratified sampling is the best approach.

Proportional stratified sampling is the process of selecting a sample so that identified subgroups in the population are represented in the sample in the same proportion in which they exist in the population. For example, a population of teachers in a district can be divided by class level. If 22% of the teachers in a district are elementary teachers, 33% are middle school teachers, and 45% are high school teachers, a researcher may want to have a sample with the same proportion in each subgroup and would thus need to select a proportionally stratified sample. Typical variables for proportional stratification include demographic variables such as race, gender, socioeconomic status, and level of education.

Stratified sampling can also be used to select equal-size (nonproportional) samples from subgroups if subgroup comparisons are desired.

Suppose, for example, that you were interested in comparing the achievement of students of different ability levels (e.g., high, average, and low) who are taught by one of two methods of mathematics instruction (e.g., teacher and computer). Simply selecting a random sample of students and assigning one half of the sample to each of the two methods would not guarantee equal representation of each ability level in each method. In fact, just by chance, one method could have only students of high and average ability, whereas the other could have students from average and low abilities; random sampling could lead to almost any combination. To solve this problem, a researcher could first identify subgroups based on ability level and then randomly select students from each subgroup, assigning half of each selected group to each of the instruction methods. Stratified sampling, used in this way, would thus guarantee equal representation of each ability level in each method. Note, however, that using proportionally sized groups requires accurate information about the size of each group. If this information is not available, proportional group studies are not recommended.

Steps for Equal-Size Groups in Stratified Sampling. The steps in stratified sampling are similar to those in random sampling except that selection is from subgroups in the population rather than the population as a whole. In other words, stratified sampling includes repeated random sampling—one random sample from each subgroup. Stratified sampling involves the following steps:

1. Identify and define the population.
2. Determine the desired sample size.
3. Identify the variable and subgroups (i.e., strata) for which you want to guarantee a specific representation.
4. Classify all members of the population as members of one of the identified subgroups.
5. Randomly select (using a table of random numbers) an equal number of individuals from each subgroup.

As with simple random sampling, after the samples from each subgroup have been randomly selected, each may be randomly divided into two or more treatment groups. For example, if we were interested in the comparative effectiveness of two methods of mathematics instruction for students with different levels of ability, the steps in sampling may be as follows:

1. The population is all 300 eighth-grade students enrolled in general math at Central Middle School.
2. The desired sample size is 45 students in each of the two methods.
3. The variable is ability, and the desired subgroups are three levels of ability—high, average, and low.
4. The 300 students are classified into the subgroups, which comprise 45 high-ability students, 215 average-ability students, and 40 low-ability students.
5. Thirty students are randomly selected (with assistance from a table of random numbers) from each of the ability subgroups; that is, a total of 90 students are selected—30 high-, 30 average-, and 30 low-ability students.
6. The 30 students in each subgroup sample are randomly assigned to one of the two methods of instruction; that is, 15 of each 30 are randomly assigned to each method. Therefore, 45 students will participate in each method of instruction—15 high-ability students, 15 average-ability students, and 15 low-ability students (see Figure 6.1).

Stratification can be done on more than one variable. In this example, we could have stratified based on math interest or prior math grades instead of ability. The following example, based on a familiar situation, should help to clarify the process of stratified sampling further.

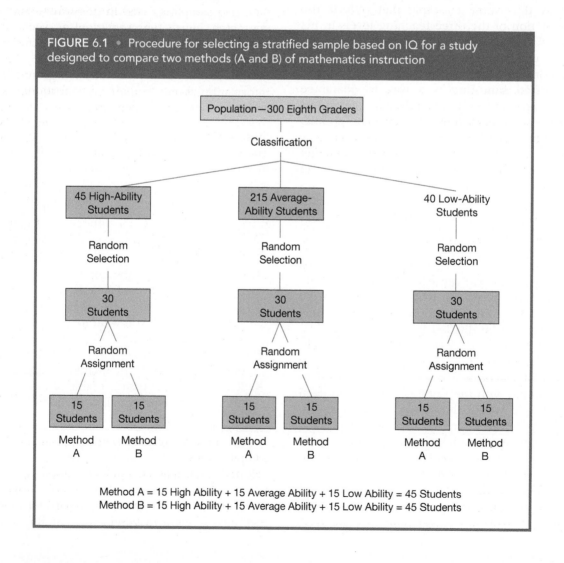

FIGURE 6.1 • Procedure for selecting a stratified sample based on IQ for a study designed to compare two methods (A and B) of mathematics instruction

Method A = 15 High Ability + 15 Average Ability + 15 Low Ability = 45 Students
Method B = 15 High Ability + 15 Average Ability + 15 Low Ability = 45 Students

An Example of Proportional Stratified Sampling. Suppose that our old friend the superintendent wants to guarantee proportional representation of teaching level in his sample of teachers. We can apply each of the five steps previously described for selecting a stratified sample:

1. The population is all 5,000 teachers in the superintendent's school system.
2. The desired sample size is 10% of the 5,000 teachers, or 500 teachers.
3. The variable of interest is teaching level, with three subgroups—elementary, middle, and high.
4. We classify the teachers into the subgroups. Of the 5,000 teachers, 65%, or 3,250, are elementary teachers; 20%, or 1,000, are middle school teachers; and 15%, or 750, are high school teachers.
5. We want 500 teachers. Because we want proportional representation, 65% of the sample (325 teachers) should be elementary teachers, 20% (100 teachers) should be middle school teachers, and 15% (75 teachers) should be high school teachers.
6. Using a table of random numbers, we randomly select 325 of the 3,250 elementary teachers (i.e., 10% of the subgroup because we want a total sample of 10%), 100 of the 1,000 middle school teachers, and 75 of the 750 high school teachers.

At the completion of this process, the superintendent will have a sample of 500 teachers (325 + 100 + 75), or 10% of 5,000, and each teaching level will be proportionally represented.

So far we have described two ways in which the superintendent could get a sample of teachers, simple random sampling and stratified sampling. Both techniques, however, would result in a sample scattered over the entire district. The interviewer would have to visit many, many schools, some of them containing only one or two teachers in the sample. If the superintendent wants the information quickly, a more expedient method of sampling is needed. For the sake of convenience, cluster sampling can be used.

Cluster Sampling

In **cluster sampling,** intact groups, not individuals, are randomly selected. Any location within which we find an intact group of population members with similar characteristics is a **cluster.** Examples of clusters are classrooms, schools, city blocks, hospitals, and department stores.

Cluster sampling may be the only feasible method of selecting a sample when the researcher is unable to obtain a list of all members of the population. It is also convenient when the population is very large or spread over a wide geographic area. For example, instead of randomly selecting from all fifth-graders in a large school district, you could randomly select fifth-grade classrooms and include all the students in each classroom. Cluster sampling usually involves less time and expense and is generally more convenient (though not necessarily as good, as we discuss later) than either simple random sampling or stratified sampling.

Cluster sampling is also advantageous for educational researchers because they frequently cannot select and assign individual participants, as they may like. For example, if the population for your quantitative study were 10th-grade biology students, it would be very unlikely that you would obtain administrative approval to randomly select and remove a few students from many classrooms for your study. You would have a much better chance of securing permission if you planned to study several intact classrooms.

Steps in Cluster Sampling. The steps in cluster sampling are not very different from those in random sampling. The major difference, of course, is that groups (i.e., clusters), not individuals, are randomly selected. Cluster sampling involves the following steps:

1. Identify and define the population.
2. Determine the desired sample size.
3. Identify and define a logical cluster (e.g., neighborhood, school, city block).
4. List all clusters (or obtain a list) that make up the population of clusters.
5. Estimate the average number of population members per cluster.
6. Determine the number of clusters needed by dividing the sample size by the estimated size of a cluster.
7. Randomly select the needed number of clusters, using a table of random numbers.
8. Include in your study all population members in each selected cluster.

Cluster sampling can be carried out in stages, involving selection of clusters within clusters. This process is called *multistage sampling*. For example, to sample classrooms for a study, a researcher can first sample from districts in a state, then schools in the district, and then classrooms in the schools.

One common misconception about cluster sampling is that it is appropriate to select only a single cluster randomly. It is not uncommon, for example, for some researchers to define a population as all fifth-graders in Knox County, to define a cluster as a school, and to select randomly only one school in the population. However, these same researchers would not dream of randomly selecting only one student! A good sample is representative of the population from which it is selected, and it is highly unlikely that one randomly selected student is representative of an entire population. Similarly, it is unlikely that one randomly selected school is representative of all schools in a population. A researcher should select a number of clusters for the results of a study to be generalizable to the population.

An Example of Cluster Sampling. Let us see how our superintendent would identify a sample of teachers if cluster sampling were used. We follow the steps previously listed:

1. The population is all 5,000 teachers in the superintendent's school system.
2. The desired sample size is 500.
3. A logical, useful cluster is a school.
4. The superintendent has a list of all the schools in the district; there are 100 schools.
5. Although the schools vary in the number of teachers per school, the average is 50 teachers per school.
6. The number of clusters (i.e., schools) to be selected equals the desired sample size, 500, divided by the average size of a cluster, 50. Thus, the number of schools needed is 500 ÷ 50, or 10.
7. Ten of the 100 schools are randomly selected by assigning a number to each school and selecting numbers from a table of random numbers.
8. All the teachers in each of the 10 schools are in the sample (i.e., 10 schools × 50 teachers per school on average = the desired sample size).

Thus, the superintendent could conduct interviews at 10 schools and interview all teachers in each school instead of traveling to a possible 100 different schools.

Although the advantages of cluster sampling are evident, it also has several drawbacks. For one thing, the chances of selecting a sample that is not representative of the population are greater than in the previously discussed methods. The smaller the sample size, the more likely that the sample selected may not represent the population. For example, the teachers in this example are from a limited number of schools. Perhaps the 10 schools selected are somehow different (e.g., in socioeconomic level of the students, or teacher experience) from the other 90 schools in the district. One way to compensate for this problem is to select a larger sample of clusters, thus increasing the likelihood that the selected schools represent all the schools adequately.

As another example, suppose our population was all fifth-graders in 10 schools, with an average of 120 students in four classes of 30 students each, and we wanted a sample of 120 students. We can select our sample in any number of ways. For example, we can (1) randomly select one school and include all the fifth-graders in that school, (2) randomly select two classes from each of two schools and include all the students in each class, or (3) randomly select 120 students from the 10 schools. In each case we wind up with 120 students, but the samples would probably not be equally representative. In the first case, we would have students from only one school. It is very likely that this school is different from the other nine in some significant way. In the second case, we would be doing a little better, but we would still have only two of the 10 schools represented. Only in the third case would we have a chance of selecting a sample containing students from all or most of the schools and from all or most of the classes within those schools. If random sampling is not feasible, as is often the case, selecting two classes from each of two schools is preferable to selecting all the students in one school, and if cluster sampling is used, it is even better to select one class from each of four schools. One way to compensate for the loss of representativeness associated with cluster sampling is to select more than four classes.

Another problem is that commonly used statistical methods are not appropriate for analyzing data resulting from a study using cluster sampling. Such statistics generally require randomly formed groups, not those selected in a cluster. The statistics that are available and appropriate for cluster samples are generally less sensitive to differences that may exist between groups. Thus, one should carefully weigh the advantages and disadvantages of cluster sampling before choosing this method of sampling.

Systematic Sampling

Systematic sampling is not used very often, but in some instances, it is the only feasible way to select a sample. **Systematic sampling** is sampling in which every Kth individual is selected from a list. The list includes all the individuals in the population, and K is a variable determined by dividing the number of individuals on the list by the number of subjects desired for the sample. If $K = 4$, selection involves taking every fourth name; if $K = 10$, every 10th name is taken, and so forth. The major difference between systematic sampling and the other types of sampling is that all members of the population do not have an independent chance of selection for the sample. After the first name is selected, all the rest of the individuals to be included in the sample are automatically determined.

Even though choices are not independent, a systematic sample can be considered a random sample if the list of the population is randomly ordered. One or the other has to be random—either the selection process or the list. Because randomly ordered lists are rarely available, systematic sampling is rarely as good as random sampling. Although some researchers argue this point, the major objection to systematic sampling of a nonrandom list is the possibility that the process will cause certain subgroups of the population to be excluded from the sample. A classic example is that many people who share a nationality have distinctive last names that tend to group together under certain letters of the alphabet; if K is large, taking every Kth name from an alphabetized list makes it possible to skip over these subgroups of people completely.

Steps in Systematic Sampling. Systematic sampling involves the following steps:

1. Identify and define the population.
2. Determine the desired sample size.
3. Obtain a list of the population.
4. Determine K by dividing the size of the population by the desired sample size.
5. Start at some random place in the population list. Close your eyes and stick your finger on a name.
6. Starting at that point, take every Kth name on the list until the desired sample size is reached.
7. If the end of the list is reached before the desired sample is reached, go back to the top of the list.

An Example of Systematic Sampling. If our superintendent uses systematic sampling, the process is as follows:

1. The population is all 5,000 teachers in the superintendent's school system.
2. The desired sample size is 500.
3. The superintendent has a directory that lists all teachers in the system in alphabetical order. The list is not randomly ordered, but it is the best available.
4. K is equal to the size of the population, 5,000, divided by the desired sample size, 500. Thus $K = (5{,}000 \div 500) = 10$.
5. Select one random name in the list of teachers.
6. Every 10th name after that point identifies a person who is automatically in the sample. For example, if the teacher selected in step 5 were the third name on the list, then the sample would include the 13th person, the 23rd, the 33rd, the 43rd, and so forth.

In this case, due to the nonrandom nature of the list, the sample may not be as representative as the samples resulting from application of the other techniques. Table 6.2 summarizes characteristics of the four quantitative random sampling approaches.

Determining Sample Size

The sampling question most frequently asked by beginning researchers is probably, "How large should my sample be?" And the answer is, "Large enough!" This answer may not be very comforting or precise, but the question is a difficult one. Knowing that the sample should be as large as possible helps, but this knowledge does not give any

TABLE 6.2 • Random sampling strategies			
Type	Process	Advantages	Disadvantages
Simple random sampling	Select desired number of sample members using a table of random numbers.	Easy to conduct; strategy requires minimum knowledge of the population to be sampled.	Need names of all population members; may over- or underrepresent sample members; difficult to reach all selected in sample.
Stratified sampling	Divide population into separate levels, or strata, and randomly sample from the separate strata.	More precise sample; can be used for both proportional and nonproportional sampling; sample represents the desired strata.	Need names of all population members; difficult to reach all selected in sample.
Cluster sampling	Select groups, not individuals; identify clusters and randomly select them to reach desired sample size.	Efficient; clusters are most likely to be used in school research; don't need names of all population members; reduces travel to sites.	Fewer sampling points make it less likely to produce a representative sample.
Systematic sampling	Using list of population members, pick a name on the list at random and select each Kth person on the list until you reach the desired sample size.	Sample selection is easy.	All members of a population do not have an equal chance of being selected; Kth person may be related to a periodic order in the population list, producing unrepresentativeness in the sample.

specific guidance about an adequate size. Suppose, for example, the population is 300 first-graders. A sample of 299, 298, or 297 students would clearly represent the population—in fact, it is almost equivalent to the population. Can a sample be too big?

On the other extreme, if we randomly select only one student, clearly that student does not adequately represent all the students. Nor could two, three, or four students, even if randomly selected. How about 10? Still too small, you say. Okay, how about 30? 75? 100? If the sample is too small, the results of the study may not be generalizable to the population, regardless of how well the sample is selected; but in many cases, the researcher does not have access to a large number of potential research participants. In fact, obtaining permission to involve students in a study or finding adults willing to participate in a study is generally not an easy task. At what point does the sample size stop being too small and become big enough? That question has no easy answer and is usually constrained by the limits of the study itself.

You can apply some guidelines to determine whether a sample is big enough. In general, the minimum sample size depends on the type of research involved. Some researchers cite a sample size of 30 as a guideline for correlational, causal–comparative, and true experimental research. For correlational studies, at least 30 participants are needed to establish the existence or nonexistence of a relation. For causal–comparative and true experimental studies, a minimum of 30 participants in each group (e.g., treatment and nontreatment groups) is recommended, although in some cases it is difficult to attain this number. However, with larger samples, the researcher is more likely to detect a difference between the different groups. We would not be very confident about the results of a single study based on small samples, but if a number of such studies obtained similar results, our confidence in the findings is generally higher. It is important to understand the consequences of a small quantitative sample size.

For survey research, it is common to sample 10% to 20% of the population, although this guideline can be misleading. In reality, the appropriate sample size depends on factors such as the specific type of research involved, the size of the population, and whether data will be analyzed for given sub-groups. For survey research as well as for other quantitative research methods, statistical techniques and related software are available for determining sample size in a precise way that takes into account relevant variables. However, the following general rules are helpful in determining sample size:

- The larger the population size, the smaller the percentage of the population required to get a representative sample.
- For smaller populations, say, $N = 100$ or fewer, there is little point in sampling; survey the entire population.
- If the population size is around 500 (give or take 100), 50% should be sampled.
- If the population size is around 1,500, 20% should be sampled.
- Beyond a certain point (about $N = 5,000$), the population size is almost irrelevant and a sample size of 400 will be adequate. Thus, the superintendent from our previous example would be relatively safe with a sample of 400 teachers, but he would be even more confident with a sample of 500.

Of course, these numbers or percentages are suggested minimums. If it is at all possible to obtain more participants, you should do so.

Even with very large samples, however, researchers can sample in such a way that the sample leads to erroneous conclusions. We turn now to the many forms of sampling bias that can affect a study, regardless of sample size.

Avoiding Sampling Error and Bias

Error, beyond that within the control of the researcher, is a reality of random sampling. Selecting random samples does not guarantee that they will be representative of the population, and no sample will have a composition precisely identical to that of the population. If well selected and sufficiently large, the sample should closely represent the population, but occasionally a sample will differ significantly from the population on some important variable (remember, *random* means out of the researcher's control and at the mercy of chance). This chance variation is called **sampling error.** If the sample is greatly underrepresented on a particular variable, the researcher should stratify on that variable (i.e., create a new sample using

stratified sampling) because stratification can provide proportional or equal-size samples.

In contrast to sampling error, which results from random differences between samples and populations, **sampling bias** is systematic sampling error that is generally the fault of the researcher. It occurs when some aspect of the sampling creates a bias in the data. For example, suppose a researcher studying college students' attitudes toward alcohol stood outside bars and asked patrons leaving the bars to answer questions regarding their attitudes toward alcohol. This sample would be biased because the study was to be about the attitudes of college students—all types of college students. By sampling outside bars, the researchers systematically omitted college students who don't go to bars. The sampling bias in the study limits the study conclusions to a different population (e.g., students who go to bars); thus, the researcher can't generalize to the original population of interest. Similarly, when a survey researcher gets a return of only 45% of questionnaires sent out, the large number of surveys that are not returned introduces a potential response bias in the results. As these examples illustrate, sample bias greatly affects the trustworthiness of a study.

Researchers should be aware of sources of sampling bias and do their best to avoid it. We've already mentioned that securing administrative approval to involve students in educational research studies is not easy. Of necessity, researchers are often forced to study whatever samples they can get (as discussed later in the section on convenience sampling) and to use whatever methods teachers and administrators will allow. Cooperating with teachers and administrators is, of course, advisable, but not at the expense of good research. If your study cannot be conducted properly under the administrators' restrictions, try hard to convince the administrators to allow the study to be conducted in a way that will provide viable results. If this fails, you should look elsewhere for participants.

If it is not possible to avoid sampling bias, you must decide whether the bias is so severe that the study results will be seriously affected. If you decide to continue with the study with full awareness of the existing bias, such bias should be reported completely in the final research report. This disclosure allows any readers of the report to decide for themselves how serious the bias is and how generalizable the findings are.

TABLE 6.3 • Nonrandom sampling strategies			
Type	Process	Advantages	Disadvantages
Convenience sampling	Also referred to as accidental sampling and haphazard sampling; the process of including whoever happens to be available in the sample.	Sample selection is simple—based on whoever is available or on whoever volunteers to participate in the study.	Difficult to describe the population from which the sample was drawn and to whom results can be generalized.
Purposive sampling	Also referred to as judgment sampling; the process of selecting a sample that is believed to be representative of a given population.	Sample selection is based on the researcher's knowledge and experience of the group to be sampled using clear criteria to guide the process.	The potential for inaccuracy in the researcher's criteria and resulting sample selection limits the ability of the researcher to generalize the results.
Quota sampling	The process of selecting a sample based on required, exact numbers, or quotas, of individuals or groups of varying characteristics.	Widely used in large-scale surveys when data are obtained from easily accessible individuals within well-defined categories.	People who are less accessible (e.g., more difficult to contact, reluctant to participate) are underrepresented.

Selecting a Nonrandom Sample

Although random sampling techniques provide the best opportunity to obtain unbiased samples, researchers can't always use random sampling due to practical constraints. For example, teachers or administrators often select the students or classes they want researchers to study to ensure a good impression or result in the study outcome, and researchers often can't find many people willing to participate in their studies. **Nonprobability sampling,** also called *nonrandom sampling,* is the process of selecting a sample using a technique that does *not* permit the researcher to specify the probability, or chance, that each member of a population has of being selected for the sample. Nonrandom sampling methods do not have random sampling at any stage of sample selection and can introduce sampling bias. See Table 6.3 for nonrandom sampling strategies.

When nonrandom samples are used, it is usually difficult, if not impossible, to describe the population from which a sample was drawn and to whom results can be generalized. To compensate for this problem, the researcher may obtain information from nonrespondents. Often, follow-up contact with nonrespondents provides the researcher with insights about potential bias provided by the respondents. For example, the researcher may determine that the majority of nonrespondents were people for whom English is a second language.

They were unable to respond to the research request because of a language barrier. This information helps a researcher identify and remedy possible bias in a study.

Nonrandom sampling approaches include convenience sampling, purposive sampling, and quota sampling. Of these methods, convenience sampling is the most used in educational research and is therefore the major source of sampling bias in educational research studies.

Convenience Sampling

Convenience sampling, also referred to as *accidental sampling* or *haphazard sampling,* is the process of including whoever happens to be available at the time. Two examples of convenience sampling are seeking volunteers and studying existing groups "just because they are there." For example, you've been part of a convenience sample if you have been stopped on the street or in a grocery store by someone who wants your opinion of an event or of a new kind of muffin. Those who volunteer to answer are usually different from nonvolunteers, and they may be more motivated or more interested in the particular study. Because the total population is composed of both volunteers and nonvolunteers, the results of a study based solely on volunteers are not likely generalizable to the entire population. Suppose you send a questionnaire to 100 randomly selected people and ask the question "How do you feel about questionnaires?" Suppose that 40 people respond, and all 40 indicate that they love questionnaires. Should you then conclude that the entire population loves questionnaires? Certainly not. The 60 who did not respond may not have done so simply because they hate questionnaires!

Purposive Sampling

Purposive sampling, also referred to as *judgment sampling,* is the process of selecting a sample that is *believed* to be representative of a given population. In other words, the researcher selects the sample using his or her experience and knowledge of the group to be sampled. For example, if a researcher plans to study exceptional high schools, she can choose schools to study based on her knowledge of exceptional schools. Prior knowledge or experience can lead the researcher to select exceptional high schools that meet certain criteria, such as a high proportion of students going to four-year colleges, a large number of advanced placement students, extensive computer facilities, and a high proportion of teachers with advanced degrees. Notice the important difference between convenience sampling, in which participants who happen to be available are chosen, and purposive sampling, in which the researcher deliberately identifies criteria for selecting the sample. Clear criteria provide a basis for describing and defending purposive samples and, as a result, the main weakness of purposive sampling is the potential for inaccuracy in the researcher's criteria and resulting sample selections.

Quota Sampling

Quota sampling is the process of selecting a sample based on required, exact numbers, or *quotas,* of individuals or groups with varying characteristics. It is most often used in wide-scale survey research when listing all members of the population of interest is not possible. When quota sampling is involved, data gatherers are given exact characteristics and quotas of persons to be interviewed (e.g., 35 working women with children under the age of 16, 20 working women with no children under the age of 16). Obviously, when quota sampling is used, data are obtained from easily accessible individuals. Thus, people who are less accessible (e.g., more difficult to contact, more reluctant to participate) are underrepresented.

MyLab Education **Self-Check 6.1**

MyLab Education **Application Exercise 6.1:** Evaluating Research Articles: Sampling in a Quantitative Study

MyLab Education **Application Exercise 6.2:** Selecting a Quantitative Sampling Technique

---

SAMPLING IN QUALITATIVE RESEARCH

Qualitative sampling is the process of selecting a small number of individuals for a study so that the individuals chosen will be good key informants (i.e., collaborators, co-researchers) who will contribute to the researcher's understanding of a given phenomenon. The characteristics of a good key informant include the ability to be reflective and thoughtful, to communicate (orally, in writing, or both) effectively with the researcher, and to be comfortable with the researcher's presence at the research site.

Qualitative research samples are generally different, smaller, and less representative compared to samples selected for quantitative research because the two approaches have different aims and needs. Because of the interest in participants' perspectives, immersion in the setting, and the research problem under study, qualitative research requires more in-depth data collection than is typically needed in quantitative research. Whereas a quantitative researcher may ask, "Are certain teacher behaviors correlated with the amount of time students will continue on a task?" a qualitative researcher may ask, "What meanings about time on task do students and teachers create together, and how are the perspectives of different students manifested when working on tasks?" To obtain the desired depth of information required by such research problems, qualitative researchers must almost always deal with small samples, normally interacting over a long period of time and in great depth.

Remember, one of the basic tenets of qualitative research is that each research setting is unique in its mix of people and contextual factors. The researcher's intent is to describe a particular context in depth, not to generalize to a context or population. Representativeness is secondary to the participants' ability to provide the desired information about self and setting. When choosing a sampling technique and the sample itself, researchers need to remember a primary goal: selecting participants who can best add to the understanding of the phenomenon under study, not participants who necessarily represent some larger population. The participants' perspectives, as described by the researcher, form the very core of a qualitative research study.

Selecting Research Participants: Purposive Sampling Approaches

Because many potential participants are unwilling to undergo the lengthy demands of participation, sampling in qualitative research is almost always purposive. The researcher relies on experience and insight to select a sample; randomness is rarely part of the process. One reason qualitative researchers spend time in the research setting before selecting a sample is to observe and obtain information that can be used to select participants whom they judge to be thoughtful, informative, articulate, and experienced with the research problem and setting.

Within the domain of purposive sampling are a number of specific approaches that are used in qualitative research. Table 6.4 illustrates the range of qualitative sampling approaches, providing an example of use and a sample strategy for each of five common techniques.

In many qualitative studies, combinations of the approaches in Table 6.4 and other purposive sampling approaches may be used to identify and narrow a sample. For example, qualitative researchers can test the robustness of their findings by purposefully selecting a few new participants and

TABLE 6.4 • Qualitative sampling strategies

Type	Example	Sample Strategy
Intensity sampling	Select participants who permit study of different levels of the research problem; for example, the researcher might select some good and poor students, experienced and inexperienced teachers, or teachers with small and large classes.	Compare differences of two or more levels of the problem (e.g., high-achieving versus low-achieving students); select two groups of about 20 participants from each of the two levels.
Homogeneous sampling	Select participants who are very similar in experience, perspective, or outlook; this produces a narrow, homogeneous sample and makes data collection and analysis simple.	Select a small group of participants who fit a narrow, homogeneous problem; collect data from the chosen participants.
Criterion sampling	Select all cases that meet some set of criteria or have some characteristic; the researcher might pick students who have been held back in two successive years or teachers who left the profession to raise children and then returned to teaching.	Identify participants who meet the defined criterion; select a group of five or so participants to collect data from.
Snowball sampling	Select a few people who fit a researcher's needs, then use those participants to identify additional participants, and so on, until the researcher has a sufficient number of participants. (Snowballing is most useful when it is difficult to find participants of the type needed.)	Decide how many participants are needed; let initial participants recruit additional participants that fit the researcher's requirements until the desired number is reached.
Random purposive sampling	Select more participants than needed for the study; for example, if 25 participants were purposively selected by the researcher but only 10 participants could take part in the study, a random sample of 10 from 25 potential participants would be chosen; this strategy adds credibility to the study, although the initial sample is based on purposive selection. (This approach is typically used with small samples.)	Given a pool of participants, decide how many of them can reasonably be dealt with in the study, and randomly select this number to participate.

determining whether they provide similar information and perspectives as the original group of participants.

After identifying a potential participant, the qualitative researcher should meet with the person. The initial communication is the start of a relationship that may continue throughout the study. Establish a day and time when you can meet to discuss the study. It will usually be more convenient to hold the visit in the research setting. This face-to-face meeting will give you a view of the setting, and it will allow you to demonstrate your interest in the potential participant and your desire to start the research relationship in a positive and professional way. It will also help you determine whether the person is able to provide the data you seek. Finally, if the potential participant is interested, understands your expectations, and can provide appropriate data, then you can arrange additional times and places for interviewing, observing, and meeting.

Determining Sample Size

All qualitative researchers, like quantitative researchers, face the inevitable question "How many participants are enough?" The answer, for qualitative researchers, is, "It depends." No hard-and-fast rules specify a "correct" number of participants. Qualitative studies can be carried out with a single participant or with as many as 60 or 70 participants representing multiple contexts. However, qualitative studies with more than 20 or so participants are rare, and many studies will have fewer. The qualitative researcher's time, money, participant availability, participant interest, and other factors influence the number of participants included in a research sample. Remember, in qualitative research, more participants does not necessarily mean the study or its results will be more generalizable or more useful.

Two general indicators are commonly used to determine if the selection of participants is sufficient. The first is the extent to which the selected participants represent the range of potential participants in the setting. For example, if the research setting is a school that includes kindergarten through sixth grade and the researcher includes teachers from only kindergarten and Grades 1 and 2, the selected participants do not represent those in the chosen setting. To rectify this problem, the researcher could change the focus to the lower grades or add participants at the higher grades. The second indicator is the redundancy of the information gathered from the participants. When the researcher begins to hear the same thoughts, perspectives, and responses from most or all participants, additional participants are not needed, at least for that particular problem or issue. This point is commonly known as **data saturation.**

MyLab Education **Self-Check 6.2**

MyLab Education **Application Exercise 6.3:** Evaluating Research Articles: Sampling in a Qualitative Study

MyLab Education **Application Exercise 6.4:** Selecting a Qualitative Sampling Technique

---

WRITING LIKE A RESEARCHER

Create a new folder called "sample selection" that will eventually find a home in the Method section of your journal article or thesis. Write a brief narrative that fully describes your sample in terms of demographic characteristics (e.g., age, sex, socioeconomic status, level of education). The more fully you describe your sample, the easier it will be for your readers to understand the results of your study and the degree to which they can be generalized. Write about your sampling procedures (as described in this chapter). Now is not the time to be brief—you can always revise this draft; your goal now is to provide a compelling argument for your readers.

SUMMARY

1. Sampling is the process of selecting a number of individuals for a study so that the individuals represent the larger group from which they were selected.

SAMPLING IN QUANTITATIVE RESEARCH

2. The purpose of sampling is to gain information about a larger population. A population is the group to which a researcher would like the results of a study to be generalizable.

Defining a Population

3. The population that the researcher would ideally like to generalize results to is referred to as the target population; the population that the researcher realistically selects from is referred to as the accessible population or available population.
4. The degree to which the selected sample represents the population is the degree to which the research results are generalizable to the population.

Selecting a Random Sample

5. Regardless of the specific technique used, the steps in sampling include identifying the population, determining the required sample size, and selecting the sample.

Simple Random Sampling

6. Simple random sampling is the process of selecting a sample so that all individuals in the defined population have an equal and independent chance of selection for the sample. It is the best way to obtain a representative sample, although representation of specific subgroups is not guaranteed.
7. Random sampling involves defining the population, identifying each member of the population, and selecting individuals for the sample on a completely chance basis. Usually a table of random numbers is used to select the sample.

Stratified Sampling

8. Stratified sampling is the process of strategically selecting a sample so that it guarantees

desired representation of relevant subgroups within the sample.
9. Stratified sampling can be used to select proportional or equal-size samples from each of a number of subgroups.
10. The steps in stratified sampling are similar to those in random sampling except that selection is from subgroups in the population rather than the population as a whole. In other words, random sampling is done from each subgroup.

Cluster Sampling

11. Cluster sampling is sampling in which groups, not individuals, are randomly selected. Clusters can be communities, states, school districts, and so on.
12. The steps in cluster sampling are similar to those in random sampling except that the random selection of groups (clusters) is involved. Cluster sampling often involves selection of clusters within clusters (e.g., districts in a state, then schools in a district) in a process known as multistage sampling.

Systematic Sampling

13. Systematic sampling is sampling in which every Kth individual is selected from a list of all members in the population. K is a variable determined by dividing the number of individuals on the list by the number of subjects desired for the sample.

Determining Sample Size

14. Samples in quantitative studies should be as large as possible; in general, the larger the sample, the more representative it is likely to be, and the more generalizable the results of the study will be.
15. Minimum acceptable sample sizes depend on the type of research, but there are no universally accepted minimum sample sizes.

Avoiding Sampling Error and Bias

16. Sampling error is beyond the control of the researcher and occurs as part of random selection procedures.

17. Sampling bias is systematic and is generally the fault of the researcher. A major source of bias is the use of nonrandom sampling techniques.

18. Any sampling bias present in a study should be fully described in the final research report.

Selecting a Nonrandom Sample

19. Researchers cannot always select random samples and occasionally must rely on nonrandom selection procedures.

20. When nonrandom sampling techniques are used, it is not possible to determine the probability of selection for any member of a population; in addition, it is often difficult to describe the population from which a sample was drawn and to whom results can be generalized.

21. Three types of nonrandom sampling are convenience sampling, which involves selecting whoever happens to be available; purposive sampling, which involves selecting a sample the researcher believes to be representative of a given population; and quota sampling, which involves selecting a sample based on exact numbers, or quotas, of persons of varying characteristics.

SAMPLING IN QUALITATIVE RESEARCH

22. Qualitative sampling is the process of selecting a small number of individuals (i.e.,

key informants) who will contribute to the researcher's understanding of the phenomenon under study.

Selecting Research Participants: Purposive Sampling Approaches

23. Qualitative research most often deals with small, purposive samples. The researcher's insights, gained through firsthand experience in the research setting, guide the selection of participants.

24. Qualitative sampling approaches include intensity sampling, homogeneous sampling, criterion sampling, snowball sampling, and random purposive sampling.

Determining Sample Size

25. There are no hard-and-fast numbers that represent the correct number of participants in a qualitative study. Qualitative studies can be carried out with a single participant or, when studying multiple contexts, may have as many as 60 or 70 participants.

26. Two general indicators used to determine whether a sample is of sufficient size are representativeness and redundancy of information.

PERFORMANCE CRITERIA   TASK 5

The description of the quantitative population should include its size and relevant characteristics (such as age, ability, and socioeconomic status). The qualitative context should be stated.

The procedural technique for selecting study participants should be described in detail. For example, if stratified sampling will be used, indicate on what basis population members will be stratified, how selection from subgroups will occur, and how many will be selected from each subgroup. If snowball sampling will be used, explain how and why it was chosen. For quantitative studies, describe how selected participants will be placed into treatment groups (e.g., by random assignment).

Include a summary statement that indicates the resulting sample size for each group. For example, the following statement may appear in a quantitative plan:

> There will be two groups, each with a sample size of 30; each group will include 15 participants with above-average motivation and 15 participants with below-average motivation.

A qualitative plan may include a statement such as this one:

> Six participants will be available for in-depth interviews and observations over a period of 6 months. Participants will be chosen for their knowledge of the research context and their lengthy experience in the context studied.

Any identifiable source of sampling bias (e.g., small sample sizes) should also be discussed.

An example that illustrates the quantitative performance called for by Task 5 appears in Task 5A Example. Again, the task in the example was submitted by the same student whose Task 3A and Task 4A work was presented in earlier chapters.

1

Effect of Interactive Multimedia on the Achievement of 10th-Grade Biology Students

Participants in this study will be selected from the population of 10th-grade biology students at an upper-middle-class all-girl Catholic high school in Miami, Florida. The student population is multicultural, reflecting the diverse ethnic groups in Dade County. The student body is composed of approximately 90% Hispanic students from a variety of Latin American backgrounds, the major one being Cuban; 9% Caucasian non-Hispanic students; and 1% African American students. The population is anticipated to contain approximately 200 biology students.

Prior to the beginning of the school year, before students have been scheduled, 60 students will be randomly selected (using a table of random numbers) and randomly assigned to 2 classes of 30 each; 30 is the normal class size. One of the classes will be randomly chosen to receive IMM instruction and the other will not.

CHAPTER SEVEN

Selecting Measuring Instruments

Image Entertainment/Everett Collection

Bride of Frankenstein, 1935

"Regardless of the type of research you conduct,
you must collect data." (p. 167)

LEARNING OUTCOMES

After reading Chapter 7, you should be able to do the following:

7.1 State the relation between a construct and a variable.

7.2 Distinguish among categories of variables (e.g., categorical and quantitative; dependent and independent) and the scales to measure them (e.g., nominal, ordinal, interval, and ratio).

7.3 Describe the characteristics of measuring instruments used to collect data in qualitative and quantitative research studies.

7.4 Describe the types of measuring instruments used to collect data in qualitative and quantitative studies.

7.5 Describe the methods used to determine the reliability and validity of various instruments.

7.6 Identify useful sources of information about specific tests and provide strategies for test selection, construction, and administration.

The chapter learning outcomes form the basis for the following task, which requires you to identify and select instruments appropriate for the research plan you developed in the previous chapters.

TASK 6

For a quantitative study, you have stated a problem to investigate, formulated one or more hypotheses, and described a sample (**Tasks 3 and 5A**). Now describe three instruments appropriate for collecting data pertinent to your study. In the description of each instrument, include the following:

1. Name, publisher, and cost
2. A brief description of the purpose of the instrument
3. Validity and reliability data
4. The group for whom the instrument is intended
5. Administration requirements
6. Information on scoring and interpretation
7. Reviewers' overall impressions

On the basis of this information, indicate which instrument is most appropriate for your quantitative study, and why (see Performance Criteria, p. 197).

Whether you are testing hypotheses or seeking understanding, you must decide on a method or methods to collect your data. In many cases, this is a matter of selecting the best existing instrument. Sometimes, however, you may have to develop your own instrument for data collection. At other times, you will become your own instrument by observing, discussing, and interacting with research participants. The major point to remember is that you should select or construct an approach that will provide pertinent data relevant to the problem of your study.

In this chapter, we discuss several factors to consider when selecting a method or instrument for quantitative and for qualitative studies. To develop your understanding of the concepts presented in this chapter, we refer to the following vignette of Big Pine School District (BPSD) as a way to illustrate the kinds of decisions that need to be made when selecting measuring instruments for research conducted in school settings.

Vignette: Big Pine School District

BPSD is made up of seven schools (i.e., five elementary schools, one middle school, and one high school) and provides a comprehensive education for 3,200 students from prekindergarten through 12th grade. The district employs approximately 330 full-time teachers along with school support staff, principals, and assistant principals. The district is in compliance with the Every Student Succeeds Act (ESSA) requirements including all testing (Smarter Balanced) required to measure students' academic progress. The relationship between the district and the local university provides students and teachers at the schools with many enriched learning opportunities, as well as placements for student-teachers from the teacher education program. BPSD and the university also collaborate to offer a university-based preschool center.

CONSTRUCTS

Regardless of the type of research you conduct, you must collect data. **Data** are the pieces of information you collect and use to examine your problem, hypotheses, or observations. The scientific method is based on the collection, analysis, and interpretation of data. Before you can collect data, however, you must determine what kind of data to collect. To make this determination, you must understand the relations among constructs, variables, and instruments.

A **construct** is an abstraction that cannot be observed directly; it is a concept invented to explain behavior. Examples of educational constructs are intelligence, personality, teacher effectiveness, creativity, ability, achievement, and motivation. To be measurable, constructs must be operationally defined—that is, defined in terms of processes or operations that can be observed and measured. To measure a construct, it is necessary to identify the scores or values it can assume. For example, the construct "personality" can be made measurable by defining two personality types, introverts and extroverts, as measured by scores on a 30-item questionnaire, with a high score indicating a more introverted personality and a low score indicating a more extroverted personality. Similarly, the construct "teacher effectiveness" may be operationally defined by observing a teacher in action and judging effectiveness based on four levels: unsatisfactory, marginal, adequate, and excellent. When constructs are operationally defined, they become variables.

VARIABLES

Earlier we defined *variable* as a placeholder that can assume any one of a range of values. A variable must be able to take on at least two values or scores. Variables are an integral part of all our research studies. Gender, ethnicity, socioeconomic status (SES), test scores, age, and teacher experience are all variables; people differ on these characteristics. Can you identify the variables in the following research problems and hypotheses?

1. Is there a relation between middle school students' grades and their self-confidence in science and math?
2. What do high school principals consider to be the most pressing administrative problems they face?
3. Do students learn more from a new social studies program than from the previous one?
4. What is the relationship between parent participation and student learning outcomes in early elementary students?
5. How do the first 5 weeks of school in Ms. Foley's classroom influence student activities and interactions in succeeding months?

6. What is the relationship between years of teaching experience and the likelihood of teachers being willing to take on new courses?
7. How do ninth-grade boys and girls differ in their attitudes toward science?

The variables in these examples are as follows: (1) grades and self-confidence, (2) administrative problems, (3) learning and the new social studies program (note that the social studies program has two forms—new and old—and thus is also a variable), (4) parent participation and learning outcomes, (5) student activities and student interactions, (6) years teaching and interest in taking new courses, and (7) gender and attitudes toward science.

There are many different approaches to measuring a variable and many instruments for doing so (in educational research, an **instrument** is a tool used to collect data). For example, to measure sixth-grade students' mathematics achievement, we can choose from a number of existing measuring instruments, such as the Stanford Achievement Test or the Iowa Tests of Basic Skills. We can also use a teacher-made test to measure math achievement. Information about the instruments should be included in the procedures section of the research plan.

Variables themselves differ in many ways. For example, they can be identified as categorical or noncategorical, as quantitative or qualitative, or as dependent or independent. The following sections discuss these distinctions in greater detail.

Measurement Scales and Variables

Researchers use four types of measurement scales: nominal, ordinal, interval, and ratio scales. A **measurement scale** is a system for organizing data so that it may be inspected, analyzed, and interpreted. In other words, the scale is the instrument used to provide the range of values or scores for each variable. It is important to know which type of scale is represented in your data because, as we discuss in later chapters, different scales require different methods of statistical analysis.

Table 7.1 summarizes the measurement scales and provides examples of each. In general, a nominal scale measures nominal variables, an ordinal scale measures ordinal variables, and so on, as discussed in the following subsections.

TABLE 7.1 • Comparison of measurement scales

Scale	Description	Examples
Nominal	Categorical	Northerners, Southerners; Republicans, Democrats; brown eyed, blue eyed; males, females; public, private; gifted students, average-achieving students
Ordinal	Rank order, unequal units	Scores of 5, 6, 10 are equal to scores of 1, 2, 3
Interval	Rank order and interval units but no zero point	A score of 10 and a score of 30 have the same degree of difference as a score of 70 and a score of 90
Ratio	Rank order, intervals, and a defined zero point	Average number of calories consumed per day by male and female. Has a defined zero point and 2000 calories is twice as many as 1000

Nominal Variables

A **nominal variable** is also called a *categorical variable* because the values include two or more named categories (i.e., the word *nominal* comes from the Latin word for "name"). Nominal variables include sex (e.g., female, male), employment status (e.g., full-time, part-time, unemployed), marital status (e.g., married, divorced, single), and type of school (e.g., public, private, charter). For identification purposes, nominal variables are often represented by numbers. For example, the category "male" may be represented by the number 1 and "female" by the number 2. It is critically important to understand that such numbering of nominal variables does not indicate that one category is higher or better than another. That is, representing male with a 1 and female with a 2 does not indicate that males are lower or worse than females or that males are at a higher rank than females. The numbers are only labels for the groups. To avoid such confusion, it is often best to label the levels of nominal variables with names or letters (A, B, C, etc.).

Ordinal Variables

An **ordinal variable** not only classifies persons or objects, it also ranks them according to some criteria. The numerical value of ordinal scales indicates a ranking in order from highest to lowest or from most

to least. For example, if 50 students were placed into five reading groups, with each group representing a different reading ability, a student in reading group 1 would be in the highest-achieving group and a student in reading group 5 would be in the lowest-achieving group. Rankings make it possible to make comparisons, for example, to say that one student is achieving at a higher level than another student. Class rank is another example of an ordinal variable. In this case, higher ranked students perform better academically than lower ranked students.

Although ordinal variables permit us to describe performance as higher, lower, better, or worse, they do not indicate how much higher one person performed compared to another. In other words, intervals between ranks are not equal; the difference between rank 1 and rank 2 is not necessarily the same as the difference between rank 2 and rank 3. Consider the following example of ordinal data from BPSD where the five elementary schools were ranked based on student test scores in math (as measured by the statewide assessments):

Rank	School	Average Test Score
1	Pinecrest	84
2	Madrone	81
3	Spruce	77
4	Cedar	75
5	Poison Oak	70

The difference in average test score between rank 1 and rank 2 is 3 points; the difference between rank 2 and rank 3 is 4 points, the difference between rank 3 and rank 4 is 2 points, and the difference between rank 4 and rank 5 is 5 points. Thus, the ordinal data, although indicating that schools can be ranked in order from highest to lowest according to test score performance, does not tell us exactly how much better one school performed than another. Although an ordinal variable can be used to rank schools or students, it does not have equal scale intervals. This characteristic limits the statistical methods used to analyze ordinal variables.

Interval Variables

An **interval variable** also has values that are ranked in order, but its values also represent equal intervals. Scores on most tests used in educational research, such as achievement, aptitude, motivation, and attitude tests, are treated as interval variables. When variables have equal intervals, it is assumed that the difference between a score of 30 and a score of 40 is essentially the same as the difference between a score of 50 and a score of 60, and the difference between 81 and 82 is the same as the difference between 82 and 83. Interval scales, however, do not have a true zero point. Thus, if Roland's science achievement test score is 0 on an interval scale of 0 to 100, his score does not indicate the total absence of science knowledge. Nor does Gianna's score of 100 indicate complete mastery. Without a true zero point, we can say that a test score of 90 is 45 points higher than a score of 45, but we cannot say that a person scoring 90 knows twice as much as a person scoring 45. Variables that have, or are treated as having equal intervals have the advantage of utilizing a wide array of statistical data analysis methods.

Ratio Variables

A **ratio variable** has equal intervals in rank order and, in addition, its measurement scale has a true zero point. Height, weight, time, distance, and speed are examples of ratio scales. The concept of "no calories" for example, is a meaningful one. Because of the true zero point, we can say that the difference between an average consumption of 2,000 calories is twice as much as an average consumption of 1,000 calories. As another example, the total number of correct items on a test can be measured on a ratio scale; that is, a student can get zero items correct and a student with 20 items correct has twice as many correct answers as a student with 10 items correct.

Quantitative and Qualitative Variables

Quantitative variables exist on a numerical continuum that ranges from low to high, or less to more. Ordinal, interval, and ratio variables are all quantitative variables because they describe performance in quantitative terms. Examples are test scores, heights, speed, age, and class size.

Nominal variables do not provide quantitative information about how people or objects differ. They provide information about qualitative differences only. Nominal variables permit persons or things that represent different qualities (e.g., eye color, religion, gender, political party) but not different quantities.

Dependent and Independent Variables

As discussed earlier, the **dependent variable** in an experimental study is the variable hypothesized to depend on or to be caused or impacted by another variable, the **independent variable.** Recall this research problem from Chapter 1:

> Is there an effect of reinforcement on students' attitudes toward school?

You probably had little trouble identifying *attitudes toward school* as a variable. Because reinforcement is hypothesized to affect students' attitudes toward school, "attitudes toward school" is the dependent variable in this example. It is also a quantitative variable because it is likely measured on a numerical scale (e.g., strongly favorable toward school could be assigned a higher number, whereas strongly unfavorable could be assigned a lower one).

If the research question is rephrased as, "Do positive and negative reinforcement affect elementary students' attitudes toward school?" it is easy to see a second variable—*type of reinforcement*—which contains two levels, positive and negative. Because it has two named categories as its levels, it is a categorical variable. And because it is manipulated by the researcher (i.e., the researcher selected the two types of reinforcement and then assigned participants to experience one or the other), type of reinforcement is the independent variable. The independent variable in a research study is sometimes called the *experimental variable,* the *manipulated variable,* the *cause,* or the *treatment variable,* but regardless of the label, the independent variable is always the hypothesized cause of the dependent variable (also called the *criterion variable,* the *effect,* the *outcome,* or the *posttest*). Independent variables are primarily used in experimental research studies (and grouping variables are used in similar ways in causal–comparative studies).

It is important to remember that the independent variable must have at least two levels or conditions of treatments. Thus, neither positive nor negative reinforcement is a variable by itself. The independent variable is type of reinforcement; positive reinforcement and negative reinforcement are the two levels of the variable. Try to identify the independent and dependent variables in this research hypothesis:

> Teachers who participated in the new professional development program are less likely to express approval of new teaching strategies than teachers who did not.

MyLab Education **Self-Check 7.1**

MyLab Education **Self-Check 7.2**

MyLab Education **Application Exercise 7.1:**
Distinguishing Between Constructs and Variables

MyLab Education **Application Exercise 7.2:**
Identifying Measurement Scales

CHARACTERISTICS OF MEASURING INSTRUMENTS

In this section, we examine the range of measuring instruments used to collect data in qualitative and quantitative research studies. There are three major ways to collect research data:

1. Administer a standardized instrument.
2. Administer a self-developed instrument.
3. Record naturally occurring or already available data (e.g., make observations in a classroom or record existing grade point averages).

This chapter is concerned with published, standardized tests and teacher-prepared tests.

Qualitative studies, such as ethnographic studies, are often built around the idea that the researcher will work with naturally occurring or existing data. Although using naturally occurring or existing data requires a minimum of effort and sounds very attractive, existing data are appropriate for very few qualitative studies and, even when appropriate, available data can lead to problems. For example, two different teachers may give the same grade for different reasons (e.g., A for effort, A for achievement). The grades, then, do not necessarily represent the same standard of behavior, and conclusions based on the data may not be trustworthy. However, developing a new, high-quality instrument to collect data also has drawbacks: It requires considerable effort and skill and greatly increases the total time needed to conduct the study. At a minimum, you would need a course in measurement to gain the skills needed for proper instrument development. At times, however, constructing your own instrument will be necessary, especially if your research problem and concepts are original or not widely researched.

Selecting an appropriate instrument that is already standardized invariably takes less time than developing an instrument yourself. A standardized instrument is one that is administered, scored, and interpreted in the same way no matter where or when it is used. Standardized instruments tend to be developed by experts, who possess both knowledge of the content area and appropriate test construction skills. From a research point of view, an additional advantage of using a standardized instrument is that results from different studies using the same instrument can be compared.

Thousands of published and standardized instruments are available and yield a variety of data for a variety of variables. Major areas for which numerous measuring instruments have been developed include achievement, personality, attitude, interest, and aptitude. Each area can, in turn, be further divided into many subcategories. Personality instruments, for example, can be classified as objective or projective, as discussed later in this chapter. Choosing an instrument for a particular research purpose involves identifying and selecting the most appropriate instrument from among alternatives. To choose intelligently, researchers must be familiar with a variety of instruments and know the criteria they should apply in selecting the best alternatives. Descriptions of tests and objective reviews can be found in publications including *Tests in Print IX* (2016) and the *Mental Measurements Yearbook* (20th ed., 2017).

Instrument Terminology

Given the array of instruments available in educational research, it is important to know some of the basic terminology used to describe them. We start with the terms *test, assessment,* and *measurement.*

A **test** is a formal, systematic, paper-and-pencil or online procedure for gathering information about peoples' cognitive, social, behavioral, and affective characteristics (a **cognitive characteristic** is a mental characteristic related to intellect, such as achievement; an **affective characteristic** is a mental characteristic related to emotion, such as attitude or feeling). Tests typically produce numerical scores. A **standardized test** is one that is administered, scored, and interpreted in the same way no matter where or when it is used. For example, the SAT, ACT, Iowa Tests of Basic Skills, Stanford Achievement Test, and other nationally used tests have been crafted to ensure that all test takers experience the same conditions when taking them. Such standardization allows comparisons among test takers from across the nation. You may remember taking national standardized achievement tests in school. They probably had a stop sign every few pages that warned, "Stop! Do not turn the page until instructed." These stops are to ensure that all test takers have the same amount of time for each part of the test.

Assessment is a broad term that encompasses the entire process of collecting, synthesizing, and interpreting information, whether formal or informal, numerical or textual. Tests are a subset of assessment, as are observations and interviews.

Measurement is the process of quantifying or scoring performance on an assessment instrument. Measurement occurs after data are collected.

Quantitative and Qualitative Data Collection Methods

Researchers typically use paper-and-pencil or online methods, observations, or interviews to collect data. Observation and interviewing are used predominantly by qualitative researchers (and are discussed in detail in Chapter 20), whereas paper-and-pencil and online methods are favored by quantitative researchers.

Paper-and-pencil and online methods are divided into two general categories: selection (close-ended) and supply (open-ended). With *selection methods* (or *selection items* on an instrument), the test taker has to select from among a set of given answers; these methods include multiple-choice, true/false, and matching questions. In *supply methods* (or *supply items*), the test taker has to supply an answer; supply items include questions that require the responder to fill in the blank or write a short answer or essay.

Current emphasis on supply methods in schools has spawned the rise of so-called performance assessments. A **performance assessment,** also known as an *authentic assessment* or *alternative assessment*, is a type of assessment that emphasizes a student process (e.g., lab demonstration, debate, oral speech, or dramatic performance) or product (e.g., an essay, a science fair project, or a research report). By asking students to do or create something, educators seek to assess tasks more complex than memorization. If a researcher is conducting research in schools, it is likely that performance assessments are used to collect data.

Interpreting Instrument Data

Data from an assessment can be reported and interpreted in various ways. A **raw score** is the number or point value of items a person answered correctly on an assessment. For example, if a student at Pinecrest Elementary achieved 78 of 100 points on a science test, the student's raw score is 78. In most quantitative research, raw scores are the basic (unanalyzed) data. By themselves, however, raw scores don't give us much information. To learn more, we must put the scores into a context. In other words, we must interpret the scores in some way. Norm-referenced, criterion-referenced, and self-referenced scoring approaches represent three ways of interpreting performance on tests and measures.

In **norm-referenced scoring,** a student's performance on an assessment is compared to the performance of others. For example, if we ask how well a Pinecrest Elementary student performed in science compared to other students in the same grade across the nation, we are asking for norm-referenced information. The interpretation of the student's score of 78 is based on how the student performed compared to the class or a national group of students in the same grade. Norm-referenced scoring is also called *grading on the curve*, where the curve is a bell-shaped distribution of the percentages of students who receive each grade. Standardized tests and assessments frequently report norm-referenced scores in the form of derived scores such as standard scores and *percentile ranks* (discussed in detail in Chapter 18).

In **criterion-referenced scoring,** an individual's performance on an assessment is compared to a predetermined, external standard rather than to the performance of others. For example, a teacher may say that test scores of 90 to 100 are an A, scores of 80 to 89 are a B, scores of 70 to 79 are a C, and so on. A student's score is compared to the preestablished performance levels—to preestablished *criteria*—to determine the grade. Anyone who scores between 90 and 100 will get an A. If no one scores between 90 and 100, no one will get an A. If all students score between 90 and 100, they all will get A's. This scenario could not happen in norm-referenced scoring, which requires that different scores, even very close ones, get different grades.

Self-referenced scoring approaches involve measuring how an individual student's performance on a single assessment changes over time. Student performances at different times are compared to determine improvement or decline.

> MyLab Education **Self-Check 7.3**
>
> MyLab Education **Application Exercise 7.3:** Evaluating Research Articles: Evaluating the Measuring Instruments Used in a Quantitative Study

TYPES OF MEASURING INSTRUMENTS

Many different kinds of tests are available, and there are many different ways to classify them. The *Mental Measurements Yearbook (MMY)*, published by the Buros Institute of Mental Measurements (buros.org/mental-measurements-yearbook), is a major source of test information for educational researchers. The yearbook, which can be found in most large libraries, provides information and reviews of more than 3,000 published tests in various school subject areas (such as English, mathematics, and reading) as well as personality, intelligence, aptitude, speech and hearing, and vocational tests. Of all the types of measuring instruments available, cognitive, affective, and projective tests are the most commonly used in educational research.

Cognitive Tests

A **cognitive test** measures intellectual processes, such as thinking, memorizing, problem solving, analyzing, reasoning, and applying information. Most tests that school pupils take are cognitive achievement tests.

Achievement Tests

An **achievement test** measures an individual's current proficiency in given areas of knowledge or skill. Typically administered in school settings, achievement tests are designed to provide information about how well test takers have learned the material introduced in school. The tests are standardized, and an individual's performance is usually determined by comparing it to the norm, the performance of a national group of students in the individual's grade or age level who took the same test. Thus, these tests can provide comparisons of a given student to similar students nationally.

Standardized achievement tests typically cover a number of different curriculum areas, such as reading, vocabulary, language, and mathematics. A standardized test that measures achievement in several curriculum areas is called a *test battery,* and the assessment of each area is done with a *subtest.* The California Achievement Test, Stanford Achievement Tests, TerraNova, and the Iowa Tests of Basic Skills are examples of cognitive achievement tests commonly used in U.S. classrooms. Depending on the number of subtests and other factors, standardized achievement batteries can take from 1 to 5 hours to complete.

Some achievement tests, such as the Gates-MacGinitie Reading Tests, focus on achievement in a single subject area. Single-subject tests are sometimes used as diagnostic tests. A **diagnostic test** yields multiple scores to facilitate identification of a student's weak and strong areas within the subject area. The Stanford Diagnostic Reading Test and the Key Math Diagnostic Inventory of Essential Mathematics Test are examples of widely used diagnostic achievement instruments.

Aptitude Tests

Tests of general aptitude are also referred to as *scholastic aptitude tests* and *tests of general mental ability.* Unlike an achievement test, which is used to assess what individuals have learned, an **aptitude test** is commonly used to predict how well an individual is likely to perform in a future situation. Aptitude tests are standardized and are often administered as part of a school testing program; they are also used extensively in job hiring.

Aptitude tests usually include cognitive measures, but ones that are not normally part of classroom tests. For example, many require that participants respond to a variety of verbal and nonverbal tasks intended to measure the individual's ability to apply knowledge and solve problems. Such tests often yield three scores: an overall score, a verbal score, and a quantitative score.

Aptitude tests can be administered to groups, or they can be individually administered. A commonly used group-administered battery is the Columbia Mental Maturity Scale (CMMS). The CMMS has six versions and can be administered to school-age children, college students, and adults. It includes 12 subtests representing five aptitude factors: logical reasoning, spatial relations, numerical reasoning, verbal concepts, and memory. Another frequently administered group aptitude test is the Otis-Lennon School Ability Test, which has versions designed for children in grades K–12. The Otis-Lennon School Ability Test measures four factors: verbal comprehension, verbal reasoning, figurative reasoning, and quantitative reasoning. The Differential Aptitude Tests is another battery that includes tests of space relations, mechanical reasoning, and clerical speed and accuracy, among other areas, and is designed to predict success in various job areas.

Individually administered tests are preferred for some test takers (e.g., very young children or students with disabilities). Probably the most well known of the individually administered tests are the Stanford-Binet Intelligence Scale and the Wechsler scales. The Stanford-Binet, Fourth Edition (SB-IV), is appropriate for young children and adults. Wechsler scales are available to measure intelligence: the Wechsler Preschool and Primary Scale of Intelligence, Third Edition (WPPSI–III), is appropriate for children age 2 years through 7 years; the Wechsler Intelligence Scale for Children, Fifth Edition (WISC–V), is designed for children age 6 years through 17 years; and the Wechsler Adult Intelligence Scale, Fifth Edition (WAIS–V), is given to older adolescents and adults. As an example, the WISC is a cognitive abilities test that includes verbal tests (e.g., general information, vocabulary) and performance tests (e.g., picture completion, object assembly). Other commonly used individually administered cognitive abilities tests are the McCarthy Scales of Children's Abilities, the Wechsler Ach Test, and the Woodcock-Johnson Test.

Affective Tests

An **affective test** is an assessment designed to measure affective characteristics—mental characteristics related to emotions including attitudes, interests, and values. Affective tests are often used in educational research and exist in many different formats. Most are objective; that is, they are self-report measures in which the test taker responds to a series of questions or statements about him- or herself. For example, a question may be "Which would you prefer, reading a book or playing basketball?" Self-report tests are frequently used in survey studies (e.g., to describe the personality characteristics of various groups, such as high school dropouts), correlational studies (e.g., to determine relations among various personality traits and other variables, such as achievement), and causal–comparative or experimental studies (e.g., to investigate the comparative effectiveness of different instructional methods for different personality types).

Instruments that examine values, attitudes, interests, and personality characteristics tap the test takers' emotions, perceptions, and beliefs. *Values* are deeply held beliefs about ideas, persons, or objects. For example, we may value our free time, our special friendships, or a vase given by our great-grandmother. *Attitudes* indicate our characteristic ways of thinking about certain situations or ideas; they reflect our tendencies to accept or reject groups, ideas, or objects. For example, Greg's attitude toward Brussels sprouts is much more favorable than his attitude toward green beans (this attitude puts Greg in a distinct minority). *Interests* indicate the degree to which we seek out or desire to participate in particular activities, objects, and ideas. *Personality* is composed of a number of characteristics, traits, or dispositions that represent a person's typical demeanor or approach to life. It describes what we typically think and do across a variety of life circumstances.

Attitude Scales

An **attitude scale** is an instrument that measures what an individual believes, perceives, or feels about self, others, activities, institutions, or situations. Five basic types of scales are used to measure attitudes: Likert scales, semantic differential scales, rating scales, Thurstone scales, and Guttman scales. The first three are frequently used in educational research.

Likert Scales. A **Likert scale** requires an individual to respond to a series of statements by indicating whether he or she strongly agrees (SA), agrees (A), is undecided (U), disagrees (D), or strongly disagrees (SD). Each response is assigned a point value, and an individual's score is determined by adding the point values of all the statements. For example, the following point values are typically assigned to positive statements: SA = 5, A = 4, U = 3, D = 2, SD = 1. An example of a positive statement is "Short people are entitled to the same job opportunities as tall people." A score of 5 or 4 on this item indicates a positive attitude toward equal opportunity for short people. A high total score across all items on the test would be indicative of an overall positive attitude. For negative statements, the point values would be reversed—that is, SA = 1, A = 2, U = 3, D = 4, and SD = 5. An example of a negative statement is "Short people are not entitled to the same job opportunities as tall people." On this item, scores should be reversed; "disagree" or "strongly disagree" indicate a positive attitude toward opportunities for short people.

Semantic Differential Scales. **A semantic differential scale** requires an individual to indicate his or her attitude about a problem (e.g., property taxes) by selecting a position on a continuum that ranges from one bipolar adjective (e.g., fair) to another (e.g., unfair). Each position on the continuum has an associated score value. For example, a scale concerning attitudes toward property taxes may include the following items and values:

Necessary						Unnecessary
——	——	——	——	——	——	——
3	2	1	0	−1	−2	−3
Fair						Unfair
——	——	——	——	——	——	——
3	2	1	0	−1	−2	−3
Better						Worse
——	——	——	——	——	——	——
3	2	1	0	−1	−2	−3

This scale is typical of semantic differential scales, which usually have 5 to 7 intervals, with a neutral attitude assigned a score value of 0. A person who checks the first interval (i.e., a score of 3) on each of these items has a very positive attitude toward property taxes. Totaling the score values for all items yields an overall score. Usually, summed scores (i.e., interval data) are used in statistical data analysis.

Rating Scales. **A rating scale** may also be used to measure a respondent's attitudes toward self, others, activities, institutions, or situations. One common self-reporting rating scale used in schools to measure students' behavior is The Behavior Assessment System for Children-3. Another form of rating scale provides descriptions of performance or preference and requires the individual to check the most appropriate description.

Select the choice that best describes your actions in the first 5 minutes of the classes you teach.

_____ State lesson objectives and overview at the start of the lesson.

_____ State lesson objectives but no overview at the start of the lesson.

_____ Don't state objectives or give overview at the start of the lesson.

A second type of rating scale asks the individual to rate performance or preference using a numerical scale similar to a Likert scale.

Circle the number that best describes the degree to which you state lesson objectives and give an overview before teaching a lesson.

5 = always
4 = almost always
3 = about half the time
2 = rarely
1 = never

1   2   3   4   5

Likert, semantic differential, and rating scales are similar, requiring the respondent to self-report along a continuum of choices. However, in certain situations—such as observing performance or judging teaching competence—Likert, semantic differential, and rating scales can be used by others (e.g., a researcher, a principal, a colleague) to collect information about study participants. For example, in some studies it may be best to have the principal, rather than the teacher, use a Likert, semantic differential, or rating scale to collect data about that teacher.

Thurstone and Guttman Scales. A *Thurstone scale* requires participants to select from a list of statements that represent different points of view on a problem. Each item has an associated point value between 1 and 11; point values for each item are determined by averaging the values of the items assigned by a number of judges. An individual's attitude score is the average point value of all the statements checked by that individual. A *Guttman scale* also requires respondents to agree or disagree with a number of statements; it is then used to determine whether an attitude is *unidimensional*. An attitude is unidimensional if it produces a cumulative scale in which an individual who agrees with a given statement also agrees with all related preceding statements. For example, if you agree with Statement 3, you also agree with Statements 2 and 1.

Interest Inventories

An *interest inventory* requires participants to indicate personal likes and dislikes, such as the kinds of activities they prefer. The respondent's pattern of interest is compared to the interest patterns of others. For example, for an occupational interest inventory, responses are compared to those typical of successful persons in various occupational fields. Interest inventories are widely used in this way to suggest the fields in which respondents may be best suited and thus, most comfortable and successful.

Two frequently used interest inventories are the Strong-Campbell Interest Inventory and the Kuder Preference Record—Vocational. The Strong-Campbell Interest Inventory examines areas of interest in occupations, school subjects, activities, leisure activities, and day-to-day interactions with various types of people. Test takers are presented with many problems related to these five areas and are asked to indicate whether they like (L), dislike (D), or are indifferent (I) to each problem. The second part of the Strong-Campbell inventory consists of a choice between two options such as "dealing with people" or "dealing with things" and a number of self-descriptive statements that the individual responds to by choosing yes (like me), no (not like me), or ? (not sure). The Kuder Occupational Interest Survey addresses 10 broad categories of interest: outdoor, mechanical, computational, scientific, persuasive, artistic, literary, musical, social service, and clerical. Individuals are presented with three choices related to these categories and must select the one they most like and the one

they least like. For example, an individual may be presented with this item:

> Would you rather: dig a hole, read a book, or draw a picture? Choose the one that you most would like to do and the one that you least would like to do.

The Strong-Campbell and the Kuder are both self-report instruments that provide information about a person's interests. Scoring the instruments requires sending data to the testing companies who produce them for computer analysis. You cannot score them yourself. Information on the Strong-Campbell, the Kuder, and other attitudinal instruments may be found in the *Mental Measurements Yearbook*.

Personality Inventories

A *personality inventory* includes questions or statements that describe behaviors characteristic of certain personality traits. Respondents indicate whether or to what degree each statement describes them. Some inventories are presented as checklists; respondents simply check items they feel characterize them. An individual's score is based on the number of responses characteristic of the trait being measured. An introvert, for example, would be expected to respond yes to the statement "Reading is one of my favorite pastimes," and no to the statement "I love large parties." Personality inventories may measure only one trait or many traits.

General personality inventories frequently used in educational research studies include the Personality Adjective Checklist, California Psychological Inventory, Minnesota Multiphasic Personality Inventory, Mooney Problem Checklist, Myers-Briggs Type Indicator, and the Sixteen Personality Factors Questionnaire. The Minnesota Multiphasic Personality Inventory (MMPI-2) alone has been utilized in hundreds of educational research studies. Its items were originally selected on the basis of response differences between psychiatric and nonpsychiatric patients. The MMPI measures many personality traits, such as depression, paranoia, schizophrenia, and social introversion. It contains more than 370 items to which a test taker responds true (of me), false (of me), or cannot say. It also has nearly 200 items that form additional scales for anxiety, ego strength, anger, repression, and alcoholism, among others.

General personality instruments based on self-report, such as the MMPI, are complex and require a substantial amount of psychological and measurement knowledge to score and interpret. The publishers of these instruments require a range of qualification experiences, including completion of graduate level training courses, to be allowed to purchase these materials. Beginning researchers should avoid their use unless they have more than a passing knowledge of these areas.

Problems with Self-Report Instruments

Self-report instruments such as attitude, interest, values, and personality scales have notable limits. The researcher can never be sure that individuals are expressing their true attitudes, interests, values, or personalities. A common problem with studies that use self-report instruments is the existence of a **response set,** the tendency of an individual to respond in a particular ways to the items on the instruments. One common response set occurs when individuals select responses that are believed to be the most socially acceptable, even if they are not necessarily characteristic of the respondents themselves. Another form of a response set is when a test taker consistently responds yes, agree, or true to items because he or she believes that is what the researcher desires (also referred to as "faking good" behavior). Because scores are meaningful only to the degree that respondents are honest and select choices that truly characterize them, every effort should be made to increase honesty of response by giving appropriate directions to those completing the instruments. One strategy to overcome the problem of response sets is to allow participants to respond anonymously. It should be noted that most of these scales have built-in validity checks to identify response inconsistency.

Both affective and cognitive instruments are also subject to instrument **bias,** which results in distortion of research data that renders the data suspect or invalid. Bias is present when respondents' characteristics—such as ethnicity, race, gender, language, or religious orientation—impact or distort their performance or responses. For example, low scores on reading tests by students who speak little English or nonstandard forms of English are probably due in large part to language disadvantages, not reading difficulties. For these students, test performance means something different than it does for English-fluent students who took the same test. Similarly, if one's culture discourages competition, making eye contact, or speaking out, the responses on self-report instruments can differ according to cultural background, not personality, values, attitudes, or interests. These issues need to be recognized in selecting and interpreting the results of both cognitive and affective instruments.

Projective Tests

Projective tests were developed in part to eliminate some of the problems inherent in the use of self-report and forced-choice measures. Projective tests utilize ambiguous content, which is not obvious to respondents. Such tests are called projective because respondents project their feelings or thoughts onto an ambiguous stimulus. The classic example of a projective test is the Rorschach Inkblot Test. Respondents are shown a picture of an inkblot and are asked to describe what they see in it. The inkblot is really just that—an inkblot made by putting a dab of ink on a paper and folding the paper in half. There are no right or wrong answers to the question "What do you see in the inkblot?" (It's only an inkblot—honest.) The test taker's descriptions of such blots are believed to be projections of his or her feelings, attitudes, or personality, which the administrator interprets. Because the purpose of the test is not clear to respondents, conscious dishonesty in responding is reduced.

The most commonly used projective technique is the method of association. Presented with a stimulus such as a picture, inkblot, or word, participants respond with a reaction or interpretation. Word-association tests are probably the most well known of the association techniques. (How many movie psychiatrists deliver the line, "I'll say a word and you tell me the first thing that comes to your mind?") Similarly, in the Thematic Apperception Test, the individual is shown a series of pictures and is asked to tell a story about what is happening in each picture.

In the past, all projective tests were required to be administered individually. There have been some recent efforts, however, to develop group projective tests. One such test is the Holtzman Inkblot Technique, which is intended to measure the same variables as the Rorschach Test. There are a number of other projective tests such as Sentence Completion,

Draw-A-Person, and House-Tree-Person tests that are more commonly used in schools. However, the use of these tests is also called in to question on the basis of lack of reliability and validity data.

From the preceding discussion, it should not be a surprise that projective tests are used mainly by clinical psychologists and very infrequently by educational researchers. Administering, scoring, and interpreting projective tests require lengthy and specialized training. Because of the training required, projective testing is not recommended for beginning researchers.

There are other types and formats of measuring instruments beyond those discussed here. The intent of this section is to provide an overview of types of tests, formats for gathering data, scoring methods, interpretation strategies, and limitations. To find more information about the specific tests described in this chapter and many other tests we have not described, refer to the *Mental Measurement Yearbook*.

MyLab Education **Self-Check 7.4**

MyLab Education **Application Exercise 7.4:** Searching for Instruments

---

CRITERIA FOR GOOD MEASURING INSTRUMENTS

If researchers' interpretations of data are to be valuable, the measuring instruments used to collect those data must be both valid and reliable. The following sections give an overview of both validity and reliability. More specific information on these problems and on testing in general can be found in the *Standards for Educational and Psychological Testing*.[1]

Validity of Measuring Instruments

Validity refers to the degree to which a test measures what it is supposed to measure and thus permits appropriate interpretation of scores. Validity is therefore critically important when considering measuring instruments. When we test, we test for

a purpose, and our measurement tools must help us achieve that purpose. For example, in Big Pine School District, the curriculum director may want to conduct an experimental study to compare learning for science students taught by method A (e.g., hands-on constructivist learning) and learning for those taught by method B (e.g., textbook or rote learning). A key question for these and other such test users is "Does this test or instrument permit the curriculum director to select the best teaching method?"

Validity is important in all forms of research and in all types of tests and measures. It is best thought of in terms of degree: highly valid, moderately valid, and generally invalid. Validation begins with an understanding of the interpretation(s) to be made from the selected tests or instruments. It then requires the collection of sources of evidence to support the desired interpretation.

In some situations, a test or instrument is used for several different purposes and thus must be validated for each. For example, at Big Pine High School, a chemistry achievement test may be used to assess students' end-of-year chemistry learning, to predict students' future performance in science courses, and even to select students for advanced placement chemistry. Because each use calls for a different interpretation of the chemistry test scores, each requires its own validation. Further, the same test may be given to groups of respondents with significant differences (e.g., one group who has studied the test material and one who has not); the differences may or may not have been considered when the test was developed. Validity is specific to the interpretation being made and to the group being tested. In other words, we cannot simply say, "This test is valid." Rather, we must say, "This test is valid for this particular interpretation and this particular group."

Researchers generally discuss four types of test validity: content validity, criterion-related validity, construct validity, and consequential validity. They are viewed as interrelated, not independent, aspects of validity. Table 7.2 summarizes the four forms of validity.

Content Validity

Content validity is the degree to which a test measures an intended content area. Content validity requires both item validity and sampling validity. **Item validity** is concerned with whether the

---

[1] *Standards for Educational and Psychological Testing*, by American Education Research Association, American Psychological Association, and National Council on Measurement in Education, 2014, Washington, DC: American Psychological Association.

TABLE 7.2 • Forms of validity		
Form	Method	Purpose
Content validity	Compare content of the test to the domain being measured.	To what extent does this test represent the general domain of interest?
Criterion-related validity	Correlate scores from one instrument of scores on a criterion measure, at the same (concurrent) or a different (predictive) time.	To what extent does this test correlate highly with another test?
Construct validity	Amass convergent, divergent, and content-related evidence to determine that the presumed construct is what is being measured.	To what extent does this test reflect the construct it is intended to measure?
Consequential validity	Observe and determine whether the test has adverse consequences for test takers or users.	To what extent does the test create harmful consequences for test takers?

test items are relevant to the measurement of the intended content area. **Sampling validity** is concerned with how well the test samples the total content area being tested. For example, a test designed to measure knowledge of biology facts would have good item validity if all the items are relevant to biology, but it would have poor sampling validity if all the test items are about vertebrates. If, instead, the test adequately sampled the full content of biology, it would have good content validity. Content validity is important because we cannot possibly measure every problem in a content area, yet we want to make inferences about test takers' performance on the entire content area. Such inferences are possible only if the test items adequately sample the domain of possible items. For this reason, you should clearly identify and examine the bounds of the content area to be tested before constructing or selecting a test or measuring instrument.

Content validity is of particular importance for achievement tests. A test score cannot accurately reflect a student's achievement if it does not measure what the student was taught and is supposed to have learned. Content validity is compromised if the test covers problems not taught or if it does not cover problems that have been taught. Early studies that compared the effectiveness of "new" math with "old" math are classic cases in which achievement test validity was called into question. Scores on achievement tests suggested no differences in students' learning under the two approaches. The problem was that the "new" math emphasized concepts and principles, but achievement tests assessed computational skills. When tests that contained an adequate sampling of items measuring concepts and principles were developed, researchers began to find that the two approaches to teaching math resulted in essentially equal computational ability but that the "new" math resulted in better conceptual understanding. The moral of the story is that you should take care that your test measures what the students were expected to learn in the treatments. That is, be sure that the test has content validity for your study and for your research participants.

Content validity is determined by expert judgment (i.e., *content validation*). There is no formula or statistic by which it can be computed, and there is no way to express it quantitatively. Often experts in the subject matter covered by the test are asked to assess its content validity. These experts carefully review the process used to develop the test as well as the test itself, and then they make a judgment about how well items represent the intended content area. In other words, they compare what was taught and what is being tested. When the two coincide, the content validity is strong.

The term *face validity* is sometimes used to describe the content validity of tests. Although its meaning is somewhat ambiguous, **face validity** basically refers to the degree to which a test appears to measure what it claims to measure. Although determining face validity is not a psychometrically sound way of estimating validity, the process is sometimes used as an initial screening procedure in test selection. It should be followed up by content validation.

Criterion-Related Validity

Criterion-related validity is determined by relating performance on a test to performance on a second test or other measure purportedly measuring the same or a similar outcome. The second test or measure is the criterion against which the validity of the initial test is judged. Criterion-related validity has two forms: concurrent validity and predictive validity.

Concurrent Validity. **Concurrent validity** is the degree to which scores on one test are related to scores on a similar, preexisting test administered in the same time frame or to some other valid measure of the same outcome available at the same time. Often, for example, a test is developed that claims to do the same job as some other test but is easier or faster. One way to determine whether the claim is true is to administer the new and the old test to the same group and compare the scores.

Concurrent validity is determined by establishing a relationship or discrimination. The relationship method involves determining the correlation between scores on the test under study (e.g., a new test) and scores on some other established test or criterion (e.g., grade point average). The steps are as follows:

1. Administer the new test to a defined group of individuals.
2. Administer a previously established, valid criterion test (the criterion) to the same group at the same time or shortly thereafter.
3. Correlate the two sets of scores.
4. Evaluate the results.

The resulting correlation, or validity coefficient, indicates the degree of concurrent validity of the new test; if the coefficient is high (near 1.0), the test has good concurrent validity. For example, suppose Big Pine School District uses a 5-minute test of children's English language proficiency. If scores on this test correlate highly with scores on the American Language Institute test of English language proficiency (which must be administered to one child at a time and takes at least an hour), then the test from Big Pine School District is definitely preferable in a great many situations.

The discrimination method of establishing concurrent validity involves determining whether test scores can be used to discriminate between persons who possess a certain characteristic and those who do not or who possess it to a greater or lesser degree. For example, a test of a personality disorder would have concurrent validity if scores resulting from it could be used to classify clients who were diagnosed or not diagnosed with a mental illness.

Predictive Validity. **Predictive validity** is the degree to which a test can predict how well an individual will do in a future situation. For example, if an algebra aptitude test administered at the start of school can predict which students will perform well or poorly in algebra at the end of the school year (the criterion) fairly accurately, the aptitude test has high predictive validity.

Predictive validity is extremely important for tests that are used to classify or select individuals. An example many of you are familiar with is the use of Graduate Record Examination (GRE) scores to select students for admission to graduate school. Many graduate schools require a minimum score for admission in the belief that students who achieve that score have a higher probability of succeeding in graduate school than those scoring lower. Other tests used to classify or select people include those used to determine eligibility for special education services and the needs of students receiving such services. It is imperative in these situations that decisions about appropriate programs be based on the results of measures with predictive validity.

The predictive validity of an instrument may vary depending on a number of factors, including the curriculum involved, textbooks used, and geographic location. The Mindboggling Algebra Aptitude Test, for example, may predict achievement better in courses using the *BrainScrambling Algebra I* textbook than in courses using other textbooks. Likewise, studies on the GRE have suggested that, although the test appears to have satisfactory predictive validity for success in some areas of graduate study (such as English), its validity in predicting success in other areas (such as art education) appears to be questionable. Thus, if a test is to be used for prediction, it is important to compare the description of its validation with the situation for which it is to be used.

Of course, no test has perfect predictive validity. In other words, predictions based on the scores of any test will be imperfect. However, predictions based on a combination of several test scores will invariably be more accurate than predictions based on the scores of any single test. Therefore, when important classification or selection decisions are to be made, they should be based on data from more than one indicator.

In establishing the predictive validity of a test (called the **predictor** because it is the variable upon which the prediction is based), the first step is to identify and carefully define the **criterion,** or predicted variable, which must be a valid measure of the performance to be predicted. For example, if we want to establish the predictive validity of an algebra aptitude test, final examination scores at the completion of a course in algebra may be considered a valid criterion. As another example, if we are interested in establishing the predictive validity of a given test for forecasting success in college, the grade point average at the end of the first year would probably be considered a valid criterion, but the number of extracurricular activities in which the student participated probably would not. Once the criterion has been identified and defined, the procedure for determining predictive validity is as follows:

1. Administer the predictor variable to a group.
2. Wait until the behavior to be predicted, the criterion variable, occurs.
3. Obtain measures of the criterion for the same group.
4. Correlate the two sets of scores.
5. Evaluate the results.

The resulting correlation, or validity coefficient, indicates the predictive validity of the test; if the coefficient is high, the test has good predictive validity. You may have noticed that the procedures for determining concurrent validity and predictive validity are very similar. The major difference has to do with when the criterion measure is administered. In establishing concurrent validity, the criterion measure is administered at about the same time as the predictor. In establishing predictive validity, the researcher usually has to wait for time to pass before criterion data can be collected.

In the discussion of both concurrent and predictive validity, we have noted that a high coefficient indicates that the test has good validity. You may have wondered, "How high is high?" Although there is no magic number that a coefficient should reach, a number close to 1.0 is best. In practice it is common to accept correlations in the range of .50–.70.

Construct Validity

Construct validity is the most important form of validity because it asks the fundamental validity question: What is this test really measuring? In other words, construct validity reflects the degree to which a test measures an intended hypothetical construct. All variables derive from constructs, and

constructs are nonobservable traits, such as intelligence, anxiety, and honesty, "invented" to explain behavior. Constructs underlie the variables that researchers measure. You cannot see a construct; you can only observe its effect. Constructs do an amazingly good job, however, of explaining certain differences among individuals. For example, some students learn faster than others, learn more, and retain information longer. To explain these differences, scientists hypothesized that a construct called intelligence is related to learning, and everyone possesses intelligence to a greater or lesser degree. A theory of intelligence was born, and tests were developed to measure a person's intelligence. As it happens, students who have high intelligence scores (i.e., "more" intelligence) tend to do better in school and other learning environments than those who have lower intelligence scores (i.e., "less" intelligence). It is important to remember, however, that research studies involving a construct are valid only to the extent that the instrument selected for the study actually measures the intended construct rather than some unanticipated, intervening variable.

Determining construct validity is by no means easy. It usually involves gathering a number of pieces of evidence to demonstrate validity; no single validation study can establish the construct validity of a test. For example, if we wanted to determine whether the intelligence test developed by Big Pine School District—Big Pine Intelligence Test (BPIT)—had construct validity, we could carry out all or most of the following validation studies. We could see whether students who scored high on the BPIT learned faster, more, and with greater retention than students with low scores. We could correlate scores on the BPIT taken at the beginning of the school year with students' grades at the end of the school year. We could also correlate performance on the BPIT with performance on other, well-established intelligence tests to see whether the correlations were high. We could have scholars in the field of intelligence examine the BPIT test items to judge whether they represented typical problems in the field of intelligence. Notice how content and criterion-related forms of validity are used in studies to determine a test's construct validity.

In addition to the confirmatory evidence just described (i.e., evidence that a test is valid for a construct), we could seek disconfirmatory validity information (i.e., evidence that a test is not valid for a different, unrelated construct). For example, we would not expect scores on an intelligence test to correlate highly with self-esteem or height. If we correlated the BPIT with self-esteem and height and found low or moderate correlations, we could conclude that the test is measuring something different than self-esteem or height. We would then have evidence that the BPIT correlates highly with other intelligence tests (i.e., confirmatory validation) and does not correlate highly with self-esteem and height (i.e., disconfirmatory validation).

Consequential Validity

Consequential validity, as the name suggests, is concerned with the consequences that occur from tests. As more and more tests are being administered to more and more individuals, and as the consequences of testing are becoming more important, concern over the consequences of testing has increased. All tests have intended purposes (I mean, really, who would create these things just for *fun?*) and, in general, the intended purposes are valid and appropriate. However, some testing instances produce (usually unintended) negative or harmful consequences to the test takers. **Consequential validity,** then, is the extent to which an instrument creates harmful effects for the user. Examining consequential validity allows researchers to ferret out and identify tests that may be harmful to students, teachers, and other test users, whether the problem is intended or not.

The key question in consequential validity is "What are the effects of various forms of testing on teachers or students?" For example, how does testing students solely with multiple-choice items affect students' learning compared with assessing them with other, more open-ended items? Should non-English speakers be tested in the same way as English speakers? Can people who see the test results of non-English speakers but do not know about their lack of English make harmful interpretations for such students? Although most tests serve their intended purpose in benign ways, consequential validity reminds us that testing can and sometimes does have negative consequences for test takers or users.

Factors That Threaten Validity

A number of factors can diminish the validity of tests and instruments used in research, including:

- Unclear test directions
- Confusing and ambiguous test items
- Vocabulary too difficult for test takers
- Overly difficult and complex sentence structures

- Inconsistent and subjective scoring methods
- Untaught items included on achievement tests
- Failure to follow standardized test administration procedures
- Cheating, either by participants or by someone teaching the correct answers to the specific test items

These factors diminish the validity of tests because they distort or produce atypical test performance, which in turn distorts the desired interpretation of the test scores.

Validity Standards

The Standards for Educational and Psychological Testing manual (2014) developed by the American Educational Research Association (AERA), the American Psychological Association (APA), and the National Council on Measurement in Education (NCME) includes a comprehensive list of validity standards that, if met, allow educational researchers to make robust claims about the context-specific interpretations they make. For novice researchers interested in a comprehensive discussion of all the standards, we recommend that you read *The Standards for Educational and Psychological Testing* (2014), Part I—Validity. The discussion presented there expands our treatment of different forms of validity and provides a comprehensive discussion of generally accepted professional validity standards.

To summarize, validity is the most important characteristic that a test or measure can have. Without validity, the interpretations of the data have inappropriate (or no) meaning. In the end, the test user makes the final decision about the validity and usefulness of a test or measure. The bases for that decision should be described in the procedure section of your research plan.

Reliability of Measuring Instruments

In everyday English, *reliability* means dependability or trustworthiness. The term means the same thing when describing measurements. **Reliability** is the degree to which a test consistently measures whatever it is measuring. The more reliable a test is, the more confidence we can have that the scores obtained from the test are consistent and essentially the same scores that would be obtained if the test were readministered to the same test takers at another time or by a different person. If a test is unreliable (i.e., if it provides inconsistent information about performance), then scores will likely be quite different every time the test is administered. For example, if an attitude test is unreliable, then a student with a total score of 75 today may score 45 tomorrow and 95 the day after tomorrow. If the test is reliable, and if the student's total score is 75 on one day, then the student's score will not vary much on retesting (e.g., likely between 70 and 80). Of course, we should not expect the student's score to be exactly the same on other retestings. The reliability of test scores is similar to the reliability of sports scores, such as scores for golf, bowling, or shot put. Golfers, bowlers, and shot-putters rarely produce identical scores time after time after time. An individual's health, motivation, anxiety, luck, attitude, and attention change from time to time and influence performance of these activities, just as they affect performance on tests—this variation is known as error. All test scores have some degree of measurement error, and the smaller the amount of error, the more reliable the scores and the more confidence we have in the consistency and stability of test takers' performance.

Reliability is expressed numerically, usually as a *reliability coefficient*, which is obtained by using correlation. A perfectly reliable test would have a reliability coefficient of 1.00, meaning that students' scores perfectly reflected their true status with respect to the variable being measured, but alas, no test is perfectly reliable. High reliability (i.e., a coefficient close to 1.00) indicates minimum error—that is, the effect of errors of measurement is small. In reality, depending upon the type of

reliability being assessed, correlation coefficients in the range of .60 and above are usually sufficient to indicate acceptable reliability.

Reliability tells about the consistency of the scores produced; validity tells about the appropriateness of a test. Both are important for judging the suitability of a test or measuring instrument. *Although a valid test is always reliable, a reliable test is not always valid.* In other words, if a test is measuring what it is supposed to be measuring, it will be reliable, but a reliable test can consistently measure the wrong thing and be invalid! For example, suppose an instrument intended to measure social studies concepts actually measured only social studies facts. It would not be a valid measure of concepts, but it could certainly measure the facts very consistently. As another example, suppose the reported reliability coefficient for a test was 0.24, which is definitely quite low. This low coefficient would tell you that the validity was also low—if the test consistently measured what it was supposed to measure, the reliability coefficient would be higher. On the other hand, if the reported reliability coefficient were 0.92 (which is definitely good), you wouldn't know much about validity—the test could be consistently measuring the wrong thing. In other words, reliability is necessary but not sufficient for establishing validity.

As with validity, there are different types of reliability, each of which deals with a different kind of test consistency and is established in a different manner. The following sections describe five general types of reliability, which are summarized in Table 7.3.

TABLE 7.3 • Five types of reliability		
Name	**What Is Measured**	**Procedure**
Stability (test–retest)	Stability of scores over time	Give one group the same test at two different times, and correlate the two scores.
Equivalence (equivalent-forms)	Relationship between two versions of a test intended to be equivalent	Give alternative test forms to a single group, and correlate the two scores.
Equivalence and stability	Relationship between equivalent versions of a test given at two different times	Give two alternative tests to a group at two different times, and correlate the scores.
Internal consistency	The extent to which the items in a test are similar to one another in content	Give tests to one group, and apply split-half, Kuder-Richardson, or Cronbach's alpha to estimate the internal consistency of the test items.
Scorer/rater	The extent to which independent scorers or a single scorer over time agree on the scoring of an open-ended test	Give copies of a set of tests to independent scorers or a single scorer at different times, and correlate or compute the percentage of scorer agreement.

Stability

Stability, also called **test–retest reliability,** is the degree to which scores on the same test are consistent over time. In other words, this type of reliability provides evidence that scores obtained on a test at one time (test) are the same or close to the same when the test is readministered some other time (retest). The more similar the scores on the test over time, the more stable the test scores. Test stability is especially important for tests used to make predictions because these predictions are based heavily on the assumption that the scores will be stable over time. The procedure for determining test–retest reliability is quite simple:

1. Administer the test to an appropriate group.
2. After some time has passed, say, 2 weeks, administer the same test to the same group.
3. Correlate the two sets of scores.
4. Evaluate the results.

If the resulting coefficient, referred to as the *coefficient of stability*, is high, the test has good test–retest reliability. A major problem with this type of reliability is that it is difficult to know how much time should elapse between the two testing sessions. If the interval is too short, the students may remember responses they made on the test the first time; if they do, the estimate of reliability will be artificially high. If the interval is too long, students may improve on the test due to intervening learning or maturation; if they do, the estimate of reliability will be artificially low. Generally, although not universally, a period of from 2 to 6 weeks is used to determine the stability of a test. When stability information about a test is given, the stability coefficient and the time interval between testing should also be given.

Equivalence

Equivalence, also called **equivalent-forms reliability,** is the degree to which two similar forms of a test produce similar scores from a single group of test takers. The two forms measure the same variable and have the same number of items, the same structure, the same difficulty level, and the same directions for administration, scoring, and interpretation. Only the specific items are not the same, although they measure the same problems or objectives. The equivalent forms are constructed by randomly sampling two sets of items from the same, well-described population. If two tests are equivalent, they can be used interchangeably. It is reassuring to know that a person's score will not be greatly affected by the particular form administered. In some research studies, two forms of a test are administered to the same group, one as a pretest and the other as a posttest.

The procedure for determining equivalent-forms reliability is similar to that for determining test–retest reliability:

1. Administer one form of the test to an appropriate group.
2. At the same session, or shortly thereafter, administer the second form of the test to the same group.
3. Correlate the two sets of scores.
4. Evaluate the results.

If the resulting *coefficient of equivalence* is high, the test has good equivalent-forms reliability.

Equivalent-forms reliability is the most commonly used estimate of reliability for most tests used in research. The major problem with this method of estimating reliability is the difficulty of constructing two forms that are essentially equivalent. Even though equivalent-forms reliability is considered to be a very good estimate of reliability, it is not always feasible to administer two different forms of the same test. Imagine your instructor saying you have to take two final examinations!

Equivalence and Stability

This form of reliability combines equivalence and stability. If the two forms of the test are administered at two different times (the best of all possible worlds!), the resulting coefficient is referred to as the *coefficient of stability and equivalence.* In essence, this approach assesses stability of scores over time as well as the equivalence of the two sets of items. Because more sources of measurement error are present, the resulting coefficient is likely to be somewhat lower than a coefficient of equivalence or a coefficient of stability. Thus, the coefficient of stability and equivalence represents a conservative estimate of reliability. The procedure for determining equivalence and stability reliability is as follows:

1. Administer one form of the test to an appropriate group.
2. After a period of time, administer the other form of the test to the same group.
3. Correlate the two sets of scores.
4. Evaluate the results.

Internal Consistency

Internal consistency reliability is the extent to which items in a single test are consistent among themselves and with the test as a whole. It is measured through three different approaches: split-half, Kuder-Richardson, or Cronbach's alpha. Each provides information about items in a single test that is taken only once. Because internal consistency approaches require only one test administration, some sources of measurement errors, such as differences in testing conditions, are eliminated.

Split-Half Reliability. **Split-half reliability** is a measure of internal consistency that involves dividing a test into two halves and correlating the scores on the two halves. It is especially appropriate when a test is very long or when it would be difficult to administer either the same test at two different times or two different forms to a group. The procedure for determining split-half reliability is as follows:

1. Administer the total test to a group.
2. Divide the test into two comparable halves, or subtests, most commonly by selecting odd items for one subtest and even items for the other subtest.
3. Compute each participant's score on the two halves—each participant will have a score for the odd items and a score for the even items.
4. Correlate the two sets of scores.
5. Apply the Spearman-Brown correction formula.
6. Evaluate the results.

The odd–even strategy for splitting the test works out rather well regardless of how a test is organized. Suppose, for example, we have a 20-item test in which the items get progressively more difficult. Items 1, 3, 5, 7, 9, 11, 13, 15, 17, and 19 as a group should be approximately as difficult as items 2, 4, 6, 8, 10, 12, 14, 16, 18, and 20. In effect, we are artificially creating two equivalent forms of a test and computing equivalent-forms reliability. In split-half reliability the two equivalent forms are parts of the same test—thus the label *internal consistency reliability*.

Notice that the procedure does not stop after the two sets of scores are correlated. Because longer tests tend to be more reliable and the split-half reliability coefficient represents the reliability of a test only half as long as the actual test,

a correction formula must be applied to determine the reliability of the whole test. The correction formula used is the Spearman-Brown prophecy formula. For example, suppose the split-half reliability coefficient for a 50-item test were 0.80. The 0.80 number would be based on the correlation between scores on 25 even items and 25 odd items and would therefore be an estimate of the reliability of a 25-item test, not a 50-item test. The Spearman-Brown formula provides an estimate of the reliability of the full 50-item test. The formula is very simple and is applied to our example in the following way:

$$r_{\text{total test}} = \frac{2r_{\text{split half}}}{1 + r_{\text{split half}}}$$

$$r_{\text{total test}} = \frac{2(.80)}{1 + .80} = \frac{1.60}{1.80} = .89$$

Kuder-Richardson and Cronbach's Alpha. **Kuder-Richardson 20 (KR-20)** and **Cronbach's alpha** estimate internal consistency reliability by determining how all items on a test relate to all other test items and to the total test. Internal consistency results when all the items or tasks on a test are related or, in other words, are measuring similar things. Both techniques provide reliability estimates that are equivalent to the average of the split-half reliabilities computed for all possible halves; Cronbach's alpha is a general formula of which the KR-20 formula is a special case. KR-20 is a highly regarded method of assessing reliability but is useful only for items that are scored dichotomously (i.e., every item is given one of two scores—one for the right answer, one for the wrong answer); multiple-choice items and true/false items are examples of dichotomously scored items. If items can have more than two scores (e.g., "How many previous research classes have you taken? Select from among the following choices: 0, 1, 2, 3"), then Cronbach's alpha should be used. As another example, many affective instruments and performance tests are scored using more than two choices (e.g., with a Likert scale). If numbers are used to represent the response choices, analysis for internal consistency can be accomplished using Cronbach's alpha.

Kuder and Richardson provided an alternative, more easily computed form of their formula, called Kuder-Richardson 21 (KR-21). It requires less time than any other method of estimating reliability, although it provides a more conservative estimate of reliability. The KR-21 formula is:

$$r_{\text{total test}} = \frac{(K)(SD^2) - \overline{X}(K - \overline{X})}{(SD^2)(K - 1)}$$

where

K = the number of items in the test
SD = the standard deviation of the scores
$\overline{X}$ = the mean of the scores

In Chapter 18 you will learn how to compute the mean and standard deviation of a set of scores. For now, recognize that the mean, $\overline{X}$, is the average score on the test for the group that took it, and the standard deviation (SD) is an indication of the amount of score variability, or how spread out the scores are. For example, assume that you have administered a 50-item test and have calculated the mean to be 40 ($\overline{X} = 40$) and the standard deviation to be 4 ($SD = 4$). The reliability of the test (which in this example turns out to be rather poor) would be calculated as follows:

$$r_{\text{total test}} = \frac{(50)(4^2) - 40(50 - 40)}{(4^2)(50 - 1)}$$

$$= \frac{(50)(16) - 40(10)}{(16)(49)}$$

$$= \frac{800 - 400}{784} = \frac{400}{784} = .51$$

Scorer/Rater Reliability

Reliability must also be investigated with regard to the individuals who score the tests. Subjectivity occurs when a single scorer over time is inconsistent or different scorers do not agree on the scores of a single test. Essay tests, short-answer tests, performance and product tests, projective tests, and observations—almost any test that calls for more than a one-word response—raise concerns about the reliability of scoring. **Interjudge reliability** (i.e., interrater reliability) refers to the consistency of two or more independent scorers, raters, or observers; **intrajudge reliability** (i.e., intrarater reliability) refers to the consistency of one individual's scoring, rating, or observing over time.

Subjective scoring is a major source of errors of measurement, so it is important to determine the reliability of the individuals who score open-ended tests. It is especially important to determine

scorer/rater reliability when performance on a test has serious consequences for the test taker. For example, some tests are used to determine who will be awarded a high school diploma or promoted to the next grade. The more open-ended test items are, the more important it is to seek consensus in scoring among raters. Subjective scoring reduces reliability and, in turn, diminishes the validity of the interpretations that the researcher or tester can make from the scores.

Reliability Coefficients

What is an acceptable level of reliability? The minimum level of acceptability differs among test types. For example, standardized achievement and aptitude tests should have high reliability, often higher than 0.90. On the other hand, personality measures do not typically report such high reliabilities (although certainly some do), and a researcher using one of these measures should be satisfied with a reliability somewhat lower than that expected from an achievement test. The reason for this is that personality is typically not considered as stable a trait as something like intelligence or achievement. Moreover, when tests are developed in new areas, reliability is often low initially. The best way to evaluate the level of reliability in a test that you are using is to gather information from other, similar tests to use as a benchmark.

If a test is composed of several subtests that will be used individually in a study, then the reliability of each subtest should be evaluated. Because reliability is a function of test length, the reliability of any particular subtest is typically lower than the reliability of the total test.

Researchers should report reliability information about tests in their research plans; they must also be sure to evaluate and report reliability for their own research participants. Reliability, like validity, is dependent on the group being tested. The more heterogeneous the test scores of a group, the higher the reliability will be. Thus, if Group A and Group B both took the same test, but Group A was made up of valedictorians and Group B was made up of students ranging from low to high performers, the test would be more reliable for Group B than for Group A. Given the homogeneous nature of Group A, only slight variations in test scores would make a more noticeable difference than for Group B.

Standard Error of Measurement.

Reliability can also be expressed by stating the standard error of measurement. The **standard error of measurement** is an estimate of how often one can expect errors of a given size in an individual's test score. Thus, a small standard error of measurement indicates high reliability, and a large standard error of measurement indicates low reliability. You should be familiar with this concept because such data are often reported for a test.

If a test were perfectly reliable (which no test is), a person's test score would be the true score—the score obtained under ideal conditions. However, we know that if you administered the same test over and over to the same individual, the scores would vary, like the golf, bowling, and shot-put scores. The amount of variability is a function of the reliability of the test: Variability is small for a highly reliable test and large for a test with low reliability. If we could administer a test many times to the same individual or group of individuals, we could see how much variation actually occurred. Of course, realistically we can't do this, but it is possible to estimate this degree of variation (i.e., the standard error of measurement) using the data from the administration of a single test. In other words, the standard error of measurement allows us to estimate how much difference there may be between a person's obtained score and that person's true score. The size of this difference is a function of the reliability of the test. We can estimate the standard error of measurement using the following simple formula:

$$SE_m = SD\sqrt{1 - r}$$

where

SE_m = standard error of measurement
SD = the standard deviation of the test scores
r = the reliability coefficient

As an example, for a 25-item test, we calculate the standard deviation of a set of scores to be 5 ($SD = 5$) and the reliability coefficient to be .84 ($r = .84$). The standard error of measurement would then be calculated as follows:

$$SE_m = SD\sqrt{1 - r} = 5\sqrt{1 - .84}$$
$$= 5\sqrt{.16} = 5(.4) = 2.0$$

As this example illustrates, the size of the SE_m is a function of both the SD and the reliability coefficient. Higher reliability is associated with a smaller SE_m, and a smaller SD is associated with a smaller SE_m. If the reliability coefficient in the previous example were .64, would you expect SE_m to be larger or smaller? It would be larger: 3.0. If the standard deviation in the example were 10, what would you expect to happen to SE_m? Again, it would be larger: 4.0. Although a small SE_m indicates less error, it is impossible to say how small the SE_m should be because the size of the SE_m is relative to the size of the test. Thus, an SE_m of 5 would be large for a 20-item test but small for a 200-item test. In our example, an SE_m of 2.0 would be considered moderate. To facilitate better interpretation of scores, some test publishers present not only the SE_m for the total group but also a separate SE_m for each of a number of identified subgroups.

MyLab Education **Self-Check 7.5**

MyLab Education **Application Exercise 7.5:**
Exploring Validity and Reliability

TEST SELECTION, CONSTRUCTION, AND ADMINISTRATION

Selecting a Test

A very important guideline for selecting a test is this: Do not stop with the first test you find that appears to measure what you want, say, "Eureka! I have found it!" and blithely use it in your study. Instead, identify a group of tests that are appropriate for your study, compare them on relevant factors, and select the best one. If you become knowledgeable concerning the qualities a test should possess and familiar with the various types of tests that are available, then selecting an instrument will be a very orderly process. Assuming that you have defined the purpose of your study, the first step in choosing a test is to determine precisely what type of test you need. The next step is to identify and locate appropriate tests. Finally, you must do a comparative analysis of the tests and select the best one for your needs.

Sources of Test Information

Mental Measurements Yearbook

After you have determined the type of test you need (e.g., a test of reading comprehension for second-graders or an attitude measure for high school students), a logical place to start looking for specific tests to meet your needs is in the *Mental Measurements Yearbook (MMY)*. The *MMY* is the most comprehensive source of test information available to educational researchers. The *Nineteenth Mental Measurements Yearbook* (2014) is the latest publication in a series that includes the *MMY, Tests in Print,* and many other related works such as *Vocational Tests and Reviews*. The *MMY*, which can be found in most university libraries, is expressly designed to assist users in making informed test selection decisions. The stated purposes are to provide (1) factual information on all known new or revised tests in the English-speaking world; (2) objective test reviews written specifically for the *MMY;* and (3) comprehensive bibliographies for specific tests, including related references from published literature. Some of this information is available free of charge from the Buros Institute website, and a fee is charged for the test reviews.

Getting maximum benefit from the *MMY* requires, at the very least, that you familiarize yourself with the organization and the indexes provided. Perhaps the most important thing to know in using the *MMY* is that the numbers given in the indexes are test numbers, not page numbers. For example, in the Classified Subject Index, under "Achievement" you will find the following entry (among others): i-Ready Diagnostic and Instruction. Students in Grades K-8 (Diagnostic) and K-6 (Instruction); 86. The 86 indicates that the description of the i-Ready Diagnostic and Instruction test is entry 86 in the main body of the volume, not on page 86 (it is actually on page 360).

The *MMY* provides six indexes with information about tests: Index of Titles, Index of Acronyms, Classified Subject Index (i.e., alphabetical list of test subjects), Publishers Directory and Index (i.e., names and addresses of publishers), Index of Names (i.e., names of test developers and test reviewers), and Score Index (i.e., types of scores obtained from the tests). For example,

if you heard that Professor Jeenyus had developed a new interest test but you did not know its name, you could look in the Index of Names under "Jeenyus." There, you would find test numbers for all tests developed by Professor Jeenyus that were included in the volume.

If you are looking for information on a particular test, you can find it easily by using the alphabetical organization of the most recent *MMY*. If you are not sure of the title or know only the general type of test you need, you may use the following procedure:

1. If you are not sure of a title for a test, look through the Index of Titles for possible variants of the title or consult the appropriate subject area in the Classified Subject Index for that particular test or related ones.
2. If you know the test publisher, consult the Publishers Directory and Index and look for the test you seek.
3. If you are looking for a test that yields a particular type of score, search for tests in that category in the Score Index.
4. Using the entry numbers listed in all the sections described previously, locate the test descriptions in the Tests and Reviews section (i.e., the main body of the volume).

An example of an *MMY* entry is shown in Figure 7.1. The entry contains the suggested ages of the participants, the author and publisher, a review by a researcher in the subject area, information about validity and reliability, and other useful information about the test.

Tests in Print

A very useful supplemental source of test information is *Tests in Print (TIP)*. *TIP* is a comprehensive bibliography of all known commercially available tests that are currently in print. It also serves as a master index that directs the reader to all original reviews of tests that have appeared in all the editions of the *MMY* to date. It is most often used to determine the availability of a test. If you know that a test is available, you can look it up in the *MMY* to evaluate whether it is appropriate for your purpose. The main body of the latest *TIP* edition is organized alphabetically. *TIP* provides information on many more tests than the

---

FIGURE 7.1 • Sample entry from the *Mental Measurements Yearbook*

[6]

Assessment of Classroom Environments.

Purpose: "Identifies [teachers'] preferences [and approaches] for establishing classroom environments [by comparing] the Leadership Model, the Guidance Model, and the Integrated Model."

Population: Teachers.

Publication Dates: 2000–2008.

Acronym: ACE.

Scores: 3 models (Leadership, Guidance, Integration) for each of 8 scales: Self-Attributions, Self-Reflections, Ideal Teacher, Peers, Students, Supervisors, General Form, Comparative Form.

Administration: Group.

Forms, 8: Self-Attributions (ratings by teacher), Self-Reflections (ratings by teacher [teacher's perception of how students, peers, and supervisors view teacher]), 4 Observation Checklists (General Form [ratings by "community members, parents, visitors, [or] college students in teacher preparation programs"], Peer Form [ratings by teacher's peers], Student Form [ratings by teacher's students], Supervisor Form [ratings by teacher's supervisors]), Ideal Checklist (ratings by teacher [teacher's perception of the ideal classroom environment]), Comparative Form (ratings by teacher [comparison of the teacher's classroom environment, other professional teachers' classroom environment, and the ideal classroom environment]).

Price Data, 2009: $50 per 25 Self-Attributions forms; $50 per 25 Self-Reflections forms; $50 per 25 Observation Checklist-General forms; $50 per 25 Observation Checklist-Peer forms; $50 per 25 Observation Checklist- Student forms; $50 per 25 Observation Checklist-Supervisor forms; $50 per 25 Ideal Checklist forms; $50 per 25 Comparative forms; $40 per test manual (2008, 34 pages); $.40 per scoring/profiling per scale; $40 per analysis report.

Time: Administration time not reported.

Authors: Louise M. Soares and Anthony T. Soares (test).

Publisher: Castle Consultants.

Review of the Assessment of Classroom Environments by AMANDA NOLEN, Assistant Professor, Educational *Foundations/Teacher Education, College of Education, University of Arkansas at Little Rock, Little Rock, AR:*

DESCRIPTION. The Assessment of Classroom Environments (A.C.E.) is a group-administered battery of rating scales designed to profile an individual's teaching style as reflecting one of three models: Leadership (teacher centered), Guidance (student-centered), or Integration (information-processing). Although not specified in the test manual or test instruments, the instrument appears to be designed for teachers in the K-12 setting.

The A.C.E. consists of eight scales to be completed by the teacher, peers, students, supervisors, and community members. The Self-Attribution Scale, the Self-Reflection Scale, and the Ideal Teacher scale are all completed by the teacher. Observation checklists are completed by peer teachers, students, supervisors, and a community member such as a parent or other adult. Finally, a Comparative Scale is completed by the teacher that identifies attributes most descriptive of self, others, and the ideal teacher.

All of the scales consist of 25 identical triads of statements that demonstrate a teacher's style preference across six factors: classroom management, learning environment, instructional approach, teacher efficacy, assessment, and instructional practices. Each of the statements in a triad represents one of three teaching models identified by the test authors. The statement that is believed to be most descriptive of the teacher's approach in the classroom is given a rank of +1. The statement that is believed to be least descriptive of the teacher is given a rank of +3. The remaining statement in the triad is given a rank of +2. These rankings are additive and the model with the lowest composite score is then considered to be most indicative of that teacher's style in the classroom.

The technical manual provides instructions for administration as well as instructions for scoring and profiling.

The primary objective for the A.C.E. is to create an accurate profile of an individual teacher's instructional style using an integrated approach of self-report as well as objective observations of others.

Source: J. C. Conoley and J. C. Impara (Eds.), *The Twelfth Mental Measurements Yearbook* (1995), pp. 380–381. Lincoln, NE: Buros Institute of Mental Measurements.

MMY, but the *MMY* contains more comprehensive information for each test.

Professional Journals

A number of journals, many of which are American Psychological Association publications, regularly publish information of interest to test users. For example, *Psychological Abstracts* is a potential source of test information. Other journals of interest to test users include *Journal of Applied Measurement, Journal of Consulting Psychology, Journal of Educational Measurement,* and *Educational and Psychological Measurement.*

Test Publishers and Distributors

After narrowing your search to a few acceptable tests, you should review the manuals for the tests, which are available from the publishers. A manual typically includes detailed technical information, a description of the population for whom the test is intended, a detailed description of norming procedures, conditions of administration, detailed scoring instructions, and requirements for score interpretation.

Final selection of a test usually requires examining the test itself. A test that appears from all descriptions to be exactly what you need may not be what you need after all. For example, it may contain many items measuring content not covered, or its language level may be too high or low for your participants. Above all, remember that, in selecting tests, you must be a good consumer, one who finds an instrument that fits your needs. The feature *Digital Research Tools* discusses online

resources to help you identify useful sources of information about specific tests.

Selecting from Alternatives

After you have narrowed the number of test candidates and acquired relevant information, you must conduct a comparative analysis of the tests. Although a number of factors should be considered in choosing a test, these factors are not of equal importance. For example, the least expensive test is not necessarily the best test. As you undoubtedly know by now, the most important factor to be considered in test selection is validity. Is one test more appropriate for your sample than the others? If you are interested in prediction, does one test have a

---

Digital Research Tools

ONLINE TEST SOURCES

Many web-based, commercial test databases allow researchers to identify useful sources of information about specific tests. Three of them are described here.

ETS Test Collection Database

A joint project of the Educational Testing Service (ETS) and the Education Resources Information Center (ERIC) Clearinghouse on Assessment and Evaluation, the ETS Test Collection Database is an online searchable database containing descriptions of more than 25,000 tests and research instruments in almost all fields. In contrast to the *MMY*, the database includes unpublished as well as published tests but provides much less information on each test. To access the ETS Test Collection Database, go to ets.org/test_link/about. There, you can search for tests and research instruments by title or keyword; each entry included in the database contains the title, author, publication date, target population, publisher or source, and an annotation describing the purpose of the instrument.

Educational Research Service

The Educational Research Service (ERS) is a nonprofit organization focused on providing educators with information about testing programs and their impact on policy decisions related to student achievement. ERS provides a searchable online catalog of tests as well as research-based resources developed to provide timely information about specific testing issues and concerns. For further information visit the ERS website at education-research-services.org.

The National Board on Educational Testing and Public Policy

The National Board on Educational Testing and Public Policy (NBETPP) monitors tests for appropriate use and technical adequacy. Housed in the Lynch School of Education at Boston College, the NBETPP is an independent organization that monitors testing in the United States. The NBETPP is particularly useful for educators wishing to investigate the policy implications of any test identified for use as part of a study. For further information about the board and links to their resources go to bc.edu/research/nbetpp.

significantly higher validity coefficient than the others? If content validity is of prime importance, are the items of one test more relevant to the problem of your study than those on other tests?

If several tests seem appropriate after the validity comparisons, the next factor to consider is reliability. You would presumably select the test with the highest reliability, but other considerations may be equally important, such as ease of test use. For example, a test that can be administered during one class period would be considerably more convenient than a 2-hour test. Shorter tests generally are also preferable because they are less tiring and more motivating for test takers. However, a shorter test will tend to be less reliable than a longer one. If one test takes half as long to administer as another and is only slightly less reliable, the shorter test is probably better.

By the time you get to this point, you will probably have made a decision. The test you choose will probably be group-administered rather than individually administered. Of course, if the nature of your research study requires an individually administered test, select it, but be certain you have the qualifications needed to administer, score, and interpret the results. If you do not, can you afford to hire the necessary personnel?

Two additional considerations in test selection have nothing to do with their psychometric qualities. Both are related to the use of tests in schools. If you are planning to include school-age children in your study, you should identify any tests they have already taken so that you do not administer a test with which test takers are already familiar. Second, you should be sensitive to the fact that some parents or administrators object to a test that contains sensitive or personal items. Certain attitude, values, and personality tests, for example, contain questions related to the personal beliefs and behaviors of the respondents. If the test contains potentially objectionable items, either choose another test or acquire appropriate permissions before administering the test.

Constructing Tests

On rare occasions you may not be able to locate a suitable test. One logical solution is to construct your own test. Good test construction requires a variety of skills. If you don't have them, get some help. As mentioned previously, experience at least equivalent to a course in measurement is needed. You should buy and read one of the many useful classroom assessment test books. In addition, if you develop your own test, you must collect validity and reliability data. A self-developed test should not be utilized in a research study unless it has first been pilot-tested by a group of 5 to 10 persons similar to the group you will be testing in the actual study. The following discussion gives an overview of some guidelines to follow if you need to construct a test to administer to schoolchildren.

Writing Your Own Paper-and-Pencil Test Items

To create a paper-and-pencil (or online) test, you will need to determine what type or types of test items to include. Selection items include multiple-choice, true/false, and matching. Supply items include short-answer items, completion items, and essays. Note that scoring or judging responses is much more difficult for essays than the other types of test items. Get help if needed.

The following suggestions provide elementary strategies for constructing your own paper-and-pencil test items.[2] Table 7.4 presents additional suggestions for preparing items.

- Avoid wording and sentence structure that is ambiguous and confusing.
  Poor: All but one of the following items are not elements. Which one is not?
  Better: Which one of the following is an element?
- Use appropriate vocabulary.
  Poor: The thesis of capillary execution serves to illuminate how fluids are elevated in small tubes. True False
  Better: The principle of capillary action helps explain how liquids rise in small passages. True False
- Write items that have only one correct answer.
  Poor: Ernest Hemingway wrote _____.
  Better: The author of *The Old Man and the Sea* is _____.

[2]Test items on these pages are from *Classroom Assessment: Concepts and Applications* (7th ed., pp. 182–190), by M. Russell and P. W. Airasian, 2012, New York: McGraw-Hill. Copyright 2012 by The McGraw-Hill Companies, Inc. Reprinted with permission.

TABLE 7.4 • Preparing test items

Multiple-Choice Items

- Set pupils' task in the item stem.
- Include repeated words in the stem.
- Avoid grammatical clues.
- Use positive wording if possible.
- Include only plausible options.
- Avoid using "all of the above" or "none of the above."

Matching Items

- Use a homogeneous problem.
- Put longer options in the left column.
- Provide clear direction.
- Use an unequal numbers of entries in the two columns.

Essay Items

- Use several short-essay questions rather than one long one.
- Provide a clear focus in questions.
- Indicate scoring criteria to pupils.

True/False Items

- Make statements clearly true or false.
- Avoid specific determiners.
- Do not arrange responses in a pattern.
- Do not select textbook sentences.

Completion and Short-Answer Items

- Provide a clear focus for the desired answer.
- Avoid grammatical clues.
- Put blanks at the end of the item.
- Do not select textbook sentences.

Source: From *Classroom Assessment: Concepts and Applications* (7th ed., p. 192), by M. Russell and P. W. Airasian, 2012, New York: McGraw-Hill. Copyright 2012 by The McGraw-Hill Companies, Inc. Reprinted with permission.

- Give information about the nature of the desired answer.
  Poor: Compare and contrast the North and the South in the Civil War. Support your views.
  Better: What forces led to the outbreak of the Civil War? Indicate in your discussion the economic, foreign, and social conditions. You will be judged in terms of these three problems. Your essay should be five paragraphs in length, and spelling and grammar will count in your grade.
- Do not provide clues to the correct answer.
  Poor: A figure that has eight sides is called an
  a. pentagon
  b. quadrilateral
  c. octagon
  d. ogive
  Better: Figures that have eight sides are called
  a. pentagons
  b. quadrilaterals
  c. octagons
  d. ogives

Be sure to assess only content that has been taught. Aligning instruction and assessment will help you ensure valid results. We strongly suggest that any test you construct should be tried in advance. Ask four or five insightful teachers or individuals experienced in test-item writing to critique your test for clarity and logic. On the basis of their suggestions, you can improve your test. Also conduct a small pilot study. It is not necessary to have a large number of participants to find out if your test is valid and clear.

Test Administration

You should be aware of several general guidelines for test administration. First, if testing is to be conducted in a school setting, arrangements should be made beforehand with the appropriate persons. Consultation with the principal should result in agreement about when the testing will take place, under what conditions, and with what assistance from school personnel. The principal can be very helpful in supplying information such as dates for which testing is inadvisable (e.g., assembly days and days immediately preceding or following holidays). Second, whether you are testing in the schools or elsewhere, you should do everything you can to ensure ideal testing conditions; a comfortable, quiet environment is more conducive to participant cooperation. You should monitor test takers carefully to minimize cheating. Also, if testing is to take place in more than one session, the conditions of the sessions should be as similar as possible. Third, be prepared. Be thoroughly familiar with the administration procedures presented in the test manual, and follow the directions precisely. If the procedures are at all complicated, practice beforehand. Administer the test to some group, or stand in front of a mirror and give it to yourself.

As with everything in life, good planning and preparation usually pay off. If you have made all necessary arrangements, secured all necessary

cooperation, and are very familiar and comfortable with the administration procedures, the testing situation should go well. If some unforeseen catastrophe, such as an earthquake or a power failure, occurs during testing, make careful note of the incident. If it is serious enough to invalidate the testing, you may have to try again another day with another group. At minimum, note the occurrence of the incident in your final research report. You cannot predict every problem that may arise, but you can greatly increase the probability of all going well if you plan and prepare adequately for the big day.

MyLab Education **Self-Check 7.6**

SUMMARY

CONSTRUCTS

1. All types of research require collecting data. Data are pieces of evidence used to examine a research problem or hypothesis.
2. Constructs are mental abstractions such as personality, creativity, and intelligence that cannot be observed or measured directly. Constructs become variables when they are stated in terms of operational definitions.

VARIABLES

3. Variables are placeholders that can assume any one of a range of values.
4. Categorical variables assume nonnumerical (nominal) values; quantitative variables assume numerical values and are measured on an ordinal, interval, or ratio scale.
5. An independent variable is the treatment, cause, or preceding variable, and the dependent variable is the outcome or effect of the independent variable.

CHARACTERISTICS OF MEASURING INSTRUMENTS

6. Three main ways to collect data for research studies include administering an existing instrument, constructing an original instrument, and recording naturally occurring events (i.e., observation).
7. The time and skill it takes to select an appropriate instrument are invariably less than the time and skill it takes to develop an original instrument.
8. Thousands of standardized and nonstandardized instruments are available for researchers. A standardized test is administered, scored, and interpreted in the same way no matter when and where it is administered.
9. Most quantitative tests are paper-and-pencil tests, whereas most qualitative researchers collect data by observation and oral questioning.
10. Raw scores indicate the number of items or points a person got correct.

11. Norm-referenced scoring compares a student's test performance to the performance of other test takers; criterion-referenced scoring compares a student's test performance to predetermined standards of performance.

TYPES OF MEASURING INSTRUMENTS

12. Cognitive tests measure intellectual processes. Achievement tests measure the current status of individuals on school-taught subjects.
13. Aptitude tests are used to predict how well a test taker is likely to perform in the future. General aptitude tests typically ask the test taker to perform a variety of verbal and nonverbal tasks.
14. Affective tests are assessments designed to measure characteristics related to emotions, personal traits, and dispositions.
15. Most affective tests are objective, self-report measures in which the individual responds to a series of questions about him- or herself.
16. Five basic types of scales are used to measure attitudes: Likert scales, semantic differential scales, rating scales, Thurstone scales, and Guttman scales. The first three are the most used.
17. Attitude scales measure respondents' feelings about various objects, persons, and activities. People respond to Likert scales by indicating their feelings along a scale such as strongly agree, agree, undecided, disagree, and strongly disagree. Semantic differential scales present a continuum of attitudes on which the respondent selects a position to indicate the strength of attitude, and rating scales present statements that respondents must rate on a continuum from high to low.
18. Interest inventories allow individuals to indicate personal likes and dislikes. Responses are generally compared to interest patterns of other people, such as those in a specific occupational setting. Interest inventories are an integral part of career planning and decision-making.
19. Personality describes characteristics that represent a person's typical behavior or way of being. Personality inventories include

lists of statements describing human behaviors, and participants must indicate the degree to which each statement pertains to them.

20. Personality inventories may be specific to a single trait (introversion–extroversion) or may be general and measure a number of traits.

21. Use of self-report measures creates a concern about whether an individual is expressing his or her true attitude, values, interests, or personality.

22. Test bias in both cognitive and affective measures can distort the data obtained. Bias is present when one's ethnicity, race, gender, language, or religious orientation influences test performance.

23. Projective tests present an ambiguous situation and require the test taker to "project" her or his true feelings on the ambiguous situation.

24. Association is the most commonly used projective technique and is exemplified by having participants respond to pictures, words, and other ambiguous stimuli.

CRITERIA FOR GOOD MEASURING INSTRUMENTS

25. Validity is the degree to which a test measures what it is supposed to measure, thus permitting appropriate interpretations of test scores.

26. A test is not valid per se; it is valid for a particular interpretation and for a particular group. Each intended test use requires its own validation. Validity is measured on a continuum—tests are highly valid, moderately valid, or generally invalid.

27. Content validity assesses the degree to which a test measures an intended content area. Content validity is of prime importance for achievement tests.

28. Content validity is determined by expert judgment, not by statistical means.

29. Criterion-related validity is determined by relating performance on a test to performance on a second test or other measure.

30. Criterion validity has two forms, concurrent and predictive. Concurrent validity is the degree to which the scores on a test are related to scores on another test administered at the same time or to another measure

available at the same time. Predictive validity is the degree to which scores on a test are related to scores on another test administered in the future. In both cases, a single group must take both tests.

31. Construct validity is a measure of whether the construct underlying a variable is actually being measured.

32. Construct validity is determined by a series of validation studies that can include content and criterion-related approaches. Both confirmatory and disconfirmatory evidence are used to determine construct validity.

33. Consequential validity is concerned with the potential of tests to create harmful effects for test takers.

34. The validity of any test or measure can be diminished by factors such as unclear test directions, ambiguous or difficult test items, subjective scoring, and nonstandardized administration procedures.

Reliability of Measuring Instruments

35. Reliability is the degree to which a test consistently measures whatever it measures. Reliability is expressed numerically, usually as a coefficient ranging from 0.0 to 1.0; a high coefficient indicates high reliability.

36. Measurement error refers to the inevitable fluctuations in scores due to person and test factors. No test is perfectly reliable, but the smaller the measurement error, the more reliable the test.

37. The five general types of reliability are stability, equivalence, equivalence and stability, internal consistency, and scorer/rater.

38. Stability, also called test–retest reliability, is the degree to which test scores are consistent over time. It is determined by correlating scores from the same test, administered more than once.

39. Equivalence, also called equivalent-forms reliability, is the degree to which two similar forms of a test produce similar scores from a single group of test takers.

40. Equivalence and stability reliability are the degree to which two forms of a test given at two different times produce similar scores, as measured by correlations.

41. Internal consistency deals with the reliability of a single test taken at one time. It measures the extent to which the items in the test are consistent among themselves and with the test as a whole. Split-half, Kuder-Richardson 20 and 21, and Cronbach's alpha are the main approaches to measuring internal consistency.

42. Split-half reliability is determined by dividing a test into two equivalent halves (e.g., odd items versus even items), correlating the two halves, and using the Spearman-Brown formula to determine the reliability of the whole test.

43. Kuder-Richardson reliability deals with the internal consistency of tests that are scored dichotomously (i.e., right, wrong), whereas Cronbach's alpha deals with the internal consistency of tests that are scored with more than two choices (agree, neutral, disagree, or 0, 1, 2, 3).

44. Scorer/rater reliability is important when scoring tests that are potentially subjective. Interjudge reliability refers to the reliability of two or more independent scorers, whereas intrajudge reliability refers to the reliability of a single individual's ratings over time.

Reliability Coefficients

45. The acceptable level of reliability differs among test types, with standardized achievement tests having very high reliabilities and projective tests having considerably lower reliabilities.

46. If a test is composed of several subtests that will be used individually in a study, the reliability of each subtest should be determined and reported.

Standard Error of Measurement

47. The standard error of measurement is an estimate of how often one can expect test score errors of a given size. A small standard error of measurement indicates high reliability; a large standard error of measurement indicates low reliability.

48. The standard error of measurement is used to estimate the difference between a person's obtained and true scores. Big differences indicate low reliability.

TEST SELECTION, CONSTRUCTION, AND ADMINISTRATION

49. Do not choose the first test you find that appears to meet your needs. Identify a few appropriate tests and compare them on relevant factors.

Sources of Test Information

50. The *Mental Measurement Yearbook (MMY)* is the most comprehensive source of test information available. It provides factual information on all known or revised tests, test reviews, and comprehensive bibliographies and indexes.

51. *Tests in Print (TIP)* is a comprehensive bibliography of all tests that have appeared in preceding editions of *MMY*. Pro-Ed Publications' *Tests* describes more than 2,000 tests in education, psychology, and business.

52. The ETS Test Collection Database describes more than 25,000 tests, published and unpublished.

53. Other sources of test information are professional journals and test publishers or distributors.

Selecting from Alternatives

54. The three most important factors to consider in selecting a test are its validity, reliability, and ease of use.

Constructing Tests

55. Self-constructed tests should be pilot-tested before use to determine validity, reliability, and feasibility.

56. Be certain to align instruction and assessment to ensure valid test results.

Test Administration

57. Every effort should be made to ensure ideal test administration conditions. Failing to administer procedures precisely or altering the administration procedures, especially on standardized tests, lowers the validity of the test.

58. Monitor test takers to minimize cheating.

PERFORMANCE CRITERIA   TASK 6

All the information required for the descriptions of the tests can be found in the *Mental Measurements Yearbook*. Following the descriptions, you should present a comparative analysis of the three tests that forms a rationale for your selection of the "most acceptable" test for your study. As an example, you might indicate that all three tests have similar reliability coefficients reported but that one of the tests is more appropriate for your participants.

An example that illustrates the performance called for by Task 6 follows (see Task 6 Example). The task in the example was submitted by the same student whose work for Tasks 3, 4A, and 5A was presented in previous chapters.

1

Effect of Interactive Multimedia on the Achievement of 10th-Grade Biology Students

Test One (from an MMY, test #160)

a) High School Subject Tests, Biology—1980–1990

American Testronics

$33.85 per 35 tests with administration directions; $13.25 per 35 machine-scorable answer sheets; $19.45 per Teacher's Manual ('90, 110 pages).

b) The Biology test of the High School Subject Tests is a group-administered achievement test that yields 10 scores (Cell Structure and Function, Cellular Chemistry, Viruses/Monerans/Protists/Fungi, Plants, Animals, Human Body Systems and Physiology, Genetics, Ecology, Biological Analysis and Experimentation).

c) Reviewers state that reliability values (KR-20s) for the various subject tests ranged from .85 to .93, with a median of .88. Content validity should be examined using the classification tables and objective lists provided in the teacher's manual so that stated test objectives and research objectives can be matched.

d) Grades 9–12.

e) Administration time is approximately 40 minutes.

f) Scoring services are available from the publisher.

g) Reviewers recommend the test as a useful tool in the evaluation of instructional programs, recognizing that the test fairly represents the content for biology in the high school curriculum. However, they do caution that a match should be established between stated test objectives and local objectives.

Test Two (from an MMY, test #256)

a) National Proficiency Survey Series: Biology (NPSS:B)—1989

The Riverside Publishing Company

$34.98 per 35 test booklets including directions for administration; $19.98 per 35 answer sheets; $9 per technical manual (26 pages) (1990 prices)

b) The NPSS:B is a group-administered achievement test with 45 items designed to measure "knowledge about the living world ranging from single-celled organisms to the human body."

c) Content validity is good; items were selected from a large item bank provided by classroom teachers and curriculum experts. The manual alerts users that validity depends in large measure upon the purpose of the test. Although the standard error of measurement is not given for the biology test, the range of KR-20s for the entire battery is from .82 to .91, with a median of .86.

d) Grades 9–12.

e) Administration time is approximately 45 minutes.

f) Tests can be machine scored or self-scored. A program is available on diskette so that machine scoring may be done on site. Both percentile rank and NCE scores are used. NCEs allow users to make group comparisons.

g) The reviewer finds the reliability scores to be low if the test is to be used to make decisions concerning individual students. However, he praises the publishers for their comments regarding content validity, which state that "information should always be interpreted in relation to the user's own purpose for testing."

Test Three (from an MMY, test #135)

a) End of Course Tests (ECT) – 1986

CTB/McGraw-Hill

$21 per complete kit including 35 test booklets (Biology 13 pages) and examiner's manual.

b) The ECT covers a wide range of subjects in secondary school. Unfortunately, detailed information is not available for individual subjects. The number of questions range from 42 to 50 and are designed to measure subject matter content most commonly taught in a first-year course.

c) No statistical validity evidence is provided for the ECT and no demographic breakdown is provided to understand the representativeness of the standardization samples. However, reliability estimates were given and ranged from .80 to .89 using the KR-20 formula.

d) Secondary school students.

e) Administration time is from 45 to 50 minutes for any one subject test.

f) Both machine scoring and hand scoring are available. A Class Record Sheet is provided in the manual to help those who hand score to summarize the test results.

g) Users must be willing to establish local norms and validation evidence for effectual use of the ECT, since no statistical validity evidence is provided.

Conclusion

All three batteries have a biology subtest; The High School Subject Tests (HSST) and the NPSS:B are designed specifically for 10th-grade students, while the ECT is course, rather than grade, oriented. It is acknowledged that more data are needed for all three tests, but reported validity and reliability data suggest that they all would be at least adequate for the purpose of this study (i.e., to assess the effectiveness of the use of interactive multimedia in biology instruction).

Of the three tests, the least validity evidence is provided for the ECT, so it was eliminated from contention first. Both the HSST and the NPSS:B provide tables and objective lists in their manuals that may be used to establish a match between stated test objectives and research objectives. The HSST and the NPSS:B both have good content validity but the HSST does not cross-index items to objectives, as does the NPSS:B. Also, norming information indicates that Catholic school students were included in the battery norm group. Therefore, of the three tests, the NPSS:B seems to be the most valid for the study.

With respect to reliability, all three tests provide a comparable range of KR-20 values for battery subtests. While specific figures are not given for the biology subtests, the reported ranges (low eighties to low nineties) suggest that they all have adequate internal consistency reliability.

The NPSS:B appears to be the most appropriate instrument for the study. The items (which were provided by both classroom teachers and curriculum experts) appear to match the objectives of the research study quite well. The KR-20 reliability is good, both in absolute terms and as compared to that of the other available tests. Both machine- and self-scoring are options, but an added advantage is that machine scoring can be done on site using a program provided by the publisher.

Thus, the NPSS:B will be used in the current study. As a cross-check, internal consistency reliability will be computed based on the scores of the subjects in the study.

CHAPTER EIGHT

Survey Research

Paradise, 2013

"Turning people off is certainly not the way to get them to respond." (p. 204)

LEARNING OUTCOMES

After reading Chapter 8, you should be able to do the following:

8.1 Define survey research, and differentiate between sample surveys and census surveys, and between cross-sectional surveys and longitudinal surveys.

8.2 Describe survey research designs, including cross-sectional studies and longitudinal studies.

8.3 Describe the procedures involved in conducting survey research.

The chapter learning outcomes form the basis for the following task, which requires you to develop the method section of a research report. In addition, an example of a published study using survey methods appears at the end of this chapter.

TASK 7A

For a quantitative study, you have created research plan components (Tasks 3 and 4A), described a sample (Task 5A), and considered appropriate measuring instruments (Task 6). If your study involves survey research, you should develop the method section of the research report for this task. Include a description of participants, data collection method, and research design (see Performance Criteria at the end of Chapter 12, p. 335).

SUMMARY: SURVEY RESEARCH

Definition	*Survey research* involves collecting data to test hypotheses or to answer questions about people's opinions on some problem or issue.
Design(s)	Cross-sectional or longitudinal
Types of appropriate research questions	Questions about people's opinions on some problem or issue
Key characteristics	• Sampling from a population • Collecting data through questionnaires or interviews • Construction or identification of survey instrument for data collection • High response rate
Steps in the process	1. State the problem. 2. Construct or locate the questionnaire/survey tool. 3. Pilot-test the questionnaire. 4. Prepare the cover letter. 5. Administer the questionnaire: select participants, distribute the questionnaire, conduct follow-up activities. 6. Tabulate the questionnaire responses. 7. Analyze the results. 8. Write the report.
Potential challenges	• Response rate of 50% or greater
Example	A school superintendent wants to know how high school teachers perceive their schools.

SURVEY RESEARCH: DEFINITION AND PURPOSE

Survey research involves collecting data to test hypotheses or to answer questions about people's opinions on some problem or issue. A **survey** is an instrument to collect data that describe one or more characteristics of a specific population. For example, researchers may ask teachers with one to three years of experience a series of questions to try to gather information about the aspects of their profession that new teachers find most challenging. Survey research can be used to gather information about a group's beliefs, attitudes, behaviors, and demographic composition. Survey data are collected by asking members of a population a set of questions, which can be administered in a questionnaire that is mailed or e-mailed, or in an interview over the phone or in person.

Surveys are either sample surveys or census surveys, usually the former. In a sample survey, as the name suggests, a researcher attempts to infer information about a population based on a representative sample drawn from that population. To be able to generalize sample survey data to an entire population, the sample responding to the survey should accurately represent all the subgroups within the population. In a census survey, researchers attempt to acquire information from every member of a population. Census surveys are usually conducted when a population is relatively small and readily accessible.

Although conducting survey research may sound fairly straightforward, there is considerably more to it than just asking questions and reporting answers. Survey studies often suffer from lack of participant response: Many potential participants do not return mailed questionnaires or attend scheduled interviews. This limited sample can skew data and make it difficult for the researcher to draw accurate conclusions from the study, especially if nonrespondents feel or act differently than people who did respond or if a particular subgroup of the population (e.g., women) is underrepresented. Say, for example, that 20% of potential survey participants are vehemently opposed to the concept of year-round schooling and avail themselves of every opportunity to express their opposition to the idea, including on a survey questionnaire they received regarding the problem. The other 80% of the population, who feel neutral or positive about year-round schooling, are not as motivated to respond and throw away the questionnaire. If researchers consider the opinions of only those who responded, they may draw very wrong conclusions about the population's feelings toward year-round schooling.

Because survey researchers often seek information that is not already available, they usually need to develop an appropriate instrument (i.e., set of questions). If a valid and reliable instrument is available, researchers can certainly use it, but using an instrument just because it is readily available is not a good idea. If you want the appropriate answers, you have to ask the appropriate questions. Furthermore, survey researchers must be very careful to write or select questions that are clear and unambiguous. The researcher seldom has an opportunity to explain to participants who are filling out a questionnaire what a particular question or word really means. If researchers develop an instrument, they need to try it out and revise it as needed before collecting the research data.

SURVEY RESEARCH DESIGNS

Survey studies generally come in one of two designs—cross-sectional studies and longitudinal studies. The key difference between these two types is the number of times the survey is administered. In cross-sectional studies, a survey is administered to a population once. In longitudinal studies, surveys are administered to a population more than once, with significant periods of time elapsing between each administration of the surveys.

Cross-Sectional Surveys

A **cross-sectional survey** is one in which data are collected from selected individuals at a single point in time. It is a single, stand-alone study. Cross-sectional designs are effective for providing a snapshot of the current behaviors, attitudes, and beliefs in a population. This design also has the advantage of providing data relatively quickly—you do not have to wait for years (as is often the case in longitudinal studies) before you have your data and can begin to analyze and draw conclusions. Cross-sectional studies are not effective if the researcher's goal is to understand trends or development over time. Furthermore, a single point in time often does not provide a broad enough perspective to inform decisions about changes in processes and systems reliably (e.g., to change the math curriculum in a school).

Longitudinal Surveys

In a **longitudinal survey** study, data are collected at two or more times. These surveys are extremely useful for studying the dynamics of a problem or issue over time. Longitudinal studies require an extended commitment by the researcher and the participants—some difficulties in conducting longitudinal studies include keeping track of sample members over time and maintaining sample members' willingness to participate in the study. Attrition (i.e., participants dropping out) is common.

Longitudinal survey studies can be categorized into four basic types. All collect data multiple times; however, they differ in how the researcher samples the population and administers the survey.

1. A *trend survey* examines changes over time in a particular population defined by some particular trait or traits, such as fourth-graders, 12-year-olds, or females from California who are currently graduating from high school and who are valedictorians of their classes. Using a trend survey, the researcher can analyze changes in the attitudes, beliefs, or behaviors within that particular population over time. For example, assume a researcher wants to study trends in female valedictorians' attitudes toward gender equality. To provide information about the trend of the valedictorians' attitudes, the researcher would select a sample of the female valedictorians in the current year and then select another sample each successive year until the study is complete. In other words, the survey would be administered annually, and each annual sample would include female valedictorians graduating that year.

2. A *cohort survey* involves one population selected at a particular time period (e.g., female valedictorians of 2020—the first class to graduate after having spent four years of high school under the Every Student Succeeds Act legislation) but multiple samples taken and surveyed at different points in time. For example, the researcher could identify 1,400 female valedictorians in 2020 and send surveys to 300 randomly selected participants. Then, in 2021, the researcher would return to the same population of 1,400 valedictorians and again randomly select 300 participants to survey. Each sample could be composed of different valedictorians (although random sampling may result in some overlap), but all samples would be selected only from the population of female valedictorians from 2020.

3. A *panel survey* involves a sample in which the same individuals are studied over time. For example, in a 3-year panel study of female valedictorians of the class of 2020 who graduated from inner-city high schools in Los Angeles and San Francisco, the exact same individuals would be surveyed in each of the 3 years of the study. A frequent problem with panel studies (and cohort studies to a lesser degree) is loss of individuals from the study because of relocation, name change, lack of interest, or death. This attrition is especially problematic the longer a longitudinal study continues.

4. A *follow-up survey* addresses development or change in a previously studied population, some time after the original survey was given. For example, a researcher who wanted to study female valedictorians in California a number of years after the original study was concluded would identify individuals who had participated in the original study and survey them again to examine changes in attitudes, behaviors, or beliefs.

MyLab Education **Self-Check 8.1**

MyLab Education **Self-Check 8.2**

MyLab Education **Application Exercise 8.1:** Understanding Survey Research

---

CONDUCTING SURVEY RESEARCH

Survey research requires the collection of standardized, quantifiable information from all members of a population or of a sample. To obtain comparable data from all participants, the researcher must ask them each the same questions. Surveys generally take one of two forms, questionnaires or interviews. A **questionnaire** is a written collection of survey questions to be answered by a selected group of research participants; an **interview** is an oral, in-person, question-and-answer session between a researcher and an individual respondent. Many of the tests described in Chapter 7 are used in survey research studies and can also be classified as questionnaires or interviews.

Questionnaires are usually mailed or e-mailed to potential participants. A questionnaire administered in this way is relatively inexpensive and usually permits collection of data from a much larger sample than an interview or a personally administered questionnaire. The disadvantages are that paper-and-pencil questionnaires mailed to participants do not allow any opportunity to establish rapport with respondents and the researcher cannot explain any unclear items. Nevertheless, the advantages usually outweigh the disadvantages, especially if the sample is large or geographically scattered.

Conducting a Questionnaire Study

The steps in conducting a questionnaire study are essentially the same as for other types of research, although data collection involves some unique considerations.

Stating the Problem

The problem studied and the contents of the questionnaire must be of sufficient significance both to motivate potential respondents to respond and to justify the research effort in the first place. Questionnaires dealing with trivial issues, such as the color of pencils preferred by fifth-graders or the make of car favored by teachers, usually end up in potential respondents' garbage cans.

In defining the problem, the researcher should set specific objectives indicating the kind of information needed. Specific aspects of the problem, as well as the kind of questions to be formulated, should be described. For example, suppose a school superintendent wants to know how high school teachers perceive their schools. She wants to conduct a study to help identify areas in the high schools that can be improved. It is useful for the superintendent to begin by identifying important aspects of her general question; then she can select questions to address each aspect. She can perhaps focus on four subproblems: (1) respondent demographics (to compare the perceptions of males and females, experienced and new teachers, and teachers in different departments); (2) teacher perceptions of the quality of teaching; (3) teacher

perceptions of available educational resources; and (4) teacher perceptions of the school curriculum. Breaking the general problem into a few main areas helps to focus the survey and aid decision making in succeeding steps in the research sequence.

Constructing the Questionnaire

Development of a valid questionnaire requires both skill and time. As a general guideline, a questionnaire should be attractive, brief, and easy to respond to. Respondents are turned off by sloppy, crowded, misspelled, and lengthy questionnaires, especially ones that require long written responses to each question. Turning people off is certainly not the way to get them to respond. To meet this guideline, you must carefully plan both the content and the format of the questionnaire. No item should be included that does not directly relate to the problem of the study, and structured, selection-type items should be used if possible. It is easier to respond by circling a letter or word than by writing a lengthy response. Identifying subareas of the research problem can greatly help in developing the questionnaire. For example, the four areas our superintendent identified could make up the four sections of a questionnaire.

Many types of items are commonly used in questionnaires, including scaled items (e.g., Likert and semantic differential), ranked items (e.g., "Rank the following activities in order of their importance"), checklist items (e.g., "Check all of the following that characterize your principal"), and free-response items (e.g., "Write in your own words the main reasons you became a teacher"). Most commonly, surveys consist of structured items (also called *closed-ended items*). A **structured item** requires a respondent to choose among the provided response options (e.g., by circling a letter, checking a list, or numbering preferences). Questionnaires rarely contain large numbers of free-response items, but they may include one or two to give respondents the opportunity to add information not tapped by the closed-ended items.

An **unstructured item** format, in which the respondent has complete freedom of response (i.e., questions are posed and the respondent must construct a response), is sometimes defended on the grounds that it permits greater depth of response and insight into the reasons for responses. Although this may be true, and unstructured items are simpler to construct, their disadvantages generally outweigh their advantages. Heavy reliance on free-response items creates several problems for the researcher: Many respondents won't take the time to respond to free-response items or will give unclear or useless responses, and scoring such items is more difficult and time-consuming than scoring closed-ended items.

Reconsider the superintendent who is conducting a survey to identify areas for improvement in high schools, focusing on the demographics of high school teachers and teachers' perceptions of teaching quality, educational resources, and school curriculum. She may develop questionnaire items like the examples shown in Figure 8.1 (note that the full questionnaire would likely have more items and would not have the headings in the figure). Each group of items relates to one of the superintendent's areas of interest. She may also include a concluding open-ended question, such as "Do you have any additional comments or information you would like to share?"

In addition to the suggestions just provided, the following guidelines should help you as you construct your questionnaire:

- *Include only items that relate to the objectives of the study.*
- *Collect demographic information about the sample if you plan to make comparisons between different subgroups.*
- *Focus each question on a single concept.*

Consider this item:

Although labor unions are desirable in most fields, they have no place in the teaching profession. Agree or disagree?

The researcher is really asking two questions: Do you agree or disagree that labor unions are desirable, and do you agree or disagree that teachers' unions have no place in teaching? This type of item thus creates a problem for both respondent and researcher. If respondents agree with one part of the item but disagree with the other, how should

---

FIGURE 8.1 • Sample questionnaire items in a survey of high school teachers

DEMOGRAPHIC INFORMATION

For each of the following items, put an X beside the choice that best describes you.
1. Gender: Male ___ Female ___
2. Total years teaching: 1–5 ___ 6–10 ___ 11–15 ___ 16–20 ___ 21–25 ___ more than 25 ___
3. Department (please list) _____

CHECKLIST

Below is a list of educational resources. Put a check in front of each resource you think is adequately available in your school.
4. ___ up-to-date textbooks
5. ___ video projection systems
6. ___ classroom computers
7. ___ games
8. ___ trade books

LIKERT

Following are a number of statements describing a school's curriculum. Read each statement and circle whether you strongly agree (SA), agree (A), are uncertain (U), disagree (D), or strongly disagree (SD) that it describes your school.
In my school the curriculum:

9. is up to date	SA	A	U	D	SD
10. emphasizes outcomes more complex than memory	SA	A	U	D	SD
11. is familiar to all teachers	SA	A	U	D	SD
12. is followed by most teachers	SA	A	U	D	SD
13. can be adapted to meet student needs	SA	A	U	D	SD

FREE RESPONSE

14. Circle how you would rate the quality of teaching in your school:
    very good   good   fair   poor
15. Write a brief explanation of why you feel as you do about the quality of teaching in your school.
16. Please make any additional comments you have about this topic.

they respond? If a respondent selects "agree," can the researcher assume that the person agrees with both statements or only one—and which one?

■ *Define or explain ambiguous terms.* Any term or concept that may mean different things to different people should be defined or restated. What does *usually* or *several* mean? Be specific! Do not ask, "Do you spend a lot of time each week preparing for your classes?" because one teacher may consider one hour per day to be "a lot," whereas another may consider one hour per week to be "a lot." Instead, ask,

"How many hours per week do you spend preparing for your classes?"

or

"How much time do you spend per week preparing for your classes?"

a. Less than 30 minutes
b. Between 30 minutes and an hour
c. Between 1 and 3 hours
d. Between 3 and 5 hours
e. More than 5 hours

Underlining or italicizing key phrases may also help to clarify questions.

■ *Include a point of reference to guide respondents in answering questions.* This suggestion is similar to the last in that it is a way of soliciting specific answers. If you were interested not only in the number of hours teachers spent in preparation but also in the teachers' perceptions concerning that time, you would not ask, "Do you think you spend a lot of time preparing for classes?" Instead, you might ask, "Compared to other teachers in your department, do you think you spend a lot of time preparing for your classes?" If you don't provide a point of reference, different respondents will use different points, and the responses will be more difficult to interpret.

■ *Avoid leading questions, which suggest that one response may be more appropriate than another.* Don't use items that begin, "Don't you agree with the experts that . . ." or "Would you agree with most people that . . ."

■ *Avoid sensitive questions that the respondent may avoid or not answer honestly.* For example, asking teachers if they set high standards for achievement is like asking parents if they love their children; no matter what the truth is, the answer is going to be "of course!"

■ *Don't ask a question that assumes a fact not necessarily true.* Unwarranted assumptions may be subtle and difficult to spot. For example, a questionnaire item sent to high school foreign language teachers in a state asked, "How many hours per week do you use your foreign language laboratory?" This question assumed that all the high schools in the state had a foreign language lab. A researcher could instead ask, "Does your school have a language lab?" and "If so, how many hours per week is it used?"

To summarize, it is important to make your questions clear and unambiguous. Remember that the questionnaire must stand on its own; in most cases, you will not be present to explain what you meant by a particular word or item.

To structure the items in the questionnaire, ask general questions and then move to more specific questions. Start with a few interesting and nonthreatening items. If possible—and it often is not—put similar item types together. Don't put very important questions at the end; respondents often do not finish questionnaires. If an item format is unusual, you can provide a completed example. Don't jam items together; leave sufficient space whenever respondents must write an answer. If possible, keep an item and its response options together on a page. Number pages and items to help with organizing your data for analysis. See Table 8.1 for a summary of the important aspects of constructing a questionnaire.

After you have constructed the questionnaire items, you must write directions for respondents; standardized directions promote standardized, comparable responses. It is good practice to include a brief statement describing the study and its purpose at the top of the questionnaire, even though respondents will usually receive a cover letter (described later in this chapter) along with the questionnaire. In addition, you should provide information about how to respond to items. Typical directions include:

Select the choice that you most agree with.
Circle the letter of choice.
Rank the choices from 1 to 5, where 1 is the most desirable and 5 is the least desirable.
Darken your choice on the answer sheet provided.
Please use a pencil to record your choices.

TABLE 8.1 • Guidelines for constructing a questionnaire

- Make the questionnaire attractive and brief.
- Know what information you need and why.
- Include only items that relate to your study's objectives.
- Collect demographic information, if needed.
- Focus items on a single problem or idea.
- Define or explain ambiguous terms.
- Word questions as clearly as possible.
- Avoid leading questions.
- Avoid or carefully word items that are potentially controversial or embarrassing.
- Organize items from general to specific.
- Use examples if the item format is unusual.
- If using open-ended items, leave sufficient space for respondents to write their responses.
- Try to keep items and response options together.
- Subject items to a pretest review of the questionnaire.

Pilot-Testing the Questionnaire

Before distributing the questionnaire to participants, try it out in a pilot study. Few things are more disconcerting and injurious to a survey than sending out a questionnaire only to discover that participants didn't understand the directions or many of the questions. Pilot-testing the questionnaire provides information about deficiencies and suggestions for improvement. Having three or four individuals complete the questionnaire helps identify problems. Choose individuals who are thoughtful, critical, and similar to the intended research participants. That is, if research participants are superintendents, then individuals critiquing the questionnaire should be superintendents. Encourage your pilot-test group to make comments and state suggestions concerning the survey directions, recording procedures, and specific items. They should note issues of both commission and omission. For example, if they feel that certain important questions have been left out or that some existing problems are not relevant, they should note

this. Having reviewers examine the completeness of the questionnaire is one way to determine its content validity. All feedback provided should be carefully studied and considered. The end product of the pilot test will be a revised instrument ready to be mailed to the already selected research participants.

Preparing a Cover Letter

Every mailed and e-mailed questionnaire must be accompanied by a cover letter that explains what is being asked of the respondent and why (see Figure 8.2 for an example). The letter should be brief, neat, and, if at all possible, addressed to a specific person (e.g., "Dear Dr. Jekyll," not "Dear Sir"—database management computer programs can assist you with the chore of personalizing your cover letters).

The cover letter should explain the purpose of the study, emphasizing its importance and significance. Give the respondent a good reason for cooperating—the fact that you need the data for your thesis or dissertation is not a good reason. Good reasons relate to how the data will help the respondent and the field in general. If possible, the letter should state a commitment to share the results of the study when completed. Include a mailing address, phone number, or e-mail address where you can be reached in case potential respondents want to ask questions.

You can add credibility to your study by obtaining the endorsement of an organization, institution, group, or administrator that the respondent is likely to know or recognize. For example, if you are seeking principals as respondents, you should try to get a principals' professional organization or the chief school officer in the state to endorse your study. If you are seeking parents as respondents, then school principals or school committees are helpful endorsers. Ideally, endorsers can cosign the cover letter or at least agree to let you mention their support in the letter. If the planned respondents are very heterogeneous or have no identifiable affiliation in common, you may make a general appeal to professionalism.

As with the questionnaire itself, the cover letter should be pilot-tested. Distribute it for comments when you distribute the questionnaire to a small group of thoughtful participants similar to the intended participants for your study.

FIGURE 8.2 • Sample cover letter

SCHOOL OF EDUCATION

BOSTON COLLEGE

January 17, 2005

Mr. Dennis Yacubian
Vice-Principal
Westside High School
Westside, MA 00001

Dear Mr. Yacubian,

The Department of Measurement and Evaluation at Boston College is interested in determining the types of testing, evaluation, research, and statistical needs high school administrators in Massachusetts have. Our intent is to develop a master's level program that provides graduates who can meet the methodological needs of high school administrators. The enclosed questionnaire is designed to obtain information about your needs in the areas of testing, evaluation, research, and statistics. Your responses will be anonymous and seriously considered in developing the planned program. We will also provide you a summary of the results of the survey so that you can examine the responses of other high school administrators. This study has been approved by the university's Human Subjects Review Committee.

We would appreciate your completion of the questionnaire by January 31. We have provided a stamped, addressed envelope for you to use in returning the questionnaire. You do not need to put your name on the questionnaire, but we request that you sign your name on the enclosed postcard and mail it separately from the questionnaire. That way we will know you have replied and will not have to bother you with follow-up letters.

We realize that your schedule is busy and your time is valuable. However, we hope that the 15 minutes it will take you to complete the questionnaire will help lead to a program that will provide a useful service to school administrators.

Thank you in advance for your participation. If you have questions about the study, you can contact me at 555-555-4444.

Yours truly,

James Jones
Department Chair

Administering the Questionnaire

Selecting Participants

Survey participants should be selected using an appropriate sampling technique. Although simple random and stratified random sampling are most commonly used in survey research, cluster, systematic, and nonrandom samples are also used. In some rare cases, when the population is small, the entire group may make up the sample. The selected research participants must be able and willing to provide the desired information to the researcher. Individuals who possess the desired information but are not sufficiently interested or for whom the problem under study has little meaning are not likely to respond. It is sometimes worth the effort to do a preliminary check of a few potential respondents to determine their receptivity.

The target population for the superintendent's study is likely to be all high school teachers in the state. Such a group is too large to survey reasonably, so the superintendent must select participants from the accessible population. In this case, the likely accessible population is high school teachers from the schools in the superintendent's district. A sample, perhaps stratified by gender and department, can be randomly selected and asked to complete the questionnaire.

Distributing the Questionnaire

An important decision faced by all survey researchers is choosing the method for collecting data. There are six approaches: mail, e-mail, web-based, telephone, personal administration, and interview (summarized in Table 8.2). Each approach has its advantages and disadvantages. The bulk of educational surveys rely on snail-mailed (i.e., via the U.S. Postal Service) or e-mailed questionnaires. Mailing questionnaires is relatively inexpensive, easily standardized, and confidential, but this method

of administration is also subject to low response rates and suffers from the researcher's inability to ask probing or follow-up questions. Sending questionnaires by e-mail has become a popular alternative. In addition to being speedy and efficient, this method shares both the advantages and disadvantages of mail questionnaires, with the additional disadvantage that not all potential respondents have e-mail service. Telephone surveys tend to have high response rates and allow data to be collected fairly quickly, but they require lists of target phone numbers and administrator training as well as the willingness of a respondent to participate in a telephone survey—something that is becoming increasingly difficult in an era of outsourcing of telemarketing services. Personal administration of a prepared questionnaire is efficient if participants are closely situated, but it is time-consuming and also requires administrator training. Personal

TABLE 8.2 • Comparison of survey data collection methods

Method	Advantages	Disadvantages
Mail	Inexpensive Can be confidential or anonymous Easy to score most items Standardized items and procedures	Response rate may be small Cannot probe, explain, or follow up on specific items Limited to respondents who can read Possibility of response sets
E-mail	Speedy results Easy to target respondents Other advantages same as mail	Not everyone has e-mail Possibility of multiple replies from single participant Other disadvantages same as mail
Telephone	High response rates Quick data collection Can reach a range of locations and respondents	Requires phone number lists Difficult to get in-depth data Administrators must be trained
Personal administration	Efficient when respondents are closely situated	Time-consuming Administrators must be trained
Interview	Can probe, follow up, and explain questions Usually high return rate May be recorded for later transcription and analysis Flexibility of use	Time-consuming No anonymity Possible interviewer bias Complex scoring of unstructured items Administrators must be trained
Web-based	Speedy results Easy to target respondents if e-mail is available Clicking on a URL provides the researcher with information about the delivery and receipt status of the survey	Relies on Internet access

interviews allow rich, more complete responses, but they have the least standardization and take the longest to administer.

If you elect to mail questionnaires to potential respondents, some special considerations apply to ensure the highest return rate possible. First, you should provide a specific deadline date by which to return the completed questionnaire. Choose a date that will give participants enough time to respond but discourage procrastination; 2 to 3 weeks is usually sufficient. Second, sign each copy of the letter you send. Individually signed letters admittedly take more time to prepare than copies of one signed letter, but the signature adds a personal touch that makes a difference in a potential respondent's decision to comply or not comply. Next, the act of responding should be made as painless as possible. Include a stamped, addressed return envelope; if you do not, your letter and questionnaire will very likely be placed into the garbage can along with the mail addressed to "Occupant"!

In some cases, you may want to contact potential research participants before sending the questionnaire and cover letter. A brief letter or phone call can alert people that they will be receiving a request for participation in a study. You should briefly note the nature of the study, explain who you and fellow researchers are, and give an indication of when the formal request is likely to arrive. Sometimes it is useful to send the questionnaire to a person of authority, rather than directly to the person with the desired information. If a person's boss passes along a questionnaire and asks the person to complete and return it, that person may be more likely to do so than if the researcher asked. This strategy is a good idea only if the boss cares enough to pass along the questionnaire and if the boss's request will not influence the respondent's responses.

Regardless of your method of administration, remember to attend to basic research ethics. If the survey questions are at all threatening (e.g., if items deal with gender or attitudes toward colleagues or the local administrators), anonymity or confidentiality of responses must be assured. If the responses are anonymous, no one, including the researcher, knows who completed a given questionnaire. If they are confidential, the researcher knows who completed each survey but promises not to divulge that information. We highly recommend that one of these approaches be used and explained in the cover letter. The promise of anonymity or confidentiality will

increase the truthfulness of responses as well as the percentage of returns. One way to promise anonymity and still be able to utilize follow-up efforts with nonrespondents is to include a pre-addressed stamped postcard with the questionnaire. People can be asked to sign their name on the postcard and mail it separately from the questionnaire. The postcards tell the researcher who has and has not responded, but they don't reveal who completed each of the separately mailed questionnaires. If responses are anonymous and the researcher wants to make subgroup comparisons later, specific demographic information should be requested in the questionnaire itself.

Individuals who are comfortable using the Internet can find a veritable smorgasbord of online, web-based survey tools to support the design and analysis of survey research instruments. See the feature *Digital Research Tools* to learn more.

Conducting Follow-Up Activities

Despite your best efforts, not everyone to whom you send a questionnaire is going to return it (what an understatement!). Some recipients will have no intention of completing it; others mean to complete it but put it off so long that they either forget it or lose it. It is mainly for this latter group that follow-up activities are conducted. The higher your percentage of returned questionnaires, the improved confidence you will have in your study. Although you should not expect a 100% response rate, you should not be satisfied with whatever you get after your first mailing. Given all the work you have already done, it makes no sense to end up with a study of limited value because of low returns when some additional effort on your part can make a big difference.

An initial follow-up strategy is simply to send out a reminder postcard. Remember, if you decide on anonymity in your survey, you will have to send out reminders and questionnaires to all participants, unless you use some procedure (such as the postcard system previously mentioned) that allows you to know who has responded but not what their responses were. If responses are confidential but not anonymous, you can mail cards only to those who have not responded. Receiving a reminder will prompt those who postponed filling out the questionnaire (but have not yet lost it). It is polite to include statements such as "If you have already responded, please disregard this reminder. Thank you for your cooperation."

Digital Research Tools

WEB-BASED SURVEY TOOLS

Many web-based survey tools support the design and analysis of survey research instruments, and many commercial survey research providers have popular online products that cater to educational researchers' needs for the development and analysis of survey instruments. Universities often provide students with free access to survey tool software hosted on the university server. However, do not be lured into a false sense of security by these user-friendly online providers. Remember the guiding principle of "garbage in, garbage out"! The survey researcher must still follow the steps in the research process to ensure that a survey tool based on an existing (commercially available) instrument collects the information necessary to answer the research questions.

What follows is a brief description of five selected online survey sites. However, a simple Google search of "online survey tools" will provide a comprehensive list of free and subscriber services.

SurveyMonkey.com

SurveyMonkey.com provides templates for the development of questionnaires using a variety of response strategies (e.g., multiple-choice, rating scales, drop-down menus, etc.), as well as the ability to administer the survey using e-mail invitations, with a record of respondents and nonrespondents, and the ability to analyze results as soon as data arrive. Data are easily downloaded into statistical and spreadsheet programs such as SPSS and Excel but can also be viewed through SurveyMonkey.com in graphic or table form. For detailed information, including pricing and guided tutorials for the development of a survey instrument, visit the SurveyMonkey.com homepage. SurveyMonkey.com also provides links to other online providers so potential users can conduct a comparison of the services provided.

Zoomerang

Zoomerang provides survey researchers with a free trial to create an online survey, including the ability to pilot-test the tool on a small sample and to analyze the results of the trial. Like other commercial online survey providers, Zoomerang provides users with survey templates and the ability to conduct sophisticated statistical analyses of the results. Zoomerang charges users for its regular services but provides a discount for educational institutions. For detailed information, including pricing and a free trial, visit the Zoomerang.com homepage.

LimeSurvey

LimeSurvey is an open-source, free survey tool that the developers claim "contains everything you need for doing nearly every survey with grace." LimeSurvey has an impressive list of features, including multilingual versions of surveys currently available in 50 languages and access to 20 different question types. The words *easy* and *free* are important descriptors for this source, which is available at limesurvey.org.

eSurveyspro

eSurveyspro is another open-source, free survey tool that provides 18 different question types and the ability to export your survey data to Excel or SPSS. Like other "free" services, eSurveyspro offers subscriptions for users with advanced survey needs. Visit eSurveyspro.com for a complete list of survey features.

Qualtrics

Qualtrics is an open-source, free (up to a point) sophisticated survey tool that provides users with over 100 different question types, and uses interactive question types and rich media sources in the hope of increasing survey response rates. Qualtrics also provides access to a large library of existing surveys to save time in the development process. Visit Qualtrics.com for a complete list of survey features and a free account.

Full-scale follow-up activities are usually begun shortly after the given deadline for responding has passed. A second questionnaire, new cover letter, and another stamped envelope can be sent to each person who has not responded. The new letter may suggest that you know the recipient meant to respond but may have misplaced the questionnaire. Perhaps the questionnaire was never received. In other words, do not scold your potential respondents; provide them with an acceptable reason for their nonresponse. Repeat the significance and purpose of the study, and reemphasize the importance of their input. The letter should suggest subtly that many others are responding, thus implying that their peers have found the study to be important and so should they.

If the second mailing does not result in an overall acceptable percentage of return, be creative. Magazine subscription agencies have made a science out of developing follow-up procedures and have become very creative, using gentle reminders and "sensational one-time-only offers," as well as phone calls from sweet-voiced representatives suggesting that the mail was apparently not getting through or certainly you would have renewed your subscription. The point is that phone calls, if feasible, may be used with any other method of written, verbal, or personal communication that may induce additional participants to respond. They may grow to admire your persistence!

If your problem is of interest, your questionnaire is well constructed, and your cover letter is well written, you should get at least an adequate response rate. Research suggests that first mailings typically result in a 30% to 50% return rate, and a second mailing increases the percentage by about 20%. Mailings beyond a second are generally not cost-effective because they each increase the percentage by about 10% or less. After a second mailing, it is usually better to use other approaches to obtain an acceptable percentage of returns.

Rule of Thumb: Survey Response Rate

The rule of thumb for your survey response rate, based on a good sample, is 50%. Anything above 50% will increase the confidence with which you speak about your findings as generalizable to the population from which your sample was developed. According to the American Association of Public Opinion Research (2016)[1] the issue of an acceptable response rate for web-based surveys is confounded by variables such as the accuracy of e-mail addresses and Internet accessibility. Dillman, Smyth, and Christian (2014)[2] raise similar concerns about web-based survey response rates and the goal of a 50% or greater response rate.

Dealing with Nonresponse

Despite all your efforts and follow-ups, you may find yourself with an overall response rate of 50%. This percentage raises concern about the generalizability of results because you do not know how well the respondents represent the population from which the sample was originally selected or even whether they satisfactorily represent the sample originally contacted. If you knew that those responding were quite similar to the total sample, generalizability would be fine, but you do not know that. Those who responded may be different in some systematic way from the nonrespondents. After all, the nonrespondents chose not to reply, which already makes them different. They may be better educated, feel more or less strongly about the issue, or be more concerned about other issues than those responding.

The usual approach to dealing with nonrespondents, then, is to try to determine if they are different from respondents in some systematic way. This determination can be done by randomly selecting a small sample of nonrespondents and interviewing them, either in person or by phone. This technique allows you not only to gather demographic information to determine if nonrespondents are similar to respondents but also to obtain more responses to questionnaire items. If responses are essentially the same for the two groups, you may assume that the response group is representative of the whole sample and that the results are generalizable. If the groups are significantly different, the generalizability across both groups is not present and must be discussed in the research report. Information describing the return rate and its impact on study interpretations should be provided in the final report.

In addition to nonresponse to the questionnaire in general, you may also encounter nonresponse to individual items in the questionnaire. If respondents do not understand an item or find it offensive in

---

[1] http://www.aapor.org/AAPOR_Main/media/publications/Standard-Definitions20169theditionfinal.pdf

[2] *Internet, Phone, Mail & Mixed-Mode Surveys* by D. A. Dillman, J. D. Smyth, and L. M. Christian, 2014, Hoboken, NJ: Wiley.

some way, they may not respond to it. Nonresponse to the entire questionnaire is usually more frequent and more critical than individual item nonresponse. The best defense for item nonresponse is careful examination of the questionnaire during your pilot test, when problems with items are most likely to show up. If you follow the item-writing suggestions in Table 8.1 and subject the questionnaire to rigorous examination, item nonresponses should be few and thus should pose no problem in analysis.

Tabulating Questionnaire Responses

The easiest way to tabulate questionnaire responses is to have participants mark responses to closed-ended questions on a scannable answer sheet. This option involves locating a scanner and possibly paying a fee to have questionnaires scanned. If scannable answer sheets are not an option, then each respondent's answers will have to be entered, one by one, into a computer spreadsheet (e.g., Excel or Lotus) or a statistical program (e.g., Statistical Package for the Social Sciences [SPSS], or R). If you design a questionnaire that will be hand-tabulated, make sure that the format is easy to follow and allows respondents to mark answers clearly so that you can enter data quickly, without having to search for information.

If your questionnaire contains open-ended questions, you will need to code answers according to patterns in the responses provided. With a qualitative software program, for example NVivo, Ethnograph, and HyperRESEARCH (described in detail in Chapter 21), you can examine your textual data, code it, and generate information regarding the frequency and nature of various codes. Many qualitative software programs also allow the researcher to export coded qualitative data into statistical programs, where advanced statistical analyses can be performed.

Analyzing Results

When presenting the results of a questionnaire study, you should include the total sample size and the overall percentage of returns along with the response rate for each item because not all respondents will answer all questions. The simplest way to present the results is to indicate the percentage of respondents who selected each alternative for each item (e.g., "On Item 4 dealing with possession of a master's degree, 50% said yes, 30% said no, and 20% said they were working on one").

Although item-by-item descriptions are a simple way to report the results of a survey, they can produce an overload of information that is difficult to absorb and condense. A better way to report is to group items into clusters that address the same issue and develop total scores across an item cluster. For example, recall the four issues of concern for our school superintendent and the item types chosen for his questionnaire (see Figure 8.2). Instead of reporting the response to each Likert or checklist item separately, the scores for each item type can be summed (i.e., a total score) or averaged (i.e., a mean). For example, if the Likert items were scored from 5 (strongly agree) to 1 (strongly disagree), a score for each item could be obtained and the scores summed or averaged across the Likert items. Not only does developing and analyzing clusters of items related to the same issue make a report of survey results more meaningful, it also improves the reliability of the scores themselves—in general, the more items, the higher the reliability. Results from surveys can be easily imported into Excel, SPSS or R to facilitate the analysis of data. These statistical packages are described in detail in Chapters 18 and 19.

You can investigate comparisons in your data by examining the responses of different subgroups in the sample. For example, a survey may indicate that 80% of those reporting possession of a master's degree expressed favorable attitudes toward personalized instruction, whereas only 40% of those reporting lack of a master's degree expressed a favorable attitude. Again, you can present comparisons on an item-by-item basis or demographic comparisons can be made by presenting the average score of each subgroup of interest. Thus, possible explanations for certain attitudes and behaviors can be explored by identifying factors that seem to be related to certain responses. However, such comparisons can be made only if demographic information about the respondents is collected on the questionnaire.

MyLab Education **Self-Check 8.3**

MyLab Education **Application Exercise 8.2:** Evaluating Research Articles: Identifying Steps in the Research Process for a Survey Study

MyLab Education **Application Exercise 8.3:** Evaluating Research Articles: Evaluating a Survey Study

SUMMARY

SURVEY RESEARCH: DEFINITION AND PURPOSE

1. A survey is an instrument for collecting data that describe one or more characteristics of a specific population.
2. Survey data are collected by asking members of a population a set of questions via a questionnaire or an interview.
3. Survey research requires attention to the selection of an adequate sample and an appropriate instrument.

SURVEY RESEARCH DESIGNS

4. Surveys can be categorized as cross-sectional or longitudinal. Cross-sectional studies collect data at one point in time, whereas longitudinal studies collect data at more than one time to measure growth or change.
5. Longitudinal survey studies can be classified as trend surveys, cohort surveys, panel surveys, and follow-up surveys. Classification depends on sampling and administration of the survey.

CONDUCTING SURVEY RESEARCH

6. Survey research requires the collection of standardized, quantifiable information from all members of a population or sample.
7. A questionnaire is a written collection of self-report questions to be answered by a selected group of research participants. An interview is an oral, in-person, question-and-answer session between a researcher and an individual respondent.

Conducting a Questionnaire Study

8. A questionnaire is efficient; it requires little time and expense and permits collection of data from a large sample.

Stating the Problem

9. In developing a questionnaire study, the researcher should identify specific objectives or subproblems concerning the kind of information needed and should formulate questions that relate directly to those objectives.

Constructing the Questionnaire

10. A questionnaire should be attractive, brief, and easy to respond to. No item should be included that does not relate directly to the objectives of the study.
11. Structured, or closed-ended, items should be used if possible because they are easier for participants to respond to and for researchers to score and analyze.
12. Common structured items used in questionnaires are scaled items (e.g., Likert and semantic differential), ranked items, and checklists.
13. In an unstructured item format (e.g., essay questions), respondents have complete freedom of response. Unstructured items permit greater depth of response and thus may permit insight into the reasons for responses, but they are often difficult to analyze and interpret.
14. Each question should focus on a single concept and be worded as clearly as possible. Any term or concept that may mean different things to different people should be defined.
15. Avoid leading questions, questions that assume a fact not necessarily in evidence, and questions that do not indicate a point of reference.
16. To structure the items in the questionnaire, begin with general, nonthreatening questions and then move to more specific questions. Group similar items, if possible.
17. Questionnaires should also include directions for respondents to help standardize the administration.

Pilot-Testing the Questionnaire

18. The questionnaire should be tested by a few respondents who are similar to those in the sample for the study.
19. Pilot-testing the questionnaire provides information about instrument deficiencies as well as suggestions for improvement. Omissions or unclear or irrelevant items should be revised.
20. Pilot-testing or review by colleagues can provide a measure of content validity.

Preparing a Cover Letter

21. Every mailed or e-mailed questionnaire must be accompanied by a cover letter that explains what is being asked of the respondent and why. The cover letter should be brief, neat, and addressed to a specific individual, if possible.

22. The letter should explain the purpose of the study, emphasizing its importance and significance, and give the respondent a good reason for cooperating.

23. The endorsement of an organization, institution, group, or administrator with which the respondent is associated or views with respect (such as a professional organization) increases credibility.

Administering the Questionnaire

Selecting Participants

24. Participants should be selected using an appropriate sampling technique (or an entire population may be used), and identified participants must be persons who have the desired information and are willing to give it.

Distributing the Questionnaire

25. Questionnaires are usually distributed via one of five approaches: mail, e-mail, telephone, personal administration, and interview. Each has advantages and disadvantages.

26. If you elect to mail questionnaires to potential respondents, some special considerations apply to ensure the highest return rate possible. A specific deadline date by which the completed questionnaire is to be returned should be given, and a stamped, addressed envelope for the respondents to return their surveys should be included.

27. Regardless of your method of administration, remember to attend to basic research ethics, including assuring confidentiality or anonymity, as necessary, for the study.

Conducting Follow-Up Activities

28. If your percentage of returns is low, the validity of your conclusions may be weak. An initial follow-up strategy is to simply send a reminder postcard.

29. Full-scale follow-up activities, such as sending additional copies of the questionnaire, are usually begun shortly after the deadline for responding has passed.

Dealing with Nonresponse

30. If your total response rate is low, you may have a problem with the generalizability of your results. You should try to determine if the persons who did not respond are similar to the persons who did respond by randomly selecting a small subsample of nonrespondents and interviewing them, either in person or by phone.

Tabulating Questionnaire Responses

31. The easiest way to tabulate questionnaire responses is to have participants mark responses to closed-ended questions on a scannable answer sheet. If your questionnaire contains open-ended questions, you will need to code answers according to patterns in the responses provided.

32. The simplest way to present the results is to indicate the percentage of respondents who selected each alternative for each item. However, analyzing summed item clusters—groups of items focused on the same issue—is more meaningful and reliable.

33. You can investigate comparisons in your data by examining the responses of different subgroups in the sample (e.g., male–female).

34. Many online providers support the development, implementation, and analysis of survey research. Examples are Survey Monkey, Zoomerang, LimeSurvey eSurveyspro, and Qualtrics.

To What Extent Are Literacy Initiatives Being Supported: Important Questions for Administrators

LESLIE MARLOW
Berry College

DUANE INMAN
Berry College

CRAIG SHWERY
University of Alabama

ABSTRACT   This study examined teachers' expressed perceptions of states' provisions for instructional materials and professional development opportunities related to state literacy initiatives for K–6 classroom teachers in ten southeastern states. Approximately 400 teachers responded to a survey instrument which included the problems of materials and professional development. Generally, the survey results indicate that teachers did not express receipt of sufficient support in implementing a state/district-wide reading initiative to the extent one might deem desirable (or appropriate) by present agencies. It appears that responding teachers perceived themselves to be ill-prepared to meet accountability mandates associated with literacy and that participating teachers lacked training, had little access to sound instructional materials, and were unfamiliar with the state standards. This information results in questions that administrators must address if teachers are to effectively implement literacy initiatives proposed as a result of state mandates.

Literacy Initiative Support Systems Entering the 21st Century

(01)   The Elementary and Secondary Education Act (ESEA) (1965), Title 1, Part B, (Reading Excellence Act, P. L. 105-277) was the first broad governmental initiative to address the literacy issue by advocating that all children would be able to read by the end of third grade. In 2002, ESEA was supplemented with the "No Child Left Behind Act." Similar to the Reading Excellence Act, the "No Child Left Behind Act" focuses on research-based methods which some experts say will virtually guarantee a more structured, skills-based approach to the teaching of reading (Manzo, 2002; Ogle, 2002). This emphasis on research-based methods has led to increased attention regarding reading and literacy standards. National literacy standards suggested from both the International Reading Association (IRA) and the National Council of Teachers of English (NCTE) (1996) have provided the framework for states to develop their own literacy standards including new state policy documentation intended to assist in bringing about positive literacy changes in teaching and learning for individual states (Kuder and Hasit, 2002; Wixon and Dutro, 1999).

(02)   While various states involved in redesigning their reading initiatives are enacting specific reading goals and standards for performance, many literacy educators, along with professional teaching organizations, have questioned the validity of many of the enacted reading measures (Block, Oaker, and Hurt, 2002; Block, Joyner, Joy, and Gaines, 2001; Hoffman et al., 1998; Allington, Guice, Michelson, Baker, and Li, 1996). Those involved with improving literacy instruction must provide on-going staff development to

ensure that implementation of reading reform models will be effective (Birman, Desimone, Portor, & Garet, 2000; Joyce, 1999; Darling-Hammond, 1995; Carter & Powell, 1992). Professional development is a powerful process for enhancing the knowledge base for teaching and the pedagogical skills needed to disseminate knowledge (Kraft, 1998; Hirsh, 1999; Joyce and Showers, 1983). Access to professional development opportunities provides teachers with an important link needed to successfully implement reading initiatives and is a useful tool for improving classroom instruction, curriculum design, and the effective use of primary teaching materials (Lieberman, 1999, 2001; Blair, 2003; Birman, 2000; Westchester Institute for Human Services Research, 1998).

Because state reading initiatives are relatively new components to teaching, there appears to be a dearth of research being done which examines state-mandated literacy professional opportunities and associated materials programs being used by the states. The purpose of this study was to examine teachers' expressed perceptions regarding their states' provisions for instructional materials and professional development opportunities related to state literacy initiatives for K–6 classroom teachers.

(03)

> Problem statement: The purpose of this study was to examine teachers' expressed perceptions regarding their states' provisions for instructional materials and professional development opportunities related to state literacy initiatives for K–6 classroom teachers. Cross-sectional survey research.

Population

Using the state's public school directory for each of several southern states, each school district within each state was assigned a number. Gay's Table of Random Numbers (1996) was then used to identify 10 schools from each state. The principal of each selected school was contacted and requested to provide information from teachers who teach reading (K–6). Principals randomly contacted 10 teachers who teach reading in their schools and obtained their participation in completing the surveys.

(04)

> Participant selection of approximately 400 K–6 teachers who teach reading.
>
> *Researchers used a cluster sampling approach to randomly select clusters (schools) to participate in the study. Once the schools were identified, principals "randomly contacted 10 teachers who teach reading in their school." However, there is no information provided about whether a simple random sample of teachers was the sampling approach used by the principals. Were the 10 teachers randomly chosen in each school? Or, was a stratified random sample used in order to have a representative sample across all K–6 grades?*

Instrumentation

The survey instrument was comprised of four-point Likert Scale items ranging from Strongly Disagree to Strongly Agree. The Likert Scale items fell into two categories: professional development and reading materials. Professional development items focused on the description of the state literacy initiative, provision by the school district to provide professional development opportunities, and professional development opportunities provided by the state. The items focusing on materials targeted their appropriateness for the various grade levels, whether they effectively addressed the state's current assessment instrument, and whether there were adequate supplemental reading materials available to accompany the mandated programs. Additionally, demographic items were included to provide background information on the respondents.

(05)

The pilot study of this instrument was conducted in Spring 2001. Test–retest stability was measured to determine the reliability of scores over time. A group of approximately 100 K–6 teachers completed the survey, once in January and once in April 2001. The scores from each were correlated and the coefficient of stability was calculated to be 0.92. The pilot study results indicated the instrument to be reliable.

(06)

> Likert scale survey instrument developed and piloted on a group of 100 K–6 teachers with a coefficient of stability (test–retest reliability coefficient) calculated at 0.92.
>
> *Is the January–April time interval used to establish the coefficient of stability an acceptable interval? Is maturation a threat to reliability?*

Procedures

One thousand surveys were sent out to participating teachers within the southern states. A packet of information was sent to the principal of each identified school from the random sample. A cover letter and copy of the survey instrument were included in each packet. If the principal agreed to his/her faculty's participation in the study, the principal then distributed the survey instrument to the teachers who teach reading. The teachers were to independently complete the surveys and return the self-addressed, stamped surveys. Only those interested participated. If a principal was unwilling to allow his/her teachers to

(07)

> Survey response rate was approximately 40%.
>
> *Is 40% an acceptable response rate on which to base the study's findings? What was the impact on the sampling methodology of sending surveys to a different school in the same "geographic area"? Was the school (cluster) randomly selected from all schools in the same geographic region?*

Table 1

Demographic Information

Ethnic Origin		Years/Teaching	Classroom	Current Placement	Teaching	Perceived Student	School Enrollment
White	81%	1–5	11%	PreK/K	14%	< 250	23%
African		6–10	15%	1–4	54%	251–499	43%
American	8%						
		11–20	17%	5–6	32%	500–1,000	27%
Hispanic	7%						
		Over 20	29%			Over 1,000	6%
Native American/	2%	No Response	28%			No Response	1%
Asian							
No Response	2%						

participate, they were asked to return the surveys in the return envelope to the researchers. These materials were submitted to a different school in the same geographic area. The return rate was approximately 40%.

(08)   For those participants or principals who wanted to know the results of the survey, such information was requested by the individual providing their name and address. All information obtained by the survey was anonymously reported in group totals only.

Results

(09)   **Demographics.** As is evidenced in Table 1, the majority of the teachers were white, teaching in grades 1–4 in schools with an enrollment between 251 and 1,000. There was a wide variety among the respondents' teaching experience, with the greatest response being 29% who had taught over 20 years.

(10)   **Professional Development.** Teacher responses indicated that 34% of the respondents either agreed or strongly agreed that professional development opportunities from the school district were provided. Sixty-six percent of the respondents either disagreed or strongly disagreed that these opportunities were provided. Teachers' perceptions of the provision for professional development opportunities from the state indicated that 31% of the respondents either agreed or strongly agreed that these development opportunities were provided. Fifty-nine percent of the respondents either disagreed or strongly disagreed that these opportunities were provided. Ten percent expressed that they did not know. In addressing how thoroughly the literacy initiative of the district was described to the teachers of that district, responses were split, with 50% agreeing and 50% disagreeing that a thorough description occurred. Therefore, while teachers indicated that they perceived themselves as being knowledgeable about state standards and the mandated literacy initiative based on the information that they were provided, the majority expressed their belief that they were not provided with professional development opportunities in order to enhance their information about the reading knowledge base and pedagogy practices being used by the state and/or districts. Table 2 provides further description of the data.

(11)   **Reading Materials.** Eighty-seven percent agreed or strongly agreed that the primary reading materials available within their school were in accordance with the state literacy initiative and were appropriate for the specified grade levels. Six percent either disagreed or strongly disagreed, and seven percent didn't know. When responding to the item regarding the availability

Table 2

Responses to Likert Items Related to Professional Development Workshops

	Strongly Agree (4)	Agree (3)	Disagree (2)	Strongly Disagree (1)	Don't Know
Literacy initiative of the district was described to teachers	24%	26%	30%	20%	n/a
Workshops provided by school district	15%	19%	42%	24%	n/a
Workshops provided by state	11%	31%	10%		

of primary reading materials designed to meet the needs of specific grade levels, the majority, 87%, indicated the presence of such materials. Of those responding to the item addressing whether they perceived that the primary reading materials used by the school effectively addressed the standard evaluated by the required assessment instruments, 47% agreed or strongly agreed and 49% either disagreed or strongly disagreed. Four percent didn't know. When queried regarding the availability of adequate supplemental reading materials to enhance state literacy initiatives, 15% agreed or strongly agreed that these materials were available, while 45% disagreed or strongly disagreed. The remaining 40% expressed that they were unaware if such materials were available. Table 3 provides additional description of the data.

Discussion

The majority of respondents indicated a concern regarding the adequacy of primary materials provided in addressing the standards, and teachers were evenly mixed in their opinions of the efficacy of these materials. However, perceptions of the adequacy of supplemental reading materials revealed only 15% of the respondents in agreement that their school provided adequate supplementary reading materials, while three times as many teachers disagreed about the adequacy of such materials. Interestingly enough, 40% of the teachers expressed that they were not aware of the availability. While teachers can be unaware of information and availability of materials for many reasons, a breakdown in communication among administration and teachers, perhaps even among colleagues, is a common reason. If a breakdown in communication among the stakeholders does exist, administrators should reflect upon several questions in an attempt to disseminate information more effectively: What media is being used to present the teachers with information about the district reading initiatives? Are multiple forms of media communication being used? Is there ample opportunity for questions and responses in order for teachers to clarify their perceptions? If not, when can time be

(12)

Table 3

Responses to Likert Items Regarding Reading Materials

	Strongly Agree (4)	Agree (3)	Disagree (2)	Strongly Disagree (1)	Don't Know
Reading materials appropriate for specific grade levels	40%	47%	3%	3%	7%
Reading materials effectively address state assessment	21%	26%	30%	19%	4%
Adequate supplemental reading materials	4%	11%	27%	18%	40%

allocated to allow for clarification? Are teacher misconceptions about availability of materials addressed—and if so, how?

(13)   Only approximately 1/3 of teachers were in accord with the idea that workshops are provided. Approximately 2/3 disagreed that workshops are provided. If the lack of provision for workshops is indeed the case, administrators have some hard questions to which they must respond: How are teachers to implement new reading programs without being trained? Is it the responsibility of the teacher to train him/herself, thereby providing students with the skills necessary to read effectively and ultimately pass "the test?" If workshops were available, why did teachers select not to attend these workshops? Were the provided professional development opportunities required or optional? What motivation can be provided to encourage teachers to become more proactive learners? In considering the broad problem of materials, participating teachers indicated that the primary materials are appropriate for the specific grade levels, yet only half expressed the belief that those same materials effectively address the standards. Does this indicate that perhaps the other half concluded that the primary materials were effective teaching tools, but, they didn't address the state standards that are tested? Another possibility is that funding may have been available for primary materials but perhaps there was a lack of funding for the supplemental materials. Was there the possibility that funding was not deemed necessary for supplemental materials—since funds were spent for the primary programs, supplemental materials were not needed? An alternative explanation is that the comprehensive nature of new programs possibly precluded the necessity for the provision of supplemental materials. Teachers should be provided with specific information related to all materials and their relationship to state and national standards.

(14)   The information provided by the participating teachers raises additional questions for administrators when considering implementation of state/district-wide literacy initiatives: Was the issue of availability of supplemental materials addressed in the workshops at state and/or district levels? To what extent is collaboration occurring between the district schools and state agencies to ensure that teachers are adequately prepared for implementing district-wide literacy initiatives? How do districts ensure that schools have adequate teacher representation so that all schools will have a "specialist" with training available as a resource for other teachers—a local person to whom questions can be directed and immediately answered?

(15)   With the increasing focus on research-based methods intended to guarantee a more structured approach to the teaching of reading, as well as the finances involved, administrators and their agencies need to ensure that teachers are adequately trained and supported for the implementation of these programs. The results of this survey indicated that teachers do not perceive that they are being supported in implementing state/district-wide reading initiatives to the extent one might deem desirable (or appropriate) by present agencies. Teachers indicate that they are ill-prepared to meet accountability mandates associated with literacy. They report that they have limited access to instructional materials and do not appear familiar with the standards themselves. The results also provided a number of additional questions which need to be addressed by administrators to further analyze educational circumstances and goals related to the state reading initiatives between and among concerned stakeholders. The quality of literacy initiatives themselves can never be thoroughly investigated if the time is not taken to work through the implementation problems indicated by those involved in classroom presentation of the state literacy programs.

REFERENCES

Allington, R., Guice, S., Michelson, N., Baker, K., & Li, S. (1996). Literature-based curriculum in high poverty schools. In Block, C., Oaker, M., & Hurt, N. (2002). The expertise of literacy teachers: A continuum from preschool to grade 5. *Reading Research Quarterly, 37*(2), 178–206.

Blair, J. (Feb. 5, 2003). With support, teachers would stay put, report finds. *Education Week*, Washington.

Block, C., Joyner, J., Joy, J., & Gaines, P. (2001). Process-based comprehension: Four educators' perspectives. In C. C. Block & M. Pressley (Eds.), *Research-based Comprehension Practices*, 119–134. NY: Guilford.

Block, C., Oaker, M., & Hurt, N. (2002). The expertise of literacy teachers: A continuum from preschool to grade 5. *Reading Research Quarterly, 37*(2), 178–206.

Birman, B., Desimone, L., Porter, A., & Garet, M. (2000). Designing professional development that works. *Educational Leadership 57*(8), 28–33.

Carter, M., & Powell, D. (1992). Teacher leaders as staff developers. *Journal of Staff Development 13*(1), 8–12.

Darling-Hammond, L., & McLaughlin, M. (1995). Policies that support professional development in an era of reform. *Phi Delta Kappa*, 597–604.

Elementary and Secondary Education Act (ESEA). ed. gov/offfices/OESE/esea

Hirsh, S. (1999). Standards-based professional development. *High School Magazine, 7*(4), 31.

Hoffman, J., et al. (1998). The literature-based basals in first grade classrooms: Savior, Satan, or same-old, same-old? *Reading Research Quarterly, 33*(2), 168–197.

Joyce, B. (1999). Reading about reading: Notes from a consumer to the scholars of literacy. *The Reading Teacher, 52*(7), 662–671.

Kraft, N. (1998). A New Model for Professional Development. rmcdenver.com/eetnet/alapp.htm

Kuder, S., & Hasit, C. (2002). *Enhancing Literacy for All Students*. Upper Saddle River, New Jersey: Merrill Prentice Hall.

Lieberman, A., & Miller, L. (Eds.) (2001). *Teachers caught in the action: Professional development that matters*. NY: Teachers College Press.

Manzo, K. (Feb. 20, 2002). Some educators see reading rules as too restrictive. *Education Week, 21*(23), 1, 23.

Ogle, D., in Manzo, K. (Feb. 20, 2002). Some educators see reading rules as too restrictive. *Education Week, 21*(23), 1, 23.

Sparks, D. (1999). Real-life view: An interview with Ann Lieberman. *Journal of Staff Development, 20*(4).

Westchester Institute for Human Services Research. (1998). *The Balanced View: Professional Development, 2*(3).

Wixson, K,. & Dutro, E. (1999). Standards for primary-grade reading: An analysis of state frameworks. *The Elementary School Journal, 100*(2), 89–110.

Source: "To What Extent Are Literacy Initiatives Being Supported: Important Questions for Administrators," by L. Marlow, D. Inman, and C. Shwery, *Reading Improvement*, Vol. 42, No. 3, Fall, 2005, pp. 179–186. Copyright 2005 by Project Innovation. Reproduced with permission of Project Innovation.

CHAPTER NINE

Correlational Research

Twins, 1987

"Correlational research involves collecting data to determine whether, and to what degree, a relationship exists . . . ." (p. 224)

LEARNING OUTCOMES

After reading Chapter 9, you should be able to do the following:

9.1 Define briefly and state the purpose of correlational research.

9.2 Describe the correlational research process.

9.3 State the major purposes of relationship studies, and identify and briefly describe the steps involved in conducting a relationship study and interpreting the data.

9.4 State the major purposes of prediction studies, and identify and briefly describe the steps involved in conducting a prediction study and interpreting the data.

9.5 Describe other correlation-based analyses and when it is appropriate to use them.

9.6 Describe the problems to consider in interpreting correlation coefficients.

The chapter learning outcomes form the basis for the following task, which requires you to develop the method section for a report of a correlational study. In addition, an example of a published study using correlational research appears at the end of this chapter.

TASK 7B

For a quantitative study, you have created research plan components (Tasks 3 and 4A), described a sample (Task 5A), and considered appropriate measuring instruments (Task 6). If your study involves correlational research, develop the method section of a research report. Include a description of participants, data collection methods, and research design (see Performance Criteria at the end of Chapter 12, p. 335).

SUMMARY: CORRELATIONAL RESEARCH

Definition	*Correlational research* involves collecting data to determine whether, and to what degree, a relationship exists between two or more quantifiable variables.
Designs	The basic correlational research design is not complicated: Scores for two (or more) variables of interest are obtained for each member of the sample, and the paired scores are then correlated. The result is expressed as a correlation coefficient that indicates the degree of relation between the two variables. Correlational research may be in the forms of relationship studies or prediction studies.
Types of appropriate research questions	Correlational studies may be designed either to determine whether and how a set of variables are related or to test hypotheses regarding expected relations. Variables to be correlated should be selected on the basis of some rationale.
Key characteristics	• Variables to be investigated can be scored. • Sample size of at least 30 participants. • Outcome of the study allows the researcher to describe whether and to what degree two (or more) variables are related. • Does not establish a causal relationship.
Steps in the process	1. Problem selection. Variables to be correlated should be selected on the basis of some rationale. 2. Participant and sample selection. The sample for a correlational study is selected by using an acceptable sampling method, and a minimally acceptable sample size is generally 30 participants. 3. Procedure. Scores for two (or more) variables of interest are obtained for each member of the sample, and the paired scores are then correlated.

(continued)

	4. Data analysis and interpretation. When two variables are correlated, the result is a correlation coefficient, which is a decimal number ranging from −1.00 to +1.00. The correlation coefficient indicates the size and direction of the relation between variables.
Potential challenges	• Sample size. The larger the sample size, the smaller the value needed to reach statistical significance. • Correct choice of correlation method (Pearson *r* or Spearman rho) used to calculate the correlation. • Interpretation of data should not suggest a causal relationship.
Example	Does parental involvement affect the reading achievement of sixth-grade students?

CORRELATIONAL RESEARCH: DEFINITION AND PURPOSE

Correlational research is sometimes treated as a type of descriptive research, primarily because it describes an existing condition. However, the condition it describes is distinctly different from the conditions typically described in survey or observational studies. **Correlational research** involves collecting data to determine whether, and to what degree, a relationship exists between two or more quantifiable variables. The degree of relation is expressed as a correlation coefficient. If two variables are related, scores within a certain range on one variable are associated with scores within a certain range on the other variable. For example, intelligence and academic achievement are related; individuals with high scores on intelligence tests tend to have high grade point averages, and individuals with low scores on intelligence tests tend to have low grade point averages.

The purpose of a correlational study may be to determine relations among variables (i.e., a relationship study) or to use these relations to make predictions (i.e., a prediction study). Correlational studies typically investigate a number of variables believed to be related to a major, complex variable, such as achievement. Variables found not to be highly related to the complex variable are dropped from further examination, whereas variables that are highly related to the complex variable may be examined in causal–comparative or experimental studies to determine the nature of the relationship.

A high correlation between two variables does not imply that one causes the other. For example, a high correlation between self-concept and achievement does not mean that achievement causes self-concept or that self-concept causes achievement. However, even though correlational relations are not cause–effect ones, the existence of a high correlation permits prediction. For example, high school grade point average (GPA) and college GPA are highly related; students who have high GPAs in high school tend to have high GPAs in college, and students who have low GPAs in high school tend to have low GPAs in college. Therefore, high school GPA can be and is used by college admissions officers to predict college GPA. Rarely are two variables perfectly correlated or perfectly uncorrelated, but many are sufficiently related to permit useful predictions. Clearly, the higher the correlation, the closer the relation between the two variables and the more accurate are predictions based on the relation.

In addition, correlational procedures are used to determine various types of validity and reliability. For example, concurrent validity can involve determining the correlation between scores on a test under study (e.g., a new test) and scores on some other established test or criterion (e.g., grade point average), and test–retest reliability is determined by correlating scores from the same test, administered more than once.

MyLab Education **Self-Check 9.1**

MyLab Education **Application Exercise 9.1:** Examining the Purpose of Correlational Research

THE CORRELATIONAL RESEARCH PROCESS

Problem Selection

Correlational studies may be designed either to determine whether and how a set of variables are related or to test hypotheses regarding expected relations. Variables to be correlated should be selected on the basis of some rationale. That is, the relation to be investigated should be a logical one, suggested by theory or derived from experience. Having a theoretical or experiential basis for selecting variables to be correlated justifies the study and makes the interpretation of the results more meaningful. Correlational "treasure hunts" in which the researcher correlates all sorts of variables to see what turns up are strongly discouraged. This research strategy (appropriately referred to as a shotgun or fishing approach) is very inefficient and makes findings difficult to interpret.

Participant and Instrument Selection

The sample for a correlational study is selected by using an acceptable sampling method (see Chapter 5). Historically, a minimally acceptable sample size is generally considered to be 30 participants. If validity and reliability are low, a larger sample is needed because errors of measurement may mask a true relation. The higher the validity and reliability of the variables to be correlated, the smaller the sample can be, but not fewer than 30.

Of course, it is important to select or develop valid and reliable measures for the variables under study. If the instruments do not accurately reflect the intended variables, the resulting correlation coefficient will not accurately indicate the degree of relation. Suppose, for example, you wanted to test the relation between achievement in mathematics and achievement in physics. Even if you administered a valid, reliable test of math computational skill and a valid, reliable test of physics achievement, the resulting correlation coefficient would not be an accurate estimate of the intended relation because computational skill is only one aspect of mathematical achievement. The resulting coefficient would indicate the relation between physics achievement and only one aspect of mathematical achievement, computational skill. Thus, researchers must take care to select measures that are valid and reliable for the purposes of the specific study.

Design and Procedure

The basic correlational research design is not complicated: Scores for two (or more) variables of interest are obtained for each member of the sample, and the paired scores are then correlated. The result is expressed as a correlation coefficient that indicates the degree of relation between the two variables. Some studies investigate more than two variables, and some utilize complex statistical procedures, but the basic design is similar in all correlational studies.

Data Analysis and Interpretation

When two variables are correlated, the result is a correlation coefficient, which is a decimal number ranging from -1.00 to $+1.00$. The correlation coefficient indicates the size and direction of the relation between variables. A coefficient near $+1.00$ has a larger effect size (i.e., it represents a strong relation) and a positive direction. In other words, a person with a high score on one of the variables is likely to have a high score on the other variable, and a person with a low score on one variable is likely to have a low score on the other. If the coefficient is near 0.00, the variables are not related—a person's score on one variable provides no indication of the person's score on the other variable. A coefficient near -1.00 has a larger effect size (i.e., is a strong relation) and a negative or inverse direction. In other words, a person with a high score on one variable is likely to have a low score on the other variable. Note that equal-size correlations with opposing signs (e.g., $+0.80$ and -0.80) represent the same strength of relation. The plus and minus represent different directions of relation. Both strong positive and strong negative relations are equally useful for making predictions.

Table 9.1 presents four scores for each of eight 12th-grade students: IQ, GPA, weight, and errors on a 20-item final exam. The table shows that IQ is highly and positively related to GPA ($r = 0.95$); not related to weight ($r = 0.13$); and negatively, or inversely, related to errors ($r = 0.89$). The students with higher IQs have higher GPAs. Additionally, students with higher IQs tend to make fewer errors (makes sense!). The relations are not perfect, but variables rarely are perfectly related or unrelated. One's GPA, for example, is related to other variables besides intelligence, such as motivation.

TABLE 9.1 • Hypothetical sets of data illustrating a strong positive relation between two variables, no relation, and a strong negative relation

	Strong Positive Relation		No Relation		Strong Negative Relation	
	IQ	GPA	IQ	Weight	IQ	Errors
1. Iggie	85	1.0	85	156	85	16
2. Hermie	90	1.2	90	140	90	10
3. Fifi	100	2.4	100	120	100	8
4. Teenie	110	2.2	110	116	110	5
5. Tiny	120	2.8	120	160	120	9
6. Tillie	130	3.4	130	110	130	3
7. Millie	135	3.2	135	140	135	2
8. Jane	140	3.8	140	166	140	1
Correlation	$r = +.95$		$r = +.13$		$r = -.89$	

The data indicate, however, that IQ is a variable related to both GPA and examination errors. Knowing that Iggie has a low IQ score enables you to predict both a low GPA and a high number of errors.

Figure 9.1 shows a scatterplot for each of the three correlations shown in Table 9.1. The top left scatterplot shows that students who score low on IQ also tend to have low GPAs and that students who score high on IQ also tend to have high GPAs. This pattern illustrates a strong positive correlation. The bottom scatterplot shows that students who score high on IQ tend to have few errors and that students who score low on IQ tend to have many errors. This pattern illustrates a strong negative correlation. The top right scatterplot illustrates a lack of any systematic relation between IQ and weight.

One way to interpret correlation coefficients is shown in the following chart:

Coefficient	Relation Between Variables
Between +0.35 and −0.35	Weak or none
Between +0.35 and +0.65 or between −0.35 and −0.65	Moderate
Between +0.65 and 1.00 or between −1.00 and −0.65	Strong

These figures are approximations and should not be used blindly; often the usefulness of a correlation coefficient depends on its purpose. A correlation coefficient between zero and ±0.50 is generally useless for group prediction or for individual prediction, although a combination of several variables in this range may yield a reasonably satisfactory prediction. Coefficients of ±0.60 or ±0.70 are usually considered adequate for group prediction purposes, and coefficients of ±0.80 and higher are adequate for individual prediction purposes. A correlational criterion-related validity of 0.60 for an affective measuring instrument may be considered high because many affective instruments tend to have low validities. Conversely, we would consider a stability reliability of 0.74 for an achievement test to be low. A researcher would be very happy with observer reliabilities in the 0.90s; satisfied with the 0.80s; minimally accepting of the 0.70s; and progressively unhappier with the 0.60s, 0.50s, and so forth. Thus, a correlation coefficient of 0.40, for example, would be considered useful in a relationship study, not useful in a prediction study, and terrible in a reliability study. A coefficient of 0.60 would be considered useful in a prediction study but would probably be considered unsatisfactory as an estimate of reliability.

The meaning of a correlation coefficient is difficult to explain. However, it does *not* indicate the percentage of relation between variables. Unfortunately, many beginning researchers erroneously

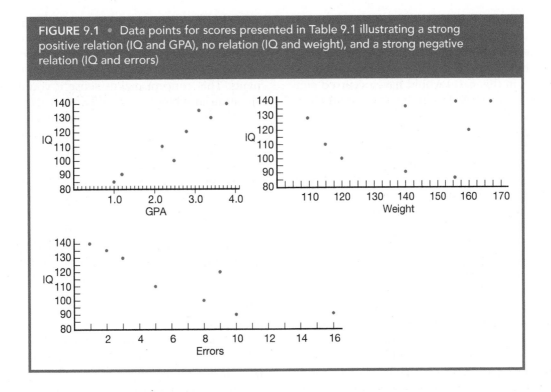

FIGURE 9.1 • Data points for scores presented in Table 9.1 illustrating a strong positive relation (IQ and GPA), no relation (IQ and weight), and a strong negative relation (IQ and errors)

think that a correlation coefficient of 0.50 means that two variables are 50% related. Not true. In the language of research, the square of the correlation coefficient indicates the amount of variance shared by the variables. In more common terms, each variable will have a range of scores, known as the score variance; that is, everyone will not get the same score. In Table 9.1, for example, IQ scores vary from 85 to 140 and GPAs vary from 1.0 to 3.8. **Common variance** (also called *shared variance*) indicates the extent to which variables vary in a systematic way. In technical terms, shared variance is the variation in one variable (e.g., in scores) that is attributable to its tendency to vary with another variable. The more systematically two variables vary, the higher the correlation coefficient. If two variables do not vary systematically, then the scores on one variable are unrelated to the scores on the other variable—no common variance, and the correlation coefficient will be near 0.00. If two variables are perfectly related (positively or negatively), then the variability of one set of scores is very similar to the variability in the other set of scores. This situation reflects a great deal of common variance, and the correlation coefficient will be near ±1.00. In simple terms, the

more the common variance, the higher the correlation coefficient. In Table 9.1, a great deal of the score variance of IQ and GPA, and IQ and errors is common, whereas the common variance of IQ and weight is quite small.

To determine common variance, simply square the correlation coefficient. A correlation coefficient of 0.80 indicates $(0.80)^2$ or 0.64, or 64% common variance. As you can see, the percentage of common variance is less than the numerical value of the correlation coefficient when the coefficient is not 0.00 or 1.00 (a correlation coefficient of 0.00 indicates $[0.00]^2$ or 0.00, or 00% common variance, and a coefficient of 1.00 indicates $[1.00]^2$ or 1.00, or 100% common variance). Thus, a correlation coefficient of 0.50 may look pretty good at first, but it means that the variables have 25% common variance; 75% of the variance is unexplained, not common, variance.

As noted previously, interpretation of a correlation coefficient depends on how it is to be used. In other words, whether a particular value is useful depends on the purpose for which it was computed. In a prediction study, the value of the correlation coefficient in facilitating accurate predictions is important. In a study designed to explore or test hypothesized relations, a correlation coefficient is interpreted in terms of its statistical significance. **Statistical significance** refers to the probability that the results (i.e., a correlation of this size, in this case) would have occurred simply due to chance. At this point, it's important to understand that, to be statistically significant, an obtained correlation coefficient must reflect a true statistical relation, not a chance one. Although no statistical tests allow you to determine whether a correlation is simply due to chance, statistical tests can indicate the probability that it is—and if the likelihood is low (i.e., it's not likely that a correlation of this size is simply due to chance), the researcher can infer a true relation between the two variables. Note carefully that *significant* does not mean *important*; rather, it is a statistical term indicating the probability that a given result is due to chance.

The standard for statistical significance is set by the researcher; convention dictates that the cutoff point is 0.05—that a correlation of this size, for this population, would occur by chance no more than 5 out of 100 times. Another way to express this idea is that the researcher is 95% confident that the results are not simply due to chance occurrences (e.g., random error, sampling techniques, etc.). For example, at the 95% confidence level (probability of chance, or $p = 0.05$), the required coefficient for a sample where $df = 10$ is 0.5760 (in this case, $df = 10$ reflects a sample size of 12—but don't worry too much about how to compute df at this point). At the 99% confidence level ($p = 0.01$), the required correlation is 0.7079. These correlation values can be retrieved from readily available statistical tables.

This example shows that if you want to be more confident that the correlation found in your sample is not simply due to chance, you should set p to be smaller, and the coefficient will need to be higher. Beware, however, of confusing significance with strength. Even if a coefficient is statistically significant (i.e., not simply due to chance), a low coefficient represents a low degree of association between two variables. The level of significance indicates only the probability that a given relation, whether weak or strong, is due to chance.

This example also illustrates another important point, that statistical significance is computed relative to the sample size. To demonstrate a significant relation, the correlation coefficients for small samples sizes must be higher than those for large sample sizes—we generally have more confidence in a correlation coefficient based on 100 participants than one based on only 10 participants. This concept makes sense if you consider a situation in which you could collect data on every member of a population. No inference would be needed because the whole population was in the sample. Regardless of how small the actual correlation coefficient was, it would represent the true degree of relation between the variables for that population. Even if the coefficient were only 0.11, for example, it would still indicate the existence of a significant relation. On the other hand, if only 10 participants from a population of 100,000 were tested, the researcher would have to infer a characteristic about the population from a very small sample. For example, as noted previously, at the 95% confidence level ($p = 0.05$), the required coefficient for a sample of 12 (where $df = 10$) is 0.5760, but the required coefficient for a sample where $df = 100$ is only 0.1946 (remember, larger df = larger sample).

To summarize, the larger the sample, the more closely it approximates the population and therefore the more probable it is that a given correlation coefficient represents a significant relation in that population. For a given sample size, the value of the correlation coefficient needed for statistical significance increases as the level of confidence increases. The level of confidence, commonly called the significance level, indicates how confident we want to be that we have identified a real relation, one that can be generalized from our sample to the population.

When interpreting a correlation coefficient, always keep in mind that you are talking about relation, not cause and effect. When a study shows a strong relation between two variables, researchers are often tempted to conclude that one variable causes the other. For example, a positive relation between self-concept and achievement could mean that having a strong self-concept causes a student to have high achievement. However, two other interpretations are equally possible: Students' experience as high achievers may cause them to have a strong self-concept, or some other factor, such as a good parent–child relationship, is responsible for an individual's strong self-concept and high achievement. A significant correlation coefficient may suggest a cause–effect relation but does not establish one. As you conduct correlation and causal–comparative research, recognize that neither correlation nor causal–comparative research provides true experimental data. The only way to establish a cause–effect relation is by conducting experimental research.

MyLab Education **Self-Check 9.2**

MyLab Education **Application Exercise 9.2:** Evaluating Research Articles: Identifying Steps in the Research Process for a Correlational Study

MyLab Education **Application Exercise 9.3:** Interpreting Correlational Data

---

RELATIONSHIP STUDIES

In a **relationship study,** a researcher attempts to gain insight into variables or factors that are related to a complex variable. Some examples of complex variables in educational research are academic achievement, motivation, and self-concept. For example, a researcher may be interested in whether a variable such as hyperactivity is related to motivation or whether parental punishment is related to elementary schoolchildren's self-concept.

Relationship studies serve several purposes. First, they help researchers identify related variables suitable for subsequent examination in causal–comparative and experimental studies. Experimental studies are costly and often time-consuming, so the use of relationship studies to suggest potentially productive experimental studies is efficient. Second, relationship studies provide information about the variables to control for in causal–comparative and experimental research studies. In other words, if researchers can identify variables that may be related to performance on the dependent variable, they can remove the influence of those variables so that the effect of the independent variable will be clear. If you were interested in comparing the effectiveness of different methods of reading instruction for first-graders, for example, you would probably want to control for initial differences in reading readiness. You could do so by selecting first-graders who were homogeneous in reading readiness or by using stratified sampling to ensure that equal numbers of children at various levels of reading readiness were assigned to each instructional method.

The strategy of attempting to understand a complex variable by identifying variables correlated with it has been more successful for some variables than others. For example, whereas a number of variables correlated with achievement have been identified, factors significantly related to success in areas such as administration and teaching have not been as easy to pin down. On the other hand, relationship studies that have not uncovered useful relations have nevertheless identified variables that can be excluded from future studies, a necessary step in science.

Data Collection

In a relationship study, the researcher first identifies the variables to be correlated. For example, if you were interested in factors related to self-concept, you might identify the variables introversion, academic achievement, and socioeconomic status. As noted previously, you should have a reason for selecting variables in the study. A shotgun approach is inefficient and often misleading. Also, the more correlation coefficients that you compute at one time, the more likely it is that you will draw a wrong conclusion about the existence of a relation. Computing 10 or 15 correlation coefficients generally doesn't cause a problem. Computing 100 coefficients, on the other hand, greatly increases the chance for error. Thus, a smaller number of carefully selected variables is much preferred to a larger number of carelessly selected variables.

After identifying variables, the next step in data collection is identifying an appropriate population of participants from which to select a sample. The population must be one for which data on each of the identified variables can be collected. Although data on some variables, such as past achievement, can be collected without direct access to participants, many relationship studies require the administration of one or more instruments and, in some cases, observations.

One advantage of a relationship study is that all the data may be collected within a relatively short time. Instruments may be administered at one session or at several sessions in close succession. In studies where schoolchildren are the subjects, time demands on students and teachers are relatively small compared to those required for experimental studies, and it is usually relatively easy to obtain administrative approval for a relationship study.

Data Analysis and Interpretation

In a relationship study, the scores for one variable are correlated with the scores for another variable, or scores for a number of variables are correlated with some particular variable of primary interest. The end result of data analysis is a number of correlation coefficients, ranging from +1.00 to −1.00.

There are a number of different methods for computing a correlation coefficient. The appropriate method depends on the type of data represented by each variable. The most common technique uses the product moment correlation coefficient, usually referred to as the **Pearson *r***, a measure of correlation that is appropriate when both variables to be correlated are expressed as continuous (i.e., ratio or interval) data. Because most scores from instruments used in education, such as achievement measures and personality measures, are classified as interval data, the Pearson *r* is usually the appropriate coefficient. And because the Pearson *r* results in the most precise estimate of correlation, its use is preferred even when other methods may be applied.

If the data for at least one variable are expressed as rank or ordinal data, the appropriate correlation coefficient to use is the *rank difference correlation,* usually referred to as the **Spearman rho.** Rank data are found in studies where participants are arranged in order of score and assigned a rank from 1 to however many subjects there are. For a group of 30 participants, for example, the subject with the highest score would be assigned a rank of 1, the subject with the second highest score 2, and the subject with the lowest score 30. When two subjects have the same score, their ranks are averaged. Thus, two participants with the identical high score are assigned the average of Rank 1 and Rank 2, namely, 1.5. If only one of the variables to be correlated is in rank order, the other variable or variables to be correlated with it must also be expressed as rank data to use the Spearman rho technique. For example, if class standing (i.e., rank data) were to be correlated with intelligence, students would have to be ranked from high to low in terms of intelligence. Actual IQ scores (i.e., continuous data) could not be used in calculating the correlation coefficients using the Spearman rho.

The Pearson *r* is more precise, but with a small number of subjects (fewer than 30), the Spearman rho is much easier to compute and results in a coefficient very close to the one that would have been obtained had a Pearson *r* been computed. When the sample is large, however, the process of ranking becomes more time-consuming, and the Spearman rho loses its advantage over the Pearson *r*.

A number of other correlational techniques are encountered less often but should be used when appropriate (see Table 9.2). A *phi coefficient* is used when both variables are expressed in terms of a categorical dichotomy, such as gender (e.g., male or female), political affiliation (e.g., Democrat or Republican), smoking status (e.g., smoker or nonsmoker), or educational status (e.g., high school graduate or high school dropout). These dichotomies are considered "true" because a person is or is not a female, a Democrat, a smoker, or a high school graduate. The two categories typically are labeled 1 and 0 or 1 and 2. Recall that, for nominal variables, a 2 does not mean more of something than a 1, and a 1 does not mean more of a something than a 0. The numbers indicate different categories, not different amounts.

Other correlational techniques are appropriate when one or both variables are expressed as artificial dichotomies. Artificial dichotomies are created by operationally defining a midpoint and categorizing subjects as falling above it or below it. For example, participants with test scores of 50 or higher could be classified as high achievers and those with scores lower than 50 would then be classified as low achievers. Such artificial classifications are typically translated into scores of 1 and 0. These dichotomies are called artificial because variables that were ordinal, interval, or ratio are artificially turned into nominal variables.

Most correlational techniques are based on the assumption that the relation under investigation is a *linear relation,* one in which an increase (or decrease) in one variable is associated with a corresponding increase (or decrease) in another variable. Plotting the scores of two variables that have a linear relation results in a straight line. If a relation is perfect (+1.00 or −1.00), the line will be perfectly straight, but if the variables are unrelated, the points will form a scattered, random plot. Refer again to Figure 9.1, which plots the data presented in Table 9.1. The top left and bottom scatterplots illustrate the concept of a linear relation.

TABLE 9.2 • Types of correlation coefficients

Name	Variable 1	Variable 2	Comments
Pearson *r*	Continuous	Continuous	Most common correlation
Spearman's rho, or rank difference	Rank	Rank	Easy to compute for small samples
Kendall's tau	Rank	Rank	Used with samples of fewer than 10
Biserial	Artificial dichotomy	Continuous	Used to analyze test items; may have r greater than 1.00 if score distribution is oddly shaped
Point biserial	True dichotomy	Continuous	Maximum when dichotomous variable split is 50-50
Tetrachoric	Artificial dichotomy	Artificial dichotomy	Should not be used with extreme splits or sample
Phi coefficient	True dichotomy	True dichotomy	Used in determining inter-item relationships
Intraclass	Continuous	Continuous	Useful in judging rater agreement
Correlation ratio, or eta	Continuous	Continuous	Used for nonlinear relationships

Not all relations, however, are linear; some are curvilinear. In a *curvilinear relation*, an increase in one variable is associated with a corresponding increase in another variable up to a point, at which further increase in the first variable results in a corresponding decrease in the other variable (or vice versa). Plotting the scores of the two variables produces a curve. For example, the relation between age and agility is a curvilinear one. As Figure 9.2 illustrates, agility increasingly improves with age, peaks, or reaches its maximum somewhere in the twenties, and then progressively decreases as age increases. Two other examples of curvilinear relations are age of car and dollar value, and anxiety and achievement. A car decreases in value as soon as it leaves the lot, it continues to depreciate over time until it becomes an antique (!), and then it increases in value as time goes by. In contrast, increases in anxiety are associated with increases in achievement to a point, but at some point, anxiety becomes counterproductive and interferes with learning; after that point, as anxiety increases, achievement decreases. If a relation is suspected of being curvilinear, then an *eta coefficient* is appropriate. If you try to use a correlational technique that assumes a linear relation when the relation is in fact curvilinear, your measure of the degree of relation will be way off base. Use of a linear correlation coefficient to determine a curvilinear correlation will reveal little or no relation.

In addition to computing correlation coefficients for a total participant group, researchers sometimes find it useful to examine relations separately for certain defined subgroups. For example,

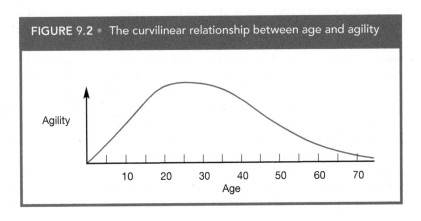

FIGURE 9.2 • The curvilinear relationship between age and agility

the relation between two variables may be different for females and males, college graduates and non-graduates, or high-ability and low-ability students. When the subgroups are combined, differential relations may be obscured. Regardless of whatever worthwhile knowledge may come from subdividing a sample and correlating the subgroups separately, a few cautions must be recognized. For example, subdivision and correlation can be carried out only if the original sample is large enough to permit sufficient numbers in the subgroups. Suppose a researcher starts with a sample of 30 participants, 15 males and 15 females, and subsequently wants to compare the correlations of males and females on the selected variables. Subgroups of only 15 participants are too small to yield stable results. Sometimes researchers recognize this problem and select a larger sample to permit analysis of subgroups. However, if subgroups have highly unequal numbers of participants (e.g., 55 females and 15 males), comparative analyses should not be carried out. If you think you want to study subgroups of your sample, select larger samples and use stratified samples to ensure similar numbers in the subgroups.

Other factors may also contribute to inaccurate estimates of relation. **Attenuation,** for example, is the reduction in correlation coefficients that tends to occur if the measures have low reliability. In relationship studies, a correction for attenuation (i.e., unreliability) can be applied that provides an estimate of what the coefficient would be if both measures were perfectly reliable. If a correction is used, it must be kept in mind that the resulting coefficient does not represent what was actually found. This type of correction should not be used in prediction studies because predictions must be based on existing measures, not hypothetical, perfectly reliable measures.

Another factor that may lead to an underestimation of the true relation between two variables is a restricted range of scores. The more variability (i.e., spread) in each set of scores, the higher the correlation coefficient is likely to be. The correlation coefficient for IQ and grades, for example, tends to decrease as these variables are measured at higher educational levels. Thus, the correlation will not be as high for college seniors as for high school seniors. The reason is that not many college seniors have low IQs—individuals with low IQs either do not enter college or drop out before their senior year. In other words, the range of IQ scores is smaller, or more

restricted, for college seniors, and a correlation coefficient based on a narrow range of scores will tend to be lower than one based on a bigger range. A correction for restriction in range may be applied to obtain an estimate of what the coefficient would be if the range of scores were not restricted, but the resulting coefficient should be interpreted with caution because, like the correction for attenuation, it does not represent what was actually found.

MyLab Education **Self-Check 9.3**

MyLab Education **Application Exercise 9.4:** Understanding Different Statistical Approaches to Correlation

---

PREDICTION STUDIES

If two variables are highly related, scores on one variable can be used to predict scores on the other variable. High school grades, for example, can be used to predict college grades, or scores on a teacher certification exam can be used to predict principals' evaluation of teachers' classroom performance. The variable used to predict (e.g., high school grades or certification exam) is called the **predictor,** and the variable that is predicted (e.g., college grades or principals' evaluations) is a complex variable called the **criterion.**

A **prediction study** is an attempt to determine which of a number of variables are most highly related to the criterion variable. Prediction studies are conducted to facilitate decision making about individuals, to aid in various types of selection, and to determine the predictive validity of measuring instruments. Typical prediction studies include those used to predict an individual's likely level of success in a specific course (e.g., first-year algebra), those that predict which students are likely to succeed in college or in a vocational training program, and those that predict the area of study in which an individual is most likely to be successful. Thus, the results of prediction studies are used not only by researchers but also by counselors, admissions directors, and employers.

More than one variable can be used to make predictions. If several predictor variables correlate well with a criterion, then a prediction based on a combination of those variables will be more accurate than a prediction based on any one of them. For example, a prediction of probable level of GPA in college based on high school grades will be less accurate than a prediction based on high school grades, rank in graduating class, and scores on college entrance exams.

Data Collection

In all correlational studies, research participants must be able to provide the desired data and must be available to the researcher. Valid measuring instruments should be selected to represent the variables. It is especially important that the measure used for the criterion variable be valid. If the criterion were "success on the job," the researcher would have to define "success" in quantifiable terms (i.e., provide an operational definition) to carry out the prediction study. For example, the size of an employee's desk would probably not be a valid measure of job success (although it might be!), whereas number of promotions or salary increases probably would be.

The major difference in data collection procedures for a prediction study and a relationship study is that, in a prediction study, the predictor variables are generally obtained earlier than the criterion variable, whereas in a relationship study, all variables are collected within a relatively short period of time. In determining the predictive validity of a physics aptitude test, for example, success in physics would probably be measured by the end-of-course grade, whereas the aptitude test itself would be administered some time before the beginning of the course. When the researcher must collect data across a lengthy time period, participant loss (i.e., attrition) can be a problem.

After the strength of the predictor variable is established, the predictive relation is tested with a new group of participants to determine how well it predicts for other groups. An interesting characteristic of prediction studies is **shrinkage,** the tendency for the prediction to be less accurate for a group other than the one on which it was originally developed. The reason for shrinkage is that the initial finding may be the result of chance relations that will not be found again with another group of participants. Thus, any predictive relation should be subject to **cross-validation** with at least one other group, and variables no longer found to be related to the criterion measure should be removed.

Data Analysis and Interpretation

Data analysis in prediction studies involves correlating each predictor variable with the criterion variable. It is beyond the scope of this text to discuss the statistical processes in detail, but we provide examples of how to interpret the results of a single prediction study, which includes a single predictive variable, and of a multiple prediction study, which includes more than one predictive variable. In both cases, data analysis is based on a prediction equation.

For single variable predictions, the form of the prediction equation is:

$$Y = a + bX$$

where

Y = the predicted criterion score for an individual

X = an individual's score on the predictor variable

a = a constant calculated from the scores of all participants

b = a coefficient that indicates the contribution of the predictor variable to the criterion variable

Suppose, for example, that we wanted to predict a student's college GPA using high school GPA. We know that the student's high school grade point average is 3.0, the coefficient b is 0.87, and the constant a is 0.15. The student's predicted score would be calculated as follows:

$$Y = 0.15 + 0.87(3.0) = 0.15 + 2.61$$
$$= 2.76 \text{ predicted college GPA}$$

We can compare the student's predicted college GPA to the student's actual college GPA at some subsequent time to determine the accuracy of the prediction equation.

Because a combination of variables usually results in a more accurate prediction than any one variable, a prediction study often results in a multiple regression equation. A **multiple regression equation,** also called a *multiple prediction equation,* is a prediction equation including two or more variables that individually predict a criterion, resulting in a more accurate prediction. For example, suppose we wanted to predict college GPA from high school GPA, SAT verbal score, and the rated quality of the student's college admission essay. The student's high school GPA is 3.0, SAT verbal score is 450, and the rating for the admission essay is 10. If *a* is 0.15 and the coefficients *b* for the three predictors are 0.87, 0.0003, and 0.02, the multiple regression equation would be as follows:

$$Y = 0.15 + 0.87(3.0) + 0.0003(450) + 0.02(10)$$
$$= 0.15 + 2.61 + 0.135 + 0.2$$
$$= 3.095 \text{ predicted college GPA}$$

We would validate the accuracy of the equation by comparing the predicted GPA of 3.095 to the student's actual college GPA.

Predictive studies are influenced by factors that affect the accuracy of prediction. For example, if the predictor and criterion variables are not reliable, error of measurement is introduced and the accuracy of the prediction is diminished. Also, prediction accuracy is lower if the length of time between the measurement of the predictor and the measurement of the criterion is long because an **intervening variable,** a variable that cannot be directly observed or controlled, can influence the link between predictor and criterion variables. Finally, general criterion variables such as success in business or teacher effectiveness tend to have lower prediction accuracy than narrower criterion variables because so many factors make up broad, general criterion variables.

Because relations are rarely perfect, predictions made by single or multiple prediction equations are not perfect. Thus, predicted scores are generally reported as a range of predicted scores using a statistic called the *standard error*. For example, a predicted college GPA of 2.20 may be placed in an interval of 1.80 to 2.60. In other words, a researcher may report that a student with a predicted GPA of 2.20 is predicted to earn a GPA somewhere between 1.80 and 2.60. Thus, for most useful interpretations, a prediction should be viewed as a range of possible scores, not as a single score. Although the predictions for any given individual may be too high or too low, predictions for the total group of applicants are quite accurate on the whole.

As in relational studies, predictive studies can provide an indication of the common variance shared by the predictor(s) and the criterion variables. This statistic, called the coefficient of determination, indicates the percentage of variance in the criterion variable that is predicted by the predictor variable(s). The *coefficient of determination* is the squared correlation of the predictor and the criterion. For example, if the correlation between high school GPA and college GPA is 0.80, the coefficient of determination is 0.80 × 0.80 = 0.64, or 64%. The higher the coefficient of determination, the better the prediction, and 0.64 is a moderately high coefficient of determination. As with relationship studies, and for similar reasons, prediction equations may be formulated for each of a number of subgroups as well as for a total group.

MyLab Education **Self-Check 9.4**

MyLab Education **Application Exercise 9.5:** Evaluating Research Articles: Evaluating a Correlational Study

MyLab Education **Application Exercise 9.6:** Understanding Correlational Research

---

OTHER CORRELATION-BASED ANALYSES

Many sophisticated statistical analyses are based on correlational data. We briefly describe a number of these analyses, recognizing that they are statistically complex.

In multiple regression, continuous predictor variables are used to predict a continuous criterion variable. Discriminant function analysis is quite similar to multiple regression analysis, with one major difference: In *discriminant function analysis,* continuous predictor variables are used to predict a categorical variable. In other words, the predictions made are about categorical group membership, such as introverted/extroverted, high anxiety/low anxiety, or achiever/nonachiever. For example, on the basis of predictor variables such as self-esteem or achievement motivation, discriminant function analysis allows us to classify whether an individual manifests the characteristics of an introvert or an extrovert. Having identified groups who are introverts and extroverts, a researcher may then want to compare the two groups on other variables.

Canonical analysis is an extension of multiple regression analysis. Whereas multiple regression uses multiple predictors to predict a single criterion variable, *canonical analysis* produces a correlation based on a group of predictor variables and a group of criterion variables. For example, we would use canonical analysis if we had a group of predictors related to achievement (e.g., GPA, SAT scores, teachers' ratings of ability, and number of advanced placement courses passed) and wanted to see how these predictors related to a group of criterion variables also related to achievement (e.g., job success, work income, and college GPA). Such analysis produces a single correlation that indicates the correlation among both groups of variables.

Path analysis also allows us to see the relations and patterns among a number of variables. The outcome of a path analysis is a diagram that shows how variables are related to one another. Suppose, for example, that we want to examine the connections (i.e., paths) between variable *X* and variables *A, B,* and *C.* A path analysis based on the correlations among the variables produces a path diagram such as the one shown in Figure 9.3. In this diagram, single arrows indicate connections among variables, and double arrows (*A* to *B*) indicate no direct link. Thus, variables *A* and *B* are individually linked to *D*, and *A* and *B* are linked to variable *C*. Variable *C* is not linked to *D*. Path analyses are useful both for showing the variables that influence a given variable (like *X*) and for testing theories about the ways in which groups of variables are related to a given variable.

An extension of path analysis that is more sophisticated and powerful is called *structural equation modeling* (or LISREL, after the computer program used to perform the analysis). Like path analysis, structural equation modeling clarifies the direct and indirect interrelations among variables relative to a given variable, but it provides more theoretical validity and statistical precision in the model diagrams it produces.

Trying to make sense of a large number of variables is difficult simply because there are so many variables to be considered. *Factor analysis* is a way to take a large number of variables and group them into a smaller number of clusters called factors. Factor analysis computes the correlations among all the variables and then derives factors by finding groups of variables that are correlated highly among each other but have weak correlations with other variables. The factors identified, rather than the many individual items within the factors, are then used as variables. Factor analysis produces a manageable number of factor variables to deal with and analyze.

MyLab Education **Self-Check 9.5**

PROBLEMS TO CONSIDER IN INTERPRETING CORRELATION COEFFICIENTS

The quality of the information provided in correlation coefficients depends on the data from which they are calculated. It is important to ask the following questions when interpreting correlation coefficients:

- Was the proper correlation method used to calculate the correlation? (See Table 9.2.)
- Do the variables have high reliabilities? Low reliabilities lower the chance of finding significant relations.
- Is the validity of the variables strong? Invalid variables produce meaningless results.
- Is the range of scores to be correlated restricted or extended? Narrow or restricted score ranges lower correlation coefficients, whereas broad or extended score ranges raise them.
- How large is the sample? The larger the sample, the smaller the value needed to reach statistical significance. Large samples may show correlations that are statistically significant but practically unimportant.

MyLab Education **Self-Check 9.6**

MyLab Education **Application Exercise 9.7:** Interpreting Correlations

---

FIGURE 9.3 • Example of a path analysis model: The connections of variables *A, B,* and *C* to variable *D*

SUMMARY

CORRELATIONAL RESEARCH: DEFINITION AND PURPOSE

1. Correlational research involves collecting data to determine whether and to what degree a relation exists between two or more variables. The degree of relation is expressed as a correlation coefficient.
2. If two variables are related, scores within a certain range on one variable are associated with scores within a certain range on the other variable.
3. A relation between variables does not imply that one is the cause of the other. You should not infer causal relations on the basis of data from a correlational study.

THE CORRELATIONAL RESEARCH PROCESS

Problem Selection

4. Correlational studies may be designed either to determine whether and how a set of variables are related or to test hypotheses regarding expected relations. The variables to be correlated should be selected on the basis of some rationale suggested by theory or experience.

Participant and Instrument Selection

5. A common, minimally accepted sample size for a correlational study is 30 participants. If the variables correlated have low reliabilities and validities, a bigger sample is necessary.

Design and Procedure

6. In the basic correlational design, scores for two (or more) variables of interest are obtained for each member of a selected sample, and the paired scores are correlated.

Data Analysis and Interpretation

7. A correlation coefficient is a decimal number between −1.00 and +1.00. It describes both the size and direction of the relation between two variables. If the correlation coefficient is near 0.00, the variables are not related.

8. A correlation coefficient near +1.00 indicates that the variables are strongly and positively related. A person with a high score on one variable is likely to have a high score on the other variable, and a person with a low score on one is likely to have a low score on the other. An increase on one variable is associated with an increase on the other.
9. If the correlation coefficient is near −1.00, the variables are strongly and negatively, or inversely, related. A person with a high score on one variable is likely to have a low score on the other variable. An increase on one variable is associated with a decrease on the other variable.
10. Correlations of +1.00 and −1.00 represent the same strength but different directions of relation.
11. A correlation coefficient much lower than 0.50 is generally not useful for group prediction or individual prediction. However, a combination of correlations below 0.50 may yield a useful prediction.
12. Coefficients in the 0.60s and 0.70s are usually considered adequate for group prediction purposes, and coefficients in the 0.80s and higher are adequate for individual prediction purposes.
13. Although all reliabilities in the 0.90s are acceptable, for certain kinds of instruments, such as personality measures, reliability in the 0.70s may be acceptable.
14. Common variance (or shared variance) indicates the extent to which variables vary in a systematic way; it is computed by squaring the correlation coefficient. The higher the common variance, the higher the correlation.
15. Statistical significance refers to the probability that the study results (e.g., a correlation coefficient of this size) would have occurred simply due to chance. To determine whether a correlation is statistically significant, researchers set a standard (e.g., 95% confident, or probability of chance = 0.05) and then compare the obtained correlation to a table that shows correlation coefficient values for particular significance levels and sample sizes.
16. Small samples require larger correlation coefficients to achieve significance. The

value of the correlation coefficient needed for significance increases as the level of confidence increases.

17. A low coefficient represents a low degree of association between the variables, regardless of statistical significance.

18. When interpreting any correlation coefficient, remember that it's an association between variables, not a cause–effect relation.

RELATIONSHIP STUDIES

19. A relationship study is conducted to gain insight into the variables or factors that are related to a complex variable, such as academic achievement, motivation, or self-concept. Such studies give direction to subsequent causal–comparative and experimental studies.

Data Collection

20. In a relationship study, the researcher first identifies the variables to be related. A smaller number of carefully selected variables is preferred to a large number of carelessly selected variables.

21. The population must be one for which data on each of the identified variables can be collected, and one whose members are available to the researcher.

22. One advantage of a relationship study is that all the data may be collected within a relatively short time.

Data Analysis and Interpretation

23. In a relationship study, the scores for one variable are correlated with the scores for another variable, or scores for a number of variables are correlated with some particular variable of primary interest.

24. Methods for computing correlation are distinguished mainly by the type of data to be correlated. The most commonly used correlation is the product moment correlation coefficient (Pearson r), which is used when both variables are expressed as continuous (i.e., ratio or interval) data. The Spearman rho correlation is used when ordinal data (i.e., ranks) are correlated.

25. Most correlational techniques are concerned with investigating linear relations in which an increase (or decrease) in one variable is associated with a corresponding increase (or decrease) in another variable. In a curvilinear relation, an increase in one variable is associated with a corresponding increase in another variable up to a point, at which further increase in the first variable results in a corresponding decrease in the other variable (or vice versa).

26. In addition to computing correlation coefficients for a total sample group, researchers may examine relations among variables for certain defined subgroups, if the sample size is large enough.

27. Attenuation is the reduction in correlation coefficients that tends to occur if the measures have low reliability. In relationship studies, a correction for attenuation can be applied to provide an estimate of what the correlation coefficient would be if both measures were perfectly reliable.

28. A narrow or restricted range of scores can lead to a correlation coefficient underrepresenting the true relation. A correction for restriction in range may be applied to obtain an estimate of what the coefficient would be if the range of scores were not restricted.

PREDICTION STUDIES

29. A prediction study is an attempt to determine which of a number of variables are most highly related to the criterion variable. Prediction studies are often conducted to facilitate decision making about individuals or to aid in the selection of individuals.

30. The variable used to predict is called the predictor, and the variable that is predicted is a complex variable called the criterion.

31. If each of several predictor variables correlates well with a criterion, then a prediction based on a combination of those variables will be more accurate than a prediction based on any one of them.

Data Collection

32. The major difference in data collection procedures for a prediction study and a relationship study is that, in a prediction study, the predictor variables are generally obtained earlier than the criterion variable, whereas in a relationship study, all variables are collected within a relatively short period of time. After the strength of the predictor variable is established, the predictive relation is tested with a new group of participants to determine how well it predicts for other groups.

33. Shrinkage is the tendency for the prediction to be less accurate for a group other than the one on which it was originally developed.

Data Analysis and Interpretation

34. Data analysis in prediction studies involves correlating each predictor variable with the criterion variable.

35. A prediction study using multiple variables results in a prediction equation referred to as a multiple regression equation, which combines all variables that individually predict the criterion to make a more accurate prediction.

36. The accuracy of prediction can be lowered by unreliable variables, length of time between gathering data about the predictor(s) and the criterion variable, and the generality of the criterion.

37. Predicted scores should be reported as a range, not as a single number.

38. The coefficient of determination indicates the percentage of variance in the criterion variable that is predicted by the predictor variable(s).

OTHER CORRELATION-BASED ANALYSES

39. More complex correlation-based analyses include discriminant function analysis, canonical analysis, path analysis, structural equation modeling, and factor analysis.

EXAMPLE: Correlational Study

Parental Involvement and Its Influence on the Reading Achievement of 6th Grade Students

CARMEN ANN HAWES
Eastmont School District

LEE A. PLOURDE
Central Washington University–Wenatchee

ABSTRACT The purpose of this study was to determine the relationship between reading achievement and parental involvement for sixth grade middle school students. The participants were forty-eight sixth grade students who completed parental involvement surveys. The parents of these students also completed a parental involvement survey. The results of the surveys were then compared with the students' reading level as determined by the McLeod Reading Comprehension Test. The data were then statistically compared to determine a correlation utilizing the Pearson Product Moment Correlation formula. Results of the study indicated a slight positive correlation but failed to reject the null hypothesis that there was no relationship between parental involvement and the reading comprehension and achievement of sixth grade students. Implications for further studies are discussed.

An increasingly important view among educators and professionals today is that parents and schools must work in partnership with each other (Alldred & Edwards, 2000). According to the Department of Education and Employment (1998) a child's first-longstanding teacher is his or her parent(s). Research provided by Alldred and Edwards finds that increased participation from parents can only enhance a child's ability to succeed. Regardless of socio-economic status or race, studies show a direct correlation between parental involvement and a child's academic achievement (Baumrind, 1991; Walberg, 1984; Wentzel, 1994; Williams, 1994). (01)

Parental involvement is now recognized as essential not only within the world of education, but by lawmakers as well. The U.S. Department of Education in 1994 stated that, "policymakers recognized the importance of involving parents in schools by incorporating federal legislation into the Goals 2000 Educate America Act" (Kohl, Lengua, & McMahon, 2000, p. 502). According to the eighth U.S. educational goal in Goals 2000, "every school will promote partnerships that will increase parental involvement and participation in promoting the social, emotional, and academic growth of children" (U.S. Department of Education, 1994). Is it happening? Does it make a difference even if it is happening? In an age when students are graduating from high school without being able to read; entering middle school unable to decipher a geography text book; leaving elementary school without the necessary skills to decode a math problem (Dymock, 1993); is this partnership with parents happening? Is a partnership between parents and teachers the key to reading comprehension success? Should we worry about the reading achievement of America's youth? (02)

The slow decline in students' ability to read is valid (Chall, 1996). Research with these findings is abundant today. A September 2000 article from the *Reading Research Quarterly* reported that Harvard-Carnegie conducted a study on reading at the elementary level and found public schools "mediocre at best" (Austin & Morrison, 2000, p. 235). This is a real and immediate problem. Can we look to parents as a valid source of help? (03)

Purpose of the Study

(04) Not only teachers and parents but also other community members must become involved in the movement to establish a strong parent–school connection. The purpose of this study was to show the importance of this movement, and to show actual success in reading comprehension when reading achievement is a priority both in the home and at school. This is an issue that is and will continue to affect society. In an essay written in 1996 by Jeanne Chall, she stated, "I was not to be concerned with whether or not students read as they should since we all know they do not" (p. 303). This is alarming. Teachers see a decline in reading skills, parents see a decline in reading skills, and the public sees a decline in reading skills. Parental involvement appears to be one tool that can be used to improve these skills.

(05) While many studies have been conducted on the affects of parental involvement on children's success in school and even reading achievement (Alldred & Edwards, 2000; Desimone, 1999; Miedel & Reynolds, 1999), little has been done that specifically targets middle school students or higher reading levels. De Jong and Leseman (2001) find that one issue that still remains under researched is that of parental involvement and its effects on more advanced readers. Manning (2000) finds that young adults are at an interesting point in their development, not yet adults no longer children and their specific needs must be dealt with in special ways. This study attempted to look at these unique needs. Is reading achievement affected by parental involvement even in middle school?

> Problem statement: Does parental involvement affect the reading achievement (specifically comprehension) of sixth grade students? The researchers will test a hypothesis regarding the expected relationship between parental involvement and sixth grade students' reading comprehension achievement.

(06) This is a vital issue for educators and parents alike. A burning question in education is how to improve reading skills and comprehension. There is a sense of urgency for services to better address children's failure in school (National Commission on Excellence in Education, 1991). A recent report from the Commission on Excellence in Education finds that 40% of students in this country are at risk to fail in school (1991). This is a prevalent and increasingly tough problem; however, parental involvement has proven a successful start in many studies.

Research Question

> The study investigated an expected relationship between two variables: 1) Parental participation in their child's education as measured by surveys administered to parents and their children (with results averaged), and 2) Reading level (as determined through the McLeod Reading Comprehension Test).
>
> *Are these reliable and valid measures for each of the variables?*

(07) This study attempted to research this problem and answer the question: Does parental involvement affect the reading achievement (specifically comprehension) of sixth grade students?

(08) To decipher the effects of parental involvement on reading achievement in sixth grade students, this study examined parent participation in their child's education through a set of surveys. One was given to parents and one was given to the student. The results of these surveys were averaged, and compared to the reading level of the student (as determined through the McLeod Reading Comprehension Test).

(09) The study looked at factors in the home such as time spent on homework with parental help, time spent reading at home with guidance, time spent by parents conferencing with teachers, etc. "Evidence appears to support a relationship between higher student achievement levels and parents who strive to provide school-based learning materials and books to their young children at home" (Shaver & Walls, 1998). This study aimed to find if this applied to sixth graders as well.

Hypothesis

(10) The following null hypothesis was utilized for this study: There is no relationship between parental involvement and the reading comprehension and achievement of sixth grade students (parental involvement measured through a survey, and reading achievement measured through the McLeod Reading Comprehension Test).

Review of Related Literature

As mentioned previously, reading comprehension is an important and controversial issue in education today. Add to the mix parental involvement and you have an extremely explosive problem for teachers, administrators, and community members alike. Parental involvement and its effect on students' achievement in school is part of school reform plans all over the country (Miedel & Reynolds, 1998). Governors in all 50 states have made parental involvement a priority. Are reading and other aspects of schooling part of the parent's responsibility? Does parental involvement play a role in reading achievement at all? This review will look at previous studies and articles to examine current views on three key issues: reading comprehension and achievement, parental involvement in schooling, and the connection between reading achievement and parental involvement in schooling. (11)

Reading Achievement and Comprehension

"Reading matters: being able to read is both a means and an end to enhancing life materially and intellectually. For this reason, concern about reading standards is an ever-present feature of our society" (Davies, 1999, p. 203). Throughout history, students' reading achievement has remained at the forefront of educational reform. Much literature exists on this problem (Bettencourt, 1982; Chall, 1996; Miedel & Reynolds, 1998). In particular, a divisive issue is reading comprehension. Are students reading for meaning? According to Dymock (1993), this has been and will continue to be a real concern for educators and parents. (12)

Reading achievement, particularly comprehension, is a complex part of education, with discussions on how best to teach reading, how best to assess reading, and how to bring low readers up to standard, being only small parts of the issue. Practices, methods, materials, and teacher training are also keys in this debate (a debate that does not have two clearly opposing sides). Michael Bettencourt (1982) said of reading achievement and other educational problems, " . . . these sort of problems have occurred many times in the history of American education. Each time they have occurred, people have expended enormous energy trying to understand where the problems have come from" (p. 47). There is no easy answer to this dilemma as children continue to decline in their ability to read for understanding. (13)

From declining scores on the verbal portion of the SAT's (Chall, 1996) to a recent report that 24% of elementary students are below grade level in reading ability (Ann, Baumann, Duffy-Hester, Hoffman, & Ro, 2000), it is obvious that this problem must be addressed. Dymock (1993) found that "remedial reading classes are filled with youngsters in late elementary and secondary school who can sound out words but get little meaning from their reading" (p. 86). Reading achievement is a high priority of Goals 2000, a governmental program looking at school reform, and if you ask just about any teacher today they will tell you they struggle with reading instruction in their own classroom. How do we as a society provide extra assistance to those who need it? How do we challenge those who are ready for a challenge? (14)

Middle school students in particular may have reading comprehension problems and therefore increased needs. Broaddus and Ivey (2000) find that not only may students enter middle school unable to read content area text purposefully, but they often are so frustrated by this stage that they won't read either. (15)

According to Chall (1996), when you get a look at the entire picture of reading achievement in this country, the outlook is bleak. Some research finds whole language is the answer, some find a return to phonics and vocabulary instruction is the answer, some find parental involvement is an answer to increased reading comprehension (Shaver & Walls, 1998). The connection between parents and school achievement is real. (16)

Parental Involvement in Schooling

(17)   Parental involvement means different things to different people. Parental involvement has a different degree of importance to different people. According to Adams and Christenson in 1999, " . . . the alliance between home and school has dramatically changed throughout the history of formal education, as have the roles and functions that parents and teachers are expected to fulfill" (p. 477). Throughout time, parents have been "portrayed as both friend and foe in the course of educational reform" (Peressini, 1998, p. 571). Historically, parental involvement wasn't always a welcomed addition to the school community, and even today some view parent–school relations as a power struggle (Peressini, 1998). In the 1840's a school committee in Concord, Massachusetts, found that parents were impeding their children's success in school and made distancing parents from their children's education one of their primary goals (Bettencourt, 1982). Parents at this time were seen as a hindrance to their children's academic success because they were not educated and they did not value the same things that the school did. Has this changed? Are parents still kept at a distance from schools? Do they negatively affect their children's education? In recent educational documents, Peressini (1998) found that parents are typically characterized as obstacles and are in the way of school reform efforts. Shaver and Walls (1998) reported that some research found little to no effect of parental involvement on school achievement for middle age students. For the most part, however, teachers and administrators welcome a helping hand in the overcrowded classrooms of the public schools and agree that parental involvement is one way to bridge reading comprehension gaps.

(18)   Today, it is widely recognized that parents play an essential role in their children's school life. Many types of parental involvement have been shown to develop cognitive growth and success in school (Shaver & Walls, 1998). Rather than ushering parents out, schools are now opening their doors wide to parents and welcoming the partnership. According to Alldred and Edwards (2000), parents and schools are seen by policy makers as having similar functions when it comes to children. This requires them to work in constant partnerships. Over the last 15 years, much time and money have been spent developing parent–school programs, including those that simply educate parents, those that give parents tools to work with their children, and those that put into place actual programs at school for parents and students together (Chapman 1991; D'angelo & Alder, 1991; Epstein, 1991; Nardine & Morris, 1991; Soloman, 1991).

(19)   Why don't parents stay more involved in the education of their children? According to Mannan and Blackwell (1992), there are many different reasons why parents don't participate in their child's education. Some of these barriers are lack of education, feeling unwelcome, and time constraints. This is especially true of ethnic minority parents. Alldred and Edward (2000) found that involving parents from working class and minority groups was difficult because they felt uncomfortable or were put off by language barriers. Do these barriers deter students from performing at their best? Are academics declining because parents are not involved? Is this lack of involvement an even greater blockade at the middle school level? Further research conducted by Alldred and Edwards (2000) found a barrier specific to middle school students was their ability to resist and modify the extent to which their parents participated in their education. "Children and young people can actively shape, and work toward encouraging or discouraging, ensuring or preventing, their parents' involvement in their education for their own reasons" (Alldred & Edwards, 2000, p. 440).

Reading Achievement and Parental Involvement in Schooling

(20)   Where do these two vital issues come together? According to current research this question yields mixed results. It is clear from recent studies that parental involvement does impact education, but what does that mean?

Most recent studies have focused on the consequence of parental involve- (21)
ment with young children and their school experience. In fact, there are
few studies that look at the effects of parent–school relationships on a
child's later development (Olmstead, 1991; Taylor & Machida, 1994). "Further
research is needed to determine the impact of such involvement [parental]
on special student groups and at various age levels . . . " (Shaver & Walls,
1998, p. 90). Research is fairly conclusive as far as early interventions and
involvement of parents. Henderson and Berla (1994) found there to be a
positive relationship between a parent's involvement and a child's early success in school. A review of research in this area by Shaver and Walls (1998)
finds a substantial relationship between a parent's behaviors at home and
his or her child's performance at school. These findings were clear regardless of socioeconomic status. As well, parent participation in preschool and
kindergarten was related to greatly increased scores on ITBS reading tests in
kindergarten (Miedel & Reynolds, 1998). Studies have also shown that parental involvement can be especially beneficial for students in poverty (Alldred
& Edwards, 2000). In broader terms, parental responsibility helps students
to gain knowledge, skills, and attitudes to become productive citizens with
a strong self-concept. Along these lines, evidence has shown a relationship
between parents who support school efforts through learning materials at
home and students' success (Shaver & Walls, 1998).

Summary and Conclusions

Research indicates that reading comprehension is an area in which American (22)
public schools are suffering; children are no longer prepared for the challenges they will face. Students are expected to read " . . . purposefully in
their content area classes by the time they reach the middle grades" (Broaddus & Ivey, 2000, p. 68). Teachers contend that many of these students cannot!
This is a complex educational issue today as it has been throughout history.
Parental involvement has been welcomed and shunned (Bettencourt, 1982).
Reading scores have increased and decreased as methods and materials have
changed over the years. Yet, there is no clear answer. Studies do, however,
indicate that parental involvement can, in some situations, be a positive factor
to academic success, specifically reading (Kohl, Lengua, & McMahon, 2000:
De Jong & Leseman, 2001).

Methods and Procedures
Methods

This was a non-experimental, correlational study designed to determine (23)
the relationship between parental involvement and reading achievement
in sixth grade students. The study did not determine a causal relationship
between the independent variable (parental involvement) and the dependent variable (reading achievement), but rather attempted to find a correlation between the two.

Data were collected in the form of surveys to measure parental involvement (24)
and the McLeod Reading Comprehension test to measure reading level. Descriptive statistics were used to compare the independent and dependent variables.
The data were analyzed using the Pearson Product-Moment Correlation.

Procedures

Data Required. As previously stated, the level of parental involvement, (25)
referred to as x, was measured through the use of a Parental Involvement
Survey developed by the researcher.

As well, a survey was developed and administered to students in order (26)
to portray a more realistic view of actual parental involvement. The parent survey was sent home to the parents of fifty-seven, sixth-grade students

> Is this researcher-developed sur-
> vey instrument valid and reliable?
> How do you know? What evi-
> dence is presented in the article?

243

and was to be returned within one week. The student survey was given in class by an outside observer. No names were used on the surveys; an outside observer coded them. The parent and student surveys were each scored by the researcher and then the scores averaged. This determined the parent involvement score. Reading achievement, referred to as y, was measured through the McLeod Reading Comprehension Test. Each student was given a reading level, roughly equivalent to a grade level, based on his or her performance on the McLeod test.

(27) **Study Sample.** The subjects selected for this study were sixth-grade students from a middle school in East Central Washington. This sample was selected based on the convenience method as the researcher used all students in her Language Arts classes. Fifty-seven students participated. The other participants, parents and guardians, were selected for obvious reasons; their son or daughter was part of the study. The study took place during the 2001–2002 school year.

(28) **Data Collection.** The parent involvement survey was sent to parents and guardians of fifty-seven students. The survey was sent home from school with each participant and then a follow-up call was made to all parents in an attempt to ensure a high return rate. A survey in Spanish was sent home with students whose home language was Spanish as well. The survey was to be returned to the classroom teacher with the student within one week of the send home date.

(29) The student survey, as previously stated, was given in class by an outside observer. Students were given a survey with their code on it and asked to complete it. The surveys were then returned to the classroom teacher for scoring. The survey contained six questions with 4 choices as a possible response. The possible responses were never, almost never, sometimes, and frequently. Each response of *never* was worth 1 point, *almost never* 2 points, *sometimes* 3 points, and *frequently* 4 points, for a possible score of 24. The total from the student survey (out of 24) was added to the total of the parent survey (out of 24), and then an average was determined and used as the parent involvement score for each student.

(30) The instrument used to measure each student's reading ability was the McLeod Reading Comprehension test. This is the test given to all incoming 6th and 7th grade students in many school districts to determine reading level. The McLeod works as a cloze test, one in which students must use context clues and reading strategies in order to fill in missing words. It is a test for understanding. This test is a part of the CORE reading program. CORE is a teaching resource for grades kindergarten through eighth and was developed by Bill Honig, Linda Diamond, and Linda Gutlohn. The test was given individually, and a quiet testing environment was used whenever possible.

Data Analysis

(31) The data in this study were analyzed using the Pearson Product-Moment Correlation. The Pearson is a statistical test used to determine if a relationship exists between two variables. The means for the independent and dependent variables were computed and compared to determine if a relationship existed between the two. When a high correlation is found between two variables, it indicates that an increase in one variable accompanies an increase in another that shows a direct relationship. When a negative correlation is found, it indicates that as the value of one variable increases, the other decreases and no relationship exists. As well, variables may be found to have weak or moderate correlation relationships.

Results

(32) The examiner administered the McLeod Reading Comprehension Test to the student subjects. The results of this test gave each student his/her reading comprehension level (a grade equivalent) ranging from pre-k to level 7. This

---

Is the McLeod Reading Comprehension Test instrument valid and reliable? How do you know? What evidence is presented in the article?

Sample size = 57 sixth grade students.

Sample size exceeds the minimum requirement of 30 participants.

Pearson r is used to determine if a relationship exists between parental participation and reading comprehension. Test is appropriate given that both variables are continuous (ratio or interval data).

comprehension level was known as the dependent variable (y). This variable was then compared to the independent variable (x), which was the parental involvement level.

Parental involvement level, as previously stated, was the average of the score on the student survey and the parent survey. Possible scores ranged from 6 (very little parent involvement) to 24 (frequent parent involvement). Forty-eight out of the original fifty-seven students returned their parent surveys and therefore participated in the study. (33)

The independent and dependent variables were compared using the Pearson Product-Moment to determine if a correlation existed. The correlation score between parental involvement and reading comprehension for these forty-eight students was $r = 0.129$. This number, the correlation coefficient, indicated the direction and strength of the relationship between the two variables and can range from -1 to $+1$. For a positive correlation to occur, there must be an increase in one variable accompanied by an increase in the other variable. A positive correlation coefficient will have a positive value. A negative correlation indicates that as one variable increases, the other decreases. This correlation coefficient will have a negative value. The greater the number is, the stronger the relationship. Therefore, the correlation between parental involvement and reading achievement with these sixth grade students, 0.129, shows a slight positive correlation or relationship. (34)

Summary, Conclusions, and Recommendations
Summary

Reading achievement, especially comprehension, is declining in the U.S. The National Commission on Excellence in Education reported in 1991 that there is an urgency to connect families with children support services to more effectively address academic achievement problems. Baumann, Hoffman, Duffy-Hester, and Ro (2000) reported that " . . . accommodating struggling or underachieving readers is a teacher's greatest challenge" (p. 338). Children no longer have the necessary skills to compete in a global market. What are schools doing to overcome this hurdle? What can society do to alleviate the burden that schools are facing? Parental involvement may be an answer. (35)

Research conducted on children at the primary level tends to be clear. A home–school partnership is necessary. "The home is the first institution of leaning" (McClain, p. 22, 2000). Across racial and social groups, parental involvement has a positive influence on reading comprehension and achievement. Miedel and Reynolds (1999) reported that " . . . although we realize that the relation between family factors and children's school success is complex, the positive influence of parent involvement is consistent . . . " (p. 396). It is generally agreed that direct parental involvement in a child's learning affects that learning in positive ways. It stimulates both academic success and cognitive growth (Epstein, 1991; Wentzel, 1994). Research is less decisive, however, when discussing students at the middle school level. In fact, few studies have even been conducted on the effects of parental involvement on children's later development and achievement in school (Olmsted, 1991; Taylor & Machida, 1994). This study was less than decisive as well. It is known that there is a relationship between parents being involved in their children's education and the success that child achieves, but just how strong that relationship is, is still unknown. (36)

Conclusions

This study found a slight positive correlation between a child's reading comprehension level and the amount of parental involvement in their schooling. The correlation was $r = 0.129$. This correlation is not significant, however, in determining a relationship between the independent and dependent variables. (37)

What correlation value would be required to establish a statistically significant relationship between parental participation and reading comprehension given a sample size of 56?

(38)   Sixth grade students (and middle school students in general) have needs and attributes unique to that age group. They themselves can affect the amount of parental involvement occurring in their education. As well, many other outside factors influence parental involvement. It is known that a child's success can be enhanced by involved parents, however, this study produced unclear results.

Recommendations

(39)   It is abundantly clear after reviewing the results of this study and the literature on this problem that more research must be done on parental involvement at the middle school level. There is no conclusive data and therefore no authority on the issue. It is widely recognized that parental involvement is both valid and influential at the primary level; therefore, it remains a top priority with regards to education reform in the United States. Since middle school students have special considerations, there is a need to focus on the specific needs and characteristics of these burgeoning young adults (Clark & Clark, 1994). Many are not performing at grade level standards and something must be done. It is still unclear if parental involvement is that something, or at least a start.

Limitations of Study

(40)   This study was limited in the fact that one sixth grade was examined. Participants were chosen based solely on the convenience method (the researcher's students were used). Students and their parents from this class only were surveyed and tested, and in this way results are not generalizable. As well, it is often found that not all participants return surveys or spend adequate time in filling them out. Questions contained in the survey dealt with the present practices of parents with regards to their child's education as well as questions dealing with early experiences (retroactive questions). According to Finney (1981), when parents report early experiences about their involvement in their child's education, the results tend to be a bit more favorable than they truly were.

(41)   Of course, a large limitation in this study was outside factors (extraneous variables). These variables, such as motivation, previous teachers, and learning style could also influence reading level and there is no way to account for all of these.

(42)   According to research conducted by Cambourne (2001), there are many factors that contribute to a student's failing to read. From faulty demonstrations, to limited exposure to quality literature, to inadequate feedback from educators, to lack of effort, many things determine whether or not a child learns to read. There is simply no way to have a controlled group of students because their literacy experiences can differ for many reasons.

REFERENCES

Adams, K., & Christenson, S. (2000). Trust and the family-school relationship: Examination of parent-teacher differences in elementary and secondary grades. *Journal of School Psychology, 38* (5), 477–497.

Alldred, P., & Edwards, R. (2000). A Typology of parental involvement in education centering on children and young people: Negotiating familiarisation, institutionalisation and individualisation. *British Journal of Sociology of Education, 21* (3), 435–455.

Ball, S., & Goc, J. (1999). Increasing parental involvement to improve academic achievement in reading and math. Unpublished doctoral dissertation, Saint Xavier University & IRI Skylight, Chicago.

Baumann, J., Duffy-Hester, A., Hoffman, J. & Ro, J. (2000). The first *r* yesterday and today: U.S. elementary reading instruction practices reported by teachers and administrators. *Reading Research Quarterly, 35* (3), 338–379.

Bettencourt, M. (1982). The present in the past: The Concord Public Schools. *The Educational Forum, 1,* 47–57.

Broaddus, K., & Ivey, G. (2000). Tailoring the fit: Reading instruction and middle school readers. *The Reading Teacher, 54* (1), 68–78.

Cambourne, B. (2001). Conditions for literacy learning: Why do some students fail to learn to read? Ockham's razor and the conditions of learning. *The Reading Teacher, 54* (8), 784–786.

Chall, J. (1996). American reading achievement: Should we worry? *Research in the Teaching of English, 30* (3), 303–310.

Ciotti, H. (2001). Including parents in the fun: Sharing literacy experiences. *English Journal, 90* (5), 52–59.

Clark, D., & Clark, S. (1994). Meeting the needs of young adolescents. *Schools in the Middle, 4* (1), 4–7.

Consortium on Reading Excellence, Inc. (1999). Multiple measures: for kindergarten through eighth grade, 112–126.

Davies, J. (1999). Decline in average reading scores in year 6 in one area. *Journal of Research in Reading, 22* (2), 203–208.

De Jong, P., & Leseman, P. (2001). Lasting effects of home literacy on reading achievement in school. *Journal of School Psychology, 39* (5), 389–414.

Desimone, L. (1999). Linking parent involvement with student achievement: Do race and income matter? *Journal of Educational Research, 93* (1), 11–36.

Dymock, S. (1993). Reading but not understanding. *Journal of Reading, 37* (2), 88–91.

Faires, J., Nichols, W., & Rickelman, R. (2000). Effects of parental involvement in developing competent readers in first grade. *Reading Psychology, 21*, 195–215.

Kohl, G., Lengua, L., & McMahon, R. (2000). Parent involvement in school conceptualizing multiple dimensions and their relations with family and demographic risk factors. *Journal of School Psychology, 38* (6), 501–523.

Manning, L. (2000). A brief history of the middle school. *Clearing House, 73* (4), 192.

Metsala, J. (1996). Early literacy at home: Children's experiences and parents' perspectives. *The Reading Teacher, 50* (1), 70–72.

Miedel, W., & Reynolds, A. (1998). Parent involvement in early intervention for disadvantaged children: Does it matter? *Journal of School Psychology, 37* (4), 379–402.

McClain, V. (2000). Lisa and her mom: Finding success in reading the word world. *Language Arts, 78* (1), 21–28.

Peressini, D. (1998). The portrayal of parents in the school mathematics reform literature: Locating the context for parental involvement. *Journal for Research in Mathematics Education, 29* (5), 555–584.

Shaver, A., & Walls, R. (1998). Effect of Title I parent involvement on student reading and mathematics achievement. *Journal of Research and Development in Education, 31* (2), 91–97.

Solo, L. (1999). Adding extras for reading achievement. *Principal, 10* (3), 48–50.

U.S. Department of Education. (1994). Goals 2000 legislation and related items [On-line]. Available: ed.gov/G2

Source: "Parental Involvement and Its Influence on the Reading Achievement of 6th Grade Students," by C. A. Hawes and L. A. Plourde, *Reading Improvement*, Vol. 42, No. 1., Spring, 2005, pp. 47–57. Copyright 2005 by Project Innovation. Reproduced with permission of Project Innovation.

CHAPTER TEN

Causal–Comparative Research

Everett Collection

Multiplicity, 1996

"… [T]he resulting matched groups are identical or very similar with respect to the identified extraneous variable." (p. 254)

LEARNING OUTCOMES

After reading Chapter 10, you should be able to do the following:

10.1 Briefly state the purpose of causal–comparative research and describe the similarities and differences among causal–comparative, correlational, and experimental research.

10.2. Describe the causal–comparative research process.

The chapter learning outcomes form the basis for the following task, which requires you to develop the method section of a research report. In addition, an example of a published study using causal–comparative design appears at the end of this chapter.

TASK 7C

For a quantitative study, you have created research plan components (Tasks 3 and 4A), described a sample (Task 5), and considered appropriate measuring instruments (Task 6). If your study involves causal–comparative research, now develop the method section of a research report. Include a description of the participants, data collection methods, and research design (see Performance Criteria at the end of Chapter 12, p. 335).

SUMMARY: CAUSAL–COMPARATIVE RESEARCH

Definition	In *causal–comparative research*, the researcher attempts to determine the cause, or reason, for existing differences in the behavior or status of groups or individuals.
Design(s)	The basic causal–comparative design involves selecting two groups that differ on some variable of interest and comparing them on some dependent variable. The researcher selects two groups of participants that are sometimes referred to as *experimental* and *control groups* but should more accurately be referred to as *comparison groups*. The groups may differ in two ways: Either one group possesses a characteristic that the other does not, or both groups have the characteristic but to differing degrees or amounts.
Types of appropriate research questions	Questions focused on independent variables that are organismic (e.g., age, sex, ethnicity), ability (e.g., intelligence, aptitude, ability), personality (anxiety, self-esteem), family-related (income, socioeconomic status [SES], family environment), and school-related (preschool attendance, type of school, size of school).
Key characteristic	• Established groups are already different on some variable and the researcher attempts to identify the major factor that has led to this difference.
Steps in the process	1. Develop research questions.
	2. Select two groups that differ on the variable(s) of interest (experimental and control groups/comparison groups). Minimum sample size of 15 in each group. The more homogeneous the groups are on everything but the variable of interest, the better.
	3. Determine the equality of the groups by collecting information on a number of background variables.
	4. Use control procedures (matching, comparison of homogeneous groups and subgroups, and analysis of covariance) to correct for identified inequalities between the groups.
	5. Analyze and interpret the data using descriptive statistics (mean and standard deviation) and inferential statistics (*t* test, analysis of variance, chi square, and analysis of covariance).

(continued)

| Potential challenges | • Because the groups being studied are already formed at the start of the study, the researcher has limited control over the study. Extreme caution must be applied in interpreting results.
• An apparent cause–effect relationship may not be as it appears. In causal–comparative research, only a relation, not necessarily a causal connection, is established.
• Lack of randomization, manipulation, and control are all sources of weakness of causal–comparative research. |
| Example | What differences exist between full-day kindergarten and half-day kindergarten students in mathematics and reading abilities as they progress through elementary school? |

CAUSAL–COMPARATIVE RESEARCH: DEFINITION AND PURPOSE

Like correlational research, causal–comparative research is sometimes treated as a type of descriptive research because it too describes conditions that already exist. Causal–comparative research, however, also attempts to determine reasons, or causes, for the existing condition. Causal–comparative is thus a unique type of research, with its own research procedures.

In **causal–comparative research,** the researcher attempts to determine the cause, or reason, for existing differences in the behavior or status of groups or individuals. In other words, established groups are already different on some variable, and the researcher attempts to identify the major factor that has led to this difference. Such research is sometimes called *ex post facto,* which is Latin for "after the fact," because both the effect and the alleged cause have already occurred and must be studied in retrospect. For example, a researcher may hypothesize that participation in preschool education is the major factor contributing to differences in the social adjustment of first graders. To examine this hypothesis, the researcher would select a sample of first graders who had participated in preschool education and a sample of first graders who had not, and would then compare the social adjustment of the two groups. If the children who participated in preschool education exhibited the higher level of social adjustment, the researcher's hypothesis would be supported. Thus, the basic causal–comparative approach involves starting with an effect (i.e., social adjustment) and seeking possible causes (i.e., did preschool affect it?).

A variation of the basic approach starts with a cause and investigates its effect on some variable. Such research is concerned with questions of "What is the effect of *X*?" For example, a researcher may investigate the long-range effect of failure to be promoted to the seventh grade on the self-concept of children. The researcher may hypothesize that children who are socially promoted (i.e., promoted despite failing grades) have higher self-concepts at the end of the seventh grade than children who are retained or held back to repeat the sixth grade. At the end of a school year, the researcher would identify a group of seventh graders who had been socially promoted to the seventh grade the year before and a group of sixth graders who had repeated the sixth grade (i.e., the cause). The self-concepts of the two groups (i.e., the effect) would be compared. If the socially promoted group exhibited higher scores on a measure of self-concept, the researcher's hypothesis would be supported. The basic approach, which involves starting with effects and investigating causes, is sometimes referred to as **retrospective causal–comparative research.** The variation, which starts with causes and investigates effects, is called **prospective causal–comparative research.** Retrospective causal–comparative studies are much more common in educational research.

Beginning researchers often confuse causal–comparative research with both correlational research and experimental research. Correlational and causal–comparative research are probably confused because of the lack of variable manipulation common to both and the similar cautions regarding interpretation of results. There are definite differences, however. Causal–comparative studies *attempt* to identify cause–effect relations; correlational studies do not. Causal–comparative studies typically involve two (or more) groups of participants and one dependent variable, whereas correlational studies typically involve two (or more) variables and one group of participants. Also, causal–comparative studies focus on differences between groups, whereas correlational studies involve relations among variables. A common misconception held by beginning and even more experienced researchers is that causal–comparative research is somehow better or more rigorous than correlational research. Perhaps this misconception arises because the term *causal–comparative* sounds more official than *correlation*, and we all have heard the research mantra: "Correlation does not imply causation." In fact, however, both causal–comparative and correlation methods fail to produce true experimental data—a point to remember as you continue your causal–comparative and correlational research.

It is understandable that causal–comparative and experimental research are at first difficult to distinguish; both attempt to establish cause–effect relations, and both involve group comparisons. The major difference is that, in experimental research, the independent variable, the alleged cause, is manipulated by the researcher, whereas in causal–comparative research, the variable is not manipulated because it has already occurred (as a result, researchers prefer the term *grouping variable* rather than the term *independent variable*). In other words, in an experimental study, the researcher selects a random sample from a population and then randomly divides the sample into two or more groups. In this way, the researcher manipulates the independent variable; that is, the researcher determines who is going to get what treatment. Any participant's group assignment is independent of any characteristic he or she may possess. In causal–comparative research, in contrast, individuals are not randomly assigned to treatment groups because they are in established

groups (e.g., male/female; college graduates/nongraduates) before the research begins. In causal–comparative research the groups are *already formed* and already differ in terms of the key variable in question. The difference was not brought about by the researcher; it is not independent of the participants' characteristics.

Grouping variables in causal–comparative studies cannot be manipulated (e.g., socioeconomic status), should not be manipulated (e.g., number of cigarettes smoked per day), or simply are not manipulated but could be (e.g., method of reading instruction). Indeed, it is impossible or not feasible to manipulate an independent variable for a large number of important educational problems. For instance, researchers can't control an **organismic variable,** which is a characteristic of a subject or organism. Age and sex are common organismic variables. Additionally, ethical considerations often prevent manipulation of a variable that *could be* manipulated but *should not be*, particularly when the manipulation may cause physical or mental harm to participants. For example, suppose a researcher were interested in determining the effect of mothers' prenatal care on the developmental status of their children at age 1. Clearly, it would not be ethical to deprive a group of mothers-to-be of prenatal care for the sake of a research study when such care is considered to be extremely important to the health of both mothers and children. Thus, causal–comparative research permits investigation of a number of variables that cannot be studied experimentally.

Figure 10.1 shows grouping variables often studied in causal–comparative research. These variables are used to compare two or more levels of a dependent variable. For example, a causal–comparative researcher may compare the retention of facts by participants younger than age 50 to the retention of facts by participants older than age 50, the attention span of students with high anxiety to that of students with low anxiety, or the achievement of first graders who attended preschool to the achievement of first graders who did not attend preschool. In each case, preexisting participant groups are compared.

Like correlational studies, causal–comparative studies help to identify variables worthy of experimental investigation. In fact, causal–comparative studies are sometimes conducted solely to identify the probable outcome of an experimental

| FIGURE 10.1 • Examples of independent variables investigated in causal–comparative studies |

ORGANISMIC VARIABLES	PERSONALITY VARIABLES	FAMILY-RELATED VARIABLES	SCHOOL-RELATED VARIABLES
Age	Anxiety level	Family income	Preschool attendance
Sex	Introversion/extroversion	Socioeconomic status	Size of school
Ethnicity	Aggression level	Employment status (of)	Type of school (e.g., public vs. private)
	Self-concept	Student	Per pupil expenditure
ABILITY VARIABLES	Self-esteem	Mother	Type of curriculum
Intelligence	Aspiration level	Father	Leadership style
Scholastic aptitude	Brain dominance	Marital status of parents	Teaching style
Specific aptitudes	Learning style (e.g.,	Family environment	Peer pressure
Perceptual ability	field independence/	Birth order	
	field dependence)	Number of siblings	

Note: A few of the variables *can be* manipulated (e.g., type of curriculum) but are frequently the object of causal–comparative research.

study. Suppose, for example, a superintendent were considering implementing computer-assisted remedial math instruction in his school system. Before implementing the instructional program, the superintendent might consider trying it on an experimental basis for a year in a number of schools or classrooms. However, even such limited adoption would require costly new equipment and teacher training. Thus, as a preliminary measure, to inform his decision, the superintendent could conduct a causal–comparative study to compare the math achievement of students in school districts currently using computer-assisted remedial math instruction with the math achievement of students in school districts or classrooms not currently using it. Because most districts have yearly testing programs to assess student achievement in various subject areas, including math, obtaining information on math achievement would not be difficult. If the results indicated that the students learning through computer-assisted remedial math instruction were achieving higher scores, the superintendent would probably decide to go ahead with an experimental tryout of computer-assisted remedial math instruction in his own district. If no differences were found, the superintendent would probably not go ahead with the experimental tryout, preferring not to waste time, money, and effort.

Despite its many advantages, causal–comparative research has some serious limitations that should be kept in mind. Because the groups are already formed at the start of the study, the researcher has limited control over the study, and

extreme caution must be applied in interpreting results. An apparent cause–effect relation may not be as it appears. As with a correlational study, only a relationship is established, and not necessarily a causal one. The alleged cause of an observed effect may in fact be the effect itself, or a third variable may have caused both the apparent cause and the effect. For example, suppose a researcher hypothesized that self-concept is a determinant of reading achievement. The researcher would compare the achievement of two groups, one comprising individuals with strong self-concepts and one comprising individuals with weak self-concepts. If the strong self-concept group indeed performed better on reading measures, the researcher could be tempted to conclude that self-concept influences reading achievement. However, this conclusion would be unwarranted. Because the participants arrived at the start of the study with an established self-concept and an established level of reading achievement, it is not possible to determine which came first and thus which influenced the other. Imagine if the variables in the study were reversed—the researcher selected a group of high achievers and a group of low achievers and measured their self-concepts. If the groups had different self-concept scores, the same temptation to infer causality exists, but in the reverse direction— simply by swapping the grouping and dependent variables, the apparent causal relation reverses, and now it appears that high achievement causes strong self-concept! Moreover, it's very plausible that some third variable, such as parental attitude, is the main influence on both self-concept and achievement. For example, parents who praise and encourage their children may have children who have strong self-concepts *and* high academic achievement.

To summarize, caution must be exercised in claiming cause–effect relations based on causal–comparative research. Nevertheless, despite the limitations, causal–comparative studies permit investigation of variables that cannot or should not be investigated experimentally, facilitate decision making, provide guidance for experimental studies, and are less costly on all dimensions.

> MyLab Education **Self-Check 10.1**
>
> MyLab Education **Application Exercise 10.1:** Evaluating Research Articles: Evaluating a Causal–Comparative Study

THE CAUSAL–COMPARATIVE RESEARCH PROCESS

The basic causal–comparative design is quite simple and, although the grouping variable is not manipulated, control procedures can be implemented to improve interpretation of results. Causal–comparative studies also involve a wider variety of statistical techniques than the other types of research discussed so far.

Design and Procedure

The basic causal–comparative design involves selecting two groups that differ on some variable of interest and comparing them on some dependent variable. As Table 10.1 indicates, the researcher selects two groups of participants, which are sometimes referred to as *experimental* and *control groups* but should more accurately be referred to as *comparison groups*. The groups may differ in two ways: Either one group possesses a characteristic that the other does not (Case A), or both groups have the characteristic but to differing degrees or amounts (Case B). An example of Case A is a comparison of two groups, one composed of children with brain injuries and the other composed of children without brain injuries. An example of Case B is a comparison of two groups, one composed of individuals with strong self-concepts and the other composed of individuals with weak self-concepts. Another Case B example is a comparison of the algebra achievement of two groups, those who had learned algebra via traditional instruction and those who had learned algebra via computer-assisted instruction. In both Case A and Case B designs, the performance of the groups is compared using some valid measure selected from the types of instruments discussed in Chapter 7.

Definition and selection of the comparison groups are very important parts of the causal–comparative procedure. The variable differentiating the groups must be clearly and operationally defined because each group represents a different

TABLE 10.1 • The basic causal–comparative design			
	Group	Grouping Variable	Dependent Variable
Case A	(E)	(X)	0
	(C)		0
Case B	(E)	(X_1)	0
	(C)	(X_2)	0
Symbols:			

Symbols:

(E) = experimental group; ( ) indicates no manipulation

(C) = control group

(X) = grouping variable

0 = dependent variable

population, and the way in which the groups are defined affects the generalizability of the results. If a researcher wanted to compare a group of students with an unstable home life to a group of students with a stable home life, the terms *unstable* and *stable* would have to be operationally defined. An unstable home life could refer to any number of things, such as life with a parent who abuses alcohol, who is violent, and/or who neglects the child. It could refer to a combination of these or other factors. Operational definitions help define the populations and guide sample selection.

Random selection from the defined populations is generally the preferred method of participant selection. The important consideration is to select samples that are representative of their respective populations. Note that, in causal–comparative research, the researcher samples from two already existing populations, not from a single population. The goal is to have groups that are as similar as possible on all relevant variables except the grouping variable. To determine the equality of groups, information on a number of background and current status variables may be collected and compared for each group. For example, information on age, years of experience, gender, and prior knowledge may be obtained and examined for the groups being compared. The more similar the two groups are on such variables, the more homogeneous they are on everything but the variable of interest. This homogeneity makes a stronger study and reduces the number of possible alternative explanations of the research findings. Not surprisingly, then, a number of control procedures correct for identified inequalities on such variables.

Control Procedures

Lack of randomization, manipulation, and control are all sources of weakness in a causal–comparative study. In other study designs, random assignment of participants to groups is probably the best way to try to ensure equality of groups, but random assignment is not possible in causal–comparative studies because the groups are naturally formed before the start of the study. Without random assignment, the groups are more likely to be different on some important variable (e.g., gender, experience, age) other than the variable under study. This other variable may be the real cause of the observed difference between the groups.

For example, a researcher who simply compared a group of students who had received preschool education to a group who had not may conclude that preschool education results in higher first-grade reading achievement. However, if all preschool programs in the region in which the study was conducted were private and required high tuition, the researcher would really be investigating the effects of preschool education combined with membership in a well-to-do family. Perhaps parents in such families provide early informal reading instruction for their children. In this case, it is very difficult to disentangle the effects of preschool education from the effects of affluent families on first-grade reading. A researcher aware of the situation could control for this variable by studying only children of well-to-do parents. Thus, the two groups to be compared would be equated with respect to the extraneous variable of parents' income level. This example is but one illustration of a number of statistical and nonstatistical methods that can be applied in an attempt to control for extraneous variables.

The following sections describe three control techniques: matching, comparing homogeneous groups or subgroups, and analysis of covariance.

Matching

Matching is a technique for equating groups on one or more variables. If researchers identify a variable likely to influence performance on the dependent variable, they may control for that variable by *pair-wise matching* of participants. In other words, for each participant in one group, the researcher finds a participant in the other group with the same or very similar score on the control variable. If a participant in either group does not have a suitable match, the participant is eliminated from the study. Thus, the resulting matched groups are identical or very similar with respect to the identified extraneous variable. For example, if a researcher matched participants in each group on IQ, a participant in one group with an IQ of 140 would be matched with a participant with an IQ at or near 140 in the other group. A major problem with pair-wise matching is that invariably some participants have no match and must therefore be eliminated from the study. The problem becomes even more serious when the researcher attempts to match participants on two or more variables simultaneously.

Comparing Homogeneous Groups or Subgroups

Another way to control extraneous variables is to compare groups that are homogeneous with respect to the extraneous variable. In the study about preschool attendance and first-grade achievement, the decision to compare children only from well-to-do families is an attempt to control extraneous variables by comparing homogeneous groups. If, in another situation, IQ were an identified extraneous variable, the researcher could limit groups only to participants with IQs between 85 and 115 (i.e., average IQ). This procedure may lower the number of participants in the study and also limit the generalizability of the findings because the sample of participants includes such a limited range of IQ.

A similar but more satisfactory approach is to form subgroups within each group to represent all levels of the control variable. For example, each group may be divided into subgroups based on IQ: high (e.g., 116 and above), average (e.g., 85 to 115), and low (e.g., 84 and below). The existence of comparable subgroups in each group controls for IQ. This approach also permits the researcher to determine whether the target grouping variable affects the dependent variable differently at different levels of IQ, the control variable. That is, the researcher can examine whether the effect on the dependent variable is different for each subgroup.

If subgroup comparison is of interest, the best approach is not to do separate analyses for each subgroup but to build the control variable into the research design and analyze the results with a statistical technique called factorial analysis of variance. A **factorial analysis of variance** (discussed further in Chapter 18) allows the researcher to determine the effects of the grouping variable (for causal–comparative designs) or independent variable (for experimental designs) and the control variable both separately and in combination. In other words, factorial analysis of variance tests for an interaction between the independent/grouping variable and the control variable such that the independent/grouping variable operates differently at each level of the control variable. For example, a causal–comparative study of the effects of two different methods of learning fractions may include IQ as a control variable. One potential interaction between the grouping and control variable would be that a method involving manipulation of blocks is more effective than other methods for students with lower IQs, but the manipulation method is no more effective than other methods for students with higher IQs.

Analysis of Covariance

Analysis of covariance is a statistical technique for adjusting initial group differences on variables used in causal–comparative and experimental studies. In essence, **analysis of covariance** adjusts scores on a dependent variable for initial differences on some other variable related to performance on the dependent variable. For example, suppose we planned a study to compare two methods, X and Y, of teaching fifth-graders to solve math problems. When we gave the two groups a test of math ability prior to introducing the new teaching methods, we found that the group to be taught by Method Y scored much higher than the group to be taught by Method X. This difference suggests that the Method Y group will be superior to the Method X group at the end of the study just because members of the group began with higher math ability than members of the other group. Analysis of covariance statistically adjusts the scores of the Method Y group to remove the initial advantage so that, at the end of the study, the results can be fairly compared, as if the two groups started equally.

Data Analysis and Interpretation

Analysis of data in causal–comparative studies involves a variety of descriptive and inferential statistics. All the statistics that may be used in a causal–comparative study may also be used in an experimental study. Briefly, however, the most commonly used descriptive statistics are the *mean*, which indicates the average performance of a group on a measure of some variable, and the *standard deviation*, which indicates the spread of a set of scores around the mean—that is, whether the scores are relatively close together and clustered around the mean or widely spread out around the mean. The most commonly used inferential statistics are the *t test,* used to determine whether the scores of two groups are significantly different from one another; *analysis of variance*, used to test for significant differences among the scores for three or more groups; and *chi square*, used to compare group frequencies—that is, to see if an event occurs more frequently in one group than another. Chapters 18 and 19 provide comprehensive coverage of descriptive and inferential statistics.

Again, remember that interpreting the findings in a causal–comparative study requires considerable caution. Without randomization, manipulation, and control factors, it is difficult to establish cause–effect relations with any great degree of confidence. The cause–effect relation may in fact be the reverse of the one hypothesized (i.e., the alleged cause may be the effect, and vice versa). Reversed causality is not a reasonable alternative in every case, however. For example, preschool training may affect reading achievement in third grade, but reading achievement in third grade cannot affect preschool training. Similarly, one's gender may affect one's achievement in mathematics, but one's achievement in mathematics certainly does not affect one's gender! When reversed causality is plausible, it should be investigated. For example, it is equally plausible that excessive absenteeism produces, or leads to, involvement in criminal activities as it is that involvement in criminal activity produces, or leads to, excessive absenteeism. The way to determine the correct order of causality—which variable caused which—is to determine which one occurred first. If, in the preceding example, a period of excessive absenteeism were frequently followed by a student getting in trouble with the law, then the researcher could reasonably conclude that excessive absenteeism leads to involvement in criminal activities. On the other hand, if a student's first involvement in criminal activities were preceded by a period of good attendance but followed by a period of poor attendance, then the conclusion that involvement in criminal activities leads to excessive absenteeism would be more reasonable.

The possibility of a third, common explanation is also plausible in many situations. Recall the example of parental attitude affecting both self-concept and achievement, presented earlier in the chapter. As mentioned, one way to control for a potential common cause is to compare homogeneous groups. For example, if students in both the strong self-concept group and the weak self-concept group could be selected from parents who had similar attitudes, the effects of parents' attitudes would be removed because both groups would have been exposed to the same parental attitudes. To investigate or control for alternative hypotheses, the researcher must be aware of them and must present evidence that they are not better explanations for the behavioral differences under investigation.

MyLab Education **Self-Check 10.2**

MyLab Education **Application Exercise 10.2:** Evaluating Research Articles: Identifying Steps in the Research Process for a Causal–Comparative Study

MyLab Education **Application Exercise 10.3:** Planning a Causal–Comparative Study

SUMMARY

CAUSAL–COMPARATIVE RESEARCH: DEFINITION AND PURPOSE

1. In causal–comparative research, the researcher attempts to determine the cause, or reason, for existing differences in the behavior or status of groups.
2. The basic causal–comparative approach is retrospective; that is, it starts with an effect and seeks its possible causes. A variation of the basic approach is prospective—that is, starting with a cause and investigating its effect on some variable.
3. An important difference between causal–comparative and correlational research is that causal–comparative studies involve two (or more) groups of participants and one grouping variable, whereas correlational studies typically involve two (or more) variables and one group of participants. Neither causal–comparative nor correlational research produces true experimental data.
4. The major difference between experimental research and causal–comparative research is that, in experimental research, the researcher can randomly form groups and manipulate the independent variable. In causal–comparative research the groups are already formed and already differ in terms of the variable in question.
5. Grouping variables in causal–comparative studies cannot be manipulated, should not be manipulated, or simply are not manipulated but could be.
6. Causal–comparative studies identify relations that may lead to experimental studies but only if a relation is established clearly. The alleged cause of an observed causal–comparative effect may in fact be the supposed cause, the effect, or a third variable that may have affected both the apparent cause and the effect.

THE CAUSAL–COMPARATIVE RESEARCH PROCESS

Design and Procedure

7. The basic causal–comparative design involves selecting two groups differing on some variable of interest and comparing them on some dependent variable. One group may possess a characteristic that the other does not, or one group may possess more of a characteristic than the other.
8. Samples must be representative of their respective populations and similar with respect to critical variables other than the grouping variable.

Control Procedures

9. Lack of randomization, manipulation, and control are all sources of weakness in a causal–comparative design. It is possible that the groups are different on some other major variable besides the target variable of interest, and this other variable may be the cause of the observed difference between the groups.
10. Three approaches to overcoming problems of initial group differences on an extraneous variable are matching, comparing homogeneous groups or subgroups, and analysis of covariance.

Data Analysis and Interpretation

11. The descriptive statistics most commonly used in causal–comparative studies are the mean, which indicates the average performance of a group on a measure of some variable, and the standard deviation, which indicates how spread out a set of scores is—that is, whether the scores are relatively close together and clustered around the mean or widely spread out around the mean.
12. The inferential statistics most commonly used in causal–comparative studies are the *t* test, which is used to determine whether the scores of two groups are significantly different from one another; analysis of variance, used to test for significant differences among the scores for three or more groups; and chi square, used to see if an event occurs more frequently in one group than another.
13. Interpreting the findings in a causal–comparative study requires considerable caution. The alleged cause–effect relation may be the effect, and vice versa, or a third factor may be the cause of both variables. The way to determine the correct order of causality is to determine which one occurred first.

Comparing Longitudinal Academic Achievement of Full-Day and Half-Day Kindergarten Students

JENNIFER R. WOLGEMUTH
R. BRIAN COBB[1]
MARC A. WINOKUR
Colorado State University

NANCY LEECH
University of Colorado–Denver

DICK ELLERBY
Poudre School District

ABSTRACT   The authors compared the achievement of children who were enrolled in full-day kindergarten (FDK) to a matched sample of students who were enrolled in half-day kindergarten (HDK) on mathematics and reading achievement in Grades 2, 3, and 4, several years after they left kindergarten. Results showed that FDK students demonstrated significantly higher achievement at the end of kindergarten than did their HDK counterparts, but that advantage disappeared quickly by the end of the first grade. Interpretations and implications are given for that finding.

Key words: academic achievement of full and half-day kindergarten students, mathematics and reading success in elementary grades.

(01)   Coinciding with increases in pre-kindergarten enrollment and the number of parents working outside of the home, full-day kindergarten (FDK) has become exceedingly popular in the United States (Gullo & Maxwell, 1997). The number of students attending FDK classes in the United States rose from 30% in the early 1980s (Holmes & McConnell, 1990) to 55% in 1998 (National Center for Education Statistics, 2000), reflecting societal changes and newly emerging educational priorities. Whereas kindergarten students were required to perform basic skills, such as reciting the alphabet and counting to 20, they are now expected to demonstrate reading readiness and mathematical reasoning while maintaining the focus and self-control necessary to work for long periods of time (Nelson, 2000).

(02)   In contrast, the popularity of half-day kindergarten (HDK) has decreased for similar reasons. For example, parents prefer FDK over HDK for the time it affords (Clark & Kirk, 2000) and for providing their children with further opportunities for academic, social, and personal enrichment (Aten, Foster, & Cobb, 1996; Cooper, Foster, & Cobb, 1998a, 1998b).

(03)   The shift in kindergarten preferences has resulted in a greater demand for research on the effects of FDK in comparison with other scheduling approached (Gullo & Maxwell, 1997). Fusaro (1997) cautioned[,] . . . that "Before a school district decides to commit additional resources to FDK

Address correspondence to R. Brian Cobb, College of Applied Human Sciences, Colorado State University, 222 West Laurel Street, Fort Collins, CO 80521. (E-mail: cobb@cahs.colostate.edu) Copyright © 2006 Heldref Publications.

classes, it should have empirical evidence that children who attend FDK manifest greater achievement than children who attend half-day kindergarten" (p. 270). According to the literature, there is mounting evidence that supports the academic, social, and language development benefits of FDK curricula (Cryan, Sheehan, Wiechel, & Bandy-Hedden, 1992; Hough & Bryde, 1996; Karweit, 1992; Lore, 1992; Nelson, 2000). Successful FDK programs specifically extend traditional kindergarten objectives and use added class hours to afford children more opportunities to fully integrate new learning (Karweit, 1992). Furthermore, most education stakeholders support FDK because they believe that it provides academic advantages for students, meets the needs of busy parents, and allows primary school teachers to be more effective (Ohio State Legislative Office of Education Oversight [OSLOEO], 1997).

Length of School Day

According to Wang and Johnstone (1999), the "major argument for full-day kindergarten is that additional hours in school would better prepare children for first grade and would result in a decreased need for grade retention" (p. 27). Furthermore, extending the kindergarten day provides educational advantages resulting from increased academic emphasis, time on task, and content coverage (Karweit, 1992; Nelson, 2000; Peck, McCaig, & Sapp, 1988). Advocates of FDK also contend that a longer school day allows teachers to provide a relaxed classroom atmosphere in which children can experience kindergarten activities in a less hurried manner (McConnell & Tesch, 1986). Karweit (1992) argued that consistent school schedules and longer school days help parents to better manage family and work responsibilities while providing more time for individualized attention for young children. (04)

Critics of FDK express concern that "children may become overly tired with a full day of instruction, that children might miss out on important learning experiences at home, and that public schools should not be in the business of providing 'custodial' child care for 5-year-olds" (Elicker & Mathur, 1997, p. 461). Peck and colleagues (1988) argued that some FDK programs use the extra time to encroach on the first-grade curriculum in an ill-advised attempt to accelerate children's cognitive learning. However, in a 9-year study of kindergarten students, the Evansville-Vanderburgh School Corporation (EVSC, 1988) found that school burnout and academic stress were not issues for FDK students. Others conclude convincingly that the events that occur in classrooms (e.g., teacher philosophy, staff development), rather than the length of the school day, determine whether curricula and instruction are developmentally appropriate for young students (Clark & Kirk, 2000; Elicker & Mathur, 1997; Karweit, 1994). (05)

Parent Choice

A critical factor driving the growth of FDK is greater parent demand for choice in kindergarten programs. Although surveys of parents with children in HDK often mention the importance of balancing education outside the home with quality time in the home, Elicker and Mathur (1997) found that a majority of these parents would select an FDK program for their child if given the opportunity. However, Cooper and colleagues (1998a) found that parents of FDK students were even more supportive of having a choice of programs than were parents of HDK students. (06)

Although some parents expressed concern about the length of time that children were away from home, most were content with her option of FDK (Nelson, 2000): In addition to the belief that FDK better accommodates their work schedules (Nelson), "parents of full-day children expressed (07) higher levels of satisfaction with program schedule and curriculum, citing benefits similar to those expressed by teachers: more flexibility; more time for child-initiated, in-depth, and creative activities; and less stress and frustration" (Elicker & Mathur, 1997, p. 459). Furthermore, Cooper and colleagues (1998a) found that parents of full-day students were happy with the increased opportunities for academic learning afforded by FDK programs.

Student Achievement

(08) Most researchers who compared the academic achievement levels of FDK and HDK kindergarten students found improved educational performance within FDK programs (Cryan et al., 1992; Elicker & Mathur, 1997; Holmes & McConnell, 1990; Hough & Bryde 1996; Koopmans, 1991; Wang & Johnstone, 1999). In a meta-analysis of FDK research, Fusaro (1997) found that students who attended FDK demonstrated significantly higher academic achievement than did students in half-day programs. Hough and Bryde (1996) matched six HDK programs with six FDK programs and found that FDK students outperformed HDK students on language arts and mathematics criterion-referenced assessments. In a study of 985 kindergarten students, Lore (1992) found that 65% of the students who attended an FDK program showed relatively stronger gains on the reading and oral comprehension sections of the Comprehensive Test of Basic Skills. In a 2-year evaluation of a new FDK program, Elicker and Mathur (1997) reported that FDK students demonstrated significantly more progress in literacy, mathematics, and general learning skills, as compared with students in HDK programs. However, some researchers have not found significant differences between the academic achievement of students from FDK and HDK programs (e.g., Gullo & Clements, 1984; Holmes & McConnell, 1990; Nunnally, 1996).

Longitudinal Student Achievement

(09) Evidence supporting the long-term effectiveness of FDK is less available and more inconsistent than is its short-term effectiveness (Olsen & Zigler, 1989). For example, the EVSC (1988) reported that FDK students had higher grades than did HDK students throughout elementary and middle school, whereas Koopmans (1991) found that the "significance of the differences between all-day and half-day groups disappears in the long run [as] test scores go down over time in both cohorts" (p. 16). Although OSLOEO (1997) concluded that the academic and social advantages for FDK students were diminished after the second grade, Cryan and colleagues (1992) found that the positive effects from the added time offered by FDK lasted well into the second grade.

(10) Longitudinal research of kindergarten programming conducted in the 1980s (Gullo, Bersani, Clements & Bayless, 1986; Puleo, 1988) has been criticized widely for its methodological flaws and design weaknesses. For example, Elicker and Mathur (1997) identified the noninclusion of initial academic abilities in comparative models as a failing of previous longitudinal research on the lasting academic effects of FDK.

Study Rationale

(11) In 1995, the Poudre School District (PSD) implemented a tuition-based FDK program in addition to HDK classes already offered. Although subsequent surveys of parent satisfaction revealed that FDK provided children with further opportunities for academic enrichment (Aten et al., 1996; Cooper et al., 1998a, 1998b), researchers have not determined the veracity of these assumptions. Thus, we conducted the present study to address this gap in the empirical evidence base.

Research Questions

Because of the inconclusiveness in the research literature on the longitudinal academic achievement of FDK versus HDK kindergarten students, we did not pose a priori research hypotheses. We developed the following research questions around the major main effects and interactions of the kindergarten class variable (full day vs. half day), covariates (age and initial ability), and dependent variables (K–5 reading and mathematics achievement).

1. What difference exists between FDK and HDK kindergarten students in their mathematics and reading abilities as they progress through elementary school, while controlling for their initial abilities?
2. How does this differential effect vary, depending on student gender?

Method
Participants

The theoretical population for this study included students who attended elementary schools in moderately sized, middle-to-upper class cities in the United States. The actual sample included 489 students who attended FDK or HDK from 1995 to 2001 at one elementary school in a Colorado city of approximately 125,000 residents. Because this study is retrospective, we used only archival data to build complete cases for each student in the sample. Hence, no recruitment strategies were necessary.

Students were enrolled in one of three kindergarten classes: 283 students (57.9%) attended half-day classes (157 half-day morning and 126 half-day afternoon) and 206 students (42.1%) attended full-day classes. Students' ages ranged from 5 years 0 months to 6 years 6 months upon entering kindergarten; overall average age was 5 years 7 months. The total study included 208 girls (44.0%) and 265 boys (56.0%). The majority of students received no monetary assistance for lunch, which was based on parent income (89.0%, $n = 424$); 49 students (10.0%) received some assistance. Twenty-six students (5.3%) spoke a language at home other than English. The majority of students (90.5%, $n = 428$) were Caucasian; 31 students (6.3%) were Hispanic; and 14 students (2.8%) were African American, Native American, or Asian American. Those data reflect the community demographics within the school district. Because of the potential for individual identification based on the small numbers of students within the various ethnic groups and those receiving lunch assistance, our analyses excluded ethnicity and lunch assistance as control variables.

Intervention

We excluded from the study students who switched during the academic year from FDK to a HDK (or vice versa). FDK comprised an entire school day, beginning at 8:30 a.m. and ending at 3:00 p.m. HDK morning classes took place from 8:30 a.m. to 11:15 a.m.; HDK afternoon classes occurred from 12:15 p.m. to 3:00 p.m. FDK recessed at lunch and provided a 30-min rest period in the afternoon when students typically napped, watched a video, or both. HDK student also recessed but did not have a similar rest period. Both kindergarten programs employed centers (small ability-based groups) as part of their reading and mathematics instruction, and all kindergarten teachers met weekly to discuss and align their curriculum. The amount of time spent on reading instruction was two or three times greater than that dedicated to mathematics.

Reading Curriculum. The kindergarten reading curriculum was based predominantly on the Open Court system, which emphasizes phonemic awareness. Students learned to segment and blend words by pronouncing and repronouncing words when beginnings and endings were removed. Teachers also included daily "letters to the class" on which students identified the

(12)

Research questions are appropriate given the focus on the variable of full-day kindergarten versus half-day kindergarten and the effects of these two program choices on student achievement in mathematics and reading abilities as they progress through elementary school. It would not be ethical to randomly assign children to FDK and HDK programs. Researchers are also interested in whether the organismic variable of gender plays a role in student achievement.

(13)

Participant selection of 489 students provided a substantial sample that far exceeds the minimum requirement of 15 participants per group.

(14)

Researchers relied on archival data to build complete cases for each student in the sample.

The researchers chose not to include participants from various ethnic groups represented in the population and those receiving lunch assistance from the study. What potential impact could this decision have on the outcomes of the study?

(15)

(16)

letters of the day and circled certain words. Teachers also read stories to students, helped students write capital and lowercase letters and words, and encouraged them to read on their own and perform other reading activities. Teachers expected the students to know capital and lowercase letters and their sounds, and some words by sight when they completed kindergarten.

(17)   **Mathematics Curriculum.** The kindergarten mathematics curriculum was predominantly workbook based and integrated into the whole curriculum. Students worked with mathematics problems from books, played number games with the calendar, counted while standing in line for lunch and recess, and practiced mathematical skills in centers. Once a week, the principal came into the kindergarten classes and taught students new mathematics games with cards or chips. The games included counting-on, skip-counting, and simple addition and subtraction. Students were expected to leave kindergarten knowing how to count and perform basic numerical operations (i.e., adding and subtracting 1).

Measures

(18)   **Initial Reading Ability Covariate.** When each participant entered kindergarten, school personnel (kindergarten teacher or school principal) assessed them for their ability to recognize capital and lowercase letters and to produce their sounds. This letter-knowledge assessment requested that students name all uppercase and lowercase letters (shown out of order) and make the sounds of the uppercase letters. Students received individual testing, and school personnel recorded the total number of letters that the student identified correctly out of a possible 78 letters. Letter-name and sound knowledge are both essential skills in reading development (Stage, Sheppard, Davidson, & Browning, 2001). Simply put, theory suggests that letter-name knowledge facilitates the ability to produce letter sounds, whereas letter-sounding ability is the foundation for word decoding and fluent reading (Ehri, 1998; Kirby & Parrila, 1999; Trieman, Tincoff, Rodriguez, Mouzaki, & Francis, 1998). Predictive validity is evidenced in the numerous studies in which researchers have reported high correlations ($r = .60$ to $r = .90$) between letter-naming and letter-sounding ability and subsequent reading, ability and achievement measures (Daly, Wright, Kelly, & Martens, 1997; Kirby & Parrila, 1999; McBride-Chang, 1999; Stage et al., 2001).

> Control measures for the study included; initial reading ability, initial mathematics ability, and K–2 reading fluency.

(19)   **Initial Mathematics Ability Covariate.** When the students entered kindergarten, school personnel (kindergarten teacher or school principal) assessed their initial mathematics ability. The assessment consisted of personnel asking students to identify numbers from 0 to 10. They recorded the total number that the student named out of a possible 11. The ability to recognize numbers and perform basic numerical operations, such as counting to 10, is recognized as important indicators of kindergarten readiness (Kurdek & Sinclair, 2001). Researchers have shown that basic number skills (counting and number recognition) in early kindergarten predict mathematics achievement in first grade (Bramlett, Rowell, & Madenberg, 2000) and in fourth grade (Kurdek & Sinclair, 2001).

(20)   **K–2 Reading Fluency Dependent Variable: One–Minute Reading (OMR) Assessment.** The school principal assessed K–2 reading achievement by conducting 1-min, grade-appropriate reading samples with each student at the beginning and end of the school year. The kindergarten reading passage contained 67 words, the first-grade passage had 121 words, and the second-grade passage included 153 words. Students who finished a passage in less than 1 min returned to the beginning of the passage and continued reading until the minute expired. The principal recorded the total number of words that a student read correctly in 1 min. Students who read passages from grades higher than their own were excluded from subsequent analyses.

The OMR is a well-known curriculum-based measure of oral fluency (21) that is theoretically and empirically linked to concurrent and future reading achievement (Fuchs, Fuchs, Hosp, & Jenkins, 2001). Scores on the OMR correlate highly with concurrent criteria (r = .70 to .90; Parker, Hasbrouck, & Tindal, 1992). Evidence of oral fluency criterion validity includes high correlations with teacher student-ability judgments (Jenkins & Jewell, 1993), standardized student achievement test scores (Fuchs, Fuchs, & Maxwell, 1988; Jenkins & Jewell), reading inventories (Parker et al., 1992), and reading-comprehension tests (Hintze, Shapiro, Conte, & Basile, 1997; Kranzler, Brownell, & Miller, 1998).

Dependent Variables for Reading- and Mathematics-Achievement-Level Tests: Reading and Mathematics Levels. The Northwest Evaluation Association (NWEA) developed standardized reading-, mathematics-, and science-level tests for the Poudre School District. NWEA generated the tests from a large data bank of items that were calibrated on a common scale using Rasch measurement techniques. The tests measure student performance on a Rasch unit (RIT) scale that denotes a student's ability, independent of grade level. The elementary school conducted reading- and mathematics-level tests once a year in the spring with all second- through sixth-grade students who could read and write. NWEA (2003) reported that the levels tests correlate highly with other achievement tests, including the Colorado State Assessment Program test (r = .84 to .91) and the Iowa Tests of Basic Skills (r = .74 to .84). Test–retest reliability results were similarly favorable, ranging from .72 to .92, depending on grade level and test (NWEA). (22)

Results

Rationale for Analyses. We considered several alternatives when we analyzed the data from this study. Our first choice was to analyze the data by using three multiway mixed analyses of covariances (ANCOVAs) with kindergarten group and gender as the between-groups factors and the repeated measurements over time as the within-subjects factor. However, we rejected that analytic technique for two reasons. First and foremost, all three analyses evidenced serious violations of sphericity. Second, this analytic design requires that all cases have all measures on the dependent variable (the within-subjects factor). That requirement reduced our sample size by as much as 75% in some of the analyses when compared with our final choice of separate univariate, between-groups ANCOVAs. (23)

Our second choice was to analyze the data with three 2 × 2 (Kindergarten Group [full day vs. half day] × Gender) between-groups multivariate analyses of variance (MANCOVAs) with the multiple dependent variables measures included simultaneously in the analysis. Field (2000) recommended switching from repeated-measure ANCOVAs to MANCOVAs when sample sizes are relatively high and violations of sphericity are fairly severe, as in our situation. Unfortunately, there also are difficulties when researchers use MANCOVAs. First, the analysis and interpretation of MANCOVA are extraordinarily complex and cumbersome. More important, a number of statisticians (e.g., Tabachnick & Fidell, 1996) have counseled against using MANCOVA when strong intercorrelations exist between the dependent measures. Finally, our data violated the homogeneity of covariance matrices, which is an additional assumption of MANCOVA. (24)

Our final choice was to conduct separate univariate ANCOVAs with appropriate Bonferroni adjustments to prevent inflation in the Type I error rate. For the OMR, we began our analyses with five 2 × 2 (Kindergarten Group × Gender) ANCOVAs, with initial reading ability as the covariate. We measured OMR at the end of kindergarten and at the beginning and end of first and second grades. The alpha level was set at .01 for each of the five analyses. (25)

> The authors introduce us to a new term here: *sphericity*. In statistical analysis (which we haven't covered yet!), sphericity relates to the equality of the variances of the differences between levels of the repeated measures. In the case of this study, the repeated measures of reading and mathematics levels were found to have unequal variances and covariances. More to follow on this in Chapter 19. This resulted in a reduction of the sample size by up to 75%.

(26)   For the reading-level analyses, we conducted three 2 × 2 ANCOVAs because reading achievement tests were given in the spring of the second, third, and fourth grades. The alpha level was set at .017 for each of the analyses. For the mathematics levels analyses, we conducted three 2 × 2 ANCOVAs with the mathematics achievement tests given in the spring of the second, third, and fourth grades. The alpha level was also set at .017 for those analyses.

(27)   **Assessing Assumptions.** We began our univariate ANCOVA analyses by testing for univariate and multivariate normality. Univariate normality existed in all 11 analyses, at least with respect to skewness. There were two instances in which univariate kurtosis exceeded acceptable boundaries for normality. Although there were a limited number of instances in which multivariate normality was mildly violated, visual inspection of the histograms and Q-Q plots suggested no substantive deviations from normality, except for the OMR test given at the end of kindergarten. Hence, we eliminated the test from our final set of analyses. Given the large sample sizes and the relative robustness of ANCOVA against violations of normality, we proceeded with the remaining 10 ANCOVAs.

(28)   We next assessed the assumption of homogeneity of regression slope, which, if violated, generates much more difficulty in the interpretation of the results of the analyses. Neither of the five OMR analyses nor any of the three mathematics levels analyses violated that assumption. However, the third-grade reading-level analysis violated the assumption. Hence, we removed that analysis from the study, leaving only two analyses of reading achievement, at the second- and fourth-grade levels.

(29)   Finally, we assessed the correlation between the covariate and the dependent variable. We began by assuming that the participant's age (measured in months) might be correlated significantly with the dependent variables and should be included in our analyses as a covariate. Tables 1 and 2 show the results of this analysis and that none of the correlations were statistically significant. Hence, we did not include age in the analyses as a covariate.

(30)   Initial reading and mathematics abilities were the other covariates included in the analyses. Our a priori assumption was that those covariates had to correlate significantly with their appropriate dependent variable to the included in the analyses. As Tables 1 and 2 show, all of the final correlation were statistically significant, confirming the propriety of their use as covariates.

(31)   **Findings.** Tables 3, 4, and 5 show the source tables for the OMR, the reading levels, and the mathematics levels, respectively. In each table, the kindergarten grouping independent variable is included in the table, regardless

Table 1

Correlations of Dependent Variables with Initial Reading Ability and Age

Variable	OMR end kindergarten		OMR beginning Grade 1		OMR end Grade 1		OMR beginning Grade 2		OMR end Grade 2		Level 2		Level 4	
	r	n	r	n	r	n	r	n	r	n	r	n	r	n
Initial reading ability	.47**	403	.50**	265	.40**	198	.39**	97	.41**	182	.40**	234	.30**	103
Age	.05	453	.03	301	.01	231	.03	105	.07	208	.03	266	−.10	127

Note: OMR = One-Minute Reading.
** $p < .01$.

Table 2

Correlations of Dependent Variables with Initial Mathematics Ability and Age

Variable	Level 2	Level 3	Level 4
Initial mathematics ability			
r	.35**	.30**	.22*
n	194	180	120
Age			
r	.03	−.02	−.09
n	264	189	127

* $p < .05$.
** $p < .01$.

of whether it achieved statistical significance. Gender, on the other hand, is included in the source tables only in those analyses in which it achieved statistical significance (second-grade mathematics achievement).

Table 3 shows that kindergarten class was statistically significant at the end of kindergarten, $F(1, 400) = 35.08$, $p < .001$, at the beginning of first grade, $F(1, 261) = 11.43$, $p < .01$, and at the end of first grade, $F(1, 194) = 6.26$, $p < .05$. The covariate, as expected, was strongly significant at all levels, (32)

Table 3

Analysis of Covariance Results for OMR Fluency Tests as a Function of Kindergarten Class, Controlling for Initial Reading Ability

Variable and source	df	MS	f	p
OMR (end kindergarten)				
Kindergarten class	1	14,405.36	32.79	<.001
Initial reading ability	1	59,031.95	134.37	<.001
Error	398	439.33		
OMR (beginning Grade 1)				
Kindergarten class	1	10,339.87	10.76	.001
Initial reading ability	1	96,556.42	100.43	<.001
Error	260	961.42		
OMR (end Grade 1)				
Kindergarten class	1	5,261.69	5.73	.018
Initial reading ability	1	39,604.41	43.15	<.001
Error	193	917.79		
OMR (beginning Grade 2)				
Kindergarten class	1	185.25	.22	.64
Initial reading ability	1	14,922.39	17.45	<.001
Error	92	855.23		
OMR (end Grade 2)				
Kindergarten class	1	100.23	.14	.71
Initial reading ability	1	25,530.89	35.52	<.001
Error	177	718.73		

Note: OMR = One-Minute Reading.

Table 4

Analysis of Covariance Results for Reading Achievement Tests as a Function of Kindergarten Class, Controlling for Initial Reading Ability

Variable and source	df	MS	f	p
Level 2 reading				
Kindergarten class	1	43.82	.37	.55
Initial reading ability	1	5,496.21	45.79	<.001
Error	228	120.02		
Level 4 reading				
Kindergarten class	1	12.85	.10	.76
Initial reading ability	1	1,265.53	9.50	.003
Error	98	133.22		

and gender was not statistically significant at any level in the analyses. Significance levels and the estimates of effect size declined as the participants progressed in school within and across academic years.

(33)   Table 4 shows that the covariate was highly significant (as expected) but with no statistically significant effect for either kindergarten class or gender. Table 5 shows a similar pattern in the two preceding tables, with (a) a statistically significant covariate, (b) absence of statistical significance for the kindergarten class, and (c) declining estimates of effect size as time in school increased. Gender was statistically significant at the second grade.

(34)   Table 6 shows the subsample sizes, means, standard deviations, and corrected effect sizes for each of the two kindergarten alternatives across all dependent measures. The only effect size estimate whose magnitude approaches Cohen's (1998) standard for minimal practical significance (.25) is the first one reported in Table 6 (.44). That effect size indicates that FDK confers a small-to-moderate advantage on reading ability at the end of the Kindergarten experience. At the beginning and end of first grade, that advantage is no longer practically significant, although it is still positive. Beginning in second grade, the advantage in reading and mathematics is neither practically significant nor positive for FDK students.

Table 5

Analysis of Covariance Results for Kindergarten and Mathematics Achievement Tests as a Function of Kindergarten Class, Controlling for Initial Mathematics Ability

Variable and source	df	MS	f	p
Level 2 mathematics				
Kindergarten class	1	22.53	.22	.64
Gender	1	707.76	6.87	.009
Initial mathematics ability	1	3,485.92	33.82	<.001
Error	248	103.08		
Level 3 mathematics				
Kindergarten class	1	29.74	.34	.56
Initial mathematics ability	1	1,464.35	16.66	<.001
Error	175	87.89		
Level 4 mathematics				
Kindergarten class	1	12.47	.11	.75
Initial mathematics ability	1	756.59	6.37	.013
Error	115	118.79		

Table 6

Descriptive Information for Statistically Significant Comparison for Full-Day Versus Half-Day Kindergarten, on All Dependent Variables

Dependent variable	Kindergarten class						
	Half-day			Full-day			
	N	M^a	SD	N	M^a	SD	$ES(d)$
OMR (end Kindergarten)	220	25.33	23.72	183	37.52	25.03	.50
OMR (beginning Grade 1)	156	44.62	36.57	109	57.61	36.47	.36
OMR (end of Grade 1)	120	84.56	33.50	78	95.87	33.77	ns
OMR (beginning Grade 2)	65	62.31	29.96	32	65.54	34.65	ns
OMR (end of Grade 2)	108	95.81	28.47	74	97.43	30.53	ns
Reading achievement (Grade 2)	137	195.95	12.05	96	196.86	11.77	ns
Reading achievement (Grade 4)	70	214.90	11.01	33	214.11	14.11	ns
Mathematics achievement (Grade 2)	151	199.71	11.08	102	199.09	10.86	ns
Mathematics achievement (Grade 3)	109	212.60	9.78	71	213.45	10.09	ns
Mathematics achievement (Grade 4)	82	218.94	11.14	38	219.64	11.09	ns

Note: OMR = One-Minute Reading.
[a]Covariate adjusted means.

Follow-Up Interviews

As a follow-up to our analyses, we interviewed the four kindergarten teachers in January 2004, for their views on (a) the kindergarten curriculum, (b) their perceived differences between FDK and HDK programming, and (c) their explanations for the findings that we observed between FDK and HDK students in reading and mathematics achievement. The teachers were women who had taught for 14, 9, 8, and 6 years, respectively. They had previously taught FDK and HDK kindergarten and had been teaching kindergarten at the elementary school research site for 10, 9, 6, and 4 years, respectively. Two of the teachers were still teaching kindergarten; the other two teachers were teaching second and sixth grades, respectively. One teacher admitted that she had a "half-day bias," whereas another teacher was a "proponent of full-day kindergarten." (35)

> The researchers added follow-up interviews to their research design. Note the use of interviews in a causal–comparative study is not part of the design, however their use adds another lens to the findings of the study. In Chapter 15 we will discuss mixed methods research and how the use of an explanatory mixed methods design can contribute to our understanding of the research results.

All interviews consisted of open-ended questions and lasted between 30 min and 1 hr. The interviews were tape-recorded and transcribed and returned to the teachers for review. After approval of the transcripts, we coded the interviews by using constant comparative analytic techniques (Strauss & Corbin, 1994), which involved inductively identifying themes and developing written summaries. (36)

When questioned about the differences between FDK and HDK, all teachers stated that they would have expected FDK students, in general, to perform better academically than HDK students at the end of kindergarten. They attributed the difference to the increased time that FDK students spent reviewing and practicing material. However, consistent with our findings, all teachers were equally doubtful that the differences would last. They believed that the academic disparity between FDK and HDK students would disappear during first through third grades. For example, one teacher stated that "kids, by third grade, catch up or things kind of level out so I don't think there'd be much of a difference." (37)

Although teachers agreed that the FDK advantage probably did not extend past early elementary education, their explanations for the ephemeral differences varied and fell into three general categories: (a) effects of differentiated instruction, (b) individual student development, and (c) individual student attributes. (38)

(39) **Differentiated Instruction.** All teachers, in various ways, suggested that differentiated instruction would need to occur in every grade subsequent to kindergarten to, at least partially, maintain higher achievement levels evidenced by FDK students. When asked to define *differentiated instruction*, one teacher said:

> What it means to me is that I need to meet that child where they are. I mean I need to have appropriate material and appropriate instruction for that child. . . . I need to make sure that they're getting what they need where they are. . . . But, I think you need to set the bar pretty high and expect them to reach that; on the other hand, I think you need to not set it so high that you're going to frustrate the kids that aren't ready.

(40) However, the kindergarten teachers recognized the challenges of using differentiated instruction and were careful not to place blame on first- through third-grade teachers. One teacher stated, "I'm not saying that not everyone does differentiated instruction. But I think that you have to be careful you don't do too much whole group teaching to a group of kids that's way past where they're at." Although all of the teachers agreed that differentiated instruction would be necessary to maintain differences after kindergarten, not all of them believed that this technique would be singularly sufficient. Some teachers believed strongly that the "leveling out" was predominantly a result of individual student development or student attributes, or both, rather than teaching methods.

(41) **Students' Development.** Two teachers felt that the leveling out of academic differences between FDK and HDK students by second grade resulted from natural developmental growth occurring after kindergarten. They explained:

> You have kids that cannot hear a sound. They cannot hear, especially the vowel sounds. They are not ready to hear those. They are not mature enough to hear those sounds. You could go over that eight billion times and they just aren't ready to hear those sounds. They go into first grade and they've grown up over the summer and . . . it clicks with them. And they might have been low in my class, but they get to first grade and they're middle kids. They've kind of reached where their potential is.
>
> I mean, there's big developmental gap in K, 1, 2 and by third grade the kids that look[sic] behind, if they're going to be average or normal, they catch-up by then. . . . Like some kids in second grade, they still struggle with handwriting and reversal and by now it's a red flag if they're still doing that, developmentally everything should be fitting together in their little bodies and minds and they should be having good smooth handwriting and writing in the right direction. And if that's not happening then that's a red flag. And by third grade . . . if they're not forming like an average student then there's something else that needs to be looked at. So it's a development thing and it's just when kids are ready.

(42) Yet, both of those teachers acknowledged that HDK students do have to work to catch up to FDK students, citing (a) less time spent on material, (b) differences in FDK and HDK teachers' instructional philosophies, and (c) lack of familiarity with all-day school as disadvantages that HDK students must overcome in first grade to equal their FDK counterparts.

(43) *Student attributes.* A final explanation that teachers offered for the leveling out of differences suggested that individual student attributes accounted for student differences in subsequent grades. Three teachers believed that, no matter what kindergarten program students attended, their inherent level of academic ability or level of parent involvement, or both, were most important in eventually determining how individual students would compare with other students. For example,

> I think they get to where their ability is, regardless of. . . . You can give them a good start and I think that can make a difference, but a high kid

is going to be high whether they were in full or half. And those gray kids, you can give them a boost and they can be higher than maybe they would have been in half-day, you know you can give them a better start.

Thus, these three teachers believed that student attributes, such as inherent ability or degree of parent involvement in their schooling, would ultimately play a more significant role in how students would eventually compare with one another in second and third grades, regardless of whether they attended FDK or HDK programs. (44)

Discussion

What can be determined about the effects of FDK versus HDK kindergarten as a result of our analyses? Children who attend FDK can and do learn more through that experience than do their HDK counterparts. Nonetheless, the additional learning appears to decline rapidly, so much so that by the start of first grade, the benefits of FDK have diminished to a level that has little practical value. That effect was consistent across two measures of reading and one measure of mathematics. The effect also was consistent across gender, given that there was a gender by kindergarten-group interaction in only one of the analyses. (45)

Our findings are consistent with past meta-analytic research (Fusaro, 1997) and high-quality empirical studies (e.g., Hough & Bryde, 1996) in that FDK confers initial benefits on academic achievement but that these benefits diminish relatively rapidly (OSLOEO, 1997). We are unclear why the rapid decline occurs, but we offer this insight from several school administrators and teachers with whom we interacted in our discussions of these data: (46)

> Teachers in the first few grades are so concerned with students who enter their classes [with] nonexistent reading and math skills that they spend the majority of their time bringing these students up to minimal math and reading criteria at the expense of working equally hard with students whose reading and math achievement are above average. Hence, the high-achieving students' gains at the end of kindergarten gradually erode over the next few years with lack of attention.

We concur with Fusaro (1997) that districts must make their choices involving FDK with a full understanding of what the benefits may be for academic achievement and nonachievement outcomes. Our findings of initial gains place the onus of maintaining those gains on schools and teachers through their own internal policies, procedures, and will to sustain those gains. (47)

Our study, of course, is not without limitations. We studied only one school, albeit over a relatively long period of time, with well-established measures and with reasonably well-equated groups. The greatest reservation we have about the generalizability of our findings clearly focuses on the predicted decline in long-term benefits of FDK for schools, making it a priority to assure that teachers provide differentiated instruction to all students to advance each one as far as possible during the academic year rather than to move all students to a common set of expected learning at the end of the academic year. We recognize that school policies, procedures, and culture play important roles in the variability in student achievement, regardless of the skill levels of students entering first grade. Although our results will likely generalize to a wide variety of elementary school children, they also will likely generalize to those children who attend schools whose instructional policies and practices in the early grades are similar to the school in this study. (48)

NOTE

The authors appreciate the thoughtful participation of Suzie Gunstream and the other elementary teachers whose invaluable practitioner insights helped us make sense of the findings.

REFERENCES

Aten, K. K., Foster, A., & Cobb, B. (1996). *Lopez full-day kindergarten study*. Fort Collins, CO: Research and Development Center for the Advancement of Student Learning.

Bramlett, R. K., Rowell, R. K., & Madenberg, K. (2000). Predicting first grade achievement from kindergarten screening measures: A comparison of child and family predictors. *Research in Schools, 7*, 1–9.

Clark, P., & Kirk, E. (2000). All-day kindergarten. *Childhood Education, 76*, 228–231.

Cohen, J. (1988). *Statistical power and analysis for the behavioral sciences* (2nd ed.). Hillsdale, NJ: Erlbaum.

Cooper, T., Foster, A., & Cobb, B. (1998a). *Half- or full-day kindergarten: Choices for parents in Poudre School, District*. Fort Collins, CO: Research and Development Center for the Advancement of Student Learning.

Cooper, T., Foster, A., & Cobb, B. (1998b). *Full- and half-day kindergarten: A study of six elementary schools*. Fort Collins, CO: Research and Development Center for the Advancement of Student Learning.

Cryan, J. R., Sheehan, R., Wiechel, J., & Brandy-Hedden, I. G. (1992). Success outcomes of all-day kindergarten: More positive behavior and increased achievement in the years after. *Early Childhood Research Quarterly, 7*, 187–203.

Daly, E. J., III, Wright, J. A., Kelly, S. Q., & Martens, B. K. (1997). Measures of early academic reading skills: Reliability and validity with a first grade sample. *School Psychology Quarterly, 12*, 268–280.

Ehri, L. C. (1998). Grapheme-phoneme knowledge is essential for learning to read words in English. In J. L. Metsala & L. C. Ehri (Eds.), *Word recognition in beginning reading* (pp. 3–40). Mahwah, NJ: Erlbaum.

Elicker, J., & Mathur, S. (1997). What do they do all day? Comprehensive evaluation of a full-day kindergarten. *Early Childhood Research Quarterly, 12*, 459–480.

Evansville-Vanderburgh School Corporation. (1998). *A longitudinal study of the consequences of full-day kindergarten: Kindergarten through grade eight*. Evansville, IN: Author.

Field, A. (2000). *Discovering statistics using SPSS for Windows*. London: Sage.

Fuchs, L. S., Fuchs, D., Hosp, M. K., & Jenkins, J. R. (2001). Oral fluency as an indicator of reading competence: A theoretical, empirical, and historical analysis. *Scientific Studies of Reading, 5*, 239–256.

Fuchs, L. S., Fuchs, D., & Maxwell, L. (1998). The validity of informal measures of reading comprehension. *Remedial and Special Education, 9*, 20–28.

Fusaro, J. A. (1997). The effect of full-day kindergarten on student achievement: A meta-analysis. *Child Study Journal, 27*, 269–277.

Gullo, D. F., Bersani, C. U., Clements, D. H., & Bayless, K. M. (1986). A comparative study of "all-day," "alternate-day," and "half-day" kindergarten schedules: Effects on achievement and classroom social behaviors. *Journal of Research in Childhood Education, 1*, 87–94.

Gullo, D. F., & Clements, D. H. (1984). The effects of kindergarten schedule on achievement, classroom behavior, and attendance. *The Journal of Educational Research, 78*, 51–56.

Gullo, D. F., & Maxwell, C. B. (1997). The effects of different models of all-day kindergarten on children's development competence. *Early Child Development and Care, 139*, 119–128.

Hintze, J. M., Shapiro, E. S., Conte, K. L., & Basile, I. A. (1997). Oral reading fluency and authentic reading material: Criterion validity of the technical features of CBM survey-level assessment. *School Psychology Review, 26*, 535–553.

Holmes, C. T., & McConnell, B. M. (1990, April). *Full-day versus half-day kindergarten: An experimental study*. Paper presented at the annual meeting of the American Educational Research Association, Boston, MA.

Hough, D., & Bryde, S. (1996, April). *The effects of full-day kindergarten on student achievement and affect*. Paper presented at the annual meeting of the American Educational Research Association, New York.

Jenkins, J. R., & Jewell, M. (1993). Examining the validity of two measures for formative teaching: Reading aloud and maze. *Exceptional Children, 59*, 421–432.

Karweit, N. L. (1992). The kindergarten experience. *Educational Leadership, 49*(6), 82–86.

Karweit, N. L. (1994). Issues in kindergarten organization and curriculum. In R. E. Slavin, N. L. Karweit, & B. A. Wasik (Eds.), *Preventing early school failure: Research, policy and practice*. Needham Heights, MA: Allyn & Bacon.

Kirby, J. R., & Parrila, R. K. (1999). Theory-based prediction of early reading. *The Alberta Journal of Educational Research, 45*, 428–447.

Koopmans, M. (1991). *A study of the longitudinal effects of all-day kindergarten attendance on achievement*. Newark, NJ: Board of Education, Office of Research, Evaluation, and Testing.

Kranzler. J. H., Brownell, M. T., & Miller, M. D. (1998). The construct validity of curriculum-based measurement of reading: An empirical test of a plausible rival hypothesis. *Journal of School Psychology, 36*, 399–415.

Kurdek, L. A., & Sinclair, R. J. (2001). Predicting reading and mathematics achievement in fourth-grade children from kindergarten readiness scores. *Journal of Educational Psychology, 93*, 451–455.

Lore, R. (1992). *Language development component: Full-day kindergarten program 1990–1991 find evaluation report*. Columbus, OH: Columbus Public Schools, Department of Program Evaluation.

McBride-Chang, C. (1999). The ABC's of the ABCs: The development of letter-name and letter-sound knowledge. *Merrill-Power Quarterly, 45*, 285–308.

McConnell, B. B., & Tesch, S. (1986). Effectiveness of kindergarten scheduling. *Educational Leadership, 44*(3), 48–51.

National Center for Education Statistics. (2000). *America's kindergartens*. Washington, DC: Author.

Nelson, R. F. (2000). Which is the best kindergarten? *Principal, 79*(5), 38–41.

Northwest Evaluation Association. (2003). *Reliability estimates and validity evidence for achievement level tests and measures of academic progress*. Retrieved March 30, 2003, from nwea.org/Research/NorthingStudy.htm

Nunnally, J. (1996). *The impact of half-day versus full-day kindergarten programs on student outcomes: A pilot project*. New Albany, IN: Elementary Education Act Title I. (ERIC Document Reproduction Service No. ED396857)

Ohio State Legislative Office of Education Oversight. (1997). *An overview of full-day kindergarten*. Columbus, OH: Author.

Olsen, D., & Zigler, E. (1989). An assessment of the all-day kindergarten movement. *Early Childhood Research Quarterly, 4*, 167–186.

Parker, R., Hasbrouck, J. E., & Tindal, G. (1992). Greater validity for oral reading fluency: Can miscues help? *The Journal of Special Education, 25*, 492–503.

Peck, J. T., McCaig, G., & Sapp, M. E. (1988). *Kindergarten policies: What is best for children?* Washington, DC: National Association for the Education of Young Children.

Puleo, V. T. (1988). A review and critique of research on full-day kindergarten. *The Elementary School Journal, 88*, 427–439.

Stage, S. A., Sheppard, J., Davidson, M. M., & Browning, M. M. (2001). Prediction of first graders' growth in oral reading fluency using kindergarten letter fluency. *The Journal of School Psychology, 39*, 225–237.

Strauss, A., & Corbin, J. (1994). Grounded theory methodology: An overview. In N. K. Denzin & Y. S. Lincoln (Eds.), *Handbook of qualitative research* (pp. 273–285). Thousand Oaks, CA: Sage.

Tabachnick, B. G., & Fidell, L. S. (1996). *Using multivariate statistics* (3rd ed.). New York: Harper & Row.

Trieman, R., Tincoff, R., Rodriguez, K., Mouzaki, A., & Francis, D. J. (1998). The foundations of literacy: Learning the sounds of letters. *Childhood Development, 69*, 1524–1540.

Wang, Y. L., & Johnstone, W. G. (1999). Evaluation of a full-day kindergarten program. *ERS Spectrum, 17*(2), 27–32.

Note: "Comparing Longitudinal Academic Achievement of Full-Day and Half-Day Kindergarten Students," by J. R. Wolgemuth, R. B. Cobb, & M. A. Winokur, *The Journal of Educational Research 99*(5), pp. 260–269, 2006. Reprinted with permission of the Helen Dwight Reid Educational Foundation. Published by Heldref Publications, 1319 Eighteenth St., NW, Washington, DC 20036–1802, Copyright © 2006.

CHAPTER ELEVEN

Experimental Research

The Evil of Frankenstein, 1964

Warner Bros./Everett Collection

"When well conducted, experimental studies produce the soundest evidence concerning cause–effect relations." (p. 275)

LEARNING OUTCOMES

After reading Chapter 11, you should be able to do the following:

11.1 Briefly define and state the purpose of experimental research.

11.2 Briefly explain the threats to validity in experimental research.

11.3 Define and provide examples of group experimental designs.

These chapter learning outcomes form the basis for the following task, which requires you to develop the method section of a research report for an experimental study.

TASK 7D

For a quantitative study, you have created research plan components (Tasks 3 and 4A), described a sample (Task 5A), and considered appropriate measuring instruments (Task 6). If your study involves experimental research, now develop the method section of a research report. Include a description of participants, data collection methods, and the research design (see Performance Criteria at the end of Chapter 12, p. 335).

SUMMARY: EXPERIMENTAL RESEARCH

Definition	In *experimental research,* the researcher manipulates at least one independent variable, controls other relevant variables, and observes the effect on one or more dependent variables.
Design(s)	An experiment typically involves a comparison of two groups (although some experimental studies have only one group or even three or more groups). The experimental comparison is usually one of three types: (1) comparison of two different approaches (A versus B), (2) comparison of a new approach and the existing approach (A versus no A), and (3) comparison of different amounts of a single approach (a little of A versus a lot of A).
	Group experimental designs include: pre-experimental designs (the one-group posttest only design, the one-group pretest–posttest design, and the posttest-only design with nonequivalent groups), true experimental designs (the pretest–posttest control group design, the posttest-only control group design, and the Solomon four-group design), quasi-experimental designs (the nonequivalent control group design, the time-series design, the counterbalanced designs), and factorial designs.
Types of appropriate research questions	In experimental educational research, the types of research questions are often focused on independent variables such as method of instruction, type of reinforcement, arrangement of learning environment, type of learning materials, and length of treatment.
Key characteristics	• The manipulation of an independent variable is the primary characteristic that differentiates experimental research from other types of research. • An experimental study is guided by at least one hypothesis that states an expected causal relation between two variables. • In an experiment, the group that receives the new treatment is called the *experimental group,* and the group that receives a different treatment or is treated as usual is called the *control group.* • The use of randomly formed treatment groups is a unique characteristic of experimental research.

(continued)

Steps in the process	**1.** Select and define a problem. **2.** Select participants and measuring instruments. **3.** Prepare a research plan. **4.** Execute procedures. **5.** Analyze the data. **6.** Formulate conclusions.
Potential challenges	• Experimental studies in education often suffer from two problems: a lack of sufficient exposure to treatments and failure to make the treatments substantially different from each other. • An experiment is valid if results obtained are due only to the manipulated independent variable and if they are generalizable to individuals or contexts beyond the experimental setting. These two criteria are referred to, respectively, as the internal validity and external validity of an experiment. • Threats to internal validity include history, maturation, testing, instrumentation, statistical regression, differential selection of participants, mortality, selection–maturation interactions, and other interactive effects. • Threats to external validity include pretest–treatment interaction, multiple-treatment interference, selection–treatment interaction, specificity of variables, treatment diffusion, experimenter effects, and reactive arrangements.
Example	What are the differential effects of two problem-solving instructional approaches (schema-based instruction and general strategy instruction) on the mathematical word-problem-solving performance of 22 middle school students who had learning disabilities or were at risk for mathematics failure?

EXPERIMENTAL RESEARCH: DEFINITION AND PURPOSE

Experimental research is the only type of research that can test hypotheses to establish cause–effect relations. It represents the strongest chain of reasoning about the links between variables. In **experimental research,** the researcher manipulates at least one independent variable, controls other relevant variables, and observes the effect on one or more dependent variables. The researcher determines who gets what; that is, the researcher has control over the selection and assignment of groups to treatments. The manipulation of an independent variable is the primary characteristic that differentiates experimental research from other types of research. The independent variable, also called the *treatment,* *causal,* or *experimental variable,* is that treatment or characteristic believed to make a difference. In educational research, independent variables that are frequently manipulated include method of instruction, type of reinforcement, arrangement of learning environment, type of learning materials, and length of treatment. This list is by no means exhaustive. The dependent variable, also called the *criterion, effect,* or *posttest variable,* is the outcome of the study, the change or difference in groups that occurs as a result of the independent variable. It gets its name because it is dependent on the independent variable. The dependent variable may be measured by a test or some other quantitative measure (e.g., attendance, number of suspensions, time on task). The only restriction on the dependent variable is that it must represent a measurable outcome.

Experimental research is the most structured of all research types. When well conducted, experimental studies produce the soundest evidence concerning cause–effect relations. The results of experimental research permit prediction, but not the kind that is characteristic of correlational research. A correlational study predicts a particular score for a particular individual. Predictions based on experimental findings are more global and often take the form, "If you use Approach X, you will probably get different results than if you use Approach Y." Of course, it is unusual for a single experimental study to produce broad generalization of results because any single study is limited in context and participants. However, replications of a study involving different contexts and participants often produce cause–effect results that can be generalized widely.

The Experimental Process

The steps in an experimental study are basically the same as in other types of research: selecting and defining a problem, selecting participants and measuring instruments, preparing a research plan, executing procedures, analyzing the data, and formulating conclusions. An experimental study is guided by at least one hypothesis that states an expected causal relation between two variables. The experiment is conducted to test the experimental hypothesis. In addition, in an experimental study, the researcher is in on the action from the very beginning, selecting the groups, deciding how to allocate treatment to the groups, controlling extraneous variables, and measuring the effect of the treatment at the end of the study.

It is important to note that the experimental researcher controls both the selection and the assignment of the research participants. That is, the researcher randomly selects participants from a single, well-defined population and then randomly assigns these participants to the different treatment conditions. This ability to select and assign participants randomly to treatments makes experimental research unique—the random assignment of participants to treatments, also called *manipulation of the treatments*, is the feature that distinguishes it from causal–comparative research. Experimental research has both random selection and random assignment, whereas causal–comparative research has only random selection,

not assignment, because random assignment to a treatment from a single population is not possible in causal–comparative studies. Rather, participants in causal–comparative studies are obtained from different, already existing populations.

An experiment typically involves a comparison of two groups (although some experimental studies have only one group or even three or more groups). The experimental comparison is usually one of three types: (1) comparison of two different approaches (A versus B), (2) comparison of a new approach and the existing approach (A versus no A), and (3) comparison of different amounts of a single approach (a little of A versus a lot of A). An example of an A versus B comparison is a study that compares the effects of a computer-based approach to teaching first-grade reading to a teacher-based approach. An example of an A versus no A comparison is a study that compares a new handwriting method to the classroom teacher's existing approach. An example of a little of A versus a lot of A comparison is a study that compares the effect of 20 minutes of daily science instruction on fifth-graders' attitudes toward science to the effect of 40 minutes of daily science instruction. Experimental designs are sometimes quite complex and may involve simultaneous manipulation of several independent variables. At this stage of the game, however, we recommend that you stick to just one!

In an experiment, the group that receives the new treatment is called (not surprisingly) the **experimental group,** and the group that receives a different treatment or is treated as usual is called the **control group.** A common misconception is that a control group always receives no treatment, but a group with no treatment would rarely provide a fair comparison. For example, if the independent variable were type of reading instruction, the experimental group may be instructed with a new method, and the control group may continue instruction with the method currently used. The control group would still receive reading instruction; members would not sit in a closet while the study was conducted—if they did, the study would be a comparison of the new method with no reading instruction at all. Any method of instruction is bound to be more effective than no instruction. An alternative to labeling the groups as control and experimental is to describe the treatments as comparison groups, treatment groups, or groups A and B.

The groups that are to receive the different treatments should be equated on all variables that may influence performance on the dependent variable. For example, in the previous example, initial reading readiness should be very similar in each treatment group at the start of the study. The researcher must make every effort to ensure that the two groups are similar on all variables except the independent variable. The main way that groups are equated is through simple random or stratified random sampling.

After the groups have been exposed to the treatment for some period, the researcher collects data on the dependent variable from the groups and tests for a significant difference in performance. In other words, using statistical analysis, the researcher determines whether the treatment made a real difference. For example, suppose that, at the end of an experimental study evaluating reading method, one group had an average score of 29 on a measure of reading comprehension and the other group had an average score of 27. Clearly the groups are different. But is a 2-point difference a meaningful difference, or is it just a chance difference produced by measurement error? Statistical analysis allows the researcher to answer this question with confidence (see Chapter 19 for a discussion of inferential statistics).

Experimental studies in education often suffer from two problems: a lack of sufficient exposure to treatments and failure to make the treatments substantially different from each other. Regarding the first problem, no matter how effective a treatment is, it is not likely to be effective if students are exposed to it for only a brief period. To test a hypothesis concerning the effectiveness of a treatment adequately, an experimental group would need to be exposed to it long enough that the treatment has a chance to work (i.e., produce a measurable effect). Regarding the second problem (i.e., difference in treatments), it is important to operationalize the variables so that the difference between groups is clear. For example, in a study comparing team teaching and traditional lecture teaching, team teaching must be operationalized in a manner that clearly differentiated it from the traditional method. If team teaching simply meant two teachers taking turns lecturing in the traditional way, it would not be very different from so-called traditional teaching, and the researcher would be very unlikely to find a meaningful difference between the two study treatments.

Manipulation and Control

As noted several times previously, direct manipulation by the researcher of at least one independent variable is the characteristic that differentiates experimental research from other types of research. Manipulation of an independent variable is often a difficult concept to grasp. Quite simply, it means that the researcher selects the treatments and decides which group will get which treatment. For example, if the independent variable in a study were number of annual teacher reviews, the researcher may decide to form three groups, representing three levels of the independent variable: one group receiving no review, a second group receiving one review, and a third group receiving two reviews. Having selected research participants from a single, well-defined population (e.g., teachers at a large elementary school), the researcher would randomly assign participants to treatments. Independent variables that are manipulated by the experimenter are also known as active variables.

Control refers to the researcher's efforts to remove the influence of any variable, other than the independent variable, that may affect performance on the dependent variable. In other words, in an experimental design, the groups should differ only on the independent variable. For example, suppose a researcher conducted a study to test whether student tutors are more effective than parent tutors in teaching first graders to read. In this study, suppose the student tutors were older children from higher grade levels, and the parent tutors were members of the PTA. Suppose also that student tutors helped each member of their group for 1 hour per school day for a month, whereas the parent tutors helped each member of their group for 2 hours per week for a month. Finally, suppose the results of the study indicate that the student tutors produced higher reading scores than the parent tutors. Given this study design, concluding that student tutors are more effective than parent tutors would certainly not be fair. Participants with the student tutors received 2½ times as much help as that provided to the parents' group (i.e., 5 hours per week versus 2 hours per week). Because this researcher did not control the time spent in tutoring, he or she has several possible conclusions—student tutors may in fact be more effective than parent tutors, longer periods of tutoring may be more effective than shorter periods regardless of type of tutor, or the combination of more time/student tutors may be more effective than the combination of less time/parent tutors. To make the comparison fair and interpretable, both students and parents should tutor for the same amount of time; in other words, time of tutoring must be controlled.

A researcher must consider many factors when attempting to identify and control extraneous variables. Some variables may be relatively obvious; for example, the researcher in the preceding study should control for reading readiness and prior reading instruction in addition to time spent tutoring. Some variables may not be as obvious; for example, both student tutors and parent tutors should use similar reading texts and materials. Ultimately, two different kinds of variables need to be controlled: participant variables and environmental variables. A **participant variable** (such as reading readiness) is one in which participants in different groups in a study may differ; an **environmental variable** (such as learning materials) is a variable in the setting of the study that may cause unwanted differences between groups. A researcher should strive to ensure that the characteristics and experiences of the groups are as equal as possible on all important variables except the independent variable. If relevant variables can be controlled, group differences on the dependent variable can be attributed to the independent variable.

Control is not easy in an experiment, especially in educational studies, where human beings are involved. It certainly is a lot easier to control solids, liquids, and gases! Our task is not an impossible one, however, because we can concentrate on identifying and controlling only those variables that may really affect or **interact** with the dependent variable. For example, if two groups had significant differences in shoe size or height, such differences would probably not affect the results of most education studies. Techniques for controlling extraneous variables are presented later in this chapter.

MyLab Education **Self-Check 11.1**

MyLab Education **Application Exercise 11.1:**
Evaluating Research Articles: Identifying Steps in the Research Process for an Experimental Study

---

THREATS TO EXPERIMENTAL VALIDITY

As noted, any uncontrolled extraneous variables affecting performance on the dependent variable are threats to the validity of an experiment. An experiment is valid if results obtained are due only to the manipulated independent variable and if they are generalizable to individuals or contexts beyond the experimental setting. Validity can also be thought of as the "approximate truth of an inference."[1] Researchers focus on four types of experimental validity, which we describe in greater detail next.

Statistical conclusion validity refers to the appropriate use of statistics to infer whether the presumed independent and dependent variables co-vary in the experiment. Threats to statistical conclusion validity include low statistical power, and violated assumptions of statistical tests. As Shadish and colleagues[2] suggest "An insufficiently powered experiment may incorrectly conclude that the relationship between treatment and outcome is not significant" with resulting implications for Type I and Type II errors. Similarly, "violations of statistical test assumptions can lead to either overestimating or underestimating the size and significance of an effect."

Internal validity refers to the degree to which observed differences on the dependent variable are a direct result of manipulation of the independent variable, not some other variable. In other words, an examination of internal validity focuses on threats or rival explanations that influence the outcomes of an experimental study but are not due to the independent variable. In the example of student tutors and parent tutors, a plausible threat or rival explanation for the research results is the difference in the amount of tutoring time. The degree to which experimental research results are attributable to the independent variable and not to another rival explanation is the degree to which the study is internally valid.

Construct validity is "the degree to which inferences are warranted from the observed

---

[1] *Experimental and Quasi-Experimental Designs for Generalized Causal Inference* (p. 34), by W. R. Shadish, T. D. Cook, and D. T. Campbell, 2002, Belmont, CA: Wadsworth Cengage Learning, p. 34.
[2] Shadish, Cook, and Campbell, p. 45.

persons, settings, and cause and effect operations included in a study to the constructs that these instances might represent,"[3] that is, the validity of inferences about the variables (constructs) in a study.

External validity, also called *ecological validity*, is the degree to which study results are generalizable, or applicable, to groups and environments outside the experimental setting. In other words, an examination of external validity focuses on threats or rival explanations that disallow the results of a study to be generalized to other settings or groups. A study conducted with groups of gifted ninth-graders, for example, should produce results that are applicable to other groups of gifted ninth-graders. If research results were never generalizable outside the experimental setting, then no one could profit from research. An experimental study can contribute to educational theory or practice only if its results and effects are replicable and generalize to other places and groups. If results cannot be replicated in other settings by other researchers, the study has low external, or ecological, validity.

Thus, all one has to do to conduct a valid experiment is to maximize statistical conclusion validity, internal validity, construct validity, and external validity, right? Wrong. Unfortunately, a "catch-22" complicates the researcher's experimental life. For example, to maximize internal validity, the researcher must exercise very rigid controls over participants and conditions, producing a laboratory-like environment. However, the more a research situation is narrowed and controlled, the less realistic and generalizable it becomes. A study can contribute little to educational practice if techniques that are effective in a highly controlled setting are not also effective in a less controlled classroom setting. On the other hand, the more natural the experimental setting becomes, the more difficult it is to control extraneous variables. It is very difficult, for example, to conduct a well-controlled study in a classroom. Thus, the researcher must strive for balance between control and realism. If a choice is involved, the researcher should err on the side of control rather than realism[4] because a study that is not internally valid is

worthless. A useful strategy to address this problem is to demonstrate an effect in a highly controlled environment (i.e., with maximum internal validity) and then redo the study in a more natural setting (i.e., to examine external validity). In the final analysis, however, the researcher must seek a compromise between a highly controlled and highly natural environment.

In the following pages, we describe the many threats to validity. Some extraneous variables are threats to internal validity, some are threats to external validity, and some may be threats to both. How potential threats are classified is not of great importance; what is important is that you be aware of their existence and how to control for them. As you read, you may begin to feel that there are just too many threats for a researcher to control. However, the task is not as formidable as it may appear at first because experimental designs can control many or most of the threats you are likely to encounter. Also, remember that each threat is a potential threat only—it may not be a problem in a particular study. Probably the most authoritative sources on experimental design and threats to experimental validity are the work that was done over 50 years ago by Donald Campbell, Julian Stanley, and Thomas Cook,[5] and most recently, the work by William Shadish.[6] And while the typology used by these authors has expanded over the years to include statistical conclusion validity and construct validity, our discussion here will focus on the two primary threats to experimental validity: internal validity and external validity.

Threats to Internal Validity

There are eight main threats to internal validity: history, maturation, testing, instrumentation, statistical regression, differential selection of participants, mortality, and selection–maturation interaction, which are summarized in Table 11.1. Before describing these threats to internal validity, however, we note the role of experimental research

---

[3] Shadish, Cook, and Campbell, p. 38.
[4] This is a clear distinction between the emphases of quantitative and qualitative research.

[5] *Experimental and Quasi-Experimental Designs for Research*, by D. T. Campbell and J. C. Stanley, 1971, Chicago, IL: Rand McNally; *Quasi-Experimentation: Design and Analysis Issues for Field Settings*, T. D. Cook and D. T. Campbell, 1979, Chicago, IL: Rand McNally.
[6] *Experimental and Quasi-Experimental Designs for Generalized Causal Inference* by W. R. Shadish, T. D. Cook, and D. T. Campbell, 2002, Belmont, CA: Wadsworth Cengage Learning.

TABLE 11.1 • Threats to internal validity

Threat	Description
History	Unexpected events occur between the pre- and posttest, affecting the dependent variable.
Maturation	Changes occur in the participants, from growing older, wiser, more experienced, and so on, during the study.
Testing	Taking a pretest alters the result of the posttest.
Instrumentation	The measuring instrument is changed between pre- and posttesting, or a single measuring instrument is unreliable.
Statistical regression	Extremely high or extremely low scorers tend to regress to the mean on retesting.
Differential selection of participants	Participants in the experimental and control groups have different characteristics that affect the dependent variable differently.
Mortality	Different participants drop out of the study in different numbers, altering the composition of the treatment groups.
Selection–maturation interaction	The participants selected into treatment groups have different maturation rates. Selection interactions also occur with history and instrumentation.

in overcoming these threats. You are not rendered helpless when faced with them. Quite the contrary, the use of random selection of participants, the researcher's assignment of participants to treatments, and control of other variables are powerful approaches to overcoming the threats. As you read about the threats, note how random selection and assignment to treatments can control most threats.

History

When discussing threats to validity, **history** refers to any event occurring during a study that is not part of the experimental treatment but may affect the dependent variable. The longer a study lasts, the more likely it is that history will be a threat. A bomb scare, an epidemic of measles, or global current events are examples of events that may produce a history effect. For example, suppose you conducted a series of in-service workshops designed to increase the morale of teacher participants. Between the time you conducted the workshops and the time you administered a posttest measure of morale, the news media announced that, due to state-level budget problems, funding to the local school district was to be significantly reduced, and promised pay raises for teachers would likely be postponed. Such an event could easily wipe out any effect the workshops may have had, and posttest morale scores may well be considerably lower than they otherwise may have been.

Maturation

Maturation refers to physical, intellectual, and emotional changes that naturally occur within individuals over a period of time. In a research study, these changes may affect participants' performance on a measure of the dependent variable. Especially in studies that last a long time, participants become older and perhaps more coordinated, less coordinated, unmotivated, anxious, or just plain bored. Maturation is more likely to be a problem in a study designed to test the effectiveness of a psychomotor training program on 3-year-olds than in a study designed to compare two methods of teaching algebra. Young participants typically undergo rapid biological changes, raising the question of whether changes on the dependent variable are due to the training program or to maturation.

Testing

Testing, also called *pretest sensitization*, refers to the threat of improved performance on a posttest that results from a pretest. In other words, simply taking a pretest may improve participants' scores on a posttest, regardless of whether they received any treatment or instruction in between. Testing is more likely to be a threat when the time between the tests is short; a pretest taken in September is not likely to affect performance on a posttest taken in June. The testing threat to internal validity is most likely to occur in studies that measure factual information that can be recalled. For example, taking a pretest on solving algebraic equations is less likely to improve posttest performance than taking a pretest on multiplication facts would.

Instrumentation

The **instrumentation** threat refers to unreliability, or lack of consistency, in measuring instruments that may result in an invalid assessment of performance. Instrumentation may threaten validity in several different ways. A problem may occur if the researcher uses two different tests, one for pretesting and one for posttesting, and the tests are not of equal difficulty. For example, if the posttest is more difficult than the pretest, improvement may be masked. Alternatively, if the posttest is less difficult than the pretest, it may indicate improvement that is not really present. If data are collected through observation, the observers may not be observing or evaluating behavior in the same way at the end of the study as at the beginning. In fact, if they are aware of the nature of the study, they may record only behavior that supports the researcher's hypothesis. If data are collected through the use of a mechanical device, the device may be poorly calibrated, resulting in inaccurate measurement. Thus, the researcher must take care in selecting tests, observers, and mechanical devices to measure the dependent variable.

Statistical Regression

Statistical regression usually occurs in studies where participants are selected on the basis of their extremely high or extremely low scores. **Statistical regression** is the tendency of participants who score highest on a test (e.g., a pretest) to score lower on a second, similar test (e.g., a posttest) and of participants who score lowest on a pretest to score higher on a posttest. The tendency is for scores to regress, or move, toward a mean (i.e., average) or expected score. Thus, extremely high scorers regress (i.e., move lower) toward the mean, and extremely low scorers regress (i.e., move higher) toward the mean. For example, suppose a researcher wanted to test the effectiveness of a new method of instruction on the spelling ability of poor spellers. The researcher could administer a 100-item, four-alternative, multiple-choice spelling pretest, with questions reading, "Which of the following four words is spelled incorrectly?" The researcher could then select for the study the 30 students who scored lowest. However, perhaps none of the students knew any of the words and guessed on every question. With 100 items, and four choices for each item, a student would be expected to receive a score of 25 just by guessing. Some students, however, would receive scores much lower than 25 due simply to rotten guessing, and other students, equally by chance, would receive much higher scores than 25. If all these students took the test a second time, without any instruction intervening, their expected scores would still be 25. Thus, students who scored very low the first time would be expected to have a second score closer to 25, and students who scored very high the first time would also be expected to score closer to 25 the second time. Whenever participants are selected on the basis of their extremely high or extremely low performance, statistical regression is a viable threat to internal validity.

Differential Selection of Participants

Differential selection of participants is the selection of participants who have differences before the start of a study that may account at least partially for differences found in a posttest. The threat that the groups are different before the study begins is more likely when a researcher is comparing already-formed groups. Suppose, for example, you receive permission to invite two of Ms. Hynd's English classes to participate in your study. You have no guarantee that the two classes are equivalent. If your luck is really bad, one class may be the honors English class and the other class may be the remedial English class—it would not be too surprising if the honors class did much better on the posttest! Already formed groups should be avoided if possible; when they are included in a study, the researcher should select groups that are as similar as possible and should administer a pretest to check for initial equivalence.

Mortality

First, let us make it perfectly clear that the mortality threat is usually not related to participants dying! **Mortality,** or *attrition,* refers to a reduction in the number of research participants; this reduction occurs over time as individuals drop out of a study. Mortality creates problems with validity particularly when different groups drop out for different reasons and with different frequency. A researcher can assess the mortality of groups by obtaining demographic information about the participant groups before the start of the study and then determining if the makeup of the groups has changed at the end of the study.

A change in the characteristics of the groups due to mortality can have a significant effect on the results of the study. For example, participants who drop out of a study may be less motivated or uninterested in the study than those who remain. This type of attrition frequently occurs when the participants are volunteers or when a study compares a new treatment to an existing treatment. Participants rarely drop out of control groups or existing treatments because few or no additional demands are made on them. However, volunteers or participants using the new, experimental treatment may drop out because too much effort is required for participation. The experimental group that remains at the end of the study then represents a more motivated group than the control group. As another example of mortality, suppose Suzy Shiningstar (a high-IQ-and-all-that student) got the measles and dropped out of your control group. Before Suzy dropped out, she managed to infect her friends in the control group. Because birds of a feather often flock together, Suzy's control-group friends may also be high-IQ-and-all-that students. The experimental group may end up looking pretty good when compared to the control group simply because many of the top students dropped out of the control group. The researcher cannot assume that participants drop out of a study in a random fashion and should, if possible, select a design that controls for mortality. For example, one way to reduce mortality is to provide some incentive to participants to remain in the study. Another approach is to identify the kinds of participants who drop out of the study and remove similar participants from the other groups in equal numbers.

Selection–Maturation Interaction and Other Interactive Effects

The effects of differential selection may also interact with the effects of maturation, history, or testing, with the resulting interaction threatening internal validity. In other words, if already formed groups are included in a study, one group may profit more (or less) from a treatment or have an initial advantage (or disadvantage) because of maturation, history, or testing factors. The most common of these interactive effects is **selection–maturation interaction,** which exists if participants selected into the treatment groups matured at different rates during the study. For example, suppose that you received permission to include two of Ms. Hynd's English classes in your study; both classes are average and apparently equivalent on all relevant variables. Suppose, however, that for some reason Ms. Hynd had to miss one of her classes but not the other (maybe she had to have a root canal) and Ms. Alma Mater took over Ms. Hynd's class. As luck would have it, Ms. Alma Mater proceeded to cover much of the material now included in your posttest (i.e., a problem with history). Unbeknownst to you, your experimental group would have a definite advantage, and this advantage, not the independent variable, may cause posttest differences in the dependent variable. A researcher must select a design that controls for potential problems such as this or make every effort to determine if they are operating in the study.

Threats to External Validity

Several major threats to external validity can limit generalization of experimental results to other populations. Building on the work of Campbell and Stanley, Bracht and Glass[7] refined and expanded the discussion of threats to external validity and classified these threats into two categories. Threats affecting "generalizing to whom"—that is, threat affecting the groups to which research results can be generalized—make up threats to population validity. Threats affecting "generalizing to what"—that is, threats affecting the settings, conditions, variables, and contexts to which results can be generalized—make up threats to ecological validity. The following discussion incorporates the contributions of Bracht and Glass into Campbell and Stanley's (1971) conceptualizations; the threats to external validity are summarized in Table 11.2.

---

[7] "The External Validity of Experiments," by G. H. Bracht and G. V. Glass, 1968, *American Educational Research Journal*, 5, pp. 437–474.

TABLE 11.2 • Threats to external validity

Threat	Description
Pretest–treatment interaction	The pretest sensitizes participants to aspects of the treatment and thus influences posttest scores.
Selection–treatment interaction	The nonrandom or volunteer selection of participants limits the generalizability of the study.
Multiple-treatment interference	When participants receive more than one treatment, the effect of prior treatment can affect or interact with later treatment, limiting generalizability.
Specificity of variables	Poorly operationalized variables make it difficult to identify the setting and procedures to which the variables can be generalized.
Treatment diffusion	Treatment groups communicate and adopt pieces of each other's treatment, altering the initial status of the treatment's comparison.
Experimenter effects	Conscious or unconscious actions of the researchers affect participants' performance and responses.
Reactive arrangements	The fact of being in a study affects participants so that they act in ways different from their normal behavior. The Hawthorne and John Henry effects are reactive responses to being in a study.

Pretest–Treatment Interaction

Pretest–treatment interaction occurs when participants respond or react differently to a treatment because they have been pretested. Pretesting may sensitize or alert participants to the nature of the treatment, potentially making the treatment effect different than it would have been had participants not been pretested. Campbell and Stanley illustrated this effect by pointing out the probable differences between two groups—participants who view the anti-prejudice film *Gentleman's Agreement* after taking a lengthy pretest dealing with anti-Semitism and participants who view the movie without a pretest. Individuals not pretested could conceivably enjoy the movie as a good love story, unaware that it deals with a social issue. Individuals who had taken the pretest, in contrast, may be much more likely to see a connection between the pretest and the message of the film. If pretesting affects participants' responses on the dependent measure, the research results are generalizable only to other pretested groups; the results are not even generalizable to the population from which the sample was selected.

For some studies, the potential interactive effect of a pretest is a more serious consideration than others. For example, taking a pretest on algebraic algorithms would probably have very little impact on a group's responsiveness to a new method of teaching algebra, but studies involving self-report measures, such as attitude scales and interest inventories, are especially susceptible to this threat. The pretest–treatment interaction is also minimal in studies involving very young children, who would probably not see or remember a connection between the pretest and the subsequent treatment. Similarly, for studies conducted over a period of months or longer, the effects of the pretest would probably have worn off or be greatly diminished by the time a posttest is given.

When a study is threatened by pretest–treatment interaction, researchers should select a design that either controls for the threat or allows the researchers to determine the magnitude of the effect. For example, the researcher can (if it's feasible) make use of **unobtrusive measures**—ways to collect data that do not intrude on or require interaction with research participants—such as reviewing school records, transcripts, and other written sources.

Multiple-Treatment Interference

Sometimes the same research participants receive more than one treatment in succession. **Multiple-treatment interference** occurs when carryover effects from an earlier treatment make it difficult to assess the effectiveness of a later treatment. For example, suppose you were interested in comparing two different approaches to improving classroom behavior, behavior modification and corporal punishment (admittedly an extreme example we're using to make a point!). For 2 months, behavior modification techniques were systematically applied to the participants. At the end of this period, you found behavior to be significantly better than before the study began. For the next 2 months, the same participants were physically punished (with hand slappings, spankings, and the like) whenever they misbehaved, and at the end of the 2 months, behavior was equally as good as after the 2 months of behavior modification. Could you then conclude that behavior modification and corporal punishment are equally effective methods of behavior control? Certainly not. In fact, the goal of behavior modification is to produce self-maintaining behavior—that is, behavior that continues after direct intervention is stopped. The good behavior exhibited by the participants at the end of the corporal punishment period could well be due to the effectiveness of previous exposure to behavior modification; this good behavior could exist in spite of, rather than because of, exposure to corporal punishment. If it is not possible to select a design in which each group receives only one treatment, the researcher should try to minimize potential multiple-treatment interference by allowing sufficient time to elapse between treatments and by investigating distinctly different types of independent variables.

Multiple-treatment interference may also occur when participants who have already participated in a study are selected for inclusion in another, apparently unrelated study. If the accessible population for a study is one whose members are likely to have participated in other studies (e.g., psychology majors), then information on previous participation should be collected and evaluated before participants are selected for the current study. If any members of the accessible population are eliminated from consideration because of previous research activities, a note should be made in the research report.

Selection–Treatment Interaction

Selection–treatment interaction, another threat to population validity, occurs when study findings apply only to the (nonrepresentative) groups involved and are not representative of the treatment effect in the extended population. This interaction occurs when study participants at one level of a variable react differently to a treatment than other potential participants in the population, at another level, would have reacted. For example, a researcher may conduct a study on the effectiveness of computer-assisted instruction on the math achievement of junior high students. Classes available to the researcher (i.e., the accessible population) may represent an overall ability level at the lower end of the ability spectrum for all junior high students (i.e., the target population). If this is true, the positive effect shown by the participants in the sample may be valid only for lower-ability students rather than for the target population of all junior high students. Similarly, if computer-assisted instruction appears ineffective for this sample, it may still be effective for the target population.

Selection–treatment interaction, like the problem of differential selection of participants associated with internal validity, mainly occurs when participants are not randomly selected for treatments. But this threat can occur in designs involving randomization as well, and the way a given population becomes available to a researcher may threaten generalizability, no matter how internally valid an experiment may be. For example, suppose that, in seeking a sample, a researcher is turned down by nine school systems before finally being accepted by a tenth. The accepting system is very likely to be different from the other nine systems and also from the population of schools to which the researcher would like to generalize the results. Administrators and instructional personnel in the tenth school may have higher morale, less fear of being inspected, or more zeal for improvement than personnel in the other nine schools. In the research report, researchers should describe any problems they encountered in acquiring participants, including the number of times they were turned down, so that the reader can judge the seriousness of a possible selection–treatment interaction.

Specificity of Variables

Like selection–treatment interaction, specificity of variables is a threat to generalizability of research results regardless of the particular experimental design. Any given study has **specificity of variables;** that is, the study is conducted with a specific kind of participant, using specific measuring instruments, at a specific time, and under a specific set of circumstances. We have discussed the need to describe research procedures in sufficient detail to permit another researcher to replicate the study. Such detailed descriptions also permit interested readers to assess how applicable findings are to their situations. When studies that supposedly manipulated the same independent variable get quite different results, it is often difficult to determine the reasons for the differences because researchers have not provided clear, operational definitions of their independent variables. When operational definitions are available, they often reveal that two independent variables with the same name were defined quite differently in the separate studies. Because such terms as *discovery method*, *whole language*, and *computer-based instruction* mean different things to different people, it is impossible to know what a researcher means by these terms unless they are clearly defined. Generalizability of results is also tied to the clear definition of the dependent variable, although in most cases the dependent variable is clearly operationalized as performance on a specific measure. When a researcher has a choice of measures to select from, he or she should address the comparability of these instruments and the potential limits on generalizability arising from their use.

Generalizability of results may also be affected by short- or long-term events that occur while the study is taking place. This threat is referred to as the *interaction of history and treatment effects* and describes the situation in which events extraneous to the study alter the research results. Short-term, emotion-packed events, such as the firing of a superintendent, the release of district test scores, or the impeachment of a president may affect the behavior of participants. Usually, however, the researcher is aware of such happenings and can assess their possible impact on results, and accounts of such events should be included in the research report. The impact of long-term events, such as wars and economic depressions, however, is more subtle and tougher to evaluate.

Another threat to external validity is the *interaction of time of measurement and treatment effect*. This threat results from the fact that post-testing may yield different results depending on when it is done. A posttest administered immediately after the treatment may provide evidence for an effect that does not show up on a posttest given

some time after treatment. Conversely, a treatment may have a long-term but not a short-term effect. The only way to assess the generalizability of findings over time is to measure the dependent variable at various times following treatment.

To summarize, the researcher must deal with the threats associated with specificity by defining variables operationally, in a way that has meaning outside the experimental setting, and must be careful in stating conclusions and generalizations.

Treatment Diffusion

Treatment diffusion occurs when different treatment groups communicate with and learn from each other. When participants in one treatment group know about the treatment received by a different group, they often borrow aspects from that treatment. When such borrowing occurs, the study no longer has two distinctly different treatments but rather has two overlapping ones. The integrity of each treatment is diffused. Often, the more desirable treatment—the experimental treatment or the treatment with additional resources—is diffused into the less desirable treatment. For example, suppose Mr. Darth's and Ms. Vader's classes were trying two different treatments to improve spelling. Mr. Darth's class received videos, new and colorful spelling texts, and prizes for improved spelling. In Ms. Vader's class, the students were asked to list words on the board, copy them into notebooks, use each word in a sentence, and study at home. After the first week of treatments, the students began talking to their teachers about the different spelling classes. Ms. Vader asked Mr. Darth if she could try the videos in her class, and her students liked them so well that she incorporated them into her spelling program. The diffusion of Mr. Darth's treatment into Ms. Vader's treatment produced two overlapping treatments that did not represent the initial intended treatments. To reduce treatment diffusion, a researcher may ask teachers who are implementing different treatments not to communicate with each other about the treatments until the study is completed or may carry out the study in more than one location, thus allowing only one treatment per school.

Experimenter Effects

Researchers themselves also present potential threats to the external validity of their own studies. A researcher's influences on participants or on study procedures are known as **experimenter effects.** Passive experimenter effects occur as a result of characteristics or personality traits of the experimenter, such as gender, age, race, anxiety level, and hostility level. These influences are collectively called *experimenter personal-attributes effects*. Active experimenter effects occur when the researcher's expectations of the study results affect his or her behavior and contribute to producing certain research outcomes. This effect is referred to as the **experimenter bias effect.** An experimenter may unintentionally affect study results, typically in the desired direction, simply by looking, feeling, or acting a certain way.

One form of experimenter bias occurs when the researcher affects participants' behavior or is inaccurate in evaluating behavior because of previous knowledge of the participants. For example, suppose a researcher hypothesizes that a new reading approach will improve reading skills. If the researcher knows that Suzy Shiningstar is in the experimental group and that Suzy is a good student, she may give Suzy's reading skills a higher rating than they actually warrant. This example illustrates another way a researcher's expectations may contribute to producing those outcomes: Knowing or even believing that participants are in the experimental or the control group may cause the researcher—unintentionally—to evaluate their performances in a way consistent with the expectations for that group.

It is difficult to identify experimenter bias in a study, which is all the more reason for researchers to be aware of its consequences on the external validity of a study. The researcher should strive to avoid communicating emotions and expectations to participants in the study. Experimenter bias effects can also be reduced by blind scoring, in which the researcher doesn't know whose performance is being evaluated.

Reactive Arrangements

Reactive arrangements, also called *participant effects*, are threats to validity that are associated with the way in which a study is conducted and the feelings and attitudes of the participants involved. As discussed previously, to maintain a high degree of control and obtain internal validity, a researcher may create an experimental environment that is highly artificial and not easily generalizable to nonexperimental settings; this is a reactive arrangement.

Another type of reactive arrangement results from participants' knowledge that they are involved in an experiment or their feeling that they are in some way receiving special attention. The effect that such knowledge or feelings can have on participants was demonstrated at the Hawthorne Plant of the Western Electric Company in Chicago some years ago. As part of a study to investigate the relation between various working conditions and productivity, researchers investigated the effect of light intensity and worker output. The researchers increased light intensity and production went up. They increased it some more and production went up some more. The brighter the place became, the more production rose. As a check, the researchers decreased the light intensity, and guess what, production went up! The darker it got, the more workers produced. The researchers soon realized that it was the attention given the workers, not the illumination, that was affecting production. To this day, the term *Hawthorne effect* is used to describe any situation in which participants' behavior is affected not by the treatment per se but by their awareness of participating in a study.

A related reactive effect, known as *compensatory rivalry* or the **John Henry effect,** occurs when members of a control group feel threatened or challenged by being in competition with an experimental group and they perform way beyond what would normally be expected. Folk hero John Henry, you may recall, was a "steel drivin' man" who worked for a railroad. When he heard that a steam drill was going to replace him and his fellow steel drivers, he set out to beat the machine. Through tremendous effort he managed to win the ensuing contest, dropping dead at the finish line. In the John Henry effect, research participants who are told that they will form the control group for a new, experimental method, start to act like John Henry. They decide to challenge the new method by putting extra effort into their work, essentially saying (to themselves), "We'll show them that our old ways are as effective as their newfangled ways!" By doing this, however, the control group performs atypically; their performance provides a rival explanation for the study results. When the John Henry effect occurs, the treatment under investigation does not appear to be very effective because posttest performance of the experimental group is not much (if at all) better than that of the control group.

As an antidote to the Hawthorne and John Henry effects, educational researchers often attempt to achieve a placebo effect. The term comes from medical researchers who discovered that any apparent medication, even sugar and water, could make participants feel better; any beneficial effect caused by a person's expectations about a treatment rather than the treatment itself became known as the **placebo effect.** To counteract this effect, a placebo approach was developed in which half the participants in an experiment receive the true medication and half receive a placebo (e.g., sugar and water). The use of a placebo is, of course, not known by the participants; both groups think they are taking real medicine. The application of the placebo effect in educational research is that all groups in an experiment should appear to be treated the same. Suppose, for example, you have four groups of ninth-graders, two experimental and two control, and the treatment is a film designed to promote a positive attitude toward a vocational career. If the experimental participants are to be excused from several classes to view the film, then the control participants should also be excused and shown another film whose content is unrelated to the purpose of the study (e.g., *Drugs and You: Just Say No!*). As an added control, all participants may be told that there are two movies and that eventually everyone will see both movies. In other words, it should appear as if all the students are doing the same thing.

Another reactive arrangement, or participant effect, is the **novelty effect,** which refers to the increased interest, motivation, or engagement participants develop simply because they are doing something different. In other words, a treatment may be effective because it is different, not because it is better. To counteract the novelty effect, a researcher should conduct a study over a period of time long enough to allow the treatment novelty to wear off, especially if the treatment involves activities very different from the participants' usual routine.

Obviously there are many internal and external threats to the validity of an experimental (or causal–comparative) study. You should be aware of likely threats and strive to nullify them. One main way to overcome threats to validity is to choose a research design that controls for such threats. We examine some of these designs in the following sections.

Control of Extraneous Variables

The validity of an experiment is a direct function of the degree to which extraneous variables are controlled. If such variables are not controlled, it is difficult to interpret the results of a study and the groups to which results can be generalized. The term *confounded* is sometimes used to describe a situation in which the effects of the independent variable are so intertwined with those of extraneous variables that it becomes difficult to determine the unique effects of each. Experimental design strives to reduce this problem by controlling extraneous variables. Good designs control many sources that affect validity; poor designs control few.

As discussed in previous chapters, two types of extraneous variables in need of control are participant variables and environmental variables. Participant variables include both organismic variables and intervening variables. Organismic variables are characteristics of the participants that cannot be altered but can be controlled for; the sex of a participant is an example. Intervening variables intrude between the independent and the dependent variable and cannot be directly observed but can be controlled for; anxiety and boredom are examples.

Randomization

Randomization is the best way to control for many extraneous variables simultaneously. This procedure is effective in creating equivalent, representative groups that are essentially the same on all relevant variables. The underlying rationale for randomization is that if participants are assigned at random (by chance) to groups, there is no reason to believe that the groups will be greatly different in any systematic way. In other words, they should be about the same on participant variables such as ability, gender, or prior experience, and on environmental variables as well. If the groups are the same at the start of the study and if the independent variable makes no difference, the groups should perform essentially the same on the dependent variable. On the other hand, if the groups are the same at the start of the study but perform differently after treatment, the difference can be attributed to the independent variable.

As noted previously, the use of randomly formed treatment groups is a unique characteristic of experimental research; this control factor is not possible with causal–comparative research. Thus, randomization is used whenever possible—participants are randomly selected from a population and randomly assigned to treatment groups. If subjects cannot be randomly selected, those available should at least be randomly assigned. If participants cannot be randomly assigned to groups, then at least treatment conditions should be randomly assigned to the existing groups. Additionally, the larger the groups, the more confidence the researcher can have in the effectiveness of randomization. Randomly assigning six participants to two treatments is much less likely to equalize extraneous variables than randomly assigning 50 participants to two treatments.

To ensure random selection and assignment, researchers use tools such as a table of random numbers and other randomization methods that rely on chance. For example, a researcher could flip a coin or use odd and even numbers on a die to assign participants to two treatments; heads or an even number would signal assignment to treatment 1, and tails or an odd number would signal assignment to treatment 2.

If groups cannot be randomly formed, a number of other techniques can be used to try to equate groups. Certain environmental variables, for example, can be controlled by holding them constant for all groups. Recall the example of the student tutor versus parent tutor study. In that example, help time was an important variable that had to be held constant, that is, made the same for both groups for them to be fairly compared. Other environmental variables that may need to be held constant include learning materials, prior exposure, meeting place and time (e.g., students may be more alert in the morning than in the afternoon), and years of teacher experience.

In addition, participant variables should be held constant, if possible. Techniques to equate groups based on participant characteristics include matching, comparing homogeneous groups or subgroups, participants serving as their own controls, and analysis of covariance.

Matching

Matching is a technique for equating groups on one or more variables, usually variables highly related to performance on the dependent variable. The most commonly used approach to matching involves random assignment of pairs, one participant to each group. In other words, the researcher attempts to find pairs of participants similar on the variable or variables to be controlled. If the researcher is matching on gender, obviously the matched pairs must be of the same gender. If the researcher is matching on variables such as pretest, Graduate Record Examination (GRE), or ability scores, the pairing can be based on similarity of scores. Note, however, that unless the number of participants is very large, it is unreasonable to try to make exact matches or matches based on more than one or two variables.

Once a matched pair is identified, one member of the pair is randomly assigned to one treatment group and the other member to the other treatment group. A participant who does not have a suitable match is excluded from the study. The resulting matched groups are identical or very similar with respect to the variable being controlled.

A major problem with such matching is that, invariably, some participants will not have a match and must be eliminated from the study. One way to combat loss of participants is to match less stringently. For example, the researcher may decide that if two ability test scores are within 20 points, they constitute an acceptable match. This approach may increase the number of participants, but it can defeat the purpose of matching if the criteria for a match are too broad.

A related matching procedure is to rank all the participants from highest to lowest, based on their scores on the variable to be matched. The two highest ranking participants, regardless of raw score, are the first pair. One member of the first pair is randomly assigned to one group and the other member to the other group. The next two highest ranked participants (i.e., third and fourth ranked) are the second pair, and so on. The major advantage of this approach is that no participants are lost. The major disadvantage is that it is a lot less precise than pair-wise matching.

Comparing Homogeneous Groups or Subgroups

Another previously discussed way to control an extraneous variable is to compare groups that are homogeneous with respect to that variable. For example, if IQ were an identified extraneous variable, the researcher may select only participants with IQs between 85 and 115 (i.e., average IQ). The researcher would then randomly assign half the selected participants to the experimental group and half to the control group. This procedure also lowers the number of participants in the population and restricts the generalizability of the findings to participants with IQs between 85 and 115. As noted in the discussion of causal–comparative research, a similar, more satisfactory approach is to form different subgroups representing all levels of the control variable. For example, the available participants may be divided into subgroups with high (i.e., 116 and above), average (i.e., 85 to 115), and low (i.e., 84 and below) IQ. Half the participants from each subgroup could then be randomly assigned to the experimental group and half to the control group. This procedure should sound familiar; it is stratified sampling. If the researcher is interested not just in controlling the variable but also in seeing if the independent variable affects the dependent variable differently at different levels of IQ, the best approach is to build the control variable into the design. Thus, the research design would have six cells: two treatments by three IQ levels. Diagram the design for yourself, and label each cell with its treatment and IQ level.

Participants as Their Own Controls

When participants serve as their own controls, the design of the study involves a single group of participants who are exposed to multiple treatments, one at a time. This strategy helps to control for participant differences because the same participants get both treatments. In situations in which the effect of the dependent variable disappears quickly after treatment, or in which a single participant is the focus of the research, participants can serve as their own controls.

This approach is not always feasible; you cannot teach the same algebraic concepts to the same group twice using two different methods of instruction (well, you could, but it would not make much sense). Furthermore, a problem with this approach is a carryover effect from one treatment to the next. To use a previous example, it would be very difficult to evaluate the effectiveness of corporal punishment for improving behavior if the group receiving corporal punishment were the same group that had previously been exposed to behavior modification. If only one group is available, a better approach, if feasible, is to divide the group randomly into two smaller groups, each of which receives both treatments but in a different order. The researcher could at least get some idea of the effectiveness of corporal punishment because one group would receive it before behavior modification.

Analysis of Covariance

The analysis of covariance is a statistical method for equating randomly formed groups on one or more variables. Analysis of covariance adjusts scores on a dependent variable for initial differences on some other variable, such as pretest scores, IQ, reading readiness, or musical aptitude. The covariate should be related to performance on the dependent variable.

Analysis of covariance is most appropriate when randomization is used; the results are weakened when a study deals with intact groups, uncontrolled variables, and nonrandom assignment to treatments. Nevertheless, in spite of randomization, the groups may still differ significantly prior to treatment. Analysis of covariance can be used in such cases to adjust posttest scores for initial pretest differences. However, the relation between the independent and covariate variables must be linear (i.e., represented by a straight line). Table 11.3 provides a summary of the controls used for extraneous variables.

> MyLab Education **Self-Check 11.2**
>
> MyLab Education **Application Exercise 11.2:** Evaluating Research Articles: Evaluating an Experimental Study

GROUP EXPERIMENTAL DESIGNS

The experimental design dictates to a great extent the specific procedures of a study. Selection of a given design influences factors such as whether a control group will be included, whether participants will be randomly selected and assigned to groups, whether the groups will be pretested, and how data will be analyzed. Particular combinations

TABLE 11.3 • Controls used for extraneous variables	
	Description
Control randomization	This is the best way to control for many extraneous variable simultaneously. This procedure is effective for creating equivalent, representative groups that are essentially the same on all relevant variables.
Matching	Matching is a technique for equating groups on one or more variables, usually variables highly related to performance on the dependent variable.
Comparing homogeneous groups or subgroups	Another way to control an extraneous variable is to control groups that are homogeneous with respect to that variable.
Participants as their own controls	When participants serve as their own controls, the design of the study involves a single group of participants who are exposed to multiple treatments, one at a time.
Analysis of covariance	The analysis of covariance is a statistical method for equating randomly formed groups on one or more variables.

of such factors produce different designs that are appropriate for testing different types of hypotheses. In selecting a design, first determine which designs are appropriate for your study and for testing your hypothesis, then determine which of these are also feasible given the constraints under which you may be operating. For example, if you must use existing groups, a number of designs will be automatically eliminated. From the designs that are appropriate and feasible, select the one that will control the most threats to internal and external validity and will yield the data you need to test your hypothesis or hypotheses. Designs vary widely in the degree to which they control various threats to internal and external validity, although no design can control for certain threats, such as experimenter bias.

There are two major classes of experimental designs: single-variable designs and factorial designs. A **single-variable design** is any design that involves one manipulated independent variable; a **factorial design** is any design that involves two or more independent variables, at least one of which is manipulated. Factorial designs can demonstrate relations that a single-variable design cannot. For example, a variable found not to be effective in a single-variable study may interact significantly with another variable.

Single-Variable Designs

Single-variable designs are classified as pre-experimental, true experimental, or quasi-

experimental, depending on the degree of control they provide for threats to internal and external validity. *Pre-experimental designs* do not do a very good job of controlling threats to validity and should be avoided. In fact, the results of a study based on a pre-experimental design are so questionable they are not useful for most purposes except, perhaps, to provide a preliminary investigation of a problem. *True experimental designs* provide a very high degree of control and are always to be preferred. *Quasi-experimental designs* do not control as well as true experimental designs but do a much better job than pre-experimental designs. The less useful designs are discussed here only so that you will know what not to do and so that you will recognize their use in published research reports and be appropriately critical of their findings.

Pre-Experimental Designs

Here is a research riddle for you: Can you do an experiment with only one group? The answer is yes, but not a really good one. As Figure 11.1 illustrates, none of the pre-experimental designs (designs without control group[s]) does a very good job of controlling extraneous variables that jeopardize validity.

The One-Group Posttest-Only Design. The **one-group posttest-only design** involves a single group that is exposed to a treatment (*X*) and then tested (*O*). No threats to validity are controlled in this design except those that are automatically

FIGURE 11.1 • Threats to validity for pre-experimental designs

Designs	Threats to Validity									
	Internal								External	
	History	Maturation	Testing	Instrumentation	Regression	Selection	Mortality	Selection Interactions	Pretest-X Interaction	Multiple-X Interference
One-Group Posttest-Only Design $X\ O$	−	−	(+)	(+)	(+)	(+)	−	(+)	(+)	(+)
One-Group Pretest–Posttest Design $O\ X\ O$	−	−	−	−	−	(+)	+	(+)	−	(+)
Posttest-Only Design with Nonequivalent Groups $X_1\ O$ $X_2\ O$	+	−	(+)	(+)	(+)	−	−	−	(+)	(+)

Each line of Xs and Os represents a group.

Note: Symbols: X or X_1 = unusual treatment; X_2 = control treatment; O = test, pretest, or posttest; + = factor controlled for; (+) factor controlled for because not relevant; and − = factor not controlled for.

Figures 11.1 and 11.2 basically follow the format used by Campbell and Stanley and are presented with a similar note of caution: The figures are intended to be supplements to, not substitutes for, textual discussions. You *should not* totally accept or reject designs because of their pluses and minuses; you *should* be aware that the design most appropriate for a given study is determined not only by the controls provided by the various designs but also by the nature of the study and the setting in which it is to be conducted.

Although the symbols used in these figures, and their placement, vary somewhat from Campbell and Stanley's format, the intent, interpretations, and textual discussions of the two presentations are in agreement (personal communication with Donald T. Campbell, April 22, 1975).

controlled because they are irrelevant in this design (see Figure 11.1). The threats that are relevant, such as history, maturation, and mortality, are not controlled. Even if the research participants score high on the posttest, you cannot attribute their performance to the treatment because you do not know what they knew before you administered the treatment. If you have a choice between using this design and not doing a study, don't do the study. Do a different study with a better controlled design.

The One-Group Pretest–Posttest Design. The **one-group pretest–posttest design** involves a single

group that is pretested (*O*), exposed to a treatment (*X*), and then tested again (*O*). The success of the treatment is determined by comparing pretest and posttest scores. This design controls some threats to validity not controlled by the one-shot case study, but a number of additional factors relevant to this design are not controlled. For example, history and maturation are not controlled. If participants do significantly better on the posttest than on the pretest, the improvement may or may not be due to the treatment. Something else may have happened to the participants that affected their performance, and the longer the study takes, the more likely it is that this "something" threatens validity. Testing and instrumentation are also not controlled; the participants may learn something on the pretest that helps them on the posttest, or unreliability of the measures may be responsible for the apparent improvement. Statistical regression is also not controlled. Even if participants are not selected on the basis of extreme scores (i.e., high or low), a group may do very poorly on the pretest just by poor luck. For example, participants may guess badly on a multiple-choice pretest and improve on a posttest simply because, this time, their guessing produces a score that is more in line with an expected score. Finally, the external validity threat of pretest–treatment interaction is not controlled in this design. Participants may react differently to the treatment than they would have if they had not been pretested.

To illustrate the problems associated with this design, consider a hypothetical study. Suppose a professor teaches a statistics course and is concerned that the high anxiety level of students interferes with their learning. The professor prepares a 100-page booklet in which she explains the course, tries to convince students that they will have no problems, and promises all the help they need to complete the course successfully, even if they have a poor math background. The professor wants to see if the booklet helps to reduce anxiety. At the beginning of the term, she administers an anxiety test and then gives each student a copy of the booklet with instructions to read it as soon as possible. Two weeks later she administers the anxiety scale again, and the students' scores indicate much less anxiety than at the beginning of the term. The professor is satisfied and prides herself on the effectiveness of the booklet for reducing anxiety. However, a number of alternative factors or threats may explain the students' decreased anxiety. For example, students are typically more anxious at the beginning of a course because they do not know exactly what they are in for (i.e., fear of the unknown). After a couple of weeks in the course, students may find that it is not as bad as they imagined, or if it turns out to be as bad or worse, they will drop it (i.e., mortality). In addition, the professor doesn't know whether the students read the booklet!

The only situations for which the one-group pretest–posttest design is appropriate is when the behavior to be measured is not likely to change by itself. Certain prejudices, for example, are not likely to change unless a concerted effort is made.

The Posttest-Only Design with Nonequivalent Groups. The **posttest-only design with nonequivalent groups** involves at least two nonrandomly formed groups, one that receives a new or unusual treatment (i.e., the experimental treatment) and another that receives a traditional treatment (i.e., the control treatment). Both groups are posttested. The purpose of the control group is to indicate what the performance of the experimental group would have been if it had not received the experimental treatment. This purpose is fulfilled only to the degree that the control group is equivalent to the experimental group.

In a posttest-only design with nonequivalent groups, the terms *experimental* and *control* are commonly used to describe the groups, but it is probably more appropriate to call them both comparison groups because each serves as the comparison for the other. Each group receives some form of the independent variable (i.e., the treatment). For example, if the independent variable is a type of drill and practice, the experimental group (X_1) may receive computer-assisted drill and practice, and the control group may receive worksheet drill and practice. Occasionally, but not often, the experimental group may receive something while the control group receives nothing. For example, a group of teachers may receive some type of in-service education while the comparison group of teachers receives nothing. In this case, X_1 is in-service training, and X_2 is no in-service training.

The posttest-only design with nonequivalent groups can be expanded to deal with any number of groups. For three groups, the design takes the following form:

$$X_1 \quad O$$
$$X_2 \quad O$$
$$X_3 \quad O$$

Each group serves as a control or comparison group for the other two. For example, if the independent variable were number of minutes of review at the end of math lessons, then X_1 may represent 6 minutes of review, X_2 may represent 3 minutes of review, and X_3 may represent no minutes of review. Thus, X_3 would help us to assess the impact of X_2, and X_2 would help us to assess the impact of X_1.

Again, the degree to which the groups are equivalent is the degree to which their comparison is reasonable. In this design, participants are not randomly assigned to groups and no pretest data are collected; thus, it is difficult to determine the extent to which the groups are equivalent. That is, posttest differences may be due to initial group differences in maturation, selection, and selection interactions, rather than the treatment effects. Mortality is also a problem; if you lose participants from the study, you have no information about what you have lost because you have no pretest data. On the positive side, the presence of a comparison group controls for history because events occurring outside the experimental setting should affect both groups equally.

In spite of its limitations, the posttest-only design with nonequivalent groups is occasionally employed in a preliminary or exploratory study. For example, one semester, early in the term, a teacher wondered if the kind of test items given to educational research students affects their retention of course concepts. For the rest of the term, students in one section of the course were given multiple-choice tests, and students in another section were given short-answer tests. At the end of the term, group performances were compared. The students receiving short-answer test items had higher total scores than students receiving the multiple-choice items. On the basis of this exploratory study, a formal investigation of this issue was undertaken, with randomly formed groups.

True Experimental Designs

True experimental designs control for nearly all threats to internal and external validity. As Figure 11.2 indicates, all true experimental designs have one characteristic in common that the other designs do not have: random assignment of participants to treatment groups. Ideally, participants should be randomly selected and randomly assigned; however, to qualify as a true experimental design, random assignment (R) must be involved. Also, all the true designs have a control group (X_2). Finally, although the posttest-only control group design looks like the posttest-only design with nonequivalent groups design, random assignment in the former makes it very different in terms of control.

The Pretest–Posttest Control Group Design. The **pretest–posttest control group design** requires at least two groups, each of which is formed by random assignment. Both groups are administered a pretest, each group receives a different treatment, and both groups are posttested at the end of the study. Posttest scores are compared to determine the effectiveness of the treatment. The pretest–posttest control group design may also be expanded to include any number of treatment groups. For three groups, for example, this design takes the following form:

$$R \quad O \quad X_1 \quad O$$
$$R \quad O \quad X_2 \quad O$$
$$R \quad O \quad X_3 \quad O$$

The combination of random assignment and the presence of a pretest and a control group serve to control for all threats to internal validity. Random assignment controls for regression and selection factors; the pretest controls for mortality; randomization and the control group control for maturation; and the control group controls for history, testing, and instrumentation. Testing is controlled because if pretesting leads to higher posttest scores, the advantage should be equal for both the experimental and control groups. The only weakness in this design is a possible interaction between the pretest and the treatment, which may make the results generalizable only to other pretested groups. The seriousness of this potential weakness depends on the nature of the pretest, the nature of the treatment, and the length of the study. When this design is used, the researcher should assess and report the probability of a pretest–treatment interaction. For example, a researcher may indicate that possible pretest interaction was likely to be minimized by the nonreactive nature of the pretest (e.g., chemical equations) and by the length of the study (e.g., 9 months).

The data from this and other experimental designs can be analyzed to test the research hypothesis regarding the effectiveness of the treatments in several different ways. The best way is to compare the posttest scores of the two treatment groups. The pretest is used to see if the groups are essentially the same on the dependent variable at the start of the study. If they are, posttest scores can be compared directly using a statistic called the t test. If the groups are not essentially the same on the pretest (i.e., random assignment does not guarantee equality), posttest scores can be analyzed using analysis of covariance, which

FIGURE 11.2 • Threats to validity for true experimental designs and quasi-experimental designs

Designs	Threats to Validity									
	Internal								External	
	History	Maturation	Testing	Instrumentation	Regression	Selection	Mortality	Selection Interactions	Pretest-X Interaction	Multiple-X Interference
TRUE EXPERIMENTAL DESIGNS										
1. Pretest–Posttest Control Group Design $R\ O\ X_1\ O$ $R\ O\ X_2\ O$	+	+	+	+	+	+	+	+	−	(+)
2. Posttest-Only Control Group Design $R\quad X_1\ O$ $R\quad X_2\ O$	+	+	(+)	(+)	(+)	+	−	+	(+)	(+)
3. Solomon Four-Group Design $R\ O\ X_1\ O$ $R\ O\ X_2\ O$ $R\quad X_1\ O$ $R\quad X_2\ O$	+	+	+	+	+	+	+	+	+	(+)
QUASI-EXPERIMENTAL DESIGNS										
4. Nonequivalent Control Group Design $O\ X_1\ O$ $O\ X_2\ O$	+	+	+	+	−	+	+	−	−	(+)
5. Time-Series Design $O\ O\ O\ O\ X\ O\ O\ O\ O$	−	+	+	−	+	(+)	+	(+)	−	(+)
6. Counterbalanced Design $X_1O\ X_2O\ X_3O$ $X_3O\ X_1O\ X_2O$ $X_2O\ X_3O\ X_1O$	+	+	+	+	+	+	+	−	−	−

Note: Symbols: X or X_1 = unusual treatment; X_2 = control treatment; O = test, pretest, or posttest; R = random assignment of participants to groups; $+$ = factor controlled for; $(+)$ = factor controlled for because not relevant; and $-$ = factor not controlled for. This figure is intended to be a supplement to, not substitute for, textual discussions. See note that accompanies Figure 11.1.

adjusts posttest scores for initial differences on any variable, including pretest scores. This approach is superior to using gain or difference scores (i.e., posttest minus pretest) to determine the treatment effects.

A variation of the pretest–posttest control group design involves random assignment of members of matched pairs to the treatment groups. There is really no advantage to this technique, however, because any variable that can be controlled through matching can be better controlled using other procedures such as analysis of covariance.

Another variation of this design involves one or more additional posttests, for example:

$$R \quad O \quad X_1 \quad O \quad O$$
$$R \quad O \quad X_2 \quad O \quad O$$

This variation has the advantage of providing information about the effect of the independent variable both immediately following treatment and at a later date. Recall that the interaction of time of measurement and treatment effects is a threat to external validity because posttesting may yield different results depending on when it is done— a treatment effect (or lack of one) that is based on the administration of a posttest immediately following the treatment may not be found if a delayed posttest is given after treatment. Although adding multiple posttests does not solve this problem completely, it minimizes it greatly by providing information about group performance subsequent to the initial posttest.

The Posttest-Only Control Group Design. The **posttest-only control group design** is the same as the pretest–posttest control group design except there is no pretest—participants are randomly assigned to at least two groups, exposed to the different treatments, and posttested. Posttest scores are then compared to determine the effectiveness of the treatment. As with the pretest–posttest control group design, the posttest-only control group design can be expanded to include more than two groups.

The combination of random assignment and the presence of a control group serves to control for all threats to internal validity except mortality, which is not controlled because of the absence of pretest data on participants. However, mortality may or may not be a problem, depending on the duration of the study. If it isn't a problem, the researcher may

report that, although mortality is a potential threat to validity with this design, it did not prove to be a threat because the group sizes remained constant or nearly constant throughout the study. If the probability of differential mortality is low, the posttest-only design can be very effective. However, if the groups may be different with respect to pretreatment knowledge related to the dependent variable, the pretest–posttest control group design should be used. Which design is best depends on the study. If the study is short, and if it can be assumed that neither group has any knowledge related to the dependent variable, then the posttest-only design may be the best choice. If the study is to be lengthy (i.e., good chance of mortality), or if the two groups potentially differ on initial knowledge related to the dependent variable, then the pretest–posttest control group design may be the best.

A variation of the posttest-only control group design involves random assignment of matched pairs to the treatment groups, one member to each group, to control for one or more extraneous variables. There is really no advantage to this technique, however, because any variable that can be controlled by matching can be better controlled using other procedures.

What if you face the following dilemma: The study is going to last 2 months, information about initial knowledge is essential, the pretest is an attitude test, and the treatment is designed to change attitudes? This is a classic case where pretest–treatment interaction is probable. One solution is to select the lesser of the two evils by taking our chances that mortality will not be a threat. Another solution, if enough participants are available, is to use the Solomon four-group design, which we discuss next.

The Solomon Four-Group Design. As Figure 11.2 shows, the **Solomon four-group design** is a combination of the pretest–posttest control group design and the posttest-only control group design. The Solomon four-group design involves random assignment of participants to one of four groups. Two groups are pretested and two are not, one of the pretested groups and one of the groups not pretested receive the experimental treatment, and all four groups are posttested. The combination of the pretest–posttest control group design and the posttest-only control group design results in a design that controls for pretest-treatment interaction and for mortality.

In this example, the design has two independent variables, each with two levels: group assignment (i.e., treatment or control) and pretest status (i.e., yes or no). The correct way to analyze the data resulting from this application of the Solomon four-group design is to use a 2×2 factorial analysis of variance. The 2×2 factorial analysis tells the researcher several things. First, if the participants who received the treatment (regardless of whether they took the pretest) perform differently than the participants who did not receive treatment (i.e., were in a control group), the researcher can conclude the treatment has an effect. Second, if the participants who took the pretest (regardless of whether they were in the treatment or the control groups) perform differently than the participants who did not take the pretest, the researcher can conclude that simply taking the pretest affects the dependent variable. Finally, if the participants who took the pretest *and* received the treatment perform differently on the posttest than those in the experimental group but did not receive the treatment, a pretest–treatment interaction is likely present. If the two experimental groups perform equally well on the posttest (i.e., no pretest–treatment interaction) but better than the two control groups, the researcher can conclude with more confidence that the treatment had an effect that can be generalized to the population.

A common misconception is that, because the Solomon four-group design controls for so many threats to validity, it is always the best design to choose. It isn't. This design introduces other challenges that must be considered. For example, it requires twice as many participants as most other true experimental designs, and participants are often hard to find. If mortality is not likely to be a problem and pretest data are not needed, then the posttest-only design may be the best choice. If pretest–treatment interaction is unlikely and testing is a normal part of the participants' environment (such as when classroom tests are used), then the pretest–posttest control group design may be best. Thus, which design is the best depends on the nature of the study and the conditions under which it is to be conducted.

Quasi-Experimental Designs

Sometimes it is just not possible to assign individual participants to groups randomly. For example, to receive permission to include schoolchildren in a study, a researcher often has to agree to keep existing classrooms intact. In other words, entire classrooms, not individual students, are assigned to treatments. When random assignment is not possible, a researcher may choose from a number of quasi-experimental designs that provide adequate controls. As you review the following discussion of three quasi-experimental designs, keep in mind that designs such as these are to be used only when it is not feasible to use a true experimental design.

The Nonequivalent Control Group Design. This design is very much like the pretest–posttest control group design discussed previously. In the **nonequivalent control group design,** two (or more) treatment groups are pretested, administered a treatment, and posttested. The difference is that it involves random assignment of intact groups to treatments, not random assignment of individuals. For example, suppose a school volunteered six intact classrooms for a study. Three of six classrooms may be randomly assigned to the experimental group (X_1) and the remaining three assigned to the control group (X_2). The inability to assign individuals to treatments randomly (as opposed to assigning whole classes) adds validity threats such as regression and interactions between selection, maturation, history, and testing.

To reduce some of the threats and strengthen the study, the researcher should make every effort to include groups that are as equivalent as possible. Comparing an advanced algebra class to a remedial algebra class, for example, would not be comparing equivalent groups. If differences between the groups on any major extraneous variable are identified, analysis of covariance can be used to equate the groups statistically. An advantage of the nonequivalent control group design is that, because established classes or groups are selected, possible effects from reactive arrangements are minimized. Groups may not even be aware that they are involved in a study.

The Time-Series Design. This design is an elaboration of the one-group pretest–posttest design. In the **time-series design,** one group is repeatedly pretested until pretest scores are stable. The group is then exposed to a treatment and, after treatment implementation, repeatedly posttested. If a group performs essentially the same on a number of pretests and then significantly improves following a

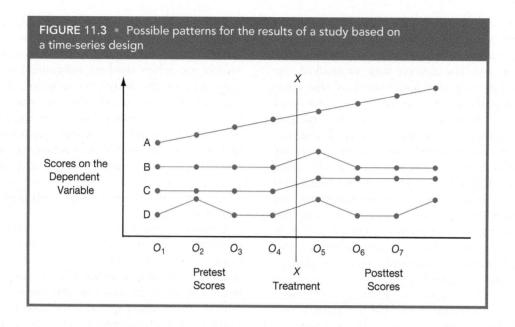

FIGURE 11.3 • Possible patterns for the results of a study based on a time-series design

treatment, the researcher can be more confident about the effectiveness of the treatment than if just one pretest and one posttest were administered. For example, if the statistics professor we discussed earlier in the chapter measured anxiety several times before giving the students her booklet, she could see if anxiety was declining even before receiving her booklet.

History is a problem with the time-series design because some event or activity may occur between the last pretest and the first posttest. Instrumentation may also be a problem, but only if the researcher changes measuring instruments during the study. Pretest–treatment interaction is certainly a possibility; if one pretest can interact with a treatment, more than one pretest can only make matters worse. If instrumentation or pretest–treatment interaction threatens validity, however, you will probably be aware of the problem because scores will change prior to treatment.

Determining the effectiveness of the treatment involves analysis of the pattern of the test scores, although statistical analyses appropriate for a time-series design are quite advanced. Figure 11.3 illustrates some of the possible patterns that may be found. The vertical line between O_4 and O_5 indicates the point at which the treatment was introduced. Pattern A suggests no treatment effect; performance was increasing before the treatment was introduced and continued to

increase at the same rate following introduction of the treatment. In fact, pattern A represents the reverse situation to that encountered by our statistics professor with her booklet. Patterns B and C indicate a treatment effect, with pattern C being more permanent than pattern B. Pattern D does not indicate a treatment effect even though student scores are higher on O_5 than O_4; the pattern is too erratic to make a decision about treatment effect. Scores appear to be fluctuating up and down, so the O_4 to O_5 fluctuation cannot be attributed to the treatment. These four patterns illustrate that comparing O_4 and O_5 is not sufficient; in all four cases, O_5 indicates a higher score than O_4, but only in two of the patterns does it appear that the difference is due to a treatment effect.

A variation of the time-series design is the multiple time-series design, which involves the addition of a control group to the basic design, as shown here:

$$O \quad O \quad O \quad O \quad X_1 \quad O \quad O \quad O \quad O$$
$$O \quad O \quad O \quad O \quad X_2 \quad O \quad O \quad O \quad O$$

This variation eliminates history and instrumentation as validity threats and thus represents a design with no likely threats to internal validity. The multiple time-series design can be used most effectively in situations where testing is a naturally occurring event, such as in research involving school classrooms.

Counterbalanced Designs. In a **counterbalanced design,** all groups receive all treatments but in a different order, and groups are posttested after each treatment. Although the example of a counterbalanced design in Figure 11.2 includes three groups and three treatments, any number of groups (more than one) may be studied. The only restriction is that the number of groups be equal to the number of treatments. The order in which the groups receive the treatments is randomly determined. This design is usually employed with intact groups when administration of a pretest is not possible, although participants may be pretested. The pre-experimental posttest-only design with nonequivalent groups can also be used in such situations, but the counterbalanced design controls for several additional threats to validity.

Figure 11.3 shows the sequence for three treatment groups and three treatments. The first horizontal line indicates that Group A receives Treatment 1 and is posttested, then receives Treatment 2 and is posttested, and finally receives Treatment 3 and is posttested. The second line indicates that Group B receives Treatment 3, then Treatment 1, and then Treatment 2, and is posttested after each treatment. The third line indicates that Group C receives Treatment 2, then Treatment 3, and then Treatment 1, and is posttested after each treatment. To put it another way, the first column indicates that at Time 1, while Group A is receiving Treatment 1, Group B is receiving Treatment 3 and Group C is receiving Treatment 2. All three groups are posttested, and the treatments are shifted as shown in the second column—at time 2, while Group A is receiving Treatment 2, Group B is receiving Treatment 1 and Group C is receiving Treatment 3. The groups are then posttested again, and the treatments are again shifted so that at time 3, Group A receives Treatment 3, Group B receives Treatment 2, and Group C receives Treatment 1. All groups are posttested again. To determine the effectiveness of the treatments, the average performance of the groups on each treatment can be calculated and compared. In other words, the posttest scores for all the groups for the first treatment can be compared to the posttest scores of all the groups for the second treatment, and so forth, depending on the number of groups and treatments. Sophisticated analysis procedures that are beyond the scope of this text can be applied to determine both the effects of treatments and the effects of the order of treatments.

A unique weakness of the counterbalanced design is potential multiple-treatment interference that results when the same group receives more than one treatment. Thus, a counterbalanced design should be used only when the treatments are such that exposure to one will not affect the effectiveness of another. Unfortunately, few situations in education meet this condition. For example, you cannot teach the same geometric concepts to the same group using several different methods of instruction.

Factorial Designs

Factorial designs are elaborations of single-variable experimental designs to permit investigation of two or more variables, at least one of which is manipulated by the researcher. After a researcher has studied an independent variable using a single-variable design, it is often useful to study that variable in combination with one or more other variables because some variables work differently when paired with different levels of another variable. For example, one method of math instruction may be more effective for high-aptitude students, whereas a different method may be more effective for low-aptitude students. The purpose of a factorial design is to determine whether the effects of an independent variable are generalizable across all levels or whether the effects are specific to particular levels.

The term *factorial* refers to a design that has more than one independent variable (or grouping variable), also known as a factor. In the preceding example, method of instruction is one factor and student aptitude is another. Method of instruction has two levels—there are two types of instruction; student aptitude also has two levels, high aptitude and low aptitude. Thus, a 2×2 (two by two) factorial design has two factors, and each factor has two levels. This four-celled design is the simplest possible factorial design. As another example, a 2×3 factorial design has two factors; one factor has two levels, and the other factor has three levels (e.g., high, average, and low aptitude). A study with three factors—homework (required homework, voluntary homework, no homework), ability (high, average, low), and gender (male, female)—is a $3 \times 3 \times 2$ factorial design. Note that multiplying the

FIGURE 11.4 • An example of the basic 2 × 2 factorial design

Type of Instruction

		Personalized	Traditional
IQ	High	Group 1	Group 2
	Low	Group 3	Group 4

factors yields the total number of cells (i.e., groups) in the factorial design. For example, a 2 × 2 design has 4 cells, and a 3 × 3 × 2 design has 18 cells.

Figure 11.4 illustrates the simplest 2 × 2 factorial design. One factor, type of instruction, has two levels: personalized and traditional. The other factor, IQ, also has two levels: high and low. Each group represents a combination of a level of one factor and a level of the other factor. Thus, Group 1 is composed of high-IQ students receiving personalized instruction (PI), Group 2 is composed of high-IQ students receiving traditional instruction (TI), Group 3 is composed of low-IQ students receiving PI, and Group 4 is composed of low-IQ students receiving TI. To implement this design, high-IQ students would be randomly assigned to either Group 1 or Group 2, and a similar number of low-IQ students would be randomly assigned to either Group 3 or Group 4. This approach should be familiar; it involves stratified sampling. In fact, this study does not necessarily require four classes; it could include only two classes, the personalized class and the traditional class, and each class could be subdivided to obtain similar numbers of high- and low-IQ students.

In a 2 × 2 design, both variables may be manipulated, or one may be a manipulated variable and the other a nonmanipulated variable. The nonmanipulated variable is often referred to as a **control variable.** Control variables are usually physical or mental characteristics of the participants (e.g., gender, years of experience, or aptitude). In the example shown here, IQ is a nonmanipulated control variable. When describing and symbolizing factorial designs, the manipulated variable is traditionally placed first. Thus, a study with two factors, type of instruction (three types,

manipulated) and gender (male, female), would be symbolized as 3 × 2, not 2 × 3.

Figure 11.5 illustrates two possible outcomes for an experiment involving a 2 × 2 factorial design. The number in each box, or cell, represents the average posttest score for that group. Thus, in both examples, the high-IQ students under Method A had an average posttest score of 80. The row and column numbers outside the boxes represent average scores across boxes, or cells. In the top example, the average score for high-IQ students was 60 (i.e., the average of the scores for all high-IQ participants regardless of treatment; 80 + 40 = 120/2 = 60), and the average score for low-IQ students was 40. The average score for students under Method A was 70 (i.e., the average of the scores of all the participants under Method A regardless of IQ level; 80 + 60 = 140/2 = 70), and for students under Method B, 30. The cell averages suggest that Method A was better than Method B for high-IQ students (i.e., 80 versus 40), and Method A was also better for low-IQ students (i.e., 60 versus 20). Thus, Method A was better, regardless of IQ level; there was no interaction between method and IQ. The high-IQ students in each method outperformed the low-IQ students in each method, and the participants in Method A outperformed the participants in Method B at each IQ level. The parallel lines in the top graph in Figure 11.5 illustrate the lack of interaction.

The bottom example of Figure 11.5 shows an interaction. For high-IQ students, Method A was better (i.e., 80 versus 60); for low-IQ students, Method B was better (i.e., 20 versus 40). Even though high-IQ students did better than low-IQ students regardless of method, how well they did depended on which method they were in. Neither method was generally better; rather, one method was better for students with high IQs, and one was better for students with low IQs. Note that if the researcher had simply compared two groups of participants, one group receiving Method A and one group receiving Method B, without separating high- and low-IQ students in the factorial design, the researcher would likely have concluded that Method A and Method B were equally effective because the overall average score for Methods A *and* B was 50. The factorial design allowed the researcher to see the interaction between the variables—the methods were differentially effective depending on the IQ level of the participants. The

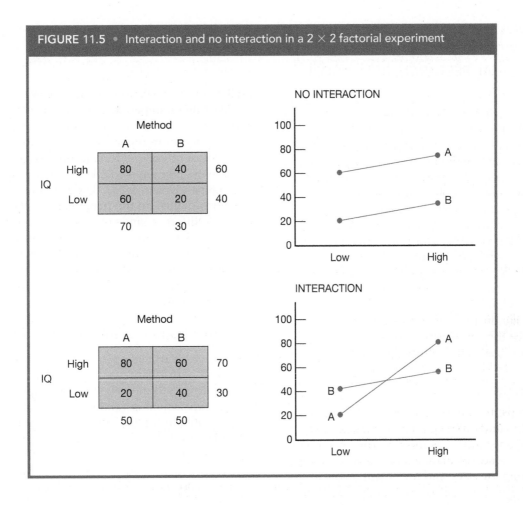

FIGURE 11.5 • Interaction and no interaction in a 2 × 2 factorial experiment

crossed lines in the bottom graph in Figure 11.5 illustrate the interaction.

Many factorial designs are possible, depending on the nature and the number of independent variables. Theoretically, a researcher could simultaneously investigate 10 factors in a 2 × 2 × 2 × 2 × 2 × 2 × 2 × 2 × 2 × 2 design. In reality, however, more than 3 factors are rarely used because each additional factor increases the number of participants needed to complete the study. A 2 × 2 design with 20 participants per cell (a relatively small number) requires at least 80 participants (2 × 2 × 20 = 80). It is easy to see that as the number of cells increases, things quickly get out of

hand. Reducing the number per cell doesn't help because as sample size decreases, so does representativeness. And interactions involving many factors are difficult if not impossible to interpret. For example, how would you interpret a five-way interaction between teaching method, IQ, gender, aptitude, and anxiety?

MyLab Education **Self-Check 11.3**

MyLab Education **Application Exercise 11.3:** Designing an Experimental Study

SUMMARY

EXPERIMENTAL RESEARCH: DEFINITION AND PURPOSE

1. In an experimental study, the researcher manipulates at least one independent variable, controls other relevant variables, and observes the effect on one or more dependent variables.

2. The independent variable, also called the experimental variable, cause, or treatment, is that process or activity believed to make a difference in performance. The dependent variable, also called the criterion variable, effect, or posttest, is the outcome of the study, the measure of the change or difference resulting from manipulation of the independent variable.

3. When conducted well, experimental studies produce the soundest evidence concerning hypothesized cause–effect relations.

The Experimental Process

4. The steps in an experimental study include selecting and defining a problem, selecting participants and measuring instruments, preparing a research plan, executing procedures, analyzing the data, and formulating conclusions.

5. An experimental study is guided by at least one hypothesis that states an expected causal relation between two variables.

6. In an experimental study, the researcher forms or selects the groups, decides how to allocate treatments to each group, controls extraneous variables, and observes or measures the effect on the groups at the end of the study.

7. The experimental group typically receives a new treatment, and the control group either receives a different treatment or is treated as usual.

8. The two groups that are to receive different treatments are equated on all other variables that influence performance on the dependent variable.

9. After the groups have been exposed to the treatment for some period, the researcher measures the dependent variable and tests for a significant difference in performance.

Manipulation and Control

10. Direct manipulation by the researcher of at least one independent variable is the characteristic that differentiates experimental research from other types of research.

11. Control refers to efforts to remove the influence of any variable, other than the independent variable, that may affect performance on the dependent variable.

12. Two different kinds of variables need to be controlled: participant variables, on which participants in the different groups may differ, and environmental variables, variables in the setting that may cause unwanted differences between groups.

THREATS TO EXPERIMENTAL VALIDITY

13. Any uncontrolled extraneous variables that affect performance on the dependent variable are threats to the validity of an experiment. An experiment is valid if results obtained are due only to the manipulated independent variable and if they are generalizable to situations outside the experimental setting. Threats to validity include statistical conclusion validity, internal validity, construct validity, and external validity.

14. Internal validity is the degree to which observed differences on the dependent variable are a direct result of manipulation of the independent variable, not some other variable. External validity is the degree to which study results are generalizable to groups and environments outside the experimental setting.

15. The researcher must strive for a balance between control and realism, but if a choice is involved, the researcher should err on the side of control.

Threats to Internal Validity

16. History refers to any event occurring during a study that is not part of the experimental treatment but may affect performance on the dependent variable.

17. Maturation refers to physical, intellectual, and emotional changes that naturally occur within individuals over a period of time and affect

participants' performance on a measure of the dependent variable.

18. Testing refers to the possibility that participants show improved performance on a posttest because they took a pretest.

19. Instrumentation refers to unreliability, or lack of consistency, in measuring instruments that may result in invalid assessment of performance.

20. Statistical regression refers to the tendency of participants who score highest on a pretest to score lower on a posttest and the tendency of those who score lowest on a pretest to score higher on a posttest.

21. Differential selection is the selection of participants who have differences at the start of a study that may influence posttest differences. It usually occurs when already-formed groups are used.

22. Mortality, or attrition, refers to a reduction in the number of research participants as individuals drop out of a study. Mortality can affect validity because it may alter the characteristics of the treatment groups.

23. Selection may interact with factors related to maturation, history, and testing. If already formed groups are included in a study, one group may profit more (or less) from a treatment or have an initial advantage (or disadvantage) because of maturation, history, or testing factors.

Threats to External Validity

24. Threats affecting to whom research results can be generalized make up threats to population validity.

25. Pretest–treatment interaction occurs when participants respond or react differently to a treatment because they have been pretested. The pretest may provide information that influences the posttest results.

26. Multiple-treatment interference occurs when the same participants receive more than one treatment in succession and when the effects from an earlier treatment influence a later treatment.

27. Selection–treatment interaction occurs when findings apply only to the (nonrepresentative) groups involved and are not representative of the treatment effect in the extended population.

28. Specificity is a threat to generalizability when the treatment variables are not clearly operationalized, making it unclear to whom the variables generalize.

29. Generalizability of results may be affected by short-term or long-term events that occur while the study is taking place. This potential threat is referred to as interaction of history and treatment effects.

30. An interaction of time of measurement and treatment effects may occur when posttesting yields different results depending on when it is done.

31. Treatment diffusion occurs when different treatment groups communicate with and learn from each other.

32. A researcher's influences on participants or on study procedures are known as experimenter effects; these effects can be passive or active.

33. Reactive arrangements are threats to external validity that are associated with participants performing atypically because they are aware of being in a study. The Hawthorne, John Henry, and novelty effects are examples of reactive arrangements.

34. The placebo effect is sort of the antidote for the Hawthorne and John Henry effects. Its application in educational research is that all groups in an experiment should appear to be treated the same.

Control of Extraneous Variables

35. The validity of an experiment is a direct function of the degree to which extraneous variables are controlled.

36. Participant variables include organismic variables and intervening variables. Organismic variables are characteristics of the subject or organism that cannot be altered but can be controlled for. Intervening variables intrude between the independent variable and the dependent variable and cannot be directly observed, but they can be controlled for.

37. Randomization is the single best way to control for extraneous variables and should be used whenever possible. Participants should be randomly selected from a population and randomly assigned to groups, and treatments should be randomly assigned to groups.

38. Certain environmental variables can be controlled by holding them constant for all groups.

39. Matching commonly involves finding pairs of similar participants and randomly assigning each member of a pair to a different group. Participants who do not have a match must be eliminated from the study.

40. Another way of controlling an extraneous variable is to compare groups that are homogeneous with respect to that variable. A similar but more satisfactory approach is to form subgroups representing all levels of the control variable.

41. If the researcher is interested not just in controlling the variable but also in seeing if the independent variable affects the dependent variable differently at different levels of the control variable, the best approach is to build the control variable right into the design.

42. Participants can serve as their own controls if the same group is exposed to the different treatments, one treatment at a time.

43. The analysis of covariance is a statistical method for equating randomly formed groups on one or more variables. It adjusts scores on a dependent variable for initial differences on some other variable related to the dependent variable.

GROUP EXPERIMENTAL DESIGNS

44. Selection of a given design dictates factors such as whether participants will be randomly selected and assigned to groups, whether the groups will be pretested, and how data will be analyzed.

Single-Variable Designs

45. Single-variable designs involve one independent variable (which is manipulated) and are classified as pre-experimental, true experimental, or quasi-experimental, depending on the control they provide for threats to internal and external validity.

Pre-Experimental Designs

46. The one-group posttest-only design involves one group that is exposed to a treatment (X) and then tested (O). No relevant threat to validity is controlled.

47. The one-group pretest–posttest design involves one group that is pretested (O), exposed to a treatment (X), and tested again (O).

48. The posttest-only design with nonequivalent groups involves at least two groups. One group receives a new or unusual treatment, and both groups are posttested. Because participants are not randomly assigned to groups and there are no pretest data, it is difficult to determine whether the treatment groups are equivalent.

True Experimental Designs

49. True experimental designs control for nearly all threats to internal and external validity. True experimental designs have one characteristic in common that no other design has: random assignment of participants to groups. Ideally, participants should be randomly selected and randomly assigned to treatments.

50. The pretest–posttest control group design involves at least two groups, both of which are formed by random assignment. Both groups are administered a pretest, one group receives a new or unusual treatment, and both groups are posttested. A variation of this design seeks to control extraneous variables more closely by randomly assigning members of matched pairs to the treatment groups.

51. The posttest-only control group design is the same as the pretest–posttest control group design except there is no pretest. Participants are randomly assigned to at least two groups, exposed to the independent variable, and posttested to determine the effectiveness of the treatment. A variation of this design is random assignment of matched pairs.

52. The Solomon four-group design involves random assignment of participants to one of four groups. Two of the groups are pretested, and two are not; one of the pretested groups and one of the unpretested groups receive the experimental treatment. All four groups are posttested. This design controls all threats to internal validity.

53. The best way to analyze data resulting from the Solomon four-group design is to use a 2×2 factorial analysis of variance. This procedure indicates whether there is an interaction between the treatment and the pretest.

Quasi-Experimental Designs

54. When it is not possible to assign participants to groups randomly, quasi-experimental designs are available to the researcher. They provide adequate control of threats to validity.

55. The nonequivalent control group design is like the pretest–posttest control group design except that the nonequivalent control group design does not involve random assignment. If differences between the groups on any major extraneous variable are identified, analysis of covariance can be used to equate the groups statistically.

56. In the time-series design, one group is repeatedly pretested, exposed to a treatment, and then repeatedly posttested. If a group scores essentially the same on a number of pretests and then significantly improves following a treatment, the researcher has more confidence in the effectiveness of the treatment than if just one pretest and one posttest were administered.

57. The multiple time-series design is a variation that involves adding a control group to the basic design. This variation eliminates all threats to internal validity.

58. In a counterbalanced design, all groups receive all treatments but in a different order, the number of groups equals the number of treatments, and groups are posttested after each treatment. This design is usually employed when intact groups are included and when administration of a pretest is not possible.

Factorial Designs

59. Factorial designs involve two or more independent variables, at least one of which is manipulated by the researcher. The 2×2 is the simplest factorial design. Factorial designs rarely include more than three factors.

60. A factorial design is used to test whether the effects of an independent variable are generalizable across all levels or whether the effects are specific to particular levels (i.e., there is an interaction between the variables).

Effects of Mathematical Word Problem–Solving Instruction on Middle School Students with Learning Problems

YAN PING XIN
Purdue University

ASHA K. JITENDRA
Lehigh University

ANDRIA DEATLINE-BUCHMAN
Easton Area School District

ABSTRACT   This study investigated the differential effects of two problem-solving instructional approaches—schema-based instruction (SBI) and general strategy instruction (GSI)—on the mathematical word problem–solving performance of 22 middle school students who had learning disabilities or were at risk for mathematics failure. Results indicated that the SBI group significantly outperformed the GSI group on immediate and delayed posttests as well as the transfer test. Implications of the study are discussed within the context of the new IDEA amendment and access to the general education curriculum.

(01)   Mathematics is integral to all areas of daily life; it affects successful functioning on the job, in school, at home, and in the community. The importance of mathematics literacy and problem solving is emphasized in the Goals 2000: Educate America Act of 1994 and National Council of Teachers of Mathematics' *Principles and Standards for School Mathematics* (NCTM, 2000; Goldman, Hasselbring, & the Cognition and Technology Group at Vanderbilt, 1997). Increasing evidence suggests that high levels of mathematical and technical skills are needed for most jobs in the 21st century. Therefore, it is important to ensure that all students, not just those planning to pursue higher education, have sufficient skills to meet the challenges of the 21st century (National Education Goals Panel, 1997). In addition, one of the provisions of the 1997 amendments to the Individuals with Disabilities Education Act (IDEA) is that students with disabilities have meaningful access to the general education curriculum. In fact, these students are held accountable to the same high academic standards required of all students (No Child Left Behind Act, 2002).

(02)   As part of the mathematics reform and standards-based reform movements, the NCTM (2000) developed the *Principles and Standards for School Mathematics*. The focus of the NCTM standards is on "conceptual understanding rather than procedural knowledge or rule-driven computation" (Maccini & Gagnon, 2002, p. 326). This emphasis has significant implications for classroom practice because special education typically has focused on arithmetic computation rather than higher-order skills such as reasoning and problem solving (Cawley, Parmar, Yan, & Miller, 1998). Students with learning disabilities often manifest serious deficits in mathematics, especially problem solving (Carnine, Jones, & Dixon, 1994; Cawley & Miller, 1989; Cawley, Parmar, Foley, Salmon, & Roy, 2001; Parmar, Cawley, & Frazita, 1996). Specifically, these students perform at significantly lower levels than students without disabilities on all problem types, especially problems that involve indirect language, extraneous information, and multisteps (Briars & Larkin, 1984; Cawley et al., 2001; Englert, Culatta, & Horn, 1987; Lewis & Mayer, 1987; Parmar et al., 1996). While problems in reading and basic computation skills may account for these students' poor performance,

difficulties in problem representation and failure to identify relevant information and operation may exacerbate their poor performance (Hutchinson, 1993; Judd & Bilsky, 1989; Parmar, 1992).

(03) In addition, ineffective instructional strategies may explain the poor problem-solving performance of students with learning disabilities. One commonly used instructional approach is the "key word" strategy, in which students are taught key words that cue them as to what operation to use in solving problems. For example, students learn that *altogether* indicates the use of the addition operation, whereas *left* indicates subtraction. Similarly, the word *times* calls for multiplication, and *among* indicates the need to divide. However, Parmar et al. (1996) argued that "the outcome of such training is that the student reacts to the cue word at a surface level of analysis and fails to perform a deep-structure analysis of the interrelationships among the word and the context in which it is embedded" (p. 427). That is, the focus is on whether to add, subtract, multiply, or divide rather than whether the problem makes sense. Another commonly employed problem-solving strategy is the four-step (read, plan, solve, and check) general heuristic procedure. Unfortunately, this procedure may not facilitate problem solution for students with learning disabilities, especially when the domain-specific conceptual and procedural knowledge is not adequately elaborated upon (Hutchinson, 1993; Montague, Applegate, & Marquard, 1993).

(04) For students with learning disabilities, explicit teaching for conceptual understanding is critical to establish the necessary knowledge base for problem solution. Recent reviews provide empirical support for problem-solving instruction, such as a schema-based strategy instruction, that emphasizes conceptual understanding of the problem structure, or schemata (Xin & Jitendra, 1999). Successful problem solvers typically create a complete mental representation of the problem schema, which, in turn, facilitates the encoding and retrieval of information needed to solve problems (Didierjean & Cauzinille-Marmeche, 1998; Fuson & Willis, 1989; Marshall, 1995; Mayer, 1982). Problem schema acquisition allows the learner to use the representation to solve a range of different (i.e., containing varying surface features) but structurally similar problems (Sweller, Chandler, Tierney, & Cooper, 1990).

(05) Schema-based strategy instruction is known to benefit both special education students (e.g., Jitendra & Hoff, 1996; Jitendra, Hoff, & Beck, 1999) and students at risk for math failure (e.g., Jitendra et al., 1998; Jitendra, DiPipi, & Grasso, 2001) in solving arithmetic word problems. However, previous research on the effects of schema-based strategy instruction is limited, for the most part, to algebra problems (Hutchinson, 1993) and addition and subtraction (e.g., change, combine, additive compare) arithmetic problems. Although the effects of semantic representation training in facilitating problem solving have been demonstrated with college students with and without disabilities, the studies are limited to a sample of comparison problems only (Lewis, 1989; Zawaiza & Gerber, 1993). Furthermore, neither the study by Lewis nor the study by Zawaiza and Gerber emphasized key components (compared, referent, and scalar function) pertinent to the compare problem schemata. In addition, the rules for figuring out the operation (e.g., if the unknown quantity is to the right of the given quantity on the number line, then addition or multiplication should be applied) cannot be directly applied to solve multiplication or division compare problems when the relational statement involves a fraction or when the unknown is the scalar function (i.e., the multiple or partial relation between two comparison quantities).

(06) A more recent exploratory study by Jitendra, DiPipi, and Perron-Jones (2002) employed a single-subject design to reach four students with learning disabilities to solve word problems involving multiplication and division using the schema-based strategy. However, one of the limitations of the study is that "the single-subject design employed in this investigation does not help clarify whether the study findings are attributable to specific schema-based nature

Selection and definition of a problem:
The purpose of this study is to evaluate and compare the effectiveness of
two problem-solving instructional
approaches, schema-based and general
strategy instruction, in teaching multiplication and division word problems to
middle school students with learning disabilities or at risk for mathematics failure.

(07)

Experimental research design: a
pretest-posttest control group design
with random assignment
R   O X_1 O
R   O X_2 O

(08)

Sample size = 22

*Does this sample size pose any threats
to the statistical conclusion validity of
the study?*

of the instruction" (p. 37) or to the generally carefully designed one-on-one intensive instruction on two problem types. The purpose of the present investigation was to evaluate and compare the effectiveness of two problem-solving instructional approaches, schema-based and general strategy instruction, in teaching multiplication and division word problems to middle school students with learning disabilities or at risk for mathematics failure.

Method
Design

A pretest–posttest comparison group design with random assignment of subjects to groups was used to examine the effects of the two word problem–solving instructional procedures—schema-based instruction (SBI) and general strategy instruction (GSI)—on the word problem–solving performance of middle school students with learning problems.

Participants

Participants were 22 students with learning problems, including 18 who were school-identified as having a learning disability, 1 with severe emotional disorders, and 3 who were at risk for mathematics failure, attending a middle school in the northeastern United States. Specifically, participant selection was based on (a) teacher identification of students who were experiencing substantial problems in mathematics word problem solving and (b) a score of 70% or lower on the word problem–solving criterion pretest involving multiplication and division word problems. To determine sample size, a power analysis using an alpha level of .05 and an effect size based on existing schema-based instruction research studies (e.g., Jitendra et al., 1998) was conducted, which indicated that a minimum of 10 participants in each group is sufficient to obtain a power of .90 for a 2 × 4 repeated measures analyses of variance (Friendly, 2000). Table 1 presents demographic information with respect to participants' gender, grade, age, ethnicity, special education classification, IQ level, and standardized achievement scores in math and reading. It is important to note that IQ and achievement data from school records were available for only nine students.

Procedure

(09) Instructors were two doctoral students in special education and two experienced special education teachers. The two doctoral students taught the first cohort of 8 students (4 in each treatment group), and the two special education teachers taught the second cohort of 14 students (7 in each treatment group). Students in both cohorts were randomly assigned to the two treatment groups. To control for teacher effects, each pair of instructors (i.e., the two doctoral students or the two special education teachers) were randomly assigned to the two conditions, and they switched treatment groups midway through the intervention. The first author developed the teaching scripts for both conditions and piloted them prior to employing them in the study. Instructors received two 1-hour training sessions to familiarize them with lesson formats, the suggested teacher wording, and lesson materials when implementing the two instructional approaches.

(10) Students in both conditions received their assigned strategy instruction three to four times a week, each session lasting approximately an hour. The SBI group received 12 sessions of instruction, with 4 sessions each on solving *multiplicative compare* and *proportion* problems and 4 sessions on solving mixed word problems that included both types. Students in the GSI group also received 12 sessions of instruction, but they solved both types of problems in each session. Unlike the SBI group, students in the GSI group did not receive instruction in recognizing the two different word problem types. Students in the two groups solved the same number and type of problems.

Table 1

Demographic Information

Variable	SBI group	GSI group
Gender		
Male	5	6
Female	6	5
Grade		
6	6	4
7	2	6
8	3	1
Mean age in months (*SD*)	153.8 (8.6)	156.7 (8.7)
Ethnicity		
Caucasian	4	3
Hispanic	5	7
African American	2	1
Classification		
LD	10	8
SEN	0	1
NL	1	2
IQ[a]		
Verbal		
M	95	93
SD	8.5	5.7
Performance		
M	92	92
SD	2.5	2.1
Full Scale		
M	92	92
SD	2.9	3.1
Achievement[b]		
Math		
M	84	88
SD	10.4	3.9
Reading		
M	90	93
SD	2.0	2.4

Note: SBI = schema-based instruction; GSI = general strategy instruction; LD = learning disabled; SED = seriously emotionally disturbed; NL = not labeled.

[a]IQ scores were obtained from the Wechsler Intelligence Scales for Children—Revised (Wechsler, 1974).

[b]Achievement scores in math and reading were obtained from the Metropolitan Achievement Test (Balow, Farr, & Hogan, 1992), with the exception of scores for one student that were obtained from the *Stanford Achievement Test*, 9th ed. (1996). IQ and achievement scores were available for only 9 of the 22 students.

Both Conditions

(11)   Across both SBI and GSI conditions, the teacher first modeled the assigned strategy with multiple examples. Explicit instruction was followed by teacher-guided practice and independent student work. Corrective feedback and additional modeling were provided as needed during practice sessions. It should be noted that students in both groups were allowed to use calculators during instruction and testing conditions, because computation skills were not the focus of this study. Table 2 summarizes the problem-solving strategy steps across two conditions.

(12)   Overall, both groups were taught to follow the four-step general problem-solving procedure of reading to understand, representing the problem, and planning, solving, and checking. However, the fundamental differences between the two conditions involved the second and third steps, with regard to how to plan and solve the problem. Specifically, the SBI group was taught to identify the problem structure and use a schema diagram to represent and solve the problem, whereas the GSI group learned to draw semiconcrete pictures to represent information in the problem and facilitate problem solving. A detailed description of the two instructional conditions, with an emphasis on how to "plan" and "solve" the problem, is presented in the next section.

Schema-Based Instruction Condition

(13)   Instruction for the SBI group occurred in two phases: problem schemata instruction and problem solution instruction. During problem schemata instruction, students learned to identify the problem type or structure and represent the problem using a schematic diagram. In this phase, story situations with no unknown information were presented. The purpose of presenting story situations was to provide students with a complete representation of the problem structure of a specific problem type. In contrast, the problem solution instruction phase used story problems with unknown information. Below is a general description of instruction employed to teach the two problem types investigated in this study.

(14)   **Multiplicative Compare Problems.** When teaching the multiplicative compare problem schema, instruction emphasized several salient features. That is, students learned that a multiplicative compare problem always includes (a) a referent set, including its identity and its corresponding quantity; (b) a compared set, including its identity and corresponding quantity; and (c) a statement that relates the compared set to the referent set. In short, the multiplicative compare problem describes one object as the referent and expresses the other as a part or multiple of it. Students first learned to identify the problem type using story situations such as the following: "Vito earned $12 from shoveling snow over the weekend. He earned 1/3 as much as his friend Guy did. Guy earned $36 from shoveling snow." This story situation, because the amount Vito earned (compared set) was compared to what Guy earned (referent set), was deemed to be a comparison problem situation. Moreover, students learned that the comparison implies a *multiplicative* relationship (i.e., multiple or part) rather than an *additive* compare (more or less) situation.

(15)   A prompt sheet that contained information describing the salient features of the problem type and the five strategy steps was designed to facilitate

Table 2

General Problem-Solving Steps Employed in the SBI and GSI Conditions

Schema-based instruction (SBI)	General strategy instruction (GSI)
• Read to understand	• Read to understand
• Identify the problem type, and use the schema diagram to represent the problem	• Draw a picture to represent the problem
• Transform the diagram to a math sentence, and solve the problem	• Solve the problem
• Look back to check	• Look back to check

problem solving. Step 1 of the strategy required identifying and underlining the relational statement in the problem. For example, students were taught that the relational statement in the above sample story was, "He earned 1/3 as much as his friend Guy did," because it describes the compared as a part of the referent. Step 2 involved identifying the "referent" and "compared" and mapping that information onto the multiplicative compare diagram. Students were instructed to examine the relational statement and note that the second subject or object, that following a phrase such as "as many as" or "as much as," indicates the referent (i.e., "Guy"), whereas the subject or object preceding the referent indicates the compared. Step 3 entailed finding the corresponding information related to the compared, referent, and comparison relation and mapping that information onto the diagram. Instruction emphasized rereading the story to find information about the compared (Vito earned $12), the referent (Guy earned $36), and their relation (1/3), as well as writing the corresponding quantities with the labels onto the diagram (see Figure 1).

In sum, students learned to identify the key problem features and map (16) the information onto the diagram during problem schema analysis instruction. Next, they learned to summarize the information in the problem using the completed diagram. Instruction emphasized checking the accuracy of the representation by having students transform the information in the diagram into a meaningful mathematics equation, for example,

$$\frac{12}{36} = \frac{1}{3}.$$

Students learned that when the representation does not establish the correct (17) equation, for example,

$$\frac{36}{12} \neq \frac{1}{3}.$$

Multiplicative Compare

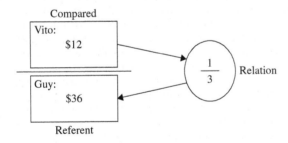

Proportion

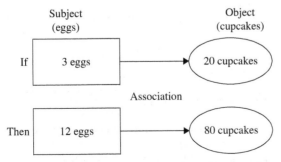

Figure 1 General problem-solving steps employed in the schema-based instruction and general strategy instruction conditions.

(18)   they should check the completed diagram by reviewing the information related to each component (i.e., the referent, compared, and relation) of the multiplicative compare problem. In addition, the instructor provided a rationale for learning the problem schema. For example, the schematic diagram used to represent the story situation reflected the mathematical structure of the problem type, which could be used eventually to solve problems that involve an unknown quantity.

(19)   During the problem-solving instruction phase, students learned to solve for the unknown quantity in word problems. For example, in the following problem, "Vito earned $12 from shoveling snow over the weekend. He earned 1/3 much as his friend Guy did. How much did Guy earn from shoveling the snow?" students were asked to solve for the unknown quantity. Instruction focused on representing the problem using the multiplicative compare schematic diagram, as in the problem schema instruction phase. The only difference was that students were taught to use a question mark to flag the unknown quantity (i.e., the amount Guy earned) in the diagram. Next, students learned to transform the information in the diagram into a math sentence and solve for the unknown (Step 4). That is, they derived the following math equation,

$$\frac{12}{?} = \frac{1}{3},$$

(20)   directly from the schematic representation. They then used cross multiplication to solve for the unknown (i.e., $? = 12 \times 3 = 36$). For Step 5, students had to write a complete answer on the answer line and check the reasonableness of their answer. Instruction required checking the accuracy of both the representation and the computation.

(21)   **Proportion Problems.** When teaching the proportion problem schema, the following salient features were emphasized: (a) The proportion problem describes an association (i.e., a ratio) between two things; (b) there are two pairs of associations between two things that involve four quantities; and (c) the numerical association (i.e., the ratio) between two things is constant across two pairs (see Marshall, 1995). Typically, the proportion problem involves an "if . . . then" relationship. That is, one pair of associations is the *if* statement, and the other is the *then* statement. The *if* statement declares a per-unit value or unit ratio in one pair, whereas the *then* statement describes the variation (enlargement or decrement) of the two quantities in the second pair. In addition, the unit ratio remains constant across the two pairs of associations (i.e., if 1 shelf holds 12 books, then 4 shelves will hold 48 books). Students first learned to identify the problem type using the following sample story: "A recipe for chocolate cupcakes uses 3 eggs to make 20 cupcakes. If you want to make 80 cupcakes, you need 12 eggs." Because this situation describes the association between eggs and cupcakes and involves two pairs of associations with the unit ratio unchanged, it is considered a proportion story.

(22)   The instructor provided a prompt sheet that contained information about the features of the proportion problem and included four problem-solving strategy steps. Step 1 required identifying the two things that formed a specific association or ratio in the story situation, and defining one as the subject and the other as the object. In the sample story described above, "eggs" and "cupcakes" illustrate the ratio relationship. Students learned to identify one as the subject (i.e., "eggs") and the other as the object (i.e., "cupcakes") and to write them in the diagram under the "subject" and "object" dimensions, respectively (see Figure 1). Step 2 consisted of identifying the two pairs of numerical associations (involving four quantities) and mapping the

information onto the proportion diagram. Instruction in representation and mapping emphasized the correct alignment of the two dimensions (subject and object) with their corresponding quantities. That is, while the first pair describes the association of "3 eggs" for "20 cupcakes," the second pair describes "12 eggs" for "80 cupcakes" rather than "80 cupcakes" for "12 eggs." Finally, instruction required checking the correctness of the representation by transforming the diagram into a math equation; that is,

$$\frac{3}{12} = \frac{12}{80}.$$

If the equation was not established in their representation, students were instructed to check the accuracy of their mapping (i.e., whether the two pairs of associations were correctly aligned). Instruction also highlighted the importance of the schematic diagram to solve proportion problems. (23)

In the problem-solving instruction phase, problems with unknown information were presented. Students were instructed to first represent the problem using the schematic diagram as they did in the problem schema instruction phase. The only difference was that they used the question mark to flag the unknown. Next, they used Step 3 to transform the diagram into a math equation and solve for the unknown. Instruction emphasized that, because the proportion problem schema entails a constant ratio across two pairs of association, the math equation can be derived directly from the diagram. For example, in the problem "A recipe for chocolate cupcakes uses 3 eggs to make 20 cupcakes. If you want to make 80 cupcakes, how many eggs will you need?" the math equation would be (24)

$$\frac{3}{20} = \frac{?}{80}.$$

Students then used cross multiplication to solve for the missing value in the equation. That is, ? = (3 × 80) ÷ 20 = 12. The last step, Step 4, required writing a complete answer on the answer line and checking it. Students not only were taught to check the accuracy of the computation, they also learned to use reasoning and critical thinking to determine whether they correctly paired the quantities of the subject and object (i.e., "3 eggs" for "20 cupcakes" and "? eggs" for "80 cupcakes"). (25)

Initially, one type of word problem with the corresponding schema diagram appeared on student worksheets. After students learned how to solve both types of problems, mixed word problems with both diagrams were presented. When mixed word problems were presented, the sameness and difference between the multiplicative compare and proportion problems were discussed to help differentiate one type of problem from another. (26)

General Strategy Instruction Condition. Strategy instruction for the GSI group was derived from that typically employed in commercial mathematics textbooks (e.g., Burton et al., 1998). A four-step general heuristic problem-solving procedure used in this study required students to (a) read to understand, (b) develop a plan, (c) solve, and (d) look back. The instructor employed a Problem-Solving Think-Along sheet to guide group discussion of the four-step problem-solving procedure. For the first step, *understand*, the instructor asked students, "What are you asked to find in the problem?" and "What information is given in the problem?" In addition, students were encouraged to retell the problem in their own words and list the information given to check their understanding of the problem. For the second step, *plan*, several strategies (e.g., draw a picture, make a table, make a model, write a math equation, act it out) were listed on the Think-Along sheet, and students were questioned as follows: "What problem-solving strategies could you use to solve this problem?" (27)

Problem 1

If Ann uses 5 lemons for every 2 quarts of lemonade, how many lemons does she need to make 8 quarts of lemonade? (* = 1 lemon; @ = 1 quart of lemonade)

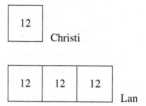

Problem 2

Christi collected 12 bottle caps for the art class. She collected 1/3 as many caps as Lan. How many caps did Lan collect for the art class?

Figure 2 Schematic representations of multiplicative compare and proportion problems.

Because students in this study commonly selected the "draw a picture" strategy, teacher instruction explicitly focused on modeling use of pictures to represent information in the problem (see Figure 2) followed by counting up the drawings to get the solution. In addition, students were encouraged to use reasoning to predict their answer. For the third step, *Solve*, students had to show their drawing, articulate how they solved the problem, and write their answer in a complete sentence. For the last step, *Look Back*, students were asked to justify whether their answer was reasonable and to indicate whether they could have solved the problem using an alternate method. During the modeling and guided practice portions of instruction, practice worksheets included the four strategy steps. Although worksheets during independent practice did not contain the strategy steps, students were given a separate prompt sheet with the four steps.

Measures

(28) Four parallel word problem–solving test forms, each containing 16 one-step multiplication and division word problems (i.e., multiplicative compare and proportion) were developed for use as the pretest, posttest, maintenance test, and follow-up test. Target problems were designed to include each of several variations of multiplicative compare and proportion problems that were similar to those used during the treatment. Multiplicative compare problems varied in terms of the position of the unknown. That is, the unknown quantity might involve the compared, referent, or scalar function. Proportion problems ranged from some in which the unit value was unknown to some in which the quantity of either one of two dimensions (i.e., subject or object) was unknown. The four tests differed only in terms of the story context and numerical values in the problem. The two types of word problems were presented in a random order on all four tests. In addition, a generalization test that comprised 10 transfer problems derived from commercially published mathematics textbooks and standardized achievement tests (e.g., the *Woodcock-Johnson Test of Achievement*) was designed. The test assessed students' transfer of learned skills to structurally similar but more complex problems (e.g., problems with irrelevant information and multiple steps).

Reliability of the four parallel test forms was established by testing a (29) group of eight sixth-grade students from the same school as the participants in the study. Students were divided into four groups. Each group received each of four forms of testing on four consecutive days. The order in which each group received the forms of testing was counterbalanced to control for the effects of testing sequence. The mean parallel form reliability of the four tests was 0.84 (range = 0.79 − 0.93). To demonstrate equivalency of the four forms, mean scores were calculated. The scores for forms 1, 2, 3, and 4 averaged 60%, 55%, 63%, and 56%, respectively. In addition, the internal consistency reliability of the generalization test was 0.88 (α).

Testing and Scoring

All testing was conducted in small groups in a quiet room. The instructors had (30) students read each problem and encouraged them to do their best. Students were assisted if they had difficulty reading words on the test. Instructions also required students to show their complete work. No feedback was given regarding the accuracy of their solution or work. All students were provided with sufficient time to complete the tests. Students in both groups completed (a) the pretest and generalization test prior to their respective strategy instruction; (b) the posttest and generalization test immediately following instruction; (c) the maintenance test, with a 1- to 2-week lapse after the termination of instruction; and (d) the follow-up test, with a lapse time ranging from 3 weeks to about 3 months. To ensure that they used their assigned strategy during the maintenance and follow-up testing, students in each condition were provided with a brief review of the respective strategy immediately before the tests.

Items on the word problem tests were scored as correct and awarded (31) 1 point if the correct answer was given. Partial credit (i.e., one half point) was given if only the mathematics sentence or equation was correctly set up. Percentage correct was used as the dependent measure for word problem–solving performance and calculated as the total points earned divided by the total possible points (i.e., 16 for pre- and posttreatment tests and 10 for the generalization test). A graduate student who was naive to the purpose of the study scored all tests using an answer key. A second rater rescored 30% of the tests. Inter-rater reliability was computed by dividing the number of agreements by the number of agreements and disagreements and multiplying by 100. Mean scoring reliability was 100% for all tests across the two independent raters.

Treatment Fidelity

For each instructional condition, a checklist that contained critical instruc- (32) tional steps was developed to assess the instructor's adherence to the assigned strategy instruction. A doctoral student in special education observed and evaluated the completeness and accuracy of instruction. The adherence of the instructor's teaching to the assigned instructional strategy was judged on the presence or absence of each critical component. Fidelity of implementation was assessed for about 30% of the lessons in both conditions. Fidelity observations were followed by feedback to the instructors, whenever procedural implementation was less than 85% accurate or complete. Overall, fidelity was 100% for the GSI group and 94% for the SBI group (range = 76% − 100%).

Results

Given that our sample included a group of students with and without dis- (33) abilities, we conducted a two-step analysis process in which we first analyzed the data for all 22 participants. To identify potential mediating effects of the presence of a disability, we conducted subsequent analyses of only the data for the 16 students with learning disabilities who completed all tests in the study. Because results of the analyses for the sample of students with learning disabilities revealed the same findings as those for the entire sample of students with and without learning disabilities, we report only the

Table 3

Percentage of Correct On-Target and Transfer Problems by the SBI and GSI Groups

Test	M		SD		N		
	SBI	GSI	SBI	GSI	SBI	GSI	ES*
Pretest	25.19	29.85	22.52	21.36	11	11	−0.21
Posttest	79.41	47.55	13.92	22.70	11	11	+1.69
Maintenance	87.29	45.45	14.51	17.97	9	11	+2.53
Follow-up	91.68	46.06	13.79	19.04	9	10	+2.72
Gen. pretest	25.45	35.00	29.11	22.69	11	11	−0.37
Gen. posttest	62.43	45.50	21.52	15.89	11	10	+0.89

Note: SBI = schema-based instruction; GSI = general strategy instruction; ES = effect size; Gen. == generalization. "Effect size was calculated as the two conditions' mean difference divided by the pooled standard deviation (Hedges & Olkin, 1985).
* A positive ES indicates a favorable effect for the SBI condition; a negative ES indicates a favorable effect for the GSI condition.

results of the primary analyses for the entire sample of 22 students. Table 3 presents means, standard deviations, and effect size indexes for all pretests and posttests on target and transfer problems for all participants in the two conditions (SBI and GSI).

Pretreatment Group Equivalency

(34) Separate one-way ANOVAs were performed to examine pretreatment group equivalency on target and transfer problems. Results indicated no significant differences between the two groups on either target problems, $F(1, 20) = .237, p = .632$, or transfer problems, $F(1, 20) = .736, p = .401$.

Acquisition and Maintenance Effects of Word Problem–Solving Instruction

(35) A 2 (group) × 4 (time of testing: pretest, posttest, maintenance test, and follow-up test) ANOVA with repeated measures on time was performed to assess the effects of instruction on students' word problem–solving performance. It must be noted that 2 participants in the SBI group did not complete the maintenance and follow-up tests, and 1 in the GSI group did not complete the follow-up test. As such, this analysis was based on the data for the 9 students in the SBI group and 10 students in the GSI group who completed all four times of testing. Results indicated significant main effects for group, $F(1, 17) = 14.906, p < .001$, and time of testing, $F(3, 15) = 33.276, p < .001$. In addition, results indicated a statistically significant interaction between group and time, $F(3, 15) = 9.507, p < .01$. Furthermore, post hoc simple-effect analyses indicated significant group differences on posttest, $F(1, 20) = 15.747, p < .01$; maintenance test, $F(1, 18) = 31.755, p < .001$; and follow-up test, $F(1, 17) = 35.032, p < .001$, all favoring the SBI group (see Table 3).

(36) Post hoc results based on the data for those who completed all four times of testing using paired-samples tests indicated that the SBI group significantly improved its performance (mean difference = 54.22, $SD = 17.17$) from pre- to posttest, $t(8) = 10.473, p < .001$; maintained the improved performance (mean difference = 5.17, $SD = 12.10$) from post- to maintenance test, $t(8) = 1.281, p = .236$; and further improved its performance (mean difference = 9.56, $SD = 12.52$) from posttest to follow-up test, $t(8) = 2.290, p = .051$. The GSI group improved its performance (mean difference = 17.590, $SD = 12.91$) from pre- to posttest, $t(9) = 4.791, p < .01$, and maintained the improved performance (mean difference = −2.94, $SD = 10.29$) from post- to maintenance test, $t(9) = -.903, p = .390$, and to follow-up test (mean difference = −4.37, $SD = 19.22$), $t(9) = -.719, p = .490$.

Transfer Effects of Word Problem–Solving Instruction

A 2 (group) × 2 (time of testing: pretest and posttest) ANOVA with repeated measures on time was performed to examine the two groups' performance on the generalization test. Results indicated that the main effect for group, $F(1, 19) = .054$, $p = .819$, was not significant. However, there was a significant main effect for time, $F(1, 19) = 18.465$, $p < .001$, and a statistically significant interaction between group and time, $F(1, 19) = 8.579$, $p < .01$. Post hoc paired-samples tests indicated that the SBI group significantly improved its performance (mean difference = 36.97, $SD = 24.82$) from pre- to posttreatment, $t(10) = 4.940$, $p < .01$, whereas the GSI group's performance on the generalization test did not show a statistically significant change (mean difference = 7.00, $SD = 21.76$) from pre- to posttreatment, $t(9) = 1.017$, $p = .336$.

Discussion

The present investigation compared the differential effects of schema-based and general strategy instruction on the mathematical problem–solving performance of middle school students with learning problems. Results showed that students in the SBI group performed significantly better than students in the GSI group on all measures of acquisition, maintenance, and generalization. These findings support and extend previous research regarding the effectiveness of schema-based strategy instruction in solving arithmetic word problems (e.g., Hutchinson, 1993; Jitendra & Hoff, 1996; Jitendra et al., 1998, 1999, 2002).

In general, results of this study indicated significant differences between the SBI and GSI groups on the posttest, maintenance, follow-up, and generalization tests. The effect sizes comparing the SBI group with the GSI group were 1.69, 2.53, 2.72, and .89 for posttest, maintenance, follow-up, and generalization tests, respectively. These effect sizes are much larger than the effect sizes reported in the Jitendra et al. (1998) study (.57, .81, and .74 for acquisition, maintenance, and generalization, respectively). In that study, elementary students with mild disabilities or at risk for mathematics failure learned to use schema diagrams to represent and solve addition and subtraction problems (i.e., change, group, and compare). After students represented the problem using schema diagrams, they had to figure out which part in the diagram was the "total" or "whole." Next, they had to apply a rule (i.e., "When the total [whole] is not known, we add to find the total; when the total is known, we subtract to find the other [part] amount"; p. 351) to decide whether to add or subtract to solve the problem. It might be the case that the schema diagrams for multiplication and division problems (i.e., multiplicative compare and proportion) in our study made a more straightforward link between the problem schema representation and its solution than those in the Jitendra et al. study and that errors were minimized once students correctly represented the problem in the diagram.

Although these findings confirm prior research on schema-based instruction by Jitendra and colleagues, an explanation regarding the more positive findings in our study when compared to previous research on semantic representation only (Lewis, 1989; Zawaiza & Gerber, 1993) is warranted. In the studies by Lewis and Zawaiza and Gerber, the diagram strategy was effective in reducing students' reversal errors, but it did not improve their overall word problem–solving scores. Participants in those studies were taught to use the diagram (i.e., a number line) as an external visual aid to check the operation for the purpose of preventing reversal errors.

Unlike the Lewis (1989) and Zawaiza and Gerber (1993) studies, this study used a schema-based instruction to systematically teach the structure of different problem types and directly show the linkage of the schematic diagram to problem solution. An examination of students' pretest performance

(37)

Data analysis included the use of separate one-way ANOVAs to examine pretreatment group equivalency on target and transfer problems, the use of ANOVA with repeated measures on time was performed to assess the effects of instruction on students' word problem–solving performance, and the use of ANOVA with repeated measures on time was performed to examine the two groups' performance on the generalization test.

(38)

Drawing and stating conclusions: Results showed that students in the SBI group performed significantly better than students in the GSI group on all measures of acquisition, maintenance, and generalization. These findings support and extend previous research regarding the effectiveness of schema-based strategy instruction in solving arithmetic word problems.

(39)

(40)

(41)

in both groups indicated a lack of conceptual understanding: Students typically grabbed all the numbers in the problems and indiscriminately applied an operation to get the answer, regardless of the nature of the problem. Following instruction in the assigned strategy, most students in the GSI group drew pictures to represent information in the problem and then counted their drawings to get the solution. However, when numbers in the problems got larger or the problem relation was complex (e.g., the scalar function in a multiplicative compare problem was 2/3 or 3/4), students found their drawings and counting to be cumbersome, and their work was prone to errors. In contrast, the performance pattern of students in the SBI group reversed following instruction. Those students used higher-order thinking, such as identifying problem structure or type and applying schema knowledge to represent and solve problems.

(42)   The intensive training in problem structure in the current study may have contributed to students' conceptual understanding and maintenance of word problem–solving skills. At the same time, it should be noted that students in both the SBI and GSI groups were reminded about the assigned strategy before completing the maintenance and follow-up tests. Specifically, students in the SBI group were shown the two schemata diagrams and asked to use them to solve problems. Students in the GSI group were provided with a review of the four-step strategy of reading to understand the problem, drawing a picture to represent the problem, solving the problem using the selected strategy ("draw a picture"), and looking back to check the solution. This review ensured that students in both groups used the assigned strategy and served to validate the differential effects of the two problem-solving strategies on students' performance. The further boost in students' performance in the SBI group on the follow-up tests compared to the posttests may be attributed to the coherent representation of the word problem and subsequent internalization of the schema-based strategy that was lacking in the general strategy. In contrast to the findings regarding maintenance in our study, only four of the six students in the Zawaiza and Gerber (1993) study maintained their posttest performance. One plausible explanation for the large effects found in our study is that participants in the SBI condition systematically learned the problem schemata and problem-solving procedures in twelve 1-hour sessions. However, community college students with learning disabilities in the Zawaiza and Gerber study received semantic structure representation training to solve compare problems during two 35- to 40-min sessions only.

(43)   The results of this study also indicated that only the SBI group significantly improved their performance on the generalization measure after the schema-based instruction. This finding confirms previous research (e.g., Hutchinson, 1993; Jitendra et al., 1998, 1999, 2002; Jintendra & Hoff, 1996), in that students in the SBI group transferred the learned skills to new tasks that included structurally similar but more complex problems when compared to the target problems. It may be that the emphasis of the schema strategy on conceptual understanding of the problem structure in conjunction with the diagram mapping helped students differentiate relevant from irrelevant information during problem representation and planning to accurately solve novel problems (Schoenfeld & Herrmann, 1982).

(44)   In summary, findings document the efficacy of the schema-based instruction over general strategy instruction in enhancing problem-solving performance for middle school students with learning difficulties. Given that "learners' 'true' math deficits are specific to mathematical concepts and problems types" (Zentall & Ferkis, 1993, p. 6), this study provides further support for schema-based instruction in enhancing students' conceptual understanding of mathematical problem structures and problem solving in general.

(45)   At the same time, several limitations of the study require cautious interpretation of the findings. First, due to missing data in school records, we did not have complete descriptive information for all participants. This presents problems in terms of accurately identifying the sample in the study, a common

struggle that researchers encounter when conducting applied research in the classroom. Second, the participant sampling procedure in this study did not control for students' reading levels. Reading comprehension is an important contributing factor to students' word problem–solving performance (Zentall & Ferkis, 1993). As such, it is not clear to what extent reading comprehension skills contributed to the findings in this study. While we ensured that the two groups' entry skills with respect to problem-solving skills were comparable, it is important that future research investigate the effects of the two instructional strategies while controlling for students' reading skills.

Third, the large standard deviation scores indicate great variation in pretest (46) performance within each group on both target and transfer problems. Pretest scores for students in both groups ranged from 0%–68% correct. Therefore, future research should employ more homogeneous groups (e.g., students with learning disabilities, students with mathematics disabilities only) and increase the sample size to examine the differential effects of strategy instruction.

Fourth, the "pull-out" nature of instruction employed in this investigation (47) may be a limitation. Because instruction did not occur during the regularly scheduled math period in the school, there is a possible disconnect between the strategy instruction provided in this study and regular classroom instruction. It is important for future research to examine the effects of schema-based instruction in regular classroom settings and to facilitate students' broad application of the strategy. A fifth limitation is the use of standard text-based word problems rather than real-world problem-solving tasks. An area for future research is to investigate the effects of the schema-based instruction to solve real-world problems. Finally, our study did not address the relative efficacy of the schema-based strategy when compared to problem-solving treatment procedures that employ manipulatives and other empirically validated strategies (e.g., cognitive–metacognitive strategy) described in the literature (Jitendra & Xin, 1997).

Implications for Practice

Overall, findings from this study have several implications for practice. First, (48) the effectiveness of the schema strategy instruction in this study suggests that classroom instruction should emphasize systematic domain-specific knowledge in word problem solving to address the mathematical difficulties evidenced by students with learning disabilities (Montague, 1992, 1997). Schema-based instruction teaches conceptual understanding of problem structure, which facilitates higher-order thinking and generalizable problem-solving skills. Although the "draw a picture" strategy in the GSI condition emphasized understanding of the problem, the representation step of the strategy focused more on the surface features of the problem and did not allow students to engage in the higher-level thinking necessary to promote generalizable problem-solving skills. The general heuristic strategy, such as the four-step approach (e.g., read, plan, solve, and check) typically found in commercial mathematics textbooks may be "limited unless it is connected to a conceptual knowledge base" (Prawat, 1989, p. 10). One of the key differences between the schema-based strategy and traditional instruction is that only the former emphasizes pattern recognition and schema acquisition. The schema-based strategy in this study provided students with explicit instruction in problem schemata and problem solving.

Second, the effectiveness of the schema strategy instruction in this study (49) suggests that students with disabilities are able to learn strategies involving higher-order thinking to improve their problem-solving skills. Many students with learning disabilities are often cognitively disadvantaged because of attention, organizational, and working memory problems (Gonzalez & Espinel, 1999; Zentall & Ferkis, 1993). Furthermore, they experience difficulties in creating complete and accurate mental problem representations (Lewis, 1989; Lewis & Mayer, 1987; Marshall, 1995). It is essential that teachers provide students with learning disabilities with scaffolds, such as schemata diagrams, when teaching conceptual understanding of key features of the problem. The schematic representation should be more than a simple semantic translation of the problem and should emphasize the mathematical relations in specific problem types to allow students to directly transform the diagrammatic representation into an appropriate math equation. Such representations may be useful aids to organize information in word problems, reduce students' cognitive load, and enhance working memory by directing resources to correctly set up the math equation and facilitate problem solution.

(50)   Overall, the findings of this study indicate the effectiveness of schema-based instruction in enhancing word problem—solving performance of middle school students with learning disabilities. Given that an increasing number of students with disabilities are currently served in general education classrooms (Cawley et al., 2001), providing them with effective strategies to access the general education curriculum as mandated by the amendment to the Individuals with Disabilities Education Act (IDEA, 1997) is critical. Schema-based instruction, with its emphasis on conceptual understanding, facilitates higher-order thinking and may be an effective and feasible option for teachers. It provides students with a tool to be successful problem solvers and to meet the high academic content standards. This has particular importance given current legislation's emphasis on "scientifically-based instructional programs and materials" (No Child Left Behind Act, 2002).

AUTHOR'S NOTES

1. This article is based on the first author's dissertation study.
2. We thank the many administrators, teachers, teacher assistants, and students at Northeast Middle School, as well as two graduate students at Lehigh University, Wesley Hickman and Erin Post, who facilitated this study. We also thank Dr. Sydney Zentall for her feedback on an earlier draft of this paper.

REFERENCES

Balow, I. H., Farr, R. C., & Hogan, T. P. (1992). *Metropolitan achievement* tests (7th ed.). San Antonio, TX: Harcourt Educational Measurement.

Briars, D. J., & Larkin, J. H. (1984). An integrated model of skill in solving elementary word problems. *Cognition and Instruction, 1,* 245–296.

Burton, G. M., Maletsky, E. M., Bright, G. W., Helton, S. M., Hollis, L. Y., Johnson, H. C., et al. (1998). *Math advantage.* Orlando, FL: Harcourt Brace.

Carnine, D., Jones, E. D., & Dixon, R. (1994). Mathematics: Educational tools for diverse learners. *School Psychology Review, 3,* 406–427.

Cawley, J. F., & Miller, J. H. (1989). Cross-sectional comparisons of the mathematical performance of children with learning disabilities: Are we on the right track toward comprehensive programming? *Journal of Learning Disabilities, 23,* 250–254, 259.

Cawley, J. F., Parmar, R. S., Yan, W., & Miller, J. H. (1998). Arithmetic computation performance of students with learning disabilities: Implications for curriculum. *Learning Disabilities Research & Practice, 13*(2), 68–74.

Cawley, J., Parmar, R., Foley, T. E., Salmon, S., & Roy, S. (2001). Arithmetic performance of students: Implications for standards and programming. *Exceptional Children, 67,* 311–328.

Didierjean, A., & Cauzinille-Marmeche, E. (1998). Reasoning by analogy: Is it schema-mediated or case-based? *European Journal of Psychology of Education, 13,* 385–398.

Englert, C. S., Culatta, B. E., & Horn, D. G. (1987). Influence of irrelevant information in addition word problems on problem solving. *Learning Disability Quarterly, 10,* 29–36.

Friendly, M. (2000). *Power analysis for ANOVA designs.* Retrieved August 7, 2002, from davidmlane.com/hyperstat/power.html

Fuson, K. C., & Willis, G. B. (1989). Second graders' use of schematic drawings in solving addition and subtraction word problems. *Journal of Educational Psychology, 81,* 514–520.

Goldman, S. R., Hasselbring, T. S., & the Cognition and Technology Group at Vanderbilt. (1997). Achieving meaningful mathematics literacy for students with learning disabilities. *Journal of Learning Disabilities, 30,* 198–208.

Gonzalez, J. E. J., & Espinel, A. I. G. (1999). Is IQ-achievement discrepancy relevant in the definition of arithmetic learning disabilities? *Learning Disability Quarterly, 22,* 291–301.

Hedges, L. V., & Olkin, I. (1985). *Statistical methods for meta-analysis.* Orlando, FL: Academic Press.

Hutchinson, N. L. (1993). Effects of cognitive strategy instruction on algebra problem solving of adolescents with learning disabilities. *Learning Disability Quarterly, 16*, 34–63.

Individuals with Disabilities Education Act of 1997, 120 U.S.C §1400 *et seq.*

Jitendra, A. K., DiPipi, C. M., & Grasso, E. (2001). The role of a graphic representational technique on the mathematical problem solving performance of fourth graders: An exploratory study. *Australian Journal of Special Education, 25*(1&2), 17–33.

Jitendra, A., DiPipi, C. M., & Perron-Jones, N. (2002). An exploratory study of schema-based word problem-solving instruction for middle school students with learning disabilities: An emphasis on conceptual and procedural understanding. *The Journal of Special Education, 36*, 23–38.

Jitendra, A. K., Griffin, C. C., McGoey, K., Gardill, M. C., Bhat, P., & Riley, T. (1998). Effects of mathematical word problem solving by students at risk or with mild disabilities. *The Journal of Educational Research, 91*, 345–355.

Jitendra, A., & Hoff, K. (1996). The effects of schema-based instruction on mathematical word problem solving performance of students with learning disabilities. *Journal of Learning Disabilities, 29*, 422–431.

Jitendra, A. K., Hoff, K., & Beck, M. M. (1999). Teaching middle school students with learning disabilities to solve word problems using a schema-based approach. *Remedial and Special Education, 20*, 50–64.

Jitendra, A. K., & Xin, Y. P. (1997). Mathematical word problem solving instruction for students with mild disabilities and students at risk for math failure: A research synthesis. *The Journal of Special Education, 30*, 412–438.

Judd, T. P., & Bilsky, L. H. (1989). Comprehension and memory in the solution of verbal arithmetic problems by mentally retarded and nonretarded individuals. *Journal of Educational Psychology, 81*, 541–546.

Lewis, A. B. (1989). Training students to represent arithmetic word problems. *Journal of Educational Psychology, 81*, 521–531.

Lewis, A. B., & Mayer, R. E. (1987). Students' miscomprehension of relational statements in arithmetic word problems. *Journal of Educational Psychology, 79*, 361–371.

Maccini, P., & Gagnon, J. C. (2002). Perceptions and application of NCTM standards by special and general education teachers. *Exceptional Children, 68*, 325–344.

Marshall, S. P. (1995). *Schemas in problem solving.* New York, NY: Cambridge University Press.

Mayer, R. E. (1982). Memory for algebra story problems. *Journal of Educational Psychology, 74*, 199–216.

Montague, M. (1992). The effects of cognitive and metacognitive strategy instruction on the mathematical problem solving of middle school students with learning disabilities. *Journal of Learning Disabilities, 25*, 230–248.

Montague, M. (1997). Students' perception, mathematical problem solving, and learning disabilities. *Remedial and Special Education, 18*, 46–53.

Montague, M., Applegate, B., & Marquard, K. (1993). Cognitive strategy instruction and mathematical problem-solving performance of students with learning disabilities. *Learning Disabilities Research & Practice, 8*, 223–232.

National Council of Teachers of Mathematics. (2000). *Principles and standards for school mathematics.* Retrieved June 28, 2005, from standards.nctm.org

National Education Goals Panel. (1997). *National Education Goals Report Summary, 1997.* Washington, DC: Author.

No Child Left Behind Act of 2001, Pub. L. No. 107–110. 115 Stat. 1425 (2002).

Parmar, R. S. (1992). Protocol analysis of strategies used by students with mild disabilities when solving arithmetic word problems. *Diagnostique, 17*, 227–243.

Parmar, R. S., Cawley, J. F., & Frazita, R. R. (1996). Word problem-solving by students with and without mild disabilities. *Exceptional Children, 62*, 415–429.

Prawat, R. S. (1989). Promoting access to knowledge, strategy, and disposition in students: A research synthesis. *Review of Educational Research, 59*, 1–41.

Schoenfeld, A. H., & Herrmann, D. J. (1982). Problem perception and knowledge structure in expert and novice mathematical problem solvers. *Journal of Experimental Psychology: Learning, Memory, and Cognition, 8*, 484–494.

Stanford Achievement Test. (9th ed.). (1996). San Antonio, TX: Harcourt Educational Measurement.

Sweller, J., Chandler, P., Tierney, P., & Cooper, M. (1990). Cognitive load as a factor in the structuring of technical material. *Journal of Experimental Psychology: General, 119*, 176–192.

The Goals 2000: Educate America Act, P.L. 103-227 (1994).

Wechsler, D. (1974). *Wechsler intelligence scale for children–Revised.* San Antonio, TX: Psychological Corp.

Xin, Y. P., & Jitendra, A. K. (1999). The effects of instruction in solving mathematical word problems for students with learning problems: A meta-analysis. *The Journal of Special Education, 32*, 40–78.

Zawaiza, T. B. W., & Gerber, M. M. (1993). Effects of explicit instruction on community college students with learning disabilities. *Learning Disability Quarterly, 16*, 64–79.

Zentall, S. S., & Ferkis, M. A. (1993). Mathematical problem solving for youth with ADHD, with and without learning disabilities. *Learning Disability Quarterly, 16*, 6–18.

Source: From "Effects of Mathematical Word Problem-Solving Instruction on Middle School Students with Learning Problems," by Y. P. Xin, A. K. Jitendra, & A. Deatline-Buchman, *The Journal of Special Education, 39*(3), pp. 181–192, 2005. Copyright 2005 by the Hammill Institute on Disability. Reprinted with permission.

CHAPTER TWELVE

Single-Subject Experimental Research

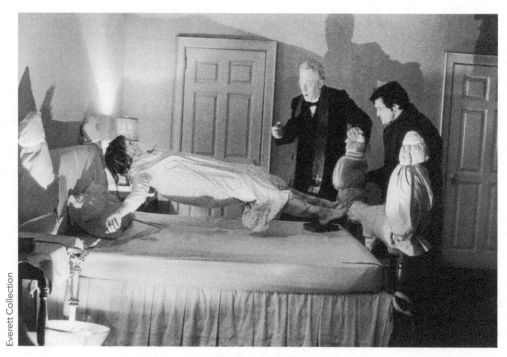

The Exorcist, 1973

Everett Collection

"[Single-subject experimental] designs . . . are typically used to study the behavior change an individual exhibits as a result of some treatment." (p. 322)

LEARNING OUTCOMES

After reading Chapter 12, you should be able to do the following:

12.1   Describe the major categories of single-subject experimental designs, and explain the benefits and challenges of this type of research.

12.2   Describe issues related to data analysis and interpretation in single-subject experimental research.

12.3   Discuss threats to validity in single-subject experimental research.

12.4   Describe the importance of replication in single-subject experimental research.

The chapter learning outcomes form the basis for the following task, which requires you to develop the method section of a research report for a study using a single-subject experimental design.

TASK 7E

For a quantitative study, you have created research plan components (Tasks 3A and 4A), described a sample (Task 5A), and considered appropriate measuring instruments (Task 6). If your study involves single-subject experimental research, now develop the method section of a research report. Include a description of participants, data collection methods, and research design (see Performance Criteria, p. 335).

SUMMARY: SINGLE-SUBJECT EXPERIMENTAL RESEARCH

Definition	*Single-subject experimental research designs* are designs that can be applied when the sample size is one or when a number of individuals are considered as one group.
Design(s)	Single-subject designs are classified into three major categories: A-B-A withdrawal, multiple-baseline, and alternating treatment designs.
Types of appropriate research questions	These designs are typically used to study the behavior change an individual exhibits as a result of some treatment. Although single-subject designs have their roots in clinical psychology and psychiatry, they are useful in many educational settings, particularly those involving studies of students with disabilities.
Key characteristics	• Study includes a sample size of one, or the study considers a number of individuals as one group. • Each participant serves as his or her own control. • In general, the participant is exposed to a nontreatment and treatment phase, and performance is measured during each phase. • Single-subject designs are applied most frequently in clinical settings where the primary emphasis is on therapeutic impact, not contribution to a research base.
Steps in the process	1. Select and define a problem. 2. Select participants and measuring instruments. 3. Prepare a research plan, including selection of the appropriate single-subject research design (A-B-A withdrawal, multiple-baseline, and alternating treatment). 4. Execute procedures. 5. Analyze the data. 6. Formulate conclusions.
Potential challenges	A major criticism of single-subject research studies is that they suffer from low external validity; in other words, results cannot be generalized to a population of interest.
Example	What is the impact of a functional mobility curriculum on five elementary-age students with severe, multiple disabilities?

SINGLE-SUBJECT EXPERIMENTAL DESIGNS

As you learned in Chapter 1, **single-subject experimental designs** (also referred to as *single-case experimental designs*) are designs that can be applied when the sample size is one or when a number of individuals are considered as one group. These designs are typically used to study the behavior change an individual exhibits as a result of some treatment. In single-subject designs, each participant serves as his or her own control, similar to participants in a time-series design. In general, the participant is exposed to a nontreatment and a treatment phase, and performance is measured during each phase. The nontreatment phase is symbolized as A, and the treatment phase is symbolized as B. For example, if we (1) observed and recorded a student's out-of-seat behavior on five occasions, (2) applied a behavior modification procedure and observed behavior on five more occasions, and (3) stopped the behavior modification procedure and observed behavior five more times, our design would be symbolized as A-B-A. Although single-subject designs have their roots in clinical psychology and psychiatry, they are useful in many educational settings, particularly those involving studies of students with disabilities.

Single-Subject versus Group Designs

Most traditional experimental research studies use group designs mainly because the desired results are intended to be generalized to other groups. As an example, if we were investigating the comparative effectiveness of two approaches to teaching reading, we would be interested in learning which approach *generally* produces better reading achievement—schools usually seek strategies that are beneficial for groups of students, not individual students. A single-subject design would not be very practical because it would focus on single students and require multiple measurements over the course of a study. For example, it would be highly impractical to administer a reading achievement test repeatedly to the same students.

For some research questions, however, traditional group designs are not appropriate, and as single-subject designs have become progressively refined and capable of addressing threats to validity, they are increasingly viewed as acceptable methods to address those questions. For example, group comparison designs are sometimes opposed on ethical or philosophical grounds because such designs include a control group that does not receive the experimental treatment. In fact, refusing to provide a potentially beneficial program to students with a demonstrated need may be prohibited, as is the case with certain federally funded programs. In addition, group comparison designs are not possible when the size of the population of interest is too small to permit the formulation of two equivalent groups. For example, if the treatment is aimed at improving the social skills of children with profound emotional disturbances, the number of such children available in any one locale is probably too small to conduct comparative research. A single-subject design is clearly preferable to the formulation of two more-or-less equivalent treatment groups composed of five children each. Finally, single-subject designs are applied most frequently in clinical settings where the primary emphasis is on therapeutic impact, not contribution to a research base. In such settings, the overriding objective is the identification of intervention strategies that will change the behavior of a specific individual—for example, one who is engaging in self-abusive or aggressive behavior.

The Single-Variable Rule

An important principle of single-subject experimental research is the **single-variable rule,** which states that only one variable at a time should be manipulated. In other words, as we move from phase to phase, only one variable should be added or withdrawn at any phase. Sometimes an attempt is made to manipulate two variables simultaneously to assess their interactive effects. This practice is not sound in single-subject designs because it prevents us from assessing the effects of either variable adequately.

Types of Single-Subject Designs

Single-subject designs are classified into three major categories: A-B-A withdrawal, multiple-baseline, and alternating treatments designs. The following sections describe these basic designs and some common variations.

A-B-A Withdrawal Designs

A-B-A withdrawal designs involve alternating phases of baseline (A) and treatment (B). The basic A-B-A withdrawal design has a number of variations, the least complex of which is the A-B design. Although this design is an improvement over the simple case study, its internal validity is suspect. In the **A-B design,** baseline measurements (O) are made repeatedly until stability is established, the treatment (X) is introduced, and an appropriate number of measurements (O) are made during treatment implementation. If behavior improves during the treatment phase, the effectiveness of the treatment can be inferred. The specific number of measurements involved in each phase varies from experiment to experiment. We can symbolize this design as follows:

O O O O | X O X O X O X O
Baseline Phase | Treatment Phase
A | B

The problem with this design is that we don't know if behavior improved because of the treatment or for some other nontreatment reason. The observed behavior change may have occurred as a result of some unknown variable, or the behavior may have improved naturally even without the treatment. Using an **additive design,** a variation of A-B design that involves the addition of another phase or phases in which the experimental treatment is supplemented with another treatment, improves the researcher's ability to make such determinations. Additive designs include the A-B-A design and A-B-A-B design.

The A-B-A Design. In **A-B-A design,** baseline measurements are made repeatedly until stability is established, treatment is introduced, a number of measurements are made, and the treatment phase is followed by a second baseline phase. This second baseline phase results in a much improved design. If the behavior is better during the treatment phase than during either baseline phase, the effectiveness of the treatment has been demonstrated. Symbolically, we can represent this design in the following way:

O O O O | X O X O X O X O | O O O O
Baseline Phase A | Treatment Phase B | Baseline Phase A

During the initial baseline phase of a study of attention, for example, we may observe on-task behaviors during five observation sessions (like the A-B design, the number of measurements depends on the experiment). We may then introduce the treatment—tangible reinforcement in the form of small toys for on-task behaviors—and observe on-task behaviors during five observation periods in the treatment phase. Next, we may stop the tangible reinforcement and observe on-task behaviors during an additional five sessions. If on-task behavior is more frequent during the treatment phase, we can conclude that the tangible reinforcement was the probable cause. A variation on this design is the **changing criterion design,** in which the baseline phase is followed by successive treatment phases, each of which has a more stringent criterion for acceptable (i.e., improved) behavior.

In a published study using an A-B-A design, researchers examined the impact of positive reinforcement on the attending behavior of an easily distracted 9-year-old boy.[1] A reinforcement program was developed for the student, and before data collection began, observers were trained until inter-rater reliability was 0.90 or above for five randomly selected, 10-minute observations of the child's attending behavior. Figure 12.1 shows the three phases of the design: baseline, treatment, and baseline. Each dot represents a data collection point. The reinforcement program established for the student improved his attending behaviors a great deal compared to the initial baseline. When the treatment was removed, attending behavior decreased; this decrease suggests the effectiveness of the reinforcement program.

It should be noted that discussions of A-B-A designs do not always use the same terminology introduced in this chapter. A-B-A withdrawal designs are frequently referred to as reversal designs, which is an inaccurate term because the treatment is generally withdrawn following baseline assessment, not reversed. You should be alert to this distinction.

The internal validity of the A-B-A design is superior to that of the A-B design. With A-B designs, it is possible that improvements in behavior are not due to treatment intervention, but it is very unlikely

[1] "The Use of Positive Reinforcement in Conditioning Attending Behavior," by H. M. Walker and N. K. Buckely, 1968, *Journal of Applied Behavior Analysis, 1*(3), pp. 245–250.

FIGURE 12.1 • Percentage of attending behavior of a subject during successive observation periods in a study utilizing an A-B-A design

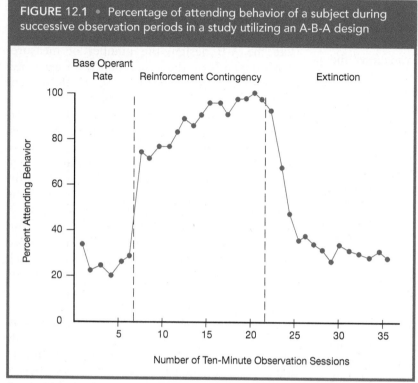

Source: From "The Use of Positive Reinforcement in Conditioning Attending Behavior," by H. M. Walker and N. K. Buckley, 1968, *Journal of Applied Behavior Analysis, 1*(3), p. 247. Reprinted with permission.

that behavior would improve coincidentally during the treatment phase and deteriorate coincidentally during the subsequent baseline phase, as could be demonstrated in A-B-A designs. The major problem with A-B-A design is an ethical one: The experiment ends with the subject not receiving the treatment. Of course, if the treatment has not been shown to be effective, there is no problem, but if it has been found to be beneficial, removing treatment may be considered unethical.

A variation of the A-B-A design that eliminates this problem is the B-A-B design, which involves a treatment phase (B), a withdrawal phase (A), and a return to treatment phase (B). Although this design provides an experiment that ends with the subject receiving treatment, the lack of an initial baseline phase makes it very difficult to assess the effectiveness of the treatment. Some studies have involved

a short baseline phase before application of the B-A-B design, but this strategy only approximates a better solution, which is application of an A-B-A-B design.

The A-B-A-B Design. In the **A-B-A-B design,** baseline measurements are made until stability is established, treatment is introduced, a number of measurements are made, and the treatment phase is followed by a second baseline phase, which is then followed by a second treatment phase. In other words, it is the A-B-A design with the addition of a second treatment phase. Not only does this design overcome ethical objections to the A-B-A design, it also greatly strengthens the research conclusions by demonstrating the effects of the treatment twice. If treatment effects are essentially the same during both treatment phases, the possibility that the effects are a result of extraneous variables is greatly reduced. The A-B-A-B design can be symbolized as follows:

$O\ O\ O\ O$	$X\ O\ X\ O\ X\ O\ X$	O	$O\ O\ O\ O$	$X\ O\ X\ O\ X\ O\ X\ O$
Baseline Phase A	Treatment Phase B		Baseline Phase A	Treatment Phase B

When application of this design is feasible, it provides very convincing evidence of treatment effectiveness.

Figure 12.2 shows a hypothetical example of the A-B-A-B design. The figure shows the summarized results of 5 days of observations in each of the four design phases. Baseline A_1 shows the student's average talking-out behavior for a 5-day period. Treatment B_1 shows the effect of a reinforcement program designed to diminish talking-out behavior: Talking-out behavior diminished

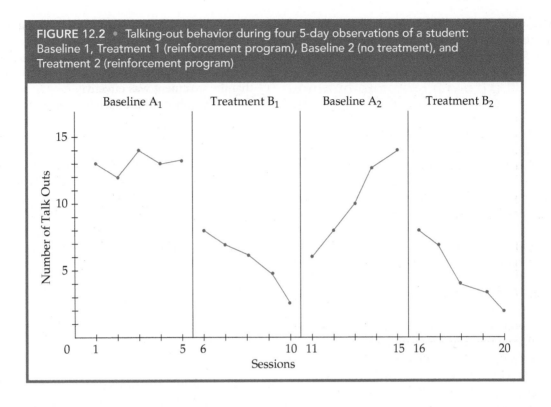

FIGURE 12.2 • Talking-out behavior during four 5-day observations of a student: Baseline 1, Treatment 1 (reinforcement program), Baseline 2 (no treatment), and Treatment 2 (reinforcement program)

greatly with the treatment. Baseline A_2 shows that removal of the treatment led to increased talking-out behavior. The reintroduction of treatment B_2 again led to diminished talking-out behavior. These patterns strongly suggest the efficacy of the treatment.

Multiple-Baseline Designs

Multiple-baseline designs entail the systematic addition of behaviors, subjects, or settings for intervention. These designs are used when it is not possible to withdraw a treatment and have performance return to baseline or when it would not be ethical to withdraw or reverse treatment. They are also used when a treatment can be withdrawn but the effects of the treatment carry over so that a return to baseline conditions is difficult or impossible. The effects of many treatments do not disappear when a treatment is removed—in fact, in many cases, it is highly desirable for treatment effects to sustain. Reinforcement techniques, for example, are designed to produce improved behavior that will be maintained when external reinforcements are withdrawn.

The "multiple" part of this design refers to the study of more than one behavior, subject, or setting, and the three basic types of multiple-baseline designs are therefore across-behaviors, across-subjects, and across-settings designs. With **multiple-baseline design,** data are collected on several behaviors for one subject, one behavior for several subjects, or one behavior and one subject in several settings. Then, over a period of time, the treatment is applied systematically to each behavior (or subject or setting) one at a time until all behaviors (or subjects or settings) are exposed to the treatment. For example, a researcher may sequentially change three different behaviors using the multiple-baseline design. If measured performance improves only after a treatment is introduced, then that treatment is judged to be effective. Of course, variations can be applied. For example, we may collect data on one target behavior for several participants in several settings. In this case, performance for the group of participants in each setting would be summed or averaged, and results would be presented for the group as well as for each individual.

The multiple-baseline design can be symbolized as follows:

Behavior 1	O O OXOXOXOXOXOXOXOXOXOXOXO
Behavior 2	O O O O O OXOXOXOXOXOXOXOXOXO
Behavior 3	O O O O O O O O OXOXOXOXOXOXOXO

In this example, a treatment was applied to three different behaviors—Behavior 1 first, then Behavior 2, and then Behavior 3—until all three behaviors were under treatment. If measured performance improved for each behavior only after the treatment was introduced, the treatment would be judged to be effective. We could symbolize examination of different participants or settings in the same manner. In all cases, the more behaviors, subjects, or settings involved, the more convincing the evidence is for the effectiveness of the treatment. Three replications are generally accepted to be an adequate minimum, although some investigators believe that four or more are necessary.

When applying treatments across behaviors, the behaviors must be independent of one another. If we apply treatment to Behavior 1, Behaviors 2 and 3 should remain at baseline levels. If the other behaviors change when Behavior 1 is treated, the design is not valid for assessing treatment effectiveness. When applying treatment across participants, the participants should be as similar as possible (e.g., matched on key variables such as age and gender), and the experimental setting should be as similar as possible for each participant. When applying treatment across settings, it is preferable that the settings be natural, not artificial. For example, we may systematically apply a treatment (e.g., tangible reinforcement) during successive class periods, or we may apply the treatment first in a clinical setting, then at school, and then at home. Sometimes it is necessary to evaluate the treatment in a contrived or simulation setting, such as when an important target behavior does not often occur naturally. For example, if we are teaching a child who is mentally challenged how to behave in various emergency situations (e.g., when facing a fire, an injury, or an intruder), simulated settings may be the only feasible approach.

Figure 12.3 shows the results of a hypothetical study using a multiple-baseline design. The treatment, a program for improving social awareness, was applied to three types of behavior: (1) social behaviors, (2) help-seeking behaviors, and (3) criticism-handling behaviors. The figure shows that for each type of behavior, more instances of the desired behavior occurred during the treatment period than during the baseline period, indicating that the treatment was effective.

Although multiple-baseline designs are generally used when the treatment makes returning to baseline conditions difficult, they can be used very effectively for situations in which baseline conditions are recoverable. For example, we could target talking-out behavior, out-of-seat behavior, and aggressive behavior, which over time could return to baseline conditions. If we applied an A-B-A design within a multiple-baseline framework, the result could be symbolized as follows:

Talking-out behavior	A-B-A-A-A
Out-of-seat behavior	A-A-B-A-A
Aggressive behavior	A-A-A-B-A

Talking-out behavior	O O OXOXOXO O O O O O O O O
Out-of-seat behavior	O O O O O OXOXOXOO O O O O O
Aggressive behavior	O O O O O O O OXOXOXO O O O

Such a design combines the best features of the A-B-A and the multiple-baseline designs and provides very convincing evidence regarding treatment effects. In essence, it represents three replications of an A-B-A experiment. Whenever baseline is recoverable and there are no carryover effects, any of the A-B-A designs can be applied within a multiple-baseline framework.

Alternating Treatments Design

The alternating treatments design is very useful in assessing the relative effectiveness of two (or more) treatments in a single-subject context. Although the design has many names (e.g., *multiple schedule design, multi-element baseline design, multi-element manipulation design,* and *simultaneous treatment design*), *alternating treatments* most accurately describes the nature of the design. The **alternating treatments design** involves the relatively rapid alternation of treatments for a single subject. The qualifier *relatively* is attached because alternation does not necessarily occur within fixed intervals of time. For example, if a child with behavior problems saw a therapist who used an alternating treatment design every Tuesday, the design would require that on some Tuesdays, the child would receive one treatment (e.g., verbal reinforcement) and on other Tuesdays, the child would

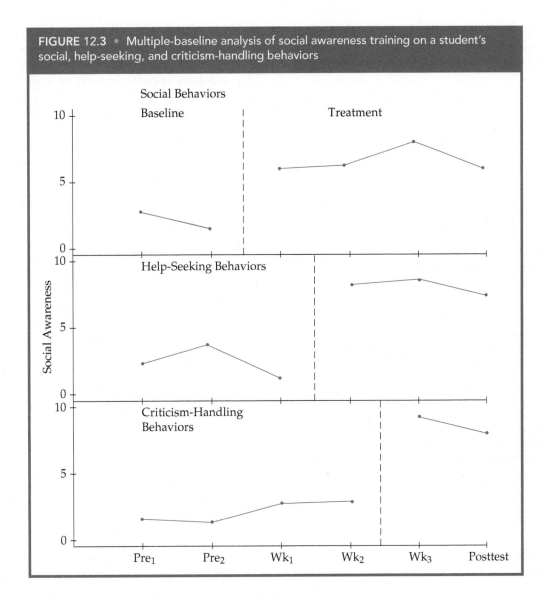

FIGURE 12.3 • Multiple-baseline analysis of social awareness training on a student's social, help-seeking, and criticism-handling behaviors

receive another treatment (e.g., tangible reinforcement). The treatments (symbolized as T_1 and T_2) would not be alternated in a regular, ordered pattern (i.e., T_1-T_2-T_1-T_2). Rather, to avoid potential threats to validity, the treatments would be alternated on a random basis (e.g., T_1-T_2-T_2-T_1-T_2-T_1-T_1-T_2). Figure 12.4 illustrates this random application of two treatments. The data points are consistently higher for T_2 than for T_1, so Treatment 2 appears to be more effective for this participant than Treatment 1. To determine whether Treatment 2 would also be more effective for other participants requires replication.

This design has several advantages that make it attractive to investigators. First, no withdrawal is necessary; thus, if one treatment is found to be more effective, it may be continued. Second, no baseline phase is necessary because the research goal is to determine which treatment is more effective, not whether a treatment is better than no treatment. Third, a number of treatments can be studied more quickly and efficiently than with other designs. However, one potential problem with this design is multiple-treatment interference—that is, carryover effects from one treatment to the other.

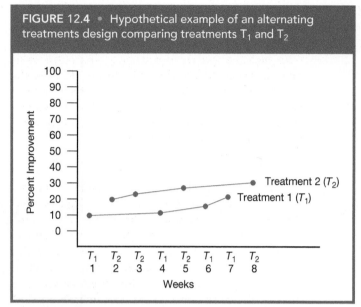

FIGURE 12.4 • Hypothetical example of an alternating treatments design comparing treatments T₁ and T₂

Source: From Barlow, D. H., & Hersen, M. *Single Case Experimental Designs*, 2nd ed. Published by Allyn & Bacon, Boston, MA. Copyright © 1984 by Pearson Education. Reprinted by permission of the publisher.

MyLab Education **Self-Check 12.1**

MyLab Education **Application Exercise 12.1:** Evaluating Research Articles: Identifying Steps in the Research Process for a Single-Subject Study

---

DATA ANALYSIS AND INTERPRETATION

Data analysis in single-subject research typically is based on visual inspection and analysis of a graphic presentation of results. First, the researcher evaluates the adequacy of the design. Second, assuming a sufficiently valid design, the researcher assesses treatment effectiveness. The primary criterion of effectiveness is typically clinical significance, not statistical significance. Clinical effects that are small may not make a noticeable or useful difference in the behavior of a participant. As an example, suppose an 8-year-old male exhibits dangerous, aggressive behavior toward other children. A treatment that produced a 5% reduction in such behavior may be statistically significant, but it is clearly not clinically significant.

A number of statistical analyses are available to the single-subject researcher, including *t* and *F* tests, but whether statistical tests should be used in single-subject research is currently debated. To date, they have not been widely used in this type of research.

MyLab Education **Self-Check 12.2**

THREATS TO VALIDITY

External Validity

A major criticism of single-subject research studies is that they suffer from low external validity; in other words, results cannot be generalized to a population of interest. Although this criticism is basically true, it is also true that the results of a study using a group design cannot be directly generalized to any individual within the group. In other words, group designs and single-subject designs each have generalizability problems. If your aim is to improve the functioning of an individual, a group design will not be appropriate.

Nonetheless, we usually are interested in generalizing the results of our research to persons other than those directly involved in the study. For single-subject designs, the key to generalizability is replication. If a researcher applies the same treatment using the same single-subject design to a number of participants individually and gets essentially the same results in every case (or even in most cases), confidence in the generalizability of the findings is increased. The more diverse the replications are (i.e., they feature different kinds of subjects, different behaviors, different settings), the more generalizable the results.

One important generalizability problem associated with many single-subject designs is the effect of the baseline phase—the phase before the experimental treatment is introduced, when initial measurements are taken—on the subsequent effects of the treatment. We can never be sure that the treatment effects are the same as they would have been if the treatment phase had come before the baseline phase. This problem parallels the pretest–treatment interaction problem associated with a number of the group designs.

Internal Validity

If proper controls are exercised in connection with the application of a single-subject design, the internal validity of the resulting study may be quite good.

Repeated and Reliable Measurement

In a time-series design, pretest performance is measured a number of times before the implementation of the treatment. In single-subject designs, similar multiple measures of pretest performance are known as **baseline measures.** When researchers obtain baseline measures over a period of time, threats to validity such as maturation are controlled in the same way that they are in the time-series design. Whereas the time-series design can be threatened by history, however, the single-subject design reduces the threat from history by measuring performance at various points in time while the treatment is being applied.

One common threat to the internal validity of most single-subject designs is instrumentation, the unreliability or inconsistency of measuring instruments. Because repeated measurement is a characteristic of all single-subject designs, it is especially important that measurements of participants' performance be as consistent as possible. Because single-subject designs often rely on some type of observed behavior as the dependent variable, it is critical that the observation conditions (e.g., location, time of day) be standardized, and every effort should be made to obtain observer reliability by clearly defining and measuring the dependent variable. If a single observer makes all the observations, intraobserver reliability should be obtained. If more than one observer makes observations, interobserver reliability should be obtained. Measurement consistency is especially crucial when moving from phase to phase. If a change in measurement procedures occurs at the same time a new phase is begun, the result can be invalid assessment of the treatment effect.

Also, the nature and conditions of the treatment should be specified in sufficient detail to permit replication. For example, one type of single-subject design has a baseline phase, a treatment phase, a return to baseline conditions (i.e., withdrawal of the treatment), and a second treatment phase. If effects at each phase are to be assessed with validity, the treatment must have the same procedures each time it is introduced. Because the key to the generalizability of single-subject designs is replication, the treatment must be sufficiently standardized to permit other researchers to apply it as it was originally applied.

Baseline Stability

The length of the baseline and treatment phases can influence the internal validity of single-subject designs. A key question is "How many measurements of behavior should be taken before treatment is introduced?" There is no single answer to this question. The purpose of baseline measurements is to provide a description of the target behavior as it naturally occurs before the treatment is applied. The baseline serves as the basis of comparison for determining the effectiveness of the treatment. If most behaviors were stable, the baseline phase would be simple to implement, but human behavior is quite variable, and the researcher must allow time for the observation of variations. For example, if a student's disruptive behavior were being measured, we would not expect that student to exhibit exactly the same number of disruptive acts in each observation period. The student would likely be more disruptive at some times than at others. Fortunately, such fluctuations usually fall within some consistent range, permitting the researcher to achieve *baseline stability* or, in other words, to establish a pattern or range of student baseline performance. We may observe, for example, that the child normally exhibits 5 to 10 disruptive behaviors during a 30-minute period. These figures then become our basis of comparison for assessing the effectiveness of the treatment. If, during the treatment phase, the number of disruptive behaviors falls well below the baseline range (e.g., fewer than 3) or steadily decreases until it reaches 0, and if the number of disruptive behaviors increases when treatment is withdrawn, the effectiveness of the treatment is demonstrated.

Three data points are usually considered the minimum necessary to identify the baseline, but more than three are often required. If the baseline behavior appears to be getting progressively worse, few measurements are required to establish the baseline pattern. If, on the other hand, the baseline behavior is getting progressively better, there is no point in introducing the treatment until, or unless, the behavior stabilizes. Normally, the length of the treatment phase and the number of measurements taken during the treatment phase should parallel the length and measurements of the baseline phase. If baseline stability is established after 10 observation periods, then the treatment phase should include 10 observation periods.

MyLab Education **Self-Check 12.3**

MyLab Education **Application Exercise 12.2:**
Evaluating Research Articles: Evaluating a Single-Subject Design Study

MyLab Education **Application Exercise 12.3:**
Designing Single-Subject Studies

---

the third type of replication, clinical replication. **Clinical replication** involves the development of a treatment package, composed of two or more interventions that have been found to be effective individually, designed for persons with complex behavior disorders. Individuals with autism, for example, often exhibit a number of characteristics, including apparent sensory deficit, mutism, and self-injurious behavior. Clinical replication would utilize research on each of these characteristics individually to develop a total program to apply to individuals with autism.

MyLab Education **Self-Check 12.4**

MyLab Education **Application Exercise 12.4:**
The Importance of Replication

REPLICATION

Replication is the repetition of a study or new test of its hypothesis. Replication is vital to all research, especially single-subject studies, whose initial findings are generally based on one person or a small number of participants. As results are replicated, we can have more confidence in the procedures that produced those results. Replication also serves to establish the generalizability of findings by providing data about participants and settings to which results are applicable.

Single-subject experiments are subject to three types of replication: direct, systematic, and clinical. **Direct replication** is replication by the same investigator, in a specific setting (e.g., a classroom), with the same or different participants. Generalizability is promoted when replication includes other participants who share the same problem, matched closely on relevant variables. When replication includes a number of participants with the same problem, at the same location and same time, the process is known as simultaneous replication. **Systematic replication** follows direct replication and involves different investigators, behaviors, or settings. Over time, techniques are identified that are consistently effective in a variety of situations. We know, for example, that teacher attention can be a powerful factor in behavior change. At some point, enough data are amassed to permit

SINGLE-SUBJECT EXPERIMENTAL RESEARCH DESIGN IN ACTION

At this point, some of you may feel confident in your ability to interpret and conduct single-subject experimental design research, but if you are still experiencing some confusion, don't worry, you are certainly not alone. Single-subject experimental design with its many variations can seem complex to the new researcher or to the classroom teacher. At the end of this chapter you will find a published example of a research study using a single-subject experimental designs, but before you get to that, let's consider a more practitioner-oriented example.

In the field of education, single-subject experimental design is best associated with special education research. As pointed out earlier in this chapter, even the population of students with a high incidence disability in a local district may not constitute a large enough sample to consider group designs. Because of this, special education teachers and researchers often rely on single-subject experimental designs in order to pursue the research required to support students. However, with the inclusion movement, special education students are no longer educated only by special educators, but are largely educated in the general education environment. With the implementation of Response to Intervention (RTI) all teachers, not just special education teachers, find themselves responsible for a great deal of rigorous data collection as well as with offering interpretations of the data they collect.

So, let's look at when a classroom teacher may want to use single-subject experimental design to learn more about how to best support students. A straightforward example should help you better understand the process and should help you to analyze the study at the end of this chapter. Let's start with a problem behavior every teacher has faced: verbal outbursts.

Meet Byron. Byron is a wonderful, brilliant 10-year old boy who has frequent verbal outbursts in class. Byron typically shouts out during independent work in math class. The teacher, Ms. Adeline, is at her wits' end. Byron's behavior severely disrupts the classroom at a time when Ms. Adeline needs to be available to work independently with all of her students. Ms. Adeline expressed her concerns to one of her colleagues who suggested that perhaps Byron's verbal outburst were a function of math anxiety. Well-versed in single-subject experimental designs, Ms. Adeline decided to conduct research that would allow her to better understand, and reduce, Byron's verbal outbursts.

Ms. Adeline decided she would use a basic AB single-subject design. Ms. Adeline has strong, positive relationships with her students, and she knows that Byron loves to write: something at which he excels. Ms. Adeline decided to use a math journal as an intervention with Byron and developed the following research question: "In what way does the use of a math journal impact Byron's verbal outbursts during independent work?"

Ms. Adeline implemented an AB single-subject experimental design and collected baseline data (the first A) and then collected data with an intervention in place (the B phase). The independent variable, or the variable being manipulated in this example, is the math journal intervention. The dependent variable, or the outcome variable, is the number of verbal outbursts.

Ms. Adeline designed her study to take place over two weeks. For the first week she only collected baseline data: Her classroom reflected "business as usual." Because Ms. Adeline is interested in reducing the number of times Byron has a verbal outburst during independent math work, she only

collected data during this time of his class. Since Ms. Adeline will be actively working with students and does not have the luxury of being simply an observer, she plans to collect simple frequency data. Every time Byron has a verbal outburst during independent math work she will simply make a tally mark on a piece of paper. She will do this for five consecutive days.

At the end of the first week, Ms. Adeline had collected the baseline data she needed for her study. At the beginning of the next week, Ms. Adeline explained to Byron that she is introducing a strategy that may help him feel less of the need to blurt out during independent math instruction. Ms. Adeline explained to Byron that she wants him to use some of the great skills he has in writing to help with math and explained to him the math journal intervention. Byron was open to the idea of a math journal and agreed to give it a try. This marked the beginning of the intervention phase, or the "B" in the AB design. Again, Ms. Adeline proceeded as normal in her teaching and data collection, continuing to take tally marks when Byron had a verbal outburst during independent math work Ms. Adeline collected data for two weeks and charts her frequency data of verbal outbursts. Table 12.1 is a display of the raw data on Byron's verbal outbursts during independent math instruction.

Following the traditions of single-subject experimental design, Ms. Adeline graphed her data in a line graph (Figure 12.5) in order to better visualize the results.

A quick interpretation of the line graph suggests that the math journal was a successful intervention for reducing Byron's verbal outbursts as the number of outbursts were drastically reduced

TABLE 12.1 • Byron's verbal outbursts during independent math instruction			
Date	Baseline Outbursts	Date	Intervention Outbursts
11/3	7	11/10	3
11/4	5	11/11	2
11/5	8	11/12	3
11/6	6	11/13	0
11/7	5	11/14	1

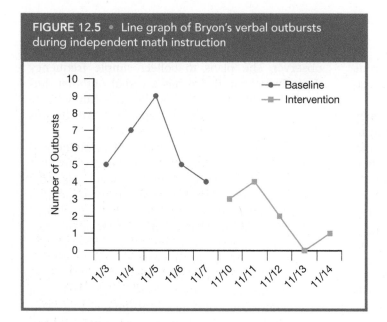

FIGURE 12.5 • Line graph of Bryon's verbal outbursts during independent math instruction

when the intervention was in place. Given this outcome, Ms. Adeline considered extending her research and implementing another week without the math journal (ABA design), and then following that with another week with the math journal (ABAB design). However, given the apparent success of the intervention Ms. Adeline decided that it would not be ethical to remove an intervention that seems to be helping a student. It is worth remembering that the goal of most single-subject experimental design studies is to identify supportive treatment and intervention options.

Word of warning: Ms. Adeline may now feel empowered to use math journals with all of her students and declare that all teachers should do the same, but she would be getting a little ahead of herself. Single-subject research design studies rarely make claims of external validity. In other words, Ms. Adeline cannot assume that just because this intervention worked for Byron that it will work for everyone. Ms. Adeline's goal was to find a supportive intervention for Byron and to collect, analyze, and interpret the data in order to better understand the impact of the math journal intervention on Byron's verbal outburst behavior. By using a single-subject experimental design, Ms. Adeline was able to identify a successful intervention that she could confidently continue to use with Byron in the future. This practical example is intended to help you as you read the study found at the end of this chapter. More importantly, perhaps, this example helps you feel more empowered to conduct your own single-case studies!

SUMMARY

SINGLE-SUBJECT EXPERIMENTAL DESIGNS

1. Single-subject experimental designs, also referred to as single-case experimental designs, can be applied when the sample size is one; they are typically used to study the behavior change an individual exhibits as a result of some intervention or treatment.

2. In this design, the participant is alternately exposed to a nontreatment and a treatment condition, or phase, and performance is repeatedly measured during each phase. The nontreatment condition is symbolized as A, and the treatment condition is symbolized as B.

Single-Subject versus Group Designs

3. Single-subject designs are valuable complements to group designs. Single-subject designs are applied most frequently in clinical settings where the primary emphasis is on therapeutic outcomes.

The Single-Variable Rule

4. Only one variable at a time should be manipulated (i.e., added or withdrawn at any phase).

Types of Single-Subject Designs

5. In the A-B design, baseline measurements are made repeatedly until stability is established, treatment is then introduced, and multiple measurements are made during treatment. If behavior improves during the treatment phase, the effectiveness of the treatment can be inferred. This design is open to many threats to internal and external validity.

6. The A-B-A design adds a second baseline phase to the A-B design, which makes its internal validity superior to that of the A-B design. A problem with this design is the ethical concern that the experiment ends with the treatment being removed.

7. The B-A-B design involves a treatment phase (B), a withdrawal phase (A), and a return to treatment phase (B). Although the B-A-B design ends with the subject receiving treatment, the lack of an initial baseline phase makes it difficult to assess the effectiveness of treatment.

8. The A-B-A-B design is the A-B-A design with the addition of a second treatment phase. This design overcomes the ethical objection to the A-B-A design and greatly strengthens the conclusions of the study by demonstrating the effects of the treatment twice. When application of the A-B-A-B design is feasible, it provides very convincing evidence of treatment effectiveness. The second treatment phase can be extended beyond the termination of the study to examine stability of treatment.

9. Multiple-baseline designs are used when it is not possible to withdraw treatment or return behavior to baseline, or when it would not be ethical to withdraw it or reverse it. They are also used when treatment can be withdrawn but the effects of the treatment carry over into other phases of the study.

10. In a multiple-baseline design, data are collected on several behaviors for one subject, one behavior for several subjects, or one behavior and one subject in several settings. The three basic types of multiple-baseline designs are, therefore, across-behaviors, across-subjects, and across-settings designs.

11. In a multiple-baseline design, a treatment is applied to each behavior (or subject or setting), one at a time, until all behaviors (or subjects or settings) are exposed to treatment. If performance improves only after a treatment is introduced, then the treatment is judged to be effective.

12. When applying a treatment across behaviors, the behaviors must be independent of each other. When applying treatment across participants, they and the setting should be as similar as possible. When applying treatment across settings, it is preferable that the settings be natural, if possible.

13. Whenever baseline is recoverable and there are no carryover effects, any of the A-B-A designs can be applied within a multiple-baseline framework.

14. The alternating treatments design involves the relatively rapid alternation of treatments for a single subject; it represents a highly valid approach to assessing the relative effectiveness of two (or more) treatments

within a single-subject context. To avoid potential validity threats, treatments are alternated on a random basis.

15. The alternating treatments design is attractive to investigators because no withdrawal is necessary, no baseline phase is necessary, and a number of treatments can be studied quickly and efficiently. One potential problem is multiple-treatment interference (i.e., carryover effects from one treatment to the other).

DATA ANALYSIS AND INTERPRETATION

16. Data analysis in single-subject research usually involves visual and graphical analysis, sometimes supplemented with statistical analysis. Given the small sample size, the primary criterion is the clinical significance of the results. Effects that are small but statistically significant may not make a useful difference in the behavior of a subject.

THREATS TO VALIDITY

External Validity

17. Results of single-subject research cannot be generalized to the population of interest without replication. A main threat to these designs is the possible effect of the baseline phase on the subsequent effects of the treatment.

Internal Validity

18. Single-subject designs require repeated and reliable measurements or observations. Pretreatment performance is measured or observed a number of times to obtain a stable baseline. Performance is also measured at various points while the treatment is being applied. Measurement or observation of performance must be standardized, and intraobserver and interobserver reliability should be obtained.

19. The nature and conditions of the treatment should be specified in sufficient detail to permit replication. The treatment must involve the same procedures each time it is introduced.

20. The establishment of a baseline pattern is referred to as achieving baseline stability. The baseline measurements provide a description of the target behavior as it naturally occurs prior to the treatment and provide the basis of comparison for assessing the effectiveness of the treatment.

21. Normally, the length of the treatment phase and the number of measurements taken during it should parallel the length and measurements of the baseline phase.

REPLICATION

22. As results from a single-subject design are replicated, we can have more confidence in the procedures that produced those results. Replication serves to set limits on the generalizability of findings.

23. Direct replication is replication by the same investigator, with the same or different subjects, in a specific setting (e.g., a classroom). Systematic replication involves different investigators, behaviors, or settings. Clinical replication involves the development of a treatment package, composed of two or more interventions that have been found to be effective individually, designed for persons with complex behavior disorders.

SINGLE-SUBJECT EXPERIMENTAL RESEARCH DESIGN IN ACTION

24. In the field of education, single-subject experimental design is best associated with special education research.

25. Special education teachers and researchers often rely on single-subject experimental designs in order to pursue the research required to support students.

PERFORMANCE CRITERIA   TASK 7

The description of participants should describe the population from which the sample was selected (hypothetically, of course), including its size and major characteristics.

The description of the instrument(s) should describe the purpose of the instrument (i.e., what it is intended to measure) and available validity and reliability coefficients.

The description of the design should indicate why it was selected and include potential threats to validity associated with the design and aspects of the study that are believed to have minimized their potential effects. A figure should be included to illustrate how the selected design was applied in the study. For example:

> Because random assignment of participants to groups was possible, and because administration of a pretest was not advisable due to the reactive nature of the dependent variable (i.e., attitudes toward school), the posttest-only control group design was selected for this study (see Figure 1).

The description of procedures should describe in detail all steps that were executed in conducting the study. The description should include (1) the manner in which the sample was selected and the groups were formed, (2) how and when pretest data were collected (if applicable), (3) the ways in which the groups were different (i.e., the independent variable, or treatment), (4) aspects of the study that were the same or similar for all groups, and (5) how and when posttest data were collected. If the dependent variable was measured with a test, the specific test or tests administered should be named. If a test was administered strictly for selection-of-subjects purposes—that is, not as a pretest of the dependent variable—it too should be described.

The example on the following pages illustrates the performance called for by Tasks 7A–E. Although the example pertains to an experimental study, the components shown would also be presented in a similar way for the other types of quantitative studies. The task in the example was prepared by the same student whose work was previously presented. You should therefore be able to see how Task 7 builds on previous tasks. Note especially how Task 4A, the method section of the research plan, has been refined and expanded. Keep in mind that Tasks 4A, 5A, and 6 will not appear in your final research report; Task 7 will. Therefore, all the important points in those previous tasks should be included in Task 7.

Group	Assignment	n	Treatment	Posttest
I	Random	25	Daily homework	So-so Attitude Scale
II	Random	25	No homework	So-so Attitude Scale

Figure 1. Experimental design.

1

Effect of Interactive Multimedia on the Achievement of 10th-Grade Biology Students

Method

Participants

The sample for this study was selected from the total population of 213 10th-grade students at an upper middle class all-girls Catholic high school in Miami, Florida. The population was 90% Hispanic, mainly of Cuban-American descent, 9% Caucasian non-Hispanic and 1% African-American. Sixty students were randomly selected (using a table of random numbers) and randomly assigned to two groups of 30 each.

Instrument

The biology test of the National Proficiency Survey Series (NPSS) was used as the measuring instrument. The test was designed to measure individual student performance in biology at the high school level but the publishers also recommended it as an evaluation of instructional programs. Content validity is good; items were selected from a large item bank provided by classroom teachers and curriculum experts. High school instructional materials and a national curriculum survey were extensively reviewed before objectives were written. The test objectives and those of the biology classes in the study were highly correlated. Although the standard error of measurement is not given for the biology test, the range of KR-20s for the entire battery is from .82 to .91 with a median of .86. This is satisfactory since the purpose of the test was to evaluate instructional programs not to make decisions concerning individuals. Catholic school students were included in the battery norming and its procedures were carried out in April and May of 1988 using 22,616 students in grades 9–12 from 45 high schools in 20 states.

Experimental Design

The design used in this study was the posttest-only control group design (see Figure 1). This design was selected because it provides control for most sources of invalidity and random assignment to groups was possible. A pretest was not necessary since the final science grades from June 1993 were available to check initial group equivalence and to help control mortality, a potential threat to internal validity with this design. Mortality, however, was not a problem as no students dropped from either group.

Group	Assignment	n	Treatment	Posttest
1	Random	30	IMM instruction	NPSS:B[a]
2	Random	30	Traditional instruction	NPSS:B

[a]National Proficiency Survey Series: Biology

Figure 1. Experimental design.

Procedure

Prior to the beginning of the 1993–94 school year, before classes were scheduled, 60 of the 213 10th-grade students were randomly selected and randomly assigned to two groups of 30 each, the average biology class size; each group became a biology class. One of the classes was randomly chosen to receive IMM instruction. The same teacher taught both classes.

The study was designed to last eight months beginning on the first day of class. The control group was taught using traditional methods of lecturing and open class discussions. The students worked in pairs for laboratory investigations which included the use of microscopes. The teacher's role was one of information disseminator.

The experimental classroom had 15 workstations for student use, each one consisting of a laser disc player, a video recorder, a 27-inch monitor, and a Macintosh computer with a 40 MB hard drive, 10 MB RAM, and a CD-ROM drive. The teacher's workstation incorporated a Macintosh computer with CD-ROM drive, a videodisc player, and a 27-inch monitor. The workstations were networked to the school library so students had access to online services such as Prodigy and Infotrac as well as to the card catalogue. Two laser printers were available through the network for the students' use.

In the experimental class the teacher used a videodisc correlated to the textbook. When barcodes provided in the text were scanned a section of the videodisc was activated and appeared on the monitor. The section might be a motion picture demonstrating a process or a still picture offering more detail than the text. The role of the teacher in the experimental group was that of facilitator and guide. After the teacher had introduced a new topic, the students worked in pairs at the workstations investigating topics connected to the main idea presented in the lesson. Videodiscs, CD-ROMs, and online services were all available as sources of information. The students used HyperStudio to prepare multimedia reports, which they presented to the class.

Throughout the study the same subject matter was covered and the two classes used the same text. Although the students of the experimental group paired up at the workstations, the other group worked in pairs during lab time, thus equalizing any effect from cooperative learning. The classes could not meet at the same time as they were taught by the same teacher, so they met during second and third periods. First period was not chosen as the school sometimes has a special schedule that interferes with first period. Both classes had the same homework reading assignments, which were reviewed in class the following school day. Academic objectives were the same for each class and all tests measuring achievement were identical.

During the first week of May, the biology test of the NPSS was administered to both classes to compare their achievement in biology.

Effects of Functional Mobility Skills Training for Young Students with Physical Disabilities

STACIE B. BARNES
University of West Florida

KEITH W. WHINNERY
University of West Florida

ABSTRACT The Mobility Opportunities Via Education (MOVE®) Curriculum is a functional mobility curriculum for individuals with severe disabilities. This study investigated the effects of the MOVE Curriculum on the functional walking skills of five elementary-aged students with severe, multiple disabilities. The MOVE Curriculum was implemented using a multiple-baseline across-subjects design. Repeated measures were taken during baseline, intervention, and maintenance phases for each participant. All students demonstrated progress in taking reciprocal steps during either intervention or maintenance. Results for each participant are discussed as well as implications and future directions for research.

(01) Since the passage of P. L. 94-142, students served in special education programs have had the right to related services (e.g., occupational therapy and physical therapy) as needed to benefit from their educational program (Beirne-Smith, Ittenbach, & Patton, 2002). Therapists in educational settings who are typically trained under the medical model of disability traditionally have provided therapy services separate from educational goals (Craig, Haggart, & Hull, 1999; Dunn, 1989; Rainforth & York-Barr, 1997). Treatment within this traditional approach is based on the developmental model in which therapists attempt to correct specific deficits and remediate underlying processes of movement to promote normalization (Campbell, McInerney, & Cooper, 1984; Fetters, 1991). As a result, these treatment programs typically do not focus on the development of functional motor skills in natural environments because students often are viewed as *not ready* to perform such high level skills (Rainforth & York-Barr). Until recently, this traditional approach to therapy was considered acceptable in school settings because educational programming for students with disabilities also relied on a developmental model. It has been only in the past 15 to 20 years that educational programs for individuals with disabilities have begun to move away from instruction based on a developmental model to curriculum approaches emphasizing functional outcomes (Butterfield & Arthur, 1995).

(02) Current educational practices promote the use of a *support model* that emphasizes an individual's future potential rather than an individual's limitations (Barnes, 1999). While earlier practices that focused on deficits often limited an individual's access to environments and activities (Brown et al., 1979), current practices employ a top-down approach to program planning designed to teach an individual to function more independently in his or her natural environments. Top-down program planning typically incorporates the concept of *place then train*, promoting instruction in the environments in which the skills will be used (Beirne-Smith et al., 2002). Individuals served under a support model are not excluded from activities because they lack prerequisite skills; rather, they are supported to participate to their highest potential. A support model approach to programming provides a framework for identifying adult outcomes, determining current levels of functioning, and identifying supports needed to achieve the targeted outcomes.

As educational practices change, therapy approaches that stressed remedia- (03) tion of individual skills in isolated environments are being replaced by the practice of integrated therapy in which services are provided in natural settings where skills will be functional and performance meaningful for individual students (Rainforth & York-Barr, 1997). Integrated therapy breaks from the more traditional, multidisciplinary model where team members conduct assessments and set goals in relative isolation (Orelove & Sobsey, 1996). Parents, teachers, and therapists collaborate as a team to assess the student, write goals, and implement intervention. The team develops the IEP together by setting priorities and developing child-centered goals through consensus (Rainforth & York-Barr). In this way, all team members are aware of the IEP goals and can work cooperatively to embed them into the child's natural activities.

As the fields of physical therapy, occupational therapy, and education have (04) begun to move away from a developmental approach toward a functional model that emphasizes potential and support, the link between special education and pediatric therapy has been strengthened (McEwen & Shelden, 1995). Recent research suggests that when therapy is integrated into the student's natural environments, treatment is just as effective as traditional therapy and that the integrated approach is more preferred by the school team (Giangreco, 1986; Harris, 1991). The benefits of providing therapy in integrated settings include (a) the availability of natural motivators (Atwater, 1991; Campbell et al., 1984), (b) repeated opportunities for practicing motor skills in meaningful situations (Campbell et al., 1984; Fetters, 1991), and (c) increased generalization of skills across different environmental settings (Campbell et al., 1984; Craig et al., 1999; Harris, 1991). "Although intervention has historically focused on deficient skills with the assumption that isolated skills must be learned and then eventually transferred to functional activities, we now know that for learners with severe disabilities, task-specific instruction must take place in the natural environment for retention to occur" (Shelden, 1998, p. 948).

In response to the shortcomings of traditional motor treatment (05) approaches, the MOVE (Mobility Opportunities Via Education) Curriculum was developed to teach functional mobility skills to students with severe disabilities (Kern County Superintendent of Schools, 1999). MOVE is a top-down, activity-based curriculum designed to link educational programs and therapy by providing functional mobility practice within typical daily activities in the natural context. Individuals using the MOVE Curriculum follow a top-down approach to program planning, rather than selecting skills from a developmental hierarchy. A transdisciplinary team that includes parents, educators, and therapists works collaboratively to assess the student's skills, design an individualized program, and teach targeted skills while the student participates in school and community activities (for additional information on the MOVE Curriculum see Bidabe, Barnes, & Whinnery, 2001).

Since the inception of the MOVE Curriculum in 1986, this seemingly success- (06) ful approach has spread to a great number of classrooms, rehabilitation facilities, and homes for students with disabilities across the United States as well as throughout Europe and Asia. Although testimony from practitioners and families as well as informal studies have praised the effectiveness of MOVE, there has been no systematic research related to the effectiveness of this approach to teaching functional mobility skills. While the great number of anecdotal reports of student successes in the MOVE Curriculum should not be disregarded, there is a critical need for demonstrable data to support the efficacy of the program. Therefore, this study asked the following question: Do functional mobility skills in students with physical disabilities improve as a result of direct training using the MOVE Curriculum and will these skills be maintained over time?

Method
Participants

Five children with severe, multiple disabilities between the ages of 3 and 9 (07) were selected to participate in this study. All of the children attended a public

The research problem focuses on answering the question: "Do functional mobility skills in students with physical disabilities improve as a result of direct training using the MOVE Curriculum and will skills be maintained over time?" The researchers define the dependent variable of "functional mobility skills" and independent variable of "MOVE curriculum" as part of the preceding review of literature.

Participants in the study described as five children with severe, multiple disabilities between the ages of 3 and 9. Selection criteria for research participants clearly stated.

elementary school located in an urban, southeastern school district, were served in special education classes, and received occupational and physical therapy as related services. Four of the participants were served in a pre-school classroom for students with severe, multiple disabilities. The remaining participant was served in a varying exceptionalities classroom for students with moderate to severe disabilities.

(08) The following criteria were used to select participants for the study: (a) diagnosis of a severe, multiple disability including a physical impairment, (b) parental consent, (c) medical eligibility, (d) willingness of the school team to participate and to be trained in MOVE, and (e) no prior implementation of the MOVE Curriculum. Five of the 17 students served in the two classes met all the selection criteria.

(09) The primary means of mobility for all participants was either being pushed in a wheelchair or being carried. Participant 1, Kim, was a 7-year-old female diagnosed with Down syndrome, severe mental retardation, general hypotonia in all extremities, and a seizure disorder for which she took anticonvulsant medication. Kim was able to bear her own weight in standing while holding a stationary object and could move her feet reciprocally while being supported for weight shifting and balance. Although she demonstrated these skills on rare occasions in physical therapy, she typically refused to use them.

(10) Participant 2, Melissa, was a 4-year-old female diagnosed with a developmental delay and cerebral palsy with hypotonia. Melissa was able to bear weight in standing while holding a stationary object and move her legs reciprocally while being supported for balance and weight shifting in physical therapy, but she also refused to use these skills.

(11) Participant 3, Kevin, was a 3-year-old male diagnosed with cerebral palsy with hypotonia, right hemiparesis, cortical blindness, and a seizure disorder for which he took medication. Kevin was unable to bear weight in standing unless his knees, hips, and trunk were held in alignment by a standing device.

(12) Participant 4, David, was a 9-year-old male diagnosed with spastic quadriplegic cerebral palsy and asthma for which he took medication. David had the ability to maintain hip and knee extension when supported by an adult and to tolerate fully prompted reciprocal steps when supported in a walker.

(13) Participant 5, Caleb, was a 4-year-old male diagnosed with global developmental delays, spastic quadriplegic cerebral palsy, chronic lung disorder, and a seizure disorder for which he took medication. Additionally, Caleb had a tracheostomy that required frequent suctioning, a gastrostomy tube, and occasionally had breathing distress. He required a one-on-one nurse in attendance at all times, and his medical complications sometimes resulted in extended absences. Caleb had the ability to maintain hip and knee extension when supported by an adult and to tolerate fully prompted reciprocal steps when supported in a walker.

Research Methodology

(14) A single-subject, multiple-baseline across subjects study was employed. The independent variable was the MOVE Curriculum that consists of six steps: (1) Testing, (2) Setting Goals, (3) Task Analysis, (4) Measuring Prompts, (5) Reducing Prompts, and (6) Teaching the Skills. The dependent variable was the number of reciprocal steps. A reciprocal step was defined as a step within a time interval of not more than 10 seconds between initial contact of one foot and initial contact of the opposite foot in a forward motion.

Research design described as a single-subject, multiple-baseline across subjects study. This design can be annotated as follows: A-B-A-B.

Setting

(15) Mobility practice was conducted in the natural context in accordance with the principles of the MOVE Curriculum. Meaningful and relevant activities that naturally occur during the school day were selected for each participant. These activities occurred throughout the school campus.

(16) The study was conducted over the course of one school year beginning in the third week of the fall term and lasting until the 27th week in spring. Maintenance data was collected over a 2-week period 2 years following the intervention year.

Staff Training

Two special education teachers, a physical therapist, and an occupational (17)
therapist from the selected school participated in a 2-day MOVE International
Basic Provider training on the MOVE Curriculum. Basic Provider training
incorporates 16 hrs of instruction on the six steps of the MOVE Curriculum
including hands-on instruction in assessment, goal setting, and adaptive
prompts and equipment with families and individuals with disabilities.

Materials and Equipment

The Rifton Gait Trainer (Community Playthings, 1999) was used during inter- (18)
vention. The Gait Trainer, also known as the Front Leaning Walker, provides
support for an individual to learn to take reciprocal steps. The Gait Trainer is
designed to provide total support (if needed) for individuals who are just
beginning to bear weight in standing. The prompts can be removed as an individual requires less support with the long-term goal of independent walking.

Procedures
Baseline

During the baseline phase, repeated measures of the number of reciprocal (19)
steps were taken twice a week until a pattern of stable performance was
established. Baseline measures began by the fifth week of the school year.
Due to the multiple-baseline design, baseline was collected for 1½ weeks for
the first participant, Kim, and continued for 12 weeks for the last participant,
Caleb. Each participant was given the least amount of adult assistance (i.e.,
one or two hands held or support at trunk) necessary for weight bearing in
standing and verbal directions to walk. No assistance was provided for taking
reciprocal steps. Baseline measures of reciprocal stepping were taken with
adult support for all participants. Additional measurements without assistance were taken for Kim and Melissa because they had demonstrated the
ability to bear weight in standing while holding a stationary object. Baseline
measures occurred within the participants' normal school environments;
however, no measures were taken using the Gait Trainer or within functional
activities because these were considered to be part of the intervention.

> Research procedures for the A-B-A-B study included baseline data collection, twice weekly, of the number of reciprocal steps taken.

Data Collection

Although practice of walking skills occurred throughout the day, measure- (20)
ment of the number of reciprocal steps was taken twice a week during specifically targeted activities to provide consistency of measurement. Measurement
was taken at the first walking opportunity during each activity.

For the purpose of data collection, three general levels of support were used (21)
for participants according to their abilities and needs. Support was defined as (a)
no outside assistance or *independent*, (b) *adult assistance* for postural control
with independent weight bearing (e.g., one or two hands held or support at
trunk), and (c) use of the *Gait Trainer* to provide postural control and partial
weight bearing support when necessary. As students' reciprocal stepping skills
increased, the level of support decreased progressively from the use of the Gait
Trainer to adult assistance to no assistance as appropriate. Therefore, measurements were taken in multiple ways for each participant because it was not possible to predict changing levels of necessary support during intervention or the
eventual level of independent mobility after intervention. For all participants,
data were collected concurrently at the level of support required at the beginning
of intervention and at the next more independent level. In addition, measurements were taken for Melissa at all three levels of support. Although Melissa
required the use of the Gait Trainer, measurements were taken for independent
walking because she had previously demonstrated the ability to bear her own
weight and occasionally take one or two reciprocal steps with both hands held.
Because Kim began to take reciprocal steps independently during the second
trial of intervention, data collection with "adult assistance" was discontinued.

Interobserver Agreement

(22) Although the intervention was implemented by all team members, measurements were taken by the first author to increase reliability. In addition, interobserver agreement checks were made by the second author to ensure accurate measurement. For each participant, a minimum of two checks was conducted for each targeted behavior. Percentage of agreement was calculated by dividing the total number of agreements by the sum of agreements and disagreements and multiplying that number by 100 (White & Haring, 1980). Agreement for the number of reciprocal steps taken equaled 100%.

Intervention Phase

(23) The intervention consisted of the implementation of the six steps of the MOVE Curriculum for each participant. Using the information obtained during Step 1, Testing, the team was able to identify each participant's consistent use of mobility skills and to select functional activities during Step 2. These activities were task analyzed in Step 3 in order to identify the critical mobility skills to be addressed in each activity.

(24) Once meaningful daily activities were identified for mobility practice, the level and type of physical support needed to accomplish the activity were determined in Step 4, Measuring Prompts. A critical component of the MOVE program is to provide the necessary but minimal prompts (physical support) needed for functional mobility within an activity. This level was determined for each individual based upon assessment data collected in Step 1. Therefore, not all participants required assistance and all three levels of support.

(25) As is advocated in Step 5 of MOVE, physical support was faded as soon as the students demonstrated an increase in skill level as indicated by the data. The reduction of prompts differed for participants according to their individual rate of progress.

(26) During Teaching the Skills, Step 6 of MOVE, instruction of skills was embedded into typical daily activities in order to provide meaningful, intensive, and consistent practice of reciprocal stepping. An important component of this step is the identification of practice activities that are relevant and motivating to the individual to encourage active participation. From these practice opportunities, one activity per participant was selected for data collection. Data were collected twice a week.

Maintenance Phase

(27) After a period of 2 years, maintenance measures were taken on dependent variables for 4 of the 5 participants. David had moved from the area and was unavailable. Data were collected during the participants' natural activities at the time. Some students had moved into new classrooms and many were participating in different activities than those used during the initial intervention phase.

(28) Measurements were taken for participants at their current level of support necessary for functional walking (e.g., independent walking for Kim and Melissa, walking with adult assistance for Caleb, and walking with the use of the Gait Trainer for Kevin).

Results
Data Analysis

(29) Data were analyzed using visual inspection of the graphs including changes in means, levels, and trends as well as percentage of overlap across phases (Kazdin, 1982). Performance data for intervention and maintenance are presented in Figures 1–3.

Data analysis for each participant in the study is represented with a visual display that captures the changes in the number of reciprocal steps taken across the baseline, intervention, and maintenance phases of the study.

(30) **Kim.** A stable baseline with a mean and range of 0 steps was observed for walking forward independently (see Figure 1). The mean for intervention phase was 5.25 steps with a range from 0 to 14 steps. There was only a 9% overlap of data points (4 of 45 data points) from baseline with a 5.25-point increase in the

mean. There was an upward trend in reciprocal steps observed in intervention phase with one notable decrease coinciding with an increase in seizure episodes.

During the maintenance phase, there was a sizable increase in the number (31) of independent reciprocal steps recorded. All measurements during maintenance revealed that Kim was able to walk over 500 ft independently. This resulted in a 494.74-point increase in the mean number of steps taken with a 0% overlap of data points from intervention phase to the maintenance phase.

Melissa. A stable baseline with a mean and range of 0 steps was observed (32) for walking (see Figure 1). Intervention included the use of the Gait Trainer (see Figure 3) and adult support (see Figure 2). As Melissa required less support, the Gait Trainer was discontinued (after the 37th trial). For adult support, there was a general increase in the number of steps with a mean of 30.16 with a range from 0 to 100 steps. A 38% overlap of data points (10 of 26 data points) was noted from baseline to intervention.

During the maintenance phase, measurements were taken on independent (33) reciprocal steps since Melissa no longer required the use of the Gait Trainer or adult support. All measurements during maintenance showed that Melissa was able to walk over 500 ft independently. A 500-point increase in the mean with a 0% overlap of data points from intervention to maintenance was observed.

Kevin. For walking forward with adult support, Kevin was unable to bear (34) weight or to take any steps during baseline or intervention (see Figure 2). Additionally, he would not accept being placed into the Gait Trainer during intervention (see Figure 3). During maintenance, however, Kevin was taking reciprocal steps both with adult support and while using the Gait Trainer. The mean for walking forward with adult support during maintenance was 3.33 steps with a

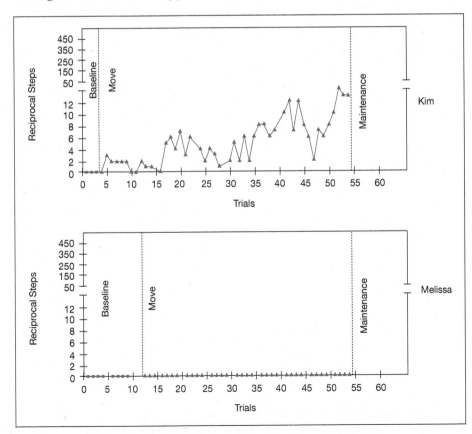

Figure 1 Independent walking for Kim and Melissa across baseline, intervention, and maintenance phases

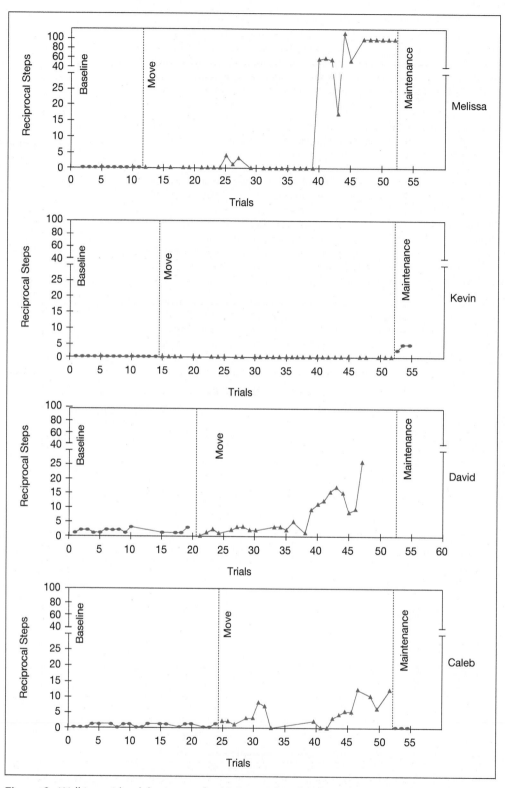

Figure 2 Walking with adult support for Melissa (2-hand assistance), Kevin (support from behind at trunk), David (2-hand assistance), and Caleb (support from behind at trunk) across baseline, intervention, and maintenance phases

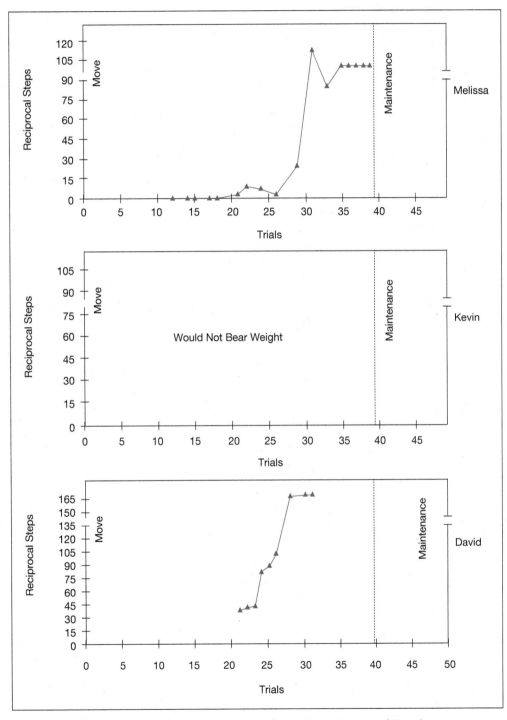

Figure 3 Walking with the use of the gait trainer for Melissa, Kevin, and David across baseline, intervention, and maintenance phases

range from 2 to 4 steps. This showed a slight upward trend and a mean of 3.33 steps. There was also a 0% overlap of data points (0 of 3 points) between intervention and maintenance. While using the Gait Trainer, Kevin consistently was able to take independent reciprocal steps for a minimum of 100 steps.

(35)   **David.**   For walking forward with adult support, there was a stable baseline with a mean of 1.64 steps and a range from 1 to 3 steps (see Figure 2). An upward trend was noted during the intervention phase with a mean of 6.91 steps and a range from 0 to 26 steps. A 55% overlap of data points (12 of 22 data points) from baseline to intervention with a 5.27-point increase in the mean was observed.

(36)   Initially, measurements of reciprocal steps while walking in the Gait Trainer were taken since David was unable to walk the 70-ft distance from the bathroom to the classroom (see Figure 3). However, once David was able to consistently walk the entire distance, the measurement of distance was discontinued and the measurement of time was added (after the 30th trial). For the duration of the study, measurements of time indicated a steady decrease from 9 min 20 sec to 4 min 54 sec by the 53rd trial. David was unavailable during the maintenance phase due to a family move.

(37)   **Caleb.**   For walking forward with adult support, a stable baseline with a mean of .60 steps and a range from 0 to 1 was observed (see Figure 2). The mean for the intervention phase was 4.47 steps with a range from 0 to 12 steps. However, after the 33rd trial, all walking was discontinued for 3 weeks due to medical complications. This resulted in a substantial decrease in walking skills following this period. A reintroduction of the intervention was followed by another upward trend. There was a 3.87-point increase in the mean from baseline to intervention with a 21% overlap of data points (4 of 19 data points). There was a significant decrease in skill level in the maintenance phase demonstrated by a mean of 0 steps. This represented a 4.47-point decrease from the intervention phase with a 0% overlap of data points.

Discussion

(38)   The current study investigated the effects of the MOVE Curriculum on functional mobility skills (e.g., walking forward) with 5 students with severe, multiple disabilities. The results of this study provide support for the use of the MOVE Curriculum to increase functional mobility skills for students with severe disabilities. A clear functional relationship between the target behaviors and the intervention procedures was demonstrated. Four of the 5 participants showed increases in walking skills from baseline to intervention. Although the fifth participant, Kevin, did not make any gains during intervention, he did show a dramatic increase in walking during the maintenance phase.

Conclusion: The results of this study provide support for the use of the MOVE Curriculum to increase functional mobility skills for students with severe disabilities.

(39)   In general, prior to intervention none of the participants was able to demonstrate functional walking skills either independently or with support. David and Caleb did demonstrate the ability to take a few steps with support during baseline, but these minimal levels did not increase their functional participation in daily activities. By the end of intervention, however, Kim was able to walk short distances independently. Melissa, David, and Caleb were able to walk with adult support to participate more fully in their selected activities. As the students gained functional walking skills, they were able to participate in other school and community activities without the use of their wheelchairs.

(40)   Although Kim demonstrated very little interest in her environment and would not attempt to take any independent steps during baseline, the addition of a motivating activity appeared to have a positive impact. Initially, Melissa resisted all attempts at walking and required the use of the Gait Trainer as well as full physical prompting to move her legs reciprocally. By the end of the intervention phase, however, she no longer required the use of the Gait Trainer and did not need to use her wheelchair during the school day. Despite Kevin's inability to take reciprocal steps during the intervention phase, the transdisciplinary team continued to practice supported weight

bearing in standing and transfers from sitting to standing with the expectation that reciprocal stepping would develop. This was found to be true when measurements were taken during maintenance.

Although David was able to take a few steps with adult support during (41) baseline, he used the Gait Trainer to practice walking for longer distances during intervention. David's ability to walk forward with adult support also improved significantly during intervention. This new skill allowed David to walk short distances without the use of his wheelchair, allowing increased participation in crowded environments.

Caleb showed a fairly steady increase in reciprocal steps with adult sup- (42) port during intervention. There was a 3-week period when Caleb's nurse restricted all walking due to medical complications. After this break, Caleb experienced a temporary regression in walking skills followed by progress beyond earlier achievements.

During the maintenance phase, only 4 of the 5 participants were avail- (43) able. Three of the 4 participants not only maintained the gains made in walking skills, but they also continued to make improvements beyond the intervention year. The remaining participant, Caleb, experienced a significant setback in walking skills.

Kim was consistently walking over 500 ft on a variety of surfaces (e.g., sand, (44) grass) and no longer used her wheelchair at school. Melissa was able to walk independently over 500 ft on a variety of surfaces, and her mother reported that she had greater access to the community. Kevin was consistently walking over 100 ft in the Gait Trainer and was bearing his own weight to take some steps with adult support. This was in sharp contrast to his performance during intervention when he was unable to bear his own weight. Caleb experienced numerous medical complications during the time period between intervention and maintenance. Walking skill practice was not a regular component of Caleb's education program resulting in regression in reciprocal stepping. During maintenance data collection, Caleb could bear his own weight for short periods of time, but was not strong enough to independently take reciprocal steps.

This study has limitations including a small sample size, variability of (45) data, and difficulty in establishing a cause and effect relationship. The first issue of small sample size is characteristic of single-subject designs. The limitations of this design were reduced by the use of repeated measurements over time and multiple baselines. Additionally, the dramatic effects required of single-subject designs may be more generalizable across individuals than are larger group designs that meet relatively weaker statistical standards (Gall, Borg, & Gall, 1996; Kazdin, 1982).

A second limitation of this study is the variability of the data that makes (46) interpretation of treatment effects difficult. The variety of influences in the natural environment and the characteristics of individuals with severe disabilities (i.e., frequent illnesses and absences, medical complexities, etc.) typically result in variations in the data. While traditional research methods consider variability to be a weakness, researchers studying the multiple factors affecting skill development advocate for the preservation of variability because it provides valuable information about behavior changes (Kamm, Thelen, & Jensen, 1990; Kratochwill & Williams, 1988).

A third limitation of this study is the difficulty in establishing a causal relation- (47) ship between MOVE and increases in reciprocal stepping. In single-subject multiple-baseline designs, causal relationships can be inferred when performance changes at each point that intervention is introduced (Kazdin, 1982; Tawney & Gast, 1984). In this study, some participants did not demonstrate immediate increases in skill with the introduction of the intervention. The slow rate of change of some participants also resulted in introduction of the curriculum for some students prior to significant increases of the previous participant. Although this violation of multiple-baseline design lessens the degree of experimental control, the decision was made to expose all participants to the intervention within the school year. However, a slow rate of behavior change is characteristic for the population studied (Beirne-Smith et al., 2002; Shelden, 1998). Additionally, a visual inspection of the data indicates that participants made dramatic changes in reciprocal stepping skills in either intervention or maintenance. Such dramatic changes in behavior provide more support for a causal relationship between the intervention and an increase in behavior (Kazdin, 1982; Tawney & Gast, 1984).

(48)   A second consideration related to the inference of causal relationships is the effect of external variables in relation to the intervention. In this study stable and staggered baselines helped to reduce the influence of competing variables such as maturation and historical events. Further, there were no gains in functional mobility skills for any participant until after the intervention was introduced for that individual.

(49)   The results of this preliminary study suggest that systematic mobility training programs, such as MOVE, can lead to an increase in functional mobility skills. Additional research investigating the effects of the MOVE Curriculum is warranted. Systematic direct replication should be conducted to help establish reliability and generalizability and could be replicated across at least five dimensions (e.g., subjects, behaviors, settings, procedures, and processes). In addition to replication of initial outcomes of this study, future research should investigate the criticality of specific components of the MOVE Curriculum (e.g., levels of family involvement, student-selected versus adult-selected activities, and systematic prompt reduction).

Implications for Practice

(50)   This study emphasizes the importance of environmental support in the development of new skills. The importance of supports was obvious with David who was unable to walk independently, but could walk short distances with adult support and even greater distances with the use of the Gait Trainer. This discrepancy would suggest that without assistance, David would not have had the opportunity to practice walking skills. Kevin not only required postural support, but he also needed to develop weight-bearing skills before he experienced gains in walking. As muscle strength and proprioceptive awareness developed, he eventually was able to walk proficiently in the Gait Trainer. The implications of this study are significant for individuals with severe disabilities who may not have opportunities to participate in meaningful life activities without environmental support.

(51)   A second implication of this study was related to motivation. In addition to a lack of postural balance and strength, some of the participants appeared to have no interest in walking. This seemed to be the case with Melissa who showed no signs of progress for over 2 months before making rather rapid and dramatic gains in her walking skills. The use of the Gait Trainer as well as full physical prompting allowed the school team to provide Melissa with the experience of walking to many different environments until she became actively engaged in walking. Thus, it appeared that once Melissa was motivated to walk within meaningful activities, she made dramatic increases in her functional walking abilities. Motivation was a factor with Kim's program, also. Once Kim developed walking skills, she would walk only to the table to eat or when returning to the "safety" of her classroom. As she became more excited about the freedom walking gave her, she began to generalize this skill across many environments and activities. The natural motivation associated with activity-based instruction is a key component of the MOVE Curriculum, and this study supports the importance of practice during motivating activities.

(52)   A third implication relates to the need for increased opportunities to practice new skills. For many individuals with severe disabilities, these opportunities do not always naturally occur. The results from this study support the use of practice opportunities that are both meaningful and continuous. Melissa appeared to have the potential to walk, but not the motivation. The continuous opportunities for practice seemed to be related to her increased desire to walk. With Caleb and Kevin who appeared to lack both the skill and the will to walk, increased

mobility opportunities provided the consistent practice necessary for the acquisition of walking skills. When progress is not immediately apparent, as with Melissa and Kevin, educational teams must be committed to continuous meaningful practice. In both cases, the participants initially appeared to be unaffected by the intervention, but eventually made significant gains in functional walking. Regardless of whether lack of progress is due to limited skills or low motivation, continuous opportunities for practice should be a critical component of mobility training.

REFERENCES

Atwater, S. W. (1991). Should the normal motor developmental sequence be used as a theoretical model in pediatric physical therapy? In J. M. Lister (Ed.), *Contemporary management of motor control problems: Proceedings of the II Step Conference* (pp. 89–93). Alexandria, VA: The Foundation for Physical Therapy.

Barnes, S. B. (1999). The MOVE Curriculum: An application of contemporary theories of physical therapy and education. (Doctoral dissertation, University of West Florida, 1999). *Dissertation Abstracts International*, 9981950.

Beirne-Smith, M., Ittenbach, R. F., & Patton, J. R. (2002). *Mental retardation*. (5th ed.). Upper Saddle River, NJ: Prentice-Hall.

Bidabe, D. L., Barnes, S. B., & Whinnery, K. W. (2001). M.O.V.E.: Raising expectations for individuals with severe disabilities. *Physical Disabilities: Education and Related Services, 19*(2), 31–48.

Brown, L., Branson, M. B., Hamre-Nietupski, S., Pumpian, I., Certo, N., & Gruenewald, L. (1979). A strategy for developing chronological age-appropriate and functional curricular content for severely handicapped adolescents and young adults. *The Journal of Special Education, 13*(1), 81–90.

Butterfield, N., & Arthur, M. (1995). Shifting the focus: Emerging priorities in communication programming for students with a severe intellectual disability. *Education and Training in Mental Retardation and Developmental Disabilities, 30*(1), 41–50.

Campbell, P. H., McInerney, W. F., & Cooper, M. A. (1984). Therapeutic programming for students with severe handicaps. *The American Journal of Occupational Therapy, 38*(9), 594–602.

Community Playthings. (1999). *Rifton equipment* (Catalog). Rifton, NY: Community Products LLC.

Craig, S. E., Haggart, A. G., & Hull, K. M. (1999). Integrating therapies into the educational setting: Strategies for supporting children with severe disabilities. *Physical Disabilities: Education and Related Services, 17*(2), 91–109.

Dunn, W. (1989). Integrated related services for preschoolers with neurological impairments: Issues and strategies. *Remedial and Special Education, 10*(3), 31–39.

Fetters, L. (1991). Cerebral palsy: Contemporary treatment concepts. In J. M. Lister (Ed.), *Contemporary management of motor control problems: Proceedings of the II Step Conference* (pp. 219–224). Alexandria, VA: The Foundation for Physical Therapy.

Gall, M. D., Borg, W. R., & Gall, J. P. (1996). *Educational research: An introduction* (6th ed.). White Plains, NY: Longman.

Giangreco, M. F. (1986). Effects of integrated therapy: A pilot study. *Journal of the Association for Persons with Severe Handicaps, 11*(3), 205–208.

Harris, S. R. (1991). Functional abilities in context. In J. M. Lister (Ed.), *Contemporary management of motor control problems: Proceedings of the II Step Conference* (pp. 253–259). Alexandria, VA: The Foundation for Physical Therapy.

Kamm, K., Thelen, E., & Jensen, J. L. (1990). A dynamical systems approach to motor development. *Physical Therapy, 70*, 763–775.

Kazdin, A. E. (1982). *Single-case research designs*. New York: Oxford.

Kern County Superintendent of Schools. (1999). *MOVE: Mobility Opportunities Via Education*. Bakersfield, CA: Author.

Kratochwill, T. R., & Williams, B. L. (1988). Perspectives on pitfalls and hassles in single-subject research. *Journal for the Association of Persons with Severe Handicaps, 13*(3), 147–154.

McEwen, I. R., & Shelden, M. L. (1995). Pediatric therapy in the 1990's: The demise of the educational versus medical dichotomy. *Occupational and Physical Therapy in Educational Environments, 15*(2), 33–45.

Orelove, F. P., & Sobsey, D. (1996). *Educating children with multiple disabilities: A transdisciplinary approach*. Baltimore: Paul H. Brookes.

Rainforth, B., & York-Barr, J. (1997). *Collaborative teams for students with severe disabilities: Integrating therapy and educational services*. Baltimore: Paul H. Brookes.

Shelden, M. L. (1998). Invited commentary. *Physical Therapy, 78*, 948–949.

Tawney, J. W., & Gast, D. L. (1984). *Single subject research in special education*. Columbus, OH: Merrill.

White, O. R., & Haring, N. G. (1980). *Exceptional teaching* (2nd ed.). Columbus, OH: Merrill.

Source: "Effects of Functional Mobility Skills Training for Young Students with Physical Disabilities," by S. B. Barnes and K. W. Whinnery, *Exceptional Children, 68*, pp. 313–324. Copyright © 2002 by The Council for Exceptional Children. Reprinted with permission.

CHAPTER THIRTEEN

Narrative Research

House of Frankenstein, 1944

Miramax/Everett Collection

"If you are a person who does not interact well with others, narrative research is probably not for you!" (p. 354)

LEARNING OUTCOMES

After reading Chapter 13, you should be able to do the following:

13.1 Briefly state the definition and purpose of narrative research.

13.2 Describe the narrative research process.

13.3 Describe the key characteristics of narrative research.

13.4 Describe narrative research techniques, including restorying, oral history, examining artifacts, storytelling, letter writing, and autobiographical and biographical writing.

13.5 Outline the steps involved in writing a narrative.

The chapter learning outcomes form the basis for the following task, which requires you to develop the research procedures section of a research report for a narrative research study.

TASK 8A

For a qualitative study, you have already created research plan components (Tasks 3 and 4B) and described a sample (Task 5B). If your study involves narrative research, now develop the research procedures section of the research report. Include in the plan the overall approach and rationale for the study, site and sample selection, the researcher's role, data collection methods, data management strategies, data analysis strategies, trustworthiness features, and ethical considerations (see Performance Criteria at the end of Chapter 16, p. 438).

SUMMARY: NARRATIVE RESEARCH

Definition	*Narrative research* is the study of how different humans experience the world around them, and it involves a methodology that allows people to tell the stories of their "storied lives."
Design(s)	Narrative studies usually focus on the experiences of individuals and their chronology and context using the technique of restorying to collaboratively construct a narrative account. The goal of a narrative research design is to collaboratively explore a phenomenon of interest with an individual in an effort to understand how individuals' past experiences impact the present and, potentially, the future.
Types of appropriate research questions	Narrative research can contribute to our understanding of educational issues such as adolescent drug use, cultural differences in diverse urban school settings, and the achievement gap that separates children raised in poverty from children who are less economically disadvantaged.
Key characteristics	• A focus on the experiences of individuals • A concern with the chronology of individuals' experiences • A focus on the construction of life stories based on data collected through interviews • Restorying as a technique for constructing the narrative account • Inclusion of context and place in the story • A collaborative approach that involves the researcher and the participants in the negotiation of the final text • A narrative constructed around the question "And then what happened?"

(continued)

Steps in the process	The narrative research process is a highly personal, intimate approach to educational research that demands a high degree of caring and sensitivity on the part of the researcher.
	1. Identify the purpose of the research study, and identify a phenomenon to explore.
	2. Identify an individual who can help you learn about the phenomenon.
	3. Develop initial narrative research questions.
	4. Consider the researcher's role (e.g., entry to the research site, reciprocity, and ethics) and obtain necessary permissions.
	5. Negotiate entry to the research setting in terms of a shared narrative with the research participant.
	6. Establish a relationship between researcher and participant that is mutually constructed and characterized by an equality of voice.
	7. Collaborate with the research participant to construct the narrative and to validate the accuracy of the story.
Potential challenges	• Trust • Developing and maintaining a mutually constructed relationship that is characterized by caring, respectfulness, and equality of voice
Example	How do teachers confront, and deal with, high school students who have drug problems?

NARRATIVE RESEARCH: DEFINITION AND PURPOSE

Narrative research is the study of how different humans experience the world around them, and it involves a methodology that allows people to tell the stories of their "storied lives."[1] Narrative researchers collect data about people's lives and, with the participants, collaboratively construct a narrative (i.e., written account) about the experiences and the meanings they attribute to the experiences.

Narrative research has a long history in diverse disciplines such as literature, history, art, film, theology, philosophy, psychology, anthropology, sociology, sociolinguistics, and education, and as such it does not fit neatly into a single scholarly field. Within the field of education, a number of recent trends have influenced the development of narrative research:

■ The increased emphasis in the past 15 years on teacher reflection, teacher research, action research, and self-study
■ The increased emphasis on teacher knowledge—for example, what teachers know, how they think, how they develop professionally, and how they make decisions in the classroom
■ The increased emphasis on empowering teachers by giving them voices in the educational research process through collaborative educational research efforts

These trends in education have resulted in a changing landscape of educational research and the promotion of scientifically based research practices to address social, cultural, and economic issues.

We live (and perhaps teach or work in schools in some other capacity) in a time when we are being challenged by educational issues such as adolescent drug use, cultural differences in diverse urban school settings, and the achievement gap that separates children raised in poverty from children who are less economically disadvantaged.

---

[1] "Stories and Experience and Narrative Inquiry," by F. M. Connelly and D. J. Clandinin, 1990, *Educational Research*, *19*(5), p. 2.

There are no silver bullets to solve these (and many other) issues that have come to the forefront of political and educational policy in the late 20th and early 21st centuries, but we can try to understand them better. By using narrative research in education, we attempt to increase understanding of central issues related to teaching and learning through the telling and retelling of teachers' stories. Narrative research provides educational researchers with an opportunity to validate the practitioner's voice in these important political and educational debates.

To visualize what *narrative* and *research* in the same sentence really mean, consider an example:

Hilda, a teacher at High High School, has students in her class who appear "distracted" (which is perhaps teacher code for under the influence of drugs). As an educational researcher, you decide that it would be helpful to know more about how Hilda deals with this significant educational issue and what she does to work with the distracted, possibly drug-using adolescents in her classroom. You think of a research question: "What have been Hilda's experiences in confronting and dealing with a student who has a drug problem?" To study this question, you plan to interview Hilda and listen to stories about her experiences working with one particular distracted student. You will talk to the student, the student's parents, other teachers, administrators, and counselors, all of whom are stakeholders in the student's educational experience. You also want to know about Hilda's life and any significant events that have affected her ability to work effectively with adolescent drug users. Perhaps Hilda

holds economic, social, cultural, or religious beliefs and values that affect her ability to deal with the drug culture in her school.

From the information you collect in interviews, you will slowly construct a story of Hilda's work with the troubled student. You will then share (i.e., retell) the story and, with Hilda's help, shape the final report of the narrative research. This final report will be Hilda's story of working with a student who is troubled by drug use, and it will contribute to our understanding of what it takes, on the part of a teacher, to work with adolescent drug users in our schools.

This example shows how narrative research allows the researcher to share the storied lives of teachers to provide insights and understandings about challenging educational issues as well as to enrich the lives of those teachers. Narrative research can contribute to our understanding of the complex world of the classroom and the nuances of the educational enterprise that exist between teachers and students. It simply is not always possible, nor desirable, to reduce our understanding of teaching and learning to numbers.

Types of Narrative Research

Like other types of qualitative research, narrative research may take a variety of forms. Some of these forms are listed in Figure 13.1.

How a particular narrative research approach is categorized depends on five characteristics: who authored the account (e.g., the researcher or the participant; note that the researcher is the participant in an autobiography), the scope of the

---

FIGURE 13.1 • Examples of types of narrative research forms

- Autobiographies
- Biographies
- Life writing
- Personal accounts
- Personal narratives
- Narrative interviews

- Personal documents
- Documents of life
- Life stories and life histories
- Oral histories
- Ethnohistories
- Ethnobiographies

- Autoethnographies
- Ethnopsychologies
- Person-centered ethnographies
- Popular memories
- Latin American *testimonios*
- Polish memoirs

Source: Creswell, John W., *Educational Research: Planning, Conducting, and Evaluating Quantitative and Qualitative Research*, 5th Edition, © 2015, p. 506. Reprinted by permission of Pearson Education, Inc., Upper Saddle River, NJ.

narrative (e.g., an entire life or an episode in a life), who provides the story (e.g., teachers or students), the kind of theoretical/conceptual framework that has influenced the study (e.g., critical or feminist theory), and whether all these elements are included in one narrative.[2] The nuances that distinguish the different forms of narrative research listed in Figure 13.1 are embedded in the disciplines in which they originated. If one specific style of narrative research piques your interest, you would do well to focus on the discipline-based literature to guide your research efforts.[3]

Narrative Analysis and the Analysis of Narrative

It is important to distinguish between narrative analysis and the analysis of narrative, which, despite their similar terminology, reflect unique processes.[4] In narrative analysis, the researcher collects descriptions of events through interviews and observations and synthesizes them into narratives or stories, similar to the process of restorying. In this type of narrative research, the story is the outcome of the research, an attempt by the researcher to answer how and why a particular outcome came about. Analysis of narrative is a process in which the researcher collects stories as data and analyzes common themes to produce a description that applies to all the stories captured in the narratives. Using this approach, the researcher develops a statement of themes as general knowledge about a collection of stories, but in so doing, underemphasizes the unique aspects of each story.

In this chapter, the focus of discussion is narrative analysis. That is, we are describing the development of a narrative or story that focuses on particular knowledge about how or why an outcome occurred rather than the development of a collection of stories and the search for themes to develop general knowledge about the collection of stories.

MyLab Education **Self-Check 13.1**

MyLab Education **Application Exercise 13.1:** Understanding the Purpose of Narrative Research

THE NARRATIVE RESEARCH PROCESS

The narrative research process is a highly personal, intimate approach to educational research that demands a high degree of caring and sensitivity on the part of the researcher. Although negotiating entry to the research setting is usually considered an ethical matter with assurances of confidentiality and anonymity, in narrative research it is necessary to think about this negotiation in terms of a shared narrative. That is, narrative research necessitates a relationship between the researcher and the participant more akin to a close friendship, where trust is a critical attribute. However, this friendship quality is not easily attained in an educational research setting (let alone in our lives in general). It is not uncommon for teachers, for example, to be cynical about any educational research, especially a style of research whose success relies on a friendship between the researcher and participant. Imagine how you would feel if approached by one of your educational research classmates (or colleagues at school) with a proposition such as this one: "I heard you talking about the difficulty you were having teaching kids who come to school stoned and wondered how you would feel about spending a lot of time talking to me about it. Maybe by working on the problem together, we can gain a greater understanding of the issues involved." Think about the kind of person you would trust to undertake this kind of research in your workplace; for your narrative study to succeed, you need to become that person. If you are a person who does not interact well with others, narrative research is probably not for you!

As Connelly and Clandinin[5] have suggested, it is important that the relationship between

---

[2] *Educational Research: Planning, Conducting, and Evaluating Quantitative and Qualitative Research* (5th ed.) by J. W. Creswell, 2015, Upper Saddle River, NJ: Pearson Education, Inc.

[3] For examples of how narrative research has been applied to a wide range of contexts (e.g., school-based violence, Holocaust survivors, undocumented immigrant families, and other challenging social problems), consider reading *Narrative Analysis: Studying the Development of Individuals in Society*, by C. Dauite and C. Lightfoot (Eds.), 2004, Thousand Oaks, CA: Sage.

[4] "Narrative Analysis in Qualitative Research," by D. E. Polkinghorne, 1995, in *Life History and Narrative* (pp. 5–23), by J. A. Hatch and R. Wisniewski (Eds.), London: Falmer Press.

[5] "Stories," by Connelly and Clandinin, 1990, pp. 2–14; *Narrative Inquiry: Experience and Story in Qualitative Research*, by D. J. Clandinin and F. M. Connelly, 2000, San Francisco, CA: Jossey-Bass.

researcher and participant be a mutually constructed one that is caring, respectful, and characterized by an equality of voice. If the researcher is unable to let go of the control that is typical in many styles of educational research, the narrative research process is not likely to succeed. The educational researcher using a narrative research methodology must be prepared to follow the lead of the research participant and, in the immortal words of *Star Trek,* go where "no man [or woman] has gone before!" In a very real sense, narrative research is a pioneering effort that takes a skilled researcher committed to living an individual's story and working in tandem with that individual.

Equality of voice is especially critical in the researcher–participant relationship because the participant (in all likelihood a teacher) must feel empowered to tell the story. Throughout the research process, the researcher must leave any judgmental baggage at home. The first hint of criticism or "ivory tower" superiority will be a nail in the research coffin. The researcher's intent must be clear: to empower the participant to tell the story and to be collaborative and respectful in the process. The researcher should listen to the participant's story before contributing his or her own perspective—even if asked. That is, the narrative researcher must not become an informant. After all, it is the participant's story we are trying to tell. As a patient listener, the researcher has an opportunity to validate the participant's voice and allows the participant to gain authority during the telling of the story.

A researcher interested in a narrative study must thus decide if he or she has the time, access, experience, personal style, and commitment to undertake this particular style of on-site research. Once the decision is made, the researcher can begin planning the study. Each study will have unique requirements, and the steps that follow are meant simply as guideposts, but you should notice a parallel between the steps and the outline for writing a qualitative research proposal.

To illustrate the steps in planning and conducting narrative research, we build on the example of our teacher, Hilda.

1. Identify the purpose of the research study, and identify a phenomenon to explore.
   The purpose of the study at High High School is to describe Hilda's experiences in confronting and dealing with a student who has a drug problem. The specific phenomenon that will be explored is that of adolescent drug use in high school.

2. Identify an individual who can help you learn about the phenomenon.
   Hilda, a teacher at High High School, has volunteered to work collaboratively with the researcher.

3. Develop initial narrative research questions.
   What have been Hilda's experiences in confronting and dealing with a student who has a drug problem? What life experiences influence the way Hilda approaches the problem?

4. Consider the researcher's role (e.g., entry to the research site, reciprocity, and ethics) and obtain necessary permissions.
   The researcher should seek permission from the Institutional Review Board (IRB), as well as any other permission required by the school or school district. In addition, the researcher must ask Hilda to sign an informed consent form.

5. Develop data collection methods, paying particular attention to interviewing, and collect the data.
   A narrative researcher utilizes a variety of narrative research data collection techniques, including interviewing and examining written and nonwritten sources of data.

6. Collaborate with the research participant to construct the narrative and to validate the accuracy of the story.
   The researcher and Hilda participate collaboratively in *restorying* the narrative and then validating the final written account (restorying—a writing process that involves synthesizing story elements—is described later in this chapter).

7. Write the narrative account.

MyLab Education **Self-Check 13.2**

MyLab Education **Application Exercise 13.2:** Evaluating Research Articles: Identifying Steps in the Research Process for a Narrative Study

KEY CHARACTERISTICS OF NARRATIVE RESEARCH

Narrative research can be characterized by the following elements:[6]

- A focus on the experiences of individuals
- A concern with the chronology of individuals' experiences
- A focus on the construction of life stories based on data collected through interviews
- Restorying as a technique for constructing the narrative account
- Inclusion of context and place in the story
- A collaborative approach that involves the researcher and the participants in the negotiation of the final text
- A narrative constructed around the question "And then what happened?"

The narrative research process is similar to the construction of a biography in that the educational researcher does not have direct access to observational data but must rely on primary data sources (e.g., the participant's recollections) and secondary sources (e.g., written documents by the participant); data are collected primarily through interviews and written exchanges. As mentioned previously, narrative research places considerable emphasis on the collaborative construction of the written account—the narrative text. Although researchers using other styles of on-site research may share accounts with research participants as a way to test the trustworthiness of those accounts, they place little emphasis on the restorying process that is quite unique to narrative research.

MyLab Education **Self-Check 13.3**

MyLab Education **Application Exercise 13.3:**
The Key Characteristics of Narrative Research

---

[6] Elements of narrative research were adapted from those in *Educational Research*, Creswell, 2015, and "Narrative Analysis," by C. K. Riessman, 2002, in *The Qualitative Researcher's Companion*, by A. M. Huberman and M. B. Miles, Thousand Oaks, CA: Sage.

NARRATIVE RESEARCH TECHNIQUES

Empirical data are central to narrative research in spite of the inevitable interpretation that occurs during the data collection process (e.g., during the telling and restorying activities). However, interpretation does not mean that the outcome of the process is fiction. The narrative researcher, like researchers using other on-site research approaches, must be prepared to use multiple data sources to counteract challenges that narratives could be written without ever leaving home. Accordingly, Clandinin and Connelly[7] recommend that data be in the form of field notes on shared research experiences. These experiences occur as the researcher collects data through journal and letter writing and documents such as lesson plans and class newsletters.

The immensity of the writing task for the narrative researcher becomes clear if you consider what is involved—for both the researcher and the participant—in "living the story." The main challenge involves the participants' abilities to live their lives while telling their stories. Picture yourself as Hilda, the teacher focused on coping with adolescent drug users in her classroom. Can you imagine yourself fully engaged in living the daily life of a classroom teacher while relaying the story of your daily events and the meaning of your actions to a researcher? You might feel as if you were having a kind of out-of-body experience in which you had to look down on yourself from above. As Connelly and Clandinin noted, "A person is, at once, engaged in living, telling, retelling, and reliving stories."[8] Now imagine yourself as the researcher who is faced with the task of recording and communicating Hilda's story. It is no wonder that the researcher and the research participant must establish a high degree of trust and respect akin to the kind of relationship we all expect in a close friendship.

As with other methods used in qualitative research, narrative research relies on the triangulation of data to address issues of trustworthiness. As noted earlier, the data collection techniques used in narrative research are sometimes criticized as

[7] *Narrative Inquiry*, Clandinin and Connelly, 2000.
[8] "Stories," Connelly and Clandinin, 1990, p. 4.

leading to fictitious, romanticized versions of life in schools. Researchers can best counter this criticism by ensuring the use of multiple data sources as well as the collaborative negotiation of the written narrative account.

In the following sections, we focus on data collection techniques somewhat unique to narrative research (e.g., storytelling, letter writing, autobiographical and biographical writing, and other narrative sources). In writing about personal experience methods, Clandinin and Connelly described these data collection techniques as "field texts"[9] that are focused on capturing the essence of collaboratively created artifacts of the field experience of the researcher and the participant.

Restorying

A characteristic of narrative research that distinguishes it from other on-site research approaches is the technique of restorying the stories that individuals tell about their life experiences. According to Creswell, **restorying** is "the process in which the researcher gathers stories, analyzes them for key elements of the story (e.g., time, place, plot, and scene), and then rewrites the story to place it in a chronological sequence."[10] Often, individuals share stories about their experiences with researchers but without attention to the real-time order of events. For example, participants may share specific details of a vacation in a somewhat random sequence, backtracking to fill in earlier omissions (e.g., "Oh, I forgot to tell you that before we got to the campsite. . .") or jumping forward as certain details of the event call to mind other, related events (e.g., "Telling you about this trip makes me think of the one we took last year, when the bear showed up. . ."). With each interview, the researcher records these recollections, amassing many pages of notes, which serve as the raw data for the narrative account. Although the notes contain many interesting stories and details, they do not constitute a narrative account of the participant's experiences because they lack chronology and coherence. The researcher must go through the process of restorying to provide that coherence.

The restorying process has three steps:[11]

1. The researcher conducts the interview and transcribes the audio recording to provide a written record of the raw data from the interview. This process involves noting not just the spoken words but also the nuances of the interview—for example, humor, laughter, anger, and so on.

2. The researcher retranscribes the data (i.e., condenses and annotates the transcripts) based on the key elements that are identified in the story. For example, suppose that Hilda (our teacher at High High School) described how she copes with students who come to class under the influence of drugs. From her comments, we may identify and highlight certain themes, such as seeking assistance from a school nurse or counselor and establishing individual educational plans and contracts.

3. The researcher organizes the story into a chronological sequence with attention to the setting, characters, actions, problems, and resolutions. For example, Hilda's story may be set in the context of her classroom with the adolescents who use drugs (i.e., characters) and may be focused on the actions of the students (e.g., their off-task behavior and other relevant classroom behavior), the problems caused by the actions (e.g., other students distracted, teacher time focused on a few students), and any resolutions to the problems that Hilda employed (e.g., seeking assistance from outside the classroom, establishing learning contracts with students).

After restorying is completed, the researcher invites the participant to collaborate on the final narrative of the individual's experiences. For example, the educational researcher and Hilda would collaboratively construct a narrative that describes Hilda's experiences working with adolescent drug users, as well as the meanings these experiences had for Hilda. This collaboration between researcher and participant is critical to ensure that there is no gap between the "narrative told and

[9] "Personal Experience Methods," by D. J. Clandinin and F. M. Connelly, 1994, in *Handbook of Qualitative Research* (p. 419), by N. K. Denzin and Y. S. Lincoln (Eds.), Thousand Oaks, CA: Sage.
[10] *Educational Research* (p. 511), Creswell, 2015.

[11] Ibid.

narrative reported."[12] One test of the trustworthiness of the narrative account is the participant's validation that the account is representative of the individual's lived experiences, as relayed in the interviews. A valid and clear narrative should increase our collective understanding of the phenomenon under study—in Hilda's case, how a teacher confronts and deals with adolescent drug users in the classroom.

Oral History

One method for creating field texts is to have participants share their oral histories. An oral history may be obtained by the researcher during a structured interview schedule with predetermined questions (and hence with the researcher's agenda clearly stated) or through an open-ended approach in which the researcher asks participants to tell their own stories in their own ways. In constructing an oral history, a researcher may ask a participant to create a time line (also known as a chronicle) that is divided into segments of significant events or memories. An oral history of a teacher working with adolescents who use drugs, for example, may include a time line from the beginning of the year (or previous years) that indicates significant events related to student drug use, such as when students were suspended from school because they violated a zero tolerance policy or when students were arrested for drug possession. The time line is a helpful tool for the narrative researcher attempting to make sense of the importance of these events in the teacher's overall story. The teacher may also be asked to expand on these significant events and to write a description in a journal. Together, the chronicle and journal of the teacher's experiences provide the narrative researcher with a powerful descriptive tool.

Examining Photographs, Memory Boxes, and Other Artifacts

Teachers have a proclivity for acting like pack rats. The materials they collect, apart from the obvious curriculum materials, often include cards from former students, newspaper clippings, yearbooks, photographs, and audio and video recordings of student performances. Often, these artifacts adorn a teacher's desk and bulletin board as badges of honor. The narrative researcher can use these artifacts as prompts to elicit details about the teacher's life in school and in particular the phenomenon under investigation. For example, a teacher may share thank-you cards from students who, due to the teacher's intervention, were able to kick a drug habit.

Storytelling

Narrative research affords many opportunities to engage participants in storytelling. Teachers, by nature, are master storytellers, and many will happily share stories about their experiences in school as "competent narrators of their lives."[13] The manner in which narrative researchers engage participants in storytelling sessions has a great impact on the nature of the story. That is, when storytelling is a routine part of the narrative research process, researchers can regularly add to their understanding of a "day in the life" of a teacher who is focused on finding a resolution to a challenging educational problem. Often, stories are shared when a recorder is not handy, and the researcher will have to record field notes and verbatim accounts as necessary. These stories are critical in providing insights into teachers' work and explanations of their actions.

Letter Writing

Letter writing (or e-mail exchange) is another way to engage participants in writing about their lived experiences and to engage the narrative researcher and participant in a dialogue. The commitment of thought to text helps both the researcher and the participant. Because e-mail is widely available, this kind of dialogue can be easily initiated and maintained. The dialogue serves as a working chronicle of the participant's thoughts on issues related to the research phenomenon and thus provides the narrative researcher with valuable insights into the evolving, tentative interpretations that the participant may be considering. Further, if each e-mail includes previous messages, the narrative researcher and the participant can reflect on the evolution of the themes by reading the increasing record of the narrative dialogue.

[12] Ibid. p. 514.

[13] *The Active Interview* (p. 29), by J. A. Holstein and J. F. Gubrium, 1995, Thousand Oaks, CA: Sage.

Autobiographical and Biographical Writing

Engaging a participant in constructing or collaboratively constructing a life history through autobiographical or biographical writing has the potential to broaden the narrative researcher's understandings about past events and experiences that have affected the participant's experiences with the phenomenon under investigation. Perhaps Hilda, for example, has had other professional or personal experiences with adolescent drug users that would contribute to an understanding of how she operates in her current educational environment. Autobiographical or biographical writing about Hilda's life could bring these experiences to light. Again, the use of e-mail could provide a wonderful electronic record of the emerging narrative.

Other Narrative Data Sources

A researcher can access many other narrative data sources that can contribute to the construction of the written narrative. For example, documents such as lesson plans, parent newsletters, and personal philosophy statements are readily available. These sources provide windows into a world of classrooms that is not easily accessible to outsiders.

Narrative research relies heavily on interviewing and observing, which comes with the challenges of transcribing recorded interviews and recording field notes. Thus, the use of readily accessible digital dictation tools is described in the Digital Research Tools feature.

MyLab Education **Self-Check 13.4**

MyLab Education **Application Exercise 13.4:** Evaluating Research Articles: Evaluating a Narrative Study

MyLab Education **Application Exercise 13.5:** Collecting Narrative Data

WRITING THE NARRATIVE

The final step in the narrative research process is writing the narrative, which is again a collaboration between participant and researcher. Many data collection techniques used in narrative research result in products—such as e-mail, letters, and a participant's biography—that often end up as part of the final written account. Given the collaborative nature of narrative research from the beginning until the end, the negotiation of the final narrative account should be relatively easy to achieve. However, it is worth remembering that the goal in conducting narrative research is to "learn about the general from the particular."[14] As such, we should be modest in the claims we make for the collaboratively constructed written narrative that is the final product of our research efforts.

[14] "Narrative Analysis," Riessman, 2002, p. 262.

Digital Research Tools

DRAGON MOBILE ASSISTANT, DRAGON DICTATION, AND DRAGON PROFESSIONAL INDIVIDUAL FOR MAC AND PC

Speech recognition programs have been available for many years but were often cumbersome to use and expensive to purchase. However, there are now many smartphone and computer applications available that will save the narrative researcher some of the time spent writing field notes and transcribing interviews.

Dragon Mobile Assistant

An app for your smartphone, Dragon Mobile Assistant combines the easy-to-use voice recognition software application with a host of other tools for the on-the-go researcher. Need help scheduling an interview? Check your calendar and send an e-mail to your research participants while driving to

(continued)

another research site. This free app can help record your field notes, send e-mails and texts, and make your dinner reservations while automatically detecting the need for hands-free operation. For more information visit www.dragonmobileapps.com.

Dragon Dictation

Dragon Dictation is an easy-to-use voice recognition application that allows you to speak and instantly see your content in a text form that can be edited, e-mailed, or even posted to blogs. With a little practice, Dragon Dictation gives the researcher the potential to record observations, field notes, and interviews at five times the speed of typing on a keyboard. This is also a great tool to use to record your thoughts in the car while you are driving to your home or office, and best of all, it's a free application for smartphone users. As Dragon Dictation claims, "Turn talk into type while you are on the go." Dragon Dictation is available for Apple iOS platforms and can also be used on the Android operation system.

Dragon Professional Individual for Mac and PC

If you're not comfortable with talking and driving and you are looking for a more advanced software package, Dragon Professional Individual for Mac and PC allows you to convert talk to type at a computer. This program could be used to record interviews with research participants and would therefore save the researcher time spent transcribing. Dragon claims to leverage a next generation speech engine called "deep learning technology" that allows users to also transcribe voice recordings from smartphones or portable voice recorders to text with 99% accuracy. Unlike Dragon Dictation, it is not free, but it may become your favorite computer application and narrative research time-saving tool. For further information visit www.nuance.com.

MyLab Education **Self-Check 13.5**

SUMMARY

NARRATIVE RESEARCH: DEFINITION AND PURPOSE

1. Narrative research is the study of the lives of individuals as told through the stories of their experience, including a discussion of the meaning of those experiences for the individual.
2. Narrative research is conducted to increase understanding of central issues related to teaching and learning through the telling and retelling of teachers' stories.

Types of Narrative Research

3. How a narrative research approach is characterized depends on who authored the account, the scope of the narrative, the kind of theoretical/conceptual framework that has influenced the study, and whether all these elements are included in the one narrative.

Narrative Analysis and the Analysis of Narrative

4. In narrative analysis, the researcher collects descriptions of events through interviews and observations and synthesizes them into narratives or stories. Analysis of narrative is a process in which the researcher collects stories as data and analyzes common themes to produce a description that applies to all the stories captured in the narratives.

THE NARRATIVE RESEARCH PROCESS

5. The relationship between researcher and participant must be a mutually constructed one that is caring, respectful, and characterized by an equality of voice. Participants in narrative research must feel empowered to tell their stories.
6. A narrative researcher first identifies a phenomenon to explore, selects an individual, seeks permissions, and poses initial research questions. After determining the role of the researcher and the data collection methods, the researcher and participant collaborate to construct the narrative, validate the accuracy of the story, and write the narrative account.

KEY CHARACTERISTICS OF NARRATIVE RESEARCH

7. Narrative research focuses on the experiences of individuals and their chronology.
8. Narrative research uses the technique of restorying to construct a narrative account based on data collected through interviews.
9. Narrative research incorporates context and place in the story.
10. The construction of a narrative always involves responding to the question "And then what happened?"

NARRATIVE RESEARCH TECHNIQUES

11. Narrative researchers employ a number of unique data collection techniques, including restorying, oral history, examination of artifacts, storytelling, letter writing, and autobiographical and biographical writing.

WRITING THE NARRATIVE

12. Writing the narrative is a collaboration between participant and researcher.

For Whom the School Bell Tolls: Conflicting Voices Inside an Alternative High School

JEONG-HEE KIM
Kansas State University

ABSTRACT This article is a study of conflicting voices inside an alternative high school in Arizona. Voices of alternative schools are, quite often, not included in the discourse of curriculum reform even though the number of alternative schools is growing every year. Bakhtinian novelness of polyphony, chronotope, and carnival are incorporated into an arts-based, storied form of representation to provoke empathic understanding among readers. Multiple voices (polyphony) of the school are juxtaposed within a certain time and space (chronotope) while all the different voices are valued equally (carnival) to represent conflicting views on public alternative school experiences. The purpose of the article is to provide readers with vicarious access to tensions that exist in an alternative school, so that they may engage in questioning the nature and purpose of these spaces. In so doing, the study aims to promote dialogic conversations about "best practice" for disenfranchised students who are subject to experiencing educational inequalities in the current era of accountability and standardization.

Introduction

(01)   One of the school experiences that are available for teenagers who dropped out or were expelled from traditional high schools is the alternative school. One of its goals is to provide students with a second chance at school success. Although definitions or characteristics of alternative schools vary by state or even school district, one of the commonalities they share is that students who attend an alternative school did not do well in traditional schools. These students tend to be labeled as "at risk" of school failure no matter how much potential they may have, and are likely to be excluded in the discourse of curriculum reform. As Oakes points out in the forward for Kelly (1993), alternative schooling tends to perpetuate social, political, economic, and educational inequalities and continues to be an undercurrent of education without scrutiny. While many alternative education programs serving the growing population of at-risk students are run by school districts, little research has been done to evaluate the success or the failure of the public alternative schools or programs (Conley, 2002).

(02)   This article is a case study of Borderlands Alternative High School (pseudonym) in Arizona, which is a public school that serves about 250 students. Five different voices of its inhabitants: the principal, the security guard, a teacher, and two students, are presented in arts-based, narrative inquiry. These voices reveal tensions and conflicts that exist inside Borderlands, which may reflect issues and problems that exist in other alternative schools. Rather than to provide a final solution, the purpose of the article is to promote dialogic conversations among educators about ways in which educators can better serve a growing number of students who are at risk of school failure. The article begins with a brief review of the literature on alternative education, then specific research methods are considered, next the theoretical framework of Bakhtinian novelness is briefly explicated, this is followed by the voices of the five protagonists, finally in the epilogue, the voice of the researcher is presented.

> The purpose of this research is to promote dialogic conversations among educators about ways in which educators can better serve a growing number of students who are at risk of school failure. Specifically, the research uses an arts-based narrative research approach to capture the voices of five participants ("inhabitants") of the alternative high school.
>
> *Is this purpose statement clear enough to allow the reader to understand the research questions that will be investigated?*

Review of the Literature on Alternative Education

Alternative education proliferated in the United States in the late 1960s and the early 1970s as educational priorities shifted back to the progressive education movement. People who were unhappy with traditional curriculum hailed alternative public schools that subscribed to the ideas of progressive education, which called for a free, open policy that emphasized the development of self-concept, problem solving, and humanistic approaches (Conley, 2002; Goodman, 1999; Raywid, 1995; Young, 1990). These alternative schools attempted to offer places where students would have greater freedom and opportunities for success than in traditional schools, affirming that one unified curriculum could not be sufficient for all (Conley, 2002). Many disgruntled parents transferred their children to alternative schools that incorporated the concepts of "Free School" and "Open School" into the school curricula in order to meet students' different learning styles, needs, and interests. However, most alternative schools of this era were short-lived for various reasons, e.g., internal financial mismanagement, public pressure for school accountability and the "Back to Basics" movement that followed in the 1980s (Marsh & Willis, 2003). (03)

In the mid 1990s, alternative learning programs and schools including public and private voucher programs, charter schools, and magnet programs, started emerging in an effort to solve issues of poor student achievement, ineffective pedagogical methods, and the increasing inability to meet the needs of diverse families (Conley, 2002). Alternative schools in this era "satisfy the need to provide choice and diversity within a monopolistic bureaucratic giant of public education" (Conley, 2002, p. 177). For instance, alternative schools in Washington State have been successful as an alternative to traditional public education, with schools effectively meeting students' different needs (see Billings, 1995). Billings states: (04)

> Experiential learning, off-campus course work, learning contracts, democratic decision making, new learning environments, restructuring of time, outcome-based credit, parental involvement, project based learning, sensitivity to diverse learning styles, process focused curriculum, and small size are just a few of the features that have long characterized alternative schools in Washington. (p. 1)

Other recent research on alternative education, however, shows that the public views alternative schools as places for students whose behaviors are disruptive, deviant, and dysfunctional (see Dryfoos, 1997; Howell, 1995; Leone, Rutherford, & Nelson, 1991; Mcgee, 2001). Rather than being recognized as alternative solutions for students whose needs are not being met by traditional schools, alternative schools are believed to exist to keep all the "trouble makers" in one place in order to protect the students who remain in traditional schools (Mcgee, 2001; National Association of State Boards of Education, 1994). They also tend to work to keep the expelled students off the streets in order to prevent them from committing a crime (Sprague & Tobin, 2000). Furthermore, Nolan and Anyon (2004) raise a concern that some alternative schools serve as "an interface between the school and the prison," calling it the "school/prison continuum" (p. 134). (05)

According to the first national study about public alternative schools and programs conducted by the National Center for Educational Statistics (NCES), there were 10,900 public alternative schools and programs serving approximately 612,900 at-risk students in the nation during the 2000–2001 school year (National Center for Educational Statistics, 2002). NCES also reported that alternative schools were disproportionately located in urban districts, districts with high minority students, and districts with high poverty concentrations. This situation, in some cases, has rendered alternative schools as "enclaves for black, Latino, native American, and poor white students" (06)

(Arnove & Strout, 1980, p. 463), and "warehouses for academically underprepared sons and daughters of working-class families or single parents receiving welfare" (Kelly, 1993, p. 3).

(07)   More specifically, in the State of Arizona, the State Department of Education announced formal definitions of alternative schools in 1999. According to the Arizona Department of Education (ADE), the school must intend to serve students exclusively in one or more of the following categories: students with behavioral issues (documented history of disruptive behavior); students identified as dropouts; students in poor academic standing who are more than one year behind on academic credits, or who have a demonstrated pattern of failing grades; pregnant and/or parenting students; and adjudicated youth (Arizona Department of Education, 2002). Every alternative school must meet the "achievement profile" provided by the ADE in the information packet on Standards and Accountability. This profile includes: ninety-five percent (95%) of students taking Arizona's Instrument to Measure Standards (AIMS), which is a state exit exam that all high school students have to pass to be able to graduate with a high school diploma; decreasing dropout rate; and increasing percentage of graduates who demonstrate proficiency on the Standards via AIMS. Every alternative school is expected to have 100% of graduates demonstrate proficiency on the Standards via AIMS by 2006 (Arizona Department of Education, 2002).

(08)   The research site, Borderlands Alternative High School, is one of the twelve public alternative schools in the East Valley school district in Arizona. Borderlands houses students from ninth through twelfth grade and accepts students only by referrals from principals of conventional public schools. Enrollment at Borderlands has increased every year since the school opened in 1999. One hundred and fifty-two students enrolled at Borderlands during the 1999–2000 school year, 291 students during the 2000–2001 school year, and 350 students during the 2001–2002 school year.

Research Methods and Methodology

(09) Fieldwork was conducted from August through December 2003. Data were collected Monday through Thursday, about five hours each day, by means of observation and participant observation. I took part in classroom activities, interacted with students and faculty, helped students with schoolwork, and invited them to talk about their school and life experiences while having lunch. A main approach to the fieldwork was "conversation as research" (Kvale, 1996), in which conversations about school experiences and daily life with students, teachers, and the school staff were made during break time, lunch hours, and in class. This approach not only helped me build informal relationships with each member of the school community, but also helped me understand the ways the school was perceived by them.

    More formal conversations with students and staff took the form of semi-structured interviews with open-ended questions. The five protagonists in this study: Mrs. Principal, Mr. Hard (pseudonym, school security guard), Holly (pseudonym, female student), Jose (pseudonym, male student) and Ms. Bose (pseudonym, teacher), were interviewed individually during their school hours except for Ms. Bose. Ms. Bose invited me to her home for dinner where the interview was conducted. Each interview lasted about an hour and a half. The interviewees were asked to talk about their backgrounds, views on the alternative schooling, and their school experiences. Interviews were tape-recorded and then transcribed.

(11)   In terms of research methodology, this study employs narrative inquiry, which has become an increasingly influential technique within teacher education during the last decade (Goodson, 1995). Using narrative inquiry, educational researchers interrogate the nature of the dominant stories through which we have shaped our understandings of education, and challenge the view of schooling framed in a predictable, fragmented, and paradigmatic

---

(10)

> Researcher's role in the study was as an observer and participant observer. The researcher participated in "classroom activities, interacted with students and faculty, helped students with schoolwork, and invited them to talk about their school and live experiences while having lunch."
>
> *How does the researcher's role reflect the goals of narrative research?*

> Data collection methods included the use of semi-structured interviews with open-ended questions.

way (Casey, 1993; Connelly & Clandinin, 1990; Goodson, 1995, 1992; Munro, 1998; Sparkes, 1994). In this study, data are analyzed through *narrative analysis* or *narrative configuration*. This is the "procedure through which the researcher organizes the data elements into a coherent developmental account" (Polkinghorne, 1995, p. 15). That is, in the process of narrative analysis, the researcher extracts an emerging theme from the fullness of lived experiences presented in the data themselves and configures stories, making a range of disconnected research data elements coherent, so that the story can appeal to the reader's understanding and imagination (Kerby, 1991; Polkinghorne, 1995; Spence, 1986).

> Data were analyzed through narrative analysis that resulted in a narrative that captured themes from the lived experiences of the study's participants.

This narrative analysis creates arts-based research texts as an outcome of research. According to Barone and Eisner (1997), some qualities that make educational stories arts-based texts include: the use of expressive, contextualized, and vernacular forms of language; the promotion of empathic understanding of the lives of characters; and the creation of a virtual reality. A virtual reality means that the stories seem real to the reader so that the reader is able to identify the episodes in the text from his/her own experiences, and thus believe in the possibility or the credibility of the virtual world as an analogue to the "real" one (Barone & Eisner, 1997). Virtual reality is an important element of an arts-based text as it promotes empathic understanding of the lives of the protagonists. (12)

In this article the five protagonists share their backgrounds, views, emotions, and reflections about their alternative school experiences using their expressive, contextualized, and vernacular language. Their stories are constructed in the first person. When stories are told in the first person, they can give the reader the illusion of spontaneous speech, that is, "the impression of listening to an unrehearsed, rambling monologue" (Purcell, 1996, p. 277), contributing to the creation of a virtual reality. (13)

> Researcher collaborated with participants to construct first-person accounts of their experiences.
>
> ---
>
> *Did the researcher employ restorying as the technique for constructing the participants' narratives?*

Theoretical Framework: Bakhtinian Novelness

Through narrative inquiry, educational researchers try to understand the lived experiences of teachers or students and transform this understanding into significant social and educational implications (Phillion, He, & Connelly, 2005). Using Bakhtinian novelness as a theoretical framework is particularly important in the story-telling nature of narrative inquiry as it facilitates the understanding of human experiences in a social and educational context. It allows each protagonist to speak for him- or herself, while there is no single, unified point of view that dominates (Tanaka, 1997). (14)

According to Bakhtin (1975/1981), all stories are not the same. Depending on what kind of purpose a story has, it becomes either an epic or a novel. In an epic, stories are told from one point of view in one language, outside of considerations of time and particular places. There is only one world, one reality that is ordered and complete. On the other hand, a novel represents many languages competing for truth from different vantage points. The world of the novel is incomplete and imperfect. There is not a sense of formal closure in a novel: "One may begin the story at almost any moment, and finish at almost any moment" (Bakhtin, 1975/1981, p. 31). This "impulse to continue" and "impulse to end" are found in novels and they are possible only in a world with open-endedness. (15)

Bakhtin posits three concepts to specify the nature of the novel, or "novelness": polyphony, chronotope, and carnival. First, polyphony, or a language of heteroglossia, refers to "a plurality of independent, unmerged voices and consciousness" (Bakhtin, 1963/1984, p. 6). The polyphonic, dialogized heteroglossia of the novel involves a special multivoiced use of language, in which no language enjoys an absolute privilege. Different languages are used and different voices are heard without having one voice privileged over the others. Each language or voice is continually tested and retested in relation to others, any one of which may turn out to be capable of becoming as (16) good or better a language of truth—if only tentatively, on a specific set of occasions, or with respect to particular questions (Morson & Emerson, 1990). In this way, the novel can offer rich images of languages. The creation of images of languages is, in turn, a form of sociological probing and an exploration of values and beliefs, and these images are tools for understanding the social belief systems (Morson & Emerson, 1990).

(17)   The second concept of novelness, chronotope, emphasizes time and space. For Bakhtin, polyphony is not enough to promote dialogic conversations. A chronotope is a way of understanding experiences; it is a specific form-shaping ideology for understanding the nature of events and actions (Morson & Emerson, 1990). For the voices to reflect believable individual experiences, they should be put in particular times and particular spaces. Bakhtin (1975/1981) states that "time, as it were, thickens, takes on flesh, becomes artistically visible; likewise, space becomes charged and responsive to the movement of time, plot and history" (p. 84, cited in Morson & Emerson, 1990). Chronotope, therefore, becomes important in understanding our lives as individuals and social beings.

(18)   The third concept of the dialogic nature of "novelness" is the concept of carnival or "the carnivalesque." Carnival, according to Bakhtin (1975/1981), is a concept in which everyone is an active participant, openness is celebrated, hierarchy is invisible, and norms are reversed, like in popular festivals. The carnivalesque novel, through "laughter, irony, humor, and elements of self-parody" (Bakhtin 1975/1981, p. 7), offers an unofficial truth, where the symbols of power and violence are disturbed and counter-narratives are promoted with equal value. The novel is indebted to the spirit of carnival in creating a genuine dialogue. Bakhtin believes that the novel should play the same role in literature that carnival is alleged to play in the real life of cultures (Morson & Emerson, 1990). One formal and privileged way of life or way of thinking is discarded, but different views and styles are valued by representing the wide range of languages and experiences in the novel. In the carnival, voices of the marginalized or silenced are promoted and respected.

(19)   In brief, using Bakhtinian novelness of polyphony, chronotope, and carnival as a theoretical framework is particularly effective for the issues of power, resistance, tensions, and conflicts that occur in schools (Tanaka, 1997). As such, conflicting voices heard in a text with Bakhtinian novelness may "raise important questions about the topics under discussion, challenging the reader to rethink the values that undergird certain social practices" (Barone, 2001, p. 157).

(20)   In the following narratives, you will hear five different voices: first, Mr. Hard is the school security guard, a big, White, middle-class, former police officer, who has been working at Borderlands for two years; second, Holly is a ninth grader, White, working-class girl, who wants to be a lawyer; third, Ms. Bose is a White, Italian descent and ninth grade science and math teacher, who has been working with at-risk students for 25 years; fourth, Jose is a half-Hispanic and half-White male student, who wants to be a great musician; and finally, Mrs. Principal is a White, middle-class administrator, who is devoted to making her school an "achieving" school.

The Voice of Mr. Hard, the Security Guard

(21)   I am the security guard at this alternative high school. I got retired from a police department where I worked for 20 years before I came here. My wife is a director at a hospital here in Phoenix. Her job brought us here from Pittsburgh two years ago. I have two sons and a daughter. Two of them are happily married, and my youngest son is in college. My hobby is fixing and building stuff around the house on weekends, and Home Depot is my favorite shopping place.

This is my second year in this school, and I've been enjoying my job so (22) far. My main responsibility is to make sure that our school is a safe place. As you know, kids these days can be dangerous. Especially kids in this school have a lot of problems that regular schools don't want to deal with. That's why they are here. A lot of kids have a criminal history. Some kids have already been to jail. My previous career working as a cop has helped me a lot dealing with these kids who have a potential to commit a crime. That's why I got hired so quickly. Our principal whom I'm closely working with gave me the authority to be in charge of the student discipline. My position here is to be a hard-liner. I'm the final set of rules that students have to abide by. That's my background. I spent a lot of money on my education at the police academy and I'm bringing that knowledge to discipline these kids. That's what I like about my job. I try to help them succeed by using my resources. If a student fails to go by rules, then he or she has to deal with me. You know, they're here because they can't control their attitudes. They can't control what they're saying. They are violent, throw temper tantrums, and talk back. There are different ways to deal with them and they are not in the textbook.

Teachers can be flexible. When they don't want to deal with disruptive (23) students, they can send them to me. My job here is to inculcate rules to kids. Some of you go to football games Sunday afternoon. When there are no referees, what kind of game is it? It's going to be a mess, right? With referees and rules, we have an organized game. Likewise, I'm the referee here. I'm the rules. Students have to face me if they don't follow the rules. I'm the one who keeps the game organized, and keeps the game from getting out of hand. My responsibility is to maintain the rules. We're trying to help these kids become successful young adults in the society. In that sense, we've been very productive. I've seen a lot of difference among students since I started working here.

Kids try to avoid me at school. Out of sight, out of fight. I know they (24) don't like me. That's fine with me. I don't want to be liked. I just want to be respected. Don't get me wrong. I'm not saying that I don't have sympathy for them. I do feel sorry for these kids because they have a lot of baggage. They come from broken, poor, and abusive families. They don't fit the mainstream. They have lost the idea of where the main road is. So, our job is to put them back on the right track. It can be done only by strict discipline. They need to learn how to behave so that they can function in a society as a cashier or something. If they don't follow the rules, we kick them out of school. In fact, we suspended a lot of students this year. It's our way of showing them they are wrong.

As you can imagine, we have a zero-tolerance policy for students who (25) violate school rules. Holly has been my target these days. She is just impossible. I don't know what she's gonna turn into in the future. She's violent and gets into trouble every other day. She smokes, violates dress codes, and talks back to teachers, just to name a few. We have given her several warnings. She's quite smart, but being smart doesn't count here. What matters is whether or not one obeys the rules. On the first week of October, I caught her smoking in the restroom again. When I asked her to come with me, she wouldn't. So I tried to call the police, but Holly picked up a handful of rocks and started throwing them at me. She was ferocious! We gave her a five-day suspension.

And then, our school threw a Halloween party for students three weeks (26) later. Teachers and staff donated money to buy hamburger patties, sausages, and other stuff for students. I brought my own barbeque grill and tools from home and took charge of barbequing. I was happy to be the chef of the day. I was happy to see students relaxing, having fun, and enjoying food that I cooked. It was so nice to see students and teachers mingling together, playing basketball and other games. It was a nice change. The party was going well for the most part. But, right before the party was over, Holly got into an argument with this Black girl, Shawnee. Holly got mad at her and mooned Shawnee who was with other ninth graders. This incident was reported to the principal, who called Holly's mom to ask her to appear at the school the next day. Holly got expelled after the "happy" Halloween party. Hope this expulsion will teach her something!

The Voice of Holly, the Goofy Snoopy

(27) My name is Holly. I just turned fifteen in July. I was born in Mesa, Arizona, and have never moved out of Arizona. I'm a White girl with a little bit of Native American descent from my mom's side. I heard my mom's great-grandma was some sort of a Native American. I don't know what tribe, though. I'm tall, about five feet seven inches, and have long blonde hair with red highlights. I like to wear tight, low-rise jeans and a black "dead-rose" shirt that has a picture of a human skull surrounded by roses. I used to wear the Gothic style of clothes in my junior high, all in black from head to toe, wearing heavy, clumpy army boots. But I got tired of it, so, now I'm into Punk. I have a tattoo on my lower back and have a silver ring on the center of my tongue. I got my tongue pierced on my 15th birthday. I like it a lot. My mom hates it, though. But I don't care. She hates whatever I do, anyway. She's a bitch. She works at a car body shop, buffing and painting old cars with her boyfriend who is living with us. I can't wait to leave home. As soon as I turn 18, I'll say bye to them and leave home. I'm tired of them ordering me to do this and that.

(28) Anyways. . . My nickname is Snoopy. I got it in eighth grade for jumping and dancing like Snoopy at the Fiesta Shopping Mall. I just felt like doing it. People gathered around me and shouted, "Snoopy, Snoopy!" I did that for an hour. I didn't feel embarrassed at all. Since then, my friends started calling me Snoopy. They think I'm goofy. Yes, I am goofy. I don't care what others think about me. If I feel like doing something, I just do it. No second thought. But at school, I get into trouble because of that. Teachers don't like my personality. They think I'm just acting out. In fact, I was very upset when Ms. Bose told me the other day to change my personality. Do you know what she told me? She said, "I don't like your personality. You need to stop acting out. You need to change your personality. Then, your school life will be a lot easier." I said to myself, '*Bullshit*!' Change my personality? It took me fifteen years to develop it, for Christ's sake! I don't care if she likes it or not. I'm unique. I'm different. I have my own opinions unlike other kids. But teachers think I'm acting out, disruptive, unruly, and rude. Because I like to speak up, I have a history of being kicked out of classrooms and sent to ALC (Alternative Learning Center) where other "disruptive" kids are isolated, supposedly working on their individual assignments.

(29) My friends like to talk to me about their personal issues because I give them a solution. Having said that, I think I have a leadership personality. I want to be a lawyer. I like to argue with people: my mom, her boyfriend, teachers, and my classmates. I win them all. Teachers are actually my worst enemies, but I'm not scared of them. A lot of times, they don't make sense. Last week, for example, I whistled in Ms. Bose's math class because I was happy to finish my work sheet earlier than other kids. Well, we're supposed to be ninth graders, but we were learning things that I had already learned in seventh grade. So this worksheet was super easy for me. So, I whistled to let everybody know that I finished my assignment. But here goes Ms. Bose. "Holly! Stop whistling. You're getting a zero point for today for being disruptive." "What? I'm getting a zero point even though I finished my assignment? That doesn't make sense!" "Yes, you're getting a zero point no matter what, because you are being disruptive." "Fine! If I'm getting a zero point for the day, I might as well keep whistling. What the hell!" I just kept whistling. Ms. Bose started yelling at me, "Holly, stop whistling right now! Otherwise,

I'm gonna call the office." "Whatever!" It was one heck of a yelling match. Finally, Ms. Bose called the office. Five minutes later, Mr. Hard came to our classroom to get me. He took me to the ALC. So, the day became another "do-nothing-at-school" day.

This school sucks, if you ask me. They put a bunch of "bad" kids here all (30) together like a warehouse. There is nothing attractive here. Look at these ugly portable buildings without any windows. They are called "classrooms." We don't have a cafeteria, so we have to eat our lunch at outdoor picnic tables near the restrooms. We get to enjoy this picnic every single day even under the hot temperature of one hundred five degree heat of the desert. Go figure. We use old, "hand-me-down" textbooks that came from a neighboring high school. It's like we are the disposables of education. We don't mean much. Our classes have six or seven students. I like this small class. But we don't really cover all the stuff in the textbook. We learn easy stuff, and I get bored with that. I had to do the multiplication table again because our Mexican boy, Guillermo, didn't know how to do multiplications! When I run into difficult stuff, I just copy answers from the textbook to fill out the worksheets without understanding. And I get a good point format as long as I behave. I want to be a lawyer. But I don't know if I will ever be able to achieve my dream. I know I'm not stupid. But there is no counselor I can talk to about it.

There are more rules and regulations here than regular schools. Look at (31) Mr. Hard, the old, fat, security guard who retired from the police department. I hate that guy. He is obsessed with rules. He goes, "Follow the rules, follow the rules. That's the rule number one here, otherwise you deal with me." We try to avoid running into him because he will make sure to find something wrong with us. He randomly calls one or two kids into his office and starts searching their backpacks. We hate it.

It's such an insult. Recently, Mr. Hard has been watching me like a hawk. (32) I don't know when I became his target. Somehow, he decided to pick on me. On a gloomy day in October, I felt like smoking. The weather was weird, and I had a fight with my mom again that morning. I was having a bad day, you know. I needed to smoke to release my stress. When I was smoking in the restroom, Mr. Hard caught me on the spot. He asked me to come with him to his office. I said no. He asked me again. I said no again. Then, he started calling the police. I quickly grabbed some rocks on the ground and threw them at the son of a bitch. He ran away like a chicken with his head chopped off. I beat him finally! That night, I had a dream of him. I had a screw driver and shoved it into his neck, saying, "Leave me alone!" He was scared of me!

The Voice of Ms. Bose, the Boss

"Hey, guys. There are times when I'll be asking you to leave the classroom (33) if you get on my nerves. When I say 'Leave,' I want you to get out of here. Get out of my sight for five minutes or so, go walk around or something and come back in, instead of fighting me. I'm the boss here. I'm the dictator. It's me who makes a decision for you guys. So you have to follow my order. They pay me a lot of money to keep me here. I get paid more than any other teachers here. Yes. I make a lot of money for educating you to become a good person. So when you and I have an argument and when I say to you to get out of here, you need to leave the classroom for five minutes."

This is what I usually say to my students in the first day of class. It is (34) important to let them know who is the boss here. Otherwise, they will be out of control. I've been teaching for almost 25 years including five years of teaching at a prison in St. Louis before I moved to Arizona. After taking a break from teaching for a couple of years to raise my boys, I volunteered to teach at the poorest and worst school where there was nothing but gangsters. I never wanted to teach at a "nice" school where all the good kids attended. It is my strength that I can easily be sympathetic with kids who have issues and problems, like gang members, because I have been there. I myself came from a poor immigrant family background from Italy. I grew up in a poor area where crimes took place every day. I know what it is like to live in poverty. My father was a cop, but his paycheck was not thick enough to feed seven family members in the 50s and 60s. I still remember those days when our family had to skip meals as often as we ate. From that kind of environment, I learned to be tough. I needed to be as tough as iron to be able to survive. I also learned to control rather than being controlled.

(35) I enjoy teaching at-risk kids. I have never been afraid of those kids even though some of them are gangsters. I believe that we, human beings, are basically the same, no matter how stupid or how smart we are. We are all vulnerable and fragile. We all make mistakes and regret. We tend to repeat the cycle. But I need to teach these kids to break the cycle. I have to be a therapist first rather than a teacher in order to be able to do that. Teaching how to read and write can't be a main focus. What they need is a mental therapy, not an education, because they are "emotionally handicapped." It is their poor emotional well-being and low self-esteem that causes them to get into trouble.

(36) But under the No Child Left Behind of 2001, terms like achievement, accountability, standardization, and testing, have become our every day language at schools. Alternative schools are not an exception. In the year 2003, we got a new principal who believed that these kids needed to be taught to standardized tests. According to Mrs. Principal, my therapeutic method was not helpful in raising students' test scores. She said teachers need to focus on teaching kids how to take the standardized test, especially AIMS, if we don't want our school to be shut down under the NCLB. But, look, these kids are former drop-outs from regular schools. They are way behind their grade level because they have been skipping classes. There is no way we can make them pass the AIMS test until we subdue these kids' acting-out behaviors first. That's why Mr. Vee, our former principal, left this school. He couldn't stand the pressure from the school district about these alternative kids meeting the standards. He was the kind of liberal educator—too liberal for me, by the way—who emphasized students' personal growth. Portfolio assessment was one of his initiatives that tried to help students to reflect on their growth. But Mrs. Principal got rid of that. I didn't care for the portfolio assessment anyway, but it just shows how our school is changing under this accountability and standards movement.

(37) My perspective on educating these kids is different from both principals. My focus here is to get them to listen, that is, to make them behave and make them be positive. A lot of kids have ADHD (Attention Deficit Hyperactivity Disorder). A good example is Holly. She cannot sit still for a minute; she's loud, annoying, and disturbing. She's pretty smart, at least smarter than other kids here, but her problem is that she likes to argue with everybody. She knows it all. She tries to get tough with me, but I am tougher. I let her know who is the boss here. I have a firm belief that resistance from students like Holly needs to be controlled by strong authority. I can be as warm as freshly baked bread when students listen to me, but I can also be as tough as iron when they don't listen. I believe that a good education for these kids is to teach them to behave and have a good positive attitude, so that they can function well in this society. I mean, what kind of boss would want to have an employee like Holly who talks back and is disobedient? It's my responsibility to teach my students to have good attitudes, which will eventually lead them to get a job after graduation. Here's my phrase for my students: "Attitude, attitude, attitude. You gotta have a good attitude."

The Voice of Jose, the Silent Rebel

(38) I am 17 years old, about five feet ten inches tall. I was born in California on April 23rd. I'm half-Hispanic, half-White. My biological dad is Hispanic

from Mexico. I haven't seen him since my parents got divorced when I was three. My mom got remarried when I was five, and that's when we moved to Arizona. Since then, my mom went through two more divorces, and now she's with her fourth husband. Right now, I'm living with my mom, my older brother, my fourth step-dad, and two of his children. My mom changed jobs several times, and she currently works as a gate-keeper for a housing company. Her current husband is a construction worker. I'm supposed to be a senior but am taking junior classes due to the lack of credits. I have attended Borderlands for two years to catch up with credits. I was in and out of school during my freshman and sophomore years because I was struggling with a lot of personal issues. My mom's frequent divorces and remarriages have badly affected me. I went to jail a couple of times for doing drugs, which I started when I was fifteen, and I'm on probation because of that. In addition, I was in a rehabilitation center for eight weeks for being depressed and suicidal. I used to be in serious depression, and used to cut myself with a razor. But the rehabilitation program didn't do much good for me because I'm still depressed most of the day and not talking to anybody.

There is one thing that keeps me going, though. It is music. Whenever I (39) feel frustrated and depressed, I play the guitar. Bass guitar. That's what keeps me sane. I express myself through music. I write a song, sing, and play. I also organized a band with my friends like six months ago. The garage of my house is our practice room. We get together once a week, sometimes twice a week for practice. We're planning to play at a bar on Saturdays when we play better. Actually, some kids at school asked us to play at the Halloween party. We asked Mrs. Principal for her permission, but she said 'no' after she examined our lyrics. Her reason was that our music was not appropriate for a school environment. She said there were too many cuss words in our songs, so students would be badly influenced by our music. We were pissed off when we heard it. Kids would have loved it! What does she know about pop music, hard rock, or punk rock? Nothing!

I bet she doesn't know who Jim Morrison is. I'm sure she has never heard (40) of the legendary band, the Doors. Morrison is my idol, although he died even before I was born. Morrison and his music influenced me so much. It was Jim Morrison who taught me how to see the world, not the teachers, not my parents. I see the world through Morrison's eyes and his music. I wanna be a great musician like him. He wrote songs and poems. I love his poetry. Through his poetry, some of which became the lyrics of his songs, he criticized the society for destroying people's souls with money, authority, and momentary pleasure. His songs are about the feeling of isolation, disconnectedness, despair, and loneliness that are caused by the problems of society. He was a free soul who was against authority. He taught me to stand up for myself to be able to survive in this world. He taught me to stand against authority. Maybe that's why I cannot stand Mr. Schiedler, our social studies teacher. I call him a "lost soul." Whenever I say something that challenges what he says, he goes, "Be quiet!", "Shut up!" He is a BIG controlling dude. He has to make an issue about everything I do. He doesn't understand students at all. He just thinks we are a bunch of losers.

In fact, many teachers are lost souls. I've been attending this school for (41) two years, but I find teachers to be so annoying. They are only interested in keeping their job, so they just regurgitate the stuff they are supposed to teach and show no compassion. A lot of things they teach are biased and pointless. Just straight facts that have nothing to do with life. There is so much going on in the world, and there are so many other things we need to learn about. But all we do, like in Mr. Schiedler's social studies class, is to copy a bunch of god damn definitions of terms from the textbook and take a test that has 150 questions on it. One hundred fifty questions! I don't even read the questions. I just choose answers in alphabetical order: A, B, C, D, A, B, C, D. . . .

(42)   Teachers expect us to believe whatever they say. It's like going against them is a sin. I think it's propaganda that brainwashes and pollutes students' minds. But not mine. Jim Morrison taught me not to believe everything that adults say. That's why I get into so many arguments with teachers. I give them a piece of my mind. I have gotten suspended and kicked out of school many times, but I don't care. Schools don't mean much to me. I have a tattoo on my right arm. It is one red word, "Revolution."

The Voice of Mrs. Principal

(43)   How did I get here? Umm, it was last year, November 2002, when my district office contacted me and asked if I wanted to transfer to Borderlands as principal. I was told that Mr. Vee had to resign because he was having some issues with the district office. At that time, I was an assistant principal at a junior high, which was also an alternative school for 6th thru 8th grade. Of course, I happily accepted the offer because it was a promotion for me. For 20 years of my involvement with education, I always liked working with those at-risk kids who were struggling in every way. It's a challenge, but it's a good challenge that I enjoy because I feel much more successful and much more needed.

(44)   I started my job here in January this year. My district superintendent told me that our school would be a "referral basis only" starting spring semester. It means that our school is not a choice school any longer. If there are students who are deviant, unruly, disruptive, skipping classes, and violating school rules, a school principal refers them to me. It has made my job more difficult especially under the NCLB because we have to spend a lot of time dealing with students' behavioral problems when we can use that time for preparing them for the tests.

(45)   I brought several teachers with me from my previous school because it's easy for me to work with teachers whom I know and trust. They are like my buddies. And they know me well. They know I have a ranch home far away from the school with three horses. They know my 15-year-old daughter is into horseback riding and enters a horse race every spring. Actually my husband and I took her to a horse show held in the West World close to Scottsdale two weeks ago. Yea, we like horses. That's an important part of my personal life.

(46)   Sorry about the digression. Anyway, the teachers who came with me are very cooperative in making the school run smooth. They are not only teaching subject matter but also teaching kids social and life skills. They work on disciplining the students. We have a zero tolerance policy for anybody who violates the school rules and regulations. Mr. Hard has been playing a key role in implementing the policy. He's really good at taking care of kids who have issues of drugs, violence, smoking, fighting, etc., all kinds of problems our students have. Since he started working with us, discipline issues got a lot better. Kids are scared of him. They try to follow the rules as much as they can, so that they don't need to face him. Holly and Jose have been exceptions, though. They tend to act out too much, making a bad influence on others. The other day, Jose was trying to bring his band to school for the Halloween party, but I flatly said no. Their songs were full of "F" words, talking about getting high, going against authority, and revolt, all kinds of bad stuff. And I know his band members do drugs. No way we would allow them to play at school.

(47)   On September 23, 2002, two months before I got a phone call from the school district office, Arizona Department of Education announced the achievement profile formula that will determine which school is underperforming, maintaining, improving, and excelling in terms of standards and accountability. We have to have ninety-five percent of our students take AIMS, and make 100% of our graduates demonstrate proficiency of the Standards via AIMS by 2006! With the NCLB, our state standards and accountability, and

AIMS, we, as an alternative school, have to cope with two main issues. It's like a double-edged sword. While trying to correct students' bad behaviors, we also have to strive to improve their academic skills. We recently got rid of the portfolio assessment that Mr. Vee started. In our monthly faculty meeting two weeks ago, we had a vote on whether we would keep the portfolio assessment or not. Our teachers said it was putting a lot of burden on the faculty's shoulders because they had to read students' essays, give them written feedback, read their revisions again and again until they improved. In addition, we had to invite three community leaders to interview our graduating students to see their personal growth. It's a good thing to do, but this Achievement Profile doesn't give us time to do such an "ideal" thing. You know what I mean. So after a short debate, teachers decided to abolish the portfolio. They came to an agreement that what our students need is to focus on basic skills that will help them pass the AIMS test such as basic vocabulary, reading, and basic math skills. And that's what our district wants us to do anyway.

Right now, our school is rated as "Improving," according to our state (48) report. It's amazing, isn't it? Well, in order for us to get there, we had to "bribe" our students to come to take a state test which took place early this spring. The formula for deciding a school as performing or underperforming is quite complicated. It is not just about how well students did on the test. But students' attendance plays a huge role in that formula. We did a campaign for a week before the test, telling students that they have to come to school to take the test. We told them we would provide lunch and snack and play time the next day if they came to school to take the test. You know what? We had almost 98% of students who showed up for the test! It was crazy but it worked. You know what I mean.

Epilogue: The Voice of the Researcher

Listening to all these "unmerged voices" (Bakhtin, 1963/1984, p. 30) among (49) different power relations and subject positions about pedagogical practice, readers may find themselves trying to understand each protagonist's standpoint. Further, readers who view "their existence as multiple selves" (Noddings, 1990, p. x) may find themselves left with more questions than answers.

While respecting and valuing the voices equally, I am reminded of an (50) Aesop's fable, *The Fox and the Stork:*

> At one time the Fox and the Stork were on visiting terms and seemed very good friends. So the Fox invited the Stork to dinner and put nothing before her but some soup in a very shallow dish. This the Fox could easily lap up, but the Stork could only wet the end of her long bill in it, and left the meal as hungry as when she began. "I am sorry," said the Fox, "the soup is not to your liking." "Pray do not apologize," said the Stork. "I hope you will return this visit, and come and dine with me soon." So a day was appointed when the Fox should visit the Stork; but when they were seated at table all that was for their dinner was contained in a very long-necked jar with a narrow mouth, in which the Fox could not insert his snout, so all he could manage to do was to lick the outside of the jar (Aesop's Fables, 1975, p. 66).

It is obvious that Mr. Hard, Ms. Bose, and Mrs. Principal care about their (51) students in their own terms. As an act of "caring," they invite students like Holly and Jose "to dinner" as a favor. The "dinner table" is filled with their favorite dishes of control, rules, authority, discipline, irrelevant teaching and learning, and test scores, without considering the guests' appetites. They believe their guests are well-fed. Unfortunately, constant conflicts, tensions, resentment, and resistance at Borderlands reveal that students are not happy with what is served and how it is served, just as the Stork could not eat the "soup in a very shallow dish." Students seem to penetrate what is going on in schools (Willis, 1977), as we heard from Holly, "This school sucks, if you ask me," and from Jose, "Schools don't mean much." Students return the favor with dishes that teachers cannot enjoy: acts of resistance such as talking back to the teacher, violating the rules and regulations, or being disruptive in class. In the different power relationship between the teacher/administrator and the student, however, it is the latter who has to leave "the meal as hungry as when she began." Students' hunger for caring, hunger for meaningful, relevant education, hunger for respect and being valued, and hunger for success, still remain unsatisfied. As a result, our students' at-risk-ness of school failure remains unresolved, if not exacerbated, causing them to be farther left behind.

(52)   Under the No Child Left Behind legislation, all schools in the nation feel the pressure of increased accountability, and Borderlands is not an exception. It seems that teachers and administrators at Borderlands are working hard to make the school accountable. But for whom are they trying to make the school accountable? Why does it seem that students' "appetites" and "needs" are not taken into consideration in that effort? Why do I see a clear line of distance, disconnection, and dissonance between the administration and the students? What happened to the ideas of progressive education to which alternative public schools in the late 1960s and 70s subscribed? Why are these "unmerged voices" heard as a cacophony, rather than, as Bakhtin would call it, "an eternal harmony of unmerged voices" (1963/1984, p. 30)? Ultimately; for whom does/should the school bell toll? I wonder.

(53)   In this article, I have presented different voices of an alternative school employing Bakhtinian novelness of polyphony, chronotope, and carnival. Although they are synopses of what is going on in the alternative school, the five voices of Mr. Hard, Holly, Ms. Bose, Jose, and Mrs. Principal, may be considered a metaphor of the possible life inside other public alternative schools experiencing similar tensions and struggles. The carnival of these multiple voices, including the epilogue, remains open-ended as it serves as a starting point of genuine dialogue among educators. A dialogue in which our taken-for-granted thoughts are disturbed, and counter-narratives that challenge one dominant view are promoted with compassion. I hope that this, in turn, will encourage questions as to the nature and purpose of alternative schooling that serves disenfranchised students, and to work together to provide true, meaningful, and equitable education that students like Holly and Jose deserve.

REFERENCES

Aesop's Fables. (1975). *The fox and the stork*. Grosset & Dunlap Inc.

Arizona Department of Education. (2002). Arizona LEARNS: Information Packet. Retrieved from ade.az.gov/azleams/2001-2002/Board9-23 submitted.pdf

Arnove, R. F., & Strout, T. (1980). Alternative schools for disruptive youth. *Educational forum, 44*, 452–471.

Bakhtin, M. M. (1963/1984). *Problem of Dostoevski's poetics*. Minneapolis, MN: University of Minnesota Press.

Bakhtin, M. M. (1975/1981). *The dialogic imagination: Four essays by M. M. Bakhtin*. Austin, TX: University of Texas Press.

Barone, T. (2001). *Touching Eternity: The enduring outcomes of teaching*. New York: Teachers College Press.

Barone, T., & Eisner, E. (1997). Arts-based educational research. In R. M. Jaeger (Ed.), *Complementary methods for research in education* (2nd ed., pp. 75–116). Washington, DC: American Educational Research Association.

Billings, J. A. (1995). *Educational options and alternatives in Washington State*. Olympia, WA: Office of Superintendent of Public Instruction.

Casey, K. (1993). *I answer with my life: Life histories of women teachers working for social change*. New York: Routledge.

Conley, B. (2002). *Alternative schools: A reference handbook*. Santa Barbara, CA: ABC-CLIO, Inc.

Connelly, F. M., & Clandinin, D. J. (1990). Stories of experience and narrative inquiry. *Educational Researcher, 19*(4), 2–14.

Dryfoos, J. G. (1997). Adolescents at risk: Shaping programs to fit the need. *Journal of Negro Education, 65*(1), 5–18.

Goodman, G. (1999). *Alternatives in education: Critical pedagogy for disaffected youth*. New York: Peter Lang.

Goodson, I. (1995). The story so far: Personal knowledge and the political. In J. A. Hatch & R. Wisniewski (Eds.), *Life history and narrative* (pp. 86–97). London: Falmer Press.

Goodson, I. (Ed.). (1992). *Studying teachers' lives*. New York, NY: Teachers College Press.

Howell, E. C. (Ed.). (1995). *Guide for implementing the comprehensive strategy for serious, violent, and chronic juvenile offenders*. Washington, DC: Office of Juvenile Justice and Delinquency Prevention.

Kelly, D. M. (1993). *Last chance high: How girls and boys drop in and out of alternative schools*. New Haven, CT: Yale University Press.

Kerby, A. T. (1991). *Narrative and the self*. Bloomington, IN: Indiana University Press.

Kvale, S. (1996). *Interviews*. Thousand Oaks, CA: Sage Publications.

Leone, P. E., Rutherford, R. B., & Nelson, C. M. (1991). *Special education in juvenile corrections*. Reston, VA: Council for Exceptional Children.

Marsh, C., & Willis, G. (2003). *Curriculum: Alternative approaches, ongoing issues* (3rd ed.). Upper Saddle River, NJ: Merrill Prentice Hall.

Mcgee, J. (2001). A Kappan special section on alternative schools: Reflections of an alternative school administrator. *Phi Delta Kappan, 82*(8), 585–588.

Morson, G. S., & Emerson, C. (1990). *Mikhail Bakhtin: Creation of a prosaics*. Stanford, CA: Stanford University Press.

Munro, P. (1998). *Subject to fiction: Women teachers' life history narratives and the cultural politics of resistance*. Philadelphia, PA: Open University Press.

National Association of State Boards of Education. (1994). Schools without fear: The report of the NASBE study group on violence and its impact on schools and learning, from nasbe.org/Educational_Issues/Reports/Schools%20without%20Fear.pdf

National Center for Educational Statistics. (2002). Retrieved from nces.ed.gov/surveys/frss/publications/2002004/6.asp

Noddings, N. (1990). Foreword. In J. T. Sears & D. J. Marshall (Eds.), *Teaching and thinking about curriculum: Critical inquiries* (pp. viii–x). New York: Teachers College Press.

Nolan, K., & Anyon, J. (2004). Learning to do time: Willis's model of cultural reproduction in an era of postindustrialism, globalization, and mass incarceration. In N. Dolby & G. Dimitriadis (Eds.), *Learning to labor in new times* (pp. 129–140). New York: Routledge Falmer.

Phillion, J., He, M. F., & Connelly, F. M. (Eds.). (2005). *Narrative & Experience in Multicultural Education*. Thousand Oaks, CA: Sage Publications.

Polkinghorne, D. E. (1995). Narrative configuration as qualitative analysis. In J. A. Hatch & R. Wisniewski (Eds.), *Life history and narrative* (pp. 5–25). London, UK: Falmer Press.

Purcell, W. (1996). Narrative voice in J. D. Salinger's "Both Parties Concerned" and "I'm Crazy." *Studies in Short Fiction, 33*(2), 270–282.

Raywid, M. A. (1995). Alternative schools: The state of the art. *Educational Leadership, I* (September), 26–31.

Sparkes, A. C. (1994). Self, silence and invisibility as a beginning teacher: A life history of lesbian experience. *British Journal of Sociology of Education, 15*(1), 93–118.

Spence, D. P. (1986). Narrative smoothing and clinical wisdom. In T. R. Sarbin (Ed.), *Narrative psychology: The storied nature of human conduct* (pp. 211–232). New York: Praeger.

Sprague, J., & Tobin, T. (2000). Alternative education strategies: Reducing violence in school and the community. *Journal of Emotional and Behavioral Disorders, 8*(3), 177–191.

Tanaka, G. (1997). Pico College. In W. Tierney & Y. Lincoln (Eds.), *Representation and the text* (pp. 259–299). Albany, NY: State University of New York Press.

Willis, P. (1977). *Learning to labor: How working class kids get working class jobs* (Revised ed.). New York: Columbia University Press.

Young, T. W. (1990). *Public alternative schools: Options and choice for today's schools*. New York, NY: Teachers College Press.

Source: From Kim, Jeong-Hee, "For Whom the School Bell Tolls: Conflicting Voices Inside an Alternative High School," *International Journal of Education & the Arts*, 7(6), 2006.

CHAPTER FOURTEEN

Ethnographic Research

Everett Collection

Good Will Hunting, 1997

"Ethnographic research . . . is the study of the cultural patterns and perspectives of participants in their natural settings." (p. 378)

LEARNING OUTCOMES

After reading Chapter 14, you should be able to do the following:

14.1 Briefly state the definition and purpose of ethnographic research.

14.2 Describe the ethnographic research process.

14.3 Describe the key characteristics of ethnographic research.

14.4 Identify and describe the different types of ethnographic research.

14.5 Describe the use of ethnographic research techniques.

The chapter learning outcomes form the basis for the following task, which will require you to write the research procedures section of a qualitative research report.

TASK 8B

For a qualitative study, you have already created research plan components (Tasks 3 and 4B) and described a sample (Task 5B). If your study involves ethnographic research, now develop the research procedures section of the research report. Include in the plan the overall approach and rationale for the study, site and sample selection, the researcher's role, data collection methods, data management strategies, data analysis strategies, trustworthiness features, and ethical considerations (see Performance Criteria at the end of Chapter 16, p. 438).

SUMMARY: ETHNOGRAPHIC RESEARCH

Definition	*Ethnographic research* (also called *ethnography*) is the study of the cultural patterns and perspectives of participants in their natural settings. The goal of ethnographic research is to describe, analyze, and interpret the culture of a group, over time, in terms of the group's shared beliefs, behaviors, and language.
Design(s)	• Critical ethnography • Realist ethnography • Ethnographic case study
Types of appropriate research questions	Questions focused on describing and interpreting cultural patterns and perspectives in a natural setting.
Key characteristics	• It is carried out in a natural setting, not a laboratory. • It involves intimate, face-to-face interaction with participants. • It presents an accurate reflection of participants' perspectives and behaviors. • It uses inductive, interactive, and repetitious collection of unstructured data and analytic strategies to build local cultural theories. • Data are collected primarily through fieldwork experiences. • It typically uses multiple methods for data collection, including conducting interviews and observations and reviewing documents, artifacts, and visual materials. • It frames all human behavior and belief within a sociopolitical and historical context. • It uses the concept of culture as a lens through which to interpret results. • It places an emphasis on exploring the nature of particular social phenomena rather than setting out to test hypotheses about them. • It investigates a small number of cases, perhaps just one case, in detail. • It uses data analysis procedures that involve the explicit interpretation of the meanings and functions of human actions. Interpretations occur within the context or group setting and are presented through the description of themes.

(continued)

- It requires researchers to be reflective about their impact on the research site and the cultural group.
- It offers interpretations of people's actions and behaviors that must be uncovered through an investigation of what people do and their reasons for doing it.
- It offers a representation of a person's life and behavior that is neither the researcher's nor the person's. Instead, it is built on points of understanding and misunderstanding that occur between researcher and participant.
- It cannot provide an exhaustive, absolute description of anything. Rather, ethnographic descriptions are necessarily partial, bound by what can be handled within a certain time, under specific circumstances, and from a particular perspective.

Steps in the process	1. Identify the purpose of the research study and frame it as a larger theoretical, policy, or practical problem.
	2. Determine the research site and the sample for the study.
	3. Secure permissions and negotiate entry to the research site.
	4. Collect data, including the use of participant observation, field notes, interviews, and the examination of artifacts such as school policy documents and attendance records.
	5. Analyze data.
	6. Write an ethnographic account that is usually a narrative capturing the social, cultural, and economic themes that emerge from the study.
Potential challenges	• Developing and maintaining an intimate face-to-face interaction with participants
	• Sustaining lengthy fieldwork for a "full cycle" of the phenomenon under investigation
	• Using the concept of culture as an interpretive lens
Example	What are the factors that affect adolescent drug use in high schools?

ETHNOGRAPHIC RESEARCH: DEFINITION AND PURPOSE

Ethnographic research (also called *ethnography*) is the study of the cultural patterns and perspectives of participants in their natural settings. Ethnographers engage in long-term study of particular phenomena to situate understandings about those phenomena into a meaningful context. With origins in cultural anthropology, ethnographic research involves multiple data collection techniques and demands prolonged time in the research setting. Most commonly, ethnographers engage in intensive participant observation: By participating in varying degrees in the research setting, the researcher attempts to discern patterns and regularities of human behavior in social activity. Ethnographic research thus requires the researcher to appreciate the tension caused by bringing together contrasting and perhaps incompatible perspectives, all in the spirit of describing and understanding what is actually going on in a specific context.

The goal of ethnographic research is to describe, analyze, and interpret the culture of a group, over time, in terms of the group's shared beliefs, behaviors, and language. **Culture** is the set of attitudes, values, concepts, beliefs, and practices shared by members of a group. As you begin to think about your own ethnographic research studies, keep the concept of culture in your mind as an organizing principle for your work. It is tempting to talk in generalities about the "culture of the school" or the "culture of adolescent drug users." In qualitative research, however, statements about culture are bold assertions that can be made about a group only after the group has been studied over an extended period of time. Use of the word *cultural* can help you clarify, in more concrete terms, what you are attempting to describe in the ethnographic research setting. Wolcott[1] suggested thinking in terms of three broad conceptual areas that focus on tangible behaviors: cultural orientation (i.e., where the people under study are situated in terms of physical space and activities), cultural know-how (i.e., how a group goes about its daily activities), and cultural beliefs (i.e., why a group does what it does). This strategy helps ethnographic researchers to identify the phenomena that are at the heart of an ethnographic research enterprise and, in so doing, capture the culture of the group.

To picture what an ethnographic research study may look like, imagine that you have been asked by a teacher (Hilda) working at a secondary school (High High School) to help her and her colleagues look into adolescent drug use at the school. You ask yourself, "What kind of research approach is appropriate to investigate this problem?" Could you structure an experiment to look at the impact of a particular treatment on the outcome of reducing drug use? What treatment would you choose? What do you really know about the drug culture of this school community? Would students really be willing to be assigned to a control group and an experimental group? (Perhaps your head hurts just thinking about these issues!)

As we think about social problems such as adolescent drug use in high schools, it becomes clear that we probably know very little about what is really going on in the drug culture that exists right under our noses. Indeed, although scientifically based approaches and school policies (such as zero tolerance policies) attempt to address the problem of adolescent drug use, we may be surprised to learn that a universal panacea for adolescent drug use in our schools probably does not exist. We may do well to think about an ethnographic study of adolescent drug use to understand the problem and how we may address it.

A unique type of understanding can be gained by implementing a research approach that focuses on everyday, taken-for-granted behaviors such as adolescent drug use. Our aim in ethnographic research is not to "prove" that a particular intervention (e.g., drug treatment) "solves" a particular "problem" (e.g., adolescent drug use) but rather to understand "what's going on" in a particular setting (e.g., high school). It should be clear that the goal of an ethnographic study is quite different from the goals of survey, correlational, causal–comparative, and experimental studies and that the methodology we use dictates the kind of research we conduct.

> MyLab Education **Self-Check 14.1**

THE ETHNOGRAPHIC RESEARCH PROCESS

An individual interested in conducting an ethnographic study must first decide if he or she has the time, access, experience, personal style, and commitment to undertake this style of research. In this section we describe some basic steps that can serve as guideposts in the process of conducting an ethnographic study. In discussing the steps, we will use the example of an ethnographic study on adolescent drug use in a secondary school (High High School).

From the start, we need to be clear about the purpose of the research. For the scenario chosen, suppose we identify the following purpose:

> The purpose of this study is to understand the social, cultural, and economic influences affecting the use of drugs at High High School.

Not a bad start. Next, the researcher should demonstrate the relevance of the proposed study using

[1] *Ethnography: A Way of Seeing*, by H. F. Wolcott, 1999, Walnut Creek, CA: AltaMira Press.

a frame of reference that the reader will be able to relate to. Given a national preoccupation with illegal drug use, it is not difficult to frame the importance of this study in terms of a larger societal, cultural, and economic study on adolescent drug use, whether it occurs in or outside school. It follows, then, that you can express the overall approach and rationale for the study as follows:

> The overall approach for this study of adolescent drug use in secondary schools will be ethnographic. The rationale for the study is based on society's need to understand how teachers cope with adolescent drug users in their classrooms and the social, cultural, and economic influences affecting the widespread use of drugs at High High School.

With the topic and design in hand, the researcher must decide on the site and the sample for the study. In this case, suppose you have been invited by a teacher, Hilda, to participate in a collaborative ethnographic research study that she hopes will ultimately contribute to her (and perhaps others') understanding of adolescent drug use in high schools. It is likely that your role as researcher in this study would need to be negotiated carefully in terms of entry to the school setting and the ethical dilemmas that would likely be faced. In this study in particular, issues of confidentiality and anonymity would be crucial, especially if illegal behavior were observed. You would also need to consider what you would do if you observed unhealthy behavior, such as cigarette smoking, which, although legal, is a violation of school policy. The very intimate nature of ethnographic research makes the possibility of facing an ethical dilemma omnipresent, but that doesn't mean we should shy away from doing it!

Having negotiated your entry to the research setting, your next step is to establish rapport with your collaborators in the research process—the key informants, also known as subjects or active participants. Researchers identify participants in many ways. For example, school counselors, teachers, administrators, and community law enforcement officers would probably be able to provide names of likely drug users or students who have a history of drug use. A good starting point would be to establish a trusting relationship with one or more of these students and then, after explaining the purpose of your study, ask for volunteers who would be willing to be observed. For students under legal age, you would need to obtain approval from parents for the students to participate in the study. You would also want to assure students and parents that students' identities would be kept confidential.

After negotiating entry and identifying participants, you can begin data collection. Your primary data collection techniques in the study of High High would likely be participant observation, field notes, interviews, and the examination of artifacts such as school policy documents and attendance records.

As a participant observer, you should ease into the research setting and refrain from asking questions until you have done some initial observation of the setting and participants. However, you should arrive with some initial ethnographic research questions in mind. Beginning researchers are often challenged when they try to make the decision about what they will ask when they arrive at the research setting. Guided by the overriding goal of describing what's going on at the research site, you could enter the site with this initial research question in mind: "How do teachers describe the effects of students' drug use on the classroom/academic setting?" Such a question naturally suggests other questions that you may want to ask the teachers and administrators:

- How do you know that students in your class are using drugs?
- What are the school policies on drug use, drug possession, and intoxication in school?
- What social services are available to help students deal with drug-related problems?

The questions just listed would be good ones to start with. If you followed up by prompting the participant to "tell me a little bit more about that," or to describe who, what, where, when, or how, you will never be at a loss for questions to ask in your study.

Following data collection, you'll need to analyze and interpret the data and write an ethnographic account of your experience. For example, you could analyze your field notes for themes emerging from the data that help you increase understanding of what is going on at High High School. Your final ethnographic account will likely be a narrative that captures the social, cultural, and economic themes that emerge from the study. The account should include a description of the limitations of the study and recommendations for what you would do differently next time. The account should also acknowledge the incomplete nature of the story given; qualitative researchers craft an "end" to a story while knowing full well that the story continues beyond their involvement.

It should be noted that one of the challenges for time-strapped educational researchers planning to do ethnographic research is the length of time in the field (i.e., usually a "full cycle," comprising a calendar year) and the length of the written account. If you are a graduate student, conducting ethnographic research could lengthen the time you spend in your graduate program and add cost to your education. Researchers in all circumstances need to consider whether they have the time to spend in the field before making the decision to undertake an ethnographic research study.

MyLab Education **Self-Check 14.2**

MyLab Education **Application Exercise 14.1:**
Evaluating Research Articles: Identifying the Steps of Ethnographic Research

---

KEY CHARACTERISTICS OF ETHNOGRAPHIC RESEARCH

There is a pretty good chance that you have already read an ethnographic account but may not have recognized it as such. Ethnographic research possesses the following characteristics:[2]

- It is carried out in a natural setting, not a laboratory.
- It involves intimate, face-to-face interaction with participants.

[2] Characteristics were adapted from those in "Ethnography and Participant Observation," by P. Atkinson and M. Hammersley, 1994, in *Handbook of Qualitative Research* (pp. 249–261), by N. K. Denzin and Y. S. Lincoln (Eds.), Thousand Oaks, CA: Sage; *Educational Research: Planning, Conducting, and Evaluating Quantitative and Qualitative Research* (5th ed.), by J. W. Creswell, 2015, Upper Saddle River, NJ: Pearson Education, Inc., *Conceptualizing Qualitative Inquiry: Mindwork for Fieldwork in Education and the Social Sciences*, by T. H. Schram, 2003, Upper Saddle River, NJ: Merrill/Prentice Hall; and *Ethnographer's Toolkit: Vol. 1. Designing and Conducting Ethnographic Research*, by J. J. Schensul and M. D. LeCompte (Eds.), 1999, Walnut Creek, CA: AltaMira Press.

- It presents an accurate reflection of participants' perspectives and behaviors.
- It uses inductive, interactive, and repetitious collection of unstructured data and analytic strategies to build local cultural theories.
- Data are collected primarily through fieldwork experiences.
- It typically uses multiple methods for data collection, including conducting interviews and observations and reviewing documents, artifacts, and visual materials.
- It frames all human behavior and belief within a sociopolitical and historical context.
- It uses the concept of culture as a lens through which to interpret results.
- It places an emphasis on exploring the nature of particular social phenomena rather than setting out to test hypotheses about them.
- It investigates a small number of cases, perhaps just one case, in detail.
- It uses data analysis procedures that involve the explicit interpretation of the meanings and functions of human actions. Interpretations occur within the context or group setting and are presented through the description of themes.
- It requires that researchers be reflective about their impact on the research site and the cultural group.
- It offers interpretations of people's actions and behaviors that must be uncovered through an investigation of what people do and their reasons for doing it.
- It offers a representation of a person's life and behavior that is neither the researcher's nor the person's. Instead, it is built on points of understanding and misunderstanding that occur between researcher and participant.
- It cannot provide an exhaustive, absolute description of anything. Rather, ethnographic descriptions are necessarily partial, bound by what can be handled within a certain time, under specific circumstances, and from a particular perspective.

These characteristics will help you recognize ethnographic research studies. They will also help you determine if this approach to educational research feels like a good fit for your individual personality and the problems you want to investigate.

FIGURE 14.1 • Types of ethnographies

- Realist ethnography—an objective, scientifically written ethnography
- Confessional ethnography—a report of the ethnographer's fieldwork experiences
- Life history—a study of one individual situated within the cultural context of his or her life
- Autoethnography—a reflective self-examination by an individual set within his or her cultural context
- Microethnography—a study focused on a specific aspect of a cultural group and setting
- Ethnographic case study—a case analysis of a person, event, activity, or process set within a cultural perspective

- Critical ethnography—a study of the shared patterns of a marginalized group with the aim of advocacy
- Feminist ethnography—a study of women and the cultural practices that serve to disempower and oppress them
- Postmodern ethnography—an ethnography written to challenge the problems in our society that have emerged from a modern emphasis on progress and marginalizing individuals
- Ethnographic novels—a fictional work focused on cultural aspects of a group

---

Source: Creswell, John W., *Educational Research: Planning, Conducting, and Evaluating Quantitative and Qualitative Research,* 5th Edition, p. 468. © 2015. Reprinted by permission of Pearson Education, Inc., Upper Saddle River, NJ.

MyLab Education **Self-Check 14.3**

MyLab Education **Application Exercise 14.2:** Identifying the Characteristics of Ethnographic Research

TYPES OF ETHNOGRAPHIC RESEARCH

Ethnographic research comes in many forms. Figure 14.1 is a comprehensive list of the types of ethnographies you are likely to encounter in your studies or likely to produce as a result of your fieldwork.

Although examples of all these types of ethnography can be found in educational research, the three most common are the critical ethnography, the realist ethnography, and the ethnographic case study. One feature that distinguishes these types of research from one another is the product (i.e., the written account) itself, the **ethnography.** However, the researcher's intent in conducting the research is an equally important distinguishing feature. A **critical ethnography** is a highly politicized form of ethnography written by a researcher to advocate against inequalities and domination of particular groups that exist in society (including schools). The researcher's intent is to advocate "for the emancipation of groups marginalized in our society."[3] These ethnographies typically address issues of power, authority, emancipation, oppression, and inequity—to name a few. Realist ethnographies are most commonly used by cultural and educational anthropologists who study the culture of schools. A **realist ethnography** is written with an objective style and uses common categories for cultural description, analysis, and interpretation; such categories include "family life, work life, social networks, and status systems."[4] Case studies, as a type of ethnographic research design, are less likely to focus on cultural themes. Instead, an **ethnographic case study** focuses on describing the activities of a specific group and the shared patterns of behavior the group develops over time. It is important that beginning ethnographic researchers recognize the different ways in which they can focus their research to distinguish it as a particular type of ethnography. The literature provides numerous examples of ethnographic research that can serve as models of particular designs and that illustrate the final written accounts.

MyLab Education **Self-Check 14.4**

MyLab Education **Application Exercise 14.3:** Designing an Ethnographic Study

---

[3] *Educational Research: Planning, Conducting, and Evaluating Quantitative and Qualitative Research*, 5th ed., p. 471, by J. W. Creswell, 2015, Upper Saddle River, NJ: Merrill/Prentice Hall.
[4] Ibid., p. 468.

ETHNOGRAPHIC RESEARCH TECHNIQUES

Like other qualitative researchers, an ethnographic researcher collects descriptive narrative and visual data. As mentioned previously, the researcher is engaging in an activity to answer the question, "What is going on here (at this research site)?" It is not a mysterious quest but is quite simply an effort to collect data that increase our understanding of the phenomenon under investigation.

Wolcott reminds us that "the most noteworthy thing about ethnographic research techniques is their lack of noteworthiness."[5] Although the techniques may not be noteworthy, they are systematic and rigorous, and over an extended period of time they allow the researcher to describe, analyze, and interpret the social setting under investigation. In the following sections, we focus on participant observation and field notes as the primary data collection techniques used in ethnographic research.

Participant Observation

A researcher who is a genuine participant in the activity under study is called a participant observer. Participant observation is undertaken with at least two purposes in mind:[6] (1) to observe the activities, people, and physical aspects of a situation and (2) to engage in activities that are appropriate to a given situation and that provide useful information. The participant observer is fully immersed in the research setting in an effort to get close to those studied and thus understand what their experiences and activities mean to them. This immersion provides a window through which the researcher can see how participants in the study lead their lives and carry out their daily activities. It also provides an opportunity for the researcher to determine what is meaningful to participants, and why.

Depending on the nature of the problem, ethnographic researchers have many opportunities to participate actively and observe as they work. However, the tendency with observing is to try to see it all! A good rule of thumb is to try to do less, but do it better. As you embark on some degree of participant observation, do not be overwhelmed. It is not possible to take in everything that you experience. Be content with furthering your understanding of what is going on through manageable observations. Avoid trying to do too much, and you will be happier with the outcomes.

Participant observation can be done to varying degrees, depending on the situation being observed and on the opportunities presented. A participant observer can be an *active participant observer;* a *privileged, active observer;* or a *passive observer.*[7]

Active Participant Observer

Ethnographic researchers, by virtue of the problems they choose to investigate, are likely to have opportunities to be active participant observers. For example, when doing educational research, researchers often negotiate roles as teacher's aides, student teachers, or even substitute teachers to gain access to schools and classrooms (i.e., the research settings). When actively engaged in teaching, teachers naturally observe the outcomes of their teaching. Each time they teach, they monitor the effects of their teaching and adjust their instruction accordingly. Teacher-researchers who plan to observe their own teaching practices, however, may become so fully immersed in teaching that they don't record their observations in a systematic way during the school day. Such recording is a necessary part of being an active participant observer.

Privileged, Active Observer

Ethnographic researchers may also have opportunities to observe in a more privileged, active role. For example, a researcher may observe children in classrooms during a time when he or she is not participating in the instructional setting as the teacher. During these times, the researcher can work as a teacher's aide and, at the same time, withdraw,

[5] "Ethnographic Research in Education" by H. F. Wolcott, 1988, in *Complementary Methods for Research in Education* (p. 191), by R. M. Jaegar (Ed.), Washington, DC: American Educational Research Association.
[6] *Participant Observation*, by J. Spradley, 1980, New York: Holt, Rinehart & Winston.

[7] *Anthropological Research: The Structure of Inquiry*, by P. J. Pelto and G. H. Pelto, 1978, Cambridge, MA: Cambridge University Press; *Participant Observation*, Spradley, 1980, Belmont, CA: Wadsworth; "Differing Styles of On-Site Research, or 'If It Isn't Ethnography, What Is It?'" by H. F. Wolcott, 1982, *Review Journal of Philosophy and Social Science*, 7, pp. 154–169; and "Ethnographic Research in Education," by H. F. Wolcott, 1997, in *Complementary Methods for Research in Education* (2nd ed.) (pp. 325–398), Washington, DC: American Educational Research Association.

stand back, and watch what is happening during a teaching episode. As a privileged, active observer, the ethnographer can move in and out of the roles of teacher's aide and observer.

Passive Observer

When a researcher takes on the role of passive observer, he or she assumes no responsibilities in the classroom setting but rather focuses on data collection. A researcher may spend time in the setting as a passive observer only or may enter the setting as a privileged, active observer and then, on occasion, choose to act as a passive observer by making explicit to the students and teaching colleagues that the "visitor" is present only to "see what's going on around here."

According to Wolcott,[8] success as a participant observer depends on the personal characteristics of the researcher, as evidenced by what the researcher is thinking and how the researcher behaves in the field. While in the research setting, you need to conduct yourself in a manner that will allow you to build rapport with research participants; otherwise, you will learn little from the field-based experience. Everyday courtesy and common sense go a long way in helping you establish your fit in the field. When was the last time you were approached by someone (maybe a telemarketer or pollster) and asked for a "few minutes of your time" (which, of course, turned into many minutes of your time!)? Was the person pleasant, patient, and genuinely interested in what you had to say? Or was the person pushy, inconsiderate, and relatively uninterested in what you had to say? Were you tempted to hang up or walk away? When you work as a researcher, you need to be accepted into the research setting as a person who can be trusted.

Guidelines for Participant Observation

Some guidelines in certain areas of social behavior encourage researchers to think about how they carry themselves in the participant observation experience. We discuss these guidelines in the following subsections.

Gaining Entry and Maintaining Rapport. During the early stages of the ethnographic research process, you will negotiate your entry into the research setting. In educational research, you will most likely make arrangements with key players in the setting, such as teachers, principals, and superintendents. You will need to describe clearly to these educators what you are planning to do, what kinds of time constraints will be placed on them, how the research will add value to the educational process, and other important details. Furthermore, you will need to maintain a good working rapport with the people in the setting. Be considerate of others and thoughtful about how you are perceived. If in doubt, ask for feedback from a highly trusted person at the research setting.

Reciprocity. Reciprocity in the ethnographic study of education can take many forms. As the researcher, you may be asked by teachers to assist with classroom tasks. Because of your connection to a university, you may be asked to provide some kind of curriculum resource or access to teaching materials. You may even be asked to pay for informants' time for interviews if such activities require time beyond informants' contracted hours (i.e., the regular workday). It is best to address these matters during your initial request for access to the setting. Unless you have a large, funded research study, it is unlikely that you will be in a position to pay teachers for their time. Reciprocity for educational ethnographic researchers more commonly takes the form of a willingness to share personal information and professional courtesy. Participants who are going to spend considerable time with you want to know something about who you are as a person. They may also look to you as an educational expert—after all, you are probably working at the university on an advanced degree, so you must know something about teaching and learning! As you negotiate your degree of participation in the setting, be sure to set your boundaries about what you are willing and able (i.e., qualified) to do.

A Tolerance for Ambiguity. Fieldwork does not always (or perhaps ever) proceed at the speed or intensity we may want it to. We may enter the field with a naïve view that something exciting will be occurring at every moment and it will be related directly to what we are investigating. The reality is, many times you will find yourself frustrated with

---

[8] *The Art of Fieldwork* (p. 90), by H. F. Wolcott, 1995, Walnut Creek, CA: AltaMira Press.

the life of an ethnographic researcher. Rather than offering perfect examples of interesting, relevant behavior, most episodes you observe are likely to be ambiguous in meaning. You must learn patience, if you are not already blessed with this trait.

Personal Determination Coupled with Faith in Oneself. Wolcott[9] offered ethnographic researchers this valuable advice: "Self-doubt must be held in check so that you can go about your business of conducting research, even when you may not be sure what that entails." At some time during your fieldwork, you may experience what is commonly termed culture shock—that is, you will encounter an unexpected set of events that challenge everything you assumed about your research setting and the participants. This situation may be both exciting and frightening. If you find yourself in this kind of situation, concentrate on simply writing down what you are seeing, hearing, experiencing, and feeling. You will inevitably make sense of it over time. Have faith in what you are doing, and hang in there!

Letting Go of Control. Just as we need to tolerate ambiguity, ethnographic researchers need to be able to let go of control. Fieldwork can be challenging and stressful, especially when our future academic lives (e.g., theses, dissertations, contracts, grades) rest on the outcome of our work. In all likelihood, we have entered the field with an approved research plan and feel in control of the situation. However, ethnographic researchers must be prepared to relinquish control of the research time line and agenda to take advantage of the emergent nature of the ethnographic research process. For example, you should be prepared to abandon your plans to talk to a participant at a certain time and place. Unanticipated events will occur, and you need to be willing to go with the flow. Wonderful things can happen when you let go of control!

Field Notes

Field notes are gathered, recorded, and compiled on-site during the course of a study. For an ethnographic researcher, field notes provide a record of the researcher's understandings of the lives, people, and events that are the focus of the research. In all likelihood, you will embark on a research journey that thrusts you into an educational setting, and you will spend considerable time and energy trying to understand what is going on. A critical component of this research journey will be the data you collect as a trained observer. You will need to capture your experiences in a way that will enable you eventually to craft a narrative about those experiences. Your primary tool is your field notes. Emerson and colleagues provide several insights into the use and nature of field notes in ethnographic research:

> (1) What is observed and ultimately treated as "data" or "findings" is inseparable from the observational process. (2) In writing field notes, the field researcher should give special attention to the indigenous meanings and concerns of the people studied. (3) Contemporaneously written field notes are an essential grounding and resource for writing broader, more coherent accounts of others' lives and concerns. (4) Such field notes should detail the social and interactional processes that make up people's everyday lives and activities.[10]

In the past, the craft of recording field notes was learned in a constructivist graduate school environment. In other words, students learned how to write field notes through folklore and on-the-job training; little in the literature helped them prepare for entering the research setting with trusty notebook and pencil in hand. The literature now has some helpful guidelines that suggest ways to record field notes and the process to use to move from writing scribbles on a table napkin to writing cohesive narratives that can ultimately find their way into the ethnographic research account.

We begin with an example of how *not* to record field notes. During his studies at the University of Oregon, one of the authors (Geoff Mills) took a class entitled Ethnographic Research in Education and was required to conduct a beginning ethnography of something that was "culturally different" for him. As an Australian studying in the United States, Geoff had a number of opportunities to study a culturally different phenomenon while having fun with the project. He chose to study a sorority. As part of this study, he participated in

---

[9] Ibid., p. 94.

[10] *Writing Ethnographic Field Notes* (2nd Ed., p. 11), by R. M. Emerson, R. I. Fretz, and L. L. Shaw, 2011, Chicago, IL: University of Chicago Press.

one of the regular ceremonies that was part of the sorority members' lives: a formal dinner held each Monday night at which members were required to wear dresses and male guests were expected to wear a jacket and tie. During the course of the dinner, Geoff frequently excused himself to visit the restroom, stopping along the way to take out his notebook so he could record quotes and reconstruct events as they were happening—trying to capture in great detail all that he was observing. Of course, the irony in this strategy was that he was missing a great deal of the dinner by removing himself from the setting. The ridiculousness of the situation became evident when a dinner host asked him if he was feeling well or if the meal was to his satisfaction. After all, why did he keep leaving the dinner table? The message for ethnographic researchers who use field notes as part of their data collection efforts is clear: You cannot record everything that is happening during an observation, nor should you try to.

Guidelines for Recording Field Notes

Some general guidelines should help you combat the naïvety exhibited by Geoff in the preceding example. You should write your field notes as soon as possible after the observational episode. You will find that you rely heavily on the mental notes, or *headnotes*, that you have made during the day, and you should record your thoughts while they are fresh in your mind.

Depending on the setting you are researching and the degree of participation you are engaged in, the detail you record in your field notes will vary considerably. You may find by the end of the day that you have a pocket full of scrap paper with jottings from the day to augment your more detailed notes. Sometimes these jottings will capture keywords and phrases without a whole lot more to explain them. It is a good habit to let research participants know that you will be scribbling things down in your notepad; soon, they will become accustomed to your writing, and it will not cause a distraction. Your jottings will serve as mnemonic devices to help you reconstruct the events of the day. In short, when combined with your headnotes, these jottings can be a crucial aid in reconstructing and writing your observations.

Your jottings and expanded field notes are for your own use, so you needn't worry about editorial concerns or journalistic conventions. They are not intended to be polished text. Your goal in recording field notes should be to describe, not analyze or interpret. It is helpful to think of field notes as a way to capture a slice of life while acknowledging that all descriptions are selective because they have been written by a researcher trying to capture it all. Once you accept that the purpose is to describe and that through your descriptions will come understandings, you can easily focus on the task of creating field notes without concerns for style and audience.

Sometimes beginning researchers are troubled by how to begin summarizing their field notes for the day. A simple approach is to trace what you did during the day and to organize the notes in chronological order. That is, start at the beginning and finish at the end of the day. You should avoid the temptation to re-create the dialogue. Use quotation marks only when the words were taken down at the time of the observation; anything else should be paraphrased. Although a recording device is appropriate for structured ethnographic interviews, in your day-to-day observations you should stick with the convention of recording the quote on the spot or paraphrasing after the event.

Whether taken in the actual setting or recorded as soon as possible after leaving the setting, field notes describe as accurately as possible and as comprehensively as possible all relevant aspects of the situation observed. They include what was observed and the observer's reactions. What was observed represents the who, what, where, and when portion of the field notes. To appreciate the enormity of the task, imagine yourself trying to describe, in writing, in excruciating detail, even one of your current research class meetings. What was the physical setting like? What did it look like? Who was present? What did they look like? How did they act? What about your instructor? How did he or she look and act? What was said? What interactions took place? The task appears even more awesome when you consider that descriptions must be very specific. Patton[11] provided several good examples that clearly illustrate the difference between "vague and overgeneralized notes" and "detailed and concrete notes." One of them is presented below:

[11] *Qualitative Evaluation and Research Methods* (2nd ed., pp. 240–241), by M. Q. Patton, 1990, Newbury Park, CA: Sage.

Vague and overgeneralized notes: The next student who came in to take the test was very poorly dressed.

Detailed and concrete notes: The next student who came into the room was wearing clothes quite different from the three students who'd been in previously. The three previous students looked like they'd been groomed before they came to the test. Their hair was combed, their clothes were clean and pressed, the colors of their clothes matched, and their clothes were in good condition. This new student had on pants that were soiled with a hole or tear in one knee and a threadbare seat. The flannel shirt was wrinkled with one tail tucked into the pants and the other tail hanging out. Hair was disheveled and the boy's hands looked like he'd been playing in the engine of a car.

What constitutes being "very poorly dressed" may vary from observer to observer, but the detailed description speaks for itself, and most people who read it will have a similar mental picture of what the boy looked like.

In addition to describing what was seen and heard, the observer also records personal reactions in reflective field notes. These notes include interpretations and other subjective thoughts and feelings, but they are clearly differentiated from the more objective, descriptive field notes; typically they are identified with a special code (e.g., PC for personal comment or OC for observer's comments). In these notes, the observer is free to express any thoughts regarding how things are going, where things are going, and what may be concluded. Reflective field notes may include statements such as the following:

PC I have the feeling that tension among faculty members has been growing for some time.

PC I think Mr. Haddit has been egging on other faculty members.

PC I'm finding it hard to be objective because Mr. Hardnozed is rather abrasive.

PC I think the transition would have been smoother if key faculty members had been informed and involved in the process.

Such insights add a significant dimension to the observations and thus contribute to producing a rich description, which is the objective of ethnographic research.

Observing and Recording Everything You Possibly Can

At the start of an observation, researchers begin with a broad sweep of the setting and gradually narrow focus to get a clearer sense of what is most pressing. Engaging in an effort to record everything will quickly attune you to the topics and behaviors that most interest you. You can also decide on your strategies for recording observations. You may decide to record verbatim conversations, make maps and illustrations, take photographs, make video or audio recordings, or even furiously write notes. Recording observations is a very idiosyncratic activity, so try to maintain a running record of what is happening in a format that will be most helpful for you. For example, in his ethnographic research study of a school district attempting multiple change efforts,[12] Geoff Mills attended the teacher in-service day for the district. Following are some of his field notes from this observation:

8:30 a.m. An announcement is made over the public address system requesting that teachers move into the auditorium and take a seat in preparation for the in-service. As the teachers file into the auditorium, the superintendent plays a song that speaks to his desire to see teachers be role models for their students.

8:41 a.m. The Assistant Superintendent welcomes the teachers to the in-service with the conviction that it is also the "best district with the best teachers." The brief welcome is then followed by the Pledge of Allegiance and the introduction of the new Assistant Superintendent.

8:45 a.m. The Assistant Superintendent introduces the Superintendent as "the Superintendent who cares about kids, cares about teachers, and cares about this district."

The next hour of the in-service was focused on the introduction of new teachers to the district (there were 60 new appointments) and

---

[12] *Managing and Coping with Multiple Educational Change: A Case Study and Analysis,* by G. E. Mills, 1988, unpublished doctoral dissertation, University of Oregon, Eugene.

the presentation of information about at-risk children becoming a new focus for the district.

10:00 a.m. The Superintendent returns to the lyrics of the song he was playing and suggests that the message from the song may be suitable as the district's charge. He compels the teachers to be the heroes for their students and wishes them a successful school year before closing the in-service.

As you can see from this abbreviated example, there is nothing mystical about field notes. They serve as a record of what a researcher attended to during the course of an observation and help guide subsequent observations and interviews. These notes were taken at the beginning of Geoff's year-long fieldwork in the McKenzie School District, and this initial observation helped him to frame questions that guided his efforts to understand how central office personnel, principals, and teachers manage and cope with multiple innovations.

Looking for Nothing in Particular; Looking for Bumps and Paradoxes

While working in the field, you should try to see routines in new ways. If you can, try to look with new eyes and approach the scene as if you were an outsider. Wolcott[13] offered helpful advice for teachers conducting observations in classrooms that are so familiar that everything seems ordinary and routine:

> Aware of being familiar with classroom routines, an experienced observer might initiate a new set of observations with the strategy that in yet another classroom one simply assumes "business as usual". . . The observer sets a sort of radar, scanning constantly for whatever it is that those in the setting are doing to keep the system operating smoothly.

You should consider the environment you are observing as if it were metaphorically flat or, in other words, with nothing in particular standing out to you. This strategy gives you an opportunity to look for the bumps in the setting. In ethnographic research studies focused in classrooms, these bumps may be unexpected student responses to a new curriculum or teaching strategy or an unexpected response to a new classroom management plan, seating arrangement, monitoring strategy, or innovation. For example, a teacher concerned with gender inequity in the classroom may notice that one or two boys seem to be controlling the classroom. Upon noticing this bump, he keeps a tally of the number of times students command his attention by answering or asking questions, and it becomes painfully evident that one or two boys are regularly the focus of attention during a lesson.

Ethnographic researchers should also look for contradictions or paradoxes in their classrooms. Like a bump, a paradox often stands out in an obvious way to the researcher who has taken the time to stand back and look at what is happening in the classroom. Teacher-researchers using ethnographic techniques often comment on the unintended consequences of a particular teaching strategy or a curriculum change that has become evident only when they have had an opportunity to observe the results of their actions. These consequences often present themselves in the form of a paradox—a contradiction in terms. For example, one teacher-researcher had recently incorporated manipulatives (e.g., tiles, blocks, etc.) into her math instruction in a primary classroom. After observing her students, she commented, "I thought that the use of manipulatives in teaching mathematics would also lead to increased cooperation in group work. Instead, what I saw were my kids fighting over who got to use what and not wanting to share."

Figure 14.2, which represents an adaptation of Patton's guidelines, provides a useful summary of fieldwork and field notes in ethnographic research. If you undertake this intimate and open-ended form of research, you may be faced with a set of personal (and perhaps interpersonal) challenges, but you may also find yourself engaged in a meaning-making activity that belies description and that redefines your life as an educational researcher.

An example of ethnographic research appears at the end of this chapter.

---

[13] *Transforming Qualitative Data: Description, Analysis, and Interpretation* (p. 162), by H. F. Wolcott, 1994, Thousand Oaks, CA: Sage.

MyLab Education **Self-Check 14.5**

MyLab Education **Application Exercise 14.4:** Conducting Ethnographic Research

FIGURE 14.2 • Summary guidelines for fieldwork and field notes

1. Be descriptive in taking field notes.

2. Gather a variety of information from different perspectives.

3. Cross-validate and triangulate by gathering different kinds of data (e.g., observations, documents, interviews) and by using multiple methods.

4. Use quotations; represent people in their own terms. Capture their experiences in their own words.

5. Select "key informants" wisely and use them carefully. Draw on the wisdom of their informed perspectives, but keep in mind that their perspectives are limited.

6. Be aware of and sensitive to different stages of fieldwork.
   a) Build trust and rapport at the beginning. Remember that the observer is also being observed.
   b) Stay alert and disciplined during the more routine, middle phase of fieldwork.
   c) Focus on pulling together a useful synthesis as fieldwork draws to a close.

7. Be disciplined and conscientious in taking field notes at all stages of fieldwork.

8. Be as involved as possible in experiencing the situation as fully as possible while maintaining an analytical perspective grounded in the purpose of the fieldwork.

9. Clearly separate description from interpretation and judgment.

10. Include in your field notes and report your own experiences, thoughts, and feelings.

Source: From M. Q. Patton, *Qualitative Evaluation and Research Methods*, pp. 272–273, copyright © 1990 by Sage Publications, Inc. Adapted by permission of Sage Publications, Inc.

SUMMARY

ETHNOGRAPHIC RESEARCH: DEFINITION AND PURPOSE

1. Ethnographic research is the study of the cultural patterns and perspectives of participants in their natural settings.
2. Ethnography produces a picture of a way of life of some identifiable group of people using a process (primarily participant observation) that enables the researcher to discern patterns of behavior in human social activity.
3. Ethnographers describe and interpret culture—the set of attitudes, values, concepts, beliefs, and practices shared by the members of a group.

THE ETHNOGRAPHIC RESEARCH PROCESS

4. In ethnographic research, the researcher first identifies the purpose of the research study and frames it as a larger theoretical policy or practical problem. The researcher then decides on the site and the sample for the study, secures permissions and negotiates entry, and begins data collection.
5. The primary data collection techniques in ethnographic research are participant observation, field notes, interviews, and the examination of artifacts such as school policy documents and attendance records.
6. Following analysis of the data, the researcher writes an ethnographic account, which is usually a narrative that captures the social, cultural, and economic themes that emerge from the study.

KEY CHARACTERISTICS OF ETHNOGRAPHIC RESEARCH

7. Ethnographic research is carried out in a natural setting, not a laboratory.
8. It involves intimate, face-to-face interaction with participants.
9. It presents an accurate reflection of participants' perspectives and behaviors.
10. It uses inductive, interactive, and repetitious collection of unstructured data and analytic strategies to build local cultural theories.

11. Data are collected primarily through fieldwork experiences.
12. It typically uses multiple methods for data collection, including conducting interviews and observations and reviewing documents, artifacts, and visual materials.
13. It frames all human behavior and belief within a sociopolitical and historical context.
14. It uses the concept of culture as a lens through which to interpret results.
15. It places an emphasis on exploring the nature of particular social phenomena rather than setting out to test hypotheses about them.
16. It investigates a small number of cases, perhaps just one case, in detail.
17. It uses data analysis procedures that involve the explicit interpretation of the meanings and functions of human actions.
18. It requires that researchers be reflective about their impact on the research site and the cultural group.
19. It offers interpretations of people's actions and behaviors that must be uncovered through an investigation of what people do and their reasons for doing it.
20. It offers a representation of a person's life and behavior that is built on points of understanding and misunderstanding that occur between researcher and participant.
21. Ethnographic descriptions are necessarily partial, bound by what can be handled within a certain time, under specific circumstances, and from a particular perspective.

TYPES OF ETHNOGRAPHIC RESEARCH

22. A critical ethnography is a highly politicized form of ethnography written by a researcher in order to advocate against inequalities and domination of particular groups that exist in society.
23. A realist ethnography is written with an objective style and using common categories (e.g., "family life") for cultural description, analysis, and interpretation.
24. An ethnographic case study focuses on describing the activities of a specific group and the shared patterns of behavior the group develops over time.

ETHNOGRAPHIC RESEARCH TECHNIQUES

25. A researcher who is a genuine participant in the activity under study is called a participant observer. The participant observer is fully immersed in the research setting as a way to get close to those studied and thus understand what their experiences and activities mean to them.

26. A participant observer can be an active participant observer; a privileged, active observer; or a passive observer.

27. Field notes are the written records of participant observers.

28. Field notes are characterized by headnotes and jottings. The observer records literal, objective descriptions and personal reactions, generally referred to as reflective field notes.

29. Ethnographic researchers try to look with new eyes and approach the scene as if they were outsiders. Ethnographic researchers also look for contradictions or paradoxes that stand out.

Preparing Preservice Teachers in a Diverse World

SUSAN DAVIS LENSKI
Portland State University

KATHLEEN CRAWFORD
Wayne State University

THOMAS CRUMPLER AND CORSANDRA STALLWORTH
Illinois State University

ABSTRACT This study was designed to develop more effective ways to address culture and cultural differences in the preparation of preservice teachers. Its purpose was to provide a more adequate preparation for working in high-need schools by assisting educators in the development of "habits of mind" that incorporate an understanding and valuing of students' cultures and a recognition of the need to consider those cultures in teaching practices. This paper reports data from the second year of a five-year study that examined the experience of six preservice teachers. The data indicate that using ethnography as an observational tool helps preservice teachers become more aware of cultural differences.

(01) The teaching force in the United States is becoming increasingly White during a time when the student population is becoming increasingly diverse. The percentage of preservice teachers of diverse races ranges from 7% to 68% per state while the national percentage of White teachers remains over 90% (Hodgkinson, 2002). Because of the disparities between the backgrounds of teachers and those of students, multicultural education in schools is essential because the "classroom is a meeting ground of cultures where the worlds of the students meet the worldview of schools and teachers" (Cumrot, 2002, p. 14). The meeting of cultures in schools, however, can result in a cultural clash when the culture of students is different from that of the teacher. Since the way that teachers address cultural differences can influence student learning, it is imperative that preservice teachers learn to become culturally responsive to students from diverse backgrounds (Garcia & Willis, 2001).

(02) Teachers need to become culturally responsive whether the teachers themselves are White or from other cultural backgrounds (Gay, 2000). Over the course of their careers, teachers can expect to teach students who come from dozens of different cultural groups, so it is unrealistic to expect teachers to have a deep understanding of all of the cultures that are represented in their classrooms (Nieto, 2002). Instead, teachers need to learn new ways of thinking about cultural differences, and this learning should begin in teacher preparation programs. According to Darling-Hammond and Garcia-Lopez (2002), "it is impossible to prepare tomorrow's teachers to succeed with all of the students they will meet without exploring how students' learning experiences are influenced by their home languages, cultures, and contexts; the realities of race and class privilege in the United States; the ongoing manifestations of institutional racism within the educational system; and the many factors that shape students' opportunities to learn within individual classrooms" (p. 9).

(03) Past efforts at preparing future teachers to become culturally responsive through traditional multicultural courses have shown mixed results. Some researchers have indicated that preservice teachers in multicultural courses had improved racial attitudes (Delany-Barmann & Minner, 1997; Ross &

Smith, 1992), while others reported few or even negative changes (Bollin & Finkel, 1995; Cannella & Reiff, 1994; Haberman & Post, 1990; McDiarmid & Price, 1993; Zeichner et al., 1998). On the whole, multicultural courses have tended to reinforce the idea of "difference blindness," which suggests that a neutral image of students promotes equality (Cochran-Smith, 2004). Recent research, however, has indicated that teachers who believe that they are "color blind" and treat all students equally, actually privilege mainstream students in subtle but important ways (Lewis, 2001; Reeves, 2004).

(04) Because preservice coursework in multicultural education has not made enough of an impact on future teachers, teacher educators have recently been working to redefine multicultural education (Cochran-Smith, 2003; Vavrus, 2002). In an outline of a new curriculum for multicultural education, Villegas and Lucas (2002) argue that preservice teachers need to become socio-culturally conscious. In order for that to occur, some researchers believe that White preservice teachers need to come to an understanding of their own White culture and that they should examine their identity in relation to other cultures (Johnson, 2002; Howard, 1999; Tatum, 1994). This change in directions has shown promise. Studies conducted by Schmidt (1998) and Xu (2001) indicated that asking teachers and preservice teachers to examine their own cultural beliefs and compare them with the beliefs of someone outside their cultural group helps them become more aware of cultural differences.

(05) Studies for preparing future teachers to become culturally responsive have not previously taken into account the observational tools ethnographers use to learn about new cultures. Ethnography is sometimes discounted in educational circles because it is traditionally a long-term, labor-intensive activity. However, some ethnographers believe that ethnographic practices can be used in short-term projects (Handwerker, 2001) since ethnography is "a way of seeing" the community and the cultures of students' classrooms (Wolcott, 1999). For example, Moll and Gonzalez (1994) used ethnography to help practicing teachers learn about the funds of knowledge of families of their students. Other studies indicate that student teachers and practicing teachers can become ethnographers in order to learn about their students (Dixon, Frank, & Green, 1999; Frank, 1999; Frank & Uy, 2004). These studies influenced our work as we developed a project that would help our preservice teachers become culturally responsive teachers.

Beyond Awareness Project

(06) The Beyond Awareness Project was a five-year program designed to move preservice teachers from being aware of cultural differences to the development of "habits of mind" that incorporate an understanding and valuing of students' cultures and recognition of the need to consider those cultures in teaching practices. As we developed the program, we decided to implement an ethnography project for preservice teachers thinking that ethnography would help preservice teachers become aware of the cultural complexities of the school communities where they would student teach. The goals of the ethnography were to promote the constructivist dispositions necessary to work with diverse populations and to move beyond awareness of other cultures to a real sensitivity toward differences. During the ethnography project, we repeatedly discussed the numerous non-visible types of diversity such as gender issues, religious diversity, and socioeconomic (SES) influences to bring about an awareness of the complexities of the populations that would constitute the future classrooms of preservice teachers.

> The purpose of the study was to describe the impact of an ethnography project (the Beyond Awareness Project) on preservice teachers' awareness of the cultural complexities of the schools and communities in which they student-teach.

Method

(07) Before and during the ethnography the preservice teachers were instructed how to conduct ethnographic research. This process was based on Spradley's

book (1980) *Participant Observation*. During the fall semester, an anthropologist, Rob, a literacy educator, Susan, and an on-site teacher, JoNancy, instructed the preservice teachers in the steps of ethnography. The steps in the ethnographic process included learning about ethnography, conducting participation observation, making descriptive observations, analyzing the data, and writing a report.

(08)   Every two weeks the preservice teachers held information sharing discussions with Rob, Susan, and JoNancy. During these sessions, the steps of eth nography were discussed and modeled. During the yearlong project, Susan also completed an ethnography and used her work to illustrate the ethnographic process. Before beginning their projects, however, the preservice teachers practiced their observation skills in a school setting. They completed walks around the neighborhood and the school, took a school bus ride, made observations in their schools, and wrote reflections. The goal of pre-ethnography activities was to increase the preservice teachers' confidence in ethnographic tools.

(09)   After the preservice teachers grew comfortable with their role as observer and were adept at taking field notes, they formed groups to choose a community site for the ethnography. Community sites were chosen with the help of an advisory group composed of community members, teachers, and administrators. The preservice teachers were encouraged to make at least 10 visits to their site, first observing and taking field notes and then becoming participant observers.

(10)   During the data-gathering period, the preservice teachers continued to receive instruction on ethnographic research. The project was designed with the assumption that to learn to conduct ethnographic research, it is necessary for individuals to develop into a researcher while simultaneously grasping how the process evolves. The preservice teachers took field notes and wrote reflections throughout the year and discussed them every week in class. Upon completion of the fieldwork, the preservice teachers wrote a final paper and prepared presentations for their classmates and for a state reading conference.

Participants

(11)   The participants of this study were enrolled in an elementary education program at a large Midwestern university. The group included 28 preservice teachers, 26 females and 2 males. Of the participants, 25 were of European American background and one was Hispanic. All of the participants attended a Professional Development School (PDS) that was located in a suburb of a metropolitan center. The PDS was a partnership between the university and a school district that has a large number of students from diverse backgrounds. During the PDS year, the preservice teachers took courses from university faculty on site, and they also spent two or three days each week in schools.

Data Sources

(12)   Over the course of this five-year project, an ethnographically informed approach to data collection was used (Lecompte & Priessle, 1993). The first year of the project was a pilot year. We collected and analyzed data and learned how to tailor the project to better serve the preservice teachers (see Lenski, Crawford, Crumpler, & Stallworth, in press). Data from the second year of the study were collected on multiple levels. Data sources included 1) neighborhood observations, 2) reflections of a school bus ride, 3) observations of school sites, 4) observational field notes and reflections of community sites, 5) interviews of six preservice teachers during the project, 6) student papers describing ways to address cultural issues in classrooms, and 7) final ethnographic papers. The data from the second year of the project will be described in this paper.

Ethnographically informed data collection strategies included observations (and field notes) of neighborhoods, school sites, and community sites; reflections of a school bus ride; interviews with six preservice teachers; analysis of student papers addressing cultural issues in classrooms; and final ethnographic papers.

Data Analysis

All twenty-eight of the preservice teachers were participants in the study. However, after a preliminary analysis of the neighborhood observation and school bus ride, a sub-group of six students were chosen to be interviewed. This group was chosen as representative of the larger group of preservice teachers and was viewed as a variation of the concept of "key informants" (Lecompte & Preissle, 1993). While they did not have "specialized knowledge" that is often attributed to individuals who are members of the community where research was conducted, as members of the community of preservice teachers, they did provide researchers access to more in depth information about issues of diversity (Lecompte & Preissle, 1993, p. 166). The interviews spanned the year and included three formal interviews and five informal interviews.

The data from these participants were separated from the larger data set. Interviews were transcribed and copies of all of the data were given to the research team. At bi-monthly meetings, the researchers discussed their overall perceptions of the data. Discussions led to the formulation of four non-overlapping themes indicative of patterns that surfaced throughout the review of the data. In each of the four areas, sample comments were selected to illustrate the pattern of responses. The themes were then reformulated into questions that framed the next stages of data analysis. The questions were:

1. How do participants view themselves as cultural beings?
2. How do participants view issues of diversity?
3. In what ways do participants "step into the community," or actually become a participant observer?
4. How do the participants use the experiences they had in the ethnography project to represent themselves as an emerging teacher?

The researchers used these questions to delve back into the data and to analyze it more thoroughly. The multiple data sources were used as triangulation for validity and reliability purposes (Yin, 1994). Based on this analysis, codes were developed by each of the four researchers independently, using a system of "open coding," and then the research team met, compared, and refined these initial codes to arrive at consensus (Strauss, 1987; Strauss & Corbin, 1990). Using these revised codes, the researchers re-examined the data to ensure theoretical rigor and to ground their analysis in conceptual precision.

Results

One of the primary goals of this study was to look at ways that preserice teachers view themselves as cultural beings. Since examining one's own culture is a prerequisite for understanding differences, we were interested in knowing whether our students were able to understand their own privileged position as future teachers in a diverse community. One way we approached the data was to look for ways students were able to confront their assumptions of culture and to look at the ways in which they could be open to new ways of thinking.

Views of Self as a Cultural Being by Confronting Cultural Assumptions

One of the purposes for asking students to conduct ethnography was to help them sharpen their observation skills and learn about communities before jumping to conclusions. The data indicated that the students in our study had made a variety of assumptions while during their observations.

(13)

Sample selection included all 28 preservice teachers in the study with a sub-group of six "key informants" chosen to be interviewed as representative of the larger group of preservice teachers.

What do we know about these key informants that would lead us to the same conclusion that they are representative of the larger group of preservice teachers?

(14)

Data analysis was conducted by the research team at bimonthly meetings, where they identified four nonoverlapping themes indicative of patterns that surfaced throughout the review of the data. In each of the four areas, sample comments were selected to illustrate the pattern of responses.

(15)

(16)

(17)

One of the activities that illustrated the assumptions students automatically made was during their walk around the neighborhood. As students observed houses, stores, and people, they tended to make unwarranted assumptions. For example, Inez (all names are pseudonyms) observed a school neighborhood that was near a bus station and power lines, so she concluded that the neighborhood was low income. She also assumed that the neighborhood was violent after seeing "neighborhood watch" signs. Inez wrote, "I thought that you don't need a neighborhood watch unless your area had some violence or vandalism." Another assumption Inez made about the neighborhood was that it had "many elderly people living in it along with a new crowd that moved there within the last couple of years." The basis for her assumption was that many houses were older and were neatly kept while other houses looked "run down." Inez, therefore, used brief snatches of observation to make assumptions and draw conclusions about the community and the people in that community.

(18)   Although the assumptions students made about a community may be benign, other assumptions they made could be potentially damaging to the students they would teach. For example, Taylor recorded, "most bilingual-Hispanic homes are single parent or combined households." She also wrote, "many teachers have a narrow mind when it comes to diversity." These comments seem to indicate that Taylor, like many other preservice teachers, tend to over generalize information. The school where Taylor was observing had a large Hispanic population in an area of low-cost houses and apartments where the parents of some of the students from her class were living. Taylor met some of the parents from her class who did not live in traditional families and she heard teachers denigrating these families. From this small sample of information, Taylor concluded that many Hispanics lived in the same situations and that teachers tended to be narrow-minded.

(19)   After reading these comments, we were concerned that the ethnographic process was leading students to use small bits of observations and making assumptions about people based on limited information. Therefore, we began examining students' assumptions in class and holding discussions about ways in which previous beliefs color observations. We also emphasized that ethnography was not intended to have investigators draw conclusions quite as rapidly as our students seemed to do. As we worked with students, we saw rapid growth and understanding.

(20)   By the time students had spent two or three visits at their community sites, they began viewing themselves in a different light. Taylor, who spent her time observing an after-school program, stated, "This project is making me aware of my own culture and that of other students. Before this, I didn't think of myself as having a culture." Like many people, Taylor had previously considered herself "just an American." Lynch and Hanson (2004) have found this lack of cultural understanding to be common among White teachers. They also suggest that not understanding one's own cultural background is an obstacle to understanding the cultural backgrounds of their students. As the project progressed through the year, the preservice teachers continued to grow in their understanding of themselves as a cultural being.

Issues of Diversity

(21)   The preservice teachers learned to expand their ideas of diversity through this project. In classroom conversations, they focused on race as the only aspect of diversity. As students visited a variety of community sites, however, they found that diversity can be found in other areas. Bob, for example, stated, "Teachers need to be aware of gender, ethnic, and socio-economic differences." This statement was a major breakthrough for him; he had described diversity in an earlier class as ethnic heritage.

An example of ways students learned to expand their internal definition (22) of diversity was illustrated by the students who visited an Asian Mexican grocery store. In the store, they found many religious icons for sale. Jodi, who was observing at the store, wrote, "This informed us how important Catholicism is to the Hispanic culture." Another student visited a Hebrew Saturday school. During class discussions, the discussions of religion as a component of diverse cultures helped some of the preservice teachers expand their views of diversity to include issues of religion, gender, and socio-economic status.

Near the end of the project, the preservice teachers wrote about diversity (23) in their final papers. Jodi wrote, "Diversity is far reaching. . .It's not just race/ ethnicity. My classroom will be full of children who are diverse and I want to be aware and sensitive of all kinds of diversity (race, gender, academics, economics, etc.) to be an effective teacher." In group discussions of the ideal classroom, Taylor said, "It calls to mind a classroom of different genders, race, religions, cultures, and all kinds of different people; all the things that make people unique."

Becoming a Participant Observer

The preservice teachers voiced concerns throughout the project about being (24) asked to conduct ethnographies. One of the concerns of the researchers was that the preservice teachers would see the project as one more teaching activity, where they, as student teachers, would find themselves in situations where they were considered an "authority." Instead, students were encouraged to make observations as researchers or ethnographers. We thought that by asking students to position themselves as ethnographers, they would be able to distance themselves from their role as teachers and actually learn about a cultural group.

Most of the students found that it took some time to learn how to (25) observe community sites without making judgments. However, they found that stepping into the role of participant observer helped them look at their students differently. For example, Bob said that observing students on the bus "brought back a lot of memories and reminded me of when I was in school." Bob continued, "I have a better idea of where the students live and what their neighborhoods are like." As Jodi began her ethnography of an Asian Mexican store, she said in her interview, "I began to feel very comfortable in the store, even helping other customers find items." Jodi moved from being an uncomfortable observer to a participant observer.

Although it was difficult for the preservice teachers to "step into the (26) community," time at the site helped them feel comfortable. Other studies support this notion. Kidd, Sanchez, and Thorp (2004) found that having preservice teachers learn about family stories helped them become more culturally aware, and Garmon (2004), in his study of a White preservice teacher, hypothesized that learning about a different culture can be the basis for potential change about views of diversity. In our study, we found that all six of the preservice teachers moved from being mildly afraid in their new surroundings to becoming enthusiastic champions of the people at their site.

Emergence as Teachers

One of the strongest areas of the ethnography project was the preservice (27) teachers' ability to apply the knowledge of their experiences and learning to future classroom instruction. In every area of the project, students attempted to make sense of the activity through the lens of a teacher. We encouraged this kind of thinking. In the first year of the ethnography project, we asked preservice teachers to think like "researchers." The preservice teachers, however, could see little value in looking at teaching as a researcher and balked at the entire notion (Lenski, Crawford, Crumpler, & Stallworth, in press). Learning that preservice teachers believed they needed to apply every activity in their methods courses to teaching, we emphasized applications to teaching during the second year of the project.

(28)   We found that our preservice teachers were able to apply their experiences to teaching easily. For example, as Jodi spent time in the Asian Mexican grocery store talking with the owners and patrons, she concluded, "The traditions of the Filipino culture we learned will aid us in giving our students the best experience possible, by carrying on some of the traditions in school. This knowledge we have gained will help us to be more culturally sensitive teachers." In this case, Jodi realized that they had little knowledge of the Filipino culture before spending time interacting with people with Filipino heritage. She realized that learning about the culture of their students is one of the prerequisites of becoming a culturally responsive teacher (Gay, 2000).

(29)   Our data were replete with such specific examples, and we also found that students were able to generate their own teaching principles about teaching and learning. For example, Inez wrote, "we must connect learning to personal experience for all students to comprehend what's happening." In their final papers, many students used language similar to Inez's by discussing the ways to connect curricula to students' lives, to help students apply their background knowledge, and to differentiate instruction. Some of the practical applications of these principles included learning words in students' native languages, researching authors from the students' culture, having books read in students' native language, posting students' native language alphabet in the classroom if it's not the Roman alphabet, and valuing students' funds of knowledge (e.g., Moll & Gonzalez, 1994). Perhaps the most telling comment from the preservice teachers, though, was Jennifer's comment: "I don't want to see them as a group of children; I want to see them as individuals."

Discussion

(30)   Analysis of the data indicated three trends. First, while the preservice teachers valued the ethnographically informed work, there was a tension between looking for specifics and using the observations as a way to learn how to see. In other words, the preservice teachers seemed to want to be told specifically what to look for, while the researchers were interested in the preservice teachers opening themselves to the dynamics and interactions of the chosen observational site. While this could be viewed as part of the challenge of the "dual purposes of participant observation" (Spradley, 1980, p. 54), it also suggested how ethnographic work in diverse settings might help faculty in teacher education courses encourage preservice teachers to examine their own views about diversity education. Second, data indicated that all six preservice teachers concluded that as they prepared to pursue teaching jobs in schools, participating in this project had shifted their thinking about diversity. Individuals described how they had moved beyond being aware of the need for dealing with diversity to actually planning strategies for bringing students' communities into their classrooms. This shift from general concern to specific plans suggested that the project impacted these preservice teachers' views about instruction. We hypothesize that the process of learning about people from different backgrounds and becoming personally engaged in their culture was one reason for this change. Third, preservice teachers reported that the writing component of this project was a burden, given the challenges of their methods coursework. We are committed to continuing participant observation in this project; however, as our larger goal is reforming aspects of teacher education, we must be sensitive to how we build this approach into an already full curriculum for preservice teachers.

Conclusions

(31) Many teacher educators recognize that recruiting and preparing teachers who can be effective to work with preservice teachers from diverse backgrounds is at a crisis level. Haberman (2003) argues that securing and retaining effective teachers is of utmost importance because conditions in education are becoming increasingly more challenging for students in urban centers. Effective urban teachers believe they are focused on their students' learning and development. "They do not stay in teaching because they want to function as educational change agents, community organizers or system reformers" (Haberman, p. 21) but instead they stay for their students. Effective teachers need to continually examine the relationships between students and the curriculum. "Being a critical multicultural educator is as much a philosophy and way of life as it is implementation of quality curriculum" (Page, 2004, p. 8). As teacher educators have learned ways to teach preservice teachers about cultural differences, new ideas for multicultural education have been developed. In keeping with this new movement in moving beyond multicultural education to influencing preservice teachers' habits of mind, we developed the Beyond Awareness Project.

(32) The data from the second year of the study suggest that participant observation and ethnographically informed approaches embedded within teacher preparation courses could be key elements to developing more effective ways to address culture and cultural diversity in teacher education. By having preservice teachers use ethnographically informed methods to learn about the community, they began to interact with perspectives different from their own. From this interaction the six preservice teachers that we studied moved "beyond awareness" of cultural differences to thinking about ways to effectively teach all students in their classrooms—especially those who have been overlooked because of their cultural background. The preservice teachers in our study learned to be problem posers through real life experiences within ethnographic inquiry. They learned to examine more critically the situations they observed and question their beliefs and understandings of the community.

(33) The data from this study suggest that participant observation and ethnographically informed approaches embedded within teacher preparation courses could be key elements in developing more effective ways to address culture and cultural diversity in teacher education. However, this study has taken place in one PDS with preservice teachers who self-selected into the site so cannot be generalizable to other groups. Our findings, however, indicate that an ethnographic approach could have the potential to impact views of diversity and needs to be tested in a larger arena.

(34) Our goal for the future of this project is to take the knowledge gained from this project back to the main campus program with the hope of transforming the methods courses and experiences for a larger number of preservice teachers. We will continue our research in this broader context to progressively refine our approaches to educating preservice teachers about diversity. Such an approach may allow more insights into preservice teachers' "habits of mind" about diversity and that lead to even more effective ways to encourage inclusive and transformative teaching for a wider audience in deeper, more meaningful ways.

REFERENCES

Bollin, G. G., & Finkel, J. (1995). White racial identity as a barrier to understanding diversity: A study of preservice teachers. *Equity & Excellence in Education, 28*(1), 25–30.

Cannella, G. S., & Reiff, J. C. (1994). Teacher preparation for diversity. *Equity & Excellence in Education, 27*(3), 28–33.

Cochran-Smith, M. (2003). The multiple meanings of multicultural teacher education. *Teacher Education Quarterly, 30*(2), 7–26.

Cochran-Smith, M. (2004). *Walking the road: Race, diversity, and social justice in teacher education.* New York: Teachers College Press.

Cumrot, T. Z. (2002). What is diversity? In L. Darling-Hammond, J. French, & S. P. Garcia-Lopez (Eds.), *Learning to teach for social justice* (pp. 13–17). New York: Teachers College Press.

Darling-Hammond, L. D., & Garcia-Lopez, S. P. (2002). What is diversity? In L. Darling-Hammond, J. French, & S. P. Garcia-Lopez (Eds.), *Learning to teach for social justice* (pp. 9–12). New York: Teachers College Press.

Delany-Barmann, G., & Minner, S. (1997). Development and implementation of a program of study to prepare teachers for diversity. *Equity and Excellence in Education, 30*(2), 78–85.

Dixon, C., Frank, C., & Green, J. (1999). Classrooms as cultures. *Primary Voices K–6, 7*(3), 4–8.

Frank, C. (1999). *Ethnographic eyes: A teacher's guide to classroom observation.* Portsmouth, NH: Heinemann.

Frank, C. R., & Uy, F. L. (2004). Ethnography for teacher education. *Journal of Teacher Education, 55*, 269–283.

Garcia, G. E., & Willis, A. I. (2001). Frameworks for understanding multicultural literacies. In P. R. Schmidt & P. B. Mosenthal (Eds.), *Reconceptualizing literacy in the new age of multiculturalism and pluralism* (pp. 3–31). Greenwich, CT: Information Age Publishing.

Garmon, M. A. (2004). Changing preservice teachers' attitudes/beliefs about diversity: What are the critical factors? *Journal of Teacher Education, 55*, 201–213.

Gay, G. (2000). *Culturally responsive teaching: Theory, research, & practice.* New York: Teachers College Press.

Haberman, M. (2003). *Who benefits from failing urban school districts? An essay on equity and justice for diverse children in urban poverty.* Houston, TX: Haberman Education Foundation.

Haberman, M., & Post, L. (1990). Cooperating teachers' perception of the goals of multicultural education. *Action in Teacher Education, 12*(3), 31–35.

Handwerker, W. P. (2001). *Quick ethnography.* Walnut Creek, CA: AltaMira.

Hodgkinson, H. (2002). Demographics and teacher education: An overview. *Journal of Teacher Education, 53*, 102–105.

Howard, G. R. (1999). *We can't teach what we don't know: White teachers multiracial schools.* New York: Teachers College Press.

Johnson, L. (2002). "My eyes have been opened": White teachers and racial awareness. *Journal of Teacher Education, 53*, 153–167.

Kidd, J. K., Sanchez, S. Y., & Thorp, E. K. (2004). Gathering family stories: Facilitating preservice teachers' cultural awareness and responsiveness. *Action in Teacher Education, 26*(1), 64–73.

LeCompte, M., & Priessle, J. (1993). *Ethnography and qualitative design in educational research.* San Diego: Academic Press.

Lenski, S. D., Crawford, K. M., Crumpler, T. P., & Stallworth, C. (In press). Beyond Awareness: Preparing culturally responsive preservice teachers. *Teacher Education Quarterly.*

Lewis, A. E. (2001). There is no "race" in the schoolyard: Color-blind ideology in an (almost) all-white school. *American Educational Research Journal, 38*, 781–811.

Lynch, E. W., & Hanson, M. J. (2004). *Developing cross-cultural competence: A guide for working with children and their families* (3rd ed.). Baltimore, MD: Brookes.

McDiarmid, G. W., & Price, J. (1993). Preparing teachers for diversity: A study of the student teachers in a multicultural program. In M. J. O'Hair & S. J. Odell (Eds.), *Diversity and teaching: Teacher education yearbook I* (pp. 31–59). Fort Worth, TX: Harcourt Brace Jovanovich.

Moll, L. C., & Gonzalez, N. (1994). Critical issues: Lessons from research with language-minority children. *Journal of Reading Behavior: A Journal of Literacy Research, 26*, 439–456.

Nieto, S. (2002). *Language, culture, and teaching.* Mahwah, NJ: Lawrence Erlbaum.

Page, M. (2004). Going beyond the book: A multicultural educator in the English language arts classroom. *Voices from the Middle, 12*(1), 8–15.

Reeves, J. (2004). "Like everybody else": Equalizing educational opportunity for English Language Learners. *TESOL Quarterly, 38*(1), 43–66.

Ross, D. D., & Smith, W. (1992). Understanding preservice teachers' perspectives on diversity. *Journal of Teacher Education, 43*(2), 94–103.

Schmidt, P. R. (1998). The ABC Model: Teachers connect home and school. In T. Shanahan & F. Rodriguez-Brown (Eds.), *47th Yearbook of the National Reading Conference* (pp. 194–208). Chicago, IL: National Reading Conference.

Spradley, J. P. (1980). *Participant observation.* New York: Harcourt Brace.

Strauss, A. L. (1987). *Qualitative analysis for social scientists.* New York: Cambridge University Press.

Strauss, A., & Corbin, J. (1990). *Basics of qualitative research: Grounded theory procedures and techniques.* Newbury Park, CA: Sage.

Tatum, B. D. (1994). Teaching white preservice teachers about racism: The search for White allies and the restoration of hope. *Teachers College Record, 95*, 462–476.

Vavrus, M. (2002). *Transforming the multicultural education of teachers.* New York: Teachers College.

Villegas, A. M., & Lucas, T. (2002). Preparing culturally responsive teachers: Rethinking the curriculum. *Journal of Teacher Education, 53,* 20–32.

Wolcott, H. F. (1999). *Ethnography: A way of seeing.* Walnut Creek, CA: AltaMira.

Xu, H. (2001). Preservice teachers connect multicultural knowledge and perspectives with literacy instruction for minority preservice teachers. In P. R. Schmidt & P. B. Mosenthal (Eds.), *Reconceptualizing literacy in the new age of multiculturalism and pluralism* (pp. 323–340). Greenwich, CT: Information Age Publishing.

Yin, R. K. (1994). *Case study methodology* (2nd ed.). Newbury Park, CA: Sage.

Zeichner, K. M., Grant, C., Gay, G., Gillette, M., Valli, L., & Villegas, A. M. (1998). A research informed vision of good practice in multicultural education: Design principles. *Theory into Practice, 37,* 163–171.

Source: From "Preparing Preservice Teachers in a Diverse World," S. D. Lenski, K. Crawford, T. Crumpler, and C. Stallworth, *Action in Teacher Education, 27*(3), pp. 3–12, 2005. Reprinted with permission from *Action in Teacher Education,* the official journal of the Association of Teacher Educators, Manassas, Virginia. Website www.ate1.org.

CHAPTER FIFTEEN

Case Study Research

Jonathan Wenk/Columbia Pictures/Everett Collection

The Wizard of Oz, 1939

"Case study research is appropriate when the researcher wants to answer a descriptive question (e.g., what happened?) or an explanatory question (e.g., how or why did something happen?)." (p. 405)

LEARNING OUTCOMES

After reading Chapter 15, you should be able to do the following:

15.1 Define and explain the purpose of case study research.

15.2 Describe the characteristics of case study research.

15.3 Describe the processes involved in designing case study research.

15.4 Describe the issues related to sample selection in case study research.

15.5 Describe how to conduct and analyze multiple case studies.

The chapter learning outcomes form the basis for the following task, which requires you to develop the research procedures section of a qualitative research report.

TASK 8C

For a qualitative study, you have already created research plan components (Task 4B) and described a sample (Task 5B). If your study involves case study research, now develop the research procedures section of the research report. Include in the plan the overall approach and rationale for the study, site and sample selection, the researcher's role, data collection methods, data management strategies, data analysis strategies, trustworthiness features, and ethical considerations (see Performance Criteria at the end of Chapter 16, p. 438).

SUMMARY: CASE STUDY RESEARCH

Definition	*Case study research* is a qualitative research approach in which researchers focus on a unit of study known as a bounded system (e.g., individual teachers, a classroom, or a school).
Design(s)	The process of designing case study research involves determining the research questions, defining the case, determining the role of theory development in case selection, determining the theoretical and conceptual framework for the study, and deciding whether a single case study, multiple case study, or collective case study is appropriate.
Types of appropriate research questions	Case study research is appropriate when the researcher wants to answer a descriptive question (e.g., what happened?) or an explanatory question (e.g., how or why did something happen?).
Key characteristics	• Case studies can be described as *particularistic, descriptive*, and *heuristic*. • Case studies are focused on a bounded system or unit of study. • Case study research is a narrative account that provides the researcher (and reader of the case study) with new insights into the way things are and into the kinds of relationships that exist among participants in the study.
Steps in the process	1. State the purpose of the research. 2. Develop initial research questions. 3. Review related literature. 4. Develop a rationale for the selection of the case (i.e., unit of analysis) including sample selection. 5. Determine data collection strategies. 6. Conduct data analysis and interpretation.
Potential challenges	• Sample selection/case selection/unit of analysis. • Data analysis of multiple cases.
Example	How do central office personnel, principals, and teachers manage and cope with multiple innovations?

CASE STUDY RESEARCH: DEFINITION AND PURPOSE

As discussed in Chapter 1, **case study research** is a type of qualitative research design in which researchers focus on a unit of study known as a bounded system (e.g., individual teachers, a classroom, or a school). A number of researchers have addressed the definition of a case, which is a concept that is sometimes difficult to grasp. Merriam[1] explained, the case is "a thing, a single entity, a unit around which there are boundaries. I can 'fence in' what I am going to study." Stake[2] further pointed out, "case study is not a methodological choice but a choice of what is to be studied." Similarly, Miles and Huberman[3] described a case study as an investigation of a phenomenon that occurs within a specific context. In other words, if the phenomenon you want to study is not bounded, not identifiable within a specific context, it is not appropriately studied as a case study. Yin[4] went beyond the definition of *case* to define *case study research* as a research strategy that is an all-encompassing method covering design, data collection techniques, and specific approaches to data analysis. Taken together, these statements suggest that case study research is

- A qualitative approach to studying a phenomenon
- Focused on a unit of study, or a bounded system
- Not a methodological choice, but a choice of what to study
- An all-encompassing research method

Furthermore, the term *case study* is used not only for the research design but also for the product of case study research.

Case study research is unique because it leads to a different kind of knowledge compared to other kinds of research. It is more concrete—case study

knowledge resonates with the readers' experiences because it is tangible and illuminative. It is rooted in the context of the study and is also related to the readers' knowledge, experience, and understandings as they compare and contrast the case to their own life experiences. Case study knowledge is interpreted by readers who are affected not only by the context but also by the populations the reader has in mind. Most important, what we learn from a single case depends on the ways in which the case is like and unlike other cases. This idea is sometimes called the "epistemology of the particular."[5] That is, the context of the case and the reader's prior knowledge and experiences affect how the reader is able to scaffold the case study and apply the findings to a similar context.

For an example of case study research, consider Mills's[6] study of educational change, which is discussed throughout this chapter. Mills described and analyzed how change functioned and what functions it served in an American school district. The function of change was viewed from the perspectives of central office personnel (e.g., superintendent, director of research and evaluation, program coordinators), principals, and teachers as they coped with and managed multiple innovations, including the introduction of kindergartens to elementary schools, the continuation of a students-at-risk program, and the use of the California Achievement Test (CAT) scores to drive school improvement efforts. Mills's study focused on the question "How do central office personnel, principals, and teachers manage and cope with multiple innovations?" and he used qualitative data collection techniques including participant observation, interviewing, written sources of data, and nonwritten sources of data.

This study showed the characteristics of case study research outlined previously. The focus was on a school district as the unit of study, or bounded system. Qualitative data collection techniques included participant observation, interviewing, written sources of data, and nonwritten sources of data to answer the question "How do central office personnel, principals, and teachers manage and cope with multiple innovations?" Subcases of central office personnel,

[1] *Qualitative Research and Case Study Applications in Education* by S. B. Merriam, 1998, San Francisco, CA: Jossey-Bass, p. 27.

[2] "Qualitative Case Studies" by R. E. Stake, 2005, in *The Handbook of Qualitative Research* (3rd ed.), N. K. Denzin and Y. S. Lincoln (eds.), pp. 443–466.

[3] *Qualitative Data Analysis: An Expanded Sourcebook* (2nd ed.) by M. B. Miles and A. B. Huberman, 1994, Thousand Oaks, CA: Sage.

[4] *Case Study Research: Design and Methods* (3rd ed.) by R. K. Yin, 2003, Thousand Oaks, CA: Sage.

[5] "Qualitative Case Studies," Stake, p. 454.

[6] *Managing and Coping with Multiple Educational Change: A Case Study and Analysis* by G. E. Mills, 1988, unpublished doctoral dissertation, University of Oregon, Eugene.

principals, and teachers were studied to understand how personnel within the school district–bounded system managed and coped with multiple innovation and educational change writ large, and the product of the research was a case study.

When to Use Case Study Research

Like other qualitative research designs, case study research allows a researcher to study phenomena that are not easily or appropriately studied by other research designs. Case study research is appropriate when the researcher wants to answer a descriptive question (e.g., what happened?) or an explanatory question (e.g., how or why did something happen?). For example, Mills started his investigation of the change processes at the McKenzie School District by focusing on an explanatory question, "How do central office personnel, principals, and teachers manage and cope with multiple innovations?" Closely related to this question was a descriptive question, "What happened in the process of managing and coping with multiple innovations?"

Case study research is also an appropriate choice if the researcher is interested in studying process. Case studies are useful when describing the context of the study and the extent to which a particular program or innovation has been implemented. They are also useful for researchers interested in providing causal explanations, such as describing the process by which a particular innovation had a particular effect on the participants in the setting. For example, Mills wanted to describe the change processes at work in the McKenzie School District and to provide an explanation of the outcomes for the study. The case study account, therefore, provided rich descriptions of how central office personnel, principals, and teachers managed and coped with multiple innovations as well as a statement of the strategies used in the process. This research resulted in a taxonomy of managing and coping strategies that represented the gamut of behaviors used at different levels in the school district (see Table 15.1). Finally, Merriam (1998) asserts that case study might be an appropriate research design to use when a researcher studies a unique phenomenon and in so doing provides

TABLE 15.1 • Taxonomy of managing and coping strategies

School District Level	Strategies Used for Coping With Multiple Changes
Central office personnel	Using the committee structure, keeping in touch with the "real world," administrative posturing: "the façade," inaction
Principals	Maintaining the status quo: fine-tuning instructional programs; using personal beliefs, values, and goals; accountability
Teachers	Using compliance and resistance behaviors, seeking motivation for a career in teaching

knowledge about "atypical cases" (p. 33) that help us explore a wide range of human behavior.

So why is the Mills study not classified as narrative research or ethnographic research? As defined in Chapter 13, narrative research is the study of how different humans experience the world around them and results in the "storied lives" of individuals. The McKenzie School District study was focused on groups such as central office personnel, principals, and teachers, not individuals per se. Similarly, the Mills study did not meet the critical tenets of ethnographic research described in Chapter 14: describing and *interpreting* cultural patterns and perspectives in a natural setting. That is, the McKenzie School District case study did not involve cultural interpretation but rather focused on describing a bounded system—a school district.

Characteristics of Case Study Research

Case studies can be described as *particularistic, descriptive*, and *heuristic*.[7] To say a case study is particularistic means that it is focused on a particular phenomenon, such as a situation or event. That is, a case study researcher may specifically choose a particular instance of a phenomenon under investigation to understand a specific problem that occurs in everyday practice. For example, a teacher may choose to conduct a case study of a child with special needs to understand the effectiveness of a specified Individualized Education Program (IEP). The case study can then supplement any data about the child gathered through standardized

---

[7] See *Qualitative Research and Case Study Applications*, Merriam, for further discussion.

testing procedures. To say that a case study is descriptive means that the end result of the case study, the narrative, includes "thick description"[8] of the phenomenon that was the focus of the case study research—inclusion of many variables and analyses of their interactions. The term *heuristic* refers to the fact that case studies "illuminate the reader's understanding of the phenomenon under study,"[9] beyond the reader's original knowledge. In short, one outcome of case study research is a narrative account that provides the researcher (and reader of the case study) with new insights into the way things are and into the kinds of relationships that exist among participants in the study.

Case study research can also be characterized by the disciplinary orientation the researcher brings to the case study. That is, different disciplinary fields use case study research for different purposes. Educational researchers frequently rely on the disciplines of anthropology, history, psychology, or sociology for their conceptual frameworks and for techniques for data collection, data analysis, and data interpretation. Anthropological case studies on educational topics, for example, are influenced by the techniques commonly used in ethnographic research—Mills' study of the culture of change in the McKenzie School District was an ethnographic case study. In historical case studies, researchers use techniques commonly used in historical research. For example, researchers collect data from primary and secondary source materials. In education, this type of case study research has tended to focus on descriptions of institutions, programs, and practices, including how they have changed over time. Psychological case studies focus on the individual. Although Freud is most commonly associated with psychological case study research, the case studies conducted in psychology with an emphasis on learning are the ones most commonly cited by educational researchers. Sociological case study research typically focuses on the constructs of society and socialization in studying educational phenomena. For a classic example of a sociological case study, see William F. Whyte's *Street Corner Society*.[10]

Regardless of the disciplinary orientation underpinning case study research, case studies can be characterized in terms of their overall intent. For example, is the case study researcher intending to be largely descriptive, or is the goal to contribute to existing theory or to evaluate an existing program? Although most case study research in education tends to be descriptive, the use of case studies in program evaluation has been well established: "Case studies are particularly valuable in program evaluation when the program is individualized, so the evaluation needs to be attentive to and capture individual differences among participants, diverse experiences of the program, or unique variations from one program setting to another. . . . Regardless of the unit of analysis, a qualitative case study seeks to describe that unit in depth and detail, holistically, and in context."[11]

MyLab Education **Self-Check 15.1**

MyLab Education **Self-Check 15.2**

MyLab Education **Application Exercise 15.1:** Evaluating Research Articles: Evaluating a Case Study

---

CASE STUDY RESEARCH DESIGN

The process of designing a case study research project shares many of the design features of other qualitative designs discussed in previous chapters. As with other qualitative designs, a good case study research design includes a statement of the purpose of the research, initial research questions, review of related literature, and a rationale for the selection of the case (i.e., unit of analysis). Specifically, the case study researcher should:[12]

- *Determine the research questions.* This step is probably the most important step taken in the case study research process. As is the case

---

[8] *The Interpretation of Cultures: Selected Essays* by C. Geertz, 1973, New York: Basic Books, p. 6.
[9] *Qualitative Research and Case Study Applications*, Merriam, p. 30.
[10] *Street Corner Society: The Social Structure of an Italian Slum* by W. F. Whyte, 1955, Chicago, IL: University of Chicago Press.

[11] *Qualitative Research and Evaluation Models* (3rd ed.) by M. Q. Patton, 2002, Thousand Oaks, CA: Sage, p. 55.
[12] Adapted from "Case Study Methods" by R. K. Yin, 2006, in the *Handbook of Complementary Methods in Education Research*, J. L. Green, G. Camilli, and P. B. Elmore (eds), pp. 111–122, Mahwah, NJ: Lawrence Erlbaum Associates; "Qualitative Case Studies" Stake, pp. 443–466; *Case Study Research, Yin; and Qualitative Research and Case Study Applications*, Merriam.

with all research, the questions asked by the researcher will determine the appropriateness of the research method. Questions that address *who, what, how,* and *why* provide the case study researcher with good starting points.

- *Define the case under study.* This step is similar to that in other research designs where the researcher defines the variables under investigation (i.e., in quantitative research) or a specific educational innovation being implemented to improve student performance (i.e., in action research). For example, in Mills' study, the case was the McKenzie School District. More specifically, the school district cases were focused on central office personnel, principals, and teachers—all of which were units of analysis.

- *Determine the role of theory development in case selection.* This step in the design process involves deciding whether or not to use theory development to select your cases. Clearly, no researcher is atheoretical, and case study researchers should make explicit the theoretical/conceptual framework that supports the choice of participants. For example, a case study researcher can use the review of related literature process and the development of explicit propositions related to the research. In his study, Mills developed a comprehensive list of propositions based on his review of related literature that included statements related to educational change processes, educational leadership, and change theory (e.g., Merton's[13] discussion of manifest function, latent function, and the unanticipated consequences of change).

- *Determine the theoretical and conceptual framework of the case study.* No researcher, regardless of disciplinary orientation, enters a research setting as a tabula rasa, unencumbered by preconceived notions of the phenomenon that he or she seeks to understand. Theory can be defined as a set of formal propositions or axioms that explain how part of the world operates. In the field of education, for example, well-known theories include Kohlberg's theory of moral development and Piaget's theory of child development. However, theory can also be characterized as a general set of ideas that guide actions. We all have theories that affect

the way we view the world, and as William James is reported to have said: "You can't pick up rocks in a field without a theory"[14] (for a comprehensive discussion of the role of theory in qualitative research, see work by Flinders and Mills[15]). These theoretical frameworks are derived from our disciplinary orientations, which in turn inform what we are studying and how we are studying it. For example, an educational sociologist and an educational anthropologist look at children and classrooms quite differently based on their disciplinary orientations: The sociologist is likely to focus on social interactions, and the anthropologist is likely to focus on the culture of the classroom.

One way to help you identify your conceptual or theoretical framework is to attend to the literature you are reading related to your research interest. Reflecting on the literature and developing a list of propositions about your research problem helps you identify the predominant theories and concepts that have emerged over a period of time. Invariably, these theories and concepts emerge as significant influences on the way you conduct your own research.

- *Determine whether a single case study, multiple case study, or collective case study is appropriate.* The decision about the number of cases to be studied should not be related to any preconceived notion that more is necessarily better or that more cases lead to greater generalizability or external validity. This is a seductive trap for new case study researchers who have come out of a quantitative tradition or who have faculty members urging them (inappropriately) to do more so that they can increase the rigor of the study. New researchers should resist the temptation to do more unless the use of subcases will strengthen the understanding or even theorizing of the phenomenon under investigation. For example, as noted previously, Mills focused on three subcases (i.e., central office personnel, principals, and teachers) to contribute to his understanding of the educational change

---

[14] As cited by Agar in *The Professional Stranger: An Informal Introduction to Ethnography* by M. Agar, 1980, p. 23.
[15] *Theory and Concepts in Qualitative Research: Perspectives from the Field* by D. J. Flinders and G. E. Mills (eds.), 1993, New York: Teachers College Press.

[13] *On Theoretical Sociology: Five Essays, Old and New* by R. K. Merton, 1967, New York: Free Press Paperback.

processes at work in the McKenzie School District. A focus on any one of these cases alone would not have provided a broad picture of how change functions in an American school district from the perspectives of the players (i.e., participants) intimately involved in the process. The challenges of conducting and analyzing multiple case studies are discussed later in this chapter.

MyLab Education **Self-Check 15.3**

MyLab Education **Application Exercise 15.2:** Evaluating Research Articles: Identifying the Steps in Case Study Research

SAMPLE SELECTION IN CASE STUDY RESEARCH

Qualitative sampling is the process of selecting a small number of individuals for a study so that the individuals chosen will be able to help the researcher understand the phenomenon under investigation. In case study research, the researcher is charged with selecting the unit of analysis; the educational researcher's unit of analysis may be a child, a classroom of children, or an entire school district, depending on the research question. In case study research, the most common form of sampling is purposive or purposeful sampling "based on the assumption that the investigator wants to discover, understand, and gain insight and therefore must select a sample from which the most can be learned."[16] The benefit of this approach to sampling for case study research is the purposeful selection of cases that are "information-rich"[17] or those from which the researcher can learn a great deal about the research problem.

Another consideration in the selection of the case or cases is the viability of the case. That is, the case study researcher should consider a screening procedure to avoid the problems associated with choosing a particular case or cases, only to discover once the research has been initiated that the case study participants withdraw from participation in the study. Screening also helps the case study researcher determine whether the case study participant has the necessary experience or knowledge of the phenomenon under investigation.

A screening procedure may include the following steps:[18]

■ Review documents about the proposed case study site to determine whether it is an appropriate choice. For example, local newspaper stories, school board minutes, and department of education publications can provide a wealth of historical information about a particular school or district.

■ Conduct informal interviews of key participants in the study to determine their willingness to participate in the study and to ensure that they understand fully the nature of their commitment over the length of the study.

■ Determine whether the case study participants have the necessary experience and knowledge of the phenomenon under investigation and the ability to provide information. For example, selecting someone who provides only monosyllabic responses to questions to be a key informant can make for very long interviews! Not all interviewees will be conversational in the way they interact with the researcher. Very shy participants who are unwilling to converse with the researcher or who are uncomfortable with such conversation may not be the best choice.

Data Collection Techniques

Like other qualitative researchers, case study researchers use the same data collection techniques used by researchers conducting other genres of qualitative research (e.g., ethnographic research and narrative research) with the aim of seeking understanding about the case under investigation—a case study researcher collects descriptive narrative and visual data to answer *how* and *why* questions. Furthermore, like other qualitative researchers, case study researchers are aware of the need to triangulate their data through the use of multiple data sources. A detailed discussion of qualitative data collection techniques and triangulation can be found in Chapter 20.

---

[16] *Qualitative Research and Case Study Applications*, Merriam, p. 61.

[17] *Qualitative Evaluation and Research Methods*, Patton, p. 169, cited by S. B. Merriam in *Qualitative Research and Case Study Applications in Education*, 1998, San Francisco, CA: Jossey-Bass.

[18] Adapted from "Case Study Methods," Yin, pp. 111–122.

MyLab Education **Self-Check 15.4**

MyLab Education **Application Exercise 15.3:**
Conducting Case Study Research

CONDUCTING AND ANALYZING MULTIPLE CASE STUDIES

In educational research, it is common to find case study research undertaken about the same phenomenon but at multiple sites. These studies are commonly referred to as collective case studies, multicase or multisite studies, or comparative case studies.[19] The use of multiple case studies in educational research is a common strategy for improving the external validity or generalizability of the research. Multisite case studies allow the researcher to make claims that the events described at one site are not necessarily idiosyncratic to that site and thus contribute to the researcher's understanding about contextual variations, or lack thereof, across sites. However, the traditional claims with respect to external validity are still limiting for the case study researcher. For example, the case study researcher may have limited ability to generalize the events from one site to other sites with similar characteristics.

Multiple case studies require cross-site analysis. In fact, an essential skill for case study researchers, and perhaps for all qualitative researchers who are concurrently involved in observation and interview activities that inform each other, is the ability to undertake data collection and data analysis activities together. For example, the case study researcher may, in the course of interviewing and observing an informant, identify inconsistencies between what the informant describes as "business as usual" and what the researcher observes in the setting. Conducting the interviews and observations is data collection, but recognizing the discrepancies between the two sources is data analysis. That is, the case study researcher is attempting to make sense of the data that have been collected and, in so doing, is identifying new questions and issues that will drive further data collection and analysis.

Miles and Huberman, in their seminal work on qualitative data analysis, provided case study researchers with helpful strategies for cross-site analysis, noting, "By comparing sites or cases, one can establish the range of generality of a finding or explanation, and at the same time, pin down the conditions under which that finding will occur. So there is much potential for both greater explanatory power and greater generalizability than a single-case study can deliver."[20] Their comprehensive list of strategies to be used for cross-site analysis can assist the case study researcher with the challenging data analysis task unique to multiple case study research, especially as he or she moves from a descriptive/narrative mode to an increasing level of abstraction while undertaking data analysis and interpretation. We present a brief summary of these strategies, along with examples to illustrate how the techniques may be applied, and recommend that prospective case study researchers using multiple case studies read the original source.

Unordered Meta-Matrix

Simply put, an unordered meta-matrix is a data management tool that enables the case study researcher to assemble master charts with descriptive data from each site on one large sheet, known as a monster dog. This phrase is a helpful way to think of one large piece of paper where the case study researcher attempts to lay out, site by site, all relevant data under organizing headings. For example, Mills constructed such a chart for each subgroup (i.e., central office personnel, principals, and teachers), shown in Figure 15.1. This chart was the starting point for Mills's management of the volumes of qualitative data collected over the course of a school year and his analysis of the themes that emerged from the study.

Site-Ordered Descriptive Matrix

The site-ordered descriptive matrix differs from the unordered meta-matrix because it includes descriptive data for each site but orders the sites on the variable of interest so that the researcher can see differences between high, medium, and low sites. For example, using this second strategy, Mills ordered the data from the principals in his study on the basis of how they dealt with change. In this example, principals ranged from "doing nothing" (i.e., ignoring central office directions) to "working with faculty to develop action plans" to deal with the change. The

---

[19] *Qualitative Research and Case Study Applications*, Merriam, p. 40.

[20] *Qualitative Data Analysis*, Miles and Huberman, p. 151.

FIGURE 15.1 • Unordered meta-matrix				
Principal	Feelings about educational change	Interactions with central office	Interactions with teachers	Strategies for dealing with change
1				
2				
3				
4				
5				

site-ordered descriptive matrix helped show the full range of responses to the challenges of managing and coping with educational change.

Site-Ordered Predictor-Outcome Matrix

A site-ordered predictor-outcome matrix moves the case study researcher from working descriptively and deductively to a more explanatory and interpretive mode. In this mode, the researcher attempts to order the case study sites in a manner that allows the researcher to understand the variables that appear to contribute most directly to the outcomes. For example, Mills was most interested in the factors that appeared to contribute to whether the principals under study chose to do nothing or to work with faculty as a response to the superintendent's mandate to implement educational change based on student performance on standardized tests. From the study emerged the revelation that individual principals made their choices based on whether they believed that taking action carried consequences and whether they believed the results of the standardized tests were valid.

Time-Ordered Meta-Matrix

A time-ordered meta-matrix extends the cross-site analysis to include chronology as an organizing variable, with the specific purpose of enabling the case study researcher to display descriptive data from several sites with respect to events that occurred over time and that may have contributed to the outcomes of the study. For example, by developing a time-ordered meta-matrix, Mills was able to see the chronology of events that led some principals

to adopt a "do nothing" response to a district mandate for change. Specifically, the time-ordered meta-matrix revealed that the superintendent consistently delayed implementation time lines and school site visits to collect evidence of action plan implementation, leading some principals to the conclusion that the superintendent was not serious about the need for school improvement plans.

Scatterplots

Scatterplots are visual displays of data from all the case study sites based on dimensions or themes of interest that appear to be related to each other. With a scatterplot, the case study researcher can see how different cases are aligned and where clustering of themes and trends occur. For example, Mills developed a scatterplot that suggested a relation between different change strategies used by central office personnel, principals, and teachers and change in the school system. A visual display is a useful tool for case study researchers as they continue to narrow their analytical focus and to triangulate their understandings of the research phenomenon with other data sources and displays.

Site-Ordered Effects Matrix

A site-ordered effects matrix is used by case study researchers to sort through the research sites and to display probable cause–effect relations between the focus of the study (i.e., the action) and the outcomes of the action. For example, Mills used a site-ordered effects matrix to identify potential relations among educational change strategies used at different levels within the school district (e.g., central office personnel, principals, teachers) and the resulting manifest functions, latent functions, and unintended consequences of the change efforts. Manifest functions are objective consequences contributing to the adjustment or adaptation of a system (in this case, a school district) that are intended or recognized.[21] On the other hand, latent functions are neither intended nor recognized. The unintended consequences of latent functions can be categorized as functional, dysfunctional, and irrelevant and unimportant to a system.

For each change strategy used at different levels in the school district, Mills was able to describe the corollary manifest functions, latent functions, and unintended consequences that accompanied each action. The manifest function of using so-called hard data (i.e., standardized test scores) as the basis for instructional improvement was to provide nationally normed, statistical data on which to build instructional improvement programs and enlist school board and community support for innovative instructional initiatives in the district. These data also provided central office personnel with baseline achievement test scores that principals and teachers were expected to improve as a result of the implementation of local school-based instructional improvement plans. However, the latent function of the central office effort to use hard data and their efforts to convince principals and teachers that they were still in touch with the real world (i.e., of schools, teachers, and children) was to validate the superior (i.e., better informed) status of central office personnel in the evaluation of schools and teachers. In other words, claiming to be in touch with the real world was seen as an attempt to validate the status of the district administrators in evaluative roles. The unintended

consequences of the testing movement were to develop an anti-testing and anti-evaluation attitude among principals and teachers in the district and to unify school personnel against the development and implementation of the plans for improvement.

Causal Models

A causal model continues to extend the case study analysis and to assist the case study researcher to identify how things go together. Causal models, like the site-ordered effects matrix, display the probable causal connections between the variables under study. Mills's causal model contributed to building a theory of educational change using Merton's[22] discussion of manifest functions, latent functions, and unintended consequences, as shown in Figure 15.2.

Regardless of the specific case study data analysis techniques used, the case study researcher should present the evidence systematically and clearly so that an independent reader of the case study will be able to follow the analysis and interpretations of the data. As Yin[23] stated, "In doing your case study, you should follow the classic way of presenting evidence: arraying data through tables, charts, figures, other exhibits (even pictures), and vignettes." In so doing, the case study researcher will be able to build a compelling narrative that informs and engages the reader.

MyLab Education **Self-Check 15.5**
MyLab Application **Exercise 15.4:** Designing a Case Study

---

[21] *On Theoretical Sociology: Five Essays, Old and New* by R. K. Merton, 1967, New York: Free Press Paperback.

[22] Ibid.
[23] Adapted from "Case Study Methods," Yin, p. 117.

FIGURE 15.2 • Causal model									
School District Levels				Change Strategy					
	Committee Structures	Keeping in Touch	The Façade	Inaction	Status Quo	Personal Beliefs	Accountability	Compliance	Motivation
Central Office	X	X	X	X					
Principals					X	X	X		
Teachers								X	X

SUMMARY

CASE STUDY RESEARCH: DEFINITION AND PURPOSE

1. Case study research is qualitative research design in which researchers focus on a unit of study known as a bounded system. It is an all-encompassing method covering design, data collection techniques, and specific approaches to data analysis.
2. The term *case study* is also used for the product of case study research.
3. What we learn from a single case depends on the ways in which the case is like and unlike other cases.

When to Use Case Study Research

4. Case study research is appropriate when a researcher wants to answer a descriptive question (e.g., what happened?) or an explanatory question (e.g., how or why did something happen?), or when the researcher is interested in studying process.

Characteristics of Case Study Research

5. Case studies can be described as particularistic, descriptive, and heuristic.
6. Different disciplinary fields use case study research for different purposes, and specific characteristics of the study are determined by the discipline.
7. Regardless of the disciplinary orientation, case studies can be characterized in terms of their overall intent.

CASE STUDY RESEARCH DESIGN

8. The process of designing case study research involves determining the research questions; defining the case; determining the role of theory development in case selection; determining the theoretical and conceptual framework for the study; and deciding whether a single case study, multiple case study, or collective case study is appropriate.

SAMPLE SELECTION IN CASE STUDY RESEARCH

9. The researcher is charged with selecting the unit of analysis.
10. The most common form of sampling is purposive or purposeful sampling.
11. Screening helps the researcher determine whether a case study participant has the necessary experience or knowledge of the phenomenon under investigation.

Data Collection Techniques

12. Case study researchers use the same data collection techniques used by researchers conducting other genres of qualitative research with the aim of seeking understanding about the case under investigation.
13. Case study researchers must also be concerned with triangulation.

CONDUCTING AND ANALYZING MULTIPLE CASE STUDIES

14. In educational research, it is common to find case study research undertaken about one phenomenon but at multiple sites. These studies are commonly referred to as collective case studies, multicase or multisite studies, or comparative case studies.
15. Multiple case studies require cross-site analysis.
16. An unordered meta-matrix is a data management tool that enables the case study researcher to assemble master charts with descriptive data from each site on one large sheet of paper.
17. In a site-ordered descriptive matrix, sites are ordered on a variable of interest so that the researcher can see differences.
18. A site-ordered predictor-outcome matrix moves the case study researcher from working descriptively and deductively to a more explanatory and interpretive mode.

19. A time-ordered meta-matrix extends the cross-site analysis to include chronology as an organizing variable.

20. Scatterplots are visual displays of data from all the case study sites based on dimensions or themes of interest that appear to be related to each other.

21. A site-ordered effects matrix is used by case study researchers to sort through the research sites and to display probable cause–effect relations.

22. Causal models extend the case study analysis and assist the case study researcher in identifying how things go together.

EXAMPLE: Case Study Research

Using Community as a Resource for Teacher Education: A Case Study

MARI E. KOERNER
NAJWA ABDUL-TAWWAB
University of Massachusetts–Amherst

ABSTRACT   This is an account of a teacher education program's attempt to connect with a neighboring community in order to better prepare faculty to teach about the urban context in which their preservice teacher education students practice. Taking a feminist perspective, the two authors discuss their goals—the processes of using a community organization to lead the discussion and obstacles inherent to university settings. Knowledge about urban communities is an area that is often neglected in teacher preparation and one that needs to be more fully considered.

> "We do not really see through our eyes or hear through ears, but through our beliefs."
>
> —Delpit (1988, p. 297)

Case study of a teacher education program and community organization working together to improve teacher preparation.

(01)   Most teachers in urban classrooms instruct students who are very different from themselves, and often teach in communities that they have never previously even visited (Wirt, Choy, Rooney, Hussar, Povasnik, & Hampden-Thompson, 2005). It is important that teacher preparation programs address these issues of diversity by helping their education students understand the value of making connections with their PreK–12 students' families and communities. The following study, written from a holistic and feminist perspective, tells the story of a teacher education program and a community organization working together to institutionalize a partnership whose main objective is to improve teacher preparation.

(02)   In the Graduate College of Education at the University of Massachusetts–Boston, those of us who prepare students to be effective urban school teachers, know that many of our students have never visited the communities in which they will student teach and (perhaps eventually) work. Yet, as Delpit (1988) points out, they do come to their preparation programs with beliefs about children and families who live in urban neighborhoods. According to the U.S. Department of Education, 84% of U.S. teachers are white and middle-class with limited experience with people of backgrounds different from their own (Wirt et al., 2005). A new teaching reality for which we need to prepare students in the 21st century is that "multiculturalism is simply a fact" (Oakes & Lipton, 2003). Another fact is that children spend only 1000 hours per year in schools as compared with 5000 hours spent in their communities and with their families (Berliner, 2005). These sheer numbers alone speak to the issue of the strong impact of the neighborhood. It is a force influencing children's learning that has to be recognized.

(03)   When these new teachers face a classroom of children who may be different from themselves (for example, in race, ethnicity, or language), how do they see and relate to the students and their families? Ayers (1996) believes that school people need to understand and respond to the conditions that shape students' lives rather than trying to "fix" community and family problems. It is important that these teachers be prepared to work

effectively with children they may perceive to be "at risk" and therefore, perhaps unteachable (Haberman, 1995). They have to be prepared to be effective in teaching children from a wide range of diversity. This is contrary to the idea that the culture of the students is irrelevant. As Ladson-Billings (2001) points out, in a "middle-income, white, English-speaking school community, teachers *do* use student culture as a basis for learning" (p. 99). That culture is invisible. It is only when the children's home culture is different from the school norms and school culture that it becomes visible and often seemingly problematic. In order for all teachers, and especially teachers in urban areas, to be successful, they have to take responsibility for learning about the culture and the community of the children they teach (Ladson-Billings, 2001). Prospective teachers, particularly those who are white and middle-class, need cross-cultural opportunities with families and students who are neither white nor middle-class and who often speak a language other than English at home. It can be argued that without connection to diverse schools and local communities, bias and stereotyping of children by teachers may go unexamined (Cochran-Smith, 1995) and interfere with the success of the children in school. Schools cannot work successfully in isolation from students' families and communities (Chrispeels & Rivero, 2001; Comer, 2005; Epstein, Sanders, Simon, Salinas, Jansom, & Van Voohis, 2002; Henderson & Mapp, 2002; Sheldon & Epstein, 2002; Taylor & Adelman, 2000). Epstein (1995) talks about the overlapping spheres of influence determining a child's achievement. Teachers play the central role in the overlapping spheres of family, community, and school. It is clear that teacher candidates must learn about the inclusion of children's social context in the school experiences.

We are arguing that teacher education programs need to take the lead (04) in showing how to build a bridge between the school (in this case, the university) and the families and cultures of PreK–12 students whom their preservice teachers will be instructing. Teacher education is under constant scrutiny (Cochran-Smith, 2001; Fullan, 1998; Goodlad, 1990) because there are doubts that it can meet the needs of teachers who are coming into schools.

> Although most new teachers have positive things to say about teacher education, and they believe it is a necessary part of becoming a teacher, many feel that teacher education needs to be rethought and reconfigured to provide prospective teachers with opportunities to spend more time in classrooms and communities. (Ladson-Billings, 2001, p. 3)

It is not surprising that these teachers "are often ill prepared to connect (05) with students, families, and communities" (Oaks & Lipton, 2003, p. 432). This is especially true for those teachers who work in schools where there are students of color who live in poverty.

> [Changed] social and political circumstances mean that for teacher education to matter it too will have to change. It will have to offer new teachers a fighting chance to both survive and thrive in schools and classrooms filled with students who are even more dependent on education to make the difference in their life circumstances. (Ladson-Billings, 2001, p. 6)

It is clear that teacher education faculty, the people who plan and create (06) the curriculum for would-be teachers, need to see the big picture of how to relate to families. They also need to know about the specific communities in which they place their students and where many of their students will work and some may live: What are the names of the schools? Where do families shop? Go to church? Play?

(07)   Often, in responding to issues of diversity, teacher education programs offer courses about sociocultural perspectives, multicultural education, and anti-bias curriculum with no consistent focus on the role of the community (Villegas & Lucas, 2002). Clearly, there is a need for teachers and teacher educators to connect with the communities where the children and their families reside. Historically, it has been difficult to find a way to connect communities and public schools (Honig, Kahne, & McLaughlin, 2002). These links are ill-defined and often put the parents in a "helping" role rather than in a full partner position (Ayers, 1996). If we extend the notion of community involvement to university programs, it becomes even more of a stretch. However, the practicum experience within the school-community setting is a good starting point and may be the most important element of teacher education (Bullough et al., 2002; Guyton & McIntyre, 1990). Knowledge of the community in which schools reside and in which our students will work is an obviously important element in the success of preservice teachers.

(08)   There is very little incentive for teacher education programs to change (Ladson-Billings, 2001). Even teacher licensure, which drives much of what is taught in preparation programs, rarely looks at content in relation to knowledge about community. With state licensing agencies increasingly focusing on alternative routes to teacher preparation, the requirements become more focused on minimum literacy and content requirements (Berliner, 2000). As a result, teacher education programs often lack a comprehensive family involvement practicum. Little is known about alternative ways to prepare prospective teachers to interact with families and students outside the structured and traditional parent-teacher conference or parent-teacher sessions regarding disciplinary actions. Since most teacher educators do not have knowledge about the local urban communities, they are not able to be a resource for their student teachers. If prospective teachers need opportunities to visit and interact with families and community members, it makes sense that teacher educators need to lead the way.

Building Bridges

(09)   This is an account of a teacher education program struggling to find a way to connect with the surrounding community through a grassroots, neighborhood organization. Our story has a feminist view as a theoretical perspective. The feminist view embraces the value of multiple perspectives, erases the distinction in hierarchy between "researcher" and "researched" (Lather, 1991) and values both "subjectivity and personal experience" (Black, 1989, p. 75). We researchers are participants as well, and in telling authentic stories, there is a comfort with "unfinished stories" (Black, 1989, pp. 4–5). That is, the story continues after the study is completed; this is only one moment in time. It also means that it may be the telling of the story that makes the most sense to the readers and that they, the consumers of the research, make sense of it for use in their own lives. It becomes applicable in the lives of teacher educators as they read and think about it, perhaps applying pieces of it to themselves and their situations. In addition, "feminist research strives to represent human diversity" (Reinharz, 1992, p. 252). All of these characteristics describe the value system that underlies both the project and the research about the project. The validity is internal validity, which means that it makes sense in its own context. We hope to be part of the conversation. The few tentative steps we have taken may spark interest and possibility for other teacher education programs.

(10)   As researchers and teacher educators, we have these firm beliefs: The overarching and most important objective for teacher educators is to improve the teaching and learning of students in urban schools; this can be done through improved instruction of teacher candidates. It is the responsibility of Colleges of Education to enhance teacher education programs

> The case study uses a feminist view as a theoretical perspective for the conduct of the research. "The feminist view embraces the value of multiple perspectives, erases the distinction in hierarchy between 'researcher' and 'researched,' and values both 'subjectivity and personal experience.'"
>
> *What are the advantages of using a feminist theoretical framework to study teacher preparation programs and community programs, and their impact on the effectiveness of teacher preparation?*

through community bridging, making and sustaining authentic collegial relationships with parents of students in urban schools and community organizations.

We at the University of Massachusetts–Boston's (UMB) Graduate College (11) of Education began to look closely at how our teacher education programs were addressing education in urban public schools. We could not help but notice that there was an almost complete lack of knowledge about the specific social context of the surrounding urban communities. We decided to try to integrate community members in our ongoing discussion as informants, as people who had knowledge we lacked. At the same time, we were at the beginning of a Title II (Higher Education Amendments of 1998) Teacher Enhancement grant, which gave us even more opportunities to shape and reshape our programs. The Director of the grant, Najwa Abdul-Tawwab (the second author of this article), was also the president of the board of a local community organization. We wanted a renewed focus on preparing teachers for urban public schools.

Research Question

A compelling issue for those of us who work in teacher education is to pre- (12) pare our students for the context of the community in which they will teach (Murrell, 2001). The question for this research project is: How can an urban university's teacher education program begin to form a relationship with its surrounding communities in order to improve the preparation of teachers?

> Research question: How can an urban university's teacher education program begin to form a relationship with its surrounding communities in order to improve the preparation of teachers?

Our goal was to bridge the gap between the teacher preparation pro- (13) grams and preservice student teachers' clinical placements, pre-practicum, and practicum experiences, where they may eventually teach. This is a documentary account of how the discussions began and how the context of the teacher education program changed. Included are its successes and failures to value and accommodate the views, as well as the knowledge of members of the community organization.

Methodology

Because of the myriad purposes of educational research, it is important to (14) select the methodology that best suits not only our feminist perspective but also informs practice and policies (Lagemann & Shulman, 1999). The qualitative method is a naturalistic approach that respects the context of research (Denzin & Lincoln, 1994). Specifically, for this inquiry, we are "qualitative researchers studying things in their naturalistic settings, attempting to make sense of or interpret phenomena in terms of the meanings people bring to them" (p. 2).

Case Study Method

The specific qualitative methodology we used was case study, with purpose- (15) ful selection (Stake, 1995) of participants from UMB and the Dudley Street Neighborhood Initiative (DSNI). Using Lincoln and Guba's (1985) case study structure, we have included in this report: the issue, the problem, the context, and the lessons learned. But first, it is necessary to situate the case within the context of its social setting (Stake, 1995), so the account describes the university setting. The case study fits well with our feminist viewpoint because both share the goals "to establish collaborative and non-exploitative relationships, to place the researcher within the study so as to avoid objectification and to conduct research that is transformative" (Creswell, 1998, p. 83). Stake (1995) stresses that a qualitative, holistic case study is highly personal research. He notes that "the quality and utility of the research is not based on its reproducibility but on whether or not the meanings generated by the researcher or the reader are valued. Thus a personal valuing of the work is expected" (p. 135).

> Single case study of participants from UMB and DSNI using purposeful selection.

Certainly the work was valued by the people involved in the study and in the project. Specifically this is considered a holistic case study, which is a "highly subjective affair and includes the personal value system of the case study team" (Scholz & Tietje, 2002, p. 21). Holistic nature means that there is a description of the case, and in-depth understanding is a desirable outcome. Even this written account illustrates a feminist influence as it becomes more personal when it moves away from the formal presentation of the methodology and moves toward our story. Another important feature of this methodology that was also attractive to us for our purposes is that the case itself can be a "significant communication device" (Yin, 2003, p. 144).

(16)   Extending this description of case study, it further fits into the feminist perspective because both of us (the researchers) were closely affiliated with the problem so that "being insiders of the experience enables . . . [us] to understand in a way that no other person could" (Reinharz, 1992, p. 260). During this project, we explored ways to talk about teacher preparation with community members, who are typically outside the process. Our account is written with the understanding that we bring our values to the project and to the inquiry. Agreeing with Freire (1985), "All educational practice implies a theoretical stance on the educator's part" (p. 43), we are making our values explicit. These values include the desire for the regeneration of urban schools; the preparation of teachers who can be successful with urban children; the recognition of varied voices of "expertise" that exist in urban areas; and a "culture of conversation" (Oakes & Lipton, 2003, p. 419) within the university. We open the traditional paradigm of "expertise" to legitimize the voices of those outside the university who are involved in the achievement of children in urban schools. Our goal was to accomplish Stovall and Ayers' (2005) description of a project in Chicago, "The 'experts' [university faculty] engaged community members as equals" (p. 37). This view sees the urban community as a context for faculty to develop relevant objectives based on students' lives. We also understand that the reality of all institutions is that much action, including our project, is person-dependent, and as the "players" change, so too the project may change and become inactive or even disappear.

Data and Analyses

(17)   There are multiple sources of data that reflect the nature of a case study: "an exploration of a 'bounded system' [using] in-depth data collection involving multiple sources of information rich in context" (Creswell, 1998, p. 61). Bounded in time, our study spanned about two years (or four semesters) at the University of Massachusetts—Boston. The data included minutes from all Department meetings, Title II meetings, seminars and workshops with participants from DSNI and UMB, reflective journals, and informal interviews with faculty and members of DSNI. Because we see this as an issue-oriented case study (Stake, 1995), all of the data were limited to the stated question of how the UMB teacher training program can connect with a local community organization. The strategy for data analysis was suggested by Yin (1984): The original theoretical proposition, which led to the study and shaped the data collection, served as the guiding strategy to focus on some of the data and ignore other irrelevant data. This proposition helps to organize the entire case study and is especially effective when used with inquiries that have a "how" question.

> Data collection strategies included: meeting minutes, field notes from seminars and workshops, reflective journals, and informal interviews with faculty members and members of DSNI.

Our Story

(18)   Before we begin our story, we will give a brief description of the values and goals of the University, the Curriculum and Instruction Department, and the Dudley Street Neighborhood Initiative. The University of Massachusetts—Boston identifies as a "model of excellence for urban universities" (UMB, 2004, Mission Statement, ¶1). Its core values include meeting the needs of

both traditional and non-traditional students and its intent is to "dedicate itself especially to understanding and improving the environment and well being of the citizens of this region" (UMB, 2004, Vision Statement §, ¶2). From the Chancellor's Office to Student Affairs, there is a stated public commitment that the surrounding community, meaning the neighborhoods around the university and Boston as a whole, are important in both research and academic programs.

The Curriculum and Instruction Department houses most teacher educa- (19) tion, including initial and professional licensure programs. At the time of the study, there were about 100 undergraduate students and 500 graduate students in all licensure programs. There were about 22 full-time faculty in the Department and 3 full-time staff. The College is National Council for Accreditation of Teacher Education (NCATE) approved and many, although not all, faculty are involved directly in the teacher education programs through teaching, research, and/or service.

Dudley Street Neighborhood Initiative (DSNI) is a nonprofit community- (20) based organization committed to revitalizing "environmental, economic and human" (DSNI, 2005, Mission Statement, ¶1) resources in the Roxbury/North Dorchester neighborhood in Boston. It began in 1984 with residents who wanted to revive their community "nearly devastated by arson, disinvesti-ture" and who wanted "to protect it from outside speculators" (¶1). It has a diverse population whose major accomplishments have been to "create a shared vision of the neighborhood and bring it to reality" by working with "individuals and organizations in the private, government and nonprofit sectors" (¶6).

After the Director of DSNI was hired to lead the Title II project, we began (21) to look more closely at how we might use DSNI as a resource for the teacher education program. Because Ms. Abdul-Tawwab also had been a teacher in the Boston Public Schools, we were able to strengthen ties with many of the surrounding public schools for clinical placements and professional development sites, which the grant enabled us to fund. We then began to look at how to involve more members of the Department in the Title II Teacher Quality Enhancement grant. One specific goal of the grant, and one that fell within our interests and expertise was to "[e]xpand the school- and-community-based nature of teacher education to provide greater practical experience" (Massachusetts Coalition for Teacher Quality and Student Achievement, 2004, p. I).

After having just successfully gone through an NCATE review, the UMB (22) teacher education programs were ready to go to a higher standard of practice than the required "minimum" expectations of national and state requirements. In order to move the grant forward and in order to go deeper into the issues of urban diversity, we decided to look at an area where little or nothing has been written—the direct connection between teacher education and community organizations.

The two of us, Mari Koerner and Najwa Abdul-Tawwab, discussed many (23) options of how to institutionalize the notions of community. Because we had little guidance, our discussion began to focus on monthly Department meetings, the one time all the faculty and staff are together. We liked the idea of enlarging Department meetings, at least one or two of them, to include members of the community and parents of students in our Title II partnership schools. We intentionally did not use the Advisory Board model. This, historically, has not been seen as a source for information about the larger community, but rather an almost pro forma structure to meet the needs of accreditation. We also discussed the membership of Advisory Boards and how this relates to community involvement. Often the membership of Advisory Boards is slanted to only include people who can be guaranteed to show up at meetings or who are publicly known for their expertise. Because both of us have served on these Boards, we knew that there is limited discussion and often the purposes are diffused because the participants may have little in common. We were looking for a more comprehensive engagement model for Advisory Boards that calls upon community members and parents to be valued peers in the education of urban teachers (Stovall & Ayers, 2005). This was based on our deeply held belief, supported by research showing positive outcomes of community/school partnerships for PreK–12 education (Comer, 2005; Sheldon & Epstein, 2002), that linking a university teacher education program with urban parents and community would eventually enhance PreK–12 education.

(24)   We believed that "insufficient knowledge about the circumstances, neighborhoods, and supports of their students hampers teachers' effectiveness with many students, most particularly, with students who come from backgrounds different than the teacher's" (Honig et al., 2002, p. 1017). For us, this meant that we needed to heighten faculty's awareness of the importance of community and family in the lives of children. Because of lack of familiarity with urban neighborhoods, it became clear that many faculty members could benefit from more knowledge about the communities in which their students had clinical experiences and in which these students might work. We thought that if we could provide opportunities for faculty to learn firsthand about the context in which urban children live, play, and work, they would be able to more effectively include this knowledge about community in courses and develop a disposition to emphasize its importance. Delpit (1988) notes that it is through our beliefs that we see the world, and a teacher education program has many opportunities to stretch, examine and shape each individual's perception that exists with and results from these beliefs (Schubert, 1991). Hopefully, this can create a sensitization of preservice teachers to the positive impact of the urban neighborhood.

(25)   Our story continued as our discussions led to action steps. All of our activities (some of them funded by the grant) were led by the Director of Title II (Abdul-Tawwab) and the Department Chair (Koerner). Parenthetically, the Dean was supportive but not actively involved in the process. We spent a lot of time talking to faculty, staff, community members, and each other to decide on the steps we could take to engage and teach faculty. Specifically, we decided to highlight the community in the curriculum and content of preservice teacher education courses and in the required clinical experience by using funds from the Title II grant to provide materials and the stated goals of the project to push the dialogue along.

(26)   We began this practice by scheduling a meeting with Department faculty and staff with a panel of school principals, teachers, faculty, and community organizers, who made a presentation about the community (both current and historical perspectives) and its importance in the education of children. The presentation was engaging and informative because it was given by a community organizer who brought a real, clear, and urgent focus about the importance of schools and teachers to his neighborhood (an expertise and framework that was lacking within our own Department). A recommendation that came out of this meeting was that community members should be invited to attend future scheduled Department meetings when relevant. The Department of Curriculum and Instruction revised their constitution to say that at least one meeting per semester should include community partners and parents as part of the discussion portion that deals with pedagogical practices or licensure. The constitution was revised so as to institutionalize the inclusion of community people in department meetings.

(27)   To ensure that everyone understood the role of DSNI as an example of a community organization linked with families of PreK–12 students, we planned a Department meeting at the community center itself. When we

invited staff and faculty to attend the meeting, we decided to make it a special event by having a lunch provided by a local caterer. We emphasized that it was very important that each person come who had promised to be a part of the event because poor attendance might be regarded as indifference on the part of the university people. Colleagues from another university in the Title II consortium were invited as well. There were some questions about directions and facilities for parking and some slight discomfort with issues of safety but, in the end, there was 100% attendance.

We set an agenda that highlighted the personnel and accomplishments of (28) the organization. The meeting included a tour of the neighborhood (the houses and the school), which had been dramatically improved because of the work of DSNI (Medoff & Slar, 1994). In addition, a copy of the book recounting the history of the community organization, *Streets of Hope: The Fall and Rise of an Urban Neighborhood* (Medoff & Slar, 1994) was given to each person attending the meeting. As a consequence of the meeting, goodwill was generated between the organization and the Department, and it was recommended that a mission statement, which we had been writing to represent the overall values of the Department, be revised to include the goal of inclusion of community.

Along with a movie, the walking tour, and presentations, the staff and (29) members of DSNI had specific suggestions for the teacher education program. One of them was to encourage faculty to become actively involved in community and model ways in which inservice teachers see their role in the community development process. This was a unique experience for Curriculum and Instruction faculty: professional development, done intentionally and done through a regular Department meeting.

Because this was such an unusual event, many people talked to us, both (30) informally after the meeting and through e-mail. There was a positive feeling about the connection with each other and with the community people, and there also was a strong feeling of respect for the work of the community people. It was suggested by several participants that the Department expand meeting places to include community locations. Several faculty also made the suggestion that they collaborate with community members on papers and presentations at local and national conferences. This paper came about as a result of the community-based meeting as well.

Title II funds provided opportunities for professional development. (31) Najwa Abdul-Tawwab asked for volunteers to participate in an ongoing book discussion group to meet monthly. Ten faculty and staff members volunteered to be part of the group and Title II funding provided books. The books, *Streets of Hope: The Fall and Rise of an Urban Neighborhood* (Medoff & Slar, 1994) along with Peter Murrell's (2001) book, *The Community Teacher*, provided common ground for the discussions. By allowing an extended time for deep conversation, this allowed faculty and teachers a safe place in which to talk about and critique practice by looking at research on community involvement, with an actual case study of a neighborhood that reformed itself.

Another simple suggestion that arose from the meeting was to keep reading materials about community works available to students and faculty. We (32) collected them from both DSNI and the Coalition of Asian Pacific American Youth (CAPAY), an Asian American student organization that is sponsored by a professor in the Department—and left them in the Department reception area as well as in the student advising office.

These ideas focused on how to enhance some of the procedures and (33) practices in the Department to encourage community participation. There were additional ideas that came from faculty and staff in subsequent Department meetings for how to enhance the design of the teacher education curriculum. Some faculty met as a study group to talk about how our new ideas could inform teaching and curriculum. These recommendations, although made for our teacher education programs, can apply to any program. They include:

- Having preservice teachers do lesson plans and make curriculum materials that use the neighborhood as the source and focus of content for student learning. Be sure family and community are used almost like a text; that is, included in every area of the curriculum.
- Taking a critical stance, continuing within a feminist perspective, and providing work in courses where students examine school policies and practices that impact lives of children in urban schools. For example, collect the parents' stories about how their children are not served well on days when their teachers are absent. Many of the preservice students work as substitute teachers, so this is an issue that is particularly relevant to a graduate teacher education program.
- Being creative in course offerings. An example of this creativity is part of our story. A special topics course about Islam and what it means to teachers and schools was proposed. Access to the local community provided the opportunity to recruit a leader of a local mosque who was respected in the community and who would not have been in the traditional academic "expert" circles.
- Preparing practicum supervisors to look at how student teachers use the community and families as resources. They need to ask questions like: Do students invite parents into the classroom? What is the language that preservice students use to describe the children's families? Do the student teachers know about the district's policies that deal with the place of family and community in the curriculum? In the school? In the classroom?

(34)   A central positive result of working together was the opening of a new subject for discussion among faculty about teaching practices and issues central to urban education. Part of this collegial conversation led to dispelling the myth that community and parents have little interest in or knowledge of how teachers are trained for urban classrooms. There was also the recognition that the consistent revision and reformation of syllabi (course content) was needed to improve the preparation of teachers for urban classrooms.

(35)   There is no question that these issues can have a direct impact on the area that has the closest relationship to the community: clinical or practicum placements. It is here that the future teachers come to know about classroom and community experiences and integrate that knowledge into future learning experiences. This is the culminating experience in teacher education programs (Koerner, Rust, & Baumgartner, 2002). Many of the faculty who supervise student teachers continued these discussions with part-time people who attend a monthly discussion group for supervisors.

(36)   Another suggested step was to create an alternative field experience for pre-practicum teacher education students. This would help to dispel students' self-reported notions that parents of color and those who may live in poverty do not care about their children. For example, an internship at DSNI or Association of Community Organizations for Reform Now (ACORN) would help the teacher education students to see urban parents as more than abstract concepts by working with and having conversations with families. This would provide opportunities for a deep understanding of the overlapping spheres of influence that contribute to a child's achievement (Epstein, 1995)—the spheres of family, school, and community. This is not possible in a traditional field experience, which tends to be only in schools. It would provide space for collegial conversations among faculty, students, and community members—a conversation about preconceived ideas, assumptions, and prejudices.

Other Outcomes

Two clear outcomes that arose from this project were: to create a substitute (37) training program with the Boston Public Schools (BPS); and to establish an oral history project with CAPAY.

We were contacted by Najwa Abdul-Tawwab's colleague from the commu- (38) nity group, ACORN, to find out how we could join forces in getting the public school system to look at the substitute teacher workforce. After going to a community meeting, we were asked by the Superintendent to meet with the head of BPS Human Resources. Following a series of meetings, the university, through the grant, planned and funded a substitute teacher training workshop. Then with representatives from ACORN, many of whom were parents, we petitioned the district office to start the training. The schools welcomed the ideas and were working on their own plan. All three constituencies worked together to change the policies for substitute recruitment and training and also requested additional funding to do a pilot program. ACORN became part of the invited guest list for future teacher education Department meetings.

Because of the success of the trip to DSNI, many faculty members asked (39) if we could have another community group talk to the Department members in the next semester. We decided to ask the faculty advisor of CAPAY to bring some of the members of his organization, which is housed in the College, to a meeting. The group who attended consisted of the Director of CAPAY and several high school student members of the organization who talked about their experiences with racism. There were faculty discussion groups following their presentations. Because their stories were so personal and powerful, we decided to ask them to write five case studies describing their experiences in high school that would be available for use by faculty in their college classrooms.

Lessons Learned

We resonate with Stovall and Ayers (2005) in how they described their proj- (40) ect, "These lessons are neither manifesto, nor 10 step program, neither blueprint, nor map. Instead, they serve as points of departure and dialogue" (p. 37). Because this study looks at the case holistically, our stories represent a change in the culture of the university and alternative sources in addition to traditional knowledge. In universities, expertise often resides in the professoriate and although there is acknowledgment that teachers in the field possess a practical knowledge, it is rare that respect extends to families and communities—especially those who reside in urban areas. There is much research that points to the importance of connecting teachers with the families of their students (Epstein et al., 2002; Henderson & Mapp, 2002; Sheldon & Epstein, 2002), but there is virtually no research about the importance of families and community in the education of teachers. Knowledge about this important aspect or circle of influence in a child's life and its relationship to the effectiveness of teacher preparation is ignored in the formal inquiries done by university faculty.

Many of our discussions and panel presentations shed light on why this (41) happens. We found there are numerous barriers that prevent collaboration of teacher education programs, community organizations, and parents of students in public schools. We received feedback from both DSNI and ACORN members that the university often appears to be a well defended fortress with little access to anyone from the outside. They felt this was especially true because of the difference in status between community people and faculty's levels of education.

It is difficult to make changes in the culture of a university, and it is even (42) more difficult to institutionalize changes. A big problem and, ultimately the piece that can lead to failure, is that new policies and practices often depend on one or two people and when those individuals are gone, the changes go with them. Making changes permanent, independent of who is in charge and that extend beyond the life of the grant is a constant struggle. Another issue that makes change difficult is that colleges are places where courses are the top priority and schedules are arranged around those classes. The main responsibility of faculty is to teach those classes. Community organizations meet during regular business hours or in the evening at the same time as classes are scheduled. Just changing meeting times to accommodate community people as well as public school teachers would help to build bridges.

(43)   We talked about the values that underlie all of the work we view as important and that drives our work. Again, we think that the overarching objective is to improve the teaching and learning of students in urban schools. We think this can be done through improved instruction of teacher candidates. We further believe it is the responsibility of Colleges of Education to enhance teacher education programs through community bridging—making and sustaining authentic collegial relationships with parents of students in urban schools and community organizations. A summary of our goals in this project, which we tried to implement and that we think are portable to other institutions, include:

1. Make institutional and systemic changes in order to build the connection for community input into teacher education instruction and curriculum.
2. Provide a forum for discussion of the expectations and issues surrounding the preparation of teachers for urban children.
3. Make faculty aware of community resources for their inclusion in their courses.
4. Use community organizations to help recruit future teachers.
5. Open up discussions so that faculty can have greater knowledge of community and greater understanding of the home and school life of urban students.
6. Validate and value community members and parents in the training of teachers.
7. Make community members and partnership schools more aware of and part of the underlying values of college of education conceptual framework.

Significance

(44) A feminist perspective includes issues of diversity and power relationships. This case has pointed to problems with barriers that have been set up to recognize academic knowledge over and above practical experiences and common sense. Research shows that it is necessary to include outside experts, families, and community members in the education of their children (Epstein, 1995). We hope that our account highlights the necessity of building on families' cultural and linguistic capital. Further, this case has raised issues of equity, its meaning, and the role educators play in the goal of achieving an understanding of social justice, stated in the College's Conceptual Framework ("Conceptual Framework," 2002). How we infuse it into the curriculum for our students is vital.

(45)   Because awareness of, and intentional experiences with, issues of diversity tend to be outside the experiences of many students as they enter their clinical experiences, it is good practice to have them placed in settings where their preconceptions and biases are challenged. It is often difficult to provide positive experiences for students to view activists working toward social justice and see its validity in classroom practices. The nontraditional field experience of placement in a community center would enable students to see what they had previously only experienced through readings and

lectures. The partnership with DSNI and ACORN would give prospective teachers opportunities to learn firsthand how an organization works with families and how a community center can help parents actively participate in the education of their children. It would also provide future teachers opportunities to interact with families and find out what it means for them to be involved in their children's education.

When universities and communities are linked, it expands the possibility (46) of the resources typically available to teacher education programs. An urban focus broadens the perspective of the educational goals and content. It also can provide advantages for the faculty who teach the classes in the college program. Teacher educators can establish a professional network that provides opportunities to connect with a different set of "experts" as an aide to their teaching and research. These relationships can provide opportunities to do action research. For example, many of the parents involved in the community organization can provide information about how schools align themselves with home life. As one example, studies about the urban neighborhood and their views of the required achievement tests are needed. An additional benefit to faculty who work in universities is the opportunity to be a vital part of community through volunteer work. This is especially true for faculty who have an interest in social justice. They may perhaps work with the PreK–12 students who will be in the classrooms of their university students.

Conclusion

"Those teachers must be willing to travel new highways and byways of teach- (47) ing and learning to ensure that all of the children they teach experience academic, cultural, and social sciences" (Ladson-Billings, 2001, p. 9). The new highways for teacher education and colleges of education have to be found in work outside of the university classrooms. The enterprise of preparing people to become teachers for urban classrooms is a complicated business. It takes more than good intentions; it takes expert knowledge from many different sources; it takes valuing children and their lives. Through our work, we received glimpses of different paradigms for doing this work.

In explaining the best outcomes of a feminist approach to research, it (48) is important to note that, "for many feminists, research is obligated to contribute to social change through consciousness-raising or specific policy recommendations" (Reinharz, 1992, p. 251). Therefore, the goal of this inquiry is to be part of a conversation at UMB and also to stimulate a conversation beyond our teacher education program. Because "feminist research strives to create social change" (Reinharz, 1992, p. 240), we think it is important that through a critical perspective, various parts of teacher education programs need to be investigated. We hope to expand the conversation about how to think about these new voices in education and then take steps in making them a part of children's learning and the preparation of their teachers.

REFERENCES

Ayers, W. (1996). Democracy and urban schooling for justice and care. *Journal for a Just and Caring Education*, *2*(1), 85–92.

Berliner, D. C. (2000). A personal response to those who bash teacher education. *Journal of Teacher Education*, *51*(5), 358–371.

Berliner, D. (2005). Our impoverished view of educational reform. Retrieved from tcrecord.org

Black, N. (1989). *Social feminism*. Ithaca, NY: Cornell University Press.

Bullough, R. V., Jr., Young, J., Erickson, L., Birrel, J. R., Clark, D. C., Egan, M. W., Berrie, C. F., Hales, V., & Smith, G. (2002). Rethinking field experience: Partnership teaching versus single-placement teaching. *Journal of Teacher Education*, *53*(1), 68–80.

Chrispeels, J. H., & Rivero, E. (2001). Engaging Latino families for student success: How parent education can reshape parents' sense of place in the education of their children. *Peabody Journal of Education, 76*(2), 119–169.

Cochran-Smith, M. (1995). Color blindness and basket making are not the answers: Confronting the dilemmas of race, culture and language diversity in teacher education. *American Education Research Journal, 32*(3), 493–522.

Cochran-Smith, M. (2001). Desperately seeking solutions. *Journal of Teacher Education, 52*(5), 347–349.

Comer, J. P. (2005). The rewards of parent participation. *Educational Leadership, 62*(6), 38–42.

Conceptual Framework. (2002). Boston: University of Massachusetts, Graduate College of Education.

Creswell, J. W. (1998). *Qualitative inquiry and research design: Choosing among five traditions.* Thousand Oaks, CA: Sage.

Delpit, L. (1988). The silenced dialogue: Power and pedagogy in educating other people's children. *Harvard Education Review, 58*(5), 280–298.

Denzin, N. K., & Lincoln, Y. S. (1994). *Handbook of qualitative research.* Thousand Oaks, CA: Sage.

Dudley Street Neighborhood Initiative. (2005). Retrieved from dsni.org

Epstein, J. L. (1995). School/family/community partnerships: Caring for the children we share. *Phi Delta Kappan, 76*(9), 701–712.

Epstein, J., Sanders, M. G., Simon, B. S., Salinas, K. C., Jansom, N. R., & Van Voohis, F. (2002). *School, family, and community partnerships: Your handbook for action* (2nd ed.). Thousand Oaks, CA: Corwin.

Freire, P. (1985). *The politics of education: Culture power and liberation* (D. Macedo, Trans.). Hadley, MA: Bergin & Garvey.

Fullan, M. (1998). The meaning of educational change: A quarter century of learning. In A. Hargreaves, A. Lieberman, M. Fullan, & D. Hopkins (Eds.), *The international handbook of educational change* (pp. 214–228). Boston: Kluwer.

Goodlad, J. (1990). *Teachers for our nation's schools.* San Francisco: Jossey-Bass.

Guyton, E., & McIntyre, D. J. (1990). Student teaching and school experiences. In W. R. Houston (Ed.), *Handbook of research of teacher education* (pp. 514–534). New York: Macmillan.

Haberman, M. (1995). *Star teachers of children in poverty.* West Lafayette, IN: Kappa Delta Pi.

Henderson, A. T., & Mapp, K. L. (2002). *A new wave of evidence: The impact of school, family and community connections on student achievement.* Austin, TX: Southwest Educational Development Laboratory.

Higher Education Amendments of 1998. Pub. L. No. 105–244, 112 Stat. 1581, 20 U.S.C. §§1001 et seq.

Honig, M. I., Kahne, J., & McLaughlin, M. W. (2002). School-community connections: Strengthening opportunity to learn and opportunity to teach. In W. R. Houston (Ed.), *Handbook of research on teaching* (pp. 998–1028). Washington, DC: American Education Research Association.

Koerner, M., Rust, F. O., & Baumgartner, F. (2002). Exploring roles in student teaching placements. *Teacher Education Quarterly, 29*(2), 35–58.

Ladson-Billings, G. (2001). *Crossing over to Canaan: The journey of new teachers in diverse classrooms.* San Francisco: Jossey-Bass.

Lagemann, E. C., & Shulman, L. S. (1999). The improvement of education research: A complex, continuing quest. In E. C. Lagemann & L. S. Shulman (Eds.), *Issues in education research: Problems and possibilities* (pp. xiii–xxi). San Francisco: Jossey-Bass.

Lather, P. A. (1991). *Getting smart: Feminist research and pedagogy with/in the postmodern.* New York: Routledge.

Lincoln, Y. S., & Guba, E. G. (1985). *Naturalistic inquiry.* Beverly Hills, CA: Sage.

Massachusetts Coalition for Teacher Quality and Student Achievement. (2004). *Working together to prepare teachers so that students in our urban schools receive a high quality education, 1999–2004.* Report funded by the U.S. Department of Education.

Medoff, P., & Slar, H. (1994). *Streets of hope: The fall and rise of an urban neighborhood.* Boston: South End Press.

Murrell, P. C., Jr. (2001). *The community teacher: A new framework for effective urban teaching.* New York: Teachers College Press.

Oakes, J., & Lipton, M. (2003). *Teaching to change the world* (2nd ed.). Boston: McGraw Hill.

Reinharz, S. (1992). *Feminist methods in social research.* New York: Oxford University Press.

Scholz, R. W., & Tietje, O. (2002). *Embedded case study methods: Integrating quantitative and qualitative knowledge.* Thousand Oaks, CA: Sage.

Schubert, W. (1991). Teacher lore: A basis for understanding praxis. In C. Witherell & N. Noddings (Eds.), *Stories lives tell: Narrative and dialogue in education* (pp. 207–233). New York: Teachers College Press.

Sheldon, S. B., & Epstein, J. L. (2002). Improving student behavior and school discipline with family and community involvement. *Education and Urban Society, 35*(1), 4–26.

Stake, R. E. (1995). *The art of case study research.* Thousands Oaks, CA: Sage.

Stovall, D., & Ayers, W. (2005). The school a community built. *Educational Leadership, 62*(6), 34–37.

Taylor, L., & Adelman, H. S. (2000). Connecting schools, families and communities. *Professional School Counseling, 3*(5), 298–308.

University of Massachusetts Boston. (2004). Mission statement. Available at: umb.edu/about_umb mission.html

Villegas, A. M., & Lucas, T. (2002). Preparing culturally responsive teachers: Rethinking the curriculum. *Journal of Teacher Education, 53*(1), 20–32.

Wirt, J. G., Choy, S., Rooney, P., Hussar, W., Povasnik, S., & Hampden-Thompson, G. (2005). *The condition of education 2005*. Washington, DC: National Center for Education Statistics.

Yin, R. K. (1984). *Case study research: Design and methods*. Beverly Hills, CA: Sage.

Yin, R. K. (2003). *Case study research: Design and methods* (3rd ed.). Beverly Hills, CA: Sage.

Source: Mari E. Loemer, Najwa Abdul-Tawwab, Using Community as a Resource for Teacher Education: A Case Study, *Equity and Excellence in Education,* 39, pp. 37–46. Reprinted by permission of the publisher. (Taylor & Francis Group, informaworld.com)

CHAPTER SIXTEEN

Mixed Methods Research: Integrating Quantitative and Qualitative Research Designs

Patrick Ecclesine/Fox Television /Everett Collection

Julie and Julia, 2009

"Mixed methods research designs involve the collection, analysis, and "mixing" of quantitative and qualitative research designs." (p. 430)

LEARNING OUTCOMES

After reading Chapter 16, you should be able to do the following:

16.1 Define mixed methods research, and describe the purpose of a mixed methods study.

16.2 Distinguish among the three basic mixed methods research designs.

16.3 Describe the processes involved in conducting mixed methods research.

16.4 Identify studies that use mixed methods designs.

16.5 Evaluate a mixed methods study using a series of questions and criteria.

The chapter learning outcomes form the basis for the following task, which requires you to develop the research procedures section of a research report.

TASK 8D

For a qualitative and/or quantitative study, you have already created research plan components (Tasks 3 and 4), and described a sample (Task 5). If your study involves mixed methods research, now develop the research procedures section of the research report. Include in the plan the overall approach and rationale for the study, site and sample selection, the researcher's role, data collection methods, data management strategies, data analysis strategies, trustworthiness features, and ethical considerations (see Performance Criteria at the end of this chapter, p. 438).

SUMMARY: MIXED METHODS RESEARCH

Definition	*Mixed methods research* combines quantitative and qualitative research designs by including both quantitative and qualitative data in a single study. The purpose of mixed methods research is to understand a phenomenon more fully than is possible using either quantitative or qualitative designs alone.
Design(s)	There are three basic types of mixed methods research design: • Explanatory sequential (also known as the QUAN → qual) design • Exploratory sequential (also known as the QUAL → quan) design • Convergent parallel (also known as the QUAN + QUAL) design
Types of appropriate research questions	Questions that involve the collection and analysis of both quantitative and qualitative data in order to better understand the phenomenon under investigation.
Key characteristics	The differences among the basic designs are related to the priority given to the following areas: • The weight given to the type of data collected (i.e., qualitative and quantitative data are of equal weight, or one type of data has greater weight than the other) • The sequence of data collection (i.e., both quantitative and qualitative data are collected during the same time period, or one type of data is collected in each sequential phase of the project) • The analysis techniques (i.e., either an analysis that combines the data or one that keeps the two types of data separate)

(continued)

Steps in the process	1. Identify the purpose of the research.
	2. State research questions that require both quantitative and qualitative research designs.
	3. Determine the priority to be given to the type of data collected.
	4. Determine the sequence of data collection (and hence the appropriate mixed methods design).
	5. Collect data.
	6. Conduct data analysis appropriate for each kind of data.
	7. Write a report that draws conclusions based on both qualitative and quantitative data and analysis.
Potential challenges	• Few researchers possess all the knowledge and skills needed to master the full range of research techniques encompassed in quantitative and qualitative research approaches.
	• Researchers who undertake a mixed methods study must have the considerable time and resources needed to implement such a comprehensive approach to research.
	• A high level of skill is required to analyze quantitative and qualitative data sources concurrently or in sequence and to find both points of intersection and discrepancies.
Example	What are college students' attitudes toward and use of birth control measures?

In this chapter, we present an introduction to mixed methods research, focusing on how to integrate both qualitative and quantitative designs.

MIXED METHODS RESEARCH: DEFINITION AND PURPOSE

Mixed methods research designs involve the collection, analysis, and "mixing" of quantitative and qualitative research designs to understand a research problem. They include both quantitative and qualitative data collection strategies within the same study. The main purpose of mixed methods research is to use the advantages of both quantitative and qualitative research designs and data collection strategies to understand a phenomenon more fully than is possible using either quantitative or qualitative design alone. Although the benefits of this approach to a research may appear obvious (i.e., of course we want a complete understanding of any phenomenon worthy of investigation), mixed methods research can be challenging because it requires a thorough understanding of both quantitative and qualitative research

procedures. The choice of a mixed methods design also assumes that the research problem, and hence the research questions, cannot be answered adequately by either a qualitative or a quantitative research design alone.

For example, let's say that you are interested in students' attitudes toward and use of birth control. To answer this question with a mixed methods design study, you might collect quantitative data in the first phase and then follow up with qualitative data in the second phase. For the initial quantitative phase, your research question might be, "What are the factors that affect college students' attitudes toward and use of appropriate birth control measures?" and you might administer a survey to a random sample of college students. In the follow-up qualitative phase, your research question may be "When students mention alcohol as an 'influencing factor' with respect to their use of birth control, what do they mean?" This phase might include a series of interviews with individual college students, with the interview questions arising from the results of the earlier survey. Alternatively, you could begin with a qualitative interview or focus group of college students to help determine the areas of concern related to attitudes and use of birth control among sexually active college students and then use the themes that emerge from the interviews or focus group to develop a quantitative survey instrument to be administered to a random sample of college students. This mixed methods study would provide an understanding both broad (i.e., from survey results) and deep (i.e., from interview data); one that would not be possible to achieve using either a quantitative design or a qualitative design by itself.

MyLab Education **Self-Check 16.1**

MyLab Education **Application Exercise 16.1:** Identifying the Purpose of Mixed Methods

---

TYPES OF BASIC MIXED METHODS RESEARCH DESIGNS

Our discussion in this chapter focuses on three basic mixed methods designs:

- **Explanatory sequential** (QUAN → qual)
- **Exploratory sequential** (QUAL → quan)
- **Convergent parallel** (QUAN + QUAL)

Basic mixed methods designs are most commonly used in education and should be viewed as a good starting point for educational researchers who seek to combine the strengths of quantitative and qualitative research designs and data collection strategies. Figure 16.1 provides a summary of basic mixed methods designs.

In the nomenclature for mixed methods designs, our use of uppercase and lowercase letters follows the conventions presented by Morse.[1] This lettering system consists of three important distinctions:

1. Whether the research is qualitatively (QUAL) or quantitatively (QUAN) oriented
2. Which aspect of the mixed methods design is dominant, as indicated through the use of uppercase letters, and which aspect of the

design is less dominant, as indicated through the use of lowercase letters
3. Whether mixed methods designs are conducted simultaneously, as designated by a plus sign (+) or sequentially, as designated by an arrow (→)

The Explanatory Sequential (QUAN → qual) Design

In the *explanatory sequential mixed methods design*, quantitative data are collected first and are more heavily weighted than are qualitative data. In the first study or phase, the researcher formulates a hypothesis, collects quantitative data, and conducts data analysis. The findings of the quantitative study then determine the type of data collected in a second phase, which includes data collection, analysis, and interpretation of qualitative data. The researcher can then use the qualitative analysis and interpretation to help explain or elaborate on the quantitative results. When quantitative methods are dominant, researchers may enliven their quantitative findings by collecting and writing case vignettes.

Let's return to our earlier example: *What are college students' attitudes toward and use of birth control measures?* What might an explanatory sequential mixed methods design that attempted to answer this question look like? In a study using this design, you would collect quantitative data in the first phase and then, in the second phase, collect and analyze qualitative data to explain the findings from the first phase. As we discussed earlier, you would likely first administer a quantitative survey to a simple random sample of college students, then analyze the data to show the percentage of students who agreed or disagreed with particular statements about using birth control. In the second phase of the design, you could include qualitative interviews or focus groups of college students selected from the group who participated in the survey, with the questions focused on explanations for common patterns seen in the analysis of the quantitative data. For example, if a large percentage of students disagreed with one particular statement in the questionnaire, you could use the interview to explore more deeply the reasons for that disagreement. The qualitative data would then be analyzed, and the themes that emerge from the analysis could be used to help understand and

---

[1] "Principles of mixed methods and multimethod research design," by J. M. Morse, 2003. In A. Tashakkori & C. Teddlie (Eds.), *Handbook of mixed methods in social and behavioral research* (pp. 189–208). Thousand Oaks, CA: Sage.

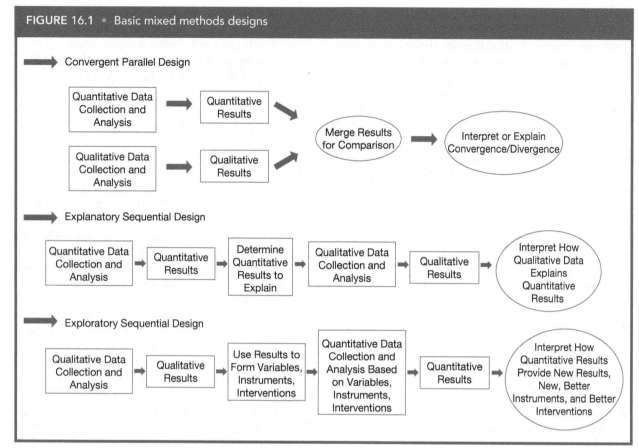

FIGURE 16.1 • Basic mixed methods designs

Source: *Educational Research: Planning, Conducting, and Evaluating Quantitative and Qualitative Research*, 5th Edition, by J. W. Creswell, 2015, Upper Saddle River, NJ: Pearson. Reprinted by permission.

perhaps even challenge initial interpretations of the survey data.

The Exploratory Sequential (QUAL → quan) Design

In the *exploratory sequential mixed methods design*, qualitative data are collected first and given more emphasis or attention than the quantitative data. When the qualitative study (or phase in a study) comes first, it is typically an exploratory study in which observation and open-ended interviews with individuals or groups are conducted. Analysis of these qualitative data helps the researcher identify key concepts and potential hypotheses to explore and test with quantitative techniques such as survey, census, and Likert-scale data that can be analyzed along with narrative data. With this study design, the validity of the qualitative results can be enhanced by the quantitative results.

In the exploratory sequential design, the researcher usually begins by working inductively, collecting qualitative data from a purposive sample (as described in Chapter 6) with a goal of increasing understanding of the phenomenon under investigation. Data collection would be followed by analyses appropriate for qualitative data (e.g., coding, identifying themes and categories, concept mapping, and visually displaying the data), and the researcher would identify key unanswered questions. The second phase of the study would then build on the findings of the qualitative phase of the study, involving quantitative data collection (e.g., a survey) with a large, randomly chosen sample (as described in Chapter 6). Ideally, analyses of the quantitative data would ultimately lead to results that are generalizable to a larger population. Each phase of the study must adhere to the methodological assumptions for the qualitative and quantitative processes and designs used in the mixed methods study if the findings of the study are to be generalizable.

We return to our earlier example, *What are college students' attitudes toward and use of birth control measures?* What might an exploratory sequential mixed methods design that attempted to answer this question look like? You could begin with a series of qualitative interviews or a focus group of college students to help determine the areas of concern related to attitudes and use of birth control. You would then analyze the data and use the themes that emerge to help understand the concerns and attitudes related to the use of birth control in this sample of students. In the second phase of the study, you could use those themes to develop and administer a quantitative survey. For example, if students indicated that they preferred not to use condoms in the qualitative phase, you could develop quantitative survey questions that ask students to rate whether they agree or disagree with statements about condom use, such as "The use of condoms for 'safe sex' is the only responsible thing to do." The resulting survey could be administered to a simple random sample of college students from the same population or from a different or larger population. The findings from the survey could then be compared to the themes identified during the qualitative phase of the study, providing both a check on validity and a more complete understanding of the phenomenon.

The Convergent Parallel (QUAN + QUAL) Design

In the *convergent parallel mixed methods design,* quantitative and qualitative data are given equal attention and emphasis and are collected concurrently throughout the same study—the data are not collected in separate studies or distinct phases, as in the other two basic designs. The main advantage of this design is that the strengths of qualitative data (e.g., data about the context) offset the weaknesses of quantitative data (e.g., ecological validity), and the strengths of quantitative data (e.g., generalizability) offset the weaknesses of qualitative data (e.g., context dependence). The fully integrated convergent parallel design is the most challenging type of mixed methods research because it requires that the researcher place equal emphasis and attention on concurrently collected quantitative and qualitative data and that the

researcher look critically at the results of the quantitative and qualitative analysis to determine if the datasets reveal similar findings.

A convergent parallel mixed methods design focused on the research question, *What are college students' attitudes toward and use of birth control measures?* might look like the following: You would likely begin by designing a quantitative survey and developing questions for qualitative interviews and/or focus groups simultaneously, based on a review of the literature. Then you would collect both types of data at the same time, although not necessarily from the same sample (e.g., the survey could be sent to a large sample from many colleges and universities, while the focus groups might be conducted with a smaller, purposive sample of students from one college). After completing all the data collection (both quantitative and qualitative), you would then merge the two datasets together for analysis, using each type of data as a check or an expansion of the other. For example, the percentages of students agreeing with particular statements could be computed and then annotated or enhanced with quotes from individual students.

To summarize, the differences among the basic designs are related to the priority given to the type of data collected (i.e., qualitative and quantitative data are of equal emphasis, or one type of data has greater emphasis than the other), the sequence of data collection (i.e., both types of data are collected during the same time period, or one type of data is collected in each sequential phase of the project), and the analysis techniques (i.e., either an analysis that combines the data or one that keeps the two types of data separate).

MyLab Education **Self-Check 16.2**

MyLab Education **Application Exercise 16.2:** Evaluating Research Articles: Evaluating a Mixed Methods Study Part 1

CONDUCTING MIXED METHODS RESEARCH

Your research question(s) dictate whether a mixed methods study is appropriate for your research, and the decision about whether one type of data will be primary and one will be secondary determines the basic design. Whether or not you tackle a problem within an overarching framework determines whether you need an advanced design, and the particular framework guides your final selection. Regardless of the design you select, you need to adhere to the basic principles for quantitative and qualitative research that relate to the procedures you choose. For example, a review of previous literature plays a different role for qualitative research than it does for quantitative research (see Chapter 4). Thus, when conducting a mixed methods study, a researcher needs to consider how and when to conduct a literature review, whether or not to let it guide hypotheses or other expectations for the study, and how to present it in a final report (see Chapter 22).

Additionally, all procedures to be used in a study must be reviewed by an Institutional Review Board (IRB) prior to data collection for that phase (see Chapter 2). Thus a researcher conducting a concurrent mixed methods study should submit an initial proposal, including both the qualitative and the quantitative components of the study, but a researcher conducting an explanatory mixed methods study may need to submit an initial proposal for the first, quantitative phase of the study and then, after that phase is complete, a second proposal for the qualitative phase of the study. Two (or more) proposals are likely necessary if the second phase of the study is based on the findings from the first phase.

Sampling (i.e., selecting participants; see Chapter 6) is a particularly important consideration when conducting a mixed methods study because sampling for each phase of the study (qualitative and quantitative) must be compatible with the assumptions belonging to that part of the design. Consider the sampling procedures needed for an explanatory mixed methods design. The first phase is quantitative, and quantitative research generally requires some type of random sample so that the findings can be generalized to the broader population. For the second (qualitative) phase, however, purposive sampling is appropriate. The researcher may choose a sample that provides useful data most effectively, and in many cases that purposive sample is a subset of the original sample that was randomly selected for the quantitative phase—as long as the participants give consent for this phase of the study as well (see Chapter 2). After all, the goal is often to have

the individuals who participated in the quantitative study explain their responses in more detail or discuss their experience as a participant in the study. On the other hand, consider the exploratory mixed methods design. Because the primary phase of the design is qualitative, purposive sampling is appropriate, but the individuals in that sample are not appropriate participants for the second quantitative phase, which will likely require a larger, random sample.

Let's return to our example from earlier in the chapter. Students who participate first in a focus group about their attitudes toward birth control may be influenced by the other participants in the focus group; or perhaps they may be influenced by a subtle response by the experimenter. If these students are then given a survey, they may—intentionally or unknowingly—change their answers. Moreover, they may be concerned that their responses to the survey would not be anonymous, given their previous interactions with the researcher, and thus not give honest responses. In this type of mixed methods design, an entirely new random sample may be needed for the second phase of the study.

Adherence to the sampling requirements for each phase of the mixed methods study is also crucial so that the researcher can use the statistical tests and analysis methods appropriate for each type of data. For example, if you conduct an ethnography as the qualitative component of an exploratory design, you would transcribe the data and organize it to look for themes. If you conducted a survey as the quantitative component, you'd tabulate the responses and summarize them with some type of descriptive statistics (in Chapters 18 to 21, we discuss basic principles and procedures for analysis in more detail). Note that, in many mixed methods studies, the researcher analyzes both types of data together, looking for points of intersection and possible discrepancies.

For a more expansive discussion of the nuts and bolts of conducting mixed methods research designs and the inherent methodological challenges of these designs, we recommend the work of Morse and Niehaus,[2] which will help to guide you through the nuances of these designs. For a comprehensive discussion of data analysis considerations in mixed

---

[2] *Mixed Method Design: Principles and Procedures* by J. M. Morse and L. Niehouse, 2009, Walnut Creek, CA: Left Coast Press.

methods designs, we encourage you to review Teddlie and Tashakkori's[3] guidelines.

> MyLab Education **Self-Check 16.3**
>
> MyLab Education **Application Exercise 16.3:** Evaluating Research Articles: Identifying Steps in the Research Process for a Mixed Methods Study

IDENTIFYING STUDIES USING MIXED METHOD DESIGNS

You now have the tools to identify a mixed methods study. When reading a study that may use mixed methods, look for the following characteristics:

1. The study title includes terms such as *quantitative* and *qualitative, mixed methods, convergent parallel, explanatory, exploratory, simultaneous, sequential*, or other terms that suggest a mixture of methods.
2. The purpose statement or the research questions indicate that a mixed methods design was used, or, if the researcher does not explicitly state the design(s), you recognize that the questions can be answered only with a combination of quantitative and qualitative data.
3. The researcher states that both qualitative and quantitative methods were used for collecting and analyzing data, or it is clear from the description of the method and the results that both narrative and numerical data were collected and analyzed.

Once you've identified a study as a mixed methods study, you can also tell from the research report which type of basic mixed methods design was used for the study. A researcher using a basic mixed methods design directly or indirectly specifies an overarching framework. The focus of the framework determines which basic mixed methods design has been implemented. If no framework is provided or implied, you can identify the type of basic design by looking at both sequencing and the weight or priority given to the phases of data collection.

Figure 16.2 shows an example of an abstract for a combined qualitative and quantitative research study. The abstract provides an overview of how combined quantitative and qualitative research can work together to broaden educational research from a single to a multiple perspective.

> MyLab Education **Self-Check 16.4**

EVALUATING A MIXED METHODS STUDY

When reading a mixed methods study, you should ask yourself the following questions:[4]

- Does the study include a rationale for using a mixed methods research design?
- Is the correct type of mixed methods research design used?
- Does the study use both quantitative and qualitative data collection techniques appropriately?
- Is the priority given to quantitative and qualitative data collection and the sequence of their use reasonable given the research question?
- Was the study feasible given the amount of data to be collected and concomitant issues of resources, time, and expertise?
- Does the study identify qualitative and quantitative data collection techniques clearly?
- Does the study use appropriate data analysis techniques for both qualitative and quantitative data?

Armed with answers to these questions, you will be prepared to evaluate a mixed methods study should you encounter one during a review of related literature. You will also be able to evaluate potential designs for your own research. Given the complexity of planning and conducting a mixed methods study, a novice researcher interested in this type of research is advised to team up with a colleague who possesses a skill set, in either qualitative or quantitative research, that complements that of the novice.

> MyLab Education **Self-Check 16.5**
>
> MyLab Education **Application Exercise 16.4:** Evaluating Research Articles: Evaluating a Mixed Methods Study Part 2

---

[3] *Foundations of Mixed Methods Research: Integrating Quantitative and Qualitative Approaches in the Social and Behavioral Sciences* (pp. 249–285) by C. Teddlie and A. Tashakkori, 2009, Thousand Oaks, CA: Sage.

[4] Questions adapted from *Educational Research* (p. 559), Creswell.

FIGURE 16.2 • Abstract of a mixed methods study

Note that the title indicates that the research involves both qualitative and quantitative methods.

The topic states that the study "considered the impact"—not "determined the impact"—giving the abstract a distinct qualitative flavor.

Note that the study used both questionnaires (quantitative) and interviews (qualitative) to collect data. It is common in mixed method studies to combine these two data-collection methods.

AUTHOR	Holbrook, Allyson; Bourke, Sid; Owen, John M.; McKenzie, Phil; Ainley, John
TITLE	Mapping Educational Research and Exploring Research Impact: A Holistic, Multi-Method Approach.
PUB DATE	2000
NOTE	31P.; Paper presented at the Annual Meeting of the American Educational Research Association (New Orleans, LA, April 24–26, 2000). "Mapping Educational Research and Its Impact on Schools" was one of three studies of the "Impact of Educational Research" commissioned and funded by the Australian Federal Dept. of Education, Training, and Youth Affairs in 1999 (Minister: The Honorable Dr. David Kemp, MP).
PUB TYPE	Reports—Research (143)—Speeches/Meeting Papers (150)
EDRS PRICE	MFOI/PCO2 Plus Postage.
DESCRIPTORS	Administrator Attitudes; Databases; Educational Administration; Educational Policy; *Educational Research; Elementary Secondary Education; Foreign Countries; *Graduate Students; Higher Education; *Principals; *Research Utilization; *Teacher Attitudes; Theory Practice Relationship
IDENTIFIERS	*Australia
ABSTRACT	This paper discusses the main analytical techniques used in "Mapping Educational Research and Its Impact on Schools." The study considered the impact of the outcomes of educational research on the practice of teaching and learning in Australian schools and on educational policy and administration. Mixed methods were used, beginning with a review of the literature and the exploration of the Australian Education Index (AEI) educational research database. Documents were collected from faculties of education in Australia, and questionnaires about the use of educational literature were developed for postgraduate students ($n = 1,267$), school principals ($n = 73$), and representatives of 72 professional associations. Interviews were then conducted with seven policymakers and selected respondents to the postgraduate student questionnaires. The study indicates that it is possible to use an existing database to monitor educational research in Australia. A clear majority of all three groups surveyed provided evidence of the awareness, acceptance, and valuing of educational research in Australia. Interviews with policymakers also showed the use of educational research in policy formation. The multiple perspectives of this study give a picture of the links between research and its use in schools and departments of education in Australia. An appendix summarizes the database descriptors from the database investigation. (Contains 3 tables, 3 figures, and 34 references.) (SLD)

Source: Holbrook, Allyson; Bourke, Sid; Owen, John M.; McKenzie, Phil; Ainley, John. "Mapping Educational Research and Exploring Research Impact: A Holistic, Multi-Method Approach." Paper presented at the Annual Meeting of the American Education Research Associations (New Orleans, LA, April 24–28, 2000). Used with permission.

SUMMARY

MIXED METHODS RESEARCH: DEFINITION AND PURPOSE

1. Mixed methods research uses procedures for conducting research that are typically applied in both quantitative and qualitative studies to understand a research problem more fully.

TYPES OF MIXED METHODS RESEARCH DESIGNS

2. Basic mixed methods research designs are distinguished based on the order and the weight of the qualitative and the quantitative components.

3. In the explanatory sequential mixed methods design, quantitative data are collected first and are more heavily weighted than are qualitative data. The findings of the quantitative phase determine the type of data collected in the qualitative phase.

4. In the exploratory sequential mixed methods design, qualitative data are collected before quantitative data. The qualitative phase is exploratory and leads to potential hypotheses that are then tested with quantitative techniques.

5. In the convergent parallel mixed methods design, quantitative and qualitative data are given equal attention and emphasis and are collected concurrently.

CONDUCTING MIXED METHODS RESEARCH

6. It is critical that the mixed methods researcher adhere to the basic principles for quantitative and qualitative research that relate to the procedures used in the study.

7. Sampling must be compatible with the assumptions belonging to the quantitative and qualitative research designs included in the study.

IDENTIFYING STUDIES USING MIXED METHODS DESIGNS

8. Look to the title, purpose statement, and research questions for terms such as *quantitative* and *qualitative, mixed methods, convergent parallel, explanatory, exploratory, simultaneous, sequential*, or other terms that suggest a mixture of methods.

9. Look to the data collection section and the analysis section to determine whether both qualitative and quantitative data were collected and analyzed.

10. To determine the particular type of mixed methods design, identify where the researcher indicates the order and the preference given to qualitative or quantitative data collection techniques and whether the study has an overarching framework.

EVALUATING A MIXED METHODS STUDY

11. A mixed methods study can be evaluated by answering questions related to the use of at least one qualitative and one quantitative research method, the rationale for using a mixed methods research design, the priority and sequence given to qualitative and quantitative data collection, the use of qualitative and quantitative research questions and matching data collection techniques, and the use of appropriate data analysis techniques for mixed methods designs.

PERFORMANCE CRITERIA   TASK 8

The qualitative research topic or problem should be open-ended and exploratory in nature. Your qualitative research questions should be worded to illuminate an issue and provide understanding of a topic, not answer specific questions. You should mention the type of research approach you will use—for instance, you should note whether it is a case study, a grounded theory study, an ethnography, or a narrative study. The reason you chose this topic, or the nature of its importance, should be mentioned.

Qualitative studies may include literature citations in the introduction of a study to provide background information for the reader and to build a case for the need for the study. Literature relevant to the research topic should be presented in your example, and citations should follow American Psychological Association (APA) style, for example, Smith (2002). Despite the fact that your study may not require a literature review until data collection begins, cite some related texts anyway to get practice weaving the literature into the plan.

The description of participants should include the number of participants, how they were selected, and major characteristics (for example, occupation). Participants are ideally interviewed or observed in their natural setting to keep the interview or observation as authentic as possible. The description of the setting should be included.

Data collection methods should be described, and there may be more than one data collection method in a study. Qualitative data are descriptive; they are collected as words. Data may be in the form of interview notes and transcripts, observation field notes, and the like. The researcher will be immersed in the data and participate in data collection. Instruments may be video cameras, audio recorders, notepads, researcher-created observation records, and so forth. The description of the instruments should also describe their validity and reliability.

An example that illustrates the performance called for by Task 8 appears on the following pages (see Task 8 Example). The task example is representative of the level of understanding you should have after studying Chapters 13 through 16. When the researcher created her plan, she still needed to choose her core participants, carry out data collection and data analysis, and write the final study. She constructed her plan taking into consideration the six steps in the research process. Note that not all plans or proposals require a results section.

1

Research Plan for: How Do Teachers Grade Student Essays?

The Research Aim

The purpose of this study was to examine the ways that freshman and sophomore high school English teachers grade their students' essays. I chose this topic to study because students in my school complain that their essays are graded unfairly. For example, one student said, "Teachers give the same scores for essays of different length." Other comments I hear include, "Teachers don't provide enough information about the number of examples they want included in an essay" and "Teachers don't give enough information about features they want included in essays so I can never match what they expect." I wanted to understand how teachers actually grade student essays. I also wanted to find out what criteria teachers use and whether they explain their essay grading criteria to their students, or whether the students' complaints are legitimate.

At the beginning of my exploration, my topic was stated generally, but through my initial investigations, it has narrowed a bit. Because qualitative research involves recurring study and examination, the topic may narrow some more. My approach is to carry out an ethnographic study. The research context is participants' classrooms.

Literature Review

An initial concern was the decision of whether to obtain and study existing literature, and if so, at what point in the study. For this study, I have consulted two assessment books frequently read by teachers in teacher education programs, Nitko (2001) and Linn and Gronlund (2000), to find out what sort of training teachers receive in scoring essays. Having some understanding of the following will help me to recognize scoring practices in the teachers I plan to interview: forms and uses of essay questions, their advantages and limitations, how essay questions should be constructed to measure the attainment of learning outcomes, and essay question scoring criteria. Later in the study, I may find a need to examine additional literature, but for now, this has been sufficient.

Choosing Participants

I identified teachers in freshman and sophomore English classes in an urban high school as participants for the study. The high school is the context for the ethnographic setting of the study. I contacted the school principal initially to propose the study and receive her approval before proceeding and contacting potential participants. She was cordial, and asked for more information about the role that the teachers and students would have. We discussed her concerns and she consented. She indicated that she would send informed consent forms to the parents involved in the study. All but two of the students' parents agreed to let their children participate. There was no indication why the parents declined the request.

The principal of the school also provided me with copies of the school's Human Subject Review Form to give to the teachers to sign when I explained their part in the study to them. I contacted the freshman and sophomore English teachers in the school, and described the project to them as an exploratory study about how teachers plan lessons and assess their students. I also told them, and the principal concurred, that each teacher participant would be identified by a number rather than by a name in the final written study. Only I would know the identities of the teachers. I thought this would allow the teachers to be more open when providing data. All but three teachers agreed to become participants in the study. Two of these teachers asked for more information about what would be asked of them. One of the two teachers agreed to participate after more discussion, but the remaining two teachers still opted not to participate. I thought this final number, 8 teacher participants, was a good sample for the study. The principal has been a helpful gatekeeper and interested observer. In general, the school personnel are supportive.

I will identify approximately 10 students to participate in the study and provide comments about essay items and graded essays. I suspect that this number will decrease once data collection begins and I determine which participants can provide the most helpful comments.

As the research data are collected, I will note the comments of the teachers, not only to obtain their comments on grading essays, but also to identify the most articulate and conceptual teachers to focus on during data collection. Ultimately, I will have a smaller number of core participants than I began with.

Data Collection

The teachers will be studied in their own context, in each teacher's own classroom. If this is not possible, data collection will take place somewhere else in the school. Ethnographic data collection relies heavily on asking questions, interviewing, and observing participants. Each of these methods will be applied over a period of 12 weeks. I plan to collect data in the form of completed and graded student essays from the teachers. I expect to collect approximately 7 to 9 essays per teacher over the 12 weeks. I think this will be sufficient to capture and integrate the data.

I have arranged to receive a copy of each essay exam or assignment. The purpose of this form of data collection is to assess the characteristics of the essay items. I plan to examine the essay items to evaluate whether students understand what is expected of them in this type of performance assessment. I will also look at samples of the teachers' essay items that will be critiqued by students. Again, the names of the students will be confidential.

I also plan to informally interview teachers and ask questions such as "Tell me how you grade your essays and why," "What do you consider to be the best feature of your essay grading?" "What do you consider to be the weakest feature of your essay grading?" Similar questions will be asked of the students in informal interviews.

During the 12-week period, I plan to hold several focus groups, one with teachers, and one with students, in which grading is discussed. The focus groups will be audiotaped and then transcribed. Finally, I will employ observation to obtain data. I will observe teachers grading student essays, question them about why they assign the grade they do, note the time it takes them to grade the items, and so forth. If written feedback is provided for the graded essays, I will collect a copy as data, for later analysis. I will also follow these graded essays and ask the students whether they feel the essay items are fairly graded. Therefore, my data will include student artifacts, audiotapes, field notes and memos from informal questioning and interviews, and field notes from observations.

Data Analysis

As data are collected from the participants, I will examine and reexamine the data in search of themes and integration in the data to arrive at a number of themes. I anticipate that analyzing and synthesizing the data will take approximately three to four weeks, eight hours a day, after data collection ends. Triangulation among asking questions, observing, interviewing, and analyzing essays will help to integrate the analysis.

Results

The final step will be to describe the procedures and interpretation in a written format for others to examine and critique. Before writing up the study, it will be important to spend time thinking about the data analysis and interpret what the data reveal. I hope to be able to express a contribution or insight that emerges from this study.

At the request of the publisher, this article has been abridged and represents approximately 50% of the original article. The full article is available through ERIC at http://files.eric.ed.gov/fulltext/EJ786202.pdf

EXAMPLE: Mixed Methods Research

How Should Middle-School Students with LD Approach Online Note Taking? A Mixed-Methods Study

L. BRENT IGO
Clemson University

ROGER H. BRUNING
University of Nebraska

PAUL J. RICCOMINI
Clemson University

GINGER G. POPE
Special Education Teacher

ABSTRACT   This explanatory sequential mixed-methods study explored how the encoding of text ideas is affected when students with learning disabilities (LD) take notes from Web-based text. In the quantitative phase of the study, 15 students took three kinds of notes—typed, copy and paste, and written—with each kind of notes addressing a different topic. After taking notes, students performed poorly on two immediate measures of facts learning. Cued-recall test performances were best for topics noted by writing, whereas multiple-choice test performances were best for topics noted by copying and pasting. Students performed worse on the cued-recall test when it was readministered four days later. In the qualitative phase of the study, follow up interviews indicated students preferred copying and pasting their notes (for practical reasons) and found typing notes to be distracting, which made learning problematic. A textual analysis of students' notes confirmed that students took mostly verbatim notes when typing or writing, which has been linked to shallow processing, and perhaps further accounts for the low level of learning that occurred. The mixing of quantitative and qualitative data (in the qualitative data analysis phase of the study), along with learning and motivation theories, provides justification for teachers to instruct middle-school students with LD to use copy and paste to take notes from Web-based sources.

(1)   Access to the general education curriculum is mandated for students with disabilities by the Individuals with Disabilities Education Act Amendments of 1997 (*Federal Register*, 1999) and reiterated in the 2004 reauthorization (Council for Exceptional Children, 2004). The importance placed on student access and progress requires educators to provide students with disabilities instruction on the essential skills and concepts emphasized through the general education curriculum. Advances in technologies over the last decade may offer a path to improved strategies for students with learning disabilities (LD) to successfully access and progress through the general education curriculum. Note taking is an especially useful skill that can be applied to learning from Web-based sources.

(2)   Web-based note taking is increasingly common, as students are more readily using the Internet for research purposes (Dabbagh & Bannan-Ritland, 2005). However, to learn from online sources students need more than access to learning technologies; they need proper instruction related to online learning (Dabbagh & Bannan-Ritland, 2005).

Recent research has addressed this issue, suggesting that teachers can (3) improve the effectiveness of students' Web-based note taking by providing students with a cued note chart (to ensure appropriate information is gathered) or by instructing students to type their notes instead of copying and pasting them from Internet sources (Igo, Bruning, McCrudden, & Kauffman, 2003). Unfortunately, to date, only general education students have been included in Web-based note-taking research. More specific investigation is needed if generalizations are to be made to the instruction of students with LD.

The next two headings in the paper cover a review of related literature (4) focused on "Facilitation of Encoding" and "Web-Based Note Taking" and lead the authors to the statement of their hypotheses.

Although general education high-school students (Igo et al., 2003) and (5) college students (Igo et al., 2005a) learn less when they use their own copy-and-paste strategies, the same might not be true for students with LD. Finally, when students with LD take notes from the Web, it might be more beneficial for them to write their notes instead of taking electronic notes.

The purpose of this sequential, explanatory mixed-methods study was (6) to (12) explore the encoding function of Web-based note taking for middle-school students with LD. In the quantitative, first phase of the study, 15 students read Web-based text covering three topics and noted each topic in a different way: by writing, typing, or copying and pasting. In Latin-square fashion, each student took three kinds of notes, but the combinations of their topic and note-taking styles differed, so that different students pasted, typed, or wrote notes on different topics (see Figure 1). After taking notes, students were (a) immediately tested to examine any differences in encoding prompted by the three note-taking techniques and (b) given a delayed measure of recall of text ideas (four days later).

In the qualitative phase of the study, each student was interviewed to (7) explore their perspectives of the three kinds of note taking, examine how they approached using the three techniques, and further explain the quantitative findings. Finally, a textual analysis of students' notes was conducted to help explain students' strategies, learning, and mental processing.

Quantitative Hypotheses and Predictions

Based on the review of literature the authors tested the following hypotheses: (8)

The depth hypothesis: that learning will be more robust when notes are taken by typing or writing, as these two techniques allow students the opportunity to create paraphrases and deepen their processing.

The transfer-appropriate hypothesis: that when students copy and paste (9) their notes (where they must identify and select the appropriate information to note), their performances will be highest on a multiple-choice test

Students/*topics*	*bauxite*	*coal*	*uranium*
1, 7, 13	Type	Write	Paste
2, 8, 14	Type	Paste	Write
3, 9, 15	Write	Paste	Type
4, 10	Write	Type	Paste
5, 11	Paste	Write	Type
6, 12	Paste	Type	Write

Figure 1. Latin-square assignment of students (numbers) to conditions (note-taking styles x topic)

Note: The three treatment conditions (type, write, paste) were assigned randomly to each student.

Basic mixed methods design: explanatory sequential (QUAN-Squal) design. The purpose of this study was to explore the encoding function of Web-based note taking for middle-school students with LD. In the quantitative, first phase of the study, 15 students read Web-based text covering three topics and noted each topic in a different way: writing, typing, or copying and pasting. In the qualitative (second) phase of the study, each student was interviewed to explore [her or his] perspectives of the three kinds of note taking, examine how [each student] approached using the three techniques, and further explain the quantitative findings.

Is the explanatory sequential mixed methods design the best choice of design for this problem?

The quantitative phase of the mixed methods design used an experimental design that tested two competing hypotheses: the depth hypothesis and the transfer-appropriate hypothesis. The 15 students who participated in the study were from an intact, self-contained social studies classroom. The experiment occurred over one day, with the delayed test taking place four days later. Students met in their usual classroom where class roll was taken; students were then assigned randomly to one of six experimental groups that differed in the combination of topics to be noted and kinds of notes to be taken.

Does the study adhere to the methodological assumptions of experimental research? Is the sampling procedure appropriate for an experimental study?

Table 1

Summary of Participant Demographic Information

Participants	
Grade Level	
7th grade	10
8th grade	5
Gender	
Male	12
Female	3
Total	15
Age	
Mean	13 years 10 months
Range	13–14 years 6 months
Race/Ethnicity	
Anglo	9
Hispanic	1
African-American	5
SES	
High	0
Middle	1
Low	14
Disability Category	
LD	11
E/BD	2
OHI	2
Educational Placement	
Time in Sp. Ed. Placement	>60%
Level of Placement	Self-contained
Intelligence	
Mean (SD)	82 (11.8)
Range	68–100
Reading Achievement	
Mean	4th grade
Range	2nd–7th grade

Note: Intelligence as measured by WISC III, Universal Nonverbal Intelligence Test, and Stanford-Binet Intelligence Scale.

(because they are required to identify and select the appropriate information for their answers).

Method
Participants

(10) The authors described the 15 participants as 7th and 8th grade students in a rural southeast town (12 male and 3 female) ranging in age from 13 years to 14 years 6 months.

(11) The number of participants was limited to 15 by the researchers to provide experimental content consistent with the teacher's goal and the number of classes covering the same content.

(12) The students' low achievement in all areas is evident in their achieve (18) ment test scores, which were obtained at the district office. Seven students

had been assessed using the Brigance Comprehensive Inventory of Basic Skills. On math computation all 7 students scored at the 3rd-grade level and ranged from 2nd to 4th grade on problem solving. Reading scores for word recognition, oral reading, and comprehension ranged from 2nd to 7th grade. Writing scores for spelling and sentence writing ranged from 3rd to 5th grade. Five students had been assessed with the Wide Range Achievement Test. For math, reading, and spelling, their scores ranged from 2nd to 6th grade. The overall achievement of three students is not reported because of incomplete files as a result of students having recently moved into the school district.

Materials

In this section the authors describe the materials used in the study: a researcher-constructed text passage from which students took notes. The passage was 763 words long, described three native Australian minerals (coal, bauxite, and uranium), and was presented on a single, continuous Web page (HTML document) accessed through Microsoft Internet Explorer. (13)

Dependent Measures

The authors described the use of two researcher-constructed tests that were used to assess student learning of facts from the text along with inter-rater reliability for the tests. (14)

Procedure

In this section the authors outline the procedures used, prior to, and during, the experiment. For example, prior to the experiment students were given a brief, informal tutorial on how to use the type and copy-and-paste functions of a computer. (15)

Results
Immediate

ANOVA results indicated a significant effect on students' immediate cued re (27) call test performances, $F(2, 42) = 4.8, p < .05$. The strength of the relationship between kind of note taking and cued recall was strong as assessed by eta square, with the kind of note taking accounting for 17% of the variance in cued recall. Results of the LSD post-hoc test indicated that cued recall was significantly higher for topics that were noted by writing than for topics that were noted by pasting (see Table 2). Recall performances for topics that were noted by typing fell between those of writing and pasting and did not differ from either. (16)

Results also indicated a significant effect on students' multiple-choice (28) test performances, $F(2, 42) = 3.96, p < .05$. The strength of the relationship between the kind of note taking and fact identification was strong as assessed by eta square, with the kind of note taking accounting for 16% of the variance in fact identification. Results of the LSD post-hoc test indicated (17)

Table 2

Means Summary of Two Tests and Analysis of Variance

Measure and Note-Taking Style	Mean	SD	F	Power	η^2
Cued Recall					
Write	1.47*	1.35	4.51	.84	.17
Type	.87	.99			
Paste	.33	.61			
M/C Facts					
Write	2.87	1.30			
Type	2.73	1.02			
Paste	4.07*	1.31	3.96	.71	.16

*$p < .05$.

that multiple-choice performances were significantly higher for topics that were noted by pasting than for topics that were noted by writing and typing (see Table 2).

Delayed

(18) ANOVA results indicated no significant effect on students' delayed cued recall (29) test performances, $F(2, 42) = 1.6, p = .38$. Performance means for students' recall of text ideas ranged from .67 points for written topics to .53 for typed topics and .24 for pasted topics.

Discussion
Quantitative Phase

Findings from the quantitative (experimental) phase of the explanatory sequential mixed methods design: The experimental results did not support our depth hypothesis, which predicted that learning through writing and typing notes is superior to learning through pasting notes. The results do support the transfer-appropriate hypothesis, as students' test performances differed with respect to both note-taking style and test type.

Is the statistical use of ANOVA appropriate given the sample size and selection procedures?

(19) The experimental results did not support our depth hypothesis, which predicted that learning through writing and typing notes is superior to learning through pasting notes. In previous research, typing notes produced higher levels of student learning across different tests assessing learning from Web-based text. This was attributed to the use of paraphrase strategies and subsequent deepening of mental processes during note taking (Igo et al., 2003). In the present study, however, students' writing and typing behaviors (which presumably afforded them the opportunity to paraphrase) yielded inconsistent performances across tests. A deepened level of processing should have resulted in boosted performances on each test. The absence of such consistency suggests the absence of deep processing.

(20) Also in previous research, copying and pasting notes decreased learning. This was attributed to the imposition of verbatim note taking on the student, which has been linked to shallow processing in previous research (Igo et al., 2003; Slotte & Lonka, 1999). In the present study, however, copying and pasting yielded higher performances on one of the immediate tests (multiple choice). This is not to say that the students were engaging in deeper levels of processing while pasting, however, because, again, the deepened processing would have resulted in consistently higher performances across tests.

(21) Finally, the absence of deep processing is made clearer by the results of the delayed, cued recall test. On average, students recalled about half of an idea across topics noted by all three kinds of note taking. This result, coupled with the relationship between depth-of-processing theory and long-term memory (Craik, 2000), suggests students were not thinking deeply while they were taking notes.

(22) By contrast, our results do support the transfer-appropriate hypothesis, as students' test performances differed with respect to both note-taking style and test type. In transfer-appropriate fashion (Baguley & Payne, 2000), students tended to perform better when the type of engagement during a particular kind of note taking was closely matched to the type of engagement required by the test. For example, points were awarded on students' cued recall tests only if students were able to generate correct written facts in the appropriate cell of their cued recall charts. They had already done this once, during the note-taking phase of the experiment when they noted topics by writing. The cognitive engagement necessary to complete the written portion of the notes was closely related to the engagement necessary to answer the cued recall test, and performances were highest when there was such a match. The same effect was evident in the multiple-choice test, which required students to search for and then select information for their answers. Performances were highest for topics that were copied and pasted, which required students to select and paste the correct ideas into notes.

(23) This is an interesting finding because transfer-appropriate processing effects are typically regarded as weak learning effects (see, e.g., Neath, 1998), occurring in the absence of deep processing. Again, for evidence of this, see the means in Table 1, which suggest that students, in general, learned little during any of the three kinds of note taking. Specifically, 6 points were possible in the cued recall of facts test, but the mean for each kind of note taking on the immediate test was below 2 points, with pasting and typing

below 1 point. As expected, performances were even worse on the delayed test, where all means fell below 1 point.

Although the experimental findings support the transfer-appropriate (24) hypothesis, they do not explain the weak learning effects. Certain other characteristics of the results also are unexplainable in light of only the experimental findings. For example, students' performances were slightly lower for typed than for written notes. This phenomenon occurred on each dependent measure, and it is not explained by either of our theoretical hypotheses. Perhaps this finding was due to the small number of students who participated in the study. Similarly, the relatively small number of items on each dependent measure might have influenced the results. But each of these explanations might also be inconclusive. In cases where quantitative, experimental inquiry does not provide enough description of a phenomenon, researchers can use qualitative follow up procedures to aid understanding (Creswell, 2003; Newman & Benz, 1998; Tashakkori & Teddlie, 1998).

Qualitative Phase

In order to gain a more detailed view of the students' note-taking behaviors (25) and attitudes, as well as the impact of those behaviors and attitudes on test performances and processing, two kinds of qualitative data were collected and analyzed: interview data and students' notes. The interview data were analyzed to ascertain the students' least and most preferred note-taking techniques, to describe why the students subscribed to those beliefs, and to help explain the experimental results. Further, students' notes were analyzed to examine how students approached using the three kinds of notes and to explain how their approaches might account for the experimental findings.

> The qualitative phase of the study used two kinds of qualitative data: interview data and students' notes.

Analysis of Notes and QUAN–QUAL Data Mixing

Students' notes were analyzed in three ways. First, they were checked for (37) (26) completeness. As documented in previous research using cued note charts (see, e.g., Igo et al., 2003; Kiewra, 1989), students in the current study completed their note charts appropriately. All cells were filled in each student's chart. The notes also were checked for appropriateness of ideas. Again, as in previous research, the information in each note-taking cell correctly corresponded to the cues that were provided in the chart. Because the chart and cues were fit with the text's structure, the notes were appropriate to the text as well. Finally, the notes were checked for the presence or absence of paraphrases and the presence or absence of verbatim text ideas, except for topics that were noted by pasting, which were all identical to the original text.

In general, students' notes—whether typed or written—were constructed (27) in verbatim fashion. This preference has been documented in older students with LD (see, e.g., Suritsky, 1992), whereas general education students prefer to create paraphrases in lieu of verbatim notes (Igo et al., 2003). In the present study, some note-taking cells were filled with verbatim sentences from the text, but more often they contained sentence fragments from the original text (varying in length from two to seven words). In most cases, students selected sentence fragments appropriately. That is, no real meaning was lost through their choice to include fewer words rather than entire sentences.

In some cases, albeit few, students attempted to paraphrase text ideas in (28) their notes. Interesting, the paraphrases were short. In fact, in most cases, they simply took the form of word substitution rather than typical sentence or paragraph paraphrases. For example, one note cell was cued to be filled with the uses of uranium. Whereas the text presented the uses of "providing electrical power" and "used to make nuclear weapons," one student wrote "bombs." There were other similar examples of such paraphrase attempts. But unlike when students wrote or typed verbatim sentence fragments, when they attempted to paraphrase, part of the text's meaning was lost in the transition of ideas from the original text to the students' notes. In the "bombs" example given above, the student's notes were perhaps not as complete as those of another student, who chose to write verbatim each of the uses of uranium. In short, in the rare cases where students chose to take paraphrase notes, their attempts seemed to come at the expense of note quality. That is, they built notes inferior to those that contained verbatim text ideas.

(29)

The analysis of notes thus further confirmed our basis for rejecting the depth hypothesis in the quantitative phase of this study. As mentioned, in previous research, verbatim note taking has been linked to shallow levels of processing (Slotte & Lonka, 1999), and shallow levels of processing have been linked to poor memory performances (Craik, 2000). Because students in the present study performed poorly on the tests and took mostly verbatim notes, the absence of deep processing becomes an increasingly more plausible account of our results.

> The intent of the explanatory sequential mixed methods design is to explain the quantitative results with qualitative data. In this study, the analysis of notes further confirmed the basis for rejecting the depth hypothesis in the quantitative phase of this study.

Student Interviews

(30) Immediately following completion of the two tests, students were interviewed separately by the primary researcher, who typed their responses verbatim on a laptop computer. After each student's responses were recorded, they were read back to the student to ensure that they communicated what had been intended.

(31) The items to which students responded came from a protocol consisting of seven questions/prompts:

- Which type of note taking did you like the best?
- And why is that so?
- Which type of note taking did you like the least?
- And why is that so?
- Explain the process you used when you typed your notes.
- Explain the process you used when you pasted your notes.
- Explain the process you used when you wrote your notes.

(32) Additional questions were asked to further prompt answers from interviewees who at first gave brief or non-descript answers to one or more of the questions. In general, the interviews lasted from four to six minutes.

(33) After the interviews, students' responses were printed and cut into slips of paper, containing a statement addressing one of the questions. A predetermined set of coding schemes was subsequently used to sort the statements into three categories: typed, written, or pasted notes. The statements within each category then were read and examined several times for any commonality or thread. Similar coding systems have been used in previous research (Igo et al., 2005a). For example, Igo et al. (2005a) used three predetermined categories to sort statements from student interviews into categories addressing shallow, moderate, and deep processing. In this study, some of the themes were identified easily, as students' responses to the questions were in some ways quite similar. Other themes were at first more elusive, but emerged after several examinations of the statements.

(34) Following the prescriptions of Miles and Huberman (1994), an effects matrix was constructed to serve three purposes: organization of the interview data, explanation of effects, and drawing of conclusions. As shown in Table 3 (a condensed version of the matrix), the effects matrix organized the interview data by kind of note taking and student preference. Four themes emerged once the data were organized.

Explanation of Effects

(35) The authors concluded that four themes emerged from the interview data: an overwhelming note-taking preference for students in the study, two students stated that writing was the easiest way for them to take notes, that most students were concerned about spelling errors in their note taking, and that typing was problematic for some students.

Table 3

Condensed Effects Matrix That Organized the Interview Data

Note Taking	Write	Type	Paste	Theme	Exemplar Quote
Preferred Method	2	1	12	**1.** 12 students preferred pasting; 10 because it removed the need to monitor spelling and grammar. **2.** 3 students who were confident in their spelling found writing/typing notes to be the most time efficient.	"When I pasted stuff, I…took it and put it in without worrying about how it looked." "I could write faster than I could do the others."
Least Preferred	2	13	0	**3.** 11 students described the worry and stress of monitoring spelling while writing and/or typing notes. **4.** 6 students found typing notes cumbersome, as need to monitor spelling was amplified by the need to search keyboard for the correct letters.	"…sometimes I had to look back [to the text] a couple of times for the same word if I didn't know how to spell it." "It was hard to find some of the [letter keys…]" "I would forget how to spell [the word] I was typing.]"

Conclusions and QUAN-QUAL Data Mixing

The four qualitative interview themes, coupled with an analysis of student notes, offer a sound explanation of the transfer-appropriate processing effects found in lieu of depth-of-processing effects in the quantitative phase of this study. First, as indicated by the analysis of notes, most students created verbatim notes; they tended to write (or type) one or two words at a time while trying to match their notes to the main text. Verbatim note taking has been linked to shallow processing with both general-education and LD populations (Igo et al., 2003; Slotte & Lonka, 1999; Suritsky, 1992). Further, during the interviews, students consistently described the need to monitor spelling while typing and writing notes. As such, they most likely would have had to shift their mental efforts away from the meaning of the text from time to time as they took notes, which can result in diminished encoding of the text ideas (Igo, Bruning, & McCrudden, 2005b). Finally, some students described the added distraction of searching the keyboard for letters while they took notes. This, too, forces students to shift their mental efforts to a task unrelated to the message in the text. (36)

The qualitative phase of this study also helps explain why students performed slightly better on tests for topics that were noted by writing than by typing. For example, although students indicated that spelling was a concern in both the writing and typing conditions, three students noted that they were able to write their notes more quickly than typing them. Similarly, five students described feeling less pressure to spell correctly while writing than while typing. Together, these two findings could account for the slightly higher performance on written topics, as each suggests that less time was spent on distracting tasks (see, e.g., Baddeley, 1998). (37)

> The intent of the explanatory sequential mixed methods design is to explain the quantitative results with qualitative data. The qualitative phase of this study . . . helps explain why students performed slightly better on tests for topics [on which they took notes] . . . by writing [rather] than by typing.

Implications for Practice

The authors suggested the following implications for practice: students should have a good set of notes to study from, that students should use the copy and paste function in lieu of typing or writing notes that would be more a more comfortable experience when learning online. (38)

Limitations and Future Research

The authors concluded that students with LD have unique needs when it comes to gathering information from Web-based text. (39)

REFERENCES

The authors include a comprehensive list of references.

CHAPTER SEVENTEEN

Action Research

Warner Brothers/Everett Collection

Glee, 2009

"The purpose of action research is to provide teacher-researchers with a method for solving everyday problems in schools." (p. 452)

LEARNING OUTCOMES

After reading Chapter 17, you should be able to do the following:

17.1 State a definition and describe the purpose of action research.
17.2 Identify the key characteristics of action research.
17.3 Identify two types of action research.
17.4 Describe the different levels at which action research can be conducted.
17.5 Describe the steps in the dialectic action research process.

The chapter learning outcomes form the basis for the following task.

TASK 9

Develop a plan for an action research study to answer a school-based research question. Use the following steps to create the components of your written plan:

1. Write an area-of-focus statement.
2. Define the variables.
3. Develop research questions.
4. Describe the intervention or innovation.
5. Describe the membership of the action research group.
6. Describe negotiations that need to be undertaken.
7. Develop a time line.
8. Develop a statement of resources.
9. Develop data collection ideas. (see Performance Criteria, p. 461).

SUMMARY: ACTION RESEARCH

Definition	*Action research* in education is any systematic inquiry conducted by teachers, principals, school counselors, or other stakeholders in the teaching–learning environment that involves gathering information about the ways in which their particular schools operate, the teachers teach, and the students learn.
Design(s)	• Critical action research • Practical action research • Individual • Collaborative, small group • Schoolwide
Types of appropriate research questions	The types of research questions that emerge from your area of focus should involve teaching and learning and should focus on your practice and be within your locus of control. The topic should be something you feel passionate about and something you would like to change or improve.
Key characteristics	• Action research is persuasive, authoritative, relevant, and accessible. • Action research challenges the intractability of reform of the educational system and is not a fad.
Steps in the process	1. Identify an area of focus. 2. Collect data. 3. Conduct data analysis and interpretation. 4. Develop an action plan.
Potential challenges	• Generalizability of the research findings
Example	How will incorporating more meaningful discussions into my biology classroom affect my teaching and the ability of students to learn?

ACTION RESEARCH: DEFINITION AND PURPOSE

Action research in education is any systematic inquiry conducted by teachers, principals, school counselors, or other stakeholders in the teaching–learning environment that involves gathering information about the ways in which their particular schools operate, the teachers teach, and the students learn. This information is gathered with the goals of gaining insight, developing reflective practice, effecting positive changes in the school environment (and on educational practices in general), and improving student outcomes and the lives of those involved.

The purpose of action research is to provide teacher-researchers with a method for solving everyday problems in schools so that they may improve both student learning and teacher effectiveness. Action research is done by teachers, for themselves; it is not imposed on them by someone else. Action research is largely about developing the professional disposition of teachers; that is, encouraging teachers to be continuous learners—in their classrooms and of their practice. In conducting research in their own classrooms and schools, teachers have the opportunity to model for students not only the skills needed for effective learning but also curiosity and an excitement about gaining new knowledge.

Action research is also about incorporating into a teacher's daily routine a reflective stance—a willingness to look critically at one's own teaching so that it can be improved or enhanced. For example, a high-school teacher confronted with the challenges of teaching "unmotivated" students critically reflects on her teaching practices to determine the specific strategies that are most effective in improving student outcomes. Teaching students who are unmotivated and apathetic can be a difficult challenge for any teacher to overcome. This example illustrates the power of action research to empower the teacher to try different teaching strategies and to collect student outcome data (e.g., test scores, student attitudes, and on-task behavior) to help determine which teaching strategy works best for the unmotivated students in her classroom.

Action research contributes significantly to the professional stance that teachers adopt because it encourages them to examine the dynamics of their classrooms, ponder the actions and interactions of students, validate and challenge existing practices, and take risks in the process. When teachers gain new understandings about both their own and their students' behaviors through action research, they are empowered to make informed decisions about what to change and what not to change, link prior knowledge to new information, learn from experience (even failures), and ask questions and systematically find answers.[1] Teachers' goals—to be professional problem solvers who are committed to improving both their own practice and student outcomes—provide a powerful reason to practice action research.

MyLab Education **Self-Check 17.1**

MyLab Education **Application Exercise 17.1:** Evaluating Research Articles: Evaluating an Action Research Project Part 1

KEY CHARACTERISTICS OF ACTION RESEARCH

Action research exhibits five key characteristics: It is persuasive and authoritative, relevant, accessible, a challenge to the intractability of reform of the education system, and not a fad.

Action Research Is Persuasive and Authoritative

Research done by teachers for teachers involves collecting persuasive data. Because teachers are invested in the legitimacy of the data collection, they identify data sources that provide persuasive insights into the impact of an intervention on student outcomes. Similarly, the findings of action research and the recommended actions are authoritative for teacher-researchers. In doing action research, teacher-researchers develop solutions to their own problems. The teachers—not outside "experts"—are the authorities on what works in their classrooms.

---

[1] "Teacher as Researcher: A Synonym for Professionalism," by V. Fueyo and M. A. Koorland, 1997, *Journal of Teacher Education*, 48, pp. 336–344.

Action Research Is Relevant

The relevance of research published in journals to the real world of teachers is perhaps the most common concern raised by teachers when asked about the practical applications of educational research. Either the problems investigated by researchers are not the problems teachers really have, or the schools or classrooms in which the research was conducted are not similar to the teachers' own school environments.

In reviewing two decades of research on schools and teaching, Kennedy cited seminal works[2] to illustrate the relevance of the findings of these studies—classroom life is characterized by crowds, power, praise, and uncertainty. By crowds, she meant that students are always grouped with 20 or 30 others, which means that they must wait in line, wait to be called on, and wait for help. By power, she meant that teachers control most actions and events and decide what the group will do. Teachers also give and withhold praise so that students know which students are favored by the teacher. Finally, the presence of 20 to 30 children in a single classroom means there are 20 to 30 possibilities for an interruption in one's work—a lot of uncertainty.

Kennedy further argued that one aim of educational research is to increase certainty by creating predictability within the classroom. An outcome of action research is that it satisfies the desire that all teachers have to increase the predictability of what happens in their classrooms—in particular, to increase the likelihood that a given curriculum, instructional strategy, or use of technology will positively affect student outcomes. In other words, the results of action research are relevant to the work of individual teacher-researchers.

Action Research Is Accessible

Action research addresses several key concerns about accessibility. First, it addresses the concern that educational research does not affect teaching because it does not address teachers' prior beliefs and values; second, it addresses the concern

that teachers have little access to research findings; third, it addresses the concern that, even if teachers were informed of the results of studies, most would be unlikely to change their practices. Herein lay the beauty, power, and potential of action research to affect practice positively. Action researchers challenge their own taken-for-granted assumptions about teaching and learning. Research findings are meaningful to you because you have identified the area of focus. You have been willing to challenge the conventional craft culture. In short, as an action researcher, your willingness to reflect on and change your thinking about your teaching has led you to become a successful and productive member of the professional community.

Action Research Challenges the Intractability of Reform of the Educational System

In her review, Kennedy suggested that the lack of connection between research and practice can be attributed to the education system itself, not the research. She noted that the educational system can be characterized as a system that lacks agreed-on goals and guiding principles, has no central authority to settle disputes, and is continually bombarded with new fads and fancies. Furthermore, the system provides limited evidence to support or refute any particular idea, encourages reforms that are running at cross-purposes to each other, and gives teachers (in the United States) less time than those in most other countries to develop curricula and daily lessons. Given this characterization, it is little wonder that the more things change, the more they stay the same! Reform is difficult to direct or control—it is intractable. Action research gives teacher-researchers the opportunity to embrace a problem-solving philosophy and practice as an integral part of the culture of their schools and their professional disposition and to challenge the intractability of educational reform by making action research part of the system.

Action Research Is Not a Fad

Action research is decidedly not a fad for one simple reason: Good teachers have always looked systematically at the effects of their teaching on student learning. They may not have called this

[2] M. M. Kennedy, 1997, *Educational Researcher*, 26(7), pp. 4–12; the seminal works include *Life in Classrooms*, by P. W. Jackson, 1968, New York: Holt, Rinehart & Winston; *Schoolteacher: A Sociological Study*, by D. C. Lortie, 1975, Chicago, IL: University of Chicago Press.

TABLE 17.1 • Components of a critical perspective of action research

Key Concept	Example
Action research is participatory and democratic.	You have identified an area in your teaching that you believe can be improved (based on data from your students). You decide to investigate the impact of your intervention and to monitor if it makes a difference.
Action research is socially responsive and takes place in context.	You are concerned that minority children (for example, English as a Second Language [ESL] students) in your classroom are not being presented with curriculum and teaching strategies that are culturally sensitive. You decide to learn more about how best to teach ESL children and to implement some of these strategies.
Action research helps teacher-researchers examine the everyday, taken-for-granted ways in which they carry out professional practice.	You have adopted a new mathematics problem-solving curriculum and decide to monitor its impact on student performance on open-ended problem-solving questions and students' attitudes toward mathematics in general.
Knowledge gained through action research can liberate students, teachers, and administrators and enhance learning, teaching, and policy making.	Your school has a high incidence of student absenteeism in spite of a newly adopted districtwide policy on absenteeism. You investigate the perceptions of colleagues, children, and parents toward absenteeism to understand more fully why the existing policy is not having the desired outcome. Based on what you learn, you implement a new policy and systematically monitor its impact on absenteeism levels and students' attitudes toward school.

Source: Mills, Geoffrey, *Action Research: A Guide for the Teacher Researcher*, 6th Edition, © 2018, p. 8. Reprinted by permission of Pearson Education, Inc., Upper Saddle River, NJ.

practice action research, and they may not have thought their reflection was formal enough to be labeled research, but it was action research!

> MyLab Education **Self-Check 17.2**
>
> MyLab Education **Application Exercise 17.2:** Evaluating Research Articles: Evaluating an Action Research Project Part 2

TYPES OF ACTION RESEARCH

The two main types of action research are critical (or theory-based) action research and practical action research.

Critical Action Research

In critical action research, the goal is liberating individuals through knowledge gathering; for this reason, it is also known as emancipatory action research. Critical action research is so named because it is based on a body of critical theory, not because this type of action research is critical, as in *faultfinding* or *important,* although it may

certainly be both. Table 17.1 shows a summary of the most important components of critical action research.

The values of critical action research dictate that all educational research not only should be socially responsive but also should exhibit the following characteristics:[3]

1. It is *democratic*, enabling the participation of all people.
2. It is *equitable*, acknowledging people's equality of worth.
3. It is *liberating*, providing freedom from oppressive, debilitating conditions.
4. It is life *enhancing*, enabling the expression of people's full human potential.

Although this critical theory-based approach has been challenged for lack of practical feasibility,[4] it is nonetheless important to consider because it provides a helpful heuristic, or problem-solving approach, for teachers who are committed to

---

[3] *Action Research* (3rd ed, p. 11), by E. T. Stringer, 2007, Thousand Oaks, CA: Sage. [Italics in original.]
[4] "On the Teacher as Researcher," by M. Hammersley, 1993, *Educational Action Research*, 1, pp. 425–441.

TABLE 17.2 • Components of a practical perspective of action research

Key Concept	Example
Teacher-researchers have decision-making authority.	Your school has adopted a school-based decision-making approach that provides teachers with the authority to make decisions that have the most direct impact on teaching and learning. Given this decision-making authority, you decide, as part of your continued professional development, to investigate the effectiveness of a newly adopted science curriculum on students' process skills and attitudes.
Teacher-researchers are committed to continued professional development and school improvement.	Based on the results of statewide assessment tests and classroom observations, the teachers and principal at your school determine that reading comprehension skills are weak. Collaboratively, staff members determine the focus for a school improvement effort and identify the necessary professional development that will be offered to change the ways teachers teach reading.
Teacher-researchers want to reflect on their practices.	You are a successful classroom teacher who regularly reflects on your daily teaching and what areas could be improved. You believe that part of being a professional teacher is the willingness to examine your teaching effectiveness continually.
Teacher-researchers use a systematic approach for reflecting on their practice.	Given a schoolwide reading comprehension focus, you have decided to monitor the effectiveness of a new reading curriculum and teaching strategies by video-recording a reading lesson (once per month), administering reading comprehension "probes" (once per week), interviewing children in your classroom (once per term), and administering statewide assessment tests (at the end of the school year).
Teacher-researchers choose an area of focus, determine data collection techniques, analyze and interpret data, and develop action plans.	To continue the example above, you have focused on the effectiveness of a new reading curriculum and teaching strategies. You have decided to collect data using video-recordings of lessons, regular interviews ("probes"), and statewide assessment tests. During the year, you try to interpret the data you are collecting and decide what these data suggest about the effectiveness of the new curriculum and teaching strategies. When all of the data have been collected and analyzed, you decide what action needs to be taken to refine, improve, and maintain the reading comprehension curriculum and teaching strategies.

Source: Mills, Geoffrey, *Action Research: A Guide for the Teacher Researcher*, 6th Edition, © 2018, p. 9. Reprinted by permission of Pearson Education, Inc., Upper Saddle River, NJ.

investigate through action research the taken-for-granted relationships and practices in their professional lives.

Practical Action Research

Compared to critical action research, practical action research emphasizes more of a how-to approach to the processes of action research and has a less philosophical bent. An underlying assumption is that, to some degree, individual teachers or teams of teachers are autonomous and can determine the nature of the investigation to be undertaken. Other assumptions are that teacher-researchers are committed to continued professional development and school improvement and that they want to reflect on their practices systematically. Finally, the practical action research perspective assumes that, as decision makers, teacher-researchers choose their own areas of

focus, determine their data collection techniques, analyze and interpret the data, and develop action plans based on their findings. These beliefs are summarized in Table 17.2.

> MyLab Education **Self-Check 17.3**
>
> MyLab Education **Application Exercise 17.3:** Explaining the Types of Action Research

LEVELS OF ACTION RESEARCH

Educational action research can be undertaken at three levels: the single school or department level, in which small teacher groups or teams conduct the research; the schoolwide level; or the individual teacher level. It is important to note that teachers rarely carry out action research involving multiple schools because of the organizational complexity and the uniqueness of the many settings or schools.

It is likely that in a single school, action research is carried out by groups of teachers, all of whom seek to understand and improve a common issue, rather than by an individual teacher. For example, a group of high-school math teachers may work together to implement a promising hands-on math strategy for students who are lagging in math performance and then determine its impact on student math performance. At the school level, it is more common and interesting for teachers to focus their action research in their own disciplines, although some teachers collaborate across subject areas, and shared goals are surely voiced by teachers in diverse content areas. For example, elementary-school teachers may form a small group and design a study to answer questions about varied strategies such as inclusion of special education students, inquiry-based learning, or literary clubs, which cross content area and grade lines. Other teachers may be involved in collaborative or participatory research by working with university-based researchers in their classrooms. For example, teachers may study their own research questions along with similar or related questions that the university researcher has.

In schoolwide action research, the majority of the school community identifies a problem and conducts research together with a common, focused goal in mind. For example, a schoolwide emphasis on reading is a common goal of many elementary schools. As another example, counselors, teachers, and administrators may band together in a middle school and try strategies to integrate cliques or other groups of students to create a more cooperative environment.

Although a group of teachers working together is more common, individual teachers can conduct action research to improve their understanding and practice in their own classrooms. Quite often, individual teachers seek to study aspects of their classrooms that are unique to them and to their students. For example, a teacher may gather information by observing students to understand their interests or behaviors in a particular subject area. Alternatively, the teacher may select or construct simple instruments or tests to collect student information pertaining to the issue or problem under

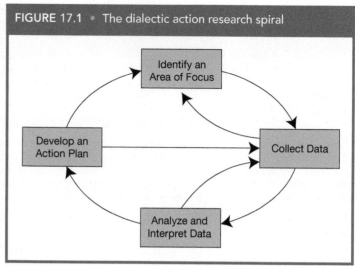

FIGURE 17.1 • The dialectic action research spiral

Source: Mills, Geoffrey, *Action Research: A Guide for the Teacher Researcher,* 6th Edition, © 2018, p. 19. Reprinted by permission of Pearson Education, Inc., Upper Saddle River, NJ.

study. Individual teacher action research can be a useful tool for solving educational problems in one's own setting.

MyLab Education **Self-Check 17.4**

THE ACTION RESEARCH PROCESS

The basic steps in the action research process are identifying an area of focus, data collection, data analysis and interpretation, and action planning. This four-step process has been termed the dialectic action research spiral[5] and is illustrated in Figure 17.1. It provides teacher-researchers with a practical guide and illustrates how to proceed with inquiries. It is a model for research done by teachers and for teachers and students, not research done on them, and as such is a dynamic and responsive model that can be adapted to different contexts and purposes. It was designed to provide teacher-researchers with "provocative and constructive ways"[6] of thinking about their work.

---

[5] *Action Research: A Guide for the Teacher Researcher* (6th ed.), by G. E. Mills, 2018, Upper Saddle River, NJ: Merrill/Prentice Hall.
[6] *Kwakiutl Village and School* (p. 137), by H. F. Wolcott, 1989. Prospect Heights, IL: Waveland Press.

Action research techniques can be viewed in terms of the dialectic action research spiral. In this section, we discuss specific action research techniques related to this model.

Identifying an Area of Focus

Finding an area of focus can be hard work for teacher-researchers who, confronted with many problems in their classrooms and schools, are not sure which one to choose. It is critical in the early stages of the action research process that the researcher take time to identify a meaningful, engaging question or problem to investigate. One technique that can help in identifying an area of focus is to ensure that four criteria are satisfied: (1) the area of focus should involve teaching and learning and should focus on your own practice, (2) the area of focus is something within your locus of control, (3) the area of focus is something you feel passionate about, and (4) the area of focus is something you would like to change or improve.

The next important step in the action research process is reconnaissance, or preliminary information gathering. More specifically, reconnaissance is taking time to reflect on your own beliefs and to understand the nature and context of your general idea. Doing reconnaissance involves gaining insight into your area of focus through self-reflection, descriptive activities, and explanatory activities.

Gaining Insight through Self-Reflection

You can begin reconnaissance by exploring your own understandings of the theories that affect your practice, the educational values you hold, how your work in schools fits into the larger context of schooling and society, the historical contexts of your school and schooling and how things got to be the way they are, and the historical contexts of how you came to believe what you believe about teaching and learning.[7] For example, suppose that your general idea for your action research inquiry is the question "How can I improve the integration and transfer of problem-solving skills in mathematics?" Your exploration and self-reflection may include the following observations:

- In my reading of the subject, I have been influenced by Van de Walle's[8] theory about teaching and learning mathematics developmentally. In particular, the goal of mathematics is relational understanding, which is the connection between conceptual and procedural knowledge in mathematics. This theory of mathematics directly affects the ways I think about teaching mathematics to my children.
- I hold the educational value that children ought to be able to transfer problem-solving skills to other areas of mathematics as well as to life outside school. That is, I am committed to relevancy of curricula.
- I believe that mathematical problem solving, and problem solving in general, fits the larger context of schooling and society by providing children with critical lifelong learning skills that can be transferred to all aspects of their lives.
- The historical context of mathematics teaching suggests a rote method of memorizing facts and algorithms. Although this approach to teaching mathematics worked for me (as a child and young teacher), it no longer suffices as a teaching method today.
- The historical context of how I came to believe in the importance of changing how I teach mathematics to children has grown out of my own frustration with knowing what to do to solve a problem but not knowing why I need to use a particular approach or algorithm.
- Given this self-reflection on an area of focus related to the integration and transfer of problem-solving skills in mathematics, I can now better understand the problem before I implement an intervention that addresses my concern for how best to teach a relevant problem-solving curriculum.

Gaining Insight through Descriptive Activities

To continue in the reconnaissance process, you should try to describe as fully as possible the situation you want to change or improve by focusing on *who, what, where,* and *when*. Grappling with these

---

[7] *The Action Research Reader* (3rd ed.), by S. Kemmis and R. McTaggart (Eds.), 1988, Geelong, Victoria, Australia: Deakin University Press.

[8] *Elementary School Mathematics: Teaching Developmentally*, by J. A. Van de Walle, 1994, New York: Longman.

questions to clarify the focus area for your action research efforts keeps you from moving ahead with an investigation that was too murky at the start. For example, in this stage, you may ask yourself a series of questions, such as "What evidence do I have that this (the problem-solving skills of math students) is a problem?" "Which students are not able to transfer problem-solving skills to other mathematics tasks?" "How is problem solving presently taught?" "How often is problem solving taught?" "What is the ratio of time spent teaching problem solving to time spent teaching other mathematics skills?" The answers you develop provide a framework for the research.

Gaining Insight through Explanatory Activities

After you've adequately described the situation you intend to investigate, you can try to explain it. Focus on the *why*. Can you account for the critical factors that have an impact on the general idea? In essence, in this step you develop hypotheses about the expected relations among variables in your study. For example, you may hypothesize that students are struggling with the transfer of problem-solving skills to other mathematics tasks because they are not getting enough practice, because they lack fundamental basic math skills, or because the use of math manipulatives has been missing or they have not been used to their full potential. Given these possible explanations for why children have not been transferring problem-solving skills to other areas of mathematics successfully, you may further hypothesize that the use of a mathematics curriculum that emphasizes the children's knowledge of what to do and why to do it is related to children's abilities to transfer problem-solving skills; you may further hypothesize that the use of a mathematics curriculum that emphasizes the use of manipulatives to help children create meaning is related to children's abilities to transfer problem-solving skills.

Reconnaissance activities such as self-reflection, description, and explanation help teacher-researchers to clarify what they already know about the proposed focus of the study; what they believe to be true about the relations among the factors, variables, and contexts that make up their work environments; and what they believe can improve the situation.

Data Collection, Analysis, and Interpretation

The type of data collected for an action research study is largely determined by the nature of the problem. A teacher-researcher must determine how the data will contribute to the understanding and resolution of a given problem. Hence, data collection during action research is often idiosyncratic, fueled by the desire to understand one's practice and to collect data that are appropriate and accessible. Therefore, data collection strategies (and hence research design) are chosen on the basis of the type of research problem confronted by the action researcher. No single method is better (or worse) than another; it is chosen on the basis of the research questions.

The literature on action research supports the assertion that qualitative data collection methods are more often applied to action research problems than are quantitative methods and designs. In part, this choice can be attributed to the fact that teachers and administrators do not routinely assign children to an experimental group that receives a treatment or to a control group that does not. However, action researchers do not—and should not—avoid numerical data. Clearly, many quantitative data sources are readily available for collection by teacher-researchers. For example, standardized test scores are increasingly important to justify state and federal funding for academic programs.

For the most part, numerical data collected as part of an action research study are appropriately summarized with descriptive statistics, such as measures of central tendency (i.e., mean, mode, median) and variability (e.g., standard deviation). Our advice here is simple: Count what counts! If it makes sense to tally and count events, categories, occurrences, or test scores, use an appropriate descriptive statistic. However, do not feel compelled to include elaborate statistical measures simply to add a perceived sense of rigor or credibility to your inquiry.

Action Planning

One of the final tasks in action research is for the researcher to share the findings with others, in both formal and informal settings. For example, results can be shared with other teachers, both in the researcher's school or in other schools, and results may be presented verbally—in formal presentations and informal conversations—or in written reports. Writing can lead to further analysis, improved interpretation, and deeper understanding of the problem—as well as suggestions for how to act on the findings. Writing also creates a permanent record of the research that others may use. Other teachers, administrators, researchers, and current or potential investors in the program may be in a position to benefit from the results.

As the name suggests, action research is action-oriented, and it is directed toward both understanding and improving practice. Thus, the last step in the research process is deciding what steps, if any, need to be taken to alter or improve practice. For example, study results can be used in the classroom, school, or district to improve instruction, procedures, and outcomes of education or to aid teacher understanding of instruction and applications. Often, action research leads to new questions to examine, thus forging new forms of understanding and deeper insights in practice. The practical nature of action research fosters much of the teacher-based improvement in schools.

MyLab Education **Self-Check 17.5**

MyLab Education **Application Exercise 17.4:**
Evaluating Research Articles: Identifying Steps in the Action Research Project

MyLab Education **Application Exercise 17.5:**
Planning an Action Research Study

SUMMARY

ACTION RESEARCH: DEFINITION AND PURPOSE

1. Action research in education is any systematic inquiry conducted by teacher-researchers, principals, school counselors, or other stakeholders in the teaching–learning environment that involves gathering information about the ways in which their particular schools operate, the teachers teach, and the students learn.

2. The purpose of action research is to provide teacher-researchers with a method for solving everyday problems in schools so that they may improve both student learning and teacher effectiveness.

3. Action research is research done by teachers, for themselves; it is not imposed on them by someone else.

KEY CHARACTERISTICS OF ACTION RESEARCH

4. Action research is persuasive, authoritative, relevant, and accessible.

5. Action research challenges the intractability of reform of the educational system and is not a fad.

TYPES OF ACTION RESEARCH

6. Critical action research is based on a body of critical theory and has a goal of liberating individuals through knowledge gathering. It is also known as emancipatory action research.

7. Practical action research emphasizes a how-to approach to the processes of action research. An assumption is that teachers are autonomous and can determine the nature of the investigation to be undertaken.

LEVELS OF ACTION RESEARCH

8. Education action research can be undertaken at three levels: the individual teacher level, the single school or department level, or the schoolwide level.

THE ACTION RESEARCH PROCESS

9. The action research process includes identifying an area of focus, data collection, data analysis and interpretation, and action planning. These four steps form a process known as the dialectic action research spiral.

10. The area of focus for action research should involve teaching and learning, focus on your practice, and be within your locus of control. It should be something you feel passionate about and something you would like to change or improve.

11. Insight into an area of focus can be gained through self-reflection, descriptive activities, and explanatory activities.

12. Data collection techniques used in action research depend on the area of focus.

13. Qualitative data collection techniques are more often applied to action research problems than are quantitative methods and designs. Teachers do not routinely assign children on a random basis to an experimental group that receives a treatment or to a control group that does not.

14. Action research is action-oriented. Action researchers follow through with their action plans to ensure that lessons learned are implemented in the classroom or school setting.

PERFORMANCE CRITERIA AND EXAMPLES   TASK 9

Write an Area-of-Focus Statement

An area-of-focus statement identifies the purpose of your study. To start, write a statement that completes the following sentence: "The purpose of this study is to . . ." Here are some examples:

> The purpose of this study is to describe the effects of an integrated problem-solving mathematics curriculum on student transfer of problem-solving skills and the retention of basic math facts and functions.

> The purpose of this study is to describe the impact of bringing audience members into an interactive relationship with teen theater productions on participants' abilities to identify issues and incorporate solutions to similar problems in their own lives.

> The purpose of this study is to describe the effects of student-led conferences on parent and student satisfaction with the conferencing process.

Define the Variables

As part of the area-of-focus statement construction process, write definitions of what you will focus on in the study. These definitions should accurately represent what the factors, contexts, and variables mean to you. A variable is a characteristic of your study that is subject to change. That is, a variable may be how you teach, the curriculum you use, or student outcomes. Definitions may also emerge from the literature, but you should commit to your definitions and communicate them clearly. In the preceding examples, the researchers should define what they mean by "an integrated problem-solving mathematics curriculum," "transfer of problem-solving skills," "the retention of basic math facts and functions," "interactive relationship with teen theater productions," "student-led conferences," and "parent and student satisfaction with the conferencing process." If you are clear about what you are examining, it will be easy to determine how you will know it when you see it. That is, your data collection ideas will flow more freely, and you will have no confusion when you communicate with your action research collaborators about your purpose.

Develop Research Questions

Develop questions that breathe life into the area-of-focus statement and help provide a focus for your data collection plan. These questions will also help you validate that you have a workable way to proceed with your investigation. Here are some examples:

> How does incorporating math manipulatives into problem-solving activities affect student performance on open-ended problem-solving tests?

> In what ways do students transfer problem-solving skills to other areas of mathematics?

> How do students incorporate problem-solving skills into other curriculum areas?

> How do students transfer problem-solving skills to their lives outside school?

Describe the Intervention or Innovation

Describe what you will do to improve the situation you have described. For example, you may say, "I will implement a standards-based integrated problem-solving mathematics curriculum," "I will include audience improvisation as part of the teen theater performances I direct," or "I will incorporate student participation in student-parent-teacher conferences." You need to provide only a simple statement about what you will do in your classroom or school to address the teaching–learning issue you have identified.

Describe the Membership of the Action Research Group

Describe who belongs to your action research group, and discuss why the members are important. Will you be working with a site council team? A parent group? What will be the roles and responsibilities of the participants? Here is one example:

> I will be working with seven other high-school math teachers who are all members of the math department. Although we all have different teaching responsibilities within the department, as a group we have decided on problem solving

as an area of focus for the department. Each of us will be responsible for implementing curriculum and teaching strategies that reflect the new emphasis on problem solving and for collecting the kinds of data that we decide will help us monitor the effects of our teaching. The department chair will be responsible for keeping the principal informed about our work and securing any necessary resources we need to complete the research. The chair will also write a description of our work to be included in the school newsletter (sent home to all parents), thus informing children and parents of our focus for the year.

Describe Negotiations That Need to Be Undertaken

Describe any negotiations that you will have to undertake with others before implementing your plan. Do you need permission from an administrator? Parents? Students? Colleagues? It's important that you control the focus of the study and that you undertake the process of negotiation to head off any potential obstacles to implementation of the action plan. It's very frustrating to get immersed in the action research process only to have the project quashed by uncooperative colleagues or administrators.

Develop a Time Line

In developing a time line, you need to decide who will be doing what and when. You can also include information on where and how your inquiry will take place. This information, although not strictly part of a time line, helps you in this stage of your planning. For example:

Phase 1 (August–October). Identify area of focus, review related literature, develop research questions, do reconnaissance.

Phase 2 (November–December). Collect initial data. Analyze video-recordings of lessons, do first interviews with children, administer first problem-solving probe.

Phase 3 (January–May). Modify curriculum and instruction as necessary. Continue ongoing data collection. Schedule two team meetings to discuss early analysis of data.

Phase 4 (May–June). Review statewide assessment test data and complete analysis of all data. Develop presentation for faculty members. Schedule team meeting to discuss and plan action based on the findings of the study. Assign tasks to be completed prior to year 2 of the study.

Develop a Statement of Resources

Briefly describe the resources you need to enact your plan. This step is akin to listing materials in a lesson plan—there is nothing worse than starting to teach and finding you don't have all the materials you need to achieve your objectives. For example, to participate in the study of math problem-solving skills, a team may determine that it needs teacher release time for project planning, reviewing related literature, and other tasks; funds to purchase classroom sets of manipulatives; and a small budget for copying and printing curriculum materials. After all, there is no sense developing a study that investigates the impact of a new math problem-solving curriculum if you don't have the financial resources to purchase the curriculum.

Develop Data Collection Ideas

Give a preliminary statement of the kinds of data that you think will provide evidence for your reflections on the general idea you are investigating. For example, brainstorm the kind of intuitive, naturally occurring data that you find in your classroom or school, such as test scores, attendance records, portfolios, and anecdotal records. As you learn more about other types of data that can be collected, this list will grow, but in the early stages, think about what you already have easy access to and then be prepared to add interviews, surveys, questionnaires, video- and audio-recordings, maps, photos, and observations as the area of focus dictates.

The tasks just described can be undertaken whether you are working individually, in a small group, or as part of a schoolwide action research effort. The resolution of these issues early in the action research process ensures that you do not waste valuable time backtracking.

"Let's Talk": Discussions in a Biology Classroom: An Action Research Project

PENNY JUENEMANN

Introduction

Action research has provided me with the opportunity to engage in profes- (01)
sional development enabling me to reflect upon my teaching and determine
whether I am living up to my values. In this action research project I have
been studying how my teaching has changed in order to facilitate meaningful
discussions in the classroom, and I have been assessing how these changes
impact my students. The motivation for this study came from my desire to
have students make connections between what they already know and new
knowledge they encounter in biology. By reflecting upon my teaching I discovered that I was doing most of the biology related talking. As an undergraduate we discussed the importance of a student-centered classroom and
when I graduated I was confident that I would always be a student-centered
teacher. It has been almost ten years since I received my undergraduate
degree and I haven't always lived up to that value. By increasing my ability
to facilitate meaningful discussions I hope to swing the pendulum back to
the students. I teach biology to all tenth grade students and believe that it is
important that students are able to make connections between biology content we cover in the classroom and the world around them. By engaging in
more discussions I believe students' learning will become more meaningful.

Context

During the 2003–2004 school year at Two Harbors High School I taught five (02)
sections of 10th grade biology, one section of 12th grade Advance Placement
biology and one section of 11th and 12th grade physics daily. Each class
had approximately 22 students except AP biology which had 8 students. My
action research focused on my 10th grade biology students.

Research Questions

How will incorporating more meaningful discussions into my biology class- (03)
room affect my teaching and the ability of students to learn?

> Area of focus: The purpose of
> this study is to describe the
> impact of biology classroom
> discussions (as a teaching inter-
> vention) on 10th-grade stu-
> dents' knowledge of biology.

Sub-Questions

1. How do I need to change my teaching to facilitate more meaningful
   discussions in my biology classroom?
2. Will having more meaningful discussions allow students to learn
   content at a higher level?
3. Will having more meaningful discussions help students make
   connections between biology content and the world around them?
4. Will having more meaningful discussions increase students' ability
   to make informed decisions regarding socially and/or ecologically
   significant issues?

Theoretical Framework

This paper is about my journey as a teacher through action research. Action (04)
research is a process by which teachers attempt to study their problems
scientifically in order to guide, correct, and evaluate their decisions and
actions concerning their teaching and learning. Action research requires the
researcher to be reflective of his or her practice. Through action research the
researcher is striving to live his or her values in the classroom.

(05)   I feel it is important for students to make connections between what they already know and what we learn in class. To acquire a deep understanding of complex ideas (meaningful learning), students need to make connections between what they know and new knowledge that they encounter. Such an epistemology is referred to as constructivism. One of the first philosophers to explain constructivism was Piaget. The idea can be traced back even further to Giambattista Vico in 1710 who proclaimed, "To know means to know how to make." He substantiates this notion by arguing that one knows a thing only when one can explain it (Yager, 2000, p. 44).

(06)   Through better discussions, students can develop a better understanding of the content being covered in class. Lord (1994) suggests that "By attempting to explain what one knows about a problem to someone else, explainers test the fit of their understanding. Similarly, while trying to understand what a colleague is saying, listeners question and challenge their own understanding and try to fit the material into their already established cognitive foundations" (Lord, 1994, p. 346–347).

(07)   Students must talk about what they are doing, relate it to past experience and then apply it to their daily lives. By discussing problems that are relevant to students' lives, but also problems that contain the biological concepts students are required to know, students will construct their knowledge in a meaningful way. By monitoring these discussions, teachers can obtain immediate feedback. If one student is incorrectly explaining material aloud to another, the teacher can do immediate re-teaching. More optimistically, teachers can also give immediate praise.

(08)   Early on in my project I realized that it would be important to ask good questions and monitor student responses and cognition. There are three domains of learning: cognitive, affective, and psychomotor. In 1956, Benjamin Bloom defined the cognitive (the mental process or faculty of knowing) domain for educators (Henson, 1993, p. 124). He developed a taxonomy for categorizing questions, objectives, or responses. His six categories can be divided into two groups, low order and high order. The low order categories are the simplest and the least demanding, whereas high order categories require greater understanding and are thus more demanding. Low order categories are knowledge and comprehension. High order categories involve application, analysis, synthesis, and evaluation. Asking higher-order questions challenges students to think while promoting learning, as higher-order questions require students to process information in ways associated with greater comprehension and understanding. In order for me to stimulate meaningful discussions, I need to ask questions of a higher order on Bloom's taxonomy. Simple knowledge-based questions elicit little discussion. Another important concept regarding questioning is wait time. It is recommended to wait three to five seconds after asking a question, and again after the response, in order to give students a chance to think and formulate a high-order response. A third important consideration in questioning is the use of Socratic dialogue. In Socratic dialogue, teachers respond to students' questions with questions. It is also very important that students ask questions. "If we want to engage students in thinking through content we must stimulate their thinking with questions that lead them to further questions" (Elder, 1998, p. 298).

(09)   After monitoring discussions for about a month, I discovered that the make-up of the group conducting the discussion is important as people learn in different ways. The main learning styles are visual, auditory, and kinesthetic. Visual learners learn best by seeing, auditory learn best by hearing and talking, and kinesthetic learners learn best by doing. People can possess any combination of these learning styles, but often times one is dominant. Through discussions with a critical friend, I decided to try grouping students heterogeneously by their learning styles. Later on, after reading more literature, I discovered that many teachers have had success grouping their students

heterogeneously by ability. I then tried arranging my students heterogeneously by learning style and ability in an attempt to improve discussions.

Another path my action research has taken me on is cooperative learning. Cooperative learning models also recommended that groups be arranged heterogeneously. In a study conducted on cooperative learning at the college level the researcher said, "We experienced first hand that homogenous teams are a prescription for disaster in a cooperative learning driven course . . . It is important for students from different backgrounds to work together and learn from each other's perspectives and strengths" (Trempy, 2002, p. 32). To facilitate meaningful discussions, students need to work together cooperatively. This practice was reinforced by the results of a questionnaire I gave my students in which they stated that participation was important for quality discussions to take place. To address this concern, I began using some cooperative learning techniques. Cooperative learning is an approach that encourages students to collaborate with each other to achieve common learning goals. According to Johnson and Johnson (1985) one of the main elements of cooperative learning is "individual accountability," where every student is responsible for contributing to the group. This can be done by assigning and checking individual contributions to the group, assigning roles or jobs to every member, randomly quizzing every member over the material, and/or giving individual tests. Another essential element is "positive interdependence" when students feel they need each other in order to complete the task successfully. According to Holubec (1992), cooperative learning is also a style that leads toward higher-level thinking. When students are working together and discussing the material, they will work beyond the lower-order questions. Within discussion groups, students need to accept and learn from each other's opinions, strengths, and contributions. In Lotan's research she found that students can be empowered by this type of group work, "Group-worthy tasks require students to share their experiences and justify their beliefs and opinions. By assigning such tasks, teachers delegate intellectual authority to their students and make their students' life experiences, opinions and points of view legitimate components of the content to be learned" (Lotan, 2003, p. 72).

The affective domain, which addresses students' attitudes and values, is also important in the classroom. Part of my research examined socially and/or ecologically significant issues, with the hope of encouraging moral growth in my students, helping them become more aware of their values and to allow them to make connections between biology and the world around them (between new and preexisting knowledge). In addition to making necessary connections, hopefully students will improve their critical thinking skills. Woodruff explains how discussing these issues can increase students' critical thinking skills, "Ethical thinking is neither a matter of pure intellect nor of gut feelings and prejudices. What is important here is one's reasoning and critical thinking skills. Thus, by strengthening and expanding these skills, the student will be able to view our ever-changing biological world from a new perspective, and not be limited by the past or previous belief-systems" (Woodruff, 1992, p. 2).

In summary, through my action research and my desire to be more of a constructivist teacher, I have found it necessary to research good questioning skills, higher-order learning, learning styles, and cooperative learning.

Changes in My Teaching Practices

The main focus of my research is on small group discussions, as that is where more students can participate in a more comfortable environment. Though I didn't have a defined method of research as I began, I collected and analyzed data and made what I thought were appropriate changes in my teaching as I progressed through my action research. The following is a list of changes that I made.

(10)

(11)

(12)

(13)

> Teaching intervention, based on promising practices from a review of related literature, included the use of questioning skills, higher-order learning (according to Bloom's taxonomy), learning styles, and cooperative learning.

465

1. I increased the number of discussion opportunities in my classroom.
2. I administered a learning style inventory then arranged students into groups heterogeneously based on their learning style and later on arranged students heterogeneously by learning style and ability.
3. I increased the number of high-order questions. Throughout my research I tried to ask higher-order questions according to Bloom's taxonomy in hopes that students would increase their higher-order responses. When preparing discussion questions I referred to Bloom's taxonomy. Also, I tried to keep myself from directly answering a student's question but to guide them to their own understanding through an increase in Socratic dialogue.
4. I used more cooperative learning techniques. From the first questionnaire that I gave students I discovered that students wanted everyone to participate more, including themselves. I used roles or jobs within a group, the numbered heads together technique, the round robin technique, and the jigsaw technique. In the numbered heads technique, the students were numbered off within a group and told that I would randomly pick a person from their table to answer a question. They must work together to make sure everyone understands the problem. The round robin technique is when each group has one paper and it is passed around the table for everyone to contribute to. I used this technique to review the plant kingdom. Students were instructed to make a dichotomous key as a group going around the table until the key was finished. The jigsaw method uses two groups, a 'home' group (their original group) and the 'jigsaw' group. First students start in their home group to discuss the issue, then they break into their jigsaw group (students are numbered within their home group—then all like numbers get together to make the jigsaw group). Last, students return to their home group to share information they collected. While using cooperative learning groups I had a student mention that discussions should be "worth more" (referring to points) and it was suggested by a colleague to have students evaluate each other on their participation. In response to this I developed a rubric for students to evaluate each other on their participation.
5. As a way to involve students in discussions, I designed and facilitated discussions on socially and ecologically significant issues. Ten of the twenty discussions focused on socially and/or ecologically significant issues. Some discussions involved scientific articles. First, students read the articles and answered questions independently. Then they discussed their answers to the articles using a cooperative learning technique. Another type of activity I used was dilemma cards, for example, 'Deer Dilemma' modified from an activity in *Project Wild* where students had to respond to the ecological impacts that the growing deer population has in our environment and design a solution as a group. I used the jigsaw method for this activity.
6. Another way to involve students in discussions was by having them design and carryout labs as a group. I provided them with the question and with some guidelines; guided inquiry. Four of the twenty planned discussions were designing labs.

Data Collection and Analysis

(14)

Data collection for this study came from several sources. To analyze this data I read through my journal on a regular basis, analyzed student questionnaires, discussed results with my validation team while searching for themes within the data.

Data collection strategies included questionnaires, interviews, journal, audio recordings of group discussions, and test scores.

Chart 1

Triangulation of Data

| Research Questions | Data Collection Techniques | | | |
	1	2	3	4
How do I need to change my teaching to facilitate more meaningful discussions in my biology classroom?	Teacher Journal	Student Questionnaire	Student Interviews	Lesson Plan Book
Will having more meaningful discussions allow students to learn content at a higher level?	Audiotape of Discussions	Student Questionnaire	Unit Tests	
Will having more meaningful discussions help students make connections between biology content and the world around them?	Audiotape of Discussions	Student Questionnaire	Student Interviews	
Will having more meaningful discussions increase students' ability to make informed decisions regarding socially and/or ecologically significant issues?	Student Questionnaire	Mock situations where students use their biology knowledge and skills to address a social or ecological problem	Student Interviews	

Chart 2

Analysis of Biology Tests

Date	Test name	Point total for higher-order question/total point	% of points from higher-order questions	Number of tests analyzed	Students' average score on higher-order questions	% of points earned for higher-order questions
9/12/03	Microscope and Scientific Method	10/47	21%	111	6.7	67%
10/10/03	Eukarya Test	13/60	22%	95	8.1	62%
10/29/03	Animal Kingdom	7/22	32%	107	5.4	78%
11/11/03	Bacteria and Viruses	4/22	18%	99	2.6	65%

Teacher Journal

While reflecting on my journal entries I was able to verify the need for this action research project. In an early entry I was concerned about 'down time,' students not engaged and a couple months later was very excited about initiating a good discussion. Reading journal entries helped guide my teaching. (15)

Student Questionnaires

Students responded to two questionnaires. The greatest benefit from the first questionnaire was that students let me know that participation was critical for group work success. One open-ended question on the questionnaire was: What can I (the teacher) do to improve discussions in the classroom? 8% of the students responded that I should make sure everyone participated. In the second open-ended question: What can you (the student) do to improve discussions in the classroom? 46% of the students responded that they should participate more. Also, from this first questionnaire, I noticed that students (16) want to make connections between what we are doing in biology and the world around them. Two students made this comment, "Have things we may run into later in life." One student seemed to be aware of the benefit of discussions to constructivism, "Have a weekly class discussion that involves not only what we learned but what we know."

(17) In the second questionnaire I noticed that students were still concerned about participation but they noted several instances when discussions were better because everyone participated. For example, with the round robin virus articles a student said, "Everyone participated because they had different information." And with the deer dilemma some student comments were: "It got everyone involved and participating." "We had to decide something as a group." "We had good conversations." From the second questionnaire I also noticed that students enjoyed discussing socially and ecologically significant articles. A student said, "We shared our point of views and opinions on the article. So I learned others' thoughts on the article."

(18) In summary, the questionnaires helped guide me in my research by showing how important it was to the students that everyone participates. I also discovered that students feel it is necessary to make connections between the biology content and the world around them and that they felt that by engaging in these discussions helped them to do that.

Unit Tests

(19) When analyzing my tests I used Bloom's taxonomy to determine if questions were low or high order questions. Then I studied the students' responses to determine the percent of points earned on the higher order questions. The purpose was to see if increases in discussions would lead to more points earned on higher order questions throughout my research.

(20) From this data I can conclude that I still need to work on writing higher-order questions. I believe the content type influences the amount and type of questions that are asked.

Audiotapes of Discussions

(21) On seven different occasions I audiotaped discussions. Using Bloom's taxonomy I categorized the discussion questions that I designed prior to the discussions and questions that developed during the discussion. When I audiotaped more than one group I averaged the number of high- or low-order questions.

(22) From this graph I can see that I have increased the number questions that I am asking and I have increased the amount of high-order questions that I am asking. However, because this graph combines different types of activities, I graphed the difference between high-order and low-order questions in graph 2.

(23) As indicated by this graph I am making progress toward asking more high order questions compared to low order questions over time.

(24) Student responses from the audiotapes were also categorized using Bloom's taxonomy.

(25) Again it is important to note that the six discussions in these graphs are from different types of activities. 9/3 and 11/4 are when students designed and conducted their own labs within their discussion group. On 9/3 students had chosen their discussion groups and on 11/4 they were arranged heterogeneously by ability and learning style. 9/23 and 11/3 students read articles and answered questions independently and then discussed their answers. On 11/3 they answered their questions using the numbered together cooperative learning technique. On 10/2 students were analyzing data from a lichen field study. On 10/23 students solved the deer dilemma. On 1/7 students responded to an ethical dilemma based on articles they read about stem cell research.

(26) I graphed the difference between high-order and low-order questions from 3 in graph 4.

(27) I was excited when I unexpectedly noticed that students had more high-order responses to low-order responses when they were involved in student-

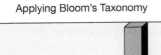

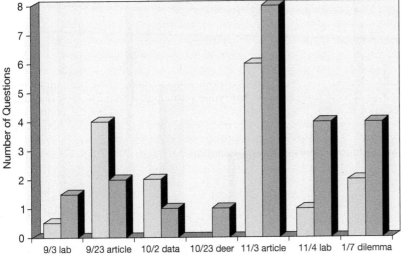

GRAPH 1 An evaluation of teacher questions

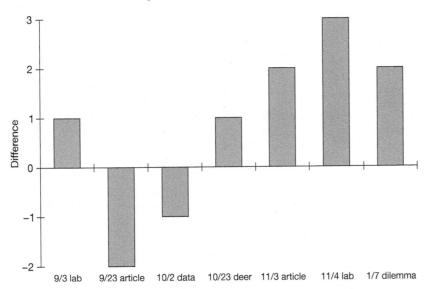

GRAPH 2 Change in higher order questions

centered activities. The three positive bars are from designing their own experiments and from the deer dilemma. Even though I increased the number of higher-order questions with the antibiotic article on 11/3/03, students responded with a higher number of low-order statements. However, I can also see that as discussions have increased, there is more being said during the discussions.

Student Interviews

From the student interviews, I found that students believe and appreciate that I am trying to get everyone involved but two of the four were still concerned that everyone doesn't always participate. In response to the question "What do you like about my teaching?" one student seemed to recognize

(28)

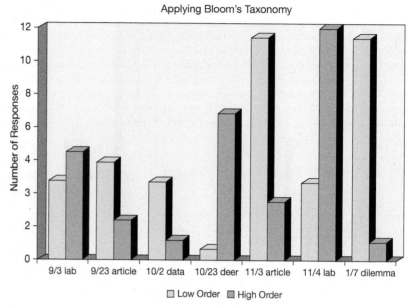

GRAPH 3 An evaluation of student responses

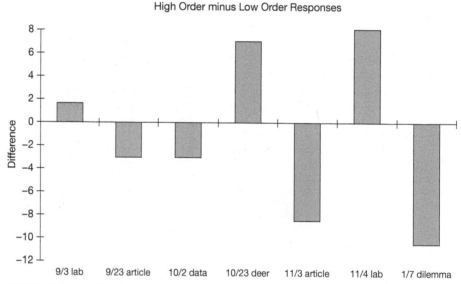

GRAPH 4 Change in higher order responses

that discussions help her make connections, "You teach from the book but then we do other things and we discuss them. It sticks really well. When I first read the chapter I think I'm never going to remember but after while it all clicks together and by the end it's stuck in my brain." Three of the four students felt that having roles during discussions helped improve the participation, and one felt that it worked really well in the deer dilemma. All four students felt that grading students on their participation would improve discussions. Three of the four students felt that discussing socially or environmentally significant issues was meaningful to them. I asked the following question: We discussed a couple of socially or environmentally controversial issues—the deer population and the antibiotics—how do you feel about discussing these types of issues—is it meaningful to you? One student responded, "I like to discuss them because it gives you more understanding of the world around you. 'Cause like I never knew there were so many antibiotic resistant bacteria. I learned a lot from that. And then with the deer it gave me different perspectives because I'm not the deer hunting type so it gave me a different perspective of where people are coming from. And it is something you could relate to in your life." A second student responded, "Oh yeah I take what I think of it and then with the deer you gave us the things that we had to be, the thing that you gave me was not what I was originally thinking so it made me think in their point of view which was a lot better than just staying focused on my point of view."

Results

As a result of this study many themes emerged. In the following chart I will triangulate the themes that emerged with the data that was collected. (29)

How Do I Need to Change My Teaching to Facilitate More Meaningful Discussions in My Biology Classroom?

With the goal of facilitating meaningful discussions in my classroom I have been more systematic when designing discussion groups and using more cooperative learning techniques. I have been more thoughtful when designing questions and have required students to be more responsible for their role within their discussion group. I have been focusing more on problems of concern to our society. The numbers of discussions that students participated in are greater this year than in the past. Students are doing more guided inquiry activities than in the past. With the greatest challenge, I have increased the number of higher order questions that I ask. (30)

Will Having More Meaningful Discussions Allow Students to Learn Content at a Higher Level?

From analyzing the audiotape transcriptions the length of student discussions has increased over time; however, this could be due to the type of discussion. Depending on the type of activity, students increased the number of higher-order responses made during discussions. Student-centered or student-directed activities seemed to elicit higher-order responses. From student responses to a questionnaire 77% of my students believe discussions help them learn biology content. I was unable to see any changes in my students' test scores by analyzing points they earned on higher-order questions. Throughout the course of this project lower-ability students have increased their participation. This could be the result of a variety of factors such as the heterogeneous grouping, maturity, the increase in discussions, and/or other factors. (31)

Will Having More Meaningful Discussions Help Students Make Connections between Biology Content and the World Around Them?

Yes. Having meaningful discussions does help students make connections between biology content and the world around them. One piece of data to support this result is from an audiotape transcription of a discussion on an article about using hydrogen produced from algae as a fuel source. The question was: Why would you want to fuel your car with pond scum? One student responded, "So we reduce carbon dioxide." Another student in the same group responded, "And we don't need to borrow it (oil) from foreign countries." The article does not discuss nor had we discussed in class where our fuel supply currently comes from. The deer dilemma clearly helped students connect biology to the world around them because many of my students hunt and there were a lot of varying strong opinions. But as students said on the questionnaires and in interviews, they found it valuable to role-play a perspective other than their own. It was rewarding to learn from parents that students were discussing these issues at home. (32)

Theme	Data source	Data source	Data source
Increase in discussion opportunities	Lesson plans	Teacher journal	Student questionnaire
Increase in cooperative learning techniques	Lesson plans	Teacher journal	Student interviews
Increase in higher-order questions being asked of students	Audiotapes of discussions	Unit tests	Teacher journal
Increase in authentic learning through discussions of socially and ecologically significant issues	Lesson plans	Audiotapes of discussions	Teacher journal
A more student-centered classroom	Audiotapes of discussions	Student interviews	Teacher journal

Will Having More Meaningful Discussions Increase Students' Ability to Make Informed Decisions Regarding Socially and/or Ecologically Significant Issues?

> Data analysis and interpretation resulted in the identification of the following themes: increasing the number of higher-order questions in group discussions increases student learning; improved in-class discussion results in improved student transfer and application of knowledge to the world around them, including the ability to make better informed decisions regarding socially and ecologically significant issues.

(33) From the second questionnaire 74% of my students felt that discussing socially and ecologically significant issues will help them make informed decisions. From the interviews I discovered that it is through these types of issues that students are really able to make the connections between biology and their life. These issues provide the hook that gets students interested in the problem of study. From interviews students agreed that it is a good idea to discuss these issues and they are glad that they are informed.

Conclusions

(34) To achieve meaningful learning, I have also considered the four commonplaces: teacher, learner, curriculum, and governance.

Teacher

(35) Through action research I have become a more reflective teacher. I have studied my teaching and used the data I collected to guide my actions while continuing to collect data for self-evaluation. Throughout my pilot study conducted last year, and my current project, action research has connected me to my students. It is their feedback combined with my journal that I have used to make changes in how I teach!

(36) Because of this project I am living closer to my values. One of the main motivations for this study was to help students make connections. I have gained a lot of satisfaction hearing students say that discussions have helped them connect biology to their world.

(37) My classroom is a more student-centered environment; I am more learner-sensitive and constructivism is taking place as I am facilitating more meaningful discussions. By monitoring students' discussions, I listen more, detecting misconceptions and giving students immediate feedback. I learn from my students.

(38) Action research has given me a systematic way to make changes in my classroom and determine if those changes are worthwhile. I will continue to facilitate meaningful discussions and use action research as a tool to evaluate the impact these discussions are having on my students and myself.

Learner

(39) Students are talking about science more in the biology classroom! These discussions give students the opportunity to share their knowledge and beliefs, which deepens their understanding through actively discussing and listening. In the course of these discussions students have acquired meaningful learning. Through cooperative learning techniques, students began helping each other in a productive way. Students can learn more in a group than individually. We are more together than alone.

Curriculum

(40) This project has not required much change in the biology curriculum. We studied the same problems while I used articles and/or activities to

compliment [*sic*] these problems. Any extra time these discussions take is worth it, because when students can discuss what they know it reinforces their learning and makes them active learners.

Governance

Currently, the state of Minnesota is in the process of developing a new set of standards, which at this time looks like biology will have to cover an even broader range of problems. As teachers are asked to cover more material in the same amount of time, it becomes more difficult to set up a learning environment that is conducive to meaningful learning. I am confident that student discussions will be integral to the meaningful learning of these new standards.

(41)

> Action plan for future teaching, specifically addressing the adoption of new state standards for biology, requires the implementation of the teaching strategies identified as being effective for improved student learning in this teacher's 10th-grade biology classroom.

Discussion

Action research has given me the opportunity to study my profession in a systematic way. The part of action research that has always been most appealing to me is the opportunity to live closer to my professional values. McNiff says, "Another difference of action research is that it has an explicit value basis. Your intention as an action researcher would be to bring about a situation that was congruent with your value position." I have long believed that students need to visualize that what they are studying fits into the broader scheme of life. Through constructivist methodologies students can connect what they know and what they have experienced to new pieces of information. Through this action research project I have been able to live closer to my values as I facilitated discussions and that helped students make the biology knowledge fit their prior experiences. Through these discussions students are able to learn content at a higher level because they are discussing the issues, formulating the information into their own words. I believe students need to think critically about the world around them, by studying and discussing social and ecological issues students are better able to relate these important issues to the biology content they are being exposed to.

(42)

The journey we make is not alone—the teacher and the student must both be active participants. Through this project I have learned a lot from my students and myself. This has been the most important lesson of action research; that I can effectively make changes in my teaching profession if I reflect on my own thoughts and the thoughts of my students.

(43)

BIBLIOGRAPHY

Council for Environmental Education. (2000). *Project Wild K12 Curriculum & Activity Guide.*

Elder, L., & R. Paul. (1998). The Role of Socratic Questioning in Thinking, Teaching, and Learning. *Clearing House, 71*(5), 297–301.

Henson, Kenneth, T. (1993). *Methods and Strategies for Teaching in Secondary and Middle Schools* (2nd ed.). New York, Longman.

Holubec, E. J. (1992). How Do You Get There From Here? Getting Started with Cooperative Learning. *Contemporary Education, 63*(3), 181–184.

Johnson, D. W., R. T. Johnson, E. J. Holubec, & Roy, P. (1985). Circles of Learning: Cooperation in the Classroom. *Association for Supervision and Curriculum Development.*

Lord, Thomas, R. (1994). Using Constructivism to Enhance Student Learning in College Biology. *Journal of College Science Teaching, 23*(6), 346–348.

Lotan, Rachel, A. (2003). Group Worthy Tasks. *Educational Leadership.* March. 72–75.

McNiff, Jean., P. Lomax, & Whitehead, J. 1996. *You and Your Action Research Project.* London, RoutledgeFalmer.

Novak, J. D., & Gowin, D. B. (1984). *Learning How to Learn.* Cambridge, Cambridge University Press.

SchoolNet Grass Roots Program. (2003). *GrassRoots Taxonomy of Thinking Skills.* Retrieved from schoolnet.ca/grassroots/e/project.centre/shared/Taxonomvy.asp

St. Edward's University Center for Teaching Excellence. (2001). *Bloom's Wheel.* Retrieved from easykayaker.com/school/reading/bloom.html

Trempy, J. E., Siebold, W. A., & Skinner, M. M. (2002). Learning Microbiology Through Cooperation: Designing Cooperative Learning Activities that Promote Interdependence, Interaction, and Accountability. *Microbiology Education, 3*(1), 26–36.

Woodruff, Brian. (1992). Woodrow Wilson Biology Institute.

Yager, Robert E. (2000). The Constructivist Learning Model. *The Science Teacher, 67*(1), 44–45.

Source: From "'Let's Talk': Discussion in a Biology Classroom: An Action Research Project" by P. Juenemann, 2004, *AR Expeditions,* arexpeditions.montana.edu. Reprinted with permission.

CHAPTER EIGHTEEN

Descriptive Statistics

Analyze That, 2002

"Looks bad, right?" (p. 479)

LEARNING OUTCOMES

After reading Chapter 18, you should be able to do the following:

18.1 Describe the process of preparing data for analysis.

18.2 Define, describe, and differentiate between types of descriptive statistics.

18.3 Describe the benefits of graphing data using statistical software packages.

THE WORD IS *STATISTICS*, NOT *SADISTICS*

Statistics is simply a set of procedures for describing, synthesizing, analyzing, and interpreting quantitative data. For example, statistical procedures can produce one number (i.e., the mean) that indicates the average SAT score of 1,000 students. As another example, suppose that we find that a group of third-grade girls has a higher average on a reading test than a group of third-grade boys from the same class. Should we be worried about the boys? Statistics can tell us if this difference between the boys and girls is something that was likely to have occurred by chance or if it is a meaningful finding, suggesting these boys may need extra help.

In this chapter, we explain how statistical procedures help describe the information gathered during a research study. These procedures, not surprisingly called descriptive statistics, provide basic information about the number of participants in a study, their characteristics, and how they did on a test or outcome. Because so many statistical approaches are available to a researcher, we address in this chapter those commonly used in educational research, and we focus on your ability to understand these descriptive statistical concepts and to apply and interpret these statistics, but not your ability to describe their theoretical rationale and mathematical derivation. It is important to understand the difference between the descriptive statistics we describe in this chapter and the inferential statistics we introduce in Chapter 19. The descriptive statistics presented in this chapter help you describe a sample or population. Think of these statistics as being statistics that leave little for the imagination. There is nothing to be inferred from these statistics. They simply offer you information needed to describe. In fact, you have worked with descriptive statistics since elementary school, you just did not call them by that name.

To help your understanding of descriptive statistics, we use the fictional Pinecrest Elementary School, which we introduced in Chapter 7, as our continuing example to show the value and relative ease of using these procedures. Pinecrest is a fictional school, but the information we have created about third-grade students in Ms. Alvarez's class represents a typical multicultural classroom on the West Coast of the United States. We use the students' scores on reading, math, and science (state tests) as required under the Every Student Succeeds Act (ESSA). As educational researchers who need to better understand student learning, we are interested in identifying possible differences among groups of students—for example, if the boys and the girls perform quite differently in one classroom at Pinecrest, we want to know so that we can further investigate and possibly eliminate or at least reduce the differences.

THE LANGUAGE OF STATISTICS

Few researchers compute statistical procedures by hand anymore; we have excellent computer programs available to make these calculations. Nevertheless, it is important to understand the basic calculations being performed by the computer. Because our goal here is to help you gain a conceptual understanding of statistical procedures, not to become statisticians, we will introduce some of the formulas and then provide examples of output from statistical programs. Although formulas for statistical procedures often appear overwhelming at first glance, they are just basic mathematical procedures. Understanding statistical procedures is like learning a new language—and in this case it is Greek: Statistical notation uses Greek letters as shorthand. For example, instead of stating that you need to add everyone's scores, the statistical notation uses the Greek symbol uppercase sigma (Σ) to mean "sum it up."

The examples in this chapter are generated from Excel and SPSS software, and for the brave at heart, we also cover the open-sourced statistical software R in a separate section. You may be familiar with Excel and probably have access to it through Microsoft Office. SPSS (Statistical Package for the Social Sciences) may be less familiar to you, but it is frequently used and available in desktop and network versions. R is a little different than Excel and SPSS in that it is open-source (read: free) but in order to operate R you need some very basic coding skills. This may frighten some of you from the start, but don't worry. We are going to send you off with a nice start to R programming and offer suggestions for future reading that will enhance your skillset. Although we do not give every step of every procedure, we refer you to additional materials in Appendix B for Excel, SPSS, and R.

PREPARING DATA FOR ANALYSIS

Scoring Procedures

After data are collected, the first step toward analysis involves converting behavioral responses into some numeric system (i.e., scoring quantitative data) or categorical organization (i.e., coding qualitative data). When a standardized instrument is used for data collection, scoring is greatly facilitated. The test manual usually spells out the steps to follow in scoring each test, and a scoring key is usually provided. It is important that data are scored accurately and consistently; each participant's test results should be scored in the same way and with one criterion. If the manual is followed conscientiously and each test is scored carefully, errors are minimized. It is usually a good idea to recheck all or at least some of the tests (say, 25%, or every fourth test) for consistency of scoring. Scoring self-developed instruments is more complex, especially if open-ended items are involved, because the researcher must develop and refine a reliable scoring procedure. If open-ended items are included, at least two people should independently score some or all of the tests as a reliability check. Steps for scoring each item and for arriving at a total score must be delineated and carefully followed, and the procedure should be described in detail in the final research report.

Tabulation and Coding Procedures

After instruments have been scored, the resulting data are tabulated and entered into a spreadsheet, usually on the computer. Tabulation involves organizing the data systematically, such as by individual subject. If planned analyses involve subgroup comparisons, scores should be tabulated for each subgroup. Table 18.1 shows the data for the Pinecrest students,

TABLE 18.1 • Excel spreadsheet of Pinecrest Elementary School data: Ms. Alvarez's third-grade class

ID	Gender	Ethnicity	Econ	ReadLevel	ReadF	ReadS	MathF	MathS
1	1	1	1	3	52.5	68.7	54.8	55.2
2	2	2	2	1	32.5	52.6	73.2	72.8
3	1	5	2	1	36.4	38.5	44.9	43
4	1	5	2	1	44.3	56.2	35.2	36.6
5	2	4	1	3	58.7	63.8	58.3	60.5
6	1	3	1	1	28.3	31.2	23.1	22
7	2	3	1	2	43.1	53.6	52.6	53.6
8	1	5	3	2	66.5	75.5	53.8	53.3
9	2	1	1	3	51.4	56.8	45.8	43.6
10	1	5	1	1	38.5	41.4	46.7	47.8
11	2	5	3	3	56	72.3	38.4	36
12	1	2	1	1	24.5	28.4	32.5	32.6
13	2	1	1	1	37.4	42.3	25.3	25.8
14	1	3	1	1	28.3	34.8	18.3	19.5
15	2	5	3	3	78.4	72.4	58.3	60.3
16	2	3	2	3	52.3	53.6	38.6	40.3
17	1	5	3	2	56.8	64.2	67.4	68.4
18	2	1	3	3	73.2	68.4	72.4	70
19	1	5	2	1	47.4	65.8	53.5	52
20	2	2	1	2	47.4	34.6	48.5	50.2
21	1	5	3	2	53.2	58.5	36.5	38.5
22	1	3	1	1	18.4	22	27.2	28
23	2	5	2	3	53.5	58.4	62.4	64
24	2	4	1	3	46.5	52.4	38.6	38
25	1	1	2	1	38.6	41.7	28.9	27

organized in an Excel spreadsheet. Each student's record is listed horizontally by student number, and then codes representing the values for each variable are placed in the vertical columns. For example, reading across the table for student 1, we find gender $= 1$ (male), ethnicity $= 1$ (African American), economic level $= 1$ (low), and so forth. The score or code for each categorical variable should be included in a code book (see Table 18.2), which serves as the key for the numerical values assigned to each variable. The ratio variables, such as ReadF (reading score for fall), are defined by their range or maximum score (e.g., student scores can range from 0 to 100 for all the tests at Pinecrest).

Following tabulation, the next step in our analysis is to describe what is happening with our students, in other words, to summarize the data using descriptive statistics. Choice of appropriate statistical techniques is determined to a great extent by your research design, hypothesis, and the kind of data you collect. Thus, different research approaches lead to different statistical analyses. Note, however, that the complexity of the analysis is not an indication of its "goodness" or appropriateness. Regardless of how well the study is conducted, inappropriate analyses can lead to inappropriate research conclusions. Data analysis is as important as any other component of research, and the statistical procedures and techniques of the study should be identified and described in detail in the research plan.

TABLE 18.2 • Pinecrest Elementary code book		
Variable	Name	Coding Values
Student ID	ID	1–25
Gender	Gender	1 = male, 2 = female
Ethnicity	Ethnicity	1 = African American
		2 = Asian, Pacific Islander
		3 = Hispanic, 4 = Native American
		5 = White
Economic level	Econ	1 = low (free/reduced lunch)
		2 = medium/working class
		3 = middle/upper class
Reading level	ReadLevel	1 = low, 2 = middle, 3 = high
Fall reading score	ReadF	0–100 scale
Spring reading score	ReadS	0–100 scale
Fall math score	MathF	0–100 scale
Spring math score	MathS	0–100 scale

MyLab Education **Self-Check 18.1**

MyLab Education **Application Exercise 18.1:** Preparing Quantitative Data for Analysis

TYPES OF DESCRIPTIVE STATISTICS

In some studies, particularly survey studies, the entire data analysis procedure may consist solely of calculating and interpreting descriptive statistics, which enable a researcher to describe many pieces of data meaningfully with a small number of indices. If such indices are calculated for a sample drawn from a population, the resulting values are referred to as statistics; if they are calculated for an entire population, they are referred to as parameters. In other words, a statistic is a numerical index that describes the characteristics of a sample or samples, and a parameter is a numerical index that describes the characteristics of a population. Many statistics used in educational research are based on data collected from well-defined samples, so most analyses deal with statistics, not parameters.

The major types of descriptive statistics discussed in the following sections are frequencies, measures of central tendency, measures of variability, measures of relative position, and measures of relationship.

Frequencies

Frequency refers to the number of times something occurs; with descriptive statistics, frequency usually refers to the number of times each value of a variable occurs. For example, we want to know the number of boys and girls in Ms. Alvarez's classroom at Pinecrest Elementary School, so we compute a frequency count (i.e., a total number) for each. Beginning our analysis with a frequency count helps to verify the data, to be sure everything has been entered into the computer correctly. For example, consider a study of school principals. The first analysis (a frequency count showing the number of principals in each age group relevant to the study) showed one of the principals was 4 years old. Assuming there is not a high probability of a precocious 4-year-old principal, the researchers rechecked the data and found the principal was really 40. The researchers would not have discovered this simple data entry error had they not conducted a frequency count of this variable (age).

Several options are available for conducting an initial frequency count of our data. Both Excel and SPSS have a variety of functions that allow you to count and display the number of individuals or occurrences for each variable. For example, for a nominal variable, such as gender, we can simply count to compute the frequency of boys (14) and girls (11) from the Pinecrest data in Table 18.1. For nominal or ordinal variables, a frequency count for each value is very descriptive.

Table 18.3 shows, for Ms. Alvarez's third-grade classroom at Pinecrest Elementary School, the number of students of each gender and of each ethnicity, presented in an Excel PivotTable. As a comparison, Table 18.4 shows the SPSS version, which is computed with the CrossTabs procedure, for the same information. The main thing to note in both tables is that they provide the distribution of the values for each variable we have selected to consider. Both tables, of course, show the same frequency counts. For example, the first cell in the table shows there are two boys (gender 1) who are African American (ethnicity 1). Reading down the column, the next cell under ethnicity 1 shows that three girls are African American—Ms. Alvarez's class thus has five students who are African

American, shown in the Grand Total/Total columns. Specific instructions for how to produce each of these analyses is included in Appendix B, Figures B.18.1 for Excel, and B.18.2 for SPSS.

Frequency is slightly more complicated when we consider interval or ratio variables (such as a test score) and when we have a much larger dataset than 25 students. Because every score or value of a ratio variable may occur only once, a simple frequency count is typically not very helpful. For example, Table 18.1 includes only one instance of 18.4 for the fall reading score, one for 24.5, one for 27.4, two for 28.3, and so on. Counting the frequency of each value of a ratio variable does not usually summarize the outcomes for us very effectively. Therefore, a calculation of the overall average, or mean, for ratio or interval data provides a much better descriptive indicator than a frequency count. Means are one measure of central tendency and are described in the next section.

Measures of Central Tendency

Measures of central tendency are indices that represent a typical score among a group of scores. They provide a convenient way of describing a set of data with a single number that represents a value generally in the middle of (i.e., central to) the dataset. The three most frequently used measures of central tendency are the mean, the median, and the mode. Each index is used with a different

TABLE 18.4 • SPSS cross-tabulation of gender by ethnicity

Gender * Ethnicity Cross-Tabulation

Count

| | | Ethnicity | | | | | |
		1	2	3	4	5	Total
Gender	1	2	1	3	0	7	13
	2	3	2	2	2	3	12
Total		5	3	5	2	10	25

TABLE 18.3 • Excel PivotTable: Gender by ethnicity

Count of ID	Ethnicity					
Gender	1	2	3	4	5	Grand Total
1	2	1	3		7	13
2	3	2	2	2	3	12
Total	5	3	5	2	10	25

scale of measurement: The mean is appropriate for describing interval or ratio data, the median for describing ordinal data, and the mode for describing nominal data.

The Mean

Because most quantitative measurement in educational research uses an interval scale, the **mean** is the most commonly used measure of central tendency. The mean is the arithmetic average of the scores. It is calculated by adding up all the scores and dividing that total by the number of scores.

The formula for the population mean, is

$$\mu = \frac{\sum_{i=1}^{N} x_i}{N}$$

Looks bad, right? However, it is really quite simple, and this formula provides a good illustration of the use of statistical symbols. The formula for the population mean (represented by the lowercase Greek letter mu, (μ) represents an individual's score (x), and Σ (as discussed previously) is the summation symbol. Thus, Σx_i asks you to add all the Xs, that is, all the scores. The number of data points (i.e., individuals or students in this example) is represented by the letter N. To calculate the mean, we sum the Xs and divide by the number of students.

The notation is slightly different when considering the mean of a sample as opposed to a population, but the idea is the same. You will see the formula for a sample mean depicted as

$$\bar{x} = \frac{\sum_{i=1}^{N} x_i}{N}$$

The math, however, is the same. You're still summing all the scores in your sample and dividing by the number of cases.

Table 18.5 shows the mean scores on the fall reading assessment for the boys and the girls in Ms. Alvarez's class. This table also shows the standard deviations, which are discussed later in this chapter. Calculation was computed with Excel by selecting Data and then PivotTable. The table is sorted by gender (boys = 1; girls = 2) and fall reading scores (ReadF).

The Median

The **median** is the midpoint in a distribution: 50% of the scores are above the median, and 50% are

TABLE 18.5 • Summary of means: Gender by fall reading scores

	Mean	Standard Deviation
Boys	41.05	14.058
Girls	52.53	13.248
Total for the class	46.56	14.612

below the median. If the total number of scores is odd, the median is the middle score (assuming the scores are arranged in order of value). If the number of scores is even, the median is the point halfway between the two middle scores. Therefore, the median is not necessarily one of the actual scores in the dataset.

The median is most useful when looking at variables that may vary widely over the distribution, such as income. For example, if we were to calculate the average or mean income of parents of children attending Pinecrest, it would likely be similar to other schools in the district. However, one parent at Pinecrest is a rock star who makes millions of dollars, significantly more than anyone else in the community. The rock star's income brings the mean income up, resulting in an index that is not a good representation of the complete dataset. In this example, we can use the median as an index of the central tendency. The outrageously high income of the rock star is just one income above the median; it doesn't matter how much higher it is than other families' incomes. The median is also the appropriate measure of central tendency when the data represent an ordinal scale.

The Mode

The **mode** is the score that is attained by more subjects than any other score. For the data presented in Table 18.6, for example, the mode is 85; more Pinecrest students (12) achieved that score than any other. The mode is not established through calculation; it is determined by looking at a set of scores or at a graph of scores and seeing which score occurs most frequently. The mode is generally of limited value and not often used in educational research. For one thing, a set of scores may have two (or more) modes, in which case the set is described as *bimodal* or *multimodal*. In addition, the mode is an unstable measure of central

TABLE 18.6 • Frequency distribution based on 85 hypothetical achievement test scores	
Score	Frequency of Score
78	1
79	4
80	5
81	7
82	7
83	9
84	9
85	12
86	10
87	7
88	6
89	3
90	4
91	1
	Total: 85 students

tendency; samples of equal size randomly selected from the same accessible population are likely to have different modes. When nominal data are being analyzed, however, the mode is the only appropriate measure of central tendency because it tells us what happened most often.

Deciding among Mean, Median, and Mode

In general, the mean is the preferred measure of central tendency. It is appropriate when the data represent either an interval or a ratio scale. It is more precise than the median or the mode because if equal-size samples are randomly selected from the same population, the means of those samples will be more similar to each other than either the medians or the modes. By the very nature of the way in which it is computed, however, the mean takes into account (i.e., is based on) each participant's score. Because all scores count, the mean can be affected by extreme scores such as the rock star's income. Similarly, in educational research, when a group of test scores contains one or more extreme scores, the median is the best index of typical performance.

As an example, suppose nine of our Pinecrest students had the following IQ scores: 96, 96, 97, 99, 100, 101, 102, 104, 195. For these scores, the three measures of central tendency are

mode   = 96 (most frequent score)
median = 100 (middle score)
mean   = 110.6 (arithmetic average)

In this case, the median clearly best represents the typical score. The mode is too low, and the mean is higher than all of the scores except one. The mean is "pulled up" in the direction of the 195 score, whereas the median essentially ignores it.

The different pictures presented by the different measures are part of the reason for the phrase *lying with statistics*. Although the calculation of a statistical procedure may be indisputable, its selection and its application are open to wide interpretations. Selecting one index of central tendency over another one may present a particular point of view in a stronger light. In a teacher-versus-administration union dispute over salary, for example, very different estimates of typical teacher salaries will be obtained depending on which index of central tendency is used. If the typical teacher salaries are $28,000, $30,000, $30,000, $33,000, $34,000, $37,000, and $78,000, the measures of central tendency are

mode   = $30,000 (most frequent score)
median = $33,000 (middle salary)
mean   = $38,571 (arithmetic average)

Both the teachers' union and administration could overstate their cases, the union by using the mode and administration by using the mean. The mode is lower than all salaries except one, and the mean is higher than every salary except one (which in all likelihood is the salary of a teacher with 30 or more years of experience). Thus, in this situation, the most appropriate index of typical salary would be the median. Remember that, in research, we are not interested in "making cases" but rather in describing the data in the most accurate way; for the majority of datasets, the mean is the appropriate measure of central tendency.

Measures of Variability

Although measures of central tendency are very useful statistics for describing a set of data, they are not sufficient. Two sets of student scores that are widely divergent could have identical means or medians. For example, if all students score 50%, the group mean and median will be 50—but if, in a second group, one student scores 100 and one scores 0, the group mean and median are also 50, and clearly the groups are not the same. To understand a situation such as this, we need measures of variability, indices of how spread out a group of scores is. The three most frequently used measures are the range, the quartile deviation, and the standard deviation. Although the standard deviation is by far the most often used, the range is the only appropriate measure of variability for nominal data, and the quartile deviation is the appropriate index of variability for ordinal data.

The Range

The **range** is simply the difference between the highest and lowest score in a distribution; it is computed by subtraction. As an example, the range of fall reading test scores (ReadF) for the Pinecrest students is 55.1 points, or from 18.4 to 73.5 points (refer to Table 18.1). Like the mode, the range is not a very stable measure, and its chief advantage is that it gives a quick, rough estimate of variability of a particular sample.

The Quartile Deviation

The **quartile deviation** is one half of the difference between the upper quartile and the lower quartile in a distribution. The upper quartile refers to the top 25% of scores, also known as the 75th percentile. Correspondingly, the lower quartile is the 25th percentile, or the lowest 25% of scores. At Pinecrest, for example, fall reading scores (ReadF in Table 18.1) above 56.8 are in the upper quartile; scores below 36.4 are in the lower quartile. By subtracting the cutoff point for the lower quartile from the cutoff point for the upper quartile and then dividing the result by 2, we get a measure of variability.

If the quartile deviation is small, the scores are close together; if it is large, the scores are more spread out. This information can tell us, for example, how the Pinecrest students are doing on the reading scores. Comparing the boys and the girls, we see the boys, as a group, are not as consistent as the girls. Likewise, we would find that the quartile deviation for the girls is smaller than for the boys. The quartile deviation is a more stable measure of variability than the range and is appropriate whenever the median is the most suitable procedure. Calculation of the

quartile deviation involves a process very similar to that used to calculate the median, which is the cutoff point for the second quartile (50%).

Variance

Variance is defined as the amount of spread among scores. If the variance is small, the scores are close together; if it is large, the scores are more spread out. Calculation of the variance is quite simple because it is a summary statistic showing, on average, how far each score is from the mean in a squared metric. For example, suppose five Pinecrest students received reading scores of 35, 25, 30, 40, and 30. The mean of these scores is 32 ($\Sigma X/n = 160/5$). The difference of each student's score from the mean is as follows:

$$35 - 32 = 3$$
$$25 - 32 = -7$$
$$30 - 32 = -2$$
$$40 - 32 = 8$$
$$30 - 32 = -2$$

There is a slight problem computing variance using these difference scores, however, because if we sum them, we get zero. Finding 0 is not especially helpful, so the most common solution is to square the differences. Squaring and then summing each difference gives:

$$35 - 32 = 3 \qquad 3^2 = 9$$
$$25 - 32 = -7 \qquad -7^2 = 49$$
$$30 - 32 = -2 \qquad -2^2 = 4$$
$$40 - 32 = 8 \qquad 8^2 = 64$$
$$30 - 32 = -2 \qquad -2^2 = 4$$

We then sum the squares of the differences and divide by the number of scores to compute the variance:

$$9 + 49 + 4 + 64 + 4 = 130$$
$$= 130/5 = 26$$

The computational formula for variance, then, is

$$\Sigma(X - \overline{X})^2/n$$

Although seldom used by itself, the variance is the calculation that gets us to the most commonly used measure of variability, the standard deviation.

Standard Deviation

Standard deviation is the square root of the variance of a set of scores. The square root of the variance in the previous example (32.5) is 5.7, which is the standard deviation of the five scores. The standard deviation, used with interval and ratio data, is by far the most frequently used index of variability. Similar to the mean, its central tendency counterpart, the standard deviation is the most stable measure of variability and includes every score in its calculation.

As an example, review the data in Table 18.5. The table shows that the mean fall reading scores (ReadF) for the girls at Pinecrest is higher overall than the score for the boys (52.53 versus 41.05), and the boys' standard deviation (14.058) is higher than the girls' (13.248). The standard deviations indicate that the girls' scores are closer together (i.e., clustered around the mean) compared to the boys' scores—there is much more variability among the boys than among the girls.

The distinct benefit of calculating the standard deviation is that it provides a standardized value to use to compare one set of scores to another. If you know the mean and standard deviation of a set of scores, you have a pretty good idea of what all the scores look like. Using both, you can describe a set of data quite well.

The Normal Curve

You have no doubt heard of "grading on the curve." But what is "the curve"? The concept comes from a normal distribution, where there are an equal but small number of As and Fs, more Bs and Ds, and then lots of Cs in the middle. Graphing the frequency of each grade results in a bell-shaped curve, with fewer grades at the extremes and most in the middle (see Figure 18.1). As another example, you probably know very few, if any, adults who are over 7 feet tall. Likewise, you probably know very few adults who are under 4 feet tall. Most people are between 5 feet and 6 feet tall, in the middle of the bell-shaped curve. A distribution with fewer people (or scores) at the extremes and more people in the middle is considered "normal." Many variables are distributed normally, including height, weight, IQ scores, and SAT and other achievement scores.

Knowing that a variable is normally distributed turns out to be quite valuable in research. If a variable is *normally distributed*, that is, forms a normal, or bell-shaped, curve, then several things are true:

1. Fifty percent of the scores are above the mean, and 50% are below the mean.

2. The mean, the median, and the mode have the same value.

3. Most scores are near the mean. The farther a score is from the mean, the fewer the number of participants who attained that score.

4. For every normal distribution, 34.13% of the scores fall between the mean and one standard deviation above the mean, and 34.13% of the scores fall one standard deviation below the mean (see Figure 18.1; find the midpoint on the curve and look at the portions under the curve marked 34.13%). In other words, 68.26% of the scores are within one standard deviation of the mean (34.13% + 34.13%). More than 99% of the scores will fall somewhere between three standard deviations above and three standard deviations below the mean.

Knowing where scores are on the normal curve helps us understand where they are placed relative to the full dataset. For example, look at the last line of Figure 18.1, marked "Deviation IQs." The average IQ score is 100; it falls in the center of the chart and directly below the peak of the normal curve above it. The normal curve shows that 50% of the population has an IQ score equal to or above 100, and 50% has a score equal to or below 100. In addition, IQ scores have a standard deviation of 15, so 34.13% of all IQ scores are between 85 and 100, and 34.13% are between 100 and 115. Overall, then, 68.26% (34.13% + 34.13%) of IQ scores are within (plus or minus) one standard deviation of the mean, or between 115 and 85.

Let us suppose we have a student at Pinecrest Elementary, Justin, who has an IQ score of 115. With your knowledge of the normal curve, you can now determine that Justin's score of 115 is quite good. An IQ score of 115 is one standard deviation above the mean of 100, and 50% of the scores are below the mean. We can thus calculate how many IQ scores are below Justin's score of 115—50% (below 100) added to 34.13% (between 100 and 115), for a total of 84.13%. In other words, Justin's score is better than 84.13% of the other IQ scores. We can also compute the percentage of students who scored higher than Justin by subtracting 84.13% from 100%: Only 15.87% of IQ scores are above Justin's score of 115. From these computations, it's clear that Justin's IQ score of 115 is relatively high; therefore, we may expect good educational outcomes from him in school.

Now suppose we have another student at Pinecrest, Dolores, who has an IQ score of 130, two

FIGURE 18.1 • Characteristics of the normal curve

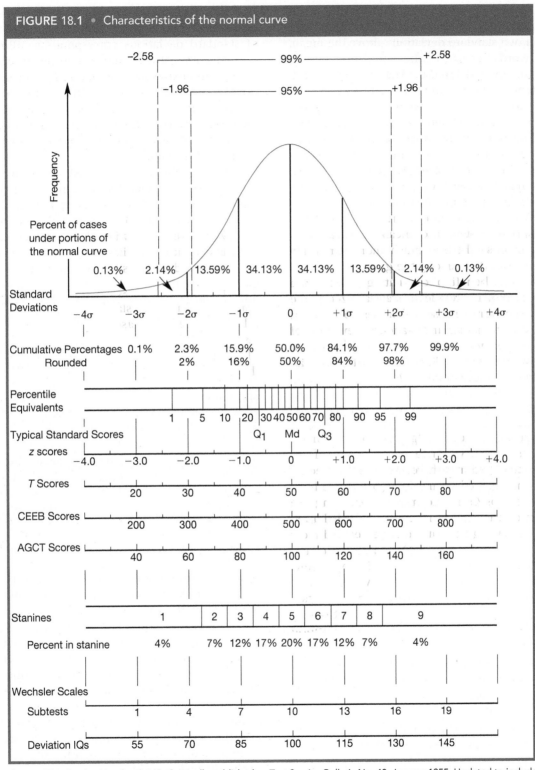

Source: *Test Service Notebook* 148. Originally published as *Test Service Bulletin* No. 48. January 1955. Updated to include Normal Curve Equivalents, September 1980 by NCS Pearson, Inc. Reproduced with permission. All rights reserved.

standard deviations (i.e., 15 + 15) above the mean of 100. Figure 18.1 shows that 47.72% of the scores are within two standard deviations above the mean. In other words, 47.72% of the population has an IQ between 100 and 130 (i.e., 34.13% between 100 and 115, and 13.59% between 115 and 130). Knowing that 50% of the population has an IQ score below 100, we can compute the percentage of people with IQ scores lower than Dolores's—50% + 47.72% = 97.72%. Looking in the other direction, we see that only 2.27% of the IQ scores are above Dolores's score of 130 (i.e., 2.14% + .13%). Obviously, we don't find many students (only 2.27%) who score as well as Dolores does on the IQ test.

With a basic understanding of the normal curve, you can understand more easily the meaning of other standardized scores, such as those for the SAT or ACT. As another example, assume Dolores has a really smart brother, Ivan, who scores 800 on the SAT math section. Figure 18.1 shows SAT scores in the line marked "CEEB Scores" (for College Entrance Examination Board)—looking up to the normal curve shows that Ivan's 800 is three standard deviations above the mean of 500, and his score places him at the 99.9% end (known as the "tail") of the curve. Only 0.1% of students scored higher than Ivan.

To summarize, if scores are normally distributed, the following statements are true:

$\overline{X} \pm 1.0\ SD$ = approximately 68% of the scores
$\overline{X} \pm 2.0\ SD$ = approximately 95% of the scores
  (1.96 SD is exactly 95%)
$\overline{X} \pm 2.5\ SD$ = approximately 99% of the scores
  (2.58 SD is exactly 99)%
$\overline{X} \pm 3.0\ SD$ = approximately 99 + % of the scores

The following are also always true:

$\overline{X} - 3.0\ SD$ = approximately the 0.1 percentile
$\overline{X} - 2.0\ SD$ = approximately the 2nd percentile
$\overline{X} - 1.0\ SD$ = approximately the 16th percentile
$\overline{X}$ = the 50th percentile
$\overline{X} + 1.0\ SD$ = approximately the 84th percentile
$\overline{X} + 2.0\ SD$ = approximately the 98th percentile
$\overline{X} + 3.0\ SD$ = approximately the 99th + percentile

Note that, in Figure 18.1, the ends of the curve never touch the baseline, and no definite number of standard deviations corresponds to 100%. The normal curve always allows for the existence of unexpected extremes at either end, and each additional standard deviation includes a tiny fraction of a percent of the scores. We need to leave room for the extremely rare person who is 8 feet tall or who has an IQ score of 160 (i.e., four standard deviations above the mean).

Most variables measured in educational research form normal distributions if enough subjects are tested. Note, however, that a variable that is normally distributed in a population may not be normally distributed in smaller samples from the population. For example, we may happen to have particularly smart students in a class one year. In this case, although intelligence may not be normally distributed in this class, intelligence will be more normally distributed if we look at the whole school district (i.e., the population). Because research studies deal with a finite number of participants, and often not a very large number, research data (from a sample) can only approximate a normal curve. To mark this difference, researchers use SD to represent the standard deviation of a sample and the symbol σ (i.e., the Greek lowercase sigma) to represent the standard deviation of the population (because the scores shown are those of populations). In the language of statistics, σ represents a *population parameter*, whereas SD represents a *sample-based statistic*.

Skewed Distributions

When a distribution is not symmetrical, it is said to be skewed. A normal distribution is symmetrical; the graph is the bell-shaped curve with the mean, the median, and the mode all the same. Remember that a normal distribution has approximately the same number of extreme scores (i.e., very high and very low) at each end of the distribution (e.g., the same number of A's and F's when grading on the curve). A skewed distribution, however, is not symmetrical; the values of the mean, the median, and the mode are different, and there are more extreme scores at one end than the other. A negatively skewed distribution has extreme scores at the lower end of the distribution, and a positively skewed distribution has extreme scores at the higher end.

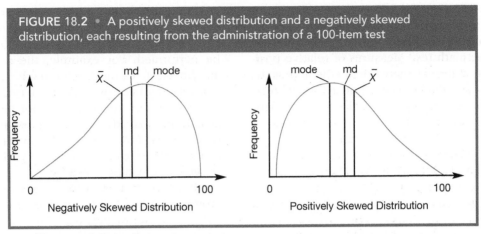

FIGURE 18.2 • A positively skewed distribution and a negatively skewed distribution, each resulting from the administration of a 100-item test

Note: $\bar{X}$ = mean; md = median.

Figure 18.2 provides two examples of skewed distributions from a 100-item test. The negatively skewed distribution on the left shows a case in which most participants did well but a few did very poorly—lower scores are on the left of the distribution and higher scores are on the right above the mean. Conversely, the second distribution in Figure 18.2 is positively skewed: Most of the participants did poorly, but a few did very well. In both cases the mean is "pulled" in the direction of the extreme scores.

In a skewed distribution, the mean is always closer to the extreme scores than the median because the mean is affected by extreme scores but the median is not. The extreme scores act like a magnet and pull the mean toward them. Thus, for a negatively skewed distribution, the mean ($\bar{X}$) is always lower, or smaller, than the median (md); for a positively skewed distribution, the mean is always higher, or greater, than the median. The mode is not affected by extreme scores. For example, consider the age at which women have babies. Most women give birth when they are relatively young (i.e., under age 30); the distribution of maternal age at childbirth is positively skewed (i.e., fewer give birth over age 40), and the mean age is greater than the median or mode for all women.

To summarize:

Negatively skewed: mean < median < mode

Positively skewed: mean > median > mode

Moreover, the farther apart the mean and the median are, the more skewed the distribution.

The shape of non-normal, skewed distributions can also be described by a measure of kurtosis; that is, whether the scores pile up at the middle or spread out to the sides of the distribution. Put another way, skewness refers to the lack of symmetry of a distribution, kurtosis refers to how peaked or flat the center is and how wide the tails of the distribution are. A high kurtosis distribution has a sharper peak and longer, flatter tails, whereas a low kurtosis distribution has a rounded or flatter peak and shorter tails.

Knowing if a distribution is skewed is important because this knowledge helps us choose other statistics to analyze our data. If the distribution is very skewed, then the assumption of normality required for many statistics is violated. For skewed distributions, researchers often use analyses designed for nominal or ordinal data, rather than ratio or interval data.

Measures of Relative Position

Measures of relative position indicate where a score falls in the distribution, relative to all other scores in the distribution; in other words, measures of relative position show how well an individual has performed compared to all other individuals in the sample who have been measured on the same variable. Earlier, this topic was addressed as *norm-referenced scoring*.

A major advantage of measures of relative position is that they make it possible to compare the performance of an individual on two or more different tests. For example, if Justin's fall reading score at Pinecrest is 40 and his fall math score is 35, it does not automatically follow that he did better in reading: A score of 40 may have been the lowest score on the reading test and 35 the highest score on the math test! Measures of relative position express different scores on a common scale. The two most frequently used measures of relative position are percentile ranks and standard scores.

Percentile Ranks

A percentile rank indicates the percentage of scores that fall at or below a given score. Knowing only that Justin scored 40 on the fall reading test does not tell us how good his score is compared to the other students. If we find that Justin's score of 40 corresponds to a percentile rank of 55, however, we know that 45% of the students scored higher than Justin. Because we know Justin's IQ score places him at a percentile rank of 84 (84%), we might be somewhat worried that his reading score is only at the 55th percentile. He is not performing as well in reading as we might expect, given the much higher percentile rank for his IQ score. We certainly would want to know if Justin is underachieving, if he is having problems with reading, or if something else is going on to account for his relatively low score.

Percentiles are appropriate for data measured on an ordinal scale, although they are frequently computed for interval data. The median of a set of scores corresponds to the 50th percentile; the median is the middle point and therefore the point below which 50% of the scores fall. Percentile ranks are not used as often in research studies, but as our example for Pinecrest shows, they are frequently used in the public schools to report students' test results in a form that is understandable to most audiences.

Standard Scores

A standard score is a calculation that expresses how far an individual student's test score is from the mean, in standard deviation units. In other words, the standard score reflects how many standard deviations a student's score is above or below the mean. A standard score is appropriate when the test data are from an interval or ratio scale. The most commonly reported and used standard scores are z scores and T scores, both of which are shown in Figure 18.1.

Standard scores allow scores from different tests to be compared on a common scale and thus permit valid mathematical operations to be performed. For example, the reading scores at Pinecrest cannot be directly compared to math scores because they are based on different scales—a 40 on reading does not mean the same as a 40 in math. By converting test scores to standard scores, however, we can average them and arrive at an indicator of average performance that is comparable across tests.

If a set of raw scores, such as student test scores, is normally distributed, then so are the standard score equivalents; similarly, the normal curve equivalencies indicated in Figure 18.1 for the various standard scores are accurate only if the distribution is normal. Raw scores can be transformed mathematically to ensure that the distribution of standard scores will be normal. Further, standard scores can be compared only if all the derived scores are based on the raw scores of the same group. For example, although both appear to have a z score of +2.0 (as discussed in the next section), a College Entrance Examination Board (CEEB) score of 700 is not equivalent to a Wechsler IQ of 130 because the tests were normed on different groups.

z Scores. A z **score** is the most basic and most used standard score. The z score expresses directly how far a score is from the mean in terms of standard deviation units. A score that is equivalent to the mean corresponds to a z score of 0. A score that is exactly one standard deviation above the mean corresponds to a z score of +1.00, and a z score of −1.00 is one standard deviation below the mean. Two standard deviations above the mean is a z score of +2.00, and so forth. To make the specific calculation of a z score, we use the following formula to convert a raw score to a z score:

$$z = \frac{X - \overline{X}}{SD}, \text{ where X is the raw score}$$

As Figure 18.1 indicates, if a set of scores is transformed into a set of z scores, the new distribution has a mean of 0 and a standard deviation of 1. Always.

The major advantage of z scores is that they allow scores from different tests or subtests to be compared across individuals. For example, consider the summary of Justin's test scores in Table 18.7 (also called raw scores) converted to z scores and percentile equivalents.

TABLE 18.7 • Justin's scores					
	Raw Score	$\overline{X}$	SD	z	Percentile
Reading	50	60	10	−1.00	16th
Math	40	30	10	+1.00	84th

We can use Figure 18.1 to estimate percentile equivalents for given z scores, but only if the scores are whole numbers or fall neatly on the scale. Estimating z scores that fall *between* the values given in the figure becomes more difficult. A more precise approach, therefore, is to use a table of standard normal curve areas (readily available on the Internet—search for "standard normal curve areas"). Typically, these tables have a column showing z scores and a column showing area under the normal curve, as shown below:

z	Area
−3.00	.0013
−2.99	.0014
−2.98	.0014
−2.97	.0015
...	
−1.01	.1562
−1.00	.1587
−0.99	.1611
...	
−0.01	.4960
−0.02	.4920
0.00	.5000
0.01	.5040
0.02	.5058
...	
0.99	.8389
1.00	.8413
1.01	.8438
...	
2.97	.9985
2.98	.9986
2.99	.9986
3.00	.9987

For any value of z, the area created to the left of that value on the x axis of the normal curve represents the proportion of cases that falls below that z score:

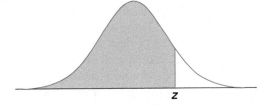

To determine the area under the curve or percentile for Justin's z score of +1.0, we simply read down the z columns until we come to +1.00 (i.e., his z score for reading); the corresponding area under the curve is 0.8413. By multiplying by 100, we see that Justin's reading score corresponds to approximately the 84th percentile (which is what we found earlier when we estimated the percentile from Figure 18.1). Similarly, for Dolores's reading score of $z = +2.00$, a complete table will show that the area under the curve is 0.9772 or 97.72%—exactly what we found before. The benefit of a standard normal curve areas table is that it allows us to make estimations from more precise z scores.

As Figure 18.1 indicates, z scores are the building blocks for a number of other standard scores. These standard scores represent transformations of z scores that communicate the same information in a more generally understandable form by eliminating negatives, decimals, or both.

T Scores. A *T* score (also called a *Z* score—notice the difference between the small z score and capital *Z* score) is nothing more than a z score expressed or transformed into an equivalent score. The **T score** is used to provide an easier-to-understand score that is standardized without pluses or minuses and is derived by multiplying the z score by 10 and adding 50. In other words, $T = 10z + 50$. Thus, a z score of +1.00 becomes a *T* score of 60 [$T = 10(1.00) + 50 = 60$], and a z score of −1.00 becomes a *T* score of 40 [$T = 10(−1.00) + 50 = 40$]. When scores are transformed to *T* scores, the new distribution has a mean of 50 and a standard deviation of 10, as shown in Figure 18.1, just below the line indicating the equivalent z score values.

A good example of converting z scores into an easier-to-understand distribution is how the SAT and other scores are calculated for the CEEB distribution, as shown in Figure 18.1. The CEEB distribution is formed by multiplying the z score by 100 (to eliminate decimals) and adding 500 (CEEB = $100z + 500$). This calculation, derived from the z score, yields a mean of 500 with a standard deviation of 100. It is much easier, for example, to say that Dolores's brother, Ivan, scored an 800 on the math section of his SATs than to say he is +3.00 standard deviations. Likewise, if Ivan's best friend, Gregg scored −1.00 standard deviations on his SAT, it is more helpful to tell Gregg he received a score of 400 on the math section of his SAT, which is below the mean of 500. Similarly, we can understand more easily now the basis for the calculations of the other standardized scales illustrated in Figure 18.1. For example, the Army General Classification Test (AGCT) distribution is formed by multiplying z scores by 20: AGCT = $20z + 100$. You can see the similarities in all these standardized scores that originate with the humble z score.

If the raw score distribution is normal, then so are the z score distribution and the T score distribution. On the other hand, if the original distribution is not normal (such as when a small sample is involved), the z and T distributions are not normal either. In either case, we can use the normal curve equivalencies to convert such scores into corresponding percentiles, or vice versa, as Figure 18.1 indicates. For example, a z score of +1.00 yields a CEEB distribution (or SAT) score of 600, an AGCT score of 120, a Wechsler score of 13, and an IQ score of 115—all at the 84th percentile. *A word of caution:* We cannot equate these scores or percentile levels across tests because the scores were obtained from different groups. Being in the 84th percentile on the SAT does not correspond to being in the 84th percentile on an IQ test.

Measures of Relationship

Measures of relationship indicate the degree to which two sets of scores are related. Correlational research, discussed in detail in Chapter 9, focuses on measures of relationship—it involves collecting data to determine whether and to what degree a relation exists between two or more quantifiable variables. This degree of relation is expressed as a correlation coefficient and is computed using two sets of scores from a single group of participants. If two variables are highly related, a correlation coefficient near +1.00 or −1.00 will be obtained; if two variables are not related, a coefficient near 0.00 will be obtained.

As stressed earlier, when interpreting measures of relationship, researchers must be careful not to make inappropriate causal assumptions. Unfortunately, this error occurs frequently, not only in research but also in the popular press. For example, National Public Radio once reported that a well-meaning organization found, after running a correlational study, that the number of trees in a neighborhood was inversely correlated with the number of crimes in that neighborhood. That is, neighborhoods with more trees had lower crime rates. The organization concluded, therefore, that planting trees will lower the crime rate. Although number of trees is a malleable variable (we can always plant more trees), it is not likely to be the solution to crime rates; the assumption that planting trees reduces the crime rate is seriously flawed. Lack of trees in crime-ridden neighborhoods is not really the problem, it is a symptom—neighborhoods with more trees are usually in nicer sections of town. It is equally easy to assume—erroneously—causal relations in educational research, and thus researchers must carefully guard against it.

A number of different statistical methods can be used to test for relationships; which one is appropriate depends on the scale of measurement represented by the data. The two most frequently used correlational analyses are the product moment correlation coefficient, known as the Pearson r, and the rank difference correlation coefficient, usually referred to as the Spearman *rho*.

The Pearson r

The Pearson r correlation coefficient is the most appropriate measure when the variables to be correlated are expressed as either interval or ratio data. Similar to the mean and the standard deviation, the Pearson r takes into account every score in both distributions; it is also the most stable measure of correlation. In educational research, most measures represent interval scales, so the Pearson r is the coefficient most frequently used for testing for relations. An assumption associated with the application of the Pearson r is that the relation between the variables is a linear one. If the relation is not linear, the Pearson r does not yield a valid indication of the relation.

Although the computational formula is somewhat complex at first glance, the Pearson r is basically a series of mathematical calculations that consider the relative association of each person, test, or occurrence (e.g., X is the person's score for the first test, and Y is that person's score for the second test).

$$r = \frac{\Sigma XY - \dfrac{(\Sigma X)(\Sigma Y)}{N}}{\sqrt{\left[\Sigma X^2 - \dfrac{(\Sigma X)^2}{N}\right]\left[\Sigma Y^2 - \dfrac{(\Sigma Y)^2}{N}\right]}}$$

If you look closely at the formula for Pearson r, you will see that you are already familiar with all the pieces of the formula except one, ΣXY, which is a symbol for the sum of the product of each person's X and Y scores (e.g., a student's first test score multiplied by the student's second score). Obviously, if we have a large dataset, multiplying and summing every score by hand is quite tedious. Fortunately, the computer arrives at the same value in much less time.

For a concrete example, we return to our analyses of the outcomes in Ms. Alvarez's third-grade class at Pinecrest Elementary School. First, we want to find the association or correlation between the fall reading and fall math scores for the students. From our experience, we expect that the reading scores and the math scores would likely be correlated; that is, students who score well on reading will also do well on math, and vice versa.

Computing the correlation using SPSS is relatively simple. We select the following options, as illustrated in Appendix A, Figure A.18.5:

Analyze
Correlate
Bivariate

Having selected the appropriate SPSS options, we then select the variables we want to analyze, as shown in Figure A.18.6: fall reading (ReadF) and fall math (MathF). SPSS then produces the output shown in Table 18.8. This output displays a 2×2 matrix with four cells. The first cell in the matrix shows the correlation coefficient of ReadF by itself: ReadF $\times$ ReadF. This is a perfect correlation (1), of

TABLE 18.8 • SPSS output of correlation: Fall reading (ReadF) by fall math (MathF) correlations

	ReadF	MathF
ReadF Pearson Correlation	1	.618(*)
Sig. (2-tailed)		.001
N	25	25
MathF Pearson Correlation	.618(*)	1
Sig. (2-tailed)	.001	
N	25	25

* Correlation is significant (sig.) at the 0.01 level (2-tailed).

course, as the table shows. If we read horizontally across the matrix to the second cell, we find the correlation between ReadF and MathF = 0.618, with a significance level of 0.001. The third cell provides the same correlation between MathF and ReadF, $r = 0.618$, only MathF is listed first. The final cell is MathF by MathF, $r = 1$, which is a perfect correlation against itself, of course. The two cells that show the perfect correlation of 1 (i.e., the first and fourth) are called the *diagonal* of the matrix. The other two cells in the matrix are called the *off-diagonal* cells. Because there are only two variables in this analysis, both off-diagonal boxes show the same correlation coefficient. Although we need only one coefficient value (0.618), SPSS prints the complete information for all the cells. Having all this information in the matrix becomes more important when we are correlating more than two variables and the matrix grows to 3×3, 4×4, or larger. In large datasets, we often compute correlations for all ratio variables in preparation for conducting multiple regression.

How do we interpret this finding of a correlation coefficient of $r = 0.618$ with a significance value of 0.001? Is this good? Does it represent a true relation? Is this correlation coefficient significantly different from 0.00? If you recall the earlier discussion, you know that a correlation coefficient of 0.618 probably indicates a strong relation between the variables. Even with our small sample size of 25, $r = 0.618$ is significant at 0.001. In other words, the likelihood of finding a correlation this large, simply by chance, is less than 1 in 1,000. We can feel confident that there is a relation between the fall reading and fall math scores; Ms. Alvarez's students have started the school year with fairly equivalent skills in reading and math. It will be important for us to test the correlation again at the end of the year; that is, to see whether the students' reading and math scores have improved at the same rates.

The ease of using SPSS to determine the correlation and level of significance is quite obvious, but remember that if we were making this calculation by hand, rather than using SPSS or other statistical software, we should arrive at the same Pearson r of 0.618. SPSS follows the same procedures you would use to compute the Pearson r (i.e., summing up the product of the X and Y scores, subtracting the sum of X times the sum of Y, dividing by N in the numerator, and then dividing by the complex calculation in the denominator). Once the Pearson r is determined, SPSS calculates the significance of this r based on the sample size and degrees of freedom and prints exactly the level of significance for those parameters. Our finding of a significance level of 0.001 in Table 18.8 assures us that the correlation we found is not very likely due to chance.

SPSS determines the level of significance automatically, but when we are conducting a correlation analysis by hand, we have to consult a table of correlation coefficients, taking into account the number of students or participants. These tables, too, are readily available on the Internet—search for "table of Pearson coefficients." They are typically organized as shown below.

		P		
df	**.10**	**.05**	**.01**	**.001**
1	0.988	0.997	0.999	0.999
2	0.900	0.950	0.990	0.999
3	0.805	0.878	0.959	0.991
...				
20	0.360	0.423	0.537	0.652
25	0.323	0.381	0.487	0.597
30	0.296	0.349	0.449	0.554
...				

The effect of the number of students on the level of significance is done through consideration of the degrees of freedom. For the Pearson r, degrees of freedom is always computed by the formula $N - 2$, with N representing the number of participants for whom we have paired data

(i.e., X and Y). Thus, for our example with Pinecrest Elementary School, degrees of freedom $(df) = N - 2 = 25 - 2 = 23$. With a level of significance set at 0.05, we would read down the column labeled .05 to the lines that correspond with df values of 20 and 25 (i.e., in the first column). The value shown in the cell is a population correlation coefficient that we use as a benchmark for comparison with our sample correlation coefficient. Although our df value falls between 20 and 25, we find that our Pearson r of 0.618 is significant if $df = 25$ ($p = 0.381$) or $df = 20$ ($p = 0.423$). Note also that if our Pearson r was negative in our example ($r = -.618$) we would still consult the table in the same way because the direction of the relation (i.e., positive or negative) does not affect the level of significance.

The Spearman Rho

Because correlational data are not always measured on an interval scale, we can use the Spearman rho coefficient to correlate ranked or ordinal data. Other measures for ordinal data include Gamma, Kendall tau, and Somer d, but Spearman rho is among the most popular. When using Spearman rho, both variables to be correlated must be ranked. For example, if intelligence were to be correlated with class rank or economic status, students' intelligence scores would have to be translated into ranks (e.g., low, medium, high). Spearman's rho has a weakness, however, when more than one individual receives the same score—there is a tie in the ranking. In these cases the corresponding ranks are averaged. For example, two participants with the same highest score would each be assigned rank 1.5, the average of rank 1 and rank 2. The next highest score would be assigned rank 3. Similarly, the 24th and 25th highest scores, if identical, would each be assigned the rank 24.5. As with most other correlation coefficients, the Spearman rho produces a coefficient somewhere between -1.00 and $+1.00$. For example, if a group of participants achieved identical ranks on both variables, the coefficient would be $+1.00$.

MyLab Education **Self-Check 18.2**

MyLab Education **Application Exercise 18.2:** Evaluating Research Articles: Understanding Descriptive Statistics

MyLab Education **Application Exercise 18.3:** Conducting Data Analysis

GRAPHING DATA

A distinct benefit of statistical software is that it provides a variety of ways to present the data in graphic form. For example, Excel and similar spreadsheet programs offer a very convenient way to graph data with commonly used pie charts and line graphs. Because the shape of the distribution may not be self-evident, especially if a large number of scores are involved, it is always helpful to provide a graphic representation of the data and, in some cases (e.g., a curvilinear relation among variables), the shape of the distribution may influence the researcher's choice of descriptive statistics.

Graphic displays of data range from simple bar graphs to more complex frequency polygons that display the shape of the data, as in a normal distribution or bell-shaped curve. Figure 18.3 shows a simple bar graph created in Excel for the distribution of Pinecrest Elementary School

students, organized by gender and economic level. The graph was created first by making a PivotTable (refer to the explanation for Figure A.18.3 in Appendix B) and then selecting Insert from the Excel menu bar and choosing Chart. Gender is on the Y axis (i.e., vertical), and economic level is on the X axis (i.e., horizontal). As the graph shows, six boys are at the low economic level, four boys are at the medium level, and so forth. Note, however, that three-dimensional graphs provide an effective illustration of data for an audience; however, the exact values are not always easy to identify from them. If precision is the goal, then a PivotTable is likely the preferable choice for displaying the data.

Another typically used method of graphing data is to construct a frequency polygon. A frequency polygon plots the frequency of each score value on the graph and then connects the dots with a line. Figure 18.4 shows a frequency polygon based on 85 achievement test scores of Pinecrest

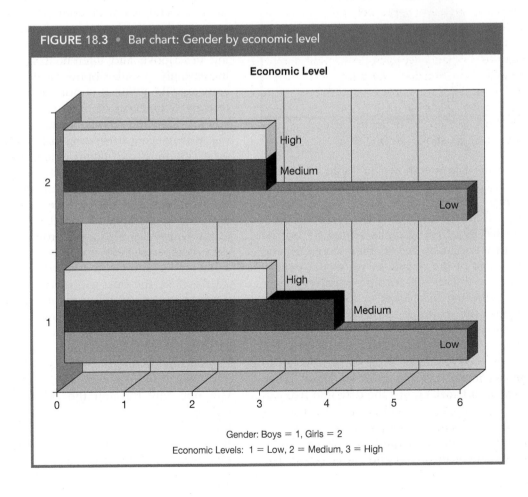

FIGURE 18.3 • Bar chart: Gender by economic level

Gender: Boys = 1, Girls = 2
Economic Levels: 1 = Low, 2 = Medium, 3 = High

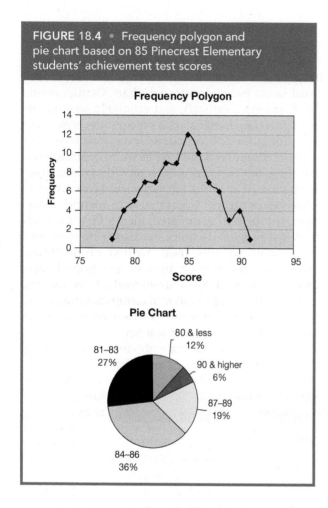

FIGURE 18.4 • Frequency polygon and pie chart based on 85 Pinecrest Elementary students' achievement test scores

next slice displays the 27% of scores found in the 81–83 range, and so forth.

Many other approaches and methods are available for displaying not only frequency data but also measures of central tendency and variance; graphs showing group means and standard deviations are among the most common. Excel, SPSS, and other programs can create scatterplots, box plots, stem-and-leaf charts, and a number of graphical and tabular formats.[1] Examining a picture of the data can give some clues about which inferential statistics, discussed in the next chapter, are appropriate.

[1] *Graphing Statistics and Data,* by A. Wallgren, B. Wallgren, R. Persson, U. Jorner, and J. Haaland, 1996, Thousand Oaks, CA: Sage.

"R" YOU READY?

At this point, you have been introduced to a wide range of descriptive statistics and you've been offered examples with both Excel and SPSS. As mentioned at the beginning of this chapter, Excel and SPSS are not the only options for calculating descriptive and inferential statistics. Another increasingly popular option is the open-sourced software "R." While R is not any more difficult to operate than Excel or SPSS it is different, and if you are someone who is not savvy with basic coding, R may seem frustrating at first. SPSS operates on a system of pull down menus and even Excel, to an extent, is filled with toolbar options. R simply offers you a blinking cursor. It is up to you to take the next step, but with a little practice and guidance this is nothing to fear. Dr. William B. Ware at the University of North Carolina at Chapel Hill once compared SPSS and R with the analogy of a bus and a sports car (personal communication, 2013). SPSS, the bus, will carry more people, has a preset route, and will certainly get you safely to your destination. R, the sports car, provides a ride for fewer people along a wide-open highway system filled with options. There is a lot of fun and a lot of danger along the way as well. We intentionally cover R in a separate section in order to walk you not only through the statistical procedures but also the steps to obtaining the R software and building your coding skills along the way. Sample R scripts will be provided in Appendix A and can be downloaded directly.

students (the data are shown in Table 18.6). The figure was created in Excel by selecting Insert and then using Chart (Figure A.18.4 in Appendix A). Various options are then used to create the polygon. Twelve Pinecrest students scored 85 on the achievement test, 10 scored 86, nine scored 84, and so forth. Most of the scores, as we would expect, group around the middle, with progressively fewer students achieving the higher or lower scores. In other words, the scores appear to form a relatively normal distribution.

Whereas the frequency polygon graphs the number of occurrences of each score from 78 to 91, the accompanying pie chart in Figure 18.4, also created in Excel, groups the data into five categories. The pie chart provides the percentage of scores in each of these categories. For example, one slice of the pie or category represents 12% of the scores falling in the 80 and lower range. The

You may be feeling a bit like Neo in *The Matrix*. If you recall, Morpheus famously gives Neo the choice of a red pill or blue pill with each offering a very different outcome. At this point you can choose to take the blue pill, if you would like. You can skip on to the next chapter and believe whatever you choose about R. However, for the brave and curious who choose the red pill, read on and welcome to the world of R.

Step 1: Installing R on Your Computer

R is an open-sourced software, meaning it is available to you free of charge. Your first step in using R will involve a simple process of downloading R onto your computer. Since R is open-sourced, many people from all over the world have contributed to the ongoing development of the R software. Because of this, think of R as an ongoing "project." In order to download R, simply go to www.r-project.org. On this page you'll see a menu of options down the left side of your screen, as shown in Figure 18.5.

If you'd like, you can take some time and read the "About R" section to learn more about R than we can cover in this text. However, if you are just ready to get down to business, simply click CRAN under the heading Download. Don't worry; CRAN isn't some fancy computer term that you need to know. It simply stands for "Comprehensive R Archive Network." The first step in obtaining R is selecting a "CRAN mirror." Again, you don't have to worry over this terminology. A "mirror" is just a copy of a server. Because there are many R users, this helps alleviate the demand on a single server. Think of it

as sharing the workload. You are only selecting the site from which you will download the R software. It is typically a good idea to pick a mirror that is close to you in terms of your physical location.

Once you have selected a CRAN mirror, you are ready to download R. At the top of the page you will see three options: Download R for Linux, Download R for (Mac) OS X, and Download R for Windows. Just choose the option that applies to the computer you are using. Each platform is a little different, but each page walks you through the process. We assume that most of you use either a Mac or a PC. On a Mac, you will simply choose the file that corresponds with your current version of OS X. On a PC, you will choose Base. The good folks that design R help you make this decision by inserting helpful hints like, "This is what you want to install R for the first time." From here, just follow the steps for installing a program just as you would with any other program you've installed on your computer.

There is much to learn about R programming, but for our purposes, you just need to know a couple of things. R works with lines of code that serve as commands called "functions." There are many functions and the best way to learn is by trial and error. Some functions are found in "packages" that are downloadable within the R platform. From here on, when we talk about "functions" we are just talking about the way in which you tell R to do what you want it to do. One of the major advantages of R is the vast support network of people who are great at helping newbies and experts alike. If you find yourself wanting R to do something, but you don't know how to tell R what to do, check out some of the many resources available to help you pinpoint the right function. We suggest www.r-bloggers.com or the R support manuals found at https://cran.r-project.org/manuals.html.

Now that you have downloaded R, let's take a look at some basic R usage using the same Pinecrest Elementary data (Table 18.1) we used earlier in the chapter.

Step 2: Getting Your Data Into R

When you open R you are going to be faced with a blinking cursor. If you were previously an SPSS user, you're going to have the reaction to look for pull down menus, but those menus don't exist in the R environment. Continuing with the sports car analogy, R is capable of doing some amazing work, but think

FIGURE 18.5 • The R homepage

The R Project for Statistical Computing

[Home]

Download
CRAN

R Project
About R
Logo
Contributors
What's New?
Reporting Bugs
Development Site
Conferences
Search

R Foundation
Foundation
Board
Members
Donors
Donate

Help With R

Getting Started

R is a free software environment for statistical computing and graphics. It compiles and runs on a wide variety of UNIX platforms, Windows and MacOS. To download R, please choose your preferred CRAN mirror.

If you have questions about R like how to download and install the software, or what the license terms are, please read our answers to frequently asked questions before you send an email.

News

• R version 3.3.3 (Another Canoe) prerelease versions will appear starting Friday 2017-02-24. Final release is scheduled for Monday 2017-03-06.

• useR! 2017 (July 4 - 7 in Brussels) has opened registration and more at http://user2017.brussels/

• Tomas Kalibera has joined the R core team.

• The R Foundation welcomes five new ordinary members: Jennifer Bryan, Dianne Cook, Julie Josse, Tomas Kalibera, and Balasubramanian Narasimhan.

• R version 3.3.2 (Sincere Pumpkin Patch) has been released on Monday 2016-10-31.

• The R Journal Volume 8/1 is available.

• The useR! 2017 conference will take place in Brussels, July 4 - 7, 2017.

of it as a sports car with a manual transmission. If you've never pressed a clutch in your life, you may have a bumpy start, but you'll get the hang of it.

The first step for working with R is to take the file filled with your data and let R know that's what we are working with. There are many ways to do this. You can read a file into R or you can create your data frame from scratch in the R platform. We can't cover all of the many ways this is possible in this text, but there are many available texts devoted to R programming. We recommend Ware, Ferron, and Miller's (2013) *Introductory Statistics: A Conceptual Approach Using R* as a text for those who find themselves interested in working with R in a more in depth level.

For our purposes, we are going to read in the file we've already been using. To begin, save your spreadsheet as a Text file. R can read an Excel file, but it takes a little more effort. To load your spreadsheet as a data frame directly into R use the read.table command. As a note, because of limited space in the textbook format, some of our lines of code will "wrap around." When you open R, you'll see that each line begins with an arrow that looks like this: >. We've added arrows in front of the code in the body of the text so you can see where one line of code stops and another begins. The arrow isn't a part of the code. It will be there for you in the R environment. With that being said, just type the following line of code:

```
>pinecrest <- read.table("path to your file",
header = TRUE)
```

This line of code says, "We are naming our file pinecrest. It is a data frame with different variables, and it is located here." You can name your file anything you want, just remember: R is case sensitive. Now that you've read in the file, you need to let R know that we will be working with this dataset. You do that through using the attach command. Simply type:

```
>attach(pinecrest)
```

You're now ready to go. Press enter and then type the word "pinecrest" at the blinking cursor. You'll see the dataset we have been working with is now in the R platform. See Figure 18.6 to make sure you are on the right track.

FIGURE 18.6 • Pinecrest data

```
Type 'demo()' for some demos, 'help()' for on-line help, or
'help.start()' for an HTML browser interface to help.
Type 'q()' to quit R.

[R.app GUI 1.68 (7288) x86_64-apple-darwin13.4.0]

[History restored from /Users/Adam/.Rapp.history]

> pinecrest <- read.table("~/Desktop/Mills Chapters/Pinecrest.txt", header = TRUE)
> attach(pinecrest)
> pinecrest
   ID Gender Ethnicity Econ ReadLevel ReadF ReadS MathF MathS
1   1      1         1    1         3  52.5  68.7  54.8  55.2
2   2      2         2    2         1  32.5  52.6  73.2  72.8
3   3      1         5    2         1  36.4  38.5  44.9  43.0
4   4      1         5    2         1  44.3  56.2  35.2  36.6
5   5      2         4    1         3  58.7  63.8  58.3  60.5
6   6      1         3    1         1  28.3  31.2  23.1  22.0
7   7      2         3    1         2  43.1  53.6  52.6  53.6
8   8      1         5    3         2  66.5  75.5  53.8  53.3
9   9      2         1    1         3  51.4  56.8  45.8  43.6
10 10      1         5    1         1  38.5  41.4  46.7  47.8
11 11      2         5    3         3  56.0  72.3  38.4  36.0
12 12      1         2    1         1  24.5  28.4  32.5  32.6
13 13      2         1    1         1  37.4  42.3  25.3  25.8
14 14      1         3    1         1  28.3  34.8  18.3  19.5
15 15      2         5    3         3  78.4  72.4  58.3  60.3
16 16      2         3    2         3  52.3  53.6  38.6  40.3
17 17      1         5    3         2  56.8  64.2  67.4  68.4
18 18      2         1    3         3  73.2  68.4  72.4  70.0
19 19      1         5    2         1  47.4  65.8  53.5  52.0
20 20      2         2    1         2  47.4  34.6  48.5  50.2
21 21      1         5    3         2  53.2  58.5  36.5  38.5
22 22      1         3    1         1  18.4  22.0  27.2  28.0
23 23      2         5    2         3  53.5  58.4  62.4  64.0
24 24      2         4    1         3  46.5  52.4  38.6  38.0
25 25      1         1    2         1  38.6  41.7  28.9  27.0
>
```

If your dataset only included numerical data, you'd be all set. But, our dataset has some categorical variables. We need to let R know which columns of our dataset are actually categorical variables. When the data are initially read into R, R assumes all of the "numbers" are actually numbers. For example, with the data we just read in, you could simply type mean(Gender) and R would give you a response of 1.48. Remember we coded our Gender variable with 1s and 2s. R just added all of those responses up and divided by the number of cases. But what is a gender of 1.48? That's nonsense. To let R know we are using categorical variables, we need to set up a factor variable for each of our categorical variables. The following code will let R know we have categorical data. In R, beginning a line of code with a # indicates that it is a comment.

```
>#Creating a factor variable for Gender

>pinecrest$f.gender = factor(pinecrest$Gender,
labels=c("male", "female"))

>#Creating a factor variable for Ethnicity

>pinecrest$f.ethnicity = factor(pinecrest$Ethnicity,
labels= c("African American", "Asian, Pacific
Islander", "Hispanic", "Native American", "White"))

>#Creating a factor variable for Economic Level

>pinecrest$f.econ = factor(pinecrest$Econ,
labels= c("low (free/reduced lunch)", "medium/
working class", "middle/upperclass"))

>#Creating a factor variable for Reading Level

>pinecrest$f.ReadLevel = factor(pinecrest$ReadLevel,
labels= c("low", "middle", "high"))
```

While the code may look complicated at first glance we are just saying, "In our dataset called

FIGURE 18.7 • Pinecrest data with factor variables

```
> pinecrest$f.gender = factor(pinecrest$Gender, labels = c("male", "female"))
> pinecrest$f.ethnicity = factor(pinecrest$Ethnicity, labels = c("African American", "Asian, Pacific Islander", "Hispanic", "Native American", "White"))
> pinecrest$f.econ = factor(pinecrest$Econ, labels = c("low (free/reduced lunch)", "medium/working class", "middle/upperclass"))
> pinecrest$f.ReadLevel = factor(pinecrest$ReadLevel, labels = c("low", "middle", "high"))
> attach(pinecrest)
The following objects are masked from pinecrest (pos = 3):

    Econ, Ethnicity, Gender, ID, MathF, MathS, ReadF, ReadLevel, ReadS

> pinecrest
   ID Gender Ethnicity Econ ReadLevel ReadF ReadS MathF MathS f.gender            f.ethnicity                  f.econ f.ReadLevel
1   1      1         1    1         3  52.5  68.7  54.8  55.2     male       African American low (free/reduced lunch)        high
2   2      2         2    2         1  32.5  52.6  73.2  72.8   female Asian, Pacific Islander      medium/working class         low
3   3      1         5    2         1  36.4  38.5  44.9  43.0     male                  White      medium/working class         low
4   4      1         5    2         1  44.3  56.2  35.2  36.6     male                  White      medium/working class         low
5   5      2         4    1         3  58.7  63.8  58.3  60.5   female        Native American low (free/reduced lunch)        high
6   6      1         3    1         1  28.3  31.2  23.1  22.0     male               Hispanic low (free/reduced lunch)         low
7   7      2         3    1         2  43.1  53.6  52.6  53.6   female               Hispanic low (free/reduced lunch)      middle
8   8      1         5    3         2  66.5  75.5  53.8  53.3     male                  White         middle/upperclass      middle
9   9      2         1    1         3  51.4  56.8  45.8  43.6   female       African American low (free/reduced lunch)        high
10 10      1         5    1         1  38.5  41.4  46.7  47.8     male                  White low (free/reduced lunch)         low
11 11      2         5    3         3  56.0  72.3  38.4  36.0   female                  White         middle/upperclass        high
12 12      1         2    1         1  24.5  28.4  32.5  32.6     male Asian, Pacific Islander low (free/reduced lunch)         low
13 13      2         1    1         1  37.4  42.3  25.3  25.8   female       African American low (free/reduced lunch)         low
14 14      1         3    1         1  28.3  34.8  18.3  19.5     male               Hispanic low (free/reduced lunch)         low
15 15      2         5    3         3  78.4  72.4  58.3  60.3   female                  White         middle/upperclass        high
16 16      2         3    2         3  52.3  53.6  38.6  40.3   female               Hispanic      medium/working class        high
17 17      1         5    3         2  56.8  64.2  67.4  68.4     male                  White         middle/upperclass      middle
18 18      2         1    3         3  73.2  68.4  72.4  70.0   female       African American         middle/upperclass        high
19 19      1         5    2         1  47.4  65.8  53.5  52.0     male                  White      medium/working class         low
20 20      2         2    1         2  47.4  34.6  48.5  50.2   female Asian, Pacific Islander low (free/reduced lunch)      middle
21 21      1         5    3         2  53.2  58.5  36.5  38.5     male                  White         middle/upperclass      middle
22 22      1         3    1         1  18.4  22.0  27.2  28.0     male               Hispanic low (free/reduced lunch)         low
23 23      2         5    2         3  53.5  58.4  62.4  64.0   female                  White      medium/working class        high
24 24      2         4    1         3  46.5  52.4  38.6  38.0   female        Native American low (free/reduced lunch)        high
25 25      1         1    2         1  38.6  41.7  28.9  27.0     male       African American      medium/working class         low
>
```

'pinecrest' create a factor variable for each of our categorical variables with appropriate labels."

Lastly, since we've made some changes to our dataset, we should again use the attach function to let R know we want to use this new and revised dataset. So, type:

>attach(pinecrest)

You'll see your new and revised dataset all ready to go! Double check your work with Figure 18.7.

Step 3: Calculating Some Descriptive Statistics

If R is a sports car, now that your data is read in it is all gassed up and ready to go, so let's calculate some of the same statistics we calculated earlier with Excel and SPSS in the R platform. If you recall from Tables 18.3 and 18.4, the first action with both Excel and SPSS was to create a frequency count. This is a simple line of code in R. To achieve this we use the "table" function in R along with the "addmargins" function. This will give us our frequency count with totals. Just type the following:

>addmargins(table(f.gender,f.ethnicity))

From here, R becomes quite a simple and powerful tool to describe your dataset if you just know

a couple of functions: "summary" and "tapply." The "tapply" function will apply the statistical procedure you want to the subgroups you indicate and give you the output in the form of a table. The "summary" function is great for summarizing data in terms of range and quartiles. Let's reproduce the results we achieved earlier with Excel and SPSS by applying just a few commands. Try the following commands on our Pinecrest dataset:

>tapply(ReadF, f.gender, mean)
>tapply(ReadF, f.gender, sd)
>tapply(ReadF, f.gender, var)

These commands gave us the breakdown of Fall Reading scores based on gender for each of the statistics we asked for: mean, standard deviation, variance. If we were interested in the ranges and quartile breakdown, we could look at each variable individually with the following commands:

>range(ReadF)
>range(ReadS)
>range(MathF)
>range(MathS)

or we could simply use the summary function and type:

>summary(pinecrest)

FIGURE 18.8 • Frequency count

```
> #Let's take a look at our frequency table
> addmargins(table(f.gender,f.ethnicity))
          f.ethnicity
f.gender African American Asian, Pacific Islander Hispanic Native American White Sum
    male                2                        1        3                0     7  13
    female              3                        2        2                2     3  12
    Sum                 5                        3        5                2    10  25
>
```

It really is that simple! You'll notice that for all of these commands the output from R matches the output we received earlier from SPSS with the exception of some rounding differences.

For one final exercise in R, let's recreate the Pearson r statistic we calculated with SPSS earlier. Recall that we were interested in the degree to which Fall reading scores and Fall math scores were correlated (see Table 18.8), and whether or not this correlation was statistically significant. In R, we just need one command:

>cor.test(ReadF, MathF)

That's it! Just as you found with SPSS, fall reading scores and fall math scores are correlated at r = .618.

If you've read this far, you undoubtedly decided to take the red pill, and we applaud you for your bravery. We hope you'll continue to explore all of the many opportunities presented by using R for your data analysis.

Postscript

Almost always in a research study, descriptive statistics such as the mean and standard deviation are computed separately for each group in the study. A correlation coefficient is usually computed only in a correlational study (unless it is used to compute the reliability of an instrument used in a causal–comparative or experimental study). Standard scores are rarely used in research studies. To test a hypothesis, however, we need more than descriptive statistics; we need the application of one or more inferential statistics to test hypotheses and determine the significance of results. We discuss inferential statistics in the next chapter.

MyLab Education **Self-Check 18.3**

MyLab Education **Application Exercise 18.4:** Graphing with R

SUMMARY

THE LANGUAGE OF STATISTICS

1. The formulas for statistical procedures are basic mathematical procedures. Statistical notation uses Greek letters as shorthand.

PREPARING DATA FOR ANALYSIS

2. The first step toward analysis involves converting behavioral responses into some numeric system or categorical organization.
3. All instruments should be scored accurately and consistently, using the same procedures and criteria. Scoring self-developed instruments is more complex than scoring standardized instruments, especially if open-ended items are involved.
4. Tabulation involves organizing the data systematically, such as by individual subject. If planned analyses involve subgroup comparisons, scores should be tabulated for each subgroup.
5. The next step following tabulation is to summarize the data using descriptive statistics.

TYPES OF DESCRIPTIVE STATISTICS

6. The values calculated for a sample drawn from a population are referred to as *statistics*. The values calculated for an entire population are referred to as *parameters*.

Frequencies

7. Frequency refers to the number of times something occurs; with descriptive statistics, frequency usually refers to the number of times each value of a variable occurs.
8. For nominal or ordinal variables, a frequency count for each value is very descriptive. Frequency is more complicated for interval or ratio variables; other measures of central tendency are preferred to describe them.

Measures of Central Tendency

9. Measures of central tendency are indices that represent a typical score among many scores.

They provide a convenient way of describing a set of data with a single number.

10. The mean is the arithmetic average of the scores and is the most frequently used measure of central tendency. It is appropriate for describing interval or ratio data.
11. The median is the midpoint in a distribution; 50% of the scores are above the median, and 50% are below the median. The median is most useful when looking at ordinal variables or datasets in which the scores vary widely over the distribution.
12. The mode is the score that is attained by more subjects than any other score (i.e., occurs most frequently). A set of scores may have two (or more) modes. When nominal data are collected, the mode is the only appropriate measure of central tendency.
13. In general, the mean is the preferred measure of central tendency. When a group of test scores contains one or more extreme scores, the median is the best index of typical performance.

Measures of Variability

14. Two sets of data that are very different can have identical means or medians, thus creating a need for measures of variability, indices that indicate how spread out a group of scores is.
15. The range is simply the difference between the highest and lowest score in a distribution and is determined by subtraction. It is not a very stable measure of variability, but its chief advantage is that it gives a quick, rough estimate of variability.
16. The quartile deviation is one half of the difference between the upper quartile (the 75th percentile) and lower quartile (the 25th percentile) in a distribution. The quartile deviation is a more stable measure of variability than the range and is appropriate whenever the median is appropriate.
17. Variance is defined as the amount of spread among scores. If the variance is small, the scores are close together; if it is large, the scores are more spread out.

18. Standard deviation is the square root of the variance of a set of scores. It is the most stable measure of variability and takes into account every score.

The Normal Curve

19. A distribution with fewer people (or scores) at the extremes and more people in the middle is considered normal. When plotted as a frequency graph, a normal distribution forms a bell shape, known as the *normal curve*.

20. If a variable is normally distributed, then 50% of the scores are above the mean, and 50% of the scores are below the mean. The mean, the median, and the mode are the same. Most scores are near the mean, and the farther from the mean a score is, the fewer the number of subjects who attained that score. For every normal distribution, 34.13% of the scores fall between the mean and one standard deviation above the mean, and 34.13% of the scores fall one standard deviation below the mean. More than 99% of the scores will fall somewhere between three standard deviations above and three standard deviations below the mean.

21. Because research studies deal with a finite number of subjects, and often a not very large number, data from a sample can only approximate a normal curve.

Skewed Distributions

22. When a distribution is not normal, it is said to be *skewed*, and there are more extreme scores at one end than at the other. If the extreme scores are at the lower end of the distribution, the distribution is said to be *negatively skewed*; if the extreme scores are at the upper, or higher, end of the distribution, the distribution is said to be *positively skewed*.

23. For a negatively skewed distribution, the mean ($\overline{X}$) is always lower, or smaller, than the median (md); for a positively skewed distribution, the mean is always higher, or greater, than the median.

Measures of Relative Position

24. Measures of relative position indicate where a score falls in the distribution, relative to all other scores in the distribution. They make it possible to compare one person's performance on two or more different tests.

25. A percentile rank indicates the percentage of scores that fall at or below a given score. Percentiles are appropriate for data measured on an ordinal scale, although they are frequently computed for interval data. The median of a set of scores corresponds to the 50th percentile.

26. A standard score reflects how many standard deviations a student's score is above or below the mean. A *z* score directly expresses how far a score is from the mean in terms of standard deviation units. A score that is equivalent to the mean corresponds to a *z* score of 0. A score that is exactly one standard deviation above the mean corresponds to a *z* score of +1.00, and a *z* score of −1.00 is one standard deviation below the mean. If a set of scores is transformed into a set of *z* scores, the new distribution has a mean of 0 and a standard deviation of 1.

27. A *T* score (also called a *Z score*) is a *z* score transformed to eliminate pluses or minuses.

Measures of Relationship

28. *Measures of relationship* indicate the degree to which two sets of scores are related. Degree of relationship is expressed as a correlation coefficient, which is computed from two sets of scores from a single group of participants. If two variables are highly related, a correlation coefficient near +1.00 or −1.00 will be obtained; if two variables are not related, a coefficient near 0.00 will be obtained.

29. The Pearson *r* is the most appropriate measure of correlation when the sets of data to be correlated are expressed as either interval or ratio scales. The Pearson *r* is not valid if the relation between the variables is not linear.

30. The Spearman rho is the appropriate measure of correlation when the variables are expressed as ranks.

GRAPHING DATA

31. It is always helpful to provide a graphic representation of the data, and in some cases (e.g., a curvilinear relation among variables), the shape of the distribution may influence the researcher's choice of descriptive statistics.

32. One common method of graphing research data is to construct a frequency polygon. Data can also be displayed in bar graphs, scatterplots, pie charts, and stem-and-leaf charts.

INTRODUCTION TO R

33. R is an open-source platform useful for conducting statistical analyses and can be downloaded directly from www.r-project.org.

Statistical Symbols and Formulas

Symbols

Symbols commonly used in statistical formulas are as follows:

X = any score

Σ = sum of; add them up

ΣX = the sum of all the scores

$\overline{X}$ = the mean, or arithmetic average, of the scores

N = total number of subjects

n = number of subjects in a particular group

The Mean

The formula for the population mean is

$$\mu = \frac{\sum\limits_{i=1}^{N} x_i}{N}$$

The formula for the sample mean is

$$\overline{x} = \frac{\sum\limits_{i=1}^{N} x_i}{N}$$

The Standard Deviation

The formula for the standard deviation of a population is

$$SD = \sqrt{\frac{SS}{N}}, \text{ where } SS = \Sigma X^2 - \frac{(\Sigma X)^2}{N}.$$

Standard Scores

The formula for a z score is $z = \dfrac{X - \overline{X}}{SD}$.

The formula for a Z score is $Z = 10z\ 1 + 50$

The Pearson r

The formula for the Pearson r is

$$r = \frac{\Sigma XY - \dfrac{(\Sigma X)(\Sigma Y)}{N}}{\sqrt{\left[\Sigma X^2 - \dfrac{(\Sigma X)^2}{N}\right]\left[\Sigma Y^2 - \dfrac{(\Sigma Y)^2}{N}\right]}}$$

CHAPTER NINETEEN

Inferential Statistics

Survival of the Dead, 2009

20th Century-Fox Film Corporation, TM & Copyright/Everett Collection

"[I]nferential statistics help researchers make calculated inferences based on information obtained from a limited number of research participants." (p. 501)

LEARNING OUTCOMES

After reading Chapter 19, you should be able to do the following:

19.1 Explain the concepts underlying inferential statistics.

19.2 Select among tests of significance and apply them to your study.

The chapter learning outcomes form the basis for the following task, which will require you to write the results section of a research report.

TASK 10

For the same quantitative study that you have been developing in Tasks 3–9, write the results section of a research report. Specifically, you must do the following:

1. Generate data for each participant in your study.
2. Summarize and describe data using descriptive statistics, computed either by hand or with the use of an appropriate statistical software package.
3. Analyze data using inferential statistics by hand or by computer.
4. Interpret the results in terms of your original research hypothesis.
5. Present the results of your data analyses in a summary table.

CONCEPTS UNDERLYING INFERENTIAL STATISTICS

Inferential statistics are data analysis techniques for determining how likely it is that results obtained from a sample or samples are the same results that would have been obtained from the entire population. Put another way, inferential statistics are used to make inferences about parameters, based on the statistics from a sample. In the simplest language, descriptive statistics show how often or how frequent an event or score occurred; inferential statistics help researchers make calculated inferences based on information obtained from a limited number of research participants.

As an example, imagine that Pinecrest Elementary School implemented an experimental third-grade reading curriculum and found that the students who used it scored significantly higher in reading comprehension than those who used the traditional curriculum (say, $\overline{X}_1 = 35$ and $\overline{X}_2 = 43$). Can this difference be generalized to the larger population or other samples within it? Would the program be equally successful at the district or state level? Perhaps, although it's possible that the difference between the original two samples occurred just by chance (possibly due to characteristics of the particular individuals or classrooms sampled). And now we get to the heart of inferential statistics, the concept of "how likely is it?"

Inferential statistics allow researchers to determine the likelihood that the difference between the old mean ($\overline{X}_1$) and the new mean ($\overline{X}_2$) is a real, significant one rather than one attributable to sampling error. Note that inferential statistics use data from samples to assess *likelihood* (i.e., inferential statistics produce probability statements about the populations), not guarantees. The degree to which the results of a sample can be generalized to a population is always expressed in terms of probabilities; analyses do not "prove" that hypotheses are true or false.

Understanding and using inferential statistics require basic knowledge of a number of concepts that underlie the analytical techniques. These concepts are discussed in the following sections.

Standard Error

Inferences about populations are based on information from samples. Obviously, a sample is not identical to the population from which it is derived because it is a subset of the larger population. Even when random samples are used, we cannot expect that the sample characteristics will be exactly the same as those of the population. For example, we can randomly select five students from Ms. Alvarez's class at Pinecrest Elementary and compute the mean of their fall reading scores. We can then randomly select five more students from the same population and compute the mean of their fall reading scores. It's very likely that the two sample means will be different from one another, and it's also likely that neither mean will be identical to the population mean (i.e., the mean for all students in Ms. Alvarez's class). This expected variation among the means is called *sampling error*. Recall that sampling error is not the researcher's fault. Sampling error just happens and is as inevitable as taxes and educational research courses! Thus, if two sample means differ, the important question is whether the difference is just the result of sampling error or is a meaningful difference that would also be found in the larger population.

A useful characteristic of sampling errors is that they are usually normally distributed, provided the samples were derived from a normally distributed population. Sampling errors vary in size (i.e., in some comparisons, sampling error is small; in others, it is large), and these errors tend to form a normal, bell-shaped curve. In other words, if we randomly select 100 different (but same-size) samples from a population and compute a mean for each sample, the means won't all be the same, but they will form a normal distribution around the population mean. It follows then that the mean of all these sample means will yield a good estimate of the population mean.[1]

To help, let's use an example. If you are familiar with the Stanford-Binet, Form L-M intelligence test you know that the population of IQ scores should have a mean of 100 with a standard deviation of 16. This means, based on a normal distribution, that about 68% of all people have an IQ that ranges from 84 to 116, or one standard deviation from the mean. Extending further to two standard deviations, about 95% of all people have an IQ that falls within the range of 68 and 132. If we extend all the way out to three standard deviations we could state with confidence that 99.7% of all people have an IQ that ranges between 52 and 148. We know the population mean in this case, but we can still demonstrate the usefulness of having multiple sample means to estimate the population mean. Even if we don't have access to the population of Stanford-Binet scores, we can simulate these data using statistical software. Using R, which was introduced in Chapter 18, we can simulate 100 means each comprised of 25 cases and having a standard

deviation of 16. If you are interested in following along, the R script used to produce this sample is provided in MyLab for Education. Just know that each time you run the script, R will randomly generate a new data set, so your results will look a little different, but not much!

Using R to simulate the mean for each of the samples with $n = 25$ yields the following 100 means:

99	105	97	98	98	99	99	100	97	98
100	103	105	99	103	97	100	97	97	101
99	102	101	97	101	97	98	100	101	100
103	106	101	100	96	93	99	99	103	103
96	90	105	96	96	96	101	98	107	100
100	98	100	94	100	101	97	96	103	100
102	98	98	97	102	106	107	97	105	97
100	99	104	103	98	99	101	101	105	96
100	99	102	102	100	103	93	99	103	97
98	100	99	99	99	101	103	95	106	101

Computing the mean of these sample means involves adding them and dividing by 100 (i.e., the number of means)—9978/100 = 99.78. This estimate of the population mean is very good as we know that the population mean is 100.

Using R we are also able to calculate the standard deviations for each of these samples with $n = 25$.

17	16	21	16	16	24	14	16	15	16
15	17	15	13	15	17	15	15	12	13
16	15	16	10	12	16	15	15	14	18
17	14	17	16	15	20	16	16	14	16
18	15	17	18	15	15	15	16	14	16
18	17	15	19	14	18	11	14	18	13
15	15	15	17	14	14	16	16	16	17
16	23	19	13	18	18	16	12	15	18
15	16	11	16	12	17	16	14	15	16
14	18	18	14	21	21	17	18	11	19

We know that the standard deviation for the Stanford-Binet is 16. Taking a look at the standard deviations for each of our samples, we can see that each of our samples are close. In fact, if we calculate the mean of these standard deviations we get 15.84. Very close!

---

[1] To find the mean of the sample means (as long as each sample is the same size), simply sum the sample means and divide by the number of means.

As with any normal distribution, a distribution of sample means has not only its own mean (i.e., the mean of the means) but also its own standard deviation (i.e., the difference between each sample mean and the mean of the means). The standard deviation of the sample means is usually called the *standard error of the mean* ($SE_{\overline{X}}$). The word *error* indicates that the various sample means making up the distribution contain some error in their estimate of the population mean. The standard error of the mean reflects how far, on average, any sample mean would differ from the population mean. According to the normal curve percentages (see Chapter 18, Figure 18.1), we can say that approximately 68% of the sample means will fall within one standard error on either side of the mean (remember that the standard error of the mean is a standard deviation), 95% will fall between ± 2 standard errors, and 99+% will fall between ± 3 standard errors. In other words, if the population mean is 100, and the standard error of the mean is 10, we can expect 68% of the sample means (i.e., means of the scores taken from each sample) to be between 90 and 110 (100 $\pm$ 10), 95% of the sample means to fall between 80 and 120 [100 $\pm$ 2(10)], and 99% of the sample means to fall between 70 and 130 [100 $\pm$ 3(10)]. Thus, in this example, it is very likely that a sample mean would be 98, but a sample mean of 135 is highly unlikely because 99% of sample means fall between 70 and 130. Given a number of large, randomly selected samples, we can quite accurately estimate population parameters (i.e., the mean and standard deviation of the whole population) by computing the mean and standard deviation of the sample means. The smaller the standard error, the more accurate the sample means as estimators of the population mean.

It is not necessary, however, to select a large number of samples from a population to estimate the standard error. The standard error of the mean can be estimated using this formula:

$$SE_{\overline{X}} = \frac{SD}{\sqrt{n}}$$

where

$SE_{\overline{X}} = $ the standard error of the mean

$SD = $ the standard deviation for the original distribution

$n = $ the sample size

Thus, in our example using the Stanford Binet Form L-M, we know the standard deviation is 16 and we had 25 means in our sample with the mean of those means being close to 100,

$$SE_{\overline{X}} = \frac{16}{\sqrt{25}} = \frac{16}{25} = 3.2$$

If you chose to run the R scripts provided in Appendix A, you'll see that our simulated sample is a good representation of the population because the mean will be close to 100, the standard deviation will be close to 16, and the standard error of the mean will be close to 3.2. Using this estimate of the $SE_{\overline{X}}$, the sample mean, $\overline{X}$, and the normal curve, we can estimate probable limits within which the population mean falls. These limits are referred to as *confidence limits*. For example, if a sample $\overline{X}$ is 100 and the $SE_{\overline{X}}$ is 3, the population mean falls between 97 and 103 ($\overline{X} \pm 1\ SE_{\overline{X}}$) approximately 68% of the time, the population mean falls between 94 and 106 ($\overline{X} \pm 2\ SE_{\overline{X}}$) approximately 95% of the time, and the population mean falls between 91 and 109 ($\overline{X} \pm 3\ SE_{\overline{X}}$) approximately 99% of the time. In other words, the probability that the population mean is less than 94 or greater than 106 is only 5/100, or 5% ($\pm 2\ SD$), and the probability that the population mean is less than 91 or higher than 109 is only 1/100, or 1% ($\pm 3\ SD$). Note that, as our degree of confidence increases, the limits get farther apart—we are 100% confident that the population mean is somewhere between our sample mean plus infinity and minus infinity.

The major factor affecting our ability to estimate the standard error of the mean accurately is the size of the sample we use for the estimate. As sample size increases, the standard error of the mean decreases—a mean computed from data from the whole population would have no sampling error at all, and a large sample is more likely than a small sample to represent a population accurately. This discussion reinforces the idea that samples should be as large as practically possible; smaller samples include more error than larger samples.

Another factor affecting the estimate of the standard error of the mean is the size of the population standard deviation. If it is large, members of the population are very spread out on the variable of interest, and sample means are also very spread out. Although researchers have no control over the size of the population standard deviation, they can control sample size to some extent. Thus, researchers should make every effort to include as many participants as practical so that inferences about the population of interest will be as free of error as possible.

Our discussion thus far has been in reference to the standard error of a *mean*. However, estimates of standard error can also be computed for other statistics, such as measures of variability, relation, and relative position. An estimate of standard error can also be calculated for the difference between two or more means. Many statistics discussed later in this chapter are based on an estimate of standard error.

Hypothesis Testing

Hypothesis testing is a process of decision making in which researchers evaluate the results of a study against their original expectations. For example, suppose we decide to implement a new reading program at Pinecrest Elementary School. The research plan for our study includes a *research hypothesis*, predicting a difference in scores for children using the new program compared to those using the old program, and a *null hypothesis*, predicting that scores for the two groups will not differ. Following data collection, we compute means and standard deviations for each group and find that children using the new program had somewhat higher reading scores than children using the old program. Because our findings could help the district superintendent decide whether to invest thousands of dollars to implement the new reading curriculum, we need to determine whether we've identified a real difference in the programs or whether our results are simply due to sampling error. Of course, we want to be reasonably certain that the difference we found between the old and the new programs is a *true* or *real* difference caused by the new reading program (i.e., the independent variable) and that it did not occur by chance. In other words, we want to know if our research hypothesis was supported—if the groups are significantly different, we can *reject the null hypothesis* and conclude that the new program is more effective. In short, hypothesis testing is the process of determining whether to reject the null hypothesis (i.e., no meaningful differences, only those due to sampling error) in favor of the research hypothesis (i.e., the groups are meaningfully different; one treatment is more effective than another). Inferential statistics offer us useful evidence to make that decision.

The concept of rejecting the null hypothesis is a complex but important one. For example, suppose our inferential statistics suggest that the scores for the two groups are different enough that the difference is likely *not* due to sampling error. Because our null hypothesis was that the scores would not differ, we can reject it—the scores for the group are different, so the null hypothesis (i.e., no difference) does not reflect the state of affairs, given this sample. Rejecting the null hypothesis can give us reasonable confidence (depending on the level of statistical significance) that the difference we have found is due to the new reading method and not other factors. Note that, although we can *reject* the null hypothesis, we can't *accept* the research hypothesis—we haven't *proven* that the new method is better; rather, we've found just one instance where the new method is better than the old. Even 1,000 tests of the new method are not enough to *prove* our hypothesis. Thus, we state that the research hypothesis was *supported* (for this sample), not that it was proven.

Similarly, suppose our inferential statistics suggest that the scores for the two groups are really not very different, that the apparent difference is likely due to sampling error. We can't conclude that the two methods for teaching reading are equally useful (or not useful) in all cases. In other words, we can't *accept* the null hypothesis; we haven't *proven* it. We've found only one instance where the difference is likely due to sampling error. Perhaps in another study, we'd find significantly different results. In this situation, we state that we have *failed to reject the null hypothesis* or that *the research hypothesis was not supported*.

Ultimately, hypothesis testing is a process of evaluating the null hypothesis, rejecting it or failing to reject it. Because we can never completely control all the factors that may be responsible for the outcome or test all the possible samples, we can never prove a research hypothesis. However, if we can reject the null hypothesis, we have supported our research hypothesis, gaining confidence that our findings reflect the true state of affairs in the population (e.g., that the new reading method leads to higher scores for our students).

Tests of Significance

In the previous example, we noted that inferential statistics can suggest that any differences between scores for comparison groups are simply due to chance or that they are likely to reflect the true state of affairs in the larger population. This process involves *tests of significance.* In the language of statistics, the term *significance* does not mean "importance." Rather, it refers to a statistical level of probability at which we can confidently reject the null hypothesis. Remember, inferential statistics tell us the likelihood (i.e., probability) that the results from our sample are just due to chance. If the probability that our results are due to chance is 50%, how much confidence can we have in them? What if that probability is 10%? 1%? Significance refers to a selected probability level that indicates how much risk we are willing to take if the decision we make is wrong. Researchers do not decide whether scores for two sample groups are different based only on their intuition or best guess. Instead, we select and apply an appropriate **test of significance.**

To conduct a test of significance, we determine a preselected probability level, known as level of significance (or *alpha*, symbolized as α). If you have any exposure to statistical procedures, you have probably heard the phrase **p-value**. Simply stated, a p-value is the probability of obtaining the data you have, given the null hypothesis is true. This probability level serves as a criterion to determine whether to reject or fail to reject the null hypothesis (remember, we never accept the null hypothesis). The standard preselected probability level used by educational researchers is usually 5 out of 100 chances that the observed difference occurred by chance (symbolized as $\alpha = .05$). Some studies demanding a more stringent level of significance set $\alpha = .01$ (i.e., probability is 1 out of 100 that results are simply due to chance), whereas other research that may be more exploratory will set $\alpha = .10$ (i.e., probability is 10 out of 100). The smaller the probability level, the less likely it is that this finding would occur by chance.

For example, at Pinecrest Elementary School, we found a difference between the reading scores of students taught with our new reading curriculum and those taught with the old curriculum. If a difference of the size we found is likely to occur only five (or fewer) times out of every 100 possible samples from our population, we can reject the null hypothesis and conclude that the difference we found is (most likely) a meaningful one—students at Pinecrest do better on reading tests after participating in the new reading program. On the other hand, if a difference of the size we found is likely to occur more than five times out of every 100 samples, simply due to chance, we cannot

reject the null hypothesis. Even if the scores for the groups appear to be different, if the probability that the difference is due to chance is greater than 5 in 100, we cannot be confident that we've found a real difference. In this case, we state that we have not found a significant difference between the programs, we state further that we have failed to reject the null hypothesis, and we tell the superintendent to keep looking for a better reading program.

With a probability criterion of five times out of 100 (5/100, or .05) that these results would be obtained simply due to chance, there is a high (but not perfect) probability that the difference between the means did *not* occur by chance (95/100, or 100 − 5): We are 95% confident. Obviously, if we can say we would expect such a difference by chance only one time in 100, we are even more confident in our decision (i.e., 99% sure that we've found a real difference). How confident we are depends on the probability level at which we perform our test of significance.

Levels of confidence can be illustrated on the normal curve, as shown in Figure 19.1. We can determine the likelihood of a difference occurring by chance at the .05 or .01 level from the normal curve. In essence, we are saying that any differences between ± 2 *SD* will be considered as chance differences at the .05 level, and any differences between ± 3 *SD* will be considered chance differences at the .01 level. Thus, real or significant differences fall outside ± 2 *SD* (.05) or ± 3 *SD* (.01).

Two-Tailed and One-Tailed Tests

How we determine our level of significance is also affected by our directional hypothesis. For example, when testing the effectiveness of a treatment program for adolescents, we predicted outcomes would be better for the residential-treatment than for the day-treatment program, but what if outcomes actually were worse? For this reason, sometimes we need to look in both directions for the outcomes of our tests. In the language of statistics, we need to conduct a *two-tailed test*.

Tests of significance can be either one-tailed or two-tailed. When we talk about "tails," we are referring to the extreme ends of the bell-shaped curve of a sampling distribution. Figure 19.2 provides an illustration. In the curve on the right, only one tail is shaded, representing 5% of the area under the curve. In the curve on the left, both tails

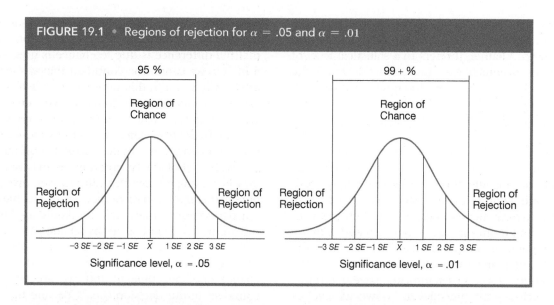

FIGURE 19.1 • Regions of rejection for $\alpha = .05$ and $\alpha = .01$

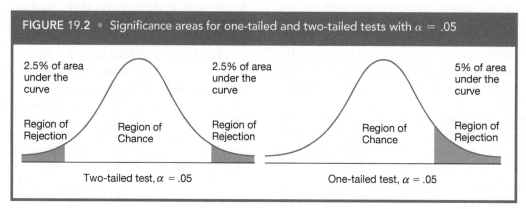

FIGURE 19.2 • Significance areas for one-tailed and two-tailed tests with $\alpha = .05$

are shaded, but each tail represents only 2.5% of the area under the curve. The entire shaded region is known as the region of rejection—if we find differences between groups that are this far from the mean, we can feel confident that our results are not simply due to chance. Note that for both bell curves, a total of 5% of the scores fall into the shaded range: Alpha is set at .05.

A concrete example is useful to help understand the graphs and the distinction between a one-tailed and a two-tailed test. Consider the following null hypothesis:

> There is no difference between the behavior during the hour before lunch of kindergarten students who receive a midmorning snack and that of kindergarten students who do not receive a midmorning snack.

What if the null hypothesis is true—the midmorning snack doesn't matter? If we take repeated samples of kindergarten children and randomly divide the children in each sample into two groups, we can expect that, for most of our samples, the two groups will have very similar behavior during the lunch hour. In other words, if we make a graph with "no difference" at the middle and "big differences" at the ends, most scores will fall into the region of chance illustrated in Figure 19.2. Sometimes, however, the two groups will appear very different (although just by chance, if the null hypothesis is true)—in some cases, the group with the snack will be better behaved (i.e., one tail on the graph), and in other cases, the group without the snack will be better behaved (i.e., the other tail on the graph).

When conducting our study, we want to know if we can reject the null hypothesis; we believe it's not true. Assume, then, we have a directional research hypothesis:

> Kindergarten children who receive a midmorning snack exhibit better behavior during the hour before lunch than kindergarten students who do not receive a midmorning snack.

To reject the null hypothesis and claim support for our research hypothesis, we need to find not just that there's a difference between groups but also that children who get snacks exhibit better behavior than their peers who don't get snacks, and we need to feel confident that our results aren't simply due to chance. We set $\alpha = .05$; a statistically significant difference between the groups (i.e., not likely to be due to chance) will be large enough to fall into the region of rejection, or the shaded region on the right tail of the bell curve on the right of Figure 19.2. We look at only one tail because, according to our hypothesis, we're interested only in seeing whether the group receiving snacks behaves better than the group without snacks.

But what if the outcome is reversed—children who get snacks behave much worse than children who don't? We haven't supported our research hypothesis (in fact, we've found the exact opposite!), and although we've found a big difference between groups, the mean difference doesn't fall into the region of rejection on our one-tailed graph. We can't reject the null hypothesis, then—but the null hypothesis clearly doesn't reflect the true state of affairs either! It should be clear that a two-tailed test of significance would help us because it allows for both possibilities—that the group that received a snack would be better behaved or that the group without a snack would be better behaved.

Tests of significance are almost always two-tailed. To select a one-tailed test of significance, the researcher has to be very certain that a difference will occur in only one direction, or the researcher is only concerned with results in one particular direction, and this is not very often the case. However, when appropriate, a one-tailed test has one major advantage: The score difference required for significance is smaller than for a two-tailed test. In other words, it is "easier" to obtain a significant difference when predicting change in only one direction. To understand this concept in more detail, reconsider

Figure 19.2. Because $\alpha = .05$, the region of rejection represents 5% of the area under the curve. In the graph for the two-tailed test, however, that 5% is split into two regions of 2.5% each to cover both possible outcomes (e.g., the children with snacks will behave better or the children without snacks will behave better). As should be clear from the graphs, the values that fall into the two shaded tails of the graph on the left are more extreme than the values that fall into the one shaded tail of the graph on the right. For example, when using a two-tailed test, the two groups of kindergarteners (i.e., with or without snacks) need to be quite different—more different than they need to be if you are using only a one-tailed test.

Type I and Type II Errors

Based on a test of significance, as we have discussed, the researcher will either reject or not reject the null hypothesis. In other words, the researcher will make the decision that the difference between the means is, or is not, likely due to chance. Because we are dealing with probability, not certainty, we never know for sure whether we are absolutely correct. Sometimes we make mistakes—we decide that a difference is a real difference when it's really due to chance, or we decide that a difference is due to chance when it's not. These mistakes are known as Type I and Type II errors, respectively.

To understand these errors, reconsider our example of the two methods of reading at Pinecrest Elementary. Our decision-making process can lead to four possible outcomes (see Figure 19.3):

1. The null hypothesis can, in reality, be true for the population (i.e., no difference between the reading methods: new method = old method). If we decide that any difference we find is just due to chance, we fail to reject the null hypothesis, and we have made a correct decision.
   - Correct: Null hypothesis is true; the researcher fails to reject it and concludes no significant difference between groups.
2. The null hypothesis, in reality, is false (i.e., new method ≠ old method). If we decide that we are reasonably confident that our results are *not* simply due to chance, we reject the null hypothesis. We have made a correct decision.
   - Correct: Null hypothesis is false; the researcher rejects it and concludes that the groups are significantly different.

FIGURE 19.3 • The four possible outcomes of decision making concerning rejection of the null hypothesis

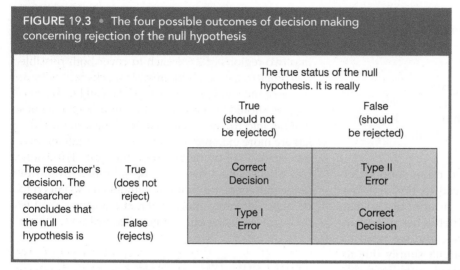

For example, at Pinecrest Elementary, we found a difference between the means of the old reading program and the new reading program; suppose our inferential statistics show that the difference is significant at our preselected level of $\alpha = .05$, and we reject the null hypothesis of no difference. In essence, we are saying that we are confident that the difference resulted from the independent variable (i.e., the new method of reading), not random error, because the chances are only 5 out of 100 (.05) that a difference in the mean of the reading scores is as large (or larger) as the one we have found would occur solely by chance. What if we are worried that we have too much at stake if we make the wrong decision about our results? For example, if we do not want to risk giving the superintendent the wrong advice, we may decide that a more stringent level of significance ($\alpha = .01$) is necessary. We are saying that a difference as large as the one we have found between the reading scores at Pinecrest would be expected to occur by chance only once for every 100 samples from our population—there's only one chance in 100 that we make a Type I error if we conclude that the new reading method is better.

3. The null hypothesis is true (i.e., new method = old method), but we reject it, believing that the results are not simply due to chance and that the methods are different. In this case, we have made an incorrect decision. We have mistakenly assumed there is a difference in the reading programs when there is none.
   ■ Incorrect: Null hypothesis is true, but the researcher rejects it and concludes that the groups are significantly different.
4. The null hypothesis is false (i.e., new ≠ old), but we fail to reject it, believing that the groups are really the same. We are incorrect because we have concluded there is no difference when indeed there is a difference.

   ■ Incorrect: Null hypothesis is false, but the researcher fails to reject it and concludes that the groups are not significantly different.

If the researcher incorrectly rejects a null hypothesis (i.e., possibility 3), the researcher has made a **Type I error.** If the researcher incorrectly fails to reject a null hypothesis (i.e., possibility 4), the researcher has made a **Type II error.**

The probability level selected by the researcher determines the probability of committing a Type I error—that is, of rejecting a null hypothesis that is really true (i.e., thinking you've found an effect when you haven't). Thus, if you select $\alpha = .05$, you have a 5% probability of making a Type I error, whereas if you select $\alpha = .01$, you have only a 1% probability of committing a Type I error.

So why not set our probability level at $\alpha = .000000001$ and hardly ever be wrong? If you select α to be very, very small, you definitely decrease your chances of committing a Type I error; you will hardly ever reject a true null hypothesis. But as you decrease the probability of committing a Type I error, you increase the probability of committing a Type II error—that is, of not rejecting a null hypothesis when you should.

Because the choice of a probability level, α, is made before execution of the study, researchers need to consider the relative seriousness of committing a Type I versus a Type II error and select α accordingly. We must compare the consequences of making each wrong decision. For example, perhaps the new method of reading at Pinecrest Elementary is much more expensive to implement than the old, traditional method of reading: If we adopt it, we will have to spend a great deal of money on materials, in-service training, and new testing. Given the expense of the new program, we can set our level of significance (α) to .01; we want to reduce the likelihood of Type I error. In other words, we want to be confident (at $\alpha = .01$) that, if we recommend the new program, it works better than the old one—that any difference we may find is not simply random error. We may be more willing to risk a Type II error (i.e., concluding the new method isn't better, although it really is) because it is such an expensive program to implement and we suspect we may find a better but cheaper program.

We're willing to take that risk because, in this example, a Type I error is the more serious error for Pinecrest Elementary. If we conclude that the new program really works, but it's not really any better than the old program (i.e., a Type I error), the superintendent is going to be very upset if a big investment is made based on our decision and the students show no difference in achievement at the end of the year. On the other hand, if we conclude that the new program does not really make a difference, but it really is better (i.e., a Type II error), it's likely that nothing adverse will happen. In fact, the superintendent would not know that the new method is better because, of course, we never implemented it. We just hope the superintendent does not find any research suggesting that the new program was effective elsewhere. Given the choice, then, we would rather commit a Type II error (i.e., rejecting a successful program) than a Type I error (i.e., going to the expense of implementing an unsuccessful program).

The choice of which type of error is worth risking may not always be so clear, however. For example, if Pinecrest Elementary is not meeting its Adequate Yearly Progress (AYP) goals for reading under the Every Student Succeeds Act (ESSA), the stakes are high. We need to find a reading program better than the old method or we risk losing funding and potentially closing the school. Under these circumstances, we may be more likely to risk committing a Type I error—we have little to lose if we select a program that is no better than the program we are now using, and a lot to gain if the program is in fact better. Therefore, we can use a level of significance that is less stringent; we can accept the greater risk that a difference of the size we find could occur by chance in 5 out of 100 studies ($\alpha = .05$) or 10 out of 100 ($\alpha = .10$).

The decision about level of significance for a particular study is based on both risk and practical significance. If the consequences of committing a Type I error are not severe or life threatening, we usually accept a lower level of significance (e.g., $\alpha = .05$ rather than $\alpha = .01$). A study conducted by one of the authors can help explain these choices further. A social service agency needed to make a choice about whether to use a day-treatment or residential-treatment program for adolescent drug abusers. A study of the two programs found the residential program was significantly better at the predetermined alpha of .10. Because the risk of committing a Type I error (i.e., claiming the residential program was better when it wasn't) was not high, $\alpha = .10$ was an acceptable level of risk. Unfortunately, the residential-treatment program, as you would imagine, was quite expensive. Even though the residential program was significantly different than the day-treatment program, the researchers recommended using the day-treatment program. This example clearly shows the difference between statistical and practical significance. The higher cost of the residential program did not justify the statistical advantage over the day-treatment program. Furthermore, the researchers subsequently found that, had they set the level of significance at a higher level ($\alpha = .01$), the difference in programs would not have been statistically significant. The researchers concluded, as did the program administrators, that the cheaper program was the better choice.

Both as researchers and as consumers, we make choices every day based on acceptable levels of risk. For example, we may choose to take vitamins each morning based on studies of their effectiveness that show only marginally significant results. But because the risk of being wrong is not severe (i.e., Type I error—so what if they might not really work? As long as they don't hurt, it's worth a try), we go ahead and take the vitamins. On the other hand, if we decided to jump out of an airplane, we would want to use a parachute that has a very high probability of working correctly and would want to know how this type of parachute performed in repeated trials. And we would want a highly stringent probability level, such as $\alpha = .000001$ or beyond. The risk of being wrong is fatal. When you are unsure what level of risk is acceptable, selecting $\alpha = .05$ is a standard practice that provides an acceptable balance between

Type I and Type II error. Otherwise, consider the risk: Are you jumping out of an airplane or are you trying to decide if you should take vitamin C? Fortunately, most choices in the fields of education and human services are not life or death.

Degrees of Freedom

After determining whether the significance test will be two-tailed or one-tailed and selecting a probability cutoff (i.e., alpha), we then select an appropriate statistical test and conduct the analysis. When computing the statistics by hand, we check to see if we have significant results by consulting the appropriate table at the intersection of the probability level and *degrees of freedom (df)* used to evaluate significance. When the analysis is conducted on the computer, the output contains the exact level of significance (i.e., the exact probability that the results are due to chance), and the degrees of freedom.

An example may help illustrate the concept of degrees of freedom, defined as the number of observations free to vary around a parameter. Suppose we ask you to name any five numbers. You agree and say, "One, two, three, four, five." In this case, N is equal to 5; you had five choices and you could select any number for each choice. In other words, each number was "free to vary;" it could have been any number you wanted. Thus, you had five degrees of freedom for your selections ($df = n$). Now suppose we tell you to name five numbers, you begin with, "One, two, three, four, . . ." and we say: "Wait! The mean of the five numbers you choose must be 4." Now you have no choice for the final number—it must be 10 to achieve the required mean of 4 (i.e., $1 + 2 + 3 + 4 + 10 = 20$, and $20/5 = 4$). That final number is not free to vary; in the language of statistics, you lost one degree of freedom because of the restriction that the mean must be 4. In this situation, you only had four degrees of freedom ($df = n - 1$).

Each test of significance has its own formula for determining degrees of freedom. For example, for the product moment correlation coefficient, Pearson r, the formula is $n - 2$. The number 2 is a constant, requiring that degrees of freedom for r are always determined by subtracting 2 from N, the number of participants. Each of the inferential statistics discussed in the next section also has its own formula for degrees of freedom, but in every case, the value for df is important in determining whether the results are statistically significant.

> MyLab Education **Self-Check 19.1**
>
> MyLab Education **Application Exercise 19.1:** Testing a Hypothesis

SELECTING AMONG TESTS OF SIGNIFICANCE

Many different statistical tests of significance can be applied in research studies. Factors such as the scale of measurement represented by the data (e.g., nominal, ordinal, etc.), method of participant selection, number of groups being compared, and number of independent variables determine which test of significance should be used in a given study. It is important that the researcher select the appropriate test because an incorrect test can lead to incorrect conclusions. The first decision in selecting an appropriate test of significance is whether a *parametric test* or a *nonparametric test* must be selected. Parametric tests are usually more powerful and generally preferable when practical. "More powerful" in this case means that, based on the results, the researcher is more likely to reject a null hypothesis that is false; in other words, use of a powerful test makes the researcher more likely to identify a true effect and thus less likely to commit a Type II error.

A parametric test, however, requires certain assumptions to be met for it to be valid. For example, the measured variable must be normally distributed in the population (or at least that the shape of the distribution is known). Many variables studied in education are normally distributed, so this assumption is often met. A second major assumption is that the data represent an interval or ratio scale of measurement, although in some cases, ordinal data, such as from a Likert-type scale, may be included. Because many measures used in education represent or are assumed to represent interval data, this assumption is usually met. In fact, this is one major advantage of using an interval scale—it permits the use of a parametric test. A third assumption is that the selection of participants is independent. In other words, the selection of one subject in no way affects selection of any other subject. Recall from Chapter 6 that, with random sampling, every member of the population has an equal and independent chance to be selected for the sample. Thus, if randomization is used in participant selection, the assumption of independence is met. Another assumption is that the variances of the comparison groups are equal (or at least that the ratio of the variances is known). Remember that the variance of a group of scores is the square of the standard deviation (see Chapter 18 for discussion of variance and standard deviation).

With the exception of independence, a small violation of one or more of these assumptions usually does not greatly affect the results of tests for significance. Because parametric statistics seem to be relatively hardy, doing their job even with moderate assumption violation, they are usually selected for analysis of research data. However, if one or more assumptions are violated to a large degree—for example, if the distribution is extremely skewed—parametric statistics should not be used. In such cases, a nonparametric test, which makes no assumptions about the shape of the distribution, should be used. Nonparametric tests are appropriate when the data represent an ordinal or nominal scale, when a parametric assumption has been greatly violated, or when the nature of the distribution is not known.

Nonparametric tests are not as powerful as parametric tests. In other words, it is more difficult with a nonparametric test to reject a null hypothesis at a given level of significance; usually, a larger sample size is needed to reach the same level of significance as in a parametric test. Additionally, many hypotheses cannot be tested with nonparametric tests. Nevertheless, we often have no choice but to use nonparametric statistics when we are dealing with societal variables that are not conveniently measured on an interval scale, such as religion, race, or ethnicity.

In the following sections, we examine both parametric and nonparametric statistics. Although we cannot discuss every statistical test available to the researcher, we describe several statistics commonly used in educational research.

The *t* Test

The ***t* test** is used to determine whether two groups of scores are significantly different at a selected probability level. A one-sample *t* test considers whether a sample mean is significantly different from a hypothesized value or population estimate. A two-sample *t* test is used to determine if two levels/values for one variable differ from each other statistically. For example, a two-sample *t* test can be used to compare the reading scores for males and females at Pinecrest Elementary School.

The basic strategy of the *t* test is to compare the *actual* difference between the means of the groups $(\overline{X}_1 - \overline{X}_2)$ with the difference *expected* by chance. For our data from Pinecrest Elementary School, we can use a *t* test to determine if the difference between the reading scores of the boys and the girls is statistically significant, that is, the likelihood that any difference we find occurred by chance. It involves forming the ratio of the scores for the boys and the girls, as shown in the formula below:

$$t = \frac{\overline{X}_1 - \overline{X}_2}{\sqrt{\left(\dfrac{SS_1 + SS_2}{n_1 + n_2 - 2}\right)\left(\dfrac{1}{n_1} + \dfrac{1}{n_2}\right)}}$$

In the formula, the numerator is the difference between the sample means $\overline{X}_1$ and $\overline{X}_2$, and the denominator is the chance difference that would be expected if the null hypothesis were true (i.e., no difference between the boys' and the girls' scores). In other words, the denominator is the standard error of the difference between the means—a function of both sample size and group variance. Smaller sample sizes and greater variation within groups are associated with greater random differences between groups. Even if the null hypothesis were true, we do not expect two sample means to be identical; there will always be some chance variation. The *t* test determines the likelihood that a difference of this size would be expected solely by chance.

If we were making the *t* test calculation by hand, we would divide the numerator by the denominator and then determine whether the resulting *t* value reflects a statistically significant difference between the groups by comparing the *t* we computed to a table of *t* values (you can easily find a table of *t* values using an Internet search). If the *t* value is equal to or greater than the table value for the required *df* (i.e., reflecting sample size) and alpha (i.e., reflecting significance level), then we can reject the null hypothesis: Our results suggest a significant difference between the groups. If the *t* value we compute is less than the table value, we fail to reject the null hypothesis: Any difference we have found is likely due to sampling error (i.e., chance).

Of course, typically, we would conduct the t test with the computer, which produces output showing the t value, its level of significance, and the degrees of freedom.

In determining significance, the t test is adjusted for the fact that the distribution of scores for small samples becomes increasingly different from the normal distribution as sample sizes become increasingly smaller. For example, distributions for smaller samples tend to be higher at the mean and at the two ends of the distribution. As a result, the t values required to reject a null hypothesis are higher for small samples. As the size of the samples becomes larger, the score distribution approaches normality. Keep in mind that, as the number of participants increases, degrees of freedom also increase, and the t value (or test statistic) needed to reject the null hypothesis becomes smaller. Furthermore, as alpha becomes smaller (e.g., .01 vs .05), a larger t value is required to reject the null hypothesis.

The t Test for Independent Samples

The t **test for independent samples** is a parametric test of significance used to determine whether, at a selected probability level, a significant difference exists between the means of two independent samples. *Independent samples* are randomly formed without any type of matching—the members of one sample are not related to members of the other sample in any systematic way other than that they are selected from the same population. If two groups are randomly formed, the expectation is that, at the beginning of a study, they are essentially the same with respect to performance on the dependent variable. Therefore, if they are also essentially the same at the end of the study (i.e., their means are close), the null hypothesis is probably true. On the other hand, if their means are not close at the end of the study, the null hypothesis is probably false and should be rejected. The key word is *essentially*. We do not expect the means to be identical at the end of the study—they are bound to be somewhat different. The question of interest, of course, is whether they are *significantly* different.

Calculating the t Test for Independent Samples Using SPSS

As we have discussed, the t test for independent samples is used when we want to compare the scores for two groups. For example, at Pinecrest Elementary School, we would want to know if the boys' reading scores are statistically different from the girls' scores. Even though we know from our previous example that the mean for the girls on the fall reading score ($\overline{X} = 52.533$) was higher than that for the boys ($\overline{X} = 41.054$), we do not know how likely it is that this difference would occur by chance or if it is a meaningful difference statistically. The t test helps us decide whether the difference between the boys' and the girls' scores is statistically significant, that is, not likely to have occurred by chance.

We can use Excel, SPSS (Statistical Package for the Social Sciences), R, or a variety of other software applications to conduct a t test. Although each program has advantages and disadvantages, dedicated statistical packages, such as SPSS and R, are set up in terms of dependent and independent variables, and as our analyses become more complex and use larger numbers of variables and cases, statistical packages offer more advantages. Although the setup procedures for analyses on different statistical software packages are slightly different, they are all somewhat similar; that is, we select the variables to be compared and the statistical test to run. To help you understand the variable selection process required in statistical tests, we present a step-by-step example of the t test procedure using SPSS. Explanations for other procedures we use in this chapter are available in Appendix A.

To perform the t test in SPSS, first click on Analyze and choose Compare Means from the pull-down menu. A submenu appears, as shown in Figure 19.4. From this submenu, choose Independent-Samples T Test. . . . In summary, the options are as follows:

Analyze
Compare Means
Independent Samples T Test

Selecting these options produces the Independent-Samples T Test window, shown in Figure 19.5.

In our example, we are comparing the fall reading test scores (ReadF) of the boys in Ms. Alvarez's third-grade class to the girls' scores. We need to move the dependent (i.e., outcome) variable, fall reading score (ReadF), into the Test Variable(s) section. Next, we need to specify that we would like to compare the group of boys and girls; we need to select the Grouping Variable, which is gender. We define the groups by selecting the Define Groups button just underneath Grouping Variable, as shown

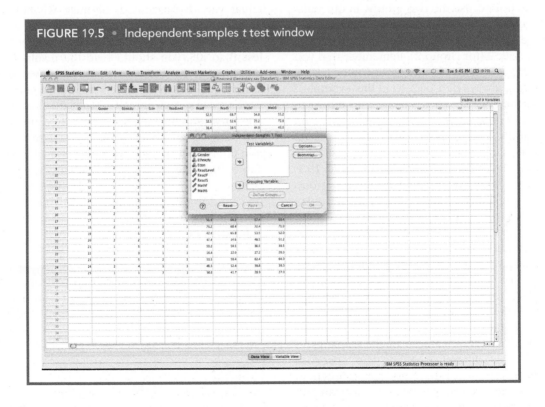

FIGURE 19.4 • SPSS menu options for independent-samples *t* test

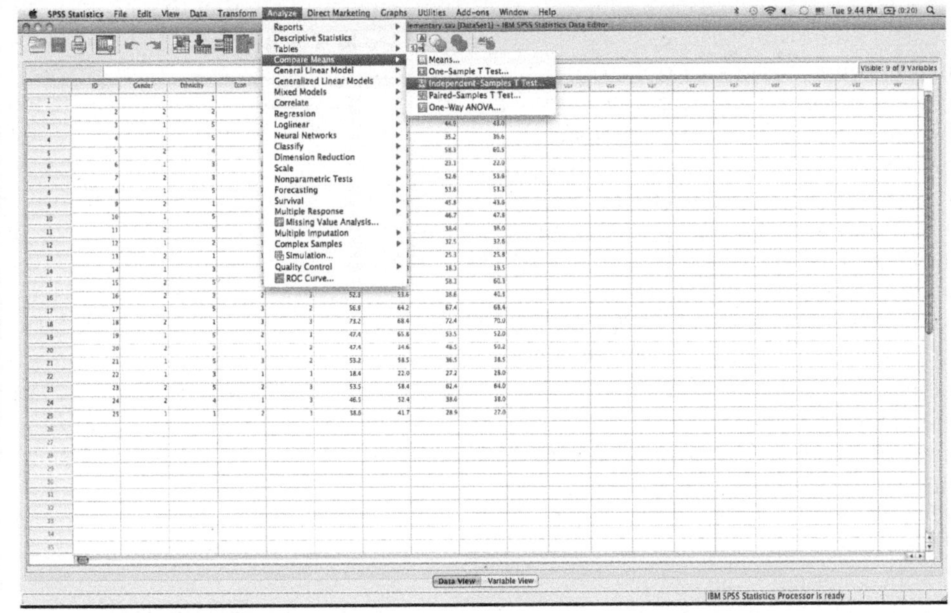

FIGURE 19.5 • Independent-samples *t* test window

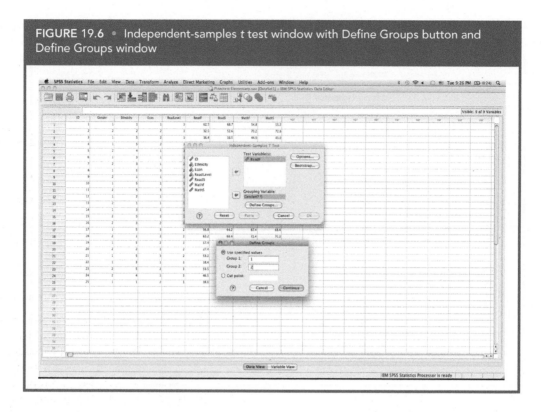

FIGURE 19.6 • Independent-samples *t* test window with Define Groups button and Define Groups window

in Figure 19.6. Because the two groups in our dataset are specified as Group 1 for boys and Group 2 for girls, we simply type the number 1 (for Group 1) and the number 2 (for Group 2). Remember that you need to specify the codes for the groups to be tested, which may not always be 1 or 2, as in this example.

To run the analysis, click Continue to return to the Independent-Samples T Test window. Click on the OK button. The analysis runs, and an output window opens, showing two tables. The first table is the Group Statistics table, shown in Table 19.1. This table shows you the sample size for each group (represented in the N column) as well as the mean test score for each group, the standard deviation, and the standard error of the mean. Table 19.2 shows the results of the independent-samples *t* test, including additional statistics to assist with the interpretation. The first set of statistics comes under the heading Levene's Test for Equality of Variances. This test determines if the variances of the two groups in the analysis are equal. If they are not, then SPSS makes an adjustment to the remainder of the statistics to account for this difference. When the observed probability value of the Levene's test (shown in the Sig. column) is greater than .05, you should read the results on the top row of *t* test statistic,

equal variance assumed, because we have found no significant difference in the variances. When the observed probability value for the Levene's test is less than .05, you should read the results from the bottom row of *t* test statistics, equal variance not assumed, because the difference between the group variances is significant. Of course, the results of Levene's test should be considered in context. If the two samples of concern have equal sample sizes, non-equivalent results would be a nonissue. In Table 19.2, the observed probability value for the Levene's test is greater than .05 (i.e., Sig. = .560, no significant difference found), so you should read from the top row of the *t* test statistic, equal variances assumed.

TABLE 19.1 • Independent-samples output

Group Statistics				
Gender	N	Mean	Std. Deviation	Std. Error Mean
ReadF 1	13	41.054	14.0581	3.8990
2	12	52.533	13.2480	3.8244

TABLE 19.2 • Independent-samples *t* test statistics									
						Independent Samples Test			
		Levene's Test for Equality of Variances				*t* test for Equality of Means			
									95% Confidence Interval of the Difference
		F	Sig.	*t*	*df*	Sig. (2-Tailed)	Mean Difference	Std. Error Difference	Lower	Upper
ReadF	Equal variances assumed	.350	.560	−2.097	23	.047	−11.4795	5.4750	−22.8055	−.1535
	Equal variances not assumed			−2.102	22.987	.047	−11.4795	5.4615	−22.7778	−.1811

Having selected the appropriate row to read, we can find the observed *t* statistic value and its corresponding probability value. In Table 19.2, the observed *t* statistic we use for equal variances is −2.097 with its observed level of significance (Sig.) = .047. The value for *t* is negative because SPSS subtracts the second number from the first, but the sign (i.e., negative or positive) has no effect on how we interpret the level of significance. The significance level of this *t* test ($p = .047$) indicates that a difference between the means this large (i.e., −11.4795) would happen by chance only 4.7 times out of 100 in repeated studies. Because .047 is smaller than the standard alpha level ($p = .05$) that we had preselected for our level of significance, this example shows a statistically significant difference between the fall reading scores of the boys and those of the girls. We can thus have confidence as we inform our colleagues at Pinecrest Elementary that the boys are entering third grade with lower reading achievement than the girls; we may suggest that the school staff accommodate for this difference using the current reading curriculum as the school year proceeds, or we may recommend new programs to benefit the boys in younger grades.

Note that, although we've used SPSS to present our example, we could use other programs and achieve the same result. For example, in Excel, we would select the appropriate *t* test in the Data Analysis menu and then define our variable range (e.g., boys' fall reading scores compared to the girls' scores) to conduct the test. The value for *t* and the probability that the results are due to chance will be the same as those generated by SPSS.

The t Test for Nonindependent Samples

The *t* test for nonindependent samples is used to compare groups that are formed by some type of matching. The nonindependent procedure is also used to compare a single group's performance on a pretest and posttest or on two different treatments. For example, at Pinecrest Elementary School, we want to know if students' reading scores improved from the beginning of the year to the end of the year. Because we have fall and spring test scores for each student, this sample has nonindependent scores. When scores are nonindependent, they are systematically related: Because at Pinecrest the reading scores are from the same students at two different times, they are expected to correlate positively with each other—students with high scores in the fall will likely have high scores in the spring, and students with low scores in the fall will likely have low scores in the spring. When the scores are nonindependent, a special *t* test for nonindependent samples is needed. The error term of the *t* test tends to be smaller than for independent samples, and the probability that the null hypothesis will be rejected is higher.

Calculating the t Test for Nonindependent Samples Using SPSS

Even though we are using the same student data for Pinecrest Elementary School in our examples, the different questions we ask allow equally different analyses. To answer our question about whether the students' readings scores improved over the school year, we conduct a *t* test of nonindependent samples, comparing fall reading scores to spring reading scores. Because we are also interested to know if the students' math scores also improved, we conduct a second comparison including MathF (i.e., fall scores) and MathS (i.e., spring scores). It is easy to conduct several analyses of nonindependent samples with SPSS—we just designate the additional variables in the *t* test.

To conduct these analyses, select Analyze in the SPSS Data Editor window. To find the nonindependent *t* test, scroll down the Analyze menu and select the Compare Means option. From the submenu, choose the option called Paired Samples T Test. This difference in designation may seem a bit confusing. One way to think of it is that we are comparing two sets of scores (i.e., fall and spring) for the same group of students. Therefore, the relation between the sets of scores is dependent on the group of people, our Pinecrest students. We are not, however, matching each student to the scores; rather, we are comparing the group means in the fall to the group means in the spring (i.e., a pair of data points for each participant).

In summary, the procedures for the SPSS analysis are as follows:

Analyze
Compare Means
Paired-Samples T Test . . .

Because this analysis is somewhat similar to the previous *t* test example, you may refer to the test menu options in Appendix A, Figures A19.1 and A19.2.

The paired samples *t* test requires that you choose the variables to include in the analysis and, as with the test for independent samples, move

them to the right section of the window, labeled Paired Variables. As you select the variables, the Current Selections section at the bottom of the window (Figure B19.2) shows them. Click the arrow button to move them into the Paired Variables section on the right of the screen, and click the OK button to conduct the analysis.

The first section of the output, showing descriptive statistics for each variable, is displayed in Table 19.3. First, the mean for each variable is shown. For ReadF, $\overline{X} = 46.564$; for MathF, $\overline{X} = 45.408$. Similarly, for ReadS, $\overline{X} = 53.964$, and for MathS, $\overline{X} = 45.560$. The next number shown is the number of cases, or the sample size (N). The output shows that 25 people—the number of students in Ms. Alvarez's class—took each of the tests. The third statistic shown is the standard deviation for each set of test scores. *SD* is used to compute the final statistic shown in the table, the standard error of the mean scores. These values are used to compute *t*, shown in the remainder of the output (Table 19.4).

TABLE 19.3 • Dependent samples output

Paired Samples Statistics		Mean	N	Std. Deviation	Std. Error Mean
Pair 1	ReadF	46.564	25	14.6123	2.9225
	ReadS	52.324	25	15.1613	3.0323
Pair 2	MathF	45.408	25	15.3108	3.0622
	MathS	45.560	25	15.3964	3.0793

TABLE 19.4 • Dependent samples *t* test output

		Mean	Std. Deviation	Std. Error Mean	95% Confidence Interval of the Difference		*t*	df	Sig. (2-tailed)
					Lower	Upper			
Pair 1	ReadF–ReadS	−5.7600	7.4184	1.4837	−8.8222	−2,6978	−3.882	24	.001
Pair 2	MathF–MathS	−.1520	1.5286	.3057	−.7830	.4790	−.497	24	.624

Paired Samples Test — Paired Differences

SPSS generates and displays the *t* value, degrees of freedom, and the significance value (i.e., *Sig.* in the output, also referred to as the *p* value) showing the probability that these results could be obtained simply by chance. The first box in the table shows the variables that are being compared. The next four boxes show the difference between the mean scores, the standard deviation, the standard error of the difference between the mean scores, and the 95% confidence interval (i.e., the range of values in which you can be 95% confident that the real difference between mean scores falls). The last three boxes show the *t* value, the degrees of freedom, and the significance value. If the value in the box labeled Sig. (2-tailed) is less than or equal to $\alpha = .05$, then the students' fall reading and math tests (i.e., ReadF and MathF) are significantly different than their spring reading and math tests (i.e., ReadS and MathS).

The finding for reading is good news for the students and Pinecrest Elementary teachers: Students' reading scores in the spring are better than their scores in the fall ($t = -3.882$, $p = .001$). We are able to reject the null hypothesis of no difference in the scores. We don't know *why*, however, the scores are different. For example, if we were testing a new reading program at Pinecrest, our findings would provide support for the new program. Or the improvement in reading scores could be due to Ms. Alvarez's skill as a teacher. The improvement could also be due to parental involvement or other variables we may have not controlled or considered. The *t* test can only tell us *if* the difference between the means is likely due to chance, not why the difference occurs.

What happened to the math scores? Table 19.4 shows that the fall math scores ($\overline{X} = 45.408$) and the spring math scores ($\overline{X} = 45.560$) were not significantly different. Without even conducting the *t* test, we can expect intuitively that this difference is not significant because the scores increased only .1520 between the fall and the spring—not much happened. The test confirms our intuition: $t = -.497$, Sig. $= .624$. In other words, we can expect this finding by chance in more than 62% of other similar studies. The students did not appear to learn very much, and we want to find out why, so we have more work to do. The *t* test cannot tell us why the math scores have not improved, but it has notified us that we have a problem.

One final note on the *t* test: In this example, the *t* value is negative because SPSS automatically subtracts the second mean score in the list from the first. If the students had done better on the fall reading test than the spring reading test (i.e., if the mean scores had been reversed), then the difference in the means and the resulting *t* test statistic would have been positive. We would hope not to have a positive *t* value for Pinecrest because a positive value would suggest that students did worse in the spring than they did in the fall.

Analysis of Gain or Difference Scores

As we noted previously, when comparing the reading and math scores for students between fall and spring, we did not match each student's score. Instead we compared the mean of all students in the fall to that of all students in the spring. Some researchers think, however, that a viable way to analyze data from two groups who are pretested, treated, and then tested again is to: (1) subtract each participant's pretest score from his or her posttest score (resulting in a gain, or difference, score), (2) compute the mean gain or difference for each group, and (3) calculate a *t* value for the difference between the two average mean differences. This approach has two main problems. First, every participant, or student in our example, does not have the same potential to gain. A participant who scores very low on a pretest has a large opportunity to gain, but a participant who scores very high has only a small opportunity to improve (the latter situation, where participants score at or near the high end of the possible range, is referred to as the *ceiling effect*). Who has improved, or gained, more—a participant who goes from 20 to 70 (a gain of 50) or a participant who goes from 85 to 100 (a gain of only 15 but perhaps a perfect score)? Second, gain or difference scores are less reliable than analysis of posttest scores alone.

The appropriate analysis for data from pretest–posttest designs depends on the performance of the two groups on the pretest. For example, if both groups are essentially the same on the pretest and neither group has been previously exposed to the treatment planned for it, then posttest scores are best compared using a *t* test. On the other hand, if there is a difference between the groups on the pretest, the preferred approach is the analysis of covariance. As discussed in Chapter 10, analysis of covariance adjusts posttest scores for initial differences on some variable (in this case, the pretest) related to performance on the dependent variable. To determine whether analysis of covariance is necessary, calculate a *t* test using the two pretest means. If the two pretest means are significantly different, use the analysis of covariance. If they are not, a simple *t* test can be computed on the post-test means.

Analysis of Variance

Analysis of variance (ANOVA) is a parametric test of significance used to determine whether scores from two or more groups are significantly different at a selected probability level. Note that, if only two groups are being compared, the analysis of variance computation will yield identical results to an independent-samples *t* test comparing those two groups.

Simple Analysis of Variance

Simple, or *one-way*, **analysis of variance (ANOVA)** is used when the comparison involves one variable with two or more levels. Because it involves only one variable, it is also known as one-way ANOVA. For our example, we introduce a new dataset composed of freshman college students at Pacific Crest College. Table A19.1 in Appendix A displays the Pacific Crest College dataset, which includes data from 125 students. Although this dataset for Pacific Crest College is still not large, it is sufficient to allow us to accomplish basic ANOVA and multiple regression analyses. We use ANOVA to test whether Pacific Crest College students' college grade point averages (CollGPA) differ for groups of students based on their economic levels (ECON). In other words, economic level is the grouping variable, with three levels (low, medium, and high), and college GPA is the dependent variable.

Three (or more) means are very unlikely to be identical; the key question is whether the differences among the means represent true, significant differences or chance differences due to sampling error. To answer this question, simple ANOVA is used: An **F ratio** is computed. Although it is possible to compute a series of *t* tests, one for each pair of means, to do so raises some statistical problems concerning distortion of the probability of a Type I error, and it is certainly more convenient to perform one simple ANOVA than several *t* tests. For example, to analyze four means, six separate *t* tests would be required ($\overline{X}_1 - \overline{X}_2$, $\overline{X}_1 - \overline{X}_3$, $\overline{X}_1 - \overline{X}_4$, $\overline{X}_2 - \overline{X}_3$, $\overline{X}_2 - \overline{X}_4$, $\overline{X}_3 - \overline{X}_4$). ANOVA is much more efficient and keeps the error rate under control.

The concept underlying ANOVA is that the total variation, or variance, of scores can be divided into two sources—variance between groups and variance within groups. Between-group variance considers, overall, how the individuals in a particular group differ from individuals in the other groups. In our example of the Pacific Crest College students, between-group variance refers to the ways in which students from different economic backgrounds differ from one another. Ultimately, between-group differences are what researchers are usually interested in. The within-group variance considers how students vary from others in the same group. Not every student in the high-economics group has the same GPA, for example. These differences are known as the within-group variance, or error variance.

To ensure that apparent group differences aren't just due to these differences among people in general (i.e., just error), ANOVA involves a ratio, known as *F*, with group differences as the numerator (i.e., variance between groups) and error as the denominator (i.e., variance within groups). If the variance *between* groups is much greater than the variance *within* groups, greater than would be expected by chance, the ratio will be large, and a significant effect will be apparent. On the other hand, if the variance between groups and the variance within groups do not differ by more than would be expected by chance, the resulting *F* ratio is small; the groups are not significantly different.

To summarize, the greater the difference in variance, the larger the *F* ratio; larger *F*'s are more likely to reflect significant differences among groups. However, a significant finding tells the researcher only that the groups are not all the same. To identify how the groups differ (i.e., which means are different from one another), additional statistics, described next, are needed.

Multiple Comparisons

In essence, multiple comparisons involve calculation of a special form of the *t* test. This special *t* adjusts for the fact that many tests are being executed. Each time we conduct a significance test, we accept a particular probability level, α. For example, we agree that if the results we find would occur by chance only five times in every 100 samples, we will conclude that our results are meaningful and not simply due to chance. However, if we conduct two tests of significance on the same dataset, the chance of finding a significant difference increases (i.e., we now have two tests that could show a significant difference), but the chance of committing a Type I error increases as well (i.e., we now have two chances to commit this error, one for each test). When multiple comparisons are involved, special statistics are needed to keep the error low.

In general, when conducting a study that involves more than two groups, researchers plan a set of comparisons between specific groups before collecting the data, based on the research hypotheses. Such comparisons are called *a priori* (i.e., "before the fact") or planned comparisons. For example, in our study of Pacific Crest College, we may predict that the GPAs of high-income students will differ from those of low-income students and plan to conduct that comparison. Often, however, it is not possible to state a priori predictions. In these cases, we can use *a posteriori*, or post hoc (i.e., "after the fact"), comparisons. In either case, multiple comparisons should not be a fishing expedition in which researchers look for any possible difference; they should be motivated by hypotheses.

Calculating ANOVA with Post Hoc Multiple Comparison Tests Using SPSS

In this example, we use SPSS to run an ANOVA to determine whether and how the college GPAs differ for students in the high, middle, and low economic groups. We selected the Scheffé test as the multiple-comparison procedure because it is somewhat conservative in its analysis, requiring a large difference between means to show significance. A number of other multiple-comparison techniques are also available to the researcher and can be selected in the SPSS analysis; the discussion of each is beyond the scope of this chapter.

Because ANOVA is an analytical method for comparing means, we begin the SPSS procedure as we have previously by selecting:

Analyze
Compare Means
One-Way ANOVA

For your reference, the menu options for ANOVA are shown in Appendix A, Figure A19.3.

TABLE 19.5 • Overall ANOVA solution

ANOVA

CollGPA

	Sum of Squares	df	Mean Square	F	Sig.
Between Groups	12.445	2	6.223	37.060	.000
Within Groups	20.484	122	.168		
Total	32.929	124			

The second step is to select the Post Hoc . . . button in the One-Way ANOVA window (shown in Figure A19.4). For this analysis, use the Scheffé multiple-comparison technique by checking the appropriate box (displayed in Figure A19.5). Click the *Continue* button to conduct the analysis.

SPSS produces a series of tables as output. The first table, shown in Table 19.5, gives the ratio of between-group variance to within-group variance, $F = 37.060$, and the associated probability value, $p = .000$. From this ANOVA, we can conclude that college GPA (CollGPA) differs for students at different economic levels (Econ). In the language of statistics, we can reject the null hypothesis of no difference between the students' GPAs; that is, students' GPAs appear to be dependent on their economic level. Notice we say "appear;" we never have definitive proof because inferential statistics simply provide an evaluation of probability. We can be quite confident of our conclusion, however, because we have a relatively high F statistic (37.060), which would occur by chance fewer than once in 1,000 samples (i.e., $p = .000$; remember that SPSS shows only three decimal places).

The Scheffé test for our comparisons is displayed in Table 19.6. This table shows the mean test score of each group compared with that for each other group. For example, the first row shows a comparison between the low and the middle economic groups, and the second row shows a comparison between the low and the high economic groups. The difference between the mean scores is shown, along with the standard error of the difference and a probability value for the test.

From this test, we can see that the GPAs of the students in the low-economic group do not differ from those of students in the middle-economic group (i.e., row 1 in the table, Sig. = .988). However, the GPAs of the students in the low-economic

TABLE 19.6 • SPSS summary table for Scheffé multiple-comparison test

					95% Confidence Interval	
		Multiple Comparisons				
Dependent Variable: CollGPA Scheffe						
(I) Econ	(J) Econ	Mean Difference (I − J)	Std. Error	Sig.	Lower Bound	Upper Bound
1	2	−.01385	.08732	.988	−.2302	.2025
	3	−.70290(*)	.08995	.000	−.9258	−.4800
2	1	.01385	.08732	.988	−.2025	.2302
	3	−.68906*	.09414	.000	−.9223	−.4558
3	1	.70290*	.08995	.000	.4800	.9258
	2	.68906*	.09414	.000	.4558	.9223

* The mean difference is significant at the .05 level.

group are significantly different from those of students in the high-economic group (i.e., row 2 in the table; Sig. = .000). The positive and negative signs for the mean differences allow us to determine further that the students in the highest economic level had the highest mean on the GPA and students at the lowest economic level had the lowest mean.

In this example, the multiple-comparison procedure allows us to identify that the overall difference shown by the ANOVA is due to the students in the higher economic level having higher GPAs than students at the middle and lower economic levels. Our findings match previously published research indicating that more economically advantaged students, as a group, are likely to have higher GPAs in college than students with fewer economic resources.

Multifactor Analysis of Variance

If a research study uses a factorial design to investigate two or more independent variables and the interactions between them, the appropriate statistical analysis is a factorial, or multifactor, analysis of variance. This analysis yields a separate F ratio for each independent variable and one for each interaction. When two independent variables are analyzed, the ANOVA is considered a two-way; when three independent variables are analyzed, it is considered a three-way ANOVA; and so forth. In some

analyses, two dependent variables are analyzed in a multivariate analysis of variance (MANOVA). For example, suppose that we want to consider whether gender and economic level both affect students' college achievement. MANOVA would allow us to consider both independent variables (i.e., economic level, gender) and multiple dependent variables (e.g., college GPA as well as other test scores we may have from math or language classes). As you can imagine, however, we need a large dataset to run increasingly complex analyses with multiple independent and dependent variables. For example, of the 125 students at Pacific Crest College, there are no women in the highest economic group who are at the lowest level of reading. Complex statistical analyses are not warranted without a larger sample size that has meaningful variation among the variables.

Although a factorial ANOVA is a more complex procedure to conduct and interpret than a one-way ANOVA, the basic process is similar. SPSS or other statistical packages provide the appropriate statistical tests; we simply specify the independent variables and dependent variable for the analysis.

Analysis of Covariance

Analysis of covariance (ANCOVA) is a form of ANOVA that accounts for the different ways in which the independent variables are measured, taking into account the design of the study. When a study has two or more dependent variables, multivariate analysis of covariance (MANCOVA) is an appropriate test. ANCOVA is used in two major ways: as a technique for controlling extraneous variables and as a means of increasing the power of a statistical test.

For controlling variables, use of ANCOVA is basically equivalent to matching groups on the variable or variables to be controlled. ANCOVA adjusts posttest scores for initial differences on a variable; in other words, groups are equalized with respect to the control variable and then compared. ANCOVA is thus similar to handicapping in bowling or golf. In an attempt to equalize teams, high scorers are given little or no handicap, and low scorers are given big handicaps. Any variable that is correlated with the dependent variable can be controlled for using covariance. Examples of variables commonly controlled using ANCOVA are pretest performance, IQ, readiness, and aptitude. By analyzing covariance, we are attempting to reduce variation in posttest scores that is attributable to another variable. Ideally, we would like all posttest variance to be attributable to the treatment conditions.

ANCOVA is used both in causal–comparative studies in which already formed but not necessarily equal groups are involved, and in experimental studies in which either existing groups or randomly formed groups are involved. Unfortunately, the situation for which ANCOVA is least appropriate is the situation for which it is used most often. Use of ANCOVA assumes that participants have been randomly assigned to treatment groups. Thus, it is best used in true experimental designs. If existing or intact groups are not randomly selected but are assigned to treatment groups randomly, ANCOVA may still be used, but results must be interpreted with caution. If ANCOVA is used with existing groups and nonmanipulated independent variables, as in causal–comparative studies, the results are likely to be misleading at best, unless the covariate is measured with very high reliability. Other assumptions associated with the use of ANCOVA are not as serious if participants have been randomly assigned to treatment groups.

A second function of ANCOVA is that it increases the power of a statistical test by reducing within-group (error) variance. **Power** refers to the ability of a significance test to identify a true research finding (i.e., there's really a difference,

and the statistical test shows a significant difference), allowing the experimenter to reject a null hypothesis that is false. In the language of statistics, increasing power reduces the likelihood that the experimenter will commit a Type II error. Because ANCOVA can reduce random sampling error by statistically equating different groups, it increases the power of the significance test. The power-increasing function of ANCOVA is directly related to the degree of randomization involved in formation of the groups. Although increasing sample size also increases power, we are often limited to samples of a given size for financial and practical reasons (e.g., Ms. Alvarez's class at Pinecrest Elementary includes only 25 students); ANCOVA thus is often the only way to increase power for a particular study.

Of course, SPSS, R, and many other statistical software packages provide the procedures for conducting ANCOVA and MANCOVA. The procedures are somewhat similar in that we designate the dependent and independent variables for analysis and the program produces tables of results. However, given the assumptions underlying the use of these complex statistics, researchers must be mindful of when and how these analyses should be employed. We cannot stress enough that analyses and their subsequent meanings need to be formulated and interpreted in relation to the research design and hypotheses you have formulated, not based exclusively on what appears on the computer screen. For example, the results of ANCOVA and MANCOVA are least likely to be valid when groups have not been randomly selected and assigned, yet in educational research, we often are faced with this situation—can you imagine trying to seek permission by assuring parents that if their child is randomly assigned to the less successful method, we could always have the student repeat the same grade again next year with the more successful method? Often, reality clashes with our knowledge of the most appropriate research and statistics methods.

Multiple Regression

The more independent variables we have measured or observed, the more likely we are to explain the outcomes of the dependent variables. Multivariate statistical analyses tell us how much of the variance found in the outcome variable is attributed to the independent variables. Whereas ANOVA is the appropriate analysis when the independent variables are categorical, multiple regression is used with ratio or interval variables. Multiple regression combines variables that are known individually to predict (i.e., correlate with) the criterion into a prediction equation known as a *multiple regression equation*. Multiple regression is an extremely valuable procedure for analyzing the results of a variety of experimental, causal–comparative, and correlational studies because it determines not only whether variables are related but also the degree to which they are related. Understanding how variables are related is beneficial both for researchers and for groups needing to make data-based decisions.

Hierarchical analysis is often used for regression because it allows us to enter predictor variables into the regression equation, or omit them, step by step (i.e., one variable at a time). We can see which of the predictor variables are making the most significant contribution to the criterion variable, and we can remove variables from our predictive model if they are not making a significant contribution.

Multiple regression is also the basis for **path analysis** that begins with a predictive model (see Figure 19.7). Path analysis identifies the degree to which predictor variables interact with each other and contribute to the variance of the dependent variables. Basically, path analysis involves multiple regressions between and among all the variables in the model and then specifies the direct and indirect effects of the predictor variables onto the criterion variable. Although somewhat more complex to calculate than a simple multiple regression, path analysis provides an excellent picture of the causal relations among all the variables in a predictive model.

As an example of multiple regression, we use the Pacific Crest College dataset (see Appendix A, Table A.19.1) that we used previously with ANOVA. A distinct advantage of multiple regression is that we must create a predictive model that posits in advance which variables predict the criterion variable or variables, as illustrated in Figure 19.7. In our example, we consider the relationship between high school math score (Math), high school language score (Lang), and high school GPA (HSGPA) and Pacific Crest College students' college GPA. We consider only the direct effects of each variable in the model on the single criterion variable.

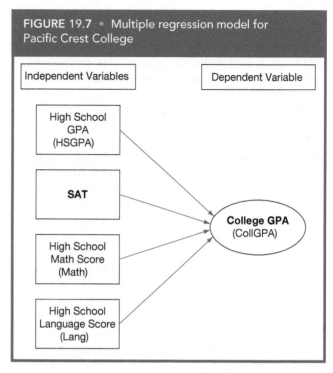

FIGURE 19.7 • Multiple regression model for Pacific Crest College

At Pacific Crest College, several groups are interested in determining the variables that best predict a student's college GPA. The admissions office at Pacific Crest College, for example, wants to make correct decisions by admitting students who will most likely be successful. High school counselors who recommend the college also would like to know what they can do at the high school level to increase a student's chance for success in college—can any of the variables that predict success be controlled (i.e., are any variables *malleable*)? In fact, two such variables may be influenced by the high school counselors, math and language scores. If our multiple regression shows that higher math or language scores are associated with a higher college GPA, we may recommend to the high school counselors that they encourage students to improve their math and language knowledge. If reading and math skills are predictors of college success, then it behooves students to improve these skills while they are still in high school.

Our basic question for the multiple regression analysis is: What are the best predictors of college GPA? If we had a large number of variables from which to choose, we would select the variables that have the greatest likelihood of predicting success, based on previous research. The results of multiple regression would give us the answer to our question and would also tell us the relative contribution of each predictor variable on the criterion variable. For example, we may find that high school GPA, language score, and SAT scores are the best predictors of college GPA, with math score as the variable contributing the least. We could then run another multiple regression excluding math score, or we could add other variables to our multiple regression equation. At this point we have a choice of procedures for the multiple regression. We can enter variables one at a time, or we can enter them all at once, as shown in the following example. The outcomes would be similar; we just have several choices of how we build and interpret them.

Calculating Multiple Regression Using SPSS

Statistical software packages such as SPSS provide various choices for conducting multiple regression, and some are quite complex. Because our goal in this chapter is to give you a conceptual understanding of inferential statistics, we provide a simplified analysis of the model illustrated in Figure 19.7. Other options for accomplishing our analysis include a complete step-wise regression where we enter independent variables one at a time to consider their cumulative effects or we could conduct a path analysis where we would consider all the multiple effects between the predictor variables and criterion variable. For the purposes of our example, we enter all the predictor variables together to consider their cumulative effect—the basic multiple regression procedure called *Enter*.

As with all statistical analyses, we specify our variables and follow the SPSS options as follows (refer to Appendix A Figure A19.6 and Figure A19.7 for the Linear Regression window):

Analyze
Regression
Linear

Once the Linear Regression window is open, we select the criterion (labeled by SPSS as dependent) variable (CollGPA) from the list of variables in the box on the left. Next, we select the four predictor (labeled by SPSS as independent) variables (HSGPA, SAT, Math, Lang) by highlighting each variable and clicking on the arrow to move the variables into the appropriate box. Underneath the independent variables box, we select a multiple regression

procedure; we have selected Enter for this analysis. Also notice the box below the independent variable is labeled Selection Variable. Although multiple regression uses ratio or interval variables, SPSS will run separate analyses using a nominal variable if it is included in the Selection Variable box. This option allows us to compare multiple regression analyses by gender or economic level, for example, both of which are included in our Pacific Crest College dataset and included in the variables window on the left in Figure A19.7. If we wanted to compare multiple regression outcomes of the males and females on college GPA, we would select gender as the selection variable and then, with the Rule button, select 1 for males as our first analysis. For the next analysis, we would then simply select 2 to conduct the multiple regression test for the females. Multiple regression also allows the user to transform a nominal variable into an interval variable, known as a **dummy variable.** For example, a nominal variable, such as gender, can be coded as 0 and 1 and entered into the multiple regression as if it were an interval variable. The interpretation of dummy variables indicates order of the variable in the multiple regression equation and has meaning only for purposes of the statistical calculation.

The multiple regression summary output of our example for predicting college GPA is shown in Table 19.7. The complete model yields an R value of .893, which is a calculation by SPSS from the multiple regression equation. This R value is quite helpful because, when it is squared ($R^2 = .798$), it provides the percentage of variance in the criterion variable explained by the predictor variables—the four predictor variables explain 79.8% of the variance in college GPA. A simple way to explain this finding is that, first, we know there are many reasons that some students have higher GPAs or lower GPAs than others (i.e., there is variance), and second, we've identified some of the reasons—not

TABLE 19.7 · Multiple regression output summary

Model Summary				
Model	R	R Square	Adjusted R Square	Std. Error of the Estimate
1	.893[a]	.798	.791	.23545

[a] Predictors: (Constant), LANG, SAT, HSGPA, MATH

all the reasons (i.e., R^2 is not 1.00), but our predictive model is quite good because our four predictor variables explain or account for about 80% of the variance in college GPA. If we can find other variables to explain the remaining 20% of the variance, we can predict college GPA with an even higher amount of certainty. Remember, of course, there is always a risk of being wrong or predicting incorrectly—we never have certainty.

Now that we know all four independent variables provide an effective predictive model, our next step is to understand which variables are the best predictors. Table 19.8 shows analysis of the variance from the SPSS Regression procedure. The SPSS output first lists the F ratio ($F = 118.494$) and the level of significance of the whole model we are testing; in this case, the probability of this finding occurring by chance is less than 1 in 1,000 (i.e., although the output notes Sig. = .000, remember that there is always a probability, very small in this example, that this finding could occur by chance). What is especially helpful about multiple regression is that it gives us information about the individual contribution each variable is making to the variance in the criterion variable. To interpret the information in Table 19.8, we look first at the t value calculation and its level of significance. This calculation gives us the individual effect of each variable in the model (including the "constant" or "Y" value, which is part of the regression equation). The strongest predictors in the model are language score (Lang; $t = 13.240$, Sig. = .000) and high school GPA (HSGPA; $t = 4.366$, Sig. = .000).

Additionally, SPSS provides individual weights or coefficients to explain the contribution each variable has on the criterion. Coefficients are calculated as unstandardized B and as standardized *beta*, which accounts for the standard error. In this example, the high *beta* weight (.792) for the language score (Lang) also shows it is the strongest

predictor. SAT, in contrast, is not a very good indicator of college GPA for these students in this particular regression model—the *beta* weight for the SAT score is quite low (.007), as is its t value (.137); the probability that the finding is due to chance is quite high (.892). Our regression model also suggests that math score is not a good predictor of college GPA (*beta* = −.016, $t = −.263$, Sig. = .793). Note, however, that the significance level of a variable in a multiple regression model is dependent on the model, and in particular the other variables included in the model, especially when there are strong relations between variables. It is important to consider all combinations of variables in order to understand the effect of each individual variable.

It is also important to remember that the results shown for Lang, HSGPA, SAT, and Math are for this sample only. Other samples using different regression models will likely show different results. The design and validity of the study are important—we want to include the variables that have the most meaning or best predict the criterion variable. Our regression models are only as good

---

TABLE 19.8 • Multiple regression: analysis of variance and of coefficients

ANOVA[b]

Model		Sum of Squares	df	Mean Square	F	Sig.
1	Regression	26.277	4	6.569	118.494	.000*
	Residual	6.653	120	.055		
	Total	32.929	124			

[a] Predictors: (Constant), LANG, SAT, HSGPA, MATH
[b] Dependent Variable: CollGPA

Coefficients[a]

Model		Unstandardized Coefficients		Standardized Coefficients		
		B	Std. Error	Beta	T	Sig.
1	(Constant)	1.068	.139		7.698	.000
	HSGPA	.196	.045	.211	4.366	.000
	SAT	3.96E-005	.000	.007	.137	.892
	MATH		.002	−.016	−.263	.793
	LANG	.022	.002	.792	13.240	.000

[a] Dependent Variable: CollGPA

as the data we collect and the choices we make regarding the variables to include in our analyses.

Nevertheless, this example suggests that students' language scores in high school and their high school GPAs are highly effective predictors of GPA at Pacific Crest College. In contrast, their SAT and math scores add very little to the accuracy of predicting their college GPAs. Based on this analysis, we can tell the admissions office that the students with the best chances of success in college are most likely those with higher language scores and high school GPAs. Of course, we make this interpretation cautiously because we did not study all variables that can possibly affect college success. Obviously, some high school students with high language scores and high GPAs will not succeed at college for other reasons; for example, psychological, personal, or family effects can contribute to college success or failure. However, considering the variables we have measured and over which we know counselors and students have some control (e.g., improving language skills), we can offer advice about two very good predictors of college success at Pacific Crest. We cannot, however, make predictions for other colleges because Pacific Crest students may be different from other college students.

Chi Square

Chi square, symbolized as χ^2, is a nonparametric test of significance appropriate when the data are in the form of frequency counts or percentages and proportions that can be converted to frequencies. It is used to compare frequencies occurring in different categories or groups. Chi square is thus appropriate for nominal data that fall into either true categories or artificial categories. A **true category** is one in which persons or objects naturally fall, independent of any research study (e.g., male versus female), whereas an **artificial category** is one that is operationally defined by a researcher (e.g., tall versus short). Two or more mutually exclusive categories are required. In educational research, we are often interested in the effects of nominal variables, such as race, class, or religion, so chi square offers an excellent analytical tool.

Simple frequency counts for the variables under consideration are often presented in contingency tables, such as those shown in Chapter 18, Tables 18.3 and 18.4. A contingency table by itself presents basic descriptive data; a chi-square analysis helps determine if any observed differences between the variables are meaningful and is computed by comparing the frequencies of each variable observed in a study to the expected frequencies. Expected proportions are usually the frequencies that would be expected if the groups were equal (i.e., no difference between groups), although occasionally they also may be based on past data. The chi-square value increases as the difference between observed and expected frequencies increases; large chi-square values indicate statistically significant differences.

As an example of a chi-square analysis, we consider the relation between gender and reading level for the students at Pacific Crest College. We use chi square because we have two nominal variables: gender (i.e., male, female) and reading level (i.e., low, medium, high). Reading level (ReadLevel) is a composite variable that considers the language score, reading fluency, and a placement assessment of reading and language ability when the students started college. Reading could be considered an ordinal variable because the reading levels are in order from low to medium to high. Because reading level is a composite of both qualitative and quantitative considerations, however, the distance between low and medium is not likely the same as between medium and high. For purposes of our example, then, ReadLevel is considered nominal and should be analyzed with a nonparametric measure, such as chi square.

As illustrated in Table 19.9, the basic contingency table shows the distribution of males and females at each of the three reading levels. We are interested in whether the pattern for the males (i.e., the distribution across reading level) is significantly different than the pattern for the females,

TABLE 19.9 • Contingency table of gender and reading level

Gender * ReadLevel Crosstabulation						
Count						
			ReadLevel			
		1	2	3	Total
Gender	1	18	34	7	59
	2	1	21	44	66
Total		19	55	51	125

and on first inspection, it appears so—only one female is at ReadLevel 1, whereas 18 males are; 44 females are at ReadLevel 3, whereas only 7 males are. Although our data suggest differences, we do not yet know if these differences are meaningful until we consider the outcome of the chi-square analysis. In the language of statistics, a significant chi square tells us that these variables (i.e., gender and reading level) are not independent.

To determine if the variables are independent or not, we compare the frequencies we actually observed (symbolized as O) with the expected frequencies (symbolized as Σ). The expected frequencies are the numbers we would find if the variables are independent—in other words, the pattern of distribution across reading level is the same for the males and the females. Therefore, the expected frequencies reflect the null hypothesis of no difference. The expected frequencies and percentage distributions are presented in the expanded cross-tabulation shown in Table 19.10.

Although we typically conduct chi square on the computer, the hand calculation is manageable when we have a simple cross-tabulation table, such as Table 19.9. The formula (which is also used by statistical programs such as SPSS) is:

$$\chi^2 = \Sigma\left[\frac{(fo - fe)^2}{fe}\right]$$

In this formula, fo is the observed frequency, and fe is the expected frequency. As with other hand calculations, we refer to a statistical table to determine whether the value computed for x^2 is significant, taking into account the degrees of freedom and probability level (i.e., the level of risk we accept that this finding would occur by chance). Degrees of freedom for chi square are computed by multiplying the number of rows in the contingency table, minus one (i.e., the number of levels of one variable, minus one) by the number of columns, minus one (i.e., the number of levels of the other variable, minus one): $df = (R - 1)(C - 1)$. In this example, then, $df = (3 - 1)(2 - 1) = 2$.

TABLE 19.10 • SPSS crosstabulation table of gender and reading level with percentages

Gender * ReadLevel Crosstabulation

			ReadLevel 1	2	3	Total
Gender	1	Count	18	34	7	59
		Expected Count	9.0	26.0	24.1	59.0
		% within Gender	30.5%	57.6%	11.9%	100.0%
		% within ReadLevel	94.7%	61.8%	13.7%	47.2%
		% of Total	14.4%	27.2%	5.6%	47.2%
	2	Count	1	21	44	66
		Expected Count	10.0	29.0	26.9	66.0
		% within Gender	1.5%	31.8%	66.7%	100.0%
		% within ReadLevel	5.3%	38.2%	86.3%	52.8%
		% of Total	.8%	16.8%	35.2%	52.8%
Total		Count	19	55	51	125
		Expected Count	19.0	55.0	51.0	125.0
		% within Gender	15.2%	44.0%	40.8%	100.0%
		% within ReadLevel	100.0%	100.0%	100.0%	100.0%
		% of Total	15.2%	44.0%	40.8%	100.0%

Calculating Chi Square Using SPSS

To specify the chi-square statistic for a given set of data, we go to the Descriptive Statistics submenu by clicking Analyze (because chi square is a nonparametric statistic, it is listed with descriptive statistics). Within this submenu, we choose the Crosstabs . . . option. Chi square is one of the few analysis procedures in SPSS that does not have a dedicated menu option. We display the SPSS menu options in Appendix A, Figure A.19.8, but they can be summarized as follows:

Analyze
Descriptive Statistics
Crosstabs . . .

Once in the Crosstabs . . . window, we need to specify the variables to go in the rows and columns of the table; in this example they are gender and reading level, as shown in Figure A.19.9.

TABLE 19.11 • Chi-square analysis of gender and reading*

Chi-Square Tests			
	Value	df	Asymp. Sig. (2-sided)
Pearson Chi-Square	44.875*	2	.000
Likelihood Ratio	51.120	2	.000
Linear-by-Linear Association	43.884	1	.000
N of Valid Cases	125		

* 0 cells (.0%) have expected count less than 5. The minimum expected count is 8.97.

To compute chi square, we click on the Statistics button at the bottom of the window and then select the Chi-square statistic button in the next screen. Finally, we click the Continue button in the upper right of this screen to complete the analysis. If we want to display the expected frequencies in each cell, we can return to the Crosstabs . . . window and click on the Cells button (shown in Figure A.19.9).

The first table that SPSS generates is the cross-tabulation table, as illustrated in Table 19.9, which shows the observed values for each cell. The next table (see Table 19.10) presents further information on the expected frequencies and percentage of students in each cell in the contingency table. These percentages are helpful to interpret the meaning of the chi-square analysis.

The outcome of the chi-square calculation is presented in Table 19.11. The first line shows a Pearson chi-square value, $\chi^2 = 44.875$, which yields a significance level of less than .001. Although SPSS provides a larger variety of statistical computations, the Pearson chi-square is adequate for our purposes of determining the relation between gender and reading level. With the significant chi-square statistic, we can conclude that gender and reading level are not independent—in other words, the patterns for the males are different than the patterns for the females. Males and females are not distributed in the same way at each reading level.

The Pearson chi-square value tells us only that the patterns are not the same; it does not tell us how they differ. In other words, we don't know if the number of males differs significantly from the number of females at each reading level or only at some of the reading levels. We need to go back to the crosstabulation table (i.e., Table 19.10), which shows that a higher proportion of the females is found at the highest level of reading. In this example, 44 females are at the highest level of reading; these 44 females account for 86.3% of the students (males and females) found at the highest level of reading. Clearly, the females greatly outnumber the males. Likewise, 18 males and only 1 female are at the lowest level of reading; that is, 94.7% of the students in the lowest level of reading are males.

To summarize, we have found from the chi-square analysis that the observed distribution of students across gender and reading level is not what we expected, simply due to chance. The two variables, gender and reading level, are not independent. From this finding with the Pacific Crest College students, we may conclude that males need additional reading help; we may consider improving the high school language curriculum, providing a remedial reading program for first-year college males, or providing support services accordingly.

Chi square may also be used with more than two variables. Because contingency tables can be of two, three, or more dimensions, depending on the number of variables, a multidimensional chi square can be thought of as a factorial chi square. Of course, as the contingency table gets larger by adding more variables, interpreting the chi square becomes more complex. We are also limited by sample size if we want to expand the number of variables to include in a contingency table. For example, because we have only 125 students in our Pacific Crest College sample, we can very easily have almost as many cells in the table as we have students. If we are interested in looking at the reading levels of students sorted by economic level, gender, and ethnicity, we quickly run out of students to fill all the cells in the contingency table. Gender has two values, reading level has three values, economic level has three levels, and ethnicity has five—this table would have 90 cells ($2 \times 3 \times 3 \times 5$), and we only have 125 students to fill the table. It's possible that some cells would have no students that fit into that combination of variables (e.g., a White, high-economic level woman at the lowest reading level). Obviously, we need more students or fewer variables to conduct an appropriate chi square.

Other Investigative Techniques: Data Mining, Factor Analysis, and Structural Equation Modeling

In addition to some of the standard statistical tests we have presented, a number of other valuable analytical tools are extremely helpful, depending on the purpose of the research and the data available. **Data mining,** as an example, uses analytical tools to identify and predict patterns in datasets or large warehouses of data that have been collected from thousands of subjects and about hundreds of variables. Data mining is used often in business and scientific research to discover relations and predict patterns among variables and outcomes. In business, for example, data-mining techniques may be used to discover purchasing patterns—who buys what products how often and for what purposes—to identify where advertisements should be placed and the products that should be sold in particular stores. Likewise, credit card companies are interested in who makes which purchases from which stores and how often. These buying patterns are also important for security reasons to detect fraudulent purchases, as when thousands of dollars of video game purchases are charged to an 80-year-old's credit card. Obviously, quite sophisticated statistical techniques are needed to test multiple hypotheses with such large databases. Among other statistical software packages, SPSS and SAS (Statistical Analysis System) offer data-mining procedures in the more advanced versions. "Clementine," for example, is the data-mining procedure available on the full version of SPSS. Newer advancements in data mining include text mining and Web mining procedures to provide predictive models beyond the data the researcher or business has collected. R has robust data mining capabilities with readily available open source packages.

Factor analysis is a statistical procedure used to identify relations among variables in a correlation matrix. Basically, factor analysis determines how variables group together based on what they may have in common. Factor analysis is commonly used to reduce a large number of responses or questions to a few more meaningful groupings, known as factors. For example, we may give our students or subjects a 100-question personality inventory. To reduce these 100 responses to a manageable number, we can perform a factor analysis to identify several key factors that the responses have in common. A number of psychological inventories, such as the Minnesota Multiphasic Personality Inventory (MMPI), were created with the assistance of factor analysis. Responses to the MMPI are scored on 10 scales that represent indicators of factors such as schizophrenia, depression, and hysteria. However, factor analysis indicates only how the responses group together; the names and meaning of the factors must be determined by the researchers. The intelligence quotient (IQ) was also created through factor analysis. Because the IQ itself represents one factor that emerged from factor analysis, a number of scholars are quite critical of how well the IQ actually measures a concept as complex as intelligence.[2] Interpreting the meaning of factors is challenging—factor analysis may be as much an art form as a statistical analysis.

Structural Equation Modeling (SEM) can be conducted by several software programs, the most widely used is LISREL (Linear Structural Relationships), which is available on SPSS. LISREL can be thought of as an ultracombination of path analysis and factor analysis: It is an extremely complicated procedure that builds a structural model to explain the interactive relations among a relatively large number of variables. The distinct advantage of LISREL is that it begins with the creation of a complex path model that considers multiple relations among independent and dependent variables as well as latent variables that are unobserved but responsible for measurement error. Factor analysis yields groupings of variables or factors that are tested with path analysis (i.e., multiple regression) to show the strength of the factors in the model. The disadvantage of LISREL is that it requires a large dataset and is quite complex to interpret. Nonetheless, for the advanced researcher it is a powerful tool that uses the best capabilities of path analysis and factor analysis.

Structural Equation Modeling (SEM) can also be conducted using R, if you are OK with doing a bit of coding. To conduct SEM with R you'll need a package called lavaan. Lavaan can do everything LISREL can, if you're patient. Conducting SEM with lavaan is beyond the scope of this text, but for the brave at heart we recommend Beaujean's (2014) *Latent Variable Modeling Using R.*

[2] See Gould, Stephen Jay. *The Mismeasure of Man.* New York: W.W. Norton, 1981, 1996. Gardner, Howard. *Frames of Mind: The Theory of Multiple Intelligences.* New York: Basic Books, 1983.

Types of Parametric and Nonparametric Statistical Tests

There are too many parametric and nonparametric statistical methods to describe in detail here. Table 19.12 provides an overview of some of the more commonly used tests and their associated purposes. The table is best used by first identifying the levels of measurement of the study. Then examine the purpose statements that fit the levels of measurement, and select the one that provides the best match. Other information in the table also helps in carrying out the appropriate significance test. Of course, researchers should use statistical tests only if they can justify their use and interpret the outcomes with confidence. Many a graduate student has needlessly suffered in a thesis defense when trying to explain an overly complex statistical procedure that is unfamiliar. Select appropriate procedures you understand and be parsimonious in your explanations.

TABLE 19.12 • Commonly used parametric and nonparametric significance tests

Name of Test	Test Statistic	df	Parametric (P) or Non-parametric (NP)	Purpose	Var. 1 Independent	Var. 2 Dependent
t test for independent samples	t	$n_1 + n_2 - 2$	P	Test the difference between means of two independent groups	Nominal	Interval or ratio
t test for dependent samples	t	$N - 1$	P	Test the difference between means of two dependent groups	Nominal	Interval or ratio
Analysis of variance	F	$SS_B =$ groups $- 1$; $SS_W =$ participants $-$ groups $- 1$	P	Test the difference among three or more independent groups	Nominal	Interval or ratio
Pearson product correlation	r	$N - 2$	P	Test whether a correlation is different from zero (a relationship exists)	Interval or ratio	Interval or ratio
Chi-square test	χ^2	rows $- 1 \times$ column $- 1$	NP	Test the difference in proportions in two or more groups	Nominal	Nominal
Median test	χ^2	rows $- 1 \times$ column $- 1$	NP	Test the difference of the medians of two independent groups	Nominal	Ordinal
Mann-Whitney U test	U	$N - 1$	NP	Test the difference of the medians of two independent groups	Nominal	Ordinal
Wilcoxon signed rank test	Z	$N - 2$	NP	Test the difference in the ranks of two related groups	Nominal	Ordinal
Kruskal-Wallis test	H	groups $- 1$	NP	Test the difference in the ranks of three or more independent groups	Nominal	Ordinal
Freidman test	χ	groups $- 1$	NP	Test the difference in the ranks of three or more dependent groups	Nominal	Ordinal
Spearman rho	ρ	$N - 2$	NP	Test whether a correlation is different from zero	Ordinal	Ordinal

CALCULATING INFERENTIAL STATISTICS USING R

For those of you that are still digesting the red pill you swallowed in Chapter 18, R is also a powerful tool for conducting inferential hypothesis testing. Let's conduct some of the same procedures we just followed in SPSS using R. If you are interested in following along, the R script used to produce this sample is provided in MyLab for Education. The first thing we need to do, if starting from scratch, is to input our data into R. If you're working right along from Chapter 18, you have already done this step. If you're starting over these procedures are identical to the ones you did in Chapter 18. As a refresher, you'll need to type the following commands after starting the R software. Remember that any command line that begins with the # symbol isn't calculated, but indicates a comment. They are included in Table 19.13 to help you make sense of what you are doing.

At this point, you're all set to work . . . with just one more piece of information.

We did not introduce the downloading of "packages" to R in Chapter 18 because R is ready right out of the box for descriptive statistics. For inferential procedures, however, you are going to need to give R a little more power. Continuing our sports car analogy from Chapter 18, think of "packages" as upgrades. Sure, your car is fast right from the factory, but if you bolt on a supercharger, it will be even better!

One of the most commonly used packages, and the one you'll need for this example, is the "car" package. No, it isn't named that because of our crafty automobile analogy. The car package stands for "Companion to Applied Regression." Remember that R is open source. The car package was designed by John Fox, Sandford Weisberg, and a host of other R contributors (see cran.r-project.org/web/packages/car/index.html). Obtaining packages varies by your operating system, which is probably either a PC or a Mac. On a PC you are going to select Packages at the top of the screen and then Install Packages. Next, select a CRAN mirror as described in the last chapter, and select your package (see Figure 19.8). Currently, there are over 10,000 packages available and they are listed in alphabetical order. Select the package you want and it will load into your R console.

On a Mac you are going to select Packages and Data from the top of the screen and then Packages Installer (see Figure 19.9). From here you will type the name of the package you want in the search bar. For us, that's the car package, so just type "car." Once you find the package from the list, just click Get List, choose the CRAN mirror you prefer, find the car package, and select Install Selected.

TABLE 19.13 • R code for calculating inferential statistics

```
> pinecrest <- read.table("insert link to your file here", header = TRUE)

> attach (pinecrest)

> #Creating a factor variable for Gender

> pinecrest$f.gender = factor (pinecrest$Gender, labels = c ("male", "female"))

> #Creating a factor variable for Ethnicity

> pinecrest$f.ethnicity = factor(pinecrest$Ethnicity, labels = c ("African American", "Asian, Pacific Islander",
    "Hispanic", "Native American", "White"))

> #Creating a factor variable for Economic Level

> pinecrest$f.econ = factor (pinecrest$Econ, labels = c ("low (free/reduced lunch)", "medium/working class",
    "middle/upperclass"))

> #Creating a factor variable for Reading Level

> pinecrest$f.ReadLevel = factor (pinecrest$ReadLevel, labels = c ("low", "middle", "high"))

> attach(pinecrest)
```

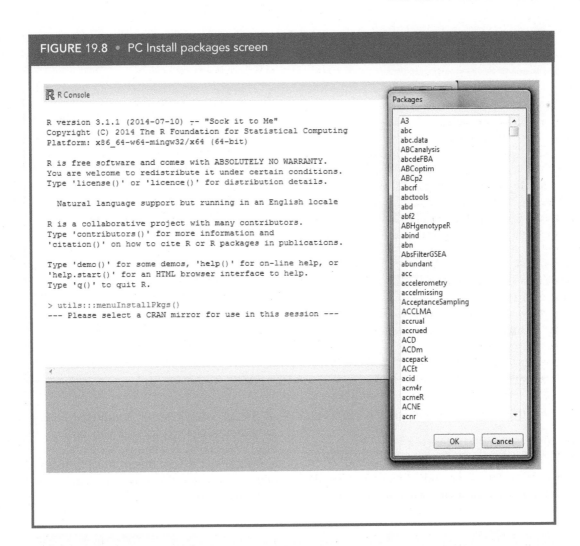

FIGURE 19.8 • PC Install packages screen

On a Mac, it is usually a good idea to go ahead and check the box that says Install Dependencies. Your download will take a little longer, but this will load everything needed to run the package you are downloading. After you've completed these steps for either a PC or a Mac you can use the command library (car) and R will activate the package into your workspace.

Calculating the *t* Test for Independent Samples Using R

Now that R is loaded and ready to go, we can conduct the statistical tests we did with SPSS in R. Let's start by calculating the *t* test for Independent samples by using two simple commands. First, to check

for homogeneity of variance via the Levene's test we conducted earlier in SPSS use the following code:

> leveneTest(ReadF ~ f.gender)

SPSS and R differ on how they calculate Levene's test. SPSS uses absolute deviations from the mean where R uses absolute deviations from the median. You'll see, though, that while our results differ slightly, our conclusions are the same. R tells us our *F*-value is .271 with a corresponding *p*-value of .6077 ($F (1, 23) = .271$, $p = .6077$). We fail to reject the null, and here failing is a good thing! See Figure 19.10 to check your status.

Now we can conduct our *t* test confidently. Remember that ReadF is our dependent variable, so it goes first followed by our grouping variable.

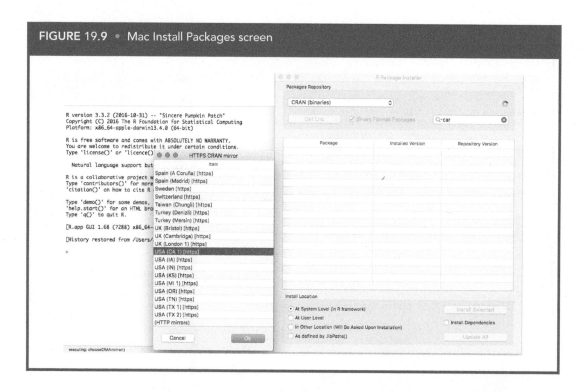

FIGURE 19.9 • Mac Install Packages screen

To conduct the *t* test for independent samples, simply type:

> t.test(ReadF ~ f.gender, var.equal = TRUE)

The last part of that command, var.equal = TRUE, is just letting R know that based on the results of the Levene's test we conducted earlier, we can assume equal variances. If you do not put this in your command, R assumes unequal variances and conducts the *t* test using Welch's method, which slightly changes the way the degrees of freedom are calculated.

FIGURE 19.10 • t test for independent samples using R

```
> pinecrest
   ID Gender Ethnicity Econ ReadLevel ReadF ReadS MathF MathS f.gender        f.ethnicity                 f.econ f.ReadLevel
1   1      1         1    1         3  52.5  68.7  54.8  55.2     male   African American low (free/reduced lunch)       high
2   2      2         2    2         1  32.5  52.6  73.2  72.8   female Asian, Pacific Islander  medium/working class        low
3   3      1         5    2         1  36.4  38.5  44.9  43.0     male              White  medium/working class        low
4   4      1         5    2         1  44.3  56.2  35.2  36.6     male              White  medium/working class        low
5   5      2         4    1         3  58.7  63.8  58.3  60.5   female    Native American low (free/reduced lunch)       high
6   6      1         3    1         1  28.3  31.2  23.1  22.0     male           Hispanic low (free/reduced lunch)        low
7   7      2         3    1         2  43.1  53.6  52.6  53.6   female           Hispanic low (free/reduced lunch)     middle
8   8      1         5    3         2  66.5  75.5  53.8  53.3     male              White      middle/upperclass     middle
9   9      2         1    1         3  51.4  56.8  45.8  43.6   female   African American low (free/reduced lunch)       high
10 10      1         5    1         1  38.5  41.4  46.7  47.8     male              White low (free/reduced lunch)        low
11 11      2         5    3         3  56.0  72.3  38.4  36.0   female              White      middle/upperclass       high
12 12      1         2    1         1  24.5  28.4  32.5  32.6     male Asian, Pacific Islander low (free/reduced lunch)    low
13 13      2         1    1         1  37.4  42.3  25.3  25.8   female   African American low (free/reduced lunch)        low
14 14      1         3    1         1  28.3  34.8  18.3  19.5     male           Hispanic low (free/reduced lunch)        low
15 15      2         5    3         3  78.4  72.4  58.3  60.3   female              White      middle/upperclass       high
16 16      2         3    2         3  52.3  53.6  38.6  40.3   female           Hispanic  medium/working class       high
17 17      1         5    3         2  56.8  64.2  67.4  68.4     male              White      middle/upperclass     middle
18 18      2         1    3         3  73.2  68.4  72.4  70.0   female   African American      middle/upperclass       high
19 19      1         5    2         1  47.4  65.8  53.5  52.0     male              White  medium/working class        low
20 20      2         2    1         2  47.4  34.6  48.5  50.2   female Asian, Pacific Islander low (free/reduced lunch)  middle
21 21      1         5    3         2  53.2  58.5  36.5  38.5     male              White      middle/upperclass     middle
22 22      1         3    1         1  18.4  22.0  27.2  28.0     male           Hispanic low (free/reduced lunch)        low
23 23      2         5    2         3  53.5  58.4  62.4  64.0   female              White  medium/working class       high
24 24      2         4    1         3  46.5  52.4  38.6  38.0   female    Native American low (free/reduced lunch)       high
25 25      1         1    2         1  38.6  41.7  28.9  27.0     male   African American  medium/working class        low
>
> #Levene's Test and independent samples t-test
> leveneTest(ReadF, f.gender)
Levene's Test for Homogeneity of Variance (center = median)
      Df F value Pr(>F)
group  1   0.271 0.6077
      23
```

Once you run this command you'll see that apart from some differences in estimation based on significant digits, we achieve the same results as we did with SPSS, $t(23) = -2.1$, $p = .047$. The boys and girls in this sample do have statistically significant differences in fall reading scores!

Calculating the *t* Test for Nonindependent Samples Using R

Much like the *t* test for independent samples, the *t* test for nonindependent samples isn't too complicated in R. Recall that for this example, we are interested in whether or not our Pinecrest Elementary students' reading and math scores improved over the course of the year. We can achieve this with essentially the same commands we used when conducing our independent samples testing. When conducting a *t* test, R defaults to the samples being independent of one another. Because we are looking at change, or essentially pre- and posttest scores that we can match, we want to let R know that. Two command lines will help us achieve our goals. With your Pinecrest data attached, type the following into R:

> t.test (ReadF, ReadS, paired = TRUE)
> t.test (MathF, MathS, paired = TRUE)

The last part of our commands, "paired = TRUE," just let's R know that these samples are dependent samples. With the exception of some rounding differences, our output gives us the same information given to us earlier by SPSS. The paired *t* test for fall and spring reading scores produces, $t(24) = -3.88$, $p = .001$, indicating that there was a statistically significant difference in these scores. Our paired *t* test for fall and spring math scores produces, $t(24) = -0.497$, $p = .624$, indicating that these scores are not statistically significant. To check your status with all of the *t* tests we have conducted, see Figure 19.11.

Calculating ANOVA with Post Hoc Multiple Comparison Tests Using R

In our earlier example using SPSS, we were interested in whether or not there were differences in the college grade point averages of students at Pacific Crest College based on their economic

FIGURE 19.11 • Calculating *t* tests using R

```
> t.test(ReadF ~ f.gender)

	Welch Two Sample t-test

data:  ReadF by f.gender
t = -2.1019, df = 22.987, p-value = 0.04672
alternative hypothesis: true difference in means is not equal to 0
95 percent confidence interval:
 -22.7778421  -0.1811323
sample estimates:
  mean in group male mean in group female
            41.05385             52.53333

> #Dependent samples t-test
> t.test(ReadF, ReadS, paired = TRUE)

	Paired t-test

data:  ReadF and ReadS
t = -3.8822, df = 24, p-value = 0.0007092
alternative hypothesis: true difference in means is not equal to 0
95 percent confidence interval:
 -8.822184 -2.697816
sample estimates:
mean of the differences
                  -5.76

> t.test(MathF, MathS, paired = TRUE)

	Paired t-test

data:  MathF and MathS
t = -0.49717, df = 24, p-value = 0.6236
alternative hypothesis: true difference in means is not equal to 0
95 percent confidence interval:
 -0.7829951  0.4789951
sample estimates:
mean of the differences
                 -0.152

>
```

level. To get the information we need, we conduct a one-way ANOVA using post-hoc testing. This was a simple procedure in SPSS, and it is a simple procedure in R as well. There are a number of ways to conduct an ANOVA using R, but we will use a procedure that only involves a few commands.

First, though, if you are working along with our examples, you'll see that we are switching to a new data set. The first thing we will need to do is read that data set into R, and just like last time, set up our factor variables. The commands are nearly identical to the commands used to set up our Pinecrest Elementary data. Type the commands found in Table 19.14 into R.

Now that R knows which data we are working with, we can conduct the same ANOVA we conducted earlier using SPSS. ANOVA is just one procedure based on the general linear model. Because of this, we let R know that we are setting up a model using college GPA and econ level. We need to name this model something so that R will know which model we are talking about when we conduct our ANOVA. You can name it anything you want, but for our purpose, we are going to call it "results" because it represents the

TABLE 19.14 • Calculating ANOVA with post hoc multiple comparison tests using R

```
> #Reading in the Pacific Crest Data Set
> pacific <- read.table ("~/Desktop/Mills Chapters/Pacific.txt",header = TRUE)
> #Creating a factor variable for Gender
> pacific$f.gender = factor (pacific$Gender, labels = c ("male", "female"))
> #Creating a factor variable for Economic Level
> pacific$f.econ = factor (pacific$Econ, labels = c ("low (free/reduced lunch)", "medium/working class", "middle/upperclass"))
> #Creating a factor variable for Reading Level
> pacific$f.ReadLevel = factor (pacific$ReadLevel, labels = c ("low", "middle", "high"))
> attach (pacific)
> #pacific is now the active dataset
```

"results" of the linear model we designed. Type the following into R:

```
> results <- aov(CollGPA ~ f.econ)
```

Now, just type the following to conduct the ANOVA:

```
> summary(results)
```

Again, you will see that our output from R matches our output from SPSS. We have an *F* statistic of 37.06 and a *p*-value rounded to .001 ($F(2, 122) = 37.06, p = .001$).

See Figure 19.12 to check your status.

As for post hoc tests, there are a number of options using R just like with SPSS. Various post hoc tests are found within various R packages. For our example here, we will use a different post hoc test than before. Just to demonstrate a post hoc test using R, we will use Tukey's HSD. Tukey's HSD is a good post hoc test to use when sample sizes are equal. It is a little less conservative than the Scheffé test, and therefore a little more powerful. It is found in the car package and therefore will work for us without downloading any additional

FIGURE 19.12 • Calculating ANOVA using R status check

```
> #Reading in the Pacific Crest Data Set
> pacific <- read.table("~/Desktop/Mills Chapters/Pacific.txt",header = TRUE)
> #Creating a factor variable for gender
> pacific$f.gender = factor(pacific$Gender, labels =c ("male", "female"))
> #Creating a factor variable for Economic Level
> pacific$f.econ = factor(pacific$Econ, labels = c("low (free/reduced lunch)", "medium/working class", "middle/upperclass"))
> #Creating a factor variable for Reading Level
> pacific$f.ReadLevel = factor(pacific$ReadLevel, labels= c("low", "middle", "high"))
> attach(pacific)
The following objects are masked from pinecrest (pos = 3):

    Econ, f.econ, f.gender, f.ReadLevel, Gender, ReadLevel

The following objects are masked from pinecrest (pos = 4):

    Econ, Gender, ReadLevel

> #pacific is now the active dataset
> #To conduct our ANOVA, we need just two commands
> results <- aov(CollGPA ~ f.econ)
> summary(results)
             Df Sum Sq Mean Sq F value  Pr(>F)
f.econ        2  12.45   6.223   37.06 2.66e-13 ***
Residuals   122  20.48   0.168
---
Signif. codes:  0 '***' 0.001 '**' 0.01 '*' 0.05 '.' 0.1 ' ' 1
>
```

TABLE 19.15 • Calculating Tukey's HSD using R				
Tukey multiple comparisons of means 95% family-wise confidence level Fit: aov(formula = CollGPA ~ f.econ $f.econ				
	diff	lwr	upr	p adj
Medium/working class –low (free/reduced lunch)	0.01384694	−0.1933254	0.2210192	0.9862328
Middle/upperclass-low(free/reduced lunch)	0.70290249	0.4894875	0.9163175	0.0000000
Middle/upperclass-medium/workingclass	0.68905556	0.4657033	0.9124078	0.0000000

packages. If you'd like to conduct the Scheffé test conducted earlier with SPSS, it is no problem to do so. It is found in the agricolae package. Just follow the steps for obtaining that package and you'll have access to the command scheffe.test. Tukey's HSD, however, is primed and ready to go because we have the car package active. To conduct this procedure, type the following:

> TukeyHSD(results)

R will then provide the following output, shown in Table 19.15.

Just like our earlier Scheffé test using SPSS, there is no statistical difference between the students in the low economic group and students in the middle-economic group. However, the other comparisons are significant.

Calculating Multiple Regression Using R

Earlier we used SPSS to conduct a multiple linear regression that considered the ability of four predictor variables, HSGPA, SAT, MATH, and LANG, to explain the variability in college GPA, or CollGPA. If you've hung with us this long, you are probably realizing that R isn't that scary once you understand some of the inner workings of the procedures you are conducting. Conducting a regression analysis in R is also a simple process. Of course, there are a number of variations and ways to go about conducting these analyses, but to achieve the same information we achieved earlier with SPSS, we again need only a couple of commands. First, we need to again set up a linear model. Remember that we are interested in the ability of our four predictor variables to explain the variability in

college GPA. Once again, we can name this model anything we want. For this example, we will just call it "regression." Type the following into the R console:

> regression <- lm (CollGPA ~ HSGPA + SAT + MATH + LANG)

If you were to read that command line aloud, it simply says: "We will create an object called 'regression' which will be a linear model of college GPA as a function of high school GPA, SAT, Math, and Language." To conduct the analysis, type the following:

> summary (regression)

You'll see that our output from R in Table 19.16 matches our earlier output from SPSS:

R also gives us a quick check for significance. This can be found in the last column with the key being the first line under the table. Just as in our earlier example using SPSS this example suggests that students' language scores in high school and their high school GPAs are effective predictors of GPA at Pacific Crest College.

Calculating Chi Square Using R

As you've likely predicted at this point, calculating chi square using R is not a complex procedure, provided you know the right commands. Remember that chi square is a nonparametric test of significance that is used to determine the level of relationship between frequency variables. In our earlier example using SPSS we were simply interested in determining whether or not gender and reading level were associated. To obtain the chi square and the associated *p*-value in R, we only need a couple of commands.

TABLE 19.16 • Calculating multiple regression using R

Call:

Lm(formula = CollGPA ~ HSGPA + SAT + MATH + Lang)

Residuals:

Min	1Q	Median	3Q	Max
−0.47649	−0.19949	0.04199	0.16197	0.55080

Coefficients:

	Estimate	Std. Error	T value	Pr(>|t|)	
(Intercept)	1.068e + 00	1.388e − 01	7.698	4.34e − 12	***
HSGPA	1.963e − 01	4.498e − 02	4.366	2.70e − 05	***
SAT	3.959e − 05	2.899e − 04	0.137	0.892	
MATH	−6.004e − 04	2.286e − 03	−.263	0.793	
LANG	2.155e − 02	1.628e − 03	13.240	< 2e − 16	***

Signif codes: 0 '***' 0.001'**' .01 '*' 0.05 '.' 0.1 ' ' 1
Residual standard error: 0.2355 on 120 degrees of freedom
Multiple R-squared: 0.798, Adjusted R-squared: 0.7912
F-statistic: 118.5 on 4 and 120 DF, p-value: <2.2e − 16

First, we need to let R know that we are only interested in using the frequency data from the variables ReadLevel and Gender. Again, we can name this anything we want. For this example, we'll just call it "chiexample." To do this, type the following:

> chiexample <- table (pacific $f. ReadLevel, pacific$f.gender)

> chiexample

You'll see in Table 19.17 that R produced a frequency table of our data:

To conduct Pearson's chi-squared test, just type the following:

> chisq.test (chiexample)

R kindly gives us the following information:

You will see that our output from R matches what we did earlier with SPSS. Of course, we can continue to look closer at our data in R just as we did with SPSS and we will see that we get the same outcomes as we did earlier. In this case, it seems that there is a statistically significant difference in reading levels between the males and females in our Pacific Crest data set.

If You "R" Still Onboard

In Chapters 18 and 19 we have demonstrated some of the basic functions of the R software. Know that this is only the tip of the iceberg and that should

TABLE 19.17 • Calculating chi square using R

	Male	Female
low	18	1
middle	34	21
high	7	44

TABLE 19.18 • Calculating Pearson's chi-squared test using R

Pearson's Chi-squared test
data: chiexample
X-squared = 44.875, df = 2, p-value = 1.801e-10

you decide to dive further into the world of statistical computing using R there are many R users and supporters who will help you along the way. You'll just need to bring some patience, humility, and a sense of adventure. Did we mention that R is free? Go ahead, give it a shot!

MyLab Education **Self-Check 19.2**

MyLab Education **Application Exercise 19.2:** Identifying the Appropriate Test of Significance

MyLab Education **Application Exercise 19.3:** Evaluating Research Articles: Understanding Inferential Statistics

SUMMARY

CONCEPTS UNDERLYING INFERENTIAL STATISTICS

1. Inferential statistics deal with inferences about populations based on the behavior of samples. Inferential statistics are used to determine how likely it is that results based on a sample or samples are the same results that would have been obtained for the entire population.

2. The degree to which the results of a sample can be generalized to a population is always expressed in terms of probabilities, not in terms of proof.

Standard Error

3. Expected, chance variation among means is referred to as *sampling error*. The question that guides inferential statistics is whether observed differences are real or only the result of sampling errors.

4. A useful characteristic of sampling errors is that they are usually normally distributed. If a sufficiently large number of equal-size large samples are randomly selected from a population, the means of those samples will be normally distributed around the population mean. The mean of all the sample means will yield a good estimate of the population mean.

5. A distribution of sample means has its own mean and its own standard deviation. The standard deviation of the sample means (i.e., the standard deviation of sampling errors) is usually called the *standard error of the mean* ($SE_{\overline{X}}$).

6. In a normal curve, approximately 68% of the sample means will fall between ± 1 standard error of the population mean, 95% will fall between ± 2 standard errors, and 99+% will fall between ± 3 standard errors.

7. In most cases, we do not know the mean or standard deviation of the population, so we estimate the standard error with the following formula:

$$(SE_{\overline{X}}) = \frac{SD}{\sqrt{N-1}}$$

8. The smaller the standard error of the mean, the less sampling error. As the size of the sample increases, the standard error of the mean decreases. A researcher should make every effort to acquire as large a sample as possible.

9. Standard error can also be calculated for other measures of central tendency, as well as for measures of variability, relationship, and relative position. Standard error can also be determined for the difference between means.

Hypothesis Testing

10. Hypothesis testing is a process of decision making in which researchers evaluate the results of a study against their original expectations. In short, hypothesis testing is the process of determining whether to reject the null hypothesis (i.e., no meaningful differences, only those due to sampling error) in favor of the research hypothesis (i.e., the groups are meaningfully different; one treatment is more effective than another).

11. Because we can never completely control all the factors that may be responsible for the outcome or test all the possible samples, we can never prove a research hypothesis. However, if we can reject the null hypothesis, we have supported our research hypothesis, gaining confidence that our findings reflect the true state of affairs in the population.

Tests of Significance

12. A test of significance is a statistical procedure in which we determine the likelihood (i.e., probability) that the results from our sample are just due to chance. Significance refers to a selected probability level that indicates how much risk we are willing to take if the decision we make is wrong.

13. When conducting a test of significance, researchers set a probability level at which they feel confident that the results are not simply due to chance. This level of significance is known as alpha, symbolized as α. The smaller the probability level, the less likely it is that this finding would occur by chance.

14. The standard preselected probability level used by educational researchers is usually five out of 100 chances that the observed difference occurred by chance (symbolized as $\alpha = .05$).

Two-Tailed and One-Tailed Tests

15. Tests of significance can be either one-tailed or two-tailed. "Tails" refer to the extreme ends of the bell-shaped curve of a sampling distribution.

16. A one-tailed test assumes that a difference can occur in only one direction; the research hypothesis is directional. To select a one-tailed test of significance, the researcher should be quite sure that the results can occur only in the predicted direction.

17. A two-tailed test assumes that the results can occur in either direction; the research hypothesis is nondirectional.

18. When appropriate, a one-tailed test has one major advantage: It is statistically "easier" to obtain a significant difference when using a one-tailed test.

Type I and Type II Errors

19. A Type I error occurs when the null hypothesis is true, but the researcher rejects it, believing—incorrectly—that the results from the sample are not simply due to chance. For example, the groups aren't different, but the researcher concludes incorrectly that they are.

20. A Type II error occurs when the null hypothesis is false, but the researcher fails to reject it, believing incorrectly that the results from the sample are simply due to chance. For example, the groups are different, but the researcher concludes incorrectly that they aren't.

21. The preselected probability level (alpha) determines the probability of committing a Type I error, that is, of rejecting a null hypothesis that is really true.

22. As the probability of committing a Type I error decreases, the probability of committing a Type II error (that is, of not rejecting a null hypothesis when you should) increases.

23. The consequences of committing a Type I error thus affect the decision about level of significance for a particular study.

Degrees of Freedom

24. Degrees of freedom are important in determining whether the results of a study are statistically significant. Each test of significance has its own formula for determining degrees of freedom based on factors such as the number of subjects and the number of groups.

SELECTING AMONG TESTS OF SIGNIFICANCE

25. Different tests of significance are appropriate for different types of data. The first decision in selecting an appropriate test of significance is whether a parametric test or nonparametric test should be selected.

26. Parametric tests are more powerful and appropriate when the variable measured is normally distributed in the population and the data represent an interval or ratio scale of measurement. Parametric tests also assume that participants are randomly selected for the study and that the variances of the population comparison groups are equal.

27. Nonparametric tests make no assumptions about the shape of the distribution and are used when the data represent an ordinal or nominal scale, when a parametric assumption has been greatly violated, or when the nature of the distribution is not known.

The t Test

28. The *t* test is used to determine whether two groups of scores are significantly different at a selected probability level. The basic strategy of the *t* test is to compare the *actual* difference between the means of the groups ($\overline{X}_1 - \overline{X}_2$) with the difference *expected* by chance if the null hypothesis (i.e., no difference) is true. This ratio is known as the *t* value.

29. If the *t* value is equal to or greater than the value statistically established for the predetermined significance level, we can reject the null hypothesis.

30. The *t* test is adjusted for the fact that the distribution of scores for small samples becomes increasingly different from a normal distribution as sample sizes become increasingly smaller.

31. The *t* test for independent samples is used to determine whether, at a selected probability level, a significant difference exists between the means of two independent samples. Independent samples are randomly formed without any type of matching.

32. The *t* test for nonindependent samples is used to compare groups that are formed by some type of matching or to compare a single group's performance on two occasions or on two different measures.

Analysis of Gain or Difference Scores

33. Subtracting each participant's pretest score from his or her posttest score results in a gain, or difference, score. Analyzing difference scores is problematic because every participant does not have the same potential to gain.

Analysis of Variance

34. Analysis of variance (ANOVA) is a parametric test of significance used to determine whether scores from two or more groups are significantly different at a selected probability level.

Simple Analysis of Variance

35. Simple, or one-way, analysis of variance (ANOVA) is used when the comparison involves one variable with two or more levels.

36. In ANOVA, the total variance of scores is attributed to two sources—variance between groups (variance caused by the treatment or other independent variables) and variance within groups (error variance). ANOVA involves a ratio, known as *F*, with variance between groups as the numerator and error variance as the denominator. If the variance *between* groups is much greater than the variance *within* groups, greater than would be expected by chance, the ratio will be large, and a significant effect will be apparent.

Multiple Comparisons

37. Because ANOVA tells the researcher only that the groups are not all the same, a test involving multiple comparisons is needed to determine how the groups differ. Multiple comparisons involve calculation of a special form of the *t* test that adjusts the error rate.

38. The comparisons to be examined should be planned before, not after, the data are collected.

39. Of the many multiple comparison techniques available, a commonly used one is the Scheffé test, which is a very conservative test.

Multifactor Analysis of Variance

40. Multifactor analysis of variance is appropriate if a research study is based on a factorial design; it investigates two or more independent variables and the interactions between them. This analysis yields a separate *F* ratio for each independent variable and one for each interaction.

Analysis of Covariance

41. Analysis of covariance (ANCOVA) is a form of ANOVA used for controlling extraneous variables. ANCOVA adjusts posttest scores for initial differences on some variable and compares adjusted scores.

42. ANCOVA is also used as a means of increasing the power of a statistical test. Power refers to the ability of a significance test to identify a true research finding, thus allowing the experimenter to reject a null hypothesis that is false.

43. ANCOVA is based on the assumption that participants have been randomly assigned to treatment groups. It is best used in conjunction with true experimental designs. If existing, or intact, groups are involved but treatments are assigned to groups randomly, ANCOVA may still be used but results must be interpreted with caution.

Multiple Regression

44. Multiple regression combines variables that are known individually to predict (i.e., correlate with) the criterion into a multiple regression equation. It determines not only whether variables are related but also the degree to which they are related.

45. Path analysis involves multiple regressions between and among all the variables in the model and then specifies the direct and indirect effects of the predictor variables onto the criterion variable.

Chi Square

46. Chi square, symbolized as χ^2, is a nonparametric test of significance appropriate when the data are in the form of frequency counts or percentages and proportions that can be converted to frequencies. It is used to compare frequencies occurring in different categories or groups.

47. Expected frequencies are usually the frequencies that would be expected if the groups were equal and the null hypothesis was not rejected.

48. Chi square is computed by comparing the frequencies of each variable observed in a study to the expected frequencies. As the number of variables and their associated values increases, the contingency table becomes geometrically larger and more complex to interpret.

Other Investigative Techniques: Data Mining, Factor Analysis, and Structural Equation Modeling

49. Data mining is an analytical technique that identifies and predicts patterns in large datasets with multiple variables.

50. Factor analysis is a statistical procedure used to identify relations among variables in a correlation matrix. Factor analysis determines how variables group together based on what they may have in common. Many personality inventories and the IQ score were developed through factor analysis.

51. Structural Equation Modeling (SEM), principally LISREL (Linear Structural Relationships), is a highly complex statistical analysis that builds a structural model to explain the interactive relations among a relatively large number of variables.

CALCULATING INFERENTIAL STATISTICS USING R

52. R is an excellent choice for conducting inferential procedures, especially when equipped with the proper packages.

PERFORMANCE CRITERIA   TASK 10

Task 10 should look like the results section of a research report. The data that you generate (scores you make up for each subject) should make sense. If your dependent variable is IQ, for example, do not generate scores such as 2, 11, 15; generate scores such as 84, 110, and 120. Unlike in a real study, you can make your study turn out any way you want.

Depending on the scale of measurement represented by your data, select and compute the appropriate descriptive statistics.

Depending on the scale of measurement represented by your data, your research hypothesis, and your research design, select and compute the appropriate test of significance. Determine the statistical significance of your results for a selected probability level. Present your results in a summary table, and relate how the significance or nonsignificance of your results supports or does not support your original research hypothesis. For example, you might say the following:

> Computation of a *t* test for independent samples ($\alpha = .05$) indicated that the group that received weekly reviews retained significantly more than the group that received daily reviews (see Table 1). Therefore, the original hypothesis that "ninth-grade algebra students who receive a weekly review will retain significantly more algebraic concepts than ninth-grade algebra students who receive a daily review" was supported.

An example of the table referred to (Table 1) appears on the right of this page.

An example that illustrates the performance called for by Task 10 appears on the following pages

(see Task 10 Example). Note that the scores are based on the administration of the test described in the Task 6 example. Note also that the student used a formula used in meta-analysis (described briefly in Chapter 3) to calculate effect size (ES). The basic formula is

$$(ES) = \frac{\overline{X}_e - \overline{X}_c}{SD_c}$$

where

$\overline{X}_e$ = the mean (average) score for the experimental group

$\overline{X}_c$ = the mean (average) score for the control group

SD_c = the standard deviation (variability) of the scores for the control group

Although your actual calculations should not be part of Task 10, they should be attached to it. We have attached the step-by-step calculations for the Task 10 example. You may also perform your calculations using Excel, SPSS, or R and attach these computations as well.

Table 1 • Means, standard deviations, and *t* for the daily-review and weekly-review group on the delayed retention test

	Review Group		
	Daily	Weekly	t
M	44.82	52.68	2.56*
SD	5.12	6.00	

Note: Maximum score = 65.
$df = 38$, $p < .05$.

Effect of Interactive Multimedia on the Achievement of 10th-Grade Biology Students

Results

Prior to the beginning of the study, after the 60 students were randomly selected and assigned to experimental and control groups, final science grades from the previous school year were obtained from school records in order to check initial group equivalence. Examination of the means and a t test for independent samples ($\alpha = .05$) indicated essentially no difference between the groups (see Table 1). A t test for independent samples was used because the groups were randomly formed and the data were interval.

Table 1

Means, Standard Deviation, and t Tests for the Experimental and Control Groups

	Group		
Score	IMM instruction[a]	Traditional instruction[a]	t
Prior Grades			
M	87.47	87.63	−0.08*
SD	8.19	8.05	
Posttest NPSS:B			
M	32.27	26.70	4.22**
SD	4.45	5.69	

Note. Maximum score for prior grades = 100. Maximum score for posttest = 40.

[a]$n = 30$.

*$p > .05$.   **$p < .05$.

At the completion of the eight-month study, during the first week in May, scores on the NPSS:B were compared, also using a t test for independent samples. As Table 1 indicates, scores of the experimental and control groups were significantly different. In fact, the experimental group scored approximately one standard deviation higher than the control group ($ES = .98$). Therefore, the original hypothesis that "10th-grade biology students whose teachers use IMM as part of their instructional technique will exhibit significantly higher achievement than 10th-grade biology students whose teachers do not use IMM" was supported.

PRIOR GRADES

	EXPERIMENTAL			CONTROL	
S	X_1	X_1^2		X_2	X_2^2
1	72	5184		71	5041
2	74	5476		75	5625
3	76	5776		75	5625
4	76	5776		77	5929
5	77	5929		78	6084
6	78	6084		78	6084
7	78	6084		79	6241
8	79	6241		80	6400
9	80	6400		81	6561
10	84	7056		83	6889
11	85	7225		85	7225
12	87	7569		88	7744
13	87	7569		88	7744
14	88	7744		89	7921
15	89	7921		89	7921
16	89	7921		89	7921
17	90	8100		90	8100
18	91	8281		91	8281
19	92	8464		92	8464
20	93	8649		92	8464
21	93	8649		93	8649
22	93	8649		94	8836
23	94	8836		94	8836
24	95	9025		95	9025
25	95	9025		96	9216
26	97	9409		96	9216
27	97	9409		97	9409
28	98	9604		97	9409
29	98	9604		98	9604
30	99	9801		99	9801
	2624	231,460		2629	232,265
	$\sum X_1$	$\sum X_1^2$		$\sum X_2$	$\sum X_2^2$

$$\overline{X}_1 = \frac{\sum X_1}{n_1} = \frac{2624}{30} = 87.47 \qquad \overline{X}_2 = \frac{\sum X_2}{n_2} = \frac{2629}{30} = 87.63$$

$$SD_1 = \sqrt{\frac{SS_1}{n_1 - 1}} \qquad\qquad SD_2 = \sqrt{\frac{SS_2}{n_2 - 1}}$$

$$SS_1 = \sum x_1^2 - \frac{(\sum x_1)^2}{n_1} \qquad SS_2 = \sum x_2^2 - \frac{(\sum x_2)^2}{n_2}$$

$$= 231{,}460 - \frac{(2624)^2}{30} \qquad\qquad = 232{,}265 - \frac{(2629)^2}{30}$$

$$= 231{,}460 - \frac{6885376}{30} \qquad\qquad = 232{,}265 - \frac{6911641}{30}$$

$$= 231{,}460 - 229{,}512.53 \qquad\qquad = 232{,}265 - 230388.03$$

$$SS_1 = 1947.47 \qquad\qquad\qquad SS_2 = 1876.97$$

$$SD_1 = \sqrt{\frac{1947.47}{29}} \qquad\qquad SD_2 = \sqrt{\frac{1876.97}{29}}$$

$$= \sqrt{67.154} \qquad\qquad\qquad = \sqrt{64.72}$$

$$SD_1 = 8.19 \qquad\qquad\qquad SD_2 = 8.05$$

$$t = \frac{\bar{x}_1 - \bar{x}_2}{\sqrt{\left(\frac{SS_1 + SS_2}{n_1 + n_2 - 2}\right)\left(\frac{1}{n_1} + \frac{1}{n_2}\right)}} = \frac{87.47 - 87.63}{\sqrt{\left(\frac{1947.47 + 1876.97}{30 + 30 - 2}\right)\left(\frac{1}{30} + \frac{1}{30}\right)}}$$

$$= \frac{-0.16}{\sqrt{\left(\frac{3824.44}{58}\right)\left(\frac{1}{15}\right)}}$$

Note: the t table does
not have $df = 58$.
To be conservative
I used $df = 40$. for $df = 40$
the table value is 2.021

$$= \frac{-0.16}{\sqrt{(65.9386)(.0667)}}$$

$$= \frac{-0.16}{\sqrt{4.398}}$$

$$= \frac{-0.16}{2.097}$$

$$t = -.08 \qquad df = 58 \qquad p < .05$$

POSTTEST   NATIONAL PROFICIENCY SURVEY SERIES: BIOLOGY

EXPERIMENTAL   CONTROL

S	X_1	X_1^2	X_2	X_2^2
1	20	400	15	225
2	24	576	16	256
3	26	676	18	324
4	27	729	20	400
5	28	784	21	441
6	29	841	22	484
7	29	841	22	484
8	29	841	23	529
9	30	900	24	576
10	31	961	24	576
11	31	961	25	625
12	31	961	25	625
13	32	1024	25	625
14	32	1024	26	676
15	33	1089	26	676
16	33	1089	27	729
17	33	1089	27	729
18	34	1156	28	784
19	34	1156	29	841
20	35	1225	29	841
21	35	1225	30	900
22	35	1225	30	900
23	36	1296	31	961
24	36	1296	31	961
25	36	1296	32	1024
26	37	1369	33	1089
27	37	1369	34	1156
28	38	1444	35	1225
29	38	1444	36	1296
30	39	1521	37	1369
	968	31808	801	22327
	ΣX_1	ΣX_1^2	ΣX_2	ΣX_2^2

$$\overline{X_1} = \frac{\Sigma x_1}{n_1} = \frac{968}{30} = 32.27$$

$$\overline{X_2} = \frac{\Sigma x_2}{n_2} = \frac{801}{30} = 26.70$$

$$SD_1 = \sqrt{\frac{SS_1}{n_1 - 1}} \qquad\qquad SD_2 = \sqrt{\frac{SS_2}{n_2 - 1}}$$

$$SS_1 = \sum x_1^2 - \frac{\left(\sum x_1\right)^2}{n_1} \qquad\qquad SS_2 = \sum x_2^2 - \frac{\left(\sum x_2\right)^2}{n_2}$$

$$= 31808 - \frac{(968)^2}{30} \qquad\qquad = 22327 - \frac{(801)^2}{30}$$

$$= 31808 - \frac{937024}{30} \qquad\qquad = 22327 - \frac{641601}{30}$$

$$= 31808 - 31234.13 \qquad\qquad = 22327 - 21386.70$$

$$SS_1 = 573.87 \qquad\qquad SS_2 = 940.30$$

$$SD_1 = \sqrt{\frac{573.87}{29}} \qquad\qquad SD_2 = \sqrt{\frac{940.30}{29}}$$

$$= \sqrt{19.789} \qquad\qquad = \sqrt{32.424}$$

$$SD_1 = 4.45 \qquad\qquad SD_2 = 5.69$$

$$t = \frac{\bar{X}_1 - \bar{X}_2}{\sqrt{\left(\frac{SS_1 + SS_2}{n_1 + n_2 - 2}\right)\left(\frac{1}{n_1} + \frac{1}{n_2}\right)}} = \frac{32.27 - 26.70}{\sqrt{\left(\frac{573.87 + 940.30}{30 + 30 - 2}\right)\left(\frac{1}{30} + \frac{1}{30}\right)}}$$

$$= \frac{5.57}{\sqrt{\left(\frac{1514.17}{58}\right)\left(\frac{1}{15}\right)}}$$

$$= \frac{5.57}{\sqrt{(26.1064)(.0667)}}$$

$$= \frac{5.57}{\sqrt{1.7404}}$$

$$= \frac{5.57}{1.3192}$$

$$t = 4.22 \qquad df = 58 \qquad p < .05$$

CHAPTER TWENTY

Qualitative Data Collection

Oscilloscope Pictures/Everett Collection

Castaway, 2006

"No one recipe explains how to proceed with
data collection efforts." (p. 549)

LEARNING OUTCOMES

After reading Chapter 20, you should be able to do the following:

20.1 Describe qualitative data collection sources and techniques.

20.2 Describe strategies to address the trustworthiness (i.e., validity) and replicability (i.e., reliability) of qualitative research.

20.3 Describe the steps for getting started as a qualitative researcher ready to begin data collection or fieldwork.

DATA COLLECTION SOURCES AND TECHNIQUES

After obtaining entry into a setting and selecting participants, the qualitative researcher is ready to begin data collection, also commonly called fieldwork. Fieldwork involves spending considerable time in the setting under study, immersing oneself in this setting, and collecting as much relevant information as possible and as unobtrusively as possible. Qualitative researchers collect descriptive—narrative and visual—non-numerical data to gain insights into the phenomenon of interest. Because the data that are collected should contribute to understanding the phenomenon, data collection is largely determined by the nature of the problem. No one recipe explains how to proceed with data collection efforts. Rather, the researcher must collect the appropriate data to contribute to the understanding and resolution of a given problem.

Observations, interviews, questionnaires, phone calls, personal and official documents, photographs, recordings, drawings, journals, e-mail messages and responses, tweets, blogs, Facebook (and other social media), and informal conversations are all sources of qualitative data. Clearly, many sources of data are acceptable as long as the collection approach is ethical, is feasible, and contributes to an understanding of the phenomenon under study. The four data collection techniques we discuss in this chapter are observing, interviewing (including the use of focus groups and e-mail), administering questionnaires, and examining records. These techniques share one aspect: The researcher is the primary data collection instrument.

Observing

When qualitative researchers obtain data by watching the participants, they are observing. The emphasis during observation is on understanding the natural environment as lived by participants, without altering or manipulating it. For certain research questions, observation is the most appropriate and effective data collection approach. If you ask teachers how they handle discipline in their classrooms, for example, you run the risk of collecting biased information—they may not remember everything, or they may tell you only about their most successful strategies. By observing the classes, you will obtain much more objective information that can be compared to the self-reports of the research participants. The two common types of observation are participant and nonparticipant observation.

Participant Observation

In **participant observation**, the observer becomes part of and a participant in the situation being observed. In other words, the researcher participates in the situation while observing and collecting data on the activities, people, and physical aspects of the setting. There are varying degrees of participant observation—a researcher can be an *active participant observer*; a *privileged, active observer*; or a *passive observer*.

A benefit of participant observation is that it allows the researcher to gain insights and develop relationships with participants that would not be possible if the researcher observed but did not participate. However, it also has drawbacks. The researcher may lose objectivity and become emotionally involved with participants, for instance, or may have difficulty participating and collecting data at the same time. In cases where the group under study is tight-knit and closely organized, participation may cause tension for both the researcher and group members. Before adopting the role of a participant observer, the researcher must evaluate the likelihood of participating in the situation and gathering the desired data simultaneously. If it is not feasible for the researcher to be a full participant observer in the group being studied, it is best to be a nonparticipant observer.

Nonparticipant Observation

In **nonparticipant observation,** the observer is not directly involved in the situation being observed. In other words, the researcher observes and records behaviors but does not interact or participate in the life of the setting under study. Nonparticipant observers are less intrusive than participant observers and less likely to become emotionally involved with participants. Nonparticipant observation may also be best if the researcher does not have the background or needed expertise to act as a true participant or if the group being observed is too closely organized for the researcher to fit in easily. For example, a middle-age researcher probably can't be a true participant in a group of fifth-graders. However, nonparticipant observers may have more difficulty obtaining reliable information about participants' opinions, attitudes, and emotional states than participant observers do.

Recording Observations

Whether you are a participant or nonparticipant observer, you will need a method to document your observations. **Field notes**—qualitative research materials gathered, recorded, and compiled (usually on-site) during the course of a study—are best. Field notes describe, as accurately and as comprehensively as possible, all relevant aspects of the situation. They contain two basic types of information: (1) descriptive information about what the observer has directly seen or heard on-site through the course of the study and (2) reflective information that captures the researcher's personal reactions to observations, the researcher's experiences, and the researcher's thoughts during the observation sessions. Because of the need for clarity and detail, notes should be made in the field whenever possible, during the observation. If necessary, the researcher may record field notes after leaving the setting, but recording should be done as soon as possible—when the interval between observing and writing field notes becomes longer, the likelihood of distortion from the original observation also increases.

Field notes are the data that will be analyzed to provide the description and understanding of the research setting and participants; they should be as extensive, clear, and detailed as possible. For example, a good researcher won't simply write, "The class was happy." Instead, the researcher should describe the activities of the students, the looks on their faces, their interactions with each other, the teachers' activities, and other observations suggesting the class was happy. It is a good rule of thumb to avoid words such as *good, happy, useful*, and other evaluative terms and replace them with words describing behaviors that were seen or heard. Figure 20.1 illustrates both the descriptive and the reflective aspects of field notes. As you read the figure, notice the clarity and level of detail in the researcher's notes as he described the physical setting, the actions of the students, and the interactions that took place. Each O.C. entry (i.e., observer's comment) represents a reflection that the researcher had while writing the descriptive field notes. These reflections represent a more personal and subjective aspect of the field notes and should be distinguished from the descriptive material in the notes themselves. In the O.C. entries, you can identify times when the researcher noted something unusual, something that had recurred, or something that had to be explored.

To aid in taking field notes in the setting, a researcher often brings a protocol, or list of issues, to guide observation. Protocols provide the researcher with a focus during the observation and also provide a common framework for field notes, making it easier to organize and categorize data across various sets of notes. For example, a simple protocol for observation may include the following topics:

- Who is being observed? How many people are involved, who are they, and what individual roles and mannerisms are evident?
- What is going on? What is the nature of the conversation? What are people saying or doing?
- What is the physical setting like? How are people seated, and where? How do the participants interact with each other?
- What is the status or roles of who leads, who follows, who is decisive, who is not? What is the tone of the session? What beliefs, attitudes, values, and so on, seem to emerge?
- How did the meeting end? Was the group divided, united, upset, bored, or relieved?

FIGURE 20.1 • Section of field notes showing detailed description and observer's comments

March 24, 1980
Joe McCloud
11:00 a.m. to 12:30 p.m.
Westwood High
6th Set of Notes

THE FOURTH-PERIOD CLASS IN MARGE'S ROOM

I arrived at Westwood High at five minutes to eleven, the time Marge told me her fourth period started. I was dressed as usual: sport shirt, chino pants, and a Woolrich parka. The fourth period is the only time during the day when all the students who are in the "neurologically impaired/learning disability" program, better known as "Marge's program," come together. During the other periods, certain students in the program, two or three or four at most, come to her room for help with the work they are getting in other regular high school classes.

It was a warm, fortyish, promise of a spring day. There was a police patrol wagon, the kind that has benches in the back that are used for large busts, parked in the back of the big parking lot that is in front of the school. No one was sitting in it and I never heard its reason for being there. In the circular drive in front of the school was parked a United States Army car. It had insignias on the side and was a khaki color. As I walked from my car, a balding fortyish man in an Army uniform came out of the building and went to the car and sat down. Four boys and a girl also walked out of the school. All were white. They had on old dungarees and colored stenciled t-shirts with spring jackets over them. One of the boys, the tallest of the four, called out, "oink, oink, oink." This was done as he sighted the police vehicle in the back.

O.C.: This was strange to me in that I didn't think that the kids were into "the police as pigs." Somehow I associated that with another time, the early 1970s. I'm going to have to come to grips with the assumptions I have about high school due to my own experience. Sometimes I feel like Westwood is entirely different from my high school and yet this police car incident reminded me of mine.

Classes were changing when I walked down the halls. As usual there was the boy with girl standing here and there by the lockers. There were three couples that I saw. There was the occasional shout. There were no teachers outside the doors.

O.C.: The halls generally seem to be relatively unsupervised during class changes.

Two black girls I remember walking down the hall together. They were tall and thin and had their hair elaborately braided with beads all through them. I stopped by the office to tell Mr. Talbor's (the principal) secretary that I was in the building. She gave me a warm smile.

O.C.: I feel quite comfortable in the school now. Somehow I feel like I belong. As I walk down the halls some teachers say hello. I have been going out of my way to say hello to kids that I pass. Twice I've been in a stare-down with kids passing in the hall. Saying, "How ya' doin'?" seems to disarm them.

I walked into Marge's class and she was standing in front of the room with more people than I had ever seen in the room save for her homeroom which is right after second period. She looked like she was talking to the class or was just about to start. She was dressed as she had been on my other visits—clean, neat, well-dressed but casual. Today she had on a striped blazer, a white blouse, and dark slacks. She looked up at me, smiled, and said: "Oh, I have a lot more people here now than the last time."

O.C.: This was in reference to my other visits during other periods where there are only a few students. She seems self-conscious about having such a small group of students to be responsible for. Perhaps she compares herself with the regular teachers who have classes of thirty or so.

There were two women in their late twenties sitting in the room. There was only one chair left. Marge said to me something like: "We have two visitors from the central office today. One is a vocational counselor and the other is a physical therapist," but I don't remember if those were the words. I felt embarrassed coming in late. I sat down in the only chair available next to one of the women from the central office. They had on skirts and carried their pocketbooks, much more dressed up than the teachers I've seen. They sat there and observed.

Source: From Robert C. Bogdan & Sari Knopp Biklen, *Qualitative Research for Education: An Introduction to Theories and Methods,* 5/e. Published by Allyn and Bacon, Boston, MA. Copyright © 2007 by Pearson Education. Reprinted by permission of the publisher.

(Continued)

FIGURE 20.1 • Section of field notes showing detailed description and observer's comments (*Continued*)

Below is the seating arrangement of the class today:

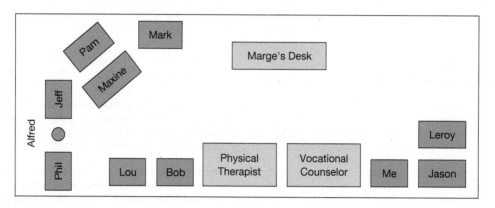

Alfred (Mr. Armstrong, the teacher's aide) walked around but when he stood in one place it was over by Phil and Jeff. Marge walked about near her desk during her talk which she started by saying to the class: "Now remember, tomorrow is a fieldtrip to the Rollway Company. We all meet in the usual place, by the bus, in front of the main entrance at 8:30. Mrs. Sharp wanted me to tell you that the tour of Rollway is not specifically for you. It's not like the trip to G.M. They took you to places where you were likely to be able to get jobs. Here, it's just a general tour that everybody goes on. Many of the jobs that you will see are not for you. Some are just for people with engineering degrees. You'd better wear comfortable shoes because you may be walking for two or three hours." Maxine and Mark said: "Ooh," in protest to the walking.

She paused and said in a demanding voice: "OK, any questions? You are all going to be there. (Pause) I want you to take a blank card and write down some questions so you have things to ask at the plant." She began passing out cards and at this point Jason, who was sitting next to me, made a tutting sound of disgust and said: "We got to do this?" Marge said: "I know this is too easy for you, Jason." This was said in a sarcastic way but not like a strong put-down.

O.C.: It was like sarcasm between two people who know each other well. Marge has known many of these kids for a few years. I have to explore the implications of that for her relations with them.

Marge continued: "OK, what are some of the questions you are going to ask?" Jason yelled out "Insurance," and Marge said: "I was asking Maxine not Jason." This was said matter of factly without anger toward Jason. Maxine said: "Hours— the hours you work, the wages." Somebody else yelled out: "Benefits." Marge wrote these things on the board. She got to Phil who was sitting there next to Jeff. I believe she skipped Jeff. Mr. Armstrong was standing right next to Phil. She said: "Have you got one?" Phil said: "I can't think of one." She said: "Honestly Phil. Wake up." Then she went to Joe, the white boy. Joe and Jeff are the only white boys I've seen in the program. The two girls are white. He said: "I can't think of any." She got to Jason and asked him if he could think of anything else. He said: "Yeah, you could ask 'em how many of the products they made each year." Marge said: "Yes, you could ask about production. How about Leroy, do you have any ideas, Leroy?" He said: "No." Mr. Armstrong was standing over in the corner and saying to Phil in a low voice: "Now you know what kinds of questions you ask when you go for a job?" Phil said: "Training, what kind of training do you have to have?" Marge said: "Oh yes, that's right, training." Jason said out loud but not yelling: "How much schooling you need to get it." Marge kept listing them.

O.C.: Marge was quite animated. If I hadn't seen her like this before I would think she was putting on a show for the people from central office.

■ What activities or interactions seemed unusual or significant?
■ What was the observer doing during the session? What was the observer's level of participation in the observation (e.g., participant observer, nonparticipant observer, etc.)?

Certainly different studies with different participants in different settings would have alternative protocol questions. The aim here is not to be exhaustive but to encourage you to develop and refine some form of protocol that will guide you in answering the overarching question, "What is going on here?" Figure 20.2 illustrates a very simple protocol.

A protocol is an important tool that provides structure for recording information from observation sessions. The following guidelines should also help you in recording information and organizing field notes successfully:

■ Start slowly. Do not assume you know what you're looking for until you have some experience in the setting and spend some time with the participants.
■ Try to enter the field with no preconceptions. Try to recognize and dismiss your own assumptions and biases and remain open to what you see; try to see things through the participants' perspectives.
■ Write your field notes as soon as possible. When you're done, list the main ideas or themes you've observed and recorded. Don't discuss your observation until the field notes are written; discussion may alter your initial perspective.
■ Include the date, site, time, and topic on every set of field notes. Leave wide margins to write your impressions next to sections of the descriptive field notes when you print. The wide margins also provide space for doing initial coding and analysis. Draw diagrams of the site.
■ List key words related to your observation, then outline what you saw and heard. Use the key words and outline to write your detailed field notes.
■ Keep the descriptive and reflective sections of field notes separate, although collected together.
■ Write down your hunches, questions, and insights after each observation. Use memos.
■ Number the lines or paragraphs of your field notes to help you find particular sections when needed.

FIGURE 20.2 • Sample of observation protocol

Setting:
Individual Observed:
Observation #: (first observation, second, etc.)
Observer Involvement:

Date/Time:
Place:
Duration of Observation (indicate start/end times):

Descriptive Notes	**Reflective Notes**
(Detailed, chronological notes about what the observer sees, hears; what occurred; the physical setting)	(Concurrent notes about the observer's thoughts, personal reactions, experiences)

Interviewing

An **interview** is a purposeful interaction in which one person obtains information from another. Interviews permit researchers to obtain important data they cannot acquire from observation alone, although pairing observations and interviews provides a valuable way to gather complementary data. Interviews can provide information that is inaccessible through observation; for example, observation cannot provide information about past events, or the way things used to be before Mr. Hardnosed became principal, or why Ms. Haddit has had it and is considering transferring to another school. In addition, interview questions can derive from observational data—you may see something and want to ask follow-up questions to understand the reasons behind particular events. Interviewers can explore and probe participants' responses to gather in-depth data about participants' experiences and feelings. Researchers can examine attitudes, interests, feelings, concerns, and values more easily than they can through observation. Interviews may range in length from a few minutes to a few hours. They may consist of a one-time session or multiple sessions with the same participant. In addition, participants may be interviewed individually or in groups.

Interviews are distinguished by their degree of formality and structure. Interviews may be formal and planned (e.g., "We'll meet Tuesday at 1:00 to discuss your perceptions") or informal and unplanned (e.g., "I'm glad I caught you in the corridor; I've been meaning to ask you. . ."). Some interviews are structured, with a specified set of questions to be asked, whereas others are unstructured, with questions prompted by the flow of the interview. Semistructured interviews combine both structured and unstructured approaches.

Unstructured Interviews

The **unstructured interview** is little more than a casual conversation that allows the qualitative researcher to inquire into something that has presented itself as an opportunity to learn about something at the research setting. The goal of informal interviews is not to get answers to predetermined questions but rather to find out the participants' perspectives and what they have experienced. Often informal interviews are used further in the study to obtain more complex or personal informa-

tion. Agar[1] suggested that researchers have a set of questions ready to ask participants by guiding the conversation around *who, what, where, when, why,* and *how.* Using these prompts, researchers will never be at a loss for a question to add to their understanding of what is happening in the research setting.

Structured Interviews

Qualitative researchers may also interview research participants formally as part of the data collection efforts. In a formal, **structured interview,** the researcher has a specified set of questions that elicits the same information from all the respondents. A major challenge in constructing any interview, however, is to phrase questions so that they elicit the desired information. Although this point may seem obvious, qualitative researchers often feel compelled by tradition to ask a lengthy set of questions, many of which stray from their focus.

When planning structured interviews, consider the following options for ensuring interview quality:

- Include both open-ended (i.e., divergent) and closed (i.e., convergent) questions in a structured interview. A closed question allows for a brief response such as yes or no, whereas an open-ended question allows for a detailed response and elaboration on questions in ways you may not have anticipated. The information gathered through open-ended questions may be more difficult to make sense of, but this type of question allows the researcher to obtain important information that may otherwise be considered discrepant.

- Pilot-test the questions with a group of respondents who share similar characteristics with your research participants to see if the questions make sense. The participants' feedback will quickly confirm or challenge the assumptions you made while writing your questions (e.g., about appropriate language). Using the feedback from this group, revise the questions before interviewing your participants.

---

[1] *The Professional Stranger: An Informal Introduction to Ethnography,* by M. H. Agar, 1980, Orlando, FL: Academic Press.

Guidelines for Interviewing

Although the concept of an interview seems straightforward, it can be a complex and difficult undertaking when the gender, culture, and life experiences of the interviewer and participant are quite different. Challenges can include control of the interview (i.e., who sets the direction or tone), the accuracy of responses provided, and the extent to which the language of the interviewee and the researcher are similar enough to permit meaningful inferences about the topic under study. For these reasons, a researcher must always take the time to enter the research setting unobtrusively and build support and trust with participants before initiating an interview. A trusting relationship is essential if participants are to answer questions—particularly about sensitive issues—with candor.

The following actions can help improve communication and facilitate the collection of interview data:

- Listen more; talk less. Listening is the most important part of interviewing.
- Don't interrupt. Learn how to wait.
- Tolerate silence. It means the participant is thinking.
- Avoid leading questions; ask open-ended questions.
- Keep participants focused and ask for concrete details.
- Follow up on what participants say, and ask questions when you don't understand.
- Don't be judgmental about participants' views or beliefs; keep a neutral demeanor. Your purpose is to learn about others' perspectives, whether you agree with them or not.
- Don't debate with participants over their responses. You are a recorder, not a debater.

Collecting Data from Interviews

Interviewers have three basic choices for collecting their data: taking notes during the interview, writing notes after the interview, and recording the interview. Although all these approaches can be used in a study, the data collection method of choice is audio or video recording, which provides a verbatim account of the session. Taking notes during the interview can be distracting and can alter the flow of the session. Writing notes after the interview is better than trying to write during the interview, but it can be difficult to remember the contents of the interview accurately. Recordings are convenient and reliable, and they ensure that the original data are available at any time. Although a few participants may balk at being recorded, most participants will not, especially if you promise them confidentiality. Make sure that the digital recorder is in good working order with new batteries or has been charged recently before entering the interview setting.

Following recorded data collection, it is useful to transcribe the recordings. A transcription is a written record of the events that were recorded. This task is time-consuming, especially for long interviews. Transcribing one 60-minute recording may take 4 or 5 hours. If you do the transcribing instead of hiring someone (a costly alternative), write the date, subject discussed, and participant (using a coded name) on the transcript. Number all pages. Make sure a different indicator is given and used to identify the various persons speaking.

The transcripts are like field notes for interview data. They should be reviewed against the recording for accuracy. Interview transcripts are voluminous and usually have to be reduced to focus on the data pertinent to the study, although sometimes this type of focus is difficult to achieve. During data analysis, the transcript should be read and important sections labeled to indicate their importance.

Focus Groups

Another valuable interview technique is the use of focus groups, which can include several individuals who can contribute to your understanding of your research problem. A focus group is like a group interview where you are trying to "collect shared understanding from several individuals as well as to get views from specific people."[2] Focus groups are particularly useful when the interaction between individuals will lead to a shared understanding of the questions posed by a teacher-researcher.

When conducting focus groups, it is important to ensure that all participants have their say and to nurture a group agreement to take turns; that is, participants should understand that the focus group is a group-sharing activity and not

[2] *Educational Research: Planning, Conducting, and Evaluating Quantitative and Qualitative Research*, (5th ed.; p. 217), by J. W. Creswell, 2015, Upper Saddle River, NJ: Pearson Education, Inc.

something to be dominated by one or two participants. Using a structured or semistructured interview schedule, a researcher can pose questions to the group and encourage all participants to respond. To use sporting metaphors, use a basketball versus a table tennis questioning style: Ask the question, elicit a response, and pass it off to another participant (i.e., basketball) versus ask the question, accept the response, and ask another question (i.e., table tennis). Get as much information out of each question as you possibly can and, in the process, ensure that all group participants have an opportunity to respond.

Ideally, the qualitative researcher conducts an interview to capture the responses from the focus group and later transcribe the discussion. This process is also time-consuming—perhaps even more so than it is for individual interviews, so be prepared to allocate time to ferreting out the nuances of the focus group interview and the shared understandings that emerge.

E-Mail Interviews

Another approach to interviewing that can be used effectively by qualitative researchers is the e-mail interview. For busy teachers, for example, engaging in an ongoing conversation using e-mail may be less intrusive—busy professionals can respond to e-mail either synchronously (i.e., akin to a real-time conversation with the researcher) or asynchronously (i.e., at some other time when researcher and participant are not both sitting at their computers).

E-mail interviews have both pros and cons. For example, one advantage of the e-mail interview is that you don't have to transcribe a recorded interview with a colleague or student—the transcription of the interview has already been done for you by the respondent! However, researchers must be attentive to the ethical issues associated with assuring respondents that their text responses will be confidential and anonymous. Most of us are not experts when it comes to technology, but in general we have concerns that e-mail directed to someone in particular may be sitting on a server somewhere, accessible to other curious folks! This worry is further enhanced by the amount of spam (i.e., junk e-mail) we receive that has been forwarded from someone else's computer. When these concerns are addressed, such interviews can be a useful tool to use in your research setting.

Questionnaires

Although face-to-face interviews provide intimate opportunities for the researcher to know how each respondent feels about a particular issue, interviewing is very time-consuming. A compromise is to use a questionnaire. A **questionnaire** is a written collection of self-report questions to be answered by a selected group of research participants. The major difference between a questionnaire and an interview is that, with a questionnaire, the participant writes the responses on the form provided. Questionnaires allow the researcher to collect large amounts of data in a relatively short amount of time. Researchers often administer questionnaires and then conduct follow-up interviews with research participants who provided written feedback that warrants further investigation.

Because a valid and reliable data collection instrument ensures useful responses, you should consider the following guidelines for developing and presenting questionnaires:

- Avoid a sloppy presentation. Make the questionnaire attractive, and consider using large print if necessary.
- Carefully proofread questionnaires before sending them out. Nothing will turn respondents off more quickly than a questionnaire littered with errors.
- Avoid a lengthy questionnaire. Pilot testing the instrument will provide a realistic sense of how long respondents need to complete the task. Remember that, no matter how much respondents want to help you, a questionnaire that's too long will find its way into the circular file instead of back in your hands.
- Do not ask unnecessary questions. Asking unnecessary questions is akin to teachers developing tests that don't match the course content—students are stumped, and teachers learn little about the effectiveness of their lessons. Likewise, as researchers, we often feel compelled to ask a great deal of trivial information on a questionnaire. Participants become frustrated, and we collect information that is tangential to our stated purpose.
- Use structured items with a variety of possible responses. Indicate what you mean by words like *often* and *frequently*, and be clear as to how they differ from each other (e.g., Do you buy chocolate often? versus Do you

buy chocolate once a week?). Otherwise, respondents may interpret the meaning of the terms in quite different ways than you intended.

■ Whenever possible, add an Additional Comments section. An Additional Comments section provides respondents with an opportunity to respond openly to your questions and to raise new questions. These comments provide an excellent source of discrepant data (e.g., "I hadn't expected a research participant to say that he or she buys chocolate every day!") and an opportunity to follow up with informal interviews to elicit more information from the respondents as your time, energy, and inquisitiveness allow.

■ Decide whether you want respondents to put their names on the questionnaires or whether you will use a number to keep track of who has responded. You should assure respondents that their confidentiality will be protected throughout the process. However, you can protect respondents while keeping track of who has responded and deciding whether they have made comments that you feel warrant a follow-up conversation. If you track respondents' identities, you must communicate that they will not suffer any negative consequences for anything they may share with you; this communication is necessary to ensure that they feel comfortable supplying honest and forthright answers.

Examining Records

Qualitative researchers examine various types of records or documents, including archival documents, journals, maps, video and digital recordings, and artifacts. Many of these data sources are naturally occurring in educational settings and require only that the researcher locate them within the research setting.

Archival Documents

Like classrooms, schools are repositories for all sorts of records—student records, standardized test scores, retention rates, minutes of meetings (e.g., faculty, PTA, school board), newspaper clippings about significant events in the community, and so on. With permission, the qualitative researcher can use these sources of data to gain valuable historical insights, identify potential trends, and explain how things got to be the way they are. Clerical assistants, school aides, and student teachers are often happy to help with uncovering archival information and organizing it in a way that is most useful to the classroom teacher if they believe that the data contribute to the collective understanding of a pressing educational issue.

Journals

Daily journals kept by teachers provide firsthand accounts of what is happening in the classroom and provide a glimpse of the school from another perspective. Students' journals can provide teachers with a window into the students' world and their daily classroom experiences, which can affect future teaching practices meaningfully. Regardless of your specific research questions, you should encourage journaling by research participants as a way to record their perceptions of what is happening in the research setting.

Maps

Qualitative researchers working in schools often find class maps and school maps useful for a number of reasons. They provide contextual insights for people who have not visited the school, and they provide the qualitative researcher with a reflective tool—a way of rethinking the way things are in schools and classrooms. For example, why are the computers in the classroom placed in a bank along one wall, and what are the effects of individual student computer time on other seatwork activities? A class map can record traffic flow in a classroom as well as teacher movement during instruction; the school map may also prove useful for teams of qualitative researchers concerned about the movement and interactions of different grade levels of students and any problems that emerge from the traffic flow. For qualitative researchers, context is everything! Figure 20.3 shows an example of a classroom map.

Digital Recordings

Digital recordings provide qualitative researchers with another valuable, although somewhat obtrusive, data source. Of course, these techniques have some downsides. For example, funny faces and bizarre comments sometimes appear as a result of

FIGURE 20.3 • Example of a classroom map

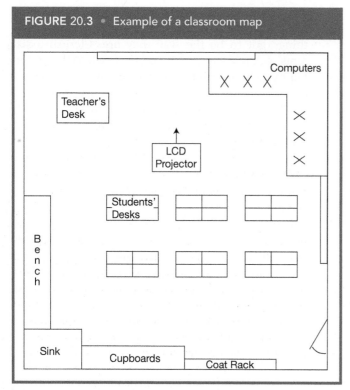

Source: Mills, Geoffrey, *Action Research: A Guide for the Teacher Researcher*, 6th Edition, © 2018, p. 87. Reprinted by permission of Pearson Education, Inc., Upper Saddle River, NJ.

the presence of such technology in a classroom for the first time. However, technologies such as digital cameras and smartphone cameras provide excellent, unobtrusive digital options that are compact, convenient, and in high-definition to boot! These unobtrusive cameras are far less likely to elicit outlandish behavior from participants, and they are part of the researcher's toolkit that can always be close at hand. Similarly, most cell phones incorporate digital voice recorder technology that provides another useful tool for spontaneous interviews or recording researcher's reflections immediately following fieldwork. However, the use of digital recording raises the serious issue of time allotment. Watching and listening to digital records and then recording observations require an enormous amount of time. This time commitment is perhaps the number-one challenge for researchers using these data sources.

Artifacts

Schools and classrooms are rich sources of what we call *artifacts*—written or visual sources of data that contribute to our understanding of what is hap-

pening in classrooms and schools. Artifacts can include almost everything else that we haven't already discussed. For example, schools have tended to move toward what administrators refer to as authentic assessment techniques, including the use of student portfolios. A portfolio is a presentation of work that captures an individual student's work samples over time to demonstrate that student's growth. Portfolios, although difficult to quantify, provide the teacher with valuable outcome data that get at the heart of the qualitatively different samples of work. Such artifacts are valuable data sources that qualitative researchers may use as starting points for conversation with research participants.

Digital research tools such as wikis, blogs, Skype, and software can contribute to your qualitative data collection strategies in an ever-changing digital environment (see the accompanying Digital Research Tools feature). These tools allow the qualitative researcher to interact with research participants (particularly those who are geographically remote) in ways that were previously not thought possible.

MyLab Education **Self-Check 20.1**

MyLab Education **Application Exercise 20.1:** Evaluating Research Articles: Collecting Data for a Qualitative Study

MyLab Education **Application Exercise 20.2:** Collecting Qualitative Data

VALIDITY AND RELIABILITY IN QUALITATIVE RESEARCH

Validity in Qualitative Research

In qualitative research, validity is the degree to which qualitative data gauge accurately what we are trying to measure. For example, teachers may ask, "Are the results of this standardized test really valid?" Or teachers may comment, "My students did poorly on the history test I gave them, but I'm not sure it's an accurate representation of what they really know." Both scenarios raise issues about the validity of the data, that is, whether or not the data reflect what they were intended to measure.

Historically, validity has been linked to numerically based quantitative research. However, as

Digital Research Tools

WIKI, BLOG, SKYPE, AND VOICE-TO-TEXT SOFTWARE?

In addition to survey tools (e.g., SurveyMonkey and Qualtrics), e-mail, and digital recordings, web-based tools can provide the qualitative researcher with additional data collection strategies and tools.

Wiki

A wiki is a website that allows the easy creation of a web page that can provide a forum for collaborative research. For example, you can create a wiki focused on an aspect of your research and invite participants (your sample) to a secure setting where they can participate in an open forum. Similarly, you can provide links to other websites, as well as use the wiki as a communication tool through which you can communicate with the study's participants. One popular, free wiki provider is Wikispaces (wikispaces.com). Creation of a wiki is simple and secure and provides a new data collection possibility for qualitative researchers who wish to invite research participants into a collaborative forum.

Blog

A blog (a blend of the term *web log*) is a type of personal website where you can share information about your research and solicit responses from participants while capturing the discourse in chronological order. It is possible to embed photos and videos within your blog as part of the creation of a collaborative research space. A popular, free blog provider is Blogger (blogger.com), and getting started is as simple as creating an account and following the template designer. Blogs provide an excellent opportunity for engaging research participants in a collaborative, secure conversation.

Skype

Skype is a proprietary software application that allows users to make voice calls and to video-conference over the Internet. Founded in 2003 by Estonian, Danish, and Swedish developers, Skype boasted 663 million registered users by 2010. By that same year, 13% of all international call minutes (54 billion minutes) were reportedly Skype calls. In short, with the proliferation of computers with cameras and cell phones, Skype provides a relatively inexpensive (if not free) qualitative data collection tool for researchers who are unable to visit a research site personally to observe or who wish to interview research participants who are located at a distance that makes face-to-face contact prohibitive.

Voice-to-Text Software

Dragon Naturally Speaking (www.nuance.com/dragon) is speech recognition software that formats voice into text. Used effectively, new generation voice-to-text programs can eliminate the need to invest time transcribing digital recordings.

---

qualitative research became more popular in the late 1970s and early 1980s, qualitative researchers felt pressure to justify and defend the accuracy and credibility of their studies. Two terms commonly used to describe validity in qualitative research are *trustworthiness* and *understanding*. Qualitative researchers can establish the **trustworthiness** of their research by addressing the credibility, transferability, dependability, and confirmability of their studies and findings.[3] First, a researcher must take into account all the complexities in the study and

address problems that are not easily explained (i.e., *credibility*). The researcher should also include descriptive, context-relevant statements so that someone hearing about or reading a report of the study can identify with the setting (i.e., *transferability*). Remember, qualitative researchers believe that everything they study is context-bound; they do not seek to draw conclusions that can be generalized to larger groups of people. Therefore, qualitative researchers should include as much detail as possible so others can see the setting for themselves. The researcher should also address the stability of the data collected (i.e., *dependability*) and the neutrality and objectivity of the data (i.e., *confirmability*).

[3] "Criteria for assessing the trustworthiness of naturalistic inquiries," by E. G. Guba, 1981, *Educational Communication and Technology Journal*, 29, pp. 75–91.

Let's look at criteria for measuring the quality of qualitative research based on these two terms, *trustworthiness* and *understanding*, and then look at strategies for increasing the validity of your qualitative research.

Guba's Criteria for Validity of Qualitative Research

Guba's article "Criteria for Assessing the Trustworthiness of Naturalistic Inquiries" (1981) speaks directly to qualitative researchers. Guba argued that the trustworthiness of qualitative inquiry could be established by addressing the following characteristics of a study: *credibility, transferability, dependability*, and *confirmability*.

Credibility. The **credibility** of the study refers to the researcher's ability to take into account the complexities that present themselves in a study and to deal with patterns that are not easily explained. To do this, Guba suggested that the following methods be used to establish credibility:

- *Do prolonged participation at the study site* to overcome distortions produced by the presence of researchers and to provide researchers with the opportunity to test biases and perceptions.
- *Do persistent observation* to identify pervasive qualities as well as atypical characteristics.
- *Do peer debriefing* to provide researchers with the opportunity to test their growing insights through interactions with other professionals. For example, most of us will be able to identify a "critical friend," a colleague, or a "significant other"—somebody who is willing and able to help us reflect on our own situations by listening, prompting, and recording our insights throughout the process.
- *Practice triangulation* to compare a variety of data sources and different methods with one another in order to cross-check data. It is generally accepted in qualitative research circles that researchers should not rely on any single source of data, whether it be an interview, observation, or survey instrument. Therefore, the strength of qualitative research lies in its multi-instrument approach, or triangulation. Triangulation is the use of multiple methods, data collection strategies, and data sources to get a more complete picture of the topic under study. It is important

that researchers apply the principle of triangulation throughout their qualitative data collection efforts.

- *Collect documents, films, digital recordings, artifacts, and other "raw" or "slice-of-life" data items.*
- *Do member checks* to test the overall report with the study's participants before sharing it in final form.
- *Establish structural corroboration or coherence* to ensure that there are no internal conflicts or contradictions.
- *Establish referential adequacy;* that is, test analyses and interpretations against documents, recordings, films, and the like, that were collected as part of the study.

Transferability. Guba's second criteria of **transferability** refers to qualitative researchers' beliefs that everything they study is context-bound and that the goal of their work is not to develop "truth" statements that can be generalized to larger groups of people. To facilitate the development of descriptive, context-relevant statements, Guba proposed that the researcher should:

- *Collect detailed descriptive data* that permit comparison of a given context (classroom or school) to other possible contexts to which transfer might be contemplated.
- *Develop detailed descriptions of the context* to make judgments about fit with other contexts possible.

The transferability of a qualitative research account depends largely on whether the consumer of the research can identify with the setting. Include as much detail as possible to allow the recipients of your work to "see" the setting for themselves.

Dependability. According to Guba, **dependability** refers to the stability of the data. To address issues related to the dependability of the data we collect, Guba recommended the following steps:

- *Overlap methods.* This step is similar to a triangulation process. Use two or more methods so that the weakness of one is compensated by the strength of another. For example, interviews with students may be used to contribute to your understanding of what you observed during a lesson.

TABLE 20.1 • Guba's criteria for ensuring the validity of qualitative research

Criteria	Definition	Strategies
Credibility	The researcher's ability to take into account all of the complexities that present themselves in a study and to deal with patterns that are not easily explained	Do prolonged participation at study site. Do persistent observation. Do peer debriefing. Practice triangulation. Collect "slice-of-life" data items. Do member checks. Establish structural corroboration or coherence. Establish referential adequacy.
Transferability	The researcher's belief that everything is context-bound	Collect detailed descriptive data. Develop detailed descriptions of the context.
Dependability	The stability of the data	Overlap methods. Establish an audit trail.
Confirmability	The neutrality or objectivity of the data collected	Practice triangulation. Practice reflexivity.

Source: From "Criteria for Assessing the Trustworthiness of Naturalistic Inquiries," by E. G. Guba, 1981, *Educational Communication and Technology Journal*, 29(1), pp. 75–91. Adapted with permission.

■ *Establish an audit trail.* This process makes it possible for an external "auditor" (maybe a critical friend, principal, or graduate student) to examine the processes of data collection, analysis, and interpretation. This audit trail may take the form of a written description of each process and perhaps even access to original field notes, artifacts, digital-recordings, pictures, archival data, and so on.

Confirmability. The final characteristic that Guba addresses is the **confirmability** of the data, or the neutrality or objectivity of the data that have been collected. Guba argues that the following two steps can be taken to address this issue:

■ *Practice triangulation,* whereby a variety of data sources and different methods are compared with one another to cross-check data.
■ *Practice reflexivity,* that is, intentionally reveal underlying assumptions or biases that cause you, as the researcher, to formulate a set of questions in a particular way and to present findings in a particular way. One technique for doing this is to keep a journal in which reflections and musings are recorded on a regular basis.

Wolcott's Strategies for Ensuring the Validity of Qualitative Research

Taken in concert with the previous discussion about validity criteria, the following strategies provide researchers with practical options for making sure their research is the best it can be.[4]

Talk Little; Listen a Lot. This strategy suggests that researchers should carefully monitor the ratio of listening to talking when they conduct interviews, ask questions, or engage children, parents, and colleagues in discussions about the problem being studied. For example, interviewing children can be difficult work—our best thought-out questions elicit painfully brief replies, and we are left wondering what to do next. Many researchers are in the business of talking for a living, so it comes quite naturally to us to jump in with our own answer for the child. The trustworthiness of our inquiries will be enhanced if we can bite our tongue, think of some other probing questions, and wait patiently (try counting one thousand?. . . two thousand. . . three thousand?. . .). The best advice to researchers

---

[4] *Transforming Qualitative Data: Description, Analysis and Interpretation* by H. F. Wolcott, 1994, Thousand Oaks, CA: Sage.

is to be patient and allow respondents time to respond. Avoid being your own best informant.

Record Observations Accurately. When conducting classroom research, recording observations while you are teaching is nearly impossible. However, you should record observations as soon as possible following a teaching episode to capture the essence of what transpired. Although digital recordings can assist with our efforts to record accurately, there will still be many occasions when, as participant observers, we have to rely on our field notes, our journals, or our memories. And for some of us, relying on memory is becoming an increasingly scary thing!

Begin Writing Early. In a workday that is already crunched by the pressures of time, finding time to write in journals is often difficult. However, if we rely solely on our memories of what has been happening in our classrooms over an extended period of time, we are likely to fall victim to writing romanticized versions of classroom and school life. Make time to write down your reflections. The act of writing your recollections of a teaching episode or observation will make evident to you what blanks need to be filled in, for example, what questions need to be asked the next day or what should be the focus of your observations.

Let Readers "See" for Themselves. Include primary data in any account to let the readers of your action research accounts (colleagues, principals, university professors) see the data for themselves. As Wolcott suggests, "In striking the delicate balance between providing too much detail and too little, I would rather err on the side of too much; conversely, between over-analyzing and underanalyzing data, I would rather say too little."[5] This is particularly true in a schoolwide action research effort in which you are seeking support for possible change based on data that you must present to colleagues who may not have had a central role in the conduct of the study. When sharing your research reports with colleagues, let them see the data. This may mean using charts, graphs, photographs, film—whatever you have collected. In doing so, you will bring the recipient of your work along in the process and perhaps earn their buy-in. Showing can be more persuasive than telling.

Report Fully. In our quest to find neat answers and solutions to our problems, it is often easy to avoid keeping track of discrepant events and data. Just when we think we know the answer, some data come along to shatter the illusion of having neatly resolved the problem! We do not need to be fearful of discrepant data. After all, it is all grist for the research mill. Although we do not need to report everything, it is helpful to keep track of the discrepant data and to seek further explanation.

Be Candid. Researchers should be candid about their work. If they are writing a narrative that they hope to publish or share with a broader audience, they should make explicit any biases that they may have about the inquiry they have undertaken. Researchers should also make explicit the things about which they have made judgments because it is easy to slip into a narrative that seeks to validate one's position. Being candid may also provide an opportunity to be explicit about events that occurred during the study and that may have affected the outcomes. For example, high student turnover rates may provide an explanation for fluctuating test scores.

Seek Feedback. It is always a good idea to seek feedback from colleagues (and perhaps even students, parents, volunteers, and administrators) on a written report. Other readers help to raise questions about what you as the writer have taken for granted. They raise questions about the accuracy of the account and help you to go back to your classroom in your quest to get the story right (or at least, not all wrong).

Write Accurately. Once you have written a description of your research, it is a good idea to read the account aloud or to ask a close colleague to read the account carefully to look for contradictions in the text. Often we are too close to the investigation to see the contradictions that may be blatantly obvious to an outsider. Nevertheless, the accuracy of the account (whether written or "performed") is critical to the validity of the study.[6]

Reliability in Qualitative Research

Reliability is the degree to which study data consistently measure whatever they measure. Although the term *reliability* is usually used to refer to instruments and tests in quantitative research, qualitative researchers can also consider

---

[5] Wolcott, 1994, p. 350.

[6] For further discussion of these points and a discussion of "When It Really Matters, Does Validity Really Matter?" see Wolcott, pp. 348–370.

reliability in their studies, in particular the reliability of the techniques they are using to gather data. For example, as qualitative researchers examine the results of their inquiry, they should consider whether the data would be collected consistently if the same techniques were utilized over time.

Reliability, however, is not the same as validity. Remember, a valid test that measures what it purports to measure will do so consistently over time, but a reliable test may consistently measure the wrong thing.

Generalizability

Historically, research in education has concerned itself with **generalizability,** a term that refers to the applicability of findings to settings and contexts different from the one in which they were obtained. That is, based on the behavior of a small group (i.e., a sample) of individuals, researchers try to describe, explain, or predict the behavior of a larger group (i.e., the population) of people. This view of generalizability, however, is not directly applicable to qualitative research.

The goal of qualitative research is to understand *what is happening* and why. Therefore, qualitative researchers are less concerned than quantitative researchers about the generalizability of their research. Qualitative researchers are not seeking to define ultimate truths or solutions to problems that can be transferred from a unique setting or sample to a broader population. Qualitative researchers do not believe that the only credible research is that which can be generalized to a larger population. The power of qualitative research is in the relevance of the findings to the researcher or the audience of the research, although the findings may have some applicability or transferability to a similar setting.

Armed with your research questions and the qualitative data collection techniques that will help you understand what is going on at your research setting, you are ready to enter the field and start collecting data. This proposition can be scary for new researchers. Following are suggestions to help smooth your entry into your first qualitative research setting.

MyLab Education **Self-Check 20.2**

MyLab Education **Application Exercise 20.3:**
Designing Qualitative Data Collection for a Research Study

GETTING STARTED

Having obtained entry into a setting and having selected participants, the qualitative researcher is ready to begin data collection, or fieldwork. Regardless of how much you read, think about, and discuss fieldwork, you will not know what it is really like until you live it. Living an experience for the first time always means uncertainty in a new role—uncertainty about how to act and interact with others. Qualitative research, by its very nature, is a very intimate and open-ended activity, and it is common to feel nervous as you learn the ropes, try to establish rapport with participants, and get a feel for the setting.

Bogdan and Biklen[7] suggested a number of cautions to make the initial days of entry into the setting less painful:

- Set up your first visit so that someone can introduce you to the participants.
- Don't try to accomplish too much in the first few days. Make your initial visit for observation short. You will have to take field notes after each data collection encounter, so start with brief data collection episodes to ease into the process of writing field notes.
- Ease your way into the context; don't storm in. Be relatively passive. Ask general, nonspecific, noncontroversial questions that allow participants to reply without being forced to provide answers they may find uncomfortable discussing with a relative stranger. The intent is for the participants to become comfortable with you gradually, and you with them. Then you can increase your degree of involvement.
- Be friendly and polite. Answer questions that participants and others ask, but try not to say too much about the specifics of your presence and purpose so that you do not influence the participants.
- Do not take what happens in the field personally.

In short, it is critical that you establish your "OKness" with the research participants with whom you will be working. Regardless of how well thought-out your study is, if your interpersonal skills are lacking, it will be difficult to develop the trust you need to be accepted into the setting.

MyLab Education **Self-Check 20.3**

---

[7] *Qualitative Research in Education*, by R. C. Bogdan and S. K. Biklen (3rd ed., pp. 79–81), 1998, Needham Heights, MA: Allyn & Bacon.

SUMMARY

DATA COLLECTION SOURCES AND TECHNIQUES

1. Qualitative data collection, or fieldwork, involves spending considerable time in the setting under study, immersing oneself in this setting, and collecting relevant information unobtrusively. Descriptive narrative and visual data are collected to gain insights into the phenomena of interest.

2. The type of data collected is largely determined by the nature of the problem.

3. Qualitative research includes data collected through observations, interviews, questionnaires, phone calls, personal and official documents, photographs, recordings, drawings, journals, e-mail messages and responses, and informal conversations.

4. In qualitative research, the researcher is the primary data collection instrument.

Observing

5. When qualitative researchers obtain data by watching the participants, they are observing.

6. A researcher who becomes part of and a participant in the situation under observation is called a participant observer.

7. A researcher can be an active participant observer; a privileged, active observer; or a passive observer.

8. A nonparticipant observer observes the situation but does not participate in the situation while observing it.

9. Field notes are the records of what the observer has seen or heard. Field notes contain literal descriptions as well as personal reactions and comments on what the observer has experienced and thought about during an observation session. Field notes may be guided by a protocol developed prior to the observation session.

Interviewing

10. An interview is a purposeful interaction in which one person obtains information from another.

11. The unstructured interview is like a casual conversation and allows the qualitative researcher to inquire into something that has presented itself as an opportunity to learn about what is happening at the research setting.

12. In a structured interview, the researcher has a specified set of questions that elicits the same information from all respondents.

13. For interviews, researchers should include convergent and divergent questions and pilot-test them with a group of respondents similar to the target sample.

14. Following basic guidelines for interviewing can help improve communication and can facilitate data collection.

15. Interviewers should take notes during the interview, write notes after the interview, or (preferably) record the interview and later transcribe it.

16. A focus group is a group interview. Researchers conducting focus groups should ensure that all participants have a chance to state their points of view.

17. An e-mail interview can be used to elicit responses from busy professionals who can respond to an e-mail either synchronously or asynchronously.

Questionnaires

18. A questionnaire is a written collection of self-report questions to be answered by a selected group of research participants.

19. Developing and presenting questionnaires takes care; questions should be relevant, and the presentation should be attractive. Be sure to protect participants' confidential information.

Examining Records

20. Useful educational records include archival documents, journals, maps, video- and audio-recordings, and artifacts.

VALIDITY AND RELIABILITY IN QUALITATIVE RESEARCH

Validity in Qualitative Research

21. Validity is the degree to which qualitative data gauge accurately what we are trying to measure.

22. Qualitative researchers can establish the trustworthiness of their research by addressing the credibility, transferability, dependability, and confirmability of their studies and findings.

Reliability in Qualitative Research

23. Reliability is the degree to which study data measure consistently whatever they measure.

24. A valid test that measures what it purports to measure will do so consistently over time, but a reliable test may consistently measure the wrong thing.

Generalizability

25. Qualitative researchers do not generally worry about the generalizability of data because they are not seeking ultimate truths. The power of qualitative research is in the relevance of the findings to the researcher or the audience of the research.

GETTING STARTED

26. Set up your first visit to the research setting so that someone is there to introduce you to the participants.

27. During the first few days in the setting, don't try to accomplish too much, be relatively passive, and be friendly and polite.

28. Do not take what happens in the field personally.

CHAPTER TWENTY-ONE

Qualitative Research: Data Analysis and Interpretation

MGM/Everett Collection

The Brooklyn Brothers Beat the Best, 2012

"[T]he thinker, imaginer, and hypothesizer—that is, the qualitative researcher—is the data analyzer . . . ." (p. 569)

LEARNING OUTCOMES

After reading Chapter 21, you should be able to do the following:

21.1 Describe the definitions and purposes of data analysis and data interpretation before, during, and after data collection.

21.2 Describe the steps involved in analyzing qualitative research data.
21.3 Describe data analysis strategies.
21.4 Describe data interpretation strategies.
21.5 Describe the steps to be followed to ensure the credibility of your qualitative research study.

DATA ANALYSIS AND INTERPRETATION: DEFINITION AND PURPOSE

Analyzing qualitative data is a formidable task for all qualitative researchers, especially those just starting their careers. Novice researchers follow the urgings of mentors who emphasize the need to collect rich data that reveal the perspectives and understandings of the research participants. After weeks (or months or years) of data collection using a variety of qualitative data collection techniques (e.g., observations, interviews), they find themselves sitting in their living rooms surrounded by boxes of data in all shapes and forms! This less-than-romantic image of qualitative researchers is a common one. Having immersed themselves in the systematic study of a significant problem, qualitative researchers are confronted with the somewhat daunting task of engaging in analysis that will represent the mountains of descriptive data accurately. There is no easy way to do this work: It is difficult, time-consuming, and challenging, and yet it is potentially the most important part of the research process; it is the part when we try to understand what we have learned through our investigations.

Data analysis in qualitative research involves summarizing data in a dependable and accurate manner and leads to the presentation of study findings in a manner that has an air of undeniability. Given the narrative, descriptive, and non-numerical nature of the data that are collected in a qualitative study, it is not possible to "number crunch" and quickly reduce the data to a manageable form, as can be done in quantitative studies. Qualitative data analysis requires that the researcher be patient and reflective in a process that strives to make sense of multiple data sources, including field notes from observations and interviews,

questionnaires, maps, pictures, audio-recorded transcripts, and video-recorded observations. On the other hand, data interpretation is an attempt by the researcher to find meaning in the data and to answer the "So what?" question in terms of the implications of the findings. Put simply, analysis involves summarizing what's in the data, whereas interpretation involves making sense of—finding meaning in—those data.

Data analysis and interpretation are critical steps in the research process that require the researcher both to know and to understand the data. When analyzing and interpreting qualitative data, challenge yourself to explore every possible angle and try to find patterns and seek out new understandings from the data. The techniques outlined in this chapter will serve as guideposts and prompts to move you through analysis and interpretation as efficiently as possible.

Data Analysis During Data Collection

Data analysis in qualitative research is not left until all data are collected, as is the case with quantitative research. The qualitative researcher begins data analysis from the initial interaction with participants and continues that interaction and analysis throughout the entire study. To avoid collecting data that are not important or that come in a form that cannot be understood, the researcher must think, "How am I going to make sense of the data?" before conducting the study. During the study, the researcher should try to narrow the topic progressively and to focus on the key aspects of the participants' perspectives. Thus, the qualitative researcher goes through a series of steps and iterations: gathering data, examining data, comparing prior data to newer data, writing field notes before returning to the research site, and making plans to gather new data. Data collection and analysis continually interact; the researcher's emerging hunches or thoughts become the focus for the next data collection period.

While gathering data, the researcher reviews everything and asks questions: "Why do participants act as they do?" "What does this focus mean?" "What else do I want to know about that participant's attitude?" "What new ideas have emerged in this round of data collection?" "Is this a new concept, or is it the same as a previous one?" This ongoing process—almost a protracted discussion with oneself—leads to the collection of new important data and the elimination of less useful data.

Anderson and colleagues[1] suggested that qualitative researchers answer two questions to guide their work and reflections:

1. Is your research question still answerable and worth answering?
2. Are your data collection techniques catching the kind of data you want and filtering out the data that you don't want?

Consciously pausing during the research process allows you to reflect on what you are attending to and what you are leaving out. Such a reflective stance will continue to guide your data collection efforts as well as to allow for early hunches about what you are seeing so far.

Although ongoing analysis and reflection is a natural part of the qualitative research process, it is important to avoid premature actions based on early analysis and interpretation of data. Researchers engaged in their first systematic study tend to collect, analyze, and interpret data zealously in rapid-fire fashion. Their efforts can go awry if they become their own best informants and jump to hasty conclusions and impulsive actions. The qualitative research process takes time; researchers must be wary of the lure of quick-fix strategies and patient enough to avoid the pitfalls of stating research outcomes on the basis of premature analysis.

Data Analysis after Data Collection

After the data have been collected, the romance of fieldwork is over, and the researcher must concentrate solely on the task of data analysis. The researcher must fully examine each piece of information and, building on insights and hunches gained during data collection, attempt to make sense of the data as a whole. Qualitative data analysis is based on induction: The researcher starts with a large set of data representing many things and seeks to narrow the set progressively into small and important groups of key data. No predefined variables help to focus analysis, as in quantitative research. The qualitative researcher constructs meaning by identifying patterns and themes that emerge during the data analysis.

A problem that faces almost all qualitative researchers is the lack of agreed-on approaches for analyzing qualitative data. Some guidelines and general strategies for analysis exist, but there are few specific rules for their application. In brief, after data are collected, the qualitative researcher undertakes a multistage process of organizing, categorizing, synthesizing, analyzing, and writing about the data. In most cases, the researcher cycles through the stages more than once in a continual effort to narrow and make sense of the data. As a result, the time frame for data analysis is difficult to determine in advance because it depends on the nature of the study, the amount of data to be analyzed, and the analytic and synthesizing abilities of the researcher.

If you conduct a qualitative study, take time to immerse yourself fully in your data—bury yourself in what you have. Read and reread, listen and relisten, watch and rewatch. Get to know intimately what you have collected. Struggle with the nuances and caveats, the subtleties, the persuasive, the incomplete. Avoid premature judgment. These goals are lofty, but they are at the heart of what we are trying to achieve in qualitative data analysis and data interpretation.

> MyLab Education **Self-Check 21.1**
>
> MyLab Education **Application Exercise 21.1:**
> Analyzing and Interpreting Qualitative Data

STEPS IN ANALYZING QUALITATIVE RESEARCH DATA

If data are to be analyzed thoroughly, they must be organized. Ideally, the researcher will have carefully managed notes, records, and artifacts as they were collected. The importance of attention to detail in

---

[1] *Studying Your Own School: An Educator's Guide to Qualitative Practitioner Research* (p. 155), by G. L. Anderson, K. Herr, and A. S. Nihlen, 1994, Thousand Oaks, CA: Corwin Press.

FIGURE 21.1 • Data-organizing activities

- Write dates (month, day, year) on all notes.
- Sequence all notes with labels (e.g., 6th set of notes).
- Label notes according to type (such as observer's notes, memo to self, transcript from interview).
- Make two photocopies of all notes (field notes, transcripts, etc.) and retain original copies.
- Organize computer files into folders according to data type and stages of analysis.
- Make backup copies of all files.
- Read through data and make sure all information is complete and legible before proceeding to analysis and interpretation.
- Begin to note themes and patterns that emerge.

---

managing data becomes all too clear when it is time to write the research. Nevertheless, some additional organization at the end of the data collection stage is usually necessary. Figure 21.1 lists some ways to "tidy up" your data, ensure their completeness, and make them easier to study. After the data are organized, the analysis can begin in earnest.

One way to proceed with analysis is to follow three iterative, or repeating, steps: reading/memoing, describing what is going on in the setting, and classifying research data. The process focuses on (1) becoming familiar with the data and identifying potential themes (i.e., reading/memoing); (2) examining the data in depth to provide detailed descriptions of the setting, participants, and activity (i.e., describing); and (3) categorizing and coding pieces of data and grouping them into themes (i.e., classifying).

- Write dates (month, day, year) on all notes.
- Sequence all notes with labels (e.g., sixth set of notes).
- Label notes according to type (such as observer's notes, memo to self, transcript from interview).
- Make two photocopies of all notes (field notes, transcripts, etc.) and retain original copies.
- Organize computer files into folders according to data type and stages of analysis.
- Make backup copies of all computer files.
- Read through data and make sure all information is complete and legible before proceeding to analysis and interpretation.
- Begin to note themes and patterns that emerge.

The interrelations among these steps are not necessarily linear. At the start of data analysis, the logical sequence of activities is from reading/memoing to description, to classifying, and finally

to interpretation. However, as a researcher begins to internalize and reflect on the data, the initial ordered sequence may lose its structure and become more flexible. If you've ever been driving home pondering some issue or problem and out of the blue had a sudden flash of understanding that provides a solution, you have a sense of how qualitative data analysis takes place. Once you are into the data, it is not the three steps that lead to understanding; it is your ability to think, imagine, create, intuit, and analyze that guides the data analysis. Knowing the steps is not enough; the thinker, imaginer, and hypothesizer—that is, the qualitative researcher—is the data analyzer, and the quality of the research analysis depends heavily on the intellectual qualities of the researcher. Let us be very clear about this process: It is a process of digesting the contents of qualitative data and finding related threads in it. You will not accomplish these tasks meaningfully with one or two or more readings of your data. To make the kinds of connections needed to analyze and interpret qualitative data, you must know your data—really know it, in your head, not just on paper. The process can be tedious, time-consuming, and repetitious; however, the steps can help you understand, describe, and classify qualitative data.

Reading/Memoing

The first step in analysis is to read and write memos about all field notes, transcripts, and observer comments to get an initial sense of the data. To begin, find a quiet place and plan to spend a few hours at a time reading through the data. Krathwohl[2] wisely pointed out that "the first

---

[2] *Methods of Educational and Social Science Research: An Integrated Approach*, by D. R. Krathwohl (2nd ed., p. 309), 1998, New York: Longman.

time you sit down to read your data is the only time you come to that particular set fresh." It is important that you write notes in the margins or underline sections or issues that seem important to you so that you have a record of your initial thoughts and sense of the data. Later, when you are deeper into the analysis, you may find that many of these early impressions are not useful; however, you may also find that some initial impressions hold up throughout. At this stage of analysis, you should also begin the search for recurring themes or common threads.

Describing

The next step, describing, involves developing thorough and comprehensive descriptions of the participants, the setting, and the phenomenon studied to convey the rich complexity of the research. The descriptions are based on your collected observations, interview data, field notes, and artifacts. The aim of this step is to provide a narrative picture of the setting and events that take place in it so you will have an understanding of the context in which the study is taking place. Attention to the research context is a common and important theme in qualitative research because the context influences participants' actions and understandings. Because meaning is influenced by context, analysis (and therefore, interpretation) is hampered without a thorough description of the context, actions, and interactions of participants.

An important concern of qualitative researchers is portraying the views of the research participants accurately. The descriptions of the research context, meanings, and social relations can be presented in a number of forms. For example, you can describe events in chronological order, create a composite of a typical day in the life of a participant in the setting, focus on key contextual episodes, or illuminate different perspectives of the participants. Regardless of the form, it is crucial that you describe thoroughly how participants define situations and explain their actions. Also, your descriptions should note how interactions and social relations among the participants may have changed during the course of the study.

Classifying

Qualitative data analysis is a process of breaking down data into smaller units, determining their import, and putting the pertinent units together in a more general, analytical form. Qualitative data are typically broken down through the process of classifying or coding; the pieces of data are then categorized. A category is a classification of ideas or concepts; categorization, then, is grouping the data into themes. When concepts in the data are examined and compared to one another, and connections are made, categories are formed.

As an example, consider a researcher who is conducting a qualitative study on characteristics of fifth-grade students' study methods. Suppose the researcher had collected 20 sets of field notes (i.e., based on observations) or 20 transcripts of interviews. The researcher's task is to read through all the notes or transcripts and categorize the meanings or understandings that emerge from the data. The categories provide the basis for structuring the analysis and interpretation. Without data that are classified and grouped, a researcher has no reasonable way to analyze qualitative studies. However, the categories identified by one researcher would not necessarily be the same as those identified by another researcher, even if they analyzed the same data. There is no single "correct" way to organize and analyze the data. Different researchers produce different categories from the same data for many reasons, including researcher biases, personal interests, style, and interpretive focus.

MyLab Education **Self-Check 21.2**

MyLab Education **Application Exercise 21.2:** Analyzing Qualitative Research Data

DATA ANALYSIS STRATEGIES

In this section we describe strategies used to analyze qualitative data: identifying themes; coding surveys, interviews, and questionnaires; asking key questions; doing an organizational review; developing a concept map; analyzing antecedents and consequences; displaying findings; and stating what is missing. Each is important in identifying research categories and patterns.

Identifying Themes

One way to begin analyzing data is to consider the big picture and start to list themes that you have seen emerge in your literature review and in the data collection. Are there patterns that emerge, such as events that keep repeating themselves, key phrases that participants use to describe their feelings, or survey responses that seem to match one another? Noting themes can be helpful during the first reading of the data, as part of memoing. In subsequent readings of the data, additional themes may emerge.

Coding Surveys, Interviews, and Questionnaires

One of the most frequent data analysis activities undertaken by qualitative researchers is coding, the process of categorically marking or referencing units of text (e.g., words, sentences, paragraphs, and quotations) with codes and labels as a way to indicate patterns and meaning. As you analyze and code, you reduce your data to a manageable form. One way to proceed when working with field notes, transcripts of recorded interviews, pictures, maps, and charts is to record important data on index cards, which are manageable and allow for sorting. As you read and reread through the data (possibly now reduced to your cards), you can compile the data in categories or themes.

Although there is nothing magical about the process of coding, it does take time and a willingness to check that the mountains of descriptive data have been analyzed accurately and reliably. The way in which you code the data, in fact, will play a large role in determining the nature of the results. For example, if you approach the data with preconceived categories and assumptions, you will likely begin analyzing the data by coding text units according to what you expect to find. Conceptually, you are beginning to construct a web of relations that may or may not appear as you thought they would. On the other hand, if you approach the data with questions you hope your research will illuminate but no clear sense about what the findings may be, you will likely start to build themes as you read.

To get an idea of the process of coding, imagine that you are organizing a deck of playing cards, but you don't know the meaning of any of the symbols on the cards. Each card in the deck contains data, and the order of the cards is random. As you initially scan the cards, you have an intuitive sense that the data on some of the cards look similar to data on other cards. You finish looking carefully at

all the cards and reshuffle the deck. Again you look through the deck, but this time you group together the cards with data that look alike. You end up with 13 collections of four cards that have some trait in common (e.g., the number or face value of the card). Again, you reshuffle the cards. This time, as you start to sort through the cards, you notice a different theme (e.g., the suit of the card) and end up with four piles of 13 cards. Puzzling. Not to be thwarted in your efforts, you again reshuffle the deck and attempt to settle on an organizing theme. You group together cards (i.e., data) that have sufficient common characteristics that you feel confident that your analysis is undeniably accurate. But there is just one problem: What do you do with the joker that found its way into the pack? And what about that wild card? Where did they come from, and where do they fit in? Just when you thought you had it all worked out, in crept something that challenges the themes you have used to organize and represent the data you have collected. The shuffling and sorting continues.

A few commonsense guidelines may make this somewhat overwhelming activity of coding mountains of data more manageable. Keep in mind that you want to be able to sort your data using whatever technology you are most comfortable that doesn't get in the way of your analytical work.

1. Gather photocopies of your original data. (Alternatively, work with electronic copies that can be "cut and paste" while retaining the integrity of your original field notes.)
2. Read through all the data and attach working labels to blocks of text. These labels should have meaning for you; they should be a kind of shorthand that will serve as reference points when you return to the text later in the process.
3. Literally cut and paste the blocks of text onto index cards so that you now have the data in a manageable form (i.e., shuffling cards is much easier than sorting through reams of paper). Use some kind of numbering system so that you can track the block of text back to the original context in which it appeared. For example, marking the date and time (e.g., 1/26 10:15) can help you locate the text in the journal or field notes from which it was excerpted. Remember, context is important. Check that you have correctly labeled the text

you are trying to funnel into a category with similar text. (This can also be managed using multiple Word files.)

4. Start to group together cards that have the same or similar labels on them.

5. Revisit each pile of cards and see if the label still fits or whether similar labels warrant their own category. Seek categories that encapsulate similar thoughts and ideas. This process is similar to brainstorming.

For example, in my study of school district change,[3] I found myself with a large pile of 3 × 5 cards that included some of the following notations:

Card 1. Assistant superintendent urges principals not to reinvent the wheel but to share ideas with each other as they attempt to deal with an identified problem. (In this case the problem was low test scores on the California Achievement Test [CAT].) The assistant superintendent states to the principals, "I don't want any of you to think that you are alone out there."

Card 2. One of the principals at the meeting comments, "Clearly, the CAT does not test what we teach in our schools. The test was designed for California, not Oregon."

Card 3. The next meeting of principals following the release of the CAT scores and the directive from the superintendent that "all schools will develop action plans to address areas of weakness identified by the test scores" does not include any discussion of action plan development.

Card 4. A principal sums up his feelings about standardized testing as follows, "The district makes us go through a whole lot of garbage for little outcome or benefit to the teachers and the students."

Card 5. Principals' meeting 3 months following the release of test scores and action plan mandate. Action plans were due to the curriculum director 7 weeks ago. Principals are instructed that they can have another 2 weeks to complete the plans.

Card 6. The assistant superintendent announces that he will be meeting with principals on an individual basis to discuss how action plans for school improvement will be implemented. It is 4 weeks before the end of the school year, and 16 weeks since the initial directive to develop school improvement action plans.

Card 7. One principal commented on the development of the action plan/school improvement plan, "Do I write plans of improvement just to let the central office know that it has been done so that they are satisfied and can get on with doing whatever it is that they do with all the paperwork? I admit that I have written plans and never followed up on them because I'm too busy getting on with the real business of school."

Following the four commonsense guidelines presented earlier in this chapter, the first step of "attaching working labels" to blocks of text that are then "cut and pasted" onto cards resulted in the following grouping of cards: Cards 1, 3, and 5 were labeled "Statement of school district approach to school change." Cards 2 and 4 were labeled "Principals' challenges to school district approach." Cards 6 and 7 were labeled "Inaction of school district approach."

These cards are indicative of the comments that were captured during interviews with individual principals and observations of principals' meetings and that collectively provided the context and understanding for the analysis, which resulted in a statement of a theme titled "inaction." In writing about school change as it related to the McKenzie School District, my data analysis included a "Taxonomy of Managing and Coping Strategies for Educational Change" with themes such as "inaction" that emerged to describe the change process; that is, one of the ways that the McKenzie School District personnel managed and coped with educational change was to do nothing! I have included this example to demonstrate how a theme emerges from the data you collect. I chose the term *inaction* as a theme because it was descriptive (to me) of what was occurring in the district. The same will be true for your own analysis—as you code your data and reduce them to a manageable form, a label will emerge that describes a pattern of behavior. You will be well on your way to making sense of your data!

Example of Coding an Interview

What follows is an annotated interview between a researcher and a bilingual education teacher as an example of the researcher's analysis of the themes

---

[3] Managing and coping with multiple educational change. Unpublished doctoral dissertation by G. E. Mills, 1998, Eugene, OR: University of Oregon.

that emerged from the interview. As this example illustrates, the process of analyzing an interview transcript involves careful reading of the transcript to identify broad themes that emerge from the data that will help answer the researcher's research questions. This in-depth, intimate knowledge and examination of the data allows qualitative researchers to categorize themes and ideas that will contribute to their understanding of the phenomenon under investigation. In this example, fear of change is a pervasive, recurring theme that contributes to the researcher's understanding of the phenomenon and possibly provides an answer to a research question.

Asking Key Questions

Another strategy used in data analysis involves asking key questions. According to Stringer,[4] working through a series of questions can enable qualitative researchers to "extend their understanding of the problems and contexts" they have investigated. Such questions may include: "Who is centrally involved?" "Who has resources?" "Which ones?" "What major activities, events, or issues are relevant to the problem?" "How do acts, activities, and events happen?" "When does this problem occur?"

[4] *Action Research: A Handbook for Practitioners* (p. 87), by E. T. Stringer, 1996, Thousand Oaks, CA: Sage.

Coding from a Sample Interview Transcript

Codes	Q: Why do you think that English-only teachers fear bilingual education?	Themes (and Other Ideas)
Culture	A: I think the fear factor is on a real gut level and personal level. Teachers feel it's kind of a one-way system in that the teachers who are in the all-English program are fearful at a real basic visceral level that their jobs and their livelihood are at risk. Not to mention their culture, their society, and their known world is at risk by this other language coming into the schools and being acknowledged in the schools. And the teacher might say, "Oh well, because I don't have Spanish that means I am going to be out of a job. Am I going to be replaced by a bilingual teacher? If you have this program in my school that means you're going to need bilingual teachers. I am not bilingual so my job is at risk."	Fear Fear of change Job stability Fear of new job
	Q: Do you think that there is resistance toward expecting all children to learn English?	
Nativistic movements Patriotic	A: I think that's an interpretation that comes out of a model like a 90/10. When the child needs to come into the first year and has 90% in Spanish and 10% in English, it's easily perceived that we are withholding English from the child. That is a perception. A 50/50 model is a little more amenable to that because it's obvious that 50% of the time the child isn't getting English.	
	Q: There is the old adage that teachers who oppose bilingual education say, "My ancestors never received bilingual education services in public schools and they did just fine." How do you respond to that kind of attitude toward bilingual education?	
	A: I say that's old thinking. I think that what your parents or your grandparents had to do when they came here from Italy or Norway, or wherever they came from, to learn another language, the language demand was less than it is today.	
	Q: What about the attitude, "Well they are in the United States and we speak English here so they can learn English. That's all there is to it." How would you respond to this attitude?	
	A: That's a big one. That's huge. I think that's a whole cultural, you know, it's based again in fear. Based again in the fact that the United States is a very isolated island in that we are closed in by two oceans and we have never had the habit of stretching out beyond our borders much, or valuing much of what is beyond our borders.	Fear
	We are xenophobic in that sense. So we haven't traditionally learned other languages, or been interested in other languages. "Why bother, we're America, the biggest, the toughest, so why would we value anybody else's culture or language?" And I think that's an old thinking as well. It's an old habit.	Fear

Although not all these questions will be applicable to any single situation, they may provide a starting point for qualitative researchers who are engaged individually or collectively in analysis.

Doing an Organizational Review

Almost any educational problem is influenced in some way by the spoken and unspoken rules of organizations, including state education departments, school districts, individual schools, teacher unions, and other similar organizations. Even in a qualitative study where the emphasis is on the personal story of a single individual or the intimate workings of a small group, it is sometimes helpful to step back and take a look at the larger setting. Researchers may consider undertaking an organizational review that focuses on several features of the organization, including the vision and mission, goals and objectives, structure and operation, and problems and concerns. As Stringer noted:[5] "As participants work through these issues, they will extend their understanding of the organization and aspects of its operation that are relevant to their problems, issues, and concerns." With these features in mind, a review of a school, for example, may provide insight into the data you have collected.

Developing a Concept Map

Stringer[6] suggested that concept maps are another useful strategy that helps action research participants to visualize the major influences that have affected the study. For example, what were the perspectives of the students? Parents? Teachers? Administrators? A concept map gives participants an opportunity to display their analysis of the problem and to determine consistencies and inconsistencies that may exist between the disparate groups. The steps for developing a concept map include the following:

1. List the major influences that have affected the study of your area of focus.
2. Develop a visual representation of the major influences (factors) connecting the influences with relationships you know exist (using solid lines) and influences you have a hunch about (using dotted lines).

3. Review the concept map to determine any consistencies or inconsistencies that exist between the influences. This forces you back to your data to see what's missing.

For example, in a study of the effectiveness of a school absenteeism policy, the researcher concluded that respectfulness, safety, conflict management, discipline, school rules, behavior, getting along, self-esteem, and academics were major indicators of success. Further, the researcher believed that some relationships (real and perceived) existed between or among these factors (see Figure 21.2).

Analyzing Antecedents and Consequences

The process of mapping antecedents (i.e., causes) and consequences (i.e., effects) is another strategy to help qualitative researchers identify the major elements of their analysis.[7] Using this framework provides a visual representation of the causal relationships that the researcher believes exist. It is also helpful to revisit the causal relationships uncovered in your review of the literature to determine challenges and support for your analysis and interpretations. The steps for analyzing antecedents and consequences are as follows:

1. List the influences that emerged from the analysis for which there appear to be a causal relationship.
2. Revisit the review of literature to determine whether the analysis of the study supports, or is challenged by, the findings of previous studies.
3. Revisit your data to determine if anything is missing and suggest how your findings may influence future research.

In the study of the effectiveness of a school absenteeism policy, for example, the concept map in Figure 21.2 could be expanded to include a mapping of antecedents (causes) and consequences (effects) as an outcome of the analysis. In this example, the researcher clearly identified (based on his analysis) that a causal relationship existed between absenteeism and academics (student performance), and absenteeism and discipline (student behavior). This framework provides

[5] Ibid., pp. 90–91.
[6] Ibid., p. 91.

[7] Ibid., p. 96.

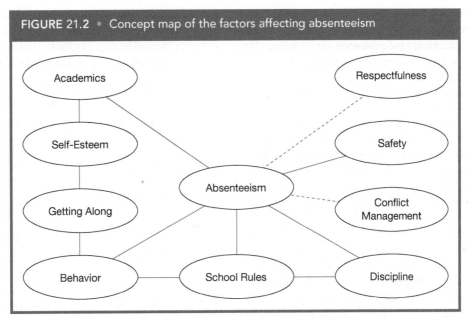

FIGURE 21.2 • Concept map of the factors affecting absenteeism

Source: Mills, Geoffrey, *Action Research: A Guide for the Teacher Researcher*, 6th Edition, © 2018. Reprinted by permission of Pearson Education, Inc., Upper Saddle River, NJ.

a visual representation of the causal relationships that the researcher has identified. It is helpful to revisit the relationships uncovered in the review of literature to determine challenges and support for the analysis and interpretations.

Displaying Findings

It is important to summarize the information you have collected in an appropriate and meaningful format that you can share with interested colleagues. To do this, it is helpful to "think display" as you consider how to convey your findings to colleagues. Displays can include matrixes, charts, concept maps, graphs, and figures—whatever works as a practical way to encapsulate the findings of the study. These visual displays of data serve an important function for researchers who want to share findings and celebrate their insights in a public forum, such as a research conference. Putting the data into a visual format can also help you see new aspects in the data.

Stating What Is Missing

Finally, as part of your full reporting, you should flag for the consumers of your research the pieces of the puzzle that are still missing and identify the

questions for which you have not been able to provide answers. Often we find ourselves wanting and needing to provide answers, to move beyond our data with unwarranted assertions that may, in some cases, ultimately lead to embarrassing questions about what we actually did. In keeping with the theme of avoiding premature judgment (i.e., arriving at answers to problems without systematic inquiry), the data analysis strategy of stating what's missing allows you to hint at what may or should be done next in your quest to understand the findings of your study.

Qualitative Data Analysis: An Example

The example that follows is intended to provide a sense of qualitative analysis. A true qualitative study would entail more data analysis than shown here, but the basic ideas represent the process that a qualitative researcher would undertake when analyzing data throughout a study.

In this example, the topics under study are the concerns of parents regarding their first child's entrance into kindergarten and the kindergarten teacher's interactions with the students and families. The participants are four parents (three female and one male, representing four families) and the first child in each of the families; the children attend the same school, and their kindergarten teacher is also a research participant. Data collection procedures include observations and interviews with students, parents, and the kindergarten teacher.

Data analysis would proceed as follows:

1. From the field notes of your classroom observations, you begin to list some common items or topics that you noticed. You recorded in your notes that during classroom instruction, the teacher was using books, videos, and handouts. You also noted that instruction was directed sometimes toward individual students, sometimes toward the whole class, and sometimes toward students who were working together in small groups.

2. From your interviews with the teacher, you realize that she gave you information about how she communicated with families about the children. You note that she talked about how she indirectly communicates through grading and report cards and how her lesson plans and tests are related to her overall assessment of the students' work. She also mentioned that she talks about report cards directly with families during conferences. She also communicates with families about their children through progress reports and phone calls.

3. From your initial analysis, you group the individual items or topics together into categories that show how the items or topics are related. For example, as shown in Figure 21.3, you could group books, videos, and handouts under a category called Teaching Materials. You could group together the ways in which the instruction was carried out— individual, small-group, and whole-class—and label this category as Classroom Interactions. Using information from the interviews, you could construct the category Indirect Communication with Families/Guardians to include grading, lesson plans, tests, and report cards. A category of Direct Communication with Families/Guardians could include family conferences, report cards, progress reports, and phone calls to parents or guardians. Notice that report cards appear in both the indirect and the direct communication categories.

4. You organize your four categories into patterns, which are made up of two or more categories. For example, the categories of Teaching Materials and Classroom Interactions indicate a pattern of Instructional Activities. The categories of Indirect Communication and Direct Communication fit together under a pattern of Teacher–Family Interactions.

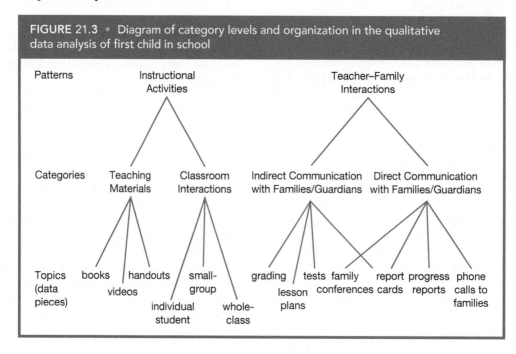

FIGURE 21.3 • Diagram of category levels and organization in the qualitative data analysis of first child in school

You then decide whether you need to collect additional data by interviewing students and parents or guardians about their experiences interacting with the teacher to confirm your categories and patterns.

The following Digital Research Tools feature discusses three common software packages available to assist qualitative researchers with the analysis of qualitative data.

Digital Research Tools

QUALITATIVE DATA ANALYSIS SOFTWARE

Software to assist with the analysis of qualitative, narrative data has been available to researchers for many years. The key word in this sentence is *assist*. This software will not do the analysis for you! It is important for novice qualitative researchers to remember that computers do not analyze or even code data. They are designed only to help expedite these operations when researchers are working with large bodies of text and other kinds of data. The process of coding, retrieving, and subsequently mulling over and making sense of data remains a laborious process completely controlled by researchers. Even if a computer is used, researchers still must go through the process of creating codes and labels and keying them into the computer as they read through their interviews, field notes, and audio and video recordings. Computers are merely handy and extremely fast labeling and retrieval tools. In addition, researchers must program the computer to retrieve and sort data in specific ways; the machines do not do these tasks automatically. Although computers can enhance and broaden qualitative research analysis, if you are not connected in some way with a research university, it is unlikely that you will have access to the software and the expertise of someone to teach you how to use it.

To help with the decision about whether or not to proceed with locating and learning a qualitative data analysis software package, ask yourself the following questions:[8]

- Are you analyzing large amounts of data (e.g., more than 500 pages of field notes and transcripts)?
- Are you or can you be adequately trained in the use of the programs and in using computers in general?

- Do you have the resources to purchase a program, or do you know someone who has the program?
- Do you need to be able to capture specific quotes from a large database?

Three common and popular qualitative analysis software packages are NVivo 11, Ethnograph v6, and HyperRESEARCH 3.7.3.

NVivo 11

NVivo 11 is designed to assist qualitative researchers with organizing, classifying, and analyzing data sources such as interviews, open-ended survey responses, articles, social media, and web-content. More information on NVivo can be found on the QSR International website at qsrinternational.com.

Ethnograph v6

Ethnograph v6 is a program designed to help qualitative researchers work with text files (in any format) and search for and code segments of interest to the researcher. More information about Ethnograph v6 can be found on the Qualis Research website at qualisresearch.com.

HyperRESEARCH 3.7.3

HyperRESEARCH 3.7.3 is an advanced software program that allows the qualitative researcher to work with text, graphics, audio, and video sources and to code and retrieve data. More information about HyperRESEARCH can be found on the ResearchWare website at researchware.com.

Remember, computer software will not do the data analysis for you, but it will help you retrieve categories from a large amount of narrative, audio, video, and photo data.

[8] List items adapted from *Educational Research: Planning, Conducting, and Evaluating Quantitative and Qualitative Research* (5th ed., p. 239), by J. W. Creswell, 2015, Upper Saddle River, NJ: Pearson Education, Inc.

MyLab Education **Self-Check 21.3**

MyLab Application **Exercise 21.3:** Evaluating
Research Articles: Qualitative Data Analysis

DATA INTERPRETATION STRATEGIES

Because the goal of data interpretation is to find meaning in the data, it is based heavily on the connections, common aspects, and links among the data, especially the identified categories and patterns. One cannot classify data into categories without thinking about the meanings of the categories. To aid interpretation, researchers must make the conceptual bases or understandings of the categories explicit and identify clearly the characteristics that make each category distinct from the others. Interpretation requires more conceptual and integrative thinking than data analysis because interpretation involves identifying and abstracting important understandings from the detail and complexity of the data.

The implicit issues in data interpretation are the answers to these four questions:

1. What is important in the data?
2. Why is it important?
3. What can be learned from it?
4. So what?

The researcher's task, then, is to determine how to identify what is important, why it is important, and what it indicates about the participants and context studied. The process for answering these four questions is idiosyncratic to a large extent. Interpretation is personal, with no hard-and-fast rules to follow as you go about the task of interpreting the meaning of data. As in most qualitative studies, success depends on the perspective and interpretive abilities of the researcher.

You may wonder why you should bother with interpretation, especially because it involves taking risks and making educated guesses that may be off base. Wolcott[9] argued for the importance of interpretation, noting that the interpretations made by qualitative researchers matter to the lives of those we study. In addition, the process of interpretation

is important because it can challenge the assumptions and beliefs that researchers have about the educational processes they have investigated.

The techniques for data interpretation that follow are adapted from those presented by Wolcott and by Stringer.[10]

Extend the analysis. One technique that is low on the data interpretation risk scale is to extend the analysis of the data by raising questions about the study, noting implications that may be drawn without actually drawing them. As Wolcott suggested, "This is a strategy for pointing the way rather than leading the way."[11]

Connect findings with personal experience. Qualitative research is very personal business, so it makes sense to personalize your interpretations. For example, you may present your findings with the prelude, "Based on my experiences in conducting this study, this is what I make of it all." Remember, you know your study better than anyone else. You have been there for every twist and turn along the way, trying to make sense of discrepant events just when you thought you had it right. Share your interpretations based on your intimate knowledge and understandings of the research setting.

Seek the advice of critical friends. If you have difficulty focusing an interpretive lens on your work, rely on your trusted colleagues to offer insights that you may have missed because of your closeness to the work. Offer your accounts to colleagues with the request that they share with you their possible interpretations. Similarly, you may ask your informants (e.g., students, parents, teachers, and administrators) for their insights. But beware! The more opinions you seek, the more you will receive, and often these suggestions will come with the expectation that you accept the advice. Over time you will develop reciprocity with a cadre of trusted, like-minded colleagues who will selflessly fulfill the role of critical friend. Take the time to build these relationships and reap the rewards they offer.

Contextualize findings in the literature. Uncovering external sources as part of the review of related literature is a powerful way for qualitative researchers to provide support for the findings of the study. Making these connections also provides a way to share with colleagues the existing knowledge base about a research problem and

---

[9] *Transforming Qualitative Data: Description, Analysis, and Interpretation,* by H. F. Wolcott, 1994, Thousand Oaks, CA: Sage.

[10] Ibid., pp. 39–46; *Action Research* (p. 87–96), Stringer, 1996.
[11] *Transforming Qualitative Data* (p. 40), Wolcott, 1994.

to acknowledge the unique contribution that the qualitative researcher has made to the understanding of the topic under study.

Turn to theory. Theory serves a number of important roles for qualitative researchers. First, theory provides a way for qualitative researchers to link their work to broader issues of the day. Second, theory allows researchers to search for increasing levels of abstraction and to move beyond a purely descriptive account. Levels of abstraction allow us to communicate the essence of our descriptive work to colleagues at research meetings. Third, theory can provide a rationale or sense of meaning to the work we do.

Know when to say when! If you don't feel comfortable offering an interpretation, don't do it. Be satisfied with making suggestions for what may be done next, and use the suggestions yourself as a starting point for the next research cycle. Restate the problem as you now see it, and explain how you think you will fine-tune your efforts as you strive to increase your understanding of the phenomenon you have investigated. As Wolcott[12] cautioned, "[D]on't detract from what you have accomplished by tacking on a wimpy interpretation."

All researchers, and qualitative researchers in particular, must face the prospect of not being able to report all the data they have collected. Rarely is every piece of data used in the report of a study. This reality is difficult for any researcher but may be more so for qualitative researchers because of the time and effort it typically takes them to obtain and understand their data. Remember, however, that the task of interpreting data is to identify the important themes or meanings in the data, not necessarily every theme.

A final piece of advice regarding data interpretation is to share your interpretations wisely. At some time we have all been exposed to what is called a fad, the pendulum swinging in the opposite direction, the bandwagon effect, and so on. As such, many of us may hesitate to embrace anything new or different that comes our way in schools, calming ourselves with the mantra, "This, too, shall pass!" If we as researchers attempt to use our qualitative research findings only as a soapbox from which we present findings that confirm our beliefs and values, then we risk being alienated by our colleagues. Avoid being evangelical about your interpretations,

connect them closely to your data and analysis, and share your newfound understandings with colleagues in an appropriate manner.

MyLab Education **Self-Check 21.4**

MyLab Education **Application Exercise 21.4:** Evaluating Research Articles: Qualitative Data Interpretation

---

ENSURING CREDIBILITY IN YOUR STUDY

Throughout this chapter, we have emphasized the centrality of the researcher as the integrator and interpreter of data. You may infer that this emphasis means that researchers have carte blanche when analyzing and interpreting data, that is, that they can rely strictly on their personal feelings or preferences. This is definitely not the case. If qualitative research were based solely on producing unsubstantiated opinions, with researchers ignoring data that did not confirm expectations and failing to examine biases of research participants, it would be of little value. Although data analysis and interpretations are heavily determined by the researcher, qualitative researchers should respect and respond to established criteria when conducting their studies. For example, Dey[13] identified six questions intended to help researchers check the quality of their data:

1. Are the data based on one's own observation or on hearsay?
2. Are observations corroborated by others?
3. In what circumstances was an observation made or reported?
4. How reliable are those providing the data?
5. What motivations may have influenced a participant's report?
6. What biases may have influenced how an observation was made or reported?

Qualitative researchers who attend to these guidelines for conducting credible data analysis and data interpretation are rewarded with trustworthy research reports that withstand the scrutiny of the research community.

[13] *Qualitative Data Analysis* (p. 224), by I. Dey, 1993, New York: Routledge.

[12] Ibid., p. 41.

MyLab Education **Self-Check 21.5**

SUMMARY

DATA ANALYSIS AND INTERPRETATION: DEFINITION AND PURPOSE

1. Data analysis in qualitative research involves summarizing data dependably and accurately. The presentation of the findings of the study thus has an air of undeniability.

2. Data interpretation is an attempt by the researcher to find meaning in the data and to answer the "So what?" question in terms of the implications of the study's findings.

3. A great deal of data analysis occurs before data collection is complete. Researchers think about and develop hunches about what they see and hear during data collection.

4. An important step in the ongoing analysis of qualitative data is to reflect on two questions:
   a. Is your research question still answerable and worth answering?
   b. Are your data collection techniques catching the kind of data you want and filtering out the data that you don't want?

5. It is important to avoid premature actions based on early analysis and interpretation of data.

6. After fieldwork has been completed, the researcher must concentrate solely on the multistage process of organizing, categorizing, synthesizing, analyzing, and writing about the data. The researcher works to narrow a large set of issues and data into small and important groups of key data.

7. It is difficult to determine, in advance, how long data analysis will take. The time frame depends on the nature of the study, the amount of data to be analyzed, and the abilities of the researcher.

STEPS IN ANALYZING QUALITATIVE RESEARCH DATA

8. Qualitative data analysis is a cyclical, iterative process of reviewing data for common topics or themes. One approach to analysis is to follow three iterative steps: reading/memoing, describing what is going on in the setting, and classifying research data.

9. Reading/memoing is the process of writing notes in the field note margins and underlining sections or issues that seem important during the initial reading of narrative data.

10. Describing involves developing thorough and comprehensive descriptions of the participants, the setting, and the phenomenon studied to convey the rich complexity of the research.

11. Classifying small pieces of data into more general categories is the qualitative researcher's way to make sense and find connections among the data. Field notes and transcripts are broken down into small pieces of data, and these pieces are integrated into categories and often into more general patterns.

DATA ANALYSIS STRATEGIES

12. Identifying themes is a strategy that relies on the identification of ideas that have emerged from the review of literature and in the data collection.

13. Coding is the process of marking units of text with codes or labels as a way to indicate patterns and meaning in data. It involves the reduction of narrative data to a manageable form to allow sorting to occur.

14. Asking key questions is a strategy that involves the researcher asking questions such as "Who is centrally involved?" and "What major activities, events, or issues are relevant to the problem?" and seeking answers in the data.

15. An organizational review helps the researcher understand the school or other organization as the larger setting. A review should focus on the vision and mission, goals and objectives, structure, operation, and issues and concerns of the organization under study.

16. Concept mapping allows the qualitative researcher to create a visual display of the major influences that have affected the study to allow for the identification of consistencies and inconsistencies between disparate groups.

17. Analyzing antecedents and consequences allows the researcher to map the causes and effects that have emerged throughout the study.

18. Displaying findings involves using matrixes, charts, concept maps, graphs, and figures to encapsulate the findings of a study.

19. Stating what's missing from the study encourages the researcher to reflect and to identify any questions for which answers have not been provided.

20. Many computer programs are available to aid in analyzing qualitative data, but it is important for novice qualitative researchers to remember that computers do not analyze or code data; researchers do.

DATA INTERPRETATION STRATEGIES

21. Data interpretation is based heavily on the connections, common aspects, and linkages among the data pieces, categories, and patterns. Interpretation cannot be meaningfully accomplished unless the researcher knows the data in great detail.

22. The aim of interpretation is to answer four questions: What is important in the data? Why is it important? What can be learned from it? So what?

23. Extending the analysis is a data interpretation strategy in which the researcher raises questions about the study, noting implications that may be drawn without actually drawing them.

24. Connecting findings with personal experience encourages the researcher to personalize interpretations based on intimate knowledge and understanding of the research setting.

25. Seeking the advice of critical friends involves inviting trusted colleagues to offer insights that may have been missed due to the researcher's closeness to the study.

26. Contextualizing the findings of the study in the related literature involves using the review of related literature to provide support for the findings of the study.

27. Turning to theory encourages researchers to link their findings to broader issues of the day and, in so doing, to search for increasing levels of abstraction and to move beyond a purely descriptive account.

28. Knowing when to say when means that the researcher refrains from offering an interpretation when he or she can offer only a wimpy interpretation.

29. As a qualitative researcher, you should share your interpretations wisely and avoid being evangelical about them. Provide a clear link among data collection, analysis, and interpretation.

ENSURING CREDIBILITY IN YOUR STUDY

30. To check the credibility (and trustworthiness) of their data, qualitative researchers should ask themselves the following six questions:
    a. Are the data based on one's own observation or on hearsay?
    b. Are observations corroborated by others?
    c. In what circumstances was an observation made or reported?
    d. How reliable are those providing the data?
    e. What motivations may have influenced a participant's report?
    f. What biases may have influenced how an observation was made or reported?

CHAPTER TWENTY-TWO

Preparing a Research Report

Paramount/Everett Collection

Legally Blonde 2: Red, White and Blonde, 2003

"The research report should be written in a clear, simple, straightforward style that reflects scholarship." (p. 585)

LEARNING OUTCOMES

After reading Chapter 22, you should be able to do the following:

22.1 Follow the guidelines for writing a research report.

22.2 Identify the key elements in formatting a research report and the appropriate style manual to satisfy your university's writing requirements.

22.3 Determine the appropriate format for your thesis or dissertation.

22.4 Identify a target professional journal and prepare a manuscript for publication in that journal.

The chapter learning outcomes form the basis for the following task, in which you prepare a complete research report.

TASK 11

You have already written many of the components of a research report through your work in previous tasks. Building on previous tasks, prepare a research report that follows the general format for a thesis or dissertation (see Performance Criteria, p. 595).

GUIDELINES FOR WRITING A RESEARCH REPORT

People conduct research for a variety of reasons. The motivation for doing a research project may be simply that such a project is a degree requirement, or maybe the researcher has a strong desire to contribute to educational theory or practice. Whatever the reason for their execution, most research studies culminate with the production of a research report. Unlike a research plan or proposal, which focuses on what will be done, a research report describes what has happened in the study and the results that were obtained. All researchers strive to communicate as clearly as possible the purpose, procedures, and findings of their studies. A well-written report describes a study in enough detail to permit replication by another researcher. The goal of this chapter is to have you, after conducting a study, integrate all your previous efforts to produce a complete report and then to turn that report into a journal article for publication.

In the early editions of this book (circa 1976–1990), the focus on writing was almost exclusively on research reports for quantitative studies. In the past two decades, however, the number of reports on qualitative research has grown steadily to include a wide spectrum of theses, dissertations, journals, and books. Although all research reports address similar topics—for example, all contain a description of the topic or problem, a review of literature, a description of procedures, and a description of results—qualitative and quantitative studies address these topics in somewhat different ways and give them different emphases. In this chapter, we emphasize the general issues and practices associated with writing a research report, whether qualitative or quantitative. You are encouraged to examine and compare the reports reprinted in previous chapters to see their differences. When you are writing your report, you should look through journals pertinent to your study to view the sections, level of detail, and types of results commonly reported to determine the appropriate format for your report. This is also a good time to revisit some of your earlier writing that was encouraged in the earlier chapters of this book—by now, you may be well on your way to developing a research report suitable for publication!

In the spirit of sharing tips for successful writing, we offer some tips in Figure 22.1 for what not to do once you finally get settled down to work. Activities such as those listed can eat up precious writing time. You may want to write down your own what-not-to-do list and stick it in a prominent place wherever it is that you write. Check it occasionally, and get the behaviors out of your system.

When you're clear on what *not* to do, focus on the following suggestions for what you *should* do when writing a research report:

- Look for progress, not perfection.
- Write whatever comes to mind. Then go back and hunt for what you are really trying to say—it's there.

> **FIGURE 22.1** • Geoff's tips for being able to avoid writing
>
> - Think about all the things at school that I need to do before tomorrow.
> - Scan my desk to see if someone has left me a note about a meeting, sports practice, birthday party that I need to go to **NOW.**
> - Check my voicemail.
> - Check my e-mail.
> - Check my checkbook to see if it is balanced.
> - Call my wife/child/colleague/friend/enemy to see what they are doing.
> - Walk down the hallway to see if I can find someone to talk to.
> - Dream about winning the lottery.
> - Make an appointment to see my dentist.

Source: Mills, Geoffrey, *Action Research: A Guide for the Teacher Researcher*, 5th Edition, © 2014, p. 180. Reprinted by permission of Pearson Education, Inc., Upper Saddle River, NJ.

- Have you ever thought to yourself, "I wish I had done that differently?" With writing, you can do it differently; editing your own work is a delight. Write boldly and then say it again—better.
- Writing is an exercise in learning about your own work. Writing, then editing, then rewriting, then editing again clarifies thoughts into a coherent package.
- With regard to editing, even a gem needs to be mined when it is in a rough state, cut ruthlessly, then buffed.
- Nobody knows your work better than you do. You'll be surprised how much better you know it when you've "discussed it with your computer" a few times.
- Write without consideration for grammar, syntax, or punctuation. Just write. Sometimes editing is an avoidance technique.
- Write at the same time every day, at a time when you know you won't be disturbed.
- Write about your research as though you're sending an e-mail to a friend. Pretend your friend needs it explained simply.

Writing is nothing more than putting thought to paper, yet many writers hold irrational beliefs about the task or even insist on rituals that must be completed if writing sessions are to be successful. An informal survey of friends and colleagues yielded examples of such rituals: One suggested that writing can occur only between the hours of 7:00 a.m. and 12:00 p.m.; another that writing can be done only in longhand, using a blue pen and white legal pad; and yet another that the house must be clean before writing can start.

There is no easy way around the pragmatic issue of time: Writing takes time, and we never have enough time to do all that we have to do, professionally and personally. The best advice we can offer is to make writing part of your professional life and responsibilities. A study is not over until the report has been completed, and the time you need for writing should be included in the schedule you create when planning your research (see Task 4 Example p. 142–144). We know of no other way, besides stealing from personal and family time, to get our writing done. In the short term, our loved ones will put up with the "I need to stay home and get this writing (grading, lesson planning, studying, etc.) done. You go ahead and enjoy the movie (dinner, picnic, hike, river rafting, skiing)." Writing need not wait until the rest of the study is complete: While you are collecting data, you can use spare time profitably to begin revising or refining the introduction and method sections of your report; after all the data are analyzed, you can turn your attention to the final sections.

The major guideline for all stages of writing is to begin with an outline. Developing an outline involves identifying and ordering major topics and then differentiating each major heading into logical subheadings. The time spent working on an outline is well worth it. It is much easier to reorganize an outline that is not quite right than to reorganize a document written in paragraph form. Your report will be more organized and logical if you think through the sequence before you actually write anything. Of course, your first draft should not be your last; two or three revisions of each section may be needed. Remember, writing inevitably uncovers issues or activities that must be rethought. Each time you read a section, you should seek ways to improve its organization or clarity. Asking others to review your report will reveal areas in need of rethinking or rewording that you have not noticed.

Fortunately, once you begin writing, it becomes easier to continue writing. You may even think of a little reward system, if you are somewhat extrinsically motivated. For example, after dedicating himself to some writing time, one of your authors (Geoff) treats himself to time on an elliptical machine or treadmill, time with family or friends, or something sweet (you know, some sugar to help with the fatigue!).

With these general guidelines for writing in mind, we next turn to some specifics about writing a research report. Probably the foremost rule of research report writing is that the writer should try to relate aspects of the study in a manner that accurately reflects what was done and what was found. Although the style of reporting may differ for quantitative and qualitative studies, the focus in all instances should be on providing accurate description for the reader. For example, in quantitative reports, personal pronouns such as *I* and *we* are usually avoided. In qualitative reports, however, the researcher often adopts a more personal tone and shares the words of the participants. Such stylistic differences do not alter the need for accurate reporting.

The research report should be written in a clear, simple, straightforward style that reflects scholarship. You do not have to be boring, just concise. In other words, convey what you want to convey and do it in an efficient way by avoiding jargon and using simple language. For example, instead of saying, "The population comprised all students who matriculated for the fall semester at Egghead University," it would be better to say, "The population was all students enrolled for the fall semester at Egghead University." Obviously the report should contain correct spelling, grammatical construction, and punctuation. Your computer probably has a spelling and grammar checker. Use it and, when necessary, consult a dictionary. It is also a good idea to have someone you know (someone who is perhaps stronger in these areas) review your manuscript and indicate errors.

The final report should be proofread carefully at least twice. Reading the report silently to yourself will usually be sufficient to identify major errors. If you have a willing listener, however, reading the manuscript out loud often helps you to identify grammatical or construction errors. Sometimes sentences do not make nearly as much sense when you hear them as when you write them, and your listener will frequently be helpful in bringing to your attention sections that are unclear. Reading the report backward, last sentence first, also helps you to identify poorly constructed or unclear sentences.

> MyLab Education **Self-Check 22.1**

FORMAT AND STYLE

Format refers to the general pattern of organization and arrangement of the report. Research reports generally follow a format that parallels the steps involved in conducting a study, although formats may vary in terms of which sections are included and how they are titled. For example, one format may call for a section titled Discussion and another format may require two separate sections, one titled Summary or Conclusions and another titled Recommendations, but all formats require a section in which the results of the study are discussed and interpreted. All research reports also include a condensed description of the study, whether it be a summary of a dissertation or an abstract of a journal article.

Style refers to the rules of grammar, spelling, capitalization, and punctuation for preparing the report. Most colleges, universities, and professional journals require the use of a specific style, either a style they have developed or one from a published style manual. Perhaps the most frequently cited manual used by education researchers is the *Publication Manual of the American Psychological Association*, also called the APA style manual. This style manual is currently in its sixth edition.

Although different style manuals emphasize different rules of writing, several rules are common to most manuals. Use of abbreviations and contractions, for instance, is generally discouraged in formal writing. For example, "the American Psychological Assn." (that may appear in an early draft) should be replaced by "the American Psychological Association." Instead of *shouldn't*, researchers write *should not*. Exceptions to the abbreviation rule include commonly used and understood abbreviations (such as IQ and GPA) and abbreviations defined by the researcher to promote clarity, simplify presentation, or reduce repetition. If the same sequence of words is used repeatedly, the researcher often defines an abbreviation in parentheses when first using the sequence and thereafter uses only the abbreviation.

Most style manuals also address the treatment of numbers. One convention is to spell out a number that comes at the start of a sentence (e.g., "Six schools were contacted…"). Another common convention is to use words if the number is nine or less (e.g., "a total of five lists…") and to use Arabic numerals if the number is greater than nine (e.g., "a total of 500 questionnaires was sent"). These guidelines hold only for the main body of the report: Tables, figures, footnotes, and references may include both abbreviations and Arabic numerals.

Style manuals also specify how to cite references and use footnotes. In APA style, for example, authors of cited references are usually referred to in the main body of the report by last name only; first names, initials, and titles are not given. Instead of writing, "Professor Dudley Q. McStrudle (2002) concluded…," researchers write, "McStrudle (2002) concluded…." A reference page at the end of the manuscript includes additional information about the author and the source of the information cited.

Check with your adviser about the style used in your institution before beginning writing—rearranging a format after the fact is tedious and time-consuming. It is also very helpful to study several reports that have been written in the style used by your institution. For example, look at existing dissertations, especially those directed by your adviser, to get an idea of format and what is expected (an institution may, in fact, be using a combination of styles and formats). If you are not bound by any particular format and style system, we recommend that you acquire and study a copy of the APA style manual, either the full publication manual or the official pocket style guide. Like other aspects of the research project, technology tools can help you manage your citations, and that will save you an enormous amount of time when it comes to preparing your research report. A few

of these tools are outlined for you in the Digital Research Tools feature.

> MyLab Education **Self-Check 22.2**
>
> MyLab Education **Application Exercise 22.1:**
> Writing Research Reports Part 1

FORMATTING THESES AND DISSERTATIONS

Although specifics vary considerably, most research reports prepared for a degree requirement follow the same general format. Figure 22.2 presents an outline of the typical contents of such a report as described by the APA for the preparation of manuscripts for publication. As the figure indicates, theses and dissertations include a set of fairly standard preliminary pages, components that directly parallel the research process, and supplementary information, which is included in appendixes. A report on a quantitative study and one on a qualitative study have similar contents except that the method section in the report of the qualitative study emphasizes the description and selection of the research site, the sampling approach, and the data collection process.

Preliminary Pages

The preliminary pages contain the title page, acknowledgments page, table of contents, list of tables and figures, and abstract. The title should communicate what the study is about. During the review of the literature for a study, researchers often make initial decisions about the relevance of a source based on its title. A well-constructed title makes it fairly easy for the reader to determine the nature of the topic; a vaguely worded title confuses the reader, who then must search through the body of the report to get more information. After you write your title, apply the communication test: Would you know what the study was about if you read the title in an index? Ask friends or colleagues to describe what they understand from your title.

Most theses and dissertations also include an acknowledgments page. This page permits the writer to express appreciation to persons who have contributed significantly to the research. Notice the word *significantly*. You cannot (and should not!)

> **FIGURE 22.2** • Common components of a research report submitted for a degree requirement
>
> ### PRELIMINARY PAGES
>
> Title Page
> Acknowledgments Page
> Table of Contents
>
> List of Tables and Figures
> Abstract
>
> ### MAIN BODY OF THE REPORT
>
> Introduction
> Statement of the Problem
> Review of Related Literature
> Statement of the Hypothesis
> Significance of the Study
> Method
> Participants
>
> Instruments
> Design
> Procedure
> Results
> Discussion (Conclusions and Recommendations)
> References (Bibliography)
>
> ### APPENDIXES

Source: Format information from *Publication Manual of the American Psychological Association* (6th ed., pp. 21–59), by the American Psychological Association, Washington, DC: Author.

Digital Research Tools

MANAGING CITATIONS

The Internet offers a variety of reference management software choices depending on the needs, operating system, and budget available to you. Here we will discuss seven of the most commonly used and accessible citation management software packages.

RefWorks (refworks.com/refworks2)

Many universities have adopted RefWorks as an online citation management tool that they make available to their students at no cost (if your university does not make it available to students, you will need to purchase a subscription). RefWorks is a commercial citation manager that provides users with the ability to manage and store references online at a personal database that can be accessed and updated from any computer. It also allows users to link to electronic editions of journals to which universities subscribe (perhaps as part of a consortium agreement) and to capture and format bibliographic information easily.

Zotero (zotero.org)

Zotero is a free plug-in for your web browser that allows users to pull bibliographic information instantly from websites into Zotero. For example, if you are browsing Amazon.com and find a book you want to add to your reference list, you simply click a button in your browser window and whatever bibliographic information is available from the site is instantly downloaded to your personal Zotero account. You can later return to your account and quickly generate citations and references in whatever format you choose. If your source is an online journal article, Zotero can store a copy of the source for you. (Did we mention that this is free?!)

EndNote (endnote.com)

EndNote is a commercial (read as "pay-to-use") reference management software package that allows users to manage bibliographies and references while writing research reports. And EndNote X8 now meets the complete APA sixth

(continued)

edition style manual requirements. It also offers quick links to create footnotes, all while creating lists of references in Word documents.

Citavi (citavi.com/en/index.html)

Citavi is a commercial comprehensive reference management system that helps researchers manage references, integrate pdfs and other documents, evaluate content, organize content, and cite sources. It also provides access to over 4800 databases and library catalogs with the ability for group work and sharing of references. A unique feature of Citavi is "The Knowledge Organizer" that allows users to structure their outline and contribute sections over time.

Colwiz (colwiz.com)

Colwiz is a free reference manager and research group manager from the University of Oxford that allows researchers to store files, maintain a reference library, annotate documents, and cite references. Users can also set up research groups on the cloud and easily share files and references. Colwiz allows users to cite as you write with co-authors using Google Docs and will auto-format in 7,000+ styles including APA, Chicago, and MLA.

Mendeley (mendeley.com/)

Mendeley is a free multi-faceted reference management, research network, data-sharing, and career network that researchers can use to create a personal library of research. Search, sort, annotate, create sticky notes, and cite using an acceptable style. And for researchers looking to share their emerging ideas with other users, Mendeley boasts a community of over 6 million users!

Qiqqa (qiqqa.com/)

Qiqqa is a free research and reference manager that researchers can use to manage references, read, annotate, tag, search, and cite pdfs and other documents and allows you to import PDFs from Mendeley while at the same time instantly creating bibliographies to share with colleagues.

---

mention everyone who had anything to do with the study or the report. It is acceptable to thank your adviser for her or his guidance and assistance; it is not acceptable to thank your third-grade teacher for giving you confidence in your ability. (Recall that the Academy Awards® starts playing music to override lengthy acceptance speeches!)

The table of contents is an outline of your report that indicates the page on which each major section (or chapter) and subsection begins. A list of tables and figures, presented on a separate page, gives the number and title of each table and figure and the page on which it can be found.

Many colleges and universities require an abstract, and others require a summary, but the current trend is in favor of abstracts. The content of abstracts and summaries is identical, but the position differs: An abstract precedes the main body of the report, and a summary follows the discussion or conclusion. Abstracts often must be limited to a specific number of words, usually between 100 and 500. Many institutions require abstracts to be no more than 350 words, which is the maximum allowed by Dissertation Abstracts International, a repository of dissertation abstracts. The APA sets a limit of 120 words for publication in its journals. Because the abstract of a report is often the only part that is read, it should briefly describe the most important aspects of the study, including the topic, the type of participants and instruments, the design, the data collection procedures, and the major results and conclusions. For example, a 100-word abstract for a study investigating the effect of a writing-oriented curriculum on the reading comprehension of fourth-grade students may read as follows:

> The purpose of this study was to determine the effect of a curriculum that emphasized writing on the reading comprehension of fourth-grade students who were reading at least one level below grade level, using a posttest-only control group design. After 8 months, students ($n = 20$) who participated in a curriculum that emphasized writing achieved significantly

higher scores on the reading comprehension subtest of the Stanford Achievement Test, Primary Level 3 (grades 3.5–4.9) than students ($n = 20$) who did not [$t(38) = 4.83, p < .05$]. The curriculum emphasizing writing was more effective in promoting reading comprehension.

The Main Body

The body of a report contains an introduction to the topic that also includes the review of the literature and the hypotheses (if any); a method or procedure section describing the participants, the instruments, and the procedures; a section presenting the results; and a discussion of the findings.

Introduction

The introduction begins with a description of the research problem. A well-written statement of a problem generally indicates the variables examined in the study, including definitions of key terms that do not have commonly understood meanings. The statement of the problem should be accompanied by a presentation of its background, including a justification for the study in terms of its significance; that is, the answer to the question "Why should anyone care about this study?"

The review of related literature indicates what is known about the problem. Its function is to educate the reader about the area under study. The review of related literature is not a series of abstracts or annotations but rather a summary and analysis of the relations and differences among relevant studies and reports. The review should flow so that the least related references are discussed first and the most related references are discussed last. The review should conclude with a brief summary of the literature and its implications.

In the report of a quantitative study, the hypothesis is presented following the literature review. A good hypothesis clearly states the expected relation or difference among the studied variables and defines those variables in operational, measurable terms. All hypotheses logically follow the review of related literature and are based on the implications of previous research. A well-developed hypothesis is testable—that is, it can be supported or disconfirmed. In a report of a qualitative study, the researcher is unlikely to state hypotheses as focused as those of a quantitative researcher but

may express some hunches about what the study may show (i.e., guiding hypotheses).

Methods and Procedures

The method section of a research report includes a description of participants, instruments, design, procedure, assumptions, and limitations. For a qualitative study, this section may also include a detailed description of the site and the nature and length of interactions with the participants. The description of participants includes information about how they were selected and, mainly for quantitative researchers, the population they represent. A description of the sample should indicate its size and major characteristics of members such as age, grade level, ability level, and socioeconomic status. A good description of the sample enables readers of the report to determine how similar study participants are to other populations of concern to the readers.

Data collection instruments or other materials used in the study should be described fully. The description should indicate the purpose of the instrument, its application, and the validity and reliability of any instrument. If a test has been developed by the researcher, its description needs to be more detailed and should also state the manner in which it was developed, any pilot-test procedures and results, revisions, steps involved in scoring, and guidelines for interpretation. A copy of the instrument, accompanying scoring keys, and other pertinent information about a newly developed test are generally placed as appendixes to the thesis or dissertation proper.

In an experimental study, the description of the design is especially important and should include a rationale for its selection and a discussion of threats to validity associated with the design, including how these threats may have been minimized in the study being reported. In other types of research, the description of the design may be combined with procedure.

The procedure section should describe the steps that the researcher(s) followed in conducting the study, in chronological order and in sufficient detail to permit the study to be replicated by another researcher. In essence, a step-by-step description of what went on during the study should be provided. It should be clear how participants were assigned to groups or treatments, if appropriate, and the conditions under which participants were observed or interviewed should be described. In many cases, qualitative researchers produce more complex and detailed procedural descriptions than do quantitative researchers.

Results

The results section describes the statistical techniques or the inferential interpretations that were applied to the data and the results of these analyses. For each hypothesis, the statistical test of significance selected and applied to the data is named, followed by the accompanying statistics indicating whether the hypothesis was supported or not supported. Tables and figures are used to present findings in summary or graphic form and should add clarity to the presentation. Tables present numerical data in rows and columns and usually include descriptive statistics, such as means and standard deviations, and the results of tests of significance, such as t tests and F ratios. Effective tables and figures are uncluttered and self-explanatory; it is better to use two tables (or figures) than one that is crowded. They should stand alone, that is, be interpretable without the aid of related text material. Tables and figures follow their related text discussion and are referred to by number, not by name or location. In other words, the text should say, "see Table 1," not "see the table with the means" or "see the table on the next page." Examine the variety of tables and figures throughout this text to get a perspective on how data can be presented.

Qualitative research reporting tends to be based mainly on descriptions and quotations that support or illustrate the themes that emerged in the study. Charts and diagrams showing the relations among identified categories and patterns are also useful in presenting the results of a study. The logic and description of the interpretations linked to qualitative charts and diagrams are important aspects of qualitative research reporting.

Discussion

All research reports have a section that discusses and interprets the results, draws conclusions and states implications, and makes recommendations. Interpretation of results may be presented in a separate section titled Discussion, or it may be included in the same section as the analysis of results. What this section is called is unimportant; what is important is how well it is constructed.

Each result should be discussed in terms of its relation to the problem and its agreement or disagreement with previous results obtained in other studies or by other researchers.

Two common errors in this section are to confuse results and conclusions and to overgeneralize results. A result is the outcome of a test of significance or a qualitative analysis; the corresponding conclusion is that the original hypothesis or problem was or was not supported by the data. In qualitative reports, the conclusion may simply be a summarizing description of what was observed. Researchers overgeneralize when they state conclusions that are not warranted by the data. For example, if a group of firstgraders receiving personalized instruction were found to achieve significantly higher scores on a test of reading comprehension than a group receiving traditional instruction, it would be an overgeneralization to conclude that personalized instruction is (always) a superior method of instruction for (all) elementary students. Similarly, if a qualitative study about teacher burnout consisted of four interviewees, it would be an overgeneralization to infer that all teachers felt the same about burnout.

The discussion of a research report should also present the theoretical and practical implications of the findings and make recommendations for future research or future action. In this portion of the report, the researcher is permitted more freedom in expressing opinions that are not necessarily direct outcomes of data analysis. The researcher is free to discuss any possible revisions or additions to existing theory and to encourage studies designed to test hypotheses suggested by the results. The researcher may discuss implications of the findings for educational practice and suggest studies designed to replicate the study in other settings, with other participants, and in other curricular areas to increase the generalizability of the findings. The researcher may also suggest next-step studies designed to investigate another dimension of the problem. For example, a study finding type of feedback to be a factor in retention may suggest that amount of feedback may also be a factor and recommend further research in that area.

References

The reference section of the report lists all the sources that were cited in the report. Every source cited in the paper must be included in the references, and every entry listed in the references must appear in the body of the paper; in other words, the citations in the manuscript and the sources in the references must correspond exactly. If APA style is used, in-text citations of secondary sources should indicate the primary source from which they were taken, and only the primary source should be included in the references. For example, an in-text citation may be, "Nerdfais (cited in Snurd, 1995) found that yellow chalk. . . ." No year would be given for the Nerdfais study, and only the Snurd source would be listed in the references. For thesis and dissertation studies, any sources consulted that were not cited directly in the main body of the report may be included in an appendix. Whatever style manual you are following will determine the form each reference must take.

Appendixes

Appendixes are usually necessary in thesis and dissertation reports to provide information and data that are pertinent to the study but are either too lengthy or not important enough to be included in the main body of the report. Appendixes commonly contain materials especially developed for the study (e.g., tests, questionnaires, and cover letters), raw data, and data analysis sheets.

> MyLab Education **Self-Check 22.3**
>
> MyLab Education **Application Exercise 22.2:** Writing Research Reports Part 2

WRITING FOR JOURNAL PUBLICATION

In the post-thesis or dissertation phase of our academic lives, we are invariably faced with the question "How can I get the word out about my research?" Rarely do novice researchers move straight from thesis or dissertation to best-selling book. An interim step is more likely to be presenting a paper at an academic conference and seeking public feedback on the study. Sooner or later, however, it will be time to bite the bullet and prepare your research for your professional community—a daunting task for all academics, even the most seasoned. This task usually involves submission of the report to an academic journal. The sixth edition of the *Publication Manual of the American Psychological Association* (2010) dedicates a new chapter to "Manuscript Structure and Content" (pp. 21–61) that is recommended reading for budding journal article authors (that would be you) who wish to transform their theses, dissertations, or research projects into publishable pieces of prose that meet the APA recommended journal article reporting standards.

Writing for a journal is somewhat different than writing a thesis or dissertation. A major difference has to do with length. Journal articles are typically shorter than theses and dissertations, although how much shorter depends on the scope of the study, the kind of research that was conducted, the audience, the time allowed for writing, and other considerations. Historically, journals limited the length of submissions to 5,000 words. It became evident during article selection for this textbook, however, that most articles are now longer—it was very difficult to find relatively short journal articles published after the year 2000. Online journals routinely publish full-length theses on the Internet. A good rule of thumb is to follow the guidelines specified in the journal itself.

Clearly, then, selecting the appropriate journal is the first step. You should become very familiar with the journal you select: Take time to read earlier volumes and pay attention to the kind of studies published, the scope of the articles published, and notification of upcoming volumes with a special guest editor or topic focus. It is possible that a journal is seeking manuscripts in your particular field—timing is everything! Journals usually contain a section for potential contributors that specify length guidelines, formatting rules, number of references, and other information specific to that journal. Comply with the requirements and "let the manuscript speak for itself, as it will have to do when published."[1]

Although journals often have idiosyncratic rules for authors to follow, the standards for good scientific writing apply for any journal you may select. In terms of content, think of a research article as telling a story within the framework specified by your style manual. Attend to the context of your study, and craft a narrative that guides

---

[1] *Writing Up Qualitative Research* by H. F. Wolcott, 2009, Thousand Oaks, CA: Sage, p. 159.

your audience to understand your goal, your procedures, your findings, and the implications. Be sure to describe data collection; analysis and interpretation; and considerations such as validity, reliability, and ethics. In terms of writing style, you should adopt a clear, reader-friendly writing style. Don't try to hide behind jargon, and don't make statements that you can't substantiate. Let your data speak for themselves. Although you may want to peruse the journals you are considering for your submissions and notice the structure and writing style of the researchers whose work has been accepted and published, don't adopt a voice that is not your own—write using the same voice that you use to tell the story of your research to your colleagues. Remember that you want to keep your readers' attention. If you are like us, you read something and make a judgment like "Not bad," "Engaging," "Pretty bad," or "I'll give it another few pages before I give up and move on." For whatever reason, we intuitively know what will keep our attention. Write your manuscripts in a way that makes them engaging for you and your audience.

When you have a complete draft, you should take one last shot at making the text as tight as possible. Wolcott[2] provided a useful analogy to help with this process:

> Some of the best advice I've ever found for writers happened to be included with the directions for assembling a new wheelbarrow: Make sure all parts are properly in place before tightening.

We've never assembled a wheelbarrow, but if our experience with assembling a barbecue grill is anything to go by, we can relate to the analogy. The directions for the barbecue grill were quite

explicit: "Ensure assembly is complete before igniting." We can apply the assembly metaphor to our writing task: Be sure to take the time to read the narrative carefully, focusing on the details. Getting a manuscript ready for publication is not the time to be in a hurry. You have spent many days, weeks, and months doing educational research. You are close to meeting your personal and professional goal and want to get the text off your desk (or hard drive). Now is not the time to be foolhardy—don't light the barbecue before all the pieces are correctly positioned and tightened! Take time to do a word-by-word edit. Stated simply, Wolcott's checklist of details to watch for in final editing include unnecessary words; passive voice, especially forms of the verb *to be*; qualifiers such as *rather, very, little,* and *pretty*; and overused phrases. Perhaps the underlying lesson here is that, if we have a story to tell and a compelling way in which to tell it, then there is a very good chance that an editorial board will agree. For an engaging discussion about writing and publishing qualitative research, we highly recommend you consult Wolcott's (2009) *Writing Up Qualitative Research*.

When the manuscript is polished and written to meet the guidelines of your chosen journal, you're almost ready to submit it. The final step is to write a cover letter to send with your manuscript. In the cover letter, briefly explain why your contribution is a good fit with the journal and how you have satisfied the criteria specified in the "Notes to Contributors" section of the journal.

Good luck in becoming a "published author"!

---

[2] Wolcott, p. 93.

MyLab Education **Self-Check 22.4**

MyLab Education **Application Exercise 22.3:**
Finding a Professional Journal

SUMMARY

GUIDELINES FOR WRITING A RESEARCH REPORT

1. All research reports contain a description of the topic or problem, a review of literature, a description of procedures, and a description of results, but qualitative and quantitative studies address these topics in somewhat different ways and give them different emphases.
2. Make writing part of your professional life and responsibilities.
3. Begin with an outline that identifies and orders major topics and then differentiates each major heading into logical subheadings.
4. Write, edit, and rewrite with an eye toward progress, not perfection.
5. Relate aspects of the study in a manner that accurately reflects what you did and what you found.
6. Use clear, simple, straightforward language. Correct spelling, grammar, and punctuation are expected.
7. Proofread the final report at least twice, or ask a friend to review the manuscript for you.

FORMAT AND STYLE

8. Format refers to the general pattern of organization and arrangement of the report. Style refers to the rules of grammar, spelling, capitalization, and punctuation followed in preparing the report.
9. The *Publication Manual of the American Psychological Association,* also called the APA style manual, specifies the style and format used by most educational researchers.

FORMATTING THESES AND DISSERTATIONS

10. The title of the report should describe the purpose of the study as clearly as possible.
11. The acknowledgments page allows the writer to express appreciation to persons who have contributed significantly to the study.
12. The table of contents is an outline of the report that indicates the page on which each major section (or chapter) and subsection begins. A list of tables and figures is presented on a separate page.
13. Most colleges and universities require an abstract or summary of the study. The number of pages for each is specified and usually ranges from 100 to 500 words. The abstract should describe the most important aspects of the study, including the topic, type of participants and instruments, design, procedures, and major results and conclusions.
14. The introduction is the first section of the main body of the report and includes a well-written description of the problem, a review of related literature, a statement of the hypothesis, and definition of terms.
15. The method section includes a description of participants, instruments, design, procedure, assumptions, and limitations.
16. The description of participants in a quantitative study includes a definition and description of the population from which the sample was selected and may describe the method used in selecting the participants. The description of participants in a qualitative study includes descriptions of the way participants were selected, why they were selected, and a detailed description of the context in which they function.
17. The description of each instrument should indicate the purpose of the instrument, its application, and the validity and reliability of any instrument.
18. The procedure section should describe the steps that the researcher(s) followed in conducting the study, in chronological order and in sufficient detail to permit the study to be replicated by another researcher.
19. The results section describes the statistical techniques or qualitative interpretations that were applied to the data and the results of these analyses.
20. Tables and figures are used to present findings in summary or graph form and add clarity to the presentation. Good tables and figures are uncluttered and self-explanatory.

21. Each research finding or result should be discussed in terms of its relation to the original research question and its agreement or disagreement with previous results obtained in other studies. A result is the outcome of a test of significance or a qualitative analysis; the corresponding conclusion is that the original hypothesis or topic was or was not supported by the data.

22. Overgeneralization occurs when researchers state conclusions that are not warranted by their research results.

23. The researcher should discuss the theoretical and practical implications of the findings and make recommendations for future research or future action.

24. The reference section of the report lists all the sources that were cited in the report. The required style manual guides the format of various types of references.

25. Appendixes include information and data that are pertinent to the study but are either too lengthy or not important enough to be included in the main body of the report.

WRITING FOR JOURNAL PUBLICATION

26. Journal articles are typically shorter than theses and dissertations, although how much shorter depends on factors such as the scope of the study and the kind of research that was conducted.

27. Selecting the appropriate journal is the first step. Follow the format and style required by that journal.

28. The standards for good scientific writing apply for any journal you may select. Craft a narrative that guides your audience to understand your goal, your procedures, your findings, and the implications. Let your data speak for themselves. Take your time.

29. The final step is to write a cover letter to send with your manuscript. In the cover letter, briefly explain why your contribution is a good fit with the journal.

PERFORMANCE CRITERIA   TASK 11

Your research report should include all the components listed in Figure 22.2, with the possible exceptions of an acknowledgments page and appendixes. For those of you who have conducted quantitative studies, Task 11 involves combining the work you have done on previous tasks, writing a discussion section, and preparing the appropriate preliminary pages (including an abstract) and references. In other words, you have already written most of the final product for Task 11. Those of you who have conducted qualitative studies should be able to build on the information you developed for your research plans as you write the report. An example that illustrates the performance called for by Task 11 appears on the following pages (see Task 11 Example). This example represents the synthesis of the previously presented tasks related to the effects of interactive multimedia on biology achievement. To the degree possible with a student paper, this example follows the guidelines of the *Publication Manual of the American Psychological Association*.

Effect of Interactive Multimedia on the Achievement
of 10th-Grade Biology Students

Sara Jane Calderin

Florida International University

Submitted in partial fulfillment of

the requirements for EDF 5481

April, 1994

Table of Contents

List of Tables and Figures

Abstract

The purpose of this study was to investigate the effect of interactive multimedia on the achievement of 10th-grade biology students. Using a posttest-only control group design and a t test for independent samples, it was found that after approximately 8 months the students ($n = 30$) who were instructed using interactive multimedia achieved significantly higher scores on the biology test of the National Proficiency Survey Series than did the students ($n = 30$) whose instruction did not include interactive multimedia, $t(58) = 4.22, p < .05$. It was concluded that the interactive multimedia instruction was effective in raising the achievement level of the participating students.

Introduction

One of the major concerns of educators and parents alike is the decline in student achievement. An area of particular concern is science education, where the higher-level thinking skills and problem solving techniques so necessary for success in our technological society need to be developed (Smith & Westhoff, 1992).

Research is constantly providing new proven methods for educators to use, and technology has developed many kinds of tools ideally suited to the classroom. One such tool is interactive multimedia (IMM). IMM provides teachers with an extensive amount of data in a number of different formats including text, sound, and video. This makes it possible to appeal to all the different learning styles of the students and to offer a variety of material for students to analyze (Howson & Davis, 1992).

When teachers use IMM, students become highly motivated, which results in improved class attendance and more completed assignments (O'Connor, 1993). In addition, students also become actively involved in their own learning, encouraging comprehension rather than mere memorization of facts (Kneedler, 1993; Reeves, 1992).

Statement of the Problem

The purpose of this study was to investigate the effect of IMM on the achievement of 10th-grade biology students. IMM was defined as "a computerized database that allows users to access information in multiple forms, including text, graphics, video and audio" (Reeves, 1992, p. 47).

Review of Related Literature

Due to modern technology, such as videotapes and videodiscs, students receive more information from visual sources than they do from the written word (Helms & Helms, 1992), and yet in school the majority of information is still transmitted through textbooks. While textbooks cover a wide range of topics superficially, IMM can provide in-depth information on essential topics in a format that students find interesting (Kneedler, 1993). Smith and Westhoff (1992) note that when student interest is sparked, curiosity levels are increased and students are motivated to ask questions. The interactive nature of multimedia allows students to seek out their own answers, and by so doing they become owners of the concept involved. Ownership translates into comprehension (Howson & Davis, 1992).

Many science concepts are learned through observation of experiments. By using IMM, students can participate in a variety of experiments which are either too expensive, too lengthy, or too dangerous to carry out in the school laboratory (Howson & Davis, 1992; Leonard, 1989; Louie, Sweat, Gresham, & Smith, 1991). While observing experiments students can discuss what is happening and ask questions. At the touch of a button teachers are able to replay any part of the proceedings, and they also have random access to related information which can be used to illustrate completely the answer to the question (Howson & Davis, 1992). By answering students' questions in this detailed way, the content becomes more relevant to the needs of the students (Smith & Westhoff, 1992). When knowledge is relevant students are able to use it to solve problems and in so doing develop higher-level thinking skills (Helms & Helms, 1992; Sherwood, Kinzer, Bransford, & Franks, 1987).

A major challenge of science education is to provide students with large amounts of information that will encourage them to be analytical (Howson & Davis, 1992; Sherwood et al., 1987). IMM offers electronic access to extensive information allowing students to organize, evaluate, and use it in the solution of problems (Smith & Wilson, 1993). When information is introduced as an aid to problem solving it becomes a tool with which to solve other problems, rather than a series of solitary, disconnected facts (Sherwood et al., 1987).

Although critics complain that IMM is entertainment and students do not learn from it (Corcoran, 1989), research has shown that student learning does improve when IMM is used in the classroom (Sherwood et al., 1987; Sherwood & Others, 1990). A 1987 study by Sherwood et al., for example, showed that seventh- and eighth-grade science students receiving instruction enhanced with IMM had better retention of that information, and O'Connor (1993) found that the use of IMM in high school mathematics and science increased the focus on students' problem solving and critical thinking skills.

Statement of the Hypothesis

The quality and quantity of software available for science classes has dramatically improved during the past decade. Although some research has been carried out on the effects of IMM on student achievement in science, due to promising updates in the technology involved, further study is warranted. Therefore, it was hypothesized that 10th-grade biology students whose teachers use IMM as part of their instructional technique will exhibit significantly higher achievement than 10th-grade biology students whose teachers do not use IMM.

Method

Participants

The sample for this study was selected from the total population of 213 10th-grade students at an upper middle class all-girls Catholic high school in Miami, Florida. The population was 90% Hispanic, mainly of Cuban-American descent. Sixty students were randomly selected (using a table of random numbers) and randomly assigned to two groups of 30 each.

Instrument

The biology test of the National Proficiency Survey Series (NPSS) was used as the measuring instrument. The test was designed to measure individual student performance in biology at the high school level but the publishers also recommended it as an evaluation of instructional programs. Content validity is good; items were selected from a large item bank provided by classroom teachers and curriculum experts. High school instructional materials and a national curriculum survey were extensively reviewed before objectives were written. The test objectives and those of the biology classes in the study were highly correlated. Although the standard error of measurement is not given for the biology test, the range of KR-20s for the entire battery is from .82 to .91 with a median of .86. This is satisfactory since the purpose of the test was to evaluate instructional programs, not to make decisions concerning individuals. Catholic school students were included in the battery norming procedures, which were carried out in April and May of 1988 using 22,616 students in grades 9–12 from 45 high schools in 20 states.

Experimental Design

The design used in this study was the posttest-only control group design (see Figure 1). This design was selected because it provides control for most sources of invalidity and random assignment to groups was possible. A pretest was not necessary since the final science grades from June 1993 were available to check initial group equivalence and to help control mortality, a potential threat to internal validity with this design. Mortality, however, was not a problem as no students dropped from either group.

Figure 1. Experimental design.

Group	Assignment	*n*	Treatment	Posttest
1	Random	30	IMM instruction	NPSS:B[a]
2	Random	30	Traditional instruction	NPSS:B

[a]National Proficiency Survey Series: Biology

Procedure

Prior to the beginning of the 1993–1994 school year, before classes were scheduled, 60 of the 213 10th-grade students were randomly selected and randomly assigned to two groups of 30 each, the average biology class size; each group became a biology class. One of the classes was randomly chosen to receive IMM instruction. The same teacher taught both classes.

The study was designed to last eight months beginning on the first day of class. The control group was taught using traditional methods of lecturing and open class discussions. The students worked in pairs for laboratory investigations, which included the use of microscopes. The teacher's role was one of information disseminator.

The experimental classroom had 15 workstations for student use, each one consisting of a laserdisc player, a video recorder, a 27-inch monitor, and a Macintosh computer with a 40 MB hard drive, 128 MB RAM, and a CD-ROM drive. The teacher's workstation incorporated a Macintosh computer with CD-ROM drive, a videodisc player, and a 27-inch monitor. The workstations were networked to the school library so students had access to online services such as Prodigy and Infotrac as well as to the card catalogue. Two laser printers were available through the network for the students' use.

In the experimental class the teacher used a videodisc correlated to the textbook. When barcodes provided in the text were scanned, a section of the videodisc was activated and appeared on the monitor. The section might be a motion picture demonstrating a process or a still picture offering more detail than the text. The role of the teacher in the experimental group was that of facilitator and guide. After the teacher had introduced a new topic, the students worked in pairs at the workstations investigating topics connected to the main idea presented in the lesson. Videodiscs, CD-ROMs, and online services were all available as sources of information. The students used HyperStudio to prepare multimedia reports, which they presented to the class.

Throughout the study the same subject matter was covered and the two classes used the same text. Although the students of the experimental group paired up at the workstations, the other group worked in pairs during lab time, thus equalizing any effect from cooperative learning. The classes could not meet at the same time as they were taught by the same teacher, so they met during second and third periods. First period was not chosen as the school sometimes has a special schedule which interferes with first period. Both classes had the same homework reading assignments, which were reviewed in class the following school day. Academic objectives were the same for each class and all tests measuring achievement were identical.

During the first week of May, the biology test of the NPSS was administered to both classes to compare their achievement in biology.

Results

Prior to the beginning of the study, after the 60 students were randomly selected and assigned to experimental and control groups, final science grades from the previous school year were obtained from school records in order to check initial group equivalence. Examination of the means and a *t* test for independent samples ($\alpha = .05$) indicated essentially no difference between the groups (see Table 1). A *t* test for independent samples was used because the groups were randomly formed and the data were interval.

Table 1

Means, Standard Deviation, and *t* Tests for the Experimental and Control Groups

	Group		
Score	IMM instruction[a]	Traditional instruction[a]	*t*
Prior			
Grades			
M	87.47	87.63	− 0.08[*]
SD	8.19	8.05	
Posttest			
NPSS:B			
M	32.27	26.70	4.22[**]
SD	4.45	5.69	

Note. Maximum score for prior grades = 100. Maximum score for posttest = 40.

[a]*n* = 30.

[*]$p > .05$. [**]$p < .05$.

At the completion of the eight-month study, during the first week in May, scores on the NPSS:B were compared, also using a *t* test for independent samples. As Table 1 indicates, scores of the experimental and control groups were significantly different. In fact, the experimental group scored approximately one standard deviation higher than the control group (ES = .98). Therefore, the original hypothesis that "10th-grade biology students whose teachers use IMM as part of their instructional technique will exhibit significantly higher achievement than 10th-grade biology students whose teachers do not use IMM" was supported.

Discussion

The results of this study support the original hypothesis: 10th-grade biology students whose teachers used IMM as part of their instructional technique did exhibit significantly higher achievement than 10th-grade biology students whose teachers did not use IMM. The IMM students' scores were 5.57 points (13.93%) higher than those of the other group. Also, it was informally observed that the IMM instructed students were eager to discover information on their own and to carry on the learning process outside scheduled class hours.

Results cannot be generalized to all classrooms because the study took place in an all-girls Catholic high school with the majority of the students having an Hispanic background. However, the results were consistent with research on IMM in general, and in particular with the findings of Sherwood et al. (1987) and O'Connor (1993) concerning the improvement of student achievement.

IMM appears to be a viable educational tool with applications in a variety of subject areas and with both cognitive and psychological benefits for students. While further research is needed, especially using other software and in other subject areas, the suggested benefits to students' learning offered by IMM warrant that teachers should be cognizant of this instructional method. In this technological age it is important that education take advantage of available tools which increase student motivation and improve academic achievement.

References

Corcoran, E. (1989, July). Show and tell: Hypermedia turns information into a multisensory event. *Scientific American, 261,* 72, 74.

Helms, C. W., & Helms, D. R. (1992, June). *Multimedia in education* (Report No. IR-016-090). Proceedings of the 25th Summer Conference of the Association of Small Computer Users in Education. North Myrtle Beach, SC. (ERIC Document Reproduction Service No. ED 357 732)

Howson, B. A., & Davis, H. (1992). Enhancing comprehension with videodiscs. *Media and Methods, 28*(3), 12–14.

Kneedler, P. E. (1993). California adopts multimedia science program. *Technological Horizons in Education Journal, 20*(7), 73–76.

Lehmann, I. J. (1990). Review of National Proficiency Survey Series. In J. J. Kramer & J. C. Conoley (Eds.), *The eleventh mental measurements yearbook* (pp. 595–599). Lincoln: University of Nebraska, Buros Institute of Mental Measurement.

Leonard, W. H. (1989). A comparison of student reaction to biology instruction by interactive videodisc or conventional laboratory. *Journal of Research in Science Teaching, 26,* 95–104.

Louie, R., Sweat, S., Gresham, R., & Smith, L. (1991). Interactive video: Disseminating vital science and math information. *Media and Methods, 27*(5), 22–23.

O'Connor, J. E. (1993, April). *Evaluating the effects of collaborative efforts to improve mathematics and science curricula* (Report No. TM-019-862). Paper presented at the Annual Meeting of the American Educational Research Association, Atlanta, GA. (ERIC Document Reproduction Service No. ED 357 083)

Reeves, T. C. (1992). Evaluating interactive multimedia. *Educational Technology, 32*(5), 47–52.

Sherwood, R. D., Kinzer, C. K., Bransford, J. D., & Franks, J. J. (1987). Some benefits of creating macro-contexts for science instruction: Initial findings. *Journal of Research in Science Teaching, 24,* 417–435.

Sherwood, R. D., & Others. (1990, April). *An evaluative study of level one videodisc based chemistry program* (Report No. SE-051-513). Paper presented at a Poster Session at the 63rd Annual Meeting of the National Association for Research in Science Teaching, Atlanta, GA. (ERIC Document Reproduction Service No. ED 320 772)

Smith, E. E., & Westhoff, G. M. (1992). The Taliesin project: Multidisciplinary education and multimedia. *Educational Technology, 32,* 15–23.

Smith, M. K., & Wilson, C. (1993, March). *Integration of student learning strategies via technology* (Report No. IR-016-035). Proceedings of the Fourth Annual Conference of Technology and Teacher Education. San Diego, CA. (ERIC Document Reproduction Service No. ED 355 937)

CHAPTER TWENTY-THREE

Evaluating
a Research Report

RGR Collection/Alamy Stock Photo

School of Rock, 2003

"A researcher critically evaluates each
reference and does not consider poorly executed
research." (p. 609)

LEARNING OUTCOMES

After reading Chapter 23, you should be able to do the following:

23.1 Evaluate each of the major sections and subsections of a research report.

23.2 For each type of research, evaluate the adequacy of a study representing that specific type of research.

These chapter learning outcomes form the basis for the following task, which requires you to evaluate a research report.

TASK 12

Given a reprint of a research report and an evaluation form, evaluate the components of the report (see Performance Criteria, p. 616).

GENERAL EVALUATION CRITERIA

Knowing how to conduct research and how to produce a research report are valuable skills, but as a professional you should also know how to consume and evaluate research. Anyone who reads a newspaper, listens to the radio, or watches television is a consumer of research. Many people uncritically accept and act on medical and health findings, for example, because the findings are presented by someone in a white lab coat or because they are labeled "research." Very few people question the procedures utilized or the generalizability of the findings. You have a responsibility to be informed about the latest findings in your professional area and to be able to differentiate good from poor research when investigating a problem to study. A researcher critically evaluates each reference and does not consider poorly executed research.

To evaluate a research study competently, you must have knowledge of each component of the research process. Your work in previous chapters has given you that knowledge. Thus, in this chapter, we discuss the criteria on which to evaluate a research report.

Many research studies have flaws of various kinds. Just because a study is published does not necessarily mean that it is a good study or that it is reported adequately. The most common flaw is a failure to collect or report validity and reliability information about data-gathering procedures and instruments such as tests, observations, questionnaires, and interviews. Other common flaws in a study itself include weaknesses in the research design and inappropriate or biased selection of participants; flaws in the report include failure to state limitations in the research and a general lack of description about the study. Watching for these problems is part of being a competent consumer of research reports; the problems also highlight common pitfalls to avoid in your own research.

At your current level of expertise, you may not be able to evaluate every component of every study. For example, you may not be able to determine whether the appropriate degrees of freedom were used in the calculation of an analysis of covariance. However, you should be able to detect a number of basic errors or weaknesses in research studies. For example, you should be able to identify the threats to validity associated with a study that has a one-group pretest–posttest design. You should also be able to detect obvious indications of experimenter bias that may have affected qualitative or quantitative research results. For example, a statement in a research report that "the purpose of this study was to prove . . ." should alert you to a probable bias.

As you read a research report, either as a consumer of research keeping up with the latest findings in your professional area or as a producer of research reviewing literature related to a defined problem, you should ask and answer a number of questions about the adequacy of a study and its components. The answers to some of these questions are more critical than the answers to others. An inadequate title is not a critical flaw; an inadequate research plan is. Some questions are difficult to answer if the study is not directly in your area of expertise. If your area of specialization is reading, for example, you are probably not in a position to judge the adequacy of a review of literature related to anxiety effects on learning. And, admittedly, the answers to some questions are more subjective than objective. Whether a study was well designed is pretty clear and objective; most quantitative researchers would agree that the randomized posttest-only control group design is a good design. On the other hand, the answer to whether the most appropriate design was used, given the problem under study, often involves a degree of subjective judgment. For example, the need for a pretest may be a debatable point; it depends on the study and its design.

Despite the lack of complete agreement in some areas, evaluation of a research report is a worthwhile and important activity. Major problems and shortcomings are usually readily identifiable, and you can formulate an overall impression of the quality of the study. In the sections that follow, we list for your consideration evaluative questions about a number of research strategies and areas. This list is by no means exhaustive, and as you read it, you may very well think of additional questions to ask. You may also note that not every criterion applies equally to both quantitative and qualitative research studies.

Introduction

Problem

- Is there a statement of the problem? Does the problem indicate a particular focus of study?
- Is the problem researchable? That is, can it be investigated by collecting and analyzing data?
- Is background information on the problem presented?
- Is the educational significance of the problem discussed?
- Does the problem statement indicate the variables of interest and the specific relations among the variables that were investigated?
- When necessary, are variables directly or operationally defined?
- Did the researcher have the knowledge and skill to carry out the research?

Review of Related Literature

- Is the review comprehensive?
- Is the review well organized? Does it flow logically so that the references least related to the problem are discussed first and those most related are discussed last? Does it educate the reader about the problem or topic?
- Is the review more than a series of abstracts or annotations? That is, have the references

been analyzed and critiqued and the results of various studies compared and contrasted?
- Are all cited references relevant to the problem under investigation? Is the relevance of each reference explained?
- Does the review conclude with a summary and interpretation of the literature and its implications for the problem under study?
- Do the implications form an empirical or theoretical rationale for the hypotheses that follow?
- Are most of the sources primary (i.e., are there only a few or no secondary sources)?
- Are references cited completely and accurately?

Hypotheses

- Are specific research questions listed or specific hypotheses stated?
- Is each hypothesis testable?
- Does each hypothesis state an expected relation or difference?
- If necessary, are variables directly or operationally defined?

Method

Participants

- Are the size and major characteristics of the population described?
- If a sample was selected, is the method of selecting the sample clearly described?
- Does the method of sample selection suggest any limitations or biases in the sample? For example, was stratified sampling used to obtain sample subgroups?
- Are the size and major characteristics of the sample described?
- If the study is quantitative, does the sample size meet the suggested guidelines for the minimum sample size appropriate for the method of research represented?

Instruments

- Do instruments and their administration meet guidelines for protecting human subjects? Were needed permissions obtained?
- Are the instruments appropriate for measuring the intended variables?

■ Was the correct type of instrument used for data collection (e.g., was a norm-referenced instrument used when a criterion-referenced one was more suitable)?

■ Is the rationale given for the selection of the instruments (or measurements) used?

■ Are the purpose, content, validity, and reliability of each instrument described?

■ If appropriate, are subtest reliabilities given?

■ Is evidence presented to indicate that the instruments are appropriate for the intended sample? For example, is the reading level of an instrument suitable for sample participants?

■ If an instrument was developed specifically for the study, are the procedures involved in its development and validation described?

■ If an instrument was developed specifically for the study, are administration, scoring or tabulating, and interpretation procedures fully described?

■ Does the researcher have the needed skills or experience to construct or administer an instrument?

Design and Procedure

■ Are the design and procedures appropriate for examining the research question or testing the hypotheses of the study?

■ Are the procedures described in sufficient detail to permit replication by another researcher?

■ Do procedures logically relate to one another?

■ Were instruments and procedures applied correctly?

■ If a pilot study was conducted, are its execution and results described? Is the effect on the subsequent study explained?

■ Are control procedures described?

■ Does the researcher discuss or account for any potentially confounding variable that he or she was unable to control?

Results

■ Are appropriate descriptive statistics presented?

■ Are the tests of significance appropriate, given the hypotheses and design of the study?

■ If parametric tests were used, is there evidence that the researcher avoided violating the required assumptions for parametric tests?

■ Was the probability level at which the tests of significance were evaluated specified in advance of the data analyses? Was every hypothesis tested?

■ Are the tests of significance interpreted using the appropriate degrees of freedom?

■ Was the inductive logic used to produce results in a qualitative study made explicit?

■ Are the results clearly described?

■ Are the tables and figures (if any) well organized and easy to understand?

■ Are the data in each table and figure described in the text of the research report?

Discussion (Conclusions and Recommendations)

■ Is each result discussed in terms of the original hypothesis or topic to which it relates?

■ Is each result discussed in terms of its agreement or disagreement with previous results obtained by other researchers in other studies?

■ Are generalizations consistent with the results?

■ Are theoretical and practical implications of the findings discussed?

■ Are the possible effects of uncontrolled variables on the results discussed?

■ Are recommendations for future action made?

■ Are the suggestions for future action based on practical significance or on statistical significance only (i.e., has the author avoided confusing practical and statistical significance)?

Abstract or Summary

Note: It is easier to review the abstract after you have read the rest of the report.

■ Is the problem stated?

■ Are the number and type of participants and instruments described?

■ Is the design identified?

■ Are procedures described?

■ Are the major results and conclusions stated?

MyLab Education **Self-Check 23.1**

MyLab Education **Application Exercise 23.1:** Evaluating Research Articles: Evaluating a Published Study

DESIGN-SPECIFIC EVALUATION CRITERIA

In addition to general criteria that can be applied to almost any study, there are additional questions you should ask depending on the type of research represented by the study. In other words, some concerns are specific to qualitative-oriented research (e.g., narrative, ethnographic, case study), some to quantitative-oriented research (e.g., survey, correlational, causal–comparative, experimental, and single-subject), some to mixed methods research, and some to action research. Both quantitative and qualitative criteria may be applied by varying degrees to mixed methods research depending on the emphasis placed on quantitative and qualitative research methods. The following sections list some of those questions for each study design.

Survey Research

- Are questionnaire validation procedures described?
- Was the questionnaire pilot-tested?
- Are pilot study procedures and results described?
- Are directions to questionnaire respondents clear?
- Does each item in the questionnaire relate to an objective of the study?
- Does each questionnaire item deal with a single concept?
- When necessary, is a point of reference given for questionnaire items?
- Are leading questions avoided in the questionnaire?
- Are there sufficient alternatives for each questionnaire item?
- Does the cover letter explain the purpose and importance of the study, and does it give the potential respondent a good reason for cooperating?
- If appropriate, is confidentiality or anonymity of responses ensured in the cover letter?
- What is the percentage of returns, and how does it affect the study results?
- Are follow-up activities to increase the number of returns described?
- If the response rate was low, was any attempt made to determine any major differences between respondents and nonrespondents?
- Are data analyzed in groups or clusters rather than in a series of many single-variable analyses?

Correlational Research

Relationship Studies

- Were variables carefully selected (i.e., was a shotgun approach avoided)?
- Is the rationale for variable selection described?
- Are conclusions and recommendations based on values of correlation coefficients corrected for attenuation or restriction in range?
- Do the conclusions avoid suggesting causal relations among the variables investigated?

Prediction Studies

- Is a rationale given for selection of predictor variables?
- Is the criterion variable well defined?
- Was the resulting prediction equation validated with at least one other group?

Causal–Comparative Research

- Are the characteristics or experiences that differentiate the groups (i.e., the grouping variable) clearly defined or described?
- Are critical extraneous variables identified?
- Were any control procedures applied to equate the groups on extraneous variables?
- Are causal relations discussed with due caution?
- Are plausible alternative hypotheses discussed?

Experimental Research

- Was an appropriate experimental design selected?
- Is a rationale for design selection given?
- Are threats to validity associated with the design identified and discussed?
- Is the method of group formation described?
- Was the experimental group formed in the same way as the control group?
- Were groups randomly formed and the use of existing groups avoided?
- Were treatments randomly assigned to groups?
- Were critical extraneous variables identified?
- Were any control procedures applied to equate groups on extraneous variables?
- Were possible reactive arrangements (e.g., the Hawthorne effect) controlled for?
- Are the results generalized to the appropriate group?

Single-Subject Research

- Are the data time-constrained?
- Was a baseline established before moving into the intervention phase?
- Was condition or phase length sufficient to represent the behavior within the phase?
- Is the design appropriate to the question under study?
- If a multiple-baseline design was used, were conditions met to move across baselines?
- If a withdrawal design was used, are limitations to this design addressed?
- Did the researcher manipulate only one variable at a time?
- Is the study replicable?

Qualitative Research (in General)

- Does the researcher give a general sense of the focus of study?
- Does the researcher state a guiding hypothesis for the investigation?
- Is the application of the qualitative method described in detail?
- Is the context of the qualitative study described in detail?
- Is the purposive sampling procedure described and related to the study focus?
- Is each data collection strategy described?
- Is the researcher's role stated (e.g., nonparticipant observer, participant observer, interviewer, etc.)?
- Are the research site and the researcher's entry into it described?
- Were the data collection strategies used appropriately given the purpose of the study?
- Were strategies used to strengthen the validity and reliability of the data (e.g., triangulation)?
- Is there a description of how any unexpected ethical issues were handled?
- Are strategies for minimizing observer bias and observer effect described?
- Are the researcher's reactions and notes differentiated from descriptive field notes?
- Are data coding strategies described and examples of coded data given?
- Is the inductive logic applied to the data to produce results stated in detail?
- Are conclusions supported by data (e.g., are direct quotations from participants used to illustrate points)?

Evaluating Validity and Reliability in Qualitative Studies[1]

Threats to Internal Validity

- Did the researcher deal effectively with problems of history and maturation by documenting historical changes over time?
- Did the researcher deal effectively with problems of mortality by using a sample large enough to minimize the effects of attrition?
- Was the researcher in the field long enough to minimize observer effects?
- Did the researcher take the time to become familiar and comfortable with participants?
- Were interview questions pilot-tested?
- Were efforts made to ensure intraobserver agreement by training interview teams in coding procedures?
- Were efforts made to cross-check results by conducting interviews with multiple groups?
- Did the researcher interview key informants to verify field observations?
- Were participants screened demographically to ensure that they were representative of the larger population?
- Were data collected using different media (e.g., audio-recordings, video-recordings, etc.) to facilitate cross-validation?
- Were participants allowed to evaluate research results before publication?
- Are sufficient data presented to support findings and conclusions?
- Were variables tested repeatedly to validate results?

Threats to External Validity

- Were constructs defined in a way that has meaning outside the setting of the study?
- Were both new and adapted instruments pilot-tested to ensure that they were appropriate for the study?
- Does the researcher fully describe participants' relevant characteristics, such as socioeconomic structure, gender makeup, level of urbanization

---

[1] The questions in this section were adapted from *Ethnographer's Toolkit: Vol. 2. Essential Ethnographic Methods: Observations, Interviews, and Questionnaires* (pp. 278–289), by S. L. Schensul, J. J. Schensul, and M. D. LeCompte, 1999, Lanham, MD: AltaMira/Rowman & Littlefield.

and/or acculturation, and pertinent social and cultural history?

■ Are researcher interaction effects addressed by fully documenting the researcher's activities in the setting?

■ Were all observations and interviews conducted in a variety of fully described settings and with multiple trained observers?

Reliability

■ Is the researcher's relationship with the group and setting fully described?

■ Is all field documentation comprehensive, fully cross-referenced and annotated, and rigorously detailed?

■ Were observations and interviews documented using multiple means (e.g., written notes and recordings)?

■ Was the interviewer's training documented, and is it described?

■ Was the construction, planning, and testing of all instruments documented, and are they described?

■ Are key informants fully described, and is information on groups they represent and their community status included?

■ Are sampling techniques fully documented and sufficient for the study?

Narrative Research

■ Does the researcher provide a rationale for the use of narrative research to study the chosen phenomenon?

■ Is there a rationale for the choice of individual to study the chosen phenomenon?

■ Does the researcher describe data collection methods and give particular attention to interviewing?

■ Does the researcher describe appropriate strategies for analysis and interpretation (e.g., restorying)?

Ethnographic Research

■ Does the written account (i.e., the ethnography) capture the social, cultural, and economic themes that emerged from the study?

■ Did the researcher spend a full cycle in the field studying the phenomenon?

Case Study Research

■ Was the phenomenon under investigation appropriate for investigation using a case study research method?

■ Is there a rationale for the selection of the case (i.e., unit of analysis)?

■ Does the researcher provide a clear description of the case?

■ Was an appropriate analysis of the case, or cross-site analysis, conducted?

■ Is there a clear link between the data presented in the case study and the themes that are reported?

Mixed Methods Research

■ Did the study use at least one quantitative and at least one qualitative data research method?

■ Did the study investigate both quantitative and qualitative research questions?

■ Is a rationale for using a mixed methods research design provided?

■ Is the type of mixed methods research design stated?

■ Is the priority given to quantitative and qualitative data collection and the sequence of their use described?

■ Are qualitative and quantitative data collection techniques clearly identified?

■ Are the data analysis techniques appropriate for the type of mixed methods design?

■ Was the study feasible given the amount of data to be collected and concomitant issues of resources, time, and expertise?

Action Research

■ Does the area of focus involve teaching and learning in the researcher's own practice?

■ Was the area of focus within the researcher's locus of control?

■ Is the area of focus something the researcher was passionate about?

■ Is the area of focus something the researcher wanted to change or improve upon?

■ Does the researcher state questions that were answerable given the researcher's expertise, time, and resources?

■ Does the researcher provide an action plan detailing the effect of the research findings on practice?

MyLab Education **Self-Check 23.2**

SUMMARY

GENERAL EVALUATION CRITERIA

1. You should be able to detect a number of basic errors or weaknesses in a research study.

2. You should be able to detect obvious indications of experimenter bias that may have affected the results.

3. As you read a research report, you should ask questions concerning the execution of the study.

4. The answers to some questions are more critical than the answers to others.

5. Major problems and shortcomings are usually readily identifiable, and you can formulate an overall impression of the quality of the study.

Introduction

6. Problem: See page 610.

7. Review of related literature: See page 610.

8. Hypotheses: See page 610.

Method

9. Participants: See page 610.

10. Instruments: See page 610.

11. Design and procedure: See page 611.

Results

12. See page 611.

Discussion (Conclusions and Recommendations)

13. See page 611.

Abstract or Summary

14. See page 611.

TYPE-SPECIFIC EVALUATION CRITERIA

15. In addition to general criteria that can be applied to almost any study, additional questions should be asked depending on the type of research represented by the study.

Survey Research

16. See page 612.

Correlational Research

17. Relationship studies: See page 612.

18. Prediction studies: See page 612.

Causal–Comparative Research

19. See page 612.

Experimental Research

20. See page 612.

Single-Subject Research

21. See page 613.

Qualitative Research (in General)

22. See page 613.

Evaluating Validity and Reliability in Qualitative Studies

23. See page 613.

Narrative Research

24. See page 614.

Ethnographic Research

25. See page 614.

Case Study Research

26. See page 614.

Mixed Methods Research

27. See page 614.

Action Research

28. See page 614.

PERFORMANCE CRITERIA   TASK 12

The research report to be evaluated appears on the following pages (see Task 12 Example). Immediately following is the form you should use in evaluating the report (see Self-Test for Task 12). Answer each question by writing one of the following on the line in the "Code" column:

Y   = Yes
N   = No
NA = Question not applicable (e.g., a pilot study was not done)
?/X = Cannot tell from information given or, given your current level of expertise, you are not in a position to make a judgment

In addition (and where possible), indicate where you found the answer to the question in the report. For example, if asked if a hypothesis is stated in the report, and the answer is yes, you may write "paragraph 7, sentences 6 and 7" as the location of the information. Write the information in the margin next to the question.

Suggested responses for the Self-Test for Task 12 appear in Appendix B.

Gender and Race as Variables in Psychosocial Adjustment to Middle and High School

PATRICK AKOS
JOHN P. GALASSI
The University of North Carolina at Chapel Hill

ABSTRACT School transition research indicates that negative outcomes (e.g., decreases in self-esteem and academic motivation) occur for a number of students in transition. Although data are not consistent, gender and race tend to play a role in school transition outcomes. The authors investigated gender and race as variables in 6th- and 9th-grade students' psychosocial adjustment (e.g., perceptions of difficulty of transition and connectedness to school) following a recent school transition and in persons who they perceived as helpful in the transition process. Results suggest differences by gender for feelings of connectedness to middle and high school following the transition. Latino students perceived the transition to middle school as significantly more difficult than did Caucasian and African American students. Additional findings and implications are presented.

> *Is the problem stated?* The authors investigated gender and race as variables in sixth- and ninth-grade students' psychosocial adjustment (e.g., perceptions of difficulty of transition and connectedness to school) following a recent school transition and in persons who they perceived as helpful in the transition process.
>
> *Are the number and type of participants and instrument described?*
>
> *Is the design identified?*
>
> *Are procedures described?*
>
> *Are the major results and conclusions stated?*

Key words: gender and race, psychosocial adjustment, transition to middle and high school[2]

(01) Most education researchers have suggested that school transitions play an important role in the developmental trajectory of students (Eccles et al., 1993; Simmons & Blyth, 1987; Wigfield, Eccles, Mac Iver, Reuman, & Midgley, 1991). The individual or personal transformations that students undergo during puberty and school changes are extensive and frequently disruptive. Researchers have identified declines in academic performance (Blyth, Simmons, & Carlton-Ford, 1983), academic motivation (Eccles et al.), self-esteem (Simmons & Blyth), extracurricular participation (Seidman, Allen, Aber, Mitchell, & Feinman, 1994), and perceived support from school staff (Seidman et al.) as well as increases in daily hassles (Seidman et al.), as some of the negative effects of school transitions.

(02) However, only a modest number of researchers have examined the influence of demographic variables in school transitions. Several researchers suggested that girls suffer greater losses in self-esteem compared with boys during the transition to middle school (Blyth et al., 1983; Eccles et al., 1993). Those findings may be due to the fact that girls experience more peer upheaval or that they experience more distress than do boys because of the greater salience of their peer networks. The combination of physical and social transitions that girls experience from elementary to middle school also may contribute to their distress. Because girls typically mature earlier than boys (Eccles et al.), they often make a distinctive physical transition (e.g., menstruation) into puberty simultaneously with a school transition. Thus, the combination of and feelings about the two transitions—physical and school—may heighten the negative outcomes that some girls experience as they enter middle school.

> Review of Related Literature
>
> *Is the review comprehensive?*
>
> *Is the review well organized?*
>
> *Does the review conclude with a summary and interpretation of the literature and its implications for the problem under study?*

(03) Researchers also have demonstrated that girls experience more depression than do boys over the transition from elementary to middle school (Blyth et al., 1983; Hirsch & Rapkin, 1987). Moreover, Diemert (1992) found that boys reported a lack of assistance with academic needs, whereas girls reported a lack of assistance with social needs in the middle school transition. In the high

[2] Address correspondence to Patrick Akos, CB #3500, The University of North Carolina at Chapel Hill, Chapel Hill, NC 27599-3500. (E-mail: pta@unc.edu)

school transition, girls exhibited more concerns in general and more intense social and academic concerns, whereas boys were concerned particularly about having longer class periods, participating in sports, and violence from gangs (Maute, 1991). Although most of the transition research has suggested differential outcomes based on gender, some researchers failed to replicate these differences (Seidman et al., 1994; Wampler, Munsch, & Adams, 2002).

(04)   In addition to gender, race has been another focus of transition research. Several researchers suggested that minority status may intensify negative transition outcomes (Cauce, Hannan, & Sargeant, 1992; Mosely & Lex, 1990). Seidman and colleagues (1994) speculated that urban minority students often are located in overcrowded classrooms in large schools that are entrenched in red tape. They hypothesized that environmental conditions of high poverty and less space intensify the contextual transition and can potentially lead to more detrimental effects such as disproportionally high rates of education failure for urban minority youth (Seidman et al.).

(05)   Gutman and Midgley (2000) also investigated transition effects on African American students and found significant achievement losses from elementary to middle school. Simmons, Black, and Zhou (1991) also suggested that grade declines may be more severe for African American students than for European American students. Simmons and colleagues discovered that African American students showed greater decreases in grade point average (GPA) and more dislike for school after the elementary to middle school transition. Maute (1991) found that in high school, Asian students and those defined as "Other" (not White, Black, or Latino) demonstrated more intense high school concerns than did other students. Students labeled "Other" were concerned especially about being with children of other races and being liked by others. In addition, gender and racial differences in transition concerns varied according to the school attended (Maute).

(06)   Wampler and colleagues (2002) examined racial differences in GPA trajectories during the transition to junior high. They discovered that grade trajectories differed for race but not for gender. Specifically, African American students' GPAs remained steady over the transition, Caucasian students experienced slight declines, and Latino students faced steep declines with some rebound effect near the end of the school year.

(07)   Although many questions remain, existing research seems to indicate that race and gender influence perceptions and outcomes of school transitions; however, the reason is unclear. One possibility might concern a student's level of engagement in school or connectedness to school. Eccles and colleagues (1993), for example, suggested that school engagement might serve as a protective factor against transitional problems. Also, Osterman's (2000) review of research revealed that students' connectedness to school or sense of belonging relates to a host of outcome variables including academic attitudes, achievement, attendance, participation in school activities, and dropping out of school. Thus, school connectedness is a variable that may affect the likelihood of a successful school transition as well as serve as an indicator of the actual success of that transition. Moreover, it seems likely that school transitions might undermine or disrupt students' sense of connectedness to school, and this impact might not be equivalent across gender and race.

(08)   In addition to feelings of connectedness, students' overall perceptions of the difficulty of the transition also seem to reflect their adjustment to a new school. Thus, students' assessment of the transition experience should provide insight into the extent to which they have adapted to the new school. Moreover, the outcome research reviewed in the previous paragraphs suggests that the difficulty of middle and high school transitions likely differs across gender and race.

(09)   Finally, if school transitions are difficult for many students, who do the students find most supportive during these times? Given that transitions often cause a disruption of social networks at the very time they are important (Barone, Aguirre-Deandreis, & Trickett, 1991) and that previous research

indicates that school transition outcomes vary as a function of gender and race, it seems likely that the persons who students perceive as most helpful also would be influenced by these variables. Determining who different groups of students find helpful during transitions should provide practitioners with useful information to facilitate more positive school transition experiences for all students.

(10) To develop effective school transition programming, school personnel may need to consider the influence of race and gender as variables in the transition process. Therefore, we explored those variables in students' psychosocial adjustment to middle and high school transitions. Perceptions of transition difficulty and of school connectedness served as gauges of adjustment to the new school because adjustment has been a significant factor in the developmental pathways of students. Moreover, the sources of support that different groups of students find helpful in transitions have rather immediate consequences in the way that students approach school as well as in the implications for future school transition programming by school personnel.

(11) The primary research question of the study was: Are race and gender significant variables in (a) overall student perception/evaluation of the difficulty of school transitions, (b) feelings of connectedness to the new school, and (c) persons who are perceived as most helpful during the transition experience?

Method

Participants

(12) All of the students came from one middle school and one high school in a medium-sized, southeastern school district. The middle school participants included 173 sixth-grade students (approximately 72% of the sixth-grade class). The sample included 83 boys (48%), 86 girls (49.7%), and 4 students (2.3%) who did not provide information about gender. By race, the student sample included 57.2% Caucasian ($n = 99$), 19.7% African American ($n = 34$), 8.7% Asian American ($n = 15$), 8.1% Latino ($n = 14$), 4% multiracial ($n = 7$), and 2.3% ($n = 4$) unspecified. The sample was reflective of the entire sixth-grade population in terms of race (57% Caucasian, 23% African American, 9% Asian American, 9% Latino, and 3% multiracial) and gender (55% boys, 45% girls).

(13) The high school sample comprised 320 ninth-grade students (approximately 71% of the ninth-grade class) in a single high school. The sample included 47.8% boys ($n = 153$), 50.3% girls ($n = 161$), and 1.9% unspecified ($n = 6$). The racial composition of the sample was 76.3% Caucasian ($n = 244$), 10.3% African American ($n = 33$), 5.6% Asian American ($n = 18$), 3.4% Latino ($n = 11$), 2.2% multiracial ($n = 7$), and 1.9% unspecified ($n = 6$). The research sample again represented the high school population ($n = 1,586$) in terms of race and gender.

(14) The middle school and high school were part of a medium-sized southern school district that included eight elementary schools, four middle schools, and two high schools. The middle school drew students primarily from three of the elementary schools; the high school attracted its students primarily from two of the middle schools. The middle school was in its first year of operation. Overall, the school district could be characterized as high performing—over 90% of the students attended postsecondary education on a regular basis.

Instrument

(15) We developed the questionnaires for the sixth grade and ninth grade to tap context-relevant considerations and student perceptions unique to each of the transitions. The School Transition Questionnaire (STQ) is a retrospective measure of student perceptions over the course of the transition (a copy of the STQ may be obtained from the first author). The questionnaire assessed a variety of information about the transition, including students' (a) overall feelings about the difficulty of the transition, (b) sense of connectedness to the new school, and (c) persons who were most helpful to them during the transition.

Problem statement

Is there a statement of the problem?

Is background information on the problem presented?

Does the problem statement indicate the variables of interest and the specific relations among the variables that were investigated?

Method

Are the size and major characteristics of the population/sample described?

Are the characteristics or experiences that differentiate the groups clearly defined or described?

Were any control procedures applied to equate the groups on extraneous variables?

Instrument

Do instruments and their administration meet guidelines for protecting human subjects?

Are the instruments appropriate for measuring the intended variables?

Are the purpose, content, validity, and reliability of each instrument described?

If an instrument was developed specifically for the study, are the procedures involved in its development and validation described?

(16)   We used a 4-point, Likert-type response format (e.g., How was the move from middle school to high school for you?) to capture students' overall feelings about the transition. The response choices were (1) *difficult*, (2) *somewhat difficult*, (3) *somewhat easy*, and (4) *easy*. *School connectedness* is a variable that assesses a student's integration and feelings of belonging to school. Extensive research has demonstrated that school connectedness is an important variable in school success (see Osterman, 2000, for a review of this literature). In this study, connectedness questions included feeling (a) close to other students, (b) a part of school, (c) that teachers care about students, and (d) happy at school. We used a 5-point, Likert-type response format: response choices were (1) *strongly disagree*, (2) *disagree*, (3) *neither agree nor disagree*, (4) *agree*, and (5) *strongly agree*. The questions were adapted from the National Longitudinal Study of Adolescent Health (1998), a study undertaken in response to a mandate by the U.S. Congress in the NIH Revitalization Act of 1993. Coefficient alpha for the 4-item connectedness measure in this study was .72 for the high school data and .71 for the middle school data.

(17)   Students also were assessed about perceived helpfulness of significant persons during the transition. Students are influenced by a variety of persons in different systems in their lives. Akos (2002) and Arowosafe and Irvin (1992) discovered that significant persons in the school environment provide support and information to students during school transitions. To determine who was most helpful in school adjustment, students rated a variety of persons including parents, peers, other family members, older students, counselors, and other adults at the school. The students used a 4-point, Likert-type scale: response choices were (1) *not helpful*, (2) *somewhat helpful*, (3) *helpful*, and (4) *very helpful*. Students also had the option of adding persons to the list and rating them.

Procedure

(18)   The STQ was administered during the fall semester to all sixth- and ninth-grade students at the participating schools. Approximately 72% of the middle school and 71% of the high school students chose to participate in the study. Homeroom or home-based teachers administered the questionnaires; no incentives were given for participation. Each questionnaire was precoded so that school personnel could not identify student responses. Students returned questionnaires anonymously in each classroom, and they were collected by a school counselor on site and delivered to the researchers. The research team worked with school personnel to gather demographic data for the participating students by precoded numbers. Researchers matched gender and race to questionnaire responses by precoded identification numbers.

Research Design and Data Analysis

(19)   Data were analyzed separately for the middle and high school samples. Gender and race represented independent or predictor variables, whereas overall perceptions of the transition, connectedness to school, and the person most helpful in the transition represented dependent or criterion variables in this causal–comparative study. A 2 × 4 (gender × race) analysis of variance (ANOVA) was planned for data analysis. Because of some low cell sizes, that analysis was contraindicated. As a result, we completed separate univariate ANOVAs to analyze gender and race differences on the variables. When we found significant F values, we used post-hoc comparisons with Tukey's Honestly Significant Differences Test to explain differences among racial categories. Because we performed multiple tests to determine who was most helpful in the transition, we used the Bonferroni adjustment to control for Type 1 errors (a = .05/3 = .016).

> **Design**
>
> *Is the design appropriate for examining the research questions?*
>
> *Does the researcher discuss or account for any potentially confounding variable that he or she was unable to control?*

Results

(20)   Tables 1 and 2 present means and standard deviations for the perceived difficulty of the transition, connectedness, and helpful person variables disaggregated by gender and race.

Table 1

Disaggregated Means and Standard Deviations for Perceptions of Difficulty, Connectedness, and Helpful Others in Transition to Middle School

Question	M	SD
Overall difficulty	3.00	.96
Boys	2.96	.11
Girls	3.09	.10
Caucasians	3.13	.16
African Americans	3.15	.16
Latinos	2.00	.27
Asians	2.71	.29
Multiracial students	2.86	.51
Connectedness	15.02	3.23
Boys	14.46	.41
Girls	15.52	.32
Caucasians	15.23	.29
African Americans	14.15	.69
Latinos	14.63	1.67
Asians	15.50	.73
Multiracial students	14.86	1.61
Helpful persons		
Parents	3.14	1.03
Other family	2.44	1.03
Students	2.84	.98
Older students	2.14	1.08
Counselors	2.23	1.02
Other adults	2.22	.99

Table 2

Disaggregated Means and Standard Deviations for Perceptions of Difficulty, Connectedness, and Helpful Others in Transition to High School

Question	M	SD
Overall difficulty	3.12	.86
Boys	3.08	.07
Girls	3.13	.07
Caucasians	3.14	.05
African Americans	3.26	.15
Latinos	2.78	.36
Asians	2.69	.34
Multiracial students	2.83	.48
Connectedness	14.98	2.60
Boys	15.65	.19
Girls	14.43	.22
Caucasians	15.04	.17
African Americans	15.16	.48
Latinos	15.22	.52
Asians	14.50	.58
Multiracial students	14.50	.72
Helpful persons		
Parents	2.56	.99
Other family	2.56	1.13
Students	2.56	.92
Older students	2.56	1.00
Teachers	2.23	.89
Counselors	1.94	.88
Other adults	1.91	.87

Overall, the results revealed that students did not perceive that the transition to middle school ($M = 3.00$, $SD = .96$) or high school ($M = 3.12$, $SD = .86$) was particularly difficult (1 = *difficult* to 4 = *easy*). Students also felt strongly connected in both middle school ($M = 15.02$, $SD = 3.23$) and high school ($M = 14.98$, $SD = 2.60$) to the new school after the transition (possible range, 4–20). Parents ($M = 3.14$, $SD = 1.03$), followed by other students ($M = 2.84$, $SD = .98$) and other family ($M = 2.44$, $SD = 1.15$), were reported as most helpful for middle school students in transition. For high school students, other students ($M = 2.77$, $SD = .92$), then parents ($M = 2.56$, $SD = .99$) and older students ($M = 2.34$, $SD = 1.00$) were rated as most helpful. The range was 1 = *not helpful* to 4 = *very helpful*. (21)

Gender as a Variable in School Transitions

(22) Gender was not a significant variable in students' overall perception of the difficulty of the transition (e.g., middle school girls, $M = 3.04$, $SD = .93$; middle school boys, $M = 2.95$, $SD = 1.00$; high school girls, $M = 3.13$, $SD = .90$; high school boys, $M = 3.10$, $SD = .83$).

(23) Yet, gender was a significant variable in students' feelings of connectedness to school in both transitions. In middle school, girls ($M = 15.6$, $SD = 2.7$) felt more connected to school than did boys ($M = 14.4$, $SD = 3.6$), $F (1, 157) = 4.59$, $p = .034$. In contrast to middle school, boys ($M = 15.7$, $SD = 2.2$) felt significantly more connected in high school than did girls ($M = 14.4$, $SD = 2.8$), $F (1, 300) = 18.52$, $p = .001$.

(24) Gender also was a significant variable in determining who was most helpful during the transition to high school. Significant differences emerged for family other than parents, $F(1, 302) = 13.07$, $p < .001$, and students, $F (1, 303) = 18.61$, $p < .001$. Boys reported that family other than parents ($M = 2.55$, $SD = 1.13$) and students ($M = 3.00$, $SD = .84$) were more helpful than that reported by girls ($M = 2.09$, $SD = 1.08$; $M = 2.56$, $SD = .94$) in high school. No other significant differences were revealed for gender.

Race as a Variable in School Transitions

(25) No significant differences were found for race in feelings of connectedness to school. Yet, a significant difference emerged for race in the perception of how difficult the transition to middle school was, $F (4, 160) = 4.54$, $p = .002$. Post-hoc tests (Tukey HSD) indicated that Latino students ($M = 2.07$, $SD = .25$) perceived the transition as more difficult as compared with Caucasian ($M = 3.12$, $SD = .09$, $p = .001$) and African American ($M = 3.15$, $SD = .16$, $p = .003$) students.

(26) Also in middle school, several differences were found for persons who were most helpful in the transition. Statistically significant differences emerged for race in terms of middle school counselors, $F(4, 153) = 7.48$, $p < .001$, and family other than parents, $F (4, 156) = 3.81$, $p = .006$. In post-hoc tests (Tukey HSD), Latino students reported that middle school counselors ($M = 3.24$, $SD = .83$) and family other than parents ($M = 3.46$, $SD = .66$) were more helpful than that reported by Caucasian ($M = 1.95$, $SD = .92$ for counselors; $M = 2.32$, $SD = 1.15$ for other family) and Asian American ($M = 2.00$, $SD = .88$ for counselors; $M = 2.20$, $SD = .94$ for other family) students. In addition, Latino students reported that other family members ($M = 3.46$, $SD = .66$) were more helpful than that reported by African American students ($M = 239$, $SD = 1.20$). Finally, African American students reported that middle school counselors ($M = 2.61$, $SD = 1.09$) were more helpful to them as compared with reports by Caucasian students ($M = 1.95$, $SD = .92$).

(27) In high school, significant differences also were found for race for help from high school counselors, $F (5, 297) = 3.54$, $p = .004$. Latino students ($M = 2.80$, $SD = .27$) reported that high school counselors were more helpful compared with reports by Caucasian students ($M = 1.86$, $SD = .06$). No other significant differences were found for race in terms of perceptions or who was helpful during the transition for the middle or high school sample.

Discussion

(28) Whereas Eccles and colleagues (1993), Seidman and colleagues (1994), and Simmons and Blyth (1987) reported negative outcomes for school transitions, students in this study perceived the transition as somewhat easy. Study participants also demonstrated a strong connection to school and found a variety of school personnel and other persons helpful during school transitions. The contextual nature of the school district (e.g., high performing) may be reflected in the perceived difficulty of the transition in this study because our results support those from previous research (Anderman, Maeher, & Midgley, 1999; Crockett, Peterson, Graber, Schulenberg, & Ebata, 1989)

Results

Are appropriate statistics presented?

Are the results clearly described?

Are the tables and figures well organized and easy to understand?

that suburban students experience fewer adverse effects in school transitions than do urban students. Implications of race and gender as variables in transition adjustment are discussed in the following paragraphs.

Gender

The results of this study demonstrate that girls felt more connected to school (29) than did boys after transition to middle school. Although the stronger connection to school may suggest more positive adaptation or orientation to middle school for girls than for boys, these findings seem incongruent with previous research (Blyth et al., 1983; Eccles et al., 1993) stating that self-esteem declines for girls. Therefore, these findings raise several questions: Do girls experience a stronger connection to middle school because of the contextual nature of elementary and middle schools? For example, does the presence of multiple female models in elementary and middle school allow girls to feel more connected to school? Academic outcomes were not measured in this study, but potentially, feelings of connectedness may relate directly to academic outcomes in transition. The lower feelings of connectedness for boys in this study may provide a possible explanation for the findings of previous studies that suggest that boys suffer more distinct academic declines in the transition to middle school (Chung, Elias, & Schneider, 1998; Elias et al., 1992).

Osterman (2000) demonstrated that a relationship exists between con- (30) nectedness or belonging and academic outcomes. Perhaps boys' academic struggles caused by the transition to middle school are related to feelings of connectedness to the new school. Boys may feel less connected to the new school and, therefore, might not apply themselves as fully academically as do girls. At the same time, connectedness may be an adjustment variable that does not capture the decline in self-esteem of girls in transition. Those relationships should be examined in future research.

In contrast to middle school transition, boys felt significantly more con- (31) nected than did girls after the transition to high school. Although that finding may reflect a cohort effect for the current sample, the results also may indicate more positive adaptation or orientation for boys at the high school level. Fewer researchers have investigated gender differences in outcomes for high school transition as compared with middle school transition. Yet, these findings may be reflective of Maute's (1991) finding that girls exhibit more concerns in general and more intense social and academic concerns than do boys in the transition to high school. Although the connection to school is strong over the transition to middle school, the peer upheaval and psychological distress experienced by girls in the transition to and over the course of middle school (Blyth et al., 1983; Crockett et al., 1989; Eccles et al., 1993; Fenzel, 1989) may present later in their feeling less connected after the transition to high school. Researchers need to examine the relationship between ecological factors (e.g., extracurricular opportunities and participation); feelings of connectedness, self-esteem, achievement, and motivation; as well as effective ways to connect students in the transition to a new school.

One common way to help students connect to school may be through (32) enhanced social support. Barone and colleagues (1991) suggested that that type of support may be particularly important during transition because social networks are usually disrupted and in flux at this time. The findings for connectedness in this study may be indicative of the gender differences in who appears helpful during school transitions. Whereas girls reported that family other than parents were more helpful at their transition into middle school, the finding was reversed when they entered high school. Even more significant, boys reported that students were significantly more helpful in the transition to high school than girls reported. Elias and colleagues' (1992) findings of the salience of peer networks in middle school and Chung and colleagues' (1998) findings of more peer-related problems for girls in middle school may culminate in lower perceived support from peers during the transition to high school. That lack of perceived social support also may relate to lower feelings of connectedness to school and highlight an important developmental need for girls when they move to high school. Programs like peer mentoring, use of students in transition programs, and building supportive peer cultures may be instrumental in helping girls feel more connected to high school.

Race

(33) Latino students perceived that the transition to middle school was significantly more difficult than did Caucasian and African American students. The results of this study may be reflective of Wampler and colleagues' (2002) finding that Latino students experience a significant decline in GPA during the transition to middle school. Although GPA was not examined in this study, the overall perception of the transition difficulty may reflect or be an indicator of difficult academic adjustment demonstrated by Latinos in previous research. One also should consider the findings (perception of difficulty of transition) and previous research (GPA declines) in light of cultural differences that may create specific challenges for Latino students in transition.

(34) The results of this study and previous research (Wampler et al., 2002) suggest that Latino students, many of whom were not born in this country, may need particular attention during the transition to middle school. Wampler and colleagues speculated that peer culture pressures and values and traditions in Latino culture might increase the struggles that those students experience in transition. For example, Latino students may experience more significant language barriers, and Latino families may believe that it is not appropriate to be involved in matters related to school (McCall-Perez, 2000). In addition, cognitive and linguistic demands are greater in secondary schools as compared with elementary schools. In secondary schools, students must understand and integrate bodies of knowledge (Lucas, 2000). The gap between language and literacy skills between Latino students and families and majority teachers may create additional barriers to achievement in the more demanding secondary schools (Osterling, Violand-Sanchez, & von Vacano, 1999).

(35) The cultural effects found in this study also may be reflected in the fact that the Latino students reported that middle school counselors and family other than parents were more helpful than that reported by Caucasian and Asian students. McCall-Perez (2000) reported that students with limited English proficiency are counselor dependent for school success because counselors contribute to more positive student outcomes, placement, credit hours earned, and smoother transitions to high school. It also may be useful to include extended family to help facilitate student transition and adjustment to middle and high school. For example, schools might offer bilingual evening transition programs with childcare to enable families and school personnel to help facilitate Latino students' transition. Schools also might offer programs delivered by diverse paraprofessionals who can bridge language and cultural barriers effectively (Lee, 2001). Lucas (2000) recommended that school personnel should help Latino students and families understand and negotiate the U.S. system of education (e.g., grading, programs, placement, parent involvement).

(36) In contrast to the middle school findings, race was not a significant factor in the perception of transition difficulty. Positive interventions by counselors and others during the transition and/or the small sample of Latino students in the high school might have made differences difficult to detect. It also is possible that Latino students might recover from initial difficulties in the transition to middle school and feel more successful by the time they make the transition to high school. Although Blyth and colleagues (1983) suggested that multiple transitions (e.g., elementary to middle to high school) exacerbate negative outcomes of transitions, perhaps Latino students are unique in that learning, and adjusting to the U.S. education system contributes to a less difficult experience in the second transition. A more likely possibility, however, with the graduation rate of Latino students near 57% (Narrid-Lacey

Results

Is each result discussed in terms of the original research question?

Is each result discussed in terms of its agreement or disagreement with previous results obtained by other researchers?

Are theoretical and practical implications of the results discussed?

Are recommendations for future action made?

& Spencer, 2000), is that many of the Latino students who would have experienced difficulty with the high school transition have already dropped out of school. Future research is clearly needed to understand the specific transition effects for Latino students in middle and high school.

Limitations

The results of this study should be considered in light of several limitations. (37) First, data were collected at only one point after the completion of the transition. We examined students' adjustment to a new level of school, but longitudinal designs may capture variables that influence adjustment prior to the transition. Also, one should interpret the data as relevant to the context of the academic achievement of students in a district in which a large majority progressed to postsecondary education. Researchers should replicate similar procedures in a variety of districts to determine whether race and gender effects are common across a variety of school contexts. Although no district is representative of all districts, our results may be particularly important because of the intense academic expectations of students in the participating district. Learning how to facilitate successful school transitions and school adjustment for Latino students in the midst of high academic expectations may be extremely informative and useful for promoting achievement for all students.

> *Are causal relations discussed with due caution?*
>
> *Are plausible alternative hypotheses discussed?*

Conclusion

To summarize, the results of this study support previous research that suggests that gender and race are influential variables in school transitions and highlight potential differences in transition programming needed for different groups of students. Therefore, it may be important to consider gender in assisting students' adjustment to school. Although orientation programs may provide the necessary procedural (e.g., how to register for classes) and organizational adjustment (e.g., how to navigate the new school) assistance for all students, researchers who investigate transition programs may need to attend to gender differences in specific needs regarding personal/social and academic adjustment. Perhaps those researchers should further examine the needs of boys when they transfer to middle school so as to foster stronger feelings of connectedness (e.g., extracurricular activities, male models) that may help prevent boys' achievement declines. Similarly, researchers should further investigate girls' needs when they transfer to high school to build stronger feelings of connectedness. Perhaps education professionals can facilitate more effective personal/social adjustment to high school with programs like peer mentoring and systematic efforts to improve female peer cultures so that girls also find other students helpful during transition.

It also may be useful to offer specific programming for Latino students (39) and families. The transition may be an influential factor in Latino students' success in school; research has demonstrated that student engagement is a predictor of achievement for Latino students (Lucas, 2000; Wampler et al., 2002). The transition to middle school may be a key point in the developmental trajectory of Latino students that can be used to prevent high rates of educational failure and dropping out. Finally, it is important that students capitalize on social support in the transition to a new school. Specifically in this study, school counselors, other students, and family other than parents appear to be most useful in helping minority students adjust to school.

NOTE

We thank the Research Triangle Schools Partnership (RTSP) and the Chapel Hill Carrboro City Schools for financial assistance with this research. We appreciate Pat Harris, Tori Lunetta, and Annie Reed for invaluable feedback and help with the research. We also thank Laura Blake, Kelley Dull, Jessica Thompson, and Sarah Doherty for preparing questionnaires and inputting the data.

REFERENCES

Akos, P. (2002). The developmental needs of students in transition from elementary to middle school. *Professional School Counseling, 5,* 339–345.

Anderman, E., Maeher, M., & Midgley, C. (1999). Declining motivation after the transition to middle school: Schools can make a difference. *Journal of Research and Development in Education, 32,* 131–147.

Arowosafe, D., & Irvin, J. (1992). Transition to a middle level school: What kids say. *Middle School Journal, 24,* 15–19.

Barone, C., Aguirre-Deandreis, A., & Trickett, E. (1991). Mean-ends problem-solving skills, life stress, and social support as mediators of adjustment in the normative transition to high school. *American Journal of Community Psychology, 19,* 207–225.

Blyth, D., Simmons, R., & Carlton-Ford, S. (1983). The adjustment of early adolescents to school transitions. *Journal of Early Adolescence, 3,* 105–120.

Cauce, A., Hannan, K., & Sargeant, M. (1992). Life stress, social support, and locus of control during early adolescence: Interactive effects. *American Journal of Community Psychology, 12,* 353–367.

Chung, H., Elias, M., & Schneider, K. (1998). Patterns of individual adjustment changes during middle school transition. *Journal of School Psychology, 36,* 83–101.

Crockett, L., Peterson, A., Graber, J., Schulenberg, J., & Ebata, A. (1989). School transitions and adjustment during early adolescence. *Journal of Early Adolescence, 9,* 181–210.

Diemert, A. (1992). *A needs assessment of fifth grade students in a middle school.* Acton, MA: Author. (ERIC Document Reproduction Service No. ED62332)

Eccles, J. S., Wigfield, A., Midgley, C., Reumam, D., Mac Iver, D., & Feldlaufer, J. (1993). Negative effects of traditional middle schools on students' motivation. *The Elementary School Journal, 93,* 553–574.

Elias, M., Ubriaco, M., Reese, A., Gara, M., Rothbaum, P., & Haviland, M. (1992). A measure of adaptation to problematic academic and interpersonal tasks of middle school. *Journal of School Psychology, 30,* 41–57.

Fenzel, L. (1989). Role strains and the transition to middle school: Longitudinal trends and sex differences. *Journal of Early Adolescence, 9,* 211–226.

Gutman, L., & Midgley, C. (2000). The role of protective factors in supporting the academic achievement of poor African American students during the middle school transition. *Journal of Youth and Adolescence, 29,* 223–248.

Hirsch, B., & Rapkin, B. (1987). The transition to junior high school: A longitudinal study of self-esteem, psychological symptomology, school life, and social support. *Child Development, 58,* 1235–1243.

Lee, C. (2001). Culturally responsive school counselors and programs: Addressing the needs of all students. *Professional School Counseling, 4,* 257–261.

Lucas, T. (2000). Facilitating the transitions of secondary English language learners: Priorities for Principals. *NASSP Bulletin, 84,* 2–16.

Maute, J. (1991). *Transitions concerns of eighth-grade students in six Illinois schools as they prepare for high school.* Unpublished doctoral dissertation, National-Louis University, Evanston, IL.

McCall-Perez, Z. (2000). The counselor as advocate for English language learners: An action research approach. *Professional School Counseling, 4,* 13–20.

Mosely, J., & Lex, A. (1990). Identification of potentially stressful life events experienced by a population of urban minority youth. *Journal of Multicultural Counseling and Development, 18,* 118–125.

Narrid-Lacey, B., & Spencer, D. (2000). Experiences of Latino immigrant students at an urban high school. *NASSP Bulletin, 84,* 43–54.

National Longitudinal Study of Adolescent Health. (1998). Codebooks. Retrieved June 19, 2002, from cpc.unc.edu/addhealth/codebooks.html

Osterling, J., Violand-Sanchez., E., & von Vacano, M. (1999). Latino families learning together. *Educational Leadership, 57,* 64–68.

Osterman, K. (2000). Students' need for belonging in the school community. *Review of Educational Research, 70,* 323–367.

Seidman, E., Allen, L., Aber, J., Mitchell, C., & Feinman, J. (1994). The impact of school transitions in early adolescence on the self-system and perceived social context of poor urban youth. *Child Development, 65,* 507–522.

Simmons, R., Black, A., & Zhou, Y. (1991). African-American versus white children and the transition into junior high school. *American Journal of Education, 99,* 481–520.

Simmons, R., & Blyth, D. (1987). *Moving into adolescence: The impact of pubertal change and school context.* Hawthorne, NY: Aldine de Gruyter.

Wampler, R., Munsch, J., & Adams, M. (2002). Ethnic differences in grade trajectories during the transition to junior high. *Journal of School Psychology, 40,* 213–237.

Wigfield, A., Eccles, J., Mac Iver, D., Reuman, D., & Midgley, C. (1991). Transitions during early adolescence: Changes in children's domain specific self-perceptions and general self-esteem across the transition to junior high school. *Developmental Psychology, 27,* 552–566.

Copyright of Journal of Educational Research is the property of Heldref Publications and its content may not be copied or emailed to multiple sites or posted to a listserv without the copyright holder's express written permission. However, users may print, download, or email articles for individual use.
Source: Akos, P., and Galassi, J. P. (2004). Gender and Race as Variables in Psychosocial Adjustment to Middle and High School. *The Journal of Educational Research, 98*(2), 102–109.

Gender and Race as Variables in Psychosocial Adjustment to Middle and High School

Self-Test for Task 12

Y = Yes
N = No
NA = Not applicable
?/X = Can't tell/Don't know

General Evaluation
Introduction

Problem	*Code*
Is there a statement of the problem? Does the problem indicate a particular focus of study?	_____
Is the problem researchable; that is, can it be investigated by collecting and analyzing data?	_____
Is background information on the problem presented?	_____
Is the educational significance of the problem discussed?	_____
Does the problem statement indicate the variables of interest and the specific relation among the variables that were investigated?	_____
When necessary, are variables directly or operationally defined?	_____
Did the researcher have the knowledge and skill to carry out the research?	_____

Review of Related Literature

Is the review comprehensive?	_____
Is the review well organized? Does it flow logically so that the references least related to the problem are discussed first and those most related are discussed last? Does it educate the reader about the problem or topic?	_____
Is the review more than a series of abstracts or annotations? That is, have the references been analyzed and critiqued and the results of various studies compared and contrasted?	_____
Have the references been critically analyzed and the results of various studies compared and contrasted (i.e., is the review more than a series of abstracts or annotations)?	_____
Are all cited references relevant to the problem under investigation? Is the relevance of each reference explained?	_____
Does the review conclude with a summary and interpretation of the literature and its implications for the problem under study?	_____
Do the implications form an empirical or theoretical rationale for the hypotheses that follow?	_____

Are most of the sources primary (i.e., are there only a few or no secondary sources)? _____

Are references cited completely and accurately? _____

Hypotheses

Are specific research questions listed or specific hypotheses stated? _____

Is each hypothesis testable? _____

Does each hypothesis state an expected relation or difference? _____

If necessary, are variables directly or operationally defined? _____

Method

Participants

Are the size and major characteristics of the population described? _____

Are the accessible and target populations described? _____

If a sample was selected, is the method of selecting the sample clearly described? _____

Does the method of sample selection suggest any limitations or biases in the sample? For example, was stratified sampling used to obtain sample subgroups? _____

Are the size and major characteristics of the sample described? _____

If the study was quantitative, does the sample size meet the suggested guidelines for the minimum sample size appropriate for the method of research represented? _____

Instruments

Do instruments and their administration meet guidelines for protecting participants? Were needed permissions obtained? _____

Are the instruments appropriate for measuring the intended variables? _____

Was the correct type of instrument used for data collection (e.g., was a norm-referenced instrument used when a criterion-referenced one was more suitable)? _____

Is the rationale given for the selection of the instruments (or measurements) used? _____

Are the purpose, content, validity, and reliability of each instrument described? _____

If appropriate, are subtest reliabilities given? _____

Is evidence presented to indicate that the instruments are appropriate for the intended sample? For example, is the reading level of an instrument suitable for sample participants? _____

If an instrument was developed specifically for the study, are the procedures involved in its development and validation described? _____

If an instrument was developed specifically for the study, are administration, scoring or tabulating, and interpretation procedures fully described? _____

Does the researcher have the needed skills or experience to construct or administer an instrument? _____

Design and Procedure

Are the design and procedures appropriate for examining the research question or testing the hypotheses of the study? _____

Are the procedures described in sufficient detail to permit replication by another researcher? _____

Do procedures relate to one another logically? _____

Were instruments and procedures applied correctly? _____

If a pilot study was conducted, are its execution and results described? _____

Is the effect on the subsequent study explained? _____

Are control procedures described? _____

Does the researcher discuss or account for any potentially confounding variables that he or she was unable to control? _____

Results

Are appropriate descriptive statistics presented? _____

Are the tests of significance appropriate, given the hypotheses and design of the study? _____

If parametric tests were used, is there evidence that the researcher avoided violating the required assumptions for parametric tests? _____

Was the probability level at which the tests of significance were evaluated specified in advance of the data analyses? Was every hypothesis tested? _____

Are the tests of significance interpreted using the appropriate degrees of freedom? _____

Was the inductive logic used to produce results in a qualitative study made explicit? _____

Are the results clearly described? _____

Are the tables and figures (if any) well organized and easy to understand? _____

Are the data in each table and figure described in the text of the research report? _____

Discussion (Conclusions and Recommendations)

Is each result discussed in terms of the original hypothesis or topic to which it relates? _____

Is each result discussed in terms of its agreement or disagreement with previous results obtained by other researchers in other studies? _____

Are generalizations consistent with the results? _____

Are theoretical and practical implications of the findings discussed? _____

Are the possible effects of uncontrolled variables on the results discussed? _____

Are recommendations for future action made? _____

Are the suggestions for future action based on practical significance or on statistical significance only (i.e., has the author avoided confusing practical and statistical significance)? _____

Abstract or Summary

Is the problem stated? _____

Are the number and type of participants and instruments described? _____

Is the design identified? _____

Are procedures described? _____

Are the major results and conclusions stated? _____

Type-Specific Evaluation Criteria

Are the characteristics or experiences that differentiate the groups (i.e., the grouping variable) clearly defined or described? _____

Were any control procedures applied to equate the groups on extraneous variables? _____

Are causal relations discussed with due caution? _____

Are plausible alternative hypotheses discussed? _____

APPENDIX A

Statistical References

PROCEDURES

1. Begin by highlighting Gender and Ethnicity and then click on "Data" in the tool bar. This is Step 1 of 3.
2. Select "Pivot Table Report," as illustrated in the screen below.
3. Click "OK" in the next window to select the Excel list or data base.
4. In the PivotTable Builder drag Ethnicity in the Column labels area and Gender in the Row labels.
5. Click on "Count of" in the Values area and then select the analysis in the PivotTable Field as shown.

6. Click on Ethnicity and drag it to "Drop Column Fields Here."
7. Click on ID, since it serves as the data count, and drag it to "Drop Data Items Here."
8. The upper left corner of the Pivot table will typically default to "Sum of ID." Change it to "Count" by going to the Pivot Table menu in the box below the table, select "Field Settings," and select "Count." You can also make a label by double-clicking above the table where it will say "Double-click to add header."

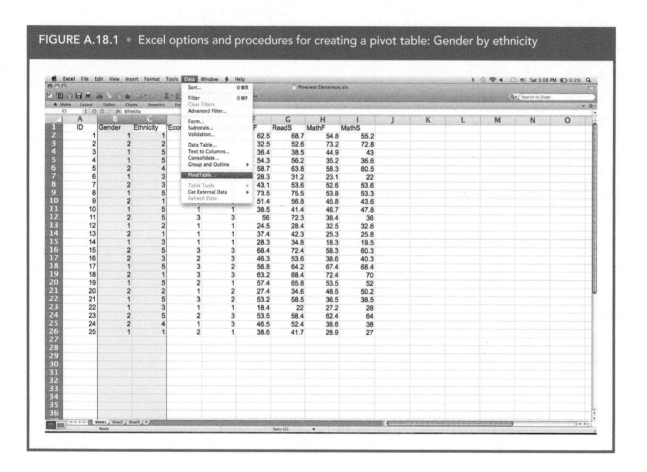

FIGURE A.18.1 • Excel options and procedures for creating a pivot table: Gender by ethnicity

FIGURE A.18.1 • *Continued*

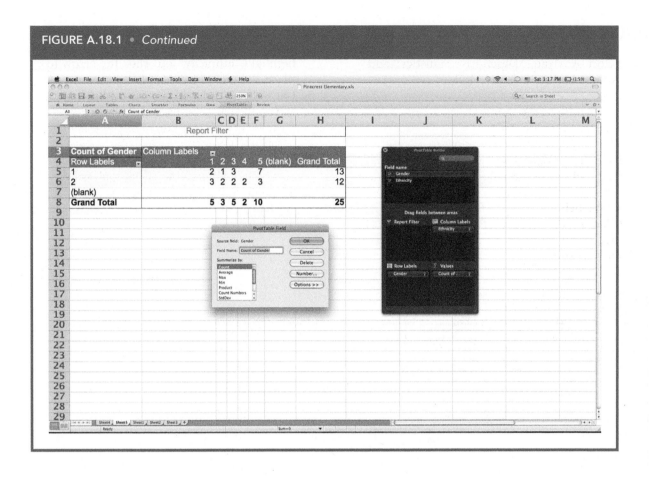

PROCEDURES

1. Select "Analyze," "Descriptive Statistics," and "Crosstabs," as illustrated below.

2. Highlight the variable "Gender" and click the arrow to place "Gender" in the row box. Then highlight "Ethnicity" and click the arrow to place "Ethnicity" in the column box.
3. Click "OK."

FIGURE A.18.2 • SPSS options for crosstab: Gender by ethnicity

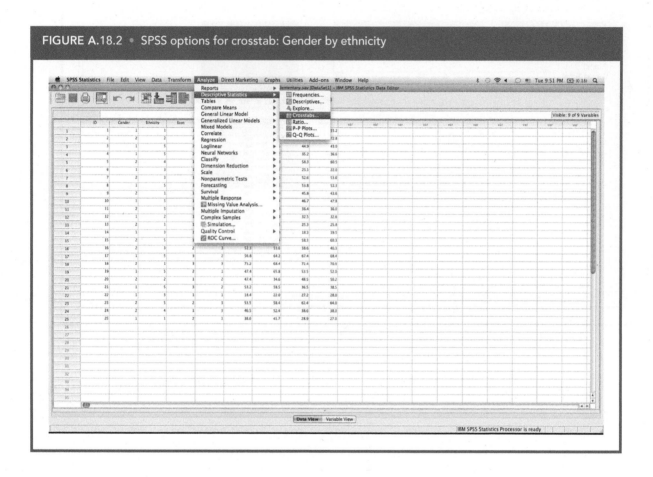

FIGURE A.18.2 • Continued

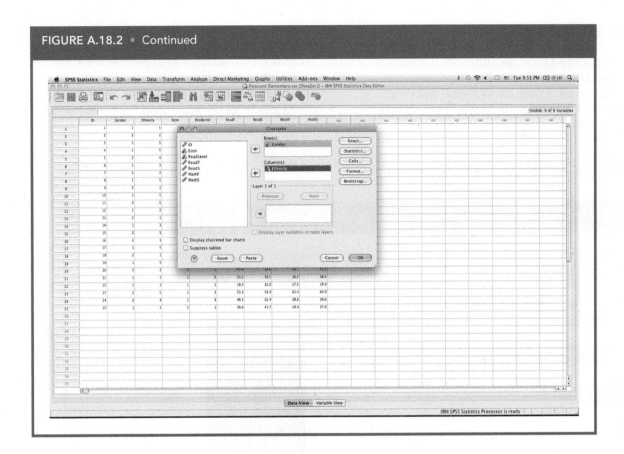

PROCEDURES

1. Create a PivotTable, as shown in the print screen below.
2. Click "Insert" in the Excel menu, and then "Chart." A bewildering array of choices will appear, as shown in the following print screen.

3. Select the chart or graphic display you wish. Also use the additional options under the Chart menu, which will appear in the Excel menu bar. In Figure A.18.3 we selected a variety of options, a 3D format, and added text labels (e.g., high, medium, low).

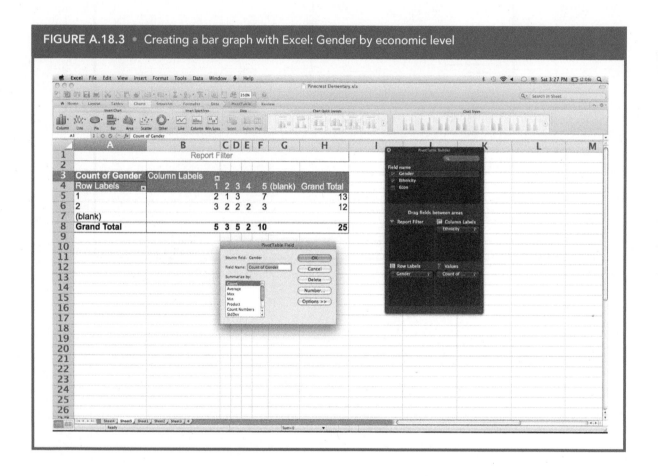

FIGURE A.18.3 • Creating a bar graph with Excel: Gender by economic level

FIGURE A.18.4 • Creating a frequency polygon in Excel of achievement test scores

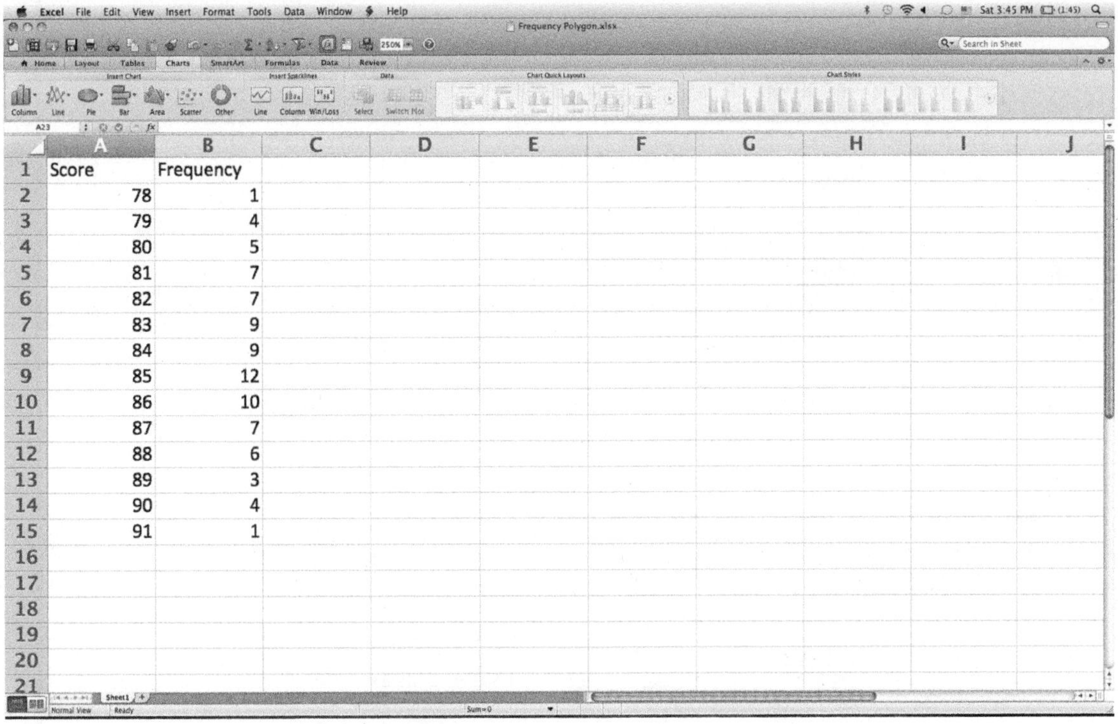

Frequency Polygon.xlsx
Score
Frequency
78 1
79 4
80 5
81 7
82 7
83 9
84 9
85 12
86 10
87 7
88 6
89 3
90 4
91 1

FIGURE A.18.5 • SPSS options for correlation

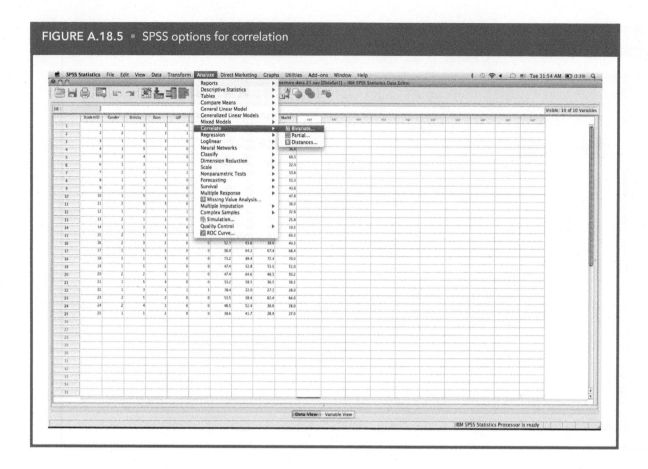

FIGURE A.18.6 • Variable selection for correlation

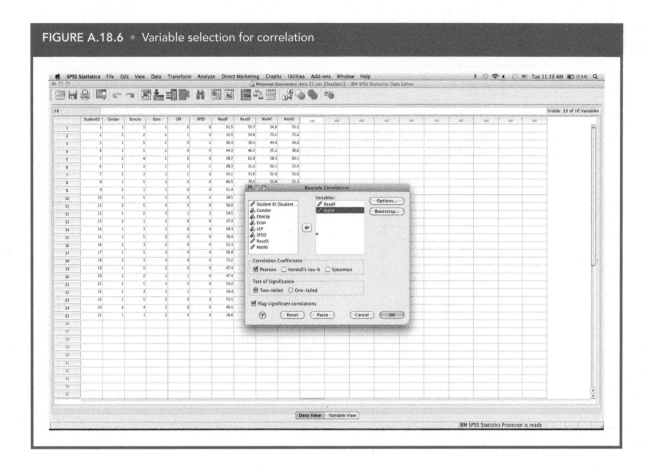

FIGURE A.19.1 • SPSS menu options for dependent (paired) samples *t* test

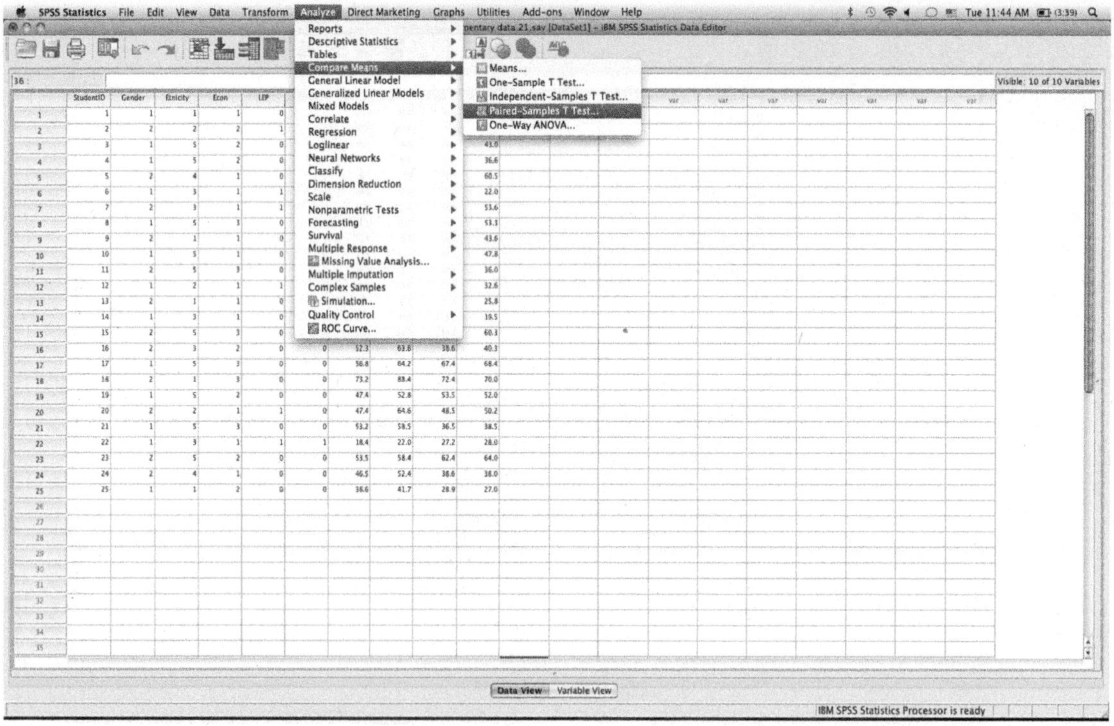

FIGURE A.19.2 • Paired-samples *t* test window

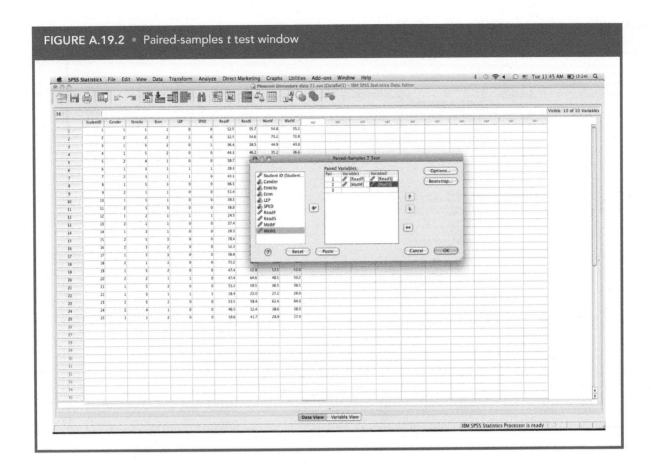

FIGURE A.19.3 • SPSS menu for ANOVA test

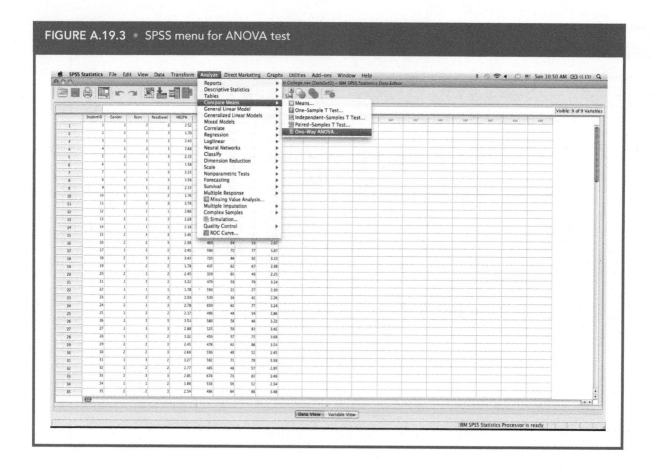

FIGURE A.19.4 • SPSS menu for ANOVA: Post hoc analysis

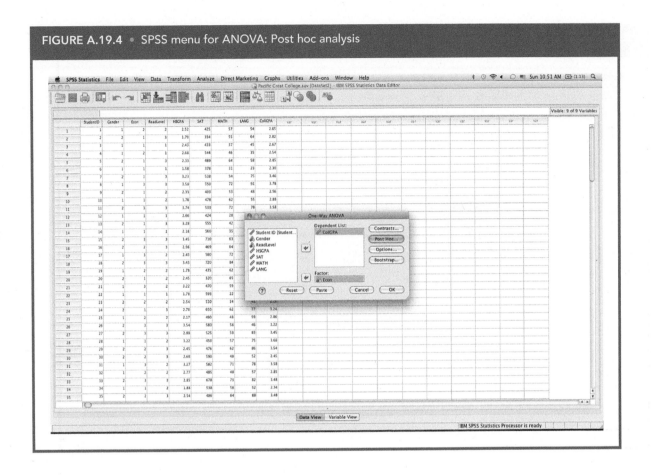

FIGURE A.19.5 • SPSS menu for ANOVA: Scheffé multiple comparison

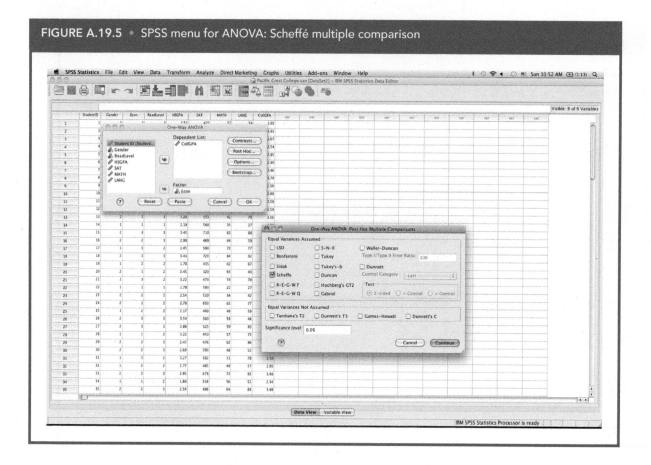

FIGURE A.19.6 • SPSS menu for multiple regression test

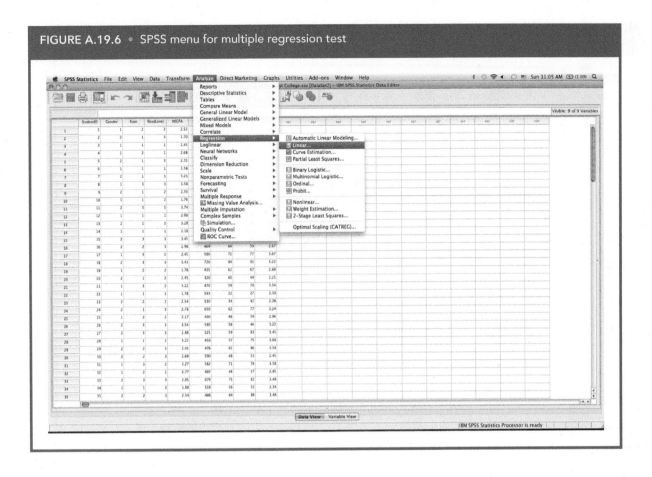

FIGURE A.19.7 • Linear regression window

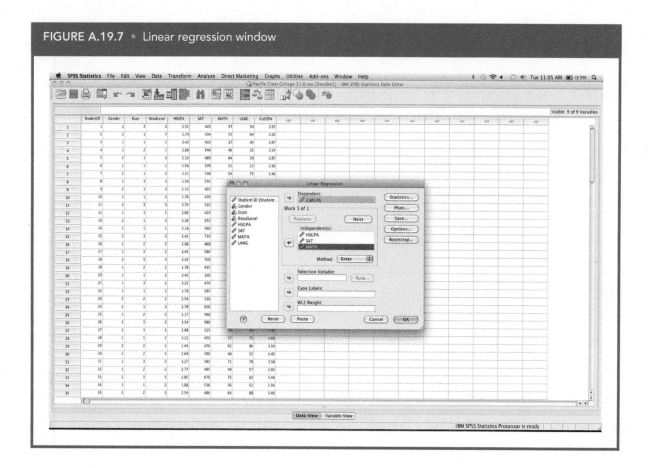

FIGURE A.19.8 • SPSS menu for chi-square analysis

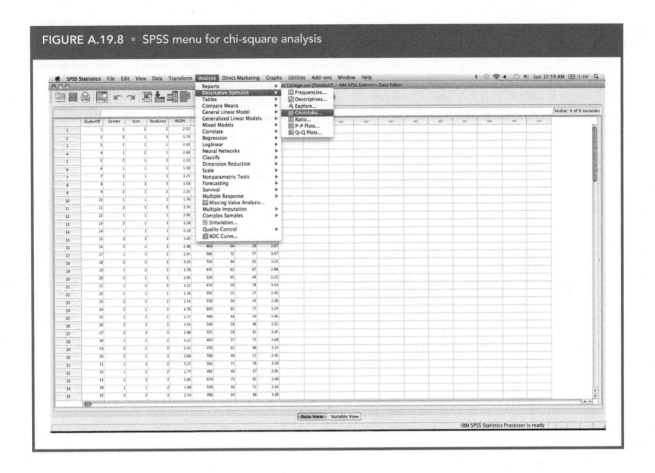

FIGURE A.19.9 • Chi-square analysis window

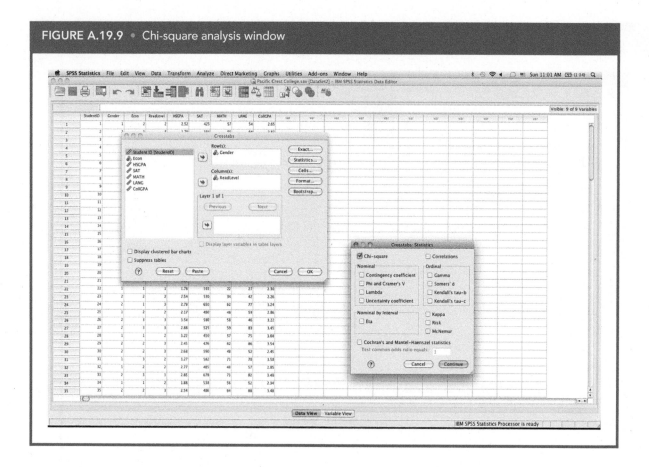

TABLE A.19.1 • Pacific Crest College dataset

StudentID	Gender	Econ	ReadLevel	HSGPA	SAT	MATH	LANG	CollGPA
1	1	2	2	2.52	425	57	54	2.65
2	2	1	3	1.7	334	54.6	64	2.82
3	1	1	1	2.43	433	37	44.9	2.67
4	1	2	1	2.68	544	46.2	35.2	2.54
5	2	1	3	2.33	489	63.8	58.3	2.85
6	1	1	1	1.58	378	31.2	23.1	2.3
7	2	1	3	3.23	538	53.6	75	3.46
8	1	3	3	3.58	550	72	91	3.78
9	2	1	2	2.33	403	53	48	2.56
10	1	1	2	1.76	478	62	55	2.88
11	2	3	3	3.74	533	72.3	78	3.58
12	1	1	1	2.66	424	28.4	43	2.59
13	2	1	3	3.28	555	42.3	78	3.56
14	1	1	1	2.18	560	34.8	27	1.88
15	2	3	3	3.45	710	63	88	3.22
16	2	2	3	2.98	469	63.6	59	2.67
17	1	3	2	2.45	580	72	77	3.67
18	2	3	3	3.43	720	84	92	3.23
19	1	2	2	1.78	435	62	67	2.88
20	2	1	2	2.45	320	64.6	48.5	2.25
21	1	3	2	3.22	470	58.5	78	3.54
22	1	1	1	1.78	593	22	27.2	2.3
23	2	2	2	2.54	530	34	42	2.26
24	2	1	3	2.78	650	62	77	3.24
25	1	2	2	2.17	490	48	59	2.86
26	2	3	3	3.54	580	58	46	3.22
27	2	3	3	2.88	525	59	83	3.45
28	1	1	2	3.22	450	57	75	3.68
29	2	2	3	2.45	476	62	86	3.54
30	2	2	3	2.68	590	48	52	2.45
31	1	3	2	3.27	582	71	78	3.58
32	1	2	2	2.77	485	48	57	2.85
33	2	3	3	2.85	678	73	82	3.48
34	1	1	2	1.88	538	56	52	2.34
35	2	2	3	2.54	486	64	88	3.48
36	2	2	2	2.33	438	38	47	2.25
37	1	3	2	3.47	498	66	73	3.25
38	1	1	2	2.54	552	52	47	2.36
39	1	3	3	2.66	620	82	85	3.54
40	2	1	3	2.34	468	43	65	2.88
41	2	1	3	1.78	432	47	72	2.65
42	1	2	2	2.53	444	53	48	2.24
43	2	3	2	3.54	585	52	48	2.85
44	2	2	3	2.88	535	54	84	3.24
45	1	2	2	2.44	588	61	73	3.16
46	2	1	3	1.78	438	43	68	2.68
47	2	2	2	3.35	450	47	38	2.48
48	1	2	1	2.55	580	36	44	2.25
49	1	3	2	2.82	465	64	82	3.54
50	2	1	3	2.94	510	48	52	2.74
51	1	2	2	2.32	435	57	54	2.65
52	2	1	3	1.75	356	45	64	2.78
53	1	1	2	2.58	487	54	44.9	2.67
54	1	2	1	2.48	454	38	42	2.64

TABLE A.19.1 • Continued

StudentID	Gender	Econ	ReadLevel	HSGPA	SAT	MATH	LANG	CollGPA
55	2	1	3	2.43	520	53	58.3	2.85
56	1	1	1	1.63	387	31.2	23.1	2.38
57	2	1	3	3.18	527	57	75	3.55
58	1	3	3	3.58	568	84	91	3.67
59	2	1	2	2.45	435	53	48	2.56
60	1	1	2	1.84	467	52	55	2.78
61	2	3	3	3.54	523	75	81	3.67
62	1	1	1	2.56	453	52	45	2.37
63	2	1	3	3.16	545	62	82	3.58
64	1	1	1	2.28	467	25	27	1.86
65	2	3	3	3.45	712	78	94	3.42
66	2	2	3	2.88	474	44	57	2.67
67	1	3	2	2.43	585	74	83	3.65
68	2	3	3	3.43	725	88.4	92	3.23
69	1	2	2	1.78	567	61	63	2.83
70	2	1	2	2.48	326	33	53	2.28
71	1	3	2	3.28	475	58.5	81	3.64
72	1	1	1	1.68	587	32	26	2.28
73	2	2	2	2.52	524	54	41	2.23
74	2	1	3	2.65	634	88	76	3.21
75	1	2	2	2.27	368	38	55	2.74
76	2	3	2	3.64	570	54	49	3.38
77	2	3	3	2.68	525	72	85	3.57
78	1	1	3	3.28	450	67	91	3.58
79	2	2	3	2.76	470	55	86	3.67
80	2	2	2	2.72	565	53	39	2.48
81	1	3	2	3.18	510	65	84	3.54
82	1	2	2	2.57	512	36	55	2.44
83	2	3	3	2.85	678	78	82	3.48
84	1	1	1	1.88	538	54	52	2.34
85	2	2	3	2.54	486	64	88	3.48
86	2	2	3	2.78	457	43	52	2.35
87	1	3	2	3.37	523	53	74	3.18
88	1	1	1	2.54	552	52	47	2.36
89	1	3	2	2.66	620	63	85	3.54
90	2	1	3	2.34	568	52	65	2.88
91	2	1	3	1.78	432	47	72	2.65
92	1	2	2	2.53	444	53	48	2.24
93	2	3	2	3.54	585	52	48	2.85
94	2	2	3	2.88	535	42	84	3.24
95	1	2	3	2.44	588	58	73	3.16
96	2	1	3	1.78	438	45	68	2.68
97	2	2	2	3.35	450	54	38	2.48
98	1	2	1	2.55	580	54	44	2.25
99	1	3	2	2.82	465	65	82	3.54
100	2	1	2	2.94	510	48	52	2.74
101	1	1	2	1.84	467	52	55	2.78
102	2	3	3	3.54	595	45	81	3.67
103	1	1	2	2.56	453	32	45	2.37
104	2	1	3	3.16	545	42.3	82	3.58
105	1	1	1	2.28	467	36	27	1.86
106	2	3	3	3.45	712	83	94	3.42
107	2	2	2	2.88	474	63.6	57	2.67
108	1	3	3	2.43	585	64.2	83	3.65
109	2	3	3	3.43	725	78	92	3.23

TABLE A.19.1 • *Continued*

StudentID	Gender	Econ	ReadLevel	HSGPA	SAT	MATH	LANG	CollGPA
110	1	2	2	1.78	567	61	63	2.83
111	2	1	2	2.48	326	57	53	2.28
112	2	1	1	2.45	320	34	48.5	2.25
113	1	3	3	3.22	570	69	78	3.54
114	1	1	1	1.78	543	22	27.2	2.3
115	2	2	2	2.54	530	58.4	42	2.26
116	2	1	2	2.78	547	47	77	3.24
117	1	2	2	2.17	498	52	59	2.86
118	2	3	2	3.54	580	58	46	3.22
119	2	3	3	2.88	525	59	83	3.45
120	1	1	2	3.22	585	57	75	3.68
121	2	2	3	2.45	476	51	86	3.54
122	2	2	2	2.68	645	48	52	2.45
123	2	3	2	3.54	585	34	48	2.85
124	1	2	1	2.48	454	38	42	2.64
125	1	2	2	2.27	525	57	59	2.86

R SCRIPTS

The following scripts are provided in order for the reader to follow along step-by-step. Each script begins with the loading of a dataset. In this command, you will see the words, "insert your file path here". In this space, you provide the path to your saved Text file. For example, "~Desktop/Pinecrest.txt". Once you change this part of the script, the rest can be pasted into your R console. Remember that commands that begin with the # symbol indicate a comment.

#CHAPTER 18

```
#You need to let R know which dataset you want to work with. To do so, type the following:
pinecrest <- read.table("insert your file path here", header = TRUE)
attach(pinecrest)
#Let's take a look at the dataset
pinecrest
#We need to let R know that some of our variables are factor variables. When we say "1 for male"
we don't literally mean the numeric value of 1. "1" is just shorthand for "male." We just need to let R
know that our categorical variables are indeed just that . . . To do so, type the following:
#Creating a factor variable for Gender
pinecrest$f.gender = factor(pinecrest$Gender, labels = c("male", "female"))
#Creating a factor variable for Ethnicity
pinecrest$f.ethnicity = factor(pinecrest$Ethnicity, labels = c("African American", "Asian, Pacific
Islander", "Hispanic", "Native American", "White"))
#Creating a factor variable for Economic Level
pinecrest$f.econ = factor(pinecrest$Econ, labels = c("low (free/reduced lunch)", "medium/working
class", "middle/upperclass"))
#Creating a factor variable for Reading Level
pinecrest$f.ReadLevel = factor(pinecrest$ReadLevel, labels = c("low", "middle", "high"))
attach(pinecrest)
#Now let's take a look at our dataset. Note that you'll see the factor variables we just created:
pinecrest
#Let's take a look at our frequency table
addmargins(table(f.gender, f.ethnicity))
#Summary of means of Fall Reading Scores by Gender
tapply(ReadF, f.gender,mean)
#Summary of standard deviation of Fall Reading Scores by Gender
tapply(ReadF, f.gender,sd)
#Range and quartile
summary(pinecrest[,3:6])
#variance
tapply(ReadF, f.gender, var)
#Correlations of Fall Reading and Fall Math
cor.test(ReadF, MathF)
```

#CHAPTER 19

```
#You need to let R know which dataset you want to work with. Remember to use a .txt file. To do
so, type the following:
pinecrest <- read.table("insert your file path here", header = TRUE)
attach(pinecrest)
#Let's take a look at the dataset
pinecrest
#We need to let R know that some of our variables are factor variables. When we say "1 for male"
we don't literally mean the numeric value of 1. "1" is just shorthand for "male." We just need to let R
know that our categorical variables are indeed just that . . . To do so, type the following:
#Creating a factor variable for Gender
pinecrest$f.gender = factor(pinecrest$Gender, labels = c("male", "female"))
#Creating a factor variable for Ethnicity
pinecrest$f.ethnicity = factor(pinecrest$Ethnicity, labels = c("African American", "Asian, Pacific
Islander", "Hispanic", "Native American", "White"))
#Creating a factor variable for Economic Level
pinecrest$f.econ = factor(pinecrest$Econ, labels = c("low (free/reduced lunch)", "medium/working
class", "middle/upperclass"))
#Creating a factor variable for Reading Level
pinecrest$f.ReadLevel = factor(pinecrest$ReadLevel, labels = c("low", "middle", "high"))
attach(pinecrest)
#Now let's take a look at our dataset. Note that you'll see the factor variables we just created:
pinecrest
#Levene's Test and independent samples t-test
#We will need to load the "car" package. If you haven't yet downloaded this package, you'll need to
do that by following the steps in the text. If you have already downloaded this package just type:
library(car)
leveneTest(ReadF, f.gender)
t.test(ReadF~f.gender)
#Dependent samples t-test
t.test(ReadF, ReadS, paired = TRUE)
t.test(MathF, MathS, paired = TRUE)
#Reading in the Pacific Crest Data Set
pacific <- read.table("insert your file path here", header = TRUE)
#Creating a factor variable for Gender
pacific$f.gender = factor(pacific$Gender, labels = c("male", "female"))
#Creating a factor variable for Economic Level
pacific$f.econ = factor(pacific$Econ, labels = c("low (free/reduced lunch)", "medium/working class",
"middle/upperclass"))
#Creating a factor variable for Reading Level
pacific$f.ReadLevel = factor(pacific$ReadLevel, labels = c("low", "middle", "high"))
attach(pacific)
pacific
#pacific is now the active dataset
#To conduct our ANOVA, we need just two commands
results <- aov(CollGPA~f.econ)
```

```
summary(results)
#Tukey's Test on Results
TukeyHSD(results)
#Regression example
regression <- lm(CollGPA~HSGPA + SAT + MATH + LANG)
summary(regression)
#Chi square example
chiexample <- table(pacific$f.ReadLevel, pacific$f.gender)
chiexample
chisq.test(chiexample)
```

APPENDIX B

Suggested Responses

SELF-TEST FOR TASK 1A (PAGE 23)

Hamre, B. K., & Pianta, R. C. (2005). Can instructional and emotional support in the first-grade classroom make a difference for children at risk of school failure?, Child Development, 76, 949–967.

Topic Studied

This study addresses how certain characteristics of the first-grade classroom affect children at risk of academic and social difficulties at school.

The Procedures

To evaluate their hypothesis that supportive classrooms would help at-risk children to succeed, Hamre and Pianta studied 910 first-graders. These children were part of a longitudinal study of 1,364 families from 10 U.S. cities. The researchers measured the children's academic and cognitive skills using a standardized psychometric test that included tests of reading, mathematics, memory, and auditory processing. They also asked the current first-grade teachers to report their perceptions of conflict with each student, using a 28-item rating scale. Additionally, trained data collectors spent a day observing each classroom to rate classroom quality and teacher behaviors.

The Method of Analysis

The primary statistical test used in this study was analysis of covariance (ANCOVA).

The Major Conclusion

Instructional support and emotional support help at-risk children achieve academic scores comparable to their lower risk peers. Emotional support, but not instructional support, also helps functionally at-risk children to relate to their teachers in a more socially appropriate way.

SELF-TEST FOR TASK 1B (PAGE 23)

Sleeter, C. (2009). Developing teacher epistemological sophistication about multicultural curriculum: A case study. Action in Teacher Education, 31(1), 3–13.

Topic Studied

How does teachers' thinking about curriculum develop in the context of teacher education coursework, and how might an analysis of a novice teacher's learning to think more complexly inform teacher education pedagogy?

The Procedures

Case study research that included the following data sources: (1) course assignments including an instructional unit, (2) researcher journal, (3) observational field notes, and (4) tape recorded interview.

The Method of Analysis

The author used qualitative analytic methods, including use of a heuristic tool for reflection (see

Table 1: Thinking Complexly About Multicultural Curriculum).

The Major Conclusions

The author concluded that: (1) reflective discussions and writings embedded in teachers' classroom work prompt thinking that can dislodge novice assumptions, (2) to facilitate development beyond novice thinking, it is essential to provide space and support for uncertaintly, and (3) teachers value opportunities to learn from peers.

SELF-TEST FOR TASK 1C (PAGE 23)

1. *Research Approach: Survey Research*. Survey research involves collecting data to answer questions about the current status of issues or topics; a questionnaire was administered to find out how teachers feel about an issue.
2. *Research Approach: Correlational Research*. Correlational research seeks to determine whether, and to what degree, a statistical relationship exists between two or more variables. Here, the researchers are interested in the similarity of the two tests.
3. *Research Approach: Causal–Comparative Research*. In causal–comparative research, at least two groups (fifth-graders from single-parent families and those from two-parent families) are compared on a dependent variable or effect (in this case, achievement of reading).
4. *Research Approach: Experimental Research*. Experimental research allows researchers to make cause–effect statements about a study. In addition, researchers have a great deal of control over the study; here the researchers determined the two groups (at random) and applied different treatments (the two methods of conflict resolution) to the two groups.

5. *Research Approach: Ethnographic Research*. Ethnographic research studies participants in their natural culture or setting; the culture of recent Armenian emigrants is examined in their new setting.

SELF-TEST FOR TASK 1D (PAGE 75)

Hamre, B. K., & Pianta, R. C. (2005). Can instructional and emotional support in the first-grade classroom make a difference for children at risk of school failure?, Child Development, 76, 949–967.

1. An ethical challenge the authors may have faced was their ability to obtain informed consent from the parents of the 910 children who made up the sample for the study. However, given that this causal-comparative study used an existing database from the NICHD Study of Early Child Care, the earlier study must have obtained consent from the parents even though it is not indicated in this article.

Sleeter, C. (2009). Developing teacher epistemological sophistication about multicultural curriculum: A case study. Action in Teacher Education, 31(1), 3–13.

1. Selection of Ann (pseudonym) as the subject for the case study was based on Ann's characteristics as a new teacher who was relatively new to multicultural education, open to learning, and teaching in a diverse classroom. It would have been critical that the researcher negotiate entry to the research site with assurances that "Ann" was not being evaluated and that there were protections in place for her and her students' anonymity and confidentiality. Informed consent would be an ongoing conversation between the researcher and Ann in order to confirm Ann's involvement in the study over an extended period of time.

SELF-TEST FOR TASK 12 (PAGES 616–617)

Akos, P., & Galassi, J. P. (2004). Gender and race as variables in psychosocial adjustment to middle and high school. The Journal of Educational Research, (98)2, 102–109.

General Evaluation Criteria

INTRODUCTION

	CODE
Problem	
A statement?	Y
Paragraph (¶)11, sentence (S)1[1]	
Researchable?	Y
Background information?	Y
e.g., ¶10	
Significance discussed?	Y
e.g., ¶10	
Variables and relations discussed?	Y
Definitions?	Y
e.g., ¶7, S4	
Researcher knowledgeable?	Y

	CODE
Review of Related Literature	
Comprehensive?	Y
Appears to be	
Well organized?	Y
Critical analysis?	Y
e.g., ¶1–10	
References relevant?	Y
Summary?	N
Rationale for hypotheses?	N
Sources primary?	Y
References complete and accurate?	Y

	CODE
Hypotheses	
Questions or hypotheses?	Y
¶11	
Testable?	Y
Expected differences stated?	Y
Variables defined?	Y

METHOD

	CODE
Participants	
Population described?	Y
Very briefly	
Accessible and target populations described?	Y
Sample selection method described?	NA
Selection method limited or biased?	NA
Sample described?	Y&Y
Size, yes; characteristics, yes	
Minimum sizes?	N

---

[1]¶7 refers to paragraph 7 of the introduction section of the article. The introduction section ends where "Method" begins.

Instruments

Guidelines met for protecting participants? Permissions obtained?	NA
Appropriate?	Y
Type of instrument correct?	Y
Rationale for selection?	N
Instrument purpose and content described?	Y
¶15, 16 & 17	
Validity discussed?	Y
Reliability discussed?	Y
¶16	
Subtest reliabilities?	N
Evidence that it is appropriate for sample?	N
Procedures for development described?	N
Performance posttest not described	
Administration, scoring, and interpretation procedures described?	N
Researcher skilled in test construction, administration?	Y

Design and Procedure

Design appropriate?	Y
Procedures sufficiently detailed?	Y
Procedures logically related?	Y
Instruments and procedures applied correctly?	Y
Pilot study described?	NA
Control procedures described?	NA
Confounding variables discussed?	NA

RESULTS

Appropriate descriptive statistics?	Y
Table 1 & 2	
Tests of significance appropriate?	Y
Parametric assumptions not violated?	Y
Probability level specified in advance?	NA
Appropriate degrees of freedom?	NA
Inductive logic explicit?	NA
Results clearly presented?	Y
Tables and figures well organized?	Y
Data in each table and figure described?	Y

DISCUSSION (CONCLUSIONS AND RECOMMENDATIONS)

Results discussed in terms of hypothesis?	Y
Results discussed in terms of previous research?	Y
e.g., ¶22–26	
Generalizations consistent with results?	Y
Implications discussed?	Y
e.g., ¶37	
Effects of uncontrolled variables discussed?	NA
Recommendations for action?	Y
e.g., ¶37 & 38	

ABSTRACT OR SUMMARY

Problem stated?	Y
Participants and instruments described?	Y&N
Participants briefly; instruments indirectly	
Design identified?	N
Procedures?	N
Results and conclusions?	Y

TYPE-SPECIFIC EVALUATION CRITERIA

Design used: Causal–comparative	Y
• Are the characteristics or experiences that differentiate the groups (i.e., the grouping variable) clearly defined or described?	
• Are critical extraneous variables identified?	Y
• Were any control procedures applied to equate the groups on extraneous variables?	Y
• Are causal relations discussed with due caution? e.g., ¶36	Y
• Are plausible alternative hypotheses discussed? e.g., ¶37	Y

Glossary

A-B design A single-subject design in which baseline measurements are repeatedly made until stability is presumably established, treatment is introduced, and an appropriate number of measurements are made during treatment.

A-B-A design A single-subject design in which baseline measurements are repeatedly made until stability is presumably established, treatment is introduced, an appropriate number of measurements are made, and the treatment phase is followed by a second baseline phase.

A-B-A-B design A single-subject design in which baseline measurements are repeatedly made until stability is presumably established, treatment is introduced, an appropriate number of measurements are made, and the treatment phase is followed by a second baseline phase, which is followed by a second treatment phase.

accessible population The population from which the researcher can realistically select subjects. *Also called* available population. *Compare* target population.

achievement test An instrument that measures an individual's current proficiency in given areas of knowledge or skill.

action research Any systematic inquiry conducted by teachers, principals, school counselors, or other stakeholders in the teaching–learning environment to gather information about the ways in which their particular schools operate, the teachers teach, and the students learn.

additive design Any of the variations of the single-subject A-B design that involve the addition of another phase or phases in which the experimental treatment is supplemented with another treatment.

affective characteristic A mental characteristic related to emotion, such as attitude, interest, and value.

affective test An assessment designed to measure mental characteristics related to emotion.

alternating treatments design A variation of multiple-baseline design that involves the relatively rapid alternation of treatments for a single participant. *Also called* multiple schedule design, multi-element baseline design, multi-element manipulation design, *or* simultaneous treatment design.

analysis of covariance A statistical method of equating groups on one or more variables and for increasing the power of a statistical test; adjusts scores on a dependent variable for initial differences on some other variable (e.g., pretest performance or IQ) related to performance on the dependent variable.

analysis of variance (ANOVA) An inferential statistics technique used to test for significant differences among the means of three or more groups.

aptitude test A measure of potential used to predict how well an individual is likely to perform in a future situation.

artificial categories Categories that are operationally defined by a researcher.

assessment General term for the process of collecting, synthesizing, and interpreting information; also, the instrument used for such purposes. A test is a type of assessment.

assumption Any important fact presumed to be true but not actually verified; assumptions should be described in the procedure section of a research plan or report.

attenuation The reduction in correlation coefficients that tends to occur if the measures being correlated have low reliability.

attitude scale A measurement instrument used to determine what a respondent believes, perceives, or feels about self, others, activities, institutions, or situations.

baseline measures Multiple measures of pretest performance conducted in single-subject research designs to control for threats to validity.

bias Distortion of research data that renders the data suspect or invalid; may occur due to characteristics of the researcher, the respondent, or the research design itself.

case study research The in-depth investigation of one unit (e.g., individual, group, institution, organization, program, or document).

causal–comparative research Research that attempts to determine the cause, or reason, for existing differences in the behavior or status of groups of individuals. *Also called* ex post facto research.

changing criterion design A variation of the A-B-A design in which the baseline phase is followed by successive treatment phases, each of which has a more stringent criterion for acceptable or improved behavior.

chi square A nonparametric test of significance appropriate when the data are in the form of frequency counts; compares proportions observed in a study with proportions expected by chance.

clinical replication The development and application of a treatment package, composed of two or more interventions that have been found to be effective individually, designed for persons with complex behavior disorders.

cluster Any location that contains an intact group with similar characteristics (e.g., population members).

cluster sampling Sampling in which intact groups, not individuals, are randomly selected.

cognitive characteristic A mental characteristic related to intellect, such as mathematics achievement, literacy, reasoning, or problem solving.

cognitive test An assessment designed to measure intellectual processes.

common variance The variation in one variable that is attributable to its tendency to vary with another variable. *Also called* shared variance.

concurrent validity The degree to which the scores on a test are related to the scores on a similar test administered in the same time frame or to some other valid measure available at the same time; a form of criterion-related validity.

confirmability The neutrality or objectivity of the data that have been collected.

consequential validity The extent to which an instrument creates harmful effects for the user.

construct An abstraction that cannot be observed directly; a concept invented to explain behavior.

construct validity The degree to which a test measures an intended hypothetical construct or nonobservable trait that explains behavior.

content validity The degree to which a test measures an intended content area; it is determined by expert judgment and requires both item validity and sampling validity.

control Efforts on the part of a researcher to remove the influence of any variable other than the independent variable that may affect performance on a dependent variable.

control group A group of participants in a research study who either receive a different treatment than the experimental group or are treated as usual.

control variable A nonmanipulated variable, usually a physical or mental characteristic of the subjects (e.g., IQ).

convenience sampling The process of including whoever happens to be available in a sample (e.g., volunteers). *Also called* accidental sampling *or* haphazard sampling.

correlation A quantitative measure of the degree of correspondence between two or more variables.

correlation coefficient A decimal number between -1.00 and $+1.00$ that indicates the degree to which two variables are related.

correlational research Research that involves collecting data to determine whether, and to what degree, a relation exists between two or more quantifiable variables.

counterbalanced design A quasi-experimental design in which all groups receive all treatments, each group receives the treatments in a different order, the number of groups equals the number of treatments, and all groups are tested after each treatment.

credibility A term used in qualitative research to indicate that the topic was accurately identified and described.

criterion The predicted variable that must be a valid measure of the performance to be predicted.

criterion-referenced scoring A scoring approach in which an individual's performance on an assessment is compared to a predetermined, external standard.

criterion-related validity Validity that is determined by relating performance on a test to performance on another criterion (e.g., a second test or measure); includes concurrent and predictive validity.

critical ethnography A highly politicized form of ethnography written by a researcher to advocate against inequalities and domination of particular groups that exist in society.

Cronbach's alpha (a) The general formula for estimating internal consistency based on a determination of how all items on a test relate to all other items and to the total test. The Kuder-Richardson 20 (KR-20) is a special case of the Cronbach's alpha general formula.

cross-sectional survey A survey in which data are collected from selected individuals in a single time period. *Compare* longitudinal survey.

cross-validation Validation of a prediction equation with at least one group other than the group on which it was developed; results in the removal from the equation of variables no longer found to be related to the criterion measure.

culture The set of attitudes, values, concepts, beliefs and practices shared by members of a group; a central construct in ethnographic research.

data (*sing.* datum) Pieces of information.

data mining The use of analytical tools to identify and predict patterns in datasets or large warehouses of data that have been collected from thousands of subjects and about hundreds of variables.

data saturation A point in qualitative research at which so much data are collected that it is very unlikely that additional data will add new information.

deductive hypothesis A hypothesis derived from theory that provides evidence to support, expand, or contradict the theory.

deductive reasoning Reasoning that involves developing specific predictions based on general principles, observations, or experiences.

dependability The stability of qualitative data.

dependent variable The change or difference in a behavior or characteristic that occurs as a result of the independent or grouping variable. *Also called* effect, outcome, *or* posttest.

design A general strategy or plan for conducting a research study; indicates the basic structure and goals of the study.

diagnostic test A type of achievement test that yields scores for multiple areas of achievement to facilitate identification of a student's weak and strong areas.

differential selection of participants Selection of subjects who have differences at the start of a study that may at least partially account for differences found on a posttest; a threat to internal validity.

direct replication Replication of a study by the same investigator, with the same subjects or with different subjects, in a specific setting.

directional hypothesis A research hypothesis that states the expected direction of the relation or difference between variables.

dummy variable Refers to multiple regression and the ability to transfer a nominal variable into an interval variable referred to as a dummy variable and only has meaning only for the purposes of the statistical calculation.

educational research The formal, systematic application of the scientific method to the study of educational problems.

environmental variable A variable in the setting of a study (e.g., learning materials) that may cause unwanted differences between groups.

equivalence The degree to which two similar forms of a test produce similar scores from a single group of test takers. *Also called* equivalent-forms reliability or alternate-forms reliability.

equivalent-forms reliability *See* equivalence.

ethnographic case study A form of ethnography that focuses on describing the activities of a specific group and the shared patterns of behavior it develops over time.

ethnographic research The study of the cultural patterns and perspectives of participants in their natural setting; a form of qualitative research. *Also called* ethnography.

ethnography Ethnographic research; also, the narrative produced to summarize the results of such research.

evaluation research The systematic process of collecting and analyzing data on the quality, effectiveness, merit, or value of programs, products, or practices for the purpose of making decisions about those programs, products, or practices.

experimental group A group of participants in a research study who typically receive the new treatment under investigation.

experimental research Research in which at least one independent variable is manipulated, other relevant variables are controlled, and the effect on one or more dependent variables is observed.

experimenter bias effect A situation in which a researcher's expectations of study results contribute to producing the outcome.

experimenter effects Threats to the external validity of an experiment caused by the researcher's unintentional or intentional influences on participants or on study procedures.

external validity The degree to which results are generalizable or applicable to groups and environments outside the experimental setting. *Also called* ecological validity.

F **ratio** A computation used in analysis of variance to determine whether variances among sample means are significantly different.

face validity The degree to which a test appears to measure what it claims to measure.

factor analysis The statistical procedure used to identify relations among variables in a correlation matrix. Factor analysis determines how variables group together bases on what they may have in common.

factorial analysis of variance A statistical technique that allows the researcher to determine the effects of independent or grouping variables and control variables on the dependent variable both separately and in combination. It is the appropriate statistical analysis if a study is based on a factorial design and investigates two or more independent or grouping variables and the interactions between them; yields a separate *F* ratio for each variable and one for each interaction.

factorial design Any experimental design that involves two or more independent or grouping variables, at least one of which is manipulated, to study the effects of the variables individually and in interaction with each other.

Family Educational Rights and Privacy Act of 1974 Federal law that protects the privacy of student educational records. *Also called* Buckley Amendment.

field notes Qualitative research material gathered, recorded, and compiled, usually on-site, during the course of a study.

formative evaluation Evaluation whose function is to form and improve a program or product under development so that weaknesses that can be remedied during implementation.

generalizability The applicability of research findings to settings and contexts different from the one in which they were obtained.

grouping variable The cause, behavior, or characteristic believed to influence some other behavior or characteristic in causal comparative research.

guiding hypotheses As used in qualitative research to describe the use of observations to guide the development of research questions.

history Any event occurring during a study that is not part of the experimental treatment but may affect performance on the dependent variable; a threat to internal validity.

hypothesis An explanation for the occurrence of certain behaviors, phenomena, or events; a prediction of research findings.

independent variable A behavior or characteristic under the control of the researcher and believed to influence some other behavior or characteristic. *Also called* experimental variable, manipulated variable, cause, *or* treatment.

inductive hypothesis A generalization based on observation.

inductive reasoning Reasoning that involves developing generalizations based on observations of a limited number of related events or experiences.

inferential statistics Data analysis techniques for determining how likely it is that results obtained from a sample or samples are the same results that would have been obtained for the entire population.

instrument In educational research, a test or other tool used to collect data.

instrumentation Unreliability in measuring instruments that may result in invalid assessment of participants' performance.

interaction A situation in which different values of the independent or grouping variable are differentially effective depending on the level of a second (e.g., control) variable.

interjudge reliability The consistency of two or more independent scorers, raters, or observers.

internal consistency reliability Internal consistency reliability is the extent to which items in a single test are consistent among themselves and with the test as a whole.

internal validity The degree to which observed differences on the dependent variable are a direct result of manipulation of the independent variable, not some other variable.

interval variable An interval variable has values that are ranked in order, but its values also represent equal intervals. Scores on most tests used in educational research, such as achievement, aptitude, motivation, and attitude tests, are treated as interval variables.

intervening variable A variable (e.g., anxiety) that intervenes between or alters the relation between an independent variable and a dependent variable but that cannot be directly observed or controlled.

interview An oral, in-person question-and-answer session between a researcher and an individual respondent; a purposeful interaction in which one person is trying to obtain information from the other.

intrajudge reliability The consistency of one individual's scoring, rating, or observing over time.

item validity The degree to which test items are relevant to the measurement of the intended content area.

John Henry effect The phenomenon in which members of a control group who feel threatened or challenged by being in competition with an experimental group outdo themselves and perform way beyond what would normally be expected. *Also called* compensatory rivalry.

Kuder-Richardson 20 (KR-20) *See* Cronbach's alpha.

Likert scale An instrument on which individuals respond to a series of statements by indicating whether they strongly agree (SA), agree (A), are undecided (U), disagree (D), or strongly disagree (SD) with each statement.

limitation An aspect of a study that the researcher knows may negatively affect the results or generalizability of the results but over which the researcher has no control.

longitudinal survey A survey in which data are collected at two or more times to measure changes or growth over time. *Compare* cross-sectional survey.

matching A technique for equating sample groups on one or more variables, resulting in each member of one group having a direct counterpart in another group.

maturation Physical, intellectual, and emotional changes that naturally occur within subjects over a period of time; poses a threat to internal validity because changes may affect subjects' performance on a measure of the dependent variable.

mean   The arithmetic average of a set of scores.

measurement   The process of quantifying or scoring performance on an assessment instrument.

measurement scale   A system for organizing data so that data may be inspected, analyzed, and interpreted.

measures of central tendency   Indices that represent the typical or average score for a group of scores.

median   The midpoint in a distribution; 50% of the scores are above the median and 50% are below.

meta-analysis   A statistical approach to summarizing the results of many quantitative studies that address basically the same problem.

mixed methods research   Research designs that include both quantitative and qualitative data in a single study.

mode   The score that is attained by more subjects in a group than any other score.

mortality   A reduction in the number of research participants that occurs over time as individuals drop out of a study; poses a threat to internal validity because subjects who drop out of a study may share a characteristic and their absence may therefore have a significant effect on the results of the study. *Also called* attrition.

multiple-baseline design   *See* alternating treatments design.

multiple regression equation   A prediction equation using two or more variables that individually predict a criterion to make a more accurate prediction. *Also called* multiple prediction equation.

multiple-baseline design   A single-subject design in which baseline data are collected on several behaviors for one subject, one behavior for several subjects, or one behavior and one subject in several settings. Treatment is applied systematically over a period of time to each behavior (or each subject or setting) one at a time until all behaviors (or subjects or settings) are under treatment.

multiple-treatment interference   Phenomenon that occurs when carryover effects from an earlier treatment make it difficult to assess the effectiveness of a later treatment; a threat to external validity.

narrative research   The study of how different humans experience the world around them; involves a methodology that allows people to tell the stories of their "storied lives."

National Research Act of 1974   Act that led to the establishment of federal regulations governing the protection of human subjects in research; mandates that activities involving human participants be reviewed and approved by an authorized group before execution of the research.

nominal variable   A nominal variable is also called a categorical variable because the values include two or more named categories, for example, employment status (full-time, part-time, unemployed).

nondirectional hypothesis   A research hypothesis that states simply that a relation or difference exists between variables.

nonequivalent control group design   A quasi-experimental design involving at least two groups, both of which are pretested; one group receives the experimental treatment, and both groups are posttested.

nonparticipant observation   Observation in which the observer is not directly involved in the situation being observed; that is, the observer does not intentionally interact with or affect the object of the observation. *Also called* external observation.

nonprobability sampling   The process of selecting a sample using a technique that does not permit the researcher to specify the probability, or chance, that each member of a population will be selected for the sample. *Also called* nonrandom sampling.

norm-referenced scoring   A scoring approach in which an individual's performance on an assessment is compared to the performance of others. *Also called* grading on the curve.

novelty effect   The increased interest, motivation, or participation participants develop simply because they are doing something different; a type of reactive arrangement.

null hypothesis   A hypothesis stating that there is no relation (or difference) between variables and that any relation/difference found will be due to chance; i.e., the result of sampling error.

one-group pretest–posttest design   A pre-experimental design involving one group that is pretested, exposed to a treatment, and posttested.

operational definitions   Operational definitions clarify important terms in a study so that all readers understand the precise meaning the researcher intends.

ordinal variable   An ordinal variable not only classifies persons or objects, it also ranks them according to some criteria. The numerical value of ordinal scales indicates a ranking in order from highest to lowest or from most to least.

organismic variable   A characteristic of a subject or organism (e.g., sex) that cannot be directly controlled but can be controlled for.

***p*-value**   See statistical significance

path analysis   Path analysis identifies the degree to which predictor variables interact with each other and contribute to the variance of the dependent variables.

participant observation Observation in which the observer becomes a part of and a participant in the situation being observed.

participant variable A variable on which participants in different groups in a study may differ (e.g., intelligence).

Pearson *r* A measure of correlation appropriate when both variables are expressed as continuous (i.e., ratio or interval) data; it takes into account every score and produces a coefficient between -1.00 and $+1.00$.

performance assessment A type of assessment that emphasizes a respondent's performance of a process or creation of a product. *Also called* authentic assessment *or* alternative assessment.

pilot study A small-scale trial of a study conducted before the full-scale study to identify problems with the research plan.

placebo effect Any beneficial effect caused by a person's expectations about a treatment rather than the treatment itself.

population General term for the larger group from which a sample is selected or the group to which the researcher would like to generalize the results of the study. *Compare* target population *and* accessible population.

posttest-only control group design A true experimental design involving at least two randomly formed groups; one group receives a new or unusual treatment, and both groups are posttested.

power The ability of a significance test to identify a true research finding (i.e., there's really a difference, and the statistical test shows a significant difference), allowing the experimenter to reject a null hypothesis that is false.

prediction study An attempt to determine which of a number of variables are most highly related to a criterion variable, a complex variable to be predicted.

predictive validity The degree to which a test is able to predict how well an individual will do in a future situation; a form of criterion-related validity.

predictor In a prediction study or analysis of concurrent or predictive validity, the variable on which the prediction is based.

pretest–posttest control group design A true experimental design that involves at least two randomly formed groups; both groups are pretested, one group receives a new or unusual treatment, and both groups are posttested.

pretest-treatment interaction Phenomenon that occurs when subjects respond or react differently to a treatment because they have been pretested; a threat to external validity.

primary source Firsthand information, such as the testimony of an eyewitness, an original document, a relic, or a description of a study written by the person who conducted it.

probability sampling The process of selecting a sample using a sampling technique that permits the researcher to specify the probability, or chance, that each member of a defined population will be selected for the sample.

problem statement *See* topic statement.

prospective causal–comparative research A variation of the basic approach to causal–comparative research; involves starting with the causes and investigating effects.

purposive sampling The process of selecting a sample that is *believed* to be representative of a given population. *Also called* judgment sampling.

qualitative research The collection, analysis, and interpretation of comprehensive narrative and visual data to gain insights into a particular phenomenon of interest. *Sometimes called* naturalistic research, naturalistic inquiry, *or* field-oriented research.

qualitative sampling The process of selecting a small number of individuals for a study in such a way that the selected individuals can help the researcher understand the phenomenon under investigation.

quantitative research The collection of numerical data to explain, predict and/or control phenomena of interest.

quartile deviation One half of the difference between the upper quartile (the 75th percentile) and the lower quartile (the 25th percentile) in a distribution.

questionnaire A written collection of self-report questions to be answered by a selected group of research participants.

quota sampling The process of selecting a sample based on required, exact numbers (i.e., quotas) of persons of varying characteristics.

range The difference between the highest and lowest score in a distribution.

rating scale A measurement instrument used to determine a respondent's attitude toward self, others, activities, institutions, or situations.

ratio variable A ratio variable has equal intervals in rank order and, in addition, its measurement scale has a true zero point. Height, weight, time, distance, and speed are examples of ratio scales.

raw score The numerical calculation of the number or point value of items answered correctly on an assessment.

reactive arrangements Threats to the external validity of a study associated with the way in which a study is conducted and the feelings and attitudes of the subjects involved. *Also called* participant effects.

realist ethnography A form of ethnography written with an objective style and using common categories (e.g., "family life") for cultural description, analysis, and interpretation.

relationship study An attempt to gain insight into the variables, or factors, that are related to a complex variable, such as academic achievement, motivation, or self-concept.

reliability The degree to which a test (or qualitative research data) consistently measures whatever it measures.

replication A repetition of a study using different subjects or retesting its hypothesis.

research The formal, systematic application of the scientific method to the study of problems.

research and development (R&D) An extensive process of researching consumer needs and then developing products specifically designed to fulfill those needs; R&D efforts in education focus on creating effective products for use in schools.

research plan A detailed description of a proposed study designed to investigate a given problem.

response set The tendency of an assessed individual to respond in a particular way to a variety of instruments, such as when a respondent repeatedly answers as he or she believes the researcher desires even when such answers do not reflect the respondent's true feelings; also, the tendency of an observer to rate the majority of observees the same regardless of the observees' behavior.

restorying A process, unique to narrative research, in which a researcher gathers stories, analyzes them for key elements, and then synthesizes them into a coherent story with a chronological sequence.

retrospective causal–comparative research The basic approach to causal–comparative research; involves starting with effects and investigating causes.

review of related literature The systematic identification, location, and analysis of documents containing information related to a research problem; also, the written component of a research plan or report that discusses the reviewed documents.

sample A number of individuals, items, or events selected from a population for a study, preferably in such a way that they represent the larger group from which they were selected.

sampling bias Systematic sampling error; two major sources of sampling bias are samples including only volunteers and sampling based on available groups.

sampling error Expected, chance variation in variables that occurs when a sample is selected from a population.

sampling validity The degree to which a test samples the total content area of interest.

scientific method An orderly process that entails recognition and definition of a problem, formulation of hypotheses, collection of data, and statement of conclusions regarding confirmation or disconfirmation of the hypotheses.

secondary source Secondhand information, such as a brief description of a study written by someone other than the person who conducted it.

selection–maturation interaction Phenomenon that occurs when already-formed groups are included in a study and one group profits more (or less) from treatment or has an initial advantage (or disadvantage) because of maturation factors; a threat to internal validity. Selection may also interact with factors such as history and testing.

selection–treatment interaction Phenomenon that occurs when nonrepresentative groups are included in a study and the results of the study apply only to the groups involved and are not representative of the treatment effect in the population; a threat to external validity.

self-referenced scoring approach A scoring approach in which an individual's repeated performances on a single assessment are compared over time.

semantic differential scale An instrument that requires an individual to indicate his or her attitude about a topic (e.g., property taxes) by selecting a position on a continuum that ranges from one bipolar adjective (e.g., fair) to another (e.g., unfair).

shrinkage The tendency of a prediction equation to become less accurate when used with a group other than the one on which the equation was originally developed.

simple random sampling The process of selecting a sample in such a way that all individuals in the defined population have an equal and independent chance of selection for the sample.

single-subject experimental designs Designs applied when the sample size is one; used to study the behavior change that an individual or group exhibits as a result of some intervention or treatment. *Also called* single-case experimental designs.

single-variable design Any experimental design that involves only one independent variable, which is manipulated.

single-variable rule An important principle of single-subject research that only one variable should be manipulated at a time.

Solomon four-group design A true experimental design that involves random assignment of subjects to one of four groups; two groups are pretested, and two are not; one of the pretested groups and one of the unpretested groups receive the experimental treatment; and all four groups are tested again.

Spearman rho A measure of correlation appropriate when the data for at least one variable is expressed as rank or ordinal data; it produces a coefficient between -1.00 and $+1.00$.

specificity of variables Refers to the fact that a given study is conducted with a specific kind of subject, using specific measuring instruments, at a specific time, and under a specific set of circumstances. These factors affect the generalizability of the results.

split-half reliability A measure of internal consistency that involves dividing a test into two equivalent halves and correlating the scores on the two halves.

stability The degree to which scores on a test are consistent, or stable, over time. *Also called* test–retest reliability.

standard deviation A measure of variability that is stable and takes into account every score in a distribution. Calculated as the square root of the variance, or amount of spread among test scores, it is the most frequently used statistical index of variability.

standard error of measurement An estimate of how often one can expect errors of a given size in an individual's test score.

standardized test A test that is administered, scored, and interpreted in the same way no matter where or when it is given.

statistic A numerical index describing the behavior of a sample or samples.

statistical conclusion validity Statistical conclusion validity refers to the appropriate use of statistics to infer whether the presumed independent and dependent variables co-vary in the experiment. Threats to statistical conclusion validity include low statistical power, and violated assumptions of statistical tests.

statistical regression The tendency of subjects who score highest on a pretest to score lower on a posttest and of subjects who score lowest on a pretest to score higher on a posttest; a threat to internal validity.

statistical significance The conclusion that results are unlikely to have occurred by chance—that is, that the observed relation or difference is probably a real one.

statistics A set of procedures for describing, synthesizing, analyzing, and interpreting quantitative data.

stratified sampling A purposive process of selecting a sample: The population is subdivided into subgroups, and participants are strategically selected from each subgroup.

structural equation modeling (SEM) Structural equation modeling is a complicated statistical procedure that builds a structural model to explain the interactive relations among a relatively large number of variables.

structured interview An interview that includes a specified set of questions to be asked.

structured item An item on a questionnaire that requires the respondent to choose from among response options (e.g., by circling a letter, checking a list, or numbering preferences). *Also called* closed-ended item.

summative evaluation Evaluation whose function is to summarize the overall quality or worth of a program or product at its completion.

survey A survey is an instrument to collect data that describe one or more characteristics of a specific population.

survey research Survey research involves collecting data to test hypotheses or to answer questions about people's opinions on some problem or issue.

systematic replication Replication that involves different investigators, behaviors, or settings.

systematic sampling Sampling in which individuals are selected from a list by taking every Kth name, where K equals the number of individuals on the list (i.e., population size) divided by the number of subjects desired for the sample.

T **score** A standard score derived from a z score by multiplying the z score by 10 and adding 50. *Also called Z* score.

t **test** An inferential statistics technique used to determine whether the means of two groups are significantly different at a given probability level. *See also t* test for independent samples *and t* test for nonindependent samples.

t **test for independent samples** A parametric test of significance used to determine whether, at a selected probability level, the means of two independent samples are significantly different.

table of random numbers A list of multidigit numbers, arranged in a table, that have been randomly generated by a computer to have no defined patterns or regularities; used in sampling. *Also called* table of random digits.

target population The population to which the researcher would ideally like to generalize study results. *Compare* accessible population.

test A formal, systematic, usually paper-and-pencil procedure for gathering information about people's cognitive and affective characteristics.

test of significance A statistical test used to determine whether or not there is a significant difference between or among two or more means at a selected probability level.

testing A threat to experimental validity in which improved performance on a posttest is the result of subjects having taken a pretest. *Also called* pretest sensitization.

test–retest reliability *See* stability.

theoretical validity How well a qualitative research report explains the phenomenon being studied in relation to a theory.

theory An organized body of concepts, generalizations, and principles that can be subjected to investigation.

time-series design A quasi-experimental design involving one group that is repeatedly pretested, exposed to an experimental treatment, and repeatedly posttested.

transferability Transferability refers to qualitative researchers' beliefs that everything they study is context-bound and that the goal of their work is not to develop "truth" statements that can be generalized to larger groups of people.

treatment diffusion A threat to external validity that occurs when individuals from different treatment groups in an experiment communicate with and learn from each other.

true categories Categories into which persons or objects naturally fall, independent of a research study.

trustworthiness Along with understanding, a feature essential to the validity of qualitative research; is established by addressing the credibility, transferability, dependability, and confirmability of study findings.

Type I error The rejection by the researcher of a null hypothesis that is actually true.

Type II error The failure of a researcher to reject a null hypothesis that is really false.

unobtrusive measures Ways to collect data that do not intrude on or require interaction with research participants; examples include observation and collecting data from written records.

unstructured interview An interview that consists of questions prompted by the flow of the interview itself.

unstructured item An item on a questionnaire that gives the respondent complete freedom of response.

variable A concept (e.g., intelligence, height, aptitude) that can assume any one of a range of values.

variance The amount of spread among scores.

z score The most basic standard score; expresses how far a score is from a mean in terms of standard deviation units.

Z score *See T* score.

Name Index

Subject Index